THE SHELL GUIDE TO SCOTLAND

THE SHELL GUIDE

TO

SCOTLAND

by

MORAY McLAREN

with a preface by Sir Compton Mackenzie

Ebury Press
in association with George Rainbird
London 1972

This book was designed and produced by George Rainbird Ltd,
Marble Arch House, 44 Edgware Road, London W2,
and was printed and bound by Jarrold & Sons Ltd, Norwich

First edition 1965
Second impression (with revisions) 1967
Third impression (with revisions) 1970
Second (fully revised) edition 1972

The revisions for the second edition were
undertaken by Donald Macnie. Readers should
note that the Ministry referred to in the
text as "of Public Building and Works" is
now reconstituted as the Department of the
Environment.

Editor: Yorke Crompton
Cartographer: John R. Flower

The maps on pages 472–80 are based on the Ordnance Survey Map with the
sanction of H.M. Stationery Office (Crown Copyright reserved)

7181 3036 7

Contents

Colour Plates

Preface

I feel that anything I can say will add little or nothing of value to the contents of this invaluable work, which will be found as useful by a visitor to the Edinburgh Festival as by a motorist or hiker.

Scotland and Greece are the two most romantic small countries in the world for what they can give of scenery and history, and both countries can add to the attraction of their mainland enchanting islands galore. To clinch the comparison, the Rock of Edinburgh and the Acropolis of Athens offer the finest combination of city landscape and seascape in Europe. Ironically, Greece is handicapped at times by too much sun and Scotland by too much rain.

Yes, it is impossible for even the most perfervid Scot to deny that in Scotland, particularly in the West, it can be very wet. Nevertheless, at frequent intervals, the West can enjoy the satisfaction of having glorious weather when the rest of Scotland, and England too, are being rained upon. Unfortunately, the weather prophets have not yet been able to forecast accurately those lovely summers in the West. That being so, a prudent topographer will refrain from advising those who wish to tour the Highlands and Islands on which months to choose.

To enjoy to the full a tour of Scotland, it is essential that the traveller should have some knowledge of its past; and, to the difficulty of compressing such a history into the space that can be allowed for it, there is added the difficulty of presenting it in such a way as to avoid controversy. I do not exaggerate when I say that for the last four centuries Scots have disagreed passionately in their interpretation of the facts of history. Was John Knox the destroyer of Scotland's independence? Was Mary Queen of Scots a martyr or a *femme fatale*? Was the Union with England a disaster or a blessing? These questions are still argued as fiercely today as once upon a time. I recommend the impartiality with which the history of Scotland has been presented in this Guide, all the more warmly because I could never have presented it myself with such impartiality.

I draw particular attention to the account of Edinburgh. This will enrich any walk taken by those who are lucky enough to be staying in the city for the Festival. I also draw attention to the account of the New Town of Cumbernauld. More and more New Towns will be rising all over Great Britain in the future; Cumbernauld sets them an enviable example.

For the last thirty years I have been receiving letters from people all over the world asking my advice about proposed visits to Scotland. I am grateful that henceforth I shall be able to reply on a postcard, "Get hold of the *Shell*

Guide to Scotland". Nevertheless, I cannot quite get out of the habit of offering advice, and I must be forgiven if I add a word or two of it here, when I beg those who drive up to spend a fortnight's holiday in Scotland to decide beforehand which part of it they most want to see. They cannot hope to enjoy the Cairngorms, Moray, Deeside, and Braemar to the full if they are set on enjoying Glenmoriston, Glengarry, and Glenlyon in the same fortnight. They cannot ever get the best out of the Borders if they are determined to get the best out of Galloway in the same fortnight.

A very short while ago motorists found it hardly worthwhile moving a car about from island to island of the Outer Hebrides. Today, thanks to bridges between North Uist, Benbecula, and South Uist and to a car-ferry service, a motorist can cover the six islands that make up what is called the Long Island in the time at his disposal. This car-ferry service will be of the greatest benefit to tourists.

Finally, if I am asked what I consider to be the pick of Scotland's scenery, I shall reply (with apologies to Loch Sunart and Moidart, to Arisaig and Morar), "From Gairloch to the isolated bens of Sutherland". Of all the lochs in Scotland, Loch Maree is most often in my mind's eye; of all the bens, Suilven. And, if it should happen to have been wet in the month you chose, the water-lilies in the lochans will make you glad that you did take your holiday then.

COMPTON MACKENZIE

Author's Foreword

No man unaided could, in one year, project a book such as this of well over 300,000 words, containing full historical and geographical essays and two appendices, as well as the 1,250 or more entries in the Gazetteer. I have, of course, leant heavily on many people's detailed and generous assistance.

First, my colleague Mrs Jean Munro, Ph.D. It was she who, with Mr John Kerr, compiled the prospective list of principal entries for the Gazetteer; as the work proceeded we found very little need to emend this list.

Even more valuable was her invention and management of what, in the jargon of our work, we have called the skeletal card system, by which all hard and relevant facts about each principal entry were inscribed on fairly full cards. No matter how well you think you know a place, there are always facts and details needed that will support your knowledge when you come to write about it. All these facts and details, and many others, were supplied by Dr Munro's assiduity while she worked (in a special room kindly placed at our disposal) in that temple of Scottish bibliography, the Scottish Department of the Central Public Library in Edinburgh. Without Mrs Munro and her assistants, the composition and the writing of this book would have been impossible even in four leap years – let alone one.

She also, under her maiden name of authorship (Jean Dunlop), contributed the Appendix on "The Clan and the Tartan". Mr Richard Feachem contributed the brief but vital account of "Prehistoric Scotland".

These my first two colleagues I salute. In saluting them I state that, insofar as my opinions or deductions from fact are expressed in this book, I am alone responsible. Responsible too am I for any errors of fact that may have crept into the text in the speed of composition. If there is any *culpa* it is *mea*; but none, I think and hope, is *maxima*. Moreover, I alone am responsible for the essay "Scotland in History".

The myth of Scottish meanness has long been moribund, but, if anyone was in at the death of it, it was the author of this work. While I claim to have travelled widely and with curiosity in all the shires of the mainland of my native country, and to have visited more of our astonishingly numerous islands than most of my compatriots, there are parts where I lack detailed knowledge – this, I think, would be true of any Scot, however widely travelled, however curious. I cannot express too strongly, then, my gratitude to those of my compatriots who have special knowledge of various districts, and who have come to my assistance. Some of these have offered scrupulous advice and criticism; some indeed have supplied me with written material, which I have edited to conform with the general style.

Let me mention first Mr Cuthbert Graham of Aberdeen. He knows in extraordinary detail that quintessential part of Lowland Scotland, the North-East – that hump of land which sticks out of Scotland south of the Moray Firth. I doubt if any man in the course of his work as a writer on the *Aberdeen Press and Journal*, and as a man who takes his holidays in his own part of the world, has a greater knowledge of our "Nor'-East". This knowledge, together with his enthusiasm and generosity, he has placed at my disposal. I mention Mr Graham first because our "Nor'-East" is the toughest nut of any part of Scotland for the author of a work such as this to crack. Mr Graham cracked it for me with skill and tenderness – the tenderness of a man who not only knows but loves the district. Though much of his valuable material has had to be condensed to meet the proportions of the book, I have endeavoured to keep his style of expression.

No one would call Galloway (that rich south-western portion of Scotland) tough. It does, however, require especially detailed treatment. This, through advice and through the written word, I have received in full measure from Mr A. E. Truckell, the Curator of the Dumfries Burgh Museum. Though I am able to cover many parts of that large and fascinating, but ill-documented, county of Perthshire myself, I also leant heavily and in the same manner on the information supplied by Mrs Margaret Stewart of Perth. Mr R. W. Munro – scholar and journalist, and husband of my chief colleague, Dr Jean Munro – was always ready with advice in the shaping of the "style and usage" of the Gazetteer. He also contributed some entries and was most generous in proof-correcting. Always was I conscious of his assisting presence, as it were, in the background; him too I thank. Mr and Mrs G. S. Burroughs gave expert assistance on certain Border and East Lothian towns.

A writer is liable to become tedious if he goes on at length thanking those who have helped him. In one sweeping gesture, then, I thank all who have come to my aid: the staff of the Central Public Library in Edinburgh; the clergy, whether ministers of the Church of Scotland or Catholic priests; and students who on our behalf and during their vacations have delved for facts and figures. And, to be done with it, I thank nearly a dozen Edinburgh ladies who, in their spare moments and in their homes, have tackled with such cheerfulness and promptness the formidable task of deciphering my handwriting and typing from it accurately in 353 days these more than 300,000 words – indeed, these more than 600,000 words; for, in the interests of thoroughness, everything had to be typed twice.

The admirable *Shell Guide to Ireland* by Lord Killanin and Professor Duignan was in form, if not in style and content, my prototype. Apart from other matters of difference, there was the enormous number of our islands – islands that to varying degrees have entered our history and in our days no less than in the past have attracted the visitor. Scotland, according to Groome's authoritative *Gazetteer*, has no fewer than seven hundred and eighty-seven islands.

It was not possible to mention in detail more than a fraction of these here. I have taken the main groups of islands, and have dealt with the main islands in each division of each group, and have tried to express their group characteristics. At various points, I have referred the reader to my preliminary essay "The Shape of Scotland". In this essay I have discussed not only Scotland's geography but also her ethnic distribution, her languages, and other matters (such as religion) that have sometimes remained with the retention of the old Gaelic tongue. I have rigorously eschewed giving a county the suffix "shire" unless it possesses a town or place within it after which it is named. Thus Argyll is not "Argyllshire", and, even more certainly, Fife is not "Fifeshire".

This book is intended not only to be a guide to Scotland, but also to be a portrait – a portrait whose subject changes in its details while the artist draws. It is thus that I have interpreted my commission to compose the book. It is thus that I have tried to catch the likeness even in its latest phase.

MORAY MCLAREN

Note by the Editor

Throughout the Gazetteer, the heading of each entry begins with the name, in capitals, of the place or other topographical element that forms the subject of the entry. After this we find, in italics, the name of the county to which the subject belongs. The third item gives (in brackets) a reference by which the subject can be located on the maps at the end of the book. The county names are included because two places may have the same name, and the counties will distinguish them; moreover, readers who wish to know the part of Scotland in which the place lies, but without turning to the maps for the exact location, may gain what they need from the name of the county alone.

About the islands, however, a warning must be given. The only groups that have separate county names are these three: Orkney, which is composed of one large island and sixty-six smaller ones, whose inhabitants refer to the large one as their Mainland; Shetland, or Zetland, which has nearly a hundred islands, including the one that, among the others, is again called the Mainland; and Buteshire, which comprises Bute, in the Firth of Clyde, and its neighbouring islands of Arran, Great and Little Cumbrae, Holy Island, Pladda, and Inchmarnock. As a contrast, the Hebrides (which the Gazetteer gives under the names of the individual islands) do not form one county; for administrative reasons, they are included in counties that divide the Scottish mainland. Thus Lewis Island, which makes part of the "Long Island" or Outer Hebrides as a whole, is composed of two islands that are physically joined; the northern one, called simply Lewis, is in the county of Ross and Cromarty, while the southern island, Harris, belongs to Inverness-shire. Where such a situation exists, we hope that inquirers from distant parts of the world will read the entry or look at the map rather than assume, from the county name, that the islands are areas on the Scottish mainland!

A further point is that, while some islands are called islands, others are popularly called isles and still others may be called either. Here, in the headings to entries, every insular piece of land is, for consistency's sake, designated "island"; while, in his descriptions, the author has, of course, been free to give whichever island he thought fit the more romantic and perhaps more common title "isle".

In each entry, the first mention of any place whose name forms the heading of another entry is printed in small capitals. Further mentions of the same name in the first entry are not so printed unless a specific reference is made. For example: if, in any entry, EDINBURGH has been mentioned already, but then a specific reference occurs, "(*see* EDINBURGH)", the name is strengthened with small capitals in this second case as well, and in every other such case later.

Readers who are not Scots may feel puzzled, when they consult the headings in the Gazetteer, by the placing of such a word as Ben (Mount) before the main name, as in "BEN NEVIS", whereas in other cases the positions of the main and of the secondary name are reversed, as in "TWEED, River". The reason for this is that Ben has become so much a part of the name in which it appears, that to transpose the words would create an odd effect, while in cases such as River the secondary

11

word is a description rather than a part of the name, and readers are more likely to look for that name under the main word than under the descriptive one. For those who, seeking the River Tweed, resort to the letter R, we do not include a dummy entry "RIVER TWEED, see TWEED, River", because, not finding what they want under "RIVER", they will know at once that it must be under "TWEED". In cases where the descriptive word forms an indivisible part of the name, as in BRIDGE OF ALLAN (which is not a bridge but a town), the whole name is printed like this.

Our attempt to help the non-Scottish reader by explaining words with which he may not be familiar does not take the form of interrupting the text to offer him such explanations, framed in brackets. If insertions were made – then, for the benefit of anyone who might refer only to a single entry, the explanation would have to follow the word wherever it appeared in various entries; and, to those others who read through several entries that happened to contain the same word, the repeated interruptions by the same gloss would be unwelcome. As an answer to this difficulty, the Author has supplied a Glossary of words that, as used in the text, are not readily comprehensible outside Scotland. Words as well understood as "bairn" for child, and local pronunciations of standard English words (such as "gowf" for golf and "doon" for down), are not included, as their meaning should be obvious from the context. Since, however, many words must after all be explained that are a commonplace for the Scot, the Author should not be held guilty of underrating his compatriots' intelligence: such explanations are given for those persons who, to their present loss, are still not as closely acquainted with the Scottish land and language as we hope this volume will inspire them to become.

Indeed, because this work attempts a standard rarely sought in guide-books, by being not only a manual to give information that the tourist will require, but also a series of essays in the Author's lively style, the question has arisen of how far abbreviations should be used. The principle followed here is that, in the Gazetteer, certain short forms that are customary for that type of work have been adopted, whereas in the Introductions, which are more expressly literary, words have always been spelt out. Even in the Gazetteer, however, shortenings have been reduced to as few as possible. Thus, for geographical directions, south-west becomes SW., but, where the description indicates an area that has some unity founded on tradition or sentiment, the words are again spelt out, so that we have then "the North" and even the "North-West": in a poetic passage, to speak about "a man of the N." would be indeed an anti-climax. Here judgement has not proved easy, and the choice of whether or not to abbreviate has depended, from one instance to another, less on rule than on the feeling of the text. Surface consistency is therefore not to be expected, but we hope that in most cases a middle way has been found, which, while not diverging too far from the letter, has done justice to the spirit where it moves.

Introduction

The Shape of Scotland

To understand Scotland, we must know something not only of its story but also of its shape. It is, incidentally, a fascinating shape, even to look at on the map, and when you get to know it you can understand how it has affected the story of her peoples. While the independent Kingdom of Scotland was establishing itself, it expanded here and contracted there, with results upon its life as a nation. Two examples from two extremes are the Border with England, and the Islands.

The border-line vacillated until after the Wars of Independence; and even then it did not, until the reign of the later native Stuarts, reach the defined position it holds today. The considerable town of Berwick, once by far Scotland's most effective and richest port, changed hands, for instance, no fewer than thirteen times until, in the words of the *Encyclopaedia Britannica*, "it was finally surrendered to England in 1482". It thus achieved the remarkable feat of giving its name to a county (Berwickshire) while slipping out of the county and out of the country in which that county exists.*

There are seven hundred and eighty-seven Scottish islands, scattered widely and at great distances around the mainland, mostly to the west and north. When Alexander III came to the throne, only about a hundred of these were attached – tenuously – to his kingdom. In just over two centuries, the remaining six hundred and seventy-eight had by peaceable agreement joined the Scottish Kingdom. In 1707 they became a part of the British Isles. But they remain Scottish in that the law of Scotland alone presides over them all.

It may well be imagined, then, that the moving southern border and the accession of an enormous number of islands – in which speech, customs, religion, and blood differ – have affected the existence of Scotland.

But it is the mainland, the indubitable mainland of Scotland, that we must consider first. Most visitors will know that the country is usually spoken of as being divided into the Highlands and the Lowlands. True; but the division is not a simple one. The Highlands do not, as is sometimes supposed, just lie to the north and the Lowlands to the south. The real, wavering line of difference stretches from the far north-east to considerably far south-west. Without going into exact geological or other details, it runs thus:

Take a point just east of the middle of the top of Scotland – the coast that runs due east and west facing the North Pole. Take it where the flat county of Caithness joins the mountainous one of Sutherland. Then come southward to the Moray Firth, wander eastwards to take in all Inverness-shire and the eastern bite of Aberdeenshire into Inverness-shire. Take in nearly all Perthshire to just south of

---

* It is interesting to note that *Chambers's Encyclopaedia* avoids the use of the word "finally" about Berwick's surrender. Let us hasten to add that there is in this no hint of a Hitleresque "liberation" of Berwick. But it would be tidier if Berwick could rejoin its county and its country – that is, if its citizens agreed!

Perth. Then swing sharply westwards to Loch Lomond. Set out to sea from the top of Loch Long, at the head of the Firth of Clyde, and take a great swing south-west and north so that you include the Mull of Kintyre and all the Hebrides up to the Butt of Lewis in the farthest Outer Hebrides. Everything west and north of that nor'-east-sou'-west wavering line is the Highlands; everything east and south is the Lowlands. To put it briefly, if crudely, the Lowland–Highland line cuts Scotland from north-east to nearly, but not quite, south-west. The extreme south-west, Galloway, is Lowland.

This is not an exact line; and there are many who would qualify it here and there, geologically, ethnologically, and from personal choice. But it will do.

By its very nature the Highland–Lowland line adds complications for the visitor. Compared with England, Scotland is, with rare exceptions, a hilly and even mountainous country all over. That is to say, there is practically no place in Scotland, including Edinburgh and Glasgow, from which you cannot see hills or even mountains. Why then, in this hilly country, call one part of it the Highlands and the other the Lowlands?

The answer is twofold. Again avoiding geology and other such details, it is true that the hills and mountains in our Highlands are usually higher – and certainly wilder, more "grand" – than those of the Lowlands; they catch the imagination more. The second answer is not about geology or mountains but about people. It was to the north and west of the Highland line and to the Western Isles that the Gaelic-speaking Celts retreated as the Kingdom of Scotland established itself. They did not retreat out of the Kingdom, but within it they did retreat into their own way of living. They left the government of the Kingdom of Scotland, except for those few occasions that will be mentioned in "Scotland in History", to the largely non-Celtic, non-Gaelic-speaking Lowlanders.

Places affect people, and people affect places. It is pointless to speculate on how much the lonely grandeur of Scotland's mountainous north and west affected the highly distinctive Highland character. One can see, however, how the Celts adapted themselves to these circumstances. They did not tend to make towns or cities; they lived in extended communities or clans, held together by family ties and by loyalty to their chiefs, to whom indeed most of them were highly conscious of being related, however remotely.

They lived by cattle-droving, by following their chiefs in war, and by hunting. Agriculture and fisheries were not highly cultivated. The crofting and sea fishing by which those who remain in the remoter parts still live were later developments. They retained their native Gaelic tongue and were lively in speech, thought, and action.

The Christian religion, when it did reach them, was to make a lasting impression on them. The extreme western Highlanders and Islanders are to this day famous for the intensity of their devotion to the purest and most traditional forms of Presbyterianism. It is characteristic, too, of the Highland character that indigenous Catholicism should have been preserved, through and after the Reformation until today, in certain mainland places and in some islands. The Catholicism thus preserved, though remote, has – again characteristically – been kept alive by the people, rather than as in England by the power of potent recusant families.

Much of this Highland human scene has been changed by emigration (*see* "Scotland in History"), by movement to the southern towns, and by other factors. It is surprising, nonetheless, in these days of mass communication and quick

J. L. Rodger

A croft on South Uist

travel, to find how much of it remains. Gaelic is declining; the remote croft is giving way to other forms of habitation. But the true Highlander, on his native ground, remains one of the most courteous and dignified of human beings.

It will not do, however, to claim that courtesy, dignity, and the power of imagination are a monopoly of the Highlanders in Scotland. The Borderers, who are very much of the Lowlands (though their country is certainly hilly enough), are the descendants of the men and women who anonymously, but out of their own life, experience, and speech, composed the deathless Border ballads.

It will be recalled that the Lowlands, beginning in Galloway in the extreme south-west, move north-east through the eastern borders by Berwickshire and thus up Scotland.

As you go northwards along the east side of Scotland and within the true Lowland country, native poetry and the power of imagination declines, as the traditional quality of hard-headedness increases. But a grave, slow courtesy remains. The speech of the Lowlands, from Ayrshire and the deep south-west in Galloway right up to Aberdeenshire, consists of local variations on the old Scots tongue used by Burns and by the great poets in the reign of James IV.

This speech is, of course, modernized and modified, and is strongest in the rural districts, but it remains as a basis even in the big towns and cities amongst the ordinary folk. In Aberdeen it is something more than a basis. The fisherwives on the quay there can, if necessary, switch from the Scots they use among themselves and their families to a Scottishly accented English; but their native speech is a different tongue. It has no affinity with Gaelic – of which ancient language more below, when we come to the Islands. Aberdeenshire in general, with its deep mysterious base of Pictish blood supporting later infusions of Norse, Teutonic, and Flemish mixtures, may be said to contain the essence of one part of Lowland culture.

Skirting round Banff, Moray, and Nairnshire, which are indubitably Lowland, by-passing the debatable lands of Easter Ross and East Sutherland, we come to the least hilly Lowland country in the far north at Caithness. There is a certain amount of agriculture there, and much moorland, and much flatness. The Caithness folk most certainly can be called Lowlanders, but their blood is mostly Norse. They are not of the essence of Lowlandism, as are the people of the more hilly Aberdeenshire.

So much for the mainland. Nothing has been said here of the great industrial belt between Edinburgh and Glasgow, for that cannot be said to conform to the traditional shape of Scotland. Nor have we yet dealt with movements of population deliberately designed, as in the overspill and New Towns policy. Such matters will occur naturally in other portions of this volume.

Leaving the mainland, we come to the apparently vast task of saying something relevant and descriptive about the seven hundred and eighty-seven islands that are so important a part of the shape of Scotland.

It must be stated at once that only about a hundred and thirty-six of these islands can strictly be described as inhabited – inhabited by people who make their living from them, as apart from lighthouse-keepers and others in lonely specific jobs. Nevertheless, these hundred and thirty-six, in the variety of human nature they have produced, have added much to the story of Scotland, and add to its attractions today. Even some of the strictly uninhabited islands play their interesting part in the story and shape of Scotland.

Here we must contract this subject, on which many books have been written, into an even briefer division of the islands as four groups; two of them contain nearly all the islands and are themselves sub-divided. We shall define the differences between these groups and, again, leave details to the Gazetteer.

First there are the Hebrides, in the Atlantic and to the west of the mainland. These are sub-divided into the Outer and Inner Hebrides. As we shall see in "Scotland in History", these joined the Kingdom of Scotland in the reign of Alexander III.

Then there are the Norse islands, sub-divided into the Orkney group and the Shetland group. These accrued to the Scottish throne in 1469 as the dowry of a royal marriage.

Finally – as the last two groups, very far behind in numbers and importance – there are the islands in the Firth of Clyde and those in the Firth of Forth.

In ascending order of importance, or (to save local or insular susceptibilities) in ascending order of fame, we begin with the Forth islands.

These ten are familiar to all Edinburgh citizens, and particularly to Edinburgh children, who regard them as their own. The only one that will catch the eye of a visitor, and will probably do so with force, is the Bass Rock, a noble hump that looms up out of the sea just to the north of the London–Edinburgh road. It is Scotland's first island welcome to the incomer from the south.

The Firth of Clyde – that great waterway of pleasure for all Glasgow – has only seven islands. But, as one of them is Arran, which probably has more devotees than any other island in Britain, it elevates this small collection to the status of a group.

To the north-east of Arran, the Firth of Clyde contains the more boisterously popular island of Bute. By a curious balancing act, it also holds something like a replica of the Bass Rock that stands in the Firth of Forth – from the Clyde rises the great hump of Ailsa Craig.

And now for the two other more famous groups, which contain the seven hundred and seventy-odd other islands. Clearly we have no space here to do more than mention by name the largest or most celebrated of these. Along with some other

Scottish Tourist Board

The Eildon Hills

minor ones, they will be listed in the Gazetteer. It is the quality of these groups, and the nature of those who live on them, that concern us here.

If, in this ascending order of importance, the Northern Islands are taken before the world-famous Hebrides, no apologies are offered to Orcadians and Shetlanders; nor indeed would they expect them. They are a highly individual group that joined Scotland only just over five centuries ago, and still feel different from Scotland – if friendlily different. In either group, what they call the Mainland is the main island. They do not regard the mainland of Scotland as their mainland; they just call it Scotland. They do not care whether they are held to be more or less important than the Scottish islands of the Hebrides.

There are forty-nine islands in Orkney, of which twenty-six are inhabited; and the Mainland of Orkney is by far the largest. Orkney contains rich arable country, and the Orcadians are famous farmers. They are a self-contained and, amongst the upper group of farmers, a prosperous people. They are not seafarers, and they seldom travel. Till the last war, there were some farmers who possessed high-powered motor-cars, and used the aeroplane to fly between their properties in the group, and yet had never been to Scotland. They had therefore never seen a railway train. They had, as it were, jumped over nineteenth-century transport.

The Orcadian is said to be a farmer who has a boat. The Shetlander is a sailor and fisherman who has a croft or small piece of land on the side. There are a hundred and seventeen islands in Shetland, of which nineteen are inhabited. Less obviously prosperous, less down-to-earth than the Orcadians, the seafaring Shetlanders are even more obviously Norse in origin. The nearest big town to Lerwick, their capital (and even more foreign-looking than Kirkwall), is Bergen in Norway. Moreover, though Scottish law rules in Shetland, the Shetlanders have retained the Norse Udal law about rights on the common foreshore between high and low tide. They are a lively, entertaining, and most hospitable people who have a dash of poetry in their make-up.

The Paps of Jura, Inner Hebrides

In both groups of these northern islands, the old Norse language was occasionally spoken till the late eighteenth century. It has left many traces in their speech today.

In both groups there is, at midsummer, an unearthly beauty in the long day that never quite dies; the Shetlanders give it, at midnight, the attractive name of the "simmer dim". You can stand at the tip of Unst, the most northerly Shetland isle, and look out to sea, conscious that you are at the most northern part of British land, and that there is no other land between you and the North Pole.

The Inner and Outer Hebrides divide the remaining large number of Scottish islands between them, with the Inner group possessing slightly the majority.

The Inner Hebrides contain some islands that are internationally known in song, legend, and history. The largest of these famous islands is Skye, striking in scenery, and strongly associated with the more romantic episodes of the '45 and of Prince Charles Edward Stuart's wanderings. A smaller famous island is Iona, which will be referred to in "Scotland in History". It was where St Columba landed in A.D. 563 to missionize Scotland.

Other large islands include Mull, Jura, and Islay. Among a host of smaller islands, there are Rum, Eigg, Canna, Tyree (or Tiree), Coll, and Colonsay. The scenery of the Inner Hebrides in fine summer or autumnal weather is rich in colour, beauty, and prospect – floating, it seems, in a pellucid sea.

If we leave out of practical account St Kilda (now inhabited only by bird-watchers and technicians) and the lonely and extraordinary obtrusion of Rockall, far out in the Atlantic, the long string of islands in the Outer Hebrides is the most westerly portion of Scotland. It begins in the north with the large Isle of Lewis, attached to the separate community – almost calling itself an island on its own – of Harris. South of this there are North Uist, Benbecula, South Uist, Eriskay, and Barra. It would be out of place to mention here the many subsidiary islands in this great outer group.

Those who love the Outer Hebrides love them for their beauty, which is indeed remarkable in its spaciousness of sea and sky and land, with its long stretches of sand in which gold and a silvery-white mingle to greet the long Atlantic rollers. It has, however, a less overwhelming scenic beauty than that of the Inner Isles. Perhaps those who are especially devoted to the Outer Isles think first of the people who live in them; or at least they think, in recollection, of the islands and the islanders together. In the people of the Outer Isles still flourishes the essence of Scottish Celtic Gaeldom.

Gaelic was once spoken as the first, often the only, language all over the region defined above as the Highlands. You may still hear it muttered at street corners in Inverness, Oban, Perth, and other towns. There are Gaelic evening services in many Highland parishes of the mainland. In the Inner Hebrides it rather more than lingers in everyday speech, but it is secondary to English (not Scots), in a particularly pleasing and soft form.

But, in the Outer Isles, more largely and strongly inhabited by indigenous islanders than the Inner Hebrides, Gaelic is still the first language among those who were born and live there.

Throughout the whole length of the Long Island, as this Atlantic stretch of many islands is popularly known in the West Highlands, Gaelic used to be spoken naturally and as the first language everywhere. You will still hear it spoken in bars, crofts, and elsewhere, but in the last decade it has sadly lost ground. When the Vikings, many centuries ago, conquered and colonized the islands, they must have despised the local Celts. But their descendants, whom you may notice by their tall bodies, fair hair, and Scandinavian appearance, speak Gaelic and are deep in the Gaelic way of life. It would be sad indeed if Gaelic should lose this power to assimilate and, in the face of increasing numbers of visitors and growing links with the mainland, ceased to be the natural form of expression of the Outer Islanders.

In many of the Protestant churches of the northern Outer Isles, Gaelic is the first language. In the southern Outer Isles, which have retained Catholicism, the Mass is now in Gaelic, and it is pleasant to think that this is an even older language than the Latin it replaced. In Gaelic, too, are the church notices about funerals, weddings, and parochial get-togethers.

This is, perhaps, the place to pay tribute to the remarkable and exemplary friendliness of the Gaelic-speaking Protestants and Catholics between islands that are of different communions, and on such an island as Benbecula, which is equally divided between Protestantism and Catholicism. Exemplary indeed! It was an example to the rest of the Christian world long before the modern ecumenical movement was heard of.

Scottish Gaelic is closely akin to Irish Gaelic, and shares with it the distinction of being one of the oldest languages in Europe. Most Irish-Gaelic speakers can understand our Gaelic. Irish Gaelic is an official second (or first) language in the Republic of Ireland, but the proportion of indigenous native Gaelic spoken in Scotland is higher.

It is impossible to close the subject of these islanders, in whatever part of the Outer Hebrides and of whatever faith, without paying tribute to the peculiar sweetness of their disposition, varying from grave courtesy to glancing Celtic wit.

Merely to mention these obvious elements in the shape of Scotland, is to do no more than hint at how important that expanding and contracting shape has been to the story of the country, and how important it is to know something of it if we are to understand and enjoy Scotland to the full.

Prehistoric Scotland

Both the start and the finish of prehistory in Scotland are ill-defined. At the beginning, the primal first-footers came in unobtrusively, here and there, over a considerable period, before anything very recognizable in the way of settlement began to show. At the end, history itself is introduced with as much hesitation and intermission. Nevertheless, the prehistoric period, during which the resources of the land were first developed and the character of the people began to take shape, lasted something over three times as long as the historical period till now.

The initial immigration was perhaps even more sporadic than those that were to follow after many years. The first-comers arrived in the western side of the country, settling on sandy shores such as Luce Bay, in Wigtownshire, or the dunes in the neighbourhood of Irvine, in Ayrshire, and at river mouths, notably the River Stinchar in southern Ayrshire. Some elements among these wandering savages came directly from what is now central northern England, others from the same source by way of a sojourn on the east coast of Ulster. They penetrated northwards to such places as Cambeltown Loch, Kilmelfort, Oban, Oronsay, and Risga. The settlers subsisted by hunting and fishing and gathering food, which in those quiet days – possibly as early as the seventh millennium B.C., certainly in the sixth and fifth – must have been plentiful. The fish-spear of bone or antler, and a considerable variety of stone knives, scrapers, hammers, and other tools and implements, together with man-high bows and flint-tipped arrows, carried them from birth to death through the recurrent seasons without starving.

Somewhat in the rear of the penetration of the west, a similar movement from southern Britain and across the North Sea led to the opening up of eastern Scotland. Traces of wandering food-gatherers occur throughout Tweeddale and along the sands of Berwickshire and East Lothian, in Clydesdale and up the River Forth.

The mesolithic dependence on catching and gathering food, without provision for more than the immediate future, may have lasted in Scotland for well over two thousand years. At some time that may have been as early as the last part of the fourth millennium B.C., however, there began a second great immigration, whose effects were to endure for over one thousand years before any considerable modification was introduced.

The word "farmer" is used to describe the people who now began to arrive, even though their practice of the art of husbandry was markedly pastoral rather than agricultural. They introduced pottery into Scotland, as well as new forms of stone tools and implements. The course of the greater part of the immigration is marked by chambered tombs, built to serve succeeding generations and comprising some of the most magnified structures ever raised in Scotland. The distribution of chambered tombs ranges from the north of Shetland to Galloway, and they number more than five hundred. The neolithic immigrants responsible for them arrived along the sheltered sea-route up the west coast of Britain and from Ireland, as well as from western Europe.

Again it was probably somewhat later that the eastern part of Scotland was entered by other neolithic peoples, who are distinguished from their western brethren by the difference in the way they disposed of their dead. Instead of the vault built to be reopened at intervals for new interments, the monument favoured in the east was a long barrow containing a grave in which several individuals were buried and sealed, not to be disturbed again. The eastern immigrants extended their occupancy of the land from Tweeddale to the Moray Firth.

At the beginning of the second millennium B.C., the third important immigration made its effect upon Scotland. To describe the immigration, we may conveniently add the word "beaker", which refers to the characteristic pottery vessel used by the newcomers, although the principal distinction between the customs already established in Scotland and those of the new arrivals lay in the method of disposing of the dead. Whereas, before, the practice of collective burial had been followed both in the chambered tombs and in the long barrows, the beaker-using peoples preferred single burial in a personal stone-lined grave, which may or may not have been covered by a cairn or a barrow.

Beaker-using, or single-grave, immigrants arrived from various directions. On the west, they came up the sea-route already familiar to earlier arrivals; on the south, overland from southern Britain; on the east, both overland and directly across the North Sea from the Low Countries. The changes in ritual practices brought about by the beaker people also included the construction of an important group of works, the "henges". A henge is a setting of upright stones in a circular space defined by a ditch with a bank. Henges occur as far north as Orkney and as far south as Annandale, Dumfriesshire.

After the entry and absorption of the beaker people, there followed a period of one thousand years or more during which no further important immigrations appear to have occurred. Perhaps the most significant change visible in the archaeological record is the return to a form of communal burial. The use of gold and copper and bronze was introduced, though perhaps not extensively. The rock-carvings known as cup-and-ring markings are attributed to the period when prospectors for ores and workers in metals first arrived, possibly from Iberia and Ireland.

Right from the start of human occupation, the remote geographical position of

A Stone Age house at Skara Brae, Orkney

Scottish Tourist Board

Scotland delayed and modified the successive cultures that were introduced. This was to apply once again at the time of the fourth principal prehistoric immigration, which, from the middle of the first millennium B.C., brought representatives of the Celtic peoples into the country and presaged the beginnings of history.

In Scotland, there is no great body of artifacts or relics to indicate that the new arrivals were, at first, really very different from the contemporary natives. But some guidance is given by various finds, and a perfectly valid explanation has been worked out from these and other sources in relation to the arrival of people, if not just of goods and ideas, from outside. Quite apart from the relics, however, there are many structural remains bearing witness to a massive immigration that eventually built up Celtic Scotland, by the end of the prehistoric period, to the country that later saw the arrival and departure of the Roman forces and the beginnings of Christianity.

The important series of timber structures, both houses and protected settlements, that are thought to represent the works of the earliest Celtic immigrants, at least in the southern part of Scotland, were followed by settlements with stone walls or ramparts and ditches, and it is among these that some of the mightiest relics of Celtic immigration are preserved. Usually called hill-forts or camps, the protected settlements are so numerous that the majority must represent the strongholds of expanded families or small communities, which may have been led by a pastoralist individual of patriarchal, or baronial, status. The few large examples – particularly the two largest, one on Traprain Law in East Lothian and the other on Eildon Hill North, in Roxburghshire, both eventually extending to forty acres – were probably developed late in the period.

In the south and east of Scotland, protected settlements were the rule. In the north and west, the dwellings of individual families predominate. These fall into two principal categories – duns and brochs. A dun is a thick-walled compound to whose safety a large family could retire during times of stress or in the winter. A broch is a circular house with a thick stone wall built in the form of two concentric skins, joined by transverse slabs. The most famous broch, at Mousa, off the main Shetland isle, still stands to a height of more than forty feet.

As the first millennium B.C. drew to a close, the distinction between the two principal Celtic peoples in Scotland became recognized. North of the Forth–Clyde isthmus there were the Picts, a conglomeration of immigrants using the Pictish variety of the Celtic language. South of the Forth–Clyde line there were the Britons, speaking the Brittonic version of the Celtic language. Among these last, one tribe was the Gododdin. Their capital, Din Eidyn, became eventually the capital of Scotland.

Prehistory into History

"They make a desert and they call it peace." This is a famous saying; yet few who are familiar with it realize that, in its original Latin form (*solitudinem faciunt pacem appellant*), it is the end of a ferociously defiant speech put by the Roman historian Tacitus into the mouth of the Pictish chieftain Calgacus, the first native whose name has come down to us of what we now call Scotland.

Calgacus was speaking of the imperial Roman troops who, close on two thousand years ago, were campaigning in Pictland, or Alba – present-day Scotland north of the Forth–Clyde isthmus. He could scarcely have entered history, and in entering it have raised the curtain on the history of his own country, with a more resounding remark. Like many sentences of its kind, it has stood the test of time; it has certainly stood that test in Scotland. It is, to take but two examples, most applicable to the story of Scotland when the armies of Edward I of England were, in the name of unity and peace, ravaging the land north of Tweed; it is applicable to the mountainous and island parts of our country in the ninteenth century when the Highland Clearances were denuding Celtic Scotland of her manpower.

Calgacus was defeated and killed; but the objectives for which he and his tribes fought successfully survived his death. He and the Pictish men who fought under him at Mons Graupius, not far from the mouth of the Spey, quite simply did not wish to become a part of the great and often beneficent machinery of the Roman Empire. At this time, fifty years before the building of Hadrian's Wall from Tyne to Solway, and seventy years before the northern *limes*, the Antonine Wall, was constructed from Forth to Clyde, no Pictish tribesmen had seen anything of the benefits or the hardships brought by the establishment of Roman rule to the Celtic British people farther south. But the Picts had doubtless heard of what was going on, may even have received reports of the heroism of Boudicca and her Iceni in A.D. 61; and they fought to keep the Romans from advancing. In due course the withdrawal of the Romans for service elsewhere left them free.

"Free"! They became aggressive. At the end of the second century the Picts made a great raid, or series of raids, southwards, sweeping through the Lowlands and through Hadrian's Wall in an overwhelming torrent, bringing death and destruction to garrisons and settlements alike. In A.D. 209, however, the Emperor Severus and his sons Caracalla and Geta launched a formidable punitive expedition northwards, and the Picts, represented by the Caledonii and the Maeatae of Perth and Angus, were saved from extermination only by the death of Severus in York in A.D. 211. Thereafter the Romans abandoned the costly occupation of the land between the walls, and substituted instead a system of strong patrols working in cooperation with the Lowland British chieftains. In this way peace was established south of the Antonine Wall for ninety years, and at the end of the fourth century the patrols were withdrawn, and the whole responsibility for keeping out the Picts was transferred to the native Celtic rulers.

If you consult the Oxford English Dictionary for a definition of the word "Scot", you will see: "A Gaelic tribe that migrated from Ireland to Scotland about the sixth century". And this indeed is the truth. It is from this tribe that Scotland received in the coming centuries her name.

In the sixth century there was a migration of Gaels from northern Ireland into the islands and mainland of what is now Argyll; some of them penetrated even farther up the "Great Glen" – that major division of Scotland which contains Loch Ness. The Caledonia that they partly penetrated was not a united country but a land loosely held by Pictish kings, by British tribes speaking a language similar to modern Welsh, and by Angles from northern England and the Germanies. Save for the sporadic if heroic missionary efforts of St Ninian and St Kentigern, it was an almost entirely heathen land. It lacked cohesion; and the incoming Irish Celts would have been unlikely to have given any form to it, less still a name that would endure, had it not been for the arrival a few years later of their remarkable compatriot, St Columba.

It was in A.D. 563 that St Columba, either because he wanted more living-room for his energy, or because he found his native island of Ireland too hot to hold

him, set sail with a band of clerical followers to Dalraida (Argyll) in Scotland. He
first set foot on what is now Scottish soil at an island just off the south-western
coast of Mull. Here he founded his community and built his humble monastic
institution; the abbey was to follow, as the island grew more famous. The name of
this small island has remained celebrated and venerated throughout the centuries.

In his account of his famous journey through the Highlands and Islands of
Scotland in 1773, Dr Samuel Johnson had this to say: "That man is little to be
envied whose patriotism would not gain force upon the plain of Marathon, or
whose piety would not grow warmer among the ruins of Iona". This is still true.

Not only Christian piety but also Scottish patriotism warms among the reconstructed and rebuilt ruins of Iona. It was from this remote western island that
there was eventually to spring the unification of the nation of Scotland. That
unification was to come first under Irish Celtic leadership, and then to merge into
a non-racial concept of nationality. But we owe the name of our land and that
concept of nationality (not only in name, but in the movement of history) to an
Irish Christian tribe in general and to St Columba in particular.

St Columba, the fiery-hearted yet humble Christian Gael, died in A.D. 597. He is
said, in the act of dying, to have blessed the island of Iona and to have prophesied
that it would be the source of the Scots' great future as the rulers of the land.

His prophecy was to come true, though perhaps not in the way he had foreseen,
and after many tribulations that were mercifully hidden from his dying eyes.

The most terrible of these tribulations were the Norse invasions and depredations.
As these Norse invasions afflicted not only the whole island of Britain but also
Ireland and much of Continental Europe, there is no need to chronicle them in
detail in Scotland, save to note two facts. The first is that many Norsemen – not
content with hit, wound, kill, burn, and run tactics – settled down in parts of
Scotland, particularly in the islands and on the east coast. Over the centuries, they
have been utterly absorbed into the racial mixture of Scotland, but you may trace
the legacy of their arrival in Scotland in the physiognomy and bodily structure of
many inhabitants of the land today.

The second important result of the Norse invasion of north Britain was the
dispersal, dissolution, and – for all practical purposes – disappearance of the Picts
from the Scottish scene. The history (insofar as it can be called history), and the
legacy in our blood, of this mysterious people who were for so long the most
important tribe in north Britain, belongs more properly to the chapter "Prehistoric
Scotland".

History Begins

Let it suffice here to say, in a historical context, that in A.D. 839 the Pictish people,
whose tenure of the land of North Britain had been growing more and more feeble,
were utterly defeated and, it was believed at the time, exterminated by the raiding
Norsemen. Their kingdom was taken over by the Gaelic Kenneth MacAlpine, who
became by this twist of history king of all the tribes in Scotland. His control of
Scotland was tenuous and vague, but it marked the first stage in the unification of
Scotland.

It did not become a fully recognized unit within the comity of European nations
in Christendom (and, equally important, it did not become internally conscious of
being a unified nation composed of a number of racial origins) until three centuries

later, when the great and wise King Alexander III ruled. That beneficent monarch was, however, a direct descendent of Kenneth MacAlpine; and Scotland would never have been Scotland had not King Kenneth seized his opportunity for Gaelicizing the land north of the River Forth at the defeat and disappearance of the Picts in A.D. 839.

The history of Scotland as it can be perceived in the form of a true nation, as it can be grasped and appreciated by the Scot or the incomer of today, begins with Alexander III in the thirteenth century. An enormously important event, however, in south Britain, so soon to be unified under the name of England, was to make its effect felt on Scotland before Alexander's reign. That event was the Norman Conquest. The Normans, save for the ruthless occupation of Edward I before the Wars of Independence, never conquered Scotland by the sword; but their presence in the southern part of the island had a strong effect on their northern neighbours.

The first effect was the introduction of the tongue we now call Scots into an exclusively Gaelic kingdom. This resulted when some northern Englishmen fled from the Normans into an unconquered territory. They brought with them a form of English that was to be transformed into one of the national languages of Scotland, a language that was eventually to be the vehicle of the great poetic renaissance under James IV expressed by Dunbar, Gavin Douglas, and others. On its incoming, however, it was called "Inglis". "Scots", to the true Scot of the period, was Gaelic.

The second effect on Scotland of the Norman Conquest in the south was the arrival of the Princess Margaret, from the royal and rightful Anglo-Saxon house that had been defeated at the Battle of Hastings and expelled from what was now known as England.

Margaret was a princess of beauty, piety, and strong determination. When Malcolm III (known familiarly by the Gaelic appellation of Malcolm Canmore), a Celtic descendant of the Kenneth MacAlpine line, took her to be his queen, he was animated by the chivalrous intention of protecting a royal maiden in distress. Her beauty, and her appealing character, soon turned this chivalrous intention into genuine love. Love and respect inspired him to give his wife complete freedom in the reform of the Celtic Church, which, since Columba's death, had retreated into the local usage that had helped to cut it off from the rest of Christendom.

It was Queen Margaret (later to be canonized) who reformed the half-isolated early Scottish Church by bringing it into line with the Church Universal. There are still those today who blame Margaret, saint and queen, for anglicizing the Celtic Church of Scotland. Another and larger point of view is that she was animating her husband's kingdom with the new religious zeal that, during the eleventh and twelfth centuries, was beginning to make itself manifest on the Continent of Europe and all over Christendom after the grim period of the Dark Ages.

Queen Margaret may have been an English princess in origin, but she was the first and most potent agent to make Scotland a true unit within the great structure of the Christian Church, as it was then universally accepted.

Her husband and eldest son were slain in battle during an invasion of northern England. The news of their death broke the heart and took the life of the Queen. In 1092 she died at Edinburgh Castle, where the chapel she caused to be built may still be seen. Her body was transferred by night to the new church she had built at Dunfermline. It is a place of pilgrimage to this day.

Malcolm may have been killed in battle across the border in England, Margaret may have perished with (in her own view) her work half done. But this is to misjudge the movement of events.

In Malcolm's second son Edgar, the next king, the succession from the Scottish and Gaelic Kenneth MacAlpine was maintained, and, in religion, Margaret's work continued. Scotland remained within Christendom, and in so doing was to strengthen her claims in the future for a loyal independence within that Christendom.

The immediate effect that the patriotic Scot of today finds most unpleasing to recall is the bloodless conquest of southern Scotland by Norman influence and control. If "conquest" be too distressing a word, none can conscientiously object to the phrase "powerful infiltration". By the beginning of the twelfth century southern Britain had, for all practical purposes, been united by Norman conquest and bore the name of England; but this was not the situation that existed north of the still not fully defined line between England and Scotland.

Before the Norman arrival on British shores, Scotland had been called the "Kingdom of Scotland". It was the unspecified aim of the Anglo-Normans to overcome north Britain and make it a part of the Norman Conquest. That they failed in this object is due to various causes, including the geography of the land and the spirit of Calgacus that survived in his Celtic successors. The Anglo-Normans never ceased, however, to try to influence Scotland with the object of making her but a province of a power seated primarily in northern France or in southern England.

They failed, and for a long time their failure persisted. Many centuries were to pass until, in 1707, they succeeded in making Scotland a province not of England but of Britain, and a Britain whose governance, let it be remembered, is conducted on the banks of the Thames in southern England. The seeds of this Anglo-Norman success were laid during and after the reign of Malcolm III and his saintly Queen Margaret.

The first tactic in the Norman attempt on Scotland was when William the Conqueror came north in peaceable style for a truly extraordinary meeting with Malcolm III, King of Scots, at Abernethy in Perthshire. Here Malcolm went through the purely diplomatic, and militarily meaningless, act of paying homage to William. The implications of this act were by both sides left deliberately vague, but it was an act that was to bedevil Scottish-English relations for centuries.

The very vagueness of the friendly relations between the two countries did allow a strong, peaceful Norman infiltration into Scotland. It was an infiltration much encouraged by David I, the youngest son of Malcolm III. David had in youth held lands in England, had had his education there, and was ambitious to lend to his country the fruits of southern civilization. He was also a genuinely pious Christian monarch who wished to carry on his mother's work in making the Church in Scotland a truly integral part of the Church Universal.

An admirable intention, no doubt. But the possession of these qualities by David King of Scots produced not only the establishment of well-regulated episcopal sees and the founding of monasteries in the continental manner; it did something more. Following the ecclesiastics from the south came many Norman barons, friendly in intention but land-hungry. Scotland offered them an opportunity for satisfying this appetite.

The largely Celtic Kingdom of Scotland to which Malcolm III had succeeded was, like all its Celtic counterparts, a land in which towns and cities did not spring up naturally. Through the centuries (if one may permit oneself to generalize), urbanization has been repugnant to the Celtic character. Into this diffuse country, lacking civic centres, the Normans came, not only establishing episcopal sees and building cathedrals and monasteries, but planting baronial castles as far as they could all over central and southern Scotland. They did this with the royal approval of a king descended from the Celtic Kenneth MacAlpine.

Their success was such that, racially speaking, they may be said to have set up the first Establishment within the Kingdom of Scotland. Their influence penetrated everywhere, but always at an Establishment level. By the time that Alexander III, the patriot King of a truly unified Scotland, had ascended the throne just under a century after the death of David I, Norman French was the language of the Court and of all the nobility and clergy south of the mountainous and Celtic parts of Scotland. Latin was the language of the Church and of the Law.

However Celtically inclined the modern Scottish patriot may be, it will not do for him to dismiss these Norman incomers purely as foreign usurpers. Scotland, as she was to do with a number of other incomers, was to absorb her Normans into the concept of Scotland.

The truth of this may be observed by recalling the names of the Scottish patriots, and of those who led Scottish troops and fought for Scotland, from the Wars of Independence against Edward I of England down to the overwhelming disaster of Flodden in 1513. Let one name, and the greatest of all, stand alone – Robert Bruce. He is the supreme example of, and justification for, the fact that Scotland was to absorb into the concept of her kingdom the Normans who began infiltrating in such strength under David I.

It is to Alexander III, however, and before Bruce that we now move directly, one century after David I.

The Kingdom of Scotland Established

The reign of Alexander III was, above all other things, a lengthy period of internal and external peace and of national hope. It was the foundation not only of the Kingdom of Scotland, but of the nation of Scotland that existed in fact until the Union of England and Scotland five centuries later, and that, in a less definable form, exists in the hearts and minds of many Scots today.

There is a case to be made for the view that our history emerged from prehistory with the immortal words said to have come from Calgacus. You may say with truth that Christian Scotland established herself as a result of St Columba's arrival at Iona, and you would be correct in claiming the foundation of Gaelic Scotland with Kenneth MacAlpine's victory over the Picts. It is also true that the modern nation of Scotland began with Alexander. It is, moreover, highly doubtful whether that nation would have appeared so clearly and definably in the European scene had it not been for the wise and benevolent personality of Alexander.

Even as a boy he resisted the wily attempts of King Henry III of England to induce him to pay homage for the Kingdom of Scotland. As a man of partly Norman blood, he was ready to pay homage for the lands he held in England; but Scotland was to be free and independent. Henry was insidious, but no man of action. His successor, the great Edward I of England, was most certainly a man of action, as he would prove after Alexander's death when he earned the name of the "Hammer of the Scots". Even Edward, however, was held firmly at bay by Alexander's policy.

It was not, at the beginning, a period of peace between Scotland and the powerful Kingdom of Norway. The Norse king maintained as the outposts of his empire all the Scottish Hebrides (*see* "The Shape of Scotland"). This was an intolerable state of affairs that Alexander tried to settle by diplomacy. When diplomacy failed, the Norse king Haakon set sail, with the largest fleet that had ever left Norway, to settle the Hebridean question by attacking the Scottish mainland.

It is sufficient to say here that, at the Battle of Largs, Alexander defeated the mighty Norse warrior by a notable blend of strategy and tactics. He lured Haakon's fleet far from its bases. He induced it to come up into the trap of the Firth of Clyde. He held off action until the inevitable equinoctial gales had forced much of Haakon's fleet on shore by Largs. He then forced the gallant but defeated old King Haakon back to sea, and back to his base in Orkney, where he died.

The Battle of Largs was an early and remarkable example of Scottish tactics and strategy – "Get the enemy on to your own ground in unfavourable conditions and tackle him where you want him to be. Never go out to meet him on his ground". This strategy was, as we shall see, to be renewed at Bannockburn.

After this decisive and resounding victory – in which, be it repeated, little blood was wantonly shed – Alexander came to terms with Haakon's son and successor. The Hebrides were ceded to Alexander's kingdom. The result was that, with the exception of the Norse Isles of Orkney and Shetland, which were to follow later, the Kingdom of Scotland assumed that shape which it was to hold for centuries.

Alexander III was known even in his lifetime, and by those who looked back on his reign after his death, as the "peaceable king". Certainly the benefits of peace began to show themselves almost for the first time since Scotland had become a recognized kingdom. No great cities or towns sprang up in this land still of Celtic background; but the burghs, where commerce and trade flourished, established themselves usually at points of geographical advantage. These burghs, which are still an integral part of Scotland's life, could never have flourished in a period of internal or external strife. Architecture in church, cathedral, and monastic building, as begun under David I, flourished. Literature, from some small gleams that survive, showed that the arts were to benefit by this reign of peace.

Peaceable though he was, King Alexander was firm not only in his relations with foreign potentates and ecclesiastics, but with the magnates of his own realm. He early perceived that the internal strife of ambitious nobles was one of Scotland's endemic evils. He enforced order amongst them without bloodshed. Nor would he suffer the common people to be idle and disputatious. More and more land came under cultivation. "If a man owned but a single ox," wrote a later chronicler, "the law bade him take land and plough it." Alexander believed that the Scots, as a later Frenchman was to put it, should "cultivate their own gardens". He had no lust for foreign conquests, and he discouraged this amongst his people.

The greatest result of this peaceable yet firm reign was an attitude of mind amongst the varying peoples of Alexander's kingdom. It was, for the future of Scotland the nation, a most important attitude of mind. "For the first time," as one of the more concise and reliable of our historians has said, "the Norman baron, the bishop who knew more Latin and French than English, the English-speaking (or, as we would now put it, the Old-Scots-speaking) traders of Fife and Lothian, the Gaelic-speaking herdsmen from the hills, began to look upon themselves as Scotsmen . . . they were no longer a collection of odds and ends; they had become a nation." At the centre of this nation, almost incarnating it, was King Alexander. All was set fair – and then suddenly, as so often happens in the affairs of men, particularly in Scotland, disaster struck.

Alexander's three children died in youth; the Prince and heir had married without issue; the Princess Margaret, who had married into the Royal House of Norway, left behind her only one baby girl; and this frail link in the royal line of Alexander was at her father's court over the seas in Norway. The succession was in peril. But all was not yet lost. The widowed Alexander married Joleta, daughter of the French Count of Dreux. The King was only in his mid-forties; and a man at that age is still virile enough to beget a second and healthy family.

But it was not to be. On the night of 19th of March 1286, Alexander attended a not very important council in the "Castle of the Maidens", which was what Edinburgh Castle was then called. At the end of it, the King, despite the urgent entreaties of his nobles and counsellors, suddenly set out in the tempest and the black night to "visit" his but newly-married and, as we now know, still unpregnant queen across the Firth of Forth at Dunfermline in the Royal Palace.

Somehow Alexander, with but three attendants, came down from the Castle Rock; somehow he managed, despite the warnings of the ferry-master, to get across the raging Firth of Forth, but somehow, somewhere between the Fife shore and the Palace of Dunfermline, where his queen lay, the relentless storm had its will of him. His horse stumbled and fell by the seashore. In the morning, his attendants, who had been separated from him in the darkness, found him dead. The rich seed of his kingly line had died unfruitful within him. The eve of Scotland's greatest disaster had begun.

The Wars of Independence

Scotland's new-found unity, it now seemed, depended on the fragile link of a little girl of three years old in Norway, Alexander's granddaughter. The nobles of Scotland did, however, agree to support her claim and did consent to her betrothal to the son and heir of Edward I of England – that son and heir who was to become Edward II and who was to meet Bruce at Bannockburn. This agreement, for what it was worth, and for what might have come of it, disappeared into one of the "if onlys" of history. The little Princess Margaret died on her journey to Scotland. The land was thrown into confusion, and Edward of England was quick to seize his new opportunity.

That opportunity lay precisely in the evil that Alexander had perceived to be endemic in his kingdom – the rivalry of ambitious nobles, all with some claims of varying degrees of remoteness to the throne of Kenneth MacAlpine. Scotland's disunity in high places gave Edward his chance. That disunity, however, when hammered at with such vigour and ruthlessness by the English king, was to produce, by paradox, the "Wars of Scottish Independence". The tale of those wars is amongst the most dramatic in European medieval history. They are dramatic not only in the fact of a nation's rebirth in what must have seemed almost impossible circumstances, but they are dramatic in the personalities involved.

Edward, the great warrior king; William Wallace, the people's hero, the near-liberator, who in the end failed, was betrayed, and was hideously done to death; and finally Robert Bruce, the scheming, apparently self-seeking, politically-minded young noble who, by the alchemy of his folly, his sufferings, his large endeavours and great ultimate achievement, was to become before he died the type of the "patriot king" – these are indeed the *dramatis personae* of history.

When news came that the little Princess Margaret, the last lawful heir of Alexander, had died, there were no fewer than twelve claimants, some by extremely remote succession, to the Scottish throne. These contentious nobles had just enough sense to decide against trying to settle the matter by civil war. They had just enough guilelessness to invite Edward, King of England, and the man who might have been the father-in-law of their queen, to arbitrate amongst them. Upon Edward's acceptance, each of these ambitious claimants had just enough short-sighted folly to agree to Edward's terms. Those were that whoever was rewarded by Edward's decision in his favour should acknowledge Edward as his overlord and do homage, not only for any lands he might hold in England, but for the whole of the Kingdom of Scotland.

At one stroke, it seemed that this competition in ignoble ambition had undone all the work of Alexander III. Yet it was from this muddle of young and old con-temptibles that the Patriot King was eventually to emerge and that Scotland was to be reborn.

Edward, in his court of decision held near the Scottish frontier, was most pains-taking and scrupulous. He examined each claim minutely, and eventually he chose the man whom the legal experts decided was most favourably placed. From Edward's point of view, too, the character and psychology of the successful claimant could not have been more suitable. He was John Balliol, a simple syco-phant whom his Scottish subjects were soon to give the nickname of the "Toom Tabard" or empty coat of arms, or, in a more modern phrase, "a king of shreds and patches".

To Edward it must have seemed that, by securing the appointment of this docile figure, he had conquered Scotland without striking a blow. After a number of humiliating cracks of the overlord's whip, Edward went too far even for Balliol; he summoned his vassal to accompany him on the invasion of France. Balliol not only refused, but entered into an alliance with the French King Philip, thus tentatively beginning the long association between Scotland and France.

Edward's angry disgust knew no bounds. The worm had turned and must be crushed. He marched north, sacked and destroyed Berwick, the richest and most powerful of the Scottish burghs. Thence he went forward into a disunited and impotent Scotland. His subjugation of the country was partly a triumphant procession, partly a contemptuous display of disciplined force, and partly a raiding expedition. He returned to London, bringing with him the celebrated Stone of Scone, on which all Scottish kings had been crowned, and many of the most important Scottish state papers. Balliol was now finished. The remainder of the contending nobles in central Scotland had sworn fealty to Edward at Berwick. As far as the Establishment was concerned, Scotland was prostrate.

She was ignominiously prostrate, but not dead. The first signs that she still lived, the first gleams of her future salvation, came very much not from the estab-lished and now subservient nobles, but from a patriot whom future generations, with a slight exaggeration, were to describe as the "kinless loon". William Wallace was not ignobly born, but he was not of the obviously upper classes and most certainly not one of those who had contended for power after Alexander's death. Equally certain, when in 1292 he "lifted up his head", slew the English Sheriff of Lanark, and gathered a small band of patriots about him to attack the English-held castles, it was in the name of the people of Scotland that he spoke, acted, and fought.

The people of Scotland commanded by an unknown guerrilla leader must have seemed an easy opposition for the English "Guardian of Scotland", Earl de Warenne, to overcome. He marched his considerable force to Stirling to crush Wallace's insolence once and for all. By a skilful tactical manœuvre, however, Wallace succeeded in cutting the English forces in two as they were crossing Stirling Bridge, and in destroying them completely.

The victory of Stirling Bridge made Wallace the master of southern Scotland, and briefly he became the true Scottish Guardian of Scotland. His tenure of the guardianship was indeed brief. Characteristically, but to their eternal disgrace, the Scottish nobles would have little or nothing to do with the people's hero. Moreover, even if the Scottish upper classes would not take him seriously, the warrior King of England had enough perspicacity to do so. In 1298, he marched into Scotland with a formidable force and defeated Wallace utterly at Falkirk.

From then, until his death in 1305, Wallace retreats, as far as history is concerned, into a mysterious, elusive, and indeed myth-like figure. As a hunted outlaw, he moved amongst humble Scottish patriots, while Edward continued his work in paying out Scotland for the crime of having bred Wallace. If, after the first triumphant procession in 1296, Scotland's Establishment had fallen prostrate, it now seemed that the spirit of the country itself was breaking in all hearts.

To all appearances, it broke utterly when in 1305 the hunted Wallace was betrayed and captured. Edward took him to Westminster, subjected him to a staged trial, condemned him to a form of death that was a mixture of vivisection and butchery, then executed him, and finally sent the portions of his dismembered body to be displayed in various parts of Scotland as a warning to all who would defy the English King.

William Wallace was, and remains, the people's hero. Alas! we who come after him know little of him save in his hour of glory, his hour of defeat, and the dreadful hours of his heroically borne end. With emotion, we salute his memory, his temporary success, his failure, and his death. In doing so, we pass on to another Scottish hero, who, at the beginning, was far less true in his motives, far more self-seeking, far more complex a character, yet who was to succeed where Wallace failed, and to achieve the impossible – the restoration of the Kingdom of Scotland that had been founded by Alexander III.

In 1305, and immediately after the death of Wallace, there were not many among his official Scottish supporters whom Edward took more for granted than the still comparatively young Robert de Brus, Earl of Carrick. We now know him simply as Robert Bruce, but, before he achieved that name in history, he was just an Anglo-Scottish-Norman with lands in England and, by heredity, possessing (amidst all the muddle that went with it) a fair claim to the Scottish throne.

Then, in 1305, events began to move that shaped not only the destiny of this man of just thirty-one, but the destiny of the nation of Scotland. Many of these events or movements in men's minds are now mysterious to us, for we do not know enough about them, only in what direction they were going.

First there can be little doubt that Bruce, though attendant upon Edward's court in London, had allowed his mind to stray northwards to Scotland. He was drawn partly by family ambition, partly by reason of mysterious negotiations with his most important rival in the confusion of claims, John Comyn, familiarly known

as the Red Comyn. Finally it appears that Edward was beginning to grow
suspicious of Bruce. Bruce was privately informed of these suspicions, and rode off
at once for Scotland in speed and in secrecy to meet his rival at Dumfries; but it
was no expedition of patriotism.

At Dumfries, Bruce met the Red Comyn by arrangement in the Franciscan
church. No one knows exactly what happened, save that a dispute arose and that
Bruce stabbed Comyn, who died immediately or soon afterwards. Did Comyn
provoke Bruce by evidence of double-dealing, or did Bruce wantonly lose his temper
and all sense of discretion? It does not matter. The only thing that concerns us is
the result.

Bruce emerged half-dazed from the church. He suddenly realized what he had
done. He had killed his most powerful rival and made blood enemies of half the
greatest families in Scotland. He had done more, and that more was dreadful. By
killing his foe in sanctuary and before the Blessed Sacrament at the high altar, he
had committed the sin and crime most abhorred in the Middle Ages – sacrilege.
At one blow, it seemed, he had utterly destroyed Scottish liberty insofar as it
existed amongst the nobles of power left in the land. To add to this, he must have
realized that his act of sacrilege, even if it had been no more than a plunge, desperate
and provoked, had made him an outlaw.

What did he do? On the advice of his impetuous brother, Edward Bruce, he at
once made his way to Scone, and, with maimed rites, had himself crowned King of
Scots in that historic place. By this apparently fantastic defiance of destiny, he now
added Edward and the whole realm of England to the half of the ruling caste of
Scotland as his enemies. On whom did he rely? On a few disaffected Scottish nobles
and perhaps (only just perhaps) those crushed people of the land who, as a legacy
from Wallace, still held the idea of Scotland in their hearts. Angry though Edward
was when the news reached him, he was as much amused as furious. "King Hob"
(as he nicknamed him) must be crushed, immediately – and it looked like an easier
job than catching the elusive Wallace.

Dr Samuel Johnson, we know, once described patriotism as the "last refuge of a
scoundrel". If it be objected that "scoundrel" is too strong a word for Bruce at
Dumfries, it must be admitted that he was at that time a complex character,
compounded largely of personal ambition and wavering duplicity, who had
by an act of reckless folly left himself only two refuges – complete flight
abroad, or patriotism. He chose patriotism, and hurled himself upon the cause of
Scotland.

None at this distance can gauge his motives at the beginning. What we can do is
to follow with fascination the course of his expiation and success. Having chosen
patriotism as the last refuge, it became in the end his prime and most dedicated
object. His character, through suffering and arduous endeavour, changed, simpli-
fied, and became dedicated.

For the next seven years (that is, until the significant date 1314), he gave himself
to the unification of Scotland by two means: first, in a guerrilla war against the
occupying English; second, in an open war upon the great Scottish families who
were opposed to him. In both he was successful. His great and formidable foe,
Edward I, died while endeavouring to lead a crushing force against him in 1307.
Thereafter, faced by the lesser determination of Edward II, he was able to bring
his war against the occupying power more into the open. By 1312 there were only
a few castles left in English hands; of these strongholds, Stirling was the most

The statue of Robert Bruce at Bannockburn

important. By this date, too, Bruce had by open warfare reduced internal Scottish opposition to negligible and remotely placed outposts. On the eve of Bannockburn he was, though the fact was not recognized outside Scotland, master of the Scotland that had been ruled over by Alexander III.

This astonishing feat, in the face of repeated disaster, which would have crushed any other man who was not in the process of thus dedicating himself, he had accomplished by three means. First, he had discovered that he was a born leader of men. Second, he had proved that he had an intuitive knowledge of the art of war, whether guerrilla or open. Third, he was winning the hearts of the people of Scotland. In achieving this last, he purified his own heart of duplicity and mere personal ambition.

He won the hearts of the people of Scotland by his outstanding personal heroism. In attack, he was always at the front; when retreat was forced upon him, he guarded the rear of his men. He won many hearts by his readiness to share the sufferings of the humblest of all his followers. King he had been proclaimed, but he would never ask the poorest soldier to endure any privation that he would not share with him.

Finally, and to put it crudely, he got things done; he was successful. In the minds of those who could recall the earlier leader, nothing could drive out the memory of one who had been much more like themselves, William Wallace; nothing could quench their devotion to that selfless patriot. But Robert Bruce, the Norman-Scottish noble of royal blood, had one quality which even the people's hero had lacked. Having repelled disaster again and again, he was continuously and growingly successful. He proved himself a victor no less than a hero.

Bruce had made himself master of Scotland, but knew that more than internal mastery was essential; he must be recognized as master from outside Scotland. And in that recognition there would lie something greater, more important: the recognition of the nation, the Kingdom of Scotland. How was this to be achieved? He may have been pondering on this question when in 1313 his impetuous brother, Edward Bruce, who had been given the task of subduing the one important English-held castle, Stirling, characteristically forced Robert Bruce's hand and threw the Kingdom of Scotland upon a huge act of self-defence.

Edward Bruce, unable to reduce Stirling by attack, wearied of the task of starving the garrison by siege. Such sit-down tactics did not appeal to him. He therefore concluded an agreement with the governor of the castle, sanctioned by the laws and customs of medieval chivalry. It was this. Should the castle not be relieved by an English force by St John the Baptist's Day (Midsummer Day) of the next year, 1314, the governor would surrender his fortress to the Scots.

When Robert Bruce heard of the agreement, he was at first much put out. In vigorous words he pointed out to his brother that Edward II *must* reply to this challenge to relieve so important an outpost of England's power. Even if only to save face, he must act, and act with all strength. At long last, by this reckless invitation, the whole force of England's arms, added to by possessions in France, Wales, and Ireland, would be launched against Scotland. This really was inviting the worst.

But when Edward Bruce said in effect (as we should put it), "Let them all come – we can take on the lot of them on our own ground", Robert's heart suddenly warmed to him. It was one of Bruce's cardinal maxims in life to "tak the ure that God wald send" (to seize each hour or opportunity of destiny thrust upon him by God). He took the flame of that hour from his brother's rash action and impetuous words; but, unlike his brother, he neither acted nor spoke impetuously.

Through the months of winter and spring, he prepared himself and all his men from all quarters of the land for the Midsummer Day that would decide the fate of Scotland and of himself as her king.

In June 1314, Edward led his splendid army of a little over 20,000 men into Scotland. He was richly served in cavalry, wherein lay his main strength. The cavalry was supported by archers and foot-soldiers carrying spears. Against this massive striking force, Bruce could effectively summon only about 5,500 trained men. For the most part, these were spearmen on foot; there was a small force mounted on what we now call garron ponies, and an even smaller body of archers. There was not the slightest hope that such an army, however well-trained, however high in morale, could withhold the full might of England upon an open battlefield on the plain.

With consummate skill, Bruce chose what we can now recognize as the one place in all Edward's northern march where there was the slightest chance that the Scottish forces would be able to meet the enemy with hope of holding them. Bruce let Edward cross into Scotland unhindered; he let him march as far north to his objective of Stirling as was possible; he encouraged Edward to stretch his communications to their utmost – then he met his challenge at a spot less than two miles from the castle that Edward had come to relieve. It was at a place we now call Bannockburn.

Bruce took up his position astraddle the only road from the south to Stirling that a large invading army could use. That spot seemed, indeed, perilously near to Stirling, but it was the spot on which to win or lose it all. It was on a slight upland and thickly wooded. To the west of it lay hills and wild moorland impenetrable by a large army. To the east lay a half-marshy plain bounded by the deep and looping River Forth, with the stream of the tributary Bannockburn on the south side of the plain.

When Edward of England came on the 23rd of June (the eve of the day on which he had agreed to relieve the castle), he paused and considered. Some skirmishing at the edge and sides of Bruce's position decided him against trying to force his great army up on to the high ground and through the wood. His massive cavalry could not charge in such conditions, and no one knew what damage these hidden savages on foot would do before he could force his way through!

He could not detour to the west. A wide flanking movement to the east was prevented by the Forth. Well, it might be a nuisance, but the only thing to do (the day being advanced), was to go down to the half-marshy plain between Forth and Bannockburn, encamp there for the brief midsummer night, and await the morrow. It was a wise decision. Protected by Forth and Bannockburn, the English army could consolidate, almost within shouting distance of their objective, Stirling Castle, and place upon the shoulders of Bruce and his men, hidden in the woods and on the upland, the burden of decision as to what to do on Midsummer Day – the day of reckoning.

When Edward, some time about midnight, had got his men encamped, he must have looked at the wooded upland where Bruce's army was hidden, and must have thought that there were only two courses open to his enemy on the next day. When Bruce had seen the full panoply and force of England stretched out below him, he would melt his army away into the west and into the wild hills and give up, or else he would be so foolhardy as to come down with his 5,500 men and try it out on the plain with Edward's 20,000-strong force. Then he would be crushed.

Edward, circumspectly though he had chosen, had left out of consideration one factor. This was that, in being led down into the hemmed-in though protected position between Forth and Bannockburn, he had gone just where Bruce had hoped he would go. By midnight of Midsummer Eve, Bruce knew that his careful planning had succeeded. He had got the enemy where he wanted him.

All depended now upon the morale of his own Scottish fighting men. It is highly characteristic of Bruce, and indeed of a later Scottish tradition, that at this supreme moment the Scottish King turned to his men and took them into his confidence. "We've got them where we want them," he said in effect. "Do you wish to go on and try the issue with them? If we lose, we lose everything, including our lives, which in any event would not be worth living in thraldom. If we gain the day, I can promise you not only glory, but something infinitely greater, more important to each of you – freedom. What is your wish? I shall abide by your decision."

With one voice all his men answered that they would "tak the ure" and would fight on the morrow. They did – and won a classic victory that has been included amongst the decisive battles of history.

This brief chronicle is not the place to describe the details of warfare. Let it be enough to say that at first light on St John the Baptist's Day, midsummer 1314, the Scottish spearmen came out of the woods and on to the plain. By using the bold and extraordinary tactic of infantrymen and, armed only with spears, advancing upon the huge mass of cavalry before it was ready or able to charge, Bruce threw the English into confusion almost at the start.

They were taken unprepared. They attempted to charge, but could get no momentum. Slowly the Scottish ate into the English position. Riderless horses turned back and caused confusion in the English rear. That rear was held by the waters of the Forth. Suddenly the entire English army disintegrated. Some tried to swim the Forth and were drowned; others tried to flee south across the other obstruction of the Bannockburn and were cut down. In the end, the whole vast force brought into Scotland by Edward was destroyed.

King Edward, himself a man of considerable courage, refused to leave the battlefield until his followers, taking his horse by the bridle, led him away. Only by the narrowest of margins did he escape capture.

Bannockburn was won; but not until another fourteen years of useless border bickering and intransigent minor warfare had passed was peace signed between England and Scotland. Peace was proclaimed at the Treaty of Northampton in 1328 between Edward III – King of England and son of Edward II, who had lost at Bannockburn – and King Robert I of Scotland, now recognized as an independent kingdom in its own right. In the next year, 1329, and just before he died, King Robert was received back into the peace and forgiveness of the Pope. He received absolution for his deed of sacrilege at Dumfries twenty-three years earlier. Scotland as a kingdom had now re-entered Christendom.

Upon his deathbed in 1329, and with his leading men all around him, King Robert Bruce sought absolution direct from God for another offence. He recalled in his last agony how his warring had caused so much blood to be shed, so much innocent life to be lost. He thanked God for giving him, in the presence of his warriors who had fought with him, these last hours of repentance, and offered up his own pains of dying in atonement.

This was the last act of expiation of the man who had once been a young self-seeking noble, no better or worse than his kind and class, yet who in the end, through ardours, sufferings, and achievements with the people of Scotland, had become their Patriot King. It is thus that we remember him – in his hour of victory, and on his deathbed.

History books, it is often alleged, are no more than the stories of kings, great men, and their fightings and achievements. A chronicle of Scotland such as is attempted here should certainly avoid this accusation. From the day of Alexander III, however, down to the moving death, in achievement and in expiation, of Bruce, the story of Scotland *is* the story of great men and of kings. It is the story of Alexander, of Wallace, and of Bruce; they made the Kingdom and nation of Scotland. Alexander did so by founding it; Wallace gave it hope again (fleeting but definite hope in the hearts of the people); and Bruce caused it to be born anew.

Before this recognized and established rebirth, before the death of King Robert Bruce, yet after his decisive victory at Bannockburn, something of the greatest importance happened, which came from the nation of Scotland. It was an utterance of the voice of Scotland that, though it may have been made by the great ones of the land, was no royal pronouncement. It was, granted the circumstances of the time, a democratic pronouncement, and thus leads into the story of Scotland of the future. We speak of it today as the Declaration of Arbroath.

In 1320, six years after Bannockburn, yet after a period when peace had not yet been officially declared between England and Scotland, and when many useless outbreaks of warfare had swayed to and fro across the Border, a self-convened assembly of nobles and ecclesiastics met at Arbroath. There they deliberated and dispatched eventually to the Pope, as head of Christendom, a noble declaration of freedom. It reads as resoundingly today as in the year it was set on paper and sent across Europe.

In splendid Latin (no unlettered country, this), it proclaims Scotland's right to freedom. It praises Bruce, but says that if he weakens in love of freedom he will be turned out, and the Scots will choose another king. Respectfully, it reminds the Pope of his fatherly duty. It founds the claim of Scotland's Kingdom upon the ancient Celtic tradition.

The Declaration of Arbroath has been acclaimed as one of the greatest pronouncements of freedom in the history of Europe. And so it is; but – as anyone who reads it will soon see, and even on the evidence of the points given above – it is a pronouncement in superb Latin, but with a strong Scottish accent of opinion and forthrightness.

The Declaration remains today for the delectation and wonderment of those Scots who take the trouble to look at it. At the time, it indubitably had its effect; but, looking back on it now, we can see it as ushering in the post-Bannockburn period of the nation. It was a period when monarchy, in the shape of considerable kings, weak kings, and infant kings, was to be the source of contention between forces in Scotland. Yet it was a period in which the reborn nation and Kingdom of Scotland grew up.

Medieval Scotland Growing Up

Bruce was succeeded by his lamentable son David II; and, despite the signing of peace between England and Scotland in 1328, warfare of an unsatisfactory kind continued. The trouble was that Scotland had been exhausted by the heroic struggle of the Wars of Independence. Disunity, the passing of the great old commanders

of the Bannockburn days, and the necessity for constant defence – all this, combined with the feckless and weakly obstinate rule of an unworthy king, threatened
Scotland with extinction not so much by subjugation as by decay.

However, David II died, perhaps fortunately, without issue, and he was succeeded
by Robert the Steward, son of Walter the Steward, one of Bruce's commanders at
Bannockburn, who had married the Patriot King's daughter, Marjorie. This
Robert II was patriotic, but elderly and not fully able to control the nobility of
Scotland, who regarded him as little more than one of themselves. However, we
owe him one great gift. Anxious to preserve the Bruce tradition, of which, through
his mother, he was the heir, he commissioned Archdeacon John Barbour of
Aberdeen to write the great epic *The Bruce*, chronicling the achievements of
Robert II's grandfather, Robert I, the Saviour of Scotland.

Some scholars, with their instinctive distaste for the arts, have dismissed this
huge and carefully composed work as "mere poetry". But this is irrelevant;
Barbour's *The Bruce* is not poetry. It is a long set of jingling verses in which
enthusiasm and beauty occasionally cannot help breaking through, but most of it
is straight narrative. It is written not in Latin nor in Establishment French, both of
which the Archdeacon knew, but in the Lowland Scots tongue. Its sources were
derived from the verbatim accounts of old warriors who had fought with Bruce. It
is a contemporary and largely accurate account intended to be memorized, in an
illiterate age. It is a kind of fourteenth-century tape-recording.

We owe it, not only to the slogging work of the good Archdeacon, but to
Robert II, who, from patriotism as well as family piety, commissioned it in the
popular tongue.

The story of Scotland – indeed the history of Europe, from the point of view of
tragedy, romance, and high drama – owes something else to the fact of Robert the
Steward's accession. With him, and as a result of taking his title as a family name,
began the long and ill-fated line of the Stewart (later corrupted by French usage to
Stuart) kings and queens. Voltaire has a well-known passage in which he marvels
at the curse of celebrated misfortune that seems to have hung over the Stuarts.
Even he, however, omits some points, one of which is that from James I of Scotland
to James VI every monarch came to the throne as a minor.

This, at a period when the "sacred person of the Monarch" was, all over Western
Europe, regarded as an invaluable possession, would have been a highly dangerous
continuing state of affairs in any country. In Scotland, with her independence but
newly regained, and with the endemic evil of disunity prevalent in her ruling
classes, it might have been disastrous. That this succession of no fewer than seven
minors to the throne did not utterly wreck the kingdom, may be ascribed to two
causes.

From James I to James VI every king, when he came of age, showed in varying
degrees the power to control; none of them were mere figureheads. The one queen
in this succession, Mary Stuart, Queen of Scots, had to abdicate and was driven
forth; but even this did not wreck her kingdom. The other reason is that, despite
the warring nobles, the Kingdom and nation of Scotland was, as a result of the
Wars of Independence, just too conscious of its all but miraculous rebirth to throw
itself away again.

Between the reign of James I and that of James IV, which ended in the disaster
of Flodden, Scotland was both consciously and, perhaps, subconsciously intent on
becoming a part of Europe. It was in this period that she attained the quality of a

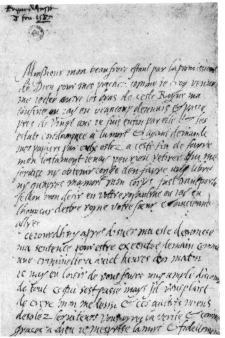

National Galleries of Scotland
Mary Queen of Scots

National Library of Scotland
The last letter of Mary Queen of Scots,
written on the eve of her execution

nation within herself. She founded her first university at St Andrews in 1412, to be followed by universities at Glasgow (1451) and at Aberdeen (1495). The University of Edinburgh opened its doors in 1583. The English visitor may reflect with interest that, until the writing of these words (when many plans are in the air), all our universities were ancient foundations, and that we had four to England's two.

During this period there was much founding and building of monasteries, in these earlier days largely free from the corruption that was to follow, and largely beneficent not only in the religious but also in the secular life of the country. In this period (painfully we must compress an important development), the merchant classes arose and made themselves felt, the burghs grew in number and importance and were, in Parliament (another development), represented as the Third Estate. Finally, at the end of this period, under James IV there was an astonishing flowering of literary talent and occasional genius expressing itself in the Scots tongue. Scotland had grown up not only to be a nation but a civilized nation.

"Civilized"! Many a visitor to our country who is shown the memorials of royal assassination and of internecine strife may smile at the word. The surprising matter is not that these things took place under the crippling period of minority succession, but that they were not worse, and that, despite them, the nation grew and established itself. The disgusted commentator on "Scotch savagery" in the Middle Ages is asked to recall that such behaviour was not a Scottish speciality at the time of the Wars of the Roses in England, of the savage quarrels of the Italian states, and of many other reprehensible happenings in Europe from which somehow, with all its imperfections thick upon it, emerged a comity of nations (an idea, if you will) called Europe.

In the space at our disposal here, it is intended to deal only with the highlights and low lights of Scotland's periods of rise and of decline. We shall move therefore directly from James I to James IV (whose reign marks a watershed), taking the reign of each Stuart king only as a tributary to the development of Scotland at this time, as already compressed in the preceding paragraphs.

James I, son of the ineffectual Robert III, had been sent as a boy and while still a prince for safety to France, thus relying on a continuance of the Franco-Scottish alliance, of which more will be said later. This child was captured at sea by the English. Within a month, he had succeeded to the throne of his father. He was nevertheless held and educated, to his considerable advantage, at the English court as the King of Scots (itself an admission from England of the rights of the Scottish Kingdom). He was returned only after the payment by the Scots of a ransom when he was nearly thirty. He was not only one of the most eminent Stuart kings, but one of the remarkable men of his time. He studied the management of men with assiduity, and was himself learned and gifted in expression. He did much to curb or manipulate the power of the nobles. He used and strengthened the legislative power of Parliament; and had he lived longer Scotland's growth might have been accelerated by the rule of a wise monarch, who, though no dictator, knew how to use as agents, to his own end and the country's good, the powerful forces in his realm.

But he was tragically assassinated at Perth in 1437; and Scotland was to face another minority rule under his six-year-old son, James II. At once the old interminable struggle broke out again, but when James II reached manhood he did much – aided by the safe advice of Bishop Kennedy of St Andrews, a true patriot – to break the power of the lawless nobles one by one. The Stuart fate struck him through his characteristic interest in mechanical devices. Eager to help the gunners at the siege of Roxburgh Castle, he was killed by an exploding cannon.

His successor, James III, was only nine, but fortunately his father's counsellor, the admirable Bishop Kennedy, was still present to guide the conduct of the kingdom through his early years. When he attained full power, however, this by no means unintelligent king dissipated it by intrigue, by reliance on favourites, and by dishonest debasement of the coin of the realm. Rebellion broke out. James III fell at the battle of Sauchieburn (just by Bannockburn), or was assassinated after it. Despite this tale of royal talent wasted in disaster or folly through three reigns, the Kingdom and nation of Scotland continued to grow up.

It was to attain something like adult status during the reign of James III's successor (who, it need hardly be said, was a minor, though one who had reached, for a Stuart successor, the comparatively advanced age of fifteen), the celebrated James IV. His reign marks a period of transition.

James IV and Flodden

James IV was so definite an individual that it is proper to discuss him as a strong factor of his age in Scotland. Certainly his reckless gamble at Flodden, when he attacked England, affected the fate of Scotland more than any action of his predecessors had done since Bruce, but in a very different way. His character, well described for us from a number of sources, is so vivid that we feel we know him. As with later descendants, he fascinates some even today as much as he repels others – and not only writers of romances, but sober historians.

This man, with all the richness of the Stuart blood in him, was also a product of the Renaissance spirit that was affecting the Europe of his time. Learned (speaking several languages, as well as the Gaelic tongue and Scots of his subjects), he had a questing and ambitious spirit. Rather than lustful, he was highly and widely amorous, gliding from mistress to mistress with as much grace as disgrace. Without being hypocritical, he was ardent in the practice of religion and suffered fits of wild repentance, in which superstition was mingled with real sorrow. He loved display, and was a capricious, though highly extrovert, patron of the arts. He liked to show himself to his people, and, as far as he was able, he dispensed justice widely and personally, and was seen to do so.

He was, of course, in that comparatively untrammelled age, popular. People liked a king who moved so freely amongst them and spoke their various tongues. They liked his Renaissance spirit. From what they could hear of it from their compatriot travellers in Europe, he was leading this northern land upon the fringes of Europe into the style and fashion of Europe. Indeed, in a sense he was. There is little evidence that he patronized the wonderful efflorescence of Scottish poetry and literature that occurred during his reign, but his attitude of mind, his proud spirit, created an intellectual and artistic climate in Scotland without which that literature would not have flowered.

Married to the sister of a king of England, James had been, for most of his reign, on superficially good terms first with his father-in-law, Henry VII, and then with his brother-in-law, Henry VIII of England. Relations had become strained; then, when Henry VIII was in France in 1513, conducting a war with the French king, James launched an attack on England that resulted in his shattering defeat at Flodden.

Most men's motives in the decisive action of their lives are mixed. This is certainly true of James's tragic folly in 1513. Idealism moved him when he saw this expedition as the first step in his project of a grand crusade against the infidel, in which the French King Louis had promised to help him. It is true that James was about the only prince in Europe to take the crusade seriously, a crusade for which Christian leaders had been asking in vain. But pride also animated his dreams.

The details of Flodden need not concern us. James mustered all the forces of Scotland at his command, and all the nobility. He proceeded into England for a few miles, and took up what he believed to be an impregnable position in the Flodden hills. His object was to draw off the English troops from France; but even in this he failed. The Earl of Surrey, who had been left to guard England in the absence of Henry VIII, by brilliant generalship outmanœuvred James, got between him and Scotland, induced him down and out of his "impregnable" position, and annihilated the Scottish army, with King James IV heading the list of the Scottish death-roll. This included a large number of the nobility and an untold number of the commonalty. What Bruce had gained at Bannockburn was recklessly thrown away.

At the time, it seemed that the blow, thus self-provoked against Scotland, had proved all but mortal; but it was not so. On his return from France, Henry had James's "sacred person" dead in England. The Scots had been thoroughly beaten; and Henry had plenty of other things to occupy his attention. Later on, he had even more: the foundation of the Church of England, the marrying and beheading of women in his feverish quest for the begetting of a male heir who should not be too much tainted by his infected blood. Let Scotland wait! The arrangement of royal marriages might yet easily absorb her into his realm after him. This was to happen, but not quite in the way Henry had thought.

France, England, the Reformation,
the Union of the Crowns

The official *casus belli* that gave James IV the excuse to invade England and nearly immolate his kingdom on the altar of Flodden, was the long-standing Franco-Scottish agreement still known as the Auld Alliance. This had officially begun with a treaty made by Bruce in 1326 before the uneasy peace had been signed with England; but, as both Scotland and France continued to suffer English invasion, it hardened into an understood alliance that was to last officially for two hundred and thirty-three years from the original treaty. It was to leave its effects, and was, after Flodden, to become a major factor, and (to many Scots who just wanted their country to be left alone) a major embarrassment.

Visitors to Scotland will hear of the Auld Alliance from guides, and will see references to it in ephemeral local leaflets. This is the place to consider what it really was.

It was an arrangement made by two hard-headed peoples who had between them an expansionist neighbour, England. Small though Scotland's population was, she was able to contribute brave fighting men to the French cause during the Hundred Years War; Joan of Arc had Scottish soldiers with her, and the royal *Garde Ecossaise* existed officially in France till the eighteenth century. But Scotland's main contribution to France's efforts in self-defence was to act as a menace at England's back door. "He that will France win must with Scotland first begin", ran a popular English saying. France could and did more massively come to Scotland's military aid – so massively, we shall see, as eventually to threaten the taking over of the smaller northern country altogether. This arrangement, useful though it might be to Scotland, could not, in its very nature as a long but temporary balancing act, work out for the benefit of the smaller nation.

And yet there are legacies from that *liaison de convenance* of nearly two and a half centuries. It is not for nothing that the very Frenchness of Calvin's theology made a direct appeal to the Scottish mind, that our greatest philosopher, Hume, was first appreciated in France, and that his style in English bears not only a Scottish cast, but the marks of a mind thinking in French. France remains today the only country in Europe where a Scot can announce his nationality and be quite sure that the statement will mean something. Linguistically there are links; we still carry a number of words of French origin in our common speech. And, as late as the spring of 1964, the French Academy was bemoaning the incursion of what it called Anglo-Saxon words (mostly Americanisms) into French usage; but they were careful to exclude those to which they had long given honourable hospitality since the days of the Scottish alliance.

It was during the reign of James V, who, in true Stuart-minority tradition, succeeded his father at the age of one, that the French influence, which was, after his death, to become so paramount as to be embarrassing, strengthened. This vigorous and socially attractive European prince was, again in the Stuart tradition, no fool, but he scarcely had a chance.

Almost the first thing he must have become aware of was that the realm to which he had succeeded had suffered a shattering defeat that had all but knocked her out. Yet his mother, Margaret Tudor, who had married James IV in such an aura of international friendship, was the sister of Henry VIII of England, whose army had dealt that defeat. As all Stuart minority monarchs had to do, he faced the inevitable disunity of his ambitious nobles who struggled for the control of his person. But, behind and greater than these nobles, there were forces outside Scotland contending for his alliance in marriage and war. Scotland may have been a small piece upon the chessboard of Europe, and James V a young untried prince, but the state of play at the time made both of value.

Of the outside powers contending for James's alliance, or maybe control of him, the only two that concern us, and concerned him, were England and France. James could not play a game of skilful neutralism. The choice before him was to ally himself with the (by then) schismatic, if not completely Protestant, England; break with the Pope; and endure the suffocating, possibly overwhelming, friendship of his unstable but still powerful uncle, Henry VIII. Or he might remain Catholic and ally himself with France.

James plumped for France. Maybe his faith had something to do with it. Maybe politics played a large part in his feeling that he was less likely to be absorbed by the remoter France. France, however, was his choice. He married first Madeleine, daughter of Francis I, King of France. This beautiful but ailing girl, upon reaching Scotland, promptly died. Wasting no time, James remarried again into France, on this occasion the physically and mentally vigorous Mary of Guise, from a family traditionally powerful. James was now committed to France.

He attempted to carry out that committal in offensive as well as defensive actions against England and Henry. He was feverishly preoccupied with these when, through his nobles' jealousy and sullen indifference, his forces suffered a humiliating defeat at Solway Moss. News of this reached the thirty-year-old king when he was in full fever at Falkland Palace. The blow was mortal. He may be said to have willed himself to die.

Just before he died, news came that Mary of Guise, his queen, had borne him a child. When he learned that the child was a girl, he made the celebrated dying speech: "It cam wi' a lass; it will gang wi' a lass". His reference was to the Stuart royal line, which had come into being through Bruce's daughter Majorie, married to Walter the Steward, and to his own daughter, who, he thought, would end it all.

He was wrong. His daughter, who set up an all-time record for Stuart minority accession by succeeding to the Scottish throne when she was less than a week old, was to be Mary Queen of Scots.

There can be few women in the last thousand years of Europe's history who have been the subject of more writing, more imaginative speculation, than Mary Stuart of Scotland. With honourable exceptions, most of the historical writing about her has been foolishly partisan or foolishly embittered; and, when it comes to imaginative writing, Mary shares with some others of her line a defeating elusiveness. She sadly lacks credibility in the innumerable novels that have been produced about her, or about the Scotland of her time; and this highly dramatic figure will not go upon the stage. Even Schiller, whose play upon her was recently seen at the Edinburgh Festival, made a fustian job of her life.

She fascinated or repelled during her lifetime; and as a figure in history she continues to fascinate. A Frenchman trying to account for this said characteristically that it was *"parce qu'elle était plus femme que les autres"*. An enthusiastic English near-contemporary of hers said, "Shee was the greatest shee that ever was". Leaving aside such outbursts of inspired infatuation, the story of her birth, life, reign, and death is indeed alluring to the feeblest imagination.

In view of the immense flood of verbiage she has been responsible for, a chronicle such as this must merely record the facts about her, and concern itself with their play upon events in Scotland.

She spent the first five years of her life closely guarded in Scotland. Despite Henry VIII's attempts to procure her betrothal to his son, later Edward VI, she was sent to the court of France, where at fifteen she was married to the Dauphin. It was a marriage that made her husband King of Scots as consort of his wife, but it contained secret clauses that, in the event of Mary's death without issue, were highly advantageous to France. Meanwhile Mary's mother, the intelligent and vigorous Mary of Guise, supported by French soldiery, was acting as Regent in Scotland. It now looked as if the Auld Alliance was going to turn Scotland into a province of France.

This improbable, impractical, and no doubt humiliating outcome was prevented by the death of Mary's husband, now Francis II of France, and Mary's consequent return in 1561 to govern her own kingdom.

Beautiful, intelligent, nurtured in the Catholic faith, exposed in her most formative years to the delicacies and refinements of an over-civilized Renaissance court, this young woman returned to her native northern country. That country, whatever attractions it may have for us today, must have appeared grim to her. It was, moreover, a country rent by internal dispute, where one event of the greatest importance had taken place in the year just before her arrival. That was the denunciation of the Catholic faith by Parliament in Scotland, and the establishment of Protestantism. To this, of course, we shall return. Here we are merely concerned with its effect on Mary's reign.

Mary was realist enough to accept the facts. As a Catholic queen, she demanded freedom to practise her own faith, but guaranteed religious freedom to her subjects. This did not please the Protestant nobles, and particularly not John Knox. The celebration of the Mass in Scotland, even behind the closed doors of the palace, was to him detestable idolatry. Mary after a fashion held her own, and her position seemed slightly strengthened when she married the half-hearted Catholic Darnley, son of the Earl of Lennox.

Darnley was vicious, idle, and filled with ambition; he made – as all parties, even his co-religionists, agreed – a highly unsatisfactory consort. He nevertheless begat by the Queen a son who was to become the future James VI of Scotland and I of England. In 1567, Darnley was murdered at the famous Kirk o' Field explosion on the outskirts of Edinburgh. Mary was strongly suspected of complicity in the crime, but this has never been proved.

At any rate, she committed a desperately impulsive act of folly that made all observers hold her guilty. She allowed herself to be captivated, captured, abducted, and finally married by the Earl of Bothwell, a man as supremely masculine as Mary was feminine. Bothwell was known by all to have been one of the murderers of Darnley. He was a Protestant, and had just been divorced; the marriage between him and Mary, conducted according to Protestant rites, took place with unseemly haste soon after Darnley's death. Mary succeeded in offending everyone in Scotland, and in calling down upon herself a denunciation by the Pope.

Abandoned by all except her new husband's followers, and those few who were still held by her fascination, she was now forced on the defensive. She was captured and imprisoned on an island in Loch Leven; she escaped, had two weeks' freedom, and then, after final defeat, abdicated in favour of her young son James.

She fled to England, hoping that Queen Elizabeth would give her refuge. Elizabeth did, but not in the way the Queen of Scots had hoped. Mary, as granddaughter of Margaret Tudor, Henry VIII's sister, was next in succession to the throne of England. Catholics in England, indeed, holding Elizabeth to be illegitimate, believed that Mary was already their rightful queen. Too dangerous a rival to be treated as a guest at liberty, she was imprisoned and, after nineteen years, executed. She died with the dignity of a queen of her race. She had long before made her peace with the Church of her birth, and her dying words proclaimed her submission to it. As her own motto proclaimed, "In her end was her beginning".

Her dramatic story has been of interest to the world. Of greater importance to Scotland were, and still are, the forces at play in the land that moulded her story. First, of course, there was the coming of the Reformed Faith to Scotland.

This huge event marks the greatest watershed in the history of the Kingdom of Scotland. It is so important, has aroused such profound feeling, and has been responsible for so many tomes, that in fairness there is only one way of dealing with it here – to give the bare facts.

The first cause of the Reformation in Scotland was the laxity and corruption of the higher clergy since just before James IV. At once it must be stated that there were some heroic exceptions (such as Bishop Elphinstone), and that attempts were made within the Church to cleanse it, but without effect. Also, among the lower clergy and the laity, there were those who lived devout lives. However, even the most patriotic and devoted Scottish Catholic of today, from those parts of the country which have retained the old faith (see "The Shape of Scotland"), can look back upon the just pre-Reformation Church with nothing but humiliation and distress, ruefully admitting his country's capacity for going to extremes. The Catholic Church, suffering from many ills in Renaissance Europe, certainly went to extremes in this matter in Scotland.

The second cause of the Reformation with us was the questing, speculative minds of Scots who went abroad and spoke with the greatest men of the Reformed Faith in Europe. Be it noted that the logical structure of the theology propounded by the Frenchman Calvin made much more impression on them than the emotional force of Luther. Scottish Protestantism has always been based on clear thought. The greatest, most potent, of these Scottish minds, and one gifted with an extraordinary power of expression, was John Knox.

The third cause of the Reformation, though less worthy and less important than the spiritual, moral, and intellectual ones mentioned above, was political. Scotland, enfeebled since Flodden, and later reduced by ineffectual rule, could not stand alone; she had to have the powerful support of one of her two traditional neighbours, England and France. Those who put their faith in France were Catholic; those who inclined to England were led to Protestantism, for Henry VIII had long broken with the Pope.

The geographical position of Scotland made the alliance with England, however distasteful to many, more practicable than one with France. Mingled with all these matters of faith, of intellect, and of practical policy, there were ignoble motives on both sides. Catholic higher clergy supported the French alliance at all costs for the sake of their own power. Many rapacious Scottish nobles were led to Protestantism by looking longingly at the wealth flowing into the purses of their kind in England as a result of Henry VIII's despoliation of the monasteries.

Menaced by England, irked by a near French occupation, there must have been Scottish patriots who cried, "A plague o' both your houses"; but it would have been an empty, irascible cry. Granted the circumstances of the time, Scotland was too weak to stand alone. This was the legacy of Flodden; the kingdom of Bruce had been thrown away.

Be that as it may, the approach to England, with the Union of the Crowns on the horizon, did occur, and with this the last obstacle to the Reformation was removed.

One final comment on the Scottish Reformation is in place here. There were seven Protestant martyrs in Scotland who officially suffered death by law for their faith before the Reformation. After the Reformation, there were two Scottish Catholic martyrs who died by process of the law. These figures contrast very favourably with those from many other countries at the time. They certainly put to shame those responsible for the fires of Smithfield, in which so many Protestants suffered under the Catholic Mary I of England. They also put to shame the policy of her Protestant half-sister Elizabeth, by which so many Catholic priests endured public butchery before death at Tyburn.

The greatest agent of the Reformation in Scotland was John Knox. Harsh yet humorous; dedicated to the system of Calvin, yet no Puritan (journalists, please note); a speaker, expounder, preacher, and writer – as all who read his words must acknowledge – of great force; he moved towards his end like some elemental power. You may receive or reject that end, as you may receive or reject his personality, but you cannot deny his achievement nor the huge force of his personality.

The greatest part of that achievement was to establish a really democratic Presbyterian Kirk in Scotland. It is true that that Kirk had to pass through many vicissitudes until, over a century after his death, it was freely and fully realized, but it was he who conceived it, made it possible. The rest of his achievement was the foundation of a Scottish system of education, the fruits of which were to be perceived until within living memory. Like so many others in our history, he is sometimes unthinkingly venerated, sometimes unthinkingly abused. He was a great man.

James VI, child of Mary Stuart and Darnley (Darnley also was a Stuart), succeeded, like all the Stuarts before him, as a minor. He was only one year old. He was also the first monarch of Scotland who was of the Protestant faith. This odd man – uncouth yet agile, pedantic yet knowledgeable, pawky yet truly humorous, learned yet superstitious, conventionally religious yet expedient, timorous yet shrewdly active – had, unlike the rest of his line, no power of personal attraction. One Stuart quality he did, however, possess. He knew his own mind. He could manage and move men to his own end.

As a boy, as a young man, as the Protestant heir of the Catholic and imprisoned Mary, he steered his course between conflicting elements in his troubled kingdom most cleverly. After his mother had died by the headsman's axe, and in his twenty-first year, he held his course with a kind of ignoble sagacity towards one great end. He knew now that, though Elizabeth of England had not admitted the fact, he was, through his great-grandmother, the heir to the throne of England as well as to the one on which he sat.

Everything must be guided to that important purpose – the long-delayed, often-avoided union of the crowns of England and Scotland, with himself, James Stuart, wearing the amalgam of them both. It was important, then, to offend as few power-ful susceptibilities as possible. He was a firm Protestant, yet (some thought) unduly lenient to prominent Catholics. He supported the Scottish Reformed Kirk; yet, even before he had left for England, he had tried to soften the differences between it and the Elizabethan Protestant compromise, the Church of England. With a mixture of intrigue, wit, and bluff, seeming to appear as an authority, this ungainly, clever man played for time. And in the end his time came.

In 1603, the indomitably virgin Queen Elizabeth died, and James VI of Scotland went south to become – in addition to what he was by native royal title – James I of England. He came back to Scotland only once again in a life that was to last another twenty-two years. His successors of the Stuart line were equally parsi-monious of their visits to their northern kingdom.

Scotland under the Union of Crowns

"The only surce [sic] and spring of our misfortunes, for thereby the seat of our Kings being removed from us, we are deprived of the golden influences which attend the Court of Princes." This is how Sir John Clerk of Penicuik, a patriotic Scot (yet one who, a little over a hundred years after the event, was to support the loss of a Scottish Parliament in a complent incorporating Union with England), described the Union of Crowns. His contention was that, when we lost the presence of the Head of State from amongst us, we lost so much of the power of government that there was little point in pretending to keep a parliament going.

"If Scotland is going to be run by a county council receiving orders from the King in London," so ran his argument, "then the sooner we join the real Establish-ment at Westminster the better."

There is – there was – a case for this point of view. Until the Settlement of 1690, just after the làst Stuart king, James VII and II, had lost his throne for ever, the Scottish Parliament was, except when it rebelled, reduced to acting as a rubber-stamp for the King's decrees. This state of affairs was brought about by James VI and I soon after 1603, when he manipulated the "Lords of the Articles" into being merely a tool of his wishes. It was characteristic of James's ingenuity and love of personal control that he was able, in removing himself four hundred miles away from Scotland, to increase his authority over his native land. He invented that bugbear of modern politics, remote control. If the shade of that sardonically humorous Stuart monarch is able to listen to modern fulminations on this theme in his native country today, it must surely smile.

Though the Kingdom of Scotland was thus officially reduced in parliamentary power on the spot, the nation of Scotland certainly was not reduced in the power of action. Throughout the stormy seventeenth century, that nation made its character felt not only at home but also in England. Reduced as an independent kingdom, Scotland grew strong in national feeling – so strong that, as we shall see, this domestically-minded people sought in the name of religion, and for the first and last time, to impose their will outside their own borders.

It began quietly enough when James VI and I, now by the law of England head of the Church of England, sought to bring John Knox's Presbyterian Kirk into line with the southern Church. He therefore strengthened the position of the more or less nominal bishops who had been introduced into the Church before he had left Scotland. He endeavoured to strengthen them against the General Assembly

National Galleries of Scotland

James VI and I

National Galleries of Scotland

John Knox, the Calvinist reformer

(the fundamentally democratic government of the Presbyterian Church), but he had had long enough experience of his countrymen to refrain from interfering too actively with the Presbyterian form of worship. Scottish hackles nonetheless were rising at the threat of episcopal domination just before James died.

More than hackles rose when Charles I came to the throne. He could scarcely remember the country he had been born in, and he tried to enforce upon the Church of Scotland Archbishop Laud's new Service Book, based on the English Book of Common Prayer. Not hackles but folding-stools, Bibles, and anything the congregation could lay their hands on, rose in the air and were hurled at the head of the Dean of Edinburgh when he tried to read from the Service Book. "Beastly belly-god" was amongst the milder epithets shouted by religiously inflamed Scottish ladies at the bishop who tried to restore order. It is said that the celebrated Jenny Geddes hurled the first stool.

The inheritors of the democratic Kirk launched by John Knox were now completely determined that their legacy should not be stolen from them by an enforced system from the King in London. After further public riots, the more sober and effective Presbyterians signed the nation-wide National Covenant, binding themselves to defend the King but utterly to reject his Church enforcements unless approved by a free Assembly and Parliament. This famous occasion was conducted in scenes not usually associated with Church of Scotland affairs today. Many men, in transports of patriotic and religious emotion, wept as they signed; others even gashed their veins and signed in their blood.

In 1638 the Assembly held at Glasgow abolished episcopacy and re-established the pure Presbyterian system. The gloves were off.

But what a predicament was thus forced on many patriotic and religious Scots! In their blood ran an inexpungeable loyalty to their King, who had not ceased to be their King even though he had been influenced by the Anglicans down there in

Plate 1 The Fish Market, Aberdeen (see p. 66)
Scottish Tourist Board

Aberdeen Press and Journal

Near Aberchirder: the Tower House of Kinnairdy Castle (see p. 60)

London. Yet, if the King were to try to force them to worship against their consciences, where lay their loyalty? This was a question that was to bedevil Scottish internal politics throughout the middle of the seventeenth century.

There followed the "Bishops' Wars", in which, by force, Charles tried to impose his system on the Scottish Kirk now supported by the Scottish Parliament. It was an absurd as well as a tragic situation, in which men fought against a king to whom they were loyal in their hearts in defence of a loyalty deeper than heart-level, in their souls. All must have been relieved when in 1646 the King promised to approve the Act of the British Parliament abolishing episcopacy.

Then the Civil War in England broke out. At first Scotland remained aloof from it. Political questions were not their concern. But, when the Royalist army had won success after success, and when the English Parliamentarians appealed to the Scots for help, the northern and absolute Presbyterians saw their chance. They, who had but recently resisted Anglican interference to defend their own form of worship, conceived the extraordinary idea of imposing pure Presbyterianism on England and Ireland. To this end they came together with English divines and signed a second Solemn League and Covenant for the establishment of Presbyterianism in the three kingdoms. For this they agreed to come in on the side of the English Parliamentarians, and they did intervene with much effect at the battle of Marston Moor. Apart from one pathetic attempt at a colonial venture at the end of the seventeenth century, this is the only example of Scottish national expansion.

At home, however, they were foiled by another and brilliant intervention of one man, in whose actions was discovered the painful division of loyalty already referred to. He was the great Marquess of Montrose who, in a series of resounding victories, fought for the Crown in Scotland, while yet remaining a loyal Presbyterian.

His prime opponent was the Earl of Argyll, the head of the powerful Clan Campbell and the greatest Highland chief. After receiving a severe drubbing in the very heart of the Campbell countryside, the forces of anti-monarchism, for which Argyll stood, conquered. Montrose was captured and suffered execution at Edinburgh.

Montrose's great fame and name, the celebrated struggle between him and Argyll, allow us, even in this compressed chronicle, to pause for four brief reflections on an interminably discussed theme. First, Montrose was an immensely attractive figure who, for subsequent generations, has had something of the allurement of Mary Stuart. The division of his policy, however, made him, while personally loyal, patriotically inconsistent. Second, his series of resounding victorious battles had not the cohesion of a campaign; he could never have won outright. Third, the unattractive Argyll, while no doubt full of personal ambition and with a disagreeable streak of cunning in him, was a consistent Scottish patriot in that he had a policy for a Scotland free of royal, episcopally-favoured control from London. Fourth, Argyll's intrusion into major Scottish politics was the first Highland venture of its kind. Hitherto, the rulers of the Scottish kingdom had regarded Gaeldom as something to be left alone or kept in control, not as a force in the policy of the kingdom.

But events moved more quickly in England than in Scotland. Cromwell defeated and executed Charles. He cared little that the axe he used for this purpose also beheaded the King of Scots. The Scots did. They were horrified, but saw an opportunity of resolving the conflict between loyalty and faith. They invited

Charles's exiled son and heir, later Charles II, to Scotland and crowned him on condition that he supported both covenants.

This was too much for Cromwell. He invaded Scotland. The Scots invaded England, but were eventually defeated. Charles escaped from the island, and, until the Restoration of the Monarchy in 1660, Cromwell ruled over Scotland as well as England. For the first time since Edward I, the land was completely subjugated by conquest. It now formed with England a single Commonwealth. Through our hindsight, we can now see that the days of an independent Scotland were numbered.

With the end of the Commonwealth, and the return of Charles II to London, the Scots at first welcomed the Restoration of the Stuart monarchy to the thrones of England and Scotland. It meant that they were rid of the Cromwellian occupation, and were, in a sense, free again. Many, too, naïvely nurtured the hope that the King, who as a youth, and almost under duress, had promised to support both covenants, would remember the promise. He did not – at least not in the form in which he was understood to have made it.

Episcopacy was restored in force, and an obsequious Scottish Parliament, only too glad to be in existence again, took away from congregations the right to choose their own ministers. Some of the ministers and members of the Church of Scotland, which was facing yet again a threat to her liberties, gave in for the sake of peace; others abstained. This abstention led to people worshipping in what were known as "conventicles", sometimes on remote hill-sides. Attendance at these conventicles had, in a rash Act of 1670, been declared treasonable. The Government then began the historic persecution of the "Covenanters" who worshipped at these conventicles.

The covenanting wars of Charles II's reign were compounded of heroism, obstinacy, persecution, genuine religious fervour, and a great deal of politics that animated these qualities on both sides. It is proper to mention that the Covenanters of the open hill-sides and the "graves of the martyrs" have joined the folklore of Scottish resistance. It is not intended here to disentangle the complicated motives that moved men in those lamentable times. We salute the brave, for whatever reason they fell, and pass on.

We can pass on through the brief reign of James VII and II, with his "Letters of Indulgence", which many Scots, weary of warfare and persecution, took at their literal value as the access to at least temporary freedom. Others suspected the indulgences as being a subtle attempt to reintroduce Catholicism, by means of "freedom for all". But the last Stuart James who occupied the united thrones settled the matter by fleeing from his kingdoms. This, however, is a matter more of English than of Scottish history.

What was of the greatest importance to Scottish history was the Settlement of the Church of Scotland in 1690 that ensued under William and Mary, who succeeded to the thrones of the last *de jure* and *de facto* Stuart king. Whether he had fled or had been turned out does not concern us here. He had gone, and his going was to keep Scotland for seventeen years (that is, until 1707 and the Union of Parliaments) in a state of heady freedom.

"Heady freedom" indeed! The national Church was now settled and democratically free. The Lords of the Articles were abolished, thus giving remarkable liberty of action to the Scots Parliament. And, if the commercial advantages of being united with England under the Commonwealth were withdrawn, it was stimulating to the nation to feel itself free to trade and move about the world independently.

It is a characteristic paradox that the withdrawal of the last Stuart king from London after the Union of the Crowns should have given Scotland more freedom than she had enjoyed for centuries.

She was on her own. But this very aloneness in a proud prickly people suffering from a readiness to take offence – and (let us be frank) from a sense of inferiority arising not only out of past oppression, but out of her obviously smaller status as compared with England in the growing Europe – marred her regained freedom. Nor did the equally proud, less prickly, but if anything more ambitious England, now successfully pushing her own way in the world, make things easier for her northern neighbour.

There were still many Jacobites in the north and Highlands and diffusely spread elsewhere in Scotland. These William III grossly offended by the tactlessness of his behaviour over the notorious Massacre of Glencoe. The offence spread to those who were not Jacobites. The big towns, the commercial classes, indeed all who possessed any money or property, attributed to England's policy (and with some justice) the ruin of Scotland's pathetic colonial venture, the Darien Scheme.

The Scottish Parliament retaliated in 1704 by passing four Acts of Independence, including the right to choose their own monarch after Queen Anne died, and the right to opt out of England's wars. It was all but serving notice on England that Scotland intended to break the Union of Crowns and to sever all connections with her southern neighbour. England, in her turn, retaliated by threatening an Alien's Act making all Scots foreigners and particularly unprivileged foreigners. War seemed possible, and the proud, disastrous story of the past centuries might have begun again.

The Union with England

Then, in 1707, the Scots Parliament, against much popular anger without its house and some strong opposition within, agreed to the Treaty of Union by which the Scots Parliament would merge (or rather sink) into the English Parliament of Westminster. The Treaty agreed that the two kingdoms, the two nations, should become one – the United Kingdom of Great Britain.

Two large questions arise. First: what prompted the proud prickly Scots to consent to this? Second: what induced England – who had shown no desire for, but indeed some aversion to, the notion of a greater union since the Union of Crowns – not only to agree to it, but suddenly and strongly to press for it?

Let us begin in a mood of generosity to produce one answer, which meets both questions. That answer is just "common sense". In both England and Scotland there must have been a number of people in power who, impelled by common sense as much as by common humanity, longed for an indissoluble agreement that would end, once and for all, the horrors of war between two nations inhabiting the same island. They were right. Maybe, in God's good time, the rest of Europe – perhaps the rest of the world – will come to the same conclusion amongst the nations. But it was the two ancient nations sharing this island who led the way.

Having proclaimed this lofty reason, let us give the more practical and immediate answers. First: why did Scotland assent? Faced with an England pressing for union, admitting the strong unpopularity of the idea in Scotland, realizing that there were only two courses open to them, complete separation or union, the Scots Parliament was upon a dilemma. If they went in with England, much would be lost; but, if they separated, where would they look for a king? There was only one inescapable answer – James Stuart, now in exile, son of James VII and II. Popular though such a choice would be amongst some Highlanders, some north-easterners and a few in the southern Lowlands, the forces of Jacobitism were diffuse.

What was not diffuse, but compact and potent, was the opinion of those in power in the big towns and in the Church of Scotland. Scots in control in this compact mass had long memories. They had had enough of the arbitrary rule of the Stuarts. Moreover, James Stuart, their *de jure* King now in France, was a devout Catholic. When, in consultation with the English framers of the Union, it was learned that Scotland could keep her own laws and liberties, and that the Church of Scotland would not only be recognized but guaranteed against interference under a Protestant succession, this decided them. They chose what to many of them must have seemed the lesser of two evils – union.

What about England and her sudden desire for union? The first answer is strategical. England was now engaged in Marlborough's crucial campaign against France. She just could not afford the prospect of an independent Scotland at her back door. She was not well informed as to the true strength of Jacobitism in Scotland, and the mere thought that the son of their James II might conceivably rule in Scotland while she was fighting France was understandably appalling.

The second answer arose from something not so acute, and less easily definable at the time. The English Establishment, having got rid of the Stuarts, having got the Monarchy more or less where they wanted it, and looking forward to a German king (George I) who could speak no English and ought to be easily managed, they wanted to define their position in these islands. The Treaty of Union offered an opportunity to define, and on paper, this position. It was a position they proposed to share with the Scots of the Establishment. To agree that the Scots should retain their legal system and their national Church was a small price to pay for union.

With the Union of England and Scotland, compounded of common sense, common humanity, and (to put it mildly) some more "realistic" motives, there was, set on paper in the Acts of the Treaty, the nearest thing we possess to a written constitution. It was a constitution establishing the Establishment. It was also the first step in the founding of the great English empire. The English empire had many benevolent qualities in common with the Roman Empire of antiquity. It dispensed justice to remote peoples, magnanimously, and was seen to do so; it never sought to mould those peoples to a central pattern. The farther it reached, the more was this kind of benevolence felt. In this, their first movement towards empire, the English showed one strong difference from the Romans. The Romans' maxim was *Divide et impera*. To the Scots, England said "Unite and be ruled". We accepted.

After the Union

The beneficent results to us of our acceptance are well known. Peace being now assured with our nearest neighbour, men in Scotland could turn their minds to industry, agriculture, and the arts. After a time wealth began to flow into Scotland, and many individual Scots became rich. With the expansion of the English empire, to which we were given full access, the Scots' capacity for adventure, and for adapting themselves to all circumstances, found satisfaction.

In the ranks of the Establishment at home, too, the Scots found no bar set against them as individuals. There have been several Scottish prime ministers at Westminster. And, even more impressive, there have been at least two Scottish archbishops of Canterbury, one of them achieving the remarkable feat of ascending to the White House of Lambeth from the log-cabin of his native manse. As individuals, we have richly benefited. As a nation, we have sadly lost.

Inevitably the nation of Scotland, as the smaller partner, declined in identity, while England, during the long period of prosperity before her, gained in national identity. The intention at the Treaty of Union was that both England and Scotland should cease to exist and the United Kingdom of Great Britain alone be born. This, of course, was an impossible assumption. Two nations can agree to unite; they cannot agree that they shall cease to exist. Did England cease to exist after 1707? Has she ceased to exist either in her own eyes or those of the world? Of course not. Did Scotland cease to exist – has she ceased? Not in her own eyes; but in much of the world she is thought of as a province not of Britain, but of England (the word "Britain" never found much favour outside this island – it sounded too much like a place inhabited by savages). But we cannot really complain of this. We were the smaller nation, and we went into the Union with our eyes open. There were plenty of people at the time to warn us of our fate.

What we could not, however, have been expected to foresee were certain effects of the Union contrary to the spirit of it, and to our disadvantage. Not six years had passed after 1707 when, less from arrogance than from a mere weight of unthinking numbers over the Scottish numbers at Westminster, two Acts were passed offensive to Scots and striking at the conditions of the Union.

The first was the arrogation by the Westminster House of Lords of the right to try appeals in civil cases originating in Scotland. Considerable ignorance of the Scots law, fundamentally different from English law, prevailed at Westminster and, until late reform, led to much injustice and northern heart-burning.

Far more grievous was an Act passed in 1712 enforcing on the Church of Scotland a system particularly odious to it. This was the system of lay patronage, an Erastian measure that deprived Presbyterian congregations of what they held to be their fundamental right – the choice of their own minister. Instead, they now had to accept the choice of the local landowner, no matter whether he was interested in the congregation or even in Church affairs. We were back to the days of James VI and I. But now it was not a crafty monarch who had had his way over Scottish democratic opinion, but the chance coming together of various politicians in England, ignorant of Scottish affairs.

The question of how ministers did or did not receive their livings, of whether they were "called" by their congregations or were appointed by lay patrons and imposed upon unwilling congregations, may seem to the southern reader a small matter in the structure of a union peacefully brought about. He is, however, asked to remember what a large part the guaranteeing of a genuinely democratic Church government played in inducing the Scots to agree to the Union, and what store they set by it.

This lamentably Erastian Act of 1712 was to bedevil the affairs of the Church of Scotland throughout the eighteenth century. The matter was not resolved until quite recently. Nor would it have been resolved, had not what might be called the last truly national action of the nation of Scotland taken place long before, in 1843. This action was the famous Disruption – of which more later.

Maybe these two Acts, occurring so soon after the Union, along with other casual rather than calculated outvoting of Scottish interests on purely domestic Scottish affairs, should have been foreseen by the Scots Parliament before it agreed to sink its identity into the larger southern body. But it did not foresee it. Those members of the last Scots Parliament who survived the five years after 1707 – and who, maybe, were amongst the representatives who went to Westminster to be outvoted – must have received a sharp lesson in being wise after the event. It is only fair to say that such an outvoting on a purely domestic Scottish issue would not occur today.

The actions of individual Scotsmen or of associations of Scots were not, of course, brought to an end by the events of 1707. Freed from the fear of neighbourly strife, there was large development in this kind. Scottish contributions to the great affairs of the Industrial Revolution, to commerce, science, education, colonial development, in what now began to be called the British Empire, were manifold and manifest. The Scottish regiments played a proud part in the British Army, and one could go on for long making a list of such examples.

One cannot, however, fail to mention the extraordinary flowering of literary and intellectual talent in southern Scotland, and particularly in Edinburgh, during the latter half of the eighteenth century. The names of Adam Smith, David Hume, Robert Burns, James Boswell (who, for all his London leanings, remained essentially native), Walter Scott, Raeburn, and the Adam brothers (who have left their indelible stamp on Edinburgh's noble neo-Georgian New Town) are only some that come to mind. An enthusiastic Englishman, Mr Amyat, said of Edinburgh at this time, "I can stand at the Mercat Cross of Edinburgh and, in half an hour, shake by the hand fifty men of genius". This was warm-hearted Englishness putting it strongly! But one knows what he meant.

These and other men drew upon the heritage of their nation's learning in science, literature, philosophy, politics, and much else to enrich the world in and from Scotland. But Scotland as a nation had, since 1707, officially ceased to exist, and it cannot be said that, as apart from individuals and strong associations of individuals, the nation of Scotland acted upon the world or upon her neighbours; she had no power to do so. This compressed chronicle is put forward as "Scotland in History"; officially, it ought to end at 1707.

But there were a few considerable events that happened within Scotland nationally and shook "North Britain", as it was now known, from end to end. These must be mentioned.

There were the two Jacobite attempts to restore the Stuarts to their ancestral thrones through Scotland. The first, in 1715, was a badly bungled affair that culminated in the apparently indecisive battle of Sheriffmuir. But it was decisive in that the Jacobites had exhausted their efforts. Poor James Stuart, the claimant to the throne (known to his opponents as the Pretender and to his supporters as James VIII and III), characteristically arrived too late, and the affair came to nothing. James was a profoundly religious man, but not one cut out to be a king. He retired from these islands, and it would have seemed that the hopes of Jacobitism, even in the still Royalist Highlands, had – save for a few sporadic movements, notably in 1719 – gone with him.

But no. In 1745 his eldest son, Charles Edward Stuart, the Bonnie Prince Charlie of song and legend, sailed from France all but unaccompanied, and set foot for the first time on the land of his ancestors at the island of Eriskay in the Outer Hebrides. Thence, despite discouragement, he moved to the mainland, met loyal greeting and

Prince Charles Edward Stuart
as a boy in Rome
National Galleries of Scotland

further discouragement. But, when Cameron of Lochiel, a considerable Highland chief, joined him with his clan, Charles unfurled the Jacobite standard at Glenfinnan, at the head of Loch Sheil, well inland, and marched south with a fair force of Highlanders, and gathering men as he went. The famous '45 had begun.

Whatever view you take of the venture (and its outcome was a major tragedy for the Highlands and, though not permanently, a crippling blow to Scotland), it carries the traditional Stuart quality of high drama – and, if you will, romance – in its most spectacular form. For some time after its failure, it was the subject in both Highlands and Lowlands of much song and folklore, eventually degenerating into a tradition infected by sentimentality.

Prince Charles's march south was at first highly successful. He took Perth and Edinburgh, and defeated the Hanoverian forces (mostly composed of English and German troops) under General Cope in a remarkably short battle at Prestonpans, near Edinburgh. The south of Scotland was in his hands. Delaying at Edinburgh, where he held court at the Palace of Holyroodhouse, he eventually marched into England; by a brilliant series of evasive moves, he reached Derby, causing much alarm. It is said that George II in London was even packing up to go.

On the advice of his Highland officers, however, Charles retreated into Scotland, where in the end he was thoroughly beaten at the battle of Culloden by the Duke of Cumberland, who undoubtedly committed various atrocities upon the wounded and dying of his defeated enemy's Highland army. These atrocities of the "Butcher" Cumberland did much to stimulate the '45 Jacobite tradition. Prince Charles's subsequent fugitive wanderings in the Highlands and Hebrides, including his celebrated rescue by Flora Macdonald, also justly added to the romantic tradition of the last Jacobite rising. A price of £30,000 was laid on his head by the Government, but none amongst those poor Highland folk was found to give him away. He escaped from Scotland five months after Culloden, and died forty-three years later disconsolate in Rome.

It was said that the campaign could never have succeeded, first because not enough English and Welsh Jacobites had joined the Prince in Derby, second because Charles could never have held London with only a Highland force. These reasons are recognized as invalid. There were Welsh and North of England Jacobites willing to join, but they did not arrive in time. Had Charles gone on to London, most loyalists to the House of Stuart would have supported him. For the rest, the then English passion for being on the winning side at all costs would have regained for Charles the thrones of his forefathers. Some people still regret that it did not.

Its real tragedy, however, was not its failure, but its effect on the Highlands. The Government, determined to "smoak out" this area of rebellious disaffection to the House of Hanover, did its best, after the troubles, to destroy the Highland tradition. It took away, in some instances, the old Highland chiefs' right of heritable jurisdiction – a thing that would have had to go, anyhow; it disarmed the Highlanders, proscribed their national dress, did its best to make Gaelic a shameful tongue, and in a general way made the Highlanders feel, whatever side they had taken, a conquered people ethnically inferior to the Saxon.

The greatest disaster that was later to flow out of this anti-Gael, anti-Celt policy was the Highland Clearances. This tragedy, the effects of which may still be seen today, had various causes. Many of them (and it is important to remember this) had their origin in events well before the '45; but it was the '45 that accelerated the disaster. The conquered Highlander, much though he loved his land, felt he was not wanted there, and he turned his eyes overseas.

Some Highland chiefs (to our shame be it admitted) found that it was more profitable to expel their clansmen, often in circumstances of great cruelty, and to bring in sheep. Later it was even more profitable to turn the great moorlands and mountain-sides into sporting property. There were honourable exceptions to this native landlord policy, such as Sir John Sinclair in the far north, and Macleod of Raasay, who ruined himself through an attempt to save his people; but these were in the minority.

The Clearances lasted till the late nineteenth century, when a series of Crofters Acts were made – projected by the great-hearted Gladstone who had already done so much for Ireland – that protected the Highland peasants' rights. The most ironically displeasing element in the Clearances policy was that its latter end coincided with the romantic revival of the once proscribed tartan and of other Highland customs. This, Queen Victoria innocently encouraged by her cult of "Balmorality".

It may seem a far step from the coloured tragedy of the '45 to a gathering of quietly and clerically clothed ministers in Edinburgh nearly a hundred years later. Nevertheless that step leads us to the next genuinely national as distinct from individual action in Scotland.

In 1843 the National Assembly of the Church of Scotland was divided on how best to deal with the offensive legacy of lay patronage (already referred to) that had been imposed on the Kirk, with disastrous results at Westminster in 1712. The outcome was that some four hundred and fifty ministers walked out of the Assembly at St Andrew's Kirk in Edinburgh to form the Free Church of Scotland. In doing

*The Rev. Thomas Chalmers,
who led the Scottish Free
Church movement*
National Galleries of Scotland

so they had walked out of their livings, the right to inhabit their manses, and their livelihood. Their courage and their tenacity of conscience were rewarded. Their Free Church was supported and maintained by the people of Scotland. At last, in 1929, the official Church of Scotland, having long got rid of lay patronage, amalgamated with the Free Church. The old dispute was over, and freedom had won. But it was the heroic action of 1843 that had achieved it. The Disruption, as it was known, was a national event within Scotland. A national event, too, was the quiet survival of Catholicism among the people of Buchan and the Western Highlands. This was something distinctively Scottish.

Much indeed – politically, industrially, commercially, and even to a certain extent artistically – has happened in Scotland since 1843. The democratic opinion in politics within Scotland has had its effect on Great Britain, and there are other trends in our country (it is still safe to call it that, at least) that have moved men's minds outside Scotland. Nothing of this, however powerful, however remarkable, can come under the head of a national movement. Tempting though it is to reflect on these things, they have no place in this brief history of the Scottish nation.

Officially, Scotland was absorbed into Great Britain in 1707; so indeed was England. But England did not become absorbed in the concept of Britain, as was for a time the fate of Scotland. Indeed, the name of England once stood for the whole island. After the First World War, however, a change set in. Scotland became conscious of herself, not only in sentiment but politically – a revival that may not be without result. Meanwhile the nations of both England and Scotland continue to live in the hearts of men and women and children within them.

The visitor to Scotland will surely recognize this when he comes amongst us. He will recognize also that there is in the land one quality – noticed so enthusiastically by de Ayala, the Spanish Ambassador to James IV, just over four and a half centuries ago – that still remains. It is hospitality.

Gazetteer

ABBEY CRAIG, *Stirlingshire* (Map 2, ref. 28²69⁵). A boulder-strewn, scrub-clad hill, 362 ft high, rising above CAUSEWAYHEAD, 1½ m. ENE. of STIRLING, on which stands the Wallace Monument. The hill was a station of Sir William Wallace's victorious army in the Battle of Stirling, on the 11th of September 1297, and the monument to the great patriot's achievement was built 1861–9. Designed by J. T. Roehead of GLASGOW, the tower stands 220 ft high; a massive statue of Wallace (d. 1305) by D. W. Stevenson, R.S.A., of EDINBURGH, was added in 1887. The monument, which contains Wallace's sword among an exhibition of other weapons and historical relics, is a prominent landmark in the FORTH Valley and commands extensive views of the adjacent Ochils and the Dunbartonshire hills. It is open daily. Historically and to a certain extent geographically, this is the heart of Scotland.

ABBEY ST BATHANS, *Berwickshire* (Map 3, ref. 37⁶66²). This hamlet on the R. Whiteadder, 7 m. NNW. of DUNS, is the site of one of the early religious settlements in the Borders. The name derives from St Baothen, the cousin and successor of Columba on IONA, to whom the 12th-cent. Cistercian nunnery was dedicated. Part of the old abbey church and a prioress's tomb are incorporated in the present parish church. From the fort and broch, 2 m. to the S., there is a fine view of Edinshall (1,066 ft). Good brown-trout fishing of the simpler kind may be had in the rivers and burns on the S. side of the Lammermuir Hills in the neighbourhood.

ABBOTSFORD, *Roxburghshire* (Map 3, ref. 35⁰63⁵). Near MELROSE, this, the celebrated home of Sir Walter Scott from 1812 until his death in 1832, is open to visitors regularly from April to October. Situated on the right bank of the TWEED, the property was a small farm called Cartley Hole when Sir Walter bought it in 1811. The baronial mansion and surrounding wooded policies are very much Scott's own creation. His rooms have remained unchanged since his lifetime, and contain his library of 20,000 rare books and his collection of well-documented historical relics, associated with Napoleon, Robert Burns, and Prince Charles Edward Stuart among others. The house is now occupied by Sir Walter's great-great-great-granddaughter, Mrs P. M. Maxwell-Scott.

Abbotsford, the last home of Sir Walter Scott

As part of the 1971 celebrations of the bicentenary of Scott's birth, Abbotsford was floodlit for a week in August.

ABBOTSINCH, *Renfrewshire* (Map 2, ref. 24⁸66⁶), 1½ m. N. of PAISLEY, as Scotland's main airport for internal and European services, now handles about 250 flights daily; PREST-WICK is used for long-range services.

ABERCHIRDER, *Banffshire* (Map 6, ref. 36²85²), is the smallest burgh in the county, and is quaint rather than exciting; but it has a most picturesque situation, riding upon a sea of country like the crest of a breaking wave. Founded in 1764, it is laid out in the form of three long parallel streets sloping gradually down from a hill-top, with a square a third of the way down Main Street. Its founder was Alexander Gordon of Auchintoul, whose grand-uncle, a previous laird, was one of Peter the Great's generals. Some 2 m. S., overlooking one of the most magnificent reaches of the DEVERON, at Bridge of Marnoch, is Kinnairdy Castle, an L-plan tower-house finely restored by its present owner, Sir Thomas Innes of Learney, who was Lord Lyon King of Arms from 1945 to 1969. About ½ m. W. of Kinnairdy is the Kirk of Marnoch, where a famous "intrusion case" set the final spark to the Disruption of 1843 (*see* "Scotland in History"), while a little to the W. of that, on the high left bank of the Deveron in an ancient graveyard, are the ruins of the pre-Reformation kirk dedicated to St Marnan. Aberchirder has a nickname, Foggieloan, meaning "mossy field", an apt description of its site.

ABERCORN, *West Lothian* (Map 2, ref. 31⁰67⁸), a small hamlet on the S. shore of the FORTH, was the seat of the first Scottish bishopric in the 7th cent. The old church, refitted in 1597 after the Reformation and restored in 1839, contains several features of antiquarian interest – part of a bishop's cross possibly dating back to Bishop Trumuini (who founded the bishopric in the 7th cent.), hog-backed stones from the graves of Danish invaders, the Hopetoun pew with painted ceiling and panelled retiring room, and the segregated Binns aisle. Abercorn is near to HOPETOUN HOUSE, The BINNS, and BLACK-NESS Castle.

ABERDEEN, *Aberdeenshire* (Map 6, ref. 39⁴80⁵), recalled to the modern poet G. S. Fraser "glitter of mica at the windy corners... a sleek sun flooding the broad, abundant dying sprawl of the Dee" and "salmon nets along a mile of shore", while the novelist Lewis Grassic Gibbon called it "the one haunting and exasperatingly lovable city in Scotland – its fascination as inescapable as its shining mail".

It is the glitter of the mica, among the crystals of quartz and felspar composing the pale blue-grey granite of which the city is so largely built, that provides the "shining mail" and is responsible for that air of timeless impersonality worn by the cliff-like façades and the steeples and turrets of its public buildings, though more than thirty housing blocks, arrayed mainly along the northern perimeter, now make the distant view restless. But Aberdeen is also a geographical curiosity. To encounter a city of 178,441 inhabitants in the English Midlands might not be worthy of remark, but Aberdeen lies well to the N. of the 57th Parallel.

The drama of Aberdeen's situation is brought home to the traveller who approaches it by road from the S. To the N. of STONEHAVEN, he crosses the Highland Boundary Fault and leaves behind the fertile red clay of the Howe of the Mearns and STRATHMORE for a land where, as Sir Alexander Gray has put it,

> A few trees, wind-twisted –
> Or are they but bushes? –
> Stand stubbornly guarding
> A home here and there.

And then, descending from the ridge of moorland that marks the seaward end of the GRAMPIAN mountain barrier, he sees laid out before him this wide-spreading, silver-veined city rising from a river's brim. Aberdeen now occupies and overspills the 2 m. of undulating land between the mouths of its rivers, DEE and DON, extending inland from its long shallow bay a distance of 3 to 4 m. It grew up, almost in defiance of the laws of nature, as two quite separate burghs, Old Aberdeen – the cathedral and university "village" at the mouth of the Don – and "New" Aberdeen (in actual fact equally ancient), the fishing and trading settlement where the creek of the Denburn entered what was then the sprawling estuary of the Dee.

As you draw nearer, there is a good example of the way in which the old and new confront one another in the Granite City. On your right, the Hill of Kincorth is now covered by a post-war residential satellite town, mostly of granite, laid out on terraced slopes gay with flower-beds, and designed on lines suggested by an international competition in 1938, though not actually carried out until the end of the Second World War. On this hill, as many of the new street names bear witness, the Army of the Covenant under Montrose and the Earl Marischal encamped in 1639 before the Battle of the Bridge of Dee, which still spans the river at its foot. That battle ended disastrously for Aberdeen's Royalist defenders. It was but one of the many reverses suffered by the inhabitants during the terrible years of the Civil War. But the bridge that bore the heat of the assault in that midsummer fray still stands as it has stood for 440 years. Although it was very carefully widened over a century ago, it still bears on its piers and abutments the coats of arms of

Bishop Gavin Dunbar (who built them between 1520 and 1527), of Bishop William Elphinstone (who planned the bridge in the previous century), of King James V, and of the Regent Albany. This graceful structure in freestone, with its seven ribbed arches, is still in use, although the main traffic artery entering the town has been diverted eastwards along the S. bank of the river to the King George VI Bridge, completed during the Second World War.

A green belt of playing-fields and parkland lines both banks of the river here. On the N. bank, close to the Bridge of Dee, is a charming miniature, the tiny three-arched Ruthrieston pack-horse bridge, also embellished with coats of arms, built in 1693–4 to improve the access from the larger bridge into the town via the ancient Hardgate, now a forgotten by-way. On the right after crossing the King George VI Bridge is the Duthie Park, one of the city's handsomest open spaces, with duck and boating pond, winter gardens and many acres of tree-lined greensward.

By Great Southern Road and Holburn Street you reach the W. end of Union Street, Aberdeen's dead straight main artery and shopping centre, 1 m. long, 70 ft wide, stately and still a source of pride to the citizens, despite the occasional excesses of shop-front commercialism.

Apart from the pleasant contrast provided by freestone churches, with spire-crowned steeples, on either side, Union Street is still entirely lined with well-dressed granite frontages, many of them the original plain Regency elevation dating from the early 19th cent. It is one of six Conservation Areas designated to preserve the original character of the city. Curiously enough, the view along both ends of the street is marked by battlemented and turreted buildings – on the W. the former Free Church College, now known as Christ's College (1850), and on the E. the grandiose Salvation Army Citadel designed by James Souttar (1896), on the right of which, rising from behind, soars the blunt tower of the 18-storey Marischal Court, a housing block. The other turreted steeple dominating the whole length of Union Street from its eastern end is that of the Town House tower, 200 ft high, completing a neo-baronial pile (designers Peddie and Kinnear, 1871). They continue a tradition of towered buildings reaching from the Middle Ages.

The architect, however, who left the most conspicuous mark on modern Aberdeen was Archibald Simpson (1790–1847), the son of an Aberdeen merchant burgess. His penchant for the neo-classic style was particularly suited to work in granite, and a dozen public buildings, two fine squares, and a plain but impressive crescent give him well-deserved local immortality. The first of these that you meet on your way eastward along Union Street is the Music Hall, with its massive pillared portico, originally built in 1820 as a group of assembly rooms. It is on the N. side of the street about a third of the way down, and was saved from demolition after a heated controversy.

A short diversion down Bon-Accord Terrace, the first cross street on the right as you move eastward from Union Street's W. end, leads to Simpson's Bon-Accord Square and Crescent, both built in the 1840s. For quiet dignity and fine proportions, they are the nearest approach in Aberdeen to the spirit of EDINBURGH's New Town. On the way there you will pass, at the corner of Bon-Accord Terrace and Hardgate, an inconspicuous square stone, built into a wall and surmounted by an inscribed plaque. This is the Crab Stane, marking the boundary of the croft that belonged to John Crab, a magistrate of Aberdeen in 1314. Crab, a Flemish immigrant, performed a service of national importance to Scotland in 1319, at the Siege of Berwick, by devising a crane to deliver the stones that shattered the roof of the English "sow". But his stone also marks the location of two notable battles – the Battle of the Crab Stane on the 20th of November 1571, and the Battle of the Justice Mills, on "Black Friday", the 13th of September 1644. In this latter fray the Marquess of Montrose, who by this time had emerged as the King's champion in the Civil War, attacked an army of Aberdeen citizens and covenanting lords. Again, as at the Battle of the Bridge of Dee, he was victorious and, enraged by the slaying of the drummer-boy who had accompanied his emissary, let loose his Irish troopers upon the city. The result was the Sack of Aberdeen, three days of rapine and carnage that marked the lowest ebb of the city's fortunes in the time of the "Troubles".

Returning to Union Street, we find that, midway along its length, it crosses, by the 130-ft single span of Union Bridge, the ravine of the Denburn Valley, which reveals on the N. side a striking natural vista.

This chasm, whose floor, now occupied by the railway, once lay open to the banks of the Den Burn, has been cultivated in a way similar to that of Edinburgh's Princes Street Gardens. Along its high western bank runs the one-sided thoroughfare of Union Terrace, while the slopes below it are laid out as a small public park where giant draught-boards, on which the pieces are moved by long poles held by the players, form a perennial attraction. The view is closed to the N. by a range of public buildings along the line of Schoolhill and its Viaduct: the Central Library, the South Church, and His Majesty's Theatre with its jaunty green dome – a trio that used to be called, by skittish Aberdonians, "Education, Salvation, and Damnation"; beyond the arches of the Viaduct stands Archibald Simpson's domed Old Infirmary, flanked on the right by the Cowdray Hall, the War Memorial, and the Art Gallery. The view of these buildings, all in granite of either grey or pink, is rounded off by the splendid brick spire of the Triple Kirks (designed by Archibald Simpson in 1843), whose stateliness makes a contrast with the glittering array.

Aberdeen is a city of many statues. Union Terrace has four: a granite King Edward VII, a bronze Robert Burns (apostrophizing his daisy, which is "removed" so often that the city authorities have to keep a regular stock), a bronze Prince Consort, and, overtopping them all, a colossal bronze of Sir William Wallace by W. Grant Stevenson that is quite the most remarkable monument to the Liberator that Scotland can show.

The Art Gallery, opened in 1885, is fortunate in having been left pictures and sums of money enabling it to amass one of the most catholic and up-to-date collections in Britain. The Old Masters are comparatively few, but the Scottish school is well represented, from George Jamesone (1588–1644), an Aberdonian acclaimed as the first portrait painter of note in these islands, to Sir William MacTaggart, John Maxwell, Robert Colquhoun, and others of our own day. Scotland was among the first of foreign countries to welcome the French Impressionists and Post-Impressionists. Aberdeen has a superb Monet, "La Falaise à Fécamp", and two Sisleys, "Les Bords du Loing" and "Une Cour aux Sablons", as well as works by his precursors and successors. Augustus John's "Lloyd George" and W. R. Sickert's "Pimlico" are only two of the many paintings that represent the modern English school, including works by Jack Yeats, Wyndham Lewis, and Ben Nicholson. As for sculpture, we should make sure of seeing the lovely Nottingham alabaster that dates from the 15th cent. The bronzes by Epstein are outstanding, and alongside one of the most happy of Degas's dancers reposes Henry Moore's "Figure on Steps". Nor must Aberdeen's collection of lithographs be missed, nor the etchings in the McBey Memorial Room.

While we are in Schoolhill (which takes its name from the ancient grammar school where Lord Byron toiled at his Latin), we can note how the arched gateway linking the Art Gallery and Gray's School of Art leads to another famous school, Robert Gordon's College, the central block of which was designed by William Adam, the father of the Adam Brothers, and completed in 1739.

We can return to Union Street by Back Wynd, an ancient street that skirts the City Kirkyard, in the centre of which stands the Parish Church of St Nicholas, the patron saint of New Aberdeen. This early medieval foundation, in which good work of the first pointed Gothic period still survives, was divided into E. and W. churches at the Reformation and has been greatly altered since. The two churches are separated from each other by the arches of the steeple and the walls of the transept.

It is in the N. transept, known as Collison's Aisle, that the early work is to be seen, including a window above which is a unique lead apron or tracery. The S. transept or Drum's Aisle, rebuilt in the 19th cent., contains a stone effigy of Sir Alexander Irvine of DRUM, who died in 1457; it has a monumental brass. The W. church (originally the nave) was rebuilt in the middle of the 18th cent. to designs by James Gibbs (1682–1754), the greatest Aberdonian architect, whose work includes Christ's College, Cambridge, the Radcliffe Library, Oxford, and St Martin-in-the-Fields, London. In the W. church are preserved four tapestries illustrating Biblical themes; they are by Mary Jamesone, the daughter of George Jamesone. The belfry houses a carillon of forty-eight bells, which regularly peal out psalm tunes that can be heard above the roar of the city's traffic. In the E. church the feature of interest is the medieval crypt, now restored and in use as St Mary's Chapel.

Back Wynd returns us to the eastern half of Union Street, which is screened off from the Kirkyard by a façade of granite pillars. This half of the street stands high above the natural level of the ground, having been built up in the first decade of the 19th cent. on a series of blind arches – an operation that proved so expensive that it led to the temporary bankruptcy of the city. On the S. side of the street, we find Market Street and the New Market, a large indoor shopping arcade with a cliff-like granite frontage; they were designed by Archibald Simpson and built between 1840 and 1842. Beyond the intersection of Market Street and St Nicholas Street, Union Street continues to Castle Street, flanked by the Town House, already mentioned, and widening out to form the Castlegate, the ancient forum of the burgh. This Square has been the heart of Aberdeen for seven centuries. It first appears in records in 1219, when the town began to supersede the lowly fishing habitation that had been raided by the Vikings in the previous century. Among its earliest known buildings was the house of the King's Justiciar, Comyn, Earl of Buchan, while William the Lion had a "palace" on the nearby green and a mint in what is now called Exchequer Row. It was called Castlegate because it led to the royal castle on Castlehill to the E. That castle, still commemorated in the burgh's coat of arms, was finally destroyed in 1308, when the pro-Bruce party in the town, rising and rallying to the cry of "Bon accord" (now the motto of the city), ejected the garrison of English soldiers left there by Edward I of England during the first War of Independence. In gratitude for this and other acts of loyalty, King Robert I in 1319 bestowed on the burgh the vast forest of Stocket, extending for many square miles to the W. of the town.

The first Town House in the Castlegate was built in 1394. It was superseded in 1622 by a square tower (surmounted by a steeple and spire in 1629), which you can still see. This is the Old Tolbooth, whose fine lead steeple rises

Aberdeen Press and Journal

King's College in Old Aberdeen

above the modern roofs at the E. end of the present municipal buildings. Here was housed the Maiden, Scotland's form of the guillotine, used in 1562 to execute Sir John Gordon, the son of the Earl of Huntly who died at the Battle of Corrichie. The tradition is that Mary Queen of Scots wept as she watched the sentence carried out; she occupied the Earl Marischal's lodging, which stood on the E. side of the Castlegate and was demolished in 1766 to make way for the present-day Marischal Street, which leads down to the harbour.

The Castlegate is no longer a market-place, thanks to the exigencies of modern traffic (provision for open-air markets is made on a cleared space off Justice Street to the E.), but the last of its many market crosses, a hexagonal structure of six open arches dating from 1686, is a real work of art. The entablature above the arches carries carved portraits of the ten Stuart sovereigns, and is surmounted by a slender shaft bearing a unicorn rampant. It was the work of a local mason, who did the job for £100.

Apart from the Salvation Army Citadel at the E. end, already mentioned, and the Town House, notable buildings include, at the corner of King Street (1842), Archibald Simpson's North of Scotland Bank, whose curving pillared portico is surmounted by a pediment bearing a coloured terra-cotta sculpture of the Goddess of Plenty; the Athenaeum, also by Simpson, at the SW. end of the square, which was built as a club and reading room in 1822 and is now a restaurant, affectionately known as "Jimmy Hay's" after the original owner, and the fine Union Bank building at the corner of Marischal Street by James Burn of HADDINGTON (1801).

At the W. end of Castlegate you can pass along the one-sided Exchequer Row to the Shiprow, probably the most ancient street in Aberdeen, now all gone save for one of the oldest houses in the city, Provost Ross's house, built in 1594 by Alexander Jamesone, father of George the portrait painter. Restored after the Second World War, it is now the local headquarters of the British Council. Returning to Union Street directly up Shiprow, and crossing it at the Town House corner, you may walk N. along Broad Street to the neo-Gothic Marischal College. The three-storey frontage and fifteen-storey tower of St Nicholas House (municipal offices, including the central information bureau) now dominate the N. side of the street. Near the main entrance a flight of steps leads down to an inner courtyard where, incapsulated in modernity, stands Provost Skene's House,

Aberdeen: Provost Skene's House
Aberdeen Press and Journal

whose W. wing dates from 1545 and was originally an L-plan mansion – a "land" and "inland". Sir George Skene of Rubislaw, a wealthy merchant who traded in Danzig and later became the Provost of the burgh, acquired it in 1669, adding the E. wing with its decorated doorway (surmounted by his coat of arms) and the two stair-turrets. The building, restored by the town council in 1951, is open to the public and contains, among other treasures, a remarkable cycle of religious paintings in tempera on the timber vault of the long gallery. Hidden for 300 years under plaster, they are believed to date from 1622. Panels depict the Annunciation, the Adoration of the Shepherds, and the Crucifixion. Other panels show how medieval religious motifs persisted in the strongly episcopalian North-East long after the Reformation. The two with-drawing-rooms on a lower floor have oak panelling of Skene's day, and there are several handsomely decorated plaster ceilings.

Across Broad Street, St Nicholas House now confronts Marischal College, founded as a specifically Protestant second university for Aberdeen by George Keith, 5th Earl Marischal, in 1593, in the old buildings of the Greyfriars Monastery. The present buildings forming the inner three sides of the quadrangle are Archibald Simpson's work and date from 1844, while the magnificently elaborate Broad Street frontage forming the fourth side of the square (designed by A. Marshall Mackenzie) was completed in 1906.

At the time of its completion, Marischal College was the second largest granite building in the world, the largest being the Escorial in Spain. The fretted pinnacles of the College – that gleaming white architectural tour-de-force – have been criticized for their over-elaboration, but they mark the highest level of ingenuity in the working of granite. Of the original building, only one stone remains. It bears the College motto ("They haif said. Quhat say they? Lat thame say"), which is supposed to have been placed there by the Earl Marischal in defiance of the critics who attacked his spoliation of the Abbey of Deer.

Inside the College the picture gallery, Mitchell Hall (where graduations are held) and the anthropological museum can be visited, and the Mitchell Tower (a later addition to Simpson's building) can be climbed. It is a natural transition from Marischal to King's College in Old Aberdeen, and one that generations of students have made daily since 1860, when the two universities (for there were two – as many as the whole of England could boast for centuries) were united. They are about 1 m. apart. To reach King's College from Marischal, the direct (though not perhaps the pleasantest) route is due N. by Gallowgate, Mount Hooly, King's Crescent, Spital, and College Bounds to the High Street of Old Aberdeen (an ecclesiastical burgh of barony created in the 15th cent. to remain an independent municipality until

fused with New Aberdeen in 1891). An alternative and perhaps simpler route is to turn E. along Queen Street from Broad Street, N. along King Street for about 1 m., then W. along University Road, which reaches High Street by skirting the E. side of King's College. Here the great flamboyant Crown Tower is unmistakable.

In front of it on the green lawn is the tomb of the founder, the great and good William Elphinstone (1431–1514), Chancellor of Scotland and Bishop of Aberdeen. He it was who in 1494 secured a Bull from Pope Alexander VI sanctioning the establishment of a *studium generale* in "the renowed City of Old Aberdeen", so that men who were until then "rude and barbarous" might have "the pearl of knowledge which shows the way to living well and happily". It was to be complete in all the faculties – theology, law, medicine, and the arts. The Crown Tower, with its "brave pourtrait of the royal diademe" of the patron King James IV, and the Chapel are the only survivors of the original building. The Chapel, completed in 1505, contains in its richly carved screen and stalls the finest example remaining of Scottish medieval ecclesiastical woodwork. To the SE. of the Chapel is the Cromwell Tower (1658). Of more recent work, the Library (1885) is a long and lofty hall with double transepts and a vaulted ceiling. It has been said that no library in Scotland is more magnificently housed.

It is impossible to give a detailed description of Old Aberdeen as a whole. Virtually all of it belongs to the University of Aberdeen, which is developing it as a "mixed village community" retaining all its old-time atmosphere and incorporating within it a *cité universitaire* with student halls of residence and new buildings for virtually all university faculties except medicine. This can be done because – while the ancient High Street, Chanonry, Dunbar Street, Don Street, and College Bounds are to remain untouched (and will in fact be carefully restored

St Machar's Cathedral, Aberdeen
Aberdeen Press and Journal

The Auld Brig o' Doon, Ayr (see p. 88)

and preserved on a plan prepared by the late Robert Hurd) – the former market lands of the burgh to the W., and existing college playing-fields, are being used for the new buildings.

And so, with a passing glance at the new buildings, like the Natural Philosophy Department with its futuristic mushroom-dome, and the Chemistry Department to the W., and the Taylor Building for Arts and Law to the E., let us pass along the High Street to the Old Town House at its N. end, which dates from 1721, noting by the way the charmingly restored tiled cottages of Grant Place and Wright's and Coopers' Place on the right. Beyond the Old Town House we cross St Machar Drive to enter the tree-girt Chanonry, now lined by the professors' houses that replaced the ancient manses of the medieval cathedral clergy. On the left, close to the Botany Department, are the Cruickshank Botanic Gardens, open to the public, and just before reaching the Cathedral itself, within a pleasant courtyard formed by low-roofed buildings on three sides of a square, is Mitchell's Hospital, originally built to maintain "five widows and five unmarried daughters" of trade burgesses of Old Aberdeen.

The twin spires of St Machar's Cathedral are graven on the hearts of innumerable Aberdonians. St Machar is said to have founded a church here in A.D. 580, on instructions from Columba to rest when he found the bend of a river that forms a shepherd's crook, as in fact the Don does at this point. Only a few stones remain of the Norman church that was built here when the see of the Bishop of Aberdeen was established in 1156. Both Old and New Aberdeen were given to the flames by Edward III in 1336, and the Cathedral had to be rebuilt. The Nave – almost all that remains in the present structure – was built between 1424 and 1440. It was formerly crested with embattled parapets, and the two western towers are still embattled like a castle. While the two pillars farthest to the E. are of sandstone and date from 1357, the 15th-cent. work is faced throughout with granite ashlar, the first instance of the large-scale use of dressed granite in the area. The twin spires of freestone that crown the W. towers were added by Bishop Gavin Dunbar, who about 1520 also installed the heraldic ceiling that is the chief glory of the interior. His carved tomb is in the ruined S. transept, but the effigy from it has now been taken inside to minimize the effects of weathering. In the various monuments within, the whole religious history of the North-East from the Middle Ages onwards can be traced, and we find also good modern stained glass.

There are many old houses in the remaining sector of the Chanonry (including No. 20 Chaplain's Court, the oldest inhabited house in Aberdeen, dating from 1519) and in Don Street, to which it leads. At the NW. corner of the Cathedral graveyard a gateway opens into Seaton Park, one of the loveliest open spaces in

Aberdeen Press and Journal

Union Street, Aberdeen

the city. Here you can walk through woods along the gradually steepening right bank of the Don to the deep gorge of the river immediately above the Brig o' Balgownie – one of the most splendid Gothic monuments in Scotland, with great buttresses and a spectacular pointed arch. It was built by Bishop Cheyne in the early 14th cent. and was so well endowed that funds from that source were more than adequate to build the new Bridge of Don farther downstream 400 years later.

From Balgownie to the new Bridge of Don you can walk along a picturesque footpath above the precipitous right bank – or motor across the old Brig and through Balgownie Village on the left bank. On the right bank on the far side of the new bridge begins the promenade, 2 m. long, that will take you all the way from the mouth of the Don to the mouth of the Dee. These 2 m. of sand forming Aberdeen Bay are responsible for making Aberdeen the largest holiday resort in Scotland. There is almost everything here that either the solitary or the gregarious could want for seaside pleasure.

Golf has been played on the Queen's Links here since 1625. There is a children's play-park, a large modern ballroom and restaurant, a bathing-station, and a carnival park with all the fun of the fair. In the summer there are organized beach games. But let us pass on to the far end of the promenade. It ends at Footdee – an 18th-cent. polite anglicization of Futty, the name of an ancient fishing hamlet whose patron was St Fotin. In 1809, harbour improvements necessitated the removal of the old village, and a new one, on "model" lines, was built by the Town Council, at the base of the N. pier at the river's mouth. It consists of three squares of cottages, which still retain the original atmosphere of an old-time fishing

Plate 2   Bass Rock, off East Lothian (see p. 97)
Scottish Tourist Board

village, although now occupied very largely by the workers in the nearby shipyards. Footdee (like Union Street, Old Aberdeen, the area of Bon-Accord and Crown Street, Rubislaw, and the Marine Terrace sector of Ferryhill) is now a Conservation Area.

Aberdeen began with a poor natural harbour, and made it a good artificial one. It still trades with the Baltic and the Scandinavian countries, and serves as the principal mainland port for ORKNEY and SHETLAND. From Footdee it is necessary to traverse the rather dreary stretch of York Street behind the shipyards, but, when you reach York Place, turn left along it, and then you can walk along the quays to Market Street, back to the city centre.

Aberdeen Fish Market on the Albert Basin off Market Street likes to be visited, and, if you can get up early enough in the morning to be there by 8 a.m., the auctioning of the catches from the trawler fleet, still one of the largest in Britain, is a spectacle you are not likely to forget. Still farther S., Market Street leads to the Victoria Bridge over the Dee, beyond which is Torry, the crowded industrial ward created by the trawling "revolution" at the end of the last century. Torry's Victoria Road leads to Balnagask, whence St Fittick's Road takes you down past the ruins of a medieval church to the Bay of Nigg. From there you can return to the city via the headland of Girdleness, with its lighthouse, along Greyhope Road, with its splendid views of the city and Aberdeen Bay.

In one other direction there are "sights" that you must not miss. Travel westwards from the W. end of Union Street via Alford Place, Albyn Place (where Archibald Simpson's fine High School for girls stands on your left), and Queen's Road to Rubislaw Quarry. This is reached by turning to the right up Royfold Crescent and then taking the first opening on the left. Here is the deepest quarry hole in Britain (465 ft), out of which in the past 200 years has come half of Aberdeen – as well as the stone for innumerable public works and buildings all over the world. Returning to Queen's Road and continuing westward, you reach (well signposted on the left) the avenue leading to Hazlehead Park, which, with its many acres of woodland, golf course, and rose and other gardens, its maze and its embryo zoo, has become an essential amenity to the city.

Something might be said about Aberdeen's complex of research institutions: the Macaulay Institute for Soil Research (near Hazlehead), the Rowett Institute for Animal Nutrition (at Bucksburn on the Don), the Torry Research Station (fish preservation), the Marine Laboratory (fishing techniques and location), and the Medical School (at Foresterhill). They are the modern scientific armoury in the war of conquest that Aberdeen has waged for centuries upon a beautiful but harsh environment – making a difficult land good. Because it is winning this war, Aberdeen has become the

Aberdeen Press and Journal

Aberdeen: Rubislaw Quarry

undisputed capital of a hinterland extending from the Dee to the SPEY and beyond.

For the motorist, here are the routes from the city, with the regions to which they lead.

From the Castlegate, A92 leads by King Street to the Bridge of Don and thence NNE. along the coast into Formartine and Buchan, "the treeless land where beeves are good".

By St Nicholas Street and George Street, A96 leads to Bucksburn, where A947 branches NNW. through the W. of Buchan to TURRIFF and BANFF, while A96 continues NW. to INVERURIE, capital of the Garioch, "the meal girnal of Aberdeenshire", and thence via the Glens of Foudland to HUNTLY, the capital of Strathbogie. This is the main N. road to INVERNESS.

By Alford Place at the W. end of Union Street, A944 leads WNW. to ALFORD, Strathdon, and the LECHT pass to TOMINTOUL and the SPEY, while, at 6 m., A974 branches due W. to TARLAND and the Howe of Cromar. By Holburn Street and the Great Western Road (right turn), A93, the main Deeside road, leads along the N. bank of the river to BANCHORY, BALLATER, BRAEMAR, and the Linn of Dee, where it ends in the heart of the Eastern CAIRNGORMS.

Finally, from the Bridge of Dee, A943, the S. Deeside road, leads up the right bank of the river through very lovely country to Banchory, where A93 may be rejoined; or a slightly longer and more roundabout route may be pursued S. of the river as far as BALMORAL. With A92, which can also be joined at the Bridge of Dee, we return to our starting-point, the main road to Stonehaven and the S.

All these roads out of the city, with the exception of A92 at its N. extension, are linked by a by-pass, known as the Ring Road or Anderson Drive, which, starting at the Bridge of Dee, encircles the greater part of the city and traverses the outskirts from Dee to Don. A connecting route between it and the northern part of A92 via Cairncry Road, Hilton Street, Leslie Road, and St Machar Drive is very clearly signposted.

Scratch an Aberdonian and you will find a countryman. While he is proud of his city, he is even more proud of the hinterland that sustains it, and to which he is, as often as not, united by ties of kinship and ancestral memory. He is anxious to share with all visitors his knowledge of its beauties even within the narrow orbit of the traditional "twal' mile roun' ": the spectacular grandeur of the rock scenery on the KINCARDINE coast to the S.; the delectable riverine scenery of Dee and Don among the hills and woods of the Province of Mar to the W.; the rolling cornlands of the Garioch; and the bare, green undulating plain of Buchan, fringed with the silver and gold of sea-spray and yellow sands that stretch northwards for a score of miles.

Aberdeen town and harbour

Aberdeen Press and Journal

ABERDOUR, *Fife* (Map 3, ref. 31⁹68⁵). An attractive small holiday resort facing S. over the Firth of FORTH. Its beach offers good sea bathing, and a sheltered harbour and anchorage have made it a popular sailing centre. The short (4,415-yd) but sporting golf course is undulating and inland compared with the coastal links of E. Fife, but has delightful views to compensate for the golfer's momentary lapses in form. Architectural and antiquarian interests are to be found in St Fillans Church, founded in the 12th cent., altered in the 16th and 17th cents., and a ruin from 1796 until restoration in 1926; and in the adjacent Aberdour Castle, dating from the 14th cent. and much extended by Regent Morton in the late 16th cent. INCHCOLM is accessible by boat from Aberdour harbour.

ABERFELDY, *Perthshire* (Map 2, ref. 28⁶74⁸). This small Highland town is an excellent touring centre surrounded by mountain scenery. The best approach is by Glen Cochill from DUNKELD. The road rises to 1,200 ft above sea level, and, before the descent to Aberfeldy, the view northwards from E. to W. includes the peaks of the Atholl Forest, Farragon, SCHIEHALLION, and BEN LAWERS. At the highest point of the road between Scotston Farm and Loch na Craig, the line of General Wade's military road can be distinctly seen running parallel over the moorland ½ m. distant to the W.

The bridge over the TAY at Aberfeldy was built by General Wade in 1733 as part of his pacification scheme for the Highlands after the Jacobite Rising in 1715. The bridge is regarded as one of the finest he built in Scotland, and in designing it he was helped by William Adam.

At the S. end of the bridge is the monument erected in 1887 to mark the enrolment of the Black Watch, 42nd regiment of the line, in May 1740. The "Watch", as it was known originally, was first raised in 1667 by various Whig clan chiefs "to be a constant guard for securing the peace in the Highlands and to watch upon the braes". The men wore dark tartan to distinguish them from the Guardsmen or Red Soldiers – hence the name Black Watch.

There is a municipal caravan site for 150 caravans, a nine-hole golf course, and good fishing. In the winter there is also access to skiing on Ben Lawers.

ABERFOYLE, *Perthshire* (Map 2, ref. 25³70¹). This modern village is now a tourist centre. To the E. and W. extends the QUEEN ELIZABETH FOREST PARK, and there is ample scope for pony-trekking and walks in the district. The Forestry Commission in the neighbourhood provides local industry.

But it is the older village, lying to the E. of the present one and near to the church, that evokes memories of the past, especially for readers of Walter Scott's *Rob Roy.* "The Clachan at Aberfoyle" is the setting of one of his most dramatic episodes in that novel, in which Bailie Nicol Jarvie figures so prominently. The present hotel stands on the site of the old clachan (Highland inn), and an old plough coulter is preserved upon a tree beside it to remind modern visitors of its fictionally historical associations.

Sir Walter Scott, apart from writing about Aberfoyle in his novel, was a frequent visitor here, and much popularized the district, including the TROSSACHS. Indeed, the Duke of Montrose in the early part of the last century felt impelled to build a road from Aberfoyle to Loch Achray for the use of tourists who flocked here after Scott's immensely popular *Lady of the Lake.* This road to the N. over the hills is still called "The Duke's Road".

ABERLADY, *East Lothian* (Map 3, ref. 34⁷67⁹). Situated on the S. side of the Firth of FORTH, Aberlady was used as the port of the county town, HADDINGTON, until the 19th cent., but is now primarily a residential village with a high proportion of daily commuters to EDINBURGH. The 18th-cent. church, with its 15th-cent. tower, is typical of ecclesiastical architecture in the county. It contains a monument by Canova to Lady Elibank, with an inscription said to have been put into Latin by Dr Johnson, but incorrectly and incomprehensibly cut by the local stonemason of the time. There are also in the village some attractive examples of early domestic buildings in cottage rows; some traditionally pantiled, others more grandly neo-Gothic. Aberlady Bay, where extensive sea-flats offer excellent wintering for waders and wildfowl, was declared a Nature Reserve (1,439 acres) in 1952, with unrestricted access for the public. The bay is not recommended for bathing or as a playground for young children.

ABERLEMNO, *Angus* (Map 6, ref. 35²75⁶), on the FORFAR–BRECHIN road, is a small village noted for some fine specimens of the ancient Pictish sculptured stones that are to be found throughout the county. A splendid upright slab, about 6 ft high, in the churchyard bears a finely ornamented cross surrounded by figures of animals, and on the reverse the representation of a battle-scene showing soldiers in action, both mounted and on foot. Two other similar stones are to be found at the farm of Flemington, ¾ m. N. of the church.

ABERLOUR, *Banffshire* (Map 6, ref. 32⁶84²). This burgh on the right bank of the SPEY is properly called Charleston of Aberlour from the name of its founder, Charles Grant of Wester Elchies, who laid out the original village in 1812. But it stands on a very ancient church site dedicated to St Drostan, and the original name of Aberlour parish was Skir-dustan – "Drostan's slice". Drostan's Well, surmounted by a simple cross, survives in the grounds of the local distillery. Opposite it on the other side of the main road is the kirkyard with the ruins of the pre-Reformation church, and here too the Lour Burn is spanned by the ruined arch of the old highway to the kirk. About 1 m. S., approached by a path along the Lour, is the Linn of Ruthrie, a fine waterfall in a wooded dell. Aberlour's mile-long, tree-shaded High Street has an attractive square and village green near its W. end, from which a road leads past the station to the banks of the Spey, here spanned by a picturesque suspension foot-bridge. Aberlour is famous for its orphanage, founded in 1875, and run by the Scottish Episcopal Church. Attached to the orphanage is the Church of St Margaret, worth a visit for the carving on its pillars of flowers, fruit, and animals in pre-Raphaelite profusion. About ½ m. E. is the neo-classic pile of Aber-lour House, now a preparatory school for GORDONSTOUN. Overlooked by the graceful cone of Ben Rinnes on the S., and by Ben Aigan on the NE., and surrounded by finely wooded, hilly country, Aberlour, with its fishing on the Spey, has a situation of great beauty.

ABERNETHY, *Perthshire* (Map 3, ref. 31⁹71⁶). From very early times, Abernethy seems to have been a place of some importance. About 1 m. SW., on high ground overlooking the town, is Castle Law fort. This is a timber-laced fort of the Iron Age. It was excavated at the beginning of this century and yielded a bronze brooch belonging to the second half of the first millennium B.C.

A short distance NE., the Romans built a legionary fortress at Carpow. This site, which was partly examined many years ago, is now in the course of systematic excavation. Carpow was a port, and the later town of Abernethy, lying near the junction of the rivers Earn and TAY, no doubt owed its importance to its riverine position. Traditionally Abernethy is a Pictish foundation and probably one of the tribal capitals of the Pictish kingdom. It was also at an early date the site of an important religious foundation dedicated to St Bridget, and was the seat of a bishop. Towards the end of the 11th cent. Culdees were established at Abernethy, but by 1273 the Culdee monastery had become a priory of Augustinian canons and a cell of the monastery at INCHAFFRAY. In 1476 there was a Collegiate Church served by a provost and prebends, the bishopric having been transferred to ST ANDREWS.

The Round Tower is one of only two such in Scotland. The other is at BRECHIN. The tower is 74 ft high and is built of courses of hewn stone. The door stands above the base, and when guarded could make the building impregnable. Such towers are Irish in origin; they served as places of refuge for the clergy in times of danger. In Ireland they date back to the 11th cent.

Near the base of the tower is a fragmentary Pictish sculptured stone.

According to Fordoun, Malcolm Canmore did homage to William the Conqueror at Abernethy in 1072.

ABINGTON, *Lanarkshire* (Map 2 ref. 29³62³). Set amid rolling Lowland hills devoted to rough grazing and sheep-farming, this is a characteristically attractive little S. Scotland township that has happily been preserved despite its nearness to the industrial belt. It lies just S. of the point where the main road from Carlisle (A74) branches to GLAS-GOW, STIRLING, and EDINBURGH.

Now, fortunately for itself, it is by-passed with the new dual carriage-way.

ABOYNE, *Aberdeenshire* (Map 6, ref. 35²79⁸). To most folk who have made its acquaintance, the name Aboyne conjures up a vision of Games Day on the Green of Charleston, a very large grassy arena flanked on two sides by the houses of the modern village, and of the panoply of pipes and pennants as the Marquess of Huntly, the Chief of the Games, takes the field. The Games, which are held annually on the first or the second Wednesday of September, were instituted in their modern form in 1867, but it is claimed that they are merely a revival of the ancient gathering held there and suppressed after the '45 Rising. They are considered by some of the best judges to be the premier athletic meeting of the kind in Scotland, since very stringent rules have always been enforced, and the site on the level haughland below the confluence of the DEE and the Tanar is completely flat. The Aboyne Games Committee deserves credit for having banished the spectacle of girl Highland dancers arrayed in a travesty of male attire weighed down with rows of jingling medals. They have insisted on the girl dancers' wearing what is called the Aboyne Dress, a simpler, more feminine uniform based on 18th-cent. Scots peasant costume.

The Aboyne village of today is largely the creation of Sir Cunliffe Brooks of Glentanar (whose daughter had married the 11th Mar-quess of Huntly) and dates from the 1880s. It is not, however, without its architectural distinction, two notable highlights being the Victory Hall and War Memorial and St Thomas's Episcopal Church. The original Charleston of Aboyne owed its origin to Charles Gordon, 1st Earl of Aboyne, the fourth son of George, 2nd Marquess of Huntly, who in 1670 obtained a charter giving him authority to erect a burgh of barony in close proximity to Aboyne Castle.

The first Aboyne Castle, which appears in 13th-cent. records as the "castrum de Obeyn",

Aboyne, Aberdeenshire

a motte-and-bailey stronghold, was followed by a stone keep, which was replaced in the 17th cent. by a tower-house, part of which still stands at the W. end of the mansion-house built in 1801 and transformed in the 1880s by Sir Cunliffe Brooks, who added the present baronial trimmings. Preserved at the Castle is the Formaston Stone dating from between A.D. 800 and A.D. 1000, which shows the mirror symbol, part of an elaborately designed Celtic cross, and an inscription in Ogham.

ACHARACLE, *Argyll* (Map 4, ref. 16⁸76⁷). At the SW. end of Loch SHIEL Acharacle is 27 m. from the ARDGOUR car ferry on Loch Linnhe. It has two hotels. Historically it is associated with Prince Charles Edward Stuart's first venture on to the mainland of Scotland in 1745. Today this highly characteristic district of W. Highland mountain, loch, and seascape beauty is mainly devoted to forestry employment and tourism. The trout, sea-trout, and salmon fishing is both good and available. It is one of the few mainland areas where Gaelic is still the first language of the people. The existence of a common Gaelic heritage is largely responsible for the cordial relationship that exists between the indigenous Catholics in the NE. part of the place (MINGARY) and the members of the Church of Scotland in the SW., who form the majority of the inhabitants of Acharacle. The priest and the minister take it turn about to preside at local concerts.

ACHILTIBUIE, *Ross and Cromarty* (Map 5, ref. 20³90⁸). This is little more than a crofting township strung along the W. coast at the head of Loch Broom. Set amid some of the wildest W. Highland mainland scenery, it is in a small way a remote holiday resort. It has climbing and sea fishing and, westwards out to sea, a justly famed view of the SUMMER ISLES.

ACHNACARRY, *Inverness-shire* (Map 5, ref. 21⁸78⁸), has been the seat of the Camerons of Lochiel, chiefs of the Clan Cameron, since the mid-17th cent. The former castle on a nearby site was destroyed by the Duke of Cumberland in 1746 because of the adherence of the then Chief (the "gentle Lochiel") to the cause of Prince Charles Edward Stuart. The family was exiled, but eventually returned under an amnesty in 1784. The present house, begun by Gillespie Graham in 1802, was used as a commando training centre in the Second World War. It was tastefully reconstructed by Ian G. Lindsay in 1952. Nearby is Loch ARKAIG, famed for its brown-trout fishing.

The Achnacarry district, with its celebrated Dark Mile (a fine tree-lined avenue), is redolent of the more genuinely romantic associations of the '45. Popular novelists have done their best to inject it with the saccharine of their trade, but the place remains untouched.

ACHNASHEEN, *Ross and Cromarty* (Map 5, ref. 21⁶85⁷). This hamlet, with but few pretensions to architectural originality, save that its hotel is literally a part of the lonely railway station, occupies an important geographical position. It is at the point of watershed between E. and W. in this central part of the N. Highland mainland. To the W. lies Loch MAREE, noted for sea-trout; to the SE. tower the twin peaks of Sgurr a'Mhuilinn and Sgurr a'Ghlas. It is a climatic and central point of expedition for this hill and loch country.

AE, *Dumfriesshire* (Map 2, ref. 30²58⁷). Commonly known as Scotland's forest village, Ae was founded by the Forestry Commission in 1947 in co-operation with DUMFRIES County Council. Set in a conifer forest of more than 12,600 acres, the village consists of about fifty houses, a modern primary school with some sixty pupils, a village shop and post office combined, and a community hall. The valley now has a total population of around 200, compared with thirty in pre-forestry days.

Conceived at a time when strategic reserves of timber were still in fashion, the village was originally intended to be considerably larger. Output now, however, is destined for chipboard and paper-pulp industries and needs only a minimum of processing in the forest.

Experiments at Ae have resulted in notable advances in forestry techniques. Mechanized ploughing and new fertilizing methods have resulted in successful afforestation of peat bog previously classified as unplantable. Plantations have been established to a height of 1,750 ft, well above the normal tree-line; work study, pioneered here by the Commission, has brought about the introduction and development of new tools and an economical system of deploying labour. The conception of crown-thinning is another innovation evolved at Ae; and research continues into the problems of deer control, wind-blow, and replanting.

The forest itself consists mainly of Sitka spruce, but has also swatches of larch, small stands of Scots pine, and some Norway spruce. The public road from Ae Bridge to Closeburn is lined with ornamentals and exotics to break the monotony of the conifers.

The village, although young in years, sustains the full range of traditional rural social activities, and has introduced an indigenous tradition of its own – an annual race to the top of the fire-tower.

AIGAS, *Inverness-shire* (Map 5, ref. 24⁶84¹). This is in general a deep gorge in the R. BEAULY. It is now used as a dam and generating station for the STRATHFARRAR hydro-electric scheme opened in 1963. The dam is 65 ft high.

To the S. along the river is Eilean Aigas, an island that contains an unusual house. Here the Lord Lovat of the '45 used to retreat at difficult times. In the early 19th cent., Eilean Aigas House was lived in by the odd pair of brothers known as the "Sobieski Stuarts", who sincerely deluded themselves into believing that they were legitimate grandsons of Prince Charles Edward Stuart, and therefore that the elder was the *de jure* monarch of Britain. Though living in romantic if constricted circumstances, they behaved as royalty, but did not press their claim. Their amiable manners in seclusion induced some eminent Victorians to believe their pretension. Amongst these is said to have been Queen Victoria, who, when she was at the height of her Highland enthusiasm, and not fearing any serious assault on her throne, allowed herself some benevolent Gothic daydreams about this pair. Indeed, she was at times known to express ardent "Jacobite sentiments". This innocent pair of eccentrics – who incidentally, by their allegedly erudite writings on the tartan, did much to stimulate the tartan-fever of the early 19th cent. – evidently appealed to this side of her nature.

AILSA CRAIG, *Ayrshire* (Map 2, ref. 20²60⁰), is the sentinel rock of the Firth of CLYDE. Ailsa Craig is a large volcanic core over 1,000 ft high lying about 10 m. due W. of GIRVAN and about 13 m. SE. of the Island of ARRAN. It lies in the parish of DAILLY. The island is notable for its large population of sea-birds, which nowadays are allowed to breed unmolested. These include large numbers of gannets (solan geese) and puffins. At one time a thriving colony of rabbits was also present. There is a lighthouse, the ruins of an old castle, and a quarry from which comes the granite for the famous Ailsa Craig curling stones. The rock was written about by both Keats and Wordsworth but, strangely enough, mentioned by Burns only in an ironic aside in one of his songs.

AIRDRIE, *Lanarkshire* (Map 2, ref. 27⁷66⁵). Now a populous burgh with an industrial history, in the heart of Scotland's industrial belt linking GLASGOW and EDINBURGH, Airdrie is becoming more of a dormitory town, and it supplies workers for COATBRIDGE, CALDERCRUIX, and Glasgow, from which it is only 11 m. to the E. Before its industrial and important dormitory status, it had small but significant beginnings.

In 1670 it was only a farm-steading; but Robert Hamilton, who became owner of it, had ambitions for the place. He built houses for feuing, and in 1695 got through an act of parliament making it a market town, which held a weekly market and four fairs each year. It became a burgh in 1821, and extended the limitations of its burgh in 1885, 1927, 1937, and 1951. It used to be on the main turnpike road – Glasgow, BATHGATE, Carlisle, STIRLING; and, as soon as the railways began to operate in the 1820s, it was well served by them, especially at the height of its iron-founding and coal-mining prosperity.

AIRDS MOSS, *Ayrshire* (Map 2, ref. 26²62⁸). This is the name given to a stretch of high moorland, N. of LUGAR, and between Bello Water and the R. Ayr. It is associated with the Covenanters.

The monument known as Cameron's Stone marks the place where, on the 20th of July 1680, an action was fought by the Covenanters against a company of dragoons. The leaders of the Covenanters were Hackston of Rathillet and Richard Cameron, who left his name to a religious sect and to a regiment. Cameron was killed; Rathillet was taken as a prisoner to EDINBURGH and, it was alleged by his followers, tortured to death.

The original stone was a flat slab laid down about fifty years afterwards, giving the names of the Covenanters who fell, and showing an open Bible and a hand grasping a sword.

AIRTH, *Stirlingshire* (Map 2, ref. 29⁰68⁷). This village, with its castle, is an example of an ancient burgh and port that has declined in importance yet keeps its identity upon the very edge of the central Scotland industrial belt.

Founded by William the Lion as a medieval burgh, as far back as the turn of the 12th into the 13th cent., Airth evidently failed. It was refounded in 1597 in the reign of James VI as a free port on the FORTH. Thus it continued until 1760, when it was superseded by Carronshore to deal with the local ironworks. The houses of the town that remain are 18th-cent. in style and have some interesting carved stones.

Just ¼ m. NW. of Airth are Dunmore Tower and Park. The former, called the Elphinstone Tower, was built in the early 16th cent. and was acquired in 1754 by John, 4th Earl of Dunmore. In 1820–2 the 5th Earl built a Tudor-Gothic house. It has a 6-acre walled garden with the celebrated "Pineapple" as the focal point. This is a colossal pineapple carved on the stone portico of a garden retreat put up in 1761.

ALEXANDRIA, *Dunbartonshire* (Map 2, ref. 23⁹68⁰). This exotically named town lies on the R. Leven and in the Vale of Leven, associated with the Scots 18th-cent. novelist Tobias Smollett. The place's main preoccupation was the bleach business established in 1768. Later came turkey-red dyeing, of which the town had almost a world monopoly. No turkey-red dyeing is done there now, as the industry was badly hit after the First World War. This town was the site of the Argyll Motor Co., which early in this century produced the first complete motor car in Scotland. Their premises were taken over in 1936 by the R.N. torpedo factory, and in 1971 by a large electronics concern, which closed some months later, causing serious redundancy.

ALFORD, *Aberdeenshire* (Map 6, ref. 35⁸81⁵). This farming mart centre and pleasant modern village on the S. bank of the DON, in the centre of a rich arable vale sheltered by the hills, is chiefly famous for a battle and a poet. The battle took place on the 2nd of July 1645, at the height of the Marquess of Montrose's wonderful summer campaign in aid of the otherwise failing cause of Charles I. Having defeated the covenanting General Urry at AULDEARN near NAIRN, Montrose moved S. via Corgarff to try conclusions with General Baillie, and took his stand on a hill to the W. of the present village. Baillie was outnumbered and did not intend to give battle, but was drawn across the Don and into the fray by skilful manoeuvring. Cavalry and infantry became confused, and the rear of the covenanting force was enveloped and the army routed. It was a victory that cost Montrose dear, for he lost in it his devoted friend and ally, Lord George Gordon, the eldest son of the Marquess of Huntly.

The poet of Alford was Charles Murray, born at Eastgate in 1864, who achieved a world-wide vogue with his nostalgic and patriotic poems in *Hamewith*, but is more justly renowned for having raised North-East dialect verse to a level of technical perfection

that has never been surpassed. Alford is still justly proud of *Hamewith*.

Alford played a notable part in the farming revolution at the end of the 18th cent., and, by the time the railway had come in 1859, the hill of Callievar was cultivated up to 950 of its 1,480 ft. The railway has gone, but the village it created continues to expand in the sunlight of agricultural prosperity. S. of the village is the now restored tower of Balfluig, and there are interesting monuments in the kirkyard of the old parish church, the centre of the original Kirkton, 1½ m. W. of the village. At Bridge of Alford (2 m. W.) lies another hamlet, with a famous anglers' inn; at Montgarrie, just N. of Alford on the N. bank of the Don, is another thriving village with an old meal mill.

ALLOA, *Clackmannanshire* (Map 2, ref. 28⁷69³). On the road between STIRLING and KINCARDINE-ON-FORTH, this go-ahead little town is the principal industrial, commercial, and administrative centre of Scotland's smallest county. In addition to brewing (started in 1784), the manufacture of yarn and woollens, and engineering, for all of which it is nationally known, the town has developed a wide variety of light industry, including the manufacture of boxes, bottles, and agricultural implements, together with bottling and whisky distilling. This growth was originally based on the town's situation as a port on the FORTH and its proximity to surrounding coalfields. The harbour and docks (approached by Lime Tree Walk, first planted in 1714) have declined with the decrease in shipping since the Second World War.

The town has good sporting facilities – for football, cricket, tennis, and particularly golf at Shawpark (an excellent inland course laid out by James Braid in 1936).

Alloa: the Church of St Columba
Scottish Tourist Board

ALLOWAY, *Ayrshire* (Map 2, ref. 23⁴61⁸), is now a residential suburb of AYR lying 3 m. S. of the town centre. It is, of course, the birthplace of Robert Burns, and the Burns Cottage is maintained as a memorial. Included in the cottage grounds is a fine museum of manuscripts and other relics, which attract both tourists and students. The average number of visitors to the cottage and museum each year is as high as 120,000. This cottage, built in 1758, is by far the oldest house in the village, which is comparatively modern, being built for the most part since the latter half of the 19th cent. During the past decade the surrounding area has been much used for private housing so that the village has become encircled with modern bungalows. Thanks to careful town-planning, however, the "atmosphere" has not been affected and Alloway remains to all appearances the same as it did 50 years ago.

The name means "the steep river bank by the cairn" and derives from the ancient burial cairn that lies about ½ m. S. of Burns Cottage and is woven into the story of Tam O' Shanter. This cairn was of some importance in past days and many of the local place-names refer to it. Close to the cairn is Mungo's Well, also referred to in the poem. In this case the name refers again to the steep river bank, not to the ancient saint, and means "the well by the steep place". Further E. and still on the bank of the river is Alloway Mote, for many centuries the place of justice for the locality. The river is, of course, the R. Doon, which is notable for having, for many miles, one steep bank (not two). Because the steep bank is invariably wooded, it still has good cause to be called "bonnie" as in the well-known song.

ALNESS, *Ross and Cromarty* (Map 5, ref. 26⁶86⁹). This village is built on both sides of the R. Averon or Alness, which flows into the CROMARTY Firth and provides excellent sport in its lower reaches for brown-trout anglers.

About 3 m. W. of INVERGORDON, it is the first village to be planned in detail to accommodate that town's greatly increasing population resulting from the development of new industries (in particular the British Aluminium smelter). It is designed to grow to some 16,000 people eventually, and facilities such as a community centre, school and playing fields are now well under way.

Near to Alness is the Black Rock of Novar, a remarkable ravine about 2 m. long. The "Indian temple" on Knock Fyrish on the S. road to Alness was built by General Sir Hector Munro of Novar (1726–1805) as work to relieve unemployment.

ALTNABREAC, *Caithness* (Map 7, ref. 30⁰94⁵). No more than a railway station, in the middle of a huge area of peat moss, 23 m. SW. of WICK, this desolate spot is interesting as the scene of an experiment conducted by the North of Scotland Hydro-Electric Board in the 1950s. The idea was to produce milled-peat electricity generation on the lines of the successful Irish plant at Ferbane (Co. Offaly). A plant for harvesting and handling peat was installed, and approximately 200 acres of bog-land were levelled and drained and about 3,000 tons of milled peat produced. A 2,000-kW gas turbine generating station was built in 1956 at Braehour and operated between 1958 and 1960.

ALTNACEALGACH, *Sutherland* (Map 5, ref. 22⁷91⁰). No more than a lonely inn on the road NW. from BONAR BRIDGE to INCHNADAMPH, and situated near to the border with Ross and Cromarty, this, one of the oldest fishing hotels in Scotland, is on the verge of the wild and unique scenery of Sutherland. There is climbing, with fine views of Benmore, Assynt, Cul Mor, Cul Beag, and the incomparable SUILVEN.

But it is the brown-trout angling that will particularly attract many to this isolated spot. The sport is varied and plentiful, varied in the size and quantity of fish, and varied in location between hill lochs and streams. Loch Veyatie is noted for large trout of the *Salmo ferox* kind.

ALTNAHARRA, *Sutherland* (Map 5, ref. 25⁷93⁵). An angling resort at the extreme W. tip of Loch NAVER, and surrounded by spectacular mountains (Ben Hope and Ben Klibreck), this village and hotel have become popular amongst anglers for salmon, sea-trout, and brown trout. Apart from Loch Naver, there is access to other nearby lochs. Recently Altnaharra has been one of the localities in which angling courses have been available in the autumn.

ALVA, *Clackmannanshire* (Map 2, ref. 28⁸69⁷), on the STIRLING–MILNATHORT road, is one of the pleasant small Hillfoots' towns that lie in the Devon valley along the base of the Ochils. Its immediate neighbours E. and W. are TILLICOULTRY and MENSTRIE. The river was the original source of power on which the town's still thriving woollens trade was developed. Shawls, scarves, and rugs, all finely woven and including a fair amount of tartan in design, are the specialities of Alva's mills. The town is also widely known as the home of a family firm of printers and publishers noted for their work in technical and foreign language books. Local benefactors have provided over the years a full complement of recreational amenities, and the glen behind the town has one of the county's leading tourist attractions. Known as the Silver Glen, from 18th-cent. mineral workings, its lower reaches have been laid out in walks and gardens where festoons of illuminations are added as a gay decoration in late summer. The glen, which has a fine waterfall cascade at its head, also offers a route to the summit of Ben Cleuch (2,363 ft), the highest of the Ochils. This hill commands far views stretching from the GRAMPIANS to Merrick in Kirkcudbrightshire, and its summit cairn was once a popular rendezvous for those who wished to see the rising of the midsummer sun.

ALVES, *Moray* (Map 6, ref. 31³86²), is the centre of a fertile parish on completely level ground, with hardly a hill in the neighbourhood except Knock Hill, which is now surmounted by York Tower. This flat land claims to be the site of the meeting between Macbeth and the witches – the "blasted heath". It scarcely deserves that description now.

Near the old military road once stood "Moray's Cairn", just by which Lochaber and Danish axes were found, the relics of Norse–Celtic warfare.

ALVIE, *Inverness-shire* (Map 5, ref. 28⁶80⁹), consists of a church and a manse built on a spit of land jutting into the 70-ft-deep Loch Alvie. The church in this romantic situation has recently been restored. At the earlier restoration in 1880, 150 skeletons were discovered beneath the floor.

Between Loch Alvie and the R. SPEY stands Kinrara House, which was once the residence of the Dukes of Richmond and Gordon. The beautiful Duchess of Gordon who used her charm as a recruiting agent at the end of the 18th cent. is buried nearby. On Tor Alvie rises a 90-ft pillar put up to the memory of the 5th Duke of Gordon; also on the hill is a monument to the Highland soldiers who fell at Waterloo. At the hamlet of Lynwilg is a former coaching inn that looks over the loch from the E. Sir George Henschel, who was so closely associated with this district at the end of his life, lived at Lynwilg.

ALYTH, *Perthshire* (Map 6, ref. 32⁵74⁸), with a stream running right through the town, lies on the edge of the counties of Perthshire and Angus, and was created a burgh in 1488. Since the 14th cent. the town has manufactured woollen goods; it is now also engaged in jute-spinning and the manufacture of linen. Alyth stands on the edge of moorland and from its borders heather stretches all the way to BRAEMAR. An indicator on the summit of the Hill of Alyth (2 m. NE. of the town) gives points that can be viewed to the S.

Arches still standing in the old kirkyard are connected with the post-Reformation church, but are probably the site of an older one.

Near the town are the ruins of Bamff Castle, a Ramsay stronghold.

A spectacular waterfall, the Reekie Linn, may be seen 4 m. N. on the road to GLEN ISLA.

Some 1½ m. NE. of the town is Barry Hill, where traditionally King Arthur's wife, Queen Guinevere, was imprisoned after having been taken prisoner by the Scots and Picts. All that remains of this vitrified fort are a massive tumbled stone wall and subsidiary ramparts.

AMISFIELD, *Dumfriesshire* (Map 2, ref. 30⁰58²). Though erected as a burgh of barony in 1613, this is but a quiet village on the EDINBURGH road, NE. of DUMFRIES, with no present burghal pretensions. In 1685, some 70 years after Sir John Charteris obtained its charter, it had fewer than 100 inhabitants.

Amisfield Tower, nearly 1 m. away, is one of the finest 17th-cent. tower-castles in Scotland; it was built just after 1600. Elschieshiels Tower, near LOCHMABEN a few miles away, was built by the same talented architect. The tower incorporates traces of an older tower, and was occupied until quite recently. The interior is in good condition. It is a tall narrow building, 30 ft square and 77 ft high, consisting of four rooms, one above the other, with the stair in a circular turret; the high expanse of plain wall contrasts sharply with the complicated corbel table and cap-house at the roof.

AMULREE, *Perthshire* (Map 2, ref. 29⁰73⁶). This airy hamlet, surrounded by noble hills, held an important position when drove routes from the N., E., and W. joined here before descending the narrow cleft of the SMA' GLEN to CRIEFF. One of General Wade's military roads, built in the 1730s, followed almost the line of the modern road from Crieff to ABERFELDY and passed Amulree.

ANCRUM, *Roxburghshire* (Map 3, ref. 36³62⁵). This village and district is a part of the Borderland much associated with past warfare, not only in the era of Border struggles between England and Scotland but possibly dating back to Roman times. The village lies on the R. Ale in the path of the northward route into Scotland. About ¾ m. N. of the village are the ruins of a fort, Little Trowpenny, which was built before the Iron Age; NW. is Castle Hill Fort, almost as old, whose more plentiful remains may, however, have been rebuilt. The Roman road runs N. and S. to the E. of the village.

Near here, at Ancrum Moor, was fought one of the last Scottish victories in the Border affrays, when, at Lilliards Edge, a strong force of English invading Borderers was put to rout in 1545. But also in that year the Duke of Hertford, upon his devastating expedition into Scotland and her capital, paused to burn the two villages of Upper and Nether Ancrum. The caves on the left bank of the Ale were probably used as human habitations about this time and as a result of Border warfare.

ANNAN, *Dumfriesshire* (Map 3, ref. 31⁹56⁵). For long a seat of the de Brus family, Annan was the caput of their Annandale lordship from about 1124 until just after 1200 when they moved to their other motte (or mound forming the site of their earlier castle) at LOCHMABEN. The town may have been a Bruce burgh. It was almost certainly a Douglas burgh in the 15th cent.; its earliest surviving charter is that as a royal burgh in 1538.

The town lies at the mouth of the R. Annan, and developed from the Bruce motte, which with its bailey lies beside the river at the head of tidal water in the grounds of the pleasant Georgina Moat House, now a community centre and museum.

Fishing in the Solway by haaf net, and stake net, and by leister was the oldest industry, and it is still carried on by the first two methods. Shrimp-netting is important, and Annan cans a considerable quantity of shrimps. The town is surrounded by rich farmland, with dairying prominent, but in the last sixty years or so new industries have come to the neighbourhood.

Annan was the home of the blind Dr Black-lock, Burns's acquaintance. Clapperton, the explorer of West Africa, and Edward Irving, the great preacher, were boyhood neighbours here; and Thomas Carlyle taught in Annan Academy, the "Hinterschlag Gymnasium" of *Sartor Resartus*.

ANSTRUTHER, *Fife* (Map 3, ref. 35⁷70³). A seaport, market town, and burgh on the N. coast of the Firth of FORTH. Locally it is known as Ainster. The burgh was created from the amalgamation of two more ancient ones separated by the Dreel Burn, Anstruther Wester (with Cellardyke), a royal burgh of 1587, and Anstruther Easter, a royal burgh of 1583.

Anstruther Wester Church has been modernized, but retains a 16th-cent. bell-tower. Anstruther Easter's church was built in 1634. Its manse, older than the church (1590), is one of the oldest inhabited manses in Scotland. Anstruther Easter was the birthplace in 1780 of Dr Thomas Chalmers of revered memory. A great-hearted worker among the GLASGOW poor in the early 19th cent., this minister of the Kirk led the heroic act of Disruption (1843), which caused the founding of the Free Kirk (*see* "Scotland in History"), happily reunited with the Church of Scotland in 1929.

Modern Anstruther was essentially a fishing community until after the Second World War. The folk of the port caught the fish and undertook all sides of marketing and complementary industries. To a lesser extent they still do. But Ainster has become more of a holiday resort. With its rocky coastline and caves, with its situation in the eye of the sun, and with its old-fashioned charm, it allures holiday-makers from across the Firth.

The Isle of MAY is in the parish of Anstruther and can be visited by motor-boat.

ANTONINUS' WALL, *Dunbartonshire/Stirlingshire* (*see* especially ROUGH CASTLE), is the most important Roman work remaining in Scotland. It was the frontier line between FORTH and CLYDE marked out by Julius Agricola in A.D. 80. In A.D. 143 the legate Lollius Urbicus, acting for Emperor Antoninus Pius, laid out what was intended to be a permanent frontier. It consisted of a wall made of sods on a stone foundation, except in the eastern section, where the wall was of clay. In front was a ditch, and in the rear a military way. The garrison inhabited some twenty forts, mostly built of turf, and the barrier is 36 m. long. This frontier was held with at least two interruptions till about the end of the 2nd cent. ROUGH CASTLE, one of the best-preserved forts, is near BONNYBRIDGE, and three lengths of wall are in the charge of the Ministry of Public Building and Works. Watling Lodge is 1¼ m. W. of FALKIRK. About 1 m. E. of Bonnybridge is the stretch at Rough Castle; Seabegs Wood is situated ½ m. W. The wall runs from Carriden on the Firth of Forth to Old Kilpatrick on the Clyde.

APPIN, *Argyll* (Map 1, ref. 19¹74⁵). This district of Scotland, famed for its scenery and for the "Appin Murder" (*see* BALLACHULISH), once covered a wider area than it does today. Now Appin is the name given to Port Appin village between Loch Laich and Airds Bay, Portnacroish on the N. shore of Loch Laich, and Strath Appin running SE. from Loch Laich towards Loch Creran.

This was the ancient land of the Stewarts of Appin who built Castle Stalker *c.* A.D. 1500 on an island in Loch Laich. It was used as a hunting lodge by James IV. Later it fell to ruins, but has now been restored. The Appin House of today is of the 17th cent.; Aird's House SE. of Port Appin was built in the mid-18th cent.

The district is occupied by small farmers rather than crofters. Their lands surround the sea-lochs, which here have a broken shore with many bays and islands, a favourite resort for Scottish family holiday-makers. There is a ferry from Port Appin to LISMORE.

The Stewarts of Appin, as readers of R. L. Stevenson's *Kidnapped* and *Catriona* will recall, lost their lands and strength after the Jacobite attempt of 1745. The Appin Regiment fought at the Battle of CULLODEN, where the Jacobite cause was forever lost. The Appin colours, the only Jacobite banner to escape being burnt by the common hangman in 1746 at EDINBURGH, is now preserved in the Scottish United Services Museum in Edinburgh Castle.

APPLECROSS, *Ross and Cromarty* (Map 4, ref. 17¹84⁴). This is a well-known but remote township upon a peninsula between Lochs TORRIDON and Kishorn. It is a place of great scenic beauty, but of declining population and strength, and is known as the most inaccessible place on the mainland of Scotland.

The road to Applecross

In A.D. 671 Maelrubha, an Irish monk from Bangor, founded a monastery in this place. It existed for about 100 years before being destroyed by the Vikings. Remains of a pre-Reformation church can still be seen, and an old cemetery containing a Celtic cross 9 ft high.

The district is still in a sense a sanctuary, as the steamer service has been withdrawn. Applecross may be reached either by daily boat from Kyle of Lochalsh to Toscaig or by the road over Bealach nam Ba, one of the highest mountain roads in Scotland – summit 2,053 ft, with steep zigzag turns.

This remote and declining place of Highland habitation still continues to exist and to look out upon the island of RAASAY and the mountains of SKYE – as fair a view as any in Scotland.

ARBIGLAND, *Kirkcudbrightshire* (Map 2, ref. 29⁸55⁸), is a pleasant country house lying near the Solway shore at Gardenfoot Bay. The gardener's cottage on the drive from the road to Powilloment, just at the S., was the birthplace of John Paul, better known as Paul Jones, one of the founders of the American Navy; his father was gardener to the Craiks of Arbigland, prosperous DUMFRIES merchants who had business and estates in America. Dr James Craik, born 1727, was a friend of George Washington and the organizer of the medical service of the American Army; it was a Craik who left Paul an estate in Virginia, thus leading him to retire temporarily from the sea – he had been at sea since he was twelve, becoming mate and captain at an early age – and to take the

American side in the War of Independence. CARSETHORN lies 1½ m. NE., and SOUTHERNESS 1 m. S. across Gillfoot Bay; young Paul, as a baby, would see Southerness Lighthouse being built in 1747–8, and would be familiar with the busy shipping at Carsethorn.

The highly contorted lower carboniferous limestone reefs along the shore are rich in fossils and are of great interest.

ARBORY HILL, *Lanarkshire* (Map 2, ref. 29⁴62⁵). On the crown of this hill (1,407 ft), 1 m. ENE.of ABINGTON, and on a promontory overlooking the CLYDE valley, are the remains of a very well-preserved and spectacular prehistoric structure. It is a fort with a walled enclosure lying inside a set of ramparts and ditches, which may or may not be of one build with it. The interior contains what are perhaps surface remains of timber-framed houses, together with an enigmatic pile of stones and a rectangular foundation. "Enigmatic" is indeed the word most applicable to this piece of fortification, which is difficult to date with accuracy.

ARBROATH, *Angus* (Map 6, ref. 36⁸74¹). Having originally been given the charter of a royal burgh in 1599, and having now become a seaside resort as well as a fishing centre and a town containing a certain amount of industry, Arbroath bustles with contemporary life. It is, however, deeply associated with our Scottish past; and the mere mention of the words "Declaration of Arbroath" can stir what remains of Scottish blood to pride and admiration – that is, if that blood flows in the veins of one whose history lessons at school were not entirely confined to English history.

The town possesses a small harbour at the mouth of the Brothock Water, from which it derives its original name of Aberbrothock, now abbreviated to its present form. Its industries are therefore largely connected with the sea. Apart from fishing, there is sailcloth-making, the manufacture of rope-soled shoes, some engineering, and the work of a small boat-yard. The tourist industry is lively here and has a number of attractions to offer. Apart from golf, there is a large open-air swimming-pool, there is sailing, and you can take motor-boat trips up the coast. There is a fine sandy beach to the W. of the town. To the NE. are red sandstone cliffs with spectacular caves and a peculiar rock-stack known as Pint Stoup. To the SE. is the BELL ROCK or Inchcape associated with the "Abbot of Aberbrothock". Arbroath is associated too with Scott's novel *The Antiquary*, and the extravagantly restored "Hospitalfield" on the N. side of the town may be the original of Monkbarn in that tale.

Arbroath has much to offer to the holiday-maker; but to the antiquarian, to the lover of old architecture even when it has suffered decay, and (of course) to the student of Scottish history, the Abbey of Arbroath is of prime importance.

Originally a Cluniac priory founded by William the Lion in 1178 (the King is buried in the present sacristy), it was taken over by Tironesian monks from KELSO after 1233 and after two fires had set back the building. It was dedicated to St Thomas à Becket of Canterbury, and continued to flourish even after the Reformation until 1606, when it was declared a "temporal lordship". Thereafter it was ruined not by violence, nor by the deliberate hand of man, but by natural decay consequent upon lack of use – the fate of many pre-Reformation ecclesiastical buildings on which we shall have cause to comment in the course of this gazetteer. It is often unjust to the reformers to attribute to them deliberate iconoclasm. They merely turned their backs upon old buildings, and let nature and pilfering

humans (without any desire to destroy or commit sacrilege) have their way.

What remains, however, is impressive and important. Dr Johnson, in his visit to Scotland, said of Arbroath, "I should scarcely have regretted my journey had it afforded nothing more than the sight of Aberbrothock". There are some who would echo his words today. Considerable portions of the Abbey and its attendant buildings remain and are only the more striking for the gradual desolation (now of course halted) around them.

What remains that is striking is of the 13th cent. The most outstanding of these relics are the S. transept gable and the W. front with a ruined tower and portal. The S. transept, with arcades and triforium intact, is famous for its fine rose window. This was called the "O of Arbroath" and was in the days of the Abbey's life illuminated to act as a guide to ships at sea. Beside the transept is a vaulted building still remarkable for its acoustics. This may have been the sacristy.

To the W. and S. of the Abbey once stood the domestic buildings. There is a large gatehouse tower by the side of the Abbey pend. The Abbot's house, until fairly recently in use as a dwelling-place, is now a museum. A headless effigy may represent William the Lion, who is buried in the sacristy. One of the rooms is still called "Bruce's Bedroom".

The Abbey pend referred to above used to have a chamber over it. It was here that the Declaration of Independence, now usually styled the Declaration of Arbroath, was eventually signed in 1320, having been outlined, prepared, and completed in the Abbey itself. The Declaration was the product of a meeting of the Estates of Scotland, and was launched toward the ear of Pope John XXII, himself in exile in Avignon. The word "ear" used above is deliberate; for this unique manifesto of freedom, this declaration of the independence of the Kingdom of Scotland after Bruce had liberated her at BANNOCKBURN, was pronounced before the Pontiff by two Scottish emissaries in the noble, echoing audience chamber still to be seen in the *Palais des Papes* at Avignon. (*See* "Scotland in History".)

On the 11th of April 1951, the world was by headlines reminded in the liveliest way of Arbroath's place in Scottish history. On that date, early in the morning, the young Scotsmen who had removed the Stone of Scone, or Stone of Destiny, from Westminster Abbey (whither it had been taken by Edward I after his campaign in Scotland), and had kept it in Scotland for over three months, surrendered it on the High Altar of the Abbey of Arbroath. The young men were not prosecuted, but the Stone was removed in a Black Maria to spend the night in FORFAR gaol on its way back to London. There continues a legend or pious belief that the real stone is still in Scotland.

Arbroath Abbey

Scottish Tourist Board

ARDCHATTAN, *Argyll* (Map 1, ref. 19⁸73³), is a ruined priory adjoining a house that is still inhabited. This was one of the three houses, founded in Scotland in 1230 (the others being PLUSCARDINE and BEAULY), of what is reconditely known as the Valliscaulian order – that is, an ascetic branch of the Benedictines. It became a private house in the 17th cent. after the Reformation. The present owner is descended from the last prior, Alexander Campbell, who remained living in the house. The church was burned by Cromwellian soldiers in 1654. In the burying ground are several monuments in the characteristic W. Highland style.

ARDCLACH, *Nairnshire* (Map 5, ref. 29⁴84⁵). This is a hamlet some 7 m. SE. of NAIRN, on the R. Findhorn, and is associated with a curiosity – a detached belfry on a promontory above the river. It was built in 1655 and was used to call worshippers to a separate church nearby in the valley; it was also employed as a watch-tower, and it bears the evidence of fortification. It is 14 ft square and has two storeys; the upper one has a fireplace and gun-loops. This odd mixture of remote rural piety and remote rural fortified architecture is now a National Monument.

ARDEER, *Ayrshire* (Map 2, ref. 22⁷64¹). A giant factory occupying the barren ground between the estuary of the R. Garnock and the sea, Ardeer was first developed industrially in 1851, when ironworks were erected to develop the coal seams, traditionally worked since the 17th cent. In 1873 Alfred Nobel built his dynamite factory here, and it now houses the largest manufacturing unit in the Nobel division of I.C.I., producing chemicals for plastics, fertilizers, paints, adhesives, and explosives. Ardeer also has a large silicone plant, an important research centre, and a nylon works.

ARDENTINNY, *Argyll* (Map 2, ref. 21⁹68⁷). This small residential village that caters for visitors is characteristic of the W. Highland scenery that lies close to GLASGOW and to the industrial West – scenery that, owing to the fretted coastline and long arms of the sea, is still largely inviolate. It is at the end of a road from DUNOON, and on the shores of Loch LONG. Though the road from Dunoon stops at Ardentinny, there is a rough narrow track leading up Glen Finart to Loch Eck. From Ardentinny itself opens a fine view of Loch Long and the ROSENEATH Peninsula. This attractive little holiday resort now lies within the Argyll National Forest Park.

ARDERSIER, *Inverness-shire* (Map 5, ref. 27⁸85⁵). An inner Moray Firth fishing village, Ardersier is sometimes locally known as Campbeltown, not to be confused with CAMPBELTOWN on Kintyre. Ardersier got this alternative name from the fact that the lands of Ardersier were acquired from the Bishops of Ross by the Campbells of Cawdor in 1574. In 1623 they obtained a charter under the Great Seal to erect a burgh of barony called Campbeltown, with a weekly market. Despite the intention of the Campbells of Cawdor, it never succeeded in achieving a higher status than that of a village. In its layout, however, you may perceive here and there the traces of greater things. The village, with its small fishing industry, has a dependence on the nearby FORT GEORGE. It was once said that "the village of Ardersier has been raised in consequence of the occasion of the garrison". A military museum at Fort George reminds us of the occasion.

ARDGARTAN, *Argyll* (Map 2, ref. 22⁸70¹), a peninsula between Glen Croe and Loch LONG, is the setting for Ardgartan House, which stands at the foot of Glen Croe and 2 m. SW. of ARROCHAR. This large house is now a Scottish youth hostel. There are also camping grounds and a caravan park. Ardgartan House is a favourite centre for pony-trekking through the Argyll National Forest Park, and is situated in characteristic SW. Highland circumstances. It is easily accessible from GLASGOW and from the industrial West.

ARDGAY, *Ross and Cromarty* (Map 5, ref. 26⁰89⁰). This small village is at the Ross end of the bridge over the Kyle of Sutherland at the head of the DORNOCH Firth. Despite its quiet circumstances, Ardgay has a curious history. In 1686, a deed was granted for erecting the place into a burgh of barony; but it never succeeded in growing into one. Nevertheless it did have an old-established winter market, which it succeeded in retaining by the energy of its inhabitants. There used in this district to be a certain quartz stone; and, wherever that stone happened to be, there the market took place. Sometimes the stone travelled as far as Assynt, and the market followed it. The inhabitants of Ardgay, however, were far-seeing enough to capture this stone and to keep it in their village. This they did by building it into the wall of the village inn. The stone, known in Gaelic as "clach eiteag", is in a prominent position nearby. It stands there to remind not only the villagers themselves, but also the passers-by, of how the winter market of Ardgay became held down and localized there.

In 1845 the churchyard of Croick, 10 m. W. of Ardgay, sheltered the people who, under the system of the Clearances, had been evicted from the nearby Glencalvie. Before their departure, these unfortunates scratched on the church windows various brief messages. These are still to be seen.

ARDGOUR, *Argyll* (Map 5, ref. 19⁹76⁴).
This hamlet is at the W. side of the narrows of
Loch Linnhe and at the S. end of the Great
Glen, which divides Scotland from NE. to
SW. This hamlet, which takes its name from the
larger and more famous district surrounding it,
is by the CORRAN Ferry, 10 m. S. of FORT
WILLIAM. For those who wish to approach
Ardgour from the E., the Corran Ferry saves a
drive of 40 m. NE., W., then SW. About ½ m.
N. of the Ferry on the western side is Ardgour
Church. This church is notable as it represents
one of those designed by Thomas Telford for
the government to build in the 1820s and 1830s.
Its action in providing Highlanders with well-
built churches at a time when their fortunes
were at an extremely low ebb was without
doubt a humane one on the part of the government. It did not, however, do much to stop the
flow of de-population that from various
causes, governmental and otherwise, had begun
in the 18th cent. About 1 m. W. of the Corran
Ferry stands Ardgour House, the seat of the
McLeans of Ardgour, who from the 15th cent.
had owned the whole district of Ardgour; the
family still owns much land in the locality.

The celebrated district of Ardgour stretches
from Loch Linnhe to Loch SHIEL. It is an
extremely mountainous area, and the mountains descend straight to the lochs; there is
therefore very little arable land. The estates are
mainly sporting, but contain also some sheep
and cattle farms. Ardgour has been further
opened up by car ferry services between
LOCHALINE and CRAIGNURE and TOBER-
MORY, on MULL, and with OBAN.

ARDLUI, *Dunbartonshire* (Map 2, ref.
23²71⁵), is the terminal point for the pleasure
steamers on Loch LOMOND, and at the very
N. end of the loch the little village is finely
situated. It lies near the junction of Dunbartonshire, Argyll, and Perthshire. It is much
dominated by mountains. To the SW. lies Ben
Vorlich; to the NW. lie the great mountains of
Perthshire, which are approached from Ardlui
by the road running through the beautiful Glen
Falloch.

ARDNAMURCHAN, *Argyll* (Map 4, ref.
15⁵76⁵). The point and the peninsula of Ardnamurchan at once catch the eye of anyone who
is looking at a map of the W. coast of Scotland,
for this is the part of the mainland that reaches
farthest out into the Atlantic. Ardnamurchan
Point might be spoken of as the Land's End of
Scotland, and the Ardnamurchan Peninsula as
the Cornwall of Scotland. They surpass, however, both Cornwall and Land's End in two
respects. First, they reach farther out into the
Atlantic; second, the view from Ardnamurchan
Point is far superior to anything seen from
Land's End. Indeed, if one excepts the prospects
seen from many mountain tops in Scotland, the
view from the shores of Ardnamurchan Point

is as magnificent as any that you will find on the
main body of Scotland itself. Standing at the
point and by the sea-shore, you have a view of
the Small Isles and of the Inner Hebrides.
COLL and TIREE lie nearby and to the W. To
the NW. is the splendid prospect of the mountains of RUM; northwards too is the sight of
the island of EIGG and the island of MUCK.
On a fine day, and without climbing any
eminence at the point, you may see the
southern Outer Hebrides far out in the Atlantic
Ocean. At Ardnamurchan Point stands a
lighthouse; it was built in 1849 and is 144 ft
high. But there is no need to ascend it if you
would see the magnificent views from this place
by the sea-shore.

The district of Ardnamurchan covers the
whole peninsula. To the W. it ends in the point.
On the E. it is bounded by the sea lochs of
Moidart and Sunart. This most westerly
district of Scotland's mainland was once owned
by the MacIans of Ardnamurchan, a branch
of the Clan Donald, which flourished until the
end of the 16th cent.; their fortress then
declined at the hands of the powerful Clan
Campbell. Later owners came from the South.
Some indeed may have come from the Borders
of Scotland. Readers of Boswell's account of
Dr Johnson's tour in the Highlands and
Islands may recall the Doctor's annoyance
when a Highland chief asked him whether he
was one of the Johnstons of Ardnamurchan.

From a geological point of view, the district
of Ardnamurchan is interesting. A comparatively recent ice-sheet at the end of the Ice Age
passed westwards over the whole of the peninsula, and in consequence there is little soil.
There are, however, good cattle stocks, including a herd of Highland cattle at MINGARY
CASTLE. The road to Ardnamurchan Point
keeps on the S. shore of the peninsula, and
there is no road along the N. side. A boat runs
regularly from TOBERMORY on the Island of
MULL to KILCHOAN on Ardnamurchan.
While Ardnamurchan peninsula and point are
not inaccessible, this lack of a circular road
keeps the peninsula remote yet renders it a good
holiday place. There is plentiful trout fishing in
the hill lochs.

ARDOCH, *Perthshire* (Map 2, ref. 28⁴70⁹).
Roman remains, excavated here in 1896–7,
showed a complicated variety of earthworks
from superimposed groups of forts. The finds
point to occupation in both Agricolan and
Antonine periods. The works were probably
(1) a road and signal post, (2) a large marching
camp, and (3) a small marching camp.

ARDRISHAIG, *Argyll* (Map 1, ref. 18⁵68⁵),
is now a seaport on Loch Gilp, which is an
inlet of Loch Fyne – that long arm of the sea
that penetrates into the SW. Highlands a mere
30 m. or so W. of GLASGOW. It owes its comparative importance, indeed possibly its

existence, to the fact that it lies at the S. end of the CRINAN CANAL. The canal was built in 1801 and connects Loch Fyne with the Sound of JURA and the Atlantic Ocean. The village and port grew up immediately after the canal was opened. Its main occupation was herring fishing in Loch Fyne, but this industry has unfortunately and unaccountably declined. Ardrishaig, however, still has a steamer service and was used as a naval base in the Second World War for anti-submarine training. In the 19th cent., many people living in the W. Highlands of the mainland S. of OBAN used the port of Ardrishaig to connect them with Glasgow and the S. on their way to England.

ARDROSSAN, *Ayrshire* (Map 2, ref. 22⁴64²). Here is an example of 19th-cent. town-planning; the town and harbour were laid out by the 12th Earl of Eglinton in 1805, but it was not until the use of sea-going steamboats that the project began to be successful. The port handles an increasing volume of imports and exports for the Scottish iron and steel industries, the great chemical works at ARDEER and passenger and freight traffic with Northern Ireland and the Scottish islands. The Shell oil refinery handles 1,000,000 tons of petroleum products annually, including fuel for PREST-WICK and ABBOTSINCH airports. But Ardrossan has extensive, clean beaches, and there are ample holidaymakers' pursuits.

ARDVRECK, *Sutherland* (Map 5, ref. 22⁵92³), is the ruins of a castle built about 1591; the remains of its three storeys stand on a rocky peninsula thrusting into Loch Assynt. It was the seat of the Macleods of Assynt, who owned this district. This ruined castle is celebrated as the place in which James Graham, Marquess of Montrose, was captured after he had lost the Battle of Carbisdale. Those who defend Macleod of Assynt claim that he found the great soldier wandering on the moors, arrested him, and sent him promptly to the authorities. A far uglier story gained credence at the time. Some people said that Montrose, exhausted and hungry, threw himself on Macleod's mercy. Macleod accepted him and entertained him with kindness. Then thoughts came to Macleod of the blood money, to the extent of £25,000, on Montrose's head. Greed overcame the Highland chief; he kept Montrose in comfort, and then sent news of his presence to the authorities. The matter is still hotly debated today. This capture was the end of Montrose's remarkable and romantic military career. Thereafter he was taken to EDINBURGH, where he was executed.

ARDWELL, *Wigtownshire* (Map 2, ref. 21¹54⁵). One of the few brochs in the SW. stands here on the precipitous W. coast of the Mull of GALLOWAY; it lies on a narrow rocky

spit cut off from the land by a wall and traversed by a ditch spanned by a built cause-way. The broch is fairly well preserved, having a normal entrance to seaward and another to landward – a very rare feature. It measures 30 ft in diameter interiorly, and its walls are 13 ft thick. Altogether apart from the broch, this wild coast is worth seeing, and the famous fish-pool and sub-tropical gardens at Logan are not far away.

ARGYLL'S BOWLING GREEN, *Argyll* (Map 2, ref. 22³69⁶), is the peninsula which lies between Loch Goil and Loch LONG, in the sea-fretted SW. Highlands near GLASGOW. It was originally given this ironical name because it is occupied by a range of rocky and precipitous mountains. A part of Ardgoil Estate, which is the more formal name for Argyll's Bowling Green, was given to the City of Glasgow by Lord Rowallan in 1906. It is now a part of the Argyll National Forest Park, founded in 1936.

ARISAIG, *Inverness-shire* (Map 4, ref. 16⁶78⁷), is a village situated upon the famous highway (sometimes known as the "Road to the Isles") that runs between FORT WILLIAM and MALLAIG. This road – which, at the time of writing, still has beside it a single-track railway – is justly famous. It takes the traveller through some of the most beautiful and characteristic W. Highland scenery; it provides him with some of the best views of the Inner Hebrides; and finally, if he is interested in such matters, it leads him into the heart of that country which is most strongly associated with the Jacobite venture of 1745. Arisaig, on the approach to the port of Mallaig, is where the road first touches the open sea.

The village is upon a low green promontory, from which the traveller will get his first view of the small isles, and of the Inner Hebrides. Most noticeable is the prospect of the island of EIGG, and of the CUILLINS of SKYE. The shore between Arisaig and MORAR is especially noted for its silver-white sand. The prospect from Arisaig and its nearby sands has often been attempted by landscape painters. It was in this part of Scotland that Prince Charles Edward Stuart first landed on the mainland, and it was from near here that he escaped.

This district from Arisaig through Morar and Mallaig is a stronghold of W. Highland Catholicism. The tower of the Arisaig Catholic church is a local landmark; in the tower is a clock put up in memory of Alasdair Mac-Mhaigstir Alasdair, who was one of the greatest and most revered of all Scottish Gaelic poets, and took part in the Rising of 1745.

ARKAIG, *Inverness-shire* (Map 5, ref. 21⁰79¹). A loch, a short river, and (through historical associations) a district, Arkaig is close by

ACHNACARRY, the seat of the Camerons of Lochiel already mentioned in the Gazetteer for its strong Jacobite associations. These same associations have caused Arkaig to be known as a district. During the Rising of '45, an unspecified but large amount of gold was sent from France to help the Jacobite cause, but it arrived too late. The treasure was buried somewhere in Arkaig and has never, as far as we know, been found. The presence of this gold in Arkaig caused much intrigue and much dissension amongst Jacobites. The political and dynastic cause for which it was sent from France to Scotland is now faded and forever lost, but the gold remains – hidden, perhaps, somewhere in Arkaig.

The Loch of Arkaig is of singular beauty and is full of sporting brown trout; few of them run to great size, but a day on Loch Arkaig when the trout are rising can give as good a day's sport as any in Scotland. The short river of Arkaig connects the loch with Loch Lochy, in the Great Glen that divides Scotland from NE. to SW. At appropriate seasons through this river and by remote connection with the sea, salmon and sea-trout run into Loch Arkaig.

ARMADALE, *Inverness-shire* (Map 4, ref. 16³80³), is on the Island of SKYE, in the Inner Hebrides (*see* "The Shape of Scotland"). This was the seat of Lord Macdonald of Sleat, who with the Macleods of DUNVEGAN are hereditary chiefs on Skye. The Gothic-style castle, which may be demolished, was built in 1815 in romantic grounds on Sleat, the southern and fertile arm of Skye reaching out to the W. end of the island opposite Knoydart and MORAR on the mainland.

By the shore stood an older house, inhabited by Macdonald of Sleat, where in 1773 Dr Johnson and James Boswell endured so chilling a reception from a Highland chief, whom Johnson later said had been "tamed into insignificance" by a southern education – Sir Alexander Macdonald, unlike his forebears, had been sent to school at Eton in England.

There is now a ferry service from Armadale to the mainland.

ARNISTON HOUSE, *Midlothian*, S. of DALKEITH, and in the neighbourhood of EDINBURGH, is the seat of the Dundases of Arniston. This family was once powerful in the affairs of SE. Scotland and eventually of Scotland itself. The statue of their most famous son, Henry Dundas, Viscount Melville, dominates the New Town of Edinburgh, at the top of its Roman column in the centre of St Andrew Square. The family, characteristic of their time in Scotland, rose in the legal profession, father and son, in the late 17th and early 18th cents. Each in turn ascended the Scottish Bench with the title of Lord Arniston. The reader should here be reminded that a Scottish "Law Lord" or Senator of the College

of Justice bears the title "Lord" but is not a peer. Sometimes a Scottish Law Lord will take his title from the name of his estate.

The Dundases of Arniston did, however, eventually procure a peerage by their political eminence; but it is an example of the power of their family name that Viscount Melville, a great man in his day, is still remembered as Dundas rather than Melville.

The Dundases bought the land of Arniston as far back as 1571. The first house was built about 1620. Upon the family achieving eminence and power in legal circles, they began to lay out grounds on a Dutch pattern in 1690. Before 1726, they commissioned William Adam to design a new house. This new house, which rose slowly but persistently, contained parts of the old within it, especially the Oak Room, which was redecorated with designs made for it by William Adam. The drawing-room and dining-room were added about 1753. A covered porch was added in the 19th cent. Arniston is characteristic of the fine 18th-cent. houses that were beginning to grow up in the neighbourhood of Edinburgh before Edinburgh's great neo-Georgian New Town had been designed.

ARRAN, Island of, *Buteshire* (Map 1, ref. 19⁵63⁵), in the Firth of CLYDE midway between Ayrshire and the Mull of Kintyre, lies 6½ m. SW. off the nearest part of BUTE. Its length is 20½ m. and its mean breadth 9 m. This exceedingly popular holiday island is best reached by ARDROSSAN, but has occasional steamers to and from GLASGOW and by FAIRLIE.

Arran, held by its devotees to be the southernmost of the Inner Hebrides, is, with Bute and the CUMBRAES, severed from the group to which it belongs in the Atlantic by the long arm of Kintyre. It is this severance that makes the purists deny it the Hebridean title. It unquestionably shares, however, many of the beauties and attractions of its oceanic island sisters to the W. of it, but is much more accessible. In consequence it has, for close on a century, been a favourite holiday resort not only for Glasgow folk, but for families from all over southern Scotland and from northern England. Its essential beauty has remained notably unspoiled.

Its northern half is mountainous; as soon as you have left the coast road that keeps close by the sea, you meet with a wild and impressively Highland Hebridean character that no amount of holiday-makers can tame. Its highest peak is GOAT FELL (2,866 ft), which is fairly easy to climb from BRODICK, the main township of Arran. The view from the summit of Goat Fell is remarkable even for Scotland. On a clear day you can see three countries – Scotland, England, and Ireland (not forgetting the Isle of Man, worthy of respect for its independence) – and many of the farthest Hebrides. It is surrounded by other peaks that, though inferior in

Isle of Arran: Glen Sannox   *Scottish Tourist Board*

height, are more jagged and arresting in appearance. Some of these are known as targets for rock-climbers.

Arran possesses three bays on the E. side. Apart from Brodick with its castle, there is LAMLASH and WHITING BAY, all containing townships that cater for holiday-makers. To the S. the island, though never completely flat, becomes more reminiscent of the Lowland agricultural scene across the Firth in Ayrshire. Here in the S., perhaps because it is less in the full stream of the island life, the Gaelic language still lives amongst the local inhabitants. There is a good ring road all round the island, and a "string" road, also in good condition, across the centre of it.

Arran has entered Scottish history on various occasions, never more resoundingly than when Robert Bruce came to it from exile on Rathlin, and mustered his men in Glen Cloy for launching his return to Carrick and the mainland of Scotland. It was a venture that, seven years later, was to culminate in the Battle of Bannockburn and the rebirth of the Kingdom of Scotland.

Today Arran is noted not only for its characteristic rural Scottish beauty of scene (Highland and Lowland on one island), but for the hospitality of its natives. There is good sea fishing and occasional brown-trout and sea-trout angling. This is not expensive, and often it is free. Sea bathing in the clear waters around the island invigorates. There is also golf. A strong local community life on Arran continues quietly underneath the surface when the visitors are there, to burst out into full display in winter. At that period of the year the climate of Arran is very mild.

Less well known than SKYE, less of a striking and remarkable island entity than LEWIS,

Arran cannot be left without repeating and stressing its appeal to visitors from all over the United Kingdom. It has its countless adherents who return there year after year, and who grow to look upon Arran as a second home. Perhaps it is this home-like quality of Arran that preserves it from being tarnished by the multitudes who enjoy it summer after summer.

Nothing less tarnished than its grand peaks, its translucent waters (particularly the Rosa river, which flows from an impressive glen of that name), its moorland and its coast of rock or sand, could be found anywhere else in Scotland. Yet Arran is by boat and train so easily reached from Glasgow and the industrial centre! How does Arran keep herself inviolate? That is her secret, and none of those who love her would try to find out that secret or to define the attraction that she never fails to exert over them.

ARROCHAR, *Dunbartonshire* (Map 2, ref. 23°70⁴), is a tourist village, and a focal centre for climbers, lying in the W. Highland district, within comparatively easy reach of GLASGOW. It is at the head of the sea-arm of Loch LONG, at the narrows to TARBET on Loch LOMOND (of which more below). It has a railway station on the W. Highland route from Glasgow, and is easily approached by road, or by water by the steamers up Loch Lomond. It is surrounded by some notable mountains. To the NW. stands a group of the finest peaks in Argyll, particularly Ben Arthur, usually styled the Cobbler, and Ben Narniam and Ben Ime, both over 3,000 ft. The first two offer facilities for rock-climbing. To the SW. lies the large Argyll National Forest Park. In the neighbourhood there is also the North of Scotland Hydro-Electric Board works which was opened in 1950. Local employment is offered at this works, and in the Argyll National Forest. In 1910 the Admiralty set up a torpedo-range on Loch Long.

Six and a half centuries before 1910, and long before such things as torpedoes were ever dreamt of, this district was the scene of one of the most remarkable achievements in naval warfare that have ever taken place within Scotland's orbit. In 1263, when King Haakon of Norway launched his great Armada against Scotland, which was to culminate in his defeat at the Battle of LARGS (see "Scotland in History"), some of his ships sailed right up to the end of Loch Long. Not content with this penetration of a sea loch, the men in charge of the boats that had come all the way from Norway dragged them across the narrow strip of land. They thus launched them upon the enclosed fresh waters of Loch Lomond and into the very heart of Scotland itself. This was a naval commando raid of the highest daring; it is still remembered in Scotland with admiration. We can afford that admiration – after all, we won the Battle of Largs.

ASHKIRK, *Selkirkshire* (Map 3, ref. 34⁷62²). This small village on the banks of Ale Water just S. of SELKIRK has its history in its remote connection with the once powerful and, from the Scottish point of view, almost independent see of the Bishops of GLASGOW. From the 12th cent., the land belonged to the Bishops of Glasgow and was used by them as a country retreat. Until the 18th cent., the ruins of the bishops' country palace were still visible, and it is said that even today local people refer to the site as "Palace Walls". Episcopal influence has long since disappeared, but a local church was rebuilt in 1790; outside the church is a 17th-cent. burial enclosure of the family of Scott of Synton. In the church we find a panel dated 1702, with the arms of Elliot of Minto and of Carre of Cavers, that may have come from Minto and may have been a part of the "Laird's loft". W. of the parish church is St Ninian's Well, where early Christians were baptized.

ATHELSTANEFORD, *East Lothian* (Map 3, ref. 35³67⁷). This pleasant and characteristic little village gets its name from remote traditional history. It is said that in the 10th cent. Athelstan, the Saxon king, suffered a severe defeat at the hands of the Picts and Scots at this spot or nearby; there is also a tradition that, as the result of this victory, the St Andrew's cross was first adopted as the Scottish national flag. Lying upon a rocky outcrop, Athelstaneford is now a well-designed village with pantiled cottages on either side of a grass-bordered street. In a street N. of the manse and bearing the date 1583, there is a particularly fine example of a stone-built and crow-stepped gabled doocot.

Athelstaneford has its literary associations.

It is believed that near here was born Sir David Lindsay, the 16th-cent. author of *Ane Satyre of the Thrie Estaits*, which after a lapse of 400 years was revived to world-wide acclaim at the EDINBURGH Festival after the last war. One of the 18th-cent. ministers who held the living of Athelstaneford was the Rev. John Home, author of *Douglas: A Tragedy*. This piece was an enormous success not only in Edinburgh but in London at the latter end of the 18th cent. Though it too was revived at the Edinburgh Festival in 1950, all that is remembered of it now is the trivial quotation "My name is Norval; on the Grampian Hills my father feeds his flocks". Opinion at that time did not approve of Scottish country ministers writing plays for the stage, no matter how successful; John Home had to resign his living of Athelstaneford. This, however, did not trouble him much. As a layman, he entered the literary and social life of his time with success. He was an amiable man, with larger social than literary talents. He was a great friend of the philosopher David Hume. The only point of difference between them on which they argued was the spelling of the surname they shared.

AUCHENCAIRN, *Kirkcudbrightshire* (Map 2, ref. 28⁰55¹). This attractive whitewashed village – the "field of the cairn" in Gaelic – climbs a steep brae facing SSE. over a sandy shallow bay, with Hestan at the S. and dominated to the N. by the steep ridge of Screel and Bengairn, rising to over 1,000 ft behind the village.

At the western uphill end of the village is the site of Ringcroft of Stocking, scene in the 1690s of a famous poltergeist "haunting", reported on in detail by a panel of ministers.

There are several fine Dark Age courtyard-forts – Suie Hill, Almorness, Dungyle, and others – on the hills in the neighbourhood.

The district is rich in a variety of minerals, including haematite.

AUCHENCROW, *Berwickshire* (Map 3, ref. 38⁵66¹). Now but a hamlet below the 860-ft Horseley Hill, Auchencrow was a flourishing village in the 17th cent. and earlier. It declined by the end of the 18th cent. Under the name of Edincraw, it figures in Border ballads about witches. The place is indeed associated with fearsome tales of witches' doings – tales of the Evil Eye, of the destruction of crops, and of the calling up of storms at sea to sink ships. There are also more reliable and even more horrific tales of the punishment meted out at Auchencrow to poor old women who were popularly believed to have been the agents of these disasters. This barbarous practice persisted well into the 18th cent.

AUCHINDRAIN, *Argyll* (Map 1, ref. 20³70²). In September 1963, a local trust was set up to transform this uninhabited township

5 m. W. of INVERARAY into a folk museum.
The township consists of stone-built houses,
byres, and outbuildings constructed in the early
19th cent., grouped together in the traditional
way, each house surrounded by its own plot of
land.

AUCHINLECK, *Ayrshire* (Map 2, ref.
25⁵62²). Today this is an upland coal-mining
village 3 m. N. of Old CUMNOCK on the trunk
road from KILMARNOCK to DUMFRIES.
Some 3 m. to the W. is Auchinleck House, the
family seat of the Boswells since early in the
16th cent. The present house was built for
Alexander Boswell, Lord Auchinleck (father of
the more famous James Boswell). There has
been some doubt as to the date on which this
house was completed. It has now been definitely
established that it was inhabited by Lord
Auchinleck in the 1760s. Therefore it was here,
in this house, that Dr Johnson was entertained
in 1773, and it was here that he had his famous
dispute (over King Charles's head, it is said)
with James Boswell's father. It will be remembered that even the frank and gossipy James
Boswell was so appalled by this dispute that he
could not bring himself to set it down in detail
in his journal. Remains of two earlier dwellings
are still to be seen.

AUCHMITHIE, *Angus* (Map 6, ref.
36⁸74⁴). This ancient fishing village, the
"Musselcrag" of Sir Walter Scott's *The Antiquary*, is said to have flourished in the 11th
cent. It is built on a rocky bank rising 150 ft
above the beach, and lies 3½ m. NNE. of
ARBROATH. There are many caves in the
neighbourhood connected with smugglers in
the 18th cent. and earlier.

AUCHTERARDER, *Perthshire* (Map 2,
ref. 29⁵71³). The barony of Auchterarder was a
crown possession and the castle a royal
residence. Today Auchterarder is one of the
royal burghs of Scotland.

In 1227 King Alexander II granted the teind
of his duties of Auchterarder to the canons of
the INCHAFFRAY ABBEY, but in 1328 Robert
Bruce reserved the liberties of the burgh to the
Montifex family, and Sir William Montifex
gave it as a dowry to his daughter Marie when
she married Sir John Drummond. The Drummond family, earls of Perth, had been associated
with Strathearn since early in the 14th cent.

The castle, traditionally a royal hunting seat,
is just N. of the town. Only the donjon keep
and the surrounding moat remain. When
Edward I invaded Scotland in 1296, he spent a
night at the Castle of Auchterarder.

In May 1559 Mary of Lorraine, widow of
James V, negotiated the Treaty of Perth from
Auchterarder, where she was staying. By its
terms John Knox gained the first State recognition of Protestantism in Scotland.

In 1716 after the Battle of SHERIFFMUIR,

the Earl of Mar ordered the town of Auchterarder to be burnt, along with several others
in the area, in order to deny shelter to the army
of the Duke of Argyll. The populace suffered
greatly, and as a result the Jacobite cause lost
support.

The main industry of the town, when rebuilt
after 1716, was hand-loom weaving, and over
500 weavers were occupied in the making of
linen. In 1838 malt barns at Castleton were converted into a weaving factory, and in 1873
power-looms were introduced. The town is now
famous for its woollen goods, including
tartan.

Auchterarder was famous for one of the chief
cases of "Patronage" that led to the Disruption
of the Church of Scotland in 1843. (*See*
"Scotland in History").

AUCHTERMUCHTY, *Fife* (Map 3, ref.
32⁴71²). This village, on account of the Lowland Scottish spelling and pronunciation of its
name, has caused our southern visitors some
difficulty. It has also been responsible for
various explosively guttural jests from those
who see the place on the map for the first time.
Nevertheless, it is a pleasing and attractive
little place. Once it was a town of standing,
but it has now sunk into the position of a
village, lying at the centre of fertile land in the
Howe of Fife. A picturesque and, for Scotland,
an unusual feature of Auchtermuchty is the
thatched roofs on some of its houses; these are
made from reeds drawn out of the R. TAY.
The visitor from England, accustomed to the
sight of thatched cottages, is unlikely to find
such upon his wanderings in Scotland except
at Auchtermuchty, and perhaps in the restored
part of the village of Swanston on the N.
slopes of the Pentlands, and on the boundaries
of EDINBURGH. These last, restored with
some taste by the Corporation, have perhaps
been designed deliberately to assume the
English manner. At Auchtermuchty they are
indigenous, and are not designed to imitate
anything.

AULDEARN, *Nairnshire* (Map 5, ref.
29⁸85⁵), is a pleasing village near to the Moray
Firth and on the ridge between the valleys of
the rivers Findhorn and Nairn. Here was the
scene of the battle between Montrose and the
Covenanters that was fought on the 9th May
1645, when with 1,500 infantry and 200 horse
he completely routed the enemy, whose
numbers were over twice his own. The Covenanters were led by General Urry. John
Buchan, in his *Life of Montrose*, describes this
battle as tactically the most brilliant one that
the great Scottish soldier ever fought. Above
the village and to the E. end of it stands, on the
site of an old castle but with more peaceful
intent, the 17th-cent. Doocot of Boath. This is
now the property of the National Trust for
Scotland.

Loch Awe and Kilchurn Castle

AULTBEA, *Ross and Cromarty* (Map 5, ref. 18⁸88⁸), is finely situated on Loch Ewe, with the island of Ewe just offshore. In both world wars the loch at Aultbea was used extensively as an anchorage by ships of the Home Fleet. Today a Royal Navy Boom Defence Depot is established on the loch side and there is a N.A.T.O. oil fuel depot.

AULTGUISH, *Ross and Cromarty* (Map 5, ref. 23⁶86⁹). This place has for a long time been the site of an inn on the road from Garve to Ullapool. Not so long ago, and certainly within the memory of the middle-aged, the inn lay on a waste of moorland. Now it lies at the foot of the Glascarnoch Dam, which has been responsible for making an entirely new and artificial loch nearly 5 m. long and running beside the Ullapool road just to the N. of it.

AVIEMORE, *Inverness-shire* (Map 5, ref. 28⁹81²), on the Perth–Inverness road, is one of the key points in the fast-developing winter-sports trade of the Cairngorms. Originally not much more than an inn on the old Wade military road, a village developed here with the opening of the railway line to Inverness in the mid-19th cent., and Aviemore gradually became a pleasant, quiet holiday resort with excellent hotels, which provided a main source of local employment. Social changes after the Second World War hit Aviemore hard, then in 1965 Lord Fraser of Allander (better known as plain Hugh Fraser) conceived the idea of creating the Aviemore Centre. He did not live to see the opening, but his son, Sir Hugh Fraser, is an equally enthusiastic member of the board. The Scottish breweries, Trust Houses, and other interests took a part in developing this multi-million-pound complex, which now has several top-flight hotels, a chalet motel, innumerable restaurants, its own 720-seat theatre and cinema, and every possible provision for indoor and outdoor sport and recreation. There are, of course, many ski-slopes and ski-lifts, but Aviemore, realizing that

Scotland's fickle climate sometimes fails to provide even a white Christmas, has concentrated on becoming a splendid all-the-year-round recreation and holiday centre for people of all ages (and pockets) in glorious surroundings. Loch-an-Eilean, 3½ m. to the S. across the river, is one of the popular touring and picnic destinations from the village. Here, on the small island from which the loch takes its name, can be seen the remains of a medieval tower-stronghold of the Wolf of Badenoch. The island was notable in the 19th cent. as the last nesting place of the osprey in Scotland. Loch Garten, where the osprey has again taken up residence in recent years, is also within easy reach of Aviemore.

AVOCH, *Ross and Cromarty* (Map 5, ref. 27¹85⁵), is now a small fishing community on the S. shore of the Black Isle with a harbour, mostly for fishing vessels.

Just to the SW. on a mound are the ruins of Ormond Castle, said to be the home of Andrew de Moray with whom William Wallace led the Scots to victory at Stirling Bridge in 1297.

Farther to the NW. is the site of Rosehaugh. This was once the seat of Sir George Mackenzie, commonly known as "Bluidy Mackenzie" for his harsh treatment of the Covenanters when he was Lord Advocate in the latter half of the 17th cent. A large, ornate house was built in 1893 on this site for James Fletcher, son of a fisherman of Avoch who had made a fortune in the South. It was demolished in July 1959.

AWE, Loch, *Argyll* (Map 1, ref. 19⁸71³). This celebrated loch is 22 m. long and in most places only about 1 m. across. It lies in the heart of the Argyll country, and, like so many of the major Highland lochs including those in the Great Glen, runs NE. to SW. At one time, when the Inveraray district of Argyll was completely ruled by the head of Clan Campbell, this long stretch of water acted as a kind of natural moat for their protection; to the S. of Inveraray lay the long sea-arm of Loch Fyne, to the N. of them lay the equally protective great inland water of Loch Awe. At first glance, and on looking at the map, it would seem that the outflow of Loch Awe is at the SW. end, where it lies near the sea; and indeed this must once have been so. In comparatively recent times, however (geologically speaking), there have been changes, and now the R. Awe flows from the N. end of the loch in a westerly direction into Loch ETIVE, thus emptying the long loch of Awe into the sea.

In the 16th and 17th cents. there were other clans than the Campbells upon the shores of Loch Awe, including the MacArthurs and the MacGregors as well as the MacNaughtons; the remains of a MacNaughton castle may be seen at Innisfroach. But Argyll, and particularly that part of it S. and E. of Loch Awe, was completely dominated by the Clan Campbell – hence the well-known Campbell saying, "It's a far cry to Lochow". This was a defiant boast of the Campbell inaccessibility behind the protection of Loch Awe.

There are various islands on Loch Awe, including KILCHURN (now largely surrounded by marshes) and Inishail, which has the ruins of a convent and chapel. Innischonell has a ruined castle that was once of royal origin under the Clan Campbell in the 16th cent., with the MacArthurs as the keepers of it. These castles, ruins, and other remains remind the visitor of Loch Awe's fortified and military past. Nothing of that past remains today in this peaceful and, after its own fashion, one of the most beautiful stretches of inland water in Scotland, set amid characteristic W. Highland scenery dominated by that peak most associated with the name of Campbell, BEN CRUACHAN. The loch is also noted for its excellent salmon and trout fishing. Trout anglers may care to note that their favourite sport begins in good condition earlier in Loch Awe than anywhere else in Scotland. The trout are indeed in good fighting trim from the end of March onwards.

At the NW. end of the loch is the site of the important Cruachan hydro-electric scheme. The North of Scotland Hydro-Electric Board's first pumped-storage scheme (1965) includes a special kind of reversible turbine never before used anywhere else in the world. Apart from the Hydro-Electric Board's activities, the Forestry Commission has erected a new village of more than 30 houses at Dalavich on the W. shore.

Finally, the W. shore of the loch contains an oddity at which the traveller may care to pause and reflect. This is a hamlet that took its name from the York Buildings Company, which endeavoured to develop Highland estates after the Jacobite Rising of 1715. The hamlet shares its name with another famous place. Those who address letters to anyone living here should be careful to add "Argyll, Scotland" after the name of the hamlet. It is called New York.

Scottish Tourist Board

Ayr: the town centre

AYR, *Ayrshire* (Map 2, ref. 23^562^2). "An ancient city by an ancient sea" – these words are particularly applicable to Ayr. They rise unbidden in your mind whenever you think of this old town, the county town of Ayrshire situated on the Firth of CLYDE, 35 m. from GLASGOW.

Even although the townsfolk and the historians disagree on the precise date of its charter, their disagreement is limited to within a year or two in the 13th cent., and no one really is much concerned whether that date is 1202, 1203, or even the extreme limit 1206. So it is ancient enough, and happily the original Charter of Erection by King William the Lion still lies safe in the custody of the Town Clerk. Other visible and tangible proofs of this antiquity are, however, sadly few.

There is, however, a fragment, and a handsome one, of the ancient church of St John the Baptist, dated by some as contemporary with the charter. Yet even here there are doubts, and the Tower of St John may well have been a latter-day addition to the original church buildings. What of the church itself? Oliver Cromwell's Model Army dealt with it in the traditional way when they requisitioned the area round it to build a citadel to overawe the remnant of the western Covenanters. Cromwell had built, in exchange, the present Auld Kirk of Ayr (1654), which is tucked away out of sight behind the modern buildings of the High Street.

The Auld Brig of Ayr on its present site probably dates back almost as far as the Church of St John, but it is not until the reign of James IV (1488–1513) that there is any proof that it was of stone. The Exchequer records of that time contain details of a gift of drink-silver to the masons at the "Brig of Air", but whether they were builders or repairers we do not know.

Loudoun Hall, overlooking the harbour from the mouth of the Boat Vennel, traces its title deeds back to 1534 and in its heyday was the town house of the hereditary Sheriff of Ayrshire. In its old age it narrowly escaped demolition as a slum, which, of course, it had become, but it is now happily restored and is one of the town's cultural centres. These, then, are the only relicts of history that the impatience of bygone generations has failed to destroy: a tower, a bridge, a house, and a 17th-cent. church. A mere scattered handful of the past. It is true that parts of the walls of Cromwell's building still remain, probably because they were too tough to be destroyed, but these are alien to the town and even yet evoke no enthusiasm among the inhabitants; of other more modern buildings of note there are few. The neo-Gothic Wallace Tower in the High Street is an 1832 throw-back to a more ancient manner, and is remarkable only as a landmark. (This is not, of course, the Wallace Tower referred to by Burns, which was pulled down to make way for this piece of 19th-cent. romanticism.) On the other hand, the town buildings and steeple at the junction of High Street and Sandgate, while dating from about the same time, are handsome, and the steeple, a feature of so many last-century Lowland towns, is considered to be one of the best in Britain. The site, however, is unfortunate, as it detracts from the loftiness of the steeple and prevents a critical appreciation of the buildings. There are one or two outstanding Georgian and Regency groups: Alloway Place and, particularly, Wellington Square with the Court House and modern County Buildings on the seaward side. These areas, however, are losing their battle with commercial interests.

One fact at least is undeniable. Ayr has vitality and excitement; it pulses with life – a life that expands in all directions. And, like the car-parking restrictions in the High Street, the excitement comes on alternate days. Tuesday's markets throng the streets with the farming folk, and the car parks are packed with sparkling automobiles. Thursdays bring them back for the week's shopping and, maybe, a hand at the curling in the ice rink. On Saturdays all the other people of the county flock in by bus, car, or scooter, and crowd the pavements of the shopping centres to exasperation point: farmers and fishers; miners and townsfolk from the outlying burghs; men and their wives; lads and their lasses; children – all with money to spend.

But this ebb and flow is most noticeable in the winter. During the holiday months, the tide of humanity flows all the time, and the local variations are swamped by the waves of holiday-makers who come from all over Scotland, from Ireland, and (very many of them) from England. In July and August it is not easy to hear an Ayrshire tongue amid the babel of varied English or Scots. But there is also peace, and beauty. Away from all the bustle of the shops, chain-stores, and supermarkets, picture houses, theatres and dance halls (and they are all there for those who want them), Ayr is a different place.

What the Ayr people are really proud of is their parks. Efficient local services of all kinds – good roads; wholesome water; clean, well-lit streets; a courteous local police force – are all taken for granted and without comment. But the parks are different. Ask an Ayr man about Belleisle or Craigie, and his face lights up.

Both were 18th-cent. estates, and on them has been lavished much care and expenditure since their acquisition by the town. Belleisle ("beautiful Belleisle", they call it) lies to the S. It has the gracious charm of mansion-house and parkland and, in addition, flower gardens and conservatories of more than special merit. Craigie on the E. has the attraction of long vistas, long walks, and a quiet river for a boundary, and its rhododendrons in the spring. Both have magnificent woodlands. Then there are the bread-and-butter parks, the Old Racecourse, and the Low Green, each of eighty acres or more, and playing-fields in addition, enough to cater for an army of children. Putting, miniature golf, boating, paddle-pools, swings, roundabouts, even a summer fairground down by the beach; a well-equipped playground, ponies on the sands, motor-boats and amphibious ducks in the sea – all go to make up an impressive total of attractions of a simple but appealing kind.

But Ayr's treasure is the shore. There are literally miles of golden sand with safe bathing and paddling. This is what brings all the holiday-makers to the town, all the school excursions, Sunday school trips, bus parties and motorists. They start coming in early May and stop in late September; and for one thing only – the shore. It is a source of much joy; to the town-planners it is a source of much wonderment that even a modern child can be happy for so long without any artificial aids.

To omit horse-racing from the catalogue would be unforgivable. Ayr's racecourse is among the finest in Britain and caters well for the fraternity. Similarly with golf; there are three good courses, two at Belleisle and one at Dalmilling, close by the racecourse. The principal Belleisle course is of professional championship standard, and the others too will test your skill. For a few shillings you may have your fill of golf. There are plenty of public bowling greens and tennis courts, and even angling in the R. Ayr. The keen fisher who does not mind moving about for his sport will find an admirable angling centre at GIRVAN, 20 m. away along the coast.

Ayr has a habit of turning its back on things – the sea, for example, and the river; and probably tradition has good reason for this.

The Burns statue, Ayr

The most remarkable example, however, is in the town's attitude to Robert Burns. No doubt the citizens would be "sore affronted" if they were taxed with this, but the fact remains. "No Stratford-on-Avon stuff here" seems to be the local motto, and certainly the minimum of fuss is made about the national bard. There's the Tam O'Shanter Inn (of dubious pedigree) in the High Street, now maintained as a museum by the Ayr Burns Club and the Town Council, and a bronze plate on a wall in the Sandgate reminds passers-by of the approximate site of Murdoch's lodgings (demolished, of course), where Robert came to school; and there is the Auld Brig. The point that Ayr almost ostentatiously makes is that these objects are left to speak for themselves.

Perhaps that is why the poet's statue in Burns Statue Square has followed the prevailing custom and turned its back on Ayr. Burns devotees will tell you that the reason for this is that Robert looks wistfully to ALLOWAY and the days of his boyhood, but this is difficult to believe, for his eyes appear to be fixed on two of the plainest buildings in the West of Scotland, which have been allowed to destroy what might have been a noble entrance to the town.

At Alloway, 2 m. to the S. and within the burgh, things are still discreet, but the people here are, to a man, staunch for Robert. No halfway here; but it will be interesting to watch the effect of the intense housing developments that threaten to inundate the village if not the villagers.

The road from Ayr to Alloway is pleasant indeed, and for the last mile traverses an avenue of beeches, part of the policies of Rozelle estate, from which tantalizing glimpses are to be had of Belleisle and its golf courses. You come upon Alloway suddenly and, after a hundred yards, just as suddenly upon the cottage, unspoiled, in spite of badly placed vending machines and "No Parking" signs. Here is William Burnes's New Garden, as he called his three acres, well laid out in turf and borders and partly occupied by a fine museum – a fitting place to commemorate the flower of Scottish genius.

A little farther S., past the exclusive housing estate of Cambusdoon, the visitor will spy the Auld Haunted Kirk glowering across the road at its successor, and beyond that to the rococo Monument and its gardens. A little further searching will reveal the Brig o' Doon, a most graceful brig, whose beauty is enhanced by the fact that at this point the R. Doon is truly bonnie. Needless to say, the view of the Brig from the Kirk is obliterated by a spurious building notable only for the fact that Robert Burns's coat of arms and motto adorn its wall. To the uninitiated, however, this will no doubt be taken for the crest and motto of the commercial firm that owns the building. "Better a wee bush than nae bield" says the motto; and it is true in this case, for, spoiled as it may be, the picture of the Brig o' Doon is still breathtaking.

The road to Alloway and the road along the coast past Doonfoot to DUNURE are comparatively untouched by the speculative builder, and in this they are distinguished from the others. The coast road is recommended as the best approach to the town, and as it sweeps round the flanks of Brown Carrick Hill it commands many views.

So seen, the town looks its best. It lies sheltered in the arms of the bay bedecked by its many trees. At this distance the scene is mellowed, and the impression, which after all is a true one, is of a mature and dignified place full of greenery, clean and fresh, and around it always the sea, undisturbed by the progress or regress of mankind upon its shore.

AYTON, *Berwickshire* (Map 3, ref. 39²66²).
The first full-sized village that the traveller on the Great North Road will reach after crossing the Border between England and Scotland, Ayton is one long double-sided street sloping up from the R. Eye. Travellers by rail as well as by road first become aware of Ayton by the sight or surprising spectacle of the large red sandstone building of Ayton Castle put up in 1851, on the site of a much older one that was destroyed by fire in 1834. The Castle is very much in the style of Victorian Scottish baronial

tradition, and has certainly excelled itself in this manner. There may come a time when, as with so many other Victoriana, it will appeal to future ages; at present it is for us but a curiosity. There is a local legend (quite without foundation) that this huge building had no plan and no architect, but was built from day to day in a quite haphazard fashion by the owner.

The present church was built in 1864, but just E. of it lie the ruins of a pre-Reformation church, in which it is said the ambassadors from English and Scottish kings used to meet at the period of the Anglo-Scottish wars.

BAILLIESTON, *Lanarkshire* (Map 2, ref. 26⁸66⁴). The origin of the name of this village lying on the E. periphery of GLASGOW is not known; it is possible, however, that some 17th- or 18th-cent. Glasgow municipal magistrate had his county residence there. The village of Baillieston as we know it grew entirely within the 19th cent., on industry – but on ever-changing industry. It started with hand-loom weaving and later turned over to coal-mining; at one time it had no fewer than 30 pits in its area. Coal-mining in this district has since declined, and assorted industry has come in to Baillieston. From the 19th cent. onwards its population was mostly immigrants, with many coming in from Ireland after the potato famine. The descendants of these immigrants largely remain, but they have adapted themselves to the circumstances that have changed so much since their forefathers were drawn or driven here through the destitution inflicted by Victorian *laissez-faire*.

BALERNO, *Midlothian* (Map 3, ref. 31⁶66⁶). A chain of villages runs along the Water of Leith and on the N. side of the Pentland Hills. The last of these villages is Balerno. Within living memory, it was considered to be deep in the country; now, however, it is so easily accessible from the capital that it has become a dormitory suburb. It is also a resort for EDINBURGH folk who wish to make a walking or climbing expedition in the Pentland Hills, or to fish the Water of Leith near its source. The village has a paper-mill dating back to the 18th cent. Balerno, for all its present position as a dormitory suburb of the capital, is highly conscious of its past as a Midlothian village.

BALFRON, *Stirlingshire* (Map 2, ref. 25⁵68⁹). This attractive little place bears much the same relation to GLASGOW as BALERNO bears to EDINBURGH; set amid hills near to the big town, it was an ancient township that later became a village. Like Balerno, it is used by commuters. Though not in the Glasgow W. Highlands, it offers an escape from the big city amidst its lesser hills; it has a fine situation facing the Campsie Fells from the slope above Strathendrick. The name Balfron means "town of sorrow"; it is derived from an ancient

tradition that at one time all the children in this neighbourhood were destroyed by wolves. The last wolf, of course, had disappeared from Scotland long before 1789, when Balfron was given the status of a village.

BALINTORE, *Ross and Cromarty* (Map 5, ref. 28⁷87⁵). Situated in the extreme E. of the county of Ross, this little fishing village is on the Tarbat Peninsula and on the Moray Firth looking across the sea to Moray. It used, in pre-Reformation times, to be known as Abbotshaven. It has fine cliff scenery to the S. and sandy beaches to the N.; it also has a small harbour, and is much used by sea anglers. Just N. of Balintore lies Hilton of Cadboll, where a sculptured 7th-cent. stone was found. It now reposes in the EDINBURGH Museum of National Antiquities.

BALLACHULISH, *Argyll* (Map 5, ref. 20⁶76⁰). The traveller who comes to this straggling village on the S. shore of the W. Highland sea-arm of Loch Leven finds himself in scenes of great landscape and seascape beauty; at the same time, as if to point and contrast with this beauty, the village itself is stained with the debris of modern industrialism. Perhaps not so modern! It was as early as 1761 that Stewart of Ballachulish opened a slate quarry on Laroch Farm in the neighbourhood. Other veins of slate continued to be found in the Ballachulish district, and they were worked until quite recently. Thus an air of slightly decrepit industrialism contrasts most vividly with all that the traveller sees around him.

He will probably approach Ballachulish for the first time through the splendid Pass of GLENCOE on his way N., and will reach Ballachulish to take the ferry across the mouth of the sea-arm of Loch Leven into Inverness-shire and on the way to FORT WILLIAM. This ingeniously worked ferry, swaying to and fro in the fast tide that runs in and out of Loch Leven, is of the greatest practical use to the motorist; it saves him, on his northward journey, a detour of more than 20 m. round the head of the loch.

Apart from the presence of Glencoe, which seems to dominate this whole district, there are splendid views and vistas to be seen from Ballachulish. Above and immediately to the S. of the village rises Ben Vair with its two peaks of 3,000 ft. Far to the N. rise the mountains of the Mamore Forest. There are the hills of ARDGOUR to the W.; and there is the presence of the sea at this the opening of the Great Glen, which divides Scotland from NE. to SW.

The two historical Highland associations that haunt this place are, first, the Massacre of Glencoe (1692), a horrible event in which the Campbells played a notorious part nearby in the reign of William III; and, second, the judicial hanging of James Stewart (James of

Ballachulish: the ferry

the Glen), who, as readers of Robert Louis Stevenson's *Kidnapped* will remember, suffered death for the murder of Colin Campbell of Glenure. They will also recall that there was considerable doubt about whether James Stewart was in fact guilty and whether his execution was not an act of political vengeance.

The district of Ballachulish has for a long time been associated with W. Highland Episcopalianism, and one of the few Scottish Episcopal Prayer Books printed in the Gaelic language is still preserved at the Episcopal church of Ballachulish.

BALLANTRAE, *Ayrshire* (Map 2, ref. 20⁹58³). A pleasant village situated on the shore at the mouth of the R. Stinchar, 13 m. S. of GIRVAN. Formerly a notorious haunt of smugglers, then a prosperous fishing port, but now a centre for agriculture and forestry, it is best known for early crops of potatoes from the seaside fields. Ruins of Ardstinchar Castle dominate the village and the fords at the mouth of the river. The old narrow bridge, which has carried the main road to STRAN-RAER for 200 years, is now being replaced. About 2 m. to the S. is Glenapp Castle, the home of Lord Inchcape, and beyond that again the road runs through Glenapp with its woods and its little church, crossing the Ayrshire–Wigtown boundary at Finnart Bay in Loch Ryan.

BALLATER, *Aberdeenshire* (Map 6, ref. 33⁷79⁶). Although the Station Square of this little town, once so familiar to most people in Britain as the much-pictured scene of royal arrivals and departures, has lost its glories since the Deeside railway closed, it is still redolent of associations linking it with nearby BALMORAL CASTLE. It is still much visited by the Queen and members of her family, and the Victoria Barracks house the royal guard of honour (chosen from the Scottish regiments in rotation) in August and September. Yet Ballater only yields up its real charms on a more prolonged and intimate acquaintance. To those who know it thus, it means the scent of pine needles, the sound of impetuous waters

rushing over the boulder-strewn bed of the DEE, and the panorama from one of the most picturesquely-sited golf courses in the world, a view embracing the twin cones of the Coyles of Muick, the long profile of Craig Cailleach ("hill of the old woman"), and that prickly inverted pudding-bowl of rock which is Craigendarroch ("hill of the oaks"). To be seen on fine days, towering over all, is the majestic snow-striped wedge of LOCHNAGAR. This loveliness was not appreciated by our ancestors until the second half of the 18th cent., when Ballater was still a black and desolate moor. Oddly enough, it was the Jacobites – after suffering for the Good Old Cause and "tholing their assize" under the disliked Hanoverian regime – who first brought out its possibilities.

Pannanich, 2 m. E. of Ballater on the high-wooded slope above the right bank of the Dee, is the clue to the holiday resort of today. It was not on the map until 1760, when a *cailleach* miraculously cured herself of scrofula by bathing in a bog to which she had been "guided" by dreams. The fame of her cure was spread abroad by Colonel Francis Farquharson, the Jacobite Laird of Monaltrie, when he returned to the land of his fathers after the 20 years' exile that followed his capture at CULLODEN and narrow escape from execution. At an old hamlet, Cobbletown of Dalmuchie, he built the inn known as Pannanich Lodge and created a spa that was soon the rage of fashionable society.

That the Dee is a real Highland torrent here can be inferred from the story told by a plaque on the present Ballater Bridge, which reads: "A bridge of stone was built 100 yards east of this site in 1783 and was swept away by flood in 1789. A second bridge of stone was built by Telford 60 feet east of this site in 1809 and was swept away by flood in 1829. It was replaced by a wooden bridge in 1834 which lasted till 6 November 1885 when this bridge built by County Road Trustees was opened by H.M. Queen Victoria who named it 'The Royal Bridge'. Long may it stand."

It would be vain to deny that Ballater's prosperity was boosted by the arrival of Queen Victoria on the scene in 1848, or that today its proximity to Balmoral is a source of profit, but it would still rank high as a Highland resort entirely on its own merits. Diva Victoria's insistence that the Deeside railway should not be carried farther W. has given Ballater a delectable amenity in the Old Line, a walk sacred to pedestrians only, along the gorge of the Dee from the golf course at the delta of the Muick to the confluence of the Gairn and the Dee 1½ m. W.

The Ballater Highland Games, traditionally held during the third week of August, and including a hill race to the top of Craig Cail-leach, have been a feature of the Deeside season for over a century.

BALLINDALLOCH, *Banffshire* (Map 6, ref. 31⁸83⁶). The township of Ballindalloch stands just below where the R. Avon joins the SPEY. Ballindalloch Castle, seat of the Grants, now the Macpherson Grant family, is a mixture of the 16th, 17th, and 19th cents. The central part is old and has a fireplace with the date 1546, while a cape-house or watch-tower was added in 1602. The wings were added in the 19th cent.

About ½ m. N. of the castle is Inveravon Church, with three early Christian symbol stones in the kirkyard. There are stone circles at Lagmore N. of Inveravon, and one near the castle to the SE.

Farming, forestry, and distilling are the chief industries of the district. There is a well-known Aberdeen Angus herd of cattle at Ballindalloch Castle. This is a part of Scotland particularly associated with the best whiskies.

BALLINGRY, *Fife* (Map 3, ref. 31⁸69⁷). This hamlet at the E. end of Benarty Hill lies in a parish vividly displaying the changes that have come over the face of rural Scotland since the middle of the last century. The parish was entirely pastoral until the 1860s, when mines were opened in the neighbourhood at Lochore, Glencraig, and Crosshill. The result was that the parish population grew to nine times its previous size between 1881 and 1911. But (almost as an oddity from the past) the hamlet of Ballingry remained isolated until a new housing plan after the Second World War linked the old and the new. The first pre-fabricated school in Scotland was built in Ballingry in 1950. The parish church, though much changed, has a pre-Reformation origin.

BALLINLUIG, *Perthshire* (Map 5, ref. 29⁸75²). This small village lies on the now busy main road from PERTH to INVERNESS.

Parts of General Wade's road built in 1738 can be seen between Ballinluig and the farm-house of Moulinearn, 1½ m. N. of the village. Moulinearn was formerly a staging inn; it was the scene of a meeting between the Earl of Mar and the Earl of Breadalbane during the first Jacobite rebellion. In 1745 Prince Charles Edward Stuart visited the inn.

A century later, in 1844, Queen Victoria called at Moulinearn during a visit to the Highlands.

BALLOCH, *Dunbartonshire* (Map 2, ref. 23⁹68¹). The town actually stands upon the R. Leven, but, for most of those who visit it, Balloch is noted for its pier upon Loch LOMOND; this is what makes Balloch the "gateway to Loch Lomond". It is the starting place for cruises right up to the N. end of the loch as far as ARDLUI, 24 m. away. The cruises may take the form of journeys by motor-boat or speed-boat or even by water-skiing. Balloch Castle was built in the 19th cent. and,

together with the grounds around it, is now owned by the GLASGOW Corporation. They are open to the public. 1½ m. NW. of Balloch stands Auchendennan House. This is now a youth hostel. As one near both to celebrated scenery and to so dense a population, it is the biggest hostel of its kind in Scotland.

BALMACARA, *Ross and Cromarty* (Map 5, ref. 18²82⁸), is both a village and 8,000-acre estate, owned by the National Trust for Scotland and covering most of the Loch Alsh promontory on the mainland side of the ferry crossing to SKYE. A tourist information centre operates in the village during the summer. Long associated with the Matheson Clan and the Seaforth Mackenzies, the estate was bequeathed to the Trust in 1946 by the widow of the late Sir Daniel Hamilton, who had bought it from the Mathesons. Recently the Trust has carried out here experiments in "roadside reception" of visitors, raising signposts to objects of local interest along the roads, providing rough-hewn log furniture at natural parking-places, and introducing a service of information in the village.

BALMACLELLAN, *Kirkcudbrightshire* (Map 2, ref. 26⁵57⁸). This picturesque village lies along a steep street below the road from DUMFRIES to NEW GALLOWAY, and is dominated by a small motte-and-bailey, probably the actual McLellan's Place which gives the village and parish its name. The village is near the NE. end of Loch Ken.

Robert Paterson, the stonemason from whom Scott drew his character of "Old Mortality", lived here for many years, and his wife kept the school until her death in 1785. A tablet in the churchyard includes his name, though he was buried at CAERLAVEROCK. In the grounds of Holm House just to the N. is a life-size sculpture of himself and his horse. Corrie (or Currie), the sculptor, had Balmaclellan connections. A copy by Currie of the same group stands in the grounds of Dumfries Museum.

BALMAHA, *Stirlingshire* (Map 2, ref. 24³69¹), is situated upon the SE. and less-frequented side of Loch LOMOND and, protected by a constellation of "inland islands", is one of the principal yachting and boating centres on Scotland's largest loch. The steamers going N. up the loch call at Balmaha, but you can also approach it by the narrow, winding road from DRYMEN. The road from Balmaha northwards and up the eastern side of the loch runs through the Pass of Balmaha to ROWARDENNAN, which is the terminus of the eastern road on the lochside and is the starting place for climbing Ben Lomond.

BALMERINO, *Fife* (Map 6, ref. 33⁶72⁴), finely set upon a hill above the southern shores of the R. TAY, has much association with past building and destruction, with past suffering, despoliation, and heroism. A Cistercian abbey was founded here in 1226 by the widow of King William the Lion – the monks coming to this new foundation from MELROSE. Today, only the ruins of the abbey survive, but we can still perceive the beauty of the 15th-cent. chapter house. The abbey suffered its first blow when it was burnt by the raiding English in 1547. It was subsequently repaired, only to be finally destroyed by the Reformers twelve years later.

But heroism, as well as destruction and despoliation, is associated with the place. Near the abbey is a block of houses built by the Earl of Dundee in memory of his brother, Lieut-Col. David Scrymgeour-Wedderburn, who was killed at Anzio in 1944.

There used to be a peerage of Balmerino granted to a cadet of the Elphinstone family in 1603 by James VI. The peerage ended in 1746 when the 6th Lord Balmerino was executed. Though officially "extinguished", the title cannot be said to have died out – at least in Scottish hearts and memories. The manner of the last lord's farewell to the world has kept his title green and fresh with us.

Though elderly ("the most natural brave old fellow I ever saw" was how Horace Walpole described him), he joined Prince Charles Edward Stuart upon his venture in 1745, and, in the gayest and most patriotic manner, suffered death for it at Tower Hill in 1746. "If I had a thousand lives," he proclaimed, "I would lay them down in the same cause." Then, as a London observer noted, "he put on a cap of Scotch plaid, saying he died a Scotchman". Whether we would have supported his cause or not, it is that Scotch bonnet on the old man's grey head just before it was hacked off his body that makes us remember the title of Balmerino.

BALMORAL CASTLE, *Aberdeenshire* (Map 6, ref. 32⁵79⁵), and estate on the upper DEE is not a state domain but the personal holiday home of the Queen, the estate having been purchased, together with the old castle, by the Prince Consort, for £31,500 in 1852. Queen Victoria and her family first came to Balmoral in September 1848, eleven months after the death of the last "civilian" tenant, Sir Robert Gordon. The estate first appears on record in 1484, when Alexander Gordon, second son of the first Earl of Huntly, paid an annual rent of £6 8s. 6d. for "Bouchmorale", as it was then called. The Gordons held Balmoral until 1662, when they sold it to the Farquharsons of Inverey. They in turn were obliged to sell it as a bankrupt estate to the Earl of Fife in 1798, who let it in 1830 to Sir Robert Gordon, brother of the Earl of Aberdeen, who was Prime Minister during the Crimean War.

Sir Robert virtually created the Balmoral

deer forest and added a kitchen wing, public rooms, bedrooms, and a turreted tower to the old castle. Among his guests at the castle were Sir Edwin Landseer, painter of "The Stag at Bay", and John Clark, the invalid son of Sir James Clark, the Queen's doctor. John had a grand time at Balmoral while the Queen and Sir James were enduring "persistent rain and mist" at Ardverikie, near Loch Laggan. It was this circumstance that first turned the Queen's attention to Deeside. Sir Robert Gordon's sudden death made possible a tenancy for the Royal Family at Balmoral, which they occupied on lease for the next four years.

When he bought the place at the end of that period, Prince Albert engaged William Smith, city architect of ABERDEEN, and son of John Smith (nicknamed "Tudor Johnny") who had rebuilt the old castle, to design the new Balmoral Castle that we know today. There is no doubt that Prince Albert's own hand was the major influence on Balmoral's design. It consists of two separate blocks of buildings connected by wings, at the E. angle of which the massive tower, 35 ft square, rises 80 ft and is surmounted by a turret with a circular stair, carrying the total height to 100 ft. The style is the Scottish baronial and the material is light grey Invergelder granite, quarried on the Balmoral estate. The hand-dressed granite work of the fabric is said to be the finest in Scotland.

Entered by the main porch, the hall opens to the main corridor that runs along the centre of the building, from which the grand staircase climbs to the royal private rooms on the first floor. The dining-room, drawing-room, billiard room, and library are on the ground floor. The ballroom, 68 ft long and 25 ft wide, has been the scene of many a famous assembly and many a' memorable Ghillies' Ball. The whole building was designed to house from 100 to 120 residents.

The Balmoral estate now extends to 24,000 acres, including Birkhall (*see* BALLATER).

Balmoral Castle

The Scotsman

The braes of Balquhidder

Those who know its beauties will feel some sympathy with Queen Victoria's almost mystical devotion to the place, which she called "this dear paradise".

BALQUHIDDER, *Perthshire* (Map 2, ref. 25⁴72⁰). The name covers a township, or small village, and a district. The Kirkton of Balquhidder, or focal point of the district, lies some 2 m. W. of the railway station named Balquhidder and the eastern end of Loch Voil in the beautiful glen known as the Braes of Balquhidder. The Kirkton contains two churches. The modern one is a little more than 100 years old, and there are also the roofless remains of a church built in 1631. Rob Roy MacGregor is buried near to the ruined church; so also are his wife and two of his five sons. Balquhidder is very much associated with the name of that celebrated outlaw, and indeed the MacGregors have had a considerable influence upon this valley. It is an influence that has been much fostered by popular romantic writing and by the indubitable fact that Rob Roy MacGregor spent his last days in the valley and died there.

In historical fact, however, rather than in romantic writing, the Braes of Balquhidder are associated with the small clan of MacLaren, who held land there continuously from the 15th cent. The last MacLaren living in the Braes of Balquhidder and farming the land there left in the 1930s. This small clan suffered much at the hands of the MacGregors. In the 16th cent. they endured a savage raid from the MacGregors of Glen Dochart that very much reduced their numbers. Later they had to act as unwilling hosts to the outlaw, Rob Roy MacGregor, who gave the impression of owning the whole glen. However, after his death, the MacLarens continued to live peacefully in the glen until, with the general drainage of manpower from the Highlands, they too left. The Chief of the MacLarens, induced by laud-

able clan and family *pietas*, has recently bought property in the Braes of Balquhidder.

Loch Voil contains salmon and trout, and also that rare fish, the char. In the hills above the loch, and to the N., are a few lochs that abound in char; the intending angler is, however, warned that the climb to these lochs is very severe. At the head of Loch Voil, Stronvar House, a 19th-cent. laird's building, is now a youth hostel. The Braes of Balquhidder are very popular as a camping site. This once peaceful but by no means deserted valley is now loud with the sound of transistor radio sets and twanging guitars and those other noises without which modern urban youth does not seem to be at ease. But this general din, which lasts most of the summer, does not affect the beauty of the mountain-side or the placid waters of the loch. And in the winter the place reverts to its primal peacefulness. That is the season for any wandering MacLaren to revisit Balquhidder.

BANAVIE, *Inverness-shire* (Map 5, ref. 21³77⁷), is a township lying near the S. end of the CALEDONIAN CANAL, which connects the lochs running NE. to SW. in the Great Glen. Banavie is at the last stage of the Canal, the part connecting Loch Linnhe with Loch Lochy to the NE. The Banavie locks – the engineering devices by which the canal is induced to rise 64 ft within 1 m. – are eight altogether and are known as Neptune's Staircase. This series of locks was one of Thomas Telford's most remarkable engineering achievements. Banavie is also noted for a famous view of BEN NEVIS. From this vantage point the celebrated mountain really does give the impression (which it does not always do) of being the highest in Scotland and in the British Isles.

BANCHORY, *Kincardineshire* (Map 6, ref. 37⁰79⁵). Although officially well to the E. of the Highland Line (which actually crosses the DEE where it meets the Burn of DINNET), Banchory, at only 18 m. W. of ABERDEEN, provides its citizens with a delightful foretaste of Highland scenery. That fact largely explains the popularity of this growing police burgh of just under 2,000 inhabitants. Straddling the North Deeside road, from which it rises up to the N. on a series of terraced streets along a steep slope known as the Brae, it descends more gently on the S. to the banks of the Dee near its confluence with the Feugh. There, sheltered by the ridge of the Hill of FARE to the N., and fronting Scolty, Clochnaben, and the Feughside hills S. of the river, it forms a delectable suntrap with a sylvan riverside golf course and splendid salmon fishings.

About ½ m. above its entry into the Dee, the Feugh crosses a sill of quartz-porphyry in a picturesque gorge spanned by the Bridge of Feugh, where the stream foams and tumbles among huge boulders. Crowds on a special footbridge watch to see the salmon leap the cascades. The parish of Banchory-Ternan (so called to distinguish it from Banchory-Devenick, also on the Dee, immediately SW. of Aberdeen) forms the pointed salient of Kincardineshire that so strangely pushes its way N. of the Dee to the summits of the Hill of Fare – a fact due to the Burnetts of Leys, who, on inheriting the Barony of Muchalls, obtained an act of parliament providing that all their lands would be in the same county.

Raemoir Hotel (2 m. W.) is an attractive example of an old Scottish "ha' hoose", while the Glen o' Dee Sanatorium (1½ m. W.) is a reminder that Banchory has a long history as a health centre. It was to the former Nordrach-on-Dee sanatorium here that the novelist Somerset Maugham came to be cured of tuberculosis, an experience he has more than once described in his autobiographical writings.

A memorial tablet in Banchory High Street commemorates Scott Skinner (1843–1927), a native of the town who became known as the "Strathspey King" for his Scottish fiddle music, one of the best-known examples of which is the Strathspey "The Miller o' Hirn". The mill lies 4 m. NE. of the town.

Banchory is the gateway to the valley of the Feugh, celebrated in the landscapes of Joseph Farquharson, R.A., a former laird of Finzean, and it also gives access to the SLUG ROAD, which crosses Cairn-monearn at 757 ft to STONEHAVEN, and the CAIRN O' MOUNT Pass from the glen of the Dye (a tributary of the Feugh) to FETTERCAIRN in the Mearns. The road over the Cairn o' Mount reaches an altitude of 1,475 ft and yields magnificent views.

A network of roads penetrates the lower part of the Feugh valley. A branch from the road that runs along the right bank of the stream to Affrusk leads to Tilquhillie Castle, a Z-plan tower-house built by the Douglas family in 1575. The road on the left bank leads to the village of Strachan (pronounced Straan) and to the Castlehill of Strachan, a severed spur on the Feugh that had a motte-and-bailey stronghold of the Durwards in the 12th cent. Above Strachan, where the Dye meets the Feugh, there is a choice of three roads, all of great interest.

BANFF, *Banffshire* (Map 6, ref. 36⁸86⁴), at the mouth of the DEVERON spanned by Smeaton's handsome seven-arched bridge, is a proud old royal burgh that has seen better days. When you consider that no fewer than 40,000 of the Banffers of old lie buried in the kirkyard between the High Shore and Church Street, you begin to realize how long its corporate life has continued without a break – bearing in mind that at the present day its population is little more than 3,000. If you have a strongly developed sense of history, you will love Banff. If not, you can still enjoy golf on its fine Duff House Royal course, and sea breezes on the glorious sandy sweep of Banff Links. The town is built on a series of terraces rising up to a cliff-top high above the old harbour, and has now been equipped with a new approach road that sweeps round to the S. and enters the town by its Georgian "West End". Having arrived on the line of High Street and Castle Street by means of this new and easy access, the visitor should park his car on the heights and descend by the stepped pavements of the Strait Path to the heart of the old town. As he does so he will retrace the centuries and find all around him the evidence of the original Banff, a trinity of castle, kirk, and commune.

Banff belonged to the Northern Hanse, or league of trading towns, before 1124. Its castle, first built to defend the coast from Viking invasion, was a royal residence early in the 12th cent. Curtain walls 144 ft long on the N. side guarded the now vanished stronghold on its plateau overlooking the sea, the same site where the 18th-cent. "castle" stands today, while the little town grew up below it in the area now comprising Low Street, Bridge Street, Carmelite Street, High Shore, and Deveronside.

Banff's first charter still extant was granted in 1372, but before 1190 a charter of the Church of Banff had been granted to the monks of ARBROATH. The Carmelites built themselves a monastery on the kirk lands, and all the houses on the S. side of Carmelite Street are built on the monastery grounds. Before the Reformation, Banff already had its beautiful mercat cross, first mentioned in 1542. The head of this shows carved effigies of the Crucifixion, with St John and the Virgin Mary in front and a figure of the Virgin and Child on the reverse. The present eight-sided shaft of the cross was probably made in 1627. There are many interesting 17th-cent. domestic buildings. Two good examples face each other at the corner of Carmelite Street and High Shore. The 18th cent. saw the high noon of Banff's vogue as a fashionable resort. By 1775, "high class citizens flitted about in their numerous private carriages paying their morning visits of compliment and sedan chairs were common". Out of this situation arose the Golden Age of Banff building.

The Town Steeple, that peculiar octagon, was built between 1764 and 1766 – despite the protests of Admiral Gordon, next door, who feared it would fall on his house. The present Banff Castle was built by Lord Deskford in 1750. St Mary's Church dates from 1789, though the fine classical spire was not finished until 50 years later, and Banff Academy, with its Ionic pillars, dates from 1838 – two years after the creation of the charming Collie Lodge. The greatest piece of architectural virtuosity of them all, Duff House, had been begun by the 1st Earl of Fife in 1735 to designs by William Adam, but only the central block was completed, at a cost of £70,000, when a crack appeared and the Earl went to law with the architect.

The quarrel between the two became so embittered that the Earl refused to live in his fine new house, which was modelled on the Villa Borghese; but it remains one of the handsomest edifices in the north of Scotland. In 1906 the Duke of Fife presented Duff House to the town councils of Banff and MACDUFF. During the Second World War, while it was housing German prisoners of war, it was bombed by the Nazis. It was handed over to the Ministry of Public Building and Works in 1953. The grounds on the haughland of the Deveron form an attractive public park alongside the Duff House Royal golf course.

The Biggar Fountain in Low Street occupies the site of the gallows where, in 1701, James Macpherson, the half-gypsy fiddler and freebooter, played defiant music in the face of death.

At the far end of the Duff House policies (2 m. S. of Banff) stretches a picturesque gorge of the Deveron, spanned by the Bridge of Alvah.

BANKFOOT, *Perthshire* (Map 6, ref. 30⁷73⁶). The villages of Bankfoot, Waterloo, and Cairniehill were built about 1800 on land feued by James Wylie of Airleywight; by 1838 most of the inhabitants lived by weaving or by employment in a linen-mill that still stands in Bankfoot village.

Beyond Bankfoot, the foothills of the Highland zone form a barrier that is not only physical but linguistic. Place-names S. of the hills are typically Lowland Scots and contrast with the Gaelic derivation of Balhomish, Tomgarrow, and Kennacoil across the watershed in Strath Brun.

At Tullybeagles Lodge are two adjacent circles of standing stones. These prehistoric burial sites may be compared with similar pairs at Sandy Road and Shianbank near SCONE.

BANNOCKBURN, *Stirlingshire* (Map 2, ref. 28¹69⁰). The village that bears this celebrated name lies just to the S. and E. of the battlefield of 1314 (*see below*). Today the village of Bannockburn is entirely supported by coal-mining and grows in prosperity and size. In the 18th cent., however, it was the centre of cottage weaving; the firm of Wilson started a tartan business and produced the first list of tartans in the 1790s. It was a coincidence – but perhaps no more than a happy coincidence – that, when Scotland (one might almost say the world) became conscious of the traditions of Scottish tartan, the firm that was most potent in propagating tartans should happen to have been based at Bannockburn.

About 1 m. S. of the Bannock Burn stands Bannockburn House. The exact date of its erection is not known, but two of the ceilings can be ascribed to 1680; it was therefore probably built in the middle 1600s. It was much altered in the 1880s. In 1745 it was the property of Sir Hugh Paterson, a strong Jacobite. He was the uncle of Clementina Walkingshaw, who became the mistress of Prince Charles Edward Stuart, who bore him his only child, and whose fortunes were much mingled with the sombre tale of his declining years. Prince Charles made Bannockburn House his headquarters on his retreat into Scotland in 1746. He stayed there from the 4th of January till the 1st of February in the same year.

The Borestane Site, where Bruce is believed to have raised his standard against the advancing English just N. of the Bannock Burn, has been acquired by the National Trust for Scotland to prevent any further encroachment of building upon it.

In 1964, the 650th anniversary of the battle, a 20-ft mounted statue of Bruce, sculpted by C. d'O. Pilkington Jackson, was set up at the Borestane. It was unveiled by H.M. the Queen.

The Battle of Bannockburn is usually included in those compendia devoted to the "Decisive Battles of History". At its time, it was indeed decisive in that, under Bruce's inspired leadership at the Battle of Bannockburn, Scotland regained her freedom. It was a freedom that she kept for centuries. That freedom may have been politically and officially abrogated in 1707; the concept of the United Kingdom of Great Britain, as promulgated in the Acts of Union passed then both in London and in Edinburgh, leave no doubt upon that score. Nevertheless, in the conspectus of history, the Battle of Bannockburn was decisive. Its decisive effect may even be said to have lingered until today. Had it not been for Bannockburn, there would not be people in Scotland still thinking of themselves and calling themselves Scots rather than North Britons. It is perhaps worth pointing out that the people who live in the southern part of the United Kingdom continue, and with equal disregard of the intentions of the Acts of Union, to call themselves English.

BARASSIE, *Ayrshire* (Map 2, ref. 23³63¹). A northern "suburb" of the burgh of TROON, this seaside resort has become a popular residential area. It is surrounded by golf courses; the Kilmarnock Club lies on the W., Western Gailes on the N., and five Troon courses extend to the S. Barassie is also involved in the great expansions following the establishment of IRVINE as the first New Town by the sea.

BARCALDINE, *Argyll* (Map 1, ref. 19⁷74¹). Though originally a township in an agricultural area, Barcaldine estate was bought by the Forestry Commission after the First World War, and large plantings now flourish there. The Alginate Industries took over a processing factory at Barcaldine that had been set up by the Ministry of Supply during the war. This industry, which processes seaweed from the Western Isles, employs about sixty workers.

Barcaldine Castle (3 m. SW. of the township) was built in the Scottish baronial style between 1579 and 1601 by Duncan Campbell of Glenorchy, on a position for defence. Today it gives superb views over Loch Creran to GLENCOE. The Campbells of Barcaldine sold the estate in 1842, but it was bought back, and the roofless Castle was restored in 1896–1910 by Sir Duncan Campbell of Barcaldine.

The Castle is now the seat of Sir Ian Campbell, the Seventh Baronet of Barcaldine, but it is occupied by his son, Mr Niall Campbell, and his family.

BAROCHAN, *Renfrewshire* (Map 2, ref. 24¹66⁹). This little place, once a town of some importance, was eventually reduced to a row of four cottages, but these have been redeveloped, and there is new life in Barochan.

There is no one living who can remember the "town of some importance", but a few people can recall the Fleming family, which for seven centuries held Barochan House. The number seven seems indeed to have had some significance for this tenacious and well-known family. In 1513 the head of the house and six of his sons were killed at Flodden. The seventh son survived to carry on the line and the estate until seven centuries were completed. The present Barochan House is a modern castellated structure built round an old house with crow-stepped gables.

Barochan Cross nearby is a fine free-standing Celtic cross 11 ft high. It is now not on the original site, but has been placed high upon a hillock.

BARR, *Ayrshire* (Map 2, ref. 22⁸59⁴). This is a secluded village, 8 m. SE. of GIRVAN, made remote by the difficulties of the roads leading to it. Barr lies in a sheltered corner where the R. Stinchar emerges from the hills. It is the centre of important forestry and sheep-farming country, and is a popular and quiet holiday resort. Close by is the mansion-house of Alton Albany, home of Sir Geoffrey Hughes-Onslow, from 1950 to 1969 Lord Lieutenant of Ayrshire. In days gone by Barr was the scene of the famous Kirkdandie Fair, where smugglers from BALLANTRAE mingled with hill-men and shepherds to indulge in a conviviality notorious even then. The smugglers knew the village well, lying as it did on the direct route from the coast via the Stinchar Glens to the security of the hill country, from which their merchandise was distributed over safe paths to towns of Ayrshire and Lanarkshire.

BARRA, Island of, *Inverness-shire* (Map 4, ref. 06⁵80⁰). This – with its satellite islands of Vatersay, Mingulay, and Berneray – lies at the southernmost and westerly end of the Outer Hebrides (*see* "The Shape of Scotland"). It is some 50 m. as the crow flies from the western mainland of Scotland. By boat the journey to Barra, the remotest inhabited part of western Scotland, takes a full day or a full night from OBAN or from MALLAIG. There is a regular air service to the island from GLASGOW. Barra is 8 m. long, 5 m. wide, and the road round its coast, rocky on the E., delicately decorated with beautiful Hebridean sand to the W., covers 14 m. The inhabitants of Barra number at least 1,400. Only about 100 people live on Vatersay.

Barra – of which CASTLEBAY, with Kisimul Castle lying on a rock just offshore, is the focal point – has a characteristic Outer Hebridean appearance. At first glance austere and bare, it soon reveals flashes of soft colouring; and its apparent bareness is relieved by the scattered crofts all over the island. It has one large hill, Ben Heaval (1,260 ft), and lesser undulations. Of its four lochs, some contain brown trout and sea-trout. Barra and its sister isles have an air of great peace and charm.

But it is the people of Barra who present the chief attraction of the place. All speak Gaelic as well as English, and are fluent, courteous, and hospitable. They live by fishing, crofting, and occasionally by taking in visitors. Nearly all of them are of Hebridean or W. Highland indigenous Catholic stock. There are three Catholic churches on the island, and one belonging to the Church of Scotland. Whether Catholic or Protestant, the Barraman is a great raconteur. Some of the most ancient Hebridean and Highland legends known to exist have been preserved over the centuries in the mouths of the Barra story-tellers. The population of Barra suffered grievously at the time of the later Highland Clearances, but the indomitable spirit they showed has won them their reward. They are still there. They have not forgotten their sufferings, but are quite unembittered. Barra was used as location for the film *Whisky Galore*. The events on which the film was based took place between Barra and South UIST.

Plate 3   Skiing in the Cairngorms (see p. 120)
Scottish Tourist Board

BARRHEAD, *Renfrewshire* (Map 2, ref. 25⁰65⁹), is a manufacturing town and burgh that began to evolve about 1773 after the establishment of textile industries on the rivers Levern and Kirkton. The town of Barrhead grew up in between the industries and the rivers, becoming a burgh in 1894. In the early part of the 19th cent. calico-printing was the main industry, and indeed it held that place until just after the end of the First World War in 1918. In the middle of the Victorian era, however, Barrhead began to cultivate another line of production that was later to outstrip that of the calico-printing.

By their energetic production of the socially beneficent industry of sanitary engineering the citizens of this little burgh in the neighbourhood of GLASGOW made the name of Barrhead familiar throughout Great Britain. As the writer of one of our popular guide-books usually given over to romantic description has put it, "hardly a street in the country but is indebted to the porcelain products of Barrhead". Strictly if philanthropically utilitarian though this industry has been, the money made by it has occasionally been used to foster the art of literature. One of the sons of the most famous firms of Barrhead sanitary engineers became a well-known Georgian poet.

BARRY, *Angus* (Map 6, ref. 35⁴73⁴). On the Buddon Ness between CARNOUSTIE and MONIFIETH, Barry has extensive links with a good E.-coast golf course. This low promontory is the site of one of Scotland's premier military training areas and has rifle and artillery ranges.

There are two lighthouses where the Firth of TAY meets the North Sea.

BARSALLOCH POINT, *Wigtownshire* (Map 2, ref. 23⁴54¹). A fine Iron Age fort, ¾ m. W. of Menteith, stands on the edge of the raised-beach bluff, at between 60 and 70 ft above the shore; it is enclosed by a horseshoe ditch 12 ft deep and 33 ft wide. The fort and point stand at the western extremity of Monreith Bay, the only sandy beach suitable for landing on a long stretch of rocky coast. The foreshore below the point is, in early summer, a mass of saxifrage blossom.

BARVAS, *Ross and Cromarty* (Map 4, ref. 13⁶94⁹), on the Island of LEWIS, Outer Hebrides (*see* "The Shape of Scotland"), is 12 m. NW. of STORNOWAY and, divided into an upper and lower village, is one of the more considerable Lewis townships. On the island, it is regarded with respect as the place of origin of the now growing policy of re-seeding – that is, the reclamation of barren moorland for pasture by the cultivation of grass. As long ago as the Napoleonic Wars, the minister of Barvas encouraged his parishioners to cut back the moorland and enrich the land by mixing with

it powdered sea-shells and other material from the shores. He had some small but definite success. The policy, however, was abandoned after Waterloo.

After the Second World War, Lewismen remembered the minister of Barvas, and, with the aid of modern chemicals (based on the sea-shell device) began re-seeding again. Barvas, as befits its history, was the first place where re-seeding was resumed. Now it has spread all over the island, notably at Garynahine and Brue. In the five years leading up to 1964, no fewer than 10,000 acres were reclaimed in Lewis. This re-seeding policy provides an example of communal effort under the crofting system. The Grazing Committee of each re-seeding locality received a toll from each croft towards the purchase of scientific material for re-seeding.

Barvas stands at the cross-roads between the main route on the W. side of Lewis southward from the Butt of LEWIS and the road from Stornoway to the E., and in appearance is a characteristic Lewis township. It straggles lengthily over the flat surface and is, by reason of its history, primarily agricultural rather than devoted to fishing. Its geographical (one is tempted to say strategical) position accounts for the fact that it contained the last licensed premises to exist outside Stornoway before the island, as apart from its capital, voted itself "dry".

BASS ROCK, *East Lothian* (Map 3, ref. 36⁰68⁸), is in the Firth of FORTH (*see* "The Shape of Scotland"). This splendid monument of nature at her most self-assertive is, for many visitors, their first introduction to Scotland's 787 islands. Its apparently huge shape looms up just off the coast by the London–EDINBURGH road in East Lothian and looks, because of its steep sides, much more than its 350 ft in height; it is 1 m. in circumference. It is of hard igneous stone, and is the last link in a chain of volcanic masses that stretch over the Lothians, having resisted the flattening glacial pressure of the Ice Age. Edinburgh Castle Rock is one of these masses, and is indeed impressive enough on land and in the centre of a city. The Bass needs no such civic setting; it happens just to stick out of the sea, and is all the more arresting and startling for that simple fact.

St Baldred, one of the few remaining Christians in the pre-Columban tradition of Scotland, had a cell on the Bass early in the 7th cent. Later this hermit-worthy rock came under the influence of the Celtic Columban Church. Thereafter its qualities as a fortress made the Bass appear and reappear in the English wars and in internecine struggles.

Under Charles II, the Bass was used as a prison to restrain covenanting ministers who had "suffered for conscience' sake". The most extraordinary episode in the Bass's history,

Above *Near Ballater: Glen Muick* (*see p.* 90)

Below *Near Beauly: Beaufort Castle, seat of Lord Lovat* (*see p.* 98)

Scottish Tourist Board

D. Whyte

however, was when, after the flight of James VII and II and the death of Claverhouse at KILLIECRANKIE, some Jacobite officers captured the Bass Rock and held it in the name of the exiled Stuart king. They succeeded in doing this for nearly three years, from June 1691 till April 1694. Thereafter the Bass retreated from history and from political intrigue, though, as readers of *Catriona* will recall, R. L. Stevenson brought it forcefully, if fictionally, back into politics as the place where David Balfour (the inconvenient witness) was incarcerated in the aftermath of the Rising of 1745.

The Bass was exclusive as a hermitage, potent as a prison, and formidable as a fortress by reason of its steep sides and the fact that it is inaccessible save at one point on the SW. An extraordinary feature is the cavernous tunnel that penetrates it from E. to W.; it was caused by natural fissure. Today the Rock's human population is four – the lighthouse-keepers. The Bass, however, is the haunt of innumerable sea-birds; pre-eminent among them is the Bass Solan goose. The rock indeed has given a name to these gannets, which are known among ornithologists as *Sula bassana*. There are regular trips by motor-boat from the mainland at NORTH BERWICK round the rock to see the gannets nesting, and permission to land is occasionally granted.

BATHGATE, *West Lothian* (Map 2, ref. 29⁸66⁹). Now and for some time a prominent industrial town in the eastern centre of Scotland's industrial belt, Bathgate's history reaches further back. It was made a burgh of barony in 1663, and its first fortunes were founded on weaving. In the mid-19th cent., Dr James Young set up a refinery at Whitehead nearby and first made paraffin for commercial use. These ventures were sustained by the coal-mining in the district; an iron foundry followed the paraffin works.

A large car-manufacturing company has founded and developed a factory near the town. Motorists travelling on the road between EDINBURGH and GLASGOW will see evidence of its activities as they pass.

At Bathgate, in 1811, was born Sir James Y. Simpson, who invented the use of chloroform as an anaesthetic.

BEARSDEN, *Dunbartonshire* (Map 2, ref. 25⁴67¹), a modern burgh NW. of GLASGOW, was until the mid-19th cent. a small village called New Kilpatrick or "New Kirk". With the railway's arrival in 1863 it attracted Glasgow residents, and development followed the line of the Antonine Wall of A.D. 143, and the town became Bearsden. Created a burgh in 1958, it now has 26,000 inhabitants, exceptionally spacious parks, three golf clubs, a swimming-pool, ample sports facilities, and good shops.

BEATTOCK, *Dumfriesshire* (Map 2, ref. 30⁸70¹). Beattock-Beathaich, the birchy place, lies at the junction of the main GLASGOW and EDINBURGH road to England down Annandale with the road from DUMFRIES; until recently a spur line went to MOFFAT from the main railway line, which passes through Beattock. The railway station was built in 1847–8 and is celebrated in Cunninghame Graham's *Beattock for Moffat*, a classic example of the short story technique in any language, and the best one this splendid old Scottish-Spanish hidalgo, laird, and supporter of the early Scottish Socialists, ever wrote.

The Glasgow–Carlisle road is now a great dual carriage-way, and the village has been growing rapidly, but the pleasant Upper Annandale surroundings are unchanged.

BEAULY, *Inverness-shire* (Map 5, ref. 25³84⁵). Traditionally the name of this town and that of the river on which it stands, as well as of the district, comes from the French words *beau lieu*. The tradition may well be correct, for the Frasers of Lovat, in whose country Beauly lies, were originally Normans; and they were, from the time of their first possession of land in Scotland, highly conscious of their French and aristocratic blood. They encouraged the use of Norman French amongst themselves even in the far places of the North.

The priory of Beauly was founded by Sir John Bisset of Lovat in 1230. All that remains of it now is a roofless shell of the church, some of which dates from the 13th cent. and other parts from the 14th, 15th, and 16th cents. The ruins, which stand at the N. end of the village, were allowed to fall into their state of decay after the Reformation.

About 4 m. SSW. of Beauly stands Beaufort Castle, the seat of the Frasers of Lovat (the Lords Lovat). Their original residence was Castle Dounie, which had been built about 1400. This castle was destroyed by the Duke of Cumberland in 1746 after his victory over Prince Charles Edward Stuart at CULLODEN MOOR; it is now a ruin in a terraced garden. The present Beaufort Castle was built in the Scots baronial style about 1880; there was a fire in 1936, after which a new wing was added.

The ruins of Dounie Castle, Beauly, and the Fraser country in general are much associated with the memory of Simon, Lord Lovat, who was executed on Tower Hill in 1747 for his participation in the Jacobite Rising of 1745. He is sometimes remembered as "Lovat of the '45", and sometimes, because of his twistings and turnings and many political attitudes, as the "old fox of the '45". He was an extraordinary character who was perhaps a throwback, being more of a princeling of the Italian States of the Renaissance than a Highland chief in 18th-cent. Scotland. But in his ending he redeemed many of his faults.

We surely cannot withhold from the old man

our admiration for the jocular bravery with which he met his death when he, the last peer to be executed for high treason in these islands, faced the headsman's axe.

"You'll get that nasty head of yours chopped off you ugly old Scotch dog," screamed a Cockney woman at him in the London crowds as he went to his end. His reply is remembered in our country with a Celtic relish. It is one for which we can forgive him much: "I believe I shall, you ugly old English bitch."

BEINN EIGHE, *Ross and Cromarty* (Map 5, ref. 19⁵85⁹). Lying in the western and wilder part of the county, this became the first National Nature Reserve in Great Britain: it was declared such on the 1st of November 1951. The reserve consists of 10,507 acres with altitudes varying from 30 ft to 3,000 ft. It has a wide range of vegetational types, including some alpine growths. Creatures living naturally here include the red deer, the wild cat (*Felis silvestris*, the true wild cat of Scotland), the eagle, and the pine marten. The Nature Conservancy has constructed two fascinating nature trails from the shore of Loch MAREE: there are picnic and camping areas.

BEITH, *Ayrshire* (Map 2, ref. 23⁵65⁴). Before the Union of Parliaments in 1707, this was a place of no size or importance, but early in the 18th cent. it became the centre of a woollen and then a linen and silk industry. Those industries have now been replaced by furniture-making and the manufacture of gloves. Beith sits high near the northern boundary of Ayrshire and looks more to PAISLEY and GLAS-GOW than to the towns farther S. It is on the Glasgow–ARDROSSAN road, about 11 m. from Paisley.

BELL ROCK, *Angus* (Map 6, ref. 37⁶72⁷), on which stands the Bell Rock Lighthouse, is a sunken reef, also called the Inchcape, 12 m. off the Angus coast, barely uncovered at low water and 16 ft under the sea at every tide. Lying in the track of coastal shipping and vessels making for the Firths of TAY and FORTH, it was once marked by the Abbot of ARBROATH who placed on it a bell, which was tolled by the waves as a warning signal. Southey's ballad tells the story of how it was cut away by Ralph the Rover, who later perished when his ship was lost on the unmarked reef. A wooden beacon designed by Captain Joseph Brodie, R.N., and fixed to the rock in 1803 did not survive the first winter's storms. The Bell Rock remained the scene or cause of many disastrous shipwrecks until a lighthouse was built there in 1807–11 by Robert Stevenson, the Edinburgh engineer and grandfather of R.L.S. The tower is 120 ft high, and the stones of each course were laid in a builder's yard at Arbroath before being shipped off to the Rock. It was visited by fifty members of the British Association for the Advancement of Science in 1850, and has been described as rising at high water "like a bulrush out of a pond". Since Smeaton's Eddystone (from which the design was adapted) was superseded in 1882, the Bell Rock has been the oldest sea-swept lighthouse in continuous use in the British Isles. After standing for over 150 years, the interior of the tower was recently modernized and a diesel-powered electric light installed by the Commissioners of Northern Lighthouses.

BELLSHILL, *Lanarkshire* (Map 2, ref. 27⁵66⁰), is a part of the main industrial centre of the parish of BOTHWELL, 11 m. SE. of GLASGOW, and it is often considered a part of Glasgow. It nonetheless retains its identity, which was founded during the period of 19th-cent. immigration. Its industry was mainly built up on steel and coal, but was very badly hit by the Depression of 1919. In 1934, at the very depth of the Depression, unemployment reached the scale of seventy per cent. Conditions have much improved since those days, and particularly after the Second World War. The presence of new industries in the neighbourhood of Bellshill and upon the EDIN-BURGH road has reduced unemployment considerably.

Amongst the immigrants who came to Bellshill in the middle of the 19th cent. was a small minority that had a marked influence on industrial Scotland. This unit was composed of Lithuanians who originally came to Scotland as prisoners of war in 1855 after the Crimea. The Lithuanians, in those days part of the Empire of the Tsar of All the Russias, adhered, as they still do, to the Roman and Western rite, and they were much out of favour with the strict Orthodox circles then ruling Tsarist Russia. Many of the prisoners, at the conclusion of the Crimean War, preferred to stay in Scotland. They formed a group and, indeed, after a fashion, flourished at Bellshill. By 1887 they had their own priest, who spoke to them in their own language. In 1914 they published a weekly magazine, *Iseivin Draugas*, in their language. The title of their paper in English was *Friend of Immigrants*. It continued publication until the Second World War.

BEMERSYDE, *Berwickshire* (Map 3, ref. 35⁹63³). Bemersyde House is the home of Earl Haig, and is well known as the hereditary land of the Haigs. The history of the family dates back to the 12th cent., but the present tower dates from 1535. Bemersyde suffered at the hands of the invading English in 1545; so did the abbeys of KELSO, DRYBURGH, and MELROSE. Bemersyde was at least partly rebuilt in 1581, and had a storey added at the top in 1690; the inside of the house also was altered. Stones in this restoration were used from the nearby ruins of Dryburgh. In 1790 a two-storey E. wing was added. Sir Walter Scott often visited Bemersyde House. He took a particular delight in the view from Bemersyde Hill and the sight of the winding R. TWEED with the EILDON Hills to the W. There is an indicator at this spot.

The old prophecy of Thomas the Rhymer is famous throughout Scotland, and became particularly well known after the First World War. The prophecy ran: "Tyde what may, whate'er betyde, Haig shall be Haig of Bemersyde". In the latter half of the 19th cent. the house went to a Haig of the Clackmannanshire family. In 1921, however, it was purchased by national subscription and presented to Field-Marshal Earl Haig. In the writing-room of the tower are preserved his maps and other mementoes of the war. Scotland had not forgotten the promise of Thomas the Rhymer before 1914, but she recalled it with added force in 1921, when Field-Marshal Earl Haig returned to the home of his ancestors.

The present Earl Haig who lives at Bemersyde is the son and successor of the famous Field-Marshal.

BEN ALDER, *Inverness-shire* (Map 5, ref. 25⁰77¹). In one of the wildest districts of the Central Highlands and of the GRAMPIANS, Ben Alder is part of a mountain mass over 3,000 ft high and extending between Loch Laggan to the N. and Loch Ericht to the S. Ben Alder is much associated with the name of Cluny Macpherson of the '45. This Highland chief, though out with Prince Charles Edward Stuart in his Jacobite venture in the middle of the 18th cent., did not leave Scotland after the failure of that venture. Indeed, he stayed hidden in his estate for nearly ten years after the last Jacobite hope had died. The Prince and Lochiel were with him in September 1746 when news came that a ship had arrived to take them to France. The Prince and Lochiel left Scotland, but Cluny stayed. He was enabled to do so owing to the wild and remote and, at that time, inaccessible nature of his dominions. He had built for him on the southern spur of Ben Alder a curious habitation known as "Cluny's Cage", which was said to be a two-storey artificial structure hanging on to the side of the mountain. Those who have read R. L. Stevenson's novel *Kidnapped* will remember how David Balfour and Alan Breck when they were in full flight came upon Cluny's Cage, "hanging like a wasp's nest in a green hawthorn bush". Here in seclusion partly savage, partly animated by the manners of a polite and hereditarily aristocratic society, Cluny lingered for a number of years. Nothing now remains to show us exactly where Cluny's Cage was. But Ben Alder towers as impressively as ever 3,757 ft above Loch Ericht.

BENBECULA, Island of, *Inverness-shire* (Map 4, ref. 08⁰85³), is one of the Outer Hebrides (*see* "The Shape of Scotland"). It is the most northerly island of the distinctive Southern Outer Hebrides and is certainly the flattest. Flying over it on the B.E.A. Hebridean route, you might think that there was almost more fresh water in the form of inland lochs and lochans than land itself on this not very large island. Looking down on such an "open-work shawl" of an island from a height of 2,000 ft, you wonder how the land contains the water; but it does, and most successfully, as you perceive when you land at the airport that was established there during the Second World War.

The communication between Benbecula and its sister southern isles used, until the war, to be a precarious affair of fording the passage at low tide between it and South UIST. Now, however, there is an admirable viaduct built for the R.A.F. leading directly to the larger island. It is admirable not only in its convenience but in its ability to withstand the furious W. and SW. gales that break here in the late autumn and winter. More recently a causeway linking Benbecula with its northern neighbour North UIST was opened, the building on it having been completed in 1961.

It is now possible to motor (or walk or ride, for that matter) from the tip of North Uist by way of Benbecula to Pollachar at the extreme S. of South Uist. Thence the traveller can go by ferry to ERISKAY or by boat to the BARRA islands. Nowadays the only wide break in the "Long Island" (the popular name for the Outer Hebrides) is between HARRIS and North Uist.

Benbecula has its quiet appeal for the visitor, especially the unambitious angler who just likes moving from small loch to small loch in search of eager, sporting brown trout and for occasional sea-trout. Almost as flat as TIREE in all the Hebrides, it lacks the verdant appeal of that island, but makes up for it by the vividness of its cloud effects and the changing colours of its scene.

The population of Benbecula, living as it does on an island linking the strongly Protestant and largely Free Kirk Northern Hebrides and the indigenously Catholic Southern Outer Isles, is equally divided between Protestants and Catholics. In the old days the Catholics, on Sundays and holy days, had to ford the crossing to South Uist for their Mass. Today they have a church of their own on the island. As is usual in the Hebrides and Western Highlands, the relationship between those of the two faiths is excellent, and a model to the rest of us. Perhaps the possession of the Gaelic tongue in common helps in their friendly relationship – at any rate, it is excellent.

Some of the most authentic Gaelic songs, poems, and traditional tales have come from the island and have been preserved there.

BEN CRUACHAN, *Argyll* (Map 2, ref. 20⁷73⁰). "Cruachan" is the war-cry of Clan Campbell; and one can well understand why this noble mountain has been used as a symbol of the power of this great clan, and why the sound of its name should inspire them to action. It is reputed, and even by many who do not bear the name of Campbell, to be the finest mountain in the S. Highlands; it is a collection of seven or eight peaks, of which two are considerably higher than the others; the highest is 3,689 ft. The view from any of its peaks (but of course pre-eminently from the highest) is outstanding. Its ascent, which need not be unduly strenuous or dangerous, is best tackled from TAYNUILT or DALMALLY. There is one annual event that offers evidence of the comparative accessibility of Ben Cruachan. This is a gathering of young people at the end of the ball that concludes the Highland Games at OBAN. Having danced the night through, they change into country clothes, motor to Taynuilt, and climb Ben Cruachan to meet, if not exactly the dawn, at least the middle of the morning. No one up to date has been reported as being any the worse from this youthful and ardent feat.

Cruachan is also the site of the North of Scotland Hydro-Electric Board's pumped storage scheme, already referred to as the Cruachan Hydro-electric scheme in the entry on Loch AWE.

BEN DAMH, *Ross and Cromarty* (Map 5, ref. 19⁰85¹). This mountain and the COULIN Deer Forest lie between Strathcarron and Glen Torridon in Wester Ross. W. H. Murray, the mountaineer and writer on Scottish topography, chose it as one of his twenty-one areas in *Highland Landscape*, a volume published for the National Trust for Scotland and selecting parts of the Highlands particularly worthy of preservation. The area has several rights of way that cross the region and are tracks only for walkers; no motor cars are allowed.

BENDERLOCH, *Argyll* (Map 1, ref. 20⁰73⁶), is, topographically and historically, a district between Lochs Creran and ETIVE. There was, however, a rural railway station at the western side of the district that bore the name of Benderloch. This led people to associate the name with a peninsula jutting out into Loch Linnhe and the Firth of Lorne. This peninsula is flat and is cultivated in many small farms. There is tourist attraction in the way of "bed and breakfast" supplied at crofts and farms. There is also a caravan site beside the sands at Tralee Bay immediately W. of Benderloch hamlet. Loch Nell Castle is near the SW. end of the peninsula and on Ardmucknish Bay.

On a ridge to the SW. of the former station of Benderloch are forts and a dun spuriously called Beregonium. The earliest is a timber-laced wall round the whole summit, but superseded by a rectangular vitrified fort 170 ft by 60 ft. This in turn is surrounded by a circular

and probably vitrified dun. Relics found in the neighbourhood indicate a pre-Roman and Roman Iron Age occupation. There is a tradition associating with this neighbourhood that half-mythical, half-mystical, but wholly Celtic figure, Deirdre.

BEN LAWERS, *Perthshire* (Map 2, ref. 26⁴74¹), is the highest mountain in the county, rising 3,984 ft from the road along the N. shore of Loch TAY between KILLIN and ABERFELDY. The mountain is renowned for its colonies of rare alpine plants, and is also one of Scotland's skiing areas. Some 8,000 acres of the southern slopes, with part of the neighbouring Ben Ghlas, were bought by the National Trust for Scotland in 1950. In accordance with its mountainous-property policy, the Trust maintains public access here at all times, with an injunction to visitors not to collect specimens of the rare flora. The summit, with its indicator cairn, opens up a coast-to-coast view across Scotland. Ski slopes are reached by way of the Lochan na Larige road off the road to Bridge of Balgie. This leads to a car park at an altitude of 1,400 ft. Some 2 m. on and a further 1,000 ft up, the Scottish Ski Club's hut in Coire Odhar is the usual rendezvous for skiers.

BENMORE, *Argyll* (Map 2, ref. 21²68⁵). Benmore House, on the shores of Loch Eck and between HOLY LOCH and Loch LONG, is now the Forestry Training School within the Argyll National Forest Park. In 1928 Mr G. H. Younger presented this house and this famous private forest to the Forestry Commission. Its large and extensive gardens are managed in close association with the Royal Botanic Garden in EDINBURGH; they contain the world's finest collection of rhododendrons and an extensive arboretum, and are open to the public.

The W. Highlands of Scotland are noted for their wild, grand, and somewhat barren prospects of sea-scape, landscape, and mountainscape. At Benmore the visitor may see the other side of the W. Highlands – in its luxurious and fertile capacity. This is an element in the W. Highlands (so often touched by the Gulf Stream) that people tend to forget.

BENNACHIE, *Aberdeenshire* (Map 6, ref. 36⁶82²). This little range of hills is the supreme symbol of the homeland to most Lowland countrymen of the NE. of Scotland. The highest of its six summits (Oxen Craig) rises only to 1,733 ft, but the whole group, being compact, stands out finely against the skyline when seen from any direction, but particularly from the E. or N., where it is visible for 20 to 30 m. It can be seen from Mastrick on the outskirts of ABERDEEN, from SLAINS and CRUDEN on the coast of Buchan, and from New DEER over 20 m. to the N. The most easterly peak, the Mither Tap (1,698 ft), the most prominent,

Ben Nevis

is crowned by a mighty stone fort encircling the summit tor with a circumference of 700 ft and walls 15 ft thick. Every poet of the region has written about Bennachie, from the anonymous author of "O! gin I war whaur Gadie rins" to Charles Murray, the author of *Hamewith*.

BEN NEVIS, *Inverness-shire* (Map 5, ref. 21⁸77⁰), is 4,418 ft high, and is the highest mountain in Scotland and in the British Isles. It does not always look as if it were the highest piece of land in Scotland, for its summit does not rise to a sharp peak but is rounded. Moreover, from one side it slopes gently and lengthily to near sea-level. It does, however (especially when viewed from CORPACH), present a superb cliff-face.

The safe route for those who wish to climb the highest mountain in the British Isles is by bridle track from Achintee in GLEN NEVIS, but this route is 10 m. up and down and will take between six and eight hours. Even on this fairly easy route the ordinary tourist is strongly advised not to make the ascent in winter, in bad conditions, or by himself.

The NE. face, the one you see from Corpach, gives climbers a very testing ascent; it is the most extensive cliff in Great Britain. An observatory was established on the summit in October 1883, but was abandoned in 1904. Climatic conditions in the neighbourhood of Ben Nevis are extremely uncertain, owing to the fact that the sea with its warm Gulf Stream is but 4 m. in a direct line from the summit of the mountain. These climatic conditions, perhaps, are responsible for the cloud-blanket that so often lies above this district, and through which the summit of Ben Nevis may just be seen by those flying over Scotland.

BERNERA, *Inverness-shire* (Map 5, ref. 18³82⁰). This township with the ruins of a barracks, near the village of GLENELG and opposite the S. end of SKYE, is rather a curiosity. It was built at some time between 1719 and 1722 by General George Wade as a permanent point on his road-making through the Highlands – an attempt to "civilize" the Highlands after the rising of 1715 by the making of roads to the farthest points. The now deserted barracks at Bernera were said to have been built to house 200 men. Long after the troops receded, however, in the early part of the 19th cent. (that is to say, well after the Jacobite rising of 1745), the ruined barracks did have some better reason for existence. It gave shelter to many victims of the Clearances in the neighbourhood, and particularly at Knoydart, where the Clearances were carried out with great ruthlessness and speed.

The British Government, which had erected these barracks for the comfort of redcoats and of German mercenaries employed to keep down the native Highlanders, can hardly have foreseen the uses to which they would be put. The ruins remain; the British Government that put them up has long been dead and is all but forgotten. No one knows the names of the English soldiers and German mercenaries who barracked here. The descendants of those Highlanders who sheltered in them are for the most part overseas, but are not forgotten.

BERNERA, GREAT, *Ross and Cromarty* (Map 4, ref. 11⁶93⁵), is an island in the Outer Hebrides (*see* "The Shape of Scotland"). This Bernera is off the W. coast of LEWIS. Its greatest length is 5½ m., greatest width 2¾ m. It is joined to Lewis by a handsome bridge "across the Atlantic", opened on the 22nd of

July 1953. Bernera people threatened to blow up the cliffs and create a causeway across the channel. The result was that they got their bridge – another victory for direct action.

In 1874 the crofters reacted with moderate violence against the oppressive landlords and their agents. An example of the ruthless way in which the owners treated their tenants is to be found at Bosta. On trumped-up charges, and by repeated acts calculated to make life untenable, they drove the people of this once-thriving village off their improved land, moving them *en bloc* to Kirkibost. Bosta is now a completely ruined "ghost village" in one of the loveliest parts of Lewis. Although it dates back to Viking times, its vigorous life was finally stamped out to make room for the sheep.

Berisay (or Birsay) is an island near Bernera where Neil MacLeod, the illegitimate son of Roderick X of Lewis, made his last stand against Mackenzie of Kintail. Neil is the William Wallace of Lewis. He routed the 17th-cent. Fife Adventurers and made their lives such a misery that they left. He turned pirate and brigand. He was eventually captured and executed in EDINBURGH. He died, it is said, "verie Christianlie".

BETTYHILL, *Sutherland* (Map 5, ref. 27¹96²). This small village stands at the mouth of the R. Naver, which runs due N. into the N. Atlantic Ocean on the N. coast of Scotland. Today it is a resort for tourists, particularly anglers. There are many opportunities for brown-trout, sea-trout, and salmon fishing. The neighbourhood has many small lochs and some larger ones, with a considerable variety in kind and quality of fish for those who are prepared to walk in search of their sport. The village as now named stands in the parish of Farr. It is believed to have been named after Elizabeth, Countess of Sutherland.

The parish church has been made into a museum of local interest and contains some remarkable carved stones.

BIGGAR, *Lanarkshire* (Map 2, ref. 30⁴63⁸), is said to consider itself the capital of the upper ward of Lanarkshire, and it certainly presents the appearance of a county town. It has a spacious High Street with a double row of well-trimmed trees; it must be one of the widest country-town high streets in all Scotland.

Biggar became a royal burgh in 1451, and was under the protection of the Flemings of Boghall Castle, which stood in the marshland to the S. of the town, but only a small part of one tower of the castle remains. The High Street has many wynds or closes off it, and on the N. side are traces of crofts or narrow strips of land surviving from medieval land tenure. St Mary's Church was erected as a Collegiate Church in 1545 on the site of the earlier church of St Nicholas. It was the last Collegiate Church to be founded in Scotland before the Reformation. At the W. end of the town is a bridge called Cadger Bridge over the Biggar Burn. It gets its name from the fact that Wallace was said to have crossed this bridge disguised as a cadger before defeating Edward I of England at a battle on the moss to the S. and E. of Biggar. Today the town is the centre of an agricultural area, which grows many tomatoes, lettuces, and chrysanthemums under glass. Also, since 1948 a factory has been developed to make machinery for land cultivation and drainage.

In previous times Biggar was the centre for Scottish industries such as weaving. The crowning of the Fleming Queen in July, which ceremony still continues, commemorates Mary Fleming from Boghall Castle, who was one of Mary Stuart's four Marys. There is also a pony-trekking centre nearby.

NE. of the town lies the attractive village of Skirling. It has on the village green some oddly shaped wrought-iron work and painted animals and birds, a local decoration not known anywhere else in Scotland. The work was the product of the fertile imagination of Lord Carmichael, who lived there.

On the outskirts of Biggar now lives Hugh McDiarmid, considered by many people the greatest Scottish poet since Burns and Dunbar.

BINNS, The, *West Lothian* (Map 2, ref. 30³68⁹). This, the historic home of the Dalyell family, stands 15 m. W. of EDINBURGH on the road between South QUEENSFERRY and LINLITHGOW. The lands of The Binns are first mentioned in documents of 1335, but the house as it is now dates mainly from the early 17th cent. Handsomely-moulded plaster ceilings (1612–30) are a feature of the interior. General Tam Dalyell, who defeated the Covenanters at Rullion Green in 1666, raised the Royal Scots Greys at The Binns in 1681. Sadly but historically, the last chapter in the history of the Royal Scots Greys was also written at The Binns when in June 1971 the regiment paraded there, as they had done 290 years earlier, but this time to mark their amalgamation with the 3rd Carabineers to become the Royal Scots Dragoon Guards; and with the Colonel of the Regiment, Lt-Col. A. G. J. Readman, D.S.O., taking the salute was Mr Tam Dalyell, M.P., the direct descendant of that earlier Tam Dalyell. The Scots Greys' amalgamation ceremonies were concluded a fortnight later when at a parade at Holyrood Park, Edinburgh, the Queen presented her colours to the new regiment, and subsequently the Greys' famous guidon (forked battle standard) was laid up in the Scottish National War Memorial in Edinburgh Castle. General Tam Dalyell is commemorated in the house by a display of personal possessions ranging from his sword to his Bible. This was the first large historic house to be placed in the care of the National Trust for Scotland (in 1944).

BIRGHAM, *Berwickshire* (Map 3, ref. 37⁸63⁹). This village on the N. bank of the TWEED, and at the W. end of that stretch where the river is the boundary between Scotland and England, has historically been regarded as the ultimate land of Scotland. Of course, much of Scotland lies far farther S. than Birgham; much of the E. Borders, and DUMFRIES and Galloway, lie S. of a large part of Northumbria. Indeed, there are parts of Galloway S. of Newcastle. But insofar as the R. Tweed has been regarded as the traditional boundary, Birgham is the most southerly point in relation to that border. It has been alleged that in this neighbourhood the command "go to Birgham" is the equivalent of "go to Jericho" – the intention being the dismissal to the farthest point of Scottish soil.

It was near Birgham, yet on the S. side of the river, that Malcolm II in 1018 won, over the English armies, a victory that secured for Scotland the land of Lothian. Birgham, during the 12th and 13th cents., was used as a meeting-place for talks between the representatives of the two countries. The most important diplomatic occasion at the small village of Birgham took place in 1290; it resulted in the Treaty of Birgham, by which the marriage of Margaret, infant Queen of Scotland, with Prince Edward of England (the future Edward II) was agreed. The bride died within three months on a voyage from her father's home in Norway to Scotland. The result (*see* "Scotland in History") was a chaos of dispute over the succession to the Scottish throne – that chaos which eventually led to the Wars of Independence and to BANNOCKBURN.

BIRNAM, *Perthshire* (Map 6, ref. 30⁴74¹). A village on the W. bank of the TAY near the join of the R. Braan, Birnam is linked to DUNKELD by a bridge built in 1809. It has the railway station for Dunkeld as well as the church of Little Dunkeld, in whose churchyard Neil Gow, the great Scottish fiddle-player, is buried.

The woods have remained a feature of the district since King Malcolm used them to attack Macbeth at DUNSINANE, from which, although lying 14 m. away, Birnam Hill can be seen. On the hill itself are the ruins of a round fort, called Duncan's Camp, where King Duncan is alleged to have held his court.

Birnam Pass, on the PERTH–Dunkeld road, is a narrow wooded route known as the Mouth of the Highlands. There is much picturesque scenery including Rumbling Bridge on the R. Braan, which was painted by Millais.

BIRNIE, *Moray* (Map 6, ref. 32¹85⁸). Once a place of worship of the early Celtic Church, Birnie has been a religious site for many centuries. The present church building dates from the 12th cent. and is one of the few Norman churches in Scotland still used for worship. It has a Norman chancel arch and also a Norman font. The sculptured "Birnie Stone", dating from the 9th cent., was found on the site.

The Ronnel Bell is a relic of the Celtic church, and the ancient square-sided altar bell was traditionally believed to have been made in Rome and blessed by the Pope. Birnie was the seat of the first four bishops of Moray 1107–84.

BIRRENS, *Dumfriesshire* (Map 3, ref. 32²57⁵). The Roman fort here is situated at the junction of the Middlebie Burn and the Mein Water, ½ m. S. of Middlebie Church. It was, in 1895, the first Roman fort in Britain to be excavated and planned in a systematic way; since then there have been various other excavations – in 1936–7 and again each year since 1962 onwards; and aerial photography has added to our knowledge of the site. Evidence of several periods, from the late 1st to the late 2nd cent., has been found.

The fort, of seven acres, housed a horsed military cohort. Of these, the Nervian Cohort and the Second Cohort of Tungrians have left evidence in the form of altars and inscriptions. There is evidence also to show the presence of a detachment of the 6th Legion, the "Victorious", whose headquarters were at York. The site has yielded a great deal of detail of its plan, in the form of walls and roads, besides a great amount of pottery and many altars, inscriptions, and pieces of sculpture; some of the altars and a statue of the goddess Brigantia are in the National Museum of Antiquities in EDINBURGH, and a good selection of altars, much pottery and other material, and a fine head of an unknown goddess can be seen at DUMFRIES Museum.

As late as the 1720s the buildings still stood to a considerable height; the worst robbing of farm buildings and dykes came after 1800, but the barrack walls and the walls of the head-quarters, granaries, and commandant's house still stand several courses high when cleared of topsoil and turf. There is some hope that the fort will eventually be fully excavated and its structure left on view, as with some of the forts along Hadrian's Wall, but even now the massive platform of the fort and its entrance, complex ditch, and rampart system can easily be seen. The fort was an outpost of Hadrian's Wall, and stands opposite the end of the wall at the "Altar Stone" in the Solway.

A little NW. of Middlebie is Birrenswark or Burnswark, on a flat-topped steep-sided lava sill rising out of the low valley to nearly 940 ft. This outstanding natural feature, which dominates much of the Borders, has two Iron Age forts on its flat summit, and is flanked by two great Roman siege-forts – a complete one, with gun-platforms for the great catapults, on the S. face, and an unfinished one on the N. face. These Roman features are very clear.

BIRSAY, *Orkney* (Map 7, ref. 32⁶02⁸), is a hamlet on the Mainland of the ORKNEY

Northern Islands (*see* "The Shape of Scotland"). Situated at the extreme NW. tip of the mainland of Orkney, this attractive little outpost has been for long a favourite haunt of Orcadian holiday-makers. In this they have followed the inclinations of early Norse bishops, and later of the Scottish occupying earls. In 1580 Earl Robert Stewart attempted to build a holiday residence here in the manner of FALKLAND Palace in Scotland. It is now in ruins. Birsay is on the coast road round the W. mainland that leads the visitor past some striking cliff scenery, notably "Yesnaby Castle", which is no man-made castle but a columnar cliff cut off from the island by the force of the seas, like the Old Man of HOY.

Off these western coasts the ship bearing Lord Kitchener to Russia in 1916 was sunk by a German mine. All on board were lost. A square tower marks the place on Orkney opposite which this disaster happened.

BISHOPTON, *Renfrewshire* (Map 2, ref. 24³67²). Though the neighbourhood in which the once little village of Bishopton stands has had a long and varied history, the village itself remained obscure until this century. In 1900 it had only 21 houses, by 1959 there were over 250; before long there will be many more. Bishopton owes its 20th-cent. prosperity to a tyre factory and an ordnance works started during the First World War. The Royal Ordnance factory is still at Bishopton. After the First World War there were plans to make this district into a garden city, on the model of those in the South of England, but the plan never matured. Planning and building of new towns, whether of the garden-city variety or of another kind, did not manifest itself in Scotland until after the Second World War. The new towns that are such a characteristic development of modern Scotland were all begun in recent years. We shall come to a consideration of their unique place in Scotland's economy under the entry for CUMBERNAULD.

BLACKFORD, *Perthshire* (Map 2, ref. 28⁹70⁹). Those who love the tang of Scotch Ale may consider it worth while pausing at this village to reflect upon its history. Brewing is still its main industry, and has been since at least 1488, when James IV, King of Scots, tasted some local ale in this neighbourhood and found it good; it is still brewed here and is still good.

The village was burned in 1716 by the Earl of Mar after the Battle of SHERRIFMUIR, an indeterminate struggle that occurred during the Jacobite Rising started in 1715. Just to the SE. of Blackford are the fragmentary remains of Ogilvie Castle, once a fortress of great strength but now reduced to rubble. The village is at the northern base of the Ochil Hills.

BLACKHILL, *Lanarkshire* (Map 6, ref. 40¹84¹), is an eminence in the industrial belt of Scotland near to KIRK O' SHOTTS, and, like Kirk o' Shotts, it is associated with television. It supports, in an area that is industrial and yet is associated with much Scottish history, the mast of the Independent Television (or more properly Teleoptic) transmission station in Scotland.

BLACK ISLE, *Ross and Cromarty* (Map 5, ref. 26⁵86⁰), shares with the Islands of LEWIS and HARRIS in the Outer Hebrides (*see* "The Shape of Scotland") the fact that it denies its name by not being an island. It is a peninsula between the Firths of BEAULY and CROMARTY. It is called black because by tradition it seldom takes the white of winter snow. It is composed of rich farmland, with some forestry on the central ridge. Easily accessible from INVERNESS, it has excellent holiday centres in a number of villages. The old name of Black Isle was Ardmeanach. The central wooded ridge is still known by this name, the lordship of which was originally granted to Darnley by Mary Stuart, Queen of Scots.

BLACKLUNANS, *Perthshire* (Map 6, ref. 31⁵76⁰). A small township on the Black Water in GLEN SHEE, Blacklunans has limited accommodation available for skiers.

BLACK MOUNT, *Argyll* (Map 2, ref. 22⁵74⁸), is strictly no more than the area of high ground between RANNOCH MOOR and the Corrie of Coire Ba, but the name is also used to include the country from the Moor of Rannoch to Glen ETIVE – bounded by Loch Dochard and Loch Tulla to the S., Glen Etive to the W., and the moor to the E.

There are in the Black Mount at least seven summits of over 3,000 ft. The scenic contrasts of wild rock and moor and 22 m. of an encircling horseshoe of mountains is extremely impressive, and it reduces the road that runs partly through it and the railway that skirts by it to their proper proportions of insignificance. It is without question one of the most impressive pieces of massive landscape on the mainland of Scotland. Though it is by modern means of communication comparatively accessible from GLASGOW and even from EDINBURGH, we may say that, even with the accelerated pace of modern regress, the Black Mount is not likely ever to be despoiled.

Coire Ba, to the W. of Loch Ba and lying between Clachlet and Stob Ghabhar, is said to be the largest corrie in Scotland. It was famous as a scene of medieval and post-medieval hunting parties. The practice of the time was to drive the deer into the corrie, and then, having closed the mouth of it, to drive them back to the hunters, who slaughtered them in the fashion of a modern grouse drive. There is a most evocative description of such a hunt given by Sir James Fergusson of Kilkerran in his book *The White Hind.*

BLACKNESS, *West Lothian* (Map 2, ref. 30⁵67⁹), is now but a village on the Firth of FORTH, but was once prominent as a seaport – a considerable position at that time, when the flourishing town of Berwick, then one of the greater European ports, lay within Scottish borders, not (as it now does) in Northumbria in England. Blackness is dominated by a castle, which has a strong oblong tower and a circular staircase that was probably added later. The tower is well preserved, although much altered, and dates from the 15th cent. It was a royal castle, and was used as a prison at various times, including the period in the 17th cent. when captured Covenanters were enclosed within its walls. In the Acts of Union in 1707, when the Parliaments of England and Scotland were merged, and the concept of Great Britain was intended to absorb the nations of England and Scotland in one entity (*see* "Scotland in History"), Blackness was one of the four fortresses to be maintained at full military strength.

BLACKSHIELS, *Midlothian* (Map 3, ref. 34⁵66¹), is a small township on the main road between DALKEITH and LAUDER at the foot of SOUTRA Hill. It has two names, Fala and Blackshiels. At one time the area containing the church was called Fala, and the part where there used to be an inn extremely well known to people travelling S. was called Blackshiels – a name given to it because it was once used as a shieling for the Black Friars of Soutra. Fala Flow just S. of the township is a favourite roosting-place in winter for pink-footed geese.

BLACKWATERFOOT, *Buteshire* (Map 1, ref. 19⁰62⁷), is a hamlet on the SW. side of the Island of ARRAN (*see* "The Shape of Scotland"). This small place is popular with holiday-makers who wish to avoid the comparative crowds on other parts of this favourite island. On Drumadoon Bay, it is on the more Lowland half, and has golf, fishing, and bathing; it looks over Kilbrennan Sound to Kintyre. It is near to Shiskine church, where a crudely-carved tombstone is said to mark the burial-place of St Molaise (*see* LAMLASH and HOLY ISLAND). Near too is the "King's Cave", believed to have sheltered Bruce upon his arrival on the island. The same cave is associated with Fingal of the Ossianic legend and poem. (*See* LISMORE.)

BLAIRADAM, *Kinross-shire* (Map 3, ref. 31³69⁶), had earlier the name of Maryburgh. In this district was born William Adam, the Scottish architect and the father of the famous family of architects. In the early part of the 18th cent., the estate of Blair near here was only a wild and unsheltered moor. In 1733, however, William Adam bought the estate and, just before 1738, built a house upon it. This house was originally intended for the factor of the

estate, and the intention was that a great mansion should follow. The factor's house, however, remained sufficiently large and imposing for the architect and his successors. William Adam's eldest son John and his descendants developed the estate, did much landscape-gardening, and also laid out the village of Maryburgh as it is today. The original William Adam's younger sons, Robert and James, were the famous architects who have adorned so much of Scotland and who also built notably in London.

The character of this celebrated estate has been a good deal modified now that it is penetrated by the Kelty by-pass on the new motorway linking the FORTH Road Bridge and PERTH.

BLAIR ATHOLL, *Perthshire* (Map 5, ref. 28⁸76⁵), is a combination of a tourist centre and village situated at the junction of the Tilt and Garry rivers. Holiday facilities include pony-trekking and fishing. There are several hotels.

Glen Tilt, which runs N. and NE. and eventually connects with Deeside, is famous for the beauty of its scenery, at first heavily wooded, later dramatic and precipitous. On the S. it is dominated by the summits of Ben-y-Gloe, the highest of which is 3,671 ft. In the upper reaches the valley leads on to the vast moors of the Atholl Deer Forest. The glen is famous for marble in shades of light grey and green. In 1861 Queen Victoria and Prince Albert passed through Glen Tilt on a historic journey over the hills to BALMORAL.

Blair Castle is the seat of the Duke of Atholl, and lies just NW. of the village. This is a private residence, but parts of the building are open to the public and contain antique furnishings and a remarkable collection of china.

The oldest part of the building is known as Comyn's Tower, and the foundations of this probably date to 1269, when David Strathbogie, Earl of Atholl, complained to the king that John Comyn of Badenoch had begun to build a fortalice at Blair.

The earldom of Atholl was given to Sir John Stewart of Balvenie in 1457, but the line failed, and in 1629 the then heiress, daughter of John 5th Earl of Atholl, married John Murray, Earl of Tullibardine, on whom Charles I bestowed the earldom of Atholl.

In 1644 the Castle was occupied by the Marquess of Montrose, and was again garrisoned by Claverhouse in 1689. After Claverhouse's death at KILLIECRANKIE, his body was brought to Blair Castle, and his cuirass is among the exhibits there.

In 1745 Prince Charles Stuart and the Jacobite troops rested at Blair Castle while on their way S., and in the following year the structure was badly damaged during a bombardment aimed at dislodging some of the Duke of Cumberland's English troops accompanied by German mercenaries.

At the end of the 18th cent. the Castle was renovated, all the turrets and parapets being removed and the whole turned into a plain Georgian mansion-house. When the Scottish baronial style of architecture became fashionable in the Victorian era, the Scottish architect David Bryce was commissioned to restore the medieval appearance, and the turrets, towers, and crow-stepped gables were put back again.

BLAIRGOWRIE, *Perthshire* (Map 6, ref. 31⁸74⁵). The burgh of Blairgowrie and Rattray lies where the R. Ericht emerges from spectacular gorges into STRATHMORE. It is set in fertile country and is the centre for growing fruit, especially raspberries. Half the total crop in Scotland is produced here.

BLAIRMORE, *Argyll* (Map 2, ref. 22⁰68²). As with ARDENTINNY, this small village on the western shore of Loch LONG provides fine W. Highland scenery near GLASGOW. Lying 1 m. N. of STRONE Point, it is a favourite tourist centre, and there is almost continuous building from Blairmore round to KILMUN. This district is within the Argyll National Forest Park.

BLANTYRE, *Lanarkshire* (Map 2, ref. 27⁰65⁸). According to the *Third Statistical Account*, this is the second largest village in Scotland, the largest being CAMBUSLANG. The definition of a village in this context applies not only to size and to census figures but to details of local administration. However, Blantyre was entirely rural until 1785, when one of the first cotton-spinning factories in Scotland was established there in association with Arkwright. The Scottish mover in this concern was that wise and humane GLASGOW industrialist, David Dale, who did so much for the working people of Scotland at the beginning of the Industrial Revolution.

It is fitting that Blantyre's most famous son, David Livingstone, should have been born there at the time he was. He grew up in the middle of the Industrial Revolution when it was affecting Scotland most profoundly, yet the circumstances that surrounded him were humane. This was entirely due to the native qualities of his parents, who came from differing parts of essential Scotland. On his father's side he was descended from a Gaelic-speaking Highland and Jacobite family; on his mother's side, from Lowland covenanting stock. The family into which he was born in 1813, though coming from different parts of Scotland, and maybe showing different parts of the temperament of Scotland, were united in one thing – religion. His parents reared a family of five children and contrived to do it with decency, dignity, and Christian devoutness in the very

small and narrow circumstances of a weaver's house at the beginning of the 19th cent.

The house in which the great missionary and explorer, one of the greatest Scotsmen of his time, was born is in Shuttle Row; it is now made into a national memorial, which was opened in 1929. The late Sir Frank Mears arranged the layout of the Livingstone Memorial, showing the exact circumstances in which a working-class operative of the industrial era at the beginning of the 19th cent. lived, worked, and prayed. There are in the Livingstone Memorial a number of mementoes of David Livingstone's journeys and voyages. There are his pocket Bible, his favourite metrical psalms, his gilt-edged consular cap, his surgical instruments, his dispatch case brought back by Stanley, his journals and other writings.

BOAT OF GARTEN, *Inverness-shire* (Map 5, ref. 29⁴81⁸). A Speyside village resort well situated for holiday-making all the year round, Boat of Garten lies between GRANTOWN-ON-SPEY and AVIEMORE. The ferry across the SPEY from which the village took its name has long been replaced by a bridge that makes a convenient link with the route to the CAIRNGORMS. The golf course has been described as a miniature GLENEAGLES; its fairways are at times demandingly narrow, but its views are always generous, particularly the vistas closed by Braeriach's magnificent corries. The Club's Open Tournament, usually held in early August, is a notably sociable occasion. Tennis and fishing are other summer sports of the area, and the whole gamut of hill or forest walking in Strathspey is readily available from Boat of Garten. Loch Garten, where ospreys have nested and bred since 1959, is 2 m. E. of the village across the river. During the winter-sports season, the Boat of Garten Ski School provides hiring and teaching facilities for visitors at all the hotels and guest-houses in the villages.

BOLTON, *East Lothian* (Map 3, ref. 35¹67⁰). It would be difficult to find in the British Isles two places bearing the same name yet showing a stronger contrast than Bolton in Lancashire and the Scottish Bolton. The little village of Bolton that lies in the rich agricultural land of East Lothian is small and utterly unindustrial. Its main claim, apart from the charm of its miniscule rural appearance, lies in the fact that Robert Burns's mother and a sister and a brother of his are buried in the graveyard. This brother, Gilbert, moved from Ayrshire to become a factor first on the farm of Morham West Mains and later at Grant's Braes.

BONAR BRIDGE, *Sutherland* (Map 5, ref. 26¹89²). The village bearing this name stands at the N. end of the bridge across the narrows of the Kyle of Sutherland. The original bridge, now replaced, was built by Thomas Telford during 1811–12; it was so successful that a similar bridge was built over the SPEY at CRAIGELLACHIE. Before Telford's bridge was built, travellers to the north of this district used the ferry at MEIKLE FERRY, 9 m. to the E. In 1809, however, there was a disastrous accident at this ferry, which resulted in the loss of more than 100 lives; the building of the bridge at Bonar followed as soon as possible.

Bonar Bridge is at the centre of a good touring district. Strath Carron lies to the W. and Strath Oykell to the NW. There is also good angling in the area. Bonar Bridge is the H.Q. of the Sutherland Tourist Association, which has an information centre here.

BONAWE, *Argyll* (Map 1, ref. 20²73²). In 1753, Richard Ford & Co. of Lancashire agreed with the local proprietor, Campbell of Lochnell, to establish furnaces and forges for smelting English iron ore at Bonawe on the S. shore of Loch ETIVE. They used local timber, and carried on working until 1873. The furnace and some buildings still stand. They represent the only real success among various other attempts to industrialize this part of the Highlands. Further attempts were made in the 18th cent. to bring industry into the Highlands after their depopulation by the Clearances. Whether these attempts were animated by humane feelings, or by the avaricious desire to occupy sadly deserted glens, it is impossible to say. Most of them failed, and you may see their results staining the scenery in sombre ugliness.

But, across Loch Etive, granite quarries have been established for more than 100 years. They worked at peak pressure with 300 men when producing granite setts for streets – a surface now replaced in EDINBURGH's New Town by a smoother, modern one.

BONCHESTER BRIDGE, *Roxburghshire* (Map 3, ref. 35⁸61²). Bonchester Hill rises to the E. of Bonchester on Rule Water. It has the remains of a hill-fort with a "complex of ruinous walls, ramparts and ditches which represent several structural phases and modifications". Finds show an early occupation and the presence of foundations of several circular stone-walled houses, probably dating from the 2nd cent. A.D.

In this neighbourhood is the Wauchope Forest, which is included in the Border National Forest Park, extending across the Border into England.

BONHILL, *Dunbartonshire* (Map 2, ref. 24⁰67⁸). Across the R. Leven from ALEXANDRIA, this village now presents almost continuous building to Jamestown.

The lands of Bonhill passed after the Restoration of Charles II in 1660 to Sir James Smollett, grandfather of the novelist Tobias

Smollett, whose family is still associated with the district.

Smollett spent most of his working life as a writer in London, and seldom saw his native country again. In his last year, he retired in search of health to Italy. It was here that he indulged in nostalgic longings for Scotland by writing the ever-readable *Humphry Clinker*. He also composed his poem "To Leven Water":

Pure stream in whose transparent wave
My youthful limbs I wont to lave,
No torrents stain thy limpid source.

The stream today is not pure; the waves are less transparent. But people go on reading Smollett, and his family name is still in possession at Bonhill.

BONNINGTON, *Lanarkshire* (Map 2, ref. 28⁸64¹). Once a famous waterfall on the CLYDE, Bonnington was the uppermost of the three and had a leap of 30 ft. In 1924–6, the Clyde Valley Company constructed here the first Scottish hydro-electric development for public supply. The power stations are Bonnington and STONEBYRES.

At the falls, "the stream becomes a river" and "industry takes over from the trout".

BONNYBRIDGE, *Stirlingshire* (Map 2, ref. 28²68⁰). The centuries, indeed even the millennia, reach across time and touch hands at this place. Bonnybridge is now an industrial town within the CAMELON–FALKIRK area. Its industry is the fairly long-established one of iron foundries of the 18th cent. and brick-works of a little later. But, centuries before them, the Romans were here. Bonnybridge is on the line of the ANTONINUS' WALL, parts of which can be seen E. and W. of the modern town.

BONNYRIGG, *Midlothian* (Map 3, ref. 33¹66⁵). The village of Bonnyrig near EDINBURGH is all but contiguous with LASSWADE and shares with it the literary associations of the Walter Scott period. Now it is mostly a colliery village; but it has various manufacturing activities, which include the making of oatcakes and carpets.

BORGUE, *Kirkcudbrightshire* (Map 2, ref. 26³54⁸), is a pleasant old village near the centre of a green, fertile, mainly low-lying parish that occupies the area between the mouth of the DEE and the mouth of Fleet Bay. It has two ancient churchyards, Kirkanders or Kirkandrews, and Senwick, both fragmentary.

Little Ross Lighthouse is on an island off the SE. end of the parish; the mainly rocky coast has several Iron Age and early medieval promontory forts, "Borness Batteries" being the chief of these; but the outstanding coastal structure is the "Borgue", from which the parish takes its name. This massive castle-like

Iron Age stronghold – in form half-way between a galleried dun and a broch – stands on the shore of Castle Ha'en, a natural boat-berth; rock-cut steps lead out of a fine postern gate to the water. Ruinous, it was partly but carefully rebuilt in 1906, on the considerable height of wall found beneath the pile of rubble. Although probably built before A.D. 100, it was re-occupied in Viking times (the 1906 finds were mainly Viking), and its Norse name of Borg, meaning fortress, indicates its importance at that time.

Only 1 m. away is "Larry's Isle", a small island off the coast, one of the Isles of Fleet, on which a stone church of the Northumbrian period, probably about A.D. 800, has been found; it was preceded by a timber oratory and succeeded by a laird's hall of the 13th cent. It has yielded various fine Dark Age crosses and an inscription of the Northumbrian period.

Scottish Tourist Board

Borthwick Castle

BORROWSTOUNNESS, *West Lothian* (Map 2, ref. 30⁰68¹), its name now contracted to Bo'ness, is one of the many coastal towns on the E. coast of the Firth of FORTH that gradually declined in status as a result of the Union of Parliaments in 1707. Even at the end of the 18th cent., Bo'ness was the third seaport of Scotland, and, in trade with Holland and France, its customs house ruled the district from Cramond (*see* EDINBURGH) and DONIBRISTLE and ALLOA. This state of affairs continued till well after the Union. However, the building of GRANGEMOUTH (1810) and of the Forth–CLYDE canal (1790) reduced the importance of Bo'ness.

The shore has been reclaimed at various times, and in the last 100 years blast-furnace slag and pit-waste have been used to build barriers for holding back the water. A pottery was founded in 1784 by Dr John Roebuck, one of the founders of the CARRON ironworks, who lived at KINNEIL.

At Bridgeness, just E. of Bo'ness, was the E. end of ANTONINUS' WALL, and an inscribed stone (now in the National Museum of Antiquities in Edinburgh) commemorating the completion of this part of the wall was found buried on what used to be a headland. Thus once again in Scotland's industrial belt do the millennia mingle. The wall in this section is called Graham's Dyke.

BORTHWICK, *Midlothian* (Map 3, ref. 33⁸66⁰). Borthwick Castle is unique in several qualities. It may be securely dated at 1430, yet it remains complete and unaltered, nor has it been added to. Save for a brief spell, it has been continuously occupied until the present day. It has a rectangular tower over 100 ft high with two wings, and walls 12–14 ft thick. There is a great hall, and three floors are built above.

In 1567, Mary Queen of Scots and Bothwell, after their disastrous runaway marriage, were blockaded here by Morton and the rebel lords.

The pair escaped separately. Mary was disguised as a boy. She must have seemed an unusually tall stripling, for she is alleged to have been six feet in height. The Castle was besieged by Cromwell in 1650 and damaged slightly by his cannon – the only alteration it has suffered.

During the Second World War, the public records of Scotland were deposited in the Castle.

The Romanesque church nearby was destroyed by fire in 1775, but the 15th-cent. barrel-vaulted aisle survived, including a painted effigy of a Lord Borthwick in full knightly accoutrements. The aisle and portrait may be seen in the modern church.

BOTHWELL, *Lanarkshire* (Map 2, ref. 27¹65⁸). Across the R. CLYDE from HAMILTON, this village is now in an area of coalmines, iron and steel works, and new light industries on industrial estates at CARFIN, Chapelhall, and Newhouse. But, as with other towns and villages now in the thickly populated industrial belt, it has an old and honourable history.

The early importance of Bothwell Bridge lay in the fact that until 300 years ago it was the only one, besides GLASGOW Bridge, over the R. Clyde. It was the scene of a battle with Cromwell's troops in 1650, but the famous Battle of Bothwell Brig, where the Covenanters were defeated by Monmouth's troops, was in June 1679.

Bothwell Church is interesting in that until 1933 it was two: the old church or choir of St Bride had been built by the Earl of Douglas in 1398, and the new church was built in 1833. Exactly 100 years later, in 1933, they were combined. A plaque in the church commemorates Col. Sir Henry Hozier, whose daughter Clementine married Winston Churchill, Prime Minister 1940–5 and 1951–5, and after his death in 1965, aged ninety, became a life baroness as Lady Spencer-Churchill.

The castle at Bothwell is the largest and finest stone castle in Scotland. It dates from before the Wars of Independence and was the principal English base in western Scotland during the occupation. There is a scheme to build 500 individually designed high-quality houses blending with the environment. By summer 1971 twenty had been completed, and one of these, standing in 1½ acres with a heated swimming-pool, sold for over £40,000.

BOWLING, *Dunbartonshire* (Map 2, ref. 24⁴67⁴). This is the point at the western end where the FORTH–CLYDE Canal running from GRANGEMOUTH, 35 m. away, joins the R. Clyde. It was opened in 1790 to cut across the waist of Scotland – our Panama.

At one time it was a centre of shipbuilding and supported a graving dock. It had seemed to be the place where eastern Scottish shipping could join the western. But the increase in size and quality of ships prevented such a growth. Today it is surrounded mostly by tanks for petrol and oil, and the canal is closed.

The past, remoter than the first years of steam and of the canal vogue, lingers in the neighbourhood. Near Bowling to the W., and with the Kilpatrick Hills as a background, is the ruin of Dunglass Castle, the seat of the Colquhoun family from the 15th to the 17th cents. The even remoter past is once again represented by the remains of ANTONINUS' WALL at the western end.

BOWMORE, *Argyll* (Map 1, ref. 13¹65⁹), is on the Island of ISLAY in the Inner Hebrides (*see* "The Shape of Scotland"). The largest village and the unofficial capital of the island, it was laid out in 1768 with wide streets – the principal one leading up the hill from the shore of Lochindaal to Killarrow parish church. This was built in 1769 by Daniel Campbell of Islay, and is the only round church built in Scotland at that period. The former church was at what is now Bridgend, 3 m. NE. of Bowmore; here the churchyard contains some interesting carved stones. Islay House stands at the head of Lochindaal, just beyond Bridgend.

BRAEMAR, *Aberdeenshire* (Map 6, ref. 31⁵79¹). The parish of CRATHIE and Braemar, 24 m. long and of 183,297 acres, has been a playground for kings, nobles, and the great ones of the land since the dawn of Scottish history. With the transformation of Mar Lodge into a winter-sports centre on Swiss lines, it now becomes potentially a playground for every man. Near the centre of the parish is the village of Braemar at the base of Morrone Hill, a dual township on the banks of the Cluny Burn where it enters the DEE. Auchendryone, on the left bank, is Catholic Braemar, while Castleton, on the right bank, is the traditionally

Protestant section. Both were of course preceded in time by Kindrochit Castle, built *c.* A.D. 1390, when Robert II granted a licence to "our dear brother Malcolm de Drummond" for building a fortalice there. Now only a fragmentary ruin, the tower was, in its heyday, the fifth largest for area in Scotland. In 1618 Braemar was visited by John Taylor, the "water poet", who wrote largely about his experiences of a deer hunt. In his story the astonishing thing is not the differences from the present but the similarities: "Once in the yeire for the whole moneth of August and sometimes part of September the Nobility and Gentry of the Kingdome doe come into these highland countries to hunt, and they doe conforme themselves to the habit of the High-land-men, who for the most part speak nothing but Irish, their garters being wreathes of hay or straw, with a plead about their shoulders which is a mantle of divers colours. . . ."

A deer hunt with an *arrière pensée* resulted in the most momentous event in Braemar's history. The "hunt" assembled on the 26th of August 1715. It was in fact a conclave of Jacobites convened by the Earl of Mar. The fateful decision was taken, and on the 6th of September the standard was raised for King James VIII on a knoll to the E. of the old Barony Courthouse of Kindrochit – on the spot now covered by the lounge of the Invercauld Arms Hotel. Braemar Castle (open to the public) is still occupied by the Farquharsons of Invercauld; it stands 1½ m. E. of the village on a knoll above the Dee. It was built by the Earl of Mar in 1628. In 1689, during Claverhouse's campaign, it was burnt by the Farquharsons of Inverey after they had outwitted the Government troop of General Mackay.

After many adventures it was leased for ninety-nine years to the War Office, as a barracks for keeping watch on the still turbulent Highlands.

To this five-storeyed, turreted, L-plan house, the War Office added a rectangular rampart or curtain-wall with salients projecting from each face so as to form an eight-pointed star – one of the most remarkable extant examples of a Hanoverian fort. At a later date the turrets were raised a storey higher and given "gingerbread" battlements. The inscriptions on the woodwork inside, made in boredom by 18th-cent. foot-soldiers of the garrison, can still be examined.

Braemar's most famous modern institution, the Gathering, dates from 1832, when it was initiated by the Braemar Wrights' Friendly Society. Queen Victoria attended her first Gathering in 1848. Today the Braemar Gathering, held in September in the Princess Royal Park, draws an annual gate of 50,000. Piping is its strong suit, with the usual "heavy" athletic events climaxed by the tossing of the caber. The arrival of the Queen and her party, who take their places in the royal pavilion in the afternoon, is the high point of the day.

The Invercauld Studios and Galleries were first opened in 1952 in a disused old church and other buildings. Here are given exhibitions of Scottish arts and crafts, and an annual festival of music and drama is held in August and September. Robert Louis Stevenson spent a winter in Braemar and wrote *Treasure Island* there.

Standing over 1,100 ft above sea-level, Braemar, at the point of junction of the roads from ABERDEEN, and from PERTH via the CAIRNWELL Pass and the DEVIL'S ELBOW, gives access to a large area of the Eastern CAIRNGORMS.

BRANDER, Pass of, *Argyll* (Map 2, ref. 20⁶72⁷). This cuts its short way between Loch AWE and Loch ETIVE, with BEN CRUACHAN rising steeply from the river. In 1308 the pass was the scene of an unsuccessful attempt by the MacDougalls to ambush Bruce. This is graphically described by Barbour in *The Bruce*. (*See* "Scotland in History".)

BRECHIN, *Angus* (Map 6, ref. 36⁰76⁰). Standing on the South Esk river, and built of the local red sandstone in continuous use from the 13th to the 19th cents., Brechin lies at the heart of the agricultural land of STRATH-MORE. Looking up the valley of that name, you may see a background of hills that culminate in the Eastern GRAMPIANS. The best view of the precipitous streets of the old town is from the river bridge on the ARBROATH road. It was created a royal burgh in 1641, and is essentially an E.-coast town with its roots deep in the ancient good farming land of Angus.

Its roots too are deep in history. It was here that the "Toom Tabard", the ignoble John Balliol, on the 10th of July 1296, with an obsequious solemnity, handed over the realm of Scotland to Bishop Bek of Durham for him to pass on to his master, Edward I of England (*see* "Scotland in History"). It was near Brechin, too, that what might be called a battle of mixed Border and Highland clans was fought in 1452. The chief participants were the Douglases and the clansmen of Huntly.

The small cathedral, now the parish church, is mainly 13th cent. in construction, but exists upon a foundation of King David I of 1150. Before this there had been an early Culdee abbey of which few, if any, physical remains still exist. The cathedral was woefully, one might almost say wantonly, treated in 1807 in a fit of early 19th-cent. "cleaning up". It was on this occasion that the transepts were completely demolished. The authorities, however, salvaged what they could in a wise restoration and part-reconstruction during 1900–2. The choir, a pleasing and delicate example of lancet work, had been left in near-ruins after the Reformation. The restorers in the early years of this century, however, were able to roof it over and put in windows. They were compelled to rebuild the transepts entirely, but were guided as to their dimensions by excavation.

Among the older features that were thus uncovered and preserved is a fine old W. window, and a broad projecting tower, surmounted by a spire, which had been built by Bishop Patrick around 1360. The piers in the nave come from two periods in the 13th cent. In the N. aisle we go back to the earliest stones of the building in the form of a notable cross-head in the Northumbrian style of *c.* A.D. 900.

The "round tower" is attached to the church and is believed to date from the 10th or 11th cents. It is 87 ft in height, 15 ft in diameter at the base, and 12½ ft at the top. Its interest lies in the fact that, both in the decorations of its doorway and in its shape and design, it is very like those Celtic medieval towers found in Ireland, occasionally in Scotland, and nowhere else in the world.

Brechin Castle lies close to the cathedral, and used to be extremely well fortified. It stood out for three weeks against Edward I of England during his overwhelming campaign of 1303, and fell only after the death of its Governor, Sir Thomas Maule.

The Castle was rebuilt in 1711, and is still the seat of the Earl of Dalhousie, who is head of the Maule family, descending from the heroic Sir Thomas Maule.

BRESSAY, *Shetland* (Map 8, ref. 45⁰13⁴), is near the Mainland of SHETLAND Northern Islands (*see* "The Shape of Scotland"). It is less than 1 m. E. of LERWICK, and acts as a protective barrier to the harbour and capital of Shetland. It contains the Lerwick golf course and a cave celebrated for its echo. Just E. of Bressay is the smaller isle of Noss, now a nature reserve, the nesting-place of innumerable birds. Bressay, a kind of insular suburb of Lerwick, is well worth a visit.

BRIDGE OF ALLAN, *Stirlingshire* (Map 2, ref. 28⁰69⁷), is a small, primarily residential burgh between STIRLING and DUNBLANE, once a Victorian spa and now benefiting from its proximity to the new Stirling University. Its well-built villas date from the discovery of medicinal properties in the Airthrey mineral springs in 1820. Within easy distance of the TROSSACHS and neighbouring scenic attractions, the town is a popular centre for touring holiday-makers. Strathallan Games is one of the notable athletic meetings of the summer season. The Allan Water itself was celebrated romantically by Burns in new words he wrote for an old air, ". . . I listen'd to a lover's sang, An' thought on youthfu' pleasures monie, And ay the wildwood echoes rang: 'O, my love Annie's very bonnie' . . . ." Among the other pleasures not listed by the poet are trout fishing and golf at GLENEAGLES.

BRIDGE OF CALLY, *Perthshire* (Map 6, ref. 31⁴75¹). This is but a township at the meeting of roads from GLENSHEE and Strath Ardle. The Blackwater flows into the R. Ardle in a deep hollow nearby. There is a hotel for skiing participants and holiday-makers. To the W. lies the Clunie Forest, to the E. the Forest of Alyth. This is one of the mountain and winter-sport resorts most accessible to EDINBURGH and the SE. of Scotland. It is not the only "gateway to the Highlands", but it makes a particularly pleasing one.

BRIDGE OF EARN, *Perthshire* (Map 3, ref. 31⁴71⁸). This sizeable village stands in the wide Strath of Earn, and is built at a bridge. Pitkeathly, 1 m. W., has five mineral wells, which are reputed to contain the oldest natural medicinal waters in the country.

Moncreiffe Hill stands N. of the village between the Earn and the TAY, giving those who climb it an excellent view. On the summit is a hill-fort with a smaller dun-like structure within the outer walls; possibly this was occupied later in post-Roman times.

Moncreiffe House was burnt in 1957, but the new laird and chief of the family lives at Easter Moncreiffe hard by the old house. He is Sir Iain Moncreiffe of that Ilk.

Some 2½ m. SE., on the slopes of the Ochil Hills, stands Balmanno Castle, built 1570–80. It has changed hands many times, and was used as a farmhouse until 1916, when it was bought by Mr W. Miller, who commissioned the well-known Scottish architect Sir Robert Lorimer to restore it. This reconstruction is considered to have been one of Sir Robert's most tasteful, authentic, and successful.

BRIDGE OF ORCHY, *Argyll* (Map 2, ref. 23⁰73⁹). This village is at the head of Glen Orchy, and it marks the place where the new road across the Moor of RANNOCH to GLEN-COE diverges from the old one. It was formerly famous for its pine forest, but most of the trees were cut down in the 19th cent. Some trees, however (believed to be relics of the ancient Caledonian Forest), are still standing on the E. side of Loch Tulla.

The eye here constantly turns to the splendid cone of Ben Doran (3,523 ft). Its dominating yet symmetrical shape with its long sweeping sides gives it a poetic appearance. Indeed, it has inspired poetry. Duncan Ban MacIntyre, the famous Gaelic poet, who came from near here, wrote what some scholars hold to be his masterpiece. It is in evocative Gaelic addressed to and descriptive of Ben Doran: a pure example of Gaelic "natural poetry", yet with undertones of spiritual character.

BRIG O' TURK, *Perthshire* (Map 2, ref. 25⁴70⁷). A show-place of the TROSSACHS, this township lies between Loch Vennachar and Loch Achray. The picturesque old bridge crosses the Turk or Finglas Water, recalling the scene of Walter Scott's strange ballad *Glenfinlas, or Lord Ronald's Coronach*. This place is now a resort of artists in search of the more "popular" Scottish paintable material.

A former inn here was kept in the earlier part of the 19th cent. by a well-known local character, Kate Ferguson (the Fergusons are, or were, numerous in this part of Perthshire). Queen Victoria, at the height of her enthusiasm for Scotland, paid a visit to Brig o' Turk and enjoyed making the acquaintance of the local innkeeper.

BRIDGE OF WEIR, *Renfrewshire* (Map 2, ref. 23⁹66⁵). This village, popular with professional and business people, is set in pleasant surroundings with facilities for golf and fishing. It has several leather factories, but is noted for the nearby Quarrier Homes, founded in 1871 by William Quarrier for orphan and destitute children, though nowadays most of the children come from broken families. It is now a model village of almost ninety buildings, and more than 26,500 children have been looked after there. In 1969 the Hunter House Assessment Unit was completed, with facilities for twenty-four epileptics and for assessing their disability. In 1965 Quarrier Homes achieved their own heated, indoor swimming-bath. Financed entirely from private funds, the Homes are open to interested visitors on weekday afternoons.

BROADFORD, *Inverness-shire* (Map 4, ref. 16⁵82³), is a village on the Island of SKYE in the Inner Hebrides (*see* "The Shape of Scotland"). About 8 m. W. of KYLEAKIN, this is the first township that the visitor to Skye by the ordinary route from the mainland will reach. It stands at the junction of the road N. to PORTREE, W. to ELGOL, and S. to Sleat. It has a pier, a few shops, a hotel, and a pleasant small stream that flows into Broadford Bay. It is a good touring centre for the S. of the island.

At the foot of the hills and at the end of a short by-road lie the ruins of Coirechatachan farmhouse. Readers of Boswell will recall that it was here Johnson warmed as nowhere else to true Highland hospitality. It was here, at some spot now covered by rubble, that Mistress Mackinnon embraced the sage from London and exclaimed, "What is it to live and not to love?"

BRODICK, *Buteshire* (Map 1, ref. 20²63⁶), is a small town on the Island of ARRAN (*see* "The Shape of Scotland"). At the centre of the E. coast, and in a bay of particular beauty, it stands as the island capital. Daily steamers from the mainland touch at it first. At Brodick you find boating, bathing, sea fishing, and some of the finest views in Arran. It is also well placed for walking or climbing expeditions. GOAT FELL, which overstands the N. of the

Corrieshalloch Gorge: the Falls of Measach (see p. 140)

Brodie Castle: the Red Drawing Room,
now used to display art treasures

bay, can be climbed in one day from Brodick.

Brodick Castle is now owned by the National Trust for Scotland and is open to the public daily in summer except on Sundays. The castle, parts of which date from the 14th cent., was enlarged in the 17th and 19th cents. Its gardens, which contain rare rhododendrons, semi-tropical plants and shrubs, and a walled rock-garden, are much admired.

Sir James Douglas stormed Brodick Castle at the beginning of Bruce's campaign, and it was from Brodick that Bruce launched his liberation of the mainland, which seven years later was to lead to the Battle of BANNOCK-BURN in 1314.

BRODIE, *Moray* (Map 5, ref. 29⁸85⁷). The village of Brodie is on the main FORRES–NAIRN road. N. of the village stands Brodie Castle, the seat of Brodie of Brodie, whose family has owned the land in this neighbourhood since at least the mid-11th cent.

The tower of this imposing structure dates from the 15th cent.; there is another section from the 16th cent. The Castle was burnt in 1645 by Lord Lewis Gordon on behalf of Montrose during the Marquess's northern campaign for Charles I, but the earlier parts survived to be included in the rebuilding. An addition was made in 1840.

In the Castle is a fine private collection of Dutch, English, and Flemish paintings.

Brodie of Brodie is the head of one of the oldest untitled landed families in the United Kingdom. In the Scottish fashion, it is an act of courtesy to address him simply as "Brodie" in the vocative and without any prefix of Mr. It is thus that his servants and tenantry as well as all his neighbours and friends, indeed any knowledgeable Scot, would speak of him or to him. There is no familiarity in this use, but merely custom and respect.

BRORA, *Sutherland* (Map 5, ref. 29¹90⁴). Now a holiday centre at the mouth of the R.

Brora, with fine salmon and trout fishing, an extensive sandy beach, and a golf course, Brora has an oddly contrasting past history of industrialism.

The coal mine, dating from 1529, the oldest in Scotland, and formerly privately owned, was acquired by the miners themselves as a co-operative enterprise some years ago and continues to be run successfully by them. The distillery at Clyneleish was started in 1819 and produces excellent whisky, and the woollen mills, which have an international reputation for tweeds and yarns, attract hundreds of welcome visitors. In 1961 the brickmaking industry, using a rich deposit of Dover clay, was revived with help from the Highland Fund and was visited by the Duke of Edinburgh in 1963.

The small harbour used to be the centre of a fishing industry, but is now not much used. It was from there that the first settlers for New Zealand left the north of Scotland.

BROUGHTON, *Peeblesshire* (Map 3, ref. 31⁰63⁸), is a village on the threshold of the beautiful TWEED valley, and is situated on Biggar Water ¾ m. above its junction with the Tweed. The village has two parts, the old and the new, which are separated by ½ m. of road.

The old church, in ruins, has an ancient cell (of a missionary from Candida Casa in the 7th cent.), which was ruined in the 14th cent. and restored in the 1920s.

Broughton Place, the house built in 1938 on the site of the old home (burnt 1775) of "Mr Evidence" John Murray of Broughton, was designed by Sir Basil Spence on 17th-cent. Scottish baronial lines. There are notable gardens planned round the old trees, which escaped the conflagration of 1775. John Murray is especially detested in Jacobite memory. He was one of the foremost to encourage Prince Charles Edward Stuart in his ill-fated venture of 1745, and indeed became the Prince's secretary during the campaign. Yet after the failure of the Rising he turned (Hanoverian) King's evidence to the cost of many Jacobite lives.

Higher up on the moorland above Broughton there is, above the farm of Thriepland, a large hole, the remains of a mine from which Scottish kings in the past extracted lead and gold.

BROUGHTY FERRY, *Angus* (Map 6, ref. 34⁷73¹). Now a residential suburb of DUNDEE and a holiday resort with a sandy beach facing towards Fife, Broughty Ferry has had a longer past. At the end of the 19th cent., when the jute trade was at its height, the "jute princes" of Dundee moved here to be near their works yet partly in a country district. Within it, this suburb was said, at the period of jute's greatest prosperity, to contain more

Plate 4 Edinburgh: Holyroodhouse (see p. 201)
Albert Barber

wealth than any area of corresponding size in Scotland. Its purely golden glory has somewhat declined, but there is still much wealth there. The jute princes in their time were notable patrons of the arts.

In the remoter past Broughty Ferry was associated with Broughty Castle, a battlemented oblong structure erected about the beginning of the 16th cent. It was restored later, and has been used for military training. Claverhouse ("Bonnie Dundee"), the notable Scottish cavalier general, once owned it.

BROXBURN, *West Lothian* (3 m. E. of Uphall). This manufacturing village in the shale-oil belt is on the FORTH and CLYDE Canal and is near the main EDINBURGH–GLASGOW road. Shale having suffered recession, nothing is left of this industry save the coloured "bings" or slag-heaps. However, the village has been revived by the incoming of a considerable number of new light industries.

At Kirkhill Farm, just W. of the village, is an inscribed "solar stone", erected as part of a solar system in the grounds of his house by the 11th Earl of Buchan, who founded the Society of Antiquaries in the 18th cent.

Mentioning the Buchan family brings to mind the strange story of the pre-Reformation font in the Broxburn–UPHALL parish church. This was ejected from the church at the Reformation, and was discovered by a local farmer, who used it as a watering-trough for his cattle. When he realized what it was (this was at the end of the 19th cent.), he gave the font to the then Countess of Buchan. She, being a devout Catholic, gave it to the new Catholic church that had come to the neighbourhood with the Irish immigrants and the flood of industry. The old pre-Reformation font, therefore, is now in use again, but in circumstances very different from the rural ones for which it was designed.

BRUAR, *Perthshire* (Map 5, ref. 28²76⁶). There are three spectacular waterfalls on the Burn of Bruar in the last 2 m. of its descent to the R. Garry.

The upper fall, which is the principal one, is threefold, with a combined height of 200 ft. The second, ½ m. lower down, is a single leap of 50 ft, and the third a series of cascades that run under a natural bridge at the foot of the fall.

Larches were planted on the banks of the Bruar after Burns wrote his "Humble Petition of Bruar Water" addressed to the then Duke of Atholl.

Bruar with its falls lies to the W. of BLAIR ATHOLL, and is easily approached from there. It is advisable to visit the falls when there is plenty of water in the burn.

BUCHAN NESS, *Aberdeenshire* (Map 6, ref. 41³84³). The lighthouse was built on this,

the most easterly point of Scotland, a few miles SE. of PETERHEAD, in 1827; but it is now one of the most powerful and modern in Britain. A beach of round stones joins the rock on which it stands to the mainland and the village of Boddam, and separates the two small fishing harbours of Boddam, officially designated a port by Act of Parliament in 1845. Although originally an important fishing station, it is now virtually a suburb of Peterhead.

By the nature of things, the name Buchan must appear many times in this book. It connotes the province, originally a Celtic mormaerdom and later a feudal earldom, extending from the R. Ythan to the R. DEVERON, and thus including the rounded knuckle of Scotland nearest to Norway, sometimes called the North-East Neuk; a land that has a physical and ethnographic individuality so great that it is almost a synonym for Lowland character carried to its most eccentric extreme.

It is a low plateau, much subdivided by ridges and hollows (usually called "the Howes o' Buchan"), treeless in the main, windswept, and much subject to chilling blankets of haar or "Scotch mist". But this austere countryside, hallowed by centuries of back-breaking human toil, which has converted what was very largely a wilderness of peat bogs into a land of plenty, has its own peculiar and piercing beauty, founded on purity of line and colour. The most acute characterizations of Buchan that have been written are in the "Buchan Doric", its own richly idiosyncratic dialect.

There is perhaps a racial explanation for the stubborn individuality of the "Buchan loon" (not lunatic, but lad). The plateau was invaded about 2000 B.C. by a race of men from Holland, tall, powerfully built, with round skulls, square jaws, and broad faces. They are called the Beaker Folk because of their peculiar burial customs, and they have been traced back from the mouth of the Rhine to central Europe. Their skeletons have been the subject of intensive anatomical study at ABERDEEN University. This has brought out the interesting fact that the Beaker Folk remain the basic and original strain in the physical make-up of the present Aberdeenshire peasantry.

BUCHLYVIE, *Stirlingshire* (Map 2, ref. 25⁸69⁴). This village on the S. edge of the remaining section of FLANDERS MOSS was the scene of resistance by villagers to one of Rob Roy's earliest exploits – the "hership of Kippen" in 1691.

In the *First Statistical Account*, weaving is mentioned, with agriculture, as an industry of the locality in the 1790s. Hand-weaving is still carried on at Auchentroig, 2 m. W. of Buchlyvie.

BUCKHAVEN, *Fife* (Map 3, ref. 33⁷69⁸). There is a tradition that the inhabitants of Buckhaven were originally foreigners; if so, they were either Vikings or more probably Brabanters, landing in the 16th cent.

Originally Buckhaven was a fishing village; the harbour was built in 1838, but, after joining with METHIL and Inverleven in 1891, the fishing declined in place of coal, as in so much of this part of Fife.

The Church of St Andrew is something of an oddity. It is said to be about ninety years old, yet a glance at the defaced statues, and the empty niches that once held the images of saints, makes it clear that the building had some connection with pre-Reformation times. A close examination of tradition reveals a story that accounts for this. The church had originally stood in North Street at ST ANDREWS, where it had suffered defacement at zealous Reforming hands. Eventually it became too small for its congregation in St Andrews, was sold to Buckhaven, and was transported there stone by stone. The folk of Buckhaven then rebuilt their purchased church as it had originally stood – reforming a jig-saw puzzle, as it were. They called their rebuilt church after St Andrew, and kept the pre-Reformation stones exactly as before. They tell the tale of pre- and post-Reformation times as accurately in their new situation as they had done in their old one.

BUCKIE, *Banffshire* (Map 6, ref. 34³86⁵). This long straggling port, a burgh since 1888, is really a conurbation rather than a coherent entity, but it has been for long the largest town in the county, and its harbour is the busiest on the whole of the Moray Firth. When Robert Burns visited the area in 1787, the villages of Easter and Nether Buckie had between them a population of 700, and most of the houses were thatched but-and-bens. Today the population of Buckie, which has in the interim absorbed the hamlets of Buckpool, Gordonsburgh, Ianstown, Portessie, and Strathlene, amounts to 7,666 – a considerable drop from the peak of 8,897 reached in 1911, when the herring-fishing boom was at its height. It was John Gordon of Cluny who in 1872 took the decisive step that, with the completion of the Cluny harbour, raised Buckie to its pre-eminence as the greatest line-fishing port in Scotland, and soon afterwards to the centre of the busiest herring-fishing district in Britain. Now the herring fishing is in eclipse, and the harbour is packed with neat, colourful, dual-purpose boats.

In the centre of the town, laid out on top of a cliff beneath which the fish market and the basins of the harbour lie, is the Cluny Square while at its western end is another square, dominated by the tall spires of St Peter's Catholic Church, a great cathedral-like building erected in 1857. This is a reminder that the parish of Rathven, in which Buckie lies, has been a stronghold of the Catholic religion ever since the Reformation.

There was an interesting historical reason for this. Rathven, with the adjoining parish of Bellie, across the Burn of Tynet in Moray, formed the province of the Enzie, largely belonging to the pro-Catholic Marquess of Huntly, the head of the House of Gordon and its scions.

The influence of the Gordons was so strong that, from the Reformation onwards, the inhabitants continued to cling to the traditional faith, and as late as 1617 there were over 1,000 known Catholics in Banffshire, as compared with only fifty in GLASGOW. Ten years later, the Catholics of the Enzie built, in the ancient kirkyard of St Ninian's at Chapelford (6 m. SW. of Buckie) on the right bank of the Tynet Burn, the first Catholic church to be erected in Scotland since the Reformation. A time of trial was coming for them. The House of Gordon deserted its faith, and the Jacobite Rising of '15 resulted in intense anti-Catholic feeling, so that in 1728 the church was wrecked by an armed band of Protestants.

Today its site is marked by a cross erected in memory of Bishop Nicholson, the first Vicar Apostolic of Scotland, who died in 1718. With him lie the remains of twenty-six priests who laboured in the area.

A barn near the Bridge of Tynet was the next refuge of the Catholic faithful, but it was burnt down after the '45. In 1755 the laird of Tynet offered the use of a but-and-ben that had been converted into a sheep-cot. It is this long, low, whitewashed building, with square windows and a slated roof – distinguished only by a ball of stone on the western gable – that is today revered as the "Banffshire Bethlehem" of the Catholics. Outside, where sheep still graze around its walls, it still maintains its disguise. Inside it has been very beautifully restored and is in regular use. As times improved, a somewhat larger and more conventional type of church – St Gregory's, Presshome – was built by the Enzie Catholics in 1788.

About 2 m. W. of Buckie, not far from the mouth of the Burn of Tynet, is Portgordon, founded by the 4th Duke of Gordon in 1797. It was built as a trading port for the export of the grain from the Enzie, and it continued to do a considerable amount of trade by sea until the end of last century, by which time there was a large herring-fishing fleet. Today the harbour is derelict, but, with that loyalty to the old hearth which is so characteristic of the Banffshire fishermen, the village is still the home, if not the working base, of a large fishing community.

BUNCHREW, *Inverness-shire* (Map 5, ref. 26²84⁶). This house on the shores of the BEAULY Firth was the birthplace and favourite retreat of Duncan Forbes of CULLODEN (1685–1747). Duncan Forbes was one of the greatest Lord Presidents of the Scottish Court of Session. He opposed the Jacobites in their Rising of 1745, but was a humane and patriotic

Highlander who did his best to mitigate the truly appalling severity of the Duke of Cumberland's revenge upon the Highlands after his victory at Culloden. He was not very successful. Cumberland, despite all the support he had received from Duncan Forbes, dismissed him as "that old maid". Forbes was a genial host and one of the greatest claret fanciers and dispensers of claret at his table in an age when claret was the Scotsman's favourite refreshment. Alas! the British Government's preference, on "duty grounds", for port, led to claret's partial dismissal from Scotland. Its passing was mourned by John Home:

Firm and erect the Caledonian stood;
Old was his mutton and his claret good.
You shall drink port, the Saxon cried;
He took the poison and his spirit died.

BUNESSAN, *Argyll* (Map 1, ref. 13⁹72²), is on the Island of MULL, in the Inner Hebrides (*see* "The Shape of Scotland"). With its sheltered harbour used by fishing boats and yachts, this village lies near the W. end of the Ross of Mull.

The once-famed granite quarries of Camus and Tormore, on the N. shore of the ross or peninsula, used to be fully worked, but the demand has declined. There is also access to many attractive sandy bays, with some crofting townships, on the S. peninsula. This is one of the more cheerful parts of Mull.

Mull is one of the islands that have suffered most strongly from depopulation. But there is some crofting on the Ross of Mull, and tourism on the island is developing.

BURG, *Argyll* (Map 1, ref. 14⁵72⁸), is a headland on the Island of MULL, in the Inner Hebrides (*see* "The Shape of Scotland"). These 2,000 acres of headland at the NW. promontory of Mull, bequeathed to the National Trust for Scotland in 1932 by Mr A. Campbell Blair, include a typical W. Highland farm where bracken-clearing experiments have been conducted with the Department of Agriculture. Further S. on this side of the island at Ardmeanach the world-famous fossil remains in basalt columns include the "MacCulloch's Tree", 50 ft tall and believed to be 35 million years old.

BURGHEAD, *Moray* (Map 6, ref. 31²86⁸). This little town, on the promontory that marks the extreme western tip of the northernmost "bulge" on the southern shores of the Moray Firth, was laid out in the first years of the 19th cent. It has many claims to attention. From here the B.B.C. transmits its programmes to a great area of the N. of Scotland. It is the home of the Outward Bound Moray Sea School, where boys from all over Britain and from abroad discover the thrills of adventurous team-work. It is also the site of the fire festival known as the Burning of the Clavie, which is held annually on the 11th of January at this, the place of so many remarkable discoveries. Pictish sculptured stones bearing incised bulls, a mysterious "Roman" well, and an elaborate ancient fort on the headland that is sometimes identified as the Ptoroton of the Romans and sometimes as the Torfness of the Vikings.

The two things that must be seen at Burghead are the view from the cliff-top, with its great grassy plateau within the foundations of the ancient fort, and the characterful waterfront of the harbour, with its striking four-storey warehouses – where, if you are at all lucky, you will encounter the tall masts and rig of the training-ship *Prince Louis II*. Burghead is still a busy commercial port, bringing in coal from Poland and timber from the White Sea, supplying the farmlands of the Laigh of Moray with lime and exporting their grain. It also has a small fleet of seine-net fishing boats. The view from the headland is of the great curving sweep of Burghead Bay, which extends SW. to FINDHORN and the CULBIN Sands, now very largely a Forestry Commission plantation, while on the northern horizon are the mountains of Sutherland and the ORD OF CAITHNESS.

In the harbour-master's office you may inspect replicas of the famous Burghead bulls. The originals are in the British Museum. At the landward end of the cliff-top plateau is the smoke-blackened Dourie Pillar, a 19th-cent. freestone erection on which the Clavie is enthroned during the Aul Eel ceremony, which itself appears to have been carried on for at least 300 years. The Clavie is made from half a tar-barrel fixed to a stout shaft 5 ft long by a hand-wrought nail hammered in with a stone. At six o'clock precisely on the evening of the 11th of January, it is lit at the Manse Wall of the old United Presbyterian church with a peat from a household fire by the Clavie King. Then follows the march around the burgh to the Dourie Hill – from which, after blazing with glorious vigour, it is felled, to cascade in fiery wreckage down the grassy slope. The embers, treasured as keepsakes and sent to "exiled" Burgheadians all over the world, are known as "witches".

Off a quiet street on the headland, and under a hill-slope, is the remarkable well that was rediscovered in 1809. A stair excavated in the solid rock leads down to a chamber 11 ft high, with a well or cistern, almost square and 4 ft deep, cut into the floor. Round the cistern runs a stone ledge 4 ft wide with a raised seat or "altar" at one corner. The entire cavity is cut out of solid rock. It has been suggested that the present roof, a lofty "Roman" arch built by William Young of Inverugie in 1810, replaces a medieval vaulted ceiling carved from the rock.

The fort on the headland is not now so complete as it was down to the end of the 18th cent. The northern part of Burghead promontory was then divided into two unequal terraces with a total area of more than four acres. Both were surrounded by ramparts of stone and earthwork varying from 7 to 20 ft high. The ramparts on the inner side, known as the Broch Briggs, were demolished in 1805 when the joint proprietors of Burghead swept away the old fishing village on the site and were building the modern town.

BURNMOUTH, *Berwickshire* (Map 3, ref. 39⁶66¹). This cluster of attractive fishermen's houses forming a village often attracts the eye of the traveller who comes to Scotland by rail on the E.-coast route. Indeed, if he is keeping a sharp look-out on the coast side of his carriage, it may well be the first example he will see of domestic Scottish building. Lower Burnmouth suddenly reveals itself at the foot of a steep ravine with its miniscule harbour, in which a new inner basin was constructed in 1959. No sooner does this pleasant little place show itself to the train traveller than it is gone; few have visited it.

Yet the more leisurely traveller will find it well worth while to descend the steep ravine and inspect this, the most southerly E.-coast harbour in Scotland. It has had a long tradition in Scottish history. The fisherfolk living there between the steep cliffs and the sea, often raging beneath an eastern gale, are a conservative folk, retentive of tradition, and, perhaps because they are so near the Border, all the more consciously Scots fisherfolk.

BURNTISLAND, *Fife* (Map 3, ref. 32⁵68⁵). This royal burgh, now a coaling port on the N. shore of the Firth of FORTH, is established round its harbour and around Rossend Castle. This last, which was built in the 12th cent. and added to in the 14th and 16th cents., began as the residence of the abbots of DUNFERMLINE and later became a private residence. Mary Queen of Scots stayed there in 1563, and it was the scene of the final arrest of Chastelard, her too ardent but highly poetic young French admirer. He died protesting not so much the innocence of his intentions as the impelling power of his love. Cromwell also stayed in Burntisland after having captured it in 1651. He did not wreak much vengeance on it, for after one shot from his cannon, which knocked out the Provost's shop and house, the town capitulated. The cannon is still preserved.

The parish church of St Columba, 1592, is unique in Scotland; it is a copy of the Old North Church in Amsterdam, being square with an octagonal tower added in 1749. The galleries were erected in the 17th cent., with painted guild insignia. In 1601 the General Assembly met here and proposed the Authorized Version of the Bible. Later James VI took the idea south, and it was published in 1611. It is odd to reflect that if the Union of the Crowns had taken place later there might well have been a Scottish Authorized Version as well as an English one. The Scottish one would have contained many homely words and phrases now used only by country folk, but then in all men's mouths north of the Border.

Just W. of Burntisland is Dunearn Hill, with the remains of a fort, which dominates the pass into the hinterland of Fife; it is a landmark from EDINBURGH. There are remains of two periods – an earlier fort and a later circular enclosure.

BUTE, Island of, *Buteshire* (Map 2, ref. 20⁷66⁵). Bute gives its name to the county composed of a group of islands in the Firth of CLYDE: Bute, the two CUMBRAES, and ARRAN. The only two other island shires in Scotland are ORKNEY and SHETLAND. About 15 m. long and anything from 1¼ m. to just over 5 m. across, the island lies roughly NNW. to due S. Dovetailed into the mainland of Argyll, it is separated from Cowal in Argyll by a very narrow channel, the Kyles of BUTE. Just to the westward of it lies the low little island of Inchmarnock, less than 1 m. away. The Cumbraes to the E. and Arran to the S. are all closely visible from the southern end of Bute, their maternal island, as it were, in the county or shire sense.

Though Bute has been for a century (that is, since the rise of GLASGOW's huge industrial population) associated with holiday-makers, it has a long and honourable place in Scottish history and, once you get away from ROTHESAY, it can show agreeable island scenery with some outstanding views.

Long before Bute attracted the "doon-the-watter" excursionists, there were incursions on to this naturally well-protected island. St Blane's Church is a Culdee foundation in what must have been far more accessible circumstances than were those surrounding most insular monks in the early years of Christianity in Scotland. Bute has been the scene of invasion of Norsemen and of Lowland Scots. And as we shall see later, the capital, Rothesay, was closely associated with the early Stuart Kings.

Edmund Kean, the early 19th-cent. actor, delighted in Bute, and built himself a country retreat by the shore of Loch Fad, the largest inland water on the island. His pleasing Regency-style house, as the author of one of the best and most readable books on Scottish islands has put it, "did not set an architectural fashion that was followed by the island" – indeed, far from it.

The very first cotton mill to be built in Scotland was put up in Bute in 1788 by the humane Glasgow 18th-cent. industrialist, David Dale, of whose activities we have already spoken under BLANTYRE, David Livingstone's birthplace. The cotton industry still continues in Bute.

The mention of this leads on to the economy of Bute. Apart from tourism, the essentially

Lowland island set in grand Highland circumstance lends itself to farming. With the decline of fishing in recent years, the agricultural interests transcend all others. The main source of income is dairying. The bulk of the milk is taken to a creamery in Rothesay built by the Scottish Milk Marketing Board and opened in 1954.

It is simpler to think of Bute as being divided into three parts: North, Middle, and South. The N. end lies close to Argyll. It is largely of high wild moorland, stretches of bog, and steep but not high hills, the largest being Windy Hill (911 ft). S. of this lies the broad, sandy Ettrick plain, of a soil rich and well-farmed, rising to the middle portion. The middle and broadest part undulates with hills and lochs. As you go S., you see a broad extent of moorland running down the centre. Nearer the shores, you find rich agricultural land. The S. end of Bute rises on a steep escarpment to a high plateau hollowed and dissected by ravines, and finishes in the S. with abrupt hills, green crags, and the cliffs of Garroch Head.

At the S. end of the island, hard by the model village of Kerrycroy, stands the sumptuous, and by now magnificent, Victorian residence of Mount Stuart, the seat of the marquesses of Bute, who descend from the Stuart hereditary Keepers of Rothesay Castle.

BUTE, Kyles of, *Argyll/Buteshire* (Map 1, ref. 20⁰67⁵). This long, narrow, curved stretch of sea-water goes E. and W. round the N. side of the Island of BUTE, separating it from the mainland. It is a favourite resort of CLYDE yachtsmen, and for steamer excursions. Loch Riddon leads off the Kyles into the S. Highlands of Argyll at the N. end. Loch Striven, another sea-arm, is further to the E. These sheltered waters provide not only sport for the yachtsmen but some fine vistas as well.

BUTTERSTONE, *Perthshire* (Map 6, ref. 30⁷74⁵), is a small village and mansion-house on the N. bank of a loch of the same name – the fourth in a chain of six lochs that stretch between BLAIRGOWRIE and DUNKELD, and are linked by the Lunan Burn. The district is one of great scenic beauty. The lochs vary in size and character, but are wooded and largely unspoilt, and for this reason are haunted by all kinds of birds and are a paradise for the botanist. Around Butterstone you can find the original wild lily of the valley, Solomon's Seal.

Clunie Loch has an island with a castle said to have been the home of the Admirable Crichton, and on the W. shore is a fine example of a Norman motte and bailey.

CABRACH, The, *Aberdeenshire* (Map 6, ref. 33⁷82⁷), is an extraordinary upland plateau of heath-covered hills, barren moors, and far-stretching rugged deer forests. An excellent motor road traverses it today, rising up to well

over the 1,300-ft contour across the moors from Rhynie and LUMSDEN and descending after 10 m. to Inverharroch, where the DEVERON is crossed, then rising once more at close on 1,200 ft to that spectacular pass called the Glacks of Balloch, and thence 4 m. NW. to DUFFTOWN. Everywhere within this remote basin you have the sense of being cut off from the rest of the world.

While Upper Cabrach on the Aberdeenshire border is largely barren moor and deer forest, ringed by magnificent mountain peaks, Lower Cabrach has many pastoral farms, though the total population of the parish, over 34,000 acres in extent, is barely 200.

CADDER, *Lanarkshire* (Map 2, ref. 26³67³), is a stretch of ANTONINUS' WALL containing what was the 6th station of the Wall from the W. It was excavated in 1929–31, revealing the likelihood of its having been occupied at three periods. The first occupation was by an Agricolan large marching camp before the Wall was built; the second was during the Antonine period; the third was about A.D. 170, for twenty years before the place was burnt.

CAERLAVEROCK, *Dumfriesshire* (Map 2, ref. 30³56⁶). The great triangular castle at Caerlaverock, built about 1290 on a sloping shelf of sandstone beside the Nith estuary, facing the great mass of Criffel and dominated by the Iron-Age and Roman forts atop the Wardlaw, is a site with a great deal of history.

The rectangular castle a few hundred yards away in the wood is now held to be a predecessor of the triangular castle (its fluted walls date it to about 1230). Moreover, the Roman road comes down the end of the ridge towards the site; there are persistent traditions of a Roman port about here, and the rectangular castle occupies, as its moat, part of a similarly shaped basin that in Roman times would have had enough water in it for shipping. One thinks, too, of the Battle of Arthuret, fought in A.D. 572 "for a Lark's Nest"–that is one of the meanings of the name Caerlaverock.

The great triangular castle, with towers at the corners and a double-towered gatehouse at the apex, was besieged by Edward I, King of England, in 1300, and his chronicler has left us an eye-witness account in Norman-French verse, "Le Siege de Karlaverok". Much of the curtain-wall is original; there were four successive drawbridges; 14th- and 15th-cent. alterations were made to the main structure; and in the 15th cent. a fine range of guest-houses was built within the courtyard. Finally, Lord Maxwell's "Daintie Fabrick", completed in 1638, is one of the finest examples of 17th-cent. Renaissance architecture in Scotland. The castle was besieged, captured, and dismantled by the covenanting forces in 1640.

The castle was from the 14th cent. one of the chief seats of the Maxwell family – the earls of

Nithsdale. The cleaning out of its ditch by the Ministry of Works in recent years has revealed a huge amount of medieval material – decorated leather horse-trappings and gauntlets, arrows complete with shafts, daggers with ornamental wooden hilts, domestic tools, large complete green-glazed pottery jars, and polychrome ware imported from Bordeaux.

CAIRNBAAN, *Argyll* (Map 1, ref. 18⁴69²), is a group of Bronze Age cup-and-ring scribings on natural rock surface, in the neighbourhood of LOCHGILPHEAD and the CRINAN CANAL, and 200 yds NW. of the Cairnbaan Hotel. Though its existence was long known, until 1860 it was not regarded as archaeologically important. It is now celebrated and is an Ancient Monument.

CAIRNBULG, *Aberdeenshire* (Map 6, ref. 40³86⁴). Eastwards from FRASERBURGH for over 2 m. stretches the wide curve of a sandy bay with links extending for ½ m. inland. Towards the E. end of this bay a small stream, the Water of Philorth, flows NE. to the sea. Sheltered by a little copse on the right bank of this burn stands Cairnbulg Castle, the home of Lord Saltoun, the modern representative of the family of Fraser of Philorth who founded Fraserburgh in the 16th cent. But their connection with Cairnbulg is much older. It came into the possession of Sir Alexander Fraser in 1375, when he married the daughter of Sir Walter Leslie, Lord of Ross.

Until quite recently it was assumed that this Sir Alexander built the Castle, or rather the oldest part of it, which consists of a rectangular tower 70 ft high, with a smaller square tower of the same height abutted to it. Some 60 ft SE. of the square tower is a lower round tower, built about 1545, at the time of the War of the Rough Wooing, for the purpose of protecting the corner of the square tower from gunfire. Between the round tower and the two rectangular towers stretches the modern main section, largely rebuilt in 1897, when the Castle, which had been abandoned in 1799, was restored by Sir John Duthie, from whose son Lord Saltoun later bought the ancient home of his race.

Recent discoveries, however, have led to the belief that the lower portion of the original rectangular keep dates from about 1260 and was built by the Comyns, Earls of Buchan. In the Harrying of Buchan it had been set on fire and its upper portions destroyed by Robert Bruce, with the result that when Fraser acquired the lands in 1375 he rebuilt the keep on a new plan.

But ancient castles are not the only features of interest in this windswept countryside. Along the coast, which turns sharply to the SE. beyond Cairnbulg Point, are three fishing villages of quite exceptional character; Cairnbulg, Inverallochy, and St Combs, with its tiny satellite hamlet Charleston. They are linked to Fraserburgh by a small branch railway built at the beginning of the present century. No more exposed beaches can be imagined than those on which these villages stand. There is no harbour, and for centuries the fishermen were accustomed to draw their boats up on to the foreshore under the gable-ends of their houses. Most of them now fish from Fraserburgh, of which the three villages might now be regarded as suburbs, save that they retain an individuality and a local tradition that apparently nothing can extinguish.

This individuality expresses itself in a great triple festival – the series of Temperance Walks, led by fife-and-drum bands, that take place annually at the turn of the year. They are held on Christmas Day (for Inverallochy), New Year's Day (for Cairnbulg), and Aul 'Eel, the 5th of January (for St Combs).

It would be a mistake to imagine that these festivals are an outlet for kill-joys. They arose out of the great temperance movement and religious revival of the 1850s, but they now completely transcend any sectarian significance. They are in fact great family occasions when the three villages mingle and rejoice in their network of kinship. The Cairnbulg and Inverallochy walks end up in St Combs, 1½ m. down the coast. The St Combs walk ends in Inverallochy and Cairnbulg, which now form a single built-up area divided only by an invisible burn that runs in pipes under a street.

When the fifers and the drummers have played some favourite air (an old Scots song, a Psalm tune, or a Moody and Sankey hymn) at virtually every door; when they have rendered instrumental solos to throngs that include nearly all the inhabitants of the three villages; when they have perambulated every street and lane and the whole length of the waterfront – then the "congregation" breaks up into groups of friends and relations. The "visitors" from one village go to dine with their in-laws or their friends in the next, and, after everyone is replete from a gargantuan repast, film shows and bun-fights are provided for the children in the nearest public hall.

There is a deep and interesting historical source for this perennial spree in which virtually every man, woman, and child in the three villages participates.

An immense transformation of life took place in the villages as a result of the 19th-cent. herring boom. The population increased rapidly, but as late as 1850 the villagers continued to live in a collection of rude clay huts with a midden in front of every door. The men spent several months of each year in the larger herring ports, where their contracts stipulated for the supply of so many gallons of whisky to each crew in addition to the price of the herring. Desperate fights among them were common. Wedding feasts lasted for the best part of a week. This rough and rather bestial life was interrupted in the middle of the century by two extremely severe cholera epidemics.

A clean-up of conditions became essential if the communities were to survive. It was accomplished with the aid of the temperance revival. New outlets had to be found for the conviviality of the community, and the temperance walks helped to provide them. At the same time great efforts were made by the small church and "dame" schools. It was part of the compulsory curriculum that pupils had to wash themselves at the village pumps every evening before going to bed. By the end of the century these reforms bore fruit. Then men were equipped with large boats in which they could sail to the East Anglian fishing grounds, and their standard of seamanship and fishing skill were so high that many of them enlisted as volunteers to act as instructors for the improvement of the Irish fisheries.

There is a high degree of prosperity in the villages today. While many of the men fish from seine-net boats in Fraserburgh or work in trawlers in ABERDEEN, about half the young men are landsmen engaged in trades ashore. But they are still fisherfolk in the deepest levels of their being.

CAIRNDOW, *Argyll* (Map 2, ref. 21⁸71⁰). Formerly called Kilmorich, which is the parish name, Cairndow is a township that stands at the W. end of Glen Kinglas just below the present road. It is farther W. and downwards from the celebrated REST AND BE THANKFUL on the road from Loch LONG to INVERARAY. Nearby is Ardkinglass estate, devoted to sheep-farming and cattle-rearing. Ardkinglass House is a modern mansion built by the well-known Scottish architect Sir Robert Lorimer, who was responsible for the world-famous war memorial on the summit of the Castle Rock at EDINBURGH. In the neighbourhood are some celebrated falls on the R. Fyne.

CAIRNGORMS, The, *Aberdeenshire/Banff-shire/Inverness-shire* (Map 5 & 6, ref. 30⁰80⁰), form a magnificent range of mountains rising between Speyside and BRAEMAR and constituting the highest mountain massif in the British Isles. The four main peaks – Ben Macdhui, 4,296 ft; Braeriach, 4,248 ft; Cairn Toul, 4,241 ft; and Cairngorm, 4,084 ft – and several more all stand above 4,000 ft. BEN NEVIS is the only higher mountain in the British Isles. In recent years a rapidly growing winter-sports industry has developed around the snow-slopes of these mountains. An access road, a tow-shieling, and chair-lifts serve the principal runs on the White Lady, Coire Cas, and Coire na Ciste. The Spey valley townships, notably the AVIEMORE Centre, cater splendidly for winter sports as well as summer visitors, and there are unlimited opportunities for hill-

walking and rock- and ice-climbing. (*See* the Scottish Mountaineering Club's Guide to the Cairngorms, and the National Forest Park Guide to Glen More and the Cairngorms.) A camping and caravan site at the base of the ski-road is operated by the Forestry Commission as part of the public access facilities in the National Forest Park, which extends for 12,500 acres around Loch Morlich and includes the main skiing grounds. Accommodation is also available nearby in the Scottish Youth Hostel Association's Loch Morlich hostel and the Scottish Council of Physical Recreation's centre at Glenmore Lodge. The Cairngorms Nature Reserve, administered by the Nature Conservancy, takes in more than 40,000 acres to the S. of GLEN MORE, including the summits of Braeriach and Cairn Toul, and is the largest in Britain. Here the principal scientific interests are the arctic-alpine plant and animal communities and the remnants of the ancient Caledonian Forest, Golden eagle, dotterel, ptarmigan, greenshank, crested tit, and capercailzie are among the birds to be found on the high tops and forest approaches. Some of the rarest of British flora, including the brook saxifrage, alpine pearlwort, wavy meadow grass, and alpine hare's-foot sedge survive in the precipitous corries. Cairngorm stones, the distinctive crystals of smoked quartz that take their name from the mountains, can be found by a knowledgeable eye along the burns. Apart from the four great peaks, which can be walked singly or in combination, one of the classic routes of Scotland is along the LAIRIG GHRU, the great pass running through the massif from N. to S. From COYLUM BRIDGE on the N. side, this leads, by way of the Sinclair Hut, across the summit of the pass (2,733 ft), to skirt the Pools of Dee and then drop to Derry Lodge, Linn of Dee, and Braemar. The distance from Coylum Bridge to Linn of Dee – the two convenient transport terminals – is 20 m. or about nine hours' walking.

CAIRN O' MOUNT, *Kincardineshire* (Map 6, ref. 36⁵78⁰). The road linking BANCHORY and FETTERCAIRN over a summit of 1,475 ft has historical associations that go back to Macbeth, Edward I of England, and Montrose, all of whom used this pass in the lower GRAMPIANS. The view to the Kincardineshire coast is fine, and the gradients are easy. But this is one of the historic passes that, whatever improvements are made on them, are still liable to be blocked by snow in winter.

CAIRNPAPPLE, *West Lothian* (Map 2, ref. 29⁸67³). Just contiguous with, yet above, Scotland's industrial belt stands on the summit of Cairnpapple Hill this important archaeological site. It consists of a group of structures. The earliest was a group of three boulders and an arc of large stones associated with a late neolithic cremation cemetery. This was replaced by a henge monument containing an oval setting of stones associated with beaker burials. In the third period the henge was destroyed and a kerbed cairn of 50-ft diameter was built. In the cist at its centre was found a food vessel inhumation. Later this cairn was enlarged to 100 ft when two cinerary urn cremations were deposited. Finally four inhumation graves, possibly of the early Iron Age, were inserted into the remains. Mr Richard Feachem in his *Guide to Prehistoric Scotland* says this: "A microcosm of two-thirds of local prehistory, Cairnpapple stands alone, as befits its lofty position, as a source from which confirmation and guidance can be directed over a very wide field".

CAIRNRYAN, *Wigtownshire* (Map 2, ref. 20⁷56⁸), formerly Macherie, lies half-way along the E. side of LOCH RYAN. Here, on a long straight stretch of coast lying beneath the raised-beach bluff, the modern port of Cairnryan was built during the Second World War. Part of the famous Mulberry Harbour, used for the liberation of Normandy on D-Day, was made here. Since the services ceased to use the port installations, they have passed into the hands of a private firm, but they are little used today. There is a lighthouse on the point by the harbour.

Lochryan House was built in 1701 by the Agnew family on a very individual Dutch design, and was inherited in the late 18th cent. by the son of Mrs Dunlop of Dunlop. This man, one of Burns's correspondents, later changed his name to Wallace. There are Victorian additions to the house, but it is largely unspoilt.

CAIRNWELL, *Aberdeenshire* (Map 6, ref. 31¹77⁸). This part of the route between BLAIRGOWRIE and BRAEMAR takes its name from the hill of 3,059 ft that dominates the W. side of the pass. It is the highest main road in Britain, rising to a maximum altitude of 2,199 ft. Constructed in the mid-18th cent. by one of General Wade's military successors, it has changed little in direction since that date. It is rather narrow for modern traffic and is liable to be blocked by snow in winter. The area is becoming popular with skiers and hill-walkers, the track over the Monega Pass to GLEN ISLA being the highest right of way in the country, with a summit of 3,318 ft above sea-level.

CALDERBANK, *Lanarkshire* (Map 2, ref. 27⁷66⁴). In 1805 a small iron foundry here was taken over by an important steel company. In 1839–40 they built twenty-four puddling furnaces, claimed as the first in Scotland. The company went into liquidation in 1861, and after that there were only short periods of work.

Now all inhabitants of this place, once the site of a brave new venture, travel away to their daily work. Many are employed on the Newhouse Industrial Estate.

CALDERCRUIX, *Lanarkshire* (Map 2, ref. 28²66⁷). There was a corn-mill on the bank of the Calder Stream at Caldercruix, whose records go back to the early 17th cent. In 1846–8 a paper-mill was erected on the opposite bank of the stream. Twenty years later a textile printing venture took over the site of an old lint mill. This closed in 1932. We see here an example of the rise and fall of 19th-cent. ventures in Scotland's industrial belt. To the E. is the large reservoir of Hillend.

CALEDONIAN CANAL, *Inverness-shire* (Map 5, ref. 21⁵78⁰; Map 5, ref. 26⁰83⁷). This famous canal, for its day a noteworthy feat of engineering, runs clean across Scotland from the NE. to the SW. It begins at the BEAULY Firth near INVERNESS and debouches in Loch Linnhe near FORT WILLIAM. The canal was built to avoid the time and hazard of sailing round the N. of Scotland by the stormy Pentland Firth and CAPE WRATH. It runs through the length of the "Great Glen", or Glen of Albyn or GLEN MORE, which naturally divides the country. It was surveyed by the great Scottish engineer Thomas Telford in 1801, and work started on it in 1804. It was opened in 1822, but was not found satisfactory. It was closed from 1834 until 1847, when it was triumphantly completed.

The total length is 60½ m., of which only 22 m. is constructed canal, the other 38½ m. being Lochs Dochfour, NESS, OICH, and Lochy. The highest point is Loch Oich, with Laggan Reach, at 106 ft above high water at Inverness. Twenty-eight locks had to be constructed; the most famous series is known as "Neptune's Staircase" by BANAVIE.

The Caledonian Canal

Scottish Tourist Board

The canal is much used by fishing boats, small craft, and yachts, and the fine road that follows its course runs through some of the grandest Highland scenery. The route is well known to the hundreds who go seeking the Loch Ness "monster" every year. There are excellent hotels at DRUMNADROCHIT, INVERMORISTON, INVERGARRY, SPEAN BRIDGE, and other points between INVERNESS and FORT WILLIAM.

CALF OF EDAY, *Orkney* (Map 8, ref. 65^{8}03^9), is one of the ORKNEY Northern Islands (*see* "The Shape of Scotland"). This now uninhabited island in the Orkney group is notable only for its chambered cairn. Having removed the debris of a thick secondary wall in 1936, the excavators went on to recover the original shape of the mound and what Richard Feachem in his *Guide to Prehistoric Scotland* calls "the remarkable content thereof".

This included a stalled chamber with the overlay of a small house; its kind would later be discovered widely in SHETLAND. The stalled chamber and possibly the tomb had been robbed at some unknown date, and the whole structure was encased in an oblong mass of stone. It seems that the chamber and the casing represent one phase of construction, and the little oval building an earlier and independent one.

There are other monuments on the Calf of Eday like those found at SKARA BRAE; but this chambered cairn is the most outstanding.

CALGARY, *Argyll* (Map 4, ref. 13^{8}75^1), is on the Island of MULL, in the Inner Hebrides (*see* "The Shape of Scotland"). This township, with a fine sandy bay in the NW. corner of the island of Mull, gave its name to Calgary, Alberta; but by no means, as is usually said, through emigration from Mull to Canada. Calgary, Alberta, received its name in 1876 from Colonel J. F. Macleod, the Commissioner of the North-West Mounted Police. He was a native of SKYE, but was a relation by marriage of J. Munro Mackenzie, who owned the Mull estate; it was because of this connection that Macleod gave the Canadian town the name it now holds.

The road each way from Calgary is remarkable. To the S. are magnificent views of the TRESHNISH ISLANDS and COLL; along the coast to the N. are views towards ARDNAMURCHAN and Skye. The Inner Hebridean prospects are, in general, the most spectacular in Scotland.

CALLANDER, *Perthshire* (Map 2, ref. 26^{4}70^8). This tourist centre is commonly described as one of the natural gateways to the Highlands, and a gateway it certainly is to the Central Highlands of Perthshire. "Gateway" is the significant word, for, though surrounded and dominated by the beautiful mountains and hills of south central Perthshire, Callander unquestionably lies just outside the Highlands. Its appearance is more that of a Lowland town than of a Highland one. It is continually growing, but its main features are its ample street and bold, simple square. Its houses are for the most part gracefully built, in the Regency style, and some of them have attractive bow-windows on the first floor that jut out into the street, giving those sitting within the windows a full prospect of the life in this little busy town below them.

Originally, and long before its rise as a tourist centre, the town was built by the Commissioners for the Forfeited Estates on the Drummond lands after the 18th-cent. Jacobite risings. The first bridge was built here in 1764 and lasted till 1907. Originally it must have been designed for cattle-drovers or for occasional visitors to the North. By 1907, however, Callander was becoming sufficiently popular, and the influence of the motor-car was becoming sufficiently felt, for a more adequate bridge to be built across the R. Teith. The R. Leny joins the Teith just W. of Callander, and the combined rivers flow through distinctly Lowland-looking, indeed one might even say English-looking, meadows into the town.

Callander is a comfortable place in which to pass a holiday on the edge of the Highlands. There are plenty of excursions to such celebrated places as the TROSSACHS. The well-known Ben Ledi (2,875 ft) is easily accessible in a little more than three hours' walk, and it is not over-difficult to climb.

Just to the NW. of Callander stands a curiously-named little township called Kilmahog, which has a tweed-mill, a fishing-rod factory, and the pretty remains of an old toll-house.

It is difficult to describe Callander's charm. It is so obviously not a Highland town, yet its ambience is Highland. The names above most of the shop-doors are Highland and Celtic. Certainly it would be difficult to find a place from which you could get easier access to most forms of Highland holiday exercise or relaxation. Yet Callander (for all its associations with forfeited estates or the Jacobite past) is, let it be repeated, as downright and honest a Lowland town in appearance as you could wish to find.

CALLERNISH, *Ross and Cromarty* (Map 4, ref. 12^{2}93^3), is a village on the Island of LEWIS in the Outer Hebrides (*see* "The Shape of Scotland"), 14 m. W. of STORNOWAY. This township, which contains some interesting survivals of converted blackhouses, or primitive Hebridean dwelling-places, is of major importance as lying adjacent to one of the most perfectly preserved megalithic temples in the United Kingdom. It is believed to have been put up by pre-Celtic Iberians about 3,000 years ago. A circle of tall standing stones surrounds a chambered cairn, which may have been an altar for human sacrifice. It is, however, clear that, whether sacrificial or not, the circle and the altar-like centre were connected with sun-worship. The avenue stretching due S. that leads to this circle is 270 yds long.

There is much that is forever hidden in this strange collection of gaunt and large stones. Not the least of its secrets is the question of how these huge blocks, some of them nearly 16 ft high, were transported thither and were set up without mechanical aid. Over the millennia they had sunk partly into the peat. Sir James Matheson caused them to be dug round and cleared of peat in the middle of last century. You may see the marks of the peat half way up the taller stones. These standing stones form one of the most impressive remains of remote human prehistory in Scotland. They are finely situated upon a small hill, and strike the eye mysteriously and forbiddingly no matter in what weather one sees them. They have lived enigmatically yet successfully through three millennia of Hebridean storm, sun, rain, and wind.

CALLY, *Kirkcudbrightshire* (Map 2, ref. 25⁹55⁵). The fine mansion-house of Cally, close to GATEHOUSE OF FLEET, was built in 1763, being designed by Robert Milne, of the famous family of Scottish architects, for William Murray of BROUGHTON and Cally, who tried to develop industries in Gatehouse. Murray of Broughton (and later of Cally) was that same Murray to whom we have already referred under BROUGHTON – that is, "Mr Evidence". Murray was Prince Charles Edward Stuart's secretary during the 1745 Jacobite Rising. He subsequently stained his name by betraying many of his former comrades in arms, when he gave judicial evidence in London. It is possible that he added the "of Cally" to his style of address to escape the odium of his reputation. An impressive portico was added to the house about 1830. The whole building is in Creetown granite. Now a hotel, its beautiful surroundings – parkland, lake, woods, fine vistas – and large size make it very suitable for conferences.

Sandgreen, on the estate, is a rapidly-expanding bungalow and caravan resort on a fine sandy beach.

The stump of a tower-house stands in the woods near the house. The fine parkland is open to visitors. The National Trust for Scotland has a restrictive agreement with the owner over nearly 7,000 acres, including thirteen farms.

CAMBUS, *Clackmannanshire* (Map 2, ref. 28⁷69⁴), is a small village at the confluence of the Devon and the FORTH, on the road between ALLOA and STIRLING. It is remarkable in that it contains two distilleries. Good wildfowling can be had by the river.

CAMBUSKENNETH ABBEY, *Stirling-shire* (Map 2, ref. 28¹69⁴), situated on the links of the R. FORTH, and among the winding loops of the river just E. of STIRLING, was founded about 1140 by David I as a house of Augustinian canons. It was the scene in 1326 of an important Parliament of Robert I (Robert Bruce) in which representatives of burghs appear to have taken part for the first time.

It was by Cambuskenneth too that Bruce had kept his reserves of stores and arms during the Battle of BANNOCKBURN.

James III is buried here. A large slab of blue stone uncovered during excavations in 1864 is the only fragment of a medieval royal tomb in Scotland.

A detached 13th-cent. bell-tower survives complete, and is 67 ft high; but the church and conventual buildings are little more than foundations.

CAMBUSLANG, *Lanarkshire* (Map 2, ref. 26³66⁰). A parish, though one without a burgh, Cambuslang is a densely populated district on the outskirts of GLASGOW. It was formerly farming country with a cluster of villages and, in the 18th cent., a colony of hand-loom weavers. There is still a little dairy-farming, but coal-mining and heavy industry arrived in the 19th cent. to drive out rural activities. The coal-mining is now in decline, but the steel industry is growing.

Cambuslang was the scene of a gigantic religious revival known as the "Cambuslang Wark" in 1742; it took place in the open air and lasted for six months.

The only old building surviving is an unusual hexagonal dovecot on the Westburn golf course; it has landing perches made of slate.

CAMBUS O' MAY, *Aberdeenshire* (Map 6, ref. 34²79⁸), is the place where the R. DEE emerges from the Highlands through a narrow pass and becomes a part of the ordinary Aberdeenshire scene. The beauty of the scenery in this neighbourhood, especially the richly wooded parts that include many birches, is celebrated in poetry. Lord Byron spent a part of his childhood in this district; literary critics and professional biographers often forget that he was half Scots.

It was not that he ever forgot this himself. He was capable of castigating the Scots from a fairly intimate knowledge of them, as in his *English Bards and Scotch Reviewers*. In other poetical works he refers with nostalgia to the Scottish scene, and especially to Aberdeenshire, where he had spent so much of his boyhood.

CAMELON, *Stirlingshire* (Map 2, ref. 28⁶68⁰). This is the place where the early Roman forts guarded the point at which the main road from York to ARDOCH and beyond crossed the R. Carron. Much of it has been destroyed by industrial development and by the railway line, and lies between the STIRLING and GLASGOW roads W. of the railway station.

There are traces of work of three periods – Agricolan, Flavian, and Antonine.

CAMPBELTOWN, *Argyll* (Map 1, ref. 17²62⁰). At the SE. end of that long projection of the mainland, Kintyre, Campbeltown has an excellent anchorage at the head of a bay. The town was founded under James VI's policy of establishing places in distant parts to civilize the natives. Taken over by the Earl of Argyll about 1618, the burgh of Lochhead was recognized as Campbeltown in 1667; it got this designation from the family name of the Argylls. In 1700 it was raised to the status of a royal burgh.

For centuries Campbeltown has had herring fishing and coal-mining and other industries; at the end of the 19th cent. it possessed about 650 boats and thirty distilleries. Boats and distilleries are now vastly reduced. In the 18th cent. the town – through its position, prominent yet attached to the mainland – had a thriving export trade, and was later connected with whaling. A creamery was founded in 1919, and a clothing factory in 1953-7. It was a centre of R.N. Asdic training during the Second World War.

The local museum has recently been overhauled and now contains traces of much prehistory of the Kintyre district. St Kiaran was an early missionary from Ireland who arrived in Scotland before St Columba. He gave his name to the loch, and that name still lingers on the SW. shore, which is called Kilkerran. St Kiaran's cave is on the shore 3 m. S. of Campbeltown, and at the Old Quay Head stands a 15th-cent. Celtic cross.

Davaar Island at the mouth of Campbeltown Loch has a lighthouse. On the same island, but on the southern shore, there is a cave, on the rock of which Archibald MacKinnon painted the Crucifixion scene in 1887. The cave and painting are illuminated only by a shaft of daylight from a natural hole in the rock. Protected though it is, the painting was retouched by the artist later in his life, and again by a local artist in 1956.

Campbeltown is very much a tourist holiday centre. It has a mild climate and a rocky beach with plenty of sea angling. There is excellent golf. For some decades listeners to the radio in Scotland have been familiar with the excellent singing of the Campbeltown Gaelic Choir.

Kintyre, with Campbeltown as its biggest centre, is the longest and most distinctive promontory from the Scottish mainland. From S. Argyll, and between the Atlantic Ocean and the Firth of CLYDE, it stretches due S. for 40 m. Its population is largely engaged in agriculture and fishing.

It is joined to the mainland by the isthmus of TARBERT, and by the tenuous connection only just fails to be one of the largest of the Hebrides. Indeed, King Haakon of Norway claimed Kintyre as one of his Hebridean possessions. He lost it to Scotland at the Battle of LARGS (*see* "Scotland in History").

CAMSERNEY, *Perthshire* (Map 2, ref. 28¹75⁰), is an attractive and unspoilt village lying just N. of the main road from WEEM to COSHIEVILLE. Several of the cottages are thatched; there is an old mill on the Camserney Burn; and many of the houses are cruck-built. Cruck building was a means of supporting the roof in early stone structures. It involved the use of specially shaped natural branching timber, which was set into the thickness of the drystone wall and overhung to support a roof of divots or heather or thatch.

In the western part of Camserney the Russell Trust for Scotland have taken over one of these cruck-built cottages. Here is still preserved the massive hooded fire-place and iron swey for the chain that carried the cooking-pots.

CAMSTER, *Caithness* (Map 7, ref. 32⁵94⁶). "The Grey Cairns of Camster" is the name given to these ancient monuments in the far N. of the mainland.

The first is a round cairn that is the prototype of the Camster chambered cairns. It is a structure of loose stones measuring 55 ft in diameter and 12 ft in height. A passage 20 ft long leads from the SE. The chamber is in three parts. Only one is roofed with flat slabs; the other two lie together beneath a single corbelled roof.

The second cairn is long and horned; it fits into a space 200 ft by 65 ft and is one of the largest in the country. The main chamber is also in three parts. It has a small cell 5 ft in diameter with a corbelled roof 6 ft from the floor reached by a 20-ft passage.

The third cairn is 140 yds W. of the round grey cairn; it measures only 27 ft in diameter and 2 ft in height.

CANISBAY, *Caithness* (Map 7, ref. 33⁵97³). This is the most northerly parish in the mainland of Scotland. The church is a plain, strong, harled building similar to the one at DUNNET. Though altered at various unknown periods, it is believed to date from the 15th cent. The oldest parts of it are in the plain square tower with walls 2 ft 6 in. thick. The church is attended by the Queen Mother when she is in residence at her home at the CASTLE OF MEY.

A monument on the S. wall of the S. transept in red sandstone is dated 1568 and commemorates members of the Groat family, so much associated with this NE. district of Scotland; it was found under the floor of the church in 1894. Other stones in the churchyard include one to Finlay Groat in 1601.

From the rising ground to the S. of the church, and on a clear day, you can enjoy a fine panorama of the Pentland Firth with the island of Stroma and those of ORKNEY in the distance.

CANNA, Island of, *Inverness-shire* (Map 4, ref. 12⁵80⁵), is one of the Inner Hebrides (*see* "The Shape of Scotland"). For almost the last thirty years Canna has in the human sense been a living island – living indeed under the woeful heritage of its past distresses, but nonetheless living and struggling to go on living in the traditional way. Its neighbour, RUM, has had humanity crushed out of it. Its preservation and use by the Nature Conservancy may be worthy of praise – indeed, this is a much better state of affairs than used to exist when this large island was the private sea-girt sporting park of a southern landlord – but as far as Hebridean humanity goes it is finished.

What, therefore, primarily holds the respect and affection of Hebridean Gaeldom to this island is not the fact that (because of its fertility) it is sometimes popularly spoken of as the "garden of the Hebrides" – an attractive if hackneyed phrase; it is not that it combines a quiet beauty inland with spectacular rocky coasts and caves on its edge; it is not that it is rich in bird and fish life; nor even that, among the Inner Hebrides (which can offer some of the finest views of landscape, seascape, and mountains in Western Europe), Canna can offer the best. It is the fact that Canna, contemporaneously, is the solitary example of an island owned by a Gaelic-speaking laird of Scottish birth who, with the assistance of his American Gaelic-speaking wife (both of them are Gaelic scholars), is endeavouring to preserve Gaeldom economically and culturally. How far they can succeed in stemming a decline that is common to all the Hebrides, remains to be seen. At present the island is reasonably prosperous and happy, but its population is low. There are other islands of the West owned by benevolent lairds, but the unique point about Canna is that its laird, Mr John Lorne Campbell, and his wife are closely associated in language, religion, and outlook with the island community.

Canna lies NW. of Rum, and is, along with its satellite of Sanday (a satellite joined to it at low tide), situated in the centre of the Minch, the sea between the Outer Hebrides and the mainland, almost exactly between MALLAIG and South UIST. The protection of Sanday gives it a fine harbour, the rendezvous of many fishing boats and lesser craft. The coast is mostly rocky with some impressive caves, but there are one or two sandy bays. At the NE. there is the famous "Compass Hill", supposed, as on ERISKAY, to affect the magnetic compasses of passing vessels. Just to the W. of this is the plateau from which you may enjoy views unparalleled elsewhere, even in the Hebrides.

About 6 m. long, it lies E. and W., instead of N. and S. like nearly all the other Hebrides. This unusual orientation protects it from the spring N. and NE. cold winds. The result is not only that spring comes to Canna always two weeks earlier than to the rest of the Hebrides, but that almost anything grows there. The only difficulty is to harvest the crops if the weather breaks too early. The island is also rich in seafood, and there are many flying visitors, moths as well as birds. There is a Catholic church for the island people and the laird, and a Protestant one for visitors; both are served from neighbouring islands or the mainland.

The fact that Canna has had to struggle to survive even under so benevolent a proprietorship is due to increasing difficulty of communication with the other islands. The carferry service with the Outer Isles, for instance, now completely cuts Canna off from direct communication with South Uist and BARRA – and both are islands that have strong affinities with Canna. The place, in the eyes of the authorities, has grown too small for them to bring it into the stream of modern sea-traffic. This is all very well for a hermit population, but it is not good for an island such as Canna, surrounded as it is by many places of a like culture, language, and faith. What Canna needs is more houses for the young folk or for Gaelic incomers; and this is beyond the benevolence of the laird's purse. Above all, it needs a strong fishing industry independent of the laird. This it would have had if the Sea Fisheries (Scotland) Act, 1895, protecting the rights of Hebridean fishermen, had ever been carried out. This Act, having passed both Houses and having received the Royal Assent, was mysteriously allowed to drop from sight. Still, life does go on there, and every effort to make the island as fruitful and as habitable as possible continues.

There is no hotel on Canna, though occasionally one of the crofters does take in guests. However, the island, its people and its laird, welcome campers and yachtsmen and all others who are sufficiently interested in Gaelic culture, and in scenic beauty, to visit this enchantingly beautiful little island.

CANNICH, *Inverness-shire* (Map 5, ref. 23⁵83¹). Now much increased in size on account of the houses built for the Hydro-Electric Board, Cannich village stands at the mouth of Glen Cannich near the W. bank of the R. Glass. These houses are well grouped, and give the appearance of being built to last; they are made of stone.

Some 2 m. SW., Fasnakyle power station is situated on the banks of the R. Glass and at the mouth of GLEN AFFRIC. It was opened in 1952 and is built of golden-yellow sandstone from Greenbrae quarries at HOPEMAN. In order to make this highly modern development consonant with its surroundings, it bears plaques representing symbols of the type found on old Celtic stones.

CANONBIE, *Dumfriesshire* (Map 3, ref. 33⁹57⁶). Canonbie village lies in a picturesque situation on the W. bank of the Esk where it flows out of a narrow wooded channel.

Coal was mined at Byreburnfoot, just N. of the village, before 1860, and later at Rowan-burn, to the E. of the village, where a new community sprang up; the mine, however, was closed in 1922. Extensive coal reserves have since the war been proved in the area, but there is no plan to work them; so the countryside remains rich farmland, mainly dairying, on a limestone soil – lime is quarried and burnt for farm use at Harelawhill in Canonbie parish.

The Canonbie area was the centre of the Armstrong surname in Border War days. Johnnie Armstrong's Tower of Gilnockie, on a rocky promontory above the Esk, 2 m. N. of Canonbie, has long been demolished; its stone was used to build a bridge. But well-preserved Holehouse (Hollows) Tower on the bank of the Esk was also an Armstrong castle.

In the Middle Ages there was an Augustinian priory at Canonbie. Traces of it linger in such local names as Priorlinn, where, above the present farmhouse, is a cruck-framed long-house made of clay and straw, now used as a hay-shed. Of the priory itself, the only relic is a fragment of sculpture in the churchyard.

CAPE WRATH, *Sutherland* (Map 5, ref. 22⁶97⁵). This celebrated and well-named headland lies in the NW. extremity of the mainland of Scotland, reaching an altitude of 370 ft. Its lighthouse, 400 ft above the sea at high tide, is visible at a distance of 27 m. There are dangerous reefs near the base of the cliffs. Cape Wrath was called by the Norsemen a "hvarf", which meant in their language a turning-point, because the coast, which hitherto runs N., here turns towards the E.

Cape Wrath is one of the finest places on the Scottish coast from which to watch the gannets. From March until autumn, and indeed at times in the winter, they are to be seen in an almost continuous stream, possibly flying from the nesting sites at ST KILDA, Sula Sgeir, and Sule Skerry to their fishing-grounds.

CARDENDEN, *Fife* (Map 3, ref. 32²69⁴). This large village is mostly a mining community, which developed rapidly after the opening of Bowhill Colliery in 1895. It suffered a relapse after 1914, but a development in coal-mining took place after 1945.

There is also some interest in agriculture here. The Forestry Commission has planted in the district Scotch and Corsican pine, and Japanese and European larch.

CARDONESS CASTLE, *Kirkcudbright-shire* (Map 2, ref. 25⁸55³), is a particularly fine 15th-cent. tower-house, well proportioned, with four storeys and a vaulted basement; the fireplaces in the great hall and solar are especially notable. The Castle, atop a high rocky knoll and in a very commanding position overlooking Fleet Bay, stands within a few hundred yards of Green Tower Motte, where, in the time of Roland of Galloway, was settled David, son of Terri, Lord of Over Denton in Gilsland. He was the progenitor of the family of de Cardines, and held his land by ward relief and marriage; the McCullochs, to whom the land had passed before 1450, held it by the same service as late as 1528. The 12th-cent. cross-stone in Anwoth Churchyard may well be David's.

Local tradition has it that the whole family of de Cardines disappeared through the ice of a frozen loch nearby while celebrating – with music, dancing, drink, and feasting on a Sabbath – the birth of an heir.

CARDOW, *Moray* (Map 6, ref. 31⁹84³). Those interested in one of Scotland's major unique products, which she exports all over the world, may care to look at Cardow. Here, near KNOCKANDO, is a famous distillery producing malt whisky for a large distillery company. It has made the celebrated Speyside "Single Whisky" since 1824, and was almost completely rebuilt in 1961. Real "Scotch" is made in Scotland only.

CARDROSS, *Dunbartonshire* (Map 2, ref. 23⁵67⁷). The site of the old Cardross Castle where Robert I (Robert Bruce) died in 1329 lies 3 m. E. of the modern village of Cardross and is near the mouth of the R. Leven in the outskirts of DUMBARTON. It was from this castle that Sir James Douglas set out to take the heart of Bruce to the Holy Land. Douglas began his crusade by fighting the Moors in Spain, where he fell in battle. Bruce's heart in its casket was recovered and brought back to Scotland and to MELROSE Abbey. Now the site is the property of the National Trust for Scotland, to whom it was presented by R. B. Cunninghame Graham. A year after Cunninghame Graham's death, a memorial cairn was set up here, out of gratitude to him, in 1937. Cunninghame Graham lived not only at GARTMORE, the family seat, but at an 18th-cent. house at Cardross on the banks of the CLYDE.

Cardross parish church was destroyed by an incendiary bomb during the blitz. Kilmahew Chapel near Cardross is on the site of one of the first churches established in Strath Clyde, which was rebuilt in 1467. It was used as a school from 1640 to 1843; it then fell into disuse, but was restored and reopened at St Peter's College for Roman Catholic priests.

CARFIN, *Lanarkshire* (Map 2, ref. 27⁷65⁸). This was an entirely rural district until, in the mid-19th cent., the mines brought people from Poland and the Baltic, and from Ireland after the potato famine there. The Industrial Estate at Carfin has now turned towards light industries; moreover, many people living in Carfin travel to their work at MOTHERWELL and GLASGOW.

Among Catholics in southern Scotland, Carfin is celebrated for its grotto, which is dedicated to St Thérèse of Lisieux. It is said that a party of pilgrims returning from Lourdes in 1920 decided to build a local shrine here. This may be so; but what is probably the true story of how the Carfin Grotto was built is more remarkable. During the depression that hit this part of Scotland in the 1920s, most of the menfolk in Carfin and the nearby district were "on the dole", and were exposed to the malady of hopeless idleness. The parish priest of Carfin could not, of course, put money into their pockets or increase their "dole"; he could, however, offer them something to do. He said to his parishioners, and indeed to any parishioners in the locality who were finding time hanging heavily on their hands, that he would get them work. He did so. He was able by appeals to procure materials for the building of the Carfin Grotto, and the largely Catholic male population of the district fell eagerly to work upon it. To some travellers in Scotland, accustomed to little else than the grey expanse of the Industrial Belt, Carfin with its grotto may seem a trifle garish. Before they condemn it as being out of place here, they should reflect that it was built as a labour of love by workingmen who would otherwise have been condemned to idleness, and who were led to that labour by the inspiration of their priest.

The Grotto and its gardens now cover fifty acres, visited by people from many countries.

CARFRAEMILL, *Berwickshire* (Map 3, ref. 35²65⁶). An attractive township at the junction of roads from EDINBURGH and LAUDER and GREENLAW at the S. foot of SOUTRA, Carfraemill was formerly a coaching stage. It is said to have marked the end of one day's march for Jacobite forces from DALKEITH in 1745 when they were on their way to England.

At the end of the 18th cent. Mr Robert Hogarth, tenant of Carfrae, introduced turnips and clover to the district and later also potatoes.

CARLINGWARK, *Kirkcudbrightshire* (Map 2, ref. 27⁷56²). This pleasant Lowland loch lies on the outskirts of CASTLE DOUGLAS (called Carlingwark until 1792), and is now surrounded by a public park and caravan site. The loch was originally larger than it is today, being held in by an earth bank, probably dating from the Iron Age, but it was almost emptied for a time in 1765, when the marl from its bed was carted away for agricultural purposes. At this time four crannogs, two dams, and a

causeway were revealed, and Bronze Age daggers and swords and other prehistoric objects were found in the lake-bed.

A spread of iron waste where the road from the town reaches the lake shore is perhaps of early medieval date. Its presence suggested the legend that Brawny Kim, the blacksmith, forged Mons Meg here in 1455. This famous piece of siege artillery may be seen on the battlements of the Castle at EDINBURGH today.

CARLOPS, *Peeblesshire* (Map 3, ref. 31⁷65⁷). This village is but a string of cottages along the EDINBURGH–BIGGAR road; it was founded in 1784 to house weavers in the district. It is now a weekend resort from Edinburgh, and is the start and finish of several walks amongst Edinburgh's Pentland Hills.

The district figures in Allan Ramsay's *The Gentle Shepherd*, published in 1725. This work is not only a charming fantasy, but also a literary curiosity. It is a conventional 18th-cent. pastoral comedy written by an educated Scotsman of the Augustan age, but not in the "polite writing" in Scotland. It is in the old broad Scots – and all the more authentic for that. The comedy was revived and successfully presented at the third Edinburgh Festival.

The poet was one of a group of friends who visited Newhall, just N. of Carlops, which then belonged to a cousin of Forbes of CULLODEN. The house was rebuilt in the early 18th cent., and a painted ceiling shows Ramsay and his friends. Habbie's Howe, also mentioned in the poem, is a further mile NE. on the Edinburgh road.

CARLOWAY, *Ross and Cromarty* (Map 4, ref. 12²94²), is a village 24 m. W. of STORNO-WAY on the Island of LEWIS in the Outer Hebrides (*see* "The Shape of Scotland"). Carloway, lying at the head of a narrow sea-inlet to the far W. of Lewis, would have been in Norse times a highly exposed place for raiders. It is this fact that accounts for the presence, on an obvious hill, of one of the best preserved and most remarkable of brochs, locally known as duns, in the Hebrides.

One half of the Carloway broch is now reduced, but what remains is impressive and clearly indicates how secure a refuge it must have been for the Picts or Celts who originally built it. They built it, not to hide themselves, but to retreat impregnably. Part of the neatly built and most workmanlike wall rises to 30 ft and is 11 ft thick. The courtyard is 25 ft in diameter. The internal structure is clearly visible, with slabs forming the bond between the two skins and floors of the galleries. A narrow entrance was easily defended from a strategically placed guardroom between the inner and outer walls.

Whether built as a defence against Roman slave-raiders, as some archaeologists believe, or later against the Norsemen, this is outstanding evidence of the architectural defensive power possessed by some of the earliest historical inhabitants of the Hebrides.

CARLUKE, *Lanarkshire* (Map 2, ref. 28⁵65⁰). This town, with a magnificent site overlooking the lower basin of the CLYDE, was in the 17th cent. a burgh named Kirkstyle, but it later declined to a few cottages, and then rose again in the 19th cent. on the establishment of cotton-weaving in the district. Now, and for many years, this neighbourhood is best known for fruit-growing. Orchards of plum, apple, and pear attract visitors to see the blossoms in spring. Strawberries were introduced about 1870; more recently tomatoes grown under glass flourished here. Much jam is made.

At Miltonhead (2 m. W. of Carluke) a plaque marks the birthplace of Gen. William Roy (1729–90), the "father of the Ordnance Survey". The Rev. Peter Kid was minister of Carluke in the 17th cent.; he was one of the clergy imprisoned on the BASS ROCK during the covenanting period. A memorial by the church on a table stone recalls him in rustic but touching verse.

CARMYLLIE, *Angus* (Map 6, ref. 35⁵74²). At the main centre of quarries supplying sandstone for building, Carmyllie became in the 19th cent. the chief works in the county for "Arbroath pavement" – employing by the end of the century about 300 people in quarrying and polishing, and other work with stone. The Rev. Patrick Bell (d. 1869), who invented the first reaping machine, was minister here for a time.

CARNOUSTIE, *Angus* (Map 6, ref. 35⁶73⁴). Known all over the golfing world for its two championship courses (one long and arduous), Carnoustie is a blend of holiday resort and industry. Jute, preserves, and crane-building are the main industries. The holiday resort is built round a bay of beautiful sand. There are all the usual seaside recreations for family holidays, in the E. coast Scottish style.

CARNWATH, *Lanarkshire* (Map 2, ref. 29⁸64⁶). One long street, stretching for ¾ m. and set amongst miles of open moorland, makes up the village of Carnwath. The market cross dated 1516 gives details of routes and distances, including those to "Air". The old Tolbooth also dates from the 16th cent. St Mary's Aisle, a fragment of the N. transept of the church of 1424, is the mausoleum of the Somervilles, who owned Cowthally Castle, now a ruin (just N. of the village), where they entertained James III, IV, and V on hunting parties. The Red Hose Race, the earliest foot-race in the United Kingdom, is run in August and is traditionally connected with the charter of 1500.

The industry in the district was at first connected with the earliest ironworks in Lanarkshire at WILSONTOWN, 6 m. N. of the village, but these closed down in 1842 and coal-mining began to take its place. Carnwath, in its lonely moorland situation, is placed half-way between evidences of Scotland's agricultural past and of her industrial past and present.

CARRADALE, *Argyll* (Map 1, ref. 18²63⁸). Standing on the E. coast of Kintyre, the village of Carradale looks across the Kilbrennan sound at the narrowest part (3 m. wide) to the island of ARRAN. Carradale has a new harbour completed in 1959, but its fishing fleet, like that of other W.-coast ports, has lately declined. It is now largely a holiday centre in the spring and summer, with a mild, moist climate. Carradale Water, which debouches into Carradale Bay, is an excellent salmon river. The Forestry Commission have begun planting in the area.

A vitrified fort occupies the central part of Carradale Point, a narrow peninsula that may be isolated at high water. The fort is oval and measures about 190 ft by 75 ft.

CARRBRIDGE, *Inverness-shire* (Map 5, ref. 29²82³), is a village on the main N. road between AVIEMORE and INVERNESS, at its junction with the road leading to GRANTOWN-ON-SPEY. It is one of the most prominent skiing resorts associated with the CAIRN-GORMS, and a popular *après*-ski rendezvous. Several hotels and guest-houses cater for a long tourist season with fishing and touring as main attractions in summer months. Pleasant walks can be found along the Dulnain valley from the village towards the old Wade military road; the ruin of Inverlaidnan House where Prince Charles Edward Stuart stayed on the eve of the Rout of Moy in 1746, and a moorland route to Aviemore, are points of interest. The village is well situated as a base for touring in all

Carrbridge

directions: NW. to Inverness and the BLACK ISLE; N. to the Moray coast; or S. into the mountains and the SPEY valley, where a hump bridge that has often been remarked upon was built beside the main road in 1775–6. At Duthil, 2½ m. away, the church and mausoleum have been the burial-place of the chiefs of Clan Grant since 1585.

CARRINGTON, *Midlothian* (Map 3, ref. 33²66⁰). The village church of Carrington is set among old sandstone cottages, with red pantiles. The church tower has, however, been converted into a dovecot, and the cottages have been augmented with council houses.

CARRON, *Stirlingshire* (Map 2, ref. 29⁰68⁴). The name of Carron leapt suddenly into fame in the latter half of the 18th cent., for, at a site on the Carron Water just N. of FALKIRK, two Englishmen, Samuel Garbett and John Roebuck, and one Scot, William Cadell, decided to set up a new ironworks. This was to be the major iron-producing company in Britain. It began operations in 1760, and is still working strongly, though no longer pre-eminent. It started by making grates, stoves, engineer work, iron pipes, and nails. In 1776 the Carron Iron Works was responsible for a new light gun called Carronade, which was very quickly accepted. Carron continued with ordnance work until 1852, and still makes a wide variety of products.

CARSEBRECK, *Perthshire* (Map 2, ref. 28⁷70⁹). The Grand Match – the national Curling Bonspiel between Scotland North, and Scotland South, of the FORTH – was first held in 1847 on a loch in the grounds of PENICUIK House outside EDINBURGH, the home of Sir George and Lady Clerk. But there was difficulty in getting a suitable stretch of ice. In 1850 the match was arranged at LOCHWINNOCH in Renfrewshire, but, through a misunderstanding, permission was withdrawn by the owner at the last moment, and Colonel McDowall of Garthland flooded 200 acres of his property so that the match could go on.

At a meeting of the Royal Caledonian Curling Club in 1851, Sir John Ogilvy moved that the club should have its own piece of ground, which could be flooded and which would form a safe sheet of ice for the Grand Matches.

At Carsebreck, near BLACKFORD station, sixty-three acres were bought, and Sir John Ogilvy presented a six-pounder gun captured by one of his ancestors. The gun was placed on Kilnknowe overlooking the site, and was fired as a signal to start and end the game.

At the first Grand Match on the 15th of February 1853, 1,400 curlers took part. An office, a bridge over the Allan Water, a special railway station, and sidings were built, but since 1935 Carsebreck has fallen into disuse. The 1959 Grand Match was held on Loch LEVEN, and that of 1963 on the Lake of MENTEITH.

CARSETHORN, *Kirkcudbrightshire* (Map 2, ref. 29⁹55⁹), is a pleasant little fishing village for salmon and flounder on the lower Nith estuary, with whitewashed limestone houses and fuchsia hedges. Its ruinous wooden jetty recalls busier days. Into the 1920s there was a brisk coastal schooner trade; in 1850 10,000 emigrants left the jetty for Canada, 7,000 for Australia, and 4,000 for New Zealand. The emigrant trade, started long before, continued until the 1870s.

Carsethorn appears as an outport of DUMFRIES in 1562, when a ship loaded there for Rochelle and Bordeaux. This was evidently a long-standing trade there, for the mention is a routine one, with no suggestion of anything new about it.

In the 1660s the merchants of Dumfries built a 13-m. cobbled wagon-road to Carsethorn, the first of its kind in Scotland. Much smuggling went on in the 18th cent., and the coastguard barracks still stands.

CARSLUITH, *Kirkcudbrightshire* (Map 2, ref. 24⁸55⁵). This roofless 16th-cent. tower-house stands among the farmsteadings beside the main road and overlooking the sea. It is on the usual L-plan, but differs from most of its class in that the staircase jamb was added in 1568; the original square tower had an open parapet with angle-towers. The castle belonged to the Brouns of Carsluith, and the family is still prominent on the other side of Fleet Bay around Knockbrex, as it was in the 16th cent. It also had extensive holdings around NEW ABBEY, and the famous Abbot Gilbert Broun of that abbey and his predecessor were both Brouns; Kinharvie was their chief New Abbey holding.

Carsluith tower lies not far from Ravenshall Rocks, a very striking stretch of wooded rocky coast, and the large cave known after Scott as "Dirk Hatteraick's", where, to hide brandy bottles and small casks, pigeon-holes have been cut in the walls.

Barholm, a charming small tower-castle, stands above the coastal road not much more than 2 m. E. of Carsluith Castle.

CARSPHAIRN, *Kirkcudbrightshire* (Map 2, ref. 25⁶59³). This pleasant village lies in surprisingly fertile arable land in the midst of a huge area of high land, with Cairnsmore of Carsphairn (2,612 ft) on the NE., and to the SW., Corserine (2,668 ft), the highest point of the 5-m. ridge, and the Rhinns of Kells, which never fall below 2,000 ft.

The district was prominent in the covenanting period from the 1660s to the 1680s; it formed part of the lands of the Griersons of Lagg, and Sir Robert Grierson concentrated his persecutions on this area.

The McAdam family estates were near here, and John Loudon McAdam, the great road-builder (1756–1836), is commemorated by a tablet in the church – he is buried in MOFFAT, and, though he spent his childhood in the Carsphairn district, he was born in AYR owing to a fire at the family home of Lagwine NW. of the village.

The route up the Ken-Deugh valley from DALRY has been transformed and greatly improved by afforestation and the formation of the large lochs of Earlston, Carsfad, and Kendoon by the Galloway power scheme.

CARSTAIRS, *Lanarkshire* (Map 2, ref. 29⁴64⁶), was a name very familiar to travellers at the height of the Railway Age; for it was here in this wide moorland that the Caledonian Railway came in 1845–7 to form a junction for the EDINBURGH and GLASGOW rail traffic to London. Indeed, a new village sprang up around the railway junction to house the workers at the station and in the industry.

However, the old village, which had been here long before the power of steam was discovered, stands above and to the SE. of the junction village. It is 700 ft above sea-level and is in farming country. It has a village green in the centre, bordered by trees, and now by-passed by much traffic. The church was built in 1794, but was altered in the 19th cent. In the vestibule are two old stones – a T-shaped Crucifixion stone and another with elaborate carving; they are rare rather than beautiful. Both date back to the 15th cent.

CARTER BAR, *Roxburghshire* (Map 3, ref. 37⁰60⁷). The name of this houseless and un-inhabited place is very familiar to motorists who prefer to take the more leisurely and picturesque route into England and the South. Carter Bar stands on the summit of the Cheviot Hills, where the JEDBURGH–Newcastle road leaves Scotland to enter England. The view from this eminent Border spot extends over much of the Lowlands of Scotland to the EILDON Hills.

CARTLAND, *Lanarkshire* (Map 2, ref. 28⁹64⁷). This district is noted for its precipitous cliffs or crags (200 to 400 ft), which hang over a remarkable chasm near the Mouse Water. These crags are a geological feature of the district and are like similar formations over the CLYDE at BONNINGTON and STONEBYRES. In the mid-19th cent. the botanist John Hutton Balfour recorded some interesting plants here.

There is a small village of Cartland. A bridge over the water, built in 1823 after designs by Thomas Telford, with three arches and 129 ft high, is still in use.

CASTLEBAY, *Inverness-shire* (Map 4, ref. 06⁷79⁷), is the chief town on the Island of BARRA in the Outer Hebrides (*see* "The Shape of Scotland"). It has two hotels, a few shops, a large if rather austere 19th-cent. Catholic church and, of course, a pier, which is designed to receive the steamships from the mainland three days a week; it is thus the gathering-place for the island. In the township of Castlebay there is little of architectural or archaeological appeal, but the place has a life of its own, which visitors who are present upon Sundays or Holy Days of obligation will not easily forget. Castlebay must be one of the easiest places in Scotland in which to find congenial and casual conversation. All inhabitants speak English, though Gaelic is their native tongue.

More famous than the town itself is Kisimul Castle, immediately within the bay. The ancient piece of clan fortification, and later residence of the chiefs of the Clan MacNeil, lies upon a small, rocky island, scarcely 200 yds from the pier at Castlebay. This castle on a small island in the bay of a remote Atlantic island presents an appearance at once romantic, appealing, and slightly touching – touching because of its small size. It has recently also acquired a pleasingly domestic appearance. The more enthusiastic votaries of the Clan MacNeil maintain that Kisimul Castle has been in MacNeil hands for 1,000 years or more. Historians not bearing the name MacNeil have cast doubt upon this early date and prefer a slightly later one. Recent researches, however, do support a fairly early MacNeil occupation, probably in the early Middle Ages. From the late Middle Ages until about 120 years ago the chiefs of the Clan MacNeil inhabited Kisimul Castle. After the decline in the fortunes of the Highlands and Islands that took place at the end of the 18th and beginning of the 19th cents., the chiefs left their ancient castle and went across the seas to the Americas.

Just before the Second World War, however, Robert Lister MacNeil, a descendant of the chiefs of the MacNeils, returned from America, bought Kisimul Castle, and began to restore it. After the war, the reconstruction was completed, and in 1960 the castle-restorer and Chief held a gathering at Kisimul Castle at which he welcomed back MacNeils from all over the world. The next Chief, Robert Lister MacNeil, was an architect by profession and used his architectural skills to restore Kisimul Castle with taste and discretion as well as piety towards the past. On his death in June 1970 his son Ian Roderick, the distinguished Professor of Law at Cornell University, became the 46th Chief of the MacNeils of Barra. He continues the family's interest in the past and in this ancient castle.

CASTLE CAMPBELL, *Clackmannanshire* (Map 2, ref. 29⁷69⁹), stands on a rock outcrop in the glen running into the Ochils behind the hillfoots burgh of DOLLAR. The great tower, built towards the end of the 15th cent. by the

Earl of Argyll, added to during the 16th and 17th cents., and burnt by Montrose in 1645, is now maintained by the Ministry of Public Building and Works, and is regularly open to the public. The glen approaches to the Castle, which commands a panoramic view of the FORTH valley, are owned by the National Trust for Scotland and make a pleasant circuit of paths and bridges.

CASTLECARY, *Stirlingshire* (Map 2, ref. 27⁸67⁸). The Roman fort excavated here in 1902 was discovered to have been raided for building materials. It was mutilated in 1841, when the railway between EDINBURGH and GLASGOW was taken right across it. The fort stands beside the ANTONINUS WALL; it was also an Agricolan station.

Just SW. of the fort rises the Castle, a 15th-cent. tower-house with an E. wing or hall-house that was added in the 17th cent.; it too was built partly of Roman stones from the fort. It held an important position on the communication routes and was burnt by the High-landers in the Rising of 1715, but the interior is now restored and modernized; it is still occupied.

CASTLE DOUGLAS, *Kirkcudbrightshire* (Map 2, ref. 27⁷56³). This pleasant modern town lies in rich, gently-rolling farmland; the oldest part of it was the village of Causewayend, near CARLINGWARK Loch. This village began to increase in importance; it had the name of Carlingwark until 1792, when it became a burgh of barony and changed its name in honour of Sir William Douglas of Gelston, a merchant who had made a fortune in the Virginia trade, and who had bought the village in 1789.

Castle Douglas has long been a market centre; Kelton Fair was one of the principal fairs of the South-West throughout the 18th cent., being held on a hillock just outside the town. Its present flourishing cattle-market is more than a century old, and is still a main centre for sales of Ayrshire and Galloway cattle.

Every year, the town holds a civic week, which includes a re-enactment of the gift of the Charter in 1792. It is fortunate in having Carlingwark Loch and its shores as a civic park, which now includes a large caravan site. Boating, golf, bowls, tennis, and fishing are available on the spot, and the town is a good centre for trips to the hills and coast. There is also a small art gallery.

Castle Douglas is regarded as the commercial capital of the county, and it won a Saltire Society award in 1962 for its enterprise.

CASTLEDYKES, *Lanarkshire* (4 m. E. of LANARK). This Roman fort was occupied in Flavian, Agricolan, and Antonine periods. Standing on a plateau that overlooks the

R. CLYDE, with a wide view, it covers 6½ acres and is one of the largest forts in SW. Scotland. It obviously had a large and elaborate ditch system.

CASTLE LAW, *Midlothian* (3 m. NW. of PENICUIK). On the summit of Castle-Knowe, a small hill on the southern slopes of the Pentland Hills near EDINBURGH, stands this interesting but now denuded fort. It shows a series of structural modifications, from a single palisade trench to a single rampart, thus growing to a standard multivallate fort of the period immediately before the arrival of the Roman armies in A.D. 79 or 80 in this part of Scotland.

The interesting element in the fort is the later addition of a well-preserved souterrain constructed in a ditch between two ramparts, dating from the end of the local Roman occupation, probably in the 3rd cent. Only a few other features of this kind in the Eastern Lowlands remain from the Roman occupation.

CASTLE OF MEY, *Caithness* (Map 7, ref. 32⁸97⁴). Now well known as the holiday home of the Queen Mother since her purchase of it in 1952, the Castle of Mey was formerly called Barrogill Castle. It stands near the most northerly sea by the mainland of Britain and overlooks the Pentland Firth to ORKNEY.

Barrogill was first built as a grange or fortified storehouse by the Bishop of Caithness; it was then, upon the eve of the Reformation, acquired by the 4th Earl of Caithness in 1556 and converted to a castle by the addition of dwelling-rooms above the grange. It was inherited by the Sinclairs of Mey, who later succeeded to the earldom of Caithness. In 1762 it had eighteen fire-rooms, but at the end of the 18th cent. and in the 19th cent. it was altered inside and sham battlements were added.

The Sinclair family left the Castle in 1889 after more than 400 years of occupation; it was threatened with demolition when saved by the Queen Mother's purchase of it.

CASTLE SWEEN, *Argyll* (Map 1, ref. 17³67⁸). Situated on the rocky W. coast of Knapdale, Castle Sween is of high architectural importance, as it appears to be typologically the earliest stone castle in Scotland. It was probably built in the mid-12th cent., for the main structure is Norman in aspect with large pilaster and angle buttresses. There is a great oblong tower-house, with pointed loopholes, and a cylindrical angle-tower, which are later additions. The Castle was destroyed as a habitation in 1647 by Sir Alexander Macdonald, Montrose's commander, but its proportions and structure remain.

CASTLE TIRRIM, *Inverness-shire* (Map 4, ref. 16⁷77²), sometimes spelt Castle Tioram. The ancient seat of the Macdonalds of Clanranald, Castle Tirrim was built in the early 13th cent. on a site of extraordinary scenic splendour; it is on a rocky hill at the end of a sand spit projecting into Loch Moidart, and at high tide it is an island.

The original curtain-wall part of the Castle has walls 8 ft thick and 30 ft high with a straight open stair to the wall-walk. About 1600 a domestic range of buildings was added against the S. wall, including a high tower with corbelled angle-turrets.

The Castle was partly burnt at Clanranald's orders after he had set out to join the Jacobite Rising in 1715. But it appears to have remained habitable, as Lady Grange was taken there in 1732 on her way to ST KILDA and occupied a small room high up in the S. range, which was then still panelled and furnished.

Poor Lady Grange was the termagant and possibly slightly unbalanced wife of a Judge of the Court of Session. He banished her by force to the ultimate Hebridean island, where she remained for years scarcely able to communicate with the monoglot Gaelic-speaking people of St Kilda. Her husband allowed her a large package of snuff and a large jar of whisky twice a year. They were each rapidly consumed on arrival. She eventually escaped to SKYE.

CASTLETOWN, *Caithness* (Map 7, ref. 32⁰96⁸). Founded in 1824, when Castlehill quarries began large-scale production of flag for paving, the village of Castletown stands near the head of DUNNET Bay. A small harbour was soon developed to meet the needs of the trade from this, the first large quarry in the county. The quarry was started by James Traill (1758–1843) of Castlehill, who planted his property at Castlehill with trees (a very unusual feature in Caithness) that still survive; he also undertook agricultural improvements in company with Sir John Sinclair, one of the humane Highland lairds at the time of the Clearances.

So large was the production of paving-stones from Caithness at one time that it was said that a Caithness man exiled in EDINBURGH or GLASGOW still trod the stones of his native county wherever he went in these two cities.

CATERTHUN, *Angus* (Map 6, ref. 35⁷76⁸). White Caterthun, 5 m. NW. of BRECHIN, is an oval fort 500 ft by 220 ft held within the most imposing ruined wall in Britain, which may well have been 40 ft thick. Outside is another wall about 20 ft thick and a combined tumble of two walls covering 100 ft. The outside walls and the low rampart encircle the hill-top. Farther outside this are remains of two ramparts and traces of two more, possibly incomplete. There was apparently little taken away, so that White Caterthun, though now notable for its voluminous space, may not have originally been greater than many other forts of the time.

Brown Caterthun, 1 m. NE. of White Caterthun, contains six lines of defence. The innermost is very ruinous, enclosing 260 ft by 200 ft. Thereafter you find a heavy rampart or even wall with nine entrances; two ramparts and a ditch with nine entrances; and two outer ramparts with eight entrances. The total enclosure is 1,000 ft by 900 ft. This suggests three separate structural phases.

CATRINE, *Ayrshire* (Map 2, ref. 25³62⁶), was the product of the Industrial Revolution, and was founded by Sir Claude Alexander of Ballochmyle as late as 1787. Here, in concert with David Dale, the humane GLASGOW industrialist of the 18th cent., he set up a cotton industry that has enjoyed more or less uninterrupted prosperity. The mills are the only Scottish example of a factory carrying through all processes from yarn to finished goods.

Ballochmyle House is situated on an eminence overlooking the village, and was the scene of Burns's song "The Lass of Ballochmyle" – the lass being the sister of Sir Claude. The song was not well received by the lady, although in later years she was not unwilling to acknowledge herself as the inspiration that had kindled the poet's genius.

CAUSEWAYHEAD, *Stirlingshire* (Map 2, ref. 28⁰69⁶), is a mainly residential area N. of STIRLING at the junction of the roads to DUNBLANE and PERTH, to MILNATHORT via the Hillfoots, and to ALLOA. Overlooking the village from ABBEY CRAIG is the great tower of the Wallace Monument, one of the outstanding landmarks of the district. An organization that specializes in light industry for disabled persons has a factory here.

CAWDOR, *Nairnshire* (Map 5, ref. 28⁵85⁰). The name of Cawdor, its castle, and its thane are known to all who have read or seen Shakespeare's *Macbeth*. The present village of Cawdor stands at the foot of the impressive castle. The keep as we see it now dates certainly from 1454, when a royal licence was granted to the Thane of Cawdor to erect and fortify the castle, but parts of it may be earlier. Alterations were made in the 16th cent., which include enlarged windows in the keep; and in the 17th cent. the N. and W. wings were enlarged and much carving was added. The absence of the lairds for 100 years after 1716 (when they settled on their lands in Wales) saved much alteration, although some was done in the 19th cent. to the interior. There is a drawbridge, an iron yett, and notable gardens.

CERES, *Fife* (Map 3, ref. 34⁰71²). Often described as the "prettiest village in Scotland", Ceres stands at the meeting- and crossing-places of old Fife highways. Lying, however, in its quiet valley undisturbed by modern traffic, it has retained its individuality.

It has managed to keep its village green (that comparative rarity in Scotland) and an old hump-backed bridge, with attractive groups of traditionally red-roofed cottages. One wall in the village shows built into it the statue of the Provost of Ceres of 1578; it was the work of a local man who also, it is believed, sculpted the left-handed piper on a cottage gable near the church. Games and horse-racing are held each June in Ceres; these are traditionally believed to commemorate the Ceres men who returned home after midsummer and from the victory they had helped to win at BANNOCKBURN.

The old tiny Barony Court House became the weigh-house and has scales; "God Bless the Just" is carved over the doorway. The church on the hill contains the mausoleum of the earls of Crawford in what may be the remains of the old church. Ceres was formerly a centre for weaving, but is now almost entirely supported by agriculture.

CHAPELCROSS, *Dumfriesshire* (Map 3, ref. $32^2 56^9$). During the Second World War the Royal Air Force took over a large area of what had been farmland in the Creca–Chapelcross district some 2 m. NE. of ANNAN, and for some years after the war the land lay partly derelict, with the hutments still standing.

A great change then took place; hundreds of workmen descended upon the site, with great earth-moving machines, and four tall broch-like cooling-towers rose to dominate both coasts of the Solway. This is the electricity-producing station for the Atomic Energy Authority enterprise in Scotland.

The reactors are graphite-moderated and produce plutonium and electricity, more than 180 mW. being supplied to the grid. The potable water supply for the station comes from the Black Esk, large quantities being taken daily, and cooling water is pumped from the R. Annan at an average rate of 6,000,000 gallons per day.

The staff includes a number of scientists and specialists from outside the area, and they have had a great influence on the social and cultural life of Annan. Many of the station staff live in a large new housing scheme near the works.

This great atomic fuel power station project was started in 1955 and has been in production since 1962.

CHAPEL OF GARIOCH, *Aberdeenshire* (Map 6, ref. $37^2 82^3$). Garioch is an ancient district and a lordship associated with that of Mar, from the time of Bruce, whose sister was Lady of Garioch, and married to the Earl of Mar.

The Chapel of Garioch was originally a private one dedicated to St Mary. It was confirmed as a regular chapel by the Abbot of LINDORES in 1195, but almost certainly existed earlier; it is built on the height of

Dundurno on an outlying ridge of BEN-NACHIE. The chapel became a parish church of the Reformed Faith in 1583.

Balquhain Tower, the seat of the Lindsay family, dating from 1530, is just SE. of Chapel of Garioch.

CHIRNSIDE, *Berwickshire* (Map 3, ref. $38^8 65^7$). A village of two streets in a T-shape lying between AYTON and DUNS, Chirnside is situated on the brow of Chirnside hill looking S. over the streams of Blackadder and of Whiteadder, and also over the R. TWEED; it has a fine position and view. Crosshill at the junction of the T in the village was the scene of the sackcloth sale every year in November. The church was originally Norman in type dating from the 13th cent., but has been much altered.

Ninewells, SW. of Chirnside, was the birthplace of David Hume. His elder brother was the laird there. The philosopher never obtruded the fact, but also (and rightly) he never forgot that he came from the landed gentry of Scotland.

An oddity lies near Ninewells on the Duns–Berwick road. It is "Rock House", so called because the back of the house is hewn from solid rock in the hill.

CHURCHILL BARRIERS, The, *Orkney* (Map 7, ref. $34^8 99^9$), of ORKNEY Northern Islands (*see* "The Shape of Scotland"), form a causeway constructed out of cement blocks during the Second World War. It links the S. of the Mainland of Orkney with the islands of South Ronaldsay, Burray, Glimps, and Lamb Holm. In war this was a useful blockage of one entrance to the famous naval base of SCAPA FLOW. Now in peacetime it is used as a method of quick transport between islands once completely severed from each other by high seas. On Lamb Holm stands a striking little chapel built by Italian prisoners of war, who between

The Churchill Barrier

Scottish Tourist Board

1940 and 1945 were engaged on what must have seemed the strangely northern task of constructing barrier fortification causeways between these (to them) ultimate islands.

CLACHNAHARRY, *Inverness-shire* (Map 5, ref. 26⁵84⁵), is a NW. suburb of INVERNESS, and stands where the CALEDONIAN CANAL reaches the Beauly Firth. Muirtown House, described as "one of the oddest houses in Scotland", was built in the 18th and early 19th cents. and is a mixture of castellated, Roman Doric, Moorish, and Gothic architecture; it stands above the canal, E. of Clachnaharry village. A plaque by the poet Robert Southey is built into the wall of the canal offices on the S. side of the main road.

A monument stands at the W. end of the village commemorating the clan battle between the Mackintoshes and the Munros fought in 1454.

CLACKMANNAN, *Clackmannanshire* (Map 2, ref. 29²69²), between ALLOA and KINCARDINE Road Bridge, is in name the county town of Scotland's smallest county, but does not in fact function as a burgh. Noted historically for associations with the Bruce family, the town contains some interesting architectural antiquities. Clackmannan Tower, built and altered between the late 14th and 17th cents., is still relatively well preserved, under the care of the Ministry of Public Building and Works, despite some structural deterioration due to subsidence. King's Seat Hill, on which the tower stands, was the site of a royal hunting lodge in medieval times. In a later mansion-house (now demolished) that stood beside the tower, Mrs Bruce of Clackmannan, in 1787, "knighted" Robert Burns with the sword of King Robert Bruce. Within the town, a few examples of attractive domestic architecture have been restored. The bell-tower of a 17th-cent. tolbooth survives in the main street, and adjoining it are the Burgh Cross and Clack-Mannan or King's Stone. (Clack-Mannan is sometimes derived as Stone of Manau – the ancient name of the district around the upper reaches of the Firth of FORTH.)

CLASHNESSIE, *Sutherland* (Map 5, ref. 20⁶93⁰). Formerly a prosperous crofting township, Clashnessie is now reduced in population. The small township stands on the W. coast of Sutherland 8 m. N. of LOCHINVER. There is a fine sandy bay with good bathing and extensive views of the coast and of the mainland mountains. The "Long Island" (the Outer Hebrides) may be seen far out in the Atlantic from the road by Clashnessie.

CLATTERINGSHAWS, *Kirkcudbright-shire* (Map 2, ref. 25⁵57⁶). Where formerly the shallow Black Water of Dee flowed over a gravel bed as it left Moss Raploch, now much

of this remote valley among the high Galloway hills – flanked on the S. by Cairnsmore of Fleet – is filled by a great lake held back by the Galloway hydro-electric dam, 1,470 ft long and looming 78 ft above the NEW GALLOWAY to NEWTON STEWART road. The water goes by tunnel and pipeline 4 m. to Glenlee Power Station on the banks of the Ken, which came into commercial production in 1935.

Westward from here the road runs through a long winding valley among fine hill scenery, now improved by afforestation, and near the line of the 18th-cent. Military Road.

Some 4½ m. SW. of Clatteringshaws a monument to Alexander Murray, D.D., stands on a roadside hillock. A shepherd boy, he became the foremost linguist of his day and Professor of Oriental Languages at EDINBURGH University, having acquired much of his knowledge by reading while still a shepherd. He had little formal education. Born in 1775, he became Minister of Urr in 1806, and was appointed Professor at Edinburgh in 1812. He died, still young, of tuberculosis.

A fine waterfall, named (like several others in S. Scotland) the Grey Mare's Tail, can be seen near the monument.

CLAVA, *Inverness-shire* (Map 5, ref. 27⁶84⁴). At Balnuaran of Clava is a group of three chambered tombs that gives the name Clava to fifty or so similar structures in the district. They lie on the SE. bank of the R. Nairn, 6 m. SE. of INVERNESS and 1 m. SE. of CULLODEN MOOR.

The centre is an annular cairn enclosing an apparently unroofed area into which there is no formal means of access. The outer ones are corbelled passage graves in round cairns. All three are set within circles of free standing stones of heights varying from 1 ft to 7 ft 6 in.

CLEISH, *Kinross-shire* (Map 2, ref. 30⁸69⁸), is a village that stands in the valley of Gairney Water below the Cleish hills. The site of the church is thought to date from a very early connection with the Culdees settlement at St Serf's Island on the nearby Loch LEVEN. A building older than the present one, and later destroyed by fire, was much visited by Sir Walter Scott when at BLAIRADAM as the guest of John Adam, a descendant of the great architectural family.

The obelisk at the side of the Kelty–KINROSS road at Gairneybridge, 2 m. E. of Cleish village, marks the site of an inn where, under the leadership of Ebenezer Erskine, minister of the West Kirk of STIRLING, the Act was signed in 1733 that founded the "Associate Presbytery" and brought about the "Original Secession", after the Establishment of the Church of Scotland under the Union of 1707.

CLICKHIMIN, *Shetland* (Map 8, ref. 44⁸14¹), is a loch and broch on the S. outskirts of LERWICK, on the Mainland, SHETLAND Northern Islands (*see* "The Shape of Scotland"). Recent excavation has discovered an early settlement by this loch. It forms a memorial of the remote past nearly as impressive as those at JARLSHOF (also on Shetland). The ruins are now under the preservation of the Ministry of Public Building and Works, and to the visitor are the most easily understood of all Shetland's remains. There is an official guide-book.

CLOCH POINT, *Renfrewshire* (Map 2, ref. 22⁰67⁷). This lighthouse, 76 ft high, built in 1796, and run by the Clyde Lighthouse Trust, stands on the roadside between GOUROCK and INVERKIP and looks across to the light on the Gantock rocks of DUNOON. In wartime the boom from Cloch to the Gantocks regulated and defended CLYDE shipping.

CLOVENFORDS, *Selkirkshire* (Map 3, ref. 34⁵63⁷). The township of Clovenfords, 3 m. W. of GALASHIELS, stands off Caddon Water. The inn now in use there replaces an older one in which Walter Scott used to stay, when he acted as Sheriff of SELKIRK and before he had a home of his own in the Border country, first at Ashiestiel and then at ABBOTSFORD. He used to come down from EDINBURGH to the Sheriff Court, and a statue of him to commemorate his visits stands outside. Wordsworth also stayed there in 1803. Nearby was the famous TWEED vineyard started by William Thomson, then gardener to the Duke of Buccleuch, in 1868, and carried on by the Thomson family until it was closed.

From Clovenfords can be seen Ashiestiel, the house on the S. bank of the Tweed where Scott lived as Sheriff 1804–12.

CLYDE, River, *Lanarkshire* to *Buteshire* (Map 2, ref. 28²65⁰), with its odd combination of beauty and industrial ugliness does not fall far short of the TWEED in the romantic feelings it arouses, especially amongst the folk of GLASGOW. In a sense they made it, by deepening it and shaping it. It made them by opening up for their city the great trade to the Americas after the Union of 1707.

Clyde rises in the southern uplands of Scotland by LEADHILLS as a mere trickle, yet in under 100 m. it is able to berth some of the biggest liners in the world. Its total length is 106 m., and its drainage area is about 1,481 sq. m.

In its headwaters, as soon as it achieves stream or near-river status in the moorland, Clyde is extremely pellucid. This makes it a very difficult river to angle in, for its highly worthwhile brown trout – at one time salmon used to ascend Clyde, but it must be a century and a half since any salmon was able to force its way through Glasgow. So shy, however, are the trout in the clear waters of upper Clyde, that the art of catching them is almost confined to local inhabitants who know their ways. Until recently (indeed, the practice may still be obscurely in existence), the locals found gut and nylon too coarsely visible, and they used hairs from the long tails of horses.

These they got from the famous Clydesdale horses that are bred a little lower down the river. The Clydesdale district is celebrated also for its orchards and fruit-growing.

From LANARK and NEW LANARK it begins to serve the industrial purposes of man in driving mills. Thereafter it prepares itself for the change in its style and situation that has made it world-famous.

In the 18th cent. the growing city of Glasgow realized that in Clyde it had a gateway to the New World that, if properly treated, would make it unique in Western Europe. The little salmon river in what Defoe called the "prettiest" cathedral city was (as shall be described in the entry under GLASGOW) eventually dredged, deepened, and made navigable as far as the heart of the city. It was this feat that primarily caused the conversion of the place into the great industrial centre we know today. It was this feat also that led to Clydeside's becoming in the 19th cent. the greatest shipbuilding centre in the world.

But romance did not leave the river. Glasgow folk not only took a great pride in their now industrial river, but achieved strong feelings for it as expressed in the "MacAndrew's Hymn" of Kipling. Not even the Liverpool people have quite the same devotion to the Mersey as Glasgow has for its ship-bearing, ship-making river of Clyde.

Clyde too became the great holiday outlet for the people of Glasgow. Excursions "doon the watter" were the most popular day-holiday ventures of the late 19th cent. They still are popular. The Firth of Clyde, with its islands and W. Highland scenery nearby, is one of the most attractive estuaries in the world.

Estuary or firth it may be, but the Glasgow folk still think and speak of it as the Clyde. The river thus has three forms of existence – the pellucid upper waters full of fine but unusually shy trout, the industrial city river receiving and making great ships, and finally the holiday estuary. All these are essentially of the Clyde.

CLYDEBANK, *Dunbartonshire* (Map 2, ref. 25⁰67⁰). In 1871, the now well-known site of the Clydebank was occupied only by a farm. Late in that year James and George Thomson had to move from Govan and chose this ground for a shipyard just opposite the mouth of the R. Cart; the first ship was launched in 1872, and the population began to leap in size – by 1881 there were 1,634 inhabitants. In 1882 the American firm of Singers set up a sewing-machine factory at Kilbowie, and the place grew round "the yard" and "the factory". Clydebank achieved burgh status in 1886.

In 1899 Thomson's was acquired by John Brown and Co. from Sheffield. Among the ships that were built by this famous company at Clydebank were the Lusitania (launched 1906), the Queen Mary (launched 1934), the Queen Elizabeth (launched 1938), and the revolutionary Queen Elizabeth 2, launched by Her Majesty on the 20th of September 1967.

The burgh was almost completely destroyed by bombing in 1941. Only eight houses in the burgh were undamaged; 4,300 were destroyed or damaged beyond repair. The chance to rebuild immediately after the hostilities was rapidly taken up.

CLYNDER, *Dunbartonshire* (Map 2, ref. 22⁵68⁵). Apart from farming, the main industry of this village on the W. shore of the Gare Loch opposite R H U is boat-building. The Hatton-burn yard is a family affair that has become world-famous for the making of yachts. Since 1911 it has been controlled by the family of Ewen McGruer.

In the 19th cent. Clynder was apparently a favourite place to set out beehives, as the district was especially rich in nectar and pollen.

COATBRIDGE, *Lanarkshire* (Map 2, ref. 27⁴66⁵). The prosperity of Coatbridge was originally based on coal. Early good communications, however, quickly developed its potential. In 1791 the Monkland Canal opened G L A S G O W as a market for coal, and in consequence there were 435 miners in Monkland parish in 1793. Finally, as a real stroke of luck, the first railway in Scotland to be constructed since the power of steam was discovered passed through Coatbridge in 1826.

Ironstone deposits were found here at the beginning of the last century. By 1830 there were seven blast furnaces in Coatbridge. Early workers came from Staffordshire, later from Ireland and elsewhere. The ironstone band was exhausted by about 1870. Tube-making was started in 1844, but in 1934 many employees went S. with the firm to Corby, Northants. The furnaces are now fired by local gas, which engenders much less smoke. Coatbridge achieved burgh status in 1885.

COCKBURNLAW, *Berwickshire* (Map 3, ref. 37⁷65⁹). Some 4 m. N. of D U N S, and lying on the NE. flank of the hill of Cockburn-law, is Edinshall Fort, broch, and settlement. The first structure, a fort, dates from just before or just after the Christian era and lies on a sloping site apparently without defences. The broch dates from the early 2nd cent. A.D. It is the only one here of ten similar brochs built N. of the T W E E D and lying in the country of the Votadini. The broch measures 55 ft in diameter, the walls being 17 ft thick, with three sets of chambers in addition to guardrooms at either side of the entrance passage. Finally there is an open settlement, dating from the

later 2nd cent. onwards, represented by lengths of walling and circular stone foundations.

COCKBURNSPATH, *Berwickshire* (Map 3, ref. 37⁸67¹). The village of Cockburnspath stands about 1 m. inland, and was built originally round a market square. In its centre still stands the cross; it has a carved top with thistles on the E. and W. faces, and roses on the N. and S. The church is near the S. end of the square, and, though the interior is modernized, it may date from the 14th cent. It has a round tower in the middle of the W. gable, with a wheel stair inside rising to 30 ft above the church roof, probably dating from the late 16th or early 17th cent.

A little SE. lies Pease Bay, a beautiful sandy beach at the end of the very steep valley of Pease Dean. This used to be a great danger point on the old road. Pease Bridge, built right over the valley in 1786 (300 ft long, 16 ft wide, and nearly 130 ft high), was said to have been the highest bridge in the world when built.

To the N. of the village in the grounds of Dunglass House is Dunglass Collegiate Church, founded in 1450 by Sir Alexander Hume; it has a central tower, nave, choir, transepts, and sacristy. The interior embellishments are very rich. This Collegiate Church held out against the invading English in 1544, but in the 18th cent. it declined into the status of a stable. It has now been rescued and is cared for.

COCKENZIE, *East Lothian* (Map 3, ref. 34⁰67⁵). As at H U N T E R S T O N, Scotland's traditional past mingles with the present and future at Cockenzie, a village on the Firth of F O R T H between P R E S T O N P A N S and P O R T S E T O N. As an old fishing village, it was the centre of herring, white-fish, and even whale fishing. Cockenzie also took part in the salt-manufacture for which Prestonpans was known. The village still has a boat-building yard, two harbours, and a fishing fleet. Since 1813 the Fisherman's Friendly Society has organized an annual festival or "walk" on the third Friday in September.

It is perhaps significant of the future that was (and is) to come, that Cockenzie should have had the distinction of possessing the earliest railway in Scotland; this railway, constructed on wooden blocks, was used to take coals from T R A N E N T to the boat-shore by the village. Being built in 1722, this was, of course, a railway long before the age of steam. Now Cockenzie has passed into an age in which steam power has become old-fashioned. As under H U N T E R S T O N, we here salute the future of Cockenzie and the present of electricity-generating, which has established itself here.

Cockenzie Generating Station is situated on the Firth of Forth immediately W. of the village from which it takes its name and has an installed capacity of 1,200 mW. The four turbine-boiler units were commissioned during the period 1966 to 1968, and now feed into the national 275 kW. grid system. The site of the station was selected to take advantage of the Lothian coalfields and existing railway facilities for the supply of coal to the station, which, at peak consumption, is 3,000,000 tons per year. The sea-water used for cooling purposes is drawn through culverts extending 450 ft into the Firth of Forth, and circulated at the rate of 500,000 gallons per minute. Notable features of the station are the two 500-ft-high chimneys and the public promenade round the sea-wall of the site. Adjacent ground previously occupied by Prestonlinks Colliery has been landscaped to provide additional recreational ground and links giving access to the sea.

During the life of the station, over 5,000,000 tons of ash will be produced and pumped through pipelines laid along the foreshore to settling ponds at MUSSELBURGH, where some 350 acres of ground will be reclaimed from the sea.

In the year 1970–1 Cockenzie generated 4,809,450 million units with a load factor of 47·7 per cent, and in March 1971 the station had a maximum available output capacity of 1,152,000 kW. of its 1,200,000 kW. capacity.

COCKPEN, *Midlothian* (Map 3, ref. 33¹66⁴). The church of Cockpen was originally a chapel under NEWBATTLE; in its sheltered setting, the ruined church dates from the 13th cent. John Knox's brother William and his nephew were both ministers of the kirk here after the Reformation. The first Marquess of Dalhousie (1812–60), a famous Viceroy of India, lies buried here. Dalhousie Castle, although modernized out of recognition, dates from the 12th cent.

Most people have heard of Cockpen through Lady Nairne's song "The Laird o' Cockpen". The hero of the song was probably Mark

Carse, who was a 17th-cent. laird here. History reveals that the lady married him in the end.

COLDINGHAM, *Berwickshire* (Map 3, ref. 39⁰66⁶). Desolate Coldingham moor was once a great hazard for travellers to the N. and S. The village at the S. edge of the moor clustered round a priory that had been founded by Edgar King of Scots in 1098, probably as a parish church, and becoming later a priory for Benedictines from Durham in the early 12th cent. The priory was plundered by King John of England in 1216, and fired by the English in 1544, but the wind changed in time to prevent its destruction. Cromwell in passing did, however, inflict some further damage.

The priory was originally cruciform, but only the N. and E. walls of the choir and sanctuary and some fragments of the S. transept survived its various ordeals. In 1662 the S. and W. walls of the choir were reconstructed, and the spot was again used as a place of worship. There have been further reconstructions since 1854, and in the course of them some sculptured stones were found nearby.

At Coldingham loch (famous for its very large brown trout – the record is said to have weighed 14 lbs) is a settlement showing how the pattern of grouped stone houses was developed at a disused pre-Roman Iron Age site.

COLDSTREAM, *Berwickshire* (Map 3, ref. 38⁴64⁰). This burgh on the N. bank of the R. TWEED is often the first town in Scotland visitors from the South encounter; it stands where the old ford crossed at the mouth of the R. Leet. The ford ceased to be used in 1766, when John Smeaton constructed the Coldstream Bridge, near to the "Old Marriage House" that is like the one at GRETNA.

On the N. side of the square the original H.Q. of the Coldstream Guards was established in 1659. The regiment was by no means

Coldingham cliffs

raised here; it had been with General Monk since the 1650s. From Coldstream the Guards set out for London in 1660 and brought about the restoration of Charles II. They paraded in London and formally became the King's men, but got the nickname of the place from which their march had started. The old colours were laid up in the parish church in 1921.

Some 2 m. NW. is The Hirsel, the seat of the Earls of Home. In 1963 the 14th Earl, who had been foreign secretary, relinquished the title to become Prime Minister (1963–4) as Sir Alec Douglas-Home. The Hirsel contains a lake that is a wildfowl sanctuary; and Dundock Wood, also in the policies, is said to have a greater variety of birds than any other wood of the same size in Britain.

COLINSBURGH, *Fife* (Map 3, ref. 34⁷70³). This village was founded by and named after Colin, 3rd Earl of Balcarres, about 1705, on his return from fighting in the Low Countries during voluntary exile for the Stuarts. He established the village for the soldiers who had fought with him, and he built it at the gates of Balcarres House, the seat of the Lindsays. Balcarres House dates from 1595, but was largely altered in the mid-19th cent. The formal and box gardens are second only to those at Drummond Castle.

The folly or tower on Balcarres Crag to the NW. is a notable example of 19th-cent. architectural eccentricity.

COLINTRAIVE, *Argyll* (Map 1, ref. 20⁴67⁴). This small holiday resort, on the Kyles of BUTE at their narrowest part, has a car ferry to Rhubodach at the N. end of BUTE. Traditionally this was the place where cattle swam across from Bute on the way to markets on the mainland. Feuing early in the century led to the establishment of villas along the coast.

COLL, Island of, *Argyll* (Map 4, ref. 11⁰75⁵), is one of the Inner Hebrides (*see* "The Shape of Scotland"). It lies just about halfway down this group's stretch from N. to S. Coll lies 7 m. W. from the nearest point of the large island of MULL. It is reached by steamer from OBAN. Its trend is from NE. to SW. It is 12 m. long and has an average breadth of 4 m. Its surface is undulating, but nowhere reaches a greater height than 339 ft. Its E. coast, by which the visitor usually approaches it, is forbiddingly rocky, but no sooner has one penetrated it by its small port of Arinangour (the only township on the island) than one perceives the rich, grassy, and arable – as well as mossy and peat-covered – land lying behind the eastern wall of rock. Along the W. beach stretch bays of silvery-gold sand, embracing the peacock-coloured sea, the equal of any in the Inner Hebrides.

At the S. end of the island at Breacacha stand the ruins of the old fortress-castle of the Macleans, one time lairds of Coll. Beside it there is that rarity, a dull and unpleasing 18th-cent. building. Rightly dismissed by Dr Johnson, on his famous and happy visit to Coll, as a "tradesman's box", it was put up by the Macleans in 1750 when they found their old castle uninhabitable.

Coll shares the history of the rest of the Hebrides in passing from prehistory into Scottish history by way of Norse and Gaelic possession. Many of the island lochs, in which brown trout abound, display signs of Coll's past, in the "duns", or small water-surrounded fortresses, to which inhabitants would retreat when their island was invaded from the sea.

The population of this quietly attractive island has declined. Originally the reason was eviction, but the more recent trend from this by no means unproductive land is less easy to explain. At the beginning of last century it supported nearly 2,000 people, but now it has only about 200. Today there is therefore little, if any, "taking in of visitors".

There is, however, a hotel at Arinangour, and there are various camping sites. For all its loss of population, Coll does not, after the manner of other denuded places in the W., breed an air of melancholy. It is a good place for a holiday-maker to dream away a midsummer season in angling for lively brown trout, never very small, nor very large, but just the right size.

COLLIESTON, *Aberdeenshire* (Map 6, ref. 40⁴82⁸), is a quaint and primitive fishing village in the parish of SLAINS 15 m. N. of ABERDEEN on the rocky slopes of a sandy cove, between high and picturesque cliffs with many spectacular caves. It is traditionally famous for "speldins", small fish that are split, salted, and dried in the sun. Between 1840 and 1871 the population rose from 167 to 442. The pier and small harbour were built in 1894. The speldins, at one time dried on hooks attached to rails on the Peerman Braes, and later at every cottage door, have gone for ever. But the village now flourishes as a holiday resort with many weekend cottages; as a result of which the permanent winter population has dwindled to 159.

On a mound to the N. of the village is the Kirk of Slains, a modern building erected in 1806 after a spartan period during which the congregation worshipped in the kirkyard, where, in Erroll's Aisle, the earls and countesses of Erroll were buried from 1585 to 1758. Near the door of the kirk is the gravestone of Philip Kennedy, most famous of the smugglers of the 18th cent. He was fatally injured a mile from Collieston by an exciseman who was afterwards tried and acquitted of murder in 1798. Kennedy's cloven skull, it is said, was repeatedly dug up in excavating graves for the many other Kennedys buried here. John Skelton's novel *The Crooked Meg* celebrates the most famous of the Slains smuggling luggers. Near the manse is a splendidly preserved dovecot, where pigeons were reared to supply food for the large manse household at the end of hard winters. A traditional dance known as the "lang reel of Collieston" was danced at every fisher wedding in the village. Modern Collieston owes much to a distinguished son of the village, Sir Douglas Ritchie, who was vice-chairman of the Port of London Authority from 1946 to 1955.

COLMONELL, *Ayrshire* (Map 2, ref. 21⁵58⁶). The local pronunciation of this name is "Com-mon-ell". It is a little village above the R. Stinchar about 4 m. from the estuary at BALLANTRAE. For all its comparatively small size, it boasts two kirks and two hotels and several ruined castles: Kirkhill, which bears a date 1589; Craigneil, of which only a fragment of a 13th-cent. tower remains; and Knockdolian, a ruined square tower sitting at the foot of the hill that bears the same name. This hill deserves mention in that it bears the alternative name of False Craig, and local tradition has it that this is because of its dangerous resemblance to AILSA CRAIG, the sentinel of the Firth of CLYDE and a sure guide for mariners. Alas for tradition! Seen from the sea, Knockdolian's bulk is dwarfed and occluded by the higher inland hills. It is only when viewed from the E. against the background of the sea that a resemblance can be traced.

Here is an interesting by-product of place names: Knockdolian – the knock or hill of the storms; False Craig – Follais Creag, the prominent rocky hill. Those familiar with the W. coast will remember the famous McCaig's Folley that crowns the town of OBAN. The word comes from the same root and means the same – "prominent", not "foolishness".

Colmonell is an excellent base from which to explore the lower Stinchar valley from Daljarrock to the sea; and a fascinating valley it is, with much to offer to the antiquarian, historian, and naturalist. Thanks to its disturbed history, it is strewn with interesting ruins – mostly the ancient fortresses of the Kennedies of Bargany (". . . Auld Castles grey, nod to the moon"); in scenic beauty it is unrivalled. For the angler, the salmon and sea-trout abound in waters that can be fished by payment, and, on those days when the river is "in guid order", the sport can be most gratifying.

COLONSAY and **ORONSAY,** *Argyll* (Map 1, refs. 13⁸69⁵, 13⁴68⁸), are two islands in the Inner Hebrides (*see* "The Shape of Scotland"). These small islands to the W. of JURA are separate islands only at high tide. At low water they are joined. Colonsay has a pier and is linked by steamer service to TARBERT, Argyll.

Colonsay House to the N. is noted for its characteristically W. Highland or Hebridean sub-tropical garden. On Oronsay are the ruined remains of a 14th-cent. priory. Long before the building of the priory, however, this island must have been used by the Monks of St Columba. It is an error, however, to link the name of the island with that of St Oran, an early Columban follower. The word Oronsay is Norse in origin and means "tidal place". Slightly changed, it appears in other Hebridean districts once occupied by the Norsemen.

COLVEND, *Kirkcudbrightshire* (Map 2, ref. 28⁶55⁴). A pleasant hilly, rocky, coastal parish with fine cliffs, sandy beaches, and romantic scenery culminating in the Urr estuary to the W. The little resorts of Sandyhills, ROCKCLIFFE, and KIPPFORD, with Portling and Portowarren, are its principal settlements. Barnbarroch and Caulkerbush are even smaller, Caulkerbush being in the former parish of Southwick, now amalgamated with Colvend. In the extreme W. of the joint parish is the village of Mainsriddle.

The rough little hills -- the Bainloch (900 ft), Maidenpap (1,000 ft), Cuil Hill (1,350 ft, a spur of Criffel), and the little Muckle Hill above Rockcliffe – command splendid views. The White Hill, terminating in high cliffs W. of Portowarren, is a spectacular viewpoint on a clear day, with the Cumberland mountains spread out across the Solway.

Southwick Old Church, nestling under Clifton Crags, contains some medieval work. King Edward I of England gave 15s. to "Our Lady of Suthayc" when he passed there in 1300.

Much of the inland part of the parish is now forested, and this includes the pleasant secluded lochs of Barean, Ironhash, and White Loch.

COMRIE, *Perthshire* (Map 2, ref. 27⁷72²). This attractive holiday centre lies in upper Strathearn between CRIEFF and ST FILLANS. Comrie, in Gaelic Combruith, means the coming together of streams, and one of the charms of the place is that it stands at the confluence of the Earn, the Lednock, and the Ruchill Water.

There are delightful walks. The path up the Lednock leads to the Deil's Cauldron and beyond to Spout Rollo, and there are other waterfalls in Glen Turret and Glen Boltachan.

Above the Deil's Cauldron a path leads to the summit of Dunmore Hill and the monument to Henry Dundas, Viscount Melville of Dunira. He was the son of Robert Dundas of ARNISTON, Lord President of the Court of Session. The mansion-house of Dunira, W. of Comrie, was severely damaged by fire many years ago and is now demolished.

Comrie has achieved a certain notoriety as being subject to earthquake shocks, though none have been felt for many years. The earthquakes are due to the fact that Comrie lies exactly on the Highland "fault". The first recorded earthquake occurred in 1789 and was accompanied by a great deal of noise. The worst shocks were in 1839, with twenty in twenty-four hours. But no severe damage has ever resulted, and no one has ever been killed.

In the 18th cent., and the early 19th, cattle-drovers came over the hill from Ardeonaig on Loch TAY to Glen Lednock, and Telford, in his Fifth Report to the Commissioners for Highland Roads and Bridges of 1811, refers to the "new road through Glen Lednock to Comrie". But the road was never built, and the track is now used only by pony-trekkers and hikers.

Dundurn is an isolated rock that juts out of the flat land by the Earn just over 4 m. W. of Comrie. The summit has been ingeniously fortified by a series of walls that link the rocky outcrops.

There is an almost obliterated Roman fort at Dalginross and also a group of prehistoric standing stones, one of which is cup-marked.

CONNEL FERRY, *Argyll* (Map 1, ref. 19¹73³). This village has grown from two inns originally at each side of an important ferry. The ferry was very short, but dangerously narrow, being situated at the place where Loch ETIVE enters the Firth of Lorne, thus causing a strong current at flood tide. The Atlantic positively races into the loch at ebb tide, and is responsible for the Falls of Lora.

The railway to OBAN from the N. and E. was built in 1880, and a branch line with a bridge at Connel was built in 1903. The bridge was later widened to include a toll-track for cars.

CONON BRIDGE, *Ross and Cromarty* (Map 5, ref. 25⁵85⁵). A bridge thus named stands at the crossing of the R. Conon, 2½ m. SW. of DINGWALL. The bridge, with an old toll-house at the N. end, was built in 1809 by Thomas Telford. Lately it had to be strengthened for the heavy traffic going to the atomic station at DOUNREAY in Caithness. The river is notable for salmon fishing.

About 1 m. S. of Conon Bridge is Kinkell Castle, which once belonged to the Mackenzies of Gairloch; it is a typical T-plan castle and has not had to endure alteration. Sadly, it is now unoccupied.

CONTIN, *Ross and Cromarty* (Map 5, ref. 24⁶85⁵). At the crossing of the R. Blackwater, 3 m. SW. of STRATHPEFFER, stands the village of Contin. An old coaching inn at Achilty on the W. side of the river dates back to the days when this was the start of rough routes to POOLEWE and ULLAPOOL on the W. coast. These roads were built in the 1760s and the 1790s. The Bridge at Contin was put up by Telford; the first newly-built one was swept away by flood in 1811, but was at once replaced.

There is a modern expansion of the village in the form of stone houses built by the Hydro-Electric Board for the workers on the nearby Conon, Orrin, Fannich, and Luichart schemes. They are made of the pink stone from Tarradale on the BLACK ISLE.

The horse fair at Contin once attracted buyers from the North of England, who found this fair a useful source for collecting sturdy ponies for work underground in the pits.

The Falls of Rogie, on the Blackwater 2 m. NW. of Contin, are easily reached by a path from Contin on the GARVE road.

CORPACH, *Inverness-shire* (Map 5, ref. 21⁰77⁷). This growing village lies just NW. of FORT WILLIAM and across the R. Lochy, Corpach Moss, and the CALEDONIAN CANAL. To the SE. is the modern community of Caol, and to the W. the township of Annat.

The Church of Kilmallie in Corpach has a parish unusually large even for the Highlands – 60 m. long and 30 m. across. The churchyard contains an obelisk to Colonel John Cameron of Fassifearn, killed at Quatre Bras in 1815; the inscription on it is attributed to Sir Walter Scott.

The £20,000,000 pulp and paper mill that went into production in 1966 has its own port on Loch Eil to take 16,000-ton ships and employs more than 2,000 men.

CORRAN, *Inverness-shire* (Map 5, ref. 18⁶80⁹). The Ferry here at Corran, at the narrows of Loch Linnhe, nearly 9 m. W. of FORT WILLIAM, saves a drive of over 40 m. round the head of the loch. It is used by travellers to the ARDGOUR district coming from the E. A lighthouse stands at the entrance to the narrows.

CORRIE, *Buteshire* (Map 1, ref. 20²64³), is a hamlet on the NW. coast of the Island of ARRAN (*see* "The Shape of Scotland"). This little place has considerable charm and is the haunt of Scottish artists. Its picturesque white cottages lie near to the mouth of the well-known Glen Sannox. It has a golf course and a small harbour, and, though lying on the main road round the island not far from BRODICK, is secluded. It also has a hotel. Corrie contains in miniature much that is characteristic of W. Highland and near-Hebridean scenery.

CORRIESHALLOCH GORGE, *Ross and Cromarty* (Map 5, ref. 22¹87⁸), is a spectacular geological fault by the roadside on the way W. from INVERNESS to ULLAPOOL. The ravine itself is a sheer plunge of some 200 ft and about 1 m. long. Pleasantly wooded paths lead to a suspension bridge, which gives a breathtaking bird's-eye view of the chasm and also opens up the view to the Falls of Measach sweeping down into the head of the gorge.

CORRIEVRECHAN, *Argyll* (Map 1, ref. 17°70¹). This famous ocean whirlpool lies between the island of Scarba and the N. coast of JURA, and is caused by the movement of the tides constricted between two obstinate pieces of land. Even today boats enter the strait only in dead calm and at the right state of tide. The sound of "boiling" can be heard at some distance, and has entered Celtic mythology by the legend of Breacon, Prince of Lochlann, and the daughter of the Lord of the Isles, in which that phenomenon of nature was used as a ballad by Scott. Sequences of Corrievrechan appeared in the film *I Know Where I'm Going.*

Scarba to the N. of the channel is a circular island about 3 m. across, rising to 1,500 ft.

CORRIEYAIRACK PASS, *Inverness-shire* (Map 5, ref. 23°79⁷). This famous section of the military road from DALWHINNIE to FORT AUGUSTUS was built under General Wade in 1731–4. Wade was the great road-constructor who opened up the Highlands after the failure of the Jacobite Rising of 1715. Posterity was to benefit, but many Highlanders of the time did not like the roads. They seemed to take away their privacy and render them more vulnerable. The summit of the pass rises to 2,507 ft, and on the E. the approach had seventeen traverses, later reduced to thirteen. Each was buttressed on the outside by a stone wall 10 ft to 15 ft high and flanked on the inside by a drain.

It was ironical (for the Hanoverians at least) that the pass was first put to use in any major way when Prince Charles Edward Stuart led his Jacobite Highland army through it, crossing from W. to E. after raising his standard at GLENFINNAN in August 1745.

The pass-road remained in general use for about 100 years, but Highland cattle-drovers, who had used the pass long before Wade, continued to drive their beasts through it until the end of the 19th cent.

CORRIMONY HOUSE, *Inverness-shire* (Map 5, ref. 23⁷83⁰), is at the head of Glen Urquhart, 8 m. W. of DRUMNADROCHIT. It was once the seat of the Grants of Corrimony, but it was burnt down (not in warfare) and is now a ruin.

Beside the R. Enrick is a passage grave of the Clava group excavated in 1952. It is circular, with a diameter of 60 ft and a height of nearly 8 ft. It is enclosed within a free-standing circle of eleven stones.

CORROUR, *Inverness-shire* (Map 5, ref. 24³76⁸). One of the most romantically, or perhaps one should say desolately, placed features of British Rail, this lonely railway siding stands in the centre of the huge wastes of RANNOCH MOOR with no road within 8 m. Loch Treig is to the NW. and Loch Ossian to the E. of Corrour.

CORUISK, Loch, *Inverness-shire* (Map 4, ref. 14°82⁰), is on the Island of SKYE in the Inner Hebrides (*see* "The Shape of Scotland"). This celebrated but forbidding loch lies at the S. foot of Skye's great CUILLIN Hills. It can with difficulty be approached on foot; and this method does indeed reveal it at its most awesome (the epithet usually applied). Those not capable of strong physical exertion are recommended to take the steamer up the sea-arm of Loch Scavaig from ELGOL. This will put them within easy walking distance of one of the most remarkable sheets of inland water in all Scotland.

COSHIEVILLE, *Perthshire* (Map 2, ref. 27°74⁸), is named after an inn at the junction of roads from ABERFELDY, FORTINGALL, and RANNOCH. The village near this inn is Keltneyburn. Cattle-drovers of the 18th cent. coming from the N. and NW. passed by Coshieville on their way to the FALKIRK and CRIEFF trysts.

N. of the inn is Garth Castle, recently restored and now a private residence. The Castle was one of the strongholds of the notorious "Wolf of Badenoch", son of King Robert II and ancestor of the Stewarts of Garth. The tall keep, built on the edge of a precipitous ravine in the bed of the Keltney Burn, is well seen from the road between Coshieville and KINLOCH RANNOCH.

The modern mansion house of Garth was built in 1838 on the site of the old house by Drumcharry. It now belongs to the Scottish Youth Hostel Association, having been given to them in memory of the officers and men of H.M. Submarine *Odin* lost in the Gulf of Taranto in 1940.

Comrie Castle, now a ruin, the original home of the Menzies family, stands at the bridge across the R. Lyon, a short distance E. of the inn. It was probably begun in the 14th cent. by Thomas Menzies, who died in 1380.

COULIN, *Ross and Cromarty* (Map 5, ref. 19⁸85³). This is the name of the pass leading from Glen Carron to Glen Torridon, on the western side of the watershed.

The private road is closed to motor-cars, but there is a right of way for walkers that provides unrivalled views of BEINN EIGHE, Liathach, and the surrounding country with its pine, birch, heather, bracken, river and loch.

COUPAR ANGUS, *Perthshire* (Map 6, ref. 32³73⁹), is a market town at the centre of an agricultural district that is mostly devoted to the growing of fruit and of seed potatoes.

A Cistercian Abbey (usually the sign of a good agricultural district) was founded at Coupar Angus about 1164, but only part of the gatehouse survives; in the parish church, built on the site of the monastic chapel, are the remains of the nave piers. The Tolbooth Tower

Coylum Bridge

Scottish Tourist Board

dating from 1769 has recently been renovated.

Coupar Angus is a good centre for touring and lies on the verge of the Highlands.

COVESEA, *Moray* (Map 6, ref. 32°87²). This small holiday resort lying on the coast of the Moray Firth between LOSSIEMOUTH and HOPEMAN is noted for its fine, sandy bathing beach, above which rise old red sandstone cliffs of between 60 and 100 ft high. Standing on top of these is a lighthouse built in 1844, and nearby is a popular caravan site. There are several notable caves in the district, one of which is reputed to have been the terminus of an underground passage leading to nearby GORDONSTOUN House. Another is known as the Laird's Stable, and is believed to have been used by Sir Robert Gordon to hide his horses during the Jacobite Rising of 1745. In more recent times it was occupied by a hermit. A third cave nearer Hopeman bears signs of early occupancy, for in the 19th cent. figures of Celtic art such as a half-moon and fish were discovered sculptured in its roof. Offshore a chain of skerries, which was once the scene of many shipwrecks, runs parallel to the coast.

COWDENBEATH, *Fife* (Map 3, ref. 31°69²). Until the mid-19th cent., Cowdenbeath was merely an agricultural township on the road N. from QUEENSFERRY, but about 1850 coal seams began to be worked. The result was that from 1850–1914 the population practically doubled itself every ten years; it was once called the Chicago of Fife. Cowdenbeath achieved burgh status in 1890.

There has been of late an attempt to introduce new industry and to build a new type of community with a better balance. Nearby GLENROTHES has been an inspiration in this.

The Kirk of Beath to the N. of the burgh has been the parish centre since the 13th cent.

COYLTON, *Ayrshire* (Map 2, ref. 24²61⁹). This is a mining village 6 m. E. of AYR on the trunk road to CUMNOCK. The local pit was closed long ago, but employment is maintained at the new Killoch pit 3 m. farther E. The old village has been almost entirely rebuilt by the County Council.

COYLUM BRIDGE, *Inverness-shire* (Map 5, ref. 29°81⁰), near AVIEMORE, is the key point of access to the CAIRNGORMS. From here a Forestry Commission road leads to Loch Morlich with its youth hostel, and to the neighbouring recreational centre of Glenmore Lodge. A further stretch of ski-road ascends to the Cairngorm car park and chair-lift terminal at a height of 2,000 ft. Hill-walking routes for the LAIRIG GHRU and Braeriach via Glen Einich also start at Coylum Bridge. Hotel development has made Coylum Bridge a most convenient residential base for skiers and summer tourists visiting the Cairngorms. The burns that flow out of Glen Einich and the Lairig Ghru meet here to form the R. Druie, which goes on to join the SPEY at Aviemore.

CRAIGELLACHIE, *Banffshire* (Map 6, ref. 32°84⁴), lies some 2 m. E. of ABERLOUR, at the junction of the Fiddich and the SPEY. It is a terraced village with a large hotel, a distillery, and two large cooperages. Undoubtedly the most beautiful village in Banffshire, it faces directly across meadowland and a wooded island on the river to Craigellachie Rock (the Lower Craigellachie as distinct from the Upper Craigellachie at AVIEMORE), which marks the nether boundary of Strathspey and the lands of the Clan Grant, whose war-cry "Stand fast, Craigellachie!" is famous in song and story. Dramatically placed at the base of this precipitous crag, where pine trees spring from every crevice in the naked quartz, is Thomas Telford's famous Craigellachie Bridge, a single-span iron structure forming an arch of gossamer-like tracery over a pool of the Spey, with two circular, stone, battlemented turrets at either end. The bridge, which will be retained as a monument of outstanding architectural interest, has been replaced as the main river-crossing in the area by a new bridge set some distance lower down the river.

Even more photographed than this spectacular bridge is the view up the Spey from Tunnel Brae, about ½ m. along the wooded road from Craigellachie to Aberlour – probably the most majestic of all the many majestic prospects on the Spey valley.

CRAIGENDORAN, *Dunbartonshire* (Map 2, ref. 23²68¹), was originally a pier built in 1883 at the eastern boundary of HELENSBURGH and opposite the TAIL OF THE BANK at the mouth of the CLYDE. The place developed as a result of railway competition. The North British Railway Company had a monopoly of the northern bank of the Clyde, while both the Caledonian and the Glasgow and South Western Company developed the southern bank. The steamer junction with the railway at Craigendoran produced much tourist traffic. Many houses were built after the establishment of the pier, but Craigendoran is really now a suburb of Helensburgh.

CRAIGHOUSE, *Argyll* (Map 1, ref. 15³66⁷), is on the Island of JURA in the Inner Hebrides (*see* "The Shape of Scotland"). The "capital" of the Jura – for so Craighouse may be called – has a pier, and the steamer calls regularly on its way between West Loch Tarbert and PORT ASKAIG on ISLAY. Because of its wonderfully protected anchorage, and because of the many islands in it, this almost land-locked bay is called Small Isles Bay. It is the best port in all the small islands of the Inner Hebrides.

Craighouse itself developed with the increase of the local distillery in 1884. The parish church is at Kilearnadil, just N. of Craighouse.

The "capital" is dominated by the famous Paps of Jura, which stand to the W. of the village and can be seen from many points on the mainland. At Feolin, round the southern tip of Jura, is a passenger ferry to Port Askaig.

CRAIGIE, *Ayrshire* (Map 2, ref. 24²63³). The village of Craigie sits on a crest of high land 3½ m. S. of KILMARNOCK, and is a rural community clustered round an 18th-cent. church. About 1 m. to the SW. are the ruins of Craigie Castle, dating from the early 13th cent., and close by is Barnweil Monument, to

commemorate the traditional burning of the Barns of AYR in 1297 by Sir William Wallace. This monument, which is in the custodianship of the burgh of Ayr, is a tower to which access is given and from which a very fine panoramic view of central and southern Ayrshire may be gained.

CRAIGIEVAR, *Aberdeenshire* (Map 6, ref. 35⁶81⁰). In the secluded, mild, hilly country 4 m. S. of ALFORD, this little gem is the fairy-tale castle *par excellence*. It not only pleases the popular imagination; it delights the expert. "As a testimony of taste," says Mr Stewart Cruden in his book *The Scottish Castle*, "Craigievar ranks with any representative building in Britain. As a work of art it claims a Scottish place in the front rank of European architecture." It is a simple L-plan tower-house, rising straight out of the ground for seven storeys and bursting forth into an efflorescence of delicately-corbelled turrets crowned with simple conical roofs. It was completed in 1626 for a colourful Forbes laird called "Willie the Merchant", who made his money by daring speculations in the Danzig trade. It has no additions, and has been continuously occupied by the Forbes and Forbes-Sempill family ever since, being sold by Lord Sempill to the National Trust for Scotland in 1963.

You enter Craigievar by one route only. Would-be invaders must have been faced with the ramparts, the heavily studded outer door, then the iron grille behind it, and beyond that another studded double door on the first flight of the stone stair leading to the great hall. The hall's groined vault preserves in plaster relief a decoration of raised panels, heraldry, foliage, classical portrait medallions, and elaborate pendants. They were the work of the same

Craigievar Castle

Aberdeen Press and Journal

master craftsman from London who, a few years before, had erected the similar ceiling at MUCHALLS. As at Muchalls, the fireplace in the hall is surmounted by an immense armorial tablet of the royal arms. The hall still boasts the timber screen, universal in feudal days, and the musicians' gallery where pipers or minstrels played. On the arch of the main stair is the Forbes motto: "Do not vaiken sleiping dogs". The second Forbes laird was himself a sort of watchdog. He waged war on the freebooters who infested the hill country on his flank. Seven of them were hanged together at the Cross of EDINBURGH in 1636, while Gilderoy, the most notorious of them all, was brought to book soon after. The similarity of the name has resulted in a traditional confusion, whereby Gilderoy's many exploits in Aberdeenshire are sometimes attributed to Rob Roy Macgregor. (*See* CULTER and DINNET.) The Barony Court records of Craigievar have been preserved in full. Other features of Craigievar are the Queen's bedroom, with its canopied bed and decorated ceiling, and the Blue Room lighted by the windows of the turrets; but the supreme experience at Craigievar is its external aspect.

To quote Stewart Cruden again, it has "a sort of sublimity . . . a serene assurance not communicated by any other tower-house however pleasing. Quite perfect, lightly poised upon the ground, it is the apotheosis of its type."

CRAIGNETHAN CASTLE, *Lanarkshire* (6 m. NW. of LANARK). This castle lies in a romantic situation in a dell overlooking the small R. Nethan. Craignethan was built by Sir James Hamilton of Finnart in the early 16th cent. In consequence of the fact that it became a stronghold for Mary Stuart, Queen of Scots, it was partly demolished by the Protestant party in 1579. It was the model for Tillietudlem in Scott's masterpiece *Old Mortality*.

The outer walls and towers are exceptionally well preserved. The oldest part is the large tower-house; it has an unusual design and is very ornate in its details.

CRAIGNURE, *Argyll* (Map 1, ref. 17³73⁷), is on the Island of MULL, in the Inner Hebrides (*see* "The Shape of Scotland"). At the S. end of Mull, this is now the port of the new vehicle ferry from OBAN and LOCHA-LINE; it will obviously become the point of entry to the island for many, though at present it is little more than a pier and an inn. The early entry to the island was at Grass Point, near the mouth of Loch Don, about 3 m. S. of Craignure and beyond DUART CASTLE. A ferry used to cross to Grass Point from Kerrera, the island opposite the bay of Oban, and a passenger boat still crosses occasionally. A short crossing here was much used by drovers, who made the cattle swim across. The old Drovers' Inn still stands.

CRAIGOWER HILL, *Perthshire* (Map 5, ref. 29⁵76⁰), which lies N. of PITLOCHRY, rises to a height of 1,300 ft and is reached by an easy and pleasant walk across the golf course. It commands extensive views S. as far as the Lomonds in Fife and W. to SCHIEHALLION and GLENCOE beyond. It also presents a bird's-eye view of Pitlochry with the wooded valley of the Tummel, Loch Faskally, and the Pass of KILLIECRANKIE. The National Trust for Scotland has acquired eleven acres of the hill.

CRAIG PHADRIG, *Inverness-shire* (Map 5, ref. 26¹84³). This famous hill-fort, 1½ m. W. of INVERNESS, forms a flat crown to the afforested hill that overlooks the narrows at the E. end of BEAULY Firth. The fort consists of an inner, heavily vitrified wall spread to a thickness of about 30 ft, which encloses an area of 245 ft by 75 ft. An outer wall, also heavily vitrified, lies at a distance varying between 45 ft and 75 ft. The whole hill-top is covered with scrub and bushes, and is surrounded by trees; no details are apparent, but the view from the fort is commanding.

CRAIL, *Fife* (Map 3, ref. 36²70⁷). The most easterly of Fife ports, Crail is a fishing town situated on a rocky coast. It is a highly picturesque little village in itself and has a fine view of the Lothian coast across the Firth of FORTH to the S. Many artists come here.

Crail burgh was an important trading and fishing port until the 17th cent., when it suffered a mercantile setback coupled with an attack of the plague. In the 18th cent. it was the haunt of smugglers, but in the last century it revived as a holiday resort for EDINBURGH people. It still has some crab and lobster fishing.

The parish church dates to the late 12th and early 13th cents., but it is much altered. There is an 8th-cent. Pictish cross slab inside the church, and another one set up in the Victoria Gardens. The tolbooth is partly 16th cent., the upper part having been added later. It has a Dutch bell with the date 1520 and a gilded copper salmon for a weather-vane.

Crail's wide, tree-lined Marketgate contains many small 17th-cent. houses. There is a scheme in operation by which the National Trust for Scotland buys, restores, and sells these houses gradually. The castle walk above the harbour gives views of St Abb's Head in the far E. of Berwickshire.

CRARAE, *Argyll* (Map 1, ref. 20⁰69⁸), is a magnificent woodland garden, regularly open to the public, on the shore of Loch Fyne, lying between IVERARAY and LOCHGILPHEAD. Set round the home of the Campbells of Succoth, this garden and the grounds are at their best when the brilliant variety of rhododendron colour is at its height in late spring; the autumn colours are also an attractive feature. Various

Plate 5   Glamis Castle, Angus (see p. 236)
Scottish Tourist Board

plants have been grown from seed collected on the famous botanical expeditions of Dr Rock and Reginald Farrer. The Crarae forest-garden on the higher ground, with its 100 and more specimen plots of trees growing under forest conditions, was presented to the Forestry Commission in 1955 by the late Sir George Campbell (who died in 1967 and was succeeded as 7th baronet by his son, Ilay Mark). A Neolithic chambered cairn is preserved in the grounds.

CRATHES, *Kincardineshire* (Map 6, ref. 37⁶79⁶). This L-plan tower-house, together with its magnificent early 18th-cent. formal garden and ancient yew hedges, is the most visited showplace owned by the National Trust for Scotland in the NE. The house itself was begun in 1553 and finished in 1596, though it is not now thought that it took forty years to build. The later date appears to commemorate a remodelling of the upper parts by the Bells, a famous Aberdeenshire family of masons, whose handiwork is also to be seen at MIDMAR and at Castle Fraser.

Crathes is the ancestral home of the Burnetts of Leys, and its greatest family treasure is the horn of fluted ivory, with four bands of gilt and three crystals, known as the Horn of Leys and believed to be the original horn of tenure in virtue of which Robert Bruce granted the lands of Leys in the ancient royal forest of DRUM to Alexander Burnard in 1323.

The tower room, the great hall of the Castle, has recovered its original austere dignity since, in the '30s of this century, the walls were stripped by the late Sir James and Lady Burnett. Here are works by Jamesone, the father of Scottish portrait-painting, and a portrait of Bishop Burnet, aider and abetter of Dutch William and author of *A History of My Own Times.* On the second and third floors are bedrooms with ceilings that are a blaze of colour. In 1877 these wonderful painted ceilings saw the light of day again after over a century under lath and plaster. The Chamber of the Muses and the Nine Worthies' Room on the second floor and the Green Lady's Room on the third had each been decorated by Jacobean artists on the same principle.

On the boards between the joists are gaily painted symbolic figures, and on the sides of the joists themselves are inscribed wise saws and descriptive jingles explaining the pictures and delivering little homilies in the manner beloved of James VI and his contemporaries.

At the top of the house, the Long Gallery running across the whole breadth of the building from E. to W. has an oaken ceiling without its peer in Scotland. Delicately carved heraldic shields form the centre-pieces of fine panelling.

One more treasure must be recorded. It is the bed of Alexander Burnett of Leys and Katherine Gordon, the laird and his lady who came to the Castle just after its completion. The last of the

Aberdeen Press and Journal
Crathes Castle: the Great Hall

Burnetts have gone from the ancestral home. But it will always be theirs. Four centuries of an abundant life have stamped an indelible character on the house that belonged to them for so long.

This character is also apparent in the garden, which the late Lady Burnett tended with loving care. The massive Irish yew hedge that encloses it is 260 years old.

CRATHIE, *Aberdeenshire* (Map 6, ref. 32⁶79⁵). This little hamlet is the nearest populated place to BALMORAL Castle, and is principally famous for the parish church attended by the Queen and her family during their residence on Deeside in August and September each year. This kirk, which stands on a high bank on the right or N. side of the North Deeside road just beyond the 49th milestone from ABERDEEN, was opened in June 1895 and was designed in a style reminiscent of the Kirk of ST MONANCE in Fife by the late A. Marshall Mackenzie, the architect of the modern frontage of Marischal College. (The royal pew and the royal porch are in the S. transept.) It replaced a plain, almost barn-like, kirk of the early 19th cent. where Queen Victoria unfailingly attended communion according to the rites of the Church of Scotland, to which she became much devoted. The church contains memorials to various members of the Royal Family, and the gates commemorate King George VI. In the kirkyard beside the ruins of a still older church by the river is the monument erected by Queen Victoria to her servant John Brown, whose house on the other side of the DEE can be seen from this point. Crowds of many thousands make pilgrimage to Crathie on Sundays during the season to see the royal party drive to

Above *The East Links at Dunbar* (*see p. 176*)

Below *Highland cattle in Glencoe* (*see p. 254*)

Aberdeen Press and Journal

Crathie Kirk

church, and an extensive official car park has now been provided for their convenience.

What is probably the best view of Balmoral Castle can be obtained from the road that climbs the hill to the N. of Crathie towards Glengairn, from which it crosses the watershed of Glaschoille (1,805 ft) to Strathdon near Cock Brig.

CRAWFORD, *Lanarkshire* (Map 2, ref. 29⁶62¹). This is yet one more example (HAD-DINGTON is another) of a village once quietly placed, later a route for traffic, and subsequently regaining its quiet by the benevolence of "by-passing"; it is now just off the main GLASGOW–Carlisle road and stands high in grazing country.

On the opposite bank of the CLYDE stands Crawford Castle in a situation to dominate the river valley. In the 13th cent. it was held by the Lindsays, and at the end of the 14th cent. they took the title of the earls of Crawford, which they still hold, coupled with that of Balcarres. In 1488 the Castle went to the Douglas family, and later briefly to James V, who used it as one of his many hunting seats. The Douglases reconstructed the Castle in the late 16th or early 17th cent.

Camps reservoir, at the head of a tributary on the E. of the Clyde, was built with the help of German prisoners of war in the First World War. A stone pillar set up in the village in the late 19th cent. is said to be connected with the Cranston family, former owners of the hotel, who ran the last mail coach in this district.

CRAWFORDJOHN, *Lanarkshire* (Map 2, ref. 28⁸62⁴). Some 4 m. W. of ABINGTON, the township of Crawfordjohn lies between Douglasdale and the CLYDE. The countryside of

grassy hills was described by Dorothy Wordsworth in 1803 as "inhabited solitude", and it has not changed much today. The district was once a favourite hunting country of James V. Some of the best Scottish curling-stones used to be produced from here.

The nomenclature is a unique mixture of surname and christian name. There is record of this little place, with its name as it is today, as far back as the early 14th cent., but we have no detail of exactly how it came about.

CREETOWN, *Kirkcudbrightshire* (Map 2, ref. 24⁸55⁸). This charming village nestles beside the Cree estuary, below the raised-beach cliff and the hills; its position is explained by its older name, Ferrytown of Cree.

Its name was changed at the instance of the local laird, McCulloch of Barholm. It became a burgh of barony in 1792, and at that time it was mainly a seaport with cottage industries, including a mill where the first patent lead shot was made. Early in the 19th cent. granite quarries opened, the stone being used for the Mersey Docks and part of the Thames Embankment; much of it was shipped from nearby CARSLUITH.

Barholm Castle, a particularly charming small tower-castle above the main road near Kirkdale, for a short while sheltered John Knox. The larger Carsluith Castle stands beside the road 2 m. nearer Creetown; it was a seat of the Brouns.

Turning inland from the main road at Kirkdale Bridge, you go up the delightful wooded glen of the Kirkdale Burn to the two great Neolithic courtyard-cairns at Cairnholy. The better-preserved, Cairnholy 1 ("King Galdus's Tomb"), lies beside the road and is 170 ft by 50 ft; the other, a couple of hundred yards farther on, is 70 ft by 40 ft. Both – the survivors of a whole group in the adjoining field – were excavated in 1949.

CREICH, *Sutherland* (Map 5, ref. 26⁴88⁹). The church of Creich, 3 m. SE. of BONAR BRIDGE, serves an enormous Highland parish that stretches 31 m. from SE. to NW., and is 9 m. broad. Near the church is a 7-ft St Dernham's Cross.

A little SE. of the church is a hill-fort with a magnificent site on the peninsula 370 ft above the narrows in Dornoch Firth (*see* DORNOCH), now heavily forested. The summit of the hill is enclosed by a rampart 260 ft by 220 ft at its highest part, and is defended by an inner rampart enclosing an area of 170 ft by 100 ft. A medieval ruin is situated within the inner rampart.

CRIANLARICH, *Perthshire* (Map 2, ref. 23⁹72⁵). This small village, situated at the junction of Glen Falloch, Glen Dochart, and Strath Fillan, is at the centre of rather austere but nonetheless spectacular scenery.

Near Crieff: Loch Ochtertyre

Scottish Tourist Board

Towards the end of the 7th cent. two Celtic monasteries were established in Breadalbane, one at DULL associated with St Adamnan, and the other in Glen Dochart associated with St Fillan. At Kirkton, 3 m. NW. of Crianlarich, wall foundations of St Fillan's Priory are still extant and legend asserts that the saint is buried there.

On an island in Loch Dochart, 1 m. E. of Crianlarich, are the ruins of a castle built by Duncan Campbell of Glenorchy, who lived from 1583 to 1631. In 1645 the castle was burnt by the MacNabs.

CRICHTON, *Midlothian* (Map 3, ref. 33⁸66³). One of the largest and finest Scottish castles, Crichton, standing on a bare site, overlooks the East Lothian R. Tyne. It is a 14th-cent. plain tower-house to which, in the 15th to 17th cents., a group of buildings was added to form a quadrangular mansion enclosing a narrow courtyard. The most spectacular feature is an arcaded range, the upper frontage of which is wrought with faceted stone-work. This was added in the Italianate manner in 1581–91 by the Earl of Bothwell, and is possibly copied from the palace at Ferrara. There is a fine 15th-cent. parish church near the Castle.

An early Iron Age fort at the W. end of the village of Crichton consists of a single heavy rampart making an enclosure of 300 ft by 190 ft.

CRIEFF, *Perthshire* (Map 2, ref. 28⁹72³). Built on a hillside above the R. Earn, Crieff is a town and holiday resort with a sheltered climate. The Knock of Crieff rises to 911 ft N. of the town and has an extensive view. There is a view-indicator. Crieff is a touring centre at the gateway to the Highlands via the SMA'

GLEN and consists of very steep streets and well designed parks, besides containing facilities for golf and fishing.

The town, originally called Drummond, contains a 17th-cent. tolbooth and the octagonal market cross of Drummond, while Crieff Cross, a 10th-cent. carved slab possibly of Runic character, was transferred to its present position from the ancient barony of Strowan. Crieff was burnt to the last house by the Jacobites in January 1716, but after 1731, owing to the efforts of James Drummond, 3rd Duke of Perth, the place was repaired and improved, James Square being laid out and a large linen factory founded, although this last was destroyed in 1745 when also the Drummond estates were forfeited to the Crown (until 1784). The commissioners who were in charge of them set up several industries, such as bleaching and tanning, and the town became an industrial centre until the Industrial Revolution took this to the lowland factories. Later in the 19th cent. villas were built, as well as Strathearn House, the large hydro.

By an Act of Parliament in 1672, the Earl of Perth got an annual cattle market or tryst established. Before that date sales had been at the local markets, but Crieff now became the centre for the whole of Scotland until 1770, when the centre moved to STENHOUSEMUIR near FALKIRK, which, being well placed for both the Highlands and the Lowlands, became the hub of the whole drove-road system.

CRIMOND, *Aberdeenshire* (Map 6, ref. 40⁵85⁷). This village and parish, in flat, almost featureless, farming country on the main road between PETERHEAD and FRASERBURGH, is famous because it gives its name to a very popular psalm-tune – that to which the 23rd

Psalm was sung at the Queen's wedding. The present Crimond church was built in 1812, and it is this church that is associated with the composition of the psalm-tune; but whether by Jessie Seymour Irvine, daughter of the Rev. Alexander Irvine, minister of the parish, or by David Grant of ABERDEEN, and named "Crimond" in Jessie's honour, still remains a matter of debate

Crimond was, however, the origin of another great Scottish tune – the ballad song "Logie o' Buchan". The Logie of the song has nothing to do with the parish of Logie-Buchan near ELLON, but is Logie in Crimond, the home of a strongly Jacobite branch of the Gordon family. The hero of the ballad was the gardener at Logie House, while the heroine was Isobel Keith, who afterwards married a farmer and died in 1826 aged eighty. It is said that the gardener, after leaving or having been dismissed from his service at Logie because Isobel was too susceptible to his charms, took employment with the laird of Kinmundy.

Today Crimond is best known locally for a former R.A.F. aerodrome, now converted into a "skid pan" for racing motorists. But the parish was the site of a former royal burgh, the vanished port of RATTRAY, not far from Rattray Head Lighthouse built in 1893 on the Ron Rock to warn shipping off the notorious Rattray Briggs, a perilous reef. Before its erection, the best safeguard for mariners was the visual warning provided by the distant outline of Mormond Hill.

CRINAN CANAL, *Argyll* (Map 1, ref. 17⁸69⁴). This important canal of 8½ m., running from ARDRISHAIG on Loch Fyne to Crinan on the Sound of JURA, saves what used to be a sea voyage of 130 m. The summit of the Crinan Canal is 64 ft above sea-level and has fifteen locks. This once very useful and still used canal was designed by John Rennie; it was built in 1793–1801 for a private company of gentlemen. It became increasingly important when the CALEDONIAN CANAL was opened in 1822. The herring-fishing boats found it very useful when going from the CLYDE or Loch Fyne to the northern waters, but the canal's overriding importance declined somewhat with the growth of the larger steam vessels. Nevertheless yachts, puffers, and ring-net fishing boats still use its course (a winding one, as canals go) through lush W. Highland scenery. They primarily use it to avoid the long pull round the Mull of Kintyre.

NW. across the bay from the end of the canal stands Duntrune Castle – possibly the oldest inhabited castle in Scotland. It dates back to the late 12th or early 13th cent., and is an L-shaped dwelling with additions made in the 16th cent. It was once a Campbell stronghold, but is now occupied by Lt-Col. George Malcolm of Poltalloch, whose large 19th-cent. mansion at Poltalloch nearby (it had thirty indoor

servants at the beginning of this century) was, of necessity, demolished in 1959.

CROMARTY, *Ross and Cromarty* (Map 5, ref. 27⁹86⁷), has been the centre of administration in a small way for many centuries; it was the heart of the hereditary sheriffdom of the Urquhart family, whose castle stood on a hill above the town. Sir Thomas Urquhart was the most notable and best remembered of that family. He was a pure Scottish eccentric who, half in joke, invented all sorts of fantastic schemes including "an Universal language". He splendidly translated Rabelais, and died in 1660 in an outburst of purely happy laughter on hearing the news of Charles II's restoration.

Cromarty was once a royal burgh, but by 1672, when the port declined, the costs of upholding this status became too onerous. In the late 17th cent., however, Cromarty became the head burgh of a "vagrant, incomprehensible county" created out of the scattered estates of the Mackenzies, earls of Cromartie, which extended to the W. coast. It was united with Ross in 1891.

The place was bought in 1772 by George Ross of Pitkerie (Rosses of Cromarty still live in the town), who built the harbour, established a cloth factory, a nail and spade factory, a brewery, and the lace industry, and built the Gaelic Chapel (now roofless) and in 1782 the Court House. Much of the old-world character of Cromarty has been retrieved by the restoration of many of the old buildings in a scheme launched by the local Development Council, with help from the National Trust for Scotland and other bodies. But Cromarty has a particularly interesting group of three ancient cottages, charmingly restored and now housing craftsmen and craftswomen who produce articles in pottery, silver, and knitwear, and a small art gallery that displays the work of contemporary Scottish artists.

CROMDALE, *Moray* (Map 6, ref. 30⁷82⁸). This village on the E. bank of the R. SPEY stands on the fertile Haughs of Cromdale below the western slopes of the hills of Cromdale. The older township of Kirktown of Cromdale once stood ¼ m. S. of the present church, but its last house was demolished in 1845. Cromdale was acquired in 1609 by the laird of Grant, who persuaded James VI to erect it into a burgh of barony with courthouse and gaol, but it never achieved the importance hoped for, and it was displaced in the 18th cent. by GRANTOWN-ON-SPEY after being (so it is said) the scene of a large market brawl.

On the 1st of May 1690 the war in Scotland between James VII and William of Orange came to an end with the Battle of the Haughs of Cromdale. In this encounter, on the slopes 2 m. E. of the village, the Dragoons of Sir Thomas Livingston surprised General Buchan's sleeping Highlanders and killed over 300.

CROOKSTON CASTLE, *Renfrewshire*
(5 m. SW. of GLASGOW). A castle was built
here in 1130, probably on the same site, but all
traces of it have disappeared. In 1330 the lands
were granted to Stewart of Darnley, whose
descendants were the Earls of Lennox; it was
they who owned the present castle. Mary Queen
of Scots and Henry, Lord Darnley, son of the
Earl of Lennox, came here after their marriage.
Crookston Castle was the first property to be
acquired by the National Trust for Scotland
when in 1931 Sir John Stirling Maxwell presented it to them.

CROSSFORD, *Lanarkshire* (Map 2, ref.
28³64⁷). This village is in a fruit-growing
district. The SW. bank of the CLYDE opposite
LANARK is covered with apple, plum, and
pear orchards from Kirkfieldbank to Crossford. There are also acres of tomato-houses.
In the village itself is a canning plant for the
fruit and vegetable products of the district.
The bridge over the Clyde at Crossford is
dated 1793, and the one at Kirkfieldbank 1699.

CROSSRAGUEL, *Ayrshire* (Map 2, ref.
22⁷60⁷). Lying 2 m. SW. of MAYBOLE, Cross-
raguel is a very fine example of a Scottish
religious establishment of the 13th cent. It was
founded in 1244 by Duncan, Earl of Carrick,
for the Cluniac Order and was a benefice of
PAISLEY Abbey. Lying well out of reach of
the English borderers, the ruins are in an
excellent state of preservation, and are of high
architectural distinction. They comprise a
church, claustral buildings, an outer court with
an imposing castellated gatehouse, and an
abbot's house with a strong tower. The choir,
with its three-sided apse, is a fine specimen of
the latest phase of Scottish Gothic; the sacristy
and chapter house are contemporary and are
also very rich.

CROY, *Ayrshire* (Map 2, ref. 22⁵61³). The
name probably derives from Coire ("Corrie"),
and is taken from the fine miniature specimen
carved out of Brown Carrick Hill by the
Knoweside burn. Today, it applies to a bay and
a brae, the former being a fine sandy cove
popular with holiday-makers. It is bounded on
the N. by the cliffs of DUNURE and on the S.
by their higher counterparts at CULZEAN.
The brae has an amusing feature, in that it has
the appearance of going down when it is going
up, and vice versa. The country folk attributed
this to electricity and today the County Council
subscribe to this theory by labelling it the
Electric Brae. The number of motor-cars
engaged in testing the phenomenon are additional hazards in the normal summer Sunday
run along this lovely road, winding its way
southward from Dunure.

CRUDEN BAY, *Aberdeenshire* (Map 6, ref.
40⁸83⁵). A quarter of a century ago, we should
have had no doubt about what were the main
features here – the renowned golf course and
the palatial railway hotel. The railway and the
big hotel have both gone. The excellent golf
course is still there, and a more modest but still
excellent hostelry caters for visitors. It was there
before the railway came and went, and it
remains, with much else, to make this the most
attractive holiday centre on the entire Buchan
coast. The ancestral home of the earls of Erroll,
the "new" or second SLAINS Castle, stands in
ruins on a cliff-top to the N. of the village.

It was at this castle that Johnson and
Boswell stayed on the 24th of August 1773.
"Mr Johnson", records Boswell, "said the
prospect here was the noblest he had ever seen
– better than Mount Edgcumbe, reckoned the
first in England."

The "new" Slains Castle began to be built at
Bowness on the Bay of Cruden in 1597, when
Francis Hay, the 9th Earl of Erroll, returned
from exile after the Rising of the Catholic
earls at Slains. "The walls of one of the
towers," wrote Dr Johnson in his melodiously
Augustan prose, "seem only a continuation of
a perpendicular rock, the foot of which is
beaten by the waves . . . I would not for my
amusement wish for a storm, but as storms,
whether wished for or not, will sometimes
happen, I may say without violation of
humanity, that I would willingly look out upon
them from Slains Castle." But the Grand
Cham's enthusiasm did not end there. Let
Boswell tell what followed: "We got into the
coach and drove to Dunbuy, a rock near the
shore, just an island covered with seafowl.
Then to a circular basin of large extent, surrounded with tremendous rocks. The place is
called the Bullers of Buchan. . . . We walked
round this monstrous cauldron. In some places
the rock is very narrow, and on each side you
have a sea deep enough for a man-of-war to
ride in, so that it is somewhat horrid to move
along. However, there is earth and grass upon
the rock, and a kind of road marked out by the
print of feet. . . . It was rather alarming to see
Mr Johnson poking his way. He insisted to take
a boat and sail into the Pot. We did so. . . . As
the entry into the Buller is so narrow that oars
cannot be used as you go in, the method taken
is to row very hard when you come near it, and
give the boat such a rapidity of motion that she
glides in. . . ."

It would have been worth seeing the immortal pair from so long ago, yet in a sense
still with us, in a boatload of Bullers fishermen
shooting into the Bullers pot, while innumerable
sea-birds screamed applause! But you can
at least go there and see that the "monstrous
cauldron" is just as monstrous today (immediately N. of Cruden Bay on the main road
to PETERHEAD), while marvelling at the charm
of Bullers of Buchan village at the base of the
promontory – a charm so great that the inhabitants have refused to live elsewhere, despite the

difficulties of water supply and drainage. There were sixteen boats fishing out of Bullers in 1881, but now it is purely residential.

A little way inland from Cruden Bay, an oasis in the midst of the treeless, hummocky, wind-swept Buchan plateau, is the prosperous village of Hatton of Cruden, famous for its butter-biscuit factory; at Cruden Bay itself there is a big brick and tile works. Longhaven, just N. of Bullers, is much frequented by rock-climbers, but expert advice is essential before attempting any of its spectacular cliff-climbs. A wide range of sea-birds breed here; their clamour competes with the thunder of the breakers. Here, all the year round, is a natural symphony provided for your delight.

CUILLIN HILLS, *Inverness-shire* (Map 4, ref. 14⁵82⁰), form a range on the Island of S K Y E in the Inner Hebrides (*see* "The Shape of Scotland"). At the S. end of the central part of Skye are grouped together these impressive hills, the most precipitous in the United Kingdom. Some of their peaks remained impregnable to even the most ardent rock-climbers until the end of the last century. There are fifteen peaks of over 3,000 ft. The view from any one top, should you reach it, will reward you as finely as any other in Scotland. Merely to look at the serrated edges of this extra-ordinary range from below is an exciting prospect. The "Black Cuillins" are the main ridge and are so called to differentiate them from the less overpowering "Red Cuillins" round Loch C O R U I S K to the S. These hills, both black and red, are of great interest to geologists, mountaineers, and lovers of scenery in general. Visitors are warned, however, that the Cuillins attract mist suddenly and without warning. You should not make solitary expeditions amongst them without taking stock or receiving expert guidance in advance.

CULBIN, *Moray* (Map 6, ref. 30¹86⁴). Once known as the "Scottish Sahara", this remark-able place, now a State Forest, used to stretch as a barren sand-dune 6 m. long and more than 2 m. wide at the mouth of the R. Findhorn, on the Moray–Nairn border. There is a tradition that on this place there had originally been a fertile estate belonging to the Kinnaird family, and that it had been overwhelmed by sand-storms in the autumn of 1694.

The process may have been more gradual than tradition so dramatically asserts; but there is no doubt that a now buried barony did exist here, and that it was not so much obliterated as hidden from sight by the mysterious element (so one is tempted to describe it) of sand – an element more associated with Africa than with Scotland: ample evidence of this is provided by shifting sands over the centuries. Much of such evidence is reliable. But again tradition (not necessarily false) dramatically intrudes. It is said that, from the movement of sand, the spire

Scottish Tourist Board
The Cuillin Hills from Elgol

of the old church briefly appeared to point heavenwards as it was wont to do, only to disappear again under another soft and silent assault of sand.

Protection against the sand before the 1690s had been offered by marram grass, which was tenacious of the sand beneath it. In the 17th cent., however, this form of grass became popular for thatching in the neighbourhood, and the peasantry pulled it up avidly and with-out considering the result upon their agricul-tural economy. In the significant year of 1695, the Scottish Parliament passed an act forbid-ding the use of marram grass for thatching.

As early as 1744, landowners tried to reclaim and plant the land of Culbin, but failed. This continued until 1922, when the Forestry Com-mission took over the place and were more successful. There is access for visitors along roads and rides from Kintessack (the H.Q. of the scheme). They can see work in various stages from "thatching" the sand with birch branches in order to fix it so that trees may be planted. An astonishing place in which archaeology and tradition mingle in a ghostly fashion.

CULLEN, *Banffshire* (Map 6, ref. 35²86⁷). This ancient royal burgh is the undisputed queen of Banffshire's Moray Firth coast resorts, for reasons which must be apparent to anyone at first glimpse of the place. Even the railway, normally no bringer of beauty, has contributed to its spectacular picturesqueness by a long curving viaduct, under which the main road passes from the square to the sea-town at cliff-top altitude, framing a delectable view of headland and harbour; gaily-painted fisher cottages, close-packed, with gable-ends to the shore; and the virginal-white sands stretching for nearly 2 m. to the headland of Scar Nose, at the W. end of the bay. Some bays can be monotonous, but not Cullen Bay, thanks to its profusion of isolated rocks: the Three

Kings, the Bow Fiddle, Boar Crag, and Red Craig. Its sands are said to sing, though they are not so gifted in this way as the sands at Sunnyside in Logie Bay, to the E. Give them a glancing blow and they respond with a sonorous "Woo, woo, woo", due to the friction of their uniform spherical grains.

Modern Cullen was built between 1820 and 1830 to plans by George MacWilliam for the Earl of Seafield, to replace the ancient burgh clustered around the old parish church in the immediate surroundings of Cullen House, about 1½ m. S. Cullen's first extant charter was granted by James II in 1455, although there was probably a royal castle there in early feudal times, and it may have been there in 1327 that Queen Elizabeth, the second wife of Robert I, died. He endowed a chaplaincy at the Church of St Mary of Cullen to pray for her soul. The existing old parish church (St Anne's Aisle) dates from 1536, to which was added in 1543 one of the last Collegiate Churches to be built before the Reformation, although a solitary round arch survives to indicate a building of the period 1180–1280. There is a particularly fine sacrament house on the N. wall, and near it an elaborate sculptured monument to Alexander Ogilvy, by whose donation the Collegiate Church was erected.

Within a stones throw of the church is Cullen House, a home of the 13th Earl of Seafield, who succeeded his well known and popular mother, the Countess of Seafield, on her death in 1969. The main part of the house dates from c. A.D. 1543, but an E. wing was added in 1711, and alterations and additions were made in 1858 by David Bryce. The front hall has walls covered in linenfold oak panelling and a fireplace of 412 Dutch tiles. The fire-irons are from Findlater Castle, the ruined 15th-cent. stronghold on a cliff-top 2 m. E., where the Ogilvys lived until 1511. The main stair, with delicate wrought-metal balustrade, rises to the first floor beneath a beautiful ceiling by Robert Adam, which came to light only in 1946, when a layer of oak panelling was removed. An immense carved overmantel by Grinling Gibbons, a set of Dutch glassware given by Queen Anne to her maid-of-honour, Anne Smith, who married the 20th Laird of Grant, and the painted ceiling in the Second Salon are among the highlights in a house of many treasures. The ceiling, hidden from view for over a century, until it came to light in 1880, is a riot of decoration dominated by brilliant blue, and at the same time a flamboyant declaration of Jacobite sympathies.

CULLODEN MOOR, *Inverness-shire* (Map 5, ref. 27⁴84⁵). Culloden was the scene of the last battle fought on the soil of the United Kingdom; for this place, 5 m. SE. of INVERNESS, is the site of the last battle in the Rising of 1745. On the 16th of April 1746 the Jacobites,

under Prince Charles Edward Stuart, were defeated by a Hanoverian army under the Duke of Cumberland. The battle lasted only forty minutes, but it has never been forgotten.

Culloden stands on a high wind-swept ridge between the Moray Firth and the R. Nairn; it now has a plantation of trees, which partly obstructs the view of it. The present road, constructed in 1835, runs through the battlefield. In 1881 a memorial cairn was built by Arthur Forbes of Culloden, and headstones were erected to identify the graves of the various Jacobite clans, and to mark the "field of the English". The battlefield is now the property of the National Trust for Scotland, who have an information centre in the old Leanach Cottage at the SE. side of the battlefield.

Culloden House, 2 m. NW. from the battle-field, was the home in 1746 of Duncan Forbes of Culloden, then Lord President of the Court of Session, who, though he was opposed to the Rising, did his ineffective best to mitigate the fury of Cumberland and the Hanoverian government against the defeated Highlanders. His house was a square Renaissance building, but it was burnt later and a new Georgian one was built on the site in 1772–83. The design of it is of the Adam type but has not yet been traced to either of the famous Adam brothers. It was the seat of the Forbes family from 1626 to 1897.

The Duke of Cumberland undoubtedly committed atrocities upon the captured or wounded Highland soldiers. It was because of this that he has earned in history the name of "Butcher" Cumberland. Handel composed *See the Conquering Hero Comes* to welcome him back to London. His Christian name was William, and

The memorial cairn, Culloden

Scottish Tourist Board

it was as a compliment to him that the English named the flower "Sweet William". The same flower used to be known in Scotland as "Stinking Willie".

CULROSS, *Fife* (Map 2, ref. 29⁹68⁶). On the N. shore of the FORTH, between KINCARDINE and DUNFERMLINE, Culross is a remarkably complete survival of early Scottish architecture. In the late 16th and early 17th cents. Culross – almost a village in scale, despite its status of royal burgh – carried on a flourishing trade in salt and coal and had seafaring contacts with Scandinavia, Germany, and the Netherlands. When this trade failed, the little town declined into a backwater and was by-passed by 19th-cent. industrial development, with the result that its early character has remained virtually unchanged. Over the past thirty years a process of restoration has been pursued in the town by the National Trust for Scotland. The Palace (1597–1611), home of the industrial laird Sir George Bruce, was one of the first of the historic little houses to be saved, and is now open to visitors under the guardianship of the Ministry of Public Building and Works. Between the Palace and the Town House, the three-storey block of Sandhaven tenement has been modernized internally and let to tenants; the mercat cross area higher up has been brought back to life with the restoration of the Study and the Ark and Nunnery; and comparable work has been achieved in other old houses in the narrow, cobbled causeways leading from the shore road to the cross. The Study, with its distinctive

Culross: the old tolbooth

tower, at the head of Back Causeway, is now the home of the Trust's resident representative and contains a display of furniture, maps, pottery, and pewter, illustrating early life in Culross. The choir of a 13th-cent. Cistercian monastery founded by Malcolm, Earl of Fife, is used now as the parish church. Close by these abbey remains is Culrose House, restored as a family home by the Earl of Elgin. Near the eastern burgh boundary on the shore road are the fragmentary remains of a chapel built by Robert Blackadder, first Archbishop of GLASGOW, in 1503, to honour St Mungo, who was born in Culross and who founded Glasgow Cathedral.

CULTER, *Lanarkshire* (Map 2, ref. 30²63⁴). One of the prettiest villages in Lanarkshire, Culter stands just off the EDINBURGH–Carlisle road, well shaded by trees and beside the Culter Water. The parish church, of which some traces remain, was founded about 1170; the present church was built in 1810. As a legacy from the past, the silver communion cups are dated 1618.

Culter Fell, 100 ft higher than the more famous Tinto, lies SE. of the village; from the summit can be seen the valleys of both the CLYDE and the TWEED. This is agricultural country, once heavily wooded but much cut down in the Second World War.

Nearby stands Culter House, a characteristic and pleasing white-harled building of the kind that the Scots put up with notable success in the 17th cent.; it is approached by an avenue of trees 1 m. long. There are successful modern and post-war additions.

CULZEAN CASTLE, *Ayrshire* (Map 2, ref. 22⁴61¹), is a dream castle created by Robert Adam in the 1780s for the Earl of Cassillis. It stands on a cliff-top site overlooking the lower Firth of CLYDE, 3½ m. W. of MAYBOLE. It is a studied masterpiece complete with hand-made "ruins" for the correct romantic effect. It is now in the possession of the National Trust for Scotland, having been transferred by the Marquess of Ailsa in 1945, and is a much-visited place. The woodlands, with their famous rhododendrons, are the main attraction; but doubtless the suite of rooms in the Castle reserved for General Eisenhower as his Scottish residence, and open to inspection on selected days, also plays its part in drawing the crowds. The building contains as well a fine and comprehensive collection of Scottish weapons. The name is pronounced "Cul-ain", and refers to the caves over which the Castle is built.

No reference to Culzean could be complete without mentioning, however briefly, the remarkable family of Kennedy whose headquarters it became. Fortunately for Scotland but unfortunately for Carrick, the Kennedy family was split into two factions, those of

Douglas Scott

A footpath from the shops in Cumbernauld New Town

Cassillis (latterly Culzean) in the N., and of Bargany (pronounced "Bar-geenie") in the S., which for generations "kept the countryside in fear" with their internecine feuding. This culminated in a pitched battle near AYR in 1601 in which the laird of Bargany was killed. James VI, who was at that time particularly anxious to impress the English with his suitability as heir to Elizabeth, was forced to take a firm hand against such uncivilized goings-on, and for a time the family suffered an eclipse. When it re-emerged, the Cassillis branch was supreme, and it has been acknowledged as the senior ever since. The present chief, David, 7th Marquess of Ailsa, resides at Cassillis House, 3 m. NE. of Maybole.

CUMBERNAULD, *Dunbartonshire* (Map 2, ref. 27⁷67⁶). It is perhaps significant that the now familiar phrase "New Town", in the sense of a planned development, was first coined in Scotland – nearly 200 years ago. Right from the start, in the 1770s, the enlightened Lord Provost Drummond and his gifted young town designer, James Craig, called that fine expansion to EDINBURGH's North, that neo-Georgian heritage which we still struggle in the face of Philistinism to maintain, the "New Town". It is still a delight for us who live in it, and for some who have never seen it before it is exciting to perambulate.

For both, a visit to Cumbernauld also is a balm and an exercise in that most neglected of the three theological virtues – hope. Cumbernauld is native, pleasing, comfortable for its inhabitants, and is an effort of constructive imagination. It has in its setting and style its roots in the past, yet it is built for this age and with an eye for the future.

The Scottish New Towns

Fortunately Cumbernauld, with its initial C, comes alphabetically first of them all in this gazetteer, and this allows one to dilate here and at the beginning upon the quality and intention of the Scottish New Towns. At once let it be said that they have no relation to the New Towns in the south of England, which, in their

own setting, sprang up beneficently in the earlier years of this century. Welwyn Garden City, for instance, was a planned effort by one section of the community to build a small town in the country, not so much as an escape (certainly not from slums or poor, dilapidated houses), but as an effort to found a new community whose members were drawn largely from the professional classes, and who were to an extent united in their attitude towards modern living.

Later, English New Towns before the Second World War did have a more practical connection with new industries, and with the relief of growing pressure in great cities. Nothing, either of the garden-city type or of the more practical nature, arose in Scotland until after the recent war. When Scotland did conceive her New Towns, she may subconsciously have been moved by the example of Lord Provost Drummond and James Craig to plan for space and freedom as an escape from the overcrowded old town on the Rock of Edinburgh, but they were immediately impelled by more modern considerations.

There was the absolute necessity of finding decent accommodation for the growing population of the GLASGOW working classes in particular, and the need to find pleasant country sites for the workers in the new modern industries characteristic of our age. It was, of course, important to attract these new and modern industries to such places, easy of access and assured of accommodation for their workers in the immediate neighbourhood.

This New Town

Cumbernauld, though far from completed, is the most striking of these ventures and one of the most attractive in its novelty, yet with something of the old medieval township about it.

Situated only 13 m. NE. of Glasgow in the CLYDE valley and on the route between STIRLING and Glasgow, it is yet neatly cut off from the stream of traffic. It is built round an old estate and 18th-cent. laird's house with a park to which all who live in Cumbernauld have access. It is built as one cohesive unit on

Cumbernauld New Town: a motor approach

Douglas Scott

the slopes and summit of a slight hill, and quite overwhelming the older and undistinguished village of Cumbernauld. Houses in it do not march side by side in dull uniformity, but enfilade down or up the hill, overtopping each other, and giving to each house a fine view of the circumstanding hills, and to each the possibility of as much light and sunshine as is available.

Perhaps Cumbernauld's most remarkable achievement is that, while it gives everyone in it the right of easy access to the motor-car, it has effectively separated the pedestrian from the motorist. One cannot do better than quote from an account in the *Glasgow Herald* published (on the 2nd of July 1964) while the town was taking visible and effective shape:

"Traffic goes round – not through – the housing areas so that their layout is determined not by streets and motor roads but by the close contours of the site. Footpaths meander between the houses like streams, opening out occasionally into a garden courtyard or woodland copse. As the houses go up, the footpath routes fit into a logical pattern, taking the shortest lines and encouraging people to walk away from the roads. In the Kildrum pedestrian precinct footpaths are the main link between the primary school, medical centre, children's playground, shops and Post Office, Y.M.C.A., and Y.W.C.A., community centre and two churches.

"Eventually footpaths and motor roads will have their destination in the town centre, a multi-storey and fully covered structure."

The main impression that strikes a visitor is that here is a family town for many families. There is privacy in the way that the houses are built and aligned; yet there is ample opportunity in the play-parks for the children's recreation, safe from the traffic. There is ample opportunity for neighbours to get to know each other; yet there is equal opportunity for them to keep to themselves if they wish to do so.

The Cumbernauld Development Corporation offices are housed in and around Cumbernauld House at the northern entrance to the New

Town, and the spacious grounds have been made a public park (one of several).

In May 1967 Princess Margaret opened Phase 1 of the Town Centre, costing £2,000,000 of the whole project's estimated £15,000,000. By March 1971 the population was 34,340 and increasing at the rate of more than 3,500 a year. By 1971 almost 100 firms had established themselves in Cumbernauld, their manufactures varying from office machinery, carpets, underwear to building components and electronic devices. The eleven primary schools are so sited that no child need cross a busy main road. Cumbernauld High School takes 1,600 pupils up to the age of nineteen with advanced educational facilities, three gymnasiums, a swimming-pool, and playing fields. A second comprehensive school had been opened and a third almost completed while construction had started on a Technical College.

As in other New Towns, the emphasis is on community and social amenities, but Cumbernauld also has a cottage theatre with its own theatre group. Plans were well advanced for an 18-hole golf course and a swimming-pool of international standard while the temporary sports centre catered for numerous activities.

Since the opening of Phase 1 Cumbernauld has received many accolades, notably the R. S. Reynolds Memorial Award of $25,000 as the best example of community architecture in the world (for which twenty communities were originally considered), and it is regularly visited by study groups from many countries.

These visitors must be impressed by the absence of ugly television masts that would have marred the graceful lines of the house tops: they are banned by the Corporation, and through proximity to the main transmitting centres there is perfect reception on indoor aerials.

We do not intend to give many names of the living, especially in connection with a growing organism such as Cumbernauld, but two must be mentioned. General Sir Gordon H. A. MacMillan was first chairman of the Development Corporation but has now retired. And the architect in whose fertile mind the shape

Douglas Scott
Terraced houses, Cumbernauld New Town

of this New Town of Scotland grew was Mr L. Hugh Wilson.

CUMBRAES, The, *Buteshire* (Map 2, ref. 21⁵65⁶). Along with BUTE and ARRAN, the two Cumbraes (Great Cumbrae and Little Cumbrae) form the shire of Bute. The only other purely insular counties in Scotland are ORKNEY and SHETLAND. Though always in Buteshire, Little Cumbrae was, until 1891, included in the mainland parish of ARDROSSAN. It was perhaps this sense that one of the islands was unwarrantably and ecclesiastically tied to the mainland that led to the Rev. James Adams's famous prayer. Mr Adams was a well-known early 19th-cent. minister on the Cumbraes. He used to pray for blessings on the Great and Little Cumbraes and "for the adjacent islands of Great Britain and Ireland".

The island of Great Cumbrae lies in the Firth of CLYDE, between the island of Bute and Ayrshire, and to the S. separated by about ½ m. of water (the "Tan"), is the island of Little Cumbrae. Great Cumbrae is about 3¾ m. long and 2 m. broad, and covers an area of nearly 5 sq. m. Little Cumbrae is under 2 m. long, 1 m. broad, and 1⅛ m. in area. A ridge of hills forms the backbone of Great Cumbrae. From the top of it, magnificent views are obtained.

The town of MILLPORT lies to the S. at the head of a fine bay. The Eileans (islands) that lie in Millport Bay, not far from the promenade, add to the charms of the Cumbraes.

The earliest village on Great Cumbrae was at Kirkton, about ½ m. from the present Millport's old pier. It was about 1330 that the Bishop of GLASGOW confirmed to PAISLEY Abbey the church of LARGS and its chapel of "Cumbrayne". (Both Largs and Cumbrayne were dedicated to St Columba.) In 1612, a church built of "fine hewnstone" at Kirkton replaced "Sanct Colmis Kirke", and on the same spot in 1802 arose the last church to be erected there.

The buildings on the island of Little Cumbrae consist of an ancient ruined castle, a gentleman's house, a home farm on a bay on the E. side, and a lighthouse on the western cliffs. The light is 115 ft high. It was erected in 1794, with a fog-horn attached.

Robert II used the castle as a royal residence, and two of his charters, 1375 and 1384, were dated there. Until 1515, the Hunters of HUNTERSTON were the hereditary keepers of the castle, which passed into the hands of the Earl of Eglinton in 1577, and was burnt by the troops of Cromwell in 1653.

Great Cumbrae has one institution that is unique among Scottish resorts, the Scottish Marine Biological Station at Keppel. Scientific work there covers a broad field including chemistry of the sea, prawns and their parasites, and the life and growth of barnacles. Meteorological observations are maintained. The museum and aquarium in the station are open to the public. Classes in marine biology for university and other students are a feature of the work of the station.

(For the attractions of the Cumbraes as a holiday resort, *see* MILLPORT.)

CUMNOCK, *Ayrshire* (Map 2, ref. 25⁷62⁰). A grey mining town on the trunk road from KILMARNOCK to DUMFRIES, 16 m. E. of AYR, this police burgh is commonly referred to as Old Cumnock, although this name is more correctly attached to the parish. It is built round a square, which at one time was the churchyard; in its centre is the parish church. Cumnock was the birthplace of Keir Hardie, the father of Scottish Socialism, a statue of whom, by Benno Schotz, stands at the Council Chamber. In general, the people of the town carry on the Keir Hardie tradition flavoured with that of the Old Covenanters, and are a fine, dour, courageous community imbued with an indomitable ambition to improve the social and economic status of the burgh. Combined with the village of LUGAR and the extensive County Council housing scheme of Netherthird, both of which are close by, Cumnock might well form the nucleus of a second-tier local authority when the day comes for the reorganization of local government.

Dumfries House, built in 1757 by William Adam for the 4th Earl of Dumfries, lies 2 m. to the W.; it contains a collection of snuff boxes and similar articles, the manufacture of which was once the main industry of the town.

CUPAR, *Fife* (Map 3, ref. 33⁶71⁴). Rather surprisingly, Cupar and not ST ANDREWS is the county town of Fife. This small but important burgh may have achieved this status owing to its more central and accessible position in the county. Moreover, Cupar used to be the seat of the thanes of Fife, and was the centre of the administration of justice from the 13th cent.; it became a royal burgh during the late 14th cent.

To those interested in drama, Cupar Fife has special associations. Some 2 m. NW. of the burgh is "The Mount", the home of Sir David Lindsay, who wrote the celebrated *Ane Satire of the Thrie Estaits*, which indeed received its first open-air performance (said to have lasted nine hours) on what is now the playground of Castlehill School in Cupar in 1535. This satire – in which the state of the Catholic Church in Scotland, as well as that of the nobility and the burgesses, is held up to scorn – was, oddly enough, the subject of a command performance before the strongly Catholic Regent, Mary of Guise. There is no evidence that Sir David Lindsay ever left the Church of his baptism, however much he was distressed by the behaviour of the clerics in his time.

"Celebrated" the play remained for centuries, but only among scholars. Then, on the occasion of the first EDINBURGH festival in 1947, a cut version was revived and produced by Sir Tyrone Guthrie; only Scottish actors performed in this play, which is in the old Scots tongue. It attracted international attention, and two years later was repeated at the Festival with equally resounding success.

CURRIE, *Midlothian* (Map 3, ref. 31⁹66⁸), is one of the Pentland villages on the banks of the upper reaches of the Water of Leith. The old bridge crosses the river where the 18th-cent. church was built on the site of a pre-Reformation one. One of the silver communion cups dates from the late 16th cent. The church is something of a curiosity, with its painted false windows, which are distinctly attractive.

The Kinleith paper-mill fills the valley below Currie, and there are ruins of many other mills, including two snuff-mills, one above and one below Juniper Green, along the water. While retaining its character, Currie is now almost a suburb of EDINBURGH, and is the start for many Edinburgh walkers on their expeditions over the Pentland Hills.

DAILLY, *Ayrshire* (Map 2, ref. 22⁷60²). There are two places of this name in the lower GIRVAN valley: Old Dailly, some 3 m. NE. of Girvan, and Dailly, another 3 m. upstream. Of the two, Old Dailly is the more interesting. It has the ruins of an ancient 14th-cent. kirk surrounded by graves of Covenanters, and close to it is the old ford across the Girvan Water, which may well date from prehistoric days. Across the ford is the Baron's Stane, dropped there long ago by the last of the glaciers. This rock was a seat of justice, and the place-names in the district point to its importance.

Like the Stinchar, the Girvan has more than its share of castles – with this difference, that, whereas the Stinchar castles are for the most part ruined, those of the Girvan are mostly occupied. KILLOCHAN, Bargany, Dalquharran, Penkill, and KILKERRAN are all close to the Daillys and are all occupied.

DALBEATTIE, *Kirkcudbrightshire* (Map 2, ref. 28³56²), also called the Birch Holm, is a small 19th-cent. town built in a basin at the head of tidal water on the Urr; all its houses are of grey granite. From the ridge of Craignair just across the Urr, granite was shipped out to Liverpool, the Thames Embankment, and Ceylon – all over the world, in fact. This enterprise raised into a substantial place the village founded in 1780 on the lands of Little Dalbeattie. The farm of Meikle Dalbeattie still stands outside the town. The arrival of the railway in 1860 still further enhanced its development; in 1897 (a peak year), 1,000 tons of wholesale groceries came into Dalbeattie Harbour in a week, carried by ships returning otherwise empty after taking granite setts to Liverpool. Thus the granite trade led to the town's becoming a distribution centre of retail goods.

The quarry now produces only granite chips for road surfacing. The old-established bobbin mill, however, serving the Lancashire textile industry, is still in full production. But the harbour, so long thronged with ships, is deserted.

A fine 10th-cent. interlace-decorated bronze flask, now in the National Museum of Antiquities in EDINBURGH, comes from Barr of Spottes, 1 m. or so from the town. The area around Dalbeattie was the missionary field of St Constantine, sent there by St Kentigern "because he was a Briton" – that is, a Cymric-speaker – about A.D. 560; the church names of St Constantine of Urr, St Constantine of Edingham, and St Constantine of Colmanele, all near Dalbeattie, commemorate his activity.

DALCROSS, *Inverness-shire* (Map 5, ref. 27⁷85⁰), is the airport for INVERNESS, and lies 6 m. NE. of the town; it was opened after the last war when runways at the Longman proved too short.

About 1 m. W. of the airport is Petty Church, which is not now used but is nevertheless the traditional burial-place of the chiefs of Mackintosh. Castle Stuart stands near Petty Church, and this castle was built in 1625 after the 3rd Earl of Moray had bought lands from the Mackintoshes. It was occupied during the 17th cent., but was then allowed to fall into disrepair. Though rescued in 1860, when the 13th Earl of Moray rebuilt the roof, it was even after that not occupied. At length, in 1951, Mr Colin Mackenzie took a lease on the building and made a dwelling of it. The Castle is a remarkable survival; owing to long periods of non-occupation, it still presents a fairly accurate architectural picture of a nobleman's home in the early 17th cent.

DALGUISE, *Perthshire* (Map 2, ref. 29⁹74⁶), is a small village on the W. bank of the TAY 5 m. N. of DUNKELD. The lands of Dalguise were given to the Church of Dunkeld by King

William the Lion in 1160. In 1543 they were granted by Bishop Crichton to John Stewart of Arntully. A descendant of the same name who was born in 1689 was a Jacobite and fought at SHERIFFMUIR. He built the present House of Dalguise in 1716.

In 1950 the house was opened as a permanent training centre for boys' clubs and was the gift of the South Africa Fund to Britain.

DALKEITH, *Midlothian* (Map 3, ref. 33⁴66⁸). This growing town, much enlarged since the Second World War, serves as a centre for the mining and agricultural area immediately to the SE. of EDINBURGH. It has also a fair measure of light industry and, because of its proximity to Edinburgh, a sizeable proportion of commuting population. An indication of the town's changing purpose is reflected in the Corn Exchange, dated 1854, in the High Street, once the seat of one of the country's largest grain markets and now an outpost of one of the most influential electronics firms. The splendid new Esbank Valley Technical College was opened here in 1969.

Traditional industry is maintained in the modernized Dalkeith mills, producing flour and oatmeal and also compound feeding stuffs for agricultural use. Carpets, brushes, and sausages are other products associated with the town, and an industrial estate at Thornybank, on the MUSSELBURGH road, is attracting additional sources of employment. Dalkeith Palace (now occupied by a large computer-making concern), a property of the Duke of Buccleuch, incorporates remnants of a 12th-cent. castle and was largely rebuilt to designs by Sir John Vanburgh around 1700, for Anne, Duchess of Buccleuch and Monmouth – the Duchess of Scott's *Lay of the Last Minstrel.* Queen Victoria began her long period of devotion to Scotland by spending her first night in this country at Dalkeith Palace in 1842, as the guest of the then Duke and Duchess of Buccleuch. She came by sea to Granton, inspected Edinburgh, and then went on to Dalkeith.

St Nicholas parish church, in the High Street, is of great antiquity. The church was restored in 1852, except for the E. apse, which is roofless.

A large housing development by local authority has been made at Woodburn on the LAUDER road. Eskbank, the residential area SW. of the town centre, consists largely of Victorian and Edwardian villas.

DALLAS, *Moray* (Map 6, ref. 31³85²), is a village in the valley of the Lossie, 6 m. SE. of FORRES. The parish church was built about 1794 on the site of earlier ones. An ancient market cross, dedicated to St Michael, stands 12 ft high in the churchyard and is presumed to have been erected in the early 16th cent. This St Michael's Cross is said to mark the exact centre of the county of Moray.

The Dallas quarry is famed for slates; as far back as 1605 it provided the slates for the old tolbooth of ELGIN. The village itself dates from the 19th cent., when the land was first feued – that is, in the parlance of Scots Law, when the land was first let out at a fixed rate in perpetuity.

Dallas Lodge was built in 1688 for Sir Robert Gordon of Gordonstoun. The original plan was for a circle of buildings similar to the "Round Square" at GORDONSTOUN. But the circle never met, and the design had to satisfy itself with achieving a semicircle. This was composed of a dwelling-house and granary, linked with an archway; there is no trace of this last now remaining. There are fine gardens and trees on the estate.

DALMAHOY, *Midlothian* (Map 3, ref. 31⁴66⁸). Formerly the seat of the Earl of Morton, Dalmahoy lies 2 m. SE. of RATHO and has long been famous for its trees; it is now also known for its golf course and club.

Dalmahoy Hill, 1 m. SE. of Dalmahoy, rises to 800 ft. It contains the remains of a fort occupying the hill-top and representing two structural periods, the earlier one an enclosed hill in a system of stone walls 1,200 ft long and 400 ft wide. The later phase on the summit has an oval enclosure of 140 ft by 85 ft. The earlier works are probably pre-Roman Iron Age, but the later one may be post-Roman.

DALMALLY, *Argyll* (Map 2, ref. 21⁶72⁷). Beautifully situated in a wooded valley of the R. Orchy, Dalmally lies near where the river flows into Loch AWE. Now a holiday centre especially favoured by anglers, it is also a good starting-point for climbing BEN CRUACHAN and Ben Lui, 6 m. S. of Dalmally.

The Valley of Orchy was well-known for its great forests of Scots pine, but it was cleared by speculators for the almost incredible sum of 6d. per tree in the 1820s. Planting was resumed in 1954.

Some 2 m. SW. of Dalmally, near the hill road to INVERARAY, is a monument to the Gaelic poet Duncan Ban MacIntyre (1724–1812). The monument stands at an excellent viewpoint.

DALMELLINGTON, *Ayrshire* (Map 2, ref. 24⁸60⁶). The former character of this small mining town, 15 m. SE. of AYR on the road to CASTLE DOUGLAS, has been spoilt by a flood of council houses, and the main item of interest is an ancient moat or fort-hill in the centre of the town. Dalmellington lies at the southern edge of cultivation, and for many miles the road drives S. through desolate moorland, romanticized by its associations with the Covenanters. Amidst this wilderness lies Loch DOON Castle, rebuilt on the shore to preserve associations when the island site was inundated by the raising of the water-level to provide hydro-electric power.

DALMENY, *West Lothian* (Map 3, ref. 31⁵67⁸). This peaceful little village on the Rosebery estate, so near to EDINBURGH as almost to be in it, reminds one of an English pastoral scene. The village green strongly accounts for this. Dalmeny lies on the fringe of the approach road to the FORTH Road Bridge. The one-storey dwellings were renovated by voluntary effort in the 1930s; so too was the 12th-cent. church – one of the finest of its period in all Britain.

The Rosebery estate contains Dalmeny Woods, through which it is possible to walk from Cramond to QUEENSFERRY. Hound Point, near this walk, takes its name from a ghostly dog that, it is alleged, appeared and bayed mournfully before the death of each laird of Barnbougle. This legend arises from the fact that an earlier laird, Sir Roger Moubray, had taken his hound with him to the Crusades, and both had fallen. Barnbogle (or Barnbougle) Castle, situated right on the shore, was the old seat of the Moubrays. It was restored in 1880 by Archibald Primrose, 5th Earl of Rosebery. Basically a 17th-cent. building, it contains, however, few architectural details of note. An interesting feature is the low balustered enclosure surrounding the Castle and garden. It is habitable but not inhabited, yet encloses a fascinating library collected by the 5th Earl, the Prime Minister (1894–5) and hero of his time.

The Eagle Rock, a mass of stone near the shore, on which has been carved some sort of figure, has been attributed to the Romans.

DALMUIR, *Dunbartonshire* (Map 2, ref. 24⁸67²). This formerly busy shipbuilding and engineering district of CLYDEBANK burgh now has no shipyard and has suffered much from redundancy, but it is hoped that new factories may help the situation. Beardmore's at Dalmuir were responsible for building the R34 – the first airship to fly the Atlantic both ways. But much has happened since then with ventures more modern than the giant airship.

DALNASPIDAL, *Perthshire* (Map 5, ref. 26⁵77³). This township has the highest railway station in Scotland (1,422 ft), just below and to the S. of DRUMOCHTER summit. The name of the place means the field surrounding a spital or hospice. The original road built by General Wade in 1728–9 runs above the present road at Dalnaspidal.

Some 2 m. E. of the township, and just beside the main road, stands the Wade Stone, which was put up when the road was built.

DALRIADA, mainly *Argyll* (near DUNADD). This name was given to the Kingdom of Scots, whose headquarters were at Add – or, as it is sometimes called, DUNADD – near Kilmichael Glassary. Dalriada flourished between A.D. 503 and A.D. 843, until the King, Kenneth Mac-Alpine, either conquered and obliterated the Picts or succeeded to their crown, thus founding the Kingdom of Scotland (*see* "Scotland in History").

DALRY, *Ayrshire* (Map 2, ref. 22⁹64⁹), is a pleasant town on the R. Garnock, 3 m. N. of KILWINNING. Dalry is yet another of the weaving towns of the 18th cent., like BEITH, STEWARTON, and NEWMILNS; and, while for a time there were ironworks and coalmines, these have been abandoned and the town's main industries are again textile. Nearby is Blair House, which has been in the Blair family for 700 years. The house is built round a 15th-cent. keep.

DALRY, *Kirkcudbrightshire* (Map 2, ref. 26²58¹). On the R. Ken, the village of Dalry stands nearly 3 m. N. of NEW GALLOWAY. At the top of the street where the roads from MONIAIVE and CARSPHAIRN meet is an ancient block of stone rudely shaped into a chair and called St John's Stone; for a legend states that John the Baptist rested upon it, and indeed the village is sometimes called St John's Town of Dalry. The real reason, however, for this name lies in the fact that the land in the area was owned by the Knights Templar, whose patron saint was St John the Baptist. It was also called Old Galloway, to distinguish it from New Galloway, which in 1692 began to overshadow it.

About 3 m. E. of Dalry is Lochinvar, a small loch with ruins of a castle on an islet, said to be the home of "Young Lochinvar" of poetic fame. The Gordons built the Castle of Earlston, 2 m. N. of Dalry, in 1665. A meeting at Dalry in 1666 of four Covenanters started a chain of events that led to the Battle of RULLION GREEN, so well mourned in covenanting history.

Dalry lies at the S. end of a chain of power stations in Galloway, set up since 1929 in the Ken Valley, on a series of fine lochs that, with the forests now clothing the hillsides, have greatly improved a bleak valley.

DALSWINTON, *Dumfriesshire* (Map 2, ref. 29³58⁵). Described in the late 18th cent. as a "neat and regularly built village", Dalswinton is still the same. The estate has changed hands many times since the 13th-cent. ownership by the Comyns, but has stayed intact. The house is 1 m. SSE. of the village and within ½ m. of the R. Nith. It was built in the 18th cent. In Burns's time the owner was Patrick Millar, of the Carron Works and Bank of Scotland, a keen "improver". He had the first steamboat on his loch in 1788, and introduced the iron plough and the turnip into Scotland. He was Burns's landlord at Ellisland across the river.

On Bankhead Farm, Dalswinton, in 1949, aerial photography revealed a complex of fourteen Roman forts and other works; excavation in the 1950s showed the principal fort to be of the late 1st cent. A.D.

DALVEEN, *Dumfriesshire* (Map 2, ref. 29²60⁸), is a wild pass 1,140 ft high over the Lowther Hills from CRAWFORD in Lanarkshire to DURISDEER, and one of the finest passes in the Lowlands. From Roman times the route was by a rough track called Wall or Wald Path, which led straight into the hills from Durisdeer village, and it is still traceable in places. The old Toll House on the Dalveen road, now a shepherd's cottage, is so surrounded by hills that it gets sun only for a short period at midsummer. The pass was the scene of a famous rescue of Covenanters, who were being taken to EDINBURGH for trial.

Dalveen Castle was once the stronghold of the Douglases and stood on the right bank of the Carron, but now the only trace is a stone built into the wall of a farmhouse in 1836, with the Douglas arms on it and the date 1622.

DALWHINNIE, *Inverness-shire* (Map 5, ref. 26⁴78⁴). Though only a village on the main road between PERTH and INVERNESS N. of DRUMOCHTER, Dalwhinnie has become a holiday centre, its prime attraction being its great bare hillsides, which are excellent for the winter sports that have recently become so popular in Scotland.

To the SW. is Loch Ericht, 15 m. long and part of the Tummel Valley hydro-electric scheme started as long ago as 1927. The water from Loch Ericht is taken by tunnel to a power station on Loch Rannoch.

DARVEL, *Ayrshire* (Map 2, ref. 25⁶63⁸). Along with NEWMILNS in the centre and GALSTON on the other side, Darvel is one of the three burghs of the Upper Irvine Valley. It too, like its neighbour Newmilns, manufactures lace. Darvel was the birthplace of Sir Alexander Fleming of penicillin fame.

DAVIOT, *Aberdeenshire* (Map 6, ref. 37⁵82⁸). This is now a very small parish within which were once three stone circles; but now only one – the Loanhead Stone Circle – remains. It is the fact of this circle's existence that warrants the inclusion of the parish here. This recumbent stone circle consists basically of a ring cairn surrounded by a circle of standing stones; among them is one huge boulder placed in a horizontal position. The circle at Daviot occupies a broad shelf near the top of a gentle hill that is nonetheless visible from a fair distance in the area. Excavation of pottery suggests that the cairn was probably used as a dwelling-place in the first millennium B.C., but was originally a burial cairn about 1,000 years before that.

DAVIOT, *Inverness-shire* (Map 5, ref. 27³83⁸), is a village in Strath Nairn, on the main PERTH road, just before the final rise and fall to INVERNESS; there is a superb view here looking N. and W.

Daviot church, rebuilt in 1826, has an unusual steeple and stands high above the R. Nairn. General Wade, who built many roads in the Highlands during the first half of the 18th cent., made one crossing the river some way upstream from the present route.

Higher up the Nairn is the parish of Dunlichty, joined to Daviot in 1618. Its church lies 5 m. SW. of Daviot and was rebuilt in 1758; it has many interesting heraldic tombstones showing the arms of the Macbains, the MacGillivrays, and the Shaws. Tordarroch, 1 m. NE. of Dunlichty, was the home of one branch of the Shaws and is now the designation of their chief.

DAWYCK HOUSE, *Peeblesshire* (Map 3, ref. 31⁷63⁵). This 19th-cent. castellated mansion is in finely wooded grounds. Sir James Naesmyth (d. 1779), who succeeded in 1720, had been a pupil of Linnaeus, the botanist, and it was Naesmyth who planted the famous avenue of silver firs at Dawyck. He was also one of the contenders for the honour of introducing the larch into Scotland in the early 18th cent. A lime avenue and a fine collection of rhododendrons can be seen there.

DEE, River, *Aberdeenshire* (Map 6, ref. 38⁰79⁹). "Bright snow-fed Dee", as it has been called, rises from the Wells of Dee on the summit plateau of Braeriach at an altitude of over 4,000 ft, and flows for 85 m. in a generally easterly direction to the North Sea at ABERDEEN. It is the fifth longest river in Scotland and drains a basin of 817 sq. m.

It is also the most rapid river in Scotland. Its two tiny headstreams bubble their way up through gravel on the great plateau of disintegrated reddish granite. The two Braeriach burns unite at a height of 3,950 ft and topple over the summit, which is 2½ m. long and about 1 m. broad. They then descend into the Fuar Gharbh-choire (the cold, rough corrie) in a conspicuous waterfall, which can be seen as far away as the summit of LOCHNAGAR. "Snow-fed" is the right word, for even in July the young river frequently flows under a great arch of snow here. From its source to the sea the Dee flows almost continuously over a bed of stones and gravel. A series of cascades follow until at a height of about 1,980 ft it enters Glen Dee, where, after a course of 3 m., it is joined by the little stream flowing out of the LAIRIG GHRU pass from ROTHIEMURCHUS on Speyside. This stream itself comes from a couple of lochans known as the Pools of Dee. Glen Dee now turns southward between Ben Vrottan and Sgor Mor until – just below a celebrated landmark, a wooden

The River Dee in Aberdeenshire

structure known as the White Bridge – it is joined by the Geldie Burn.

From the Wells on Braeriach until it enters Glen Dee the river thus makes the tremendous drop of 2,000 ft, and here and in Glen Dee itself is to be found the wildest scenery in the whole basin – the corries of Braeriach and the scarped front of the Angel's Peak, Cairntoul, and the Devil's Point. It is sometimes suggested that the Dee is a river almost monopolized by "privilege". While it is true that, lower down, its valley is lined by great sporting estates, including the royal deer forests of Ballochbuie, Balmoral, and Glengairn, it should not be forgotten that in its upper reaches it penetrates the very heart of the CAIRNGORMS. It never was and never could be in this sector anyone's exclusive "preserve", although its wild life is now protected by the Nature Conservancy. To enjoy it the only restriction is that you must walk on your own two feet, for the nearest approach to a carriage road – a private one – ends at the White Bridge, where tracks turn S. and W. to Geldie and to Bynack, almost on the Perthshire border.

The famous Linn of Dee is 3 m. below the White Bridge. It is not a waterfall, in the usual sense of the word, but a chasm, a rock-bound channel in which the river seethes through a gorge as narrow as 4 ft across in places. At the Linn of Dee you reach a motor road proper, and the Linn itself is spanned by a granite bridge opened by Queen Victoria in 1857. It is the terminus of innumerable coach tour excursions.

Little more than a mile farther down the Dee valley you come to the hamlet of Inverey with its ruined castle at the mouth of Glen Ey. The stretch of the river from Inverey to BRAEMAR can only be described as majestic.

To the N. spread the massive shoulders of Ben a' Bhourd and Ben Avon (3,843 ft). In the foreground is Mar Lodge, the former home of the Duke of Fife that is now a Swiss-style ski centre. At your back a succession of cataracts come down from the slopes of Morrone and fill the air with the sound of rushing water. To the E. of Braemar the river passes under the Lion's Face Rock to Invercauld, with its two bridges. The older of the two (closed by the Prince Consort because it carried the road into Ballochbuie Forest) is known as the "Old Bridge of Dee" and was built in 1752. With its picturesque mountain background and graceful lines, it is a favourite with photographers.

Invercauld House stands on a little plateau above the river on the N. bank some distance above the Invercauld Bridge, and is sometimes said to enjoy the best view on Deeside. It has a battlemented tower 70 ft high, but the main block was reconstructed in 1875. It is the home of Capt. A. A. C. Farquharson, the present Chief of the Farquharson Clan.

At Inver, between Invercauld and BALMORAL, there is a famous inn where the Dee is joined by the Feardar Burn, the usual starting-place for the ascent of either Ben a' Bhourd or Ben Avon. About this point the valley widens out and takes on a softer, mellower aspect, and the silver birches that are its glory in its lower reaches begin to dominate the landscape. Beyond Balmoral it narrows again, winding about between the low "pudding bowl" hills produced by glacial erosion, which are a feature of the stretch immediately above and below BALLATER.

Although the Dee is officially a Lowland river E. of its confluence with the Burn of Dinnet, its entire right bank is overlooked by the high land rising to the watershed of the Mounth, or

The priory cross, Fyvie (see p. 229)

GRAMPIAN range, and indeed even at Aberdeen the ridge of moorland above Kincorth and Torry, though under 1,000 ft, is called the Grampians. This formidable mountain barrier played a most significant part in Scottish history; it is intersected by a series of passes through which armies marched in campaigns from the Celtic period to the 17th cent. Some of these passes are now represented only by drove roads and fragmentary paths and tracks; others are followed by modern motor roads. But it may be helpful to identify them.

Reading from W. to E., they were: the CAIRNWELL – the DEVIL'S ELBOW road from Braemar to BLAIRGOWRIE; the Tolmounth, leading from Braemar via Glen Callater to GLEN CLOVA, KIRRIEMUIR, and FORFAR; the Capel Mounth leading from Glenmuick also to Glen Clova; the Mounth Kean road from Ballater to Glen Esk and EDZELL; the Fir Mounth Pass from DINNET through Glen Tanar to Glen Esk; the Fungle Pass from ABOYNE, which joins Glen Esk on the county march of Angus; the CAIRN O' MOUNT road from BANCHORY to FETTERCAIRN; the Crynes Corse Mounth from Durris on Deeside to GLENBERVIE; the Elsick Mounth from Maryculter to Cowie just N. of STONEHAVEN; and the Causey Mounth Pass from Banchory to Devenick just SW. of Aberdeen. Dee is a famous water for salmon.

DEER, *Aberdeenshire* (Map 6, ref. 38°84⁷). The district of Deer is a very large area embracing thirteen parishes, the northern and much the larger part of the province of Buchan. The presbytery of Deer is roughly equivalent to this, while the former parish of Deer, originally the administrative area directly under the oversight of the Cistercian Abbey of Deer, was itself split up at the Reformation into two parishes which are themselves unusually large: Old Deer and New Deer.

To this place in its central position in the fertile and finely wooded valley of the South Water of Ugie came St Drostan about the year A.D. 520 and founded what became the Celtic monastery of Deer. Its actual size is not known, but it was not where the ruins of the later Cistercian abbey now stand. St Drostan was a Pict, but his disciples were followed in the course of time by the Celtic monks of the united Scottish kingdom. They occupied the ancient monastery and wrote the Gaelic portions of that remarkable manuscript the *Book of Deer*, which came to light in the library of Cambridge University in 1857.

By the end of the 12th cent. the monastery had fallen into ruin, but its memory was still green; and so in 1218 William Comyn, Great Justiciar of Scotland, who, eight years before, had married Marjorie, only child and heiress of Fergus, the last Celtic Earl of Buchan, founded the Cistercian Abbey of St Mary in the Vale of Deer, about ¾ m. from the old Celtic monastery, and on the opposite bank of the Ugie.

The existing ruins and foundations, which were acquired by the Catholic Church and are cared for by the Ministry of Public Building and Works, are open to the public from March to September. They include the church with its nave, choir, and presbytery, and N. and S. transepts, this last with its night stair to the dortour in which the monks slept. Separated from the church by the cloister are the kitchen, refectory, and warming-room, and beyond them the abbot's lodging and the infirmary.

The nearby village of Old Deer is full of interest. One of the monks of Deer, Gilbert Chisholm, became the first post-Reformation minister of the parish of Deer. The present parish church was built in 1788, but behind it are the ruins of the pre-Reformation parish church. For 150 years Old Deer was the scene of intense conflict between Presbyterian and Episcopalian factions, and this reached a violent climax in 1711 in the incident known as the Rabbling of Deer. Encouraged by the Keiths and other Episcopalian and Jacobite heritors of the parish, a mob attacked the reverend gentlemen of the presbytery, who had come to ordain and install John Gordon as the new minister, and forced them to retire. Today the beautiful little Episcopal Church of St Drostan stands in the main street opposite the parish kirk, and universal toleration and good feeling reign.

Until the second half of the 18th cent. Old Deer was alone in its glory as the principal populated place, not only in the parish, but in the whole valley of the South Ugie. Today that fertile vale sustains six other thriving villages, four of them founded by one remarkable man, James Ferguson of Pitfour (1734–1820). He drove turnpike roads throughout Buchan, transformed its treeless aspect by miles of hawthorn hedges, made great plantations on his own estate, constructed a lake of forty-five acres, and adorned it with a miniature facsimile of the Temple of Theseus in Athens.

Longside, which lies 6 m. W. of PETERHEAD and 4½ m. E. of Old Deer, he feued out in 1801. This beautiful tree-lined village, which vies with Old Deer itself as the most charming in Buchan, was just being built when John Skinner of Linshart, the poet of "Tullochgorum", left it for the last time (*see* BALLATER). He had survived the years of Episcopalian persecution that followed his arrival as pastor. Skinner's faith is magnificently represented at Longside today by St John's Episcopal Church, whose massive bell-tower dominates the whole village from its stance on the far side of the Burn of Linshart. The chancel window is perhaps his finest memorial.

Mintlaw, 2½ m. W. of Longside and 2 m. E. of Old Deer, was also feued out by James Ferguson in 1801. It has a spacious square, which has been transformed by the creation of

Plate 6   Glasgow: the University (see p. 249)
Scottish Tourist Board

an enormous traffic roundabout in the middle of it, for it lies at the junction of the main ABERDEEN–FRASERBURGH and Peterhead–BANFF highways. It has building and motor-engineering industries, and is still growing.

James Ferguson's first venture in the creation of a "New Town" was Fetterangus, 1½ m. NW. of Mintlaw. Founded in 1772, it has an old-world air, having been by-passed by what is now the main road to Fraserburgh. But its air of dereliction is misleading, for it has a big engineering works that exports agricultural implements all over the world.

New Deer is 5½ m. W. of Old Deer; it was founded by Ferguson in 1805 alongside the ancient hamlet of Auchriddie – "The Field of Bog Myrtle". It lies high at the head of the Ugie vale, and from the nearby Hill of Culsh there are magnificent views. From this view-point one can see the spires of Peterhead (18 m. E.), BENNACHIE (28 m. S.), the hills in the neighbourhood of Banff and CULLEN, and Ben Rinnes on the borders of Moray. New Deer's nearby antiquities are the Castle of Feddrate (15th cent.) and the Muckle Ordeal Stone of Auchmaliddie.

Stuartfield, situated 1½ m. S. of Old Deer, was founded in 1772 by John Burnett, the Laird of Crichie (who was related by marriage to Ferguson of Pitfour). Burnett named the place Stuartfield in honour of his grandfather, Captain John Stuart, who had lost a hand in the siege of Namur in 1696. But the village is still popularly called Crichie after the manorial estate. It was a weaving town, with a loom in every but-and-ben, and at one time outstripped Old Deer in prosperity. Now its only industry is the finishing shop of a local wool mill.

DENHOLM, *Roxburghshire* (Map 3, ref. 35⁷61⁸), is another village possessing that unusual feature in Scotland, a village green. On this green is an obelisk to John Leyden, scholar poet (1775–1811), who was born in the low, whitewashed, thatched cottage on the N. side of the village. Denholm was also the birthplace of John Scott, botanist (1836–80), and of Sir James Murray (1837–1915) of the Oxford English Dictionary. The village went in for stocking-weaving, and two of the early factories have survived; the one at the W. corner of the village is well preserved.

The SE. street of the village has nine 18th-cent. houses, and at the S. corner of the village is Westgate Hall, a 17th-cent. house with a lintel dated 1663; the arms of Sir Archibald Douglas and his wife Dame Rachel Skean are on a fireplace within.

DENNY, *Stirlingshire* (Map 2, ref. 28¹68³). A paper-manufacturing town on the R. Carron to the E. of the Kilsyth Hills, Denny also possesses light engineering. The town is joined with DUNIPACE in the same police burgh and parish. It is on the route to STIRLING from the

S. and also on a by-road through hilly country to FINTRY and the W. Nearly 2 m. S. of Denny lies the mining village of Dennyloanhead.

DESKFORD, *Banffshire* (Map 6, ref. 35⁰86²), is a village 4 m. inland from CULLEN. Deskford Tower, now demolished, was once the family seat of the earls of Findlater and Seafield.

The church, now unused and a ruin, has a rich sacrament house of the type peculiar to the NE. of Scotland during the early 16th cent. It bears an inscription saying that "this present lovable work of sacrament house" was provided by Alexander Ogilvy of Deskford in 1551.

The Vale of Deskford (pronounced locally "Deskert") is bounded by low hills rising to 1,000 ft on either side, and is now purely agricultural, but in the 18th cent. it was humming from end to end with the linen-spinning industry launched by James, 5th Earl of Findlater, which resulted in the building of two picturesque villages at the lower end of strath – Lintmill and Tochieneal. Every house in the vale had its spinning-wheel, and Deskford had a bleachfield. When the linen industry collapsed, Tochieneal acquired a brick-works to use a rich deposit of Jurassic clay, and also a distillery. Both these have gone, and in both villages the residents are mainly employees of the Seafield estates.

In this parish was found the Boar's Head of Leichestown, a hammered brass effigy of a boar's head now in the Scottish National Museum of Antiquities in EDINBURGH.

DEVERON, River, *Aberdeenshire*/*Banffshire* (Map 6, ref. 36⁰83⁵). Just short of 62 m. in length, the Deveron (anciently the Doveron or Black Water) rises in the wild recesses of the CABRACH, from which it emerges by a series of glens and enters Aberdeenshire to flow through the lovely Haugh of Glass to the out-skirts of HUNTLY, just N. of where it is joined by the Bogie. It now skirts the Bin forest to tryst with its largest tributary, the Isla, at Rothiemay, where it re-enters Banffshire. Once more the hills close in upon it as it flows by the Dens of Mayen, with high wooded banks on either side, to Bridge of Marnoch, after which it continues on an eastward course through tamer country to Inverkeithney, where it is joined by the Burn of Forgue, coming from storied Frendraught and Glendronach to the S.

Deveron is an elusive river. Whenever it approaches a town, it takes avoiding action; and this is what happens on the outskirts of TURRIFF, where it swings from E. to N. on receiving the Water of Idoch, and flows under a fine three-arched bridge of Delgatie sand-stone. It then passes Forglen House amid charming scenery, and by Montblairy and Deulugas to meet the Burn of King Edward. By the ruins of Eden Castle, it turns westward to enter the picturesque narrows between the Hill of Alvah and the Hill of Montcoffer, where a precipitous chasm that narrows to 17 ft is spanned by a fine bridge over a pool 50 ft deep. Below this point the valley opens out, and the river encloses the plain on which Duff House stands, to pass under the seven-arched Bridge of Banff, and reach its estuary beyond the towns of BANFF and MACDUFF.

From its source to its mouth on the Moray Firth coast, the Deveron has, in the course of centuries, gathered to itself a great harvest of popular minstrelsy and ballad lore, which ranges from the stirring "Roy's Wife of Aldivalloch" to that epic of peasant endurance, "The Hash of Drumdelgie". Drumdelgie deserves, perhaps, a special comment. This great 700-acre farm lies about 3 m. NW. of Huntly on steeply sloping fields facing S. towards a wide loop of the river. The actual farmhouse stands on top of a hill and enjoys a glorious panoramic view of the Deveron valley, with the town of Huntly and the hills of Strathbogie in the background. Through the many variations of the ballad, it has come to stand for the apotheosis of the "muckle toon" or major holding, in which, before the mechanization of farming, a very large staff of farm labourers toiled by day and slept by night in the "chaumer", where they also sang their songs to the fiddle or melodeon and enjoyed the rough and tumble of a very spartan communal life. It is this life that is described in detail in the ballad, with the emphasis on the hardships of peasant existence. It is indeed a masterpiece of invective against the misuse of the farm servant, which is now happily a thing of the distant past. But, mingled with the exposure of sweated labour, there is also pride in farming skills.

It was Robert Louis Stevenson who said that the old land was the true land – everything else was a falling away from that great elemental reality. Today at Drumdelgie the slavery of the mill is over and tractors drive the ploughs. The farm servant has become a mechanic. And above the sloping fields of Drumdelgie the leonine form of the Bin Hill is clad from base to summit with conifers. There is good salmon and trout fishing in various reaches of the Deveron.

DEVIL'S BEEF TUB, The, *Dumfriesshire* (Map 2, ref. 30⁷61³). A deep hollow in the hills at the head of Annandale, 5 m. NW. of MOFFAT, the "Devil's Beef Tub" is overshadowed by steep green slopes. The road from BROUGHTON to Moffat skirts the side of the hollow. It was used by cattle-raiders to hide their spoil, and there are many legends attached to the place, including the incident used by Scott in *Redgauntlet*. The barren and wild hillside and a monument at the roadside underline the winter hardships here. This monument is about ½ m. on the Moffat side of the summit near the head of the Devil's Beef Tub; the inscription reads: "Near the head

of this burn, on 1st February 1831, James McGeorge, Guard, and John Goodfellow, Driver, of the Dumfries to Edinburgh mail lost their lives in the snow after carrying the bags thus far. Erected 1931".

Above the road, as it climbs along the flank of the Beef Tub, is Erickstane Brae, up which the Roman road runs past a Roman signalstation. High on this stretch of road was found in the 1780s a magnificent heavy gold brooch of about A.D. 304–6, a princely object that may well have been dropped by Constantius Chlorus himself when on his Scottish campaign.

DEVIL'S ELBOW, The, *Perthshire* (Map 6, ref. 31⁴77⁷), is the name given to a series of very steep and tortuous turns near the highest part of the road leading from GLEN SHEE to BRAEMAR, and near to where the counties of Perthshire, Aberdeenshire, and Angus meet. The road and the corners have been much improved in recent years, but it is still renowned for being one of the first roads in Scotland to be blocked by snow in winter.

Nearby are high peaks – Meall Odhar (3,019 ft), the Cairnwell (3,059 ft), and Glas Maol (3,502 ft); in recent years their slopes have been developed as a ski resort. There is a chair-lift, several ski-tows, and a ski school. In winter the Elbow is now thronged with cars and buses bringing skiers from all over Scotland, while in summer the chair-lift is equally busy taking visitors up to see the incomparable view from the top.

DINGWALL, *Ross and Cromarty* (Map 5, ref. 25⁵85⁸), is the county town and derived its name from "thing", the Norse word for parliament. The town once had a royal castle, and was a stronghold of the earls of Ross until their downfall in 1476. According to some claims, it was created a royal burgh in 1226. Dingwall now consists of one long street, from which the main road to the N. branches off in the middle, the rest of the traffic going to STRATHPEFFER and the W. The tolbooth dates from 1730, and has in front of it the shaft of the old mercat cross and an iron yett from the old town gaol. Near the church at the N. side of the town is an obelisk in memory of George, 1st Earl of Cromartie (1630–1714). The tower on the hill S. of the town, put up in 1907, commemorates the birth of General Sir Hector Macdonald, "Fighting Mac" (1853–1903). The inhabitants and civic authorities are to be praised for recalling in stone the qualities of this Scottish soldier who met such a tragic end.

Dingwall is a good centre for touring the North and West.

DINNET, *Aberdeenshire* (Map 6, ref. 34⁶79⁹). When the R. DEE emerges from its close confinement between the hills at CAMBUS O' MAY, it enters the Muir of Dinnet, a wide undulating basin almost entirely covered with heather and birchen scrub, which in a less picturesque setting would probably seem monotonous and dreary. But here, ringed as it is by shapely hills (the long ridge of Culblean rising up to the towering mass of Morven on the W., and lesser hills topped by the sharp pinnacle of Mount Keen on the S.), and broken by the gleaming waters of several little lakes, the largest of which are Loch Kinord and Loch Davan, the Muir of Dinnet has a magic that never fails to capture the eye.

The village of Dinnet, in the centre of the basin, owes its existence to the coming of the Deeside railway in the middle of last century, but close by are the signs of very ancient settlement. On Loch Kinord is Crannog Island, an artificial creation dating from the Bronze Age. Based upon a raft of logs and brushwood, it was built up by successive layers of stone and earth, held together by intersecting mortised timbers, until the whole contraption grounded by its own weight; piles were then driven in all around and through the existing mass. Kinord also has its Castle Island, where a medieval peel-tower played its part in one of the decisive dramas of Scottish history, the Battle of Culblean, the turning-point in the Second War of Independence. The battle is commemorated by a granite monolith overlooking Loch Kinord on the W., erected by the Deeside Field Club in 1956 and recording the defeat of the English forces of David de Strathbogie, Earl of Atholl, by Sir Andrew de Moray, Warden of Scotland, on St Andrew's Day, the 30th of November 1335. De Moray had hurried N. on learning that Atholl with 3,000 men was besieging his wife, Christian Bruce, the aunt of King David II, in KILDRUMMY Castle. By the night of the 29th of November, de Moray reached the Ha' of Ruthven on Loch Davan, to find that opposite him on the slopes of Culblean were the camp fires of Atholl, who had withdrawn from Kildrummy and was hoping to give him the slip. But he came upon them from behind in the grey of the morning, surprised and totally routed the English forces, slaying Atholl in the process. One of Atholl's men, Sir Robert Menzies, took possession of the Castle of Kinord, where he was safe for the time being in the island fastness; but he afterwards capitulated.

On the other side of the Dee, S. of Dinnet village, is the farm of Ballaterach, where, as a little lame boy aged eight, Lord Byron recovered from an unromantic bout of scarlet fever and fell in love with the farmer's daughter, Mary Robertson, who became the subject of a poem by him – the most famous verses ever written about Culblean and Morven.

Romantic interest attaches also to the old house of Blelack, farther N., where Charles Gordon raised levies for Bonnie Prince Charlie in the '45.

DIRLETON, *East Lothian* (Map 3, ref. 35²68⁴). Standing about 3 m. from NORTH BERWICK on the road to EDINBURGH, Dirleton is claimed by many to be the most beautiful village in Scotland – though some would accord the palm to GIFFORD, also in East Lothian. Framed by mature trees, it is set around a large green, ringed on three sides by 17th- and 18th-cent. houses and cottages, and dominated on the fourth side by the Castle.

Dirleton Castle, maintained by the Ministry of Public Building and Works, stands in a lovely flower garden, and dates partly from the 13th cent.; there is a three-storey Renaissance portion still standing. The Castle's last battle was fought against Oliver Cromwell's troops; the building was dismantled by General Lambert in 1650.

In the Castle gardens are a 17th-cent. bowling-green, surrounded by ancient yew trees and still used regularly by the villagers, and a 16th-cent. circular doocot.

The parish kirk, built in the early 17th cent., lies to the N. of the village facing its own small green. It has been modernized inside, and a vestry, E. porch, and upper part of the tower added.

To the W. lies Archerfield House, also now a ruin, which took the place of the Castle as the residence of the Ruthven family. Its grounds have associations with Robert Louis Stevenson's *Pavilion on the Links*.

Dirleton lies 2 m. inland, and the coastline, which is accessible most of the way by motorcar, is unspoilt and delightful with trees and springy turf right down to the shore. It is known as "Yellowcraig", and it was left to the people of Dirleton to be enjoyed by them for ever.

The small rocky island of Fidra, with a lighthouse, lies a short way off the shore, and includes a bird sanctuary where gannets breed. Trips by boat to Fidra are organized daily in the summer months from North Berwick. It is usually possible to land, to climb slowly to the top of the lighthouse gallery, and on a fine day to enjoy what surely must be one of the finest views in southern Scotland.

DOLLAR, *Clackmannanshire* (Map 2, ref. 29⁷69⁸), is a small orderly rural town between STIRLING and MILNATHORT, and known locally as the "classic burgh". It is probably best known for its Academy, set up in 1818 with an endowment from John McNab, a local boy who made a fortune as a sea-captain. The original school building was designed by William Playfair, the architect responsible for the Royal Scottish Academy, the National Gallery, and other New Town building in EDINBURGH. Dollar Glen, on the flank of King's Seat, which is 2,111 ft high, with its ravines, paths, and bridges, makes a pleasant approach to CASTLE CAMPBELL. A hilltrack from the Castle leads N. for 3 m. to

Glendevon. The residential, academic character of the town has been preserved by a local government policy of strict control over development.

DOLPHINTON, *Lanarkshire* (Map 3, ref. 31¹64⁷). This small farming village on the road between EDINBURGH and BIGGAR is at the S. end of the Pentlands. Evidence of early settlement here was found in 1920 when a cist was discovered on Kippit Hill during the erection of the monument to Major Kenneth Mackenzie. Relics found with remnants of a human skeleton in the cist indicated that the burial dated from the early Iron Age. The village is said to take its name from Dolfin, a kinsman of the 1st Earl of Dunbar, who owned the lands in the early 12th cent.

DON, River, *Aberdeenshire* (Map 6, ref. 38°81⁶), comes sixth of the Scottish rivers in size, being 80 m. long and draining a basin of 515 sq. m. It rises on the Aberdeenshire–Banffshire border within ⅔ m. of the Avon at Inchrory at an altitude of about 2,000 ft in Coire Domhain, and flows in a generally easterly direction, entering the sea a little N. of Old ABERDEEN.

The old rhyme

> Ae mile o' Don's worth twa o' Dee
> Except for salmon, stone and tree

is still true except for the reservation about stone, for it was coined long before the granite-quarrying industry at KEMNAY, and in other Donside parishes, was born. It is the finest trouting stream in Scotland. Its comparative poverty in salmon is due to the cruives or wicker salmon-traps and other obstructions near its mouth.

The Don can scarcely rival the R. DEE in rugged Highland grandeur in its upper reaches, where the surrounding hills are lower and the enclosing glen is altogether narrower and more intimate, but its variety is superb. Although the portion of the valley above Cock Bridge, where the LECHT pass diverges to the N. over the Hill of Allargue, is rather bare, below that point a succession of quick changes from Corgarff to the Water of Deskry dazzles you with a succession of inviting vistas and delectable hamlets and historic homes.

Strathdon, as more than one observer has remarked, is a misnomer. It is not a strath in the usual sense of the word, but a closely-walled winding river valley intersected by five large glens – the Conrie, the Ernan, the Carvie, the Nochty, and the Deskry.

Much of Strathdon is traversed, on the appropriate date towards the end of August, by the Lonach Highlanders in the picturesque march that preludes the annual Lonach Games, held in front of the Lonach Hall, which stands beside Colquhonny Castle and the modern Colquhonny Hotel (45 m. W. of Aberdeen).

The clansmen who participate in the march from the head of the Strath, in the early morning before the games, calling at Inverernan, Edinglassie, Candacraig, and other big houses, where they receive tots of whisky in which to toast their patrons, are members of the venerable Lonach Highland and Friendly Society established in 1825. Prizes are awarded for the "best-dressed Highlander" and for other distinctions.

The economic pivot of this part of the valley is Candacraig estate, where the present laird has developed a great forestry enterprise, which goes hand in hand with a famous herd of Aberdeen-Angus cattle. Between Candacraig and the hamlet of Bellabeg is the beautiful Bridge of Poldhullie, with a single arch of 70 ft. It was built in 1715 by John Forbes of Inverernan, who died at Carlisle in the following year on the night before the day fixed for his execution as an officer in the Jacobite army.

Just W. of the point where the Water of Nochty sweeps out of its wide open glen into the tree-sheltered, much-winding vale of the upper Don at Bellabeg, there rises out of a little plain the green mound of the Doune of Invernochty.

This was a partly isolated junction terrace trimmed by man to provide the perfect site for a motte-and-bailey stronghold of the Earl of Mar in the early feudal period. When parishes were created, the church arose in the shelter of this moated doune and was known as the Church of Invernochty as early as the 12th cent. The present Church of Strathdon was built in 1853 on the site of four predecessors, and is one of the glories of the Strath. Its lofty ribbed interior seems more like that of a cathedral than that of a parish church, and it contains carved 17th-cent. panels from an old pew.

The portion of the Don valley between Bellabeg and the Bridge of Buchat is dominated by Ben Newe – an easy hill to climb, and one yielding a fine view despite its modest height of 1,855 ft. A short distance below the Bridge of Buchat, the Don enters the fine basin of KILDRUMMY and, after being joined by the Burn of Mossat, passes through a narrow, richly wooded stretch between the Hill of Coillebhar and Lord Arthur's Cairn (1,699 ft). Here the river is rapid and shallow, until at last it emerges into the open country of the Vale of Alford. It is spanned by the triple-arched Bridge of Alford, built in 1811.

One might suppose that now the course of the Don would be through tamer Lowland country, and that its moments of Highland grandeur were over. But in that case some very pleasant surprises are in store, for – after meandering for some 6 m. through the open farmland of the vale (which is really an alluvial basin of little more than 15 sq. m.) – the Don enters the parish of Keig and passes through the impressive gorge of the Lord's Throat between Cairn William and BENNACHIE. The

Bridge of Keig (pronounced Kegg), a single arch of 100 ft built in 1817, is at the SW. corner of the estate of Castle Forbes, the traditional seat of the Premier Baron of Scotland.

There is another attractive section of the river at Manar before it reaches INVERURIE to join its most important tributary, the Urie. Below this confluence lies a long stretch of haughland around KINTORE and Kinaldie, but at Cothal, just N. of DYCE, there is another picturesque gorge. From this sector, until it reaches the final gorge at Balgownie in Aberdeen, the Don is used by a succession of papermills, yet it never loses its contact with natural beauty, and at Persley it flows through a wooded den that is a well-known haunt of Aberdonians in search of outdoor pleasure.

The Don is a companionable river; it brings never-failing delight and refreshment of spirit.

DONIBRISTLE, *Fife* (Map 3, ref. 31⁷68³). The estate of Donibristle, on the shore of the Firth of FORTH 3 m. SW. of ABERDOUR, was originally in the possession of the abbots of INCHCOLM. After the Reformation, the land was granted to the Stuart earls of Moray, and it was here that the Bonny Earl o' Moray was slain. Dalgety, about 1 m. NE. of Donibristle, has an old chancel built by the monks of Inchcolm, with the priests' lodging at the end.

During the First World War, Lord Moray gave the land to the Royal Air Force for some experiments; in 1936 the airfield was handed over to the Fleet Air Arm. In 1962 the Admiralty finally gave it up, and it became an industrial estate, which was opened in August 1962. A new town in connection with this venture is being planned under private management.

DOON, Loch, *Ayrshire* (Map 2, ref. 25⁰59⁸), lies in the mountainous country 5 m. S. of DALMELLINGTON. It is 700 ft above sea-level, and approximately 5½ m. long, with an average width of about ½ m. In the early 1930s the level was raised by about 20 ft by the Galloway Water Power Company, the first hydro-electric company of any size in Scotland. It now forms part of the undertaking of the South of Scotland Electricity Board. The water impounded in the loch is abstracted through a tunnel into the watershed of the R. Ken in Galloway, and passes through several power stations *en route* to the Solway, but the Bonnie Doon of Robert Burns is comparatively unharmed. Loch Doon Castle, which stood on an island, was rebuilt on the loch-side to preserve it from inundation when the water-level was raised. The Castle dates from the early 14th cent.

DORES, *Inverness-shire* (Map 5, ref. 26⁰83⁴), is a village on the eastern shore of Loch NESS, almost at the northern end. The land round about it was once Macbain country, and about 2 m. NE. of the village, near Kinchyle on the road to Loch Ashie, is the clan "Memory Park", recently laid out by Hughston Macbain of Macbain.

A road going S. follows the loch-side closely for 8 m., with attractive views of water and trees, while another road climbs steeply out of Dores to the ridge above the loch and follows that, providing a remarkable series of vistas in all directions.

DORNADILLA, *Sutherland* (Map 5, ref. 24⁶94⁴). This is the site of the Dornadilla Broch on the old route between the N. coast and Strathnaver just S. of Loch Hope, now a very rough road. The broch is one of the very few in which part of the wall stands more than 20 ft high. Another item of interest is that a large triangular lintel covers the outer opening of the entrance passage – a feature noted in later rather than earlier brochs.

DORNIE, *Ross and Cromarty* (Map 5, ref. 18⁹82⁶), is the name given to the narrows where Loch Duich meets Loch LONG. There was formerly a ferry, but a bridge was completed in 1939. Near Dornie village, to the S. of the bridge, is EILEAN DONAN Castle, and from the village a path leads inland to the Falls of GLOMACH. W. Highland scenery of mountain, sea, and loch, is shown here at its finest. There are other places in the West as beautiful as Dornie – but not many.

Dornie is also a centre of the indigenous W. Highland Catholicism.

DORNOCH, *Sutherland* (Map 5, ref. 28⁰88⁹). The royal burgh of Dornoch (created 1628) is the county town of Sutherland, and was once the seat of the bishops of Caithness. The cathedral is now a parish church; it was built in the early 13th cent. on the site of what had been the centre of a Culdee community since the 6th cent. It was much damaged in 1570; the nave was rebuilt in 1835–7, and the whole wall was restored in 1924. Sixteen earls of Sutherland are said to be buried here. The church has a statue of the 1st Duke (d. 1833) and an effigy of Sir Richard de Moravia, brother of Gilbert the founder, killed by the Danes at Embo in 1248.

Dornoch possesses a world-renowned golf course, which is long established even for Scotland, having been played on in the early 17th cent. Holiday visitors will also find good sandy beaches.

In a garden near the lower links of the town is a stone to mark the spot of the last judicial execution of a witch in Scotland, in 1722. She was Janet Horn, who was tarred, feathered, and roasted, being accused of having turned her daughter into a pony and having her shod by the devil.

Some 4 m. W. of Dornoch is Skibo estate, which once belonged to the bishops of Caithness, later to the Mackays, and in the 18th cent.

to George Dempster, the "improver". Dempster, though he came originally from the Lowlands, was one of the most humane and far-seeing of Scots at the time of the "Clearance and Evictions". Later Skibo was the home of Andrew Carnegie, who built the present Castle as a holiday residence in the early part of this century.

DOUGLAS, *Lanarkshire* (Map 2, ref. 28⁴63¹), is a small town on the Douglas Water in a coal-mining area. A seam opened beneath Douglas Castle caused it to be demolished in 1938–48; only the chapel and porch remain of the house that was rebuilt in 1759. The earlier building was the scene of the Douglas Larder when, in 1307, Sir James Douglas trapped the English while they were in church on Palm Sunday and recaptured his own castle.

"The guid Schir James" Douglas has been much romanticized in Scottish history. He was undoubtedly one of Bruce's boldest and most reliable captains during the King's guerrilla warfare to regain Scotland. But Douglas was primarily a virtuoso in terrorism. The episode of the Douglas Larder is one of the most daring, the most outrageous, and (be it added) the most disgusting of his terroristic activities. The castle was rebuilt later and was Scott's "Castle Dangerous".

The Church of St Bride was founded in the 12th cent. and rebuilt in 1390; it has canopied tombs and effigies of Douglases, including Archibald Bell-the-Cat, Earl of Angus, whose heart in a leaden casket is there. It has an unusual clock-tower with a clock dated 1565, traditionally a gift of Mary Queen of Scots, and a Dutch bell cast in 1609. In 1780 the church was abandoned as a place of worship.

DOUNE, *Perthshire* (Map 2, ref. 27³70¹). This small town was once famous for the manufacture of pistols, a trade introduced in 1645 by Robert Caddell. The main attractions of the town are the Castle, once a royal palace and still the property of the earls of Moray, and the Deanston Cotton Mills, which in 1844 employed over 1,000 people, but may soon be closed. The Castle, one of the best-preserved medieval castles in Scotland, stands on the left bank of the R. Teith at its point of junction with the Ardoch. The date of the present structure is uncertain, but documents relate to the "Castle of Downe in Menteyth" at the end of the 14th cent. The Castle, as seen today, is unfinished. The strongly fortified keep rises above the entrance, but the residential apartments, which were planned for the remaining sides of a spacious courtyard with walls 40 ft high, have never been built. The Castle belonged originally to the dukes of Albany, but it was confiscated by James I and used by him and his successors as a royal residence until 1528, when it was given back to a descendant, with the title of Lord Doune, of the original owner.

Through him it came into the possession of the earls of Moray. The famous Scottish ballad, "The Bonnie Earl o' Moray", with the immortal lines

> O lang lang will his lady
> Look ower the Castle Doune
> Ere she sees the Earl o' Moray
> Come sounding through the toun,

relate to the death of the Earl murdered at DONIBRISTLE in 1591.

The Castle was last used by Prince Charles Edward Stuart to house prisoners taken after the Battle of FALKIRK in 1746.

The bridge over the Teith was built in 1535 and widened and repaired in 1866. It was built by one Robert Spittal, who is said to have been tailor to James IV of Scotland. Arriving at the ferry without money on one occasion, he was refused passage, and he built the bridge out of spite in order to take away the ferryman's living. One arch of the bridge was destroyed in 1715 by the Earl of Mar to hold up the government troops moving N. out of STIRLING.

"Old Kilmadock", upstream from the town where the Annet Burn joins the Teith, is a ruin of the original monastery of St Docus, which in 1238 was under the wing of the Priory of INCHMAHOME in the Lake of MENTEITH. The name Annet (or Annat) is one of the oldest religious terms in the Celtic Church, meaning always the Mother Church of a district. "Wherever there is an Annat there are traces of an ancient chapel. . . ."

DOUNREAY, *Caithness* (Map 7, ref. 30⁰96⁵). Owing partly to its spectacular appearance, often photographed in the Scottish and English press, partly to its extraordinary position at the extreme N. of the ultimate

The Fast Reactor at Dounreay
United Kingdom Atomic Energy Authority

county of Caithness, and, of course, largely because of its high scientific importance, the Dounreay Experimental Reactor Establishment has attracted large attention within Scotland and without.

The Reactor Establishment is situated on the rock-bound coast of Northern Scotland, 30 m. W. of JOHN O' GROATS and just about halfway between London and the Arctic Circle.

Dounreay's purpose is this. The establishment has been set up by the United Kingdom Atomic Energy Authority to develop and test advanced nuclear reactors for use in the atomic power stations of the future. The importance of this work can be judged by the fact that towards the end of this century the production of cheap and plentiful electricity from nuclear power will be vital to Britain's economy.

Dounreay's first task has been to demonstrate that what is called a "fast breeder reactor" can be built and operated safely at power. This type of reactor is being developed for inclusion in the third stage of Britain's nuclear power programme. It has been chosen for three main reasons:

1. If the development programme is successful, fast reactors will provide, for the first time, an efficient means of extracting energy from plutonium under controlled conditions.

2. Plutonium is a by-product of thermal nuclear power stations such as CHAPEL-CROSS and HUNTERSTON. If, therefore, the present system of thermal power stations can be supplemented by a system of fast reactor stations, the cost of producing electricity should be significantly reduced.

3. Fast reactors will themselves "breed" more atomic fuel than they consume.

The main features are these. The Dounreay Fast Reactor is housed in a steel sphere, 135 ft in diameter (three feet more than the dome of St Pauls), which dominates the site and is the focal point of its activities. It is this spectacular object that has so strongly appealed to the photographers and visitors. The core of the reactor – a cylinder just about the size of a dustbin – produces, at full power, 60 mW. of heat, the equivalent of 60,000 single-bar electric fires. Complex liquid metal-cooling circuits carry this concentrated heat away from the core and through the wall of the sphere to an adjacent heat-exchanger building. Here the heat is used to raise steam and drive a turbo-alternator with a maximum output of 15 mW. of electricity. If the turbine is not running, the steam is diverted into condensers cooled by sea-water, supplied by a pump-house on the cliff-edge, which can deliver up to 2 million gallons per hour.

A second reactor – the Dounreay Materials Testing Reactor – which was used to test the behaviour, under irradiation, of materials intended for use in existing and future reactors (which, of course, include fast reactors) was closed down in May 1969 after completing

over 700 major experiments. The associated fuel manufacturing plants have continued to supply fuel for other materials testing reactors in the United Kingdom and abroad.

There is an extensive range of laboratories and full supporting engineering, administrative, and health and safety services. In fact, no other atomic energy establishment in the world is so self-supporting or better equipped to carry through a reactor development programme.

Dounreay's achievements till now may be summed up thus. The Dounreay Fast Reactor was first brought into operation or "taken critical" in November 1959. Having completed its primary task of proving the safety and reliability of the fast reactor system when it reached its design power of 60 mW. in July 1963, this reactor has since been used to test fuels and materials for future fast reactor designs and more recently as a general irradiation facility for materials used in the construction of all types of reactors.

Dounreay has given Britain a substantial lead over the rest of the world in fast-reactor technology. The Dounreay Fast Reactor has operated at higher power levels than any other fast reactor in the world, and it has the additional distinction of being the first fast reactor ever to supply electricity for public use. Its turbine was linked to the National Grid in October 1962. Since then, it has supplied electricity both to the establishment itself and to a large area of the North of Scotland. By the end of 1970 the Dounreay Fast Reactor had produced over 300 million units of electricity.

Since 1966 Dounreay has been earning foreign currency by selling irradiation space in Dounreay Fast Reactors, pre- and post-irradiation services, and fuel manufacturing and reprocessing services to foreign organizations. In 1970 these sales were bringing in about £500,000 per annum.

In 1966 construction started on the Prototype Fast Reactor and it is expected it will go on power at the end of 1972. It has been constructed in order to confirm the performance of a design similar to that of future commercial fast reactor power stations and to provide a test bed for fuel and components for these reactors. In mid-1971 the U.K.A.E.A. announced that, since fast reactors showed every promise of generating electricity on the most economic basis, courses would be started in 1972 at Dounreay for British and other executives, engineers, and scientists, with a sodium technology and handling course for staff constructing and maintaining nuclear power stations.

Dounreay employs over 2,000 people, of whom half are imported key staff, including a high proportion of professional and scientific personnel. The majority of these people are housed with their families in THURSO (8 m. E. of Dounreay), where the Authority has built over 1,000 houses and a couple of hostels. This development has naturally stimulated corresponding developments by local authority and private enterprise, with the result that the town of Thurso has expanded from a population of 3,250 in 1955 to a figure of over 9,000. This unique and rapid development has been achieved with the minimum of friction, and an enriched, re-invigorated, and closely integrated community is now emerging from the fusion of the old and the new.

Casual visitors are not admitted to the Establishment, but ½ m. from the entrance there is a sign by the roadside inviting you to visit the Dounreay Exhibition. This exhibition was set up in the control tower overlooking the airfield on which Dounreay has been built, partly to satisfy the obvious interest of passing tourists and partly to provide an additional and novel tourist attraction to the North of Scotland. Since 1960, when it was opened, it has attracted over 150,000 visitors. The proportion of overseas visitors, at the peak of the tourist season, has been as high as 50 per cent, from places as far apart as Tokyo, Los Angeles, Dunedin, Reikjavik, and Vancouver. Many of these overseas visitors were people whose ancestors had left Scotland to seek their fortune abroad many years ago or who had themselves emigrated to various parts of the Commonwealth.

DREM, *East Lothian* (Map 3, ref. 35¹67⁹). A small village and a junction on the main E.-coast railway line, Drem lies in the centre of some of the best farming land in East Lothian, about 5 m. from NORTH BERWICK.

In the gardens of Drem House is the shell of a 15th-cent. chapel, once belonging to the Knights Templar. Part of the E. gable is built into the garden wall. The priests' house was SE. of Drem House, but only the site remains.

DRUIDIBEG, Loch, *Inverness-shire* (Map 4, ref. 08⁰83⁷), is on South UIST in the Outer Hebrides (*see* "The Shape of Scotland"). This large loch is now a nature reserve, notable for both birds and plants. It is the most important British breeding ground for greylag geese. The shallow waters are rich in aquatic flora.

It is swarming with small brown trout, and is much over-populated by these fish. Nevertheless it is a good water on which to teach young people how to cast a fly and catch a trout.

It was made a nature reserve in 1958, when the much-disputed rocket-range appeared to threaten this loch. Fortunately it has had no effect on it. However, the rocket-range is now spreading N. to other islands. Crofters have been evicted on BENBECULA to make room for it.

DRUM, *Aberdeenshire* (Map 2, ref. 30⁴70⁰). This castle in the secluded country between CULTER and the Hill of FARE speaks with two voices. It consists of the 13th-cent. Tower of Drum, one of the very first and certainly among the most famous of medieval Scottish tower-houses, a simple rectangle with battlements and rounded corners 70 ft high, whose walls at basement level are 12 ft thick, and linked to it a handsome Renaissance mansion with dormer windows and crow-stepped gables built in 1619.

The Tower of Drum was a royal keep in the ancient Forest of Drum, to which there is reference as early as 1247. The lands of Drum were bestowed by King Robert I on his armour-bearer and clerk-register William de Irwin in February 1323, and Irvines have inhabited the Tower and its Jacobean adjunct ever since, though arrangements have been made by the present Irvine Laird, 24th of his line, for its eventual transfer to the National Trust for Scotland.

The former banqueting-hall of the tower, now entered by a doorway cut through walls 11 ft thick from the first floor of the Jacobean wing, is a great vaulted chamber occupying one entire storey of the keep. It is in use as a library and billiard-room. On the barrel-vaulted ceiling are shields bearing the arms of families linked to the Irvines. Above it is another vaulted chamber also occupying the entire area of its storey, while, wholly within the thickness of the wall at one corner, a wheel-stair rises from the first floor to the battlements.

The Jacobean wing has much of interest and beauty. In the drawing-room, formerly the great hall, with a finely panelled ceiling, are Raeburn portraits of a former laird and his wife, a Reynolds, and other family portraits of distinction.

Drum Castle

Aberdeen Press and Journal

DRUMBEG, *Sutherland* (Map 5, ref. 21²93²). This township lies on the narrow winding road between LOCHINVER and KYLESKU. The district round about it is devoted to crofting. Drumbeg is popular amongst trout anglers; there are many lochs in the district, including one opposite the hotel full of just sizeable sporting fish. The Drumbeg area is also good for birds; red-throated divers nest on some of the small lochs.

DRUMCLOG, *Lanarkshire* (Map 2, ref. 26⁴63⁸). This tract of moorland and bog near the Ayrshire border was the scene of a battle on the 1st of June 1679 between Claverhouse and the Covenanters – the Covenanters being the victors. An obelisk commemorates the battle; and later, in 1912, a new church was built and dedicated as Drumclog Memorial Kirk. On the first Sunday of each June a special commemoration service with covenanting memories strong to the fore is now held here.

DRUMCOLTRAN, *Kirkcudbrightshire* (Map 2, ref. 28⁸56⁹). A tower situated among farm buildings, Drumcoltran is a good example of a mid-16th-cent. Scottish tower-house, being an oblong building three storeys high with garrets served by a wheel-stair in a projecting turret.

DRUMELZIER, *Peeblesshire* (Map 3, ref. 31³63⁴). This village on the S. bank of the TWEED is just downstream from where the river takes its bend eastwards. Near where Drumelzier Burn enters the Tweed is the traditional burial-place of the wizard Merlin. The ruins of Tinnis or Thanes Castle stand high above the river; the Castle was demolished in 1592 by order of James VI.

There is evidence of early and lasting occupation of Tweeddale from finds in cairns at Drumelzier and Woodend.

DRUMNADROCHIT, *Inverness-shire* (Map 5, ref. 25⁰83⁰), is a village lying on the W. side of Loch NESS at the mouth of Glen Urquhart. The road from the village up the glen leads through picturesque country to Strath Glass. A road also climbs up from the valley and crosses the high moorland to BEAULY. Across the R. Enrick is the twin village of Lewiston.

This is a good centre for holidays, walks, climbing, angling, and pony-trekking. URQU-HART CASTLE by Drumnadrochit is the spot where many claims to have seen the Monster of Loch Ness have been made (*see* Loch NESS).

DRUMOCHTER, *Inverness-shire/Perthshire* (Map 5, ref. 26³77⁸), is the summit of the pass on the main communication to the N. by both road and rail. The road, built originally by General Wade in 1729, reaches a height of 1,506 ft, and the railway reaches 1,484 ft. At the summit, the most prominent hills are the Boar of Badenoch to the N. and the Sow of Athol to the S.

In some conditions of snow, skiing is good on the hills round Drumochter and access is easy by rail or road.

DRUMTOCHTY, *Kincardineshire* (Map 6, ref. 37⁰77⁹). There are two ways of approaching this delectable glen that carries the upper reaches of the Luther Water from Loch Saugh through a wooded defile in a great semicircle between Strathfinella Hill and the foothills of the Mounth. There is the road from FETTER-CAIRN to the Clatterin Brig, which is the southern terminus of the CAIRN O' MOUNT, or the journey may be made in the reverse direction, going upstream from the village of Auchinblae and its near neighbour the ancient Kirktown of Fordoun, which form the link between this hill country and the lush green plain of the Howe of Mearns.

From Clatterin Brig, instead of continuing along B 974, which climbs over the pass, it is possible to take the road to the right (or E.) and, splashing through the ford on the Burn of Slack, climb up the hill past the experimental farm of Glensaugh. Loch Saugh is among the trees on the right, and on the left is Bright's Well, once reputed to have medicinal qualities. Then the road descends via Strath Finella into the Glen of Drumtochty. To the right is the entrance to Friar's Glen, where John of Fordoun is said to have written his Chronicle six centuries ago.

There is new life in Drumtochty Glen since the Forestry Commission acquired and planted Drumtochty Forest in 1926–7 and the Glenfarquhar Hills in 1953. The fifteen or twenty men employed there may not seem a great force, but the difference they have made to the landscape is profound.

Finally one emerges from the glen into the village of Auchinblae, founded about 1770, on the N. side of the Water of Luther, facing the far more ancient Kirktown of Fordoun on the S. side. Cross the river into tree-shaded, old-world Fordoun, dominated by the church, the school, and the Kirkton Farm on the site of a historic inn, and you are in a different world, for Fordoun was the cradle of Christianity in the Mearns. In the kirkyard is the ruined Chapel of St Palladius, a building consecrated by David de Bernham, Bishop of ST ANDREWS, on the 17th of October 1244.

In the kirkyard is a monument to George Wishart, one of Scotland's seven Reformation martyrs, burned as a heretic on the 1st of March 1546. He was one of the Wisharts of Pittarrow and probably worshipped in Fordoun Church as a boy.

DRYBURGH ABBEY, *Berwickshire* (Map 3, ref. 35⁹63³). This is one of the famous group of Border monasteries. It was founded by Hugh de Morville about 1152 for monks from Alnwick in Northumberland. It stands in a beautiful setting on a horseshoe bend of the TWEED. The cloister buildings have survived more completely than any in Scotland except at IONA and INCHCOLM. There is, however, little left of the church except the transepts. The ruinous state of the church is due to Dryburgh's nearness to the Border. It was destroyed by the English in 1322, 1344, and 1385.

Sir Walter Scott and Field-Marshal Earl Haig are buried here.

DRYMEN, *Stirlingshire* (Map 2, ref. 24⁸68⁸). This village in Strathendrick, within 3 m. of the SE. corner of Loch LOMOND, is a popular touring centre and, being less than 20 m. from GLASGOW, a lung for the citizens. The road from Glasgow suddenly opens out at Catythirsty Well, above Carbeth, and the Stockiemuir falls away towards Drymen and Loch Lomond, providing a panoramic mountain view scarcely equalled in Scotland.

Buchanan Castle, the seat of the Grahams of MONTROSE until about 1930, has now been demolished. Set in a wooded park laid out by "Capability" Brown and now containing a golf course, the Castle was acquired after the family home at Montrose had been destroyed in 1640.

James Bridie, the Scottish dramatist, lived in two houses in the Drymen area before and after the Second World War.

DUART CASTLE, *Argyll* (Map 1, ref. 17⁵73⁵), is on the Island of MULL in the Inner Hebrides (*see* "The Shape of Scotland"). It is the home of the Chiefs of the Macleans of Duart. The present (27th) Chief, Lord Maclean of Duart, was perhaps better known as Sir Charles Maclean, 11th Baronet, and Chief Scout of the Commonwealth since 1959. Made a life peer in the 1971 New Years Honours, in June 1971 he was appointed Lord Chamberlain to the Queen's Household and relinquished the Scout chieftainship.

The Castle was built in the 13th cent., with 16th- and 17th-cent. additions, on a rocky site at the entrance to the Sound of Mull, and opposite the S. end of LISMORE in a very commanding position. It was occupied by the Macleans until the 17th cent., when the Marquess of Argyll became dominant over the Maclean family. Argyll himself became forfeit in 1681, but the Macleans lost the lands finally after holding out for James VII and II on Cairnburg Mor in the TRESHNISH ISLANDS until 1691. The Castle was then garrisoned by the government until the end of the 18th cent., when it fell into decay.

In 1936 it was bought back by Sir Fitzroy Maclean and completely restored. Open to the public during the summer, it contains notable collections of Scottish historical relics and scouting records.

DUBH ARTACH Rocks, *Argyll* (Map 1, ref. 11³70³). The lighthouse on these rocks, 15½ m. SW. of IONA near the Torran Rocks, was built in 1867–72 of red granite from the Ross of MULL and was prepared at EARRAID.

In his *Memories and Portraits*, Robert Louis Stevenson has a description of the building of this lighthouse entitled "Memoir of an Islet". The lighthouse stands on a rock that is swept but not covered by the tide.

DUFFTOWN, *Banffshire* (Map 6, ref. 33²83⁹). A popular couplet sums up the industrial significance of this "capital of Scottish malt-distilling":

Rome was built on seven hills;
Dufftown stands on seven stills.

But this quaint town, laid out by James Duff, 4th Earl of Fife, in 1817, has yet the air of a quiet village, and it has many attractions apart from its renown as the home of pure malt whisky. It stands on a plateau in the centre of a great bowl amid the hills. The escarpments of the plateau are washed by the waters of the Fiddich, peat-stained from the shaggy moors of its glen, and its tributary the Dullan, bright with the snows of Glenrinnes. The burgh itself is laid out in the form of a right-angled cross with streets running N., S., E., and W. from the square in the middle, in which stands a square tolbooth tower.

Immediately S. of the town in the vale of the Dullan is the ancient parish church of Mortlach. It is said to be on this site that in 1010 King Malcolm II, after marching down the SPEY and camping with his army in the Queen's Haugh at CARRON, routed an army of Scandinavian invaders ("ramscuttered" is the word the chroniclers use), and thereafter fulfilled a pious vow to extend the existing church by three spears' length. The tradition is that St Moluag, from the island of LISMORE, had come to the spot in the year A.D. 566, setting up a church, a school, and a farm. What is called the Battle Stone is undoubtedly much older than King Malcolm's victory; it stands over 7 ft high and has Christian symbols on both sides. In 1923 a still older stone, called the Elephant Stone, was unearthed in the churchyard; it is now preserved within the church.

Mortlach is also said to have been the original site of the see of the bishopric transferred to ABERDEEN in 1124 by David I.

Dufftown's two other major antiquities are the Castles of Balvenie and Auchindoun. Balvenie, in the care of the Ministry of Public Building and Works, stands above the Fiddich (1½ m. N.) as one of the earliest stone castles in Scotland, with the form of a quadrangular court 150 ft by 130 ft enclosed by high curtain walls 7 ft thick. In the 13th cent., when it belonged to the Comyns, the living-rooms of the Castle were at the NW. and SE. sides of the courtyard. From the "Black Douglases", who owned it after the Comyns, it passed after 1455 to John Stewart, 1st Earl of Atholl. It was the Stewarts who in the 16th cent. gave Balvenie the shape it has today by demolishing the entire SE. front and building instead a three-storey Renaissance tower-house, known as the Atholl Building because it was erected by John, 4th Earl of Atholl, between 1542 and 1550. It has been roofless since 1724.

Auchindoun (3 m. SE. of Dufftown) also stands on a bluff above the Fiddich, and its grand old ruins are visible miles away as one approaches along the road from the CABRACH.

DUFFUS, *Moray* (Map 6, ref. 31⁸86⁸). Some 2 m. inland from HOPEMAN the great Norman mound of Duffus Castle – once lapped by the waters of the Loch of Spynie – rises from the Laich of Moray "like a boss on a buckler". The stone castle on the site was preceeded by a motte-and-bailey stronghold of earthwork and timber. The formidable keep was built in the 14th cent., and a range of domestic buildings was added after 1452. The ruins are now in the care of the Ministry of Public Building and Works; so too are the ruins of the ancient Church of St Peter near Duffus village. This lovely old church has a handsome decorative porch built by Alexander Sutherland, its rector in 1524, while in the churchyard is an ancient cross over 14 ft high.

DULL, *Perthshire* (Map 2, ref. 28²74⁸). This small township, lying N. of the main road through Strath Appin between WEEM and Keltneyburn, is the traditional site of the Celtic monastery founded by Adamnan, the biographer of Columba. At the centre of the cluster of houses is a mutilated stone cross, one of four that once marked the limits of the sanctuary. Two more crosses are preserved in the old church at Weem.

Adamnan's name is preserved in the name of the local market, Feill Eonan, and Strath Appin comes from the Gaelic "Strath-na-h-Apuinn", the Strath of the Abbeyland. The seat of learning founded by Adamnan flourished and its endowments were finally transferred to the University of ST ANDREWS. Eighteen bolls of black oats were payable from the Priory of St Andrews to the stipend of the minister at Dull. Today local tradition associates the monastic buildings with a gathering of stones in a field below the village. This, however, is the final vestige of a prehistoric neolithic chambered tomb.

In the immediate neighbourhood of Dull are the remains of many prehistoric monuments.

DULNAIN BRIDGE, *Inverness-shire* (Map 6, ref. 30⁰82⁵), is a village at the junction of the roads between AVIEMORE and GRANTOWN-ON-SPEY, ringed by Speyside (*see* SPEY)

farming and sporting country. Geographically it is a good base for skiing and touring, but it has no hotel and only limited private accommodation. Muckerach Castle (a ruin), built in 1598, was one of the original possessions of the Grants of ROTHIEMURCHUS. The village has an active and competitively successful rifle club.

DULSIE BRIDGE, *Nairnshire* (Map 5, ref. 29⁴84¹). This bridge over a spectacular gorge of the R. Findhorn passes above rocks, pools, and birch trees. The bridge is very high and at a steep angle. It is on a stretch of road often attributed to General Wade, but is actually a part of the highway from Deeside to FORT GEORGE built in the 1750s, when the fort was moved from INVERNESS to its present site. The LECHT ROAD is also on this route.

DUMBARTON, *Dunbartonshire* (Map 2, ref. 24⁰67⁵). An important shipbuilding royal burgh, Dumbarton is dominated by a 240-ft rock, a volcanic plug of basalt. This rock has a longer history as a stronghold than any other place in Britain; from at least the 5th cent. to 1018, it was the centre of the kingdom of Strathclyde, and was a royal castle in medieval times. Later it became a barracks, and remained such until the 20th cent.; it is now a museum. The medieval buildings have gone, but the 17th- and 18th-cent. fortifications are still visible. The Castle was taken by Thomas Crawford of Jordanhill in 1571 after holding out for Mary Queen of Scots during a longer period than anywhere except EDINBURGH Castle. The tower-arch in Church Street is all that remains of the Collegiate Church of St Mary founded in the mid-15th cent.

Boat-building (mentioned in James IV's reign) was, and is, an industry here. The Leven shipyard of Denny, a long-famous firm, started in 1844 and was liquidated in 1963; it was associated with the *Cutty Sark*, *Shamrock*

The Castle, Dumbarton

Scottish Tourist Board

Scottish Tourist Board

Dumfries: the old bridge over the River Nith

II and *Shamrock III*, and the Denny-Brown stabilizer; and finally it was the first firm in Britain to develop the hovercraft. Nowadays Dumbarton's main industry is the blending and bonding of whisky.

DUMFRIES, *Dumfriesshire* (Map 2, ref. 29⁷57⁶), which derives its name from Dum Fres, the fort of the Frisians, is the county town of Dumfriesshire and the largest burgh in SW. Scotland. With its warm red sandstone buildings, particularly pleasing in the glow of sunset, it justifiably wears the proud title "Queen of the South". Situated near the Scottish border on a route that runs through the pastoral landscape of Nithsdale, linking Carlisle (32 m.) with KILMARNOCK (59 m.) and GLASGOW (72 m.), it also serves as the gateway to beautiful Galloway and to many unspoilt villages on the shores of the Solway Firth, once the haunt of smugglers and now the delight of those who "mess about in boats". Originating on the E. bank of the Nith 5 m. from its estuary, Dumfries is the main centre of a prosperous agricultural area and the seat of several flourishing manufactures, such as the production of a new plastic, the dehydration and canning of milk, and the manufacture of rubber shoes and flooring, in addition to the town's traditional industry of high-quality hosiery and knitwear. Dumfries in 1964 earned the distinction of being the first burgh in Scotland to clear all its slums; yet it still retains something of the atmosphere of its colourful past rooted in antiquity. In 1931 an important urn-field found at Palmerston Park, Dumfries, bore witness to a Bronze Age civilization in the area, and evidence of Iron Age crannogs a few miles outside the burgh is found at Friars Carse (6½ m. NW.) and LOCHMABEN (8½ m. NE.).

It is in the 12th cent. that the town emerges into the certain, though dim, light of history. Created a royal burgh by William the Lion in 1186, and granted its oldest known charter by Robert III in 1395, Dumfries figures largely throughout the pages of Scottish history, and its people endured much strife and bloodshed as they rallied to their battle cry "A Loreburne!" (now perpetuated in the burgh motto), as well as in many bloody feuds between local families – the Maxwells, the Johnstones, and the Douglases.

In 1300 Edward I besieged and captured CAERLAVEROCK Castle, an ancient stronghold. It was in Dumfries that Robert Bruce struck the first blow for Scottish independence when, in 1306, on the high altar of the Monastery of Greyfriars, he slew Sir John Comyn (known as the "Red Comyn"), representative of the English king. A plaque in Castle Street marks the site of the famous incident when Bruce ran from the monastery crying, "I doubt I have slain the Comyn" – to which his friend Roger de Kirkpatrick replied, "You doubt! Then I'll mak siccar (sure)". The capture of Dumfries Castle, of which only traces remain at CASTLEDYKES (¾ m. SSW.), preserved now as a natural woodland with formal sunken garden below, soon followed. The War of Independence that preceded BANNOCKBURN had begun. (*See* "Scotland in History".)

The central point of Dumfries is the Midsteeple, built by Tobias Bachup of Alloa in 1707 to act as municipal offices, courthouse, and prison, until in 1867 these began to be replaced by shops. This sturdy Scottish structure, without architectural pretensions, has become a landmark to successive generations. Among embellishments on its outer walls are a plan in relief of the town in Robert Burns's day, erected to celebrate the Burns bi-centenary in 1959, and the old Scots ell measurement of 38 in. used by the tradesmen who once plied their trade around the Steeple. This ancient spire has looked down on many historic occasions. It was here that Effie Walker, sister of Helen Walker, immortalized as Jeanie

Deans in Sir Walter Scott's *The Heart of Mid-lothian*, was condemned for child murder. On its S. slope stands the County Hotel, headquarters of Prince Charles Edward Stuart, who held the town to ransom for three days in December 1745. Finding little support for his Jacobite cause, he left the burghers of Dumfries the poorer by £2,000 and 1,000 pairs of shoes for his impoverished Highland troops as well as claiming the Provost as a hostage. "Prince Charlie's Room" is still preserved in Highland decor. A few yards to the S., up a typical Dumfries "close" on the opposite side of High Street, is the Globe Inn, Burns's favourite howff, in which his chair and other relics are on view.

Undoubtedly, however, the most moving scene enacted beneath the Midsteeple's characteristic spire was the funeral of Robert Burns in July 1796. While he was still farming in Ayrshire, Dumfries acknowledged his fame by electing him a burgess in 1781, and in the following year he took up tenancy of the farm Ellisland (6 m. NNE.) on the Kilmarnock road. After striving unsuccessfully to wrest a living from its stubborn soil, while at the same time acting as exciseman, he moved to Dumfries in 1791, residing first in Bank Street and later in Mill Street (now Burns Street), where his home, with its many relics and manuscripts, is a place of pilgrimage. Close by Burns Street is St Michael's, the old parish church of Dumfries around which the town first grew, and in the adjoining churchyard is the tomb erected in 1815 to mark his resting-place.

Here one may see a somewhat idealistic sculpture of the poet standing at his plough with Coila, the muse of Scottish poesy, casting her mantle over him. For those who wish to savour the essence of Dumfries's past, a stroll through this old churchyard will be found worthwhile, with its martyrs' monument in memory of the Covenanters who died for their faith, and, most touching of all, the burial-place of the 420 citizens who lost their lives in the dread cholera plague that attacked Dumfries in 1832 and was the means of the town's obtaining a water supply, later commemorated by the erection of the ornamental fountain in High Street. The southerly route past St Michael's leads to Dumfries Infirmary, where, in November 1846, the first ether anaesthetic in Scotland was given by Dr William Fraser, son of a Dumfries surgeon, and to Crichton Royal (1½ m. SSE.), a famous mental hospital whose church and gardens give delight to visitors and patients alike.

Returning to the Midsteeple, it is against its background that the burgh re-enacts at a public ceremony held each year on "Guid Nych-burris Day" (the last Saturday in June) the granting of its charter, the crowning of its queen, and the return of the cornet and his horsemen, who have ridden, stobbed, and nogged the burgh marches – an ancient custom initiated before maps existed to pass on from old to young knowledge of the town's boundaries.

At the N. end of High Street, where the statue of Robert Burns stands in front of Greyfriars Church, first erected in 1721, the street branches on the left into Castle Street, with its graceful Georgian residences now serving as offices for medical and professional men, and leading to Buccleuch Street, the site of the Municipal Chambers opened in 1932. Here can be seen the "siller gun" presented to the town by James VI in 1617, and also the model of a Viking ship commemorating the presence of many escaping Norwegian soldiers and whalers, who made Dumfries their headquarters during the German occupation of their country in 1940–45. On the river bank, below the Municipal Chambers, stands the burgh's magnificent indoor swimming-pool opened in 1963 on Greensands. Again branching from Burns's statue, the road to the right, Academy Street, leads to what may be termed the cultural centre of Dumfries. Here is situated Dumfries Academy, a secondary school of some repute, where Sir J. M. Barrie, the author of *Peter Pan*, as well as many other distinguished men, received his pre-university education, and behind it, in Irving Street, the garden of Moat Brae Nursing Home, where the characters of Peter and Wendy were first conceived in boyhood days. In Catherine Street, opposite the Academy, is the Ewart Library, headquarters of the Dumfries County Library service, proudly wearing the name of William Ewart, M.P. for Dumfries in 1850, who pioneered the public-library movement in Great Britain. A few yards distant, in Langlands, facing the river, is Gracefield Arts Centre, opened in 1951 in celebration of Festival of Britain year, which contains a growing collection of the works of Scottish artists. This route leads on the left to Burns's Walk (2 m.), the wooded section of the river bank favoured by the poet, and on the right to Locharbriggs quarries (3 m. NNE.), which now supply half the freestone used by Scottish builders.

Returning to Burns's statue, and descending to the riverside by the picturesque Friars Vennel, you reach the most ancient of the five bridges that span the Nith, the 15th-cent. Old Bridge with its six arches (originally nine) erected by Lady Dervorguilla, the wife of John Balliol. Friars Vennel is now enjoying improvement after the manner of HADDINGTON. It is being restored and made gay and attractive by the liberal use of paint; it adds to the colour of Dumfries. Below the bridge a characteristic feature is the "Caul", a weir built to provide power for early 18th-cent. grain mills that once flanked the W. bank and now provide a pleasant spectacle on summer evenings, when fish glide like quicksilver through the shallow waters. The broad expanse leading to the bridge is Whitesands, once an ancient common, the site of horse and hiring fairs in bygone days, and still the haunt of neighbouring farmers who buy and sell at the indoor livestock marts there each market day (Wednesday). From this vantage-point one looks across at Maxwelltown, a small burgh on the W. side of the Nith amalgamated with Dumfries in 1929. At one time the haunt of Dumfries criminals, who escaped to the notorious "Brig En' ", as it was called, Maxwelltown is now almost entirely residential, and the major housing schemes of Dumfries Town Council have been carried out on its boundaries near the historic ruins of Lincluden College (2 m. NNW.), founded in the 12th cent. and later converted into a Collegiate Church by Archibald, Earl of Douglas. Enshrined within its walls is the tomb of Princess Margaret, daughter of King Robert III, and the building contains some fine examples of stone-carving, particularly the sedilia or seats for the clergy. Maxwelltown also houses Dumfries Burgh Museum (½ m. W.), a picturesque windmill, built in 1798 and occupying a commanding site in delightful grounds; it has been developed into a regional museum for Dumfriesshire and Galloway, and contains fine archaeological and natural history material, including Roman altars and early Christian monuments, as well as a collection of local costume. Its camera obscura, dated 1834, affords visitors some excellent panoramas of the town and its surroundings and is a popular amenity. As an adjunct to its museum service, Dumfries Town Council has preserved, to form a small folk museum, the ancient cottage that is part of the structure of the Old Bridge.

DUMYAT PEAK, *Perthshire* (Map 2, ref. 28²69⁸), rising 1,375 ft above MENSTRIE, between STIRLING and ALVA, at the W. end of the Ochils, is the most distinctive of this range. More of a peak than its neighbours, it stands out above the main bulk; seen from several angles in the FORTH plain, it forms part of the view also including ABBEY CRAIG and the Wallace Monument. The summit affords what has been called one of the best low-ascent vistas in Scotland, taking in the Forth and CLYDE valleys and an arc of mountains from Ben Lomond through the GRAMPIANS to the Pentlands. Normal walking ascent is from Menstrie Glen up the eastern contours; the frontal route, in places, is precipitous.

DUNADD, *Argyll* (Map 1, ref. 18³69¹), also called Add, lies near the hamlet of Kilmichael Glassary. This is the site of the ancient capital of Dalriada (*c.* A.D. 500–803), from which the Celtic Kingdom of Scotland sprang (*see* "Scotland in History"). Though it once was an important fortified place, all that remains of its great past is a hillock supporting an isolated rock 176 ft high. On this are carved the figure

Lt-Col. George Malcolm of Poltalloch
Dunadd: prehistoric wild boar cut in stone

of a boar and the sign of a footprint. This probably marks the spot where the Dalriadic kings were invested with royal power.

DUNBAR, *East Lothian* (Map 3, ref. 36⁸67⁹). The old fishing port and new holiday resort of Dunbar became a royal burgh in 1369. Dunbar Castle had played a part in the Wars of Independence; in 1339 Black Agnes, the Countess of March and Dunbar, had defended it for six weeks against the English. The town was sacked by the Earl of Hertford in 1544. The Castle was later associated with Mary Queen of Scots, who stayed there with Darnley in 1566 after the murder of Rizzio, and with Bothwell in 1567 after the murder of Darnley. The Regent Moray, who stayed there too, destroyed the Castle after the Battle of Carberry. The site of Cromwell's Battle of Dunbar in 1650 is marked by a stone SE. of the town just off the Great North Road.

The old Town House dates from 1620 and

The harbour and castle, Dunbar
Scottish Tourist Board

has a six-sided tower. The parish church, on high ground with a square tower, 108 ft high, is a landmark for fishermen. A cluster of modern fishermen's houses by Sir Basil Spence are notable beside the harbour.

Tourism is now the main industry, the wide facilities including a golf links and a large open-air swimming-pool.

DUNBEATH, *Caithness* (Map 7, ref. 31⁷92⁹), is a scattered village of considerable charm and interest. The dominating feature is the white mass of Dunbeath Castle, spectacularly poised on the cliff's edge, 1 m. S. of the village. The original keep of the Castle dates from at least 1428. The older portion of the present building, probably erected in 1633, was really only one room thick, but it was greatly enlarged on the seaward side in the 19th cent. The Castle was besieged by Montrose for three days before it surrendered, and was recaptured by General Leslie after Carbisdale.

DUNBLANE, *Perthshire* (Map 2, ref. 27⁹70¹). This attractive little town shares with the neighbouring BRIDGE OF ALLAN an early Victorian reputation as a spa and also the scenic attractions of the Allan Water. The river is spanned at Dunblane by a single-arch 16th-cent. bridge. At the old heart of the town, which is now primarily residential, stands the ancient cathedral of Dunblane, in part handsomely restored. Carved figures on the pulpit in the nave symbolize the history of the church, representing the five denominations that have used the buildings or the site over the past 1,000 years and more. The lower storeys of the tower are the oldest parts of the cathedral, dating probably from about 1100. The full Gothic flowering did not take place until the middle of the 13th cent., under Bishop Clement. After the neglect and decay that followed the Reformation, the nave remained roofless for 300 years. Restored at the end of the 19th cent. under the architectural supervision of Sir Roland Anderson, this part of the church is regularly used for public worship. During the ascendancy of the Episcopal Church in the 17th cent., Robert Leighton served as Bishop of Dunblane before his elevation to the Archbishopric of GLASGOW. His personal collection of books can be seen in the Leighton Library at the Cross. The pleasing "little houses" of Kirk Street and Sinclairs Street, which form the cathedral close or precinct, have been adapted and restored by the Ecumenical Council of Churches to serve as a retreat and conference centre.

DUNCANSBY, *Caithness* (Map 7, ref. 33⁹97³). The township of Duncansby lies at the road junction just S. of JOHN O' GROATS. From here the road (latterly gated) leads to Duncansby Head, with its lighthouse. This is the NE. point of the Scottish mainland, and

rises almost sheer in sandstone cliff to 210 ft. Grass grows right to the cliff edge, and the views are startling.

There are remains of an ancient watch-tower on the head, and underground a shelter of the Royal Observer Corps, and a new coastguard's lookout (built in 1963). To the W. of the lighthouse is the grand Long Geo, a great chasm with 200-ft vertical walls, running inland from the sea for 100 yds. A short distance further W. from Long Geo is the impressive natural bridge known as the Glupe. The bridge can be crossed easily. It has been caused by the partial collapse of the roof of a long cave.

To the S. of the lighthouse it is a short walk to another stretch of extremely fine cliff scenery. First the famous natural arch of Humlie's Hole, where a "stack" of rock is joined by a narrow bridge to the main cliff. This is at the N. corner of the dramatic Long Geo of Slaites, noted for the large number of nesting birds (best in May and June); these include cormorants, shags, gannets, puffins, and gulls.

The first stack southwards is The Knee (67 ft), with the famous tidal race called The Rispies between it and the shore. Next is Gibbs Craig (170 ft). From near here there is a grand view of the other three stacks making a total of five in this group: Tom Thumb Stack, Little Stack (218 ft), and Muckle Stack (297 ft). There is an easy walk back to the road, and also a cliff walk southward from which one gets a close view of the stacks.

Duncansby Head is the Veruvium Promontarium (clean-cut cape) mentioned by Ptolemy.

DUNDEE, *Angus* (Map 6, ref. 34⁰73⁰), stands on a hill-side on the N. bank of the Firth of TAY just far enough up the estuary to provide an anchorage safely sheltered from the eastern winds of the North Sea. Its population of a little under 200,000 makes it Scotland's third city, but its industrialists claim that in commercial importance it ranks second only to GLASGOW.

The city can boast of great antiquity, having been in existence at the time of the Roman invasion, and the surrounding district shows many remains of Roman camp sites. In A.D. 834 it was the headquarters from which Kenneth MacAlpine set out to conquer the Picts and so become the first King of the Scots. As he returned to Dundee after the battle, we can assume that he regarded the town as his capital.

Dundee's geographical situation made it a strategic point of defence for central Scotland, and it suffered much in the many affrays between the Scots and the English in the years before the Union of the Crowns. Its history can be largely epitomized in the story of its oldest standing structure, the Tower of St Mary's, locally known as the Old Steeple. The tower, now part of the City Churches, was built in the mid-15th cent. as the W. wall of the great pre-

Reformation Church of the Blessed Virgin, an ecclesiastical foundation dating back to 1198. It was built, under the blessing of a Papal Bull, by David, Earl of Huntingdon, brother of King William the Lion, and was dedicated to that knight's patron saint, St Mary.

Although many buildings have risen and fallen, and much blood has been shed, the site has remained consecrated all these years, and it is still occupied by the parish church of Dundee.

Earl David's Church took a long time to build, and it was hardly completed when, in 1296, Edward I of England, the Hammer of the Scots, drove his armies north to Dundee, sacked the town, set fire to the church, and left nothing but rubble on the holy site of St Mary's. Once again the masons chipped, the sawyers sawed, and the craftsmen added their embellishments; but in 1385 an English army once again marched over the Border and burnt and pillaged the town. This time it took longer for Dundee to recover; but faith was strong, and it was in this rebuilding that the Church of Our Lady of Dundee took on its most magnificent form – it was now (about 1450 to 1480) that the great W. wall and tower were built. This church survived for a century, but in 1547 an English fleet sailed into the Firth of Tay, and after a long siege the city was sacked and its church once more destroyed.

It was thus to a smoking ruin, with only the choir and altar standing at one end and the high tower at the other, that the Reformation came in Dundee, and there was little papal splendour left for the reformers to tear down. But again Dundee accepted the new faith, and the church was rebuilt, this time to house more than one congregation.

These frequent sackings were not due to any particular local antagonism; rather, they grew out of the fact that Dundee was a convenient turning-point for the English invaders, and, to impress their might upon the whole Scottish nation, they caused as much havoc as possible before retracing their steps.

But, even after the Union of the Crowns, trouble continued, for Dundee got involved with the second last of the Stuart kings, Charles II, and in 1651 Cromwell dispatched General Monk with a force of 4,000 men to deal with the situation. This proved to be Dundee's greatest blow, because, expecting to be safe within the sanctuary of the church, the Council removed all the city's valuables to the Old Steeple. Monk's army quickly sacked the city, gathered all the valuable old books from the church library, and set fire to them round the tower, sprinkling the blaze with water to smoke out the defenders.

Dundee is a city best looked up to or down upon, and the best points of vantage from which to be introduced to it are from the R. Tay, which sweeps past its doorstep, or from the top of its own little eminence of the Law

A. L. Hunter

Dundee: modern hotel development

Hill, once its dramatic back-cloth and now a central park.

The river view may be obtained from the two-mile railway bridge (one of the longest bridges in Europe); or from the new road bridge. From mid-stream it will be seen that the city is built in terraces round the slope of a 572-ft hill of volcanic origin, Dundee's Law. Viewed from this angle, the less pleasing factories are lost in the foreshore, and the lasting picture is of a mosaic rising from the sparkle of the river to the green of the conical hill-top.

On a day of good visibility, the prospect from the top of this Law Hill has been compared favourably with the view overlooking the Bay of Naples. To the E. you can see the curve of BROUGHTY FERRY Bay running out to its ancient castle, and farther off the sandy spit of Buddon Ness jutting out to form the N. shoulder of the firth. Across the river the woodpiles of Tayport catch the eye, and above its little harbour it is easy to pick out the full sweep of St Andrew's Bay. The ribbon of the railway bridge, with its graceful curve on to the city shore, has always impressed the visitor, and now, with two bridges, the vista is unique. To the W. and N. sit the first rolling slopes of the Sidlaw Hills, and away beyond them rises the mass of the GRAMPIANS with peaks and landmarks too numerous to mention.

Having plunged from either of these vantage-points into the city itself, you find yourself in a melting-pot in which dilapidated old properties are being demolished, cleared sites are being drained and levelled, and rather uninspiring new structures are rising that have achieved utility at the sacrifice of individuality. The town planners have assured us that these glass-and-concrete rectangles will ultimately blend well with the grey stone of our older buildings, but that is for the future to record.

Although it has now spread out to cover an area of about 20 sq. m., Dundee has always contrived to retain a very compact communal life. It is rather like a small market-town surrounded by many dormitory suburbs, but the heart of the city has always remained closely knit. Dundee has few buildings of any architectural note: the City Churches with St Mary's Tower, the museum and library and the High School at the top of Reform Street, and the remains of the Wishart Arch in the old Cowgate. These are all of interest, and all are within the compass of a ten-minute stroll, yet were an ex-Dundonian, returned from Calcutta or New York, to tour that small area, he would meet so many old acquaintances and see so many nostalgic sights that he would probably never complete the journey.

Apart from these central streets, there are down-town areas of industrial activity stretching out to engulf old residential slums that still await the bulldozer, while out in what was once the surrounding countryside there are whole townships of attractive, if over-standardized, new houses for the displaced workers. But travel from home to factory is no longer a short walk, and bus routes serving all Dundee's residential suburbs are causing the usual new-town traffic problems.

To understand the background of modern Dundee, we must consider various aspects of its early history. In common with the people of most Scottish E.-coast ports, the local inhabitants developed an interest in fishing, but, while the men from Fife and Aberdeenshire fished the neighbouring North Sea, the Dundee men went off to Iceland and the far North and developed one of Scotland's main whaling fleets. Although the Dundee Whale Fishing Company was not formed till 1756, the history of Scottish whaling goes back to the 12th cent., and individual whalers went out from Dundee in early times. While their men were away on these expeditions, the women employed themselves in spinning the local flax and weaving it into cloth. As a result of these early beginnings, Dundee became a prime supplier of whale oil and developed a textile trade in which it became customary for the women to work.

As a result of the heavy losses sustained in the final sacking by General Monk in 1651, the city spent the next 100 years in abject poverty. There was no local capital to restore the weaving industry, and merchants had to cut their

Scottish Tourist Board

Dundee: Balgay Park

costs by spinning only the cheapest of Russian flax and weaving it into the poorest grades of sacking, while they left the finer linens to the weavers of Dunfermline and Belfast.

Then, towards the end of the 18th cent., the city found a growing market in the American economy by making coarse bagging for the plantations. It was to this state of affairs that the East India Company in 1822 sent home a sample of a new fibre from India called jute. This was tried out by the flax-weavers of Dundee, but they found much difficulty in working this strange new fibre, and for a time it was neglected. Then someone had the bright idea of adding whale-oil to the batching process, and this solved the problem.

It was this combination of readily supplied whale oil and the technical skill of weaving coarse cloth cheaply, plus an abundance of skilled female workers, that established Dundee as the world centre of the jute industry. Imports from India sprang from 4,000 bales of jute in 1836 to 30,000 bales in 1840, and to 289,000 in 1850. A town of 35,000 people leapt in less than fifty years into a city of 130,000.

Jute factories were rapidly built, tenement houses appeared in crowded areas for the workers who came in from the country, and in the outskirts of the city the wealthy jute lords built themselves splendid mansions. It was said that at this time the two most wealthy residential areas in Great Britain were the homes of the jute lords in Broughty Ferry and those of the cotton kings in Bowden near Manchester.

A link developed between Dundee and Calcutta as the Indian port of dispatch, and for many years every second Dundee home had a son or brother working out on the Hooghly; the voices on the golf links at Tollygunge were more Dundee than those in the home city itself.

But the trend of trade changes; Calcutta developed its own capacity for handling jute, and, by the time independence came to India, Dundee could no longer compete for much of the cheaper end of the jute market. But once again it was the skill and adaptability of its women workers that came to the rescue. Their deft fingers were trained to many new light-engineering crafts, to make such articles as cash registers, wrist-watches, petrol-pump computers, refrigerators, and the many other new products of industries that have come to Dundee's industrial estate. Automation has brought no overspill problems to Dundee, for the influx of new industry has readily absorbed labour as it became available.

It may be that having so many women working has steadied industry in Dundee, for it has had very little trouble in labour relations. Indeed, the one trouble spot is also the only one in which no women are employed – the shipyard. Although never approaching the volume of work done on the CLYDE, shipbuilding has been carried on in Dundee for many years and, probably as a result of the old whaling days, it had the distinction of building the *Discovery* and the *Terra Nova* used in polar exploration by Shackleton and Scott. During both world wars Dundee provided a base for naval operations, in particular for submarine maintenance work.

It has often been said that Dundee is famous for jute, jam, and journalism, and this is still largely true. It was a Dundee man who first created marmalade, and this product still provides employment for many Dundonians. Allied with it is the production of other preserves and confectionery, and, as an interesting sideline, light foundries in the city have achieved world renown in the making of unusual commercial cooking appliances. In recent years they have supplied the whole factory equipment needed to introduce potato crisps to Russia; they have also made spaghetti-spinning machinery for Italy, and an orange-peeler and sorter for Spain.

Journalism continues to occupy many people in Dundee, for, in addition to providing news and views for local readers in central Scotland, a large share of the ever-growing output of weekly papers for children and teenagers has its centre in Dundee. There is also within the city the largest publisher in Britain of picture postcards, calendars, and greeting cards of every kind.

In spite of competition from Calcutta in the cheaper end of the market, jute continues to be Dundee's prime industry; many new avenues have been explored and developed for its use in specialized forms. This has been considerably helped by the setting up of the British Jute Research Association, which employs a staff of graduate research workers constantly experimenting with all aspects of the fibre. The union of jute with plastic, for example, has shown encouraging results in the production of polythene-lined jute bags that can be used for foodstuffs and other materials liable to contamination.

Forty per cent of Dundee's jute now goes into the carpet industry, and the city's own carpet-manufacturing enterprises are flourishing. An important development has been the introduction of the tufted carpet, in which the pile is introduced into a stout jute-cloth foundation, and many mills now weave this backing for export to carpet-makers all over the world.

From an educational point of view, Dundee has done well for its size and situation. The High School and three Academies bear evidence of the benevolent institutions raised by former citizens, and corporation schools are well staffed and constantly expanding. Queen's College, formerly a home for the medical, dental, law, and engineering faculties of ST ANDREWS University, has some of the most advanced lecture halls and facilities among the Scottish colleges. With the extension of higher education in prospect, Dundee's ever-growing establishment has now deservedly achieved the status of a self-contained university. Dundee School of Art is housed in a recently built unit, and the city's Technical College is continuing its process of expansion. All these spheres of higher learning are supported by visiting students, many from overseas, and youngsters of many nations appear to find Dundee a happy place in which to acquire modern training.

In the world of the arts Dundee has produced no outstanding figures, but intermittently it has shown a love for drama. Its first theatre was opened in 1806, and between 1885 and 1910 there were as many as eight theatres all producing live shows. This was at a time when the city was expanding very rapidly, but it does appear that the theatre was important to the lives of its people. Then came the cinema, and by 1928 the last of the old theatres had gone over to film; for nearly twenty years there was no professional theatre. Then Dundee Repertory Theatre was opened in the early days of the Second World War, and it was well supported by the members of the services stationed in Dundee. This interest continued to thrive till television became available in central Scotland, since when it has survived only by grants from the Arts Council and the local Corporation. There are many amateur groups of actors, musicians, playgoers, and others for those who are interested, but even they are finding loyalty difficult to maintain in these days of television.

There has always been some doubt as to whether the sobriquet "Bonnie Dundee" was originally applied to the city or to the romantic John Graham of Claverhouse, but, with a glimpse of sunshine and a fresh east breeze, there is much to be said for applying it to the douce city that sprawls along the north bank of the Firth of Tay.

DUNDONALD, *Ayrshire* (Map 2, ref. 23⁷63⁵), is an attractive rural village clustered round the ruins of an ancient castle about 4 m. inland from TROON. The present Castle was built by King Robert II, and was a favourite residence of both him and his son Robert III.

Both kings died there. The name is popularly held to mean the "Fort of Donald", but more probably it refers to the rocky hill that shelters the Castle and the village from the W. The hill is a prominent landmark in the flat coastal plain. There is a site for a new development model village at Auchans in the neighbourhood.

DUNDONNELL, *Ross and Cromarty* (Map 5, ref. 21⁰88⁷), is a village at the head of Little Loch Broom. From it there are outstanding views of the TORRIDON sandstone peaks of An Teallach, forming some of the strangest shaped mountains of the Scottish mainland.

The road from Dundonnell northwards is called "Destitution Road" (sometimes it appears as "Desolation"), taking its name from the fact that it was one of several constructed after the potato famine of 1846–7, when food and nothing more than food was provided for work.

It is sometimes forgotten that the potato famine, with all its attendant evils coming from the government's policy of *laissez faire*, struck the Highlands of Scotland as well as Ireland. It was a disaster which hit the western Celts particularly hard.

DUNDRENNAN, *Kirkcudbrightshire* (Map 2, ref. 27⁵54⁷). Dundrennan Abbey, a Cistercian Abbey founded by David I and Fergus, Lord of Galloway, in 1142, was not completed until the 1180s or later. The ruins consist of much late-Norman and transitional work, and a rich chapter house dating from the end of the 13th cent. Little remains of the church but the W. end and transepts, and a western range of cloisters. There are many fine monuments, including one to a nun and another to a murdered abbot.

The village of Dundrennan, in a most attractive setting, is built partly from stones taken from the ruined abbey. Mary Queen of Scots spent her last night in Scotland at Dundrennan, and took boat across the Solway Firth from Port Mary, just E. of Burnfoot.

Dundrennan Abbey

DUNFERMLINE, *Fife* (Map 2, ref. 31⁰68⁷). This famous royal burgh grew round the Benedictine abbey founded by Queen Margaret (*see* "Scotland in History"), the foundations of whose church are under the present nave, which is late Norman and constructed by masons from Durham. The site of the choir is now the modern parish church, but at the E. end the remains of the 13th-cent. St Margaret's shrine can be seen. This shrine is the object of a yearly pilgrimage of Scottish Catholics. King Robert I (Robert Bruce) was buried in the choir, his grave being marked by a modern brass. The ruins of some monastic buildings are still visible. The Guest House was later reconstructed as a royal palace.

The site of the great Warrior King's grave was located for certain only in 1818, when some reconstructions were being made. Before the high altar was a grave containing a skeleton in what may have been the remains of royal robes. What identified the bones as those of Bruce was the fact that the breast-bone had been neatly sawn asunder and something extracted from the body after death.

That "something" was his heart, which he had given instructions on his deathbed to be taken on a Crusade to the Holy Land. His instructions were obeyed. Douglas took the heart. He fell in battle, but the King's heart was recovered and brought back to MELROSE.

The town was almost completely destroyed by fire in 1624. Later it developed as a centre for weaving, an early branch of the British Linen Company being set up in 1749.

Andrew Carnegie (d. 1919), the son of a damask-weaver, was born in a small cottage in 1835. This cottage is now open, and it holds mementoes of him. Carnegie gave to Scotland and the world 2,500 libraries; Dunfermline, his native place, received the first. He also handed over Pittencrieff Glen to the town, and provided a fund to develop the beautiful gardens, trees, and public buildings. The beautifully restored 16th-cent. Abbot's House in Maygate is a few yards from the first Carnegie Library.

The FORTH Road Bridge has brought welcome trade.

DUNIPACE, *Stirlingshire* (Map 2, ref. 28¹68⁴), is a village on the left bank of the R. Carron, connected by a bridge with DENNY, and since 1876 has been joined with it in one burgh. It has Roman connections in the past, and some finely preserved Roman utensils have been found there.

DUNKELD, *Perthshire* (Map 6, ref. 30³74²). On the main road between PERTH and PITLOCHRY, Dunkeld is a delightful little town on the R. TAY with more than 1,000 years of recorded history. Its first monastery may have been founded before A.D. 700, when St Adamnan, the biographer of St Columba, established a settlement. Kenneth MacAlpine, who united the kingdoms of Picts and Scots in A.D. 844, made Dunkeld and SCONE his joint capitals. The majestic medieval cathedral, of which substantial remains survive, took almost two centuries to build, starting with the choir in 1318 and reaching completion with the addition of the great NW. tower in 1501. Only sixty years later it was reduced to roofless ruin in the heat of the Reformation. The town itself suffered badly in the Battle of Dunkeld (1689), which followed the rout of King William III's army by Claverhouse's Jacobite Highlanders at KILLIECRANKIE. It still, however, retains something of the character of a cathedral precinct in the scale and plan of the little houses in High Street, the Cross, and Cathedral Street. Much has been done in recent years to preserve this character through an ambitious and comprehensive programme of restoration carried out by the National Trust for Scotland. Old houses have been brought up to modern living standards, gap sites have been filled by new buildings, and the properties let to local tenants to bring them back fully into the life of the town. An area of woodland, including Stanley Hill, behind the Cross, has been presented to the Trust to secure the attractive setting of the old part of the town. Rising behind the town are the wooded slopes of Newtyle, 996 ft high, and Craigiebarns, 900 ft; and across the river stand Craig Vinean, 1,247 ft, and Birnam Hill, 1,324 ft. There is superb fishing available on the Tay (spanned here by Thomas Telford's handsome bridge); there is a fascinating variety of local walks and touring possibilities; and the Festival Theatre at Pitlochry is within easy reach.

DUNLOP, *Ayrshire* (Map 2, ref. 24¹64⁹), lies on the moorland about 5 m. NW. of KIL-MARNOCK, and is best known for its cheese. Burns students know it also as the home of Mrs Dunlop (of Dunlop), the correspondent of Robert Burns. The Dunlop family, who held the lands round the village from about 1260 to 1858, are credited with the breeding of the first Ayrshire cows.

DUNNET, *Caithness* (Map 7, ref. 32²97²). The village of Dunnet is a small scattering of houses near Dunnet Bay, which must surely be one of the most dramatic sweeps of fine sand in Britain. The simple white church has a pre-Reformation saddle-backed tower, which is possibly 14th cent., and here one of the first cartographers, Timothy Pont, was minister from 1601–8. To the N. of Dunnet is St John's Loch, a popular haunt of the trout fisherman, and 4 m. NE. is Dunnet Head. This is actually the most northerly point of the Scottish mainland, and the promontory, studded with lochans and rich in botanical specimens, is well worth a visit. From the northern end, where the lighthouse shines across the stormy waters of the

Pentland Firth, there is a fine view of ORKNEY, especially the Old Man of Hoy, doubly so for the visitor clever enough to time his trip to coincide with one of the spectacular sunsets for which Caithness is noted.

DUNNING, *Perthshire* (Map 2, ref. 30²71⁴), is an attractive village lying at the N. base of the Ochils. At the centre of the village is a thorn tree planted in 1716 to commemorate the burning of the houses by the Earl of Mar's troops after the Battle of SHERIFFMUIR in the Rising of 1715.

Dunning was held in feu by Lord Rollo of Duncrub, whose feudal obligation was to act as baron-bailie. The lands of Duncrub had been given by Robert II of Scotland to John de Rollo early in the 14th cent. He was probably of Norman stock, one of the many Normans who followed David I when he became King of Scotland.

In 1715 the Rollos came out as Jacobites, but they received a pardon and were not out again in 1745. The mansion house of Duncrub is now demolished.

The parish church of St Serf was rebuilt in 1810, but the early medieval tower was untouched and well repays a visit. This tower belonged to the church built some time between 1200 and 1219.

DUNNOTTAR, *Kincardineshire* (Map 6, ref. 38⁸78⁴). To visit this noteworthy ruin is to relive some of the darkest chapters of Scottish history. The Castle stands on a stupendous isolated rock projecting from the coast 2 m. S. of STONEHAVEN. As its name indicates, it was a "dun" or place of strength to the Pictish tribes of the Mearns. It is approached from the main road by a ravine still called St Ninian's Den. St Ninian's Well is close by, and some say that the Saint from Candida Casa did indeed found a Christian settlement in the neighbourhood. In May 1276 William Wishart, Bishop of ST ANDREWS, consecrated on the rock the parish church of Dunothyr, also dedicated to St Ninian. In 1297 Dunnottar was held by the English and stormed by William Wallace.

During the usurpation of Edward Balliol in 1336, Dunnottar was again seized by the English, but shortly afterwards it was retaken and destroyed by the Scottish Regent, Sir Andrew de Moray. By the end of the 14th cent. Dunnottar lay in the hands of Sir William Keith, Great Marischal of Scotland, who built a castle upon it.

The original nucleus of the Castle that survives is the 14th-cent. keep, a rectangular tower 41 ft by 36 ft and 50 ft high, with rubble-built walls 5 ft thick. Perched at the extreme SW. corner of the rock, it dominates all the works at the entrance. Early in the 16th cent. a new block was built E. of the keep, and in 1574 the large building known as the Priest's House was erected. To this period also belong the defensive works at the entrance. The W. wing of the quadrangle was begun shortly after 1581, and two other wings linking up with a 16th-cent. chapel were added early in the 17th cent.

In 1639 the 7th Earl Marischal declared for the Covenant and took part with Montrose in the capture of ABERDEEN. The whole story of Dunnottar's part in the Civil War is pregnant with tragic irony. Montrose, who had been the Earl Marischal's ally, tried and failed to win him over to the Royalist cause in March 1645 – largely owing to the intervention of the notorious Andrew Cant, one of sixteen ministers who fled their own houses and took refuge in the Castle with the Earl. Rebuffed, Montrose took terrible vengeance, and the Earl Marischal had to stand on his own battlements and see the fires of war devouring his broad acres. Cant "consoled" him with the remark "Trouble not, for the reek will be a sweet-smelling incense in the nostrils of the Lord".

Montrose went to his death. King Charles II signed the Solemn League and Covenant and, on the 8th of July 1650, was entertained by the Earl Marischal at Dunnottar on his way south to try the hazard for the recovery of his father's realm. He dined on fresh salmon. By May 1652, Dunnottar was the only place that still flew the royal flag in Scotland. In September 1651 the English troops under General Overton appeared before the Castle, and then began the siege that was to last for eight months until the 24th of May 1652. The Governor of Dunnottar, Sir George Ogilvy of Barras, surrendered to Colonel Morgan with all the honours of war. The prize that the English hoped to win from this accomplishment was a double one – the private papers of King Charles, and the regalia of Scotland. But it eluded their grasp. The papers, carefully stitched into a flat belt round her middle, had been smuggled through the besieging lines by Anne Lindsay, a kinswoman of Ogilvy's wife. The regalia – the Scottish crown, sceptre, and sword of state – were by this time secreted beneath the pulpit of the parish church of KINNEFF.

But the darkest chapter of Dunnottar's story was yet to be written. In May 1685, during the course of Monmouth's and Argyll's rebellion, a large body of covenanting prisoners – 122 men and 45 women – was moved for security to the fortress and herded indiscriminately into the dungeon now known as the "Whig's Vault". Many died.

But Dunnottar, as we have seen, could be used to inflict durance vile upon either side in the see-saw of power and persecution. Only fourteen years later, in Viscount Dundee's campaign, seventeen suspected Jacobites from Aberdeen, including a professor of mathematics, George Liddel, were imprisoned for over a year in the Castle. Finally, in 1715, the cannon from Dunnottar were used in the

Jacobite army. The Castle itself, with all the other possessions of the 10th Earl Marischal, was forfeited after the rising, and in 1718 was dismantled. The systematic repair and excavation of the ruins was undertaken for the late Annie Viscountess Cowdray in 1925, and they are now open to the public.

DUNOLLIE CASTLE, *Argyll* (Map 1, ref. 18⁵73²). On the northern outskirts of OBAN, the ruined Castle stands on a rock more than 80 ft high and surrounded on three sides by the sea. The keep of the Castle remains, and ivy covered fragments of other buildings. This and earlier buildings on the same site have been the seat of chiefs of the Clan Macdougall since the 11th cent.

The Castle was besieged in 1647 and again in 1715, when the chief was fighting on the Jacobite side; his wife defended it with traditional Scottish feminine courage against the Argyll militia.

To the N. of the Castle is the present house built about 1746.

DUNOON, *Argyll* (Map 2, ref. 21⁷67⁷). Now a popular holiday resort on the Firth of CLYDE, Dunoon until the early 19th cent. was a small village clustered round the Castle. This was the seat of the High Stewards from the end of the 11th cent., but after the accession of the Stuart kings, the Castle passed into the hereditary keepership of the Campbells. In the 1471 Charter the fee for this hereditary keepership was defined as "one red rose when asked for". In 1958 the Queen (without asking for it) was given this fee on her visit to Dunoon.

The early 19th cent. saw the first villas, and soon, with steamers across the Clyde from GOUROCK, the town developed into a holiday resort. It now has all the usual amenities, but also possesses a wild hinterland country; there are many cruises and tours available. Dunoon too is a yachting centre.

Burns's "Highland Mary" was born near Dunoon, and a statue of her commemorates the fact.

DUNROBIN CASTLE, *Sutherland* (Map 5, ref. 28⁶90¹), stands 1 m. N. of GOLSPIE on a natural terrace by the sea, and was the seat of the earls and dukes of Sutherland. The massive inner keep of the present building dates from before this time. Additions were made by Earl John Glas in the mid-17th cent. and around 1785. Between 1835 and 1850 Sir Charles Barry made large extensions, enclosing the old castle on the N. and E. These were burnt down in 1915, but restored by Sir Robert Lorimer, who also (in 1921) designed the library, drawing-rooms, and dining-rooms.

There are remarkable flower gardens, bordering a 100-yd terrace. In the park is a museum containing Sutherland antiquities, which include objects found in local excava-

Dunrobin Castle

tions. There are also examples of country crafts, birds, fossils, and the like.

The monument at the private railway station is that of the 2nd Duke of Sutherland. The Countess of Sutherland, who succeeded to the earldom (created 1228) in 1963 on the death of her uncle the 5th Duke (a cousin having succeeded to the dukedom), created an independent boarding school for boys at Dunrobin on the lines of GORDONSTOUN, but the castle and its Versailles-like gardens are open to the public during the summer.

DUNS, *Berwickshire* (Map 3, ref. 37⁸65⁵). Absurd though it may seem, Berwick is not the county town of the Scottish shire of Berwick. The unfortunate, once-important port of Berwick was tossed between Scotland and England many times, eventually (though perhaps not permanently) settling in Northumberland.

In the meantime the pleasing little Scottish Border town of Duns has to act as regent county town for the shire. It was originally built on the dun that rises to 713 ft on the N. side of where the town was destroyed by the English in the mid-16th cent.; the new town, founded below, was originally guarded on three sides by swamp. Duns is also a market-town. A stone on a nearby summit commemorates the camping-place in 1639 of General Leslie's covenanting army. About 1 m. NW. of the town is Duns Castle, which incorporates part of the ancient tower traditionally built in 1320 for Randolph Earl of Moray.

Duns Scotus was a religious philosopher and theologian who had much effect upon the schools of thought in the Middle Ages. He is sometimes and incorrectly claimed by the Irish, on the grounds that "Scotus" was one of the Latin names for the Irish Celts. In reality Duns Scotus was a Franciscan friar, born here at Duns in 1266. Having lectured at Oxford, Paris, and Cologne, he died and was buried in the last-named city. But he was born at Duns.

DUNSCORE, *Dumfriesshire* (Map 2, ref. 28⁶58⁵). A village in a rural agricultural area, Dunscore is notable for the literary associations of the parish.

On the banks of the Nith, some 5 m. E. of Dunscore, is Ellisland, the farm that Robert Burns rented from 1788–91, and where he lived happily for a time with Jean Armour and their children; it was here that he wrote "Tam o' Shanter".

Some 6 m. W. of Dunscore, in very bleak surroundings, is Craigenputtock Farm, where Thomas Carlyle took his wife. They lived there 1828–34, and during this time he wrote *Sartor Resartus.* On his death, the estate was bequeathed to EDINBURGH University to found bursaries.

Nearby Loch Urr has good fishing. On an artificial island in the loch stands a rectangular build-up. It is connected to the shore by a sub-merged stone causeway, and is possibly of Viking origin.

DUNSINANE HILL, *Perthshire* (Map 6, ref. 32²73¹), is a conspicuous conical summit of the Sidlaws, 1,012 ft above sea-level, from which there is a magnificent view of STRATH-MORE and BLAIRGOWRIE. Traditionally it is the site of Macbeth's Castle, and it lies only 12 m. ESE. of BIRNAM Wood. The NE. face is precipitous, but a winding road has been cut from the rock on the NW. side, and this leads by an easy gradient to the summit. The flat top is occupied by a prehistoric fort, the triple ramparts surrounding an area 210 ft by 130 ft. The site was excavated in 1857, but lack of scientific method at that period makes it difficult to interpret the report. Apparently an earth-house of Iron Age date was found within the defences, and from this is said to have come a bronze finger-ring in the form of a spiral double serpent.

The estate of Dunsinane originally belonged to the Nairne family, of whom the 5th and last baronet, Sir William, was in 1786 made a Judge of the Court of Session under the title Lord Dunsinane.

A persistent but probably apocryphal story tells how the original Stone of Destiny was hidden on top of Dunsinane Hill by the monks of SCONE Abbey, who in turn allowed King Edward I of England to take away a replica made of local stone.

DUNSTAFFNAGE CASTLE, *Argyll* (Map 1, ref. 18⁹73⁵) is on a promontory on a rocky platform in a bay 4 m. N. of OBAN, and was built to the orders of Alexander II as a spring-board for his projected attack against the Norse who then held the Hebrides. Originally it was a royal castle, but it has been in Campbell hands since at least 1470. The Earl of Argyll in 1502 gave a formal charter to a Campbell relative to hold the lands in return for service as keeper or captain.

The 13th-cent. Castle had the usual great curtain wall and round towers; it was burnt in 1685 and partially restored. The gatehouse tower was built in the 16th cent. and was the residence of the family until burnt in 1810, when they moved to the factor's house named Dunstaffnage House, 1 m. E. This too, alas, was burnt in December 1940, and Angus Campbell, Captain of Dunstaffnage, had to move to a small dwelling-place on the estate scarcely larger than a cottage. In this, until his death in 1958, he preserved in pathetic isolation some of the family treasures and fine paintings he had managed to rescue from the burnt house. Dunstaffnage (for so he was universally styled) was a cosmopolitan European figure who knew many people in all the European capitals. He once said that one of his saddest losses in the fire was his address-book, which had survived a long time. He was succeeded by his nephew the 22nd Captain of Dunstaffnage.

The chapel, a large and elaborately decorated edifice in the first point style, is now in ruins and stands outside the walls 160 yds SW. of the rock. The Castle was built on the traditional site of the early seat of the Dalriadic Kings, and is said to be the place of the Stone of Destiny before it was taken to SCONE, to become the Stone of Scone.

During the Second World War the bay by Dunstaffnage was used as a naval repair base. A temporary village sprang up in consequence; it is now replaced by a more permanent one. The old Castle dominates the village and, indeed, the whole scene round about.

DUNSYRE, *Lanarkshire* (Map 2, ref. 30⁸64⁸). This village at the S. end of the Pentland Hills, 17 m. from Lothianburn at the N. end, and in the EDINBURGH district, is a very good starting-point for numerous walks on the hills both short and long. It lies near the South Medwin river, through whose valley also runs a road to the W.

About ½ m. SE. of the village is Newholm, the seat of the Macdonald Lockharts of Lee and CARNWATH, who own most of the district. The Lockharts of Carnwath were in 1707 prominent Lowland Jacobite opposers of the Union.

Some 2 m. NE. is the "Covenanter's Grave" made for an unknown Covenanter wounded at RULLION GREEN in 1666, who, having asked to be buried within sight of Ayrshire, died next day.

DUNURE, *Ayrshire* (Map 2, ref. 22⁵61⁶), is a fishing village of the E.-coast type, yet upon the West, 9 m. S. of AYR, with a fine little harbour. Dunure Castle, built on a promontory, was a Kennedy stronghold, and in 1570 was the scene of the roasting of Allan Stewart, Commendator of CROSSRAGUEL, by Gilbert Kennedy, 4th Earl of Cassillis and "King" of Carrick. This incident aggravated the feud between Bargany

Scottish Tourist Board
Dunvegan Castle on Skye

and Cassillis, which ultimately led to the outlawing, for a time, of the Cassillis branch of the family.

DUNVEGAN, *Inverness-shire* (Map 4, ref. 12⁵84⁹), is a village with a castle of the same name on the Island of SKYE in the Inner Hebrides (*see* "The Shape of Scotland"). It stands at the head of the loch on the Bay of Dunvegan at the NW. of the islands. The village is small and picturesque, the bay full of islands. The Castle, the seat of the Macleod chiefs, is world-famous. Parts of it are reputed to date from the 9th cent. The massive four-square towered pile indubitably shows signs of building from the 15th to the 19th cents. Though some Scottish castles now inhabited are said to be older than Dunvegan, it is the oldest castle in private hands to have been in continuous occupation by the same family.

The interior of this formidable fortification now presents a cheerfully modern, inhabited air that only throws into relief the outward and visible signs of its great past. It is moated; its walls by the tower are 10 ft thick; it has a dungeon of the 15th cent. and many human relics of past Macleod achievements in battle and in hospitality. Amongst these are Rory Mor's two-handed sword, the "fairy flag" believed to have been captured from the Saracens during a Crusade. Rory Mor (the twelfth chief) also possessed a drinking-horn that held the equivalent of two modern bottles of claret; this he could drain at one draught. Other signs of past Macleod hospitality are to be seen in letters from Dr Samuel Johnson and from Sir Walter Scott. Dunvegan Castle is still the venerated centre of the Macleod clan wherever it may be dispersed over the world.

About 8 m. NW. of the Castle stands a memorial cairn to the MacCrimmons, the hereditary pipers to the Macleod chiefs and the founders and sustainers of the greatest school of piping the Highlands and Islands of Scotland have ever known.

DURISDEER, *Dumfriesshire* (Map 2, ref. 28⁹60⁴), is a pleasant hamlet nestling at the mouth of the Dalveen Pass and the Well Path; up this last still run the Roman road and the 18th-cent. coach road.

The hamlet is dominated by its late 17th-cent. church, built by the Duke of Queensberry and still containing its old box-pews. The N. wing is the Queensberry mausoleum, and it contains a fine white marble monument by Van Nost to the Duchess of Queensberry who died in 1709, and the Duke who died in 1711; this can be viewed by the public on request at a nearby cottage where the key is kept. At the mouth of the Well Path stands a large and well-preserved motte.

About ½ m. along the Well Path, leaving the main track a little way up and branching left through the fields, one comes to the well-preserved Roman road-post at the narrowest part of the pass; this was excavated in the late 1930s. Its ditch had long before yielded a bronze Roman saucepan (still surviving) and two other vessels (since lost). Durisdeer was host to several royal processions, by James III and James IV, in the 15th cent. Part of a fine Northumbrian cross-head suggests that there was a church here in the 10th cent.

DURNESS, *Sutherland* (Map 5, ref. 24°96⁸). The village nearest to CAPE WRATH, Durness is really a group of crofting townships. There are large sheep farms in the district.

To the N. is Balnakeil; the church, now in ruins, was built in 1619, but the churchyard still has a fine carved monument to Donald Macmurchov dated 1619 and a monument to the Gaelic poet Rob Donn (1714–78). The 18th-cent. Balnakeil House was formerly a seat of Lord Reay. The County Council bought the old Air Ministry buildings in 1964 with the intention of establishing a "craft-village" – that is, a community of independent craftsmen to work as individuals, but having in common a co-operative marketing scheme.

About 2 m. E. of Durness is Smoo Cave, at

Durness: Smoo Cave

the end of a deep cleft in limestone cliffs. It consists of three chambers; the first and largest is 200 ft long by 120 ft high with an entrance 53 ft high like a Gothic arch. The second cave is difficult of access and has a waterfall descending 80 ft into it.

The mention of limestone above allows one to point to the admirable trout fishing in the neighbourhood of Durness. There are half a dozen or so lochs with a limestone bottom, which is a good base for the freshwater shrimp and other small creatures on which trout flourish; and the trout of Durness certainly do flourish. Some of them, even in the small lochs, grow to a great size, but even the two-pounders fight as if they had three times that weight and muscle behind the power of their impetuous rushes.

DUROR, *Argyll* (Map 5, ref. 19°75⁴). The township of Duror in APPIN is associated with the Appin Murder of 1752, made more famous by Robert Louis Stevenson's dramatic but fictional account in his *Kidnapped*. James Stewart, who was accused of and eventually hanged for the murder, lived at Acharn and is buried near the ruined church of Keil 1 m. S. of the township. People still debate whether Stewart was properly tried and justly condemned, or whether he was merely a victim of post-1745 anti-Jacobite government policy.

About 1 m. NW. of Duror on the shores of Loch Linnhe is Ardsheal House, formerly the home of one of the most important cadet families of the Stewarts of Appin.

DYCE, *Aberdeenshire* (Map 6, ref. 38°81³). Since 1935 the site of ABERDEEN airport, this rapidly expanding industrial village is the outer tip of a continuous conurbation extending for 5 m. along the S. bank of the DON from Aberdeen, beginning with Kittybrewster, the city's mart centre and including Woodside (formerly an independent burgh), Bucksburn, Bankhead, and Stoneywood. In the 6 m. from the gorge at Cothal, just above Dyce, the Don falls 100 ft in a short distance, a fact of great economic importance, since it provides abundant water-power, which has been utilized since the 18th cent. by paper-making and textile mills of world-wide fame, while along the high land S. of the river extends a series of granite quarries. Dyce itself has a big bacon-curing factory and a chemical works. The village dates from the 1860s, when it became important as the junction of the main railway line to INVERNESS and the Buchan and Formartine railway.

But this intense industrialization has been confined to a fairly narrow strip along the Don's right bank, except at Grandholm opposite Woodside, where there is a large tweed and woollen mill. Elsewhere on the left bank of the river stretches wooded and arable country, rising up to the Scotston Moor. To the S., beyond the haugh on which the airfield lies, are two ridges, Tyrebagger Hill (823 ft, with a stone circle and view indicator), and the Hill of Marcus, on whose eastern slope the road from Pitmedden Station to Kinaldie yields one of the finest views in Aberdeenshire – across the Don and over a vast stretch of rural Formartine, with the village of Hatton of Fintry in the foreground.

The ancient ruined church of Dyce (long supplanted by others in the village) overlooks the gorge of Cothal and has two Pictish symbol stones built into the east gable.

This ancient church is dedicated to St Fergus, one of the three disciples of St Drostan, the founder of the Celtic monastery of DEER.

DYSART, *Fife* (Map 3, ref. 33¹69³). The old royal burgh of Dysart is now a part of KIRK-CALDY. Once an important harbour trading greatly with Holland, it was also one of the earliest coal-mining towns, with records of coal workings as far back as 1424 at least; and coal is indeed still the main industry. In the 18th cent. nail-making was important; at the end of that century 100 smiths made nearly 12,000,000 nails per year.

St Serf's Church at Dysart and a number of houses date back to the late 16th cent.; the church tower as well as the church was apparently used as a place of refuge.

The title, Earl of Dysart, was taken in 1643 by William Murray, former "whipping boy" to Charles I and son of the Rev. William Murray, once minister of Dysart.

EAGLESHAM, *Renfrewshire* (Map 2, ref. 25⁷65²), is a village 500 ft above sea-level and on the edge of the moors, 4 m. S. of Busby. Founded in 1796 on the site of a former village, and demolished to make way for a new planned town envisaged by the 12th Earl of Eglinton, it has two long rows of houses, very far apart, with a burn, trees, and a meadow in between. More rows were planned originally, but the cotton factory that the Earl established there was later burnt and was never replaced (the 10th Earl, incidentally, 200 years before his time, tried to dispeer himself to qualify for the House of Commons, but failed in the attempt). There was also work for 400 individual weavers in the area, but the coming of power put the hand-looms out of business. The village still retains the neat and regular appearance of the original design, with the two rows separated by some 250 yds of meadow at the lower end, converging to about 100 yds at the upper end. In 1960 Eaglesham became the first village in Scotland to be permanently listed as a place of special architectural or historical interest.

The parish church, erected by Lord Eglinton in 1790, has an eagle as a weathercock on the spire. The monument in the yard is to two Covenanters, Gabriel Thomson and Robert Lockhart, who were shot by "a party of Highlanders and dragoons under the command of Ardincaple, 1st May 1685" after the discovery of a conventicle on the moors.

A little to the W. are scanty remains of the 14th-cent. Polnoon Castle, built by the Montgomerie family, ancestors of the Eglintons. It was the 9th Baron, Sir John, who married the heiress of the Eglintons (bringing with her lands near ARDROSSAN), who built this Castle.

To the NE. of the village is Eaglesham House (formerly Polnoon Lodge), built in the baronial style; it is now used for storing dried grass. It was near to this house that in 1941 Rudolf Hess made his dramatic landing from Germany into the United Kingdom.

EARLSFERRY, *Fife* (Map 3, ref. 34⁸70⁰). On the coast and situated on the W. side of ELIE harbour, the royal burgh of Earlsferry is a popular summer resort with golf and fine sands. Traditionally it is said to have been made a burgh by Malcolm Canmore at the request of Macduff, Earl of Fife, who hid from Macbeth in a cave at Kincraig Point, and thence was ferried to DUNBAR. There are, be it admitted, no historical grounds for this legend, for the original charter, if it existed, was lost in an EDINBURGH fire. But James VI in 1589, when he granted a new charter, made the best of an insubstantial claim by describing the burgh as "old, past memory of man". It was a place of trade, with two weekly markets, rights of collecting dues and customs, and of returning an M.P. All this is now a thing of the past, despite James VI's best efforts.

Kincraig House in the town dates from 1680, and to the W. is the prominent headland of Kincraig Point, which flanks the E. side of LARGO Bay. It rises to a height of 200 ft and is of considerable geological interest, with good exposures of basalts, tuffs, greenstone, and porphyry. There are several caves on the seaward side, one of which is the legendary "Macduff's Cave".

EARLSTON, *Berwickshire* (Map 3, ref. 35⁸63⁸). On the Leader Water in the Lauderdale valley, Earlston was once known as Ercildoune. To the S. of the town stand the ivy-covered remains of the Rhymer's Tower, traditionally associated with the 13th-cent. poet and prophet Thomas the Rhymer, Sir Thomas Learmount, also known as Thomas of Ercildoune, Thomas Rimour, and True Thomas. Thomas the Rhymer lived all his life in Earlston – apart from the seven years he tarried in Elfland with the Queen of the Faeries. There are many legends about his prophecies, examples being the succession of Robert Bruce, the death of Alexander III suddenly on Kinghorn cliffs, the union of Britain under one of Bruce's blood, and the famous " 'Tide, 'tide, whate'er betide, there'll aye be Haigs of Bemersyde", which has held good despite many vicissitudes. The Russian poet Lermontov (1814–41) claimed descent from Thomas the Rhymer. The EDINBURGH Borderers' Association purchased the Rhymer's Tower in 1895, and placed a tablet on it; a National Trust examination, however, concluded that the structure was post-13th cent.

Built into the parish church is a small stone, which came from a former church and is now restored, with the lettering "Auld Rymr Race Lyees In This Place". The present building was erected in 1892 by Dr William Mair, minister for thirty-four years in Earlston, Assembly Moderator in 1897, and writer of Mair's *Digest* of Church Law. In the church tower is a bell cast by Jan Burgerhuys of Middleburg in 1609. Among many quaint tombstones in the churchyard is one saying simply:

Time how short
Eternity how long.

Earlston is a comparatively busy modern town, with sawmills, tweed and gingham mills, and quarrying. The town square was planted with a rose garden in 1953 to commemorate the Coronation of Queen Elizabeth II. A drinking fountain is set in a wall as a memorial to John Young, a celebrated local doctor for fifty years.

Some 3 m. NE. in the hills is the village of Legerwood, with its famous church, which has a fine Norman chancel arch and chancel. It was preserved by the Ker family's blocking up this part of the building, and was not revealed again until 1898, but is now fully restored. On the E. wall of the chancel is the 17th-cent. Ker Monument to the memory of John Ker of Moristoun and his wife Grizell Cochrane. She saved the life of her father, Sir John Cochrane of Ochiltree, during the political troubles of 1685, by twice waylaying the messenger bearing a warrant for his execution, until a third warrant was changed by the king to a pardon, and Sir John was saved. Just NE of the church are the remains of Corsbie Peel Tower. The ruins of Whitslaid Tower are also nearby in a strong site beside the Leader.

EARRAID, *Argyll* (Map 1, ref. $13°72°$). Readers of Stevenson's *Kidnapped* will recognize the name Earraid, this tidal island off the W. coast of MULL. It was here that David Balfour was shipwrecked, and wandered about the island not realizing that he could get off at low tide.

Earraid was used as a base for the building of DUBH ARTACH lighthouse (1867–72), and thereafter as the shore station for it, and later also as a base for SKERRYVORE until 1950; both lighthouses are visible in clear weather from a look-out point on the island.

EASDALE, Island of, *Argyll* (Map 1, ref. $17°71°$), is one of the Inner Hebrides (*see* "The Shape of Scotland"). Just to the W. of the Island of SEIL, which is connected with the mainland S. of OBAN, Easdale was famed for its slate quarrying, and, with one of its sister islands (LUING), helped to provide slate for the re-roofing of the abbey buildings at IONA. During the Second World War it supplied material for prismatic tools.

EASSIE, *Angus* (Map 6, ref. $33°74°$). In the churchyard at Eassie is a fine example of Pictish sculptured stone (an Ancient Monument under the Ministry of Public Building and Works). It is richly ornamented on the front with a cross and figures in relief. On the back the carving includes an "elephant" symbol, a double disc and Z-rod symbol, with figures of men and beasts.

EAST FORTUNE, *East Lothian* (3 m. NW. of East Linton). At this township to the S. of the main railway line from EDINBURGH to London, a monument marks the starting-point of the first double air-crossing of the Atlantic, by the airship R.34 in July 1919. This airship was built by Beardmores on the CLYDE.

An aerodrome was constructed here during the First World War; the buildings were afterwards used as a sanatorium. The sanatorium survived the Second World War and played a part in the conquering of tuberculosis.

This is a healthy place with strong fresh air, standing on good rich farmland of the characteristic East Lothian kind.

EASTHOUSES, *Midlothian* (Map 3, ref. $33°66°$). Near DALKEITH, Easthouses used to be part of the land farmed by the monks of NEWBATTLE Abbey. Since the Second World War it has been developed as a large housing estate for the mining community.

EAST KILBRIDE, *Lanarkshire* (Map 2, ref. $26°65°$) is now noted for its "New Town" – the first of Scotland's new satellite towns to be established after the Second World War. (For the policy of the post-war New Towns in Scotland, see CUMBERNAULD.)

This, one of the oldest villages in Scotland, with historical associations dating back to the 12th cent., was made a burgh of barony in the reign of Queen Anne; it then had a weekly market and three annual fairs. The name indicates that this place was one of the many Celtic foundations dedicated to St Bride or Bridget. The church dates from different periods, having the date 1774 carved above the tower entrance, with an unusual open crown tower put on during the 19th-cent. reconstruction – not unlike that of the Tolbooth at GLASGOW. There is an 18th-cent. mausoleum of the Stuarts of Torrance Castle, and near to the church entrance is an old mounting-stone. In the village the first Scottish meeting of the Society of Friends took place in 1653.

A little N. of the old village is the 13th-cent. Mains Castle, for long a ruin but recently restored. Originally it had been given to John Lindsay for his help in murdering the Red Comyn at DUMFRIES – the somewhat shady event that yet gloriously led to BANNOCK-BURN. The farm of Laigh Mains by the road-side has a model of the Castle in its garden.

Nearly 2 m. E. is Long Calderwood House, the birthplace of William and John Hunter, the 18th-cent. anatomists. To the S. is Torrance House, now the headquarters of the East Kilbride Development Corporation. The oldest parts date from the 14th cent., but there are many later additions. It was the former home of the Stuarts of Castlemilk.

About 1 m. E. is Mount Cameron Farm, home of Mrs Jean Cameron from 1746 to her death in 1773. She was associated with Prince Charles Edward Stuart in the '45, and legends in England and the South grew up about the allegedly powerful influence of Jeannie Cameron in Jacobite politics. She was amongst other accusations credited as being a "glamorous spy", a Mata Hari of the '45.

To turn from the '45 to the modern and enthusiastically growing modern town, it should be stressed that this was the first of all the post-war Scottish New Towns. It was, in a sense, experimental; and the experiment has succeeded. Its success did not mean, however, that all its features were followed in the shape and intention of the New Towns which came after it.

Cumbernauld, for instance, has emphasized its compactness, while keeping each of its houses individual. East Kilbride's wider acreage does, however, allow it a much more ample spread. With the historical centre of Torrance House as the site for its Development Council it stretches out in all directions, and really presents the appearance of a town with suburbs of its own.

By 1971 the population had reached 65,452, and the original 1946 designation target of 70,000 was raised to 100,000.

There are a great number of industrial firms now working in East Kilbride, and those who work in these concerns (mostly light industries) live in detached or semi-detached houses in various districts of the New Town. These districts are connected by principal internal routes. There are also "Residential Roads" for slow-moving traffic, and in addition to the normal roadside pavements there are in many areas separate footpaths for pedestrians only. The little valleys that cross the town have been made into landscaped parks called greenways, where the footpaths usually follow the natural line of the burns and streams.

There is a pedestrian shopping centre. This central shopping area was originally designed for a dual-carriageway road to pass between the shopping blocks. But by 1960 the decision was made to convert this to a "pedestrian precinct", and there are now safe shopping conditions under ample canopies. This precinct is provided with extensive car parks approached by the perimeter roads. Some of the sloping footpaths have under-floor heating to avoid the danger of ice in winter. There is an efficient omnibus system that connects the various residential units and leads to the shopping centre. As in other New Towns, modern archi-tects have built in the modern style pleasing churches both for the Catholic and Protestant inhabitants. It should be remembered that the vast majority of East Kilbrideans come from Glasgow, and it is from Glasgow that the younger ministers and priests have followed them.

The general impression of East Kilbride is modernity, space, comfort, a civic sense amongst its inhabitants, and perhaps above all youth. The Provost of East Kilbride is a young man full of energy and vigour. There are children wherever you walk and wherever you shop. With pleasure and gratification you look upon them and realize that, though they have the immense benefit of the motor-car, they are free from many of its dangers that lurk for young people in the crowded and older cities. The senior New Town of Scotland has, in this respect, set a pattern that will be followed in all other New Towns in this country.

EAST LINTON, *East Lothian* (Map 3, ref. 35^{9}67^7), is an old-world village on the R. Tyne, which flows here through a miniature gorge, with huge rocks, and is crossed by a 16th-cent. bridge. It is by-passed by the A1 trunk road, and this has helped to preserve its charm.

To the N. of the village is the parish kirk of Prestonkirk, built in 1733, and enlarged in 1824. It incorporates a 13th-cent. chancel, which is now a private burial-place, and a 17th-cent. square tower, which is thought to have much older foundations. In the church-yard are the graves of three men who might well be called "pioneers of agriculture in Scot-land". They were Andrew Meikle, who invented the threshing mill; John Sherriff, a pioneer in the breeding of different kinds of wheat and oats; and John Brown, who was the first editor of a farming journal in Scotland.

A little farther along the road from the church is Preston Mill, the only working water-mill to survive of the many that once dotted the banks of the R. Tyne, and thought to be the only one of its kind still able to operate in Scotland. It dates from the 17th cent. The conical roof of the kiln with its projecting wind vane, known locally as the "long arm of friend-ship", make it a very popular beauty spot and water-colour subject. In fact, all through the 19th cent. and until the present day, East Linton, its bridge, and its mill have been most popular with artists. Three whose names have survived from the artistic colony that flourished here are John Petty, who belonged to East

Linton; Martin Hardie, who is buried in the churchyard; and the most prolific of them all, Robert Noble.

Near the Mill is Phantassie Doocote, an excellent example of the traditional Scottish dovecote, which was acquired by the National Trust for Scotland in 1961. It was in Phantassie Mansion House nearby that the famous brothers George Rennie, the agriculturist, and John Rennie, the engineer and bridge-builder, were born. A memorial to John Rennie stands beside the by-pass road at East Linton, and incorporates a baluster of the Waterloo Bridge, in London, which he designed.

About 2 m. to the SW., near the river, is the beautiful ruin of Hailes Castle. It is of exceptional interest because its oldest portions date from before the War of Independence, and represent not so much a castle as a fortified manor house. It then belonged to the Gourlays, but afterwards it passed to the Hepburn family, by whom a great square tower and high curtain walls were added. There is also a fine 16th-cent. chapel. The Castle was heavily involved in the War of the Rough Wooing, and was dismantled by Cromwell in 1650. Bothwell brought Queen Mary here on their flight from BORTHWICK in 1567.

A strange feature of the Tyne at East Linton shows itself in the Lynn Pool, just by the village. Here may be seen, jumping at the falls but never overcoming them, fish that the locals have never managed to identify. The reason is simple: no one has ever been able to catch one – at least on a lure.

Tyne sea-trout are notoriously difficult to catch; but these jumping fish in the Lynn Pool are much larger than the run of Tyne sea-trout. They are certainly not salmon; they often have as much black on them as silver. The natives have speculated that they are "bull trout" – that is, brown trout that live in brackish water and sometimes grow to great size. Some East Linton folk call them "Norwegian" sea-trout.

EAST WEMYSS, *Fife* (Map 3, ref. 33³69⁶.)

This small coal-port on a rocky stretch of the coast is particularly known for its caves; about ten rock caves stretch along the coast to the SW. in the direction of WEST WEMYSS, and the towns get their name from the Gaelic word for cave, "uamh". The coastline is bold and rocky, though not very high. Some of the caves are indeed quite large, and all of them are above high-water mark. One of the largest is Glass Cave, used as one of the earliest glass-works in the country. The oddly styled Court Cave, E. of the town, derives its name from a traditional encounter that took place there between James V and some gipsies. Several caves have inscriptions, described in the 19th-cent. guide by Sir James Simpson.

To the E. of the town, just above Well Cave, are the extensive ruins of Macduff's Castle,

This is traditionally the stronghold of Macduff, and the ruins are in the characteristic red sandstone of the eastern district.

There is an old established linen-weaving factory in the town.

ECCLEFECHAN, *Dumfriesshire* (Map 3, ref. 31⁹57⁵).

This large Annandale village, in fertile farmland, at a crossroads and near HODDOM, BIRRENS, and Burnswark, is famous as the birthplace of Thomas Carlyle (1795–1881), who described it in *Sartor Resartus* under the name of Entepfuhl.

The house in which he was born, an attractive plain building, is known as "The Arched House" and stands in the middle of Main Street (the village lies to the side of the new main A74 trunk road). The house was built by Carlyle's father and uncle, both of whom were master masons, and has an archway or "pend" through it.

The room where he was born can be seen, as well as furniture from his Chelsea house, and personal relics, including correspondence with Goethe.

At the top of the village at the N. end of Main Street is a copy of Boehm's statue of Carlyle at Chelsea showing "Auld Tam Cair'll" seated. In the churchyard to the W. is the grave of the author and his parents and brother. Archibald Arnott (1772–1855), who was doctor to Napoleon in St Helena, is also buried there.

The village lies in a hollow with a burn flowing through the centre, once crossed by eighteen small bridges, as described by Carlyle. It is now largely covered in, and a plaque on the wall at the head of the village reads: "1875. 209 ft of the burn below this spott was arched over by Dr George Arnott at his own expence". The burn, however, is still above ground opposite the Carlyle House.

The village, despite much modern housing on the outskirts, keeps its highly distinctive character.

ECCLES, *Berwickshire* (Map 3, ref. 37⁵64²).

This village, 6 m. W. of COLDSTREAM, was formerly of considerable importance, for it contained St Mary's Cistercian Convent, founded in 1155 by Gospatrick, Earl of Dunbar. The town and convent were burnt by the English in Hertford's raid of 1545, and there are now only a few remains of the convent to be seen. The large parish church was built in 1774, and shows a handsome spire. The bell has on it the date of 1659.

Some 2 m. NE. is Kames, birthplace of Henry Home (1696–1782), the philosopher and judge, who took the title of Lord Kames when he was raised to the Bench in 1752.

Lord Kames had a sardonic wit. On assizes in the West he used to play chess with a hard-drinking local laird. This same laird killed a boon companion in a drunken brawl. Lord

Kames sat on the Bench at the trial. After the jury had returned a verdict of guilty, His Lordship passed sentence and then, after a pause, added, "That's checkmate to you, Matthew".

ECHT, *Aberdeenshire* (Map 6, ref. 37⁴80⁵). Those who read through Lewis Grassic Gibbon's trilogy of novels *A Scots Quair* to the somewhat bitter end will know that it concludes on the Barmekin of Echt, which occupies a symbolic place in the story, and where in fact the last pages of it were actually written by the author (*see* GLENBERVIE) in the summer of 1934, only about nine months before his death. It adds something, perhaps, to the meaning it holds in Gibbon's masterpiece to know that this flat-topped hill, the upper slopes of which are clad in heather and rich in wild berries, was of old a place of refuge, as it was to his heroine.

Here, esconced in five concentric rings of stone fortifications, the Picts who built them could look straight across country northwards, to the next big hill-fort on the Mither Tap of BENNACHIE. To the SW. of them towered the shapely ridge of the Hill of FARE, while 1 or 2 m. E. lay the shimmering mirror of the Loch of SKENE – all as described in *Grey Granite*.

A millennium after it was in use as a hill-fort, the Barmekin was the scene of signs and portents in the winter of 1637, on the eve of the Civil War. Gordon's *History of Scots Affairs* avers that "for the space of all the winter, almost every night, drums were heard beaten about four o'clock, the parade of retiring guards, their taptoes, their reveilles and marches distinctly heard". Even more prophetic of dire events to come was the fact that first Scottish marches were heard, then Irish, then English, and then the marches of French, Dutch, and Danish soldiers – an omen of the various troops that were to be used in the coming conflict. The Barmekin was in the news again in 1882, when a telescope from the Earl of Crawford's observatory at Dunecht was set up inside the ancient fort to watch a transit of Venus.

Immediately to the E. of the Barmekin lie the two small villages in the parish of Echt: the older Kirkton of Echt, with an interesting Georgian parish church and an old inn, and 2 m. N. the Waterton of Dunecht, a model village laid out at the end of the 19th cent. by A. C. Pirie, then proprietor of the estate of Dunecht and its palatial mansions. This great estate of 12,827 acres belongs to the 3rd Viscount Cowdray, whose grandfather the 1st Viscount, Weetman Dickinson Pearson, a great civil engineer magnate and former president of the Air Board in the First World War, purchased it in 1910. The vast mansion itself, with over 100 rooms and a W. front of 230 ft, was built for the Earl of Crawford after 1845 to designs by G. E. Street. When the 25th Earl of Crawford and Balcarres was buried in a special vault here in 1880, a scandal ensued that shook the Victorian world. The vault was broken open and the body removed secretly. Its whereabouts remained unknown for over a year, and Queen Victoria, who was intensely interested in the affair, wrote condolences to the widowed Countess. The missing corpse was discovered under 2 ft of soil 700 yds from the house, and a rat-catcher called Charles Soutar was tried, convicted, and sentenced in EDINBURGH for complicity in the exploit, which still remains "the Great Dunecht Mystery".

There are many prehistoric monuments in the Echt district, including the stone circle at Sunhoney to the W., but the best preserved is the Cullerlie Stone Circle about 1 m. SE. of Kirkton, now under the care of the Ministry of Public Building and Works. It consists of eight untrimmed boulders, enclosing an area consecrated by fire, on which eight small cairns were later constructed, probably in the late Bronze Age. It resembles the circle at Ford in Northumberland, where it has been suggested the child of a chieftain was buried, surrounded by the bodies of dependants slain at the funeral.

EDDERTON, *Ross and Cromarty* (Map 5, ref. 27¹88⁴). The village of Edderton stands on the S. side of the DORNOCH Firth. The Premonstratensian Abbey was founded there in 1221 by Farquhar, 1st Earl of Ross, but was removed to FEARN (10 m. SE.) in 1338.

The church dates from 1743, as an inscription on the W. gable shows; the date 1794 on the E. gable refers to repairs.

Nearly 2 m. NW. are the remains of a cairn, 50 ft in diameter, containing traces of a chamber. Another cairn stands 100 yds to the SE., but is more denuded.

On the NW. edge of the village is a Pictish symbol stone of red sandstone, standing 10 ft high and incised with double disc, Z-rod symbol, and fish symbol.

EDDLESTON, *Peeblesshire* (Map 3, ref. 32⁴64⁷). Overlooked by the Moorfoot Hills to the E. and the Cloich Hills to the W., this hamlet lies in the valley of Eddleston Water. Darnhall, a massive château-like house in fine grounds, was formerly the seat of the Murrays of Elibank and is now the Black Barony Hotel. It was originally a border tower, the seat of the Murray family from 1412, and was greatly added to in the 17th cent.

On a roadside cottage on the PEEBLES road to the S. of the village is a monument to commemorate George Meikle Kemp (1795–1844), the designer of the Scott Monument in EDINBURGH. In this cottage Kemp was apprenticed as a joiner and a wheelwright in 1809. He was a Pentland shepherd's son, and later worked as a millwright in France, studying as best he could. He was tragically drowned before the Scott Monument was finished. There is a bust of Kemp in the monument, and a bronze tablet with a miniature of the monument at the hamlet of Redscaurhead nearby.

A little NE. of the village is Portmore House built in baronial style. It was erected in 1850 and destroyed by fire in 1883, but was subsequently restored. The previous house was the birthplace of William Forbes Mackenzie (1801–62), M.P. for Peeblesshire for sixteen years; he was responsible for getting the Public House Act of 1852 passed, closing the public houses on Sundays.

The *bona fide* travellers clause, however, enabled anyone in Scotland who had travelled 3 m. to get a drink from a public house. The result was that in Scotland for more than a century after 1852 the house had (in theory) to serve any 3-m.-traveller from midnight on Saturdays to midnight on Sundays. This was indeed a freedom of which many Scottish visiting "travellers" availed themselves. The anomaly, however, was removed by Parliament in the early 1960s.

EDDRACHILLIS, *Sutherland* (Map 5, ref. 21⁶94⁰). This coastal parish includes thirty-five islands and islets (amongst them H A N D A) and a large area of rugged country with the prominent peaks of Ben Stack and Foinaven. There are many tiny lochans and very little cultivable land in this area of Lewisian gneiss. The land once belonged to the earls of Sutherland, but passed to the Morays in the 13th cent. Afterwards it was owned successively by the Kinnairs, the Macleods, and the Mackays, finally being repurchased by the Sutherland family in 1829.

EDINBURGH, *Midlothian* (Map 3, ref. 32⁵67¹). "This is pure theatre!" exclaimed a well-known dramatic critic when he saw Edinburgh for the first time. He was right; the capital of Scotland is highly dramatic in appearance. Take but one instance from its most celebrated thoroughfare. If you walk along Princes Street on a fine day and look up at the silhouette of the 1,000-year-old Castle on its rock and the Old Town stretched against the southern sky, it is as if you were looking at a drop-curtain on the stage.

This is not the only theatrical effect Edinburgh produces. Built upon hills, and with greater hills behind it, it has at its feet the sea in the shape of the Firth of F O R T H – and, as if this were not enough, it has within its boundaries, and in a royal park near the centre, a great rocky hill, Arthur's Seat, which in some eyes might pass for a mountain. From the highest point at the heart of Edinburgh, you can see half over southern Scotland and into the Highland hills. Everywhere in its streets you may come upon a corner from which you will catch unexpected glimpses of sea or hills or remote countryside. It is a superb natural city-site for building; and, on the whole, man has done well by it.

Scottish Tourist Board
Lady Stair's House, Edinburgh

The best thing he has done is to seize the advantage of the hills descending to the sea, to keep a sense of space and vista while displaying, again in theatrical form, high contrast.

That contrast is nowhere better discovered than in the fact of the Old and New Towns lying almost side by side. The Old Town

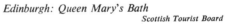

Edinburgh: Queen Mary's Bath
Scottish Tourist Board

sloping down from the Rock crowned by the Castle is on an eminence; is crowded, historic; and is a romantic jumble of buildings from past centuries going back to medieval times. The New Town is spacious, gracious, and ordered. It lies upon the slopes to the sea. It is, in contrast with the city on the hill, pure classicism. Built at the end of the 18th cent. and the beginning of the 19th, it is the finest example of neo-Georgian town-planning left in the world. Its juxtaposition to, and complementary contrast with, the romantic and antique Old Town is unique.

The Old Town huddled upon its sloping rock was, until 200 years ago, all that Edinburgh consisted of. Until just before half way through the last century, the Old and the New Town together comprised all the Edinburgh that concerned anyone. It would, perhaps, be too much to say that it contains all the Edinburgh that the modern visitor need concern himself with, but it is nearly true. In Victorian times Edinburgh spread vastly and, in character with the city, spaciously. In our own age it has, alas! spread less spaciously, even more vastly, and without doubt less graciously. But the old Edinburgh of our great (or great-great) grandfather's day, the Old and the New Town, remains the essence of Edinburgh. If you have investigated it thoroughly, you will have absorbed the real capital of Scotland.

The capital! Other towns, in particular PERTH, have claimed prior place, and with some justification, as Scotland's capital city. But now, despite the fact that Edinburgh is not the largest city in Scotland, it is indubitably the capital, and has been so for over 500 years. Without official statement, Edinburgh became the capital when James II, having taken a fancy to the place, held his parliament there upon attaining his majority in the 1450s. The name "Edinburgh" is of doubtful origin. Probably it came from Edwin's burgh, Edwin being a king of Northumbria who, in A.D. 617, held the fortress that is now the Castle, and encouraged a small cluster of houses outside its gates and on the Rock.

To return to the real, the essential Edinburgh of today springing from this cluster on the Rock, it is still possible to investigate it all on foot. Like another famous city, the real Edinburgh is built on seven hills. In Rome you can, if you do not mind walking up and down occasional steepish streets, cover the essential city of seven hills on foot – that is, if at some seasons you can bear the heat. In Edinburgh, you can do the same, if you do not mind even steeper streets – and you will not be troubled by excessive heat. In imagination, let us take such a walk through the essential Edinburgh.

There is no better place from which one could begin than from the heart of Edinburgh, St Margaret's Chapel, which at the top of the Castle Rock, stands as the oldest building in Edinburgh.

ESSENTIAL EDINBURGH

The Old Town and the New Town

St Margaret's Chapel is more than the heart of Edinburgh; all Scotland claims it. The fairly friendly, if somewhat vociferous, rivalry between Edinburgh and GLASGOW is well known, but even the most fervent Glaswegian does not think of St Margaret's Chapel – indeed, he does not think of the Castle itself – as belonging only to Edinburgh. It is Scotland's, and so is everything in it. He owns it too.

Margaret, queen and saint (see "Scotland in History" – and this is the last time that essay will be referred to in this entry on Edinburgh, for so much of Scotland's history happened here), built this chapel at the highest point of the Edinburgh Castle Rock in 1076. It is poignant in its simplicity, with space today for only twenty-six worshippers. It is a breathtaking experience to emerge from this tiny sanctified enclosure at the very heart of Edinburgh and, if the visibility is good, look out over the great Lowland scene – the sea, Fife, and the distant Highlands. Here indeed is contrast.

There is so much to see in what remains of this centuries-old fortress that the visitor is recommended to the services of the official guides who take parties round. Whether guided or not, however, he must not miss the royal apartments that Scottish monarchs used in the days of our independence. Here, in a room smaller even than St Margaret's Chapel, Mary Queen of Scots gave birth to her son who was to be James VI and I. There is a window in this room looking out on to the sheer depths, into the Grassmarket. A tradition exists that the infant James was lowered out of this window in a basket to be smuggled into safety, and possibly to be baptized in his mother's faith.

Nor should the visitor miss, in the same apartments just above Mary Stuart's room, the Crown Chamber containing the Honours of Scotland. Rich yet austere, these antique insignia of Scottish royalty the crown, the sceptre, and other objects used in the coronation of our independent monarchs since Bruce are no less beautiful than touching. But not always have they been so evident to the eye.

They were hidden at the time of Cromwell's occupation of Scotland. Patriotically saved in a wooden chest at the Union of 1707, they at last came to light in 1817 when a commission on which Sir Walter Scott served "officially discovered" them. Now, brightly gleaming or sombrely glowing, they are there for all to see and to remind some of us of "ane auld sang".

In the same Palace Square as the royal apartments is the famous Scottish national war memorial, built after the First World War to the inspired design of Sir Robert Lorimer. Completed in 1927, it might be expected, as it is of the exact period, to "date". But no. It is too

Plate 7   Edinburgh from Calton Hill (see p. 203)
Scottish Tourist Board

*The Canongate
Tolbooth, Edinburgh
(see p. 196)*

*Edinburgh:
John Knox's House
(see p. 196)*

Edinburgh Castle from the east

heartfelt an achievement in architecture to suffer that fate. It has been called a coronach in tone.

You pass out of the Castle to the E. and over a moat by means of drawbridge. Just before this is the Half-Moon Battery from which the daily one-o'clock gun is fired. Since 1861, when the idea of a time-reminding gun was borrowed from Paris, citizens have grown accustomed to his watch-setter. Visitors, especially those near the Castle just before luncheon, are warned to beware of its thunderous voice echoing amidst the rock of Edinburgh.

Passing over the wide Esplanade, where the Festival tattoos are held, you come to the head of the Lawnmarket and the beginning of the Royal Mile, which is the main channel of the Old Town, leading down from the Castle to the Palace of Holyroodhouse. To walk down the Royal Mile is to walk through much of the history of Scotland.

Kings, queens, and princes have ridden and walked in the Royal Mile; great men have gone this way to their execution. Spectacular scoundrels have lived and operated in this high, grey, slightly winding thoroughfare; so have poets, writers, and philosophers of international fame. Until recently it was all but a picturesque slum; now its last elements of squalor have been removed, and it has been effectively illuminated. We no longer sentimentalize over the Old Town's past, but take pride in its present.

To the visitor from the South, however, it still remains "picturesque", rather "foreign-looking", and – there is only one other word that will do for it – "fruity". Every yard of this Royal Mile has some history, major or minor, attached to it. In this descent of it we shall deal only with the major facets.

Immediately on the right is a tributary street leading down to the Grassmarket, the wide open mart where, amidst scenes of appalling gusto and gloom, public hangings used to take place till as late as the last century. All that remains of the West Bow or gate of this ill-omened road is now, and rather inappropriately, the church that is used as the Assembly Hall of the Free Kirk of Scotland. Nearly opposite, in the Lawnmarket, is the Outlook Tower, containing that instrument of pleasure for children of all ages up to eighty, the *camera obscura*, which gives one on a screen a peep-show of all Edinburgh below you.

Farther down on the left is James's Court, where Dr Johnson spent his first night in Scotland as the guest of the eager and nervous Boswell. David Hume, the amiable philosopher, also lived here until he led the way into the New Town (*see below*). Gladstone's Land, its interior splendidly restored to its 17th-cent. coloured richness by the National Trust for Scotland and the Saltire Society, is just next door. If you want to know what life was like in the Old Town before it became a slum, do not miss this. But we have covered only 70 yds of

Studio Brett

Edinburgh: procession from the General Assembly of the Church of Scotland

this beguiling street. We must get on and, in doing so, move well down to the next really important place.

The Lawnmarket turns into the High Street 100 yds down. Here is the real centre of the Old Town. The High Kirk of St Giles occupies the centre of the thoroughfare, which is widened here. Insofar as the democratic Church of Scotland has any official first church, this is it. Assemblies meet there; so do the Scottish judges for worship at the opening of the Court of Session. Royal Proclamations affecting the United Throne are heraldically spoken at the mercat cross by the W. door of the church. St Giles is full of the memorials of Scottish history right down to the present date. Its famous Thistle Chapel is the meeting-place of the Scottish order of the Knights of the Thistle, roughly corresponding to the Knights of the Garter.

St Giles is not a cathedral, though often referred to as such. Before the Reformation this building, said to have been established about 1120, was the Civic Church of Edinburgh, then a Collegiate Church. After the Reformation, owing to John Knox's vigorous use of it, it became the Capital Kirk. For a brief period, during the 17th-cent. episcopal imposition from the Stuarts in London, it became officially a cathedral.

But the stool hurled at the Dean of Edinburgh's "lug" in 1637 by Jeannie Geddes (the

name is a matter of pious and permitted belief, rather than *de fide*) started a movement that ended in its position as the "Hie Kirk of St Giles" within the Church of Scotland, which of course has no cathedral. The architecture of St Giles was relentlessly restored at the beginning of last century, but its essential ambience remains. It is said that, on the 1st of May 1707, when the Acts of Union came into force, someone managed to get into the belfry of St Giles and ring out over the city on the carillon the old Highland lament "Why should I be sad upon my wedding day?"

In Parliament Square, which is just by St Giles, there is the grave of John Knox, and (somewhat incongruously) a fine statue of Charles II. Parliament House, where the Scottish parliaments met from 1639 until the Union of 1707, is now the headquarters of Scottish law. The Courts of Session have their place there. This is a spot in which the history of Scotland lives on. In the Courts, Scottish judges, arrayed in the traditional Scottish robes of crimson, preside over justice administered according to the Scottish legal system – differing from the English system in that Scottish law derives from Roman law.

The visitor may care to see the Court (it is exactly as it was) where, in 1857, the celebrated Miss Madeleine Smith "tholed her assize" on the charge of having poisoned her lover. The verdict was Not Proven, and she lived until 1928. In the Parliament Hall, which once resounded to Scottish parliamentary debate before the Union, Scottish advocates (advocates with us, not barristers) stroll up and down discussing their cases with clients or solicitors, and sometimes, it is said, by silent display soliciting work from solicitors. The officials at Parliament House, though of course not paid guides like the custodians at the Castle, are highly conscious of the living traditions of Scottish law in this place, and will give courteous information to those genuinely interested.

Here at the middle of the High Street, with Parliament House and St Giles on the one side and, on the other, the City Chambers, whose early 19th-cent. classicisms contrast oddly, yet not unpleasingly, with the more antique architecture around it, one is at the heart of the Old Town, the Heart of Midlothian. Nearly every second building, however insignificant it may now look, has some historical tradition. Space would be wasted here in detailing them, and the visitor's time would be dissipated in trying to see everything.

Rather, he should wander about as he wills, in this descent to Holyroodhouse, gathering the atmosphere of this still companionable part of old Edinburgh. Most buildings of genuine interest bear a plaque. The visitor should not miss the narrow closes or wynds that lead steeply down from the Royal Mile; as he descends, surprising vistas of the classical New Town and the sea beyond can suddenly leap out upon him. If he gets the chance, too, he should look at the stone staircases, now leading often to the humblest dwellings. These circulating stairways wind from right to left, designed for defending swordsmen of long ago to use their right arms and so put the ascending attackers at a disadvantage.

This perhaps is the place to consider what an

The High Kirk of Edinburgh: St Giles

unusual place the Old Town was when it was in its heyday. Hemmed in by loch and marshland on one side, by other constrictions on the S., its citizens huddled together on the slope of the Castle Rock. Their only expansion was upwards, by building houses or what we would now call flats, on top of each other. These, in their day, were considered the first skyscrapers.

Huddled these people may have been, but they were companionable in a way that has disappeared. One winding stone staircase might be shared by a duchess, a printer, a philosopher, a poor poet, and perhaps a "lady of the town". Smollett, in his novel *Humphry Clinker*, gives an admirable description of this Old Town life in the middle of the 18th cent.

"Sir," said Dr Johnson when he met Boswell in the High Street of Edinburgh on the night of the 14th of August 1773, "I smell you in the dark". It was the Doctor's first visit to Edinburgh, in a period that is often called its Golden Age, but we know what he meant. It must be admitted that the Old Town's Golden Age was highly insanitary. The rock on which it was built offered few facilities for tunnelled drainage. Citizens were in the habit of hurling their refuse from out of their windows at night, to be taken away by the cleansing men before next morning.

The only concession to convenience was the crying of "Gardy loo" (a derivation from the French of the Auld Alliance days of *Gare de l'eau*) before hurling. But it was more than *eau* that was flung out of the high old windows; the kitchen refuse and the contents of the chamber commode went with it. Many a finely-dressed gallant, a little too much under the influence of claret to hear the warning cry (the Golden Age was also the great wine-drinking age in Edinburgh), must have reeled home not only drenching but stinking. An extraordinary period in an extraordinary place!

Today the visitor need fear no such inundation as he walks the Royal Mile, but he may

The General Assembly of the Church of Scotland, Edinburgh

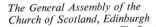

The Rev. Dr Ronald Falconer

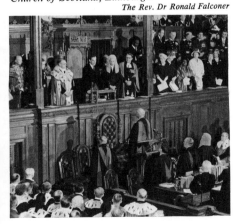

care to reflect on the odd mixture of sociability, learning, intellectual eminence, and discomfort that once marked the Old Town of Edinburgh for its own.

Leaving the Heart of Midlothian and crossing the 19th-cent. intersection of the North Bridge, you come to the lower reach of the High Street. Here the most famous building is "John Knox's House" at the farther end and on the left. This undubitably ancient building, in excellent repair, may or may not deserve its title in the sense of being the permanent or long residence of the reformer. But he did live there for a time while his manse was repairing. The study where he worked is preserved; so are some Knoxian relics.

The Royal Mile ends and flattens out into the Canongate (the entry to the city for the canons in the old days of Holyrood Abbey). The Canongate Street was used by the higher nobility in the great days of the Old Town. Huntly House, bought and gracefully preserved by the Edinburgh Corporation, is a notable example of a great noble's temporary town house, taken over, be it noted, from a civic "incorporation" or guild. Here also stands the Canongate Tolbooth. A particularly good instance of Scottish-style 17th-cent. architecture is the adjoining Canongate parish church, recently most tastefully restored. It is full of light, of delicate colouring, and shows a new tendency in the style of Church of Scotland worship and church decoration. Just before his recent and lamented death, Robert Hurd, commissioned by the Corporation, did some notable reconstruction work in the Canongate. This pleasing rehabilitation will be obvious to visitors.

We emerge from what was once the old city of Edinburgh into an open space, surrounded by small houses and ending the Royal Mile at the entrance to the Palace of Holyroodhouse. The space by the Watergate was once "in sanctuary", as being Abbey ground. Long after the Reformation, and until 1880, this sanctuary ground acted as a refuge for debtors, who could not be arrested there. The owners of the small houses did a good trade by accommodating (for ready money) debtors on the run. It is said that the great and good Sir Walter Scott – when, through no fault of his own, he had got into deep money difficulties – contemplated fleeing temporarily to this place.

This is the end of the Royal Mile, and the end of the long straggling old city on the rock which was *the* Old Town. As has been said earlier, the city could not spread N. in the direction of the Princes Street of today because of a loch and marshland. Citizens were unwilling to spread their town much S. and away from the Rock; for such an expansion would have exposed their capital to English depredation. After the Union of 1707, however, it was safe to extend in a rather unplanned sort of way in this direction. This extension is still a part of the real Old Town, though tenuously connected with it.

Immediately below the Rock and the Royal Mile to the S. is the Cowgate, an early extension. This, with its prolongation into Holyrood Road, used until recently to be a noisome slum. Rightly purged, it has also lost any antique distinction that lingered in it. It is redeemed by its two endings. To the E. it leads into Holyrood Park; to the W. it debouches into an old open mart, the Grassmarket, splendidly set under the towering heights of the Castle.

The only two other buildings in this southern extension that are essential for visitors to see are the University and George (more properly George's) Square. Edinburgh's is the youngest of the four older Scottish universities (since 1967 there have been eight) but is of respectable antiquity (1583). In the latter part of the 18th cent., and at the beginning of the 19th, its noble Old Quadrangle rose to house its growing activities. Since then the University has spread far in Edinburgh, but this fine neo-Georgian building, put up from plans made by Robert Adam, is its headquarters. Edinburgh herself now has two universities, since the Heriot-Watt College was promoted to university status in 1966.

George Square was originally named George's Square, after the architect George Brown (1722–1806). It was the farthest extension southwards of the Old Town, and was the first attempt by the citizens to escape from the overcrowded conditions of the Royal Mile. What remains of it possesses considerable charm. It is, moreover, a highly interesting, indeed all but a unique, example of indigenous Scottish architecture in a period of transition from the 17th-cent. half-medieval style to classicism.

"What remains of it"! The University, having bought up most of it, has turned it into a residential and lecture-hall quarter. They have pulled down two sides of it, and in their place have erected "contemporary" buildings, some of them jutting far into the sky. This action caused furious controversy. It is, however, worth noting that, save for this disagreeable structure, Edinburgh is the only large city in Scotland to have escaped the ugly menace of the block skyscraper building. The Town Council, under pressure from the Georgian Society, has also been at pains to stop the erosion of that unique example of neo-Georgian town-planning, the New Town. New buildings above a stated height have now been forbidden.

We left the reader at the end of the Old Town and at the entrance to the Palace of Holyroodhouse. The Palace we shall deal with later as an entity on its own. We ought not to leave the Old Town quarter, however, without mentioning two buildings in which Edinburgh takes a particular pride. These are the Central Public Library (of no architectural merit, but

Randolph Crescent in Edinburgh's Georgian New Town

containing much of literary value) and, immediately opposite it, the National Library of Scotland, a distinguished modern building. In the richness of its contents, it comes only just after the British Museum Library and the Bodleian at Oxford. Edinburgh, as capital of Scotland, is a city of the printed word. These buildings enshrine it.

As buildings, however, they are not of the Old Town, nor yet of the New. It is to the New Town we must now turn.

In the middle of the latter half of the 18th cent., Edinburgh, growing in population, prosperity, and fame, began to find the constriction of life in the Old Town on the Rock intolerable. They looked for a direction in which they could expand. After the tentative move of George's Square to the S., they found still more attractive the N. prospect laid out so temptingly below their windows. But one large obstacle lay in their way – the "Nor' Loch", a considerable sheet of water immediately below the Castle and the Old Town, where Princes Street Gardens lie today. This obstacle was further extended by marshland to the E.

The great Lord Provost Drummond and his Town Council were not daunted. They drained the loch and threw the North Bridge over the marshy land to the E. of it. They then started to build the first New Town to the inspired design of the youthful James Craig. This consisted of St Andrew Square at the E. end and Charlotte Square at the W., with the wide and lengthy thoroughfare of George Street connecting them. To the N. of George Street lay Queen Street; to the S., Princes Street.

This bold and imaginative design was begun in 1770, and was completed in the first years of the 19th cent. This first New Town was, very soon afterwards, to be followed by a second New Town in something of the same manner, and to the N., a little lower down the hill towards the sea. Thereafter, the New Town style and influence was to spread, less planned but almost equally beneficial, in all directions. But it was to the Lord Provost Drummond and to Craig's plan that this transformation in the life, style, and beauty of Edinburgh was due.

It was a transformation indeed. The noble, the rich, the prosperous – in fact, anyone who could afford to move – swarmed out of the overcrowded, companionable warren of the Old Town on the Rock, and sought and found spaciousness, graciousness, cleanliness, and (perhaps as important as anything else) light and air in the New Town. If they lost something of the traditional companionability of the Old Town, they gained so many other advantages. Moreover, the first New Town, consisting of but two squares and three streets (two of them one-sided), was sufficiently compact for people to go on knowing each other as neighbours.

One of the first to join in this huge "flitting", as we call house-moving in Scotland, was the (by then) internationally famous yet characteristically Edinburgh philosopher, David Hume. He left James's Court in the Lawnmarket, where he had been a neighbour of James Boswell, and moved to a small street off St Andrew Square.

Hume, the philosopher of doubt, the

questioner of all religious faiths, was not highly in favour amongst Edinburgh Church or eminently respectable circles, but he was the most companionable of men, and well liked. It is surely an indication of the kindliness and continuing companionability of Edinburgh in its first New Town, that, in honour of the philosopher, the Corporation named after him the street in which he chose to live, adding, with a touch of humour, the word "Saint". The little thoroughfare bears to this day the name of St David Street.

The second New Town, begun in the 1820s, reflects the ideas of the first venture. It was not able to spread its plan so extensively, but, because it has remained much more residential, it retains more of the New Town spirit. It begins with Heriot Row, facing nobly uphill into the sunshine across Queen Street Gardens, and ends at Fettes Row, down the hill. The massive and eminently satisfactory Great King Street, in between, is the George Street of this second New Town.

Edinburgh Castle, the Old Town and its extensions, and the Palace and Park of Holyroodhouse, together with the two planned New Towns and one or two inescapable extensions of that planning and style, form all of the essential Edinburgh. It is that part of the capital of Scotland which, it was earlier said, can conveniently and (from the point of view of sight-seeing) beneficially be covered on foot: a city of great and internationally-famed beauty, and one with history behind each stone or round each corner.

Before continuing to point out buildings and institutions worthy of note in the New Town, and before going on into outer Edinburgh, it is worth pausing to reflect on the idea and intention of the New Town project.

It must be understood that, as originally designed, the now world-famous Princes Street was a minor affair, playing in the first New Town third fiddle to George Street and Queen Street. People at the beginning went to the New Town to enjoy large commodious houses rather than fine prospects. Princes Street, when built, held only small Regency-type buildings contrasting humbly with the mansions of George Street and Queen Street.

Mammon was quick to perceive the usefulness of Princes Street's position, and soon turned the buildings in it into the ill-considered jumble they now present. Mammon too, but in a somewhat dignified way, entered George Street. The severely beautiful Queen Street was largely left alone, and can be enjoyed today as much as it was enjoyed when it was built. The second New Town is hardly touched by commerce. Though lacking the full inspiration of the first design, it is, by reason of its inviolability, most satisfying.

The final comment one cannot but make on the planned New Towns, on their consequent effects elsewhere in the growing Edinburgh,

Scottish Field

Ainslie Place: Edinburgh's Georgian New Town preserved

indeed all over Scotland to the edges of the Pentland Firth by THURSO in Caithness, is this. It was a wonderful stroke of good fortune for us in Edinburgh and Scotland, for all who respect that most satisfying art of architecture wherever they may be, that Edinburgh had a Lord Provost such as Drummond, a young architect such as Craig, and a Corporation with an imaginative civic sense at precisely the time it did.

Had Edinburgh waited to burst its bounds, or had she tinkered with the problem of expansion for another fifty years, while thrusting out unplanned movements towards the S. such as George's Square, one shudders to think of the probable result. The Nor' Loch would eventually have gone; there would have been building of some kind on the Northern Slopes. But what would that kind have been?

Probably, under the influence of Walter Scott romanticism (beneficial in literature but detestable in architecture), some ghastly neo-Gothic excrescence would have been spawned where Charlotte Square, George Street, Heriot Row, and Moray Place now stand. As it was, Edinburgh expanded at a period of high taste in building, when there were architects of such eminence as the Adam Brothers, William Playfair, and others. The result is our incomparable New Town, which, since the wanton bombing of Dresden, is unique in the Western world.

The mention of Moray Place above allows us to anticipate slightly and go outside the formal limits set to the essential Edinburgh. The second New Town was a little cramped in development owing to the Corporation's lack of power over private property. A notable example was the estate belonging to the Earl of Moray, just W. of Heriot Row. But these and other lands soon became free. The most notable results of this freedom were the magnificent, if a trifle overpowering, Moray Place to the W. and the superb Drummond Place to the E.

We cannot leave the subject of New Town extensions without mention of Ann Street. This delightful miniscule in the "Style" is clean outside the New Town and across the Water of Leith, yet it is in its miniature way of the essence of the New Town. It is a small, almost a doll's, two-sided street standing on its own and built to the specifications of the great Edinburgh painter, Raeburn. Ann Street also bears the distinction of being (as far as one knows) the only entire street in the world to be given to a woman as a birthday present. Raeburn was devoted to his wife, and had prepared the street for her as a surprise. On her birthday, he took her down from central Edinburgh to see it, gave it to her and named it after her.

Other extensions of the New Town style are scattered all over Edinburgh, some as far S. as Newington and Morningside (see below), some of them nearly as beautiful as anything in the New Town proper. Unfortunately there is no space to mention them in detail.

Now for places that ought to be seen, or at least places and things of interest, within the New Town.

Starting from the W. (which is not the end from which the New Town was built – but we may as well fall in with the Glasgow description of Edinburgh as being "West-Endy and east-windy"), there is Charlotte Square. It is outstanding. Designed and partly built, though not completed before his death, by Robert Adam, its finest feature is its lovely N. side, so notably cared for and rehabilitated, rather than restored, by the 4th Marquess of Bute in the earlier decades of this century, it is incomparable. Charlotte Square and its N. side are perpetually new.

Passing from Charlotte Square, with its green-domed St George's Kirk, we must proceed to the famous Princes Street, but in doing this we endure an architectural blow. The street's situation is justly world-renowned. Facing up and into the sunshine, this wide, one-sided thoroughfare looks out across Princes Street Gardens (where once the Nor' Loch was) to the dramatic sight of the Castle and the Old Town on the Rock. In Europe, only Prague can equal such a civic prospect.

Alas! The buildings on the one-sided street are (to put it mildly) unworthy of the prospect. Had the modest little Regency houses that originally stood there all survived (only two remain, dwarfed by their pretentious neighbours), it would have been tasteful. Had an arcaded shopping street, of the style and size of the Rue de Rivoli in Paris, arisen instead, the effect might have been grand as well as convenient. But no. "Money talks." And money throughout the Victorian and Edwardian eras, down to the present day, talked up a jumble of commercial buildings striving to outdo each other. Princes Street is sometimes spoken of as one of the most beautiful streets in the world. If one sadly points out that as a street it is architecturally lamentable, the reply always comes, "But look at the view from it!" To which one might answer, "You wouldn't take it as much of a compliment to your face if people were to say that the view looking away from it was fine".

Having relieved ourselves of that architectural grumble, and having paused to praise once again Princes Street's incomparable prospect, let us pass on to the places within its extent that are worthy of note.

First, there are the National Gallery of Scotland and the Royal Scottish Academy, two impressive buildings in the New Town modern Athenian style at the foot of the Mound. The R.S.A. annually shows what is best in Scottish painting and sculpture, as well as selections of contemporary works from other countries.

The National Gallery is smaller, obviously, than the one in London, yet it contains an admirably eclectic collection. Early European works include Filippino Lippi's "Nativity" and two historic panels by Hugo van der Goes known as the Holyrood Altar-piece. There are later Italian paintings, including four Titians, among which are those "triumphant masterpieces painted for Philip II of Spain", "Diana and Callisto" and "Diana and Actaeon". There is Bassano's splendid "Adoration of the Shepherds". And the great "Finding of Moses" from the 18th cent. is "probably the most important painting by Tiepolo outside Venice".

Rembrandt ("Hendrickje Stoffels in Bed"), Velasquez ("Old Woman Cooking Eggs"), El Greco ("Saviour of the World"), Goya ("El Medico"), Watteau ("Fetes Vénitiennes"), and various other representatives of Continental European paintings – including works by Chardin, Greuze, Degas, Gaugin, Monet, and others – go to make up a richly representative gathering of paintings from abroad.

Naturally Scottish painting from native artists, except those still living, is' well represented. Raeburn predominates; see his glowing "Lord Newton" and his various portraits of Highland and Lowland lairds of his time. The most touching Scottish picture in this, the largest collection of Scottish art that exists, is Allan Ramsay's exquisite portrait simply entitled "The Painter's Wife". Here is Scottish feminine beauty painted to perfection by a Scottish hand of genius.

Just by the Mound, and near to the art galleries, there is a pleasing little curiosity that has nothing to do with art but has captured the attention of countless visitors to Edinburgh. This is the large floral clock, built into the bed of the Princes Street Gardens, and hard by the street. Electrically driven, it is of ingenious design, tells the time accurately, has on its face some 20,000 plants, and holds a cuckoo that appears every quarter of an hour.

Half-way up the Mound stands the Assembly Hall of the Church of Scotland. Herein annually meet the ministers and elders of our democratic National Kirk. The Queen is represented by the Lord High Commissioner.

No one can avoid seeing the Scott Monument in East Princes Street Gardens. It was erected in honour of Scotland's greatest novelist in 1846, and is 200 ft high. You can climb to the top of it (287 steps) and get a fine view of the New Town. Most Edinburgh citizens have acquired a smiling affection for this neo-Gothic spire under which a white statue of the good Sir Walter Scott sits. At any rate, it is a matter of civic pride to have put up what must surely be the largest monument to any novelist, or indeed writer, in the world.

Clean at the E. end of Princes Street, and facing up the North Bridge into the Old Town, is the splendid building of the Register House. This is one of Robert Adam's masterpieces, and it is a pity that, owing to the overwhelming obtrusion of the North British Hotel and the nearby G.P.O., it is difficult to get a proportionate view of it save by walking up the North Bridge and then turning to look back. Even then, you do not achieve a full view of it.

The Register House contains Scottish national and historical records as well as legal documents. The documents from the past begin with a charter to the Abbey of MELROSE in 1137, and continue down to the present day, including one signed by our present monarch, Queen Elizabeth. To the historically-minded Scottish visitor, probably the most heart-stirring document on view is a contemporary copy of the great Declaration of Arbroath (1320). This manifesto of freedom is there for all to see today. There are letters from Mary Queen of Scots and a salary-book used by the poet Robert Burns in his capacity as an exciseman. But these are only a few of the thousands of Scottish written treasures, here carefully preserved and nobly housed.

George Street – running parallel with Princes Street and, as has been said, once of a much higher status than that possessed by Princes Street – has only two buildings that demand particular attention.

The first is the "Assembly Rooms and Music Hall" built exactly half-way down the S. side of the street as a gathering place for the *élite* of Edinburgh at the end of the 18th cent. It is a Scottish equivalent of the Assembly Rooms at Bath and other Augustan centres in the United Kingdom. With an arcaded portico, it contains rooms and one large hall built in the finest New Town style. It was here that Sir Walter Scott, quite late in his literary career, first publicly admitted to being the author of his world-famous novels. He did this at a banquet by rising to reply to a toast, "The author of Waverley". By that time, everyone knew that Scott was the author, but, because of his connections with the law, Scott had long officially remained anonymous as an author.

Despite the fact that this fine building is constantly in use, the visitor to Edinburgh can, if he asks, usually gain admittance to it. In Festival time, however, it is all his own, for here is established the Festival Club, especially founded for those who attend the Festival in the capital.

The other George Street building of note, but one that is often overlooked, is St Andrew's Church on the N. side and just next door to the George Hotel. This unusual and most attractive church is in the New Town style, but has an added touch of what one might call Continental decoration. It was designed by a much-travelled army officer who entered the competition to produce a design for this George Street church. On his journeys he had seen the Church of St Andrew in the Via Quirinale in Rome, and, in honour of Scotland's patron saint, decided to borrow a feature from it.

There are countless cruciform churches in the world, and various circular ones. But, until the building of this George Street church, there was only one elliptical church, the one in the Via Quirinale. After the New Town extension, in the latter half of the 18th cent., there were two: St Andrew's Catholic Church in Rome, and the Presbyterian Kirk of St Andrew in Edinburgh. St Andrew's in Edinburgh is piously remembered as the place of assembly where the heroic Act of Disruption forming the Free Church of Scotland took place in 1843.

We find, of course, other buildings of passing interest in George Street, such as the fine Athenian-style house in which are the offices of Blackwood & Co., the publishers, and the headquarters of the Northern Lighthouse Board. But the Assembly Rooms and St Andrew's Kirk are outstanding. George Street, originally altogether residential, is now largely given over to houses of business and a few shops. In contrast with Princes Street, however, it has kept its essential dignity of shape. The visitor's attention is drawn to the surprising vistas towards the sea, and to the distant county of Fife, that open up northwards at each intersection of this still grand street.

St Andrew Square at the E. end of George Street is where the New Town began. You can perceive this in the roughcast stone of some of the houses reminiscent of George's Square in the Old Town. St Andrew Square was intended to balance Charlotte Square at the W. end, as indeed it does physically. It is a fine square, but not comparable in style with the serene beauty of Charlotte Square. Devoted to banking houses and notable law firms, it is said to be one of the "richest" squares in the United Kingdom.

In the centre of the square there is a column, just on 150 ft high, intended to equal the Trajan column in Rome. Henry Dundas, Lord Melville, held to be the most important man in Scotland a century and a half ago, stands statuesquely on top of it.

Behind him is what (when it was in the hands of the Dundas family) must have been the greatest mansion of the New Town. In size, elegance, and proportion it is the equal of any of the London noble houses that the elder generation can just recall. Since 1825, this splendid Augustan building has been occupied by the Royal Bank of Scotland.

Fine though this great house is, it threw out of scale Craig's original plan for the New Town. He had intended to build a church here to face St George's Church in Charlotte Square at the other end of George Street. But the Dundas family would not move. Nevertheless they have left us a proud great house, proudly maintained by the great banking firm that occupies it today.

Queen Street, parallel to George Street and on the N. side, is, to the real addict of the New Town style, especially appealing. It has kept its building line, and the wall-head height of the houses has been little interfered with. Looking to the N., and with its grey stone, it may at first sight appear a trifle austere, but it is one of the streets in the New Town that most surely grow acceptable with time.

Queen Street contains, at No. 52, the house in which J. Y. Simpson first experimented with chloroform, to the incalculable benefit of mankind. In the same street there is the somewhat elaborate front of the Library of the Royal College of Physicians (Scottish), but behind this front there is one of the most exquisite Adam suites in Edinburgh.

Just before Queen Street reaches York Place to the E., at the borderland of the first New Town, there is the National Museum of Antiquities of Scotland. The same large building (which is distinctly not in the New Town style) holds the Scottish National Portrait Gallery.

The Museum of Antiquities is rich in relics of prehistoric times. Notable amongst these is the Traprain Treasure from TRAPRAIN LAW (or Hill) in E. Lothian. This was a collection of crushed and broken silver plate of the 4th cent., and is believed to have been a pirate hoard. It was discovered as late as 1919. In the Museum also is the "Maiden", a Scots form of

guillotine invented by us long before the French Revolution. John Knox's pulpit from St Giles, and the stool alleged to have been thrown by Jenny Geddes during the anti-episcopal disturbances, are on view with many other objects from our history.

The Scottish National Portrait Gallery begins in order of time with portraits of the earlier Stuart kings, and comes down to great Scots men and women of just after the First World War. Not only portraits are included, but also pictures of great events in Scottish history where famous figures appear. Amongst these events are the Union of Crowns (160?), the Union of Parliaments (1707), and episodes from the 18th-cent. Jacobite risings of 1715 and 1745. There is also a large collection of Scottish photographs and engravings.

The second New Town begins with the gracious Heriot Row, just across Queen Street Gardens, and continues down to Fettes Row. This district is still largely residential, and still to a large extent presents the appearance it had when it was built. Few people now can afford to live in these ample houses occupying the whole structure of them; but the native Edinburgh habit of making flats out of houses enables many families still to live here. One house in Heriot Row, at the time of writing, remains un-subdivided and in the hands of one occupier; it is No. 17, the house where Robert Louis Stevenson spent all his childhood and youth from the age of five onwards. The house is not open to the public, but ardent Stevensonians may look at its gracious front and recall that here lay the origin of *A Child's Garden of Verses*.

In Queen Street Gardens, just opposite, there is a small ornamental lake or pool containing an even smaller island. It is said (and there is ample reason to believe this) that R.L.S. took this island as the model for his island in *Treasure Island*. The map he sketched at the beginning of his delightful tale certainly bears a strong resemblance to it.

Thus we leave the Castle, the Old Town, and the New Town proper. In doing so, we leave the essential Edinburgh that holds nearly all her past, and most of her present that the visitor need concern himself with. Before going on a less detailed tour of extended Edinburgh, there is one important place, once outside the Old Edinburgh, now well within the city boundaries, that must be treated on its own. This is the celebrated Palace of Holyroodhouse and its environs. Strictly speaking, Holyrood lies to the E. of Old Edinburgh. It can therefore be taken as the first and most important subject in our next section.

Holyrood: the Palace, the Abbey, the Park

You enter the forecourt or square before Holyrood at the end of the Royal Mile and from the foot of the Canongate. At first sight, the Palace of our Stuart kings and queens may seem but a small royal residence. Perhaps, even, there is a touch of pathos in this brave display of remote royalty in a kingdom once on the fringe of Europe. Then you look up at its setting, the wide space of Holyrood Park, and the bold slopes of Arthur's Seat, and it all falls appropriately into place.

For the brief history of Holyrood is this. David I dedicated Holyrood Abbey to Christ's Rood or Cross because of what he believed was a miraculous escape he experienced while out hunting in the neighbourhood. The name may equally well derive from a relic of the True Cross that Queen Margaret brought to Scotland, and that was afterwards removed by Edward I on his subjugation of the country. The ruins of the Abbey still stand to the N. and left of the Palace as you enter the forecourt. It is a melancholy sight, but demands respectful attention.

The Abbey, richly endowed during the reign of the earlier Stuarts, became associated with royal residence, but it was not until James IV's reign that an official palace was built beside the Abbey. In 1543, the Palace and Abbey were burnt during an English invasion. Only the church and NW. tower escaped.

Mary Stuart, Queen of Scots, and her son James VI lived in the partly restored Palace; but it was again burnt badly after its occupation by Cromwellian troops during the Commonwealth. After the Restoration, Charles II ordered a large rebuilding rather than reconstruction from the plans of Sir William Bruce, King's Surveyor in Scotland. It is largely this rebuilt palace that you see today. You will perceive the strong French influence in the style of the front. This is partly a genuine relic of the Auld Alliance and partly a result of Charles II's French tastes.

James VII and II occupied the Palace when, as heir to the throne and as Duke of York, he resided in Scotland. After the fall of the Stuarts, the Palace remained until modern times largely unused save for the brief visit of Prince Charles Edward Stuart during the victorious part of his campaign of 1745. In Victorian times, Edward VII lived there as Prince of Wales. During this century, the Palace has been constantly used by monarchs of the United Kingdom when visiting Scotland. The Lord High Commissioner also lives there during the annual General Assembly of the Church of Scotland.

The public is admitted to the Palace at any time when it is not being occupied as a residence. As with the Castle, visitors are recommended to the services of the skilled and informative official guides. They are indeed essential to a proper tour of the building. Here, therefore, we shall confine ourselves to mention of the outstanding or unusual objects of interest.

The Palace – in serious history, in romance, and in popular imagination – is strongly associated with Mary Queen of Scots. You may see her audience chamber, and the supper-room where her poor Italian secretary, Rizzio, was so falsely and treacherously murdered by dissident Scots nobles. A brass tablet (no longer the famous and annually renewed bloodstain) marks the spot. You may also see Queen Mary's bedroom, in which, somewhat restored, are the remains of the Queen's bed.

In the picture gallery, the largest apartment in the Palace, there is a collection of alleged portraits of ancient Scottish kings. These were done by a hack painter, James de Witt, in 1684, and are pure invention – tasteless invention at that. The atmosphere of the gallery is somewhat relieved by the knowledge that it was here that Prince Charles Edward held the last Stuart levees in the castle of his ancestors. This room has also been used for the election of Scottish representative peers to the House of Lords.

Though on a small scale, even as compared with many other historic or noble buildings in Scotland, the general effect of Holyroodhouse, and of what remains of the Abbey, is one of melancholy pride. That sense is enlarged and, in an odd way, made contemporary by emerging from the Palace into the Park of Holyrood.

Here is that spacious height for which the capital of Scotland is famous. In the New Town, man has by his architectural efforts made a notable contribution to spaciousness and graciousness. In Holyrood Park, simply by leaving nature to be herself, Edinburgh has achieved the same effect, and on a grander scale.

At the centre of the Park stands Arthur's Seat, the near-mountain within a city. It is 822 ft high, and the parkland of wild and springy turf covers 648 acres. Arthur's Seat has often been compared, in the outline it presents to Edinburgh, to a lion couchant. To the W. of it is an odd and somewhat menacing basaltic formation or rock known as Samson's Ribs. The effect, besides that of light and air, is decidedly romantic in the better sense.

Round the Park is a fine carriage-way, now a motorway, from which you can see Edinburgh and all its views. If, however, you can bring yourself to do so, you should certainly climb to the top of Arthur's Seat, from which you can enjoy a view, both civic and rural, of landscape and seascape that is unrivalled in the United Kingdom.

As Edinburgh to the E., and only that part of it which lies in the surrounds of Holyrood, is our immediate concern here, we shall confine ourselves to drawing the visitor's attention to but two places. The other sections of Edinburgh to the E., we shall approach from a different direction.

The first of these two places is the attractive

little village of Duddingston, with its Norman church hard by Duddingston Loch. Duddingston, now well within the city boundaries, has preserved its individuality. It is below you from Arthur's Seat to the SE.

The second place is Craigmillar, containing Craigmillar Castle, just beyond Duddingston. This 14th-cent. building, only partly ruined, is open to the public. It has seen much of Scottish history, and, as with nearly everything one touches in Scottish history, Mary Stuart is involved. She often fled to the security of Craigmillar. The place well repays a visit. But take in Duddingston on your way there.

STILL TO THE EAST
Calton, Portobello, Musselburgh

The approach to Edinburgh's E. via Holyrood is from the foot of the Canongate and from the Old Town. No less important is the approach eastwards from the New Town. This is at the E. end of Princes Street just by the Register House, and where the New Town proper (though not the New Town style) ends.

Immediately on your left is the Calton Hill. Less high than Arthur's Seat and Edinburgh Castle, it yet gives what to many is the most satisfyingly detailed view of Edinburgh. It is surmounted, apart from the Observatory, by what is known as Edinburgh's Folly. This is the unfinished remains of a civic war memorial that Edinburgh intended to put up after Wellington's Peninsular campaign. It was meant (in the tradition of the modern Athens) to be a complete Parthenon. But funds ran out, and the building was never finished. Prosperous Victorian Edinburgh was ashamed of this, as it was of various other things not necessarily to its discredit, but we now have an affection for our unfinished "folly".

Passing the Calton Hill, there is on your right the large modern building of St Andrew's House, which is the headquarters of the Scottish Office in Scotland. On the left, in the purest Grecian Doric style, is the famous Royal High School of Edinburgh. When this ancient institution moved over from the Old Town, it certainly did so in style and to fine quarters. Here indeed is modern Athens.

Having passed the Royal High School, there is nothing eastwards worth pausing at until you reach the sea at Portobello, some 3 m. away. This exotic-sounding place received its name in the early 18th cent. from a Scottish sailor who had assisted in capturing the Spanish fortress of Puerto Bello in the isthmus of Darien. He called his house by the sea "Porto Bello". In Regency times, at the beginning of the last century, Portobello set up as an Edinburgh seaside resort – a kind of Scottish Brighton. It is still a seaside resort where the Firth of Forth surrenders to the North Sea, but of a humbler kind. Some pleasant little Regency buildings derivative of the New Town style remain there.

EDINBURGH TO THE NORTH
Leith, Newhaven, Granton, Inverleith

To go N. from Edinburgh, you set out from the same spot as you do on the New Town eastward journey; that is, from the Register House at the end of Princes Street. You go down Leith Street and soon find yourself in Leith Walk, which at its inception had the makings of as fine a boulevard as you could see anywhere. Apart from O'Connell Street in Dublin, it is in places the widest two-sided street in the British Isles. And at the beginning it supports this amplitude by a show of grand houses, in the New Town style, now fallen from their high estate. A little lower down on this declension to the sea, Leith Walk narrows and becomes less ambitious.

Leith Walk in its fine start possibly owes its origin to the idea that the Edinburgh of the New Town should have a splendid approach to its nearest (and then independent) seaport, Leith. But the arrival of the railway, in the late 1830s and '40s, no longer made Leith the formal approach by which royal and other important personages came to the capital of Scotland. It remains, however, the legacy of an ambitious and worthy idea.

Leith became incorporated with Edinburgh as late as 1920. In its independent history, however, as the cardinal E. of Scotland port, it is almost as old as Edinburgh. Always overshadowed by the presence of the capital on the Rock, it nevertheless prized its own identity. To this day, when you enter Leith, you feel a slightly different atmosphere about you from that of Edinburgh.

This is due not only to the presence of the sea, and the unmistakable surroundings of a port, but to the antiquity of the houses and the narrow, sometimes rather foreign-looking, streets. These streets are in process of being renovated or pulled down as Leith adapts herself to modern conditions.

Many modern buildings are going up, but Leith is careful to keep both its dignity and its antiquity. In Constitution Street are the Assembly Rooms, or Exchange Buildings, of 1788 in the style of the period. And in Baltic Street (appropriately named after the old seafaring trade) is the Corn Exchange. In Water Street – the old Water Lane that was – we find Lamb's House, the most ancient dwelling-house in Leith, well preserved and restored. Mary Stuart stayed at this historic place on her return to Scotland. Scotland's first Cardinal since the Reformation, Archbishop Gordon Joseph Gray, was born in Leith. Leith too is a centre of violent Protestant reaction.

The Water of Leith, the little Edinburgh river, runs into the sea at Leith. And near its exit are the modern docks of this ancient port.

Turning E. from Leith, we pass on the shores of the Firth of Forth the harbours of Newhaven and Granton. Before the Forth railway bridge was built in 1890, these were the harbours from which all travellers in Edinburgh set out from Fife. Newhaven is a delightful fishing village, famous for its fisherwomen's choir, and for its fish dinners. Granton is the headquarters of Edinburgh yachting.

Near Granton lies a modern housing estate. As you pass through it, you sigh and ask yourself why Edinburgh, with her fine natural site, should not have followed the example of CUMBERNAULD.

Returning to Edinburgh by the district of Inverleith, we should certainly pause to visit the Royal Botanic Garden, among the finest of its kind in the United Kingdom. The Rock Garden is famous. From the Garden, you get a superlative view of both the New and the Old Towns of Edinburgh before and above you. It is a view of the capital with which not many are familiar. Inverleith House, a stately building at the centre of the Gardens, now houses a gallery of modern art.

Coming out of the Botanic Garden to return to Princes Street and the centre of Edinburgh, you will pass two famous public schools. Fettes College in ornate neo-Gothic, known for its scholarship and its rugby football, lies to the N. And, just where the hill begins to mount into the centre of the city again, stands in severely classic style Edinburgh's famous dayschool, the Edinburgh Academy. Generations of Scottish lawyers have been schooled here. Thus we mount to Princes Street by way of the second New Town to turn towards the next quarter.

EDINBURGH TO THE WEST

The Dean, Lauriston, Cramond, Corstorphine

The most attractive way out to western Edinburgh is not to take the busier thoroughfare W. to Glasgow, though this does pass some pleasing building by Atholl Crescent and the lofty spires of the Episcopal Cathedral. It is better to leave the W. end of Princes Street by Queensferry Street. You pass the Moray Estate New Town by Randolph Crescent and its delightful gardens to cross the valley of the Dean by Telford's 1832 Dean Bridge.

The Valley of the Dean is a deep gorge showing a romantic Edinburgh in the middle of its classical side. Far below in the wooded gardens, Edinburgh's one river, the Water of Leith, chatters its way to the sea by way of the old village of Dean. From the bridge, you can see the Firth of Forth with its islands, the back of the classical town, and Fife in the distance.

Following Queensferry Road, which swings W. through suburbs, you pass through Davidson's Mains, a sturdy little Scottish village still in Edinburgh. Thus you come to the historic Lauriston Castle, bequeathed with its beautiful grounds by the late owner to the Edinburgh Corporation. The Castle's architecture runs from the 16th to the 19th cents., and the

furnishings, carefully preserved within, reflect these periods. It is domestic history set up for you to see. The public are admitted to the Castle and the gardens, which contain the Edinburgh Croquet Club's fine lawns. The view from these across the Forth is admirable.

A mile or so down the road is the picturesque and historic village of Cramond. Passing by a 17th-cent. church, you come to a street of charming whitewashed houses and a well-known inn. This leads to the minute harbour of Cramond, where the R. Almond joins the Forth. This is much used by yachtsmen. Opposite is Cramond Island, to which you can walk at low tide.

The Romans had a camp at Cramond, and some interesting finds have been made at recent excavations. Through the centuries, Cramond has been a resort for Edinburgh folk who want to "get out of the town" without leaving it. It was a favourite place of James V, who loved to go down there incognito. He had some strange adventures in Cramond, which are traditionally remembered.

At Cramond you can cross the river by ferry or walk through the Dalmeny Woods and grounds, the property of the Earl of Roseberry. From Cramond, too, you can see the world-famous Forth railway bridge (1890). Also you can catch glimpses behind it of the new road bridge (1964). But these remarkable engineering feats come more properly under the history of South QUEENSFERRY, outside Edinburgh.

The other western village now within Edinburgh, Corstorphine, can best be approached from W. end of Princes Street by the main Glasgow road. Passing by Murrayfield, a Victorian-style prosperous suburb, now well known for containing the Scottish Rugby Union's international football ground, you will find yourself under the slopes of Corstorphine Hill. Here is the Scottish Zoological Park, in ample surroundings. Edinburgh is justly proud of its Zoo.

Corstorphine really does feel like, as well as look like, a village. It has a notable 15th-cent. church with pre-Reformation tombs. There is a typically Scottish 17th-cent. circular dovecot. Nearby is Edinburgh's airport at Turnhouse. All this is in Edinburgh, but Corstorphine retains the essential village character.

EDINBURGH TO THE SOUTH

Newington, Liberton, Morningside, Colinton

Edinburgh has spread vastly towards the S., and there are many roads from the centre in this direction. It is proposed here to do no more than to take an E. to W. line covering what is worthy of mention in this quarter.

To the SE. is the village of Liberton, on a hill and with a fine parish church visible for miles around. Nearer to the city is the distinctively Edinburgh suburb of Newington. It is distinctive because this is the best example of really good Regency or neo-Georgian Edinburgh building well outside, and far away from, the New Town proper.

Morningside has been a well-to-do and growing suburb since the mid-19th cent. It is salubrious and spacious, and it leads up to the slopes of the Braid Hills, on which so many Scottish golfers have first learned their game. Here we are getting to the really hilly side of Edinburgh, and the impressive slopes of the Pentlands (of which more later) are almost immediately above us.

To approach Colinton from Morningside, you go down the Colinton Road past George Watson's College, a famous Edinburgh day-school, and then ascend the hill to turn SW. into Colinton. Just before you get there, Merchiston Castle School and its spacious playing-fields are set out on your right. This well-known Scottish public school used to be in Merchiston Castle itself (where in the 16th cent. Napier invented logarithms). The Castle is now a technical training college nearer to Edinburgh on the Colinton Road. The school of Merchiston Castle moved out here.

Colinton, by the upper reaches of the Water of Leith, is again most distinctly a village within Edinburgh. It has rural surroundings and pleasing walks. Still rural, yet strictly in Edinburgh, are the two little towns of Juniper Green and Currie.

Here to the SW., you are under the shadow of the Pentlands – quite considerable hills. On the N. slopes by Fairmilehead is the picturesque and almost self-sufficient village of Swanston, associated with the boyhood of Robert Louis Stevenson. The Edinburgh Corporation have successfully preserved the individuality and country quality of that entity within its borders.

But Edinburgh's border line does not end even here. It goes right up to the top of the northernmost part of the Pentlands. At Caerketton and at Allermuir (1,617 ft), you are still in Edinburgh, but only just. From this, surely one of the loftiest spots in any capital city, you can look down to the N., to the E., to the W., all over Edinburgh and, if visibility is good, over most of the southern half of that country of which Edinburgh is the capital.

We have attempted in this section to give a portrait, as well as a survey, of Edinburgh. No portrait of this ancient and romantic, classical yet modern, city would be complete without a mention of her International Festival of the Arts, which she has held every year since 1947. Since then her concert halls, her theatres, her galleries, her numerous public halls have opened their arms to the arts of the world.

There are plenty of other international festivals now, but Edinburgh led the way. In 1946, just after the Second World War, an exhausted Europe was inclined in each country to say "No" to any imaginative international ideas put forward. It was then that a group of people from outside Edinburgh and Scotland, as well as within the capital, put forward to the city authorities the novel and, at the time, startling idea that here in Old and New Edinburgh was a splendid locale for an international gathering and display of the arts.

It is a matter of some pride to us that, in that year 1946, when the word "No" was, perhaps understandably, on everyone's lips, Edinburgh said "Yes".

The effects of that courageous and imaginative monosyllable are still with us. So, too, are the fruits of another "Yes" obtained when Edinburgh asked to be the venue of the 1970 Commonwealth Games, the first to be held in Scotland. This entailed building the fine £2,500,000 Meadowbank Stadium (opened by the Duke of Kent in May 1970) and the truly magnificent £1,600,000 Royal Commonwealth Pool (opened by Princess Anne in January 1970), by its design and remarkable facilities voted probably the best in Europe.

EDZELL, *Angus* (Map 6, ref. 36°76°). Now an inland resort lying between STRATHMORE and the Howe of the Mearns, Edzell is situated just W. of the North Esk river. It dates from the 16th cent. but was much improved when replanning began in 1839. The picturesque valley of North Esk in Glen Esk is to the N. of the village.

A little NW. stands the ruined Edzell Castle, now an Ancient Monument. Originally it was the seat of the Stirlings, then it passed to the Lindsays of Glenesk, and became the most splendid castle in Angus. The oldest part is a fine tower-house, dating from the early 16th cent. To this a quadrangular mansion was added by the 9th Earl of Crawford in the late 16th cent., and in 1602 the buildings were completed by his son, Sir David Lindsay, Lord Edzell, who added a spacious walled garden or "pleasance" or *viridarium*. His arms and the date 1604 appear over the NE. doorway. It has a bath-house and summer-house, and the garden wall displays a wealth of heraldic and symbolic decoration unique in Britain, including a series of sculptured panels portraying the Cardinal Virtues, the Liberal Arts, and the Planetary Deities, all of German inspiration. The walls are also indented with large square holes that, when seen from a distance, form the Lindsay arms.

The Castle was visited in 1562 by Mary Queen of Scots (her bower is in the main Stirling Tower); in 1651 by Cromwell's soldiers; and in 1746 by the Campbells, who caused much devastation in the name of Hanoverian loyalty. There is a fine dovecot in a neighbouring farm.

EIGG, Island of, *Inverness-shire* (Map 4, ref. 14°78°), is one of the Inner Hebrides (*see* "The Shape of Scotland"). Here is an island easily passed over by those who deal mainly in statistics. It lies 7½ m. from the nearest point on the W. coast of Inverness-shire, forming with the islands of MUCK, CANNA, and RUM the Small Isles parish in that county. About 6 m. long, and 4 m. in extreme breadth, it contains slightly more than 5,500 acres. These figures are of little significance to anyone who knows directly the fascination of this small world in the western sea, with its rich scenery and its ancient tradition of culture.

Seen from the mainland, from ARISAIG or MORAR, Eigg has been likened to an upturned boat, so regular is the sweep of its great cliffs from N. to S., ending in the dramatic point of the Sgurr. From some other approaches the island looks less silent and mysterious, and the traveller can see clearly the depression that runs across the middle and from which it has derived its Gaelic name Eilean Eige, "the island of the notch". If he lands, it is across this depression that he will travel from the small harbour at the SE. corner to the crofting community of Cleadale, which represents, in sadly dwindling numbers, the authentic story of Eigg, going back beyond the monks of St Columba to prehistoric time.

Above, on the cliffs, is a high plateau where keen biologists may chase the Eigg vole, or search a small loch for a rare water-insect. To the S. is the ridge that runs out towards Canna from the sheer, 900-ft sides of the Sgurr. Geologists argue about how it all came to be, but the non-specialist is awed by the great walls of rock, the twisted and broken columns of pitchstone, and the small lochs high in the hills. This is a primitive laboratory of the world – a sudden glimpse, it seems, of another planet. You descend to the work and laughter and music of the crofts with a sense of having lived in another sphere. It is a shock to learn that the highest point on Eigg reaches just under 1,300 ft.

There is not much woodland on Eigg, apart from some small plantations in the SE. corner, but there are varied flora.

Until the present century and a succession of alien landlords, the religious tradition on the island was predominantly Catholic. To some extent this was due to the activity of Irish Franciscans in the 17th cent., who paid frequent visits to Eigg. It is also explained by the adherence of the chiefs of Clanranald to Rome. At the same time Eigg is happy in a tradition of ecumenical relationship illustrated in a site with three names; the building that once occupied it was known as the House of the People, the House of the Sermon, and the House of Devotion. Tradition reports that it was built by the island people and was used equally by Protestants and Catholics for their services. There are now two small churches on Eigg, one Catholic, the other belonging to the (Presbyterian) Church of Scotland; their members are on excellent terms with one another.

The island tradition is still rich in stories and folklore, although tradition-bearers are now very few. Let those find them who can. They are the legacy of a community slowly throttled by economic and political pressure, by clearance and other products of an alien landlord system. There are summer visitors, admitted on a basis of personal contact or recommendation; most of them come to recognize very quickly how privileged they are in being admitted to a community in which "everyone is still somebody", and to an island so rich in interest of every kind.

EILDONS, *Roxburghshire* (3 m. NE. of SELKIRK). The three peaks of the celebrated Eildon Hills attain 1,327 ft, 1,385 ft, and 1,216 ft, and because of their isolation form prominent features in the landscape of the Borderland and Scott country. An indicator on the highest point (the central summit) explains the panoramic view to the visitor. It was Sir Walter Scott who said, "I can stand on the Eildon Hills and point out forty-three places famous in war and verse".

There is a traditional legend that the hills were formerly one, and were split into three by Michael Scott, the Border Wizard. The legend, as told by Walter Scott, is that the wizard was embarrassed by having to find work for a demon. He first ordered him to build a dam across the TWEED at KELSO; this was done in the night. The next order was to split the single cone of the Eildon hill into three; again it was completed in a night. Finally the indefatigable demon was conquered by employing him on the endless task of spinning ropes out of sea-sand.

On the eastern slope is Eildon Tree Stone, traditionally marking the spot where Thomas the Rhymer met the Queen of Faeries, and entered into the hill, to stay for seven years in Faeryland.

Whatever experiences, real or fancied, Thomas of Ercildoune enjoyed and suffered at this place in the late Middle Ages, he made of them a marvellous poem, now usually known as "The Ballad of Thomas the Rhymer". Thomas indubitably had a mystical vision of Beauty. Most mystics find it impossible to express to other human beings in ordinary language the experiences they have passed through. Not so Thomas of Ercildoune. In pure, translucently simple poetry he tells us what he felt happening to him. We, at a distance, feel it too, even if we do not know exactly what did happen to him. The Eildon Hills are in themselves a remarkable feature of the lovely Border landscape, but it is primarily because of Thomas of Ercildoune and his ballad that they are remembered with love and affection by all Scots, Highland as well as Lowland.

EILEAN DONAN, *Ross and Cromarty* (Map 5, ref. 18⁹82⁵), near DORNIE and on the road to SKYE between KINTAIL and KYLE

OF LOCHALSH, is the picturesque island Castle. Overlooking the confluence of Loch Alsh, Loch LONG, and Loch Duich, the Castle is linked to the shore by a causeway. Dating from the Middle Ages, it is thought to occupy the site of an even earlier Caledonian vitrified fort. It was for long a stronghold of the Mackenzies of Kintail, who became earls of Seaforth. In 1539 Donald Gorm, an aspirant to the lordship of the Isles, died in an attack on the Castle. The greater part of the Castle itself was reduced to ruin in 1719 when garrisoned by Spanish troops under the 5th Earl of Seaforth, the Earl Marischal, and the Marquess of Tulli-bardine. These Jacobite sympathizers were attacked from the water by three men o' war of the English navy that sailed up Loch Alsh and knocked most of the old tower off its rock with heavy bombardment. An extensive restoration was carried out in 1932, and the Castle is open regularly to visitors.

ELDERSLIE, *Renfrewshire* (Map 2, ref. 24⁵66³). This small town on the western outskirts of PAISLEY has in tradition the honour of being the birthplace of the great patriot, the people's hero, Sir William Wallace (*see* "Scotland in History"). An old whitewashed house at the W. end of the main street is usually taken to be the family mansion.

Wallace (1270–1305) was the younger son of Sir Malcolm Wallace of Elderslie, who presumably dwelt in a kind of mansion. This house, now associated with the Wallace Mansion, cannot be the original, for it does not date back to earlier than the 16th cent. It may well, however, have been built on the site of the original, for the oldest parts of the present structure show it to have been a place of some importance. The principal room downstairs, a former kitchen with massive fireplace, is shown as the traditional birthplace; the room above is a dovecot.

The estate was granted to the Wallace family in the 13th cent. and was held by them until sold in 1729 to the Speirs family. A dense yew tree near the house is seeded from an ancient tree known as "Wallace's Yew". Along the street to the E. an inn marks the spot where Wallace's Oak once stood. There is a legendary tale of how Wallace and 300 Scots hid in its branches from English soldiers. In 1825 this tree was 21 ft in girth and 67 ft high, but was reduced by souvenir hunters to a stump, which was blown down in gales in 1856.

At the birthplace is a modern monument, a granite pillar with a crown on the top.

ELGIN, *Moray* (Map 6, ref. 32²86³). The city and royal burgh of Elgin, NW. of ABERDEEN and E. of INVERNESS, has a pivotal importance far greater than its population of 16,000 indicates. Indeed, its excellent shops do a trade normally commensurate with a town twice its size. The fertile Laich of Moray, of which it

Aberdeen Press and Journal

Elgin Cathedral

is the market town, acts today, in the way it has done for ten centuries, as a magnet to the folk of less favoured areas. Approaching the town across this mellow plain, with its cornfields and Lombardy poplars, you see miles away the soaring western towers and the magnificent E. gable of Elgin Cathedral, known of old as "the Lanthorn of the North", which was without doubt the most perfect of Scottish cathedrals. The fame of the cathedral is so great that it has tended to obscure the fact that Elgin has many other architectural glories. The character of modern Elgin as a "boom-town" of the North-East also tends to smother the plentiful evidence of its more gracious past. But old Elgin, like old EDINBURGH, is remarkably compact and can be simply described. It was cruciform, laid out upon a low ridge stretching from E. to W. above the winding R. Lossie. At the W. end of the ridge is the Lady Hill, on which a royal castle stood from the 12th to the 15th cent., having been occupied in 1296 by Edward I of England. The ruins that remain today are so fragmentary that it is impossible to assign a date to them. They are at the NE. angle of the hill, on the summit of which is a tall column in honour of the last Duke of Gordon, who died in 1836. At the E. end of the ridge is the Cathedral, founded in 1224. Between these two monuments of temporal and spiritual authority, from the S. face of Lady Hill to the S. limit of the Cathedral sanctuary, runs the ancient High Street. Parallel to it on N. and S. run two subsidiary streets originally known as the North Back Gait and the South Back Gait, now named Blackfriars Road (with North Lane), and South Street. These three long lines of streets running E. and W. were linked by a series of wynds running N. and S., of which Lossie Wynd and School Wynd (now renamed Commerce Street) formed the entries to the town from N. and S. respectively.

Elgin Cathedral was virtually complete by the end of the 13th cent. It comprised twin western towers, a nave of six bays with double aisles to N. and S., a central tower with N. and S. transepts, and a long choir flanked by N. and S. aisles, having an octagonal chapter house still farther to the N.

The N. and S. transepts are of severe Transitional work – and may have been inherited from the older Church of the Holy Trinity on the same site; but the choir is a masterpiece of early Gothic, with a double tier of lancets surmounted by a great rose window. French inspiration is traced in the W. front with its magnificent portal set between massive flanking towers, and in the double aisles of the nave.

The chapter house was reconstructed after the most notable disaster in Elgin's early history, when in May 1390 that unruly scion of King Robert II, Alexander Earl of Buchan, the notorious "Wolf of Badenoch", enraged by the sentence of excommunication passed upon him for previous misdeeds, burnt both the burgh and the Cathedral. The shame of the final ruin of this great edifice, however, must rest with the Privy Council of Scotland, who in 1567 ordered the roof to be stripped of its lead to raise funds for the paying of troops.

NW. of the Cathedral is the "Bishop's Palace", now thought to have been the precentor's manse, a house of two wings linked by a square staircase tower. It bears the date 1557, and has interesting heraldic detail. To the SE. is the Pans Port or Water Yett by the bank of the Lossie. It represents the E. gateway to the Cathedral and its college precinct. The W. front of the Cathedral faces Cooper Park, Elgin's great central open space, rich in old trees, acres of lawns, playing-fields and a boating pond. Within the park is Grant Lodge, the Georgian town house of the Grants of Grant, now the headquarters of the very efficient Moray County Library.

It is worth while trying to see the High Street of Elgin at some time when you can avoid being jostled by fellow pedestrians with urgent business, for it was during the 17th cent., the great age of Scottish burgh architecture, that most of the characteristic houses of old Elgin were built. In a district more richly endowed with good freestone than any other in Scotland, the mason-craftsmen of Moray developed what might be called an Elgin School of building, and by the opening of the 18th cent. the greater length of High Street was lined with stately stone houses with piazzas or arcades. In the 19th cent. very many were destroyed with

wanton insensitivity, but a goodly number still remain. In 1946 the Elgin Society published a record listing no fewer than twenty-eight of these historic buildings, all of which are described in the Society publication *Old Elgin*.

Along its central portion High Street widens out to enclose, in the middle of the thoroughfare, the Muckle Cross (a restoration in which only the Scottish Lion is from the original), the parish church of St Giles (a classical building designed by Archibald Simpson in 1828 to replace the ancient Muckle Kirk), a causeway, and a fountain that marks the site of the Old Tolbooth.

One historic domestic building must be mentioned; on no account should it be missed. This is Thunderton House, in a narrow lane called Thunderton Place off the S. side of High Street, just W. of the fountain. The present building, a hotel marked by a plaque erected by the Elgin Society, represents part of the old Thunderton House, once the most splendid mansion in Elgin, belonging successively to the families of Moray, Duffus, and Dunbar. Before that, in medieval times, the site was occupied by the "Great Lodging" of the Scottish kings. History repeated itself when Prince Charles Edward Stuart lodged here, prior to CULLODEN in March 1746.

Entered from Abbey Street is the Church of the Greyfriars Monastery, which moved thither from another Elgin site in the later 15th cent. A long building without an aisle, it was restored in 1896 by John Kinross for the 3rd Marquess of Bute. With its plastered walls and richly decorated screen, it recovers the true medieval feeling.

Of the four bridges crossing the Lossie, the oldest is the Bow Brig (1630–5), with its graceful single arch; next in date comes the pleasant Brewery Bridge of 1798. Elgin is a town that gròws on you and inspires well-merited affection.

ELGOL, *Inverness-shire* (Map 4, ref. 15²81³), is a hamlet on the Island of SKYE in the Inner Hebrides (*see* "The Shape of Scotland"). It lies at the tip of the most southerly peninsula in the central section. It is primarily of interest for its magnificent views. To the N. lie the CUILLINS, to the S. the mountains of RUM and its adjacent isles of CANNA and EIGG. You can also see the tip of Sleat and the peaks of the W. mainland. From Elgol, too, is the approach to the celebrated Loch CORUISK and its wild mountain circumstances.

ELIE, *Fife* (Map 3, ref. 34⁹70⁰). Situated on the coast on a bay between Chapel Ness to the W. and Elie Ness to the E., Elie, which forms a burgh with neighbouring EARLSFERRY, was formerly of some importance in trade and local affairs, but has for a long time been a popular seaside resort, having beautiful sands and excellent golfing facilities. It has a sheltered

Above One of the Grimersta lochs (*see p. 270*)

Below Taransay, Harris (*see p. 274*)

Ian Smith

J. L. Rodger

Scottish Tourist Board

Elie: the "Scottish Riviera"

natural harbour, with quays and a pier. To the E. of the harbour is Wadehaven, said to be named after General Wade who recommended it as a suitable harbour for naval ships.

Gillespie House, also known as "The Muckle Yett", in South Street, has a fine carved door, dated 1682; the original house was demolished about 1860. The parish church dates from the 17th cent.

ELLON, *Aberdeenshire* (Map 6, ref. 39⁵83⁰), which was the ancient "capital" of Buchan, but is now almost wholly a creation of the 19th and 20th cents., presents to the world a most attractive southern front, with its crisp granite buildings lining its riverside. And yet its church, its square, and its castle stand roughly where they did in the Middle Ages.

One vanished ingredient of the ancient town plan was the Moot Hill, which stood opposite the W. end of the New Inn, in a position now occupied by a small garden enclosure. On its mound rose the timbered motte of the Norman castle, where under the rule of the Comyn Earls of Buchan, in the 13th cent., the burgh of barony was organized. The motte was no doubt placed there to control the bridge, which, we can hardly doubt, spanned the Ythan at the very same point as it does now. The Moot Hill has gone, but Ellon still looks into the sun, and it is sheltered from the N. by the bold river terrace upon which the oldest part of the surviving Ellon Castle, once the fortalice of Ardgith, has stood for 400 years.

It is one of the ironies of history that the triumph of Robert Bruce in the Wars of Independence, which meant new prosperity and valued endowments to the city of ABERDEEN,

16½ m. S., meant for Ellon an end of old greatness, with the downfall of the Comyns and the subsequent Harrying of Buchan.

After much destruction, rebuilding, and decay, the Ellon Castle estate was bought by Bailie James Gordon of EDINBURGH in 1706. While you stand on the terrace and look out over one of the finest landscape gardens in the country, Bailie Gordon should be remembered, for he created this marvel. The terrace, 190 yds long and 15 yds wide, is held up by a massive stone retaining wall, 18 ft high. In the garden below is a grass lawn nearly 100 yds deep and 90 yds broad, crossed by paths; between them stand fifteen huge yew trees. Bounding the lawns on either side of the trees are clipped yew hedges 7 to 8 ft high.

Bailie Gordon's two sons were murdered by their tutor, and his widow sold the property to George, 3rd Earl of Aberdeen.

This remarkable man, sometimes called the "Wicked Earl", who was a splendid estate manager, bought three great houses, Ellon and CAIRNBULG Castles in Aberdeenshire, and Wiscombe Park in Devon, settled a brown-eyed mistress in each, and raised three flourishing families. The lady he installed at Ellon was Penelope Dering, a young girl who hailed from the village of Pett in Sussex. In 1782 he commissioned the architect John Baxter to add two great wings to the old Castle. By the time Alexander, the son of Penelope, succeeded to this great mansion, it was considered beyond repair. But more of it now survives than of its successor. The home of the present owner of Ellon Castle, Sir Edward Reid, was originally the stables and servants' quarters of the earl's Castle of 1782.

Plate 8   Glen More, Inverness-shire: Loch Morlich and the Cairngorms (see p. 259)
(see p. 259)
Scottish Tourist Board

In 1783 was built Ellon's first modern bridge over the Ythan. It still stands there, though derelict and by-passed by the road leading to the present-day bridge. Ellon became a police burgh in 1893, and today is increasingly popular as a residential centre. It has good fishing and a golf course. The Episcopal Church of St Mary's on the Rock, on high land overlooking the S. bank of the Ythan, was built in 1875 to designs by Sir George Street. It is the inheritor of a series of Episcopal meeting houses, the first of which was built in 1713 and demolished by a posse of soldiers in 1746 in the heat of the anti-Jacobite reaction.

Some 4 m. NNW. of Ellon is Arnage Castle, a charming old tower-house in finely wooded policies in the vale of the Ebrie, a tributary of the Ythan which is a famous trouting stream. It is on the Z-plan, with towers at the diagonally opposite corners of the main keep, while a modern wing was added in the 19th cent. to designs by James Matthews, an architect in Aberdeen.

The Castle was built by the Cheyne family, who held the lands of Arnage from 1380 to 1643. In 1702 it was acquired by Bailie (afterwards Provost) John Ross of Aberdeen, who in the same year took over the famous house that still bears his name in the Shiprow of that city. His portrait by Sir John Medina, preserved in the Castle for many years, shows a grave countenance, and his religious zeal was well known. The Rosses and their descendants in the female line, the Leith-Rosses, continued as lairds of Arnage down to 1937.

ELPHIN, *Sutherland* (Map 5, ref. 22²91¹). This township is on the S. border of Sutherland in the wild country of Assynt. It is situated on a limestone outcrop, which gives rise to the green fields in this district, as contrasted with the prevailing hummocks of Lewisian gneiss. To the W. in Drumrunie Forest is the fine peak of Cul Mor (2,786 ft), overlooking Loch Veyatie and the Cam Loch, and beyond is the spectacular peak of SUILVEN (2,399 ft), a narrow ridge of Torridonian sandstone forming an extraordinary, steep cone when viewed from the W. or E. There are particularly fine views of this famous mountain from Elphin.

ELPHINSTONE, *East Lothian* (Map 3, ref. 34⁰67¹). This coal-mining village, 2 m. S. of TRANENT, is mostly of interest through the proximity of Elphinstone Tower, an unusually strong 15th-cent. fortalice, square and three-storied, with eight escutcheons over the fireplace in the second-floor hall. A mansion built on to the tower in 1600 was demolished in 1865. In 1546 George Wishart, the Protestant martyr, was brought from Ormiston by the Earl of Bothwell to Cardinal Beaton at Elphinstone Tower, and thence taken for trial and execution to ST ANDREWS, where he perished in the flames outside the Castle. Scot-

land has had seven official Protestant martyrs and two official Catholic ones. But our record in inflicting martyrdom for religious belief compares favourably with most countries to the south of us.

Nearby is Carberry Tower, of the 16th cent. which was converted into a mansion in 1819 it is now a Church of Scotland youth centre Carberry Hill Battle was fought in June 1567 resulting in the abdication of Mary Queen of Scots.

ELVANFOOT, *Lanarkshire* (Map 2, ref 29⁵61⁷). Where the Elvan Water joins the R CLYDE stands this village in the upper part of Clydesdale. S. of the village, the tiny Clyde Burn is joined by the combined streams of the Daer Water and the Portrail Water. Elvanfoot is the first place on the true Clyde river. The Telford bridge over the Clyde has been replaced by a new bridge.

In the 19th-cent. church is a stained-glass window commemorating the once well-known actor-manager Wilson Barrett, who stayed frequently at Watermeetings up the Daer Valley; indeed, this district seems to have attracted the stage, for other theatrical visitors here included Ellen Terry, and Irving, and Toole. There are also three striking windows in the church in memory of three young airmen who died in the Second World War. A wall plaque commemorates a local farmer, John Willison, a staunch Covenanter who had a Shunammite chamber on his farm for a refuge of persecuted Covenanters.

Opposite the church is Glengeith, a white toll-house said to have been a favourite halt of Robert Burns on his journeys between EDINBURGH and DUMFRIES. In the burial-ground near Clyde Bridge is a plaque recording the death from cholera in 1847 of thirty-seven men working on the railway; in the 1840s and '50s, cholera was a dreaded disease in the North of England and in Scotland. It was said to have come from infected sailors on Russian ships.

The road SW. from Elvanfoot traverses the picturesque Dalveen Pass (1,140 ft) to the Nith Valley; it was called the "Lang Glen" by Burns. The land to the E. of this pass is the site of the Daer Valley water scheme.

The Daer Water Board was established in 1951 to co-ordinate various separate water undertakings by the MOTHERWELL, WISHAW, AIRDRIE, COATBRIDGE, and HAMILTON Water Boards. The new reservoir is expected to meet their needs of the next thirty years. The completed dam is an earth embankment, the largest of its kind in Britain.

EMBO, *Sutherland* (Map 5, ref. 28²89³). This coastal village on the outer DORNOCH Firth has become a popular holiday centre, with a large caravan site and water-skiing facilities.

Embo was the traditional site of a battle against the Danes, where Sir Richard de

Moravis, brother of the founder of Dornoch Cathedral, was killed. A large stone is reputed to commemorate the event. Archaeologists recently found a Neolithic chambered cairn in the neighbourhood.

ERIBOLL, *Sutherland* (Map 5, ref. 24³95⁶). This township is on the middle of the E. side of Loch Eriboll, a 10-m. fjord rather than sea-loch, which runs due S. and provides magnificent loch and mountain scenery. The former hill road from Eriboll SE. to Loch Hope is now impassable to vehicles. Loch Eriboll forms an exceptionally fine harbour with a depth ranging from fifteen to sixty fathoms, and the surrounding hills give it admirable shelter. In the Second World War it was used as a naval anchorage. The NE. point of the loch is called Whiten Head, also known as Kennageal, and on the E. shore S. from here is a series of remarkably fine cliffs and caves – again no access by road. At the head of Loch Eriboll is Craig-na-Faoilinn (934 ft), which provides a particularly fine rolling echo. Beyond are the peaks of Ben Spionnaidh, Cranstackie, and Foinaven, giving splendid mountain and moor scenery.

The Loch Eriboll district is noted for its extensive limestone outcrops, and lime kilns are found on the E. coast at Heilem. There have been various projects mooted from time to time for developing diatomite here.

ERISKAY, Island of, *Inverness-shire* (Map 4, ref. 08⁰81⁰), lies between the BARRA group of islands and South UIST in the Outer Hebrides (*see* "The Shape of Scotland"). It is only 3 m. by 1½ m. Its name, however, is known far outside Scotland, partly on account of the famous Gaelic melody known popularly as the "Eriskay Love Lilt", and partly because this barren but beautiful place happened to be the spot where Prince Charles Edward Stuart first set foot on Scottish soil at the beginning of his venture that led to the Rising of 1745. The bay where he landed is still called the Prince's Bay, and some pink convolvulus that grow there are associated with him. The adult male members of the population are nearly all fisherfolk, and in consequence the number of residents fluctuates. It is best approached by motor-ferry from the S. end of South Uist.

Despite the ubiquitous rock and thin soil, there are small crofts of cultivation preserved by a populace of singular charm and ease of manner. The island, on which little seems to have changed for centuries, is one of great beauty, soft colours, and rounded contours. It is the source of some of the finest Gaelic melodies and songs. That these were preserved is largely due to the scholarly care of Father Allan MacDonald, whose memorial in stone is the strongly built church near the centre of the island. It is dedicated to St Michael, the patron saint of the islands, and was the product of

Father Allan's energy and of his islanders' personal devotion to him and to their faith. Father Allan died in 1905, but his memory is green. Gaelic scholarship and the preservation of Gaelic song owes much to him, and to the fact that his last years as a priest were spent on the unique island of Eriskay.

ESKDALEMUIR, *Dumfriesshire* (Map 3, ref. 32⁵59⁷). Eskdalemuir Church, in Upper Eskdale, stands in the junction of the LOCKER-BIE and LANGHOLM roads, some 12 m. up the Esk from Langholm, on the road into ET-TRICK, and in the midst of what was until recently grassy moorland but now is mile after mile of forest, rising finally well above the normal tree-line and culminating in Ettrick Pen (2,270 ft) to the NW.

Beside the church, aerial photography shows a D-shaped enclosure containing hut-circles. A short distance upstream the Craikhaugh Ford, and a footbridge cross the river to the 2nd-cent. Roman fort of Raeburnfoot; this crossing marks the line of the ancient Craik-muir road. Raeburnfoot, excavated in the 1890s and again for two seasons recently, seems to have been a cavalry patrol post. From here up to Craik Cross, which rises to 1,481 ft, the 24-ft Roman road provides an astonishing example of engineering through very difficult country. It heads ultimately to Trimontium (Newstead) at MELROSE. W. of the Esk it heads for the upper Dryfe Water but is soon lost on the moors.

Some 3½ m. N. of the church is Eskdalemuir Observatory, on a moorland site at 800 ft. It was established in 1908 by the National Physical Laboratory to continue the terrestrial magnetism observations formerly made at Kew, and has been controlled since 1910 by the Meteorological Office. It has long had an international reputation as a magnetic institute, and makes continuous geomagnetic observations. It is also a first-order meteorological station, reporting internationally, and since 1958 has made hourly observations between 16.00 and 21.00 hours. Atmospheric sampling is also carried on here. Eskdalemuir Observatory has been chosen for a Government seismological station, which will replace Kew as the most important in Britain; it was built deep underground in 1963 and is, of course, far from traffic and heavy industry. The Atomic Energy Authority have had a listening post here since 1962, listening for nuclear explosions.

Also near Eskdalemuir was the traditional scene of the annual Handfasting Fair, where unmarried young people were paired off for a year's trial "marriage" until the next fair, at which it was reconsidered. If the trial was unsuccessful, they went their ways and tried again, any children of the "handfast" going to the unsatisfied party. Lord Maxwell was handfasted here in the 16th cent., and the practice lasted into the 18th cent.

ETIVE, *Argyll* (Map 2, ref. 22⁶73⁸). The narrow sea loch of Loch Etive extends from the Firth of Lorne to the foot of Glen Etive, whence a narrow road, bordered by the Dalness Forest (owned by the National Trust for Scotland) leads to Kingshouse and GLENCOE. The hills of Dalness Forest include the famous "Shepherds of Etive" – Buchaille Etive Mor, 3,345 ft, and Buchaille Etive Beg. These hills are strictly to the E. of Glencoe proper, but are always taken as being part of the Glencoe district.

There is a tradition that Deirdre was in Glen Etive, and place-names recall the connection. It should be added that others make this claim also – for instance, GLENDARUEL and BENDERLOCH.

ETTRICK FOREST, *Selkirkshire* (Map 3, ref. 33⁵62²). Now a poetic and historical name for the chief part of Selkirkshire, Ettrick Forest is a remnant of the great Caledonian Forest that formerly covered most of the county, and portions of Peeblesshire and Midlothian. The timber suffered severely during English invasions. King Robert Bruce granted the forest to the Douglases, who forfeited it in the 15th cent. when it became a royal hunting ground. In 1528 James V put 10,000 sheep into the forest instead of the 10,000 bucks that had previously been there, thus converting almost the entire forest into the sheep-pasture that it still is.

EVANTON, *Ross and Cromarty* (Map 5, ref. 26¹86⁶). This village, founded about 1810 on a waste piece of land just inland from the CROMARTY Firth where the Allt Graat river enters the sea, replaced the older village of Drummond that stood on the W. side of the river. The river itself, known farther W. as the Glass, emerges from Glen Glass and Loch Glass in the foothills of Ben Wyvis (3,429 ft). On the seaward side of the village is Balconie House, built on the site of an old fortress of the earls of Ross.

Further to the W. a path leads to the spectacular ravine known as the Black Rock of Novar, a tortuous channel cut by the Glass river, for about 2 m. through old red conglomerate. At one point the gorge is only 17 ft wide, with cliffs 110 ft high. The valley sides are covered in moss, and tangled trees grow across the ravine. The best view is to be had from the second bridge 1¾ m. farther on.

About 2 m. N. is Novar Estate, and Novar House, which is surrounded by fine woods.

EWE, Loch, *Ross and Cromarty* (Map 5, ref. 18⁵88⁸). A sea-loch about 10 m. long, with Isle of Ewe in the middle, Loch Ewe is fed by the R. Ewe, which flows into the loch after its short course from Loch MAREE; this river is particularly notable for salmon and sea-trout. At the crofting townships along the E. coast,

and at INVERASDALE on the W. shore, experimental work on crofter rehabilitation has been carried out.

In both world wars Loch Ewe was of considerable naval importance, and the entrance was, and indeed still is in part, blocked by anti-submarine nets. The naval depot of AULTBEA is on the E. side of the loch.

At the loch-side near Tournaig is a stone cairn in memory of Alexander Cameron, the Tournaig bard who died in 1933, having spent his entire life by the shores of the loch. Those who have enjoyed the beauties of this place will agree that he could have gone farther and fared worse.

EYE, Peninsula of, *Ross and Cromarty* (Map 4, ref. 15⁵93³). This extends from the Island of LEWIS, in the Outer Hebrides (*see* "The Shape of Scotland"), 3 m. E. of STORNOWAY. Eye, locally known as the "Parish of Point", will be dealt with below under two heads: (1) the peninsula itself; (2) the isthmus connecting it with Lewis.

(1) The peninsula, some 8 m. long SW. to NE., is a well-inhabited crofting and fishing community that, despite its proximity to Stornoway, keeps its individuality. The pleasing and durably constructed houses, often bearing a characteristic splash of paint, have largely been built by "Point Community" itself – a community that consists of various villages. The Gaelic spoken on this near island is distinct from that in the rest of Lewis. Eye culminates in the important Tiumpan Head lighthouse.

(2) The Eye isthmus is narrow, but has recently been made secure by concrete building against the SE. gales that were threatening to make Eye into an island. Along the isthmus are some of Lewis's most notable sand beaches; but the outstanding object in the isthmus, indeed one of the most remarkable of its kind on the island, is the roofless ruin of the pre-Reformation Chapel of Iu, as the Gaels call Eye. Owing to the fact that this early place of Christian worship shows several periods of rebuilding, it is impossible to date its unquestionably very early foundation. As it stands now, we see the remains of a late medieval chapel in which many of the Macleod chiefs were buried. Remarkable too is the Celtic Stone on the N. side commemorating Margaret Macleod, mother of John MacFingone, the last Abbot of IONA. On the S. side stands the effigy of Roderick Macleod, the 7th Chief, who is said to have cut a considerable figure in the reign of James II of Scotland, 1437–60. Having withstood the Hebridean storms for many years, this effigy is suddenly showing signs of weather defacement. Macleod societies, wherever they may be, please note. The last person to be buried in the chapel cemetery was Margaret Macleod of Bayble in 1900. She was well over 100 years old. When

Fair Isle

her grave was being dug, some ancient papers came to light, which unfortunately and immediately crumbled to dust. Let it not happen that the effigy of Roderick Macleod follows them into obscurity.

EYEMOUTH, *Berwickshire* (Map 3, ref. 39⁵66⁴), is a busy fishing town and holiday resort on the Eye Water, where it flows into the sea between Hare Point and Nestends. The beach is partly sandy and is suitable for bathing. There is rocky and picturesque coast scenery both to the N. and S. of the bay. At the entrance to the bay are the "Hurcars" rocks, which are almost awash, thus causing fierce breakers. The original harbour was built in 1768, being one of Smeaton's first designs; it was extended at the end of the 19th cent. Eyemouth suffered terrible destruction in the great gale of the 14th of October 1881, when half of the fishing fleet (24 boats) was sunk and 129 men drowned.

In 1597 a charter from James VI made Eyemouth a free burgh of barony, with the status of a free port. This led to the growth of smuggling, especially in the 18th and 19th cents. The narrow alleys and intricate pattern of the town's buildings served as a material aid in evading customs men, and the caves and caverns in the neighbouring cliffs were used as hiding places by the smugglers.

On Hare Point to the N. of the town are the remains of the fort, twice built and twice destroyed in the 16th cent. The coastguards' watch-house is built on the remains of one earthwork, called the King's Mount.

To the E. of the harbour is Gunsgreen, with Gunsgreen House, a Georgian mansion that became a centre of smuggling in the 18th cent. because of its many secret passages; it has since become a boarding house. The tower nearby, now used as Eyemouth Golf Club-house, is associated with Cromwell's visit to Eyemouth in 1650.

To the SW. of the town, overlooking the confluence of the rivers Ale and Eye, is Linthill, an early 17th-cent. mansion house with crow-stepped gables. It was once a seat of the Humes, and the scene of the gruesome and notorious murder in 1751, when the wealthy widow, Mrs Patrick Hume, was killed by her butler. He was surprised rifling her possessions, and cut her throat when she grappled with him. The old lady groped her way to the bell and summoned the other servants, whereupon Ross leapt from the window, broke his leg, was taken and hanged. Mrs Patrick Hume is buried in the old church of Bunkle.

FAIR ISLE, *Shetland* (Map 8, ref. 42¹07²), is one of the SHETLAND Northern Islands, and lies about midway between the Mainland of Shetland and the ORKNEY Isles (*see* "The Shape of Scotland"). It has achieved a two-fold international reputation for the intricate and colourful knitting patterns of the women-folk, and the island Bird Observatory's work in migration research. A small mail-boat, the *Good Shepherd*, which runs to Grutness on the Mainland of Shetland twice a week in summer and once a week in winter, is the only regular transport to the island. The isolation and other social drawbacks imposed by limited communications have been largely responsible for a drift towards depopulation; the population before 1939 was more than 100, but now is fewer than fifty. Efforts by the National Trust for Scotland, who have owned the island since 1954, to stimulate immigration and to improve conditions have met with only partial success. A deep-water pier extension has been built, piped water and electricity have been introduced, housing improvements have been encouraged, and a radio-telephone link installed. Much still depends on the viability of the mail-boat (in the absence of an air-strip or helicopter service); and, so long as the island can produce a crew, life on it will continue. Crofting (with emphasis on sheep), lobster-fishing, knitting, and some hand-loom weaving are the principal occupations. Only about 3 m. long by less than 2 m. wide, the island can be comfortably covered on foot or by bicycle from the bird observatory at the North Haven to the main crofting area in the S. The cliffs and moorlands are breeding-grounds for native species of sea-birds, and the island is frequently visited as a staging-post by other migrating birds; it has the remarkable record of 300 species observed. Limited accommodation is available at the bird observatory hostel and through the National Trust for Scotland.

FAIRLIE, *Ayrshire* (Map 2, ref. 22¹65⁵). This is a small resort on the Ayrshire coast road, 2 m. S. of LARGS. Formerly a fishing hamlet, this is now a flourishing residential and holiday resort, with a busy yacht-building yard of world-wide fame, and naturally a sailing centre. A car ferry connects it with ARRAN. Two miles offshore is the island of Great CUMBRAE, which makes Fairlie a safe anchorage in all weathers. Nearby is Kelburn Castle, the seat of the Boyle family, and the present home of the Earl of Glasgow.

FALKIRK, *Stirlingshire* (Map 2, ref. 28⁹68⁰). Now a bustling town in the industrial belt of Scotland, yet within sight of the Highland hills, Falkirk has had a long history. To begin with it was the scene of Roman activity, and there are sections of ANTONINUS' WALL to the E. and W. of the town. Lying by the Firth of FORTH, with the Campsie Hills to the W., EDINBURGH to the E., and the road into the Highlands to the N., its strategic importance led to the two battles of Falkirk. In 1298 William Wallace was overcome by great numbers of English under Edward I. This was the end of Wallace's purely military resistance to the occupying forces. The Wallace Stone is a 10-ft pillar on a hill-top 1 m. SE. of Callendar Wood.

In 1746, after his retreat from Derby and from England, Prince Charles Edward Stuart surprised his enemies by beating the Hanoverian forces under General Hawly at Falkirk. They thought they had Prince Charles Edward on the run, but Falkirk was in the Lowlands, and his Highland army was largely intact. It was after they got into the hills on their way N. to INVERNESS that the soldiery began to melt away in their own country.

In 1770 the largest cattle market in Scotland was transferred from CRIEFF to Falkirk and held there annually until the end of the 19th cent. Later, industry developed – iron founding and coal, the former particularly at nearby CARRON.

The parish church was founded as early as 1080, but was reconstructed as late as 1811, incorporating the William Adam tower of 1734; the church contains some old carved stones, a crosshead, the 15th-cent. Livingstone arms, and a pair of crudely carved effigies. In the churchyard are monuments to the dead of both battles. The monuments of Sir John Stewart of Buncle and of Sir John de Graham, who fell in 1298, recall the Wallace defeat − these monuments were reconstructed in 1773, but certainly existed well over a century earlier. The monuments to Sir Robert Munro of

Foulis and his brother Duncan recall the last Jacobite victory of 1746. The town steeple 146 ft high, was built on the site of an earlier tower in 1813.

Callendar House, SE. of the town centre, has existed in some form for 800 years. In the 14th cent. it was acquired by the Livingstone family; a later daughter of that family was one of "the Queen's Marys", and five trees in the grounds were planted by Mary Stuart and her four attendants. In 1606 Falkirk became a burgh of barony, but the earldom was forfeited in 1715. In 1783 William Forbes bought the house and estate; they remained in that family for nearly 200 years. Callendar House is an odd mixture of periods from the 14th to the 19th cent. It changed from castle-type in the 17th cent. to become a symmetrical mansion; in the 19th cent. the N. front was remodelled and the octagonal turrets disappeared.

FALKLAND, *Fife* (Map 3, ref. 32⁶70⁸), a small royal burgh between MARKINCH and STRATHMIGLO, lies at the foot of the East Lomond Hill (1,477 ft) on the fringe of the fertile Howe of Fife. Its character derives mainly from its associations with the Stuart kings who built the attractive palace that dominates the High Street, and frequented it as a hunting-lodge. Probably started by James III, on the site of the older castle of Falkland, the palace was much enlarged in the reign of James IV, and the S. range was embellished by James V during preparations for his marriage first to Magdalene, daughter of Francois I of France, and then, after her early death, to the French king's adopted daughter, Mary of Lorraine. The E. range and Cross House contain the King's Room, where it is thought James V died (of melancholy or jaundice) shortly after hearing news of the birth of his own daughter, Mary Queen of Scots. It is here he is said to have uttered his prophecy about the Stuart monarchy: "It cam wi' a lass, it will gang wi' a lass".

This room has been specially decorated and furnished by the National Trust for Scotland, who are now responsible for the upkeep of the palace. Major Michael Crichton Stuart, the hereditary constable, captain, and keeper of the palace, whose family started restoration of the fabric at the end of the last century, now lives in the S. range. Apart from the keeper's personal apartments, the palace and its extensive garden are regularly open to visitors; an admirable guide written by one of the most lively of Scottish historians, Sir Iain Moncreiffe of the Ilk, is published by the National Trust for Scotland. Adjoining the twin-towered gatehouse of the palace, St Andrew's House and Key House, typical of the dwellings occupied by courtiers and members of the Stuart royal household, have been restored by Major Crichton Stuart. The thatched Moncreif House opposite the palace was the home of Nicol Moncreif, one of King James VI's personal bodyguard, and Brunton House off Cross Wynd was at one time the home of the Simsons of Brunton who had served the Stuart kings as royal falconers.

FARE, Hill of, *Kincardineshire* (Map 6, ref. 36⁸80³). On the border of Aberdeenshire and Kincardineshire, the Hill of Fare rests on a broad base of some 17 m. circumference and rises to 1,545 ft. There was formerly much granite-quarrying here. The site of the old quarry is now a reservoir. On the SE. slopes of the hill is the marshy Howe of Corrichie; this was the site of a battle in 1562, when Royalist forces of Mary Stuart, Queen of Scots, defeated the rebellious Earl of Huntly. The Earl fell in the battle, but his son, Sir John Gordon, was captured and was later executed for treason at ABERDEEN.

FARNELL, *Angus* (Map 6, ref. 36²75⁶). The village of Farnell 3½ m. SE. of BRECHIN lacks distinction, but Farnell Castle is worthy of note. It was originally the Episcopal Palace of the bishops of Brechin, who had to leave it after the Reformation in 1566. It then came into the possession of the earls of Southesk. It was a plain three-storey pile originally in the 16th cent., but was repaired in the late 19th cent. for use as almshouses for former employees of the estate.

Kinnaird Castle, 1 m. NE. of Farnell, is now the seat of the earls of Southesk. The present building replaced former ones occupied since the early 15th cent. Extensive alterations were carried out by Playfair about 1790; it was then transformed once again by Bryce (1854–60) on the lines of a 16th-cent. French château.

FASLANE, *Dunbartonshire* (Map 2, ref. 22⁴68⁹), formerly famous for its ship-breaking yard where such notable warships as the *Malaya* and *Renown* and the liner *Aquitania* were dismantled, and for its Second World War emergency deep-water dock, is now the site of H.M.S. *Neptune*, the land base for Britain's nuclear submarine fleet and also for a squadron of conventional submarines.

FEARN, *Ross and Cromarty* (Map 5, ref. 28³87⁸). This village lies in the centre of the fertile farming district of Easter Ross. About 1½ m. W. of the village is Calrossie, formerly the home of the famous herd of Shorthorn cattle. A Premonstratensian abbey founded by Farquhar, the 1st Earl of Ross, at EDDERTON in 1221 moved here in 1298, induced by the more fertile soil. In its heyday it comprised a nave, choir, lady chapel, and two transeptal chapels completed in 1545. Its titular abbot, Patrick Hamilton, became the first Scottish martyr of the Reformation when he was burnt at ST ANDREWS in 1528. After the

Reformation the abbey was used as a parish church, but in 1742 on a Sunday, the roof fell in, killing forty-four worshippers.

About 3 m. NE. of the village is the ruin of Lochslin Castle, the family home of Sir George Mackenzie of Rosehaugh, who, as Lord Advocate of Scotland (chief Crown prosecutor), was given the undeserved description of "Bloody" Mackenzie. He is regarded as the father of modern Scottish criminal law. And as founder of the Advocates' Library (now the National Library of Scotland in EDINBURGH), he left us all a great legacy.

FENWICK, *Ayrshire* (Map 2, ref. 24⁶64³). High Fenwick and Low Fenwick combine in one village, which lies on a by-pass from the KILMARNOCK–GLASGOW trunk road about 4 m. N. of Kilmarnock. Fenwick is high on the Eaglesham Moor, and, while it serves a dairy-farming district, it is not far from the marginal land of Fenwick Moor. The village has many links with the Covenanters.

FERINTOSH, *Ross and Cromarty* (Map 5, ref. 25⁷85⁷). About 3 m. NE. of CONON BRIDGE, the township of Ferintosh is in an estate belonging, after 1667, to the family of Forbes of CULLODEN. As a compensation for damage caused to the estate in the troubles of the 17th cent., the Scots Parliament in 1690 granted Duncan Forbes the right to make whisky on the estate of Ferintosh, unrestricted by excise regulations. It was then described as "an ancient Brewery of aqua-vitae". The family were bought out of their hereditary rights in 1785 for £20,000. The whisky distilled there was famous, and "Ferintosh" became a noted trade name in the north.

FESHIE, *Inverness-shire* (Map 5, ref. 28⁶80⁴). The Glen of Feshie, leading deep into the hills from Speyside towards Deeside, is much gentler than the LAIRIG GHRU, and since the 18th cent. has been suggested as a suitable road linking the two areas. It has an excellent all-weather path for walking, with good bridges. The distance from KINGUSSIE to BRAEMAR is 22 m. by Glen Feshie, and more than 80 m. by any other route. It was surveyed because of this by General Wade, the great Highland road-maker of the 18th cent.

FETTERCAIRN, *Kincardineshire* (Map 6, ref. 36⁵77³). With its great royal arch of Rhenish–Gothic design, built in 1864 to commemorate the incognito visit of Queen Victoria and Prince Albert three years previously, the village of Fettercairn lords it over the western fringe of the Howe of the Mearns. Set amid rich woods and lush fields and within easy distance of the CAIRN O' MOUNT Pass over the GRAMPIANS to Feughside and Deeside, the present village dates from the middle of the 18th cent., but it has several links with a much

Fettercairn House   *Aberdeen Press and Journal*

more remote past, and no doubt it had its predecessor in the shadow of "Finella's Castell of Fethircarne, the chiefest fortress of all the Mearns". A very fragmentary relic known as the Green Castle on the left bank of the Devilly Burn, 2 m. NE. of Fettercairn, has been traditionally identified as Finella's Castle, the place where King Kenneth III was murdered in A.D. 994. The *Chronicle of Kings* says that Kenneth was killed by his own men in Fettercairn, through the treachery of Finella (daughter of Connacher, Earl of Angus), whose son he had put to death. But the chroniclers Fordoun and Hollinshed told a much more spectacular tale of the regicide. Feigning reconciliation with the King after the death of her son, Finella, who had married the Mormaer of the Mearns, received the monarch with lavish hospitality.

Within her Castle she caused to be built a tower covered with copper and fitted inside with rich furnishings; concealed behind them were crossbows set ready bent and loaded. In the centre of the room was a brazen image resembling the figure of the King, holding in one hand a golden apple, so artfully devised that if anyone took hold of it the crossbows would discharge their arrows upon him with great force.

After dinner the King was invited to admire this flattering representation of himself and accept the golden apple, which in all innocence he did, with the inevitably fatal result. Endless are the variants of the rest of the story. Mearns legend, which sees Finella as a witch, avers that she fled across the Howe and over the Hills of Garvock and met her end in the Den of Finella at ST CYRUS.

The most notable building in the area today is Fettercairn House, erected shortly after the Restoration of 1660 by John, 1st Earl of Middleton. Middleton had played a spectacular part in the Civil War, at first as a covenanting general, helping to defeat Montrose at Philiphaugh, and then as a Royalist at Preston and Worcester and in later adventures during the Commonwealth. On the Restoration he became the "first man in the kingdom" as Lord High

Commissioner to the Scottish Parliament, but his regime was intensely hated in Scotland, and, when the Cabal Ministry came to power, he fell from royal favour and was sent to Tangier, where he died in 1673.

The present chatelaine of Fettercairn is Mrs Diana Somervell, a cousin of the Queen. One of her ancestors, a Miss Stuart, had James Mill the philosopher as her tutor and was wooed by Sir Walter Scott. But instead she married Sir William Forbes, who brought to Fettercairn two journals by James Boswell and over 100 letters written to him that were rediscovered in 1930 by Professor Claude Collier Abbott, purchased by Yale University, and published in the famous series of Boswell Papers.

About 1 m. SW. of Fettercairn is Balbegno Castle, built in 1569 by James Wood. A hero of the family is commemorated by the sculpture of a bearded figure over the garden door, representing Admiral Sir Andrew Wood of Largo, the Scottish "Nelson" who humbled the English in a sea-fight in the Firth of FORTH. Balbegno has a rib-vaulted hall with fine painted plaster severies.

FINDHORN, *Moray* (Map 6, ref. 30⁴86⁴), is a village on the E. side of the sandy Findhorn Bay facing the Moray Firth. It was once the chief port of Moray and the centre of a big fishing industry. It is now a holiday resort with sandy beaches and fine facilities for sailing.

This is the third village to bear the name of Findhorn in this district. The earlier ones were built to the NW. and were overwhelmed by disaster. The first was obliterated by sand following the extraordinary fate of CULBIN just across the bay. The second village of Findhorn was destroyed by a great flood in 1701.

FINDOCHTY, *Banffshire* (Map 6, ref. 34⁷86⁸). "Sound judges," wrote the Rev. Francis P. Chisholm in the *Third Statistical Account of Banffshire*, "knowing both Findochty and the Cornish coast, have been said to prefer the former." Anyone who has savoured the charm of Findochty's fishertown will know why. The situation of the little harbour between its two headlands, one crowned by the old kirk, the other by a towering obelisk, is picturesque enough to satisfy all connoisseurs of the Cornish riviera. On a sunny, breezy day with the wind from the west, the Moray Firth's white horses gleam and the breakers thunder on the encircling rocks. The immaculate paintwork of the stout stone cottages that stand in rows, gable-ends to the street, glistens as if it has been applied only yesterday – and that is, in fact, quite likely, for the old salts of Findochty are never happier than when painting their homes, which they do in gay colours, outlining the mortar between the stones in spotless white and covering every square inch of masonry.

For a police burgh of 1,331 inhabitants,

Findochty can seem exceedingly quiet, with its skippers and crews fishing out of nearby BUCKIE or commuting on the trawler train from ABERDEEN, but this quietude is in a sense deceptive. For Findochty men, wherever they work, still make their homes here, as they have done since 1716, when thirteen men and four boys – their names being Flett, Campbell, and Smith – came, under a kind of contract from FRASERBURGH, to homes built for them at the Broad Hythe by Thomas Ord of Findochty Castle, and later worked for the Earl of Findlater. Even that was not the beginning, for we know by a charter of 1568 that there were then "port, customs, and fishing grounds" at Findochty, and there must have been fishermen to use them.

There has been a great decline in the forty years since Banffshire owned over a third of the total line- and herring-fishing craft in Scotland, and Findochty has suffered from the centralization that bled all the other little ports so that Buckie and MACDUFF could consolidate themselves as the major market centres. But every now and then the hope of revival flares up again. The harbour is in good shape, but is used only by lobster-boats and pleasure-craft. The spirit of the little port is symbolized by a splendid statue of a seated fisherman on the waterfront, gazing out over the waters. Inscribed on the pedestal of this modern work by Coreena Cowie are the words "They see the works of the Lord and his wonders in the deep".

Findochty clusters in its haven at the foot of lofty cliffs. On the high land behind the town is the ruin of Findochty Castle, a rectangular tower-house with a small oblong tower attached to the N. front. It was built by Thomas Ord in the 16th cent. The Muir of Findochty, now largely reclaimed and converted into farm land, was the scene of the Battle of the Bauds in A.D. 961 when the Norse, under Eric of the Bloody Axe, were routed by the Scots under King Indolphus, who was himself slain and is commemorated by the King's Cairn.

Immediately W. of Findochty is the golf course of Strathlene, one of Buckie's two municipal courses, with the massive Strathlene House Hotel – a useful hostelry, since there are no big hotels in Findochty itself.

FINDO GASK, *Perthshire* (Map 2, ref. 30°72°), is a village and parish in Strathearn.

The present House of Gask dates from 1801, but the ruins of the earlier house are in the grounds. The Oliphant family, originally called Olifard, had owned the lands of Strageath since the 12th cent., but the first mention of a house at Gask is in August 1304, when Edward I of England and his French queen stayed at West Gask. The "Auld Hoose" celebrated in song is probably the building purchased by Laurence Oliphant from his cousin in 1625.

The family were devoted Jacobites, and on the 11th of September 1745 Prince Charles breakfasted at Gask while on his way S. from PERTH. Among the Jacobite relics at Gask was a lock of the Prince's fair hair given to Marjory Robertson of Strowan on the day of his visit. In the following year the house was burnt and ransacked by the Hanoverian troops, and the old laird and his son were banished.

Carolina Oliphant (Lady Nairne) was born in 1766 and died at Gask in 1845. She wrote many famous Scots songs, including "The Laird of Cockpen", "Will Ye No' Come Back Again", and "The Land o' the Leal". She greatly admired Burns, and was one of the first of his contemporaries to recognize his genius.

One of the best authenticated stretches of Roman road in Scotland runs from W. to E. across this area. The western end hinged on the Roman camp at Strageath can be recognized all the way from just N. of INNERPEFFRAY as far as Dupplin Loch. N. of Gask House the road probably coincides with the line of the modern road. Various signal stations have been identified along the line, one of the best preserved being in the wood NE. of Gask House but on the opposite side of the road.

FINDON, *Kincardineshire* (Map 6, ref. 39¹79⁷). This tiny hamlet gave its name to the Finnan haddock, cured by splitting, drying, and colouring in a special way by the smoke of peat. By the end of the 18th cent., these were "known and esteemed in most parts of Scotland" and were publicized by Sir Walter Scott. But Findon was only one, and the smallest, of a whole string of fishing havens on the precipitous cliff-bound coast S. of ABERDEEN; Cove Bay, Portlethen, Downies, and Newtonhill with Skateraw all managed to sustain fishing villages virtually in defiance of the laws of nature, since the tiny shingle beaches were scarcely capable of accommodating the boats and only at Skateraw was it possible to build a pier. At the other coves the boats were raised and lowered out of the water by means of wooden rails forming improvised slipways. Slipways of this kind are still used at the salmon stations that survive, although the white fishing has long gone. The making of Finnan haddocks in the old way, by the smoke of cottage fires, became illegal under the Factory Act in the 19th cent., and the industry was transferred to hygienic fish-houses in Aberdeen, where it still continues. While Findon is now virtually extinct as a "populated place", Portlethen, Downies, and Newtonhill have a great vogue as suburbs of Aberdeen, and Newtonhill is in the throes of very rapid expansion. Kincardineshire County Council attempted to transfer Portlethen to a new town inland, owing to the difficulty of taking water-supply and sewage to the clifftop, but the inhabitants both there and at Downies, loving their magnificent sea-view, refused to move, and power, water, and all modern amenities have been brought to them.

Artists, scientists, and other professional people have now chosen to live in these cliff-top cottages.

FINLAGGAN, Loch, *Argyll* (Map 1, ref. 13⁸66⁸) is on the Island of ISLAY, in the Inner Hebrides (*see* "The Shape of Scotland").

This loch, lying 3 m. SW. of PORT ASKAIG, was once the famous centre of a Gaelic principality. On Eilean Mor, an island almost joined to the shore at the N. end of the loch, are the ruins of a chapel, and of a castle once described as a palace, held during the 14th and 15th cents. by Macdonald Lords of the Isles; it became ruinous by the end of the 17th cent. There are some carved stones at the ruins.

Some 50 yds S. of Eilean Mor lies the very small Council Isle, to which fourteen chief men of the lordship were summoned to a council to advise the Lord of the Isles.

FINNART, *Dunbartonshire* (Map 2, ref. 21⁹ 68⁸). On the E. shore of Loch LONG, Finnart was one of the first jetties in Britain capable of berthing giant tankers in all weathers and at all states of the tide. The natural advantages are the depth of the loch and the shelter of the hills around. Finnart is used to serve the refinery at GRANGEMOUTH by pumping the crude oil 57 m. overland by pipeline. The first jetty was built in 1951; it is now increased and called Finnart Ocean Terminal.

FINTRY, *Stirlingshire* (Map 2, ref. 26²68⁶). This village is set in a pleasant valley between the Fintry Hills to the N. and the Campsie Fells to the S., in the heart of the Lennox country.

About 1 m. N. is Culcreuch Tower, a 16th-cent. keep with late 17th-cent. additions. It was owned at one time by Napier of Merchiston, who worked there on logarithms. It is reputed to be haunted.

The old village was near the church, but the new town of Fintry lies W. of it, where sites were feued for workers' houses in 1794. A little SW. of the tower stand the remains of a large cotton factory erected by the Speirs family in 1796. It was not a financial success, and it fell into ruin before the end of the 19th cent.

To the SE. of Fintry village, the Craw Road crosses the Campsies to LENNOXTOWN, reaching a height of 1,064 ft, with fine views of the CLYDE valley. The Campsie Fells are mainly basaltic trap, and the sheets of igneous rocks can easily be seen under the scanty grass. The long ridge of the Campsies is more grandly seen from the SW., where it dominates the Blane valley between GLASGOW and LOCH LOMOND. The highest hill, Earl's Seat (1,894 ft), is within 12 m. of the centre of the city.

Some 3 m. E. of the village is the fine water-fall called the Loup of Fintry, where the End-rick Water goes over a 94-ft precipice. The

narrow hill road continues eastwards past the Carron Valley Reservoir to DENNY. Near the waterfall are scant remains of Sir John de Graham's Castle, the ancient stronghold of the Grahams of Fintry.

FIONPHORT, *Argyll* (Map 1, ref. 13¹72³) is on the Island of MULL in the Inner Hebrides (*see* "The Shape of Scotland"). This is the starting-point of the IONA ferry from the Ross of Mull. It was on the old pilgrim route over-land to Iona and must have been in use for very many centuries. The coast here is very rocky.

FLANDERS MOSS, *Perthshire* (Map 2, ref. 25⁷69⁶). In prehistoric times the heavy carse clays of the upper FORTH valley carried a particularly dense type of oak forest. This forest decayed owing to climatic changes and gave rise to extensive areas of peat moss, of which two of the best known tracts were Flanders Moss and Blairdrummond Moss. The peat, 6 to 12 ft deep, overlay rich alluvial soils, and in the latter part of the 18th cent. plans were made to strip it off and reclaim the land beneath for agricultural purposes. The origina-tor of this plan was Lord Kames, who, as Henry Home, inherited through his wife the estate of Blairdrummond in 1766. Blairdrum-mond Moss extended to some 1,800 acres, but this was only a fraction of the 10,000 acres covered by the peat.

The reclamation was slow and laborious, and tenants, attracted by the low rents, had in the first instance to work very hard to clear sufficient land to support themselves and their families. Lord Kames died in 1782, but his work was continued by his son, who extended and improved on the initial plan to wash the peat away down channels cut in the moss and fed by a constant stream of water. To maintain the flow of water a great wheel was set up at Mill of Torr on the R. Teith. Through an ingenious system of buckets the water was raised 17 ft and conveyed in wooden pipes 18 in. in diameter for a distance of 354 yds underground. It then flowed along a raised aqueduct for 1,400 yds. The Great Wheel functioned until 1839. By 1811, 1,440 acres had been reclaimed, and they supported a population of 1,000.

Today parts of Flanders Moss are still not reclaimed, and the desolate character of the area can be appreciated by motoring between KIPPEN and Thornhill.

FLANNAN ISLANDS, The, *Ross and Cromarty* (Map 4, ref. 07³94⁶), belong to the Outer Hebrides (*see* "The Shape of Scotland"), and are amongst the remotest of the Western Islands. They form a group of seven lying in the Atlantic 15 m. W. of LEWIS; at one time regarded as being of special sanctity, they were also used as grazing for sheep. On the summit of Eilean Mor, which stands 280 ft above high water, a lighthouse was completed in 1899; the rock is very steep and was almost inaccessible until steps and paths were cut in it, and during stormy weather water passes right over it. The shore station is at Breascleit, Loch Roag, and during a severe gale at Christmas 1900 the three light-keepers on duty at the rock disappeared and no trace of them was ever found. The tragedy, never fully explained, is one of the mysteries of the lighthouse service, but it has been supposed that two of the men, perhaps with the third also, were washed into the sea by an unexpectedly high wave while trying to secure some gear on the landing-stage at the base of the rock.

FLEET, *Sutherland* (Map 5, ref. 27⁵90⁰). The R. Fleet rises near LAIRG and winds for 17 m. E. until it joins the DORNOCH Firth at Little Ferry. In its upper stretches it traverses the fine glen of Strath Fleet, then expands into the tidal lagoon of Loch Fleet, contracting again at Little Ferry. The lagoon is crossed at its head by the railway on the Mound, an embankment 995 yds long, completed in 1816 at a cost of £12,500; it is pierced at the E. end by four arches and has a sluice for the river. The embankment was built by Thomas Telford, reclaiming some 400 acres of land.

FOCHABERS, *Moray* (Map 6, ref. 33⁵85⁸). Like HUNTLY in Aberdeenshire, Fochabers owes its being to the noble house of Gordon. But here the position is reversed, for while at Huntly it is the castle, though in ruins, that is their greatest monument, at Fochabers it is the town itself, an exceptionally fine example of Georgian town-planning, that remains to testify to their good taste. It was laid out by John Baxter, mason to William Adam, for Alexander, 4th Duke of Gordon, and his Duchess, Jane Maxwell, at the end of the 18th cent., when it became necessary to remove the original village, which stood in the way of the extension of Gordon Castle. Baxter designed the "New Town" in the form of a rectangle, bisected lengthways from E. to W. by the main highway from ABERDEEN to ELGIN. On this major axis is a large market square with the parish church of Bellie (1798) in the middle of its S. side. From the square, Duke Street ran N. on the alignment of Gordon Castle, but in 1852 this vista was closed by the erection of an Episcopal chapel, balancing the parish kirk at the other end of the street. The plan is completed by another cross street (Westmorland Street) and by a series of lanes. Bellie Church, with pillared portico and spire, is a splendidly proportioned building, and happily it has been saved from the threat of demolition. It is allowed its full effect by symmetrical flanking blocks, one of which houses the offices of the Crown Lands Commissioners who now administer most of the Richmond and Gordon estates. Most of the original buildings of the town remain, as well-proportioned Georgian houses, usually harled and whitewashed.

Fochabers is approached from the E. through miles of woodlands, part of the immense Forestry Commission Forest of Speymouth. At this end of the town is Milne's High School, built in the Tudor Collegiate style in 1846 from the 100,000 dollars bequest of Alexander Milne, a local boy who emigrated to America because he did not want to cut his hair in the way decreed by the 4th Duke of Gordon. It is now a state secondary school.

A handsome four-arch bridge across the SPEY was partly swept away in the "Muckle Spate" of 1829. In 1832 the space left by the two fallen arches was spanned by a single timber arch of 185 ft. In 1854 this was replaced, without stopping the traffic for a single day, by an iron arch. An entirely new Fochabers Bridge was completed in July 1971 to cope with the heavy Aberdeen–INVERNESS traffic.

There are some noteworthy monuments in Bellie kirkyard, including a Greek temple that is the tomb of Jean Christie, the Fochabers beauty who was the mistress and ultimately the second wife of the 4th Duke of Gordon; and of Adam Gordon of Newtongarrie, one of the nine children she bore the Duke.

They have heard of Fochabers in Addis Ababa and Honolulu, among the capitals of seventy-eight countries where the Gordon tartan encircles the containers of "fine foods from Scotland" marketed from Fochabers by a business founded in 1868 by a retired gardener to the Duke of Richmond and Gordon whose wife was a genius at making jam.

FORDYCE, *Banffshire* (Map 6, ref. 35⁶86⁴). Most pleasingly situated on the side roads to the S. of the main road from PORTSOY to CULLEN, Fordyce was a burgh of barony under the Earl of Seafield, and received its first charter in 1499, another in 1592. The village has gathered itself round a castle built in 1592, with later additions (now lived in) with fine corbelling and dormer windows. Fordyce Academy was a well-known secondary school with a boarding house, founded by a bequest left by an Indian magnate. It is now a junior secondary school.

About 1½ m. NW. stands the mansion house of Birkenbog, with a fine walled garden. It was the birthplace of Thomas Nicholson (1645–1718), the first Catholic Vicar-Apostolic of Scotland, after the Reformation and before the 19th-cent. restoration of Scottish sees.

FORFAR, *Angus* (Map 6, ref. 34⁵75⁰). This royal burgh, founded in the reign of David I, stands in the midst of flat fertile country at the NE. end of the Vale of STRATHMORE, here known as the Howe of Angus, with Forfar Loch to the W. and Fithie Loch to the E. It is the county town of Angus.

Tradition relates that a "parliament" was

held here in 1057, when King Malcolm Canmore conferred surnames and titles on the Scottish nobility. Certainly a royal residence existed in his time, the castle being situated on the conical Castlehill at the NE. corner of the town. The spot is marked by an octagonal turret (1684), which itself was once the town cross. A track, known as the "King's Codger's Road", formerly led to the coast at Usan and was used to bring fresh fish to the royal castle. Queen Margaret, wife of Malcolm Canmore, had a residence on an island in Forfar Loch. Tradition associates some weapons found in the loch in 1770 with the murder of King Malcolm II in GLAMIS, his murderers being drowned while trying to cross the ice-covered water.

During the 17th cent. the town acquired notoriety as a result of the number of women burnt here for witchcraft, nine being so put to death between 1650 and 1662 alone. A hollow to the N. is still known as "The Witches' Hose", and there executions were carried out. Preserved in the Town House is the gruesome Forfar "bridle", a metal collar, hinged to fit the neck, with a metal prong in front to act as a gag during executions. Noteworthy are the County Buildings, erected in 1873, and the Reid Hall, built in 1871 as a result of the generosity of Peter Reid, who made his fortune from the distinctive Forfar "rock" confectionery. The town, whose atmosphere typifies the quietly industrious spirit of the smaller Scottish burghs, has always depended to a large extent on the textile industry, and at one time possessed eight or nine large jute- and linen-mills. Even today a quarter of its working population is occupied in this trade. Forfar was famous in the past for its manufacture of wooden-soled shoes, or brogues. Its inhabitants were called the "Sutors of Forfar", as they had gained the reputation of being extremely argumentative.

FORGANDENNY, *Perthshire* (Map 6, ref. 30°71⁸). In the valley of the Earn, the village of Forgandenny is situated 1 m. S. of the river.

About 1 m. S. of the village and in the Ochils stands Culteuchar Hill (1,028 ft), also called Castle Law; to the NE. it possesses, on a slight eminence, a fort. This fort was excavated in 1891, when the sockets of beams were found, preserved entire. An area of 180 ft by 80 ft is enclosed by two walls.

FORRES, *Moray* (Map 6, ref. 30⁴85⁸), is a small burgh of great antiquity standing to the right of the R. Findhorn near where it enters Findhorn Bay, and justifiably prides itself on its sheltered situation and its reputation for healthy invigorating air. King Duncan held court at Forres, and it was on their way there that Macbeth and Banquo met on the "blasted heath" the "weird sisters" – three of the witches for whom Forres was notorious. This tradition

has, of course, been used by Shakespeare in *Macbeth*. The place where this meeting is believed to have occurred is near the boundary with Nairn and is called Hardmain or "Macbeth's Hill". It is now no longer "blasted" but cultivated and wooded. The importance of Forres declined after the foundation of the Bishopric at the Diocese of ELGIN. Various writers have claimed that Forres was a Roman station and was the mysterious *Varis* mentioned by Ptolemy.

On an elevated platform at the W. end of the High Street once stood the long-vanished castle. Its site is marked by a tall granite obelisk erected in 1857 in memory of Dr Thomson, who died in the Crimean War through his heroic efforts to help the wounded. Though well known in Forres, he was not a native. He came from CROMARTY, but the council there refused his monument. Forres was more perceptive and generous. It is worth pointing out to the visitor that the remnants on this hill are not of the ancient royal castle, but of a house started in the early 18th cent. The Falconer Museum (1870) in the High Street has an interesting collection of fossils. Forres House, at the E. end of the public park, houses a library. To the SE. of the town is Cluny Hill, the highest summit, crowned by an octagonal 70-ft tower erected in 1806 as a monument to Lord Nelson. There is a magnificent view from the top, which is reached by a spiral stair. The Cluny Hills Hydropathic Establishment on the S. side was one of the oldest in Scotland.

At the E. end of the town is the famous Sueno's Stone, 23 ft high and an Ancient Monument, one of the most remarkable early sculptured works in Scotland. Made from sandstone, it has a tall cross on one side, accompanied by elaborate figure sculptures at the base; on the other side are carved groups of figures of warriors. Possibly it commemorates a victory of Sweyn, son of Harald, over Malcolm II in 1008. In 1813 eight human skeletons were found near the pillar. Nearby to the E. is the granite Witches' Stone, the remaining one of three stones traditionally marking the place where three witches, accused of plotting the death of King Duffus, were put to death. The story is that the witches were found melting a wax image of the King. They were each placed in a barrel on top of Cluny Hill and set rolling. Where they stopped the barrels with the witches inside were burnt, and the stones set up. The one that remains was at one time broken up for building, but was replaced and held together with iron bands.

The scenery on the R. Findhorn to the S. of Forres is of exceptional beauty. The GRANTOWN road is followed to Sluie. From here walkers can go along the river gorge, eventually passing Logie House. The road is rejoined near Relugas House. Shortly farther on, a path leads to the famous Randolph's Leap, with striking views on all sides. The road continues back on the W. side of the R. Findhorn through the Darnaway Forest, which surrounds Darnaway Castle, an imposing castellated structure built in 1810, with the 15th-cent. Earl Randolph's Hall incorporated at the rear. This is a banqueting-hall, 90 by 35 ft and with an arched oaken roof. Queen Mary held court here in 1564. It was often visited by James IV, who gave it to his mistress, Lady Janet Kennedy. It is the seat of the earls of Moray. The hall has a gruesome portrait of the "Bonny Earl" gashed with wounds. From the main road nearby is an extensive view northwards across the Moray Firth to Morven and Caithness.

FORSINARD, *Sutherland* (Map 5, ref. 28⁹94²), lies in a district that has good fishing and sporting facilities. Strath Halladale, which was the former boundary between the clans of Sutherland and Mackay, runs N. from the village, bearing many scars still visible where once were thriving crofting communities. The railway, a useful adjunct to the flourishing hill lamb sales held here, curves away to the NE. lands of Caithness.

FORT AUGUSTUS, *Inverness-shire* (Map 5, ref. 23⁸80⁸), is a village in the Great Glen or large fracture that divides Scotland from NE. to SW. by way of Loch NESS, and it stands on the fine modern highway through GLEN MORE, partly on the line of General Wade's road of 1725–6. It once held a Hanoverian outpost against insurgent Jacobite Highlanders, and later a Benedictine abbey and school were founded here. It is a well-known angler's resort, situated at the SW. end of Loch Ness, near the place where it is entered by the CALEDONIAN CANAL. Once it was known as Kilcumin, which is Gaelic for the cell or church of Cumin, an early Iona abbot.

After the Jacobite rising of 1715, the Hanoverian Government decided to garrison this point, commanding Glen Tarff to the S. and thus also the CORRIEYAIRACK PASS. In 1716 the barracks was built, one wall of which still stands in the grounds of what is now the Lovat Arms Hotel. The first fort was built by General Wade in 1730; it was named after William Augustus, Duke of Cumberland. It was capable of holding 300 men. In 1746, during the last Jacobite Rising, it was captured by the Highlanders after a two-day siege during which a shell exploded the powder magazine. Reoccupied by Hanoverian troops after the Battle of CULLODEN, the fort was reconstructed and garrisoned and remained so until the Crimean War.

In 1867, by which time Jacobitism in the Highlands of Scotland was held to be no more dangerous than a romantic dream (had not Queen Victoria proclaimed herself an ardent Jacobite?), the Government sold the fort and lands to Lord Lovat for £5,000; he presented it to the Catholic Benedictine Order for the erection of an abbey and school. The foundation-stone was laid in the same year, and the college was opened in 1878. It was completed in 1880 and raised to abbey status in 1882 with the name of St Benedict's. Those who have a taste for irony may observe with some amusement that a part of the old Hanoverian fort is carefully preserved in the NW. corner. The same sort of preservation is shown in the Pantheon at Rome.

Cloisters in the Early English style, and other parts, were built by Peter Paul Pugin, son of the famous Pugin, in 1893, while the school and clock-tower were designed by Joseph Hansom, the inventor of the hansom cab. The Romanesque church by Richard Fairlie was begun in 1914. In passing, one may remark that the site was originally Benedictine property, being given in 1232 to the BEAULY Priory, then being granted by the last prior at the Reformation to Lord Lovat in 1558. A later Lord Lovat, the famous Simon of the '45, forfeited the land for his part, or suspected part, in the Rising of 1715.

The present foundation of St Benedict's was colonized by monks from the Schottenkloster at Ratisbon, which was founded by St Marianus of DUNKELD in 1074 and dissolved in 1863. After the Reformation, Ratisbon continued connections with what remained of native Scottish Catholicism; and the colonization of the new Benedictine Abbey in the Highlands from Ratisbon could not have been more appropriate. Today most of the monks are Scottish, and practically all the schoolboys who attend there come from EDINBURGH, GLASGOW, ABERDEEN, and the Catholic Highlands. In the early days, however, there were a number of continental monks. As part of their duties was to attend to remote parts of the Scottish Highlands, some of the monks learned Gaelic. One, a Slav, succeeded so well that he was able to publish a reliable Gaelic dictionary and grammar.

In the far corner of Fort Augustus's Protestant Churchyard is the grave of John Anderson, a carpenter who died here in 1832. He was an old friend of Robert Burns, and is said to have made the poet's coffin. Anderson's name lives in the poem "John Anderson, My Jo John".

There are Forestry Commission developments on the western shores of Loch Ness, which include the newly founded village of Inchnacardoch, 1 m. N. of Fort Augustus.

A little SW. along Glen More, and at the head of Loch Oich, is Aberchalder Lodge, where Prince Charles Edward Stuart reviewed 2,000 men on his march South on the 27th of August 1745.

FORTEVIOT, *Perthshire* (Map 6, ref. 30⁵71⁷). This village in Strathearn was once the capital of the Pictish kingdom of Fortrenn, and Kenneth MacAlpine died here in A.D. 860. Two centuries later there was a royal residence here and its existence is confirmed by references made in the lives of the Scottish kings of the 11th, 12th, and 13th cents. Andrew Wyntoun's tale of the Miller of Forteviot's daughter who became the mother of Malcolm Canmore may be rejected by historians, but his successors signed charters here, and in 1306, after the Battle of METHVEN, the English commander was issuing orders from Forteviot. The palace or castle stood on Halyhill to the NW. of the present village. The ruins are referred to by several writers and travellers of the 18th and 19th cents., but today no vestiges remain.

In the National Museum of Antiquities in EDINBURGH is a carved arch-stone found in the bed of the Water of May not far from the village. The carving consists of the upper part of three human figures who hold swords or staves in their right hands and a larger figure whose feet rest on an animal with a curved horn. All the figures appear to be wearing quilted armour, while the larger figure has the hem of his garment decorated with a key pattern.

There was a religious foundation of the Celtic Church at Forteviot, and tradition says that this was established as early as the 8th cent. Two Celtic crosses testify to its existence. The Dupplin Cross, magnificently carved, stands above Bankhead Farm, and a sculptured fragment of the Dronachy Cross, which once stood in the grounds of Invermay House, is now housed in the parish church. The bronze Celtic handbell belonging to Forteviot Church has been dated to the 10th cent.

Just SW. of the village on the farm of Broomhill are the outlines of a large Roman camp.

About $1\frac{1}{2}$ m. SE. is Invermay House, associated with Scott's novel *Redgauntlet*. The original fortalice of Invermay is only a ruin, but above the entrance the arms of Drummond and the date 1633 can be seen. The setting is one of great scenic beauty, and has been duly praised in the well-known song "The Birks of Invermay". When neighbouring Pitkeathley Wells was in its heyday as a spa, one of its recommendations was its proximity to Invermay, whose picturesque scenery and natural beauty were a great attraction.

Dupplin Loch lies 2 m. N. of the village and to the SE. is Dupplin Castle, built between 1828 and 1832 to replace an earlier building destroyed by fire. The Castle stands in a finely wooded park, and is the seat of Lord Forteviot, whose father, Sir John Dewar, (created Baron Forteviot in 1916), bought the estate from the Earl of Kinnoull in 1911 and in 1925 demolished the old houses and built a model village (now extended) on the site.

The Battle of Dupplin was fought in this neighbourhood on the 12th of August 1332. Edward Balliol and the "disinherited Barons", numbering some 3,000 foot and 500 horse, surprised and completely routed 30,000 men under the command of the Regent Mar; 13,000 were slain, and Balliol pursued the remnant to PERTH which capitulated.

FORT GEORGE, *Inverness-shire* (Map 5, ref. 27⁸85⁷). The fort is situated at the end of a narrow spit of land, which, with Chanonry Point on the N., divides the INVERNESS Firth from the Moray Firth. Seen from the N. and W., it is an imposing edifice.

The fort is an irregular polygon with six bastions. Built in 1748–63 to replace an earlier Fort George (built by General Wade in 1726 on Castle Hill in Inverness as part of a chain of forts in the Great Glen, including FORT WILLIAM and FORT AUGUSTUS, and blown up by the Jacobites in 1746), it is an outstanding example of 18th-cent. military architecture. It cost more than £160,000, and covered twelve acres, being defended on the landward side by a ditch, a covert way, a glacis, two lunettes, and a ravelin. It could accommodate 2,500 men, and it was the depot of the Seaforth Highlanders until 1963 when the Seaforths and the Queen's Own Cameron Highlanders were amalgamated as the Queen's Own Highlanders, a detachment of which garrisons the Fort with its Regimental Museum.

The inside of the fort belies its rather grim aspect, and you pierce the wall to find pleasant lawns overlooked by the long, low officers' buildings, in one of which Dr Johnson "made a very good figure" on the topic of manufacturing gunpowder, but afterwards confessed to Boswell that he had "talked ostentatiously".

FORTH RIVER, *Stirlingshire* SE. to *East Lothian* (Map 2, ref. 28⁹69³), is formed by two headstreams, the Duchray Water and the Avondhu, which join 1 m. W. of ABERFOYLE. The Duchray Water rises at 3,000 ft on the N. side of Ben Lomond, and has a 14-m. course before joining the Avondhu. This latter rises at 1,900 ft and flows through Loch Chon and LOCHARD. Both the parent rivers of the Forth are in fine mountainous scenery; their child for the most part meanders or widens out in flatter more prosaic surroundings.

The Forth flows, from this point of conjunction of the Duchray and Avondhu at a height of 80 ft, through a flat valley to STIRLING and beyond. The distance direct from the confluence to Stirling is $18\frac{1}{2}$ m., but measures 39 m. along the winding meanders of the river. Two important tributaries, the Teith and the Allan Water, join it above Stirling.

From here to ALLOA the distance is only $5\frac{1}{2}$ m. as the crow flies, but this stretch of river, called the "Links of Forth", measures $12\frac{1}{2}$ m. This carse land is traditionally very valuable, and gave rise to the old rhyme:

A crook o' the Forth
Is worth an earldom o' the north.

It was certainly worth more than an earldom o' the north in 1314. For it was amongst or at

Scottish Tourist Board

The Forth Bridges, road and rail

least on one side of those loops and meanders of the R. Forth that the Battle of BANNOCK-BURN was won. In this place was regained not an earldom but the Kingdom of the North.

Below Alloa the river becomes more estuarine, and opens out into the Firth of Forth. It expands here to a maximum width of 17 miles between PRESTONPANS and LEVEN – this after contracting to 1¼ m. wide at QUEENSFERRY. The firth then contracts again to 8¼ m. between DIRLETON and ELIE Ness in Fife and enters the North Sea between Fife Ness and the mouth of the R. Tyne, with a width of 17½ m.

The islands, with the exception of Inchgarvie and some rocky islets near Queensferry, are in the wider part of the firth, comprising INCH-COLM, Cramond Island, and INCHKEITH. The last is crowned by a lighthouse, and in 1881 a fort was erected. Half a dozen small islands lie off the East Lothian coast, Fidra and Craigleith being the best known, while the entrance is flanked by the BASS ROCK on the S. and the Isle of MAY on the N. In mid channel the estuary has a maximum depth of thirty-seven fathoms.

There have been many schemes for bridging or tunnelling the Firth of Forth. In 1851 Sir Thomas Bouch perfected the "floating railway" between Granton and BURNTISLAND, which enabled goods trains to be loaded on to large flat steamers. This continued successfully for many years. Then came the Forth Rail Bridge in 1890, and the Road Bridge in 1964.

The Forth, despite its Highland origins, is a Lowland waterway of immense historical importance to Scotsmen. From the days of the Romans onwards, its mere presence has affected the lives and habits of Scots people, Highland and Lowland. Any man born in EDINBURGH thinks of it in its firth form as a part of his own sea (until recently the Lord Provosts of Edinburgh held Admiral status and could, even within this century, issue pass-

ports in that capacity). The Forth and its firth are Edinburgh's sea-lung. Its islands are its own islands, familiar to all Edinburgh folk since childhood. Anyone who has sailed direct from Scotland to the Continent from the uppermost navigable portions of the Forth will not forget his sailing out, especially if he has undertaken it on a fine summer's day or evening.

Setting out from the heart of Scotland, the sight of the Highlands can be seen to the left. Later the noble silhouette of the castle-crowned Edinburgh appears to the right. Then there is the Bass Rock, and finally the Isle of May is a welcome to the open sea beyond. The pleasures of sailing "doon the watter" on the CLYDE have often been sung, but the pleasures of sailing out of the Forth from the very centre of Scotland have not been equally noted. In their own way they are just as notable.

New legislation should remove a hazard of recent years: oil slicks along the beaches of the Firth.

FORTINGALL, *Perthshire* (Map 2, ref. 27⁵74⁷), is a well-known and attractive village planned and built by Sir Donald Currie, who bought Glen Lyon House and estate in 1885.

In the churchyard is a yew tree of great age and size, now protected by a wall and railing. In 1769 Pennant reported its girth to be 56½ ft; it may well be over 2,000 years old.

At the W. end of the village is Glen Lyon House, rebuilt in 1891 but formerly the home of the Campbells. John Campbell, son of that Captain Campbell who took part in the Massacre of GLENCOE, built the first stone house on the site in 1728.

A persistent legend says that Pontius Pilate (whose father may have been a legionary in North Britain during the Roman occupation) was born at Fortingall, and that his mother was a Menzies or a MacLaren from BALQU-HIDDER! To lend plausibility to this legend, a rectangular site defended by ditches SW. of the village is referred to as the "Praetorium". It is in fact probably an early medieval fortified homestead.

Opposite the hotel is the Cairn of the Dead. A plaque records that, during a visitation of the plague in the 14th cent., the victims were buried at this spot, having been brought there on a sled drawn by a white horse and led by an old woman.

There are several important archaeological sites in the neighbourhood of the village. In the graveyard behind the yew tree is a fine example of a cup-marked stone said to have been found 8 ft below ground level. In a field between the road and the river, a short distance E. of the village, are three circles each of three standing stones. Above the farm of Balnacraig is Dun Geal, a stone ring-fort of the Iron Age similar to those in GLEN LYON. W. of the junction of the roads at Glen Lyon House, and between the Fearnan road and the river, in a wide low-lying flood plain, are a Bronze Age burial site (disc barrow) on which is a cup-marked stone that originally stood upright, a standing stone by the river, and a long earthen mound that is probably prehistoric and possibly a Neolithic burial tumulus. It is near the bridge over the R. Lyon.

FORTROSE, *Ross and Cromarty* (Map 5, ref. 27³85⁶), is a quiet resort on the BLACK ISLE facing the INVERNESS Firth. A narrow neck of land culminating in Chanonry Point with a lighthouse separates Fortrose from the outer Moray Firth. This point is only 1 m. distant from FORT GEORGE, on a spit of land S. of the firth, and a ferry used to link the two. The original name of Fortrose was Chanonry, and it was made a royal burgh in 1592. There is a golf course, and the neighbouring resort of ROSEMARKIE lies 1 m. NE.

The ruined cathedral is a mere fragment of the church founded by David I for the see of Ross. The existing remains are the S. aisle of the nave and the nearby sacristy or undercroft of the chapter house, which is probably 13th cent. The S. nave aisle is in the late 14th-cent. decorated Gothic style, while other parts are in the perpendicular style of MELROSE, the church having been completed in 1485 by Abbot Fraser, a monk of that Abbey. There is much fine detail, and among the monuments, on the N. wall, much mutilated, is the canopied tomb of Euphemia, Countess of Ross, builder of this aisle about the year 1395; and there is a later monument of a bishop. An arched compartment at the W. end is walled off as the burial-place of the Mackenzies of Seaforth. Cromwell is reputed to have used many of the stones of the already derelict building to build his fort at Inverness. In the clock-tower a bell dated 1460 is still rung daily. To the NE. is the detached chapter house, which preserved some sedilia, or seats, for the officiating clergy. In January 1880 a hoard of 1,100 silver coins was discovered buried in the cathedral green; they dated from the time of Robert III.

FORT WILLIAM, *Inverness-shire* (Map 5, ref. 21²77⁴). This important W. Highland centre, strategically placed on the eastern shore of Loch Linnhe under the shadow of BEN NEVIS, has been variously known throughout its history as Gordonsburgh, Duncansburgh, and Maryburgh. It had its origins in an earth-and-wattle fort built by General Monk in 1655 and rebuilt in stone in the reign of William III. It successfully withstood an attack during the rising of 1715, and in 1746 it held out for the Government after FORT AUGUSTUS had fallen to the Jacobites. It was demolished in 1864 to make way for a railway.

The present town, which developed largely after the coming of the railway, is mainly of Victorian and later construction. There is an urgent need for rebuilding, as the main street is a bottleneck with no by-pass between loch and hill-side. Now an important tourist centre with road and rail connections, it also serves as the terminus for steamers plying up Loch Linnhe from OBAN.

In an 18th-cent. building in Cameron Square is the West Highland Museum which contains many exhibits of local interest, including Jacobite relics.

In the neighbourhood is the pulp-mill industry at CORPACH and INVERLOCHY.

FORVIE, *Aberdeenshire* (Map 6, ref. 40²82⁷), is a former parish, 13 m. N. of ABERDEEN, that was united with SLAINS when it was overwhelmed with sands.

Dr Johnson marvelled at the fate of Forvie in 1773. Now we understand better why the calamity occurred. When the seas fell back from the land after the Ice Age, and the R. Ythan (see NEWBURGH) dwindled from a lordly flood to a shallow stream, it left great banks of silt that it was no longer able to carry beyond the coast. Dunes formed and progressed N. in a series of high parabolas on to the cliffed coastal plateau of Buchan for several miles, until the extreme edge of this little desert rested at the southern outskirts of the village of COLLIESTON. But where now the eider duck, the tern, and the grouse nest and innumerable migrant wildfowl settle, man through many millennia tilled the land and settled in a succession of hamlets, and was moved back time and again by the creeping sands. There were episodic advances of the sand. These gave rise to the many legends of catastrophe, including the tale of the Laird of Forvie whose three young daughters were rudely despoiled of their heritage, and uttered the curse:

If ever maiden's malison
Did light upon dry land,
Let naught be found on Forvie's glebes
But thistle, bent and sand.

Scottish Tourist Board

Fort William and Ben Nevis

Some 2 m. S. of Collieston, the old church of Forvie, traditionally said to have been founded by St Ninian, was partially excavated in the 19th cent., and its pre-Reformation piscina is in the National Museum of Antiquities in EDINBURGH. In 1951 Dr Sylvia Landsberg, then an Aberdeen University student of botany, discovered stone foundations. On excavation by the university geography department, they proved to mark a village of nineteen circular huts 2,000 years old. Then began a long period of further excavation and discovery, revealing many relics of the medieval village of the 13th and 14th cents. The work continues.

FOULA, *Shetland* (Map 8, ref. 39⁵14⁰), is one of the SHETLAND Northern Islands (*see* "The Shape of Scotland"). It lies 16 m. W. of Walls on the Mainland of Shetland and 35 m. N. of the nearest part of ORKNEY; it probably has a greater atmosphere of isolation than any other inhabited island off the Scottish coast. When high seas are running, the mail-boat, which should run once weekly to Walls, is restricted by the inadequacies of the island's tiny harbour, Ham Voe.

As on FAIR ISLE, this has led to a steady trend of depopulation; there are now some fifty islanders left; more than one-third are old-age pensioners. The island rises from the sea as sheer cliffs that culminate in five peaks, the highest of which is the Sneug (1,373 ft), and

on the NW. coast the Kame, the second highest sea-cliff in Britain, plunges 1,200 ft to the sea. Above Ham Voe the island shop, post office with beam radio, and school form the nucleus of one inhabited settlement, and another is grouped at Hametoon near South Ness. The bird population is of considerable interest to ornithologists and includes Arctic skuas, kittiwakes, and red-throated divers; but the most striking feature is the large colony of bonxies, or great skuas, which nest on the high ground. These large aggressive birds will, by dive-bombing flight, attack humans who approach their nest during the breeding season. One of the sights of the island is the bonxies taking their morning bath in the Mill Loch.

FOULIS CASTLE, *Ross and Cromarty* (Map 5, ref. 25⁹86⁵). Some 2½ m. SW. of EVANTON is the Clan Munro seat of Foulis Castle. The Foulis estates have been held by the Munros since early in the 12th cent., on the tenure of furnishing a snowball, if required to do so, at midsummer. They fought at BANNOCK-BURN, Halidon Hill, HARLAW, Pinkie, Fontenoy, and FALKIRK, and Robert Munro, the "Black" Baron, served under the great Gustavus of Sweden with 700 of his men, and died of wounds at Ulm in 1633. The Munro motto is "Castle Foulis in flames", and the original structure was destroyed by fire in the mid-18th cent. The present building dates from 1754–72.

Foulis Castle

This comparatively modern building (modern, that is, when one is thinking of the 12th cent.) is interesting. This "Georgian" house is not, in some of its features, an orthodox 18th-cent. mansion. The chief of the Munros at the time of the building had, according to tradition, spent much of his youth in Holland, and a certain number of Dutch elements are included. Foulis Castle is upon an ancient foundation, yet carries forward from the 18th cent. the traditional Scottish tendency to seek continental models in its construction.

FOWLIS EASTER, *Angus* (Map 6, ref. 33²73³). The township of Fowlis Easter is most noted for its restored 15th-cent. church. There is mention of a church here in 1180, but the present one was built in 1453 by Andrew, 2nd Lord Gray of Fowlis. It is dedicated to St Marnan, and measures externally 89 ft by 29 ft. There are jougs beside the SW. door.

Inside are preserved the door of the original rood-screen, four pre-Reformation paintings on oak representing the Crucifixion, the Virgin, St John the Baptist, and St Catherine, with an entombment below, and eleven saints. There is also a badly mutilated sculptured font, and (a surprising survival of the Reformation in a Presbyterian church) a tabernacle adorned with an Annunciation. Indeed, Fowlis Easter Church and its contents provide a notable and unusual feature of its kind.

In the churchyard are a cross-carved coffin slab and a plain passion cross.

FOWLIS WESTER, *Perthshire* (Map 2, ref. 29³72⁵). This quaint village lies to the N. of the CRIEFF to PERTH road, and consists of a church, manse, schoolhouse, an inn, and a few picturesque cottages.

A Pictish symbol stone stands within a railing in the village. It is 10 ft high, much eroded by the weather, but once clearly a magnificent example of Pictish sculpture. The front has a great ornamented cross, and the back a number of carved features. It is a protected Ancient Monument.

FOYERS, *Inverness-shire* (Map 5, ref. 25⁰82⁰). Immediately to the S. of this village standing on the southern side of Loch NESS lies the R. Foyers, with its famous Falls of Foyers. These waterfalls, the upper of which is 30 ft and the lower 90 ft high, have a lovely wooded setting and were formerly regarded as the most magnificent in Britain. The volume of water was much reduced when Britain's first hydro-electric scheme was installed here in 1896 for the aluminium works at the mouth of the river. These were closed down in 1968, but the North of Scotland Hydro-Electric Board installed a 5 mW. set in the power station to utilize water from Loch Mhor, 600 ft up in the hills, until a pumped storage project is completed. Near the eastern shores of Loch Mhor (which was created by uniting Lochs Garth and Farraline) is the estate of Easter Aberchalder, noted for its fine rock gardens.

Foyers is on the line of General Wade's military road linking FORT AUGUSTUS and INVERNESS, and tradition has it that the General built himself a shelter known as the "General's Hut" here. No part of it remains, and even its exact site is unknown.

FRASERBURGH, *Aberdeenshire* (Map 6, ref. 40⁰86⁷). On Kinnaird Head (see KINNAIRDS), the castle, converted into a lighthouse, forms the pivot around which Fraserburgh is built. A little rocky mound with a shelter upon it, where you may sit and contemplate both, is all that separates the lighthouse from the busy harbour. Behind them stretches the "sea-washed town between the flat land of the plain and the brief rock". Kinnaird was the "hill of watch" from which Alexander Fraser, the 7th Laird of Philorth, kept an eye on his creation. "Whereas," says the charter granted in 1546, "Alexander Fraser of Philorth, for the convenience of his neighbours has built a harbour upon the seashore in which ships overtaken by storms may be able to find refuge, we erect the town of Faithlie into a free burgh of barony. . . ." At that time there was no castle. It was built by his grandson soon after he succeeded to the barony in 1569, when he continued the work of town-building with the erection of "public buildings and fine streets". Three more charters followed, the last of which refers to "the town now called Fraserburgh" and empowers Fraser to build and endow a university.

Only the central tower (on a rectangular plan, but much altered) of the castle that the 8th Sir Alexander Fraser built in 1570 remains today. Four floors of the original house survive, but the fifth was removed in 1787 to make way for the lantern-chamber of Kinnaird Head lighthouse, the first to be built by the Commissioners of Northern Lights. But, if the castle itself has been changed almost out of recognition, the Wine Tower, on its rock at the foot

The Scotsman

The harbour, Fraserburgh

of the castle wynd, is virtually unaltered and is therefore the oldest house in Fraserburgh, for it dates from the 16th cent. and was built at the same time as, if not before, the castle. Its romantic name is a cheat; it cannot have been built as a "wine store", whether or no it was used for that purpose in after years. It was probably a watch-tower against the menace of seaborne invasion.

Fraserburgh University was erected in 1595 with a grant from the Scottish Parliament. Unfortunately the first principal incurred King James VI's displeasure by taking part in the General Assembly of 1605; he was placed under arrest, and in his absence the infant seat of learning collapsed and never recovered.

Despite its exposed position, modern Fraserburgh is a most attractive and finely planned town with a long sandy beach to the E. In the past 160 years its population has risen from under 2,000 to over 10,000. In 1914 it had a fleet of over 200 herring drifters. Today the big decline in the herring industry has been closely balanced by the compensatory development of white fishing and by food-processing plants; at the same time, its machine tool industry employs about 1,000 workers.

FRESWICK, *Caithness* (Map 7, ref. 33⁷96⁷). Freswick Bay is one of the few places along the Caithness coast, where the plateau, instead of ending abruptly with high sheer cliffs, descends softly to wide stretches of sandy beach. Freswick village is slightly inland on the road from WICK to JOHN O' GROATS, and from Warth Hill 2 m. N. can be glimpsed a fine view of the distant ORKNEY ISLANDS. The prehistoric cairn on the summit of Warth Hill must have measured 40 ft in diameter, within a double row of large blocks, at its second

millennium B.C. origin. It encased a central primary cist containing a crouched skeleton with no grave goods, and a secondary cist 3 ft away containing an uncremated burial.

Beyond Ness Head, which shelters Freswick Bay to the S., are the ruins of Bucholly Castle. There are traditions, quoted by Pennant, the early Scottish travel writer, that the original castle was built in 1155, and was occupied in the 12th cent. by a Danish nobleman. It became the seat of the Mowat family around 1300.

FRIOCKHEIM, *Angus* (Map 6, ref. 35⁹74⁹). The name of this village is pronounced "Freecum", and is said to be derived from Freke, a one-time baillie of FORFAR, and "heim", meaning home, the suffix having been added in 1830 by one John Anderson who had lived in Germany. Friockheim was founded about 1830 when the estate of Middleton granted cheap feus to operatives connected with textile manufactures. The village still has the same industry with a factory for making candlewick bedspreads.

FURNACE, *Argyll* (Map 1, ref. 20³70⁰). This small township on the N. side of Loch Fyne took its name from local iron-smelting work in the early 19th cent., but it is now best known for the large granite quarry of Dun Leacainn, started in 1841. There were famous "blasts" at the quarry in 1871, September 1876, and September 1880. The quarry is again working to produce material for roads.

FYVIE, *Aberdeenshire* (Map 6, ref. 37⁰83⁵). Fyvie Castle, in the parish of that name and close to the village of Fyvie in a pleasant wooded vale of the R. Ythan, was described by

Fyvie Castle: the wheel stair

Sir Herbert Maxwell as "the crowning glory of Scottish baronial architecture". It has a S. front 150 ft long with a full-sized, angle-turreted tower-house at each end, and an immense gatehouse tower projecting from the centre. This great façade has often been likened to that of a French château, and French influence in the design has been suggested. But there is no real evidence for this supposed borrowing. Fyvie is a purely Scottish creation that took its final form as the result of the combined inventions of five dynasties of lairds (the Prestons, the Meldrums, the Setons, the Gordons, and the Leiths), each of which has a tower or wing named after it – though it does not follow that they were its "onlie begetters". Indeed, recent discoveries have shown that the architectural history of this impressive pile – at present the home of Sir Ian Forbes-Leith, the Lord Lieutenant of Aberdeenshire – is extremely complicated.

The tradition is that the oldest part, the Preston Tower, was built about 1400 by Sir Harry Preston, who captured the English knight Ralph Percy at the Battle of Otterburn in 1388, and received the lands of Fyvie as part of the reward for the ransom of Percy. Preston died in 1433. He had two daughters: Mariota,

who was the ancestress of Lord Leith and the present-day Laird, and her sister, who married Alexander Meldrum. Meldrums inherited the Castle and built the Meldrum Tower. The Castle remained in their hands for 163 years until, in 1596, they sold the lands and barony of Fyvie to Alexander Seton, Lord Urquhart, afterwards the 1st Earl of Dunfermline. Dunfermline, who was Lord High Chancellor of Scotland, built the Seton Tower as we know it today, but, as a result of discoveries made by Dr W. Douglas Simpson in 1962, we now realize that the lower part of the tower is much older than the Seton dynasty's appearance. Many windows and gun-loops and a full range of battlements have been uncovered, which Lord Dunfermline's masterly reconstruction had hidden from view for over 300 years. It was, however, Lord Dunfermline who gave the Castle the appearance that has made it architecturally renowned, and he also gave it the wonderful wheel stair that is the chief glory of the interior.

"Fyvie lands lie broad and wide, and O but they lie bonny," says one of the innumerable versions of the ballad "Mill o' Tifty's Annie". It is a beauty that yields its full measure when the visitor is prepared to spend a quiet hour or wo in and around the modern village and up and down the vale of the Ythan from the Den of Rothie to the Braes of Fetterletter. On the arm of Lewes near the village is the Priory Cross, a monument erected in 1868 to mark the site of the ancient Priory of St Mary, founded in 1179. In 1937 the aqueduct that carried the water-supply of the monks of St Mary's was uncovered by workmen making an augmentation to the present village water-supply.

In the centre of the village, just behind the market cross, is a large boulder of white quartz called the Buchan Stone. It marks the boundary between the Earldom of Buchan and the Thanage of Formartine, which here does not follow the course of the Ythan exactly. Formartine, the territory between the DON and the Ythan, is said to have been given its name (anciently spelt Fermartyn) by St Ninian from Candida Casa, in honour of his spiritual mentor, St Martin of Tours.

Lower down the Ythan, between Fyvie and the village of Methlick, are the picturesque Braes of Gight, with the ruins of Gight Castle, the stronghold of the Gordons of Gight, whose last laird was the mother of Lord Byron. Her spendthrift husband, "mad Jack" Byron, ensured that the prophecy of Thomas the Rhymer would be fulfilled:

When the heron leaves the tree
The lairds o' Gight sall landless be.

There was at one time a great heronry here, but the herons deserted it and flew across the Ythan to nest in the lands of the earls of Aberdeen at Haddo.

GAILES, *Ayrshire* (Map 2, ref. 23³63⁵). A whistle-stop on the AYR–GLASGOW railway line, in the midst of desolate sandy machair, Gailes is known for golf courses and army camps. The Western Gailes course is deservedly famous for the high quality of its turf.

GAIRLOCH, *Ross and Cromarty* (Map 5, ref. 18¹87⁶), is a village, now a touring and holiday centre, on Gair Loch, that wide arm of the sea that is almost a bay. Amidst some of the best W. Highland scenery, Gairloch looks W. over the bay to the distant "Long Island" (the Outer Hebrides), with the majestic hills of TORRIDON to the SW., while Flowerdale towers behind the village. The small harbour is now used by fishing-boats, and there are fine beaches for bathing, especially at Big Sand 3 m. NW. on the road to the crofting township of Melvaig, lying 8 miles NW., from which a path leads to the Rudha Reidh lighthouse.

Flowerdale House was the seat of the Mackenzies of Gairloch, and was described as Tigh Dige by Osgood Mackenzie, that remarkable 19th-cent. Highland Gaelic-speaking laird and "character", in his *Hundred Years in the Highlands*.

The attractive village of Badachro, 6 m. (by road) to the SW., is in a bay sheltered by Horrisdale Island.

The main attractions of Gairloch are angling, sea fishing, stalking, and bird-watching.

GALASHIELS, *Selkirkshire* (Map 3, ref. 34⁹63⁷). Situated on both sides of the GALA WATER, and pleasantly and spaciously laid out, Galashiels is a busy Border manufacturing town, noted especially for tweeds and woollen hosiery. Wool-mills were in existence here as long ago as 1622, but main developments came in the 19th cent. with the building of the first Scottish carding-machine nearby in 1790. The Scottish Woollen Technical College was founded here in 1909, and is the centre for wool studies in Scotland. Incidentally, the word "tweed" in connection with the wool industry has nothing to do with the river, for it is a misprint of the word "tweels" – the Border name for woollen fabrics.

The mercat cross in the town dates from 1695. The war memorial comprises a fine statue of a mounted Border "Riever", or moss-trooper, with the massive clock-tower behind, designed by Sir Robert Lorimer. The granting of a charter in 1599 is celebrated annually in the early summer with the "Braw Lads' Gathering", in which a mounted procession goes to various parts of the district, including ABBOTSFORD. The town crest can be seen on the NW. façade of the municipal buildings, and shows a fox trying to reach plums hanging on a tree, with the motto "Sour Plums". This commemorates a Border foray of 1337, when some English soldiers were caught while picking wild plums, and were killed.

On the S. side of the town is Old Gala House, a 15th-cent. mansion, now the headquarters of the Gala Art Club.

The "common riding" at Galashiels
Scottish Tourist Board

A short distance SE. of the town on the MELROSE road, near Langlee, is a tablet recording Sir Walter Scott's last journey to Abbotsford on his return from Italy in 1832, shortly before his death.

A little NW. lies the fort and broch of Torwoodlea. The fort is a ruinous structure, measuring 450 ft by 350 ft inside. A broch was built on the inner rampart, probably after the Roman occupation ceased in A.D. 100; it was knocked down when the Romans returned in A.D. 140.

A stretch of the ancient earthwork known as the "Picts' Work Ditch" or the "Catrail" can be seen on the high ground to the W. of the town. This dyke extended S. over many miles; where it is now most distinct it is about 25 ft broad, with 12-ft-thick ramparts on each side standing 6 ft high, but it varies greatly, and there is no general agreement about its purpose. On the slopes of Buckholm Hill to the N. of the town stands Old Buckholm Tower, now roofless.

About 2½ m. S. of Galashiels are the striking remains of the Rink Fort. There appears to have been an early oval settlement, followed by a circular enclosure, 200 ft in diameter, formed by two concentric ramparts; there are ruins of a massive stone wall on the inside rampart.

GALA WATER, *Midlothian/Selkirkshire* (Map 3, ref. 34⁴64⁷). This river runs 21 m. from its source in the Moorfoot hills in Midlothian before joining the TWEED near MELROSE. The road S. from EDINBURGH follows the valley of the river through STOW and GALASHIELS.

Gala Water is also the name of one of eight Midlothian District Councils and covers a large but slightly populated area.

GALLOWAY, Mull of, *Wigtownshire* (Map 2, ref. 21⁵53¹). This precipitous headland forms the southernmost point of Scotland. Ireland is only 26 m. away, and the Isle of Man 22½ m.; both can be seen on a clear day.

The Mull rises to 210 ft above sea-level, being separated from the main peninsula of the Rhinns by a neck of low land, which is accentuated by a trench, probably of Viking origin. On the tip stands a 60-ft lighthouse built in 1828–30; 128 steps lead down to a fog-horn on a railed terrace that provides a fine viewpoint.

The Mull and the Rhinns in general have always been remote, and the people until recently preserved many old customs and beliefs. The place-names all down the western side of the Rhinns attest a settlement of Ulster Cruithne crofter-fishers in the 4th and 5th cents.

According to local tradition, Sawney Bane, the Scottish cannibal, and his tribe of post-medieval times, lived in a cave on the Mull (but the Ayrshire folk, oddly enough, claim him for Carrick). It is said that the "last defence" of the Picts against the Scots took place here. There is, of course, no evidence of this, but as late as Victorian times there was a popular legend that the last Pict leapt off the Mull clutching to his bosom the formula for heather ale.

About ½ m. N. of the narrow neck, on the Luce Bay shore, is St Medan's Cave and Chapel, the chapel being built into the cave. It has yielded to excavation slates, pilgrim badges, and a sandstone statue of the Virgin (or possibly the saint herself). The excavators had been employed by the Marquess of Bute who had set them to work in 1872. This young nobleman had but recently adhered, and amidst much controversy in the GLASGOW press, to the Catholic religion. This was to have an unfortunate effect on the results of his excavations at the Mull of Galloway. The day between the end of the excavations and the moving of the finds to Glasgow was a Sunday and an anti-Catholic crowd from STRANRAER threw the lot into the sea.

St Medana, after whom this parish, Kirkmaiden, is named, has another Kirkmaiden church across Luce Bay; traditionally she crossed to the Mull on a floating rock.

Several miles out in Luce Bay the great gannetry of Big Scar and its neighbouring rocks can be seen.

GALSTON, *Ayrshire* (Map 2, ref. 25⁰63⁷). This was the first of the "valley burghs": Galston, NEWMILNS, and DARVEL. Lying 5 m. E. of KILMARNOCK, in the upper Irvine Valley, Galston has little attraction as a town. Originally it was engaged in mining and cotton-weaving, but now the local pits are exhausted and the mills are the main source of employment. Burn Anne, flowing through the town, is noted for two reasons, first as a source of agates and jaspers, which are still found in quantities, and second as a good example of the anglicization of a Gaelic place-name, Anne being the rendering of "Abhainn", pronounced Ahan and meaning "river". Loudoun Castle, the seat of the former hereditary sheriffs of Ayrshire, and at one time one of the most imposing houses in the W. of Scotland, is near the town. It was largely destroyed by fire in 1941. Loudoun Golf Club, which claims to be the oldest in Scotland, has its course in part of the castle policies.

GARDENSTOWN, *Banffshire* (Map 6, ref. 38⁰86⁴). The Bay of Gamrie in which this village lies is a geological sport in which old red sandstone usurps the domain of clay slates. As spectacle, it is the high point of a 15-m. stretch of coastline of peculiar character that begins with MACDUFF and ends on the western outskirts of ROSEHEARTY. In this world apart, cliffs are not merely cliffs. They are mountainous green ledges that rise in waves out of the plain of Buchan and soar as high as 600 ft to confront the Moray Firth. Only at three points – at Aberdour, PENNAN, and Gamrie Bay – is the resulting wall of rock sufficiently broken to permit of human settlement.

It is 120 years since Alexander Whyte, the parochial schoolmaster of Gamrie, described Gardenstown, but no one has ever done it better. "At the bottom of the bay," he says, "the rocks, which are steep and rugged on either side, retire a little, leaving room for the village of Gardenstown *and no more*, and then they rise with just as much bend from the perpendicular as allows mould to lie upon them, which is closely covered with green grass, except here and there a winding foot-path like a staircase, on which few can venture without fear and trembling. . . . So abrupt is the rising of the ground that a house of three stories has them all ground floors, one entrance being at the front, another at the back and a third at the end. On the east side of the Bay the little village of Crovie lies about a mile from Gardenstown, with one gable-end of the houses to the sea and the other to the land – and this last is bored into the bank – like a brood of young seafowl, nestling with their heads under their dam. Nearly at the same distance on the west side stands the old church and churchyard, on a ledge of the hill's brow, which one would think in equal danger of being smothered by the hill hanging over it, and of being undermined by the sea below."

It is on the site of this ruined Church of St John the Evangelist, whose gable bears the startlingly improbable date 1004, that the human annals of Gamrie open with an invasion of horsemen.

The invaders were forced to a last stand and cut down to a man. "The Bloody Pits" is still the name of the site of the massacre. An observer who had visited the Kirk of St John, before it was abandoned as a place of worship in 1832, wrote: "I have seen the Norsemen's skulls grinning horrid and hollow in the wall where they had been fixed directly east of the pulpit". After the church was abandoned, the heads were pilfered bit by bit by sightseers, although one was recovered and placed in Banff Museum. There is of course an anonymity about skulls that renders their identification difficult.

Now roofless, the church of Gamrie has not been allowed to fall to pieces altogether. Indeed, a workman has inscribed on cement in a shored-up plaque: "Built 1004, repaired 1961". But the oldest authentic monument inside commemorates "an honourable man, Patrick Barclay, laird of Tolly, and Janet Oglivy his spouse, who died January 6, 1547".

The village of Gardenstown was founded by Alexander Garden of Troup in the year 1720. By 1842 the Rev. Thomas Wilson, the third in the direct line of his family to be minister of the parish, presided over a community in which an intense family spirit had developed. "With few exceptions," we are told, "the

families of the whole of the farms on the estate of Troup are related in some way to each other. This system of clanship is carried still farther among the fishing population of the villages, most of whom in Crovie or Gardenstown are of the name of Watt or Wiseman, so that they are obliged to have recourse to nicknames for the sake of distinction." This is still roughly true today. Gardenstown itself now has a population of 1,000. Ever since the traditional *Fifie* and *Zulu* fishing boats were superseded by steam drifters, the majority of Gardenstown men have sailed from Macduff or FRASER-BURGH, but they remain Gardenstown men for all that. Between thirty and thirty-five motor fishing-vessels are locally owned, and it has been estimated that, with an annual income of £500,000 a year, Gardenstown is one of the richest fishing villages in Scotland. Names of boats pass down from generation to generation. It is estimated that half of the village population belong to the Plymouth Brethren, either "Close" or "Open". As at TOBERMORY, enormous letters proclaim at the harbour entrance "God is Love".

A good centre for salmon fishing; it has a picturesque hotel and some excellent shops.

GARELOCHHEAD, *Dunbartonshire* (Map 2, ref. 22⁴69¹). This well-known resort at the head of Gare Loch (the Gare Loch comparatively near GLASGOW, and not to be confused with Gair Loch in Ross and Cromarty) is a popular centre for yachting and is also used as an anchorage for naval vessels.

A steamer service used to call at Gareloch-head until the Second World War. In 1853 the incursions of this public steamer was responsible for the so-called "Battle of Gareloch-head", when Sir James Colquhoun of Luss, with the help of his gamekeepers, unsuccessfully attempted to stop trippers from an excursion landing on Sunday.

GARGUNNOCK, *Stirlingshire* (Map 2, ref. 27¹69⁴). A small village on the slopes of the Gargunnock Hills, Gargunnock looks N. over the carse and valley of the FORTH. The highest point of the hills (1,591 ft) has an excellent view.

About ½ m. E. of the village is Gargunnock House, built in the 16th and 18th cents. and now occupied as flats. It was originally designed in the 16th cent. as an L-shaped tower-house. The 18th-cent. additions included the 1794 classical S. front, which blended well with the original. The sundial in the garden has the arms of Sir James Campbell of Ardkinglass with the date 1731.

GARLETON HILLS, *East Lothian* (Map 3, ref. 34⁸67⁸). This is a range of porphyrite hills to the N. of HADDINGTON. The highest point is 590 ft. The western spur of the hills is crowned by the monument to John, 4th Earl of

Hopetoun (1766–1823), the Peninsular War hero who took command of the British Army when Sir John Moore fell at Corunna. Despite the fact that its eminence is by Scottish standards not very great, the column is a conspicuous landmark visible throughout East Lothian, and the view from the base is very fine. It was erected in 1824.

GARLIESTON, *Wigtownshire* (Map 2, ref. 24⁸54⁷), is a small port on Garlieston Bay, an inlet of Wigtown Bay, founded about 1760 by John, 7th Earl of Galloway (Lord Garlies). About 1 m. S. of the village is Galloway House, formerly the seat of the earls of Galloway, and now a school. It was built in 1740, and has well-wooded policies.

About 1 m. to the NE. on the cliffs is the ruin of Eggerness Castle; 3 m. S., also on the cliff-top are the remains of Cruggleton Castle, chief seat of the semi-independent Fergus, later a stronghold of the Comyns, and modified in the 16th cent. against artillery. A little inland is the old Cruggleton church, now a potato store, but in good condition; it is a very early Romanesque building dating to the 12th cent. It was restored by the late Marquess of Bute.

GARMOUTH, *Moray* (Map 6, ref. 33³86⁴). Now but a village on the left bank of the SPEY, Garmouth is about 1 m. from the sea. Formerly it was a port, but the river-channel now changes too often for use. At one time, however, it had a considerable timber trade in the export of tree trunks floated down the Spey from ROTHIEMURCHUS and GLENMORE forests. Charles II landed here from Holland on the 23rd of June 1650, and a plaque on a cottage commemorates the place where he signed the Solemn League and Covenant. This signature he later regarded as being made under duress. Whether or no he was right, it was to cost him much vexation, and his Scottish subjects much suffering, after the Restoration.

Down-river, about 1 m. away, lies Kingston – founded in 1784 by two Yorkshiremen who came to buy timber, and named it after Kingston-upon-Hull. The village was badly threatened by erosion. That threat has now passed. The new mouth of the R. Spey at Tugnet has removed it. Kingston-upon-Spey was a great 18th- and early 19th-cent. ship-building centre, with several yards on the Spey, where many large sailing-vessels were built.

GARTCOSH, *Lanarkshire* (Map 2, ref. 26⁴67⁰). Over 1,000 men are employed in the Gartcosh Steel Works in this town 3 m. SW. of COATBRIDGE. The steel-rolling mills are a part of the Colville Group. There is also a brick-works, which was the main source of employment for this area in the 19th cent.

GARTMORE, *Perthshire* (Map 2, ref. 25³69⁷). This village in the upper FORTH valley, between the Forth river and Kelty Water is primarily known for Gartmore House just to the NE. of it. Now a school, it was formerly the home of the Graham family. The last laird was Robert Bontine Cunninghame Graham (1852–1936). More will be said about this remarkably attractive Scottish figure (so unlike the usual conception of a dour Scot) under MENTEITH and INCHMAHOME. This perhaps is the place to remind the reader, if such a reminder is necessary, that not only was Cunninghame Graham a Scottish-Spanish aristocratic laird, member of the Labour party and subsequently a founder of the Scottish National Party, but that he was also an eminent writer.

GARTOCHARN, *Dunbartonshire* (Map 2, ref. 24²68⁶). The village of Gartocharn, partly a dormitory village for GLASGOW, lies about 1 m. from the SE. shores of Loch LOMOND, and stands below Duncryne, an abrupt conical hill that rises to 462 ft from a base of about two acres. There is a path to the summit, from which is an excellent view of Strathendrick, the Vale of Leven, and Loch Lomond.

On the shores of the loch is Ross Priory,

A Cistercian monk welding at Nunraw Abbey
J. Partridge

D. McCrae

*Near Garvald: monks working above the new
abbey at Nunraw*

where Sir Walter Scott stayed and wrote parts
of *Lady of the Lake* and *Rob Roy*. There is a
notable yew avenue in the grounds.

GARVALD, *East Lothian* (Map 3, ref.
35⁹67¹), is a small intimate village of considerable architectural and natural charm
lying on the northern slopes of the Lammermuir Hills, and situated in a steep valley on the
Papana Water. The church dates partly from
the 12th cent., and has a sundial dated 1633,
and also ancient jougs attached to the W.
gable. The church, the cottages, and the houses
in the village are built of the attractive deep
rose-coloured East Lothian stone. Of recent
years, however, Garvald has been associated
with a new venture, the roots of which nonetheless lie locally and deeply in the past.

Just above the village to the E. stands a
15th-cent. fortified mansion, restored in a
typically Victorian style in 1864. It was established originally by Cistercian nuns. A magnificent painted ceiling dating from 1610 remains,
part of which has been removed to the National
Museum of Antiquities in EDINBURGH.

The house now belongs once again to the
Cistercian order, and the white-habited Trap-
pists came in 1946 to establish their first
monastery in Scotland since the Reformation.
In 1952 on Easter Monday, and 814 years after
the Easter Monday when the Cistercians began
the building of their first monastery in Scotland
at MELROSE, the first sod was cut, and the

thirty-five-year task of building the Abbey of
Sancta Maria begun. The new Abbey has now
been built; it stands just to the NE. of the old
house of Nunraw. The Cistercians of Sancta
Maria Abbey in Nunraw sustain their order's
custom of hospitality. They are farmers as well
as builders, have reclaimed waste moorland,
and are well liked in this predominantly
Protestant farming district.

GARVE, *Ross and Cromarty* (Map 5, ref.
24⁰86¹). This village, in dramatic scenery, has a
railway station on the line between DINGWALL
and KYLE OF LOCHALSH, and is the point at
which both road and rail split off for ULLA-
POOL. It is a good centre for touring and
fishing. Forestry is gradually encroaching on
the bare moors.

There are several hydro-electric schemes in
the district, as the high, central situation makes
it a catchment area for rivers flowing E. and W.

GARVELLOCHS, *Argyll* (Map 1, ref.
16⁵71⁰). This name is given to a chain of small
islands nearly 3 m. long at the entrance to the
Firth of Lorne W. of LUING; they are also
called the Isles of the Sea. On Eileach-an-
Naoimh, the most south-western island, is a
very interesting group of Celtic monastic
remains, including beehive cells, a chapel, and
graveyard. It is associated in local tradition
with St Brendan and St Columba, and may be
the "Hinba" to which Adamnan says St

Columba frequently retired for meditation. The northern island of the group has the ruins of Dun Chonaill castle, which was inhabited in the 13th cent.

Access is by hired motor boat from Luing or EASDALE, and landing can only be made in favourable weather conditions.

GATEHOUSE OF FLEET, *Kirkcud-brightshire* (Map 2, ref. 26°55⁷). This small Galloway town lies surrounded by exception-ally fine scenery on the Water of Fleet near its mouth on Fleet Bay, an inlet of Wigtown Bay. General Roy's map of 1759 shows a single house on the main road where the town now stands; "gate" means a road – hence the name Gatehouse. The town flourished around 1800, with a variety of light industries (one cotton factory still stands above Fleet Bridge as a picturesque ivy-covered ruin), and tried to become a commercial port, but stagnated during the 19th cent. and lost its industries.

The large clock-tower of Craignair granite (75 ft high) that dominates the main street was built in 1871. The main town has been com-pared in its plan to a miniature of the New Town of EDINBURGH.

Robert Burns is reputed to have composed "Scots Wha Ha'e" on the nearby moors, and to have written the song down in a room in the Murray Arms Hotel.

Near the town are the CALLY Hotel and CARDONESS CASTLE, and Trustee's Hill with its Pictish symbols on the native rock near the Rutherford Monument, erected to a famous scholar and writer on religion who held the parish in the early 17th cent.

Anworth Church nearby has a late Dark Age cross in its churchyard. The surrounding countryside is full of archaeological interest, such as the early Christian site on the Skyre Burn, and many groups of cup-and-ring marks, stone circles, and cairns, all within 3 or 4 m. Palace Yard at Enrick, 1 m. on the DUMFRIES side of the town, is a medieval, moated manor on which can be seen the foundations of the palace of the last Bishops of Galloway before the Reformation. About ½ m. above Gatehouse

Gatehouse of Fleet

Scottish Tourist Board

is the site of a small 1st-cent. Roman fort beside the Fleet.

There are large caravan parks at Sandgreen and Auchenlarie on the two flanks of Fleet Bay.

From the early years of this century, Gate-house o' Fleet has been much frequented by the Galloway School of Scottish artists. In this respect it is second only to KIRKCUDBRIGHT itself.

GIFFORD, *East Lothian* (Map 3, ref. 35³66⁸). Situated on the Gifford Water, with fine views S. to the Lammermuirs, this 18th-cent. village formerly had many small indus-tries, including linen-weaving and paper-making, and the Bank of Scotland notes were made from Gifford paper in the early 18th cent. However, all the industries, and the three big livestock fairs, have died out, and the village is now noted for its peacefulness and old-world charm.

The present church was built in 1708–10. It contains a 15th-cent. bell and a 17th-cent. pulpit; the church replaced a 13th-cent. Collegiate Church that is now a family burial vault in the grounds of YESTER HOUSE. This old church is well preserved and has many monuments of the Tweeddale family. The village has retained its mercat cross.

A famous personality connected with Gifford is the Rev. John Witherspoon (1722–94) who was born in the manse and emigrated to America. He became first President of New Jersey College (now Princeton University) and was one of the signatories of the American Declaration of Independence.

A narrow hilly road leads S. from Gifford into the Lammermuirs, ascending to 1,346 ft at Newlands Hill, with fine views of the Lothians. On this way out of the village, travellers may note a reed-fringed mere, rather than loch or lake, by the S. gate of Yester. This contains what is for anglers a curiosity. Nearly all the books on angling say that that strongest fight-ing fish, the carp, is not to be found in the British Isles N. of Burton-on-Trent. This is not true. This mere by Yester is full of strong and lusty carp. There is the inevitable theory that they found their way there in the old days of monasteries. Be that as it may, these carp are undoubtedly the most northern of their species in the United Kingdom.

GIGHA, Island of, *Argyll* (Map 1, ref. 16⁵65⁰) is one of the Inner Hebrides (*see* "The Shape of Scotland"). It lies about 3 m. W. of Kintyre, and is one of the most fertile of the islands, its name being properly interpreted as "Isle of God". Despite insular limitations, it is a prosperous dairy-farming centre. The island is well-known for the garden of Achamore, the home of Sir James Horlick. Azaleas, rhododen-drons, ornamental trees, and hydrangeas are among the tender plants that flourish here, protected from Atlantic winds by shelter belts

Gifford village

of trees. Achamore House, built in 1884, contains a collection of 18th-cent. English furniture and works of art. The island, which is only 6 m. long by 1½ m. wide, can be reached by the ISLAY steamer from West Loch Tarbert, or by ferry from Tayinloan. There are attractive sandy beaches on the E. coast, but little holiday accommodation is available. The island is also associated with the name of the Rev. Kenneth Macleod, its minister at the end of the last century and till the '20s of this. He was a noted Gaelic scholar from whom Mrs Kennedy Fraser got much material for her famous *Songs of the Hebrides*.

GIRVAN, *Ayrshire* (Map 2, ref. 21⁸59⁷). This is a pleasant and prosperous holiday resort 21 m. S. of AYR, lying on the coast road at the mouth of the R. Girvan. The origins of the place go back to prehistoric times, when it appears to have been of considerable importance. Knockcushion, which overlooks the harbour, was once a fort-hill and latterly a "moat" of justice and jurisdiction. The town is an important fishing centre for the CLYDE herring fleet, although its trade is being eroded by the better facilities at Ayr. The building of ring-net drifters is a main industry here. Girvan has much to offer the sportsman visitor, particularly the angler, being within easy reach of the R. Girvan and the R. Stinchar, and of at least one good loch. The R. Girvan affords probably

the best sea-trout fishing in the W. of Scotland, and, although much of it is privately owned, tickets may be obtained for one or two fine stretches. About 2 m. S. of the town is Ardmillan House, a 16th-cent mansion where Mary Queen of Scots really did stay (in August 1563).

GLADSMUIR, *East Lothian* (Map 3, ref. 34⁶67³), is a small village on the main trunk road to the W. of HADDINGTON. The brisk and Highland Jacobite victory over General Cope in 1745 was sometimes called the victory at Gladsmuir, but more accurately it is known as the Battle of PRESTONPANS.

Dr William Robertson, the Scottish historian of EDINBURGH's Golden Age, was minister of Gladsmuir for fifteen years and wrote his *History of Scotland* here. He later became Principal of Edinburgh University, and died in 1793.

George Heriot, the "jingling Geordie" of James VI's reign and wealthy philanthropist who founded George Heriot's School in Edinburgh, is claimed as a native of Gladsmuir; his family certainly came from there.

In the 17th cent. the Gladsmuir area became notorious for witchcraft. A tree near Penston in the neighbourhood was reputed to be their gathering-point. It is said that thirteen witches were burnt at the stake here in 1661.

Coal-mining in this area dates back over 500 years; there are records of pits at Gladsmuir in 1531.

GLAMIS, *Angus* (Map 6, ref. 33⁸74⁶), is probably best known for its literary, if historically vague, association with Shakespeare's *Macbeth.* The present Castle, which dates predominantly from the last quarter of the 17th cent., contains fragments of much earlier building, and the site is thought to have been occupied by a royal residence in the 11th cent. King Robert II granted the lands of Glamis to the Lyon family (Earls of Strathmore) in 1372. Queen Elizabeth the Queen Mother spent much of her childhood here, and Princess Margaret, Countess of Snowdon, was born in the Castle in 1930. It has fine collections of armour, furnishings, paintings, and tapestries.

By way of contrast, the Angus Folk Collection in Kirkwynd cottages in the village of Glamis reflects the countryman's mode of life in this neighbourhood over the past 200 years. The village jougs are preserved near the churchyard gate, and an ancient sculptured stone stands in the grounds of the manse. There are other sculptured stones at Eassie Church 2½ m. N., and near Coassans farm, some 2 m. to the W.

GLASGOW, *Lanarkshire* (Map 2, ref. 25⁸66⁴).

IN THE PAST; AND FROM WITHOUT

The first thing to be said about Glasgow is that it is an entity of long repute. Its diocese, of which Glasgow Cathedral is the seat, was established by papal consecration in 1136. In 1950 Glasgow University sent out invitations for the chief seats of learning in the world to send representatives to the celebration, in the following year, of its 500th anniversary. Perhaps some of the more venerable amongst these learned institutions may have been surprised to learn that this teeming industrial centre of the North had an academic history going back half a millennium. They ought not to have been.

But more than half a millennium before 1451, when her University was founded, Glasgow was a place of note at the crucial ford on the then shallow but important R. CLYDE, associated with the early saint now usually known as St Mungo. This was as far back as about A.D. 540. "About" that date! As a well-known historian of Glasgow has pointed out, in referring to the romantic quality of Glasgow's soft light and changing colours, "If a faint mist of romance hangs about Glasgow's origins, this is, perhaps, very much as it should be".

Glasgow's ancient origins, which make the capital city of EDINBURGH, for all her antique and statuesque beauty, appear something of a new arrival on the Scottish scene, have helped to contribute to the mixed racial sources of her people. Added to this cause, there has been, of course, the geographical position of Glasgow. It is in the lap of the Lowlands yet at the back door of the W. Highlands. It has been, since it became a navigable port well over a century and a half ago, at the head of Scotland's most important river and firth. It has looked out to the W. by water and by sea, and has invited the world into Scotland by its W. door.

Ever since she became a great trading city in the 18th cent., and later a great industrial centre, the world has accepted that invitation. Highlanders and Lowlanders from Scotland, Irishmen from across the sea in great numbers in the last century, Englishmen from the South in lesser numbers – all these, with a distinct infusion from the 19th-cent. Continent of Europe, have helped to make the character of Glasgow's population. But (and this is an important point) they have been themselves absorbed in that character. They have been as much absorbed in the character of the place they have come to as the Viking raiders were when, 1,000 years ago, they became absorbed into the Gaeldom of the Hebrides.

The Glasgow character of the inhabitants of the modern city (men, women, and children) is indefinable, yet it is as pervasive as garlic in a salad. Or – should you be averse to that delicious root – as recognizable as the scent of an orange straight from its Mediterranean tree. Jaunty, humorous, dogged, sardonic, self-assertive, tender, down-to-earth – a further dozen seemingly contradictory epithets could apply; and not one of them, nor yet all of them in a row, would suffice. The only thing to do is to mix them all together, shake them well, and something – only something – of the Glasgow character will emerge.

There are not many more large European cities that indelibly stamp the character of all their natives. Edinburgh, for instance, Glasgow's nearest great neighbour, is entirely composed of individuals. There are Edinburgh characteristics, of course, but there is no one overwhelming Edinburgh character. It is perhaps significant that Sir Walter Scott (an Edinburgh man, if ever there was one), despite his excellent Edinburgh portraits in his novels, never surpassed his creation of the Glasgow Bailie Nicol Jarvie as the prototype of the Scottish city-dweller.

Before anything more is said, let it be admitted that the writer of these introductory remarks on Glasgow's history and Glasgow's place in Scotland is an Edinburgh man, one who constantly visits Glasgow, who has briefly lived there, who loves the place, yet who feels a foreigner there. The Glasgow character is too potent for him to pretend to assimilate it, or for him to aspire to be assimilated by it. He recognizes the character of Glasgow as distinctive and, in its own kind, as unmistakable as that of Vienna, of Warsaw, or of those few remaining indigenously Cockney parts of London. He recognizes it as soon as he sets foot upon the platform of a Glasgow railway station. But, Scotsman and near neighbour of

Glasgow University

Glasgow though he is, he would no more claim to be of that character than he would assert himself to be a Varsovian, a Viennese, or a Cockney. Glasgow has created much, but it is in select company in having created a purely native character of its own.

The present Glasgow character was not manifest in the early Glasgow, or, at least, the earliest we need to consider here; that is, in the Middle Ages and the 16th and early 17th cents. It was then known as an important but "douce" little cathedral city of the West. The word "douce" (a Franco-Scottish word, the antonym of "dour" but without the excessively sweet qualities of its French origin) is the only one that will do. Glasgow, though then, as now, near to the W. Highlands, was essentially a Lowland town of respectable antiquity and authority within the Kingdom of Scotland, which it had, in the days of the great struggle for independence from England, helped to form. Bishop Wishart of Glasgow had been an intrepid supporter of Bruce.

When Scotland had regained her independence, and had settled down as a unit in the comity of European nations, Glasgow settled down too, to be a pleasing small episcopal city of the West, in appearance not unlike St Andrews in the East. Unlike St Andrews, which lay in the teeth of the east wind and in the heart of ecclesiastical controversy, it was a quiet place. Moreover, surrounded by rich agricultural land, and itself a natural market-place, its atmosphere was prosperous and peaceful. Removed from the dynastic struggles that attended the succession of infant Stuarts to the throne in the East, and largely untouched by the savage internecine warfare of the nobles, again mostly of the East, Glasgow flourished modestly but distinctly as a Lowland city of

importance, allowed to go its own peaceful and prosperous way. This is what is meant by "douce".

As such, her appearance was often praised by visitors from England and abroad, right down to the beginning of the 18th cent. and the dawn of the great trading and subsequent industrial era. Since then her romantic, vivid appearance has been praised, but for different reasons. In the days of her earlier episcopal and market-town prosperity, she was set beside the yet undeepened Clyde. This river was later to be dredged into the waterway it is now, but at that period it was no more than a Lowland salmon-stream. Around the city by the ford there were rich gardens, and behind the gardens there were fruitful farms. Amongst the many tributes to her aspect, and rather a late one for this period, there is the well-known eulogium of Daniel Defoe beginning "The beautifullest little city I have seen in Britain".

He might have added "peaceablest", for Glasgow, throughout her long existence right down until comparatively modern times, was singularly little touched by the dreadful dissensions that tore at the body politic of Scotland, and most of which had their origin in the East.

Even the great upheaval of the Reformation, which indeed changed Glasgow's official form of Christianity along with that of the rest of Scotland, had small violent effect upon her. Her ancient cathedral, as compared with the gaunt ruins that romantically or tragically stand against the sky in the rest of Scotland, has survived inviolate as a place of worship. All that has happened to it as a direct result of the Reformation is that it was stripped of its Catholic images – a process described by Andrew Fairservice in Scott's *Rob Roy* as an old dog shaking itself free of fleas.

Immediately after the Reformation Glasgow was sufficiently conscious of its status as an episcopal city to keep on its bishops under the Reformed Faith. It was not until the covenanting wars in the 17th cent., and until Glasgow, along with the rest of Scotland, began to suffer from the intolerable arbitrary rule of the Stuarts when they had removed to London, that Glasgow really threw in her whole-heartedly with the non-Episcopalian, democratic Kirk of Scotland as we know it today.

Indeed, the South-West of Scotland was the centre of the heroic anti-Episcopalian resistance that Glasgow supported. But it is in key with Glasgow's own curiously peaceful resistance that the city itself did not suffer in the wars. She suffered humiliation, again along with the rest of Scotland, under the English Commonwealth when Cromwell briefly subjugated Scotland; but she did not suffer the devastation of war. Nor, be it added, was this immunity earned by silent subjection. The Glasgow ministers from their pulpits certainly let Cromwell know what they thought of him, and while he was in their presence.

At the end of the 17th and the beginning of the 18th cents., the New World of the North Americas was beginning to infringe on the trading interests of Western Europe. Glasgow, as one of the most important western cities all but touching on the Atlantic, saw her opportunity. Remotely northern as she was then held to be, there was no doubt that she could, if she had made the effort, become the ultimate "great gateway of civic Europe towards the New World". She did make that effort.

After the Union, and until the revolt of the American colonies, there arose the fantastic Glasgow period of the "tobacco lords". These were industrious Glaswegian overseas traders who became the middlemen for the tobacco trade not only for Great Britain, but for much of Europe. With their gold-headed canes, their scarlet coats, their easy right-of-way through the Glasgow streets (everyone got off the Glasgow "plainstanes" to let a tobacco lord pass), they became the northern equivalent of the one-time Florentine merchant princes.

Their period of glory vanished with the revolt of the American colonies in 1775, but they had left their mark on Glasgow and given an impetus to the great trading city of the North-West of Great Britain that was not to cease. Architecturally, nearly all that they achieved in Glasgow disappeared with their glory. One notable exception remains – the mid-18th-cent. Church of St Andrew's off the Saltmarket. It is in its style superior to any church of Edinburgh's New Town, save perhaps, and by a coincidence of nomenclature, the Edinburgh Kirk of the Disruption (see "Scotland in History"), St Andrew's in George Street.

It was during the period of the tobacco lords' glory that Glasgow suffered her one full-scale invasion and occupation by soldiery. Yet it was an invasion that was to emphasize the curious consistency of Glasgow's immunity from physical harm in warfare. This invasion was the occupation of the city by the army of Prince Charles Edward Stuart upon return from his unsuccessful sally from Scotland into England in 1745. Glasgow was then an entirely Whig city (the remains of the Whiggish temperament may still be noted among the more prosperous of the citizens today), and deeply resented this Stuart and Highland occupation. But, beyond a certain expense to which she was put (and for which she was later recompensed by the Government in London), she suffered nothing.

The rest of Scotland in varying degrees suffered from the results of this sad venture of the last of the Stuarts, but Glasgow, almost a "city republic" within Scotland, did not suffer.

But this brief and, to Glasgow, disagreeable irruption was soon forgotten in the excitement of planning the dredging, widening, and deepening of the shallow Clyde that was eventually to make the river navigable to ocean-going ships right up to the centre of the city.

International commerce was, despite all plans for the re-making of Glasgow's great river, to receive a severe blow when, in 1775, the Americans revolted. The tobacco trade in Glasgow seemed to vanish overnight. But Glasgow was already too big, too inherently wealthy, too forward-looking (and this last-mentioned quality is relevant today) to surrender beneath such a purely political blow.

Glasgow now turned her attention to the weaving of cotton and the export of cloth all over Europe. She carried on with her schemes for the Clyde, and continued as an exporting city republic now within Britain, rather than solely within Scotland. Perhaps a little under the influence of example from Edinburgh with her noble New Town (see EDINBURGH), she began to build Augustan squares, places, and streets, in the centre and W. centre. Some of these, as in Blythswood Square, notably remain; others were swept aside in the forthcoming Industrial Revolution, the coming Railway Age, and the emergence of Glasgow as the shipbuilding centre of the world.

When one speaks of Glasgow as the "second city of the Empire" and as the city republic "now within Great Britain, rather than solely within Scotland", this is not to say that the great and growing city of that era forgot its national roots. Far from it. As soon as Glasgow began to feel its great strength, she began also to feel that she comprehended all Scotland. Edinburgh, the capital city, the headquarters of the national legal system and of the national Church (the two elements of Scottish life left officially free and independent at the Union) might give the appearance of being somewhat aloof from the rest of Scotland. Not so Glasgow.

It was at this period that she drew within

Glasgow shipyard

herself Highlanders and Hebrideans as well as Lowlanders from all parts of Scotland, including even the usually self-sufficient North-East. There was no element of Scottish life or Scottish enthusiasm, including the enthusiasm for religious sectarianism (the word is not intended pejoratively), that was not reflected in Glasgow, and reflected thereby all the more vividly.

About this time the "Glasgow character" as we know it, which has already been spoken of, began to manifest itself recognizably. And now Sir Walter Scott projected on to paper his immortal Glasgow citizen, the Bailie Nicol Jarvie. Scott's tale may have been drawn from the early 18th cent., but in his creation of the Bailie his eye was on his own present time, the era of Glasgow in the first years of last century. That was the era just before the rise of the great modern city of Victorianism, of shipbuilding and of many industries.

In its outward shell, and in its essential city character, the Glasgow of today preserves much of the signs of its largest metamorphosis till now, but it was in the era of Victorianism that Glasgow really expanded to the world. Victorian Glasgow – dark, stone-built, romantic, continually expanding, growing in vigour and in continual enterprise – is still with us. She was (and is) too powerful an entity to sink easily into the background of "modern progress".

Powerful indeed! For this was the period when Glasgow, Scottish Glasgow, the city republic in Great Britain, in the British Empire yet inescapably rooted in Scotland, for the first time opened her gates to incomers in large quantities from outside Scotland. She not only opened her gates to them but assimilated them. She gave them her own especial gift – the Glasgow character.

It was the power of steam that brought in the new Glasgow of the 19th cent. James Watt, in his laboratory, had harnessed the power of steam back in the 18th cent. in Glasgow University. Not until the dawn of the Victorian age did steam really come out into the open air of Glasgow, so tremendously to affect its development. It affected it in two ways, on water and on land.

On water, it soon became evident that the steamboat was able to manage the entry to the Clyde in ways far beyond that available to sailing-ships. Even before Waterloo had ended the Napoleonic wars, and had ushered in the great century of comparative peace, steam-driven vessels had moved upon the Clyde. In 1812 the famous little *Comet* had been launched, on the Clyde, to paddle about there, if a trifle ineffectively, at least prophetically.

Now, with the age of steam getting under way, and with the *Comet*'s progeny or successors in the form of steam-tugs, ships whether under sail or not could easily and safely face the journey up and down the Clyde. The 1773 project of dredging and deepening the little salmon-stream was seen to have been in itself something more than a sound investment; it had been a prophetic venture.

It is so characteristic, too, of the go-ahead spirit of the city republic of Glasgow that the place should not have been content merely with opening its gates to the steam-vessels of the world. No. She now set about that task for which she was to become world-famous in the 19th cent.; she made her own steam-vessels and founded her own engineering yards, and with what results the world knows. Before the century had ended, there was no higher praise for a vessel that moved upon the waters of the world than to say that she had been Clyde-built.

In entering the seas of the world, and in thrusting their own railways out into the landscape of Great Britain, Glasgow, at the beginning of the Victorian and Steam Age, had to relax something of the purely civic self-sufficiency of the city republic. She was growing too big, too important, for that. Again in a fashion characteristic of her spirit, Glasgow faced this new challenge and tackled it in a Glasgow manner.

Until the 19th cent. and the increase of rapid communication, Glasgow Town Council had largely been a self-elected affair, an oligarchy again of the Florentine kind representing only the great merchants and the incorporated trades. It had worked not badly; but now, in an age of peace and quick travel, and of parliamentary reform away down in London, the people began to make their voice heard among the quiet councils of the aristocracy of wealth. The reform of parliamentary representation was quickly followed in Glasgow by the reform of the burgh. When at last the people, the ordinary people of the city republic, had a voice in the election of the city rulers, and had a potent say in the running of the city affairs, the whole of the city blazed with lights.

They were gas jets (the wonderful new invention of gas illumination, which Walter Scott had recently installed at ABBOTSFORD), lit by the ordinary folk of Glasgow. It was a far cry from the so-called "city of the Red Clyde" (a catch-phrase that was often to be exaggeratedly repeated in the years between the two world wars), but the age of democratic left-wing progressive Glasgow had begun.

A great change was now to come over the face of the quickly growing Glasgow in the age of Victoria. By the end of Queen Victoria's reign in 1901, Glasgow's population, if you included the suburbs, had multiplied itself by four. In self-contained wealth and potency, it is impossible to calculate the figures for its increase. More and more incomers came to Glasgow, to be inescapably absorbed into the Glasgow way of living, but – despite its growth in population and power, and despite its

infusions from without – Glasgow remained a distinctively itself as ever.

It was, for instance, utterly untouched in influence or fashion by the capital city of Edinburgh, only 40 m. away. Even less, is possible, was it affected by London. There were great Glaswegian merchant princes who though they may have taken their holiday with their families to the Continent of Europe or in rented mansions in the remote Highlands scarcely ever went to London, and certainly never *en famille*. Edinburgh was a place they visited only to consult lawyers or to take part in great civil cases that had to be tried at the Court of Session, in the place that they smilingly admitted was the official capital of the country in which Glasgow was situate.

Glasgow's Victorian metamorphosis made her in her outward aspect a complete Victorian city. It is in fact, of all cities in the British Isles, *the* Victorian city. In its building, it expresses Victorianism more definitely, more self assuredly, more solidly, than Manchester, Leeds, Birmingham, Halifax, Bradford, or any other of the great British cities that grew out of the Victorian Age. To wander through the centre, and even through some of the outer parts, of Glasgow today in the 1970s is to perceive Victorianism about you in its most impressive and apparently permanent form. Victorian building here, whether it be office, works, shops, trading-places of commerce, banks, railway stations, or dwelling-houses, does not appear as a museum piece, nor does it have the disagreeable if pathetic air of decline that it often wears in other cities. It is alive; in its solidness people vitally live and work.

The reason for Glasgow's triumphant assertion of Victorianism is twofold. First, unlike the other great industrial cities of Great Britain that raised their heads in the last century, Glasgow did not raise her head from nothing or from small circumstances. When, at the start of the age of the steamboat and the railway, Glasgow took on the challenge of being Victorian, it took it on from strength. It took it on from the vantage-point of its own long-prosperous, peaceful past. Glasgow, not as a newcomer but as an old hand at the game, embraced the task of being at the forefront of success.

This huge, this remarkable if sometimes alarming, expansion of Victorian Glasgow in stone may have thrust the city republic forward, but it did result in the loss of much that was gracious in the aspect of the considerably prosperous commercial city of the late 18th and early 19th cents. that came before it. Glasgow Regency and neo-Georgian ventures in building may not have been so splendidly planned as Edinburgh's, but, as we can see from the fragments that remain of it, it was not negligible. We may mourn the fact that the age of the railway and the steamboat ruthlessly destroyed much of 18th-cent. as well as earlier

Glasgow, but it did put up something long-lasting, solid, and vital in its place.

Blythswood Square, at the centre of the city and on the hill, may remind us of Glasgow's one-time Augustan ambitions. The pleasing buildings at the river end of St Enoch's Square speak of a less ambitious but nevertheless gracious style. The fact remains, however, that Glasgow could not at the time see her way to taking on the challenge of Victorianism while keeping the old buildings as museum-pieces.

Now that Glasgow has wrung the last drop out of the Victorian Age, now when she is facing, with characteristic confidence, whatever changes the modern age may bring, she has acquired a strong affection for what it would be wrong to call her Victorian remains of architecture. They are still more than remains. People still work and live in them with native gusto. There are plans for rebuilding much of Victorian Glasgow, starting very properly with the depressed slum areas, but it will take a very long time indeed before Glasgow's present Victorian aspect is abolished or even reduced. And it is likely that the last viable Victorian building in Britain to be left standing, and standing not as a mere curiosity, will be in Glasgow.

It would be improper to leave the subject of the aspect of 19th-cent. Glasgow without mentioning the name of Alexander Thomson, known in his Victorian day (and still thus referred to) as "Greek" Thomson. Alexander Thomson had a passion for the Grecian style, which, by paradox, can be admirably expressed in our grey Scottish stone. It is not the equal of Greek marble, of course, but the strength of the old dark stone speaks of the Old Testament and covenanting tradition that lay at the background of "Greek" Thomson's training. His churches – notably the St Vincent Street church built between 1857 and 1859 – are remarkably effective and satisfying.

Alas! Just about at the same time as these solid and satisfying Victorian churches, commercial palaces, and private houses for the wealthy were going up, another kind of building was being generated in Glasgow much less worthy of respect.

Having knocked down the great houses of the late 18th cent., Victorian Glasgow used the gardens and backlands of the prosperous parts as sites for dwelling-places for the poorer immigrants, who were now pouring into Glasgow in search of work. At this period an official commissioner wrote: "The wynds of Glasgow comprise a fluctuating population of from 15,000 to 20,000 persons. This quarter consists of a labyrinth of lanes, out of which numberless entrances lead into small courts, each with a dunghill reeking in the centre. Revolting as was the outside of these places, I was little prepared for the filth and destitution within. In some of these lodging houses we found a whole lair of human beings littered along the floor – sometimes fifteen and twenty, some clothed, some naked – men, women and children huddled promiscuously together."

In 1840, not long before the European revolution that was to drive fresh refugees to Glasgow, and just before the full horror of the Irish potato famine, which again was to swell the numbers of Glasgow, the British Association met there. Speaking to the dignified members, the Chief Constable said, "In the very centre of the city there is an accumulated mass of squalid wretchedness which is probably unequalled in the British Dominions". This, the worse product of the liberalizing and freedom-searching doctrine of *laissez faire*, was worse than anything to be found in Edinburgh's by now shameful Old Town. That Old Town on the Castle Rock had sunk into decay through being abandoned. Glasgow's slums seemed almost to be the deliberate product not so much of slave labour but of the needless philosophy that said, in effect, "We will leave you to get as rich as you like or to stink to death in as deep a squalor as you please, provided everyone leaves everyone else alone".

But, of course, everyone was not left alone. Official Glasgow cannot be too strongly reprehended for its neglect of its Victorian slums, but the conscience of the strongly religious covenanting spirit of Glasgow amongst individual characters was deeply stirred. But it was individual rather than corporate effort that manfully struggled to combat this dreadful problem. The greatest of these individuals was the Church of Scotland minister, Thomas Chalmers, the man who was later to lead the Church to freedom in the Act of Disruption in 1843. He organized his parish in the poorest parts of the city to bring relief to many of the wretched creatures who were officially his parishioners.

There were other clerics coming into Glasgow and its environs now who gave themselves with selfless devotion to the cause of the miserably impoverished. But they were less potent even than the heroic and much respected Thomas Chalmers to strike at the root of the disease, for they were of a band of Glasgow folk who, at that date, were not recognized as being of Glasgow. And the faith they professed and carried with them in their ministrations to the most miserable hovels was looked upon with suspicion and even hatred by decent Christian Glasgow folk of covenanting blood. Times have indeed changed in this respect.

These were the priests who came over with the starving Irish during and after the horror of the potato famine, surely one of the most dreadful results of the policy of *laissez faire* in the British Isles.

The problem of the "Glasgow Irish" was once a delicate one, which most writers on the city tended to avoid for the simple reason that they were forced to take one side or the other in a desperate partisan struggle. Those days, save on the football field when Celtic play Rangers, are largely over. Today there are few inhabitants of the city who are more civically proud, more keen on being not only Scots but Glasgow-Scots than the descendants of the Irish who descended upon Glasgow and the W. of Scotland 120 or more years ago. But it certainly was not always so.

In those far-off days when disease stalked through the slums of Glasgow, and when the dread visitation of cholera was not uncommon, the Irish priesthood did heroic work and suffered many casualties in death while bearing the Sacraments to their dying compatriots and parishioners. They acted corporately, but necessarily within a closed corporation of their faith and their race. Their heroism was conducted largely in privacy; and they could not make the open effect even of the great Presbyterian minister, Thomas Chalmers.

But the Irish were not the only Catholics who were coming in to disturb the Presbyterian and covenanting traditions of Glasgow. The Scottish Catholic Highlanders who had suffered under the Highland Clearances had been coming into Glasgow since the early days of the century. The fine interior of the little Glasgow Catholic Cathedral by the banks of the Clyde shows clearly that it was built before the mid-Victorian era. These Highlanders and Irish were joined too by Poles, Lithuanians, and Italians who had fled their native countries at the time of the European upheavals in 1848. The Protestant Catholic problem was indeed an acute one in Glasgow in those days.

Glasgow is still strong in its religious opinions, or strong sometimes in its stand against religion, but the days of religious intolerance of the mid-Victorian kind are over. Only a few days before these words were written in the mid-1960s, Glasgow's Protestant Lord Provost officially represented the city at the enthronement of the Catholic Archbishop of Glasgow in the little cathedral by the Clyde, which had been built over 130 years before mainly for the incoming Scottish Highland Catholics.

And so Glasgow marched forward in prosperity, in poverty, in strife and agreement, but all the while in growing civic pride, towards the present century. She was much more of a British (North British), and certainly more of a continental, city than the capital town of Edinburgh. Her University had moved from the centre of the city to its noble premises in the W. of the city on the ridge of Gilmorehill. Its architecture of the 1870s may have made some smile at it in the early years of this century and in the reaction from Victorian Gothic. Unlike other remnants of Victorian Gothic, however, it inspires more than affection.

This, one of the genuine masterpieces of Sir George Gilbert Scott, is a truly impressive building. Standing on its hill, dominating western Glasgow with its amplitude and its style, it really does give the impression that Oxford once claimed uniquely for itself, of "dreaming spires". Glasgow's soft air and drifting mists do much to increase this impression.

Save for the ultimate poor who still, though not so painfully, lay in the backwash of *laissez faire*, the prosperity of Glasgow affected all classes in the now "second city of the Empire" during the last thirty years of Queen Victoria's reign and of this century. The best theatres in Scotland and the best music-halls (some of the best in Britain) flourished during this period. The aeroplane was undreamt of; the motor-car, even when it began to appear, was merely a rich man's toy, a foolish ephemeral experiment. The way of getting about the world was still by the seas of the world, and by sea only. Glasgow, in her superb tradition and achievement of shipbuilding, held the key to those seas. In a sense it must have seemed to many of the Glasgow merchant princes – who, as has already been said, seldom bothered to visit London, where all those tiresome politicians went, or Edinburgh, where those lawyers congregated – that Glasgow was something more than the second city of the Empire. As the city that produced the best ships of the world, she was, in a more practical sense than Great Britain claimed, the Mistress of the Seas.

In such a community, too, the arts were encouraged to flourish. Journalism and writing were lively, architecture experimental (*see below* in this essay); but it was in painting that Glasgow became, at this period, internationally known. The wealth of the Glasgow merchants had enabled them to buy paintings extensively from abroad. And in the 1870s and '80s they made a speciality of investing in the French Impressionists. This in the days before popular reproduction, engraving, and mass communication of the arts introduced to Glasgow practising artists a school of painting that particularly appealed to them.

As a result there emerged the famous Glasgow school of impressionist painters. Their names are still in our ears – James Guthrie, John Lavery, A. E. Hornel, and others. Maybe the sometimes misty, or at least not strongly defined, outlines of the Glasgow scene provided a suitable environment in which such a school could grow. At any rate, it did grow, and grow in fame far outside its own city and country.

The ordinary Glasgow man, however indifferent to art, was proud of his city's achievement in this unfamiliar respect. Sometimes indeed he was even detected in liking the Glasgow impressionist painting for its own sake. There is a story of an ordinary Glasgow man of the period being taken rather unwillingly into a gallery exhibiting these paintings. After a little, he was heard to exclaim, "Tak' me out. Tak' me out quickly. I'm beginning to like them."

Glasgow: George Square and the City Chambers

Such a man, if indeed he ever existed, was (and is) a true example of the modern Glasgow "character" as he has emerged from the long centuries of his city's history, sketched above. Too perceptive of artistic merit, even if it were beyond him, to be called a complacent Philistine, it was such a man who, emerging from the great era of Glasgow's prosperity and poverty, at the end of the last century and at the beginning of this, who became known as a type outside his city. In the islands of Great Britain, by the end of this century, there were only two cities whose ordinary folk had established themselves in the public eye, London and Glasgow.

The ordinary Glasgow citizen, for all his apparent hard practicality (the legacy of his covenanting and strong Lowland past), has a strong infusion of imagination and sentiment (the product of Celtic infusion in his city). His city, for all its heavy architecture, for all its remains of squalid slum-building in the past, is near to some of the loveliest scenery in Britain, the West Highlands. It is at the period we are now considering that Glasgow invented its most romantic and beauty-searching popular holiday known as going "doon the watter", that is, taking a day-trip down the Clyde from the Bridge Wharf dock in the heart of the city on a pleasure-steamer. Today, in the age of the cheap motor-car and bicycle and bus, the ordinary folk of Glasgow have many other means of exploring the beauties that lie so richly round their city. At the turn of the century there was for most of them only one, a trip "doon the watter".

It was an entrancing experience. You left Glasgow right at its heart, and sailed down the stream that Glasgow's engineering has made; the stream, now river, that has made Glasgow. With a glow of pride (that is, if you were a true Glaswegian) you passed the great shipyards that have spread Glasgow's fame and name all over the world. And eventually you swung out on the broad water of the Firth of Clyde itself, to be faced with an incomparable island and mainland beauty. Its aspects are described in their proper places elsewhere in this volume. At the end of the day you turned home, the westering sun behind you, and were filled with a sense of natural loveliness, that was all your own property, and into the bustling, warm-hearted city of the Clyde.

Glasgow approached the turn of the century with supreme assurance – not to be confused with self-satisfaction. She had survived centuries of change as the city republic of Scotland, of Britain, and now (it seemed) of the Empire. Doubtless she would be able to face further changes – as indeed she is, in this terrifying century of ours – with her customary ability. But this is a matter to be dealt with by a more native pen later in this essay, in the description of Glasgow today.

At any rate, it must have seemed to the

Glaswegian at the end of Queen Victoria's reign that his city's position was unassailable. In true Glasgow fashion he did not want to assail or expand, or to take over the property of anyone else. Glasgow just wanted to go on being Glasgow. And that is precisely what she has been doing ever since.

A part of the business of being Glasgow at that period was a legacy from the immediate and less happy past of the early and mid-Victorian period. The Glasgow working man, as he was then called, had never forgotten the time of the slums, the desperate overcrowding and the incoming of new blood into his ancient city. It was in Glasgow that the rights of the working man were first put forward not only from the heart but from the head. The Labour movement in Britain owes much that is most valuable and genuine in its tradition to Glasgow and to such figures as Keir Hardie. They are not forgotten.

In 1901, Glasgow held a Great Exhibition to mark its industrial progress, to include much that was Scottish and outside the bounds of the city republic. Nor was this Exhibition hampered by the fact that an age was obviously ending. The sign of this was the death of the old Queen Victoria in that year. Glasgow faced the future with confidence. Had she but known what was to happen in 1914 and 1939, and (an important fact for Glasgow) what was to come in the inter-war years to affect Glasgow, she might not have faced that future with quite such confidence. But she did. And largely that confidence has been justified.

In that year there appeared, in order to mark the Glasgow Exhibition's date, a book with the rather uninspiring title of *Glasgow in 1901*, by James Hamilton Muir. This pseudonym concealed the identity of three young Glasgow journalists, two of whom were to attain considerable fame in the world of writing and of the arts, far beyond Glasgow and (to use a Scottish word that the English reader might do well to learn) far "furth" of Scotland.

It would be too much to claim for this book, as some of its admirers do, that it is the best book ever written on Glasgow. Memories of certain chapters in *Rob Roy* forbid that. Since 1901, moreover, there has been a great deal of writing on Glasgow, notably from the late George Blake, and from J. M. Reid, and Jack House, that concerns the Glasgow of this century – the Glasgow that was to emerge after the catastrophic events of 1914 – and is the equal of the fine little book that hailed the Glasgow Exhibition at the dawn of our era. Still, it remains a memorable work of art and affection, giving us a portrait of Glasgow and its people that is still recognizable.

In reading and re-reading *Glasgow in 1901*, you feel the pulse of life that animated this proud, emotional, yet down-to-earth city at the very peak of its self-sufficient yet partly cosmopolitan prosperity.

The city republic of Scotland, of Britain, of the Empire, though one of the richest cities in the West (including the Americas, from which the origins of her wealth had sprung), though linked by her great industry of shipbuilding with the ends of the earth, remained true to herself and her character. That she was and remained Glasgow was enough for her.

This is not to deny that Glasgow at the beginning of this century was a place where strong "progressive" movements in the form of socialism, Scottish nationalism, and new thought in politics, philosophy, and the arts could flourish. Glasgow men, whether boss or worker, were united in their city republic. The poorer classes by this time were, however, undoubtedly beginning to manifest their claim that wealth should be more equally shared among them, and that all should have a say in the government of their own city and country.

This was indeed a far cry from the days of the tobacco lords of the 18th cent.; it was also removed in kind from the growling and most understandable discontent of unemployment between the two wars of this century which earned for Glasgow the name of the "Red Clyde". In 1901, however, Glasgow may have appeared to be sufficient unto itself, but it was deeply enough rooted in the soil of Scotland never to forget the words of the landward lad from its own West of Scotland who had sung, "A man's a man for a' that". Glasgow indeed, through all its ups and downs, Glasgow in all its self-containment in Scotland, has been the place in it where that poetic maxim has been most constantly remembered.

How does the rest of Scotland look upon this great self-sufficient unity within it? It looks at her as she has done for a very long time indeed.

Scotland looks upon Glasgow with respect mingled possibly with alarm at the size of the place, at its capacity for growth and for absorbing into its very essence so much of the rest of Scotland. But this alarm is quietened by the sheer vitality of Glasgow, a vitality that is not often found, seldom if ever made so patently manifest, in other great cities in western Europe. It is a vitality that has survived the years of distress as well as the years of prosperity. Scots, and particularly those in the South-East, are sometimes surprised at the ease with which it is possible to provoke Glasgow's wit at the expense of (it would be too strong to call it contempt for) the capital city of Edinburgh, so near to it. But that wit is often so sardonic, so genuinely amusing, that it does not offend. The worst thing one can say about it is that Glasgow folk spend too much of their time being irritably conscious of the fact that the comparatively new city of Edinburgh has somehow got itself made into the capital of the country. They should be content (as indeed they fundamentally are) with being the city republic of Scotland.

But perhaps most of all emotions aroused by

Glasgow in the rest of Scotland is an affection for its lively and free-minded people. When the rest of us in the East or North-East of this small country of ours feel a bit depressed, we go to Glasgow briefly for enlivenment. It is a state that fills us with vitality and with affection returned. Let not the word "briefly" pass unnoticed. If we stay too long in Glasgow, it is apt to become overpowering. We who are not yet assimilated into the Glasgow "character" may find it too heady a draught for deep or sustained potation. But it is with affection and with the memory of infectious vitality that we recall it.

So much, then, of Glasgow from this Edinburgh pen! What has been written here concerns what happened to Glasgow, and how Glasgow uniquely grew and flourished over the centuries until this one. It is a view of Glasgow that can be put forward without impertinence by a Scot who lives near to Glasgow, visits her often, has affection for her, and has read much about her.

When it comes, however, to the Glasgow that emerged after the world catastrophe of 1914, the Glasgow whose shape and fact will strike the eye of the visitor, it is another matter. It is a matter that should be, and now is, written about with more close particularity by a writer of Glasgow living in the Glasgow of this day.

TODAY, TOMORROW; AND FROM WITHIN

Edinburgh grew up round a castle. Glasgow grew up round a cathedral. And so the historical way to see the city is to start in Cathedral Square and move down to Glasgow Cross. Then you go NW. to George Square and W. again to the University. That, roughly speaking, has been the development of Glasgow over the last 1,400 years.

The founder of Glasgow was St Kentigern, popularly known as St Mungo, and he established a little chapel on a green hill overlooking the Molendinar Burn in the 6th cent. Glasgow Cathedral stands on the site of that chapel. In its present form it goes back partly to the 12th cent., but most of it is 15th cent. The tomb of St Mungo is in a fan-vaulted crypt, and a light always burns there.

The Cathedral is the only example of pre-Reformation Gothic architecture on the mainland of Scotland. Official guides show visitors round, and this is a good opportunity to become acquainted with the Glasgow dialect, a tongue rich and quite easily understood once you get used to it. The things to see are the Laigh Kirk; the vaulted crypt, said to be the finest in Europe; the rood-screen depicting the Seven Deadly Sins; the East Chapel; and the well in which St Mungo baptized his converts.

If you want to see the Cathedral to the best advantage, cross the Bridge of Sighs into the Necropolis, the graveyard of the Merchants' House of Glasgow. It is built on a rocky hill,

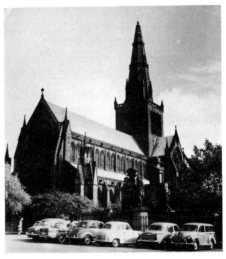

Scottish Tourist Board

The Cathedral, Glasgow

and the topmost statue is that of John Knox. You can tell what he thinks of Glasgow today by the expression on his face as he gazes over the city. The Necropolis was opened in 1832, and the first person to be buried there was a Jew – which fact is typical of Glasgow's tolerant feelings. There has been no "colour problem" in Glasgow.

The Necropolis is built in the style of the Père-la-Chaise cemetery in Paris. It contains imitations of almost every kind of architecture in the world, because each Glasgow merchant had his tomb built in the style of the place where he made his money.

Seen from Cathedral Square, the Cathedral seems dwarfed by the bulk of the Royal Infirmary, which is built on the site of the Bishop's Palace that existed in pre-Reformation days. A statue of Queen Victoria stands in front of the main door, which is hardly ever opened. This is a Glasgow peculiarity. When you visit the Cathedral, you go in by a side door. Even the famed Kelvingrove Art Galleries follow this pattern. You may think you are going in by the front door, but it is actually the back door; the front door is facing the University across the R. Kelvin, and so determined are the authorities that you must not use the front door, that they have stretched a chain across to keep people out.

There are several statues in Cathedral Square, but the only notable one is that of William of Orange. It is notable because it is believed to be the only statue in Europe with a movable part. The statue, which depicts the King in the garb of a noble Roman seated on a horse, once stood at Glasgow Cross. It was displaced to make way for a railway station, and the horse's tail was broken off. When the statue was re-erected in Cathedral Square, the tail was

Scottish Tourist Board
Provand's Lordship, the oldest house in Glasgow

attached by a ball-and-socket arrangement. It is said that, in a very strong wind, the tail actually moves. Not long ago two enthusiastic Glaswegians were discovered inside the railings that surround the statue; they were attempting to set the tail swinging.

The oldest house in Glasgow, Provand's Lordship, stands in Cathedral Square. It was built around 1471 for the priest in charge of St Nicholas Hospital. Mary Queen of Scots is supposed to have lived here in 1566, and, if she did write the notorious "casket letters", this is where she wrote them. The house is now a museum, devoted mainly to Old Glasgow relics.

'If you go down Castle Street to the High Street, you come to the Bell o' the Brae, where Sir William Wallace won a small battle against the English in the 13th cent. Duke Street, leading to the E., is said by patriotic Glaswegians to be the longest street in Britain. College Street goods station is built on the site of the ancient University of Glasgow, but only a plaque in the wall remains to show where it once stood.

At the foot of the High Street is Glasgow Cross, so much admired by Daniel Defoe and other 18th-cent. visitors. All that remains of what Defoe saw are the Tolbooth Steeple, built in 1626, and the Tron Steeple, built in 1637. The Tron Steeple was part of St Mary's Church, which was burnt down by the Hellfire Club in 1793. Its archway is typical of the surroundings of Glasgow Cross in the 17th and 18th cents. The mercat cross is a replica of the original one and was put up in 1929.

To the E. runs the Gallowgate, the way to the gallows once. Now it is the way, every Saturday and Sunday, to the famous "Barrows", probably the largest open-air market in Britain. A climbing expedition to the Himalayas was once fitted out almost entirely from material bought at the stalls and stances here.

On the S. side is the Saltmarket, near which is St Andrew's Parish Church, already mentioned, and St Andrew's-by-the-Green, the

oldest church in Glasgow. It was built in 175 by the Episcopal Church; for many years it ha the only organ in the city, and it was known a the "Whistlin' Kirk". Off the Saltmarket als is Bridgegate, which leads to another famou open-air sales place, "Paddy's Market". Nex door is the Fish Market, and the steeple here i the original one of the Merchants' House, buil in the 17th cent.

At the foot of the Saltmarket is Jocely Square. On one side are the Justiciary Buildings where High Court trials are held. On the othe is Glasgow Green, the oldest public park ir Britain. In Glasgow Green is the first monu ment ever erected to Lord Nelson (1806); the People's Palace, which contains the Old Glasgow Museum; and the Fleshers' Haugh. where Bonnie Prince Charlie reviewed his troops in 1745. It is now used for football and fairs.

Russian visitors to Glasgow are amazed when they see Templeton's carpet-factory, overlooking the Green. It reminds them of the Kremlin in Moscow. This is because the factory is built in the style of the Doge's Palace in Venice, and the Kremlin has many of the same architectural features.

Across the R. Clyde is the Gorbals, a district famous (if that is the right word) in story, cinema, theatre, and ballet. It is being completely rebuilt. Skyscrapers now stand where the characters of Alexander McArthur's *No Mean City* once flashed their razors and got drunk on Red Biddy.

There are still vestiges of the old Gorbals round Gorbals Cross, near which stands the Citizens' Theatre, now a respected repertory house but once the Royal Princess's home of the world's longest-running pantomime. Of Glasgow, famous for its pantomimes, one comedian said, "It's the only place I know where you start the run wearing a fur coat and end it wearing a straw hat."

From Glasgow Cross the street to the W. is the Trongate, where Glasgow's first pavement was laid. It runs into Argyle Street, now lined with big shops and great stores, but once the centre of Glasgow's saturnalia, as expressed in Will Fyffe's song, "I belong to Glasgow". From Argyle Street, it is only a step up Queen Street to George Square, the present-day centre of the city. On the way you pass Stirling's Library, once the Royal Exchange, and before. that, in part at least, the country house of one of the Glasgow tobacco lords, William Cuninghame of Lainshaw.

George Square is another part of Glasgow that is changing. Already it is dominated by educational skyscrapers, and eventually the whole of the N. side, except the North British Hotel, will be modernized. The Square has sometimes been described as Glasgow's Valhalla because it contained thirteen statues. Now there are twelve, because David Livingstone was removed to Cathedral Square so

Building in progress at the Gorbals, Glasgow

that a Corporation information kiosk could be built in his place. By tradition George Square has been the gathering-place of Glasgow citizens on important occasions for many years. The beginnings and the ends of wars have been celebrated here. The Riot Act has been read from the City Chambers to rebellious Glaswegians. Monarchs going in for luncheon have been cheered.

Today the Square is principally famous for the huge crowds that assemble there on sunny days in the summer to hear a variety of bands – jazz, Salvation Army, brass, and pipe. They take their picnic lunches with them, and consequently the pigeon population in George Square is growing so fast that it is becoming a menace.

The City Chambers are in the Italian Renaissance style. They were opened, appropriately, by Queen Victoria in 1888. The interior is almost oppressively grand, and this may be the reason why many Glasgow town councillors prefer to use the side doors instead of the official entrance. Or they may be just following the Glasgow habit already described.

We have noted the pigeons in George Square. They are not the chief menace. The area just W. of the Square, St Vincent Place, and Buchanan Street, and areas adjoining became known to Glaswegians, who have a phrase for everything, as "Dodge City". This was through the arrival of many hundred thousand starlings every evening at sundown. Visitors were entranced by their busy to-ings and fro-ings and their constant piping; but every now and then a message came from above, and, if it landed on your coat or hat, the only consolation was that is was supposed to be lucky. However, campaigns to get rid of the birds now seem to have proved successful, though they may return at any time.

One of the fashionable shopping centres of Glasgow is the Argyll Arcade, which was opened in 1826. When it was opened, Argyle Street (kindly observe the difference in spelling) was nearly as busy a thoroughfare as it is today, whereas Buchanan Street was little more than a country road. Anyone who opened a shop in Buchanan Street was considered to be going mad. At that time the idea in Glasgow was that the city would spread to the E. It did so for a while, and then, as more and more industries were opened up in the E., people started to to go W.

Buchanan Street, like New York's Fifth Avenue, starts well but peters out. At its best it is the Glasgow equivalent of Bond Street in London. But it is true that you will see the brave and the fair of the city more in Buchanan Street than any other thoroughfare. All the same, it has lost some of its characters. There was the tragic-looking fiddler, who had once played in the best orchestras and was now reduced to interpreting "O Sole Mio" on the pavement-edge. He made more in Buchanan

Street than he ever made from the orchestra pit. And there was the great "Clincher", a Mr Alexander Petrie, who started as a barber but became a politician and an editor of his own paper, *The Clincher*. He wore a shiny topper and a grey frock coat and a sparkling white beard, and, as he sold his paper in Buchanan Street, he would say to the passers-by, "Be kind tae yer granny an' gi'e her plenty o' whusky!"

There are still characters in Glasgow, but they are not so recognizable now. To the visitor, however, any Glaswegian will turn out to be a character. The essence of the Glasgow man is his friendliness. If you ask the way to somewhere, he will not only tell you, but insist on accompanying you to the spot, just in case you miss it. Some visitors are worried about this. They need not be. It's just that nearly all Glaswegians want every visitor to like Glasgow.

Between George Square and a line drawn S. from Charing Cross, at the end of the Sauchiehall Street shopping area, is the business and shopping centre of the city. The principal shopping streets run at a right angle, with Sauchiehall Street, straight along the top, and a line consisting of Renfield and Union Streets running down to join the other shopping centre at Argyle Street.

The streets in this area were developed along American city lines, but long before American cities were born. American visitors to Glasgow today are immediately reminded of, say, Philadelphia, because the streets make a pattern of blocks in the American style. They are laid out mathematically, and it is surprising to come across such an oasis as Blythswood Square in the middle of them.

When you are promenading the main shopping and other streets of Glasgow, there is one thing you must remember. Not all of the people you see are Glaswegians. Glasgow is the centre of a group of towns and villages whose population amounts to something over 2,500,000. Half the population of Scotland live inside a 20-m. circle round Glasgow. The Glaswegian, unlike the Cockney, is not disappearing, however. The contrary is the case. Through television and other means, including the race of Scotch comics, the Glaswegian is apt to turn the impressionable burghers outside his boundaries into quasi-Glaswegians.

Sauchiehall Street, architecturally, is every bit as bad as Princes Street, Edinburgh. Most people, however, never look above the shop-window level, and so do not notice it. The one outstanding architectural feature of the street is the School of Art, which rises behind Sauchiehall Street like a great cliff. It is the work of Charles Rennie Mackintosh, already briefly mentioned. Mackintosh was a Glasgow man ahead of his time. He was appreciated on the Continent, when he was just noticed, and no more, in his native city. He made his designs between the end of the 19th cent. and the beginning of the 20th. The School of Art is one of his finest works, and both architects and artists from all over the world come to admire it.

If Buchanan Street is the Bond Street of Glasgow (and Argyle Street is the Oxford Street), Sauchiehall Street is the Regent Street. The shopping facilities are remarkable. At night it is a great amusement centre – not that all the amusements are concentrated in Sauchiehall Street, but they are not far away. They include the biggest cinema in Europe; Green's Playhouse in Renfield Street; several theatres and dance-halls (until recently Glasgow had, in proportion to population, more dance-halls than any other city in Britain); and a variety of restaurants and public houses.

Sauchiehall Street runs right down along to Kelvingrove Park, where international exhibitions were held until the site of 85 acres was considered too small. The art galleries in Kelvingrove are thought to house the finest municipal collection in Britain. A London critic who was shown over the collection one Sunday afternoon came out saying incredulously, "Are all these pictures the originals?" The answer is that they are, and they include Rembrandt's "A Man in Armour", Giorgione's "The Adulteress Brought Before Christ", Salvador Dali's "Christ of St John of the Cross", Whistler's "Portrait of Carlyle"; paintings by Corot, Rubens, Botticelli, and Raphael; and fine examples of all the major schools.

The art galleries are now too small to hold even a fraction of the treasures that Glasgow possesses, and there is a scheme to build a Gallery of Modern Art on the bank of the R. Kelvin. There is also a plan to build a gallery

Glasgow: Argyll Arcade

Scottish Tourist Board

n Pollok Estate to house the Burrell Collection, ut many of the Burrell treasures are still tored in the cellars or lent to art galleries in ther parts of Europe.

On one side of the art galleries is the University, already mentioned, and on the other is the Kelvin Hall, where all the big indoor exhibitions and fairs in Scotland are held. There is omething in the Glaswegian that responds to exhibitions and shows, and it is seldom that an xhibition runs at a loss here. In the days of the British Industries Fair, held simultaneously in London, Birmingham, and Glasgow, the Glasgow attendances were more than those of London and Birmingham combined.

Kelvingrove Park is the best known of the fifty-eight parks in Glasgow, which has the highest proportion of parks to population of any place in Britain. The beauty of these parks bears witness to Glasgow's soft climate. Although Glasgow is on approximately the same latitude as Moscow, the difference in climate is remarkable. There are seldom any extremes in Glasgow. One Glasgow firm exports air-conditioning plants to India, so that the cotton mills there can have, artificially, the climate that exists normally in the mills in the Bridgeton district of Glasgow. At the same time, Queen's Park in Glasgow may have more flowers on show than the five royal parks of Paris put together. It is named after Mary Queen of Scots, who met defeat at the Battle of Langside (1568) nearby. Some distance away is Linn Park, which includes the Court Knowe, from which Mary watched the progress of the battle.

In the Botanic Gardens, Glasgow grows its own bananas – out W. from Sauchiehall Street and just opposite the headquarters of the B.B.C. in Scotland, where the most modern television studio in Britain is housed. Orchids are grown in the Botanic Gardens. Here also is the Kibble Palace, the largest glasshouse in Britain, where Gladstone and Disraeli delivered their rectorial addresses to the students of Glasgow University.

Of the Glasgow parks, Rouken Glen is probably the most beautiful. Victoria Park is famous for its Fossil Grove, where you can see fossil roots and parts of an extinct species of tree. These are in the exact positions in which they grew many thousands of years ago. Hogganfield Loch, to the NE. of Glasgow, is perhaps the only public park in the country where water-skiing is a popular sport.

We started this tour of parks from Kelvingrove. Let us return there. Glasgow University, on Gilmorehill, looks across the R. Kelvin, at the art galleries, the Clyde, and the city. It has a student population of nearly 8,000. The original Victorian pile is being surrounded by modern buildings, and the acquisition of ground to the N. means that a university city will eventually grow up in the middle of Glasgow.

The University moved from the High Street to Gilmorehill in 1870, but there are two remnants of the old college. Pearce Lodge, opposite the modern Students' Union in University Avenue, is made from High Street stone, and the gateway is the original one. Inside the University grounds stretches an ornamental terrace that was transported bodily from the first University.

Glasgow's first museum is housed in the University grounds. It is in the Hunterian Museum, established in 1807 and bequeathed to the University by the famed William Hunter, Doctor of Medicine of Glasgow University, Professor of Anatomy to the Royal Academy, and Physician Extraordinary to Queen Charlotte. The collection is notable for its coins, its prints, and its Whistler pictures, which are often in demand as loans to exhibitions in various parts of the world.

Next door to Glasgow University is the Western Infirmary, a hospital that, like the University, is extending N. Down at its gates is a modest little hall known as Anderson's Institution. It was founded under the will of Professor John Anderson in 1795. This professor was a typical Glasgow man. He worked for the University, but he could not abide snobbery and jobbery. He was the first person to start classes for working men in Glasgow, and he was known, from the nature of some of his experiments, as "Jolly Jack Phosphorus".

When he died, he left a will describing the kind of University that he would like to see, and he left his money to found it. Unfortunately, his entire estate amounted to little more than £1,000. But his friends carried on and founded the institution. And out of it came the Royal College of Science and Technology, chartered in 1964 as the University of Strathclyde. So "Jolly Jack Phosphorus" was vindicated, and you can see his University to the immediate NE. of the City Chambers in George Square.

Glasgow is not the type of city where the centre is deserted at night. On the contrary, it is a place where theatres, cinemas, dance-halls, and restaurants are usually crowded. This is because most of the suburbs are within easy reach of the centre by public or private transport. The older suburbs are really former villages, and the inhabitants retain the identity of the village. For example, a person who lives in Dennistoun is asked by an acquaintance in London where he comes from. Instead of replying "Glasgow", he says, quite simply, "Dennistoun". But it is possible to travel from the centre of Glasgow to anywhere in Dennistoun within fifteen minutes by bus. So a Dennistounian can leave his office, go home and have a meal, and be back in plenty of time for the theatre.

As elsewhere in Britain, the number of theatres has declined in Glasgow. But theatregoing is still very popular, as witness the pantomimes already mentioned, and the summer shows, which often run for six months. Glasgow, indeed, is in danger of becoming the theatrical equivalent of London, for bus parties come to the theatre in Glasgow from as far away as the Borders, DUNDEE and ABERDEEN, and even THURSO.

A special type of theatre comedian is brought up in Glasgow. He is a Scotch comic, and his gift is a faithful and kindly portrayal of the Glasgow man. Almost always there is at least one theatre in the city where such a Scotch comic is appearing, and visitors should not miss the experience. It is significant that, when this type of comedian is appearing outside Glasgow, he has to alter his accent so as to be understood.

Eating-places in Glasgow have changed radically since 1901. For many years the great tea-rooms held sway. There are only a few left. But there are many snack bars. There are plenty of fish-and-chip shops and Italian cafés. There are several first-class restaurants, including one that Miss Nancy Mitford described as the finest outside Paris. There has also been a tremendous increase in popular restaurants of the London type. The Glasgow waitress, however, has not changed. She still looks as if her feet hurt. But her nature is kind to an extreme.

Although all Glaswegians will appear the same to the visitor, there is a big cleavage between them. They are divided between North-Siders and South-Siders, the sides being divided by the R. Clyde. Although they do their work and have their recreation mainly in the centre of the city, which is on the N. side of the Clyde, they prefer their own side for living and playing in. Glasgow is surrounded by golf courses, but not many golfers join clubs on the other side of the river from where they live.

Strange to say, there is not the same difference in Glasgow between the East-Enders and the West-Enders. Roughly speaking, it is true that the East End is "working-class" and the West End is "well-off", but Glasgow is a democratic place, and such differences are little thought of. When the city started to grow, it went E., so that communities were established there long before there were houses at all in the W. This means that the East-Ender has a historical feeling denied the West-Ender.

Although a man will say that he comes from Govan or Springburn or Shettleston, he knows that he is really a Glaswegian. People who live in the Royal Burgh of Rutherglen, in PAISLEY or in CLYDEBANK, all contiguous with Glasgow, would deny firmly that they were Glaswegians. But there are also two groups in a transitory stage, and perhaps they should be dealt with here.

For many years the village of MILNGAVIE on the N. of Glasgow has sent its population into Glasgow to work. At one time it was connected with the city by the tram-car system. But it is an independent burgh and, though many would consider it not much more than a dormi-tory town of Glasgow, it has its own art gallery, which holds exhibitions of works by its own artists; it has its own newspaper, recreations, sporting facilities, and chamber-music club; and it even runs its own Highland Games.

It has also an amenity that draws people out from Glasgow, and that is a hotel with an especially good restaurant. This is true of various suburban places nowadays, and such an attraction simply did not exist in the Glasgow of 1901.

Adjoining Milngavie is BEARSDEN, which was once nothing more than a dormitory town for Glasgow. But Bearsden has now achieved independence as a burgh too, and is engaged in establishing its own kind of life – although, in the main, Bearsden people still come into Glasgow for their entertainment.

But places like Milngavie and Bearsden may play different parts, along with the suburbs of Glasgow, when the new city comes into being. There are elaborate plans for changing the face of Glasgow, so that the three young journalists of 1901 would hardly be able to recognize the city they loved so dearly. New ring roads and fly-overs will be driven through parts of the city, and buildings will disappear just as they did before the railways in Victorian days.

Changes are already taking place because of the influence of the Clyde Tunnel, crossing under the river between Whiteinch and Lint-house. It consists of twin tunnels, and is placed 3 m. downstream from Glasgow Bridge in the city centre. Ever since it was opened in 1963 it has been in constant use, and the change it has made now is that travellers by-pass the centre of Glasgow completely. An even greater influence on city-centre traffic has been the Kingston Bridge, opened in 1970, which forms part of the city's inner ring road. Again, much relief from heavy and tourist traffic from the SW. heading for CLYDEBANK, DUMBAR-TON, LOCH LOMOND, and other points W. was provided in July 1971 when Princess Anne opened the £9,000,000 Erskine bridge, 180 ft high, linking Renfrewshire and Dunbartonshire and replacing the often heavily congested ferry.

In the Glasgow of the immediate future, more skyscrapers are to be built because of difficulty in getting land suitable for building. It is likely that the shopping walks in the centre of the city will be raised to one storey above the street. This pattern is already visible in the new buildings along Sauchiehall Street.

St Andrew's Hall, which was the pride of Glasgow, was burnt out after a boxing match. Parts of the walls remain, and the site is to be used as an extension to the Mitchell Library alongside. The Mitchell is the chief of Glasgow's thirty-nine public libraries. It contains more than 750,000 volumes, and is said to be overflowing. Incidentally, it holds the world's largest collection of books on Robert Burns (3,500 volumes).

Glasgow is apt to boast of the various things

she has that are the largest in the world, in Europe, in Britain, or even in Scotland. Perhaps it is appropriate here to mention Hampden Park, the second largest football stadium in the world and the largest in Europe. Glasgow is football mad, and continental players have described the Glasgow football fan as "the most intelligent in Europe". It is appropriate that Glasgow has the biggest football league in the world. It is run by the Boys' Brigade and consists of more than 200 teams.

The Glasgow man is intensely interested in Glasgow. The longest queues ever seen at the Kelvingrove Art Galleries were for an exhibition showing how Glasgow was run and something of the city's history. The most popular single item of the exhibition was in the section organized by the Glasgow police. They had a large glass case showing gangsters' weapons picked up in Glasgow in the days of gang warfare just after the First World War. And the reason the crowds around this glass case were so big was that most people had never seen such things.

Ask a Glasgow man about his city's crime record, and he will reply indignantly (and rightly) that it is considerably less than most other large cities, especially including Manchester, Liverpool, and Birmingham. But in the next breath he will be telling you proudly (and again rightly) that Glasgow has the four best murder cases in the world. You cannot beat the Glasgow man.

GLEN AFFRIC, *Inverness-shire* (Map 5, ref. 22⁸82⁶). Once the old E.–W. route through the bulk of the Inverness-shire Highlands from Loch NESS, this glen has changed its use as a habitation for men but has retained its well-known beauty. The motor-road carries one from the E. as far as Loch Beneveian. Thereafter is found a right of way for walkers through to KINTAIL on the W. coast.

There has been much recent development of a modern kind on this old glen-route. The Hydro-Electric Board has raised the level of Loch Beneveian and put a dam at the E. end of it, with a power station at Farnakyle by the foot. Rock-enclosed gorges with a Dog Fall near the road are features of the lower glen. The Forestry Commission own land on both sides of the loch, and have here the laudable intention of regenerating the ancient and native Caledonian pine.

GLENALMOND, *Perthshire* (Map 2, ref. 28⁵73³). The R. Almond rises in the hilly country behind the southern shore of Loch TAY and joins the R. TAY just above PERTH. In the upper reaches it flows through rugged and mountainous country dominated by Ben Chonzie (3,048 ft). A little E. of Auchnafree, the valley widens and from there to Newton Bridge the fertile ground beside the river

contrasts with the steep heights, especially to the N. Opposite the shepherd's house at Conichan the Allt Coire Chultrain leads up past the Eagle's Rock to the "Kirk of the Grove", possibly a secret meeting-place of the Covenanters.

Just E. of the junction of Glenshervie Burn, with the Almond by the N. side of the road, is a prehistoric burial-cairn. It is a long cairn, 190 ft from E. to W., and three burial chambers lie exposed at right angles to the main axis. The Gaelic name of the site is Clach na Tiompain, which (curiously) means the "place of the cymbals". The site was excavated, and is described in the proceedings of the Society of Antiquaries of Scotland. On the opposite side of the road is a prehistoric standing stone – the last remnant of a small circle of four such stones. Just before reaching Newton Bridge, on a narrow plateau 100 ft above the road, is the deserted village of Craignavar. It is worth making the climb to see this. The lint pool, the lime-burning kiln, and the house foundations are all there.

Below Newton Bridge the Almond flows through the SMA' GLEN and emerges into flatter and more fertile country known as Logiealmond. In the upper part of this pleasantly wooded stretch of the river is Trinity College, a well-known public school for boys. It is an Episcopalian foundation opened in 1847 under the Wardenship of Charles Wordsworth, later Bishop of ST ANDREWS.

It should be noted that Glenalmond above Newton Bridge is private property, and permission to visit should be obtained.

GLEN ARTNEY, *Perthshire* (Map 2, ref. 27⁵71⁷). This beautiful wooded glen in the hills 8 m. W. of COMRIE, with Ruchill Water flowing through it, is a part of the country made famous by Sir Walter Scott's earlier romantic narrative verse.

Scott made use of this area in two of his works. It was "in lone Glen Artney's hazel shade" that the stag in *The Lady of the Lake* made his lair before the chase. In *The Legend of Montrose* he included the story of the murder in 1589 of James VI's forester by the Macgregors. Scott's verse was responsible for bringing large numbers of tourists to this region of Perthshire in the early part of the 19th cent., and indeed up till the end of the Victorian age.

GLEN BEG, *Inverness-shire* (Map 5, ref. 18⁵80⁵). This small glen extends inland from the Sound of Sleat opposite SKYE. About 1½ m. from the coast are the remains of two brochs – the best preserved in Scotland, if one excludes those at MOUSA in SHETLAND.

Dun Telve, an official Ancient Monument, has a maximum height of 33 ft 6 in. The wall measures 13 ft 6 in. thick at the base at the entrance, and the courtyard is 32 ft in diameter.

It was cleared in 1914. The broch features can be seen to great advantage.

Dun Troddan, also an Ancient Monument, is ¼ m. farther up the glen. The walls rise to 25 ft with 13½-ft thickness and possesses a 28-ft-diameter courtyard. All the usual broch features occur – the entrance passage, the mural cells, stairs, and three galleries. It was cleared in 1920.

Some 1½ m. farther up the glen is Dun Grugaig. It stands on the brink of a steep gorge, with 14-ft walls still rising to a height of 8 ft. It once formed an enclosure with mural chambers and ledges.

GLENBERVIE, *Kincardineshire* (Map 6, ref. 37⁸77⁹). This upland parish, with its neighbour to the S., Arbuthnott, is the country celebrated in the most remarkable work of fiction by a Scottish writer in the present century – *A Scots Quair*, a trilogy comprising the novels *Sunset Song*, *Cloud Howe*, and *Grey Granite*, by Lewis Grassic Gibbon, whose real name was James Leslie Mitchell. As Gibbon reminds us in *Cloud Howe*, it is also the country of the forefathers of Robert Burns.

Of James Burnes, the poet's great-grandfather, Gibbon writes: "His folk had the ups and downs of all flesh till the father of Robert Burnes grew up, and grew sick of the place, and went off to Ayr, and there the poet Robert was born, him that lay with nearly as many women as Solomon did, though not all at one time".

Bervie Water is a stream less than 20 m. long that rises in the foothills of the G R A M P I A N S and flows roughly southward to the North Sea at I N V E R B E R V I E. To the E. of the stream stand the small upland farms on which both the Burneses and the parents of the modern novelist dwelt. Although Gibbon was born (in 1901) at Hill of Seggat, in the Buchan parish of Auchterless, he spent his boyhood at Blaweary, the cottage of Bloomfield. Above it, the moor called the Reisk mounts to the Hill of Bruxie, which, with its snipe-haunted lochan, overlooks the main road from S T O N E H A V E N to L A U R E N C E K I R K. Bogjorgan and Brawlinmuir lie farther N., actually in the foothills of the Mounth where they face the Howe of the Mearns. For Glenbervie is the frontier parish, a parish between two worlds, opening out to the W. into the fertile strath that is really the northern continuation of S T R A T H M O R E, with its soil of rich red clay, and closing in to the N. and E. in rounded hills where the land is "coarse and lonely", as Gibbon put it.

A little to the NE. of the Kirkton of Glenbervie is the old-world weavers' village of Drumlithie, of which it has been said that "the only regular feature about it is its irregularity. A bird's eye view of it from a balloon would almost convince one that the houses had been shaken from the skies." Often taken to be the original of Segget, the village that is the scene of *Cloud Howe* (although Gibbon deliberately gave it some differing characteristics), Drumlithie has, in the centre of its main street, an isolated steeple built in 1777 as a bell-tower to summon the weavers to their labour. It was originally a village of long, low but-and-bens, with a loom in every ben-end. But the power-loom put an end to all that, and by 1878 only a single hand-loom weaver remained. Today the steeple bell is still rung, but only to celebrate the wedding of a villager.

The ancient centre of the parish is the Kirkton, quite different in character and diversified by wood, river, meadow, and hedgerow. Here the Water of Bervie comes down by an ancient ford, still in use, till it meets a small tributary burn in a picturesque wooded dell. On the high triangular cape of land at the meeting of the streams stands Glenbervie House, in reality a castle of the early 16th cent., the home of Mrs P. Badenoch Nicolson. Glenbervie, built on an unusual plan with two great round towers projecting at either end of the main front, was besieged by Adam Gordon of Auchindoun (the "Edom o' Gordon" of the ballad) on behalf of Mary Queen of Scots in 1572. The upper parts of the main block and of the round towers were altered and rebuilt in the 18th and 19th cents., but the basement, including the two towers, is vaulted throughout and the towers have wide-mouthed gun-loops so disposed as to cover the approaches and rake with fire the front of the main building. Glenbervie was held successively by the Melvilles, including that unpopular Sheriff of the Mearns who was "sodden and suppit in bree" (boiled alive by his obstreperous neighbours) in 1420, and by the Douglases, earls of Angus, who held it at the time of the siege.

The church and churchyard of Arbuthnott, 5 m. S. on a loop of the road (B967) that follows the left bank of the Bervie to the sea, has a naturally beautiful setting. It is here at a corner of the surrounding kirkyard wall that the ashes of Grassic Gibbon lie under a grey granite stone on which is inscribed a phrase from the peroration of *Sunset Song*. In that book, he had described the kirk itself rather irreverently. "Hidden away among their yews", he wrote, "were kirk and manse. . . . Next door the kirk was an olden tower, built in the time of the Roman Catholics, the coarse creatures, and it was fell old and wasn't used any more except by the cushat-doves. In the lower half of the tower was an effigy-thing of Cospatrick de Gondeshil, him that killed the gryphon, lying on his back with his arms crossed and a daft-like simper on his face . . . the real kirk was split in two bits, the main hall and the wee hall, and some called them the byre and turnip-shed, and the pulpit stood midway. . . ."

Anyone who visits Arbuthnott will immediately recognize the point of this highly satirical description, which must have caused shock and heart-burning in the 1930s. The "main hall" and the "wee hall" are the nave nd the chancel. The chancel (considerably restored) was built and dedicated by Bishop David de Bernham in 1242. It has three lancets, under one of which is a piscina. The "olden ower" is the aisle, a two-storey building with a ound stair-turret. It was built by Sir Robert Arbuthnott, *c*. 1471, for the purpose of housing a portable altar, which he had obtained under cence from Pope Innocent VIII. The aisle is a eautiful example of late Scottish Gothic architecture, and is built of finely hewn ashlar. he "effigy-thing" is a full-length stone statue a a reclining posture of a knight in full armour, elmet, and sword, the face looking upwards nd the feet resting on the figure of a dog. It robably represents James Arbuthnott, son of ir Robert, who died in 1521.

Readers of *Sunset Song* will be able to discover for themselves many more correspondences, and indeed one could spend days of ell-rewarded literary pilgrimage in these two arishes, which represent a complete cross-ection of the "old Scotland" that Gibbon both locked and yet deeply loved.

;LEN BRITTLE, *Inverness-shire* (Map 4, ef. 14³82⁴), lies W. of the CUILLIN Hills, on he Island of SKYE in the Inner Hebrides (*see* The Shape of Scotland"). This wild and emote spot on Loch Brittle, at the SW. of the entral body of Skye, is a meeting-place for limbers of the Cuillins that tower all around . There is now a youth hostel there. A rough oad leads N. to connect with Loch Harport; a etter road is thus reached, which leads to LIGACHAN and the main road.

;LENBUCHAT, *Aberdeenshire* (Map 6, ef. 33⁸81⁵). One of the tributary glens of the pper DON, opening out to the N. at Bridge f Buchat, this tragically depopulated valley, vhere the population has fallen from 570 in 871 to 139 today, is both scenically and istorically of absorbing interest. Just above ridge of Buchat, in the midst of the Castle 'ark, stands the ruin of Glenbuchat Castle, ow under the care of the Ministry of Public Building and Works. One of the finest examples f the Z-plan tower-house, it was built by John Jordon, younger of Cairnburrow, and his econd wife, Helen Carnegie, in 1590. Over the ntrance, with their names and the date, appears he motto "Nothing on earth remains but ame". On the staircase (but now unfortunately anished) was inscribed an eight-line "meta-hysical" poem, the translation of which reads: 'This house shows that I have a care of my ealth; as wives cherish their spouses, so I love ife: I declare death a stranger. On the contrary he godly love death, they cry that love is anity, but pain doth make them weep eternally. Then live to love, ere love is really thine, for ove as lived, or beloved, or believed, divinely hines."

Architecturally, the most unusual feature of the Castle is that trompes, or bold squinch arches, are used to carry the two stair-turrets instead of the usual corbelling. The device was given the name "trompe" by a famous French architect Philibert de L'Orme in a book published in 1567 because of its resemblance to the mouth of a trumpet.

Most famous of the Gordons of Glenbuchat was the last, the John Gordon known to history as "Old Glenbuchat of the '45". He fought at SHERIFFMUIR in the '15. When the '45 broke out he was aged 68, but he raised a little army of several hundred men and flung himself into the fray. After the march to Derby, he accompanied the Jacobite army in all its terrible retreat to the N. At CULLODEN he was in the second line of Prince Charles's force. Thereafter his sufferings were extreme. His house at St Bridget's near TOMINTOUL was burnt before his eyes. He hid under rocks and in woods in wild weather, let his hair grow to try to disguise himself, and eventually reached the Buchan coast and escaped to Norway in a small Swedish sloop, with a price of £1,000 upon his head. He died in poverty at Boulogne in 1750.

No one who goes to Glenbuchat should fail to visit the old parish kirk at the Kirkton, a perfect example of the traditional country church of 200 years ago recently taken over by ABERDEEN County Council for preservation as an Ancient Monument. Its walls are plastered, and so is the coved ceiling. Between the pews the floor is cobbled, and the alleys are laid in Correen stone. The pews are arranged on three sides of the pulpit, which is midway along the S. wall. With its laird's loft and its pews of unvarnished woodwork, it has been described as "a model of primitive but comely decency". In the early 19th cent. Glenbuchat lived by smuggling. Every man in the glen was either engaged in making whisky or transporting it to the low country, and every house had its hiding-place for the illicit still, usually under the "deece", the long seat or bench that was a feature of every farm kitchen.

GLENCAPLE, *Dumfriesshire* (Map 2, ref. 29⁹56⁸). A village of whitewashed rose-festooned cottages, Glencaple lies in a very pretty situation on the E. side of the Nith estuary, 5 m. S. of DUMFRIES, looking across at Kirkconnel Merse and Criffell.

It was founded near Dumfries on land granted by the Maxwells of Nithsdale, and the quay was built with stone from their quarries, in 1746–7. The Maxwells were granted in return free passage for their goods across Dumfries Bridge. From its foundation far into the 19th cent., it was, with the "New Quay", 3½ m. upstream (Kingholm Quay, built a few months after Glencaple, which is known locally as the "Auld Quay"), a very busy port.

Besides trade, great numbers of emigrants

left Britain from this place; but it is now silted up, road traffic having delivered the death-blow to its coastal shipping, which lasted till as late as the 1930s; in that decade, 100 to 150 ships were coming into the two quays each year. Its shipbuilding industry, active in the 1820s, has long since disappeared. Its quays and moorings are now used by local yachtsmen, power-boating being a popular sport. It has literary associations with Scott's *Guy Mannering* and with Robert Burns, who wrote some poetry when working as an exciseman here. Although the village is now largely a Dumfries dormitory and a holiday centre, local fishermen still operate their stake-nets for flounders. The haaf-net, a Solway speciality, is still used for salmon; fishermen stand in a line, deep in the water, using nets attached to a 14-ft spar, facing the current and holding the net in pockets. When a fish tugs against the net, the haafer throws net and fish over the spar, then stuns the captive fish with his "mell" and pops it into the bag on his shoulder. There are about seventy licensed haaf-net fishermen who work at it from April to September; it is a profitable part-time hobby rather than an industry.

The great expanse of salt marsh below the village is a bird sanctuary where greylag and pink-footed and barnacle geese resort.

The Iron Age and Roman forts on top of the Wardlaw (which has a fine view of the Solway and Cumberland Fells) lie about 2 m. below the village. CAERLAVEROCK Castle, 3 m. downstream, is the principal local antiquity. There is some bathing.

GLEN CLOVA, *Angus* (Map 6, ref. 33°77⁴), is the valley of the R. South Esk from its source in the LOCHNAGAR range to where it leaves the hills and enters STRATHMORE.

Glen Clova, and its western extension Glen Doll, are celebrated for their alpine flora, and for other rare plants and ferns. It is very rich in moss flora, and is the only habitat of *Oxytropis campestris* in the British Isles. The scenery in the upper part of the glen is very grand and wild, with magnificent rock-cliffs and corrie basins. There are three famous hill-paths leading from the glen across to Deeside. The Capel Mounth is the most easterly, and joins Glen Clova to Glen Muick, ascending to 2,239 ft. The Bachnagairn route goes from the head of Glen Clova up to 2,345 ft, descends to the side of Loch Muick, and then joins the other path to BALLATER. The other, western route is to BRAEMAR. It goes from Glen Clova to Glen Doll, then over Jock's Road by a stony pass ascending steeply to the summit at "Tolmount" (3,143 ft). The actual watershed is at 3,000 ft at the "Knaps of Fafernie". Having reached here the climber will enjoy magnificent views of the CAIRNGORMS. The path then descends to Loch Callater, Glen Callater, and thus to Braemar.

At the village of Clova in the glen are remains of a castle, once the seat of th Ogilvies. The historical incident known as th Start took place at Clova, for in 1650 Charle II, after landing at GARMOUTH, travelled t PERTH to meet the Presbyterian Committee o Estates. There were delays in the plans for hi coronation, and he decided to take refuge wit his Royalist friends. He escaped to Strathmore called at Cortachy Castle, and then continue up Glen Clova. A party of horsemen from Perth, under Colonel Montgomery, caught hir in a cottage there; the poor young man, havin found none of the support he expected returned to Perth and was crowned (afte having signed certain Presbyterian documents as he later claimed, under duress) at SCON three months later.

GLENCOE, *Argyll* (Map 5, ref. 21⁵75⁵). The famous pass through Glencoe from th Moor of RANNOCH to the Inverness-shir Loch Leven is known to thousands of travellers Glencoe is the most celebrated glen in Scotland – both for historical associations and for over-whelmingly magnificent mountain scenery.

The glen proper is 7½ m. long from Col a 1,011 ft to Loch Leven, but by long custom the name Glencoe is given to the whole valley running 15 m. W. of Kingshouse on the R. Etive. As many as 12,800 acres of this land were acquired in 1937 and are now owned by the National Trust for Scotland, including the site of the Glencoe Massacre and Bidean nam Biam (the highest mountain in Argyll). The new road through the glen dates from 1935, and is con-structed at a lower level than the old one; it is well engineered. In the middle of the defile, beside the old road, is a rock platform known as the Study. The name is a corruption of the old Scots "stiddie", meaning anvil, and from here is the famous view of the Three Sisters of Glencoe. These hills are Beinn Fhada, Gearr Aonach, and Aonach Dubh (from E. to W.), and are the outliers of the great Bidean nam Bian (3,766 ft) and of Stob Coire nan Lochan (3,657 ft).

High on the side of Aonach Dubh, above Loch Achtriochtan, is the deep slit of Ossian's Cave. It is reached by a moderately difficult rock climb, named Ossian's Ladder. Ossian was a Gaelic bard and hero of the 3rd cent. A.D., traditionally born in Glencoe, but there is no historical evidence for this belief, and the cave could hardly have been habitable, as the floor slopes at an angle of 45 degrees.

Below Loch Achtriochtan, the old and new roads part, the latter keeping to the S. of the R. Coe. To the N. of the river is the Clachaig Inn, and nearby the Signal Rock. From here the signal for the infamous and still remembered massacre of the Macdonalds was allegedly given in the early hours of the 13th of February 1692. The massacre was carried out under the orders of William III by Campbell of GLEN LYON and 128 soldiers, all of whom had lived

Scottish Tourist Board

Glencoe

for twelve days upon friendly terms with the inhabitants. The cause was the failure of MacIan of Glencoe to take the oath of allegiance to the King before the 1st of January 1692. MacIan reached FORT WILLIAM by the 31st of December, but was told to go to INVERARAY. With the inevitable delays, he did not take the oath until the 6th of January. Out of 200 occupants of the glen at least forty were slain; others fled to the hills to die of want and exposure. All the hamlets were burnt down by the soldiers. The monument in memory of the fallen Macdonalds stands in the strath near the old road to Invercoe. Their chief, MacIan, was buried on the island of Eilean Munde, in Loch Leven, near the entrance to the glen. This dreadful deed, though it took place in what was then a remote corner of the Highlands, created much anger all over Scotland.

On the N. side is the pinnacled ridge of Aonach Eagach (meaning the Notched Ridge). It is 6 m. long, and is one of the narrowest summit-ridges in Scotland. Continuous to the W. is the prominent Pap of Glencoe (2,430 ft). Above the Clachaig Inn, the peak of Sgor nam Fiannaidh is split by the great chasm called "Clachaig Gully" – a famous rock climb. At Altnafeadh, at the head of the glen, the Aonach Eagach is crossed by the zigzagging Devil's Staircase, which runs to KINLOCHLEVEN 6 m. away. It is an old drove route, made into a military road around 1750, and is an easy pass in fine weather; it has been used for motorcycle reliability trials.

On the S. side of Altnafeadh are the very fine mountains known as the Shepherds of Etive. To the W. is Buchaille Etive Beag, 3,129 ft, and to the E. is the magnificent Buchaille Etive Mor (summit Stob Dearg, 3,345 ft), which presents a grand rock-face 1,200 ft high to the NE. There is excellent rock-climbing, and ski-ing facilities include a chair-lift to 2,100 ft about a mile from King's House hotel.

GLENCORSE, *Midlothian* (Map 3, ref. 32⁴66³). This is a parish to the S. of EDINBURGH that contains the Glencorse Barracks, headquarters of the Lowland Brigade; these were formerly the barracks of the Royal Scots, the oldest regiment to be formed in Britain, as the nucleus was in the companies formed by Louis XIII in 1633, incorporating the famous Scots Brigade from the Swedish Army. Greenlaw mansion house was converted in 1804 to be a depot for prisoners taken in the Napoleonic

Wars. Further buildings were added in 1813. From 1845 to 1888 they served as a Military Prison for Scotland.

The central tower and chapel of the prison are incorporated in the latest barracks, which take the place that the Royal Scots had held as H.Q. for the past sixty years. The old Glencorse Kirk, to the N. of Milton Bridge, is now in ruins. Robert Louis Stevenson once worshiped there, and described it in his unfinished *Weir of Hermiston*. The kirk dates from 1699, replacing an earlier structure.

Nearby on the E. is Auchindinny House, which was the last house to be built by the famous Scottish architect Sir William Bruce. It dates from 1702 to 1707, and is one of the most charming small residences in the Queen Anne style in Scotland. From 1797 to 1807 the author Henry Mackenzie lived there, and it became the centre of a literary circle including Scott. Mackenzie's best-remembered work is that lachrymose novel, *A Man of Feeling*.

GLENDALE, *Inverness-shire* (Map 4, ref. 12⁰84⁶), is on the Island of SKYE in the Inner Hebrides (*see* "The Shape of Scotland"). On the extreme W. tip of the island, on Loch Pooltiel and on the road W. from DUNVEGAN, this remote spot was one of the scenes of the crofters' resistance in 1883. This led to the Crofters' Commission and the subsequent Crofting Act. (*See* "Scotland in History".)

GLENDARUEL, *Argyll* (Map 1, ref. 20⁰68⁴). This picturesque valley of the R. Ruel is in the district of Cowal, and is 11 m. long to the head of Loch Riddon, an inlet of the Kyles of BUTE. In Kilmodan churchyard, at Glendaruel village, is a memorial to Colin Maclaurin (1698–1746), the famous mathematician who organized EDINBURGH's defences against Prince Charles Edward Stuart during the '45. The Prince's army also contained a certain number of Maclaurins, the name now usually spelt MacLaren.

At the mouth of Glendaruel, a narrow winding and hilly road leads W. to OTTER FERRY on Loch Fyne. The road ascends to 1,026 ft, and there are fine views from it.

GLEN DEVON, *Perthshire* (Map 2, ref. 29⁵70⁶). To the N., this glen merges with GLENEAGLES and the two valleys form a dramatic passage through the Ochil Hills, rising to nearly 900 ft at their junction.

Fife County Council have established two reservoirs in this part of the Ochils, the first in the upper reaches of the R. Devon, the second in Glenquay, a western tributary.

The glen was extensively used by 19th-cent. cattle-drovers, who brought beasts from the N. to the cattle tryst at FALKIRK. In 1812–13, 863 cattle and 13,219 sheep passed this way, and no doubt many more should have been recorded at the toll-bar at the Yetts of Much-kart had not secret passages of the Ochils been made to avoid payment of the toll.

Today Glen Devon and its subsidiary valley afford wonderful walking and pony-trekking country.

Glendevon village first emerges historically in 1521 when Abbot Mylne of CAMBUSKENNETH ABBEY consecrated a new chapter house, and invited to the service "Jacobus Wilson prebandarius de Glendowane" and also "Jacobus Haldene of Glenaggls Knight". At this time the church in Glendevon was attached to DUNBLANE and served from there.

In 1643 John Brughe was tried in EDINBURGH for practising witchcraft; one of the charges against him was that "thrice he had met Satan in the Kirkyard of Glendevan". In 1649 another inhabitant of the glen, Mart. Kennard, was suspected of witchcraft.

Glendevon Castle is an early 15th-cent. fortalice. It is said to have belonged to the Douglas who was stabbed by King James II at STIRLING in 1452, after having been given a safe conduct. By the 16th cent. the Castle belonged to the Crawfords, but after 1766 the keep became the property of the Rutherfords.

GLEN DIOMHAN, *Buteshire* (Map 1, ref. 19¹64⁷), Island of ARRAN, Buteshire. These 24 acres of steep-sided gorge in Glen Catacol, in the NW. of the Island of Arran, are noted for their rare white beam trees. It is now a nature reserve.

GLENEAGLES, *Perthshire* (Map 2, ref. 29³71⁰), one of the most famous golfing resorts in Scotland, is situated on the edge of the Muir of Ochil looking towards GLEN DEVON and the summits of the Ochil hills. The hotel, which belongs to British Rail, was opened in 1923 and has a well-deserved reputation for comfort. During the Second World War, it was used as a hospital and later as a rehabilitation centre.

There are two main golf courses associated with the hotel: the King's Course and the Queen's Course. The famous Scottish golfer James Braid took part in the planning of both courses.

Gleneagles House, in Glen Eagles proper, was built in 1624, replacing the old moated castle, which since the 14th cent. had been the home of the Haldanes. In 1799 the estate was bought by Viscount Duncan of Camperdown, but has since returned to the Haldane family.

Through Glen Eagles and Glen Devon runs one of several drove roads linking the N. with the big cattle tryst at FALKIRK.

GLENELG, *Inverness-shire* (Map 5, ref. 18²81⁹). This village on Glenelg Bay is in a picturesque situation facing SKYE. It is accessible by one road only, which crosses the hills to the W. of Loch Duich by the famous MAM RATAGAN Pass. Dr Johnson and oswell reached Glenelg over this pass during their Highland tour in 1773. On the N. side of Glenelg Bay are the remains of BERNERA barracks, which were erected in 1722. There is a memorial to one of the officers dated 1730 in the old churchyard. A ferry now operates from Glenelg to Kylerhea in Skye, across the KYLE RHEA, which is noted for its exceptionally strong currents.

The narrow, rough, and hilly coast road from Glenelg around Outer Loch Hourn to Arnisdale has particularly fine views across to Skye and RUM. There are those who, having had the good fortune to see Loch Hourn on a fine summer's day, consider it to be the most spectacular of all Scotland's many sea-lochs.

GLENFARG, *Perthshire* (Map 3, ref. 31³ 71°). This picteresque and narrow glen will be much more pleasant for motorists and pedestrians when the huge and (totally unsuitable) volume of heavy traffic between Fife and Perth is by-passed on to the new section of the main trunk road, linking up with the FORTH ROAD BRIDGE and also by-passing Kelty and KINROSS. The glen is 4 m. long and in the northern half twists and turns with the course of the Farg river; the railway (now closed) ran alongside and had two tunnels within 2 m.

The village of Glenfarg at the southern end of the glen, in a sheltered position and noted for its mild climate, is a popular holiday resort. From the summit of an old road over the Wicks of Baiglie from the glen, Sir Walter Scott described the setting of PERTH in the first chapter of *The Fair Maid of Perth*.

GLENFINNAN, *Inverness-shire* (Map 5, ref. 19°78°), is one of the most beautiful and romantic places in the W. Highlands, where the "Road to the Isles" passes the head of Loch SHEIL on the way to MORAR and MALLAIG. At the head of Loch Sheil, near where the R. Finnan flows down from Glen Finnan into the loch, stands that prominent Glenfinnan Monument acquired by the National Trust for Scotland in 1938. It commemorates the raising by the Marquess of Tullibardine of Prince Charles Edward Stuart's standard on the 19th of August 1745 as a rallying-point for the clans. It was over the hill to the N. that Lochiel and his clansmen marched to join the Prince, thus convincing all who had already joined him that a march S. on the United Kingdom was feasible.

The statue was erected in 1815 by Macdonald of Glenaladale, grandson of one of the original supporters, as a tribute to the clansmen who fought and died in the Prince's cause, and who are symbolized by the statue of a Highlander, sculptured by Greenshields, that surmounts the tower. On plaques around the encircling wall is a dedication in English, Gaelic, and Latin. In the Catholic church, standing directly above Loch Sheil and overlooking the statue, is a tablet that recalls the unfortunate Prince and his venture. Whenever possible the door of the church is kept open as a symbol of greeting. The churchyard contains an old Irish church-bell hung at ground level. The bell sounds a deep note at the lightest touch.

St Finnan's Isle at the head of Loch Sheil has been a burial-place for the Macdonalds since time immemorial. A ruined chapel stands there.

Glenfinnan and the monument beside Loch Shiel

Scottish Tourist Board

GLEN ISLA, *Angus* (Map 6, ref. 32¹76⁰). The picturesque valley of the R. Isla runs for 17 m. in the eastern GRAMPIANS. The village of Kirkton of Glenisla is a third of the way up the glen. Some 4 m. farther on, the road passes the ruins of Forter Castle burnt by Argyle in 1640. It was a stronghold of the Ogilvies and was burnt at the same time as Airlie Castle.

The road continues up the glen to Tulchan Lodge, then a track goes N. up Monega Pass, a former drove road that attains the height of 3,318 ft, and is said to be the highest right-of-way in Scotland; it eventually joins the CAIRNWELL Pass. The path goes up steep Canlochan Glen, under the slopes of Monega Hill (2,917 ft) and Glas Maol (3,502 ft). Glen Isla is noted for its rare plants, and is now a State Forest.

GLENKENS, *Kirkcudbrightshire* (Map 2, ref. 25⁵59⁰). The Glenkens comprises the whole northerly district of Kirkcudbrightshire – the four parishes of CARSPHAIRN, DALRY, BALMACLELLAN, and Kells. It consists of a huge area of mountain and forest penetrated by the valleys of Ken and Deugh, and well sprinkled with the new Electricity Board reservoirs, a great improvement, with the forests, to what was rather a bleak landscape.

Population is very thin. Dalry and Carspairn are the only substantial villages.

The highest points are on the Rhinns of Kells, rising to Corserine 2,669 ft. The whole 5 m. ridge is above 2,000 ft., and in the N. part of the Ken Valley are Cairnsmore of Carsphairn, 2,612 ft, and Windy Standard, 2,287 ft.

GLEN LIVET, *Banffshire* (Map 6, ref. 32⁰83⁰). This glen, which has won world renown from the whisky associated with it, is in the N. GRAMPIANS to the NE. of TOMINTOUL. The Livet Water flows N. from the Ladder Hills to join the R. Avon. The famous distillery was founded in 1824. This was one of five started there when the Distillery Act of 1824 put an end to over 200 illicit stills in the district. "Glenlivet" is a pure malt – unblended – whisky.

Some 4 m. E. of the village is the scene of the Battle of Glenlivet, where on the 4th of October 1594 the Protestant Army, loyal to King James VI and under the Earl of Argyll, was defeated by an insurgent Catholic army under the Earl of Huntly.

Above Livet Water and near the distillery are the remains of the 16th-cent. Blairfindy Castle, the hunting-seat of the earls of Huntly, and now an Ancient Monument. At the junction of Livet Water and the Avon is a ruined ancient keep – Castle Drumin. There are also picturesque remains of an old bridge.

At Scalan, in the Braes of Glenlivet and at the head of the glen, was hidden a Catholic seminary, for training young men in Scotland, and particularly from this part of Scotland, for the Catholic priesthood. This secret spot wa founded in 1717, but it was plundered an burnt after the Duke of Cumberland's victor over the Jacobite forces at CULLODEN in 174! It was quietly removed to a place nea INVERURIE.

Catholicism, amongst the peasantry, is i Scotland usually associated with the Celti West and with the Hebrides, where it survive because of its remoteness at first from th Scottish post-Reformation Government an later, after the Union, from London. Thes mainland north-eastern Catholics who su vived, and whose descendants are still of th Old Faith, had a much harder job. Travelle in Aberdeenshire and in Banffshire ofte express surprise at finding indigenous, non Celtic, non-Irish immigrant Catholicism here.

The toleration that the British Governmen eventually extended to these north-easter. Scottish Catholics at the end of the 18th cen had its reward. Some fine soldiery (allowed t have their own Catholic chaplains) serve notably abroad. One inhabitant of this distric the well-known Abbé Macpherson, with th assistance of the British Navy, nearly pulled o a major coup during the Napoleonic Wars. H was sent on a man-o'-war to rescue Pop Pius VI, then a captive of Napoleon's. Th Pope, who knew and trusted the Scots pries had agreed to the scheme. But Napoleon gc wind of it and it came to nothing. The Britis Government, however, noted with gratitud the Abbé's readiness to assist. It is roughl from this time that increased toleration fo Scottish native Catholics began to take effect.

GLENLOCHAR, *Kirkcudbrightshire* (Ma 2, ref. 27³56⁴). Glenlochar Bridge and House li on the Dee near Crossmichael village at the S end of the Loch Ken, just below the barrage constructed in 1934, that heightens the loch Near the bridge are the foundations of a larg Roman fort discovered on an aerial photo graphy sortie by Dr St Joseph of Cambridge in 1949.

Excavation has shown it to be of 7 acres i extent and to have had two 1st-cent. and tw 2nd-cent. occupations. The fort was actuall found during the agricultural revolution in th 18th cent. (and compares with NEWSTEAD' Roman Fort and the "Redabbeystead" nea MELROSE), and until recently the wor "abbey" in Gothic type marked the site o Ordnance maps.

GLENLUCE, *Wigtownshire* (Map 2, ref 22⁰55⁷), is a pleasantly situated village – just t the N. of the sandy shores of Luce Bay. The Water of Luce flows into the bay just to the W. and the village itself climbs the steep easter slope of the valley. Gilbert Campbell, the "Devil of Glenluce", lived in the village from 1654 to 1658. Notorious throughout Scotland he terrified the villagers.

The remains of Luce Abbey, an Ancient Monument, are situated 2 m. NW. of the village, on the E. bank of the river, on a wooded site of great beauty. The Abbey was founded in 1190 by Roland, Lord of Galloway, as a Cistercian house and daughter house of DUNDRENNAN; the ruins are of much architectural interest. The Abbey church is in the first pointed style, and the fine vaulted chapter house, dating from 1470, is almost intact. The S. aisle and S. transept are the principal remains of the church.

There are some interesting tombstones and remains of medieval water-pipes, including junction-boxes, drains, and tiles; part of the site was cleared by the Ministry of Public Building and Works a few years ago, and it yielded a fine collection of medieval pottery, including polychrome ware from the Bordeaux area.

The Abbey is linked traditionally with Michael Scott, the 13th-cent. wizard, who was reputed to have lured the plague, which was then raging, to the Abbey and shut it up in the vault. James IV and his Queen Margaret visited the Abbey in 1507 on a pilgrimage to WHITHORN, as also did Mary Queen of Scots, on her pilgrimage of 1567.

A little W. of the village stands the Castle of Park, a castellated mansion built by Thomas Hay of Park in 1590, using stones from the Abbey; Thomas was the son of the last abbot of Glenluce. It is in very fine condition.

Some 2 m. NE. of the village are the ruins of Carscreugh Castle, built about 1680 by Sir John Dalrymple, later first Lord Stair and President of the Court of Session. The betrothal and marriage of his daughter, Janet (who died in 1669), gave Sir Walter Scott the theme for his novel *The Bride of Lammermoor*; Janet became his tragic heroine, Lucy Ashton.

The village of New Luce is some 5 m. N. at the junction of the Main Water of Luce with the Cross water of Luce, and is the capital of the "Moors" district of Galloway. From 1659, until his ejection in 1662, the famous Alexander Peden – "Prophet Peden" (1626–86) – was the minister. After preaching his farewell sermon, he closed the pulpit door, knocked on it with the Bible thrice and declared, "I arrest thee in My Master's name that none ever enter thee but such as come in by the door as I have done" – a prophesy that was fulfilled, as the pulpit was not preached in from then until after the Revolution.

GLEN LYON, *Perthshire* (Map 2, ref. 26°74⁷), is the longest glen in Scotland (32 m.), but has recently been curtailed by the construction of the Lubreoch Dam at the head of the glen. This has absorbed Loch Lyon, and the water is fed by pipeline to the power station in Glenlochay.

The Gaelic name for Glen Lyon is "Cromghlearn nan clach", which means the Crooked Glen of the Stones. There is a traditional Gaelic saying that Fionn or Fingal, one of the heroes of Celtic mythology, "had twelve castles in the crooked glen of the stones". The castles referred to are a series of stone-built ring-forts of the Iron Age. Strictly speaking, they are not forts, as all lie on low ground and several are close together. They represent an influx of prehistoric people from the W., who cultivated the arable land at the bottom of the glen and built fortified homesteads. The best-preserved examples are near Cashlie farm.

The entrance to Glen Lyon is dramatic. The sides of the glen rise steeply and are heavily wooded, and the river flows in a deep rocky bed. Here is Macgregor's Leap. The story relates to Gregor Macgregor of Glenstrae, who leapt the Lyon in order to escape from pursuing bloodhounds. Higher up, the glen widens considerably and provides a variety of splendid scenery.

The township of Milton Eonan at Bridge of Balgie recalls St Adamnan's mission from Iona. Adamnan or Eonan, the biographer of St Columba, died in A.D. 704. His name is closely associated with Glen Lyon and Strathtay, particularly with the early Culdee College at DULL. He is credited with having set up the first meal-mill in Glen Lyon – hence the name Milton, or Mill Town, Eonan.

The oldest part of Meggernie Castle, now privately owned, dates from the 16th cent. It was begun by Mad Colin, Colin Campbell of Glen Lyon, in about 1585. In the early 18th cent. the then owner, James Menzies, "Old Culdares", is one of those who introduced larches to Scotland, bringing them from the Tyrol, whither he had been banished for his part in the Jacobite Rising of 1715.

There are several hill routes from Glen Lyon across the watersheds between Glen Lochay to the S. and Rannoch to the N. The northernmost of these, by Glen Mearan to the Moor of RANNOCH, is associated with the famous Gaelic lament "Crodh Chailean" (Colin's Cattle).

GLEN·MORE, *Inverness-shire* (Map 5, ref. 29⁵81⁵). The National Forest Park of Glen More is in the NW. corner of the CAIRNGORMS. The forest contains 3,300 acres of pine and spruce woods, as well as 9,200 acres of mountain-side. At the heart is Loch Morlich, no less than 1,000 ft above sea-level, with sandy beaches fringed with old Caledonian pines, descendants of the immemorial Caledonian Forest, and surrounded by grand mountain scenery, including Cairngorm (4,084 ft). A footpath connects the park with AVIEMORE and NETHY BRIDGE. At the E. side of Loch Morlich are the Glen More Youth Hostel, a shop, and Glen More Lodge, the outdoor training centre of the Scottish Council for Physical Recreation.

In summer Glen More attracts ramblers, swimmers, and dinghy-sailors, and in winter it attracts skiers. There is a 2½-m. "ski-road",

Glenmore: dinghies on Loch Morlich   *Scottish Tourist Board*

which goes a farther 1,000 ft up the Cairngorm to the ski-lift; thereafter a chair-lift will take you even farther up.

GLENMORE ALBIN, *Inverness-shire* (Map 5, ref. 24⁸82³). Known also as the "Great Glen of Albin" or just the "Great Glen", this large and spectacular natural fissure extends in a straight line across Scotland from FORT WILLIAM in the SW. to INVERNESS in the NE. It is a long geological fault, and forms a remarkable physical feature that completely divides Scotland. There is a chain of lochs along the glen – Loch NESS (the largest), Loch Dochfour, Loch Oich, Lochgarry, and Loch Lochy. These are linked by the CALEDONIAN CANAL, which stretches for 22 m. of the 60-m. length of the Great Glen itself.

General Wade's road linking Fort William and Inverness traversed the glen from end to end, but the modern road only partly follows this line.

GLEN NEVIS, *Inverness-shire* (Map 5, ref. 21⁴76⁷). One of Scotland's finest and loveliest glens, Glen Nevis runs on the W. and S. flanks of BEN NEVIS (4,406 ft), with the Water of Nevis flowing through it. A narrow switchback road traverses much of the glen. Leaving FORT WILLIAM, it passes Achintee Farm, where a path branches off to the summit of Ben Nevis; then the road goes past Glen Nevis House, the headquarters of Lochiel when besieging Fort William in 1746.

Some 9 m. from Fort William is the vitrified fort of Dun Deardail. It stands on the hill to the

W. of the road at a height of 1,127 ft. It measures 150 ft by 90 ft within a massive vitrified ruin, some 50 ft thick in places. The entrance is from the NW., and there is a magnificent view from the site.

The road reaches Polldush waterfall, in the wooded gorge of the R. Nevis. Thereafter it deteriorates into a poor track, which leads to a climbing-hut at Steall and to a lofty waterfall, 450 ft high, providing once again magnificent scenery.

GLEN PROSEN, *Angus* (Map 6, ref. 33⁰76⁵). The well-wooded valley of the Prosen Water, from its source in the Braes of Mar in the E. GRAMPIANS, to where it enters STRATHMORE, is known as Glen Prosen. About 2 m. up the glen is a sandstone fountain erected in memory of the Antarctic explorers Captain Scott and Dr Wilson. It was in a bungalow near the entrance to the glen (where Dr Wilson was staying during a study of grouse) that Scott and Wilson discussed plans for that ill-fated expedition to the South Pole in 1912. The bungalow is still to be seen, bordered at the roadside by a row of birch trees planted to celebrate Queen Victoria's Jubilee in 1887.

GLEN ROSA, *Buteshire* (Map 1, ref. 19⁹63⁹), is on the Island of ARRAN (*see* "The Shape of Scotland"). Where it opens into BRODICK Bay, this is one of the most appealing glens in Scotland. Grand in its steep sides and its culminating saddle that separates it from Glen Sannox, it attracts by its elusive

G. W. Harvey

Glenrothes: the Town Centre

tints of pink. The R. Rosa, which runs through it, is particularly clear. The little trout in it, on account of their protective colouring, seem like pale flickering ghosts. The glen is easily approached from Brodick.

GLENROTHES, *Fife* (Map 3, ref. 32⁹70⁰). This, the second of Scotland's New Towns to be established (1949) after the Second World War, had a curious beginning, which has produced beneficial results not envisaged by the founders of the town. Before touching on the origins of Glenrothes and its development, the reader is referred to the general policy on the post-war Scottish New Towns that was described under CUMBERNAULD – alphabetically the first New Town in this gazetteer.

Glenrothes was at first primarily designed to provide modern housing in pleasant country circumstances for coal-miners who, it was believed, would work a new seam in this district of Fife. The intention was to provide a complete contrast to the squalid mining towns and villages that for more than a century and a half had disfigured the Lowlands of Scotland. A good and forward-looking idea, but it was (at the time unfortunately, so it seemed) made impotent by the discovery that the seam was unworkable.

Still, a good and forward-looking idea need not necessarily perish because its original *raison d'etre* is removed; it can be developed upon another basis. This is what has happened at Glenrothes. There are those who, seeing the happy state of Glenrothes today (though one would never impute such an idea to those in

charge of the place), would say that the best thing that ever happened to this growing and prosperous, yet essentially Scottish, New Town was the unworkability of the coal. Such might reflect even further that coal is becoming a thing of the past in this atomic age, and that to provide a New Town for a traditionally begrimed industry would have been inappropriate.

At any rate, what happened was that, coal being gone, the Glenrothes Development Corporation concentrated with redoubled energy on another facet of the scheme that had always been in their minds. That was the attraction of new industries (one avoids the constricting word "light") to this place already springing up as a New Town. Right from the start, there had been the intention to attract lighter industries for the employment of the womenfolk of the miners. Now the Corporation went forward with the scheme of drawing any new and suitable modern industry to the New Town for the employment of men and women. The word "suitable" is important here. "Any old industry" will not do. Diverse industries are needed to protect the town against recession, strikes, and other catastrophes. Also it is essential to select the right industries in terms of employment as the final target of population is approached.

This book is a portrait of Scotland, and this section of it is a portrait-gazetteer. We shall not, then, seek to inflict on visitors to Scotland a detailed list of the industries that Glenrothes did succeed in attracting. Let it suffice to say that they succeeded, are succeeding, and look as if they will continue to succeed. The only statistics we need to mention show that the population drawn to this entirely new venture was over 30,000 by 1971 (eventual target 70,000), and the number of industries established (coming from England, Europe, and America) was approaching fifty.

Now for a picture of the place, which, if the visitor sees it in fine weather, is bound to please and interest him. The reference to fine weather allows one in passing to point out that the climate of Fife, though bracing, is considerably superior to (say) that of Kent. This statement, which is supported by the Meteorological Office, has been useful in changing the minds of some southern industries who have traditionally feared that anywhere N. of Birmingham is verging on the Arctic Circle.

Set in circumstances of characteristic Fife rural beauty, then, with the Lomond Hills dominating it to the N., Glenrothes has not sought to be revolutionary in style. Rather it has tended to develop in a modern fashion the pleasing Fife Lowland cottage or small house. The visitor may observe this as he sees the early 19th-cent. buildings on the outskirts of the town growing into the modern domestic architecture.

This is not to say that there are not one or two buildings that are completely up-to-date. In Scotland during the last ten years, there has been some excellent experimental church-building, both Protestant and Catholic. In particular the eye lights upon the Protestant church of the Kirk of Scotland. The Catholic church in Glenrothes, admirable in its cata-comb-like severity, is not what the usual Protestant conceives a Catholic church to look like. The Protestant kirk is even more stagger-ingly unlike the usual Catholic idea of such places of worship. When a visitor enters its always open door (a Protestant innovation), he might well think for a moment that he had strayed into some modern Catholic church in the neighbourhood of Naples. It is so full of light that it seems positively luminous. At the far end of the church is a richly coloured mural painted by Alberto Morroco – an artist who has at least this connection with Scotland, that his family resides in DUNDEE – and portraying scenes from Our Lord's life. Brigadier Doyle, the resident chairman of the Development Corporation who, as his name might lead one to guess, is an adherent of the older faith, is particularly friendly with the Protestant minister, whose lively, modern, yet religiously-based work amongst the youth of Glenrothes is of the greatest civic assistance in training the young to be citizens of the future.

In a town such as this, springing up and healthily growing out of a rural area in Fife, one of the essential problems is this preparation of young people for the duties of citizenship. In it, the Church of Scotland minister and the Catholic priest combine to give their assistance to the Corporation.

The Brigadier pointed out with some pride that Glenrothes is a completely independent unit in the heart of the rich rural land of Fife. No one commutes from there, as people some-times do in other New Towns near to big cities. Glenrothes eyes are entirely upon itself – where it lives and works.

On the other hand (and this is particularly true since the completion of the FORTH Road Bridge), the place is easily accessible to EDIN-BURGH. You can get into Edinburgh within an hour, do your shopping, theatre-going, or visiting, and be back comfortably by bedtime. Incidentally Glenrothes, like CUMBERNAULD, has an airfield of its own. Industrialists from North America may fly to our Scottish airport of PRESTWICK and, by quick change of air-craft, be within Glenrothes in twenty-three minutes. The workers of Glenrothes are particularly proud of their airfield and take great interest in it.

No, Glenrothes, independent unit though it is, does not lie out on a limb. And, of course, there are other cities easily accessible, such as PERTH with its good shops, and of course ST ANDREWS, whose links are hallowed ground for visitors from America.

Glenrothes, like every expanding unit, has its growing-pains. One of these involves the adaptability of the women who may have come from crowded tenements in the cities into these rural houses of their own. But those in charge of this modern yet rurally-rooted New Town do everything they can to make the change easy for incomers.

GLEN ROY, *Inverness-shire* (Map 5, ref. 23°78⁴). The narrow valley of the Roy, in the Lochaber district, extends NE. from Roy Bridge where the R. Roy joins the R. Spean.

A rough road leads into Glen Roy, and after 4 m. provides views of the very striking and famous Parallel Roads, unsurpassed in Western Europe. These can be traced almost con-tinuously on both sides of the valley. Each forms a gently sloping shelf, 3 to 30 ft wide, and represents the natural erosion along the shores of a former lake, which in unknown antiquity varied in height. The lake was formed by glacial action, being dammed up by ice in Glen Spean. The highest "road" (1,144–1,155 ft) of the three can be traced from the col (1,151 ft), at the head of Glen Roy, to the mouth of the glen. The middle shelf (1,062–1,077 ft) runs parallel to this but continues into Glen Glaster. The lowest shelf (850–862 ft) can be traced right round Glen Roy, Glen Glaster, Bohun-tine Hill, and E. along Glen Spean. It corre-sponds to the col (848 ft) at Muckall above Loch Laggan.

Montrose made a memorable forced march through Glen Roy before the Battle of INVER-LOCHY in 1645.

At Roy Bridge, the 18th-cent. Keppoch House is a successor to an older mansion of the Macdonells of Keppoch. One of the young chiefs and his brother were murdered here in the 17th cent. The assassins, seven brothers, were slain seven years later by Iain Lom, the family bard, and their gory heads washed in the "Well of the Heads" on the W. side of Loch Oich (*see* INVERGARRY).

The last of the great clan battles took place at Mulroy, Roy Bridge, being fought between the MacDonnells of Keppoch and the Mac-Intoshes on the 4th of August 1688. The MacDonnells were victorious, but their opponents' standard-bearer jumped the R. Roy and escaped. Tradition says that it was the last time bows and arrows were used by the Highlanders. To the E. of Roy Bridge is the Achluachrach Gorge of the Spean, containing the Monessie Falls in a rocky setting.

GLENSHEE, *Perthshire* (Map 6, ref. 31¹76⁰), can properly be described as the course of the Shee water from the Spittal of Glenshee to BRIDGE OF CALLY, about 6 m. N. of BLAIRGOWRIE. In practice the name is usually taken to include the stretch N. of the Spittal known as Glen Beag that leads to the skiing grounds of Meall Odhar, Glas Maol, and the CAIRNWELL just beyond the DEVIL'S ELBOW. During the winter-sports season this area is one of the three principal skiing resorts of Scotland. Hotel and bed-and-breakfast accommodation is provided from Blairgowrie all the way up to the glen. In addition to two hotels and one hostel at the Spittal, the nearest rendezvous to the snow slopes, there are a ski-school and a sports shop. At the Cairnwell a chair-lift operates from road level, and a number of tows are also available, depending on conditions. In summer the road is an attractive touring route through to BRAEMAR and Deeside. This was yet another fashion of Highland travel set by Queen Victoria and Prince Albert on their early trips to BALMORAL; earlier the glen was primarily regarded as a stage on the military road between PERTH and FORT GEORGE. E. of the Spittal a stone circle and a tumulus, known as the Tomb of Diarmid, are associated with the ancestors of the Clan Campbell.

GLEN SHIEL, *Ross and Cromarty* (Map 5, ref. 19⁷81³), is a remarkably impressive W. Highland glen, traversed by one of the two "Roads to the Isles". No fewer than 15,000 acres of it are now owned by the National Trust for Scotland, purchased in 1944 with a gift of £7,000 made by the late Mr P. J. H. Unna. The glen extends for 10 m. from Glen Cluanie to the head of Loch Duich at Shiel Bridge, with fine mountains on both the N. and S., and with the famous ridge of the Five Sisters of KINTAIL displaying themselves to the N. Near the township of Achnangart is a boulder where Prince Charles Edward sheltered in hiding on the 22nd of July 1746, just before

Scottish Tourist Board

Glenshee

he joined the eight men who accompanied him in his flight to the remote places of Scotland.

In the heart of the glen at the Bridge of Shiel, which spans the R. Shiel, is the site of the Battle of Glenshiel on the 11th of June 1719 between 1,500 Jacobites and 1,600 Hanoverians; 274 Spaniards who had supported the Jacobites in this venture, sometimes called "the '19", surrendered the next day. They had landed in the Jacobite cause, from frigates in Loch Duich. One of the five sisters, Sgurr Nan Spainteach (3,129 ft), takes its name from this incident. It is said that some of the arms discarded by the Jacobites were recovered from the deep pool here at intervals throughout the 19th cent.

Dr Johnson and Boswell traversed the glen on horseback in 1773, and the scenery of Glen Shiel was instrumental in determining Boswell to write his *Journey*. A boulder in the glen, known as "Clach Johnson" is associated with a resting place on this adventure.

GLENTRESS, *Peeblesshire* (Map 3, ref. 33⁵64⁵), is a State Forest lying E. of PEEBLES. It includes over 2,000 acres, and is one of the first to be established by the Forestry Commission in Scotland. The Department of Agriculture operates adjacent lower ground for small-holdings. The Forest Training School was set up here in 1946, but moved to Faskally, near PITLOCHRY, in 1953.

The forest includes older stands of the Douglas fir, the Norway spruce, and the Sitka spruce. Plantings since the 1920s have been mainly pines, spruce, and larches. Over 1,000 tons of timber are produced annually from thinnings.

GLEN TROOL, *Ayrshire/Kirkcudbrightshire* (Map 2, ref. 24⁰58²). This National Forest Park is made up of five forests – Glen Trool, Carrick, Cairn Edward, Changue, and Kirroughtree. The total area covers over 116,000 acres (or over 180 sq. m.) in Galloway and Carrick, containing some of the finest and highest hill country in the South of Scotland. The forest culminates in the Merrick (2,764 ft), the highest hill in the southern uplands. It includes at least ten other hills of over 2,000 ft and several picturesque lochs, including the famous "loch-in-loch" of Loch Enoch (1,617 ft), just E. of the Merrick, which has a lochan on an island in the centre of the main loch. This is a loch feature unique in Scotland.

About 30,000 acres are under trees, this being two-thirds of the total planned for afforestation. The planting began in 1922 at Cairn Edward Forest, but now 7,000,000 plants are used annually from two nurseries. The Douglas fir, the Norway and Sitka spruce, and Scots pine are the main types planted. The new forest village of Glentrool has been established in the SW. corner of the park.

Eastwards by 3 m. the road leads to Loch Trool, with a camp site at Caldons Farm. Near here is a stone commemorating six Covenanters, who were surprised at prayer and martyred on the spot in 1685. At the E. of Loch Trool is the Bruce Memorial erected in 1929 on the sexcentenary of his death. It records the victory of Robert Bruce over the English in the Battle of Glen Trool in March 1307. This was during the period of guerrilla warfare when Bruce was on the run. The Battle of Glen Trool was a characteristic feat of his tactics at this time. With a small following, he routed superior English forces by hurling down rocks on them from the heights of Muldonach.

S. of Glentrool village is the isolated stone bridge over the Minnoch Water, the so-called "Roman Bridge". There may have been a Roman bridge here, but the present structure is 17th or 18th cent.

The whole area has many legends associated with it, and has been used to provide the setting for many novels. An example is the "Murder Hole" of the W. part of Loch Neldricken (NE of Loch Trool), which Crockett incorporates into his novel *The Raiders* as a repository for treasure and the bodies of thieves' victims. The cave on Macaterick is also celebrated in story. The granite of Craignaw, S. of Loch Trool, has produced some remarkable effects on weathering, and these have evoked such names as the "Devil's Bowling-Green".

The "Glen Trool Hoard" is preserved in the National Museum of Antiquities of Scotland in EDINBURGH. It was discovered in 1915 on the slopes to the N. of Glen Trool, dating from the middle Bronze Age about 1000 B.C.; it

includes a rapier, a spearhead, two razors, and various heads.

GLOMACH, Falls of, *Ross and Cromarty* (Map 5, ref. 20²82⁷), off the road between Cluanie and the KYLE OF LOCHALSH, lie N. of the Five Sisters of KINTAIL and are among the highest waterfalls in Britain. There is a sheer drop of 300 ft and a farther fall of 50 ft from a projecting ledge to the bottom pool; and from the top of the ravine above the falls to the pool below is a total plunge of 750 ft. The falls and an area of 2,200 acres around them are owned by the National Trust for Scotland. A good approach is from the Morvich croft at the top of Loch Duich, by the keeper's cottage at Dorusduain, through a forest track to the Bealach na Sroine (Pass of the Nose) and down sharply to the falls. An alternative route from Dorusduain is by Glen Choinneachain, round a shoulder of Beinn Fhada, through the Bealach an Sgairne (Rumbling Pass), and so by way of the burn to the head of the falls.

GOAT FELL, *Buteshire* (Map 1, ref. 19⁹64³), is the highest mountain on the Island of ARRAN (*see* "The Shape of Scotland"). This, as one of the most popular peaks in the land, is now rightly the property of the National Trust for Scotland. Innumerable holidaymakers from BRODICK, which Goat Fell (2,866 ft) dominates from the N., make the steep, but not very arduous, ascent of Goat Fell to enjoy one of the widest and most satisfying views in Scotland. On a clear day you may see Scotland, England, Ireland, and the Isle of Man. Surrounded by slightly lower but more striking peaks, Goat Fell is Arran's gift to the holiday-maker who likes getting to the top of things but is not an expert mountaineer.

GOLSPIE, *Sutherland* (Map 5, ref. 28³89⁹), a busy distributive centre for the farmlands and crofting hinterland, has a wide shopping range, a sandy beach, a good golf course, salmon and trout fishing, and many well-wooded walks on Ben Bhraggia, which is topped with the huge statue by Chantrey of the first Duke of Sutherland. Pupils attending the excellent High School are accommodated in hostels, and there is a residential Technical College. On the old bridge is a Gaelic stone marking the rallying point of the Clan Sutherland, whose slogan is "Ceann na Drochaide Bige" ("Top of the little bridge"). St Andrew's Church, early 18th-cent. but on the site of an ancient chapel, has fine wood-carving.

GORDONSTOUN, *Moray* (Map 6, ref. 31⁹86⁸), the school, founded 1934 and attended by the Prince of Wales, lies 2½ m. W. of LOSSIEMOUTH. This was until 1638 the house of Plewlands, and was given its present name when it was purchased by Sir Robert Gordon of the

Sutherland family. He remodelled the old mansion so as to give it a symmetrical frontage towards the S., but the W. wing represents the original 15th-cent. tower-house, while parts of a long 16th-cent. wing are incorporated in the central block. The classical N. front was added in the 18th cent. W. of the main building is the famous "Round Square" built by the "Warlock Laird", Sir Robert Gordon, the 3rd baronet, at the end of the 17th cent.

GOREBRIDGE, *Midlothian* (4 m. S. of DALKEITH). The mining town of Gorebridge is on the southern edge of the Midlothian coalfield; there are large open-cast pits nearby.

On the W. of the town are the ruined remains of Newbyres Castle, with its square tower dating from the 16th cent. Stobs Mills were erected in 1793 and were the first gunpowder works in Scotland. They were on the E. side of the Gore Water, but nothing now remains of the building.

Nearly 2 m. NW. of the town is a fort on the summit of Camp Wood Hill (900 ft). It is traceable only in parts, with remains of an earth rampart 20 ft broad and 3 ft high; it measured some 420 ft across.

Camp Wood is also associated with the extraordinary eccentric known locally as "Camp Meg". She was a lady in comfortable and delicate circumstances living originally in the West of Scotland. She abandoned her home and husband to become a female recluse in a hut that she built for herself in Camp Wood. Quite incidentally, as it were, she established a local reputation as an efficient horse-doctor, a profession she practised with masculine gusto. She also rode in local races wearing men's garments. Though she had retired to this odd life in the early 19th cent., her memory still lives on in the district.

GOUROCK, *Renfrewshire* (Map 2, ref. 22⁴67⁸), one of the best known of the Firth of CLYDE resorts, situated on the bay looking across the Firth to KILCREGGAN, Loch LONG and the Cowal hills, is the centre for yachting and for steamer trips in the Firth and in the Kyles of BUTE. The town extends for over 2 m. along the shore of the Firth of Clyde with houses built along the narrow shelf and backed by buildings picturesquely sited on the high ground.

There are no remains of the former Gourock Castle from which James IV sailed on his expedition to the Hebrides in 1494; the later castle was built in 1747. It was a plain building on Tower Hill and was demolished in the early years of this century, despite public condemnation of the Town Council's refusal to buy it and its grounds. On the cliff side of Gourock is "Granny Kempock's Stone", a monolith of grey schist 6 ft high, probably of prehistoric origin. It has long been regarded with superstitious awe, featuring in various

rites practised by fishermen to ensure fair winds; couples intending to get married used to encircle the stone in order to get "Granny's blessing". In 1662 Mary Lamont, a girl in her teens, was condemned with other women of Gourock and GREENOCK and burnt as a witch. She confessed amongst other things to having intended to throw the stone into the sea to cause shipwrecks.

Gourock indulged in early industrial enterprises. There was a rope-walk started in 1736, a copper mine was sunk in 1780 behind Tower Hill, and the first red herring to be cured in Britain was cured in the town in 1688. Gourock is still famous for its herring-curing, and it has other industries. The rope-walk that it so enterprisingly began has flourished at NEW LANARK.

Nearly 3 m. to the SW., on the coast, is the ruined Levan Castle. Nearby is the notable white-painted landmark of the Cloch lighthouse; it was constructed in 1797 and is 76 ft high.

GRAMPIANS, The, *Inverness-shire/Perthshire/Aberdeenshire* (Map 5, ref. 27⁵78⁵), is a range of grass and heather-covered mountains that stretch across the Highlands. The range was known earlier as the Mounth, a name still preserved in the CAIRN O' MOUNT Pass in Kincardineshire, and in the plateau of the White Mounth, S. of the R. DEE, of which the highest point is LOCHNAGAR. It is as the Mounth that Barbour speaks of this mountain mass in his *The Bruce*. Included are the high mass of the CAIRNGORMS, with large areas of flat summits exceeding 4,000 ft. A considerable number of summits in the Grampians exceed 3,000 ft, and are known to mountaineers and hillwalkers as "Munros" – the name given to all well-defined tops in Scotland of 3,000 ft and over. There are 543 Munros in Scotland, of which 276 are separate mountains. The name recalls Sir Hugh Munro, the distinguished mountaineer who was mainly responsible for their classification.

The name Grampians is essentially a literary one, having been first used in 1520 by Hector Boece, the historian. He used the term "Mons Grampius", taken from Tacitus's *Agricola* (A.D. 95), as the scene of Agricola's crushing victory over the Picts (under Calgacus) about A.D. 86. The scene of this battle is placed some distance N. of the TAY. *Solitudinem faciunt pacem appellant* (*see* "Scotland in History").

The passes across the Grampians were used by the invading armies of the Romans and the English, just as they are now used by the 20th-cent. traveller. The best known are the Pass of LENY near CALLANDER; the CAIRNWELL Pass with the DEVIL'S ELBOW, which is the highest main road in Britain; DRUMOCHTER Pass, traversed by Wade's great highway linking DUNKELD and INVERNESS; the famous LECHT road linking Cock Bridge in the

At the heart of the Grampians

The Scotsman

Don Valley with TOMINTOUL, the highest village in the Highlands; and the Cairn o' Mount from STRATHMORE to Strathdee. W. of Drumochter Pass, the Grampians intersect the ridge known as "Drum Alban", the backbone of the country situated near the main watershed. This ridge extends N. from Ben Lomond, and finally reaches Ben Hope, the most northerly "Munro" in the country.

Many of the high moors in the Grampians are shot over for grouse during the season, and deer-stalking takes place in the hills, frequently referred to as "forests". Winter snow provides scope for skiing, and this is being practised increasingly.

GRANDTULLY, *Perthshire* (Map 5, ref. $29^2 75^2$) is a village on the TAY where a bridge links the roads along the N. and S. banks. Grandtully Castle lies some 2 m. SW., and is the seat of the family of Stuart of Grandtully, who have been established there since the end of the 14th cent. The original castle, built probably about 1414, is said to have stood a mile to the eastward of the present structure.

The Castle is mainly 16th-cent.; but the main block, which incorporates a square keep, and the entrance, which has a guard-room with a prison-pit below, suggest an earlier building period. The upper part of the structure, including the turrets and dormer windows, was much altered in 1626 by Sir William Stuart, then Sheriff of PERTH, and his wife Agnes Moncrieff. Further restoration and additions were made in 1893, and the Castle, which is readily seen from the main road, is now occupied as a private residence. Among many other castles, Grandtully is claimed as the prototype of "Tullyvolan" in Sir Walter Scott's novel *Waverley*.

The park contains some magnificent elm trees. Just beyond the Castle, a signpost indicates the road to the Church of St Mary, now part of Pitcairn farm buildings. This church was known to exist in 1533. The exterior is plain; the arched ceiling, however, is vividly ornamented with painted wooden medallions. Most of these depict scriptural subjects, but represented also are the armorial bearings of the laird of Grandtully, of his wife (Dame Agnes Moncrieff), and of the Earl of Athole, and the royal arms of England, Scotland, and France.

A stone in one of the windows bears the initials of Sir William and Dame Agnes and the date 1636. This was probably the year in which he church was restored and the medallions ainted. The church is under the care of the Ministry of Public Building and Works, and he key can be obtained at the farm.

A little over a mile W. of the Castle, a road eads to the Farm of Lundin. About ½ m. up his road, and by the side of it, is a burial-place f the early Bronze Age, excavated in 1963. The ite consists of a mound on which are four tanding stones. At the centre was a pit, and round it various token cremations. The ottery found included a cord-ornamented eaker and decorated fragments from a large essel with parallels as far afield as Cornwall nd Ireland. Outside the burial area is a rostrate slab with numerous cup-markings.

GRANGEMOUTH, *Stirlingshire* (Map 2, ef. 29³68²), on the Firth of FORTH, is second only to Glasgow of Scottish seaports in cargo handled.

A flourishing and apparently ever-expanding centre of the oil and plastics industries, its population has more than doubled in the last ten years. Its architectural fabric varies from the aluminium tubular of the refineries and plastic plants on the outskirts to the 19th-cent. drab in the heart of the town, and to the landscaped, modern, with-adventure play areas in the new housing developments. In terms of rateable value the town has the seventh highest assessment in the country, but a large proportion of its industrial wages and salaries is taken out by commuting workers.

Oil-refining, the key to Grangemouth's growth, was started in 1924 and assumed the proportions of a boom industry after the Second World War. Crude oil comes by overland pipeline from FINNART on the W. coast. In addition to fine oils, petrol, paraffin, and liquid gas, the refining process produces the basic stock needed for the manufacture of chemical intermediates for the plastics industry. Synthetic rubber, resin, glue, detergents, cosmetics, film and sheet plastics, synthetic fibres, and insecticides are all products that owe something to Grangemouth's hydrocarbon plants.

In 1971 a major oil company announced a £30,000,000 scheme that will more than double the refining capacity to deal with 20,000,000 tons of crude oil a year, thus providing some 20 per cent of Britain's total refined products.

The docks, which are constantly being improved, handled 5,300,000 tons of cargo in 1970, of which oil represented 3,500,000 tons. They have accommodated ships of more than 21,000 tons deadweight, and work on enlarging the entrance dock to take even bigger ships is due for completion in 1973. Imports include timber, cement, iron ore, wood-pulp, esparto, rubber, and foodstuffs. Iron, steel, coal, whisky, sewing-machines, agricultural implements, books, and carpets are mong the regular outgoing cargoes.

A reflection of the town's importance as a port of entry for foreign timber is seen on the wood yards and sawmills that line the FALKIRK road. A combination of this trade and the development of resinous glues through petrol chemicals has given Grangemouth a pioneering lead in the production of laminated timber beams, which match steel girders for strength and fire-resistance. Industrial advances have also been made here in the realms of dye-stuffs and pharmaceuticals. As befits a town that produced the first effective steamboat (*Charlotte Dundas*, 1801), there is still a ship-yard in operation, although its function is now divided mainly between repair work and construction of components for other industries. The Forth and CLYDE canal, which has its eastern terminal at Grangemouth, was closed to navigation in 1963.

GRANTOWN-ON-SPEY, *Moray* (Map 6, ref. 30⁴82⁸), to the NE. of AVIEMORE, is one of Speyside's principal residential resorts for holidays in summer and winter. Planned by Sir James Grant, one of the improving lairds of the Highlands, the town has a pleasant, spacious aspect typical of Georgian development in the latter half of the 18th cent. It first attracted the tourist trade, which is now the basis of its economy, about a century ago when Victorian doctors began to prescribe a change of air in Grantown as a cure for most ills. In more recent times it has grown as a centre for salmon fishing on the SPEY, and has long been patronized by EDINBURGH families who walk and play golf and seek recreation in the open air. Skiing is now a major preoccupation during the winter season. More than £250,000 was spent within two years in modernizing the town's hotels to meet the demands of this new custom. A ski-school and a sports shop provide instruction and a service of equipment hire, and transport to the CAIRNGORM snow-slopes is arranged. *Après*-ski life is gay and varied; and to be sure of accommodation around the peak periods of Christmas, New Year, and Easter it is well to make reservations in advance, as the popularity of the area is increasing. There are attractive walks along the river, to the view-point NW. of the town, to Beachen Wood, among others, and such longer expeditions as the climb of Glen Beg or the 16-m. round trip to LOCHINDORB. The Moray coast between NAIRN and ELGIN is within easy reach by car, and the town is at the northern end of the TOMINTOUL–Cockbridge road that links Speyside with Deeside.

GREENLAW, *Berwickshire* (Map 3, ref. 37¹64⁶). Situated on the Blackadder Water in the foothills of the Lammermuirs, this small town takes its name from a low isolated hill, or "green law", 1 m. SE., where the original town was situated. The present town was founded towards the close of the 17th cent., and from

1696 to 1853 was the county town of Berwick-shire, then being replaced by D U N S. The market cross, which was first put up by Sir Patrick Hume of Polwarth, dates from 1696. It was taken down in 1829 to make room for the County Hall, but was discovered and re-erected in 1881 on the W. side of the town. The tower of the church dates from 1712, though it is built in the style of the late 15th cent.

Some 3 m. S. of Greenlaw, at a height of 600 ft, is the ruined Hume Castle, the ancient seat of the Home family; it has a commanding viewpoint. It probably originated in the 13th cent.; it had a stormy history, being captured in 1547 by Somerset and retaken by young Lord Home in 1549. Twenty years later the Earl of Sussex captured it, and in 1650 it surrendered to Cromwell's artillery. The defiance with which its Governor greeted the besiegers on that occasion is in the children's rhyme in which he wrote about the siege:

I, Willy Wastle, stand firm in my castle;
And a' the dogs o' your town will no'
pull Willie Wastle down.

At the end of the 18th cent. the ruins were re-erected on the old foundations and restored into their present "imitation antique".

About 3 m. N. of the town on the moor is an unusually fine example of a "kaim", a gravelly ridge formed by infilling in glacial fissures, which extends for over 2 m. and measures up to 50 ft broad and 40 ft high.

The village of Polwarth, 3 m. NE. of Green-law, has two old thorn trees, which formerly stood in the centre of the village green; for three centuries, until the 19th cent., it was the custom to dance at every wedding around these trees, and this is celebrated in many songs, especially one by Allan Ramsay. To the S. of this village is Marchmont House, a semi-Palladian mansion built about 1754 by John and Robert Adam from designs made in 1724 by their father, William Adam. The house, which superseded the earlier Redbraes Castle nearby, stands in finely wooded grounds, including an oak 128 ft tall and 15 ft in girth, and contains a fine collection of paintings.

In the grounds of Marchmont House lies Polwarth Church, which was rebuilt in 1703 by Patrick Hume, the 1st Earl of Marchmont. An inscription erected then says that its pre-decessor was erected before A.D. 900 and re-stored in 1378. In 1684 Sir Patrick Hume, a follower of Argyll, hid in the family vault and remained there for several weeks, being supplied with food by his redoubtable daughter Grizel, then only 12 years old, who later became Lady Grizel Baillie. The house was frequently searched by soldiers of Charles II, but Sir Patrick eventually escaped to Holland and was ultimately restored.

GREENOCK, *Renfrewshire* (Map 2, ref. 22⁷67⁶). The important industrial and ship-building town of Greenock is on the CLYDE estuary. The roadstead in the river immediately off Greenock is known as the TAIL OF THE BANK.

The growth of the town was greatly linked with the fortunes and activities of the Shaw family, who are first mentioned in 1589. By the 17th cent. Greenock had a pier of note, and was the port for Scottish packets going to Ireland. Later there was an agitation that resulted in a charter permitting Greenock to take part in foreign trade (hitherto reserved for royal burghs); this was granted in 1681. In the second half of the 17th cent. there was a very extensive trade in herrings, mainly to the French and Baltic ports; in consequence the town adopted the motto "Let herring swim that trade maintain". The trade declined, but at one point in the 17th cent. there were over 300 boats in the firth, of which more than half sailed from Greenock. The 18th cent. saw the construction of improved facilities, starting with a harbour and quays in 1710 – once again with the aid of the Shaw family.

The first square-rigger to be built there was launched in 1760, and the graving-dock was completed in 1786. Even more extensive developments were to come in the 19th cent. The foundation-stone of the East India Har-bour was laid in 1805, designed by John Rennie. In 1850 the Victoria Harbour was completed, and in 1862 the Albert Harbour was begun – to cost £250,000. The Garvel Graving Dock was begun in 1871, and the £350,000 James Watt Dock in 1881. By the end of the 19th cent., the total harbour was 195 acres.

The varied import and export trade con-tinues, and today Greenock produces 14 per cent of Clyde tonnage.

The lower part of the town is generally cramped and industrial. In 1818 David Reid planned an extension of the town, and the result is seen in the residential area of the "West End". Unfortunately nothing was done for the relief of overcrowding in the town centre. Greenock suffered considerable damage by bombing during the Second World War.

James Watt (1736–1819) was born in Greenock. This discoverer of the power of steam is commemorated in the Watt Monu-ment in Union Street, built by his son in 1837 to house a statue by Sir Francis Chantrey, and to accommodate the Watt Scientific Library and the Greenock Library (1753) – the second oldest subscription library in Scotland (KELSO being the oldest). Adjoining this Gothic build-ing are the Watt Museum and Lecture Hall, which were built in 1876; in 1958 an art gallery was added.

Hardly any old buildings of merit remain in Greenock, but mention must be made of Garvel House (1772), once the Georgian man-sion of Baillie Gammell, which stands amid the James Watt Dock; also there is the very

Scottish Tourist Board

Gretna Green: the blacksmith's shop

imposing classical Custom House (1818) on the sea-frontage, recalling byegone days. The Tontine Hotel, once a Georgian residence, is worth notice.

In the cemetery is a Watt Cairn, and also a tombstone of Burns's "Highland Mary" (died 789), removed from the old North Kirk. Behind the town is higher ground with fine views over the firth. On the viewpoint of Lyly Hill is a Cross of Lorraine surmounting an anchor – a monument to Free French sailors who gave their lives in the Battle of the Atlantic in the Second World War. Farther back on the moors are the waterworks, justly famous, and a memorial to the genius of Robert Thom in the early 19th cent. These remain almost unchanged since their inception and include Loch Thom with 1,780 gallons. Water-power is also generated by a system of "cuts".

Auchmountain Glen is an overgrown relic of own improvement at the end of the 19th cent. This opens off Kilmacolm Road and was "beautified" with statuary and landscaping; now virtually lost, it may be resurrected.

A new dry dock was opened at Greenock in 1964, reckoned to be amongst the six largest of its kind in the world.

GRETNA, *Dumfriesshire* (Map 3, ref. 33²56⁷). This Border village, comprising Gretna Green and Springfield, to the N. of the R. Sark, stands on the actual border between England and Scotland. It is famous as the place where runaway couples from England formerly came to be married in accordance with 18th-cent. Scots law; that is, by means of a declaration before witnesses.

These marriages took place at the Sark Toll Bridge (the King's Head Inn) till 1826, and at other inns as well as Gretna Hall (built 1710). From 1826, the smithy at Gretna Green became the most popular place for these declaratory marriages. The popularity of Scots declaratory marriages at Gretna was brought about by the passing of Lord Hardwicke's Act in 1754, which abolished irregular marriages in England. These were previously possible anywhere in the United Kingdom, and were particularly common in London's Fleet Prison. No banns or licences were needed for this style of marriage, and it could still be contracted in Scotland. After 1856, it was rendered invalid unless one party had residence of twenty-one days in Scotland prior to the ceremony. In 1939 the Marriage (Scotland) Act made the presence of a minister or registrar necessary, but runaway lovers still came to Gretna (or other parts of Scotland) to get residential qualifications and be married; this was because under Scots Law parents' consent was not required after the age of sixteen. Under the more recent Act of 1969, however, the age at which couples might marry in the rest of Britain without parental or other official consent was lowered from twenty-one to eighteen, and thus the attractions of a "runaway" marriage at Gretna were greatly reduced.

There are interesting registers of irregular marriages that have been made at Gretna Hall (where 1,134 were performed between 1826 and 1855); there are also registers at the smithy. At the Toll Inn, 1,300 marriages were carried through in a period of six years. The Lang family were prominent in performing the weddings, and their graves can be seen in the churchyard. Sark Toll Bar House is a prominent tourist site, with a marriage-room tablet above the door. It stands near the road built in 1830 and superseding the road via Springfield and Longtown.

Springfield, to the E. of Gretna, was a village founded by weavers in 1791. During the 18th cent. marriages were performed here in competition with Gretna as the main GLASGOW–

Carlisle road went through the village, crossing the R. Esk at Longtown. Springfield's "marriage trade" was lost with the building of the new Sark Bridge in 1830. The First World War saw considerable changes in Gretna, with workers arriving to work in the munitions factories established in the neighbourhood; and over 200 permanent houses were put up, along with 600 huts.

At the entrance to Gretna Green Kirk is a little house known as "Prince Charlie's Cottage", where he is believed to have spent a night in 1745 on his way back from the campaign in England. Nearby is the site of the Battle of Solway Moss, where the Scots were defeated in 1542.

On the shores of the Solway Firth is the Clochmaben Stone, 7 ft high and weighing 10 tons; this could be a remnant of a stone circle. There is a possibility that the stone is connected with a shrine to Maporos, god of youth and music in antiquity. If so, its nearness to Gretna Green is oddly appropriate. The stone was certainly a place of Border meetings and fairs through the Middle Ages. In 1398 the details of a truce between Scotland and England were discussed there.

GREY MARE'S TAIL, *Dumfriesshire* (Map 2, ref. 31⁷61⁵). This dramatic 200-ft waterfall is formed by the Tail Burn as it drops from Loch Skene to meet Moffat Water. It is seen on the main road from MOFFAT to St Mary's Loch, to the N. of the road 8 m. from Moffat. The area of more than 2,000 acres around the falls was purchased by the National Trust for Scotland in 1962. That rarity, a herd of wild goats, is to be found in the surrounding hills, and there is a wide variety of wild flowers in the neighbourhood of the falls. Just to the NE. is the summit of Birkhill Pass at 1,105 ft, overshadowed by White Coomb, 2,695 ft. In the vicinity is Dob's Linn, which was used as a refuge for the persecuted Covenanters, who much frequented this district and the South-West generally. Just below the waterfall is a hollow called the "Giant's Grave"; this and the waterfall are in Scott's *Marmion*.

There are two other waterfalls in SW. Scotland known by the same name. In Dumfriesshire on the Crichope Burn to the SE. of THORN-HILL is an impressive cascade over a 100-ft precipice. Lower down the burn is an unusual linn 20 ft wide and 100 ft deep. It is said that this too was used as a refuge in covenanting times, and was chosen as a lair for Balfour by Scott in his novel *Old Mortality*.

In the Stewartry of Kirkcudbright near DUNDRENNAN there is a 60-ft waterfall also called Grey Mare's Tail.

GRIMERSTA, River, *Ross and Cromarty* (Map 4, ref. 12¹93⁰), is on the Island of LEWIS in the Outer Hebrides (*see* "The Shape of Scotland"). About 17 m. WSW. of STORNO-

WAY, the river, with a small chain of lochs at the head of it, offers what some claim to be the finest salmon water in Scotland. It has been seriously spoken of as the finest in Europe. On a fine spring or early summer day, when the fish have just arrived and have not yet made their way into the lochs, it certainly would be difficult to rival the Grimersta for fast and exciting sport. The right to fish this notable river is not cheap, and plans should be made in advance. Anglers are referred to the Lewis Tourist Association, Stornoway.

GRUINARD BAY, *Ross and Cromarty* (Map 5, ref. 19⁵89⁵), is one of the most scenically delightful bays in this corner of the NW Highlands. The "arms" enclosing the bay are Stattic Point to the E. and the promontory of Greenstone Point to the W. A beach of fine golden sand curves alongside the road leading from INVEREWE to DUNDONNELL. From the viewpoint on Gruinard Hill, overlooking the bay is a superb panorama including the mountain ranges of An Teallach, Ben More Coigeach and the hills of Sutherland beyond. Gruinard Island, in the bay, was contaminated during wartime military experiments and is strictly prohibited. The Gruinard river and the Little Gruinard, which flow into the bay, have good salmon and sea-trout fishing.

GULLANE, *East Lothian* (Map 3, ref. 34⁹68³), is a well-known holiday village and golfing centre on the Firth of FORTH, about 18 m. from EDINBURGH. It has three 18-hole golf courses, and the Luffness course adjoins them to the S. To the E. of the village is the world-famous MUIRFIELD Championship Course, the headquarters of the Honourable Company of Edinburgh Golfers.

There is a view of the Firth of Forth from the 200-ft Gullane Hill, which rises to the W. and excellent sands and bathing in a wide bay.

St Andrew's Church, dating from the second half of the 12th cent., is now roofless and dilapidated. It was given in the 13th cent. to DRYBURGH ABBEY, and made collegiate in 1446. A zigzagged chancel arch is of Norman character. It is said that James VI dismissed the last vicar for smoking tobacco!

The village was devastated by sand blown from the W. in the 16th and 17th cents., and the church and parish centre were moved to DIRLETON, 3 m. to the E. Gullane began to develop again when golf became a popular pastime, and many fine houses were built then; its whole appearance is of a prosperous place.

Just to the S. are the fragmentary ruins of Saltcoats Castle, dating from the 16th cent. There is an unusual set of fourteen gargoyles on the tower, and a rectangular dovecote is preserved there.

The neighbourhood is described in Robert Louis Stevenson's *Catriona*.

Gullane was noted in the 19th cent. as a centre for training racehorses. It was called the Newmarket of Scotland, and traces of the old racecourse still survive.

GUTHRIE, *Angus* (Map 6, ref. 35⁷75¹), is a village in the NE. part of the Sidlaw Hills, and on the left bank of Lunan Water. Guthrie Castle stands W. of the village. Built in 1468 by Sir David Guthrie, Comptroller of the Exchequer, it has been inhabited by the Guthrie family ever since. It possesses a massive square tower, 60 ft high, with walls 10 ft thick; the tower was repaired and enlarged in 1848. The Castle contains some fine paintings, including some medieval murals, and has renowned gardens.

St Mary's Church belonged originally to ARBROATH Abbey, but was purchased by Sir David Guthrie in 1479 and became a collegiate establishment.

HADDINGTON, *East Lothian* (Map 3, ref. 35²67⁴). Because of its red sandstone, the abbey (now partly ruined as a result of the English wars, but restored and carefully tended) was known in the Middle Ages as the "Lamp of the Lothians". Today, some would give this title back to the county town of East Lothian or, as it was once called, Haddingtonshire. This is because the energy of its civic authorities has made the little town pre-eminent among Scottish Lowland burghs. It is an energy that at once guards, furbishes, and keeps alive the place's considerable architectural legacy from the past, yet plays its part in the economy of modern Scotland.

In the years just before the war, no visitor of sensibility could have failed to enjoy Haddington's spacious High Street and Market Street,

A. Barber

Haddington: the Town House

its gracious 18th-cent. architecture, and its romantic remains from an earlier age. The enfeebling word "picturesque", which would have flitted through the mind, might also have made him believe that here was an old market town and county centre that, because of its nearness to EDINBURGH, was falling gently into desuetude. He would not believe that now.

After the last war, however, and particularly in the late 1950s, Haddington by its own civic effort pulled itself up by its own boot-straps; and, if it is not straining the metaphor too far, pulled itself up in two directions.

First, by rehabilitation, and the generous use of colour and decoration, it has made the older buildings of the town really live again. Citizens who may have grown up to think of their town as little more than a pleasing museum-piece "on the way out" suddenly found it a valuable living property of which they could justly be proud. People came from other parts of Scotland to see and admire the fine Adam buildings of Haddington, and those by earlier and humbler architects, not as relics, but as things that were in vigorous use. We have much for which we should be grateful to the Civic Trust in this matter.

The other direction in which Haddington applied the upward pull was to align herself in the economy of the changing scene in modern Scotland. In 1958, Haddington was the very first burgh, or indeed place, in Scotland to offer itself as a host to families from GLASGOW

The ruined abbey at Haddington

A. Barber

Haddington: the River Tyne and the abbey

under what has come to be known as the Over-spill Agreement. By this agreement with a town very different from her and 57 m. to the W. of her, Haddington took in 178 families from Glasgow – families that were feeling the brunt of unemployment in heavy industry and of the lack of housing. Before any of the New Towns of the late 1950s and early '60s had been built to cope with Glasgow's overspill, this ancient and handsome burgh had taken the first step in practical hospitality. She has had her reward in the infusion of new blood, and of the use of hands, in small industries more suitable to Haddington than to Glasgow. Haddington has also built houses on its periphery for these newcomers, but has been careful to keep them consonant with the older buildings while not falling into the trap of pastiche.

At the risk of seeming to overpraise, one may say that what is so heartening in Haddington to those who come for Scotland's past as well as her present is this: the county town of this rich agricultural land of East Lothian, so near to Edinburgh, has shown that it is possible not only to preserve the visible signs of the past but at the same time to keep them living, to make plans for Haddington's position in the future Scotland. Considering the wanton desecration that is going on elsewhere in the name of progress, this example is, to say the least of it, encouraging.

Haddington has had a pretty stormy past, on which we need not dwell, during the English wars. Its position in the direct path of the invaders made it particularly vulnerable. Save for the damaged abbey, now joined to the

parish kirk, there is little visible sign left of this repeated violation. After the Union, and when Haddington was safe, it developed into a residential town of standing both as the capital of Haddingtonshire and as a stopping place on the London–Edinburgh route. Readers of Smollett's *Humphrey Clinker* may recall his lively description of life in Haddington in the mid-18th cent.

As Nash is associated with Bath, Adam is with Haddington. He designed the fine Town House, later to be enlarged by Gillespie Graham, the architect of Edinburgh's Moray Place. He was also responsible for a good many houses in the spacious central street. Three of them are now banks, but the best is that delightful, miniature piece of domestic Georgian building, the Bank of Scotland. It would be tedious to take the reader on a printed house-by-house tour of 17th- and 18th-cent. Haddington. He is recommended to wander as he will in the streets, wynds, and closes, and to note the lively, almost stage-scene, setting of Haddington's revived prosperity.

Haddington's past is associated with various famous people. The medieval philosopher Duns Scotus taught here. A very different theologian, John Knox, is said to have been born in Haddington; and Jane Welsh Carlyle – the wife of Thomas Carlyle, yet worthy of fame on her own merits – was also a native of Haddington. She is buried in the abbey grounds, and her birthplace has been restored and preserved.

The Lamp of Lothian Collegiate Centre was founded in 1968 to foster community life in this small, beautiful town.

Plate 9   Handa Island, Sutherland (see p. 273)

Meeting the ferry-boat on Scarp, N. Harris (see p. 274)

HALKIRK, *Caithness* (Map 7, ref. 31⁴95⁹). Sir John Sinclair planned Halkirk in the last decade of the 18th cent. as a self-supporting community. The pattern of small-holdings makes for a symmetrical and lengthy village, which runs from the railway line between Georgemas Junction and THURSO, past a stretch of the Thurso river, and on towards the sporting hinterland. There is splendid fishing in the area; lochs Calder, Scarmclett, and Watten, and many others are within easy reach.

There are prehistoric remains all round Halkirk, including stone rows between Loch Calder and Brabster.

Braal or Brawl Castle, the old part of which dates from the 14th cent., lies in ruins upstream from the village. Tradition has it that this was the site of the burning of the Bishop of Caithness in 1222, an act of revenge by the over-ythed, over-taxed people of the diocese, who had appealed in vain for help to John Earl of Caithness.

HAMILTON, *Lanarkshire* (Map 2, ref. 27²65⁵). is the administrative centre of Scotland's most populous county with, in 1971, 519,691 (this includes six large and three small burghs), although it is by no means the largest in the area. Hamilton was made a royal burgh in 1548; Mary Queen of Scots stayed in the town after her escape from Loch LEVEN and before Langside. Cromwell had his H.Q. there in 1651.

Hamilton Palace, once the seat of the Dukes of Hamilton, was built in 1822–9 on the site of an earlier house; it contained a superb collection of paintings and furniture sold by auction in 1862. It was demolished in 1927.

To the S. of the town in High Parks is the site of Cadzow Castle, picturesquely situated above the Avon. It had been a royal residence since the 10th cent. and was given by Bruce to the Hamilton family after BANNOCKBURN. In the parks there are some of the original wild white cattle of the Caledonian Forest.

At Barncluith House, built in the 16th cent., are to be seen some interesting Dutch terraced gardens planned in 1583. Chatelherault Lodge (the Duke of Hamilton is also the Duke of Chatelherault in France) was designed by William Adam, who was also the architect of the octagonal parish church of the town in 1732. Opposite the church is the Celtic Netherton Cross. The modern county buildings were opened in April 1964.

HANDA ISLAND, *Sutherland* (Map 5, ref. 21³94⁸). This uninhabited island of 766 acres has a sandy beach on the SE. and high cliffs (400 ft) on the NW. side.

Since 1962 Handa has been a nature reserve managed by the Royal Society for the Protection of Birds, and has a bothy on the island for the use of members. No specially rare birds are found here, but the spectacular sight of thousands of sea-birds nesting together on ledges of the cliff and on stack, 500 ft from the shore to the NW., is impressive. There are also fine views of mountains on the coast.

Access is by boat across the narrow Sound of Handa from the village of Tarbet, 2 m. NW. of SCOURIE.

HARLAW, *Aberdeenshire* (Map 6, ref. 37⁴82⁴). Some 3 m. N. of INVERURIE, on the road that overlooks the N. bank of the Ury, is the Harlaw Monument, a great red granite obelisk erected by the city of ABERDEEN and unveiled on the 24th of July 1911, the 500th anniversary of the "Red Harlaw", the most bloody conflict ever fought in NE. Scotland. The contestants were Donald, Lord of the Isles, and the Earl of Mar, acting on behalf of the Government. The pretext of the quarrel was a purely feudal dispute, but there were far wider issues involved, too complicated to be resolved here. Let it rest that it was one of the most savage internal encounters on Scottish soil.

HARRIS, Island of, *Inverness-shire* (Map 4, ref. 11⁰89⁵), is in the Outer Hebrides (*see* "The Shape of Scotland"). This – though always, and rightly, spoken of as an island – is firmly attached to the larger, more populous, and in many respects differing, island of LEWIS. Apart from the extraordinary feat of achieving island status though attached to another island, this Outer Hebridean entity, varying between 30 and 40 m. out W. from the mainland, does have certain qualities in common with its geographically attached twin, Lewis.

In such matters as religion, crofting, weaving, fishing, the universal knowledge of Gaelic, and other Outer Hebridean peasant qualities, the reader is referred below to the entry on Lewis, where they are dealt with in detail on the larger, more prosperous, more go-ahead island.

The immediate differences between Harris and Lewis are to be found in the wildness of the attractive scenery in Harris and the lack, in

Harris: the Macleod tomb in Rodel Church
J. L. Rodger

J. L. Rodger

Harris: Shielebost Beach

the Harris people, of a quality that we have called "latent wildness" lying beneath the courteous surface of the bold Lewisman. The Harris people are as courteous as those of Lewis, but their charm of manner is perhaps more apparent, the remote Norse blood in them being perhaps more remote.

The chief scenic appeal of Harris lies in its variety. It has – particularly in its northern end, adjacent to Lewis – far higher hills than those in its sister isle; the Clisham rises to 2,622 ft, and the forest of N. Harris is indeed ruggedly grand. The W. side of the island contains some beautiful sandy bays and pleasing prospects of satellite islands, such as Taransay and Scarp. Going down S. by the western route along the Atlantic shore until you reach the enchanted ultimate point of RODEL, you are conscious all the while of an approaching softness of climate, very different from that of Lewis. At Rodel itself the growth of grass and flower seems by contrast to be luxuriant. Rodel has its back to the N., its eyes towards the SW.; it is protected from the N. by the great hills of Harris.

Leaving Rodel to come N. again by the one other route (that is, along the eastern side),

there is presented to you a striking contrast; but it would be a striking journey even without the additional piquancy of contrast. The land through which the eastern S. Harris road passes has well been described as a moonscape, and indeed there is something lunar in its wild fantastic aspect.

Everywhere rock abounds. Grey rock, black rock, silvery-white rock thrusts itself through thin soil, not always in jagged edges, but more often in smooth, heaving shoulders. Rock reaches or tumbles down to the sea on your right and rises rolling above you on your left. The place looks not "half as old as time", but twice.

Yet within the indentations that the sea has made upon this uncompromising mass, there are small villages whose inhabitants are primarily devoted to fishing and to weaving. As a secondary support, they cultivate the oddly-named "lazy-beds", that is, small thin catches of soil held between the rocks above them. These they enrich with manure and sea-weed – their cultivation is far from lazy. Despite its fantastic appearance, through which the road winds and twists its way N., the landscape is not gloomy or overwhelming. Colour

J. L. Rodger

Home weaving on Harris

splashes here and there in the lazy-beds, in the white and painted small houses, and in the changing sea.

Nevertheless it is something of a relief to come to the end of S. Harris at TARBERT, the narrow isthmus that connects S. and N. Harris. From now onwards there is but one road N. to the Harris–Lewis border. It passes through typical W. Highland mountain and sea scenery, with a fine view of Loch Seaforth, the most deeply reaching sea-arm in all the "Long Island". Thus you go on to the small bridge across a burn that leads you into the flatter land of Lewis.

The bridge cannot be much more than 20 or 30 ft long, but you will notice the change in all around you immediately you have crossed it. Expert Gaelic speakers say there is a different "taste" to the Gaelic on the N. as distinct from the S. side of the bridge. The monoglot English speaker who cares to talk with the people on the Harris side of the bridge, and also with those on the Lewis side, may convince himself that there is a difference in their English.

The history of Harris follows the general pattern of the Outer Hebrides in the amalgam of Norse and Celt, with perhaps Celtic in-

fluence more strong than in Lewis. Harris was not subject to the depredations of the Fife Adventurers or of Cromwell (*see* STORNO-WAY), and, save acting as the scene of part of the wanderings of Prince Charles Edward Stuart in 1746, it has not impinged much on Scottish mainland history. The Macleods, as in Lewis, were the chiefs.

The car-ferry service to the Outer Isles from the mainland and via SKYE touches at Tarbert daily and at LOCHMADDY in North UIST, one day at Tarbert first, the next at Lochmaddy. There is a private ferry, not cheap if you are the only passenger, between South Harris and North UIST. For speed of travel it is best to take the overland route by bus or motor-car to the airport at Stornoway.

Apart from its striking, and as everywhere else in the Hebrides, individual scenic beauties, Harris has other attractions for the visitor. Bathing on the fine sandy beaches of the W. side offers exhilaration tempered, as in Lewis, by the beneficence of the Gulf Stream, here washing its uninterrupted way against the Atlantic side of the island. There is excellent sea-trout and some good salmon fishing. One brown-trout loch at its N. end (Loch Langavat) contains unusually large specimens. For detailed information apply to the Scottish Tourist Board.

HAWICK, *Roxburghshire* (Map 3, ref. 35°61⁵), the largest of the Border towns, is known historically for its independence; it has come to be called a women's town because of the predominance of female employment in its hosiery mills, and against the general run of play in Scotland has achieved a notable affluence in the past twenty-five years. This prosperity, like the alleged feminine superiority, is based on the knitwear industry. Almost two centuries ago knitting was established as a cottage industry in Hawick when, in 1771, a local magistrate introduced the first stocking-frames to be exploited successfully in Scotland. Mechanization came with the Industrial Revolution, and the emphasis shifted from hose to fine underwear (which, as the advertisements of the day put it, "enjoyed the patronage of many of the crowned heads of Europe"). The foundation of the modern boom was laid in the 1930s, when Hawick mills turned to production of the now classic "twin-set" combination of sweater and cardigan which has become a staple in feminine fashion. There are now some 20 firms, employing 5,000 workers, engaged in this industry − one of them alone producing more than 400 individual designs a year to meet the demands of world-wide markets.

The tradition of civic independence is essentially a male preserve dating back to 1514, when in the aftermath of Flodden the youth (callants) of the town routed an English raiding party. This achievement of arms is celebrated annually with almost pagan energy at the burgh's Common Riding in June. The marches, or boundaries, of the burgh are inspected by a mounted cavalcade of townsfolk led by an elected "Cornet", bearing a replica of the Hexham pennant captured from the English raiders in 1514. Spectacular to the point of hair-raising is that part of the main procession known as the Chase, when Cornet and his followers take a stretch of road from Haggisha towards St Leonard's at the gallop, in symbolic celebration of the triumphant return of the original callants. Tribute to the early heroes is also paid at the equestrian monument in Central Square. The day of the Common Riding is the grand climax to more than a month of preliminaries and is one of the most full-blooded festivals in the country.

Built along the walled banks of the Teviot, and its tributary the Slitrig Burn, Hawick dates visually from the latter half of the last century. The long, narrow High Street is flanked in the main by solid, plain stone buildings − busy, well-stocked shops on the ground floor with two or three storeys of housing or offices above. Housing development since the last war has been concentrated on sites away from the centre of the town. More than 1,000 new houses have

been erected in the Burnhead and Burnfoot scheme, which also has its own shopping centre and two new churches. Pre-fabricated houses built at Silverbuthall during the Second World War are being demolished and replaced by permanent development.

Although distinctively a close-knit community, tucked as it is in a fold of the Border hills, Hawick serves as a focal point for an extensive outlying farming area. It has the oldest-established auction market in the British Isles − a thriving family concern that has passed from father to son in unbroken succession since 1817. In the course of a season, more than a quarter of a million sheep and some 20,000 cattle from the surrounding hills change hands at the Hawick sales. There is, too, a more than usually active trade in hunters and ponies reflecting the enthusiastic following that hunting still commands in and around the town.

It is rugby, however, that is Hawick's abiding passion in sport. Here, as in the valleys of Wales, the game is played, watched, and discussed with intense democratic dedication. It is, in short, a mode of life. The Hawick team, colloquially called the "Greens", have maintained a high place in the records of club rugby and contributed notable players to the Scottish international side for many years. Their sociable party piece is a tumultuous rendering of the town song *Teribus ye Teri Odin*, traditionally based on an ancient Saxon invocation to the deities Thor and Odin. But anyone less likely than a Hawick man to need the intervention of the gods on a rugby field is hard to imagine.

HAWTHORNDEN, *Midlothian* (Map 3, ref. 32°66³). Some 2½ m. up the valley of the North Esk from LASSWADE is the village of Hawthornden. The river flows here through steep, thickly-wooded banks, and Hawthornden House is beautifully situated among trees on the edge of a gorge. This was the home of the poet William Drummond (1585–1649), who, says a Latin inscription, restored and largely rebuilt the house in 1638 for himself and his successors. An ancient bell-tower is incorporated in the house, and below it are artificial caves of great antiquity. Here Ben Jonson was entertained in 1618–19, after walking from London, and in the grounds stands a large sycamore known as Ben Jonson's tree.

HELENSBURGH, *Dunbartonshire* (Map 2, ref. 22°68²). This popular holiday burgh stands on the lower CLYDE near its junction with the Gare Loch, and is a centre for yachting and boat-building. The burgh began to be laid out as a residential district about 1776 by Sir James Colquhoun of Luss. During the 19th cent. it became a popular dormitory suburb of GLASGOW as well as a holiday centre. It has some good examples of Victorian architecture. Henry Bell (1767–1830), designer of the early steamboat the *Comet*, stayed in the town from 1807 and did experiments while his wife kept the principal inn. An obelisk to him stands on the sea-front. The flywheel of the *Comet* is preserved in Hermitage Park. John Logie Baird, pioneer of television, was also a native of the town.

About 1½ m. N. of the town on the road across the hill to Loch LOMOND is the entrance to Glen Fruin, where in 1603 a clan battle, or rather massacre, took place by the Macgregors against the Colquhouns. It was partly for this that the law was passed in April of the same year outlawing the whole Clan Gregor and proscribing the name. It was this outlawry of an entire clan that gave Sir Walter Scott so much of the theme of his most popular novel, *Rob Roy*.

HELMSDALE, *Sutherland* (Map 7, ref. 30³91⁵). Here the road and the railway, which have been running more or less in company since INVERNESS, part company. The railway takes the long detour by Strath Ullie then over the moors by FORSINARD and lonely ALTNA-BREAC to Georgemas Junction for WICK and THURSO. The road follows the coastline, with splendid views of cliff and ravine, the seemingly endless moors rolling inland to the heights of Morven and Scaraben.

The natural harbour now has some twenty seine-netting boats. It is overlooked from the S. by ruined 15th-cent. Helmsdale Castle, where in 1567 Isobel Sinclair poisoned the Earl and Countess of Sutherland so that her son the Earl of Caithness might succeed to the earldom of Sutherland; but he also drank the poison and perished with the Sutherlands. Helmsdale river is noted for its trout and salmon fishing; it is one of the great rivers of the N. for the angler.

HERIOT, *Midlothian* (Map 3, ref. 33⁹65²). Prettily situated on the main EDINBURGH-to-Carlisle road, this village lies just to the S. of a watershed. Heriot Water rises in the Moorfoot hills to the S. and W. of the village.

The church, which was rebuilt in 1835, stands just SW. of the village, on an attractive hill road through grass and moorland alongside Heriot Water and Dewar Burn.

HERMANESS, *Shetland* (Map 8, ref. 46⁰21⁹), is on the Island of UNST in the SHETLAND Northern Islands (*see* "The Shape of Scotland"). This hill at the northern end of Scotland's most northerly isle is 627 ft high and is now a nature reserve. Many sea-birds breed there, including the great skua. Not only naturalists, but lovers of wild scenery, will appreciate a visit to this impressive and remote promontory.

HERMITAGE CASTLE, *Roxburghshire* (Map 3, ref. 35⁰59⁶). Turning N. from the

Liddel valley, or S. from the Ewes, a winding road among fine Border hills brings one to the secluded site of Hermitage Castle, the best-preserved of all the Border keeps, 5 m. N. of NEWCASTLETON and about the same distance from the border on the Warieston Fells.

Near the little medieval hermitage that gives it its name, that great double mass of the Castle rises on comparatively flat land, its only protection being the Hermitage Water to the S. and marshy ground around the tower. The English agent's report of the 1560s calls it an "old house, not strong, but evill to be winn by the strait ground about the same", and this difficulty of access was added to by massive outworks of earth.

There was a castle here in 1296, and some fragments of the fabric near the centre of the present one may relate to this earlier building. Excluding this, four building periods can be discerned, plus an extensive early 19th-cent. restoration. The first of these is a smallish tower with an oblong central court enclosed by a cross-wing and screen-walls; this plan is foreign to Scotland, and is in fact a North English fortified mansion built by the Dacres, who were the owners at that time. The second phase was a large tower occupying the same area; in the third period, small square towers were added at the corners of the main tower, and the Castle began to assume its present form. In the fourth stage an oblong wing was incorporated and a continuous wooden hoarding ran beneath the parapet.

The Castle, founded by the Comyns, passed to the Grahams and from them to the Douglasses, passing by marriage to the Dacres and back to the Douglasses, who exchanged it in 1492 with the Earls of Bothwell; it played a large part in the Border Wars, and is chiefly known for its romantic association with Mary Queen of Scots, who in 1566 galloped from JEDBURGH to visit the wounded Bothwell at Hermitage. From the Bothwells it passed to the Scotts of Buccleuch.

HESTAN ISLAND, *Kirkcudbrightshire* (Map 2, ref. 28⁴55¹), is a small island, with a lighthouse, in AUCHENCAIRN Bay. It is connected to Almorness Point on the mainland at most low tides by a long spit of gravel. A large shell midden of oyster shells, possibly of mesolithic date, stands at the top of the raised beach coastline, beside the 19th-cent. farmhouse at the Hestan end of the spit. On the N. face of the island stands the ruin of "King" Edward Balliol's manor, which functioned as the puppet king's "capital" during much of his precarious "reign" from about 1332. Duly crowned at SCONE, Edward, after his first few months, had little hold on Scotland, but retained a tenuous hold on Galloway, the family territory; he issued grants under the Great Seal of Scotland "at our place of Estholm".

Holy Isle from Whiting Bay, Isle of Arran

HILLSWICK, *Shetland* (Map 8, ref. 42⁸17⁷), is a seaport and village on the Mainland of SHETLAND Northern Islands (*see* "The Shape of Scotland"). On an extreme NW. projection of Shetland's largest island, Hillswick can be approached by a good road from LERWICK. It lies in a bay of the Ura Firth, and is not far from the Sandwick bay. Some years ago a hotel was provided at Hillswick to accommodate anglers who seek the sea-trout in the neighbouring "voes", and the brown trout in the fresh-water locks just N. of Hillswick. (*See* description on angling in SHETLAND.)

HODDOM, *Dumfriesshire* (Map 3, ref. 31⁵57³). Hoddom Bridge lies about 1½ m. W. of ECCLEFECHAN. Itself a fine Telford bridge over a charming stretch of the R. Annan, it stands between Hoddom Castle, a massive 16th-cent. tower-castle, a seat of the Johnstones at that time, and the old churchyard, ¼ m. down the river, opposite the wooded mass of Woodcockair.

This marks the site of the great Anglian monastery founded, just before the Anglian period, by St Kentigern, and has yielded a series of crosses, the best of which comes close to the RUTHWELL Cross in style and execution.

It was here that Rhydderch of Alcluyd met Kentigern on the latter's return from Wales about A.D. 600 when Kentigern preached to a large gathering, including Angles who worshipped "Woden" – the first mention of Angles in the South-West. The monastery was an artistic centre. Many of the cross-fragments disappeared during the Second World War, and are believed to lie beneath the drive to Hoddom Castle.

HOLY ISLAND, *Buteshire* (Map 1, ref. 20⁵63⁰), small but steep, protects LAMLASH Bay in the island of ARRAN (*see* "The Shape of Scotland"). It rises to 1,030 ft and is 2 m. long. The island derives its name from the anchorite St Molaise, who had a cell on the island in Columban days. Holy Island is easily approached from Lamlash by motor boat, or on fine days by rowing-boat.

HOLY LOCH, *Argyll* (1 m. N. of HUNTER'S QUAY). This small inlet of the CLYDE estuary lying between STRONE and HUNTER'S QUAY is about 2 m. in length by 1 m. in breadth at its widest point. Now fringed with the popular resorts of the so-called "Costa Clyde", it was once the quarantine centre for infectious diseases in the area. Tradition has it that the loch received its name during the building of GLASGOW Cathedral, when a ship bearing a load of earth from the Holy Land to lay beneath the Cathedral's foundations was stranded in it. More probably, however, it was because of its connection with the ancient Columban church of KILMUN. The loch has received a great deal of publicity as the anchorage for the tender ship serving United States' submarines armed with Polaris missiles.

HOPEMAN, *Moray* (Map 6, ref. 31⁴86⁹). To the outside world the little harbour of Hopeman has a special kind of fame associated with the Prince of Wales and the Duke of Edinburgh. It is familiar to them both as the unofficial "port of GORDONSTOUN", for here the cutters of the famous school founded by Kurt Hahn have made their haven for nearly four decades. But this fishertown on its gentle slope fronting the Moray Firth, 6½ m. NW. of ELGIN, has other claims to attention. The golden freestone known as Hopeman stone, which comes from Greenbrae quarry ½ m. W. of the village, has been extensively used by the North of Scotland Hydro-Electric Board for power-stations and workers' houses, while the stone from Clashach, 1 m. E., is also an important building material. You will get a misleading idea of the village's prosperity if you judge it from the four or five lobster boats to be seen in the harbour, for almost a score of Hopeman seine-net boats fish all round the W. coast from the CLYDE in spring to LERWICK in high summer, while others fish off the Bergen banks on the Norwegian coast.

Hopeman is not an ancient village. The first house in it was built in 1805 when the village was laid out by William Young of Inverugie, the "improver" who later migrated across the Moray Firth to the Strath of Kildonan and played a key part in the most bitterly resented of the Sutherland Clearances, side by side with James Loch and Patrick Sellar.

If he had not been attracted by the prospects of profit from sheep-farming under the Marquess of Stafford in the Sutherland glens that he helped to depopulate, it is possible that Young would be remembered today as an entirely benificent influence on the economy of Moray. He transformed the estate of Inverugie

by deep ploughing, which turned up the sandy surface of the soil and brought the deep black earth beneath into cultivation, while his founding of the village of Hopeman certainly seems to have been justified by the long-term history of the place, though it had its teething troubles. The harbour was built by Admiral Archibald Duff of Drummuir after Young had left the scene. A modern benefactor, Innes Cameron, an Elgin distiller, provided the "town clock" in the tower of Hopeman church, the extensive playing-fields and the paddling-pool − created by the building of a barrier forming a lagoon.

The rich agricultural land in the hinterland of Hopeman was brought into existence by draining the Loch of Spynie, which in historic times extended all the way from LOSSIEMOUTH to BURGHEAD. By this means "an uncultivated forest, deformed almost everywhere by gloomy black pools of stagnant water" was transformed in the 18th cent. into an "unbroken arable field of deep rich clay producing weighty crops". (*See also* DUFFUS.)

HOPETOUN HOUSE, *West Lothian* (at ABERCORN). This splendid building to the W. of EDINBURGH is the seat of the Marquess of Linlithgow, and is one of the notable historic family homes in Scotland regularly open to visitors. The 1st Earl of Hopetoun commissioned Sir William Bruce, who was largely responsible for the reconstruction of the Palace of Holyroodhouse in Edinburgh, to design the original Hopetoun House, which was built between 1699 and 1703. Within the following 50 years, the house was considerably enlarged and embellished by the famous architectural family of William Adam and his sons, John and Robert. Classical symmetry of the façade, formal layout of lawns, fine Adam interior decoration, superb furniture, and an extensive collection of paintings are prominent features of the house. The surrounding parklands are landscaped to reveal vistas over the FORTH

Hopetoun House: the Adam wing

Scottish Tourist Board

to the N., and contain flocks of red and fallow deer and St Kilda sheep.

HOWGATE, *Midlothian* (Map 3, ref. 32⁵65⁸). An attractive small village, Howgate lies in rolling wooded country with fine views W. to the Pentlands. It is associated with Dr John Brown (1754–1832) and with his book *Rab and his Friends.*

Some 4 m. SE. is the large Gladhouse reservoir, a roosting-place in winter nights for large flocks of greylag and pink-footed geese. Gladhouse on the Roseberry estate is also a fine trouting loch, and is probably the best within easy reach of EDINBURGH.

HOWNAM, *Roxburghshire* (Map 3, ref. 37⁸61⁹). On the banks of Kale Water, this village lies in attractive rolling wooded country looking towards the main range of the Cheviots. Nearby is Heatherhope Loch, from which KELSO obtains its water supply; unusual in the Borders, this loch has heather growing on its banks giving it a Highland appearance.

The fort at Hownam Rings became of great importance when, in 1948, excavation showed a sequence of occupations covering more than half a millennium: the settlement defended by a palisade, then reconstruction of the same type, then conversion to a stone wall 10 ft thick, then remodelling with three ramparts and external ditches, then an open settlement without defences having circular stone-walled houses, and finally a sub-rectangular homestead with one or more similar houses.

HOY, Island of, *Orkney* (Map 7, ref. 32⁵99⁸), is one of the ORKNEY Northern Islands (*see* "The Shape of Scotland"). The most westerly of the main Orkney group, Hoy is scenically the most striking. It is the second largest of the group, being 14 m. by 6 m. It can be reached at the Longhope end by steamer daily in the summer from STROMNESS.

There is a good motoring road on this island, but the western cliffs that provide the grandest scenery in Orkney can be approached only by walkers. They will, however, be well rewarded for their energy. At the extreme western tip of the cliffs there erects itself proudly and strikingly the celebrated Old Man of Hoy. This is an isolated columnar peak standing to a height of 450 ft. It is halfway out to sea on a small peninsula, and would at first glance appear to have been put up by human labour. It is, however, a product of nature over the centuries. It is of red sandstone and is strikingly conspicuous, being visible on a clear day from the mainland of Scotland.

A road elsewhere runs round Hoy passing by Rawick, near to which is the "Dwarfie Stone" – a mass of rock hollowed out to make a corridor and two chambers. It is probably a neolithic burial chamber. This strange product of nature and of early man's devising struck the imagination of 19th-cent. romantics. It plays a large part in Walter Scott's *The Pirate.*

HUMBIE, *East Lothian* (Map 3, ref. 34⁶66³). A village at the foot of the Lammermuir Hills, with some most attractive beech hedges, Humbie is noted for its "children's village", which was founded by Mrs Stirling Boyd in 1886 and is now a holiday centre run as a public charity for needy children. Two cottages were opened in 1904, and now the hill-side is dotted with them.

In 1730, an acidulous spring was discovered in the district, and it became a constant place of resort for skin complaints.

About 1 m. NW. of Humbie, in front of Keith Marischal House, are the ruins of a pre-Reformation chapel; a tablet on the inside wall records that it was erected as a private chapel in the reign of David I (1124–53) by Hervei de Keith, King's Marischal.

There are several large houses in lovely grounds around Humbie. To the S. on the LAUDER road is Johnstounburn House, an attractive 18th-cent. house in beautiful gardens.

HUNTER'S QUAY, *Argyll* (Map 2, ref. 21⁸67⁹). This resort on the CLYDE at the S. of HOLY LOCH is the headquarters of the Clyde Yacht Club, and is the centre of the Clyde yachting fortnight in July. It takes its name from the Hunters of Hafton House to the NW. of the town.

This yacht club, founded in 1856, was the first in Scotland. The club-house was given by Mr Hunter in 1872. The original one was later destroyed by fire.

HUNTERSTON, *Ayrshire* (Map 2, ref. 21⁸ 65¹). Originally known as Hunter's-toun, this place has for centuries been associated with one of the oldest untitled landed families in Scotland, the Hunters of Hunterston. The last laird but one lived in a 19th-cent. mansion, but he notably restored the old castle, which had been the dwelling-place of his ancestors.

With its roots deep in the Scottish past, and with "finds" from the district shown in the Museum of Antiquities in EDINBURGH, Hunterston has now entered the Nuclear Age, if not with a bang at least more beneficiently and quite as spectacularly.

It was here, on the 22nd of September 1964, that the first Hunterston Nuclear Power Station was officially opened by Queen Elizabeth the Queen Mother; but much preparation and action had taken place before this.

Hunterston Nuclear Power Station, owned and operated by the South of Scotland Electricity Board, was the first civil nuclear station in Scotland and, when officially opened in 1964, was the most powerful nuclear station in the world. With an output in excess of 320 mW., it produced enough electricity to supply a city the size of Edinburgh. Together with the output

United Kindom Atomic Energy Authority

Hunterston: A Nuclear Power Station

from the United Kingdom Atomic Energy Authority's nuclear station at CHAPELCROSS in Dumfriesshire, it gave Scotland a greater nuclear generating capacity in relation to its population than any other country in the world. This claim still holds true, and will be strengthened by the presence of a second nuclear station now under construction alongside the first. This second station is known as Hunterston B, and the original station is now referred to as Hunterston A.

Progress in nuclear engineering technology has been such that the B station, on which work began in October 1967, will occupy a site area considerably less than that of Hunterston A but will produce almost four times as much electricity as the older station. Each station has two reactors, the A station's being of the first-generation magnox type and the B station's being of the advanced gas-cooled type. The esential difference in the two types lies in the nature of the fuel elements used to maintain the nuclear chain-reaction in the reactors and to supply the heat energy to run the turbo-generators.

Hunterston A has proved to be a splendid station, with a record of availability and output that is unmatched anywhere in the world. Hunterston B, whose two 660 mW. reactors are each scheduled to be in operation in 1973, will add greatly to Scotland's prospects and prestige.

The Hunterston site is on a promontory of the Ayrshire coast near WEST KILBRIDE, and, sheltered on the landward side by Goldenberry Hill, it faces out over the Firth of CLYDE to the island of Great CUMBRAE and the peaks of ARRAN. The coastal rock formation provides a firm foundation for the great weight of the reactor buildings, and the waters of the Clyde provide a plentiful supply of cooling water. At a distance of 25 m. from GLASGOW, the stations' output can be readily fed to the heavy industries of Clydeside and the mid-Scotland industrial belt.

In order to maintain the amenity value of the area, the buildings have been designed to the highest architectural standards; their massive proportions blend with their magnificent surroundings and have become something of a tourist attraction on this world-famous stretch of the Clyde.

HUNTINGTOWER, *Perthshire* (Map 6, ref. 30⁸72⁶), is the name of a castle situated some 3 m. W. of PERTH. It is a very fine castellated house of the 15th and 16th cents., standing on a site which to the N. slopes steeply to the low ground S. of the R. Almond.

The Castle is under the care of the Ministry of Public Building and Works, and should be visited to see the very fine painted wooden ceilings. It was the ancestral home of the Ruthvens (pronounced Rivens), earls of Gowrie, and in 1582 was the scene of the so-called Raid of Ruthven, when the young King James VI was kidnapped by the Earls of Mar and Gowrie and other nobles. In 1600 the mysterious Gowrie conspiracy at Perth cost the Earl of Gowrie and his brother their lives, and their heirs forfeited their estates.

Near to the Castle are the Ruthvenfield Bleach Works, which, since 1774, has been bleaching linen, though today bleaching is a small part of their work compared with dyeing and mercerizing. A village of about 90 houses has grown up around the bleach works and the firm today employs 170 men and 90 women.

HUNTLY, *Aberdeenshire* (Map 6, ref. 35²83⁹), is the capital of the province of Strathbogie, and lies in a little plain entirely surrounded by hills 39 m. W. of ABERDEEN, in the angle formed by the meeting of the R. DEVERON and its tributary the Bogie. It is a little town of 3,800 inhabitants laid out in the 18th cent. on the gridiron or draughtboard plan around two long, straight, and now painfully narrow streets with a pleasant square at their point of intersection. The town owed its

existence to the powerful family of Gordon, whose name is writ large in the annals of Scotland. From the N. end of the square, Castle Street leads directly under the arch of the Gordon Schools (founded by the last Duchess of Gordon in 1839) to the wooded drive leading in turn to the stately ruins of Huntly Castle on the high right bank of the Deveron.

Now zealously preserved by the Ministry of Public Building and Works, Huntly Castle is an epitome of the development of the Scottish castle from the earliest Norman fortress to the palace of the 17th cent. It was one of the last strongholds, and for a time the headquarters, of the Catholic faith in Scotland. These ruins are truly splendid. The green mound of the Norman motte rising high above the rock-

Huntly Castle

J. Pugh

trewn gorge of the river, the enormously thick walls of the medieval keep known as the "Auld Werk", the foundations of the courtyard, and he earthwork of the Civil War ravelin – these re now but the outlines of "old, unhappy, far-ff things". But the great Renaissance palace uilt by the first Marquess of Huntly between 597 and 1602 remains in all its glory, roofless nd tenantless, but otherwise almost entire. Its utstanding features are the stately row of irst-floor windows (inspired by those of the Château of Blois, of which during his "exile" he Marquess is said to have been governor), he grand doorway with its armorial bearings, nd the splendid carved fireplaces.

The "palace" is a large oblong building ?6 ft long, with a round tower at the SW. orner, and a smaller round tower opposite it t the NE. angle carrying the grand stair. You an see over the building and look down from he oriel windows on a scene of sylvan beauty hat is an experience in itself, but probably the memory that will remain is that of the "most plendid heraldic doorway in the British Isles", s the Lord Lyon has called it. Achievement fter achievement stretches up the side of he tower, connected with delicately-moulded panels in a series that symbolizes first human nd then divine authority: first the lord of the castle and his lady, then king and queen, then he Passion of Christ and the Resurrection. Above all is the figure of St Michael, the warrior archangel, triumphing over Satan.

Huntly Castle was the home of the Gordons from 1376 to 1752. By that time Gordon Castle, FOCHABERS, was the principal seat of the family, and in that year the widow of the 3rd Duke of Gordon used some of the stones of the stronghold to rebuild Huntly Lodge as a jointure-house. This stately 18th-cent. mansion is now, with modern additions, the Huntly Castle Hotel. It stands on rising ground about ¼ m. from the Castle on the far side of the Deveron, here spanned by a fine old bridge. It was in this period also that the ancient burgh of barony known as the Raws of Strathbogie clustered about the Castle, and was replaced by the modern town of Huntly, as its linen industry was replaced by the woollen manu-facturing one that still continues. In an old building on the W. side of the square a crafts-man named Forsyth designed the sett of the Gordon tartan when the 4th Duke of Gordon, assisted by his famous Duchess, Jane Maxwell, raised the Gordon Highlanders regiment in 1794. The Duchess, a leader of London fashion, is said to have placed the King's shilling between her lips to woo recruits with a kiss. As "Bonnie Jean", she is still revered in memory by the Gordons of today.

A tablet in Duke Street indicates the birth-place of the novelist George MacDonald (1824–1905), whose works include *David Elginbrod*, a mystical romance, and *Alec Forbes of Howglen*, a description of humble life

in Huntly. The modern reader is more likely to be familiar with his fairy tales, such as *At the Back of the North Wind*.

Huntly Town Council administers 22½ m. of burgh fishings on the Bogie and the Deveron. A fine golf course extends almost from the castle into the salient where Deveron and Bogie meet, while farther W. is a children's lido on the Deveron. Trees and hills are the natural attractions. The bare shoulder of Clashmach rises to the SW. Due W. the Deveron emerges from a charming glen through which a road runs by Kirkton of Glass to DUFFTOWN, while due N. the river – having joined forces with the Bogie – skirts the Bin Forest, a large Forestry Commission plantation, to enter Banffshire and tryst with the R. Isla in golden haughlands above the village of Rothiemay. The country to the SE., where the Bogie meanders through a long vale after emerging from the hills of the CABRACH, is plainer and barer; so too is the upland road to Aberdeen through the Glens of Foudland to the E.

INCHAFFRAY ABBEY, *Perthshire* (Map 2, ref. 29⁵72²). Very little now remains of this ancient foundation 6 m. E. of CRIEFF. Originally the site of a Celtic community it was founded as a priory by Gilbert, Earl of Strath-earn, in 1200. Here a religious house dedicated to God, St Mary, and St John the Evangelist was founded, and was served by Augustinian canons brought from the Abbey of SCONE, near PERTH. The building was thereafter richly endowed by Gilbert's successors. The house had in its possession the arm of St Fillan, and this precious relic was carried to the Battle of BANNOCKBURN by Maurice, Abbot of Inchaffray. The last abbot resigned in favour of James Drummond of INNERPEFFRAY (the second son of David, 2nd Lord Drummond), who in 1609 was created Lord Maddertie.

INCHCOLM, Island of, *Fife* (Map 3, ref. 31⁹68³), is in the Firth of FORTH (*see* "The Shape of Scotland"). Unquestionably the most attractive of the usually rather grim islands of the Firth of Forth, Inchcolm lies only 1½ m. S. of ABERDOUR and is 1 m. long. The name of the island derives since Christian times from Gaelic, meaning Colum's Isle, and Inchcolm (*see* IONA) has sometimes been called the "Iona of the East". There is no doubt that in the 12th cent. a Columban hermit inhabited the island and that Alexander I, having sought shelter on Inchcolm during a stormy passage of the Forth, in gratitude endowed and had built there an Augustinian abbey. Like Iona, Inch-colm came to be regarded as holy, so that the illustrious, even from without Scotland, sought it as their burial-place, being an island "close to heaven". Shakespeare in *Macbeth* mentions this fact.

Until the Reformation, the abbey flourished and grew despite many savage depredations during the English Wars. The abbey officially expired under the Reformed Faith in 1578, and thereafter was used as an occasional dwelling-house by the earls of Moray. Towards the end of the 19th cent. the buildings became national property.

Inchcolm may be easily visited by boat from Aberdour, and more occasionally by steamer from Granton on the EDINBURGH shore. The abbey, an interesting example of early ecclesiastical Scottish architecture, is fairly well preserved (much better than many such buildings on the mainland), and is now carefully tended. You may still see the remains of a hermit's cell that tradition associates with the Columban Culdees, who gave hospitality to the Scottish king, thus inspiring the grateful monarch over 800 years ago to found the monastery and abbey on this attractive and douce islet, of pleasant grazing ground and venerable buildings.

INCHINNAN, *Renfrewshire* (Map 2, ref. 24⁹66⁸). The village and parish of Inchinnan take the name from the site of the church, for the name means island of the rivers and the church formerly stood on an island of the R. Gryfe between two side branches of the river.

The church was given by David I to the Knights Templar; after their suppression, however, it was transferred in 1312 to the Knights of St John and held by them until the Reformation. The church was pulled down in 1827–8, and has been rebuilt twice since then. The present one in neo-Gothic style was given by Lord Blythswood and was built in 1904.

Until the First World War the parish was an agricultural one. Immediately after hostilities ceased, however, Beardmores acquired the land to erect hangars for airship construction. One of those built here made the pioneer double crossing of the Atlantic in 1919. In the late 1920s Beardmores gave up aircraft and the hangars were acquired by a tyre manufacturing company.

The churchyard contains Celtic stones and some tombs of Templars; there are many mortsafes to recall the later age of body-snatching for the anatomists.

INCHKEITH, *Fife* (Map 3, ref. 32⁹68³), an island in the Firth of FORTH (*see* "The Shape of Scotland"), is 4 m. NNE. of Leith, and is just about halfway between the Lothian and Fife coasts. The island gets its name from the illustrious family of Keith (hereditary Grand Marischal of Scotland), who once possessed it. It would indeed today be a pleasing island residence for an Edinburgh family who wished to be near enough to the capital for frequent access, yet sufficiently insulated to be protected from the more deplorable manifestations of our age. This was suggested for Inchkeith by a famous 18th-cent. traveller who visited the island. But nothing ever came of it. Inchkeith,

alas! has long proved too valuable to the military as a base for protection of the Forth to be allowed as private property. Its value in this respect was recognized by Mary of Lorraine in the middle of the 16th cent. after she, as Queen Regent, held Scotland independent from England but still under French influence. She invited her compatriots to occupy and fortify the island. After Mary of Lorraine's death, the French garrison for the most part retreated, but those that remained were faithful to the interests of the Regent's daughter, Mary Stuart, Queen of Scots. "M R" (*Maria Regina*) may be seen to this day engraved upon a stone in the present lighthouse.

The old fortress of Inchkeith has long been demolished. Gun emplacements, wireless machines, and the like have taken its place. But, for those who succeed in getting permission to visit the island from Leith, there is a reward in its historical associations, and in an incomparable view of the capital city of Edinburgh, at her proudest and set against the background of her hills.

It is alleged that that curious Renaissance Prince, James IV of Scotland, segregated two infants by placing them upon Inchkeith in the care of a dumb nurse, in order to discover what natural language they grew up to speak. It is even more improbably averred that they expressed themselves in "extremely good Hebrew". None of Edinburgh's small but intelligent Jewish minority have been inspired by this story, and by a devotion to their venerable tongue, to make Inchkeith a place of pilgrimage.

INCH KENNETH, Island of, *Argyll* (Map 1, ref. 14³73⁵), is one of the Inner Hebrides (*see* "The Shape of Scotland"). Lying NE. to SW. off the W. coast of MULL, only ¼ m. from the larger island and scarcely ½ m. long, this lovely little green island now supports a population in single figures. There is a 19th-cent. restored house that takes the place of the Old House of Inch Kenneth owned by the Macleans. The rest of the inhabitants live upon grazing and occasional fishing.

We have in this gazetteer-portrait of Scotland had to omit other of our 787 islands that are larger, more contemporarily significant, than this one. Apart from the poignant beauty of the island and of its position, the reason for including Inch Kenneth is its past. It is just as tangible for the sensitive and literate visitor as the past of RAASAY, but it goes deeper and is more holy.

After St Columba had brought Christianity to IONA (itself just off the west of Mull, and about 12 m. SW. of Inch Kenneth), the lesser island was one of Iona's first and immediate dependencies. There was a Culdee foundation, and you may still see the ruins of a church that must have been 60 ft long. There you can still find standing a Celtic cross of great antiquity.

Inch Kenneth: the remains of the Chapel

Daniell print, in the possession of Moray McLaren

Inch Kenneth, no less than the other insular Christian settlements of the West, was raided by Norsemen. Later it was tossed about in internecine Celtic clan warfare, particularly between the Macleans, who used to own much of Mull and its satellite islands, and the Campbells of Argyll. It was but a small spot of fertile land, scarcely an island (at low tide a vigorous man who knows his way amongst the quicksands may wade out to it), and can have been of only small importance. Then, like other islands of the West, it entered the substance of English, indeed of international, literature in 1773. It was in the autumn of that year that Dr Samuel Johnson and James Boswell stayed on Inch Kenneth, and each in his differing but unforgettable manner wrote of it. They fixed this green islet in the consciousness of educated literate mankind.

We need not, as in the entry under RAASAY, evoke by quotation the Johnsonian and Boswellian scene when they were entertained by Sir Allan Maclean and his two daughters at Inch Kenneth. Let anyone who visits this place and falls under its spell turn to the accounts left by the Doctor and his biographer. He will find that, for once, Johnson is more detailed than and nearly as gossipy as Boswell. Also, let him not forget to look at the Doctor's set of Latin verse "Insula Sancti Kennethi".

It is permissible, however, to take some words from Boswell's private journal, which was discovered only recently; they were omitted from his *Journal of a Tour in the Hebrides*. From the secret paper, we learn that Boswell crept out of the pleasant little party in

the laird's house, leaving the tea-table, the talk, the harpischord-playing, and the dancing, and went into the darkness of the night on Inch Kenneth to pray before the centuries-old Celtic cross. Thus he confided to himself in his private journal: "I knelt before it, and holding it with both my hands, I prayed with strong devotion while I had before me the image of that on which my Saviour died for the sins of the world". Then, after a characteristic piece of Boswellian self-excuse to himself for invoking a saint, he goes on: "I said '*Sancte Columbe, ora pro me*, O Columbus thou venerable Saint, as we have all the reason that can be to believe that thou art in heaven, I beseech thee to pray to God that I may attain everlasting felicity' ".

(Moving though this naïve account of Boswell's experience may be, one cannot let him away without a rebuke for a mistake others have made before and after him. Both in his Latin, as his vocative shows, and in his English, he was thinking of the Saint's name as Columbus, not Columba. He must somehow have got him mixed up with Christopher Columbus. This egregious error was, however, confined to his private journal intended for his own eyes only. In his published book, wherever he has to speak of St Columba, he spells his name correctly.)

The cross before which Boswell knelt still stands, its slender staff rising like the stem of a flower from the grass. Indeed, since his day, the little island, save for the quite inoffensive 19th-cent. house, has scarcely changed. It is as green as it was in 1773; and the old stones of the cross and the church (now carefully preserved) are as they were. As on ERISKAY, time on Inch Kenneth scarcely moves.

You may take the private ferry on to Inch Kenneth from Mull near the mouth of Loch na Keal. As you pass over it, the floor of the sea is never out of sight. The waters here are amongst the most pellucid in the West.

INCHMAHOME, *Perthshire* (Map 2, ref. 25⁷69⁹). This is an island in the Lake of MENTEITH – why this celebrated sheet of water is the only one of its kind in Scotland to be called a lake and not a loch will be mentioned when we come to the entry under MENTEITH.

The island in the lake has much connection with Scotland's past. There are remains on it of an ancient priory, and it is one of the most attractive memorials of monastic life that is left in Scotland. The Augustinian house on this island was founded by Walter Comyn, Earl of Menteith, in 1238, and considerable parts of the church and of thé claustral buildings remain. It is possible that its island situation helped to preserve the buildings here from post-Reformation destructive zeal; that situation too would certainly help to preserve them from that fate which has been mentioned elsewhere and which had such dire results upon so much of Scotland's ecclesiastical architecture. This was not reforming zeal but the casual pilfering of stones for secular buildings in subsequent ages. ST ANDREWS Cathedral is, of course, a prime example of this, but the Augustinian priory on Inchmahome may have been protected by the waters of the lake.

There are monuments of Walter Stewart, a later Earl of Menteith, of his Countess, and of Sir John Drummond, a 15th-cent. benefactor. Robert Bruce visited the island and priory upon one occasion, and later, in 1363, his lamentable son David II was married here for the second time.

In the stormy 16th cent. Inchmahome once again played its part in Scotland's story. After the decisive defeat of the Scots forces by the English at the Battle of Pinkie, just outside EDINBURGH, in 1547, it was believed, and probably rightly, that STIRLING Castle was not a sufficiently safe place for the infant Queen Mary. She was, of course, the daughter of the dead James V, and in later years famous as Mary Stuart, Queen of Scots. The child Mary was hastily taken away from Stirling, rowed across the waters of the lake, and hidden almost in secrecy upon Inchmahome. She stayed there only a short time before being sent for complete security to France. She set sail from DUMBARTON. On Inchmahome you may see a little garden known to this day as Queen Mary's Bower.

Robert Bontine Cunninghame Graham was buried, at his own request as stated in his will, upon the island of Inchmahome beside the remains of his Spanish wife (*see* MENTEITH).

That increasingly rare bird, the osprey, used to nest in the chestnut trees on Inchmahome; these trees are said to have been grown from chestnuts brought from Rome. Towards the end of the 17th cent. the Montrose family acquired the island and held it until 1926. Today the priory is open to the public, and there is access to it by boat from the port of Menteith, a small resort on the N. shores of the lake.

INCHNADAMPH, *Sutherland* (Map 5, ref. 22⁵92²), is now primarily an angling resort in the Assynt district, geologically an interesting part of Sutherland. The land to the NW. is Archaean gneiss rock, which is one of the oldest formations in the world and found elsewhere only in the Outer Hebrides and near the St Lawrence river in Canada.

The nature reserve of 3,200 acres of limestone country nearby includes the famous Allt nan Uamh bone caves showing traces of occupation by early man; there are also rare plants and ferns.

Just W. of the township is a massive stone cairn with a tablet in memory of Benjamin N. Peach and John Horne "who played the foremost part in unravelling the geological structure of the North-West Highlands", 1883–97.

Anglers may note that that rarity within the United Kingdom, the Gillaroo trout, is to be found in Loch Maoloch.

INCHTURE, *Perthshire* (Map 6, ref. 32⁸72⁸). This attractive village of red sandstone houses lies in the fertile Carse of Gowrie between the Sidlaw Hills and the estuary of the TAY.

The ruins of the ancient Castle of Moncur stand just to the N. of the main road between PERTH and DUNDEE, about ½ m. E .of the village.

Since 1670, the parish of Inchture has included the parish of Rossie. Two old communion cups belonging to the church are dated 1692, and the records in the parish register date from 1623. Two curious old customs are attested in these earliest records. Apparently at one time baptisms were sworn to by witnesses, and for men travelling to England as agricultural workers a certificate was supplied to the effect that they were not "rebels".

About 1½ m. N. of the village is Rossie Priory, seat of Lord Kinnaird. It was built between 1807 and 1817 from a design by John Atkinson on the site of an earlier building called Drimmie House. John Atkinson was born near Durham in 1773 and became a pupil of James Wyatt. He became very fashionable with the landed gentry and various well-known houses in Scotland were designed by him including TULLIALLAN Castle in Clackmannanshire, ABBOTSFORD for Sir Walter Scott, and Bowhill for the Duke of Buccleuch.

The original Rossie Priory was in Gothic style, but the present owner has demolished much of the building and greatly reduced its size. The old village of Rossie was destroyed when the priory was built and the model village of Baledgarno was constructed at the western entrance gates. The old village cross of Rossie still stands in the grounds, as do the ruins of the original parish church, which occupies the site of a very old religious foundation mentioned in old records as the Abbacy of Rossie. King David I gave the abbey to Matthew, Archdeacon of ST ANDREWS, who handed it over to the canons of St Andrews, and his gift was confirmed by King Malcolm IV in the 12th cent. In 1243 the church of Rossie was consecrated by David de Bernham, 4th Bishop of St Andrews. After the Reformation the lands of Rossie were made into a temporal lordship and bestowed on the Duke of Lennox in 1588.

The Family of Kinnaird first appear in Perthshire in the reign of King William the Lion and obtained a charter of the barony in 1180. Richard, the 7th laird Kinnaird, married Elizabeth, daughter of Sir John Drummond of Stobhall, who was brother to Lady Annabella Drummond, wife of Robert III, King of Scotland. Thus the Kinnaird family was linked with royalty. The family has been associated with Rossie for more than eight centuries.

Some 3 m. SW. of Inchture is Megginch Castle. It bears a Latin inscription, which says that Peter Hay built it in 1575. Since the mid-17th cent. it has belonged to the Drummonds. The Castle stands in well timbered policies and there is here a famous holly tree which has attained a height of fully 50 ft.

It is well worth while taking the road N. of Inchture into the hills and visiting the quaint villages of Kinnaird, Rait, and Kilspindie. From the latter a hill road with splendid views

of the carse crosses the watershed and joins the main Perth to COUPAR ANGUS road just S. of Balbeggie.

INCHTUTHIL, *Perthshire* (Map 6, ref. 31³73⁹). This site of a Roman legionary fortress lies 7 m. ESE. of DUNKELD on the left bank of the R. TAY. Since 1952 the site has been excavated by Sir Ian Richmond and Dr J. K. St Joseph. The fortress was in existence in A.D. 83 during the Scottish campaign of Agricola (two coins of Domitian A.D. 85 and 86 have been recovered), but it was abandoned hurriedly, and indeed before completion of some of the internal buildings. In particular the site for the legionary legate's house had been levelled but no building erected. In 1961 a cache of 12 tons of Roman nails was found. These had obviously been buried hastily to prevent them from falling into the hands of the Picts.

Inchtuthil has produced some rather surprising discoveries. Here is some of the earliest evidence for all-timber defences in Scotland, and during the 1956 season a hospital range was examined which included "a very large hall . . . flanked by smaller rooms which seems to correspond to the operating theatre. The building is the first of its kind to be discovered in Britain."

A temporary Roman camp of 40 acres has been located on the plateau W. of the fortress and a remarkable pre-Roman structure of wigwam timbers enclosing an area 170 ft by 30 ft has been found inside the fortress.

The nearby Roman baths, discovered earlier this century, have been filled in to preserve them from the effects of exposure to the weather.

INGLISTON, *Midlothian* (Map 6, ref. 38¹82²). The modern mansion of Ingliston was

Ingliston House

built in 1846 in the old baronial style. New and handsome stables and a garden-house were added later. In 1934 the grounds became a golf course with residential facilities in the mansion.

The estate was sold in 1958 to the Royal Highland and Agricultural Society, and after 1960 it became the permanent site for the Royal Highland Show. The show ground is already used for kart-racing and also for motor-racing.

INNELLAN, *Argyll* (Map 2, ref. 21⁵67⁰). GREENOCK merchant princes excelled themselves in building country villas at this pleasant resort, nearly 4 m. SW. of DUNOON. The houses are built in terraces looking across to WEMYSS BAY with uninterrupted views of shipping entering and leaving the CLYDE.

On high ground above the pier stands Knockarmillie Castle, a stronghold of the Campbells, which was probably abandoned when the mansion-house was built in 1650.

INNERLEITHEN, *Peeblesshire* (Map 3, ref. 33³63⁷). Standing where the rivers TWEED and Leithen meet, this pleasant little town, formerly a noted spa, still attracts tourists. The early 19th cent. saw the rise of Innerleithen as a watering-place. Its mineral spring on Lee Pen, called Dow or Doo's Well, was reported to be similar to the waters at Harrogate. Its popularity increased with the publication in 1823 of Scott's novel *St Ronan's Well*, the name by which the spring is now known. In 1826 Lord Traquair furnished the well with a pump-house, reading rooms, and a verandah, which were reconstructed in 1896. It became a burgh in 1868.

The town has important woollen, spinning, and knitwear industry, but it was just a hamlet until 1790, when the first woollen-mill was built by Alexander Brodie, a Traquair black-smith who had made a fortune in London. The process of dyeing wool in blue with woad was first carried out in this mill by Thomas Turnbull (d. 1803). This mill is still in existence as Caerles Mill and belongs to a famous knitwear firm.

The church was granted by Malcolm IV to the monks of KELSO in 1159; he gave it the right of sanctuary as it was here that tradition-ally the body of his son had first rested when taken from the Tweed, where he was accident-ally drowned.

The Border Games, instituted in 1827, are still held annually and since 1900 have included the "Cleikum ceremony", a pageant of St Ronan ridding the town of the devil for the next twelve months.

INNERPEFFRAY, *Perthshire* (Map 2, ref. 29⁰72⁰), is a township on the R. Earn 2¼ m. SE. of CRIEFF. During the Roman occupation of this part of Scotland there was an important

Scottish Tourist Board
Innerpeffray: a family gravestone

crossing of the river here, guarded on the farther bank by the camp at Strageath.

The original name is Innerpowfray. After the Battle of BANNOCKBURN, and in recognition of the services rendered there by Maurice, Abbot of Inchaffray, Robert Bruce ordered that the marsh around the abbey should be drained. This involved the stream known as the Pow, a tributary of the Earn, and the drained lands became known as Innerpowfray.

The laird of Innerpeffray was Sir John Drummond, who in 1508 founded here a Collegiate Church, with provost and prebend, on the site of an earlier chapel dedicated to St Mary and mentioned as early as 1342.

Today Innerpeffray is known for its library – the oldest public library in Scotland, founded in 1691 by David Drummond, 3rd Lord Madderty. The library is particularly rich in old Bibles, and it includes a copy of the so-called Treacle Bible and also a Bible carried by the Marquis of Montrose. The oldest printed books are a copy of Barclay's *Ship of Fools* dated 1508 and the Paris edition of Hector Boece's *Chronicles* printed in 1527. The books were originally housed in the attic of the adjacent chapel, but between 1750 and 1758 Archbishop Hay Drummond erected the present building and added his own library to the collection.

INSCH, *Aberdeenshire* (Map 6, ref. 36³82⁸). This pleasant granite-built village at the

Above *The Falls of Leny* (see p. 332)

Below *Loch an Eilean* (see p. 341)

Scottish Tourist Board

Scottish Tourist Board

western end of the province of the Garioch signals its whereabouts to the approaching traveller by means of an unmistakeable landmark. This is the conspicuous tower on top of the conical grassy hill of Dunnideer (876 ft), with a great irregular arch in the middle of a rough-hewn wall of masonry through which the light of day shines. This is all that remains of the medieval Castle of Dunnideer – the earliest authenticated tower-house on the mainland of Scotland. Actually there are three antiquities on the summit of Dunnideer, which is just W. of the village. They form a triple ring. On the outer circle is a multiple earthwork rampart, the origins of which are lost in the mists of prehistory. Inside is an elliptical vitrified fort of the Iron Age, while inside that again are the ruins of the medieval castle, which have now been saved for posterity by a timely restoration fund.

The story of the medieval castle is clearly authenticated. The chartulary of the Abbey of LINDORES, which held sway over wide lands in the Garioch, records that in 1260 the "Castle of Dunidor" was built by Sir John de Balliol, husband of Dervogillan, Lady of Galloway, who nine years later founded Balliol College, Oxford, in her husband's memory. This lady was the mother of the obsequious King John Balliol, the "toom tabard" whom Edward I of England so grievously humiliated. The castle was a simple rectangular tower, unvaulted, and with two narrow slit windows in the basement. It is the gable with its breached and broken lancet window that is the landmark we know today. The castle appears to have been the headquarters of the Barony of Insch and the village itself received a charter as a burgh of barony in the 16th cent. With a population of just over 800, it has never sought to enter the lists as a police burgh and consequently its provost, bailies and town council are "unofficial", but they hold regular meetings and act as a sort of village amenities association. In the kirkyard of Insch is the ruin of an early post-Reformation parish church with a beautiful belfry bearing the date 1613 and a bell that dates from 1706.

Today Insch is an important mart centre for the agricultural produce of a particularly rich farming area.

There are many antiquities of interest in the Insch area. But perhaps the most charming is Lickleyhead Castle (3 m. S.), on the banks of the Gadie near the hamlet of Auchleven, the home of Madame de Mier, who has carefully restored and refurnished this fine old Scottish tower-house.

You reach Lickleyhead through undulating country of great beauty. Just beyond the quiet village of Premnay the tree-lined drive begins. It sweeps round and across a new bridge over the Gadie to the entry to the tower, and your first impression is of the great height of the building. The effect is accentuated by the dis-position of the windows, which diminish in size from the first floor upwards. There is the grace of ornament in the heavily-corbelled stair-tower, in the turrets, in the gabled windows of the upper storeys and in turret windows of unusual ovoid form.

As Mr Stewart Cruden has remarked in his book *The Scottish Castle*, the long soaring roundel of the stair-tower, corbelled out at only a few feet above the ground, demonstrates the 16th-cent. Scottish mason's fondness for this contrivance, and his tendency to design from the wall-head down instead of from the ground up.

Above the entry to the tower are carved the initials of John Forbes, Lickleyhead's first Forbes laird, and the date 1629.

The Forbes family held Lickleyhead Castle throughout the 17th cent. and went down in history as ardent supporters of the Covenant. One of their number, William Forbes, met and challenged a famous Royalist, Alexander Irvine of Kingcausie, near the Bridge of Dee, ABERDEEN, on the 17th of August 1644. The covenanting authorities had offered an award for the arrest of Irvine, and Forbes attempted to capture him. When he resisted arrest, Forbes drew out a pistol and shot him dead. When some years later, while practising shooting in the garden at Lickleyhead, Forbes's gun burst and both his hand and arm were shattered, folk said it was "just what he deserved". After the Restoration he was arrested and executed for Irvine's murder.

At the end of the century the Castle passed out of the hands of the Forbes family and was owned in turn by Hays, Duffs, Gordons, and Oglivies, and ultimately by the Lumsdens of Auchindoir and Clova, from whom it was purchased by Madame de Mier. There are portraits by Allan Ramsay and Romney in a Georgian wing of the house which forms the third side of a paved courtyard.

INVER, *Perthshire* (Map 6, ref. 30²74²), is an attractive village on the right bank of the TAY just W. of DUNKELD. Before the building of the bridge at Dunkeld, there was an important ferry at Inver, and the old inn with its yard can still be recognized.

Neil Gow, the celebrated Scots fiddler and composer, lived here. He was born in Strathbraan in 1727, but died at Inver in 1807. His cottage is preserved, and in 1949 a bronze plaque, showing him in the characteristic attitude made familiar by Raeburn's portrait of him, was unveiled by the Duchess of Atholl. He knew Hogg, the Etrrick Shepherd, and also Burns and Lady Nairne; at the age of eighteen, during the Jacobite march south of 1745, he played before Prince Charles at an entertainment in Dunkeld House given by the Marquess of Tullibardine. Burns spent a convivial evening with him on his Highland tour in 1787. His sons were all musicians, but Nathaniel is best known

Plate 10 Isle of Islay, Argyll: Kilchoman Bay (see p. 300)
Scottish Tourist Board

Inveraray town

as a composer, especially of the melody for the song "Caller Herrin' ".

A short distance from Inver on the road to ABERFELDY is the entrance to the Hermitage, now National Trust property. This picturesque walk to the viewpoint at the Falls of Braan is well worth a visit.

INVERARAY, *Argyll* (Map 2, ref. 20⁹70⁹). The two most attractive of Scotland's historical small towns are HADDINGTON, in the E., and Inveraray, so far to the W. that it is all but enisled near the head of that arm of the sea, Loch Fyne.

The two towns have elements in common. Both were destroyed in wars of centuries ago (Haddington by the English, Inveraray in a civil war). Both were reconstructed as "New Towns" at a period of taste in the 18th cent. Both fell into a certain outer desuetude in the early years of the 20th. Both have now pulled themselves up "by their boot-straps". In both there has been a praiseworthy collaboration of civic and national effort. In both, moreover, there has been quite new building in harmony with the old. And they have both succeeded in making it clear that the graces of the past can be made triumphantly to live on into, and often surpass, the present.

In the case of Inveraray, however, the efforts of the great Campbell family and clan, of which the dukes of Argyll are the head, have combined to give impetus to the restoration. Of the Campbells of Argyll, and of their famous seat at Inveraray Castle, we shall speak below.

THE TOWN

This small, picturesque (the word is not used here as a condescending substitute for beauti-

ful) little town on Loch Fyne, and at the mouth of the salmon-abounding R. Aray, is the oldest royal burgh in Argyll. Created a royal burgh in 1648, the fishing-village portion of it was burnt by Montrose in 1644 after his astonishing descent upon the Campbell country. Again we shall see more below. In the early 18th cent., the 3rd Duke of Argyll decided to rebuild the castle, and demolished what remained of the old village to plan a new one – fortunately in an era of good taste. It was an era too in which Highland domestic architecture was turning to the use of white-washed building – the perfect contrast to the polychromatic W. Highland scene.

Roger Morris, with William Adam as his Clerk of Works, was engaged to lay plans for the new burgh and castle; and excavations were begun in 1743. Comparatively soon afterwards, however, both Morris and William Adam died. Robert Mylne (the name Mylne has been associated with Scottish architecture for centuries) is usually credited with finishing the job and carrying out the plans. This attribution, however, overlooks the fact that John Adam, the elder son of William, carried on the supervision of the works and of the whole town, except for the church, which was designed later. Several of the buildings were completed by 1751. Much of the interior decorations and the mantelpieces, particularly in the castle, were designed by John Adam.

Among these buildings stood the inn, which was afterwards destroyed by fire. This was reconstructed according to Adam's design, but possibly by Mylne, who also carried out a certain amount of the interior decoration of the castle. But this was after the 5th Duke had changed to Mylne from Adam (*see below*).

Mylne probably did build the imposing

frontage of the new inn, now the Argyll Arms. Once again readers are referred to Boswell's account of the tour of the Highlands and Islands that he and Dr Johnson made in 1773. It was here that the Doctor tasted his first and last glass of whisky ("Come, let me know what it is that makes a Scotchman happy"); it was here that he gave so severe a verbal drubbing to the Rev. John Macaulay, minister of Inveraray and grandfather of the historian ("Are you so grossly ignorant of human nature, Sir, as not to know that a man may be very sincere in good principles without having good practice?").

The old town house, now the municipal offices, was built by Mylne, though whether planned by him is not certain. It is a common error to suppose that the celebrated trial of James Stewart of the Glen for the APPIN murder took place in the old town house, the new version of which, in fact, was not built until a year after the trial – that is, in 1753. James probably "tholed his assize" in the kirk of the old town. Readers are referred to Robert Louis Stevenson's *Kidnapped* and *Catriona* for graphic if fictionalized accounts of this famous trial, which is still the source of hot dispute not only amongst novel-writers but between serious legal historians.

Another feature of the new 18th-cent. town was the tall buildings called, in the Scots fashion, "lands". These were also put up rather in the style of Edinburgh's Old Town. In 1957 the present Duke of Argyll gave up possession of these buildings in favour of the Ministry of Public Building and Works, which employed the distinguished Scottish architect, the late Ian Lindsay, to rehabilitate them. As at Haddington, the result has been most successful. Mr Lindsay's main task was less to make the outsides of these buildings agreeable

to look at – there was little need of that – than to make them habitable by the 20th-cent. people who live in Inveraray. It may well be that in the beautiful little town of Inveraray you will find the best example in all Scotland of the fact that it is possible to preserve the 18th cent. and to live in it with comfort.

The parish church (1798–1804) has a unique feature – a centrally dividing wall that once enabled services in Gaelic and in English to proceed at the same time. As there are now very few monoglot Gaelic speakers outside the Hebrides, the Gaelic half has now been converted into the church hall. The courthouse was completed in 1820, and in 1962 was sold to the Highland Industries in Inveraray, who have converted it into a centre for the training of young people. The great tower (1923–32) of the Episcopalian church, so close to the heart of the late and 10th Duke, is famous for its peal of ten bells sounding out as a memorial to the Campbells who fell in the First World War. The grammar school was founded in 1684; the new buildings, opened in May 1962, gained a Civic Trust Award.

THE CASTLE

Originally dated about 1520, the new castle, the seat of the dukes of Argyll, was replanned by Morris and Mylne in the earlier half of the 18th cent., to be completed in 1770. The old castle, which stood 80 yds from the present front door, was finally demolished only in 1773 (the year of Johnson's and Boswell's visit). The new one was roofed by 1760, but scarcely lived in by the 3rd or 4th Dukes. It was the 5th Duke who, when he was Marquess of Lorne and heir to the dukedom, modernized it and completed its decoration.

Inveraray Castle

The Duke of Argyll

The result of this modernizing and decoration in the latter half of the 18th cent. was impressive then. It remains impressive. In its kind, it is unique. It is amongst the earliest, if not the earliest, example of neo-Gothic in these islands, and was conceived and built well before Horace Walpole's Strawberry Hill. It is also, oddly enough, an extremely early example of the neo-Scottish baronial style. Yet, standing four-square, it is indubitably of the splendid 18th century and indubitably Scottish. Thus it presents itself to the onlookers from the town, who may see it in glimpses through a well-wooded park against the background of the dramatically abrupt yet domestic hill of Duniquaich. Thus it may be seen from the outside. Its interior may also be seen by visitors on set days and hours. It is not the policy of this portrait-gazetteer to give details of all great or small Scottish country houses and castles still inhabited yet open to the public. It is impossible, however, to speak of Inveraray and its castle without mentioning that its interior too may be seen. That interior provides such a wealth of 18th-cent. beauty and architectural curiosity, and so many outward signs of Scotland's past, that we do not feel inclined here to give a detailed list extending from the superb Augustan Age wall-pieces, fireplaces, chimney-pieces (many of them by Adam), to battle-axes and antique evidence of a Highland past. As with the castle at EDINBURGH, we prefer to leave the discovery of the interior of Inveraray Castle to the visitor himself, who will be well informed as he makes his way through this classic castle and country home.

What is perhaps more needful is to say a word about the Campbell Clan and their chiefs – the earls, marquesses and dukes of Argyll. Each one of these has borne in Gaelic the title of *Mac Cailein Mor*, or, in English, the "Son of Great Colin".

Visitors to Scotland will often be presented with, or more often asked to buy, innocent little items of tartan romanticism in the form of personal adornment. Often too they will be expected to accept less substantial items of tartan sentiment that are widely supposed to represent Scottish feelings on events of the past and present.

Among these will be the "Auld Alliance" between France and Scotland – a condition that undoubtedly did exist, but is now dressed up by professional romanticists to represent a profound likeness between the two people of Scotland and France. There are such likenesses (*see* "Scotland in History"), but the romantic proposition in general is unsound. There is also the revived cult of Bonnie Prince Charlie, based upon the fact of fine past loyalties, but now greatly sentimentalized. Finally, Campbell is supposed to be a distrusted name.

Above all, the admittedly unattractive figure of the Earl (later Marquess) of Argyll, of the covenanting period of Charles I, is contrasted with the indubitably attractive character of the Presbyterian and Cavalier soldier and poet, the Marquess of Montrose. English readers may wonder why we go on debating the past in this manner in Scotland; but the fact remains that, like all Celtic people, we do. In such a recollection of the warfare between Argyll and Montrose in the 17th cent., however, we in modern Scotland must ask ourselves, not who was the more attractive of the two men, but which of the two was more realistic, which had the interests of all Scotland more at heart.

We surely can have no doubt in answering this question – it was Argyll. Montrose may have been a brilliant tactician, but strategically he was less able. He won many splendid battles, but he could never have won his campaign for Charles Stuart against all Scotland. His thinking and emotions were entangled. If he had succeeded in conquering for the Royalist cause in Scotland, all he would have done would have been to impose upon Scotland the Episcopalian form of Church government, which to the people of Scotland was, if anything, more repugnant than Catholicism. No, the Earl of Argyll who fought in the cause of Mary Queen of Scots – and, by implication, in defence of Catholicism – was logically patriotic. But, Catholicism being gone, the later Argyll of the covenanting period was no less logically so.

INVERASDALE, *Ross and Cromarty* (Map 5, ref. 18²88⁷). This village on the W. side of Loch EWE 4 m. N. of POOLEWE has a beautiful situation and fine views back to the hills of the mainland.

Experiments in crofter rehabilitation were recently carried out here. The Rollo Industries engineering plant, established in 1951, has been joined by a fishery research station.

INVERBERVIE, *Kincardineshire* (Map 6, ref. 38²77³). This ancient royal burgh at the mouth of the Bervie Water has a striking situation on the right bank of the gorge through which the river forces its way from the open haughland of its lower reaches to the sea. The massive leonine form of the Bervie Brow, the hill that bars the river's way when it reaches the coast, ends in a shoulder of rounded cliff. It was given the name Craig David at some time after the 4th of May 1341, when that unfortunate monarch, David II, made a spectacular landing here after an adventurous voyage from La Rochelle in France, where he had been sent for security during the Second War of Independence.

Although for at least two centuries it had a Carmelite monastery at Friar's Dubh near the old Bervie Bridge, today the old mercat cross in the market-square is Bervie's visible link with its historic past. It is a slender pillar of stone 14 ft high with a ball on top, dated 1737, and a flight of steps at its base.

The attractions of Inverbervie include good

shing in the river and striking rock scenery N.
f the town, where, beyond the river's mouth
here is a shingle beach with a great array of
tones of brilliant colouring. Architecturally
he dominating feature of the town is the steeple
f the parish church built in 1836 and opened
n the first Sunday of 1837. The church bell
ame from the former parish kirk at Kirkburn,
he remains of which can be seen behind the
ew Bervie fire station. Just S. of the town on a
ocky terrace above the sea front is Hallgreen
'astle, an old building remodelled in the 19th
ent.

Bervie has been an industrial town since
788, when a machine for spinning linen yarn –
he first in Scotland – was set up in the Haughs
f Bervie. At the end of another 100 years there
'ere four flax and tow mills, a chemical works,
nd wincey and sacking factories. There are
till two mills for textiles, while a third has been
onverted for food processing and employs
00 workers preparing crabs.

Inverbervie is now rivalled for population by
s nearest neighbour, the thriving fishing
illage of Gourdon (1⅛ m. S.), a highly pictur-
sque haven with a good harbour enclosed by
ofty sheltering cliffs.

Gourdon grew rapidly in the 19th cent., when
nost of the houses of the sea-town round the
arbour were built, and by 1855 it had a fleet
f over 100 boats. Today it is the most pros-
erous hand-line fishing port in the United
Kingdom. There is a special reason for this.

It was the first port in Scotland to adapt the
notor boat for fishing at a time when the
team drifter seemed to be sweeping all before
. After the First World War it went through a
can time, but by tenacity and a willingness to
nnovate and experiment it has won through.
he chief factor in this success has been the
eadiness of its womenfolk to continue the hard
abour of baiting lines that used to be the lot of
very Scottish fisherman's wife. There is today
fleet of 24 dual-purpose fishing vessels. At
0.30 a.m. every day a lorry arrives in the
illage with 100 baskets of mussels. These are
elivered at every door, and the women proceed
o bait 1,200 hooks to each hand-line, ready for
heir menfolk to take to sea.

Two other factors contribute to the pre-
minence of Gourdon in its special niche in the
shing world. One is the adoption of synthetic
bre lines, which are superior to the old horse-
air ones. The other is the resource of the
ort's buyers and merchants in marketing the
sh, which never has to be dumped.

Nature herself provides a third helpful factor
the existence of good fishing grounds 11 to
6 m. offshore. There are several fish packing
nd processing plants in the village.

A visit to the harbour at the time of the fish
uctions is a tonic, and the spectacle of the
vomen in their traditional fisher garb wheeling
ne sleek modern "prams" that carry the creels
s something to lift up the heart. The boats can

be, and are, also used for seine-netting and
lobster-fishing, according to the state of the
market.

The 15th-cent. Tower of Benholm, crowned
with its parapet and angle bartizans, stands in
the neighbourhood. It is a former stronghold
of the Keiths, Earls Marischal, to which a
modern mansion was added in comparatively
recent times. A famous jewel theft took place at
Benholm Castle in 1623, in which the culprit
was the 5th Earl's widowed countess.

Another, and perhaps the most interesting
castle in the area, Allardyce Castle, stands on
the N. bank of the Bervie Water about 1 m.
above Inverbervie's Jubilee Bridge, where
Walterus de Allardus took the oath of fealty to
Edward I of England in 1297. The Castle is
thought to have been mostly built about the
time of the marriage of Sir John Allardyce to
Lady Mary Graham in 1662. It has gateway
turrets with most elaborate label corbelling.

Arbuthnott House, the ancestral home of
Viscount Arbuthnott, 3 m. NW. of Inverbervie
on the left bank of the Bervie Water, is said to
have been started in the year 1420, with many
changes and additions made in later centuries.

In October 1969 Sir Francis Chichester
unveiled the Hercules Linton Memorial to
commemorate the designer of the *Cutty Sark*,
who was born in Inverbervie.

INVERESK, *Midlothian* (Map 3, ref.
33⁵67²), is one of the most attractive villages in
all the Lothians. It has been established as a
residential community since Roman times,
when it was the site of a civil settlement as well
as a military camp. Its charm now derives from
the graceful architecture of its houses, which
have survived unspoiled from the 17th and
18th cents. The Inveresk Preservation Society
has served as a constructive watchdog in recent
years, restoring cottages and maintaining the
overall character of the place. At Inveresk
Lodge – which belongs to the National Trust
for Scotland – the garden is open to the public.
St Michael's Church (1805), at the W. end of
the village, is the lineal descendant of an
ancient place of worship said to have been
founded soon after the introduction of
Christianity. The Rev. Alexander "Jupiter"
Carlyle (1722–1805) described by Sir Walter
Scott as "the grandest demigod I ever saw",
was minister here for 57 years.

INVEREWE, *Ross and Cromarty* (Map 5,
ref. 18⁸88¹), is the famous Highland garden at
POOLEWE on Loch EWE, which was founded
by the sportsman-laird Osgood Mackenzie in
1862. Since it was presented to the National
Trust for Scotland in 1952 by the late Mrs.
Mairi T. Sawyer, daughter of the founder, the
garden has become one of the outstanding
tourist attractions in the W. Highlands, seen
by more than 100,000 visitors a year.

In the mid-19th cent. the site of Inverewe

Inverewe Gardens: a tropical corner

was a barren, rocky promontory with a single bush of dwarf willow as its only discernible vegetation. Soil imported in creels from nearby, and shelter-belts of trees to break salt-laden westerly gales from the Atlantic, established conditions in which all manner of exotic flowers and shrubs have come to flourish. As with other W. coast gardens, Inverewe benefits from a warm, moist Gulf Stream climate.

Now, with something of interest to be seen at any time of the year, the garden's variety of colour and kind ranges from Australian tree-ferns to a climbing hydrangea more than 50 ft high; from giant Chatham Island forget-me-nots to magnificent magnolias (one, 28 ft high and 75 ft in circumference, is thought to be the largest of its kind in existence); from towering eucalyptus and Monterey pines to seemingly endless variations on the theme of rhododendron.

The garden is open to visitors all the year round.

INVERGARRY, *Inverness-shire* (Map 5, ref. 23¹80¹), is a small scattering of houses that lie at the heart of the most spectacular scenery in Scotland. The road to the W. runs up the richly wooded valley of the R. Garry, then along the shores, green with birch, of Loch Garry, which has been nearly doubled in length by the hydro-electric scheme; then a new road turns N. over the hills into Glen Loyne to meet the road from INVERMORISTON, and continues by Loch Cluanie, GLEN SHIEL, and Loch Duich to Loch Alsh.

To the N. of the hamlet of Invergarry on the shores of Loch Oich is the Well of the Heads. Above a natural spring, a monument was erected in the year 1812 by Macdonell of Glengarry, inscribed in Gaelic, Latin, French,

and English, to commemorate a deed of "ample and summary vengeance" inflicted by the orders of one of his ancestors in the early 17th cent. Keppoch, chief of a branch of the Macdonell Clan, had sent his two sons to be educated in France. After his death the estate was run by his seven brothers who murdered the boys on their return. The family bard, Iain Lorn, had the murderers slain, and washed their heads in this spring before presenting them "at the feet of the Noble Chief at Glen-garry Castle".

The ruins of Invergarry Castle lie S. of the village on the shores of Loch Oich. This was for centuries the ancestral home and fortress of the Macdonells of Glengarry, two earlier build-ings having been destroyed, the first by General Monk in 1654. The next one, completed before the Battle of KILLIECRANKIE in 1689, was garrisoned again and burnt in the same year Prince Charles Edward Stuart visited the rebuilt castle before and after the Battle of CULLO-DEN, and it was burnt by the Duke of Cum-berland in revenge.

Near the old castle is Invergarry House, now a hotel. The name "Glengarry", as applied to that individual form of Highland bonnet, was adopted because Macdonell of Glengarry popularized it during the Royal visit to EDIN-BURGH in 1822.

INVERGORDON, *Ross and Cromarty* (Map 5, ref. 27¹86⁸). This seaport and holiday resort, lying on the shores of the deep, sheltered waters of the CROMARTY Firth, was known as Inverbreakie before being given its present name. As early as the 13th cent. a castle stood here, but the modern burgh grew up only after the castle and the estate had been purchased in the early 18th cent. by a local landowner, Sir

William Gordon of Embo, who drew up plans for the construction of the town and changed its name to Invergordon. His son sold the state but the new name has persisted.

The first harbour was built at Invergordon in 1828, and, with the realization that the Cromarty Firth provided one of the largest, deepest and safest anchorages in the British Isles, it became a vital Royal Navy base with dockyard and fuelling facilities for the biggest ships. Extended and vital in both world wars, it was also important in the Second World War as a base for R.A.F. flying-boats and marine craft. The naval base was closed in 1956, but Invergordon is still used for refuelling by the Royal Navy and NATO ships.

In 1961 a new grain distillery started production (there is also a long-established malt plant), and by 1970 with a production of 10,000,000 gallons yearly became the largest single distillation unit in Europe. But the big industrial change in Easter Ross came with the British Aluminium Co.'s smelter project, also attracted by the deepwater harbour, flat hinterland, and plentiful available labour.

INVERGOWRIE, *Angus* (Map 6, ref. 33³73⁰). In this village, 4 m. W. of DUNDEE, a church is said to have been founded in the 8th cent. by St Boniface, who landed here about A.D. 715; it was replaced by a now ruined 15th-cent. building. Two fine, though fragmentary, 8th-cent. sculptured stones were built into the ruin.

Bullionfield Mill began as a meal-mill in 1600; about 1800 it was converted into a spinning-mill and later a bleach-field. Finally, in the mid-19th cent. it became a paper-mill.

INVERKEITHING, *Fife* (Map 3, ref. 31³68³). A royal burgh 3¾ m. SE. of DUNFERMLINE, Inverkeithing lies on the shore of the Firth of FORTH and commands splendid views. It also occupies a position on the old route from N. to S.

Agricola set up an encampment in A.D. 78–87, and the village probably grew up beside this strategic point. As early as 1165, a charter was granted by William the Lion, and thereafter trade increased and the royal burgh prospered. In 1651 a battle was fought between Cromwell's forces and the Scottish Royalist army, and this precipitated the southward march of the Royalists to Worcester. Inverkeithing was the meeting-place of the Court of the Four Burghs, until the evolution of the Convention of Royal Burghs, which had its first official meeting in EDINBURGH in 1552.

In the 19th cent., coal-mining provided a new trade in the town; 1893 brought paper-mills; and in 1922 a ship-breaking yard was established. Substantial parts of the old wall still stand. St Peter's Church was founded in the 12th cent., but the 14th-cent. tower is all that survives of the original church which was burnt in 1825. The Gothic-style reconstruction of the following year contains a font of exceptional beauty and interest. Found buried in 1806 under the floor of the ground stage of the tower, it is thought to have been hidden at the Reformation. It bears the arms of Queen Annabella Drummond, wife of Robert III, who lived at the Hospitium of Grey Friars, part of which (dating back to the 14th cent.) still stands, and was traditionally given for the baptism of the Duke of Rothesay.

The Town House dates from 1770, but part of the building goes back as far as 1550. The Council Chamber contains original 18th-cent. chairs. The mercat cross, moved in 1799 from the High Street to the square owing to the traffic congestion, traditionally dates from 1398, and commemorates the marriage of the Duke of Rothesay.

INVERKIP, *Renfrewshire* (Map 2, ref. 22¹67²). Now a village of grey sandstone at the mouth of the R. Kip, Inverkip was at one time called Auldkirk because the GREENOCK people worshipped here before they built their own church in 1592. Inverkip church was originally granted to PAISLEY Abbey in 1170, and was held by the monks till the Reformation. The village was a notorious centre of witch mania in the 17th cent. At the end of the 18th cent. it was noted for smuggling.

To the N., above Lunderston Bay, is one of the largest summer camps in Scotland, with a Church of Scotland mission presiding.

INVERLOCHY, *Inverness-shire* (Map 5, ref. 21²77⁵). Some 2 m. NE. of FORT WILLIAM and now joined to it, the village of Inverlochy combines strong historical associations with modern development.

Its past is visible in the well-preserved 13th-cent. Castle of the Comyns. It has a quadrangular wall and round-angle towers showing the characteristic long-bow slits of the period. The eventful history of the Castle dates from the War of Independence, reaching its climax over three centuries later during Montrose's campaigns. Inverlochy was the scene of the great soldier-marquess's astonishing victory over the Campbells in 1645.

The modern Inverlochy Castle is the centre of a cattle-ranching scheme started in the 1950s by Mr J. W. Hobbs, who, using his experience of Canadian ranching, developed 10,000 acres as the Great Glen Cattle Ranch. Before his death he sold it, but cattle ranching continues here.

In the 1930s a company producing aluminium developed a factory at Inverlochy in connection with the hydro-electric scheme at LAGGAN. The same company produces ingots for further processing at the FALKIRK plant. After some problems over power supply, the factory here is going ahead well, having arranged to switch into the Hydro-Electric Board's grid to maintain continuity.

INVERMORISTON, *Inverness-shire* (Map 5, ref. 24²81⁷).

The township of Invermoriston lies on the W. side of Loch Ness and at the E. end of Glenmoriston, the traditional country of the Grants. Glenmoriston, a well-wooded glen up to Loch Cluanie, now has all the appurtenances of a hydro-electric scheme, but retains its beauty. A little E. of Torgyle, farther up the glen, a small cairn at the edge of the road leads to mysterious footprints. It is said that in 1827 an itinerant preacher, Finlay Munro, was interrupted while holding an open-air service; the preacher declared that he spoke the truth, and to prove it the very ground would bear witness from him. His two footprints still remain beisde a larger cairn.

To the W. of Torgyle on the N. bank of the river is Aonach, the site of an inn where Johnson and Boswell stayed in 1773.

Near Ceannacroc bridge on the roadside is a cairn in memory of the gallant death in 1746 of Roderick Mackenzie, who allowed himself to be identified as Prince Charles Edward Stuart and drew off the redcoats from the pursuit of the Prince. From Ceannacroc, a path leads N. up the R. Doe to a cave where the Prince hid in July 1746, guarded by the famous Seven Men of Glenmoriston.

INVERNESS, *Inverness-shire* (Map 5, ref. 26⁶84⁵).

Natural advantages have for long made Inverness the centre of a wide and distinctive region, and it is now generally and fittingly recognized as the "capital" of the Highlands It lies in a level plain at the best crossing-place of the short river that flows out of Loch Ness and forms the northern end of the Great Glen of Scotland. Easily accessible from the sea and by air, it has become the focal point of the road and rail system in the N., where the main routes from the S. across the mountains and from the E. along the Moray Firth coast converge and continue westwards and northwards into the heart of the Northern Highlands. This strategic position led to more permanent settlement earlier than has been found in the surrounding country. Carved stones, burial cairns, and hill-top forts remain to show that the site was occupied long before written history; the "boar stone" at Knocknagael and the vitrified fort on CRAIG PHADRICK are among the most notable relics of their kind in Scotland, and a ring of monoliths at Druid-temple Farm near Leys overlooks the town from the sloping ground to the S. When St Columba visited King Brude in A.D. 565, this was the capital of the Pictish kingdom, and by the 12th cent. a chartered burgh had been established, with a trading community living in the shelter of a royal castle.

Macbeth may have lived in the old castle, which has long since disappeared, but his predecessor, King Duncan, did not die there; however, the red stone product of the early Victorian era may occupy the same commanding position as the original castle held above the river crossing. And so it is with the bridges, ancient and modern: a structure of oak, which is the earliest known, was destroyed by the

Inverness Castle

ord of the Isles (Donald of HARLAW) in 411; a stone bridge of seven arches, shown in many old prints of Inverness, stood for a century and a half before being swept away by a great flood in 1849; and the suspension bridge which succeeded it was replaced in 1961 by a graceful triple-span bridge.

Most of the town's old buildings have also been superseded: the oldest, Queen Mary's House in Bridge Street – a great deal altered since the visit in 1562 which its name recalls – now faces the latest feature, a typical town-centre redevelopment such as has sprung up all over the country in the 1960s. An isolated clock-tower is all that is left of Cromwell's star-shaped fortress by the R. Ness. Abertarff House (early 17th cent.), Dunbar's Hospital (1668), the old High Church (1772 with earlier clock tower and spire), and the Steeple (1791), all in Church Street, are reminders of earlier days, and Union Street, Queensgate, Station Square, and part of Academy Street, all designed by Alexander Ross of Inverness, retain some of the formal dignity of late Victorian architecture. In the spiky Gothic Town House (1878), representing the period's more fanciful moods, members of the British Cabinet met in 1921 under Lloyd George to consider the Irish Treaty. The riverside presents a notable skyline of church spires of various denominations, and St Andrew's Cathedral (1866-9) is the centre of the modern bishopric of Moray, Ross, and Nairn.

The main part of the town and the shopping centre lie near the river, and the entrance from the E. is confined by an escarpment from which the Cameron Barracks (until recently a regimental depot) and other buildings look northwards, with a magnificent view over the sea to the BLACK ISLE and Ben Wyvis, and westwards to the hills beyond BEAULY. Road traffic passing through the town negotiates some narrow streets, overdue for widening, but for railway passengers the station's calm serenity is still ensured by the origin of the system, which dictated that no main line passes directly through it and nearly all trains enter backwards at a snail's pace. Change there has been, however, and with the recent change-over to diesel engines, one of the only two open-type steam locomotive sheds or "round houses" on the Scottish railway system, built in 1863 (within ten years of the first line reaching Inverness), just failed to reach its centenary before it was swept away.

The harbour, which occupies the right bank of the river below the Waterloo Bridge (1896), at one time had regular passenger connections with ports in the South, and it still carries on a considerable commercial traffic. The municipal airport on the Longman (now an industrial estate) has been replaced by the airport at DALCROSS, 7 m. E. of the burgh.

Inverness is not predominantly a manu-facturing town, but it has several new as well as old-established industries. A firm that exports welding equipment to many parts of the world was responsible for the "Pluto" pipe-line across the English Channel in the Second World War. The town is a shopping, distribut-ing, and marketing centre for a wide area and the headquarters of Scotland's largest adminis-trative unit, for which new County Council offices were opened in 1963. Particularly since the First World War, there has been an increasing tendency to locate in Inverness more Government and ancillary offices, for the Highlands and the North of Scotland. The forestry and agricultural services, of prime importance here, were in the forefront of this revolutionary trend, and road improvements qualifying for Treasury grants have been administered from Inverness since the start of the Crofter Counties schemes in 1936. Regionalization in the Second World War made the town a headquarters for civil defence, and for food and fuel rationing, as well as for the armed forces. Post-war development brought Tourist Board and Board of Trade offices to the town, and in 1952 a Government building was opened on the Longman estate which now houses Department of Agriculture and Inland Revenue officials. The Crofters Commission (1955) and the Red Deer Com-mission (1960) were set up with Inverness head-quarters, and the establishment of a Highland Development Board promises fresh initiative and coordination in the efforts to improve living conditions in the region and to stem depopulation.

Apart from official administration, Inverness has a special place as a centre of professional life. It has been the setting for two General Assemblies (1845 and 1888), and is the place where the High Court of Justiciary sits twice a year, and the head town of the sheriffdom of Inverness-shire, Moray, Nairnshire, and Ross and Cromarty. An important educational centre, it was one of the towns proposed for the establishment of a new university; the Royal Academy, dating from 1792, has origins going back to the foundation of a Dominican Priory in 1233; the North of Scotland College of Agriculture branch at Drummondhill (1955), and the Inverness Technical College at the Longman (1960), attract students from a wide area. There are four hospitals in the town, and future plans show the importance of Inverness as a centre of healing for the whole North of Scotland. The town also claims, in the wooded ridge of Tomnahurich, the handsomest ceme-tery in Scotland, overlooking the river and the CALEDONIAN CANAL.

With a population approaching 30,000, Inverness is well placed for further growth and increasing importance. As a popular holiday centre and a place of residence, it is a town with a character of its own to which many incomers from the South have contributed. It flourishes in a magnificent Highland setting, but yet has some of the advantages of urban life. While the number of people living in the surrounding glens and valleys has declined, the burgh has expanded; but, even if their loss has hitherto been its gain, the health of the Highland region and its capital are closely linked, and the one is not likely to flourish without benefit to the other.

INVERPOLLY, *Ross and Cromarty* (Map 5, ref. 20⁸91⁵). A nature reserve of 26,827 acres, this is a wild, remote, and almost uninhabited area on the NW. coast of the county near the Sutherland border. It includes three summits of over 2,000 ft, rising sharply from the loch-scattered moorland, and the whole of Loch Sionascaig. There is a great diversity of habitats – lochs, streams, bogs, moorland, woodland, screes, cliffs, and summits, and among animals in the area are wildcats, pine marten, red and roe deer, and golden eagles. Some relics exist of relatively untouched primitive birch-hazel woodland. On the E. is the classic geological locality of Knockan Cliff, which exposes a section of the Moine Thrust zone. The region was acquired by the Nature Conservancy in 1961–2.

A small vitrified fort, 4½ m. SSW. of LOCH-INVER – almost isolated at high tide – is at present the most northerly example, but the area is archaeologically unexplored and it may be one of several such forts.

INVERSHIN, *Sutherland* (Map 5, ref. 25⁸89⁶). At the junction of the rivers Oykell and Shin, with the power station at Inveran 1 m. to the N., stands the township of Invershin on the N. shore of the Kyle of Sutherland. About 2½ m. N. on the LAIRG road are the spectacular Falls of Shin, where from a platform can be watched the salmon jumping and swimming up the falls. Across the Kyle stands Carbisdale Castle, completed of local grey whinstone in 1914. When originally built, the rooms and galleries were arranged in different periods.

The Carbisdale district was the scene of the last battle of Montrose in 1650. The cairns on the hill-side are supposed to cover bodies, and various relics of battle have indeed been found. After defeat, Montrose escaped NW. into Assynt, but was captured there. The details of his capture or betrayal are still hotly debated.

INVERSNAID, *Stirlingshire* (Map 2, ref. 23⁴70⁸). With a pier on the E. shore of Loch LOMOND, Inversnaid has fine views of the "Arrochar Alps" on the opposite shore. From here a road runs E. to Stronachlachar on Loch KATRINE; the road from ABERFOYLE joins this route at the E. end of Loch Arklet. A little S. of the pier on the Water of Arklet is a waterfall where, in 1803, Wordsworth met the "Highland Girl".

The farmstead, still known as the Garrison,

incorporates the ruins of the Barracks built in 1718–19, the first of the four – the others being FORT AUGUSTUS, BERNERA, and RUTHVEN. The Barracks were kept in repair until the late 18th cent.; the MacGregors attacked and burnt the buildings on at least two occasions. About 1 m. N. by the loch-side is Rob Roy's cave, where he often took refuge from his enemies.

INVERURIE, *Aberdeenshire* (Map 6, ref. 37⁷82¹), is a pleasant town with wide streets, built of granite and with a spacious market place, 17 m. NW. of ABERDEEN, at the confluence of the DON and its tributary, the Ury. Burgh fishings on both rivers are available to visitors. It is an ancient royal burgh, traditionally founded by David of Huntingdon, Earl of the Garioch and great-great-grandfather of Robert Bruce; but its earliest extant charter is dated 1558. The town, with a population of 5,000, has railway locomotive works employing over 500, and marts and slaughter-house to cater for a great farming region. Its most important antiquity is the Bass, a grassy conical mound 50 ft high with a lesser mound, the Little Bass, by its side. Originally a severed spur of the Ury, it was the site of an important motte-and-bailey stronghold.

Certain it is that Inverurie was the turning-point of King Robert's fortunes. Here he lay gravely ill. In 1307 he returned, his army of 700 lying in camp near the farm of Crichie; then, pinpricked into action by the raiding tactics of Comyn, Earl of Buchan, he led it to decisive victory in the Battle of BARRA. The strategic position of the town resulted in its witnessing the opening manœuvres of the Civil War in 1639, and it was many times held by Royalists and Covenanters in turn in the years that followed. In December 1745 it became the only scene of bloodshed in Aberdeenshire during the Rebellion of that year.

On that occasion Lord Lewis Gordon, with a party of Jacobites, surprised and defeated a detachment of the Hanoverian army of Lord Loudon on its way from INVERNESS to the relief of Aberdeen.

Inverurie has many literary associations, the earliest of which is with Arthur Johnston of Caskieben, the Latin poet known as the Scottish Ovid (1587–1641). A son of George, the 7th Johnston Laird of Caskieben, he was born in the family seat, Caskieben Castle, which now forms the older portion of Keith Hall (on the SE. outskirts of the town), the home of the Earls of Kintore.

This Z-plan castle, still virtually entire, forms a dramatic contrast with the splendid Restoration mansion conjoined to it by the 1st Earl of Kintore; the S. front of this building is crested with a classical balustrade supporting urns, and is set between square pavilions capped by pointed "helmets". Standing in policies originally landscaped by "Capability" Brown, it

Iona: the restored abbey

contrives to make the best of two worlds, the medieval and the modern.

The Ministry of Public Building and Works cares for the notable ruin of Kinkell, which lies just S. of Inverurie. It is a 16th-cent. parish church with ornate details including a rich sacrament house dated 1524.

IONA, Island of, *Argyll* (Map 1, ref. 12⁸72³), is just off the extreme SW. of the large island of MULL in the Inner Hebrides (*see* "The Shape of Scotland"). The little island of Iona has, though for a different reason, a fame world-wide like that of the immense Inner Hebridean SKYE. It was on Iona that in A.D. 563 St Columba landed from Ireland and began the effective Christianization of Scotland. A place of pilgrimage and veneration throughout the centuries for reasons of faith, it has also been the cradle of the Celtic Kingdom of Scotland. (*See* "Scotland in History".)

The island is 3 m. long and 1½ m. wide. The strait that separates it from Mull, with which it is connected by ferry, is only ¾ m. wide. Steamers also call at Iona from OBAN. It has a hotel, and some of the islanders take in guests. The Iona Community was founded in 1938 by the Rev. George F. MacLeod. With a D.D. from Glasgow University he became Dr MacLeod. He succeeded to a baronetcy in 1944, but specifically asked not to be addressed by the title. As an ex-Moderator of the Church of Scotland (1957–8) he became the Very Rev., and was made a life peer in 1967 as Lord MacLeod of Fuinary.

Even if Iona were without its strong religious and historical associations, this remarkable little Hebridean island would surely attract visitors to the W. of Scotland. Remote enough to remain well off the beaten track of tourism,

it is accessible enough for all who wish to get there. Its polychromatic beauty and splendid setting have inspired some of the best Scottish painting – and also some of the feeblest.

For 34 years after his landing, St Columba, despite his successful missionary wanderings on the mainland, kept his headquarters firmly established on Iona. The buildings of his original foundation, being of daub and wattle, have long disappeared. They were probably where the later monastery buildings of stone stood. After Columba's death in A.D. 597, the foundation and the island suffered terribly from the savagery of Norse and pagan invasion, but the faith lived on in the tenacity of the monks. Their tenacity was rewarded, for, though the primitive simplicity of their rule and foundation was to go, Christianity, which they had introduced into Scotland, survived in Scotland and intensely on Iona.

Somerled, a Celtic chief of Argyll, having married into the Norwegian royal family, eventually secured recognized possession of Iona. His son established a community of Benedictine monks on the island, which, though it maintained the Christian faith in this holy place, had the sad effect of turning out the last of the genuine Columban Catholic monks. This led to friction between the Irish and Scottish Celts, but the Benedictine foundation, also called "St Columba's Monastery", continued until the establishment of the Reformation in Scotland in 1560.

Meanwhile, through the centuries of suffering, invasion, warfare, and constant devotion to the rule and memory of their saintly and vigorous founder, Columba, the monks had made of their island a place recognized in western Christendom as an unrivalled seat of holiness. It became a burial-place for kings not only from Scotland and Ireland and Norway, but, it is claimed, from France. Certainly, Kenneth MacAlpine, the first Celtic king of Scotland, lies there, as well as many chiefs of the Isles. For more than 400 years, to achieve burial in Iona was to have gained as one's last resting-place that island of the West which was held to be nearest to heaven.

During the reign of Abbot Mackinnon, the last Abbot of Iona, the island became the cathedral centre for the bishopric of the Isles. After the Reformation the monastery was suppressed, and eventually the MacLeans of Duart seized the island from the now moribund bishopric. But the Presbyterian system of worship under the reformed Kirk of Scotland continued, of course, on the island. In 1693, Iona came under the overlordship of the Campbells of Argyll, and in 1899 the 8th Duke of Argyll presented to the Church of Scotland the ruins of the abbey, expressing the hope that it might be re-roofed and made available for public worship. The first service that took place in the reconditioned building occurred in June 1910.

Just before the Second World War, Iona was much invigorated by the foundation of the Iona Community under the Rev. George MacLeod. As a result of his energetic and individual guidance, it has had a considerable influence throughout Scotland. The abbey is now a place of regular religious service; the old conventual buildings were finely restored by that sensitive and highly knowledgeable Scottish architect, the late Mr Ian Lindsay.

The remains of the old monastery, the restored abbey, the conventual buildings, and the burial place of the kings all lie within easy reach of the landing place of the ferry. Having inspected these outward and visible signs of the continuing Christian faith of Iona, and of the fact that this Celtic island was the cradle of the Kingdom of Scotland, the visitor should go into the island itself. He should certainly go to the small bay at the S. of the island where, by a tradition that we have no reason to doubt, Columba first landed on his voyage from Ireland. This place is inviolate, and looks exactly as it must have done 14 centuries ago.

The visitor should also ascend the small hill of Dun I, the highest point on the island, yet only 332 ft, where there is erected a cairn in St Columba's honour.

IRVINE, *Ayrshire* (Map 2, ref. $23^2 63^9$), the ancient royal burgh with 13th-cent. origins, one time main port for GLASGOW on the Firth of CLYDE, half-way between SALTCOATS and TROON, is now being engulfed by Scotland's fifth New Town, the first in Britain to be developed by the sea. Designated in 1967, Irvine New Town will be the largest in Scotland, covering 20 sq. m. of central Ayrshire. Bounded on the W. by the coastline between BARASSIE and ARDEER, the area stretches inland to encompass old Irvine, KILWINNING, and cer-

tain villages. By 1970, with 39,000 "pre-development" inhabitants, Irvine had the second largest population of Scotland's New Towns. With its sea front, harbour, and other natural advantages – easy accessibility, unspoiled hinterland, equable climate – it aims at becoming the major commercial, cultural, and recreational centre in the W. of Scotland. With a target population of 80,000 within twenty years, the programme aimed at 1,500 houses and at least 300,000 sq. ft of factory space yearly. But with all its new industries, thriving Irvine will not forget its past or relatively recent links with Robert Burns, who went there to learn flax-dressing in 1781, nor the fact that its Bogside racecourse, where meetings were held in 1806, is one of the oldest in the country, and that it owes much to its proximity to Eglinton Castle, ancient seat of the Montgomeries, Earls of Eglinton.

ISLAY, Island of, *Argyll* (Map 1, ref. $14^\circ 66^\circ$). The most southern of the Inner Hebrides W. of Kintyre (*see* "The Shape of Scotland"). Formerly having close and regular contact with Ireland, this was the administrative centre of the Lordship of the Isles that made the Macdonalds almost independent princes after the end of Norwegian rule in the 13th cent. FINLAGGAN was the heart of this principality, and many other places in Islay are connected with the story of the Lordship. The island is almost cut in two by shallow Lochindaal and Loch Gruineart; the green farmlands of the western half slope up to rugged cliffs N. and S. of Kilchoman (with an ancient carved cross), while the long strand and machair of Laggan Bay ends to the S. in the rugged Oa peninsula, and is backed by moors that extend right across to the isolated but picturesque E. coast, where there is another finely carved cross at Kildalton. BOWMORE is the island capital, with Bridgend as the centre of the road system. Car ferries from the mainland call daily (more frequently in summer) at PORT ELLEN and PORT ASKAIG, and there is a daily service from Glenegedale airport.

Islay Airport

Islay is notable for songs and singers, and, though less Gaelic is heard nowadays, the islanders' keen sense of music remains. There is daily air service from GLASGOW, and most of the villages have hotels and boarding-houses. Together with farming, the principal industry is distilling, and brilliantly white distillery buildings are to be seen in several parts of the island. In a generally cheerful island, there is a reminder of wartime tragedy in the American monument on the Mull of Oa commemorating the loss of 650 lives from the *Tuscania* and *Otranto* in 1918, and among earlier victims of the rocky W. coast was the emigrant ship *Exmouth*, wrecked at Sanaig in 1847. No road encircles Islay, but there are some good classified roads connecting the various villages. Islay is world famous for its malt whiskies. It also produces one of the most palatable of Scottish cheeses.

ISLE ORNSAY, *Inverness-shire* (Map 4, ref. 7⁰81²), is a village on the Island of SKYE in the Inner Hebrides (*see* "The Shape of Scotland"). Lying at the beginning of the SW. peninsula of Sleat on Skye and 9 m. SE. of BROADFORD, Isle Ornsay takes its name from St Oran's isle, just offshore. On that island there are the remains of a chapel dedicated to the Columban Oran. There is a hotel at Isle Ornsay, pleasant green countryside, and a fine view of that remarkable mainland arm of the sea Loch Hourn.

JARLSHOF, *Shetland* (Map 8, ref. 44⁰10⁹), a group of ruins on the Mainland of SHET-LAND Northern Islands (*see* "The Shape of Scotland"), situated near the extreme southern tip of Shetland and only ½ m. from the modern airport. Jarlshof presents one of the most interesting remains of early human habitation, not only in the islands but in all Scotland. It shows us a sequence of occupations, beginning with houses dating from the early or middle part of the 2nd millennium B.C. Later came occupiers of the Bronze Age, then of the early Iron Age. After an unknown interval came the builders of the broch with its walled garth. Later still came a series of structures beginning with an aisled round-house and a wheel-house.

Jarlshof displays through its monuments a view of many periods and peoples. To understand its significance, you should have the services of the official guide of the Ministry of Public Building and Works who, as at CLICK-HIMIN (also in Shetland), is on duty at specified times.

JEDBURGH, *Roxburghshire* (Map 3, ref. 36⁵62⁰). The county town of Roxburgh is situated in the valley of the Jed Water, a tributary of the Teviot, within 10 m. of the English Border. By virtue of its geographical location, it forms one of the gateways into Scotland from the S., lying as it does astride the main road running through the heart of picturesque Border country from Newcastle to EDINBURGH, via the Carter Bar, giving easy access to the road system of the TWEED basin.

The effect of time goes very deep at Jedburgh. Its history, which can be traced back to the 9th cent., has had its full influence on the

Jedburgh Abbey, "where late the sweet birds sang"

Scottish Tourist Board

present-day town that still centres around the market-place upon which the principal streets converge.

It is recorded in the annals of Lindisfarne that a church was built at Jedburgh in the 9th cent. Fragments of Celtic ornamented stonework, and of other supporting evidence found during restoration, indicate that Jedburgh Abbey occupies the site of this earlier church. A priory founded here by David I in 1118 was for the use of Augustinian canons who came from St Quentin's Abbey at Beauvais in France. In 1147 this priory was elevated to the status of an abbey. Much devastation occurred during invasions by the English, but the men of Jedburgh – each armed with a Jethart Staff, which he knew how to use with sure effect – always rallied to avenge themselves upon their enemies. In 1523, troops commanded by the Earl of Surrey bombarded the Abbey, and, in his dispatches to Henry VIII, the Earl commented on the valour of the Jedburgh fighters, saying "the strength of Teviotdale once destroyed, a small power would be sufficient to keep the borders of Scotland in subjection".

Jedburgh Castle was occupied on many occasions by the English; it was one of the five fortresses ceded to England under the Treaty of Falaise in 1174 to provide the security for the ransom of William the Lion. It subsequently became a favourite royal residence. Malcolm IV died there in 1195; 90 years later, Alexander III was married to Jolande, daughter of the Count of Dreux, in Jedburgh Abbey, and, while the wedding-feast was in progress in the castle, a spectre is said to have appeared to warn the King of his impending tragic death. He died, in fact, in the following year when he fell from his horse over the cliff at KINGHORN (*see* "Scotland in History").

The Castle was finally demolished in 1409 at national expense by order of the Scottish Parliament, after demands made by the Provost, the magistrates, and the baillies, all of whom found its periodic occupations by English forces a distinct embarrassment.

Its place is now taken by an interesting Georgian building erected in 1832 as the county jail, but still known as the "Castle".

On the 9th of October 1566, Mary Queen of Scots arrived at Jedburgh to preside at the Justice Aire, or Circuit Court, in the Tolbooth, and she stayed at what is now known as "Queen Mary's House", a picturesque old house in Queen Street, now owned by the Town Council and open to visitors as a museum of great historical interest. At the conclusion of the Courts, Mary made a hasty journey on horseback to see the Earl of Bothwell at Hermitage Castle, some 20 m. away, as he had been wounded in a skirmish. On returning to Jedburgh, she developed a fever and became so stricken that she nearly died. During her illness Lord Darnley came to visit her, but he left next morning, after he had slept at the residence of the Earl of Home, which stood in the High Street near the Spread Eagle Hotel.

It was not until a month later that Queen Mary was well enough to leave Jedburgh; she departed on the 9th of November with a retinue of nobility including Bothwell, who had by now also recovered from his wounds.

The town is rich in historical associations. Prince Charles Edward Stuart lodged in No. 11, Castlegate, during his march into England; much of this house remains unaltered to this day. (It is in this house that the famous sweets called "Jethart snails" are made today.) Sir David Brewster, the scientist and founder of the British Association, was born here in 1781, being the son of the Master of the Grammar School. Robert Burns and William Wordsworth both lodged in the town, and Sir Walter Scott frequently attended the Circuit Courts at Jedburgh; here, in 1793, he made his first appearance as an advocate in a criminal trial. It is recorded that Sir Walter Scott visited Wordsworth and his sister Dorothy after attending the Judge's dinner that followed the court proceedings. From Jedburgh Sir Walter, accompanied by his friend Sheriff Shortreed, used to go into Liddesdale to collect border ballads.

Jedburgh, however, does not live in the past. It is a thriving town and proud of being the only royal burgh in Roxburghshire. It is now a noted textile-manufacturing centre, and recently it has acquired factories for engineering and electrical goods.

It has for long been famous for its rugby football, and the popular annual "seven-a-side" matches were invented by a Jedburgh man.

The Redeswire Ride is held annually on the first Saturday in July, and ends with the 100-year-old Border Games. The traditional game of handba' is still played at Candlemas and Easter E'en between the "Uppies" and the "Doonies" all over the old town; it is reputed to date from before the Reformation and to have originated in Scots playing with the heads of their slain enemies.

JOHN O' GROATS, *Caithness* (Map 7, ref. 33⁸97⁴). The name of John o' Groats has become a household word and a favourite destination for tourists as the most northerly point of the mainland of the British Isles, although that distinction correctly belongs to Dunnet Head. Various road races terminate here, such as Maiden Kirk to John o' Groats (280 m.), and Lands End to John o' Groats (873 m.).

The name derives from a Dutchman, John de Groot, who is said to have come to run the ORKNEY ferry with two brothers in the late 15th cent. Later there were eight descendants, joint owners of the estate, and to obviate problems of precedence an octagonal house with eight doors and an octagonal table were built. The house has gone, but the site is

John o' Groats

marked by a mound and flagpole. Beside it is a hotel built in 1875–6, with an octagonal tower. There are gravestones of the Groot family in CANISBAY churchyard.

The last house in Scotland is an old white-washed fisherman's cottage built in the traditional style with a roof of Caithness flag stones. It is now a small souvenir shop. There is a fine view over to Orkney on a clear day, with Stroma Island lying off shore. On the beach may be found the pretty little European cowrie shells, known as "Groatie Buckies".

JOHNSTONE, *Renfrewshire* (Map 2, ref. 24³66³). An industrial town, Johnstone is sometimes known as the "engineering burgh". Founded in 1781 on a plan drawn up by George Houston, laird of Johnstone, on the site of a hamlet called Brig o' Johnstone, it was well

planned, but it grew too fast and became a typical product of the industrial revolution. Engineering is the staple industry, and John-stone claims to have started the first firm of its kind in Britain (founded 1815) for making machine tools.

Cochran Tower, built in 1896, marks the site of Cochran Castle, the residence of the earls of Dundonald. Johnstone Castle was demolished in 1956 when purchased by the Council for a housing estate, but the central tower survives. Chopin stayed at the castle in 1848 when he gave his recital in GLASGOW, during that strange visit of his to Scotland shortly before his death.

JURA, *Argyll* (Map 1, ref. 15⁵68⁵), just NE. of ISLAY, is one of the southern Inner Hebrides (*see* "The Shape of Scotland"). About

Isle of Jura: West Loch Tarbert

28 m. long, it is a mountainous island now largely divided into sporting estates. A road, of which the northernmost section has been allowed to disappear, connects the ferry opposite PORT ASKAIG in Islay in the S. with the northern tip of Jura, from which the whirlpool of CORRIEVRECHAN can be viewed (and its roaring sound heard at certain states of wind and tide). The highest of the three paps of Jura, which form a splendid part of the prospect both on the island itself and from neighbouring Islay and over the sea in Kintyre, is 2,569 ft. There are some fine raised beaches and caves on the W. coast, which has never been settled. There are a few small communities on the E. with CRAIGHOUSE as the only village (it has a hotel). A group of islands forms a natural breakwater across the Bay of Small Isles, where the steamer from E. Loch Tarbert on the Argyll mainland calls regularly.

KATRINE, Loch, *Perthshire* (Map 2, ref. 24⁵71⁰) is associated through Walter Scott with high romance, and in modern times with the more practical business of water-supply. This was the loch associated with Scott's *The Lady of the Lake*. Though not many people now read Scott's longer poetry, the legend of the Lady of the Lake persisted until within living memory. There are those who from their childhood can remember scenoramic displays at such places as the Waverley Market in EDINBURGH, intended to catch the atmosphere of mystery and romance surrounding the Lady of the Lake.

By the time, however, that such displays had become popular at the beginning of this century, Loch Katrine had long adopted its secondary and modern role – that of supplying fresh water to the whole of the huge city of GLASGOW. The water from the loch is induced into Glasgow by means of a submerged aqueduct 34 m. long. The presence of this aqueduct does not of course affect the scenery, but the level of the loch had to be raised by 17 ft to accommodate the aqueduct. The only unfortunate result of this has been that the Silver Strand opposite Ellen's Isle has been submerged.

The loch and its district, however, are still attractive to tourists and visitors. Steamers run its full length of 9 m. from the E. end near Loch Achray to Stronachlachar. There is a road on the N. shore for pedestrians; motorcars are allowed by permit only. Near the head of the loch at Portnellan there is an ancient graveyard of the shifting and mobile Clan Macgregor. This was moved when the loch level was raised in the 19th cent.; the oldest legible date on any stone remaining is 1609.

KEILLS, *Argyll* (Map 1, ref. 16⁹68⁰). The ruined church of Keills, 12 m. SW. of CRINAN, stands on the slope above the N. shore of Loch Keills. It was a 13th-cent. chapel dedicated to St Charmaig; its churchyard contains many

interesting and beautiful sculptured grave slabs and a notable cross 7 ft 4 in. in height. Keills was a landing place for cattle brought from Lagg in JURA across the Sound of Jura and once a ferry crossed here.

KEITH, *Banffshire* (Map 6, ref. 34³85⁰). A trim country town and agricultural centre with woollen mills and distilleries, Keith combines Old and New towns and, across the R. Isla, Fife Keith. Plans for the New Town were laid down in 1750 by the Earl of Findlater, who established three lint-mills. Horse- and cattle-fairs also became important here. The oldest working distillery in Scotland, the Milton Distillery, founded in 1786, which has changed hands several times and is now called Strath Isla, is situated here. Keith Show in the first week of August is one of the biggest in the North.

The Catholic Church of St Thomas, which has an imposing copper dome, was built in 1830 with a donation from Charles X of France, who, after his expulsion from his throne, took refuge in Scotland for a while.

Keith's oldest building is the Milton Tower, built by the Ogilvies in 1480. It stands close to the new Glen Keith Distillery. The second oldest landmark is the Auld Brig o' Keith over the R. Isla; it was built in 1609 and nowadays is much painted by artists, as it is highly picturesque. The new bridge, also a handsome structure, dates from 1770. New Keith is full of character. Its three fine parallel streets – Moss Street, Mid Street, and Land Street – are intersected by a series of narrow lanes, and the houses have a simple dignity reminiscent of the 18th-cent. part of BANFF.

KELSO, *Roxburghshire* (Map 3, ref. 37³63⁴). Situated on the rivers TWEED and Teviot, Kelso is a busy market town surrounded by parkland; it was described by Sir Walter Scott as the most beautiful, if not the most romantic, village in Scotland. In the Middle Ages ROXBURGH was the royal burgh, but Kelso became prominent by virtue of the ford of the Tweed and by the bridge over it built in 1754; later, in 1800, a five-arch bridge was begun by John Rennie. This bridge took three years to build and was the model for Waterloo Bridge, London, built in 1811 and demolished amidst the lamentations of many Londoners in 1934. The square is spacious; it is dominated by the elegant town hall, which has a plaque by Polish Forces in gratitude for the town's hospitality during the Second World War. Kelso has many fine houses including Ednam House; this was built in 1761 and, although now a hotel, the Italian ceilings have been preserved.

The greatest architectural attraction of Kelso are the ruins of Kelso Abbey, founded by David I in 1128 and destroyed by Hertford in 1545. This used to be regarded as the ruin of a small abbey, but investigations and a descripion dated 1517 in the Vatican Library now suggest that the remains are only the extreme W. end of the largest and most imposing of Border abbeys. The building is of Norman-Transitional work, unique in Scotland, with a plan having western as well as eastern transepts and a tower over both crossings.

To the NW. of the town is the magnificent Floors Castle, which has been described as the largest inhabited mansion in Britain; it was designed by Sir John Vanbrugh for the 1st Duke of Roxburghe in 1718, remodelled by Playfair in 1838–49. Golden gates and handsome lodges were added in 1929. French prisoners from the Napoleonic wars built part of a wall round the estate and also a theatre. There are extensive, very fine grounds and gardens, including a holly tree said to mark the spot where James II was killed by a bursting cannon at the siege of Roxburgh in 1460.

KELTON, *Kirkcudbrightshire* (Map 2, ref. 29⁹57¹). This parish contains the village of Keltonhill, 2 m. SW. of CASTLE DOUGLAS, which was famous in the 18th cent. as the site of many fairs, including a horse-fair, which was held in mid-June, and said to be "perhaps the largest in Scotland". In 1723, this fair was the scene of angry protests against enclosures and was the occasion when the "levellers" campaign was planned.

In the early 19th cent. the fairs were transferred to Castle Douglas.

KEMNAY, *Aberdeenshire* (Map 6, ref. 37⁴81⁵). This village on the R. DON, in a pleasant basin facing BENNACHIE, owes its existence to the granite industry, and nearly all its substantial granite houses were built by the granite workers themselves, for themselves, in the 19th cent. Kemnay House to the W. of the village dates largely from the 17th cent., with later additions. It was rifled and plundered in the Civil War, but since 1688 it has belonged to the Burnetts, a cadet branch of the Burnetts of Leys.

Thomas Burnett, the second of the Kemnay line, was a friend and adviser to Sophia, Electress of Hanover, and had a hand in preparing the ground for the Hanoverian cause in Britain. He went to Paris in 1702, and was thrown into the Bastille through the influence of the Jacobites. The Electress discovered where he was and, by exerting her influence through the Duchess of Orleans, had him set at liberty after a year and a half in durance vile.

Alexander, the fourth Burnett laird, was a friend of Frederick the Great and served as British chargé d'affaires in Berlin. It was his son John who, in 1830, opened the first quarry at Paradise Hill, one of several in the area that were to form the basis of a great industry.

Kemnay granite, a magnificent silver-grey stone that has a light tinge of brown caused by the tints of felspar, and contains both black and white mica, was soon being produced in enormous quantities. It was here that steam was first applied to the quarrying industry, and later that blasting shots were first fired by electricity.

Seven bridges over the Thames, and innumerable public buildings all over the world, were built of the stone quarried here, and Kemnay became the home of a colony of quarrymen, granite-masons, and sett-makers.

In the first decade of the present century, great numbers of skilled sett-makers and masons from Kemnay took part in an annual migration to the United States to work from spring to fall in every state from New York and Maine to the Middle West, returning to winter at home. Others went to Odessa to teach the Russians how to make setts. Setts, it should perhaps be explained, are the paving-stones for streets, not pavements.

In 1960 it was decided to close down the main quarry (400 ft deep) at Paradise Hill. So in a sense the saga of Kemnay granite proper is over, though it will be resumed in time, for another quarry is to be developed. Meanwhile the granite dust, of which there is an inexhaustible supply, is used to produce a patent material (called Fyfestone) that simulates the appearance of granite and provides blocks of great strength and hardness for building purposes. All over Britain it is extensively used in housing.

KENMORE, *Perthshire* (Map 2, ref. 27⁸74⁵). This charming village, at the E. end of Loch TAY, was added to and enhanced in 1760 by the 3rd Earl of Breadalbane. In 1774, the bridge over the TAY where the river leaves the E. end of the loch was built with the help of £1,000 from the Commissioners of Forfeited Estates.

Robert Burns visited Kenmore, and over the fire-place of the inn parlour, where it can still be seen, wrote lines in praise of the village and the view from the bridge.

Some 2 m. E. of Kenmore at Croft Moraig is the finest group of standing stones in Perthshire. A double circle of stones has been set on a specially prepared platform, 185 ft in diameter, outlined by large boulders of which one is cup-marked.

From Kenmore, a loose-surfaced road, with steep gradients, climbs above the S. shore of the loch to cross the watershed into Glen Quaich. This route is not recommended for cars, but those who do not mind a stiff climb will be rewarded by a superb panoramic view.

KENNOWAY, *Fife* (Map 3, ref. 33⁶70²). This town is in a now rapidly developing coal-mining area. Once it was a flourishing weaving community, which also practised handicraft industries, such as clock-making and the manufacture of shoes.

The first preaching of Christianity in East Fife is attributed to St Kenneth at the end of the 6th cent., there is record in 1177 of a church here, dedicated to him.

KESSOCK, *Inverness-shire/Ross and Cromarty* (Map 5, ref. 26⁵85⁷). This ferry route stretches for just under ½ m. across the Moray and BEAULY Firths from INVERNESS to the BLACK ISLE. It is one of the safest ferries in Scotland, and a magnificent view may be had from the middle of the strait. The attractive village of North Kessock with its cottages lining the shore and clinging to the steep side of wooded Ord Hill faces S. across the narrows. On top of the hill is a vitrified fort, but the remains are now difficult to identify owing to trees.

KETTINS, *Angus* (Map 6, ref. 32⁵73⁹). A church was consecrated here at Kettins in 1249, subordinate to the Abbey of St Mary's, CUPAR. In the churchyard is the 16-cent. bell preserved complete with belfry. A large sculptured stone 9 ft high by the N. wall of the churchyard served as a bridge over the nearby burn until 1860. The village possesses a green, and the church has – what is usual in England but uncommon in Scotland – a lych-gate.

KILBARCHAN, *Renfrewshire* (Map 2, ref. 24⁰66⁹). Now a town near PAISLEY, Kilbarchan was once a place of early religious significance; the original church of St Barchan was bestowed in Paisley by Walter Fitz-Allan, High Steward of Scotland. Ranfurly Castle nearby was once the home of the Knox family, from whom John Knox was descended. In the mid-18th cent. the town became a prominent centre of the weaving industry, with about 1,000 hand looms in production. A typical weaver's cottage at the Cross has been restored by the National Trust for Scotland. In summer, visitors may see the old craft in operation here, and the cottage also contains items of local interest illustrating the domestic life of those earlier days. The distinctive steeple (1755), which is an outstanding architectural feature of the centre of the town, has been given a new lease of life as council offices and public meeting rooms. Habbie Simpson, a renowned piper and local character of the late 16th cent., is commemorated by a statue mounted on the steeple.

KILBERRY, *Argyll* (Map 1, ref. 17²66³). Tradition has it that at Kilberry is the site of an early monastery; certainly there was here an ancient burial-ground, which was cleared in the 17th or 18th cent. Early medieval gravestones from it have been collected into a shelter. Kilberry Castle, built in 1497, was burnt by an English pirate about 1513 and was not rebuilt until 1844.

Some 12 m. NW. of Kilberry on the W. shore of Loch Killisport, near Ellary, is St Columba's cave at Cove, which has an altar and two crosses on a shelf of rock. Outside the cave is the ruin of a 13th-cent. chapel.

KILBIRNIE, *Ayrshire* (Map 2, ref. 23²65⁵). With its adjoining neighbour of Glengarnock, Kilbirnie is the main industrial potential in Ayrshire N. of ARDEER. There is a large steelworks here (situated at the S. end of Kilbirnie Loch), and the prosperity of the district depends on it. An object of note in the town is the parish church, part of which dates back to the 15th cent. Like many another in the country, it is a "laird's" church, having been largely built by the Cunningham and Crawford families. The Crawford Gallery in carved oak is in the Renaissance style. Coats of arms were added in the early 18th cent. when the grandson of Crawford of Kilbirnie became the 1st Viscount Garnock. Kilbirnie is on the ARDROSSAN–PAISLEY road, about 8 m. N. of KILWINNING.

KILCHATTAN, *Buteshire* (Map 2, ref. 21⁰65⁴). This village is on Kilchattan Bay, a district that lies on the Great Highland Fault running from STONEHAVEN to INNELLAN, thus showing some interesting rock formations – around the bay there is a patch of columnar sandstone, and also a mass of volcanic rock.

Kilchattan was popular in the 19th cent. when steamers called here, but it is still busy with summer visitors who now come by road.

The local industry was once fishing, but has now changed to dairying.

KILCHOAN, *Argyll* (Map 4, ref. 14⁹76⁴). The so-called "capital" of ARDNAMURCHAN is the village of Kilchoan, and it is certainly a good centre for seeing the peninsula. Ben Hiant (1,729 ft) rising to the E. of the village is an excellent viewpoint. The district is good for walking but the roads are narrow and twisty for motorists.

The ferry for passengers runs from here to TOBERMORY on MULL. There are sandy beaches and hill lochs full of brown trout.

The district is so far W. that the sundial at Ardnamurchan lighthouse records time about 25 minutes later than G.M.T.

KILCHURN CASTLE, *Argyll* (Map 2, ref. 21³72⁷). The Castle of Kilchurn stands at the NE. end of Loch AWE, on a rock that was once an island but is now surrounded by marsh. It was a stronghold of the Campbells, and the keep was built by Sir Colin Campbell of Glenorchy, founder of the Breadalbane family about 1440. The N. and S. sides were built in the 17th and 16th cents. respectively. The Campbells, who were anti-Jacobite in the 18th cent., offered the castle as a garrison for Hanoverian troops in 1746. The TAY Bridge disaster gale of 1879 blew down one of the tower tops, but the castle is still one of the finest baronial ruins in Scotland, in a wonderful etting between Loch Awe and BEN CRUA-HAN, at the mouth of Glenorchy.

KILCONQUHAR, *Fife* (Map 3, ref. 4⁸70²). The pretty village of Kilconquhar (pronounced "Kinneuchar") consists of one winding street with picturesque white cottages with red roofs. It is an agricultural centre growing mainly potatoes, sugar beet, grain, and dairy products; forestry also provides employment for some of the inhabitants.

The village stands on the NW. shore of Kilconquhar Loch, in which it is said the Witch of PITTENWEEM was drowned. This loch is now used for bonspiels in winter.

The church stands on a knoll above the village and has an 80-ft tower that dominates the scene.

KILCREGGAN, *Dunbartonshire* (Map 2, ref. 22⁴68⁰). Now a resort at the S. end of ROSNEATH peninsula, Kilcreggan faces GOUROCK and overlooks Loch LONG and HOLY LOCH. Just to the W., beyond Baron's Point, is Cove, with which Kilcreggan is joined as a burgh for administration. The district is very popular with CLYDE business men who want villas accessible for office travel and for retirement.

Knockderry Castle 3 m. NW. of Kilcreggan stands on the dungeons of an ancient tower, and is associated with Knock Dunder in Scott's *The Heart of Midlothian*.

KILDALTON, *Argyll* (Map 1, ref. 14³64⁶), is on the Island of ISLAY, in the Inner Hebrides (*see* "The Shape of Scotland"). This is a wooded district in the SE. of the island. The church was the centre of the parish until the late 17th cent.; in the churchyard are two fine Celtic crosses and other sculptured stones. One of the crosses is, justly, nearly as famous as St Martin's Cross on IONA.

To the N. of Kildalton is bare high ground with MacArthur's Head lighthouse on the cliff at the entrance to the Sound of Islay, and above it Ben Bheigeir (1,609 ft), Islay's highest hill.

KILDONAN, *Sutherland* (Map 5, ref. 29²92⁰). The village of Kildonan is on the Helmsdale river. Gold found in the Kildonan Burn led to a minor gold rush in 1868–9, but it was later found to be nearly all in dust; £6,000-worth was extracted, but the search for gold here was pronounced uneconomic.

On Learable Hill, about 1 m. up-river from Kildonan, are several rows of stones and cairns with no evident connection, also a standing stone on the summit of the hill with a cross carved on the W. face.

In the 1960s interest in panning for gold in the Kildonan burns was revived, and a number of amateurs spent their holidays seeking El Dorado. The Government's scheme announced in mid-1971 to encourage the search for minerals

of all kinds in Britain will undoubtedly turn professional eyes towards these hills and waters; it may be hoped that they do not too deeply scar this lovely strath.

KILDRUMMY, *Aberdeenshire* (Map 6, ref. 34⁸81⁷). "The noblest of northern castles", now a spectacular ruin on the summit of a ridge above the N. side of the main road to Strathdon 39 m. W. of ABERDEEN, is the magnet that draws interest to this very beautiful Donside parish in a basin of old red sandstone, which gives the landscape a softer, mellower look than the stern granite country in which it is set. It was not the first castle in the area, for there was an early Norman motte, or fortified mound, on the fluvo-glacial hillock 1 m. NE. where the parish church and the ruins of its pre-Reformation predecessor, St Bride's, now stand; but it has so much historic interest and architectural distinction that it must be considered first.

Kildrummy Castle is the best surviving example of a 13th-cent. stone castle of enceinte in Scotland, and the only one of its period that still possesses a complete articulated layout of domestic buildings – hall, kitchen, solar, and chapel – all belonging to the original design. It was the creation of St Gilbert (the last of the Scottish saints). Bishop Gilbert de Moravia, who was Bishop of Caithness from 1223 to 1245, and, as King Alexander II's treasurer of the North, was responsible for the works necessary to secure the pacification of the country after that monarch had crushed the last Celtic revolt against the Canmore dynasty.

It was conceived entirely on the pattern of the mighty Chateau de Coucy near Laon, with an enormous semicircular curtain wall, defended by five projecting round towers, the largest of which, at the NW. salient, was the Donjon, now known as the Snow Tower. At some time during the course of erection, probably about the middle of the 13th cent., the plans were altered to permit the correct orientation of a chapel, whose E. gable, with its three finely moulded windows, projects over the foundations of the curtain wall.

By the end of the century the Castle was virtually complete. Before it was finished, however, Scotland was under the heel of Edward I of England, who visited the area in 1296 and again in 1303. To the English occupation it owed a new feature, the gatehouse with two massive drum-towers, which is virtually a replica of the gatehouse of Harlech Castle in North Wales, and may well be the work of King Edward's architect, Master James St George, who is known to have been in Scotland at the time. Thus, in its finished form, Kildrummy displayed both the Donjon, which is the distinguishing sign of French military architecture, and the Gatehouse, which characterizes the English school.

In 1306 occurred the most famous event in

Kildrummy's story. After the Battle of METH-VEN, Sir Nigel Bruce, the brother of Robert Bruce, convoyed thither the royal ladies for safety in the period of danger that all knew must lie ahead. When an army under Prince Edward of Carnarvon, the future Edward II of England, and the earls of Gloucester and Hereford, approached to besiege the Castle, the Queen and her party moved on to the sanctuary at TAIN, where they were captured, but Sir Nigel remained to give battle.

The Siege of Kildrummy raged on throughout the end of August and the beginning of September. Every attempt to carry the walls by storm ended in costly failure for the English. But what fair fighting could not gain, treachery accomplished. Secretly in the pay of the English, Osbarn, the smith of the Castle, set fire to the granary. The blaze was so intense that the great gate melted in the heat, and though Sir Nigel was able to build a barrier to take its place, starvation and thirst won the day. Kildrummy fell. Sir Nigel was executed at Berwick. "Hang him on a gallows thirty feet higher than the rest!" growled King Edward, when someone protested that he was of the blood royal.

From the time of its erection, Kildrummy was the principal messuage of the earls of Mar. Disaster befell that earldom in the 15th cent. In 1402 Sir Malcolm Douglas, the husband of Isabel, Countess of Mar and Garioch in her own right, was murdered at Kildrummy by a gang of assassins in the hire of Alexander Stewart, a son of the notorious Wolf of Badenoch (*see* ELGIN). Two years later Stewart himself arrived on the scene, stormed the Castle, and forced the widowed Countess to marry him. To legitimize this atrocity, he staged a spectacular charade outside the gate of the Castle before a company including the Bishop of Ross and many local magnates. In this he presented the keys of the castle to the Countess and declared that he voluntarily gave up all right to it and to the earldom. Whereupon the persecuted Countess – already, one suspects, thoroughly intimidated – handed back the keys and declared to all beholders that she chose him to be her husband of her own free will. "Why must the wicked prosper?" The usurping earl only seven years later covered himself with glory and became a national hero as the victor in the Battle of HARLAW. But the Countess had died long before then, without bearing him any children, and when he himself died in 1435 the earldom was annexed to the Crown by King James I – in defiance of the clear right of Sir Robert Erskine, the rightful representative of the ancient Celtic line of the earldom.

The earldom was restored to the Erskines by Mary Queen of Scots in 1565, and the Castle became theirs again in 1626. The Elphinstone family, who had held it for 120 years, built the structure known as the Elphinstone Tower (a lofty pile with crow-step gables) on top of the original great hall.

In the Civil War the Castle was garrisoned by Royalists and Roundheads in turn, and in 1690 it was burnt by the soldiers of "Bonnie Dundee". Finally, in 1715, it became the headquarters from which the 10th Earl of Mar launched the Jacobite Rising of that year. Following its collapse, Kildrummy was dismantled and was used as "the common quarry of the country", but in the 19th cent. a stop was put to the spoliation, and in 1898 was begun a long series of repairs and excavations, which have continued to the present day. In 1901 a "new castle" of Kildrummy was built on the N. side of the Back Den, the picturesque defile to the N. of the Castle, for the then laird, Col. James Ogston.

The quarry from which came the stone for both castles was converted into a rock- and water-garden, and a striking bridge; a replica of the medieval Brig o' Balgownie at Aberdeen was built to span the stream. Kildrummy was handed over to the Ministry of Public Building and Works in 1951, and in 1955 the new mansion became a hotel.

Of the original burgh of barony of Kildrummy, which lay between the church and the Castle and flourished from 1377 until the 17th cent., nothing now remains but the place-name Boroughmuir.

In addition to the operations carried out at the castle itself, the Ministry of Public Building and Works excavated 1½ m. N., at Muirs of Kildrummy farm, two of over a score of eirde-houses – those remarkable stone-lined underground dwellings of the Iron Age in which this district is particularly rich.

KILKERRAN, *Ayrshire* (Map 2, ref. 23¹60²), a mansion house in the Girvan Valley, is the seat of Sir James Fergusson of Kilkerran, Baronet, chief of his name. The house was built around an older tower in 1695–1700, and enlarged in 1814–15, but the Kilkerran lands have been associated with the Fergusson family since the early 15th cent.; Sir James is one of the few landowners who today retain and occupy lands held by their family in continuous succession for more than 500 years. The Fergussons of Kilkerran played a notable part in the efflorescent intellectual life of Scotland during the latter half of the 18th cent. Lord Hermand of the Kilkerran Fergussons (the Scottish Judge) is remembered for his aphorisms and for his character, notable even in that age of highly individual characters. In modern times, three members of the family have been governors-general of New Zealand. Kilkerran lies about 2½ m. N. of DAILLY.

KILLEARN, *Stirlingshire* (Map 2, ref. 25³68⁶). This village lies to the NW. of the Campsie Fells and above Strathendrick.

In 1932 the Killearn Trust was founded to

reserve the 18th- and early 19th-cent. cottages nd bring them up to standard. It started by buying the Well Green – then followed the purchase of three but-and-bens in the Square, nd the Knowe Head, which has the date 1803 on its lintel. It finally purchased the Glebe, which has a view of Loch LOMOND and the hills from Cowal to Ben Vorlich, to prevent building.

In the village is a tall obelisk to the memory of George Buchanan (born near Killearn in 506), the Latinist and tutor of James VI and I.

The large hospital nearby has become an important centre for brain surgery.

KILLIECRANKIE, *Perthshire* (Map 5, ref. 29¹76²), is a historic spot a few miles N. of PITLOCHRY on the main INVERNESS road; it lends its name to a hamlet, a hotel, a battle, and a pass. The pass is an attractive beauty spot with 1½ m. of wooded walk along the banks of the R. Garry. Reception and information for visitors is comprehensively provided by the National Trust for Scotland, who have owned part of the pass since 1947.

The battle on the 27th of July 1689 was fought not in the pass but on higher ground near Urrard House 1 m. to the N. A force of Jacobite supporters of James VII under Graham of Claverhouse, "Bonnie Dundee", routed William III's army under General Mackay. Dundee himself was killed in the action, which lasted only a few minutes; deprived of his leadership, the Jacobite cause failed to hold the advantage gained by the victory. A detailed, illustrated description of

The Pass of Killiecrankie

Scottish Tourist Board

the battle is displayed at the National Trust for Scotland's information centre.

The Soldier's Leap, in the pass below the centre, is a formidable jump said to have been cleared in retreat by one Donald MacBean of Mackay's forces. On the way down to the leap there is a viewpoint that earned commendation in Queen Victoria's diary after a visit by her in 1844.

KILLIN, *Perthshire* (Map 2, ref. 25⁶73³). This village at the W. end of Loch TAY lies at the centre of typically beautiful Highland scenery. BEN LAWERS (3,984 ft) towers over the village, and on its slopes botanists in summer search for, but are particularly asked not to touch, the rare Alpine plants to be found there. In winter the slopes are a centre for skiing enthusiasts. Trout and salmon fishing are also available on the rivers Dochart and Lochay and on Loch Tay.

Killin is closely associated with the Clan MacNab, and their burial-place is on a small island in the river just below the falls of Dochart and can be seen from the road bridge.

On the S. side of the river facing the village is Kinnell House, which became the seat of the MacNabs in the 17th cent. but later came into the possession of the Breadalbane family. The 2nd Marquess of Breadalbane planted a black vine at Kinnell; it is said never to have missed a crop since 1832.

In the grounds of Kinnell House is a well-preserved prehistoric circle of standing stones.

Near the village are the ruins of Finlarig Castle, once a seat of the Campbells. Tradition says that near the castle is a pit where the gentry were executed, while the common people were hung on a neighbouring oak tree.

The eight healing stones of St Fillan can still be seen at the tweed-mill near the Bridge of Dochart. Each stone is supposed to resemble that part of the body for which it claimed healing powers.

KILLOCHAN, *Ayrshire* (Map 2, ref. 22²60⁰) is another of the GIRVAN castles; it lies midway between New DAILLY and Girvan, and immediately opposite Old Dailly. This castle is thought to date from about 1586. It is remarkably unchanged and was originally in the family of the Cathcarts of Carleton. (*See* LENDALFOOT.) The name appears to be connected with the Baron's Stone, which sits nearby. (*See* DAILLY.)

KILMACOLM, *Renfrewshire* (Map 2, ref. 23⁶67⁰). Now a holiday resort, Kilmacolm gives the appearance of Highland scenery isolated in the South of Scotland. It became also a residential area in the 19th cent. with the opening of a station on the GLASGOW to GREENOCK railway.

The modern church replaces earlier ones, the first one being built as far back as the 12th

Killin: the River Dochart

cent.; an aisle from an earlier church is used as a burial place for the earls of Glencairn.

About 2 m. to the SE. is the ruined Church of St Fillan with a doorway dated 1635; also nearby are a holy well once thought to cure children with rickets, and a rock on which the saint sat when baptising children.

KILMARNOCK, *Ayrshire* (Map 2, ref. 24³63⁸). With a population of about 48,000 and a considerable diversity of industry, Kilmarnock is well-named the "industrial capital of Ayrshire". The town sits in a large amphitheatre open only to the W. It is 13 m. N. of AYR, about 20 m. S. of GLASGOW, and about 5 m. inland of IRVINE; it is on the main Glasgow–DUMFRIES–London railway, and is a first-class communications centre. The principal industries of the place are whisky, carpets, boots, heavy and light engineering, agricultural machinery, tractors and harvesters, and even nylon stockings. Like its neighbour, Irvine, Kilmarnock is proud of its association with Robert Burns, because it was here that the famous Kilmarnock edition was produced by John Wilson. During his life in MAUCHLINE, the poet became friendly with the Kilmarnock folk and wrote some poems to please them: "The Ordination" and "Tam Samson's Elegy" are the best known. The Kay Park contains the well-known Burns Memorial, and there is also a worthwhile museum of manuscripts and relics.

Sir James Shaw, Baronet, the first Scottish Lord Mayor of London, was born at Kilmarnock.

KILMARTIN, *Argyll* (Map 1, ref. 18³69⁸) The village and church of Kilmartin date from the mid-19th cent., but there is much evidence of very early settlement in the district, which is fertile and is on the meeting of the routes from the W. coast and Loch Fyne and Loch AWE.

Various prehistoric remains can be found nearby. These include three large cairns S. of the village, and near Nether Largie. The one to the S. was originally 130 ft in diameter and contains a chamber 20 ft long and 3 ft wide with corbelled walls covered with huge slabs. The one to the N. is 70 ft in diameter with a capstone carved on the underside with bronze axes and cup-marks. This cairn is considered sufficiently remarkable to be locked up, but those interested can obtain the key from the Kilmartin Hotel.

At Balnacraig 1 m. SSE. of Kilmartin are cup-and-ring marks on the rock faces in an exceptionally good state of preservation. To the SW. of Nether Largie cairns is the Temple Wood stone circle.

In Kilmartin churchyard there are an interesting collection of grave-slabs and fragments of at least two crosses; one shows Christ crucified on the obverse and Christ in Majesty on the reverse. These date from the 16th cent., but the influence of the 12th-cent. ivory work- is evident.

Some 2 m. N. of Kilmartin is Carnasserie Castle on a commanding hill above the road. It consists of a tower-house and a hall-house, both built in the 16th cent. and was the home of John Carswell, the first Protestant Bishop of he Isles, who published Knox's liturgy translated into Gaelic in 1567. This is the first book to have been printed in Scotland's most ancient tongue. The castle was captured and partly blown up in 1685.

KILMAURS, *Ayrshire* (Map 2, ref. 24^{1}64^0). This is a couthy central Ayrshire town 4 m. NW. of KILMARNOCK. Like others in the neighbourhood, it has had a variety of industries – coal, horn spoons and cutlery, and bonnets; now it has hosiery and a large creamery – a fitting complement to the rich dairy-farming district in which it lies. It traces its origins to 1527, when the Earl of Glencairn gifted 200 acres, 5 acres to each of forty freemen. The town was built around the Collegiate Church, which dates back to the early 15th cent.

KILMELFORT, *Argyll* (Map 1, ref. 18^{5}70^2). A small angling resort, Kilmelfort, as its name suggest, stands at the head of Loch Melfort. This sea-loch is protected from the Atlantic ocean by many islands; it has boating, and fishing for sea-trout and mackerel is safe and easy. There are a number of hill-lochs in the district that provide fair sport among the brown trout.

The pass of Melfort is a picturesque channel cut by the R. Oude through steep rocky cliffs.

KILMORIE, *Argyll* (Map 1, ref. 17^{2}67^4). The township of Kilmorie is in Knapdale on the neck of land between Loch Sween and Loch Coaliport. The now ruined church is used to house a notable collection of carved Celtic slabs. Outside the church is the 12-ft "Macmillan's Cross", one of the finest in Scotland and to be compared with those at IONA and KILDALTON; it was elaborately carved, probably in the 15th cent. and possibly by the monks at KILBERRY.

KILMUIR, *Inverness-shire* (Map 4, ref. 12^{6}84^7), is a hamlet on the Island of SKYE in the Inner Hebrides (*see* "The Shape of Scotland"). This small place, about 5 m. N. of UIG, is chiefly celebrated as containing the graveyard in which rest the remains of Flora Macdonald, who rescued Prince Charles Edward Stuart in 1746. Her tombstone bears Dr Johnson's celebrated panegyric, which he first printed in his *Journey to the Western Isles of Scotland.*

KILMUN, *Argyll* (Map 2, ref. 21^{7}68^2). This pleasing village, on the N. shore of HOLY LOCH, is a popular holiday resort with good anchorage.

Sir Duncan Campbell of Lochawe founded a Collegiate Church here in 1442. The tower of this church still remains; it was probably at one time a residence of the Argyll family. The traditional burying-place of the house of Argyll was within the church, and the churchyard is still used as such.

On a hill above Kilmun is the arboretum, which covers 166 acres. It is used to test the suitability of unusual specimens, the plots being labelled and numbered and set in 7½ m. of pathways, but the whole place has a natural aspect. The Forestry Commission encourages visitors; it has laid out the area in a way that enables them to see everything easily.

KILRAVOCK CASTLE, *Nairnshire* (Map 5, ref. 28^{1}84^8), which stands in pleasant wooded surroundings, is the ancestral home of the Chief of the Clan Rose, who is at present Miss Elizabeth Rose of Kilravock. Begun in 1460, the present castle consists of the original tall keep, to which has been added a 17th-cent. manor house and several small cottages. It was visited by Mary Queen of Scots in 1562, by Prince Charles Edward Stuart and his pursuer, the Duke of Cumberland, in 1746, and by Robert Burns in 1787.

KILSYTH, *Stirlingshire* (Map 2, ref. 27^{2}67^8). This mining burgh at the southern foot of the Kilsyth hills was revealed in 1918 as one of the worst-housed towns in Scotland. It was fortunately almost entirely rebuilt between the two world wars.

Nearby, Montrose won his great victory of Kilsyth on the 15th of August 1645 – the last victory of his great year. Relics of the battle are on view at Colzium, a mansion now used as a community centre and lying ½ m. NE.

KILWINNING, *Ayrshire* (Map 2, ref. 23^{0}64^3). Every Freemason worthy of the name looks to Kilwinning as the Mother Lodge in Scotland. The town is an important communication centre, lying between ARDROSSAN and GLASGOW, and Ardrossan and IRVINE. It surrounds an ancient abbey, built in the reign of David I (1124–53), of which only scanty ruins remain. In days gone by, when the Scots burgher was fonder of his archery than his "gowf", an annual competition for bowmen was held at the abbey, with prizes for each part shot off the papingo that was suspended from the tower. The "shoot" is still commemorated by the Ancient Society of Kilwinning Archers, who annually shoot at a silver papingo set in the traditional place.

KINBRACE, *Sutherland* (Map 5, ref. 28^{7}93^1). The crofting township of Kinbrace stands near the junction of two burns that come together to form the R. Helmsdale, noted for its angling.

The district was turned over to sheep-farming in the early 19th cent. In 1877, however, the 3rd Duke of Sutherland spent large sums of money trying to reclaim land for agriculture, and used a steam plough as at LAIRG, but with no lasting success.

Just over 2 m. SE. of Kinbrace is the largest of a variety of chambered cairns recorded in the district; it has a tripartite chamber reached by a passage 25 ft long.

KINCARDINE, *Kincardineshire* (Map 6, ref. 36⁸77⁵). In the neighbourhood of FETTER-CAIRN there arose in the reign of William the Lion the fortress of hammer-dressed sandstone that was the royal castle of Kincardine. There, in 1296, the scroll of John Balliol's resignation of the Scottish Crown in favour of Edward I of England was written. The castle was finally demolished in 1646. In the meantime the "town" of Kincardine itself had flourished and declined. It was never more than a row of straggling clay-built hovels extending from the East Port near Kincardine Castle to the West Port near Fettercairn House. STONEHAVEN replaced it as the county town in the 17th cent. But it had its market cross, and part, at least, of that ancient monument is believed to form the shaft of Fettercairn's market cross today, having been moved there in 1730, along with the annual fair of St Catherine. Nothing remains on the site of Kincardine now but the disused kirkyard of the vanished St Catherine's Chapel.

Kincardine is almost as remote from its shire as is Berwick from Berwickshire. Berwick is buried in Northumbria in England and away from the shire to which it gives its name. Kincardine is buried in the remote past. It is perhaps this that has led local people in the NE. to refer to the "Mearns" rather than to Kincardineshire. The Mearns is a more meaningful title for them than that of a shire named after a dead county town.

KINCARDINE O'NEIL, *Aberdeenshire* (Map 6, ref. 35⁹79⁹). Pleasantly situated on the left bank of the DEE, this village was once of importance as being at the Deeside end of CAIRN O' MOUNT. There was a pass and a ferry at this point, and an early wooden bridge built by the Durward family in the 13th cent. In 1812 a bridge was built 2 m. to the SE. at Potarch. The village declined when the railway went via Torphins, but road traffic has increased prosperity once more. There is an ancient medieval church on the main street. A little to the W. the R. Dee is joined by Dess Burn on which is the Slug of Dess waterfall.

KINCARDINE-ON-FORTH, *Fife* (Map 2, ref. 29³68⁷). This once busy and ancient small port on the R. FORTH is well rooted in Scottish history. Now better known for its bridge and thermal power station, its past is seen in the 17th-cent. houses and mercat cross bearing the arms of the Earl of Kincardine, although that is now overshadowed by several enormous blocks of high-rise flats.

In 1936 Kincardine became known to road-users because its new bridge provided the only crossing of the Forth between STIRLING and the somewhat unreliable ferry at QUEENS-FERRY. With the completion of the mighty Forth Road Bridge in 1964 it seemed that Kincardine Bridge would lose its importance, but, unlike its would-be supplanter, the latter is toll-free, and, with the creation of new trunk road networks to the busy industrial belt south of the Forth and the motorway to GLASGOW, Kincardine Bridge now carries an ever-increasing volume of commuter, tourist, and heavy traffic. Until the building of those high-rise flats and other housing schemes, the most modern element in Kincardine-on-Forth was the large South of Scotland Electricity Board's generating station, opened by the Queen in 1960.

The reader's attention is here drawn to COCKENZIE and LONGANNET, where even more ambitious schemes have been undertaken by the Board. The Kincardine station in March 1971 had a maximum available output capacity of 714,000 kW of its installed capacity of 760,000 kW, ranking next to Cockenzie, 1,200,000 kW, and Longannet. (In mid-summer 1971 Longannet was forced to close following damage to turbines.)

The availability of Fife coal and Forth tidal water is the reason why Kincardine, Cockenzie, and Longannet are all sited in the E.

Those of us, however, who have seen the face of Scotland change under industrial development are prepared for changes anywhere. DOUNREAY in the far N., the hydro-electric schemes in the Highlands, and now these immense generating-stations on the Forth have accustomed us to the fact that all Scotland (and not, as was once the case, only the industrial belt) is in the process of change and is to the fore in new developments.

KINCLAVEN, *Perthshire* (Map 6, ref. 31⁵73⁷). The church and castle of Kinclaven stand on a tongue of land caused by a wide bend in the R. TAY just at its junction with the Isla.

The Castle is a magnificent example of the courtyard type of defensive structure enclosed by strong walls and defended by flanking towers, features common to the military architecture of the 13th cent.

In the reign of King Alexander II of Scotland (1214–49), it was a royal residence, and, though today it is sadly neglected and over-grown, it still retains an air of its former grandeur. Its chief claim to remembrance is in connection with William Wallace and the Wars of Independence. In 1297 Wallace had come to PERTH with some followers, but as the town was in English hands he hid in Methven Wood. Hearing that the English garrison at Kin-claven was to be reinforced by a detachment from Perth, he decided to ambush the detachment, and he did this so successfully that the English were pursued up to and into Kin-

:laven Castle. The Castle surrendered, the garrison were killed, the place looted and then burnt.

The curtain wall encloses an area of 130 ft square, and the postern gate, which gives on to the steep slope above the river, has a dog-leg passage in order to ease defence. It is interesting that the Duke of Atholl bears the hereditary title of Keeper and Constable of the Royal Castle of Kinclaven.

KINCRAIG, *Inverness-shire* (Map 5, ref. 28³80⁵). The village of Kincraig is a holiday centre near the CAIRNGORMS and at the NW. end of Loch Insh, through which the SPEY flows. On a hillock jutting into Loch Insh is Insh church that claims to stand on a site continuously used for worship since the 7th cent. The church is dedicated to St Adamnan, one of St Columba's followers and his biographer. Inside, chained to a granite basin, is a very ancient square bell of cast bronze said to have special powers of healing and to be able to find its way back from any distant parish, if removed.

Some 3 m. S. of the village stands Balavil House, built by James Macpherson of "Ossian" fame. In the grounds nearby is an obelisk to him. (For further reflections on the Macpherson–Ossian controversy *see* LISMORE.)

KINDROGAN, *Perthshire* (Map 6, ref. 30⁷76³). This large mansion house with some 10 acres of ground stands on the S. bank of the R. Ardle about 8 m. E. of PITLOCHRY. It was acquired in 1964 by the Scottish Field Studies Association with help from the Scottish Education Department, the Carnegie Trust, and the World Wildlife Fund. It is equipped as a residential centre with a qualified warden, and is Scotland's first permanent Field Studies Centre for work on biology, geology, physical and human geography, and archaeology.

KING EDWARD, *Aberdeenshire* (Map 6, ref. 37²85⁵), is a parish and castle bearing a name that is, for Scotland, a highly unusual one. It lies on the E. bank of the R. DEVERON, so noted for its salmon and trout fishing. The name did not derive from any memory of the conquests in the far north by King Edward I of England, nor is it likely that if that had been its derivation it would have been allowed to survive. The two words, as they now stand in English, are a corruption of a Gaelic phrase in sound vaguely like the words King Edward: "ceann eader", or (in a later version) "Kynedor". Authorities are puzzled; the original *may* have meant the head of the "Fedder", a word of uncertain meaning. The present inappropriate English name is said to have appeared officially first on communion cups presented to the church in 1619. The Castle was once a stronghold of the Comyns, who were foes of Robert Bruce.

KINGHORN, *Fife* (Map 3, ref. 32⁷68⁷). A royal burgh, Kinghorn faces S. and has become a holiday resort on the Firth of FORTH; it has a fine, safe beach.

The town had a royal castle in the early 13th cent., but this was granted by Robert II to his son-in-law Sir John Lyon, ancestor of the Strathmore family; Sir John called it Glamis Tower. Formerly Kinghorn was the N. end of a ferry across the Forth.

At Pettycur to the SW. of the burgh is a monument put up in 1886 to mark the spot where Alexander III was killed by a fall from his horse in 1286 (*see* "Scotland in History").

Carlin Craig at the W. end of the bay has interesting specimens of wild plant life.

KINGLASSIE, *Fife* (Map 3, ref. 32³69⁸). Surprisingly rural for a mining area, this village has an old part mellow with red pantiles; the new part towards Inchdairnie has modern cement and tiles. Kinglassie was once called Goatmilk, and a farm in the district keeps the name.

To the NW. of the village, and on the summit of Redwells Hill, is a square tower known as Blythe's Folly. Built in the early 19th cent. for no purpose and never really finished, it rises to 52 ft. Scotland is famed for these "follies"; most Scots have acquired an irrational affection for them.

KINGSBURGH HOUSE, *Inverness-shire* (Map 4, ref. 13⁹85⁵), is on the Island of SKYE in the Inner Hebrides (*see* "The Shape of Scotland"). A former house here sheltered Prince Charles Edward Stuart in 1746 when he was rescued from the "Long Island" by Flora Macdonald. The heroine of that oft-told venture subsequently married the son of the Macdonald of Kingsburgh, who was then the Prince's host and protector. After an adventurous life in America, she returned to Skye and is buried on the island.

KINGUSSIE, *Inverness-shire* (Map 5, ref. 27⁸80⁰), the capital of Badenoch, is one of the several summer-holiday and winter-sports resorts associated with the CAIRNGORMS. The town takes its modern form from development at the end of the 18th cent. when the Duke of Gordon planned to set up a centre of woollen manufacture. Its earlier history goes back to pre-Pictish times, and a priory was founded in the area by an earl of Huntly in 1490.

Across the R. SPEY, on a prominent grassy mound, stand the remains of Ruthven Barracks. Adopted as an anti-Jacobite garrison between the Risings of 1715 and 1745, the barracks was captured and destroyed by supporters of Prince Charles Edward Stuart in 1746. The clans rallied here after defeat at CULLODEN in the hope of carrying on the fight, but were instructed by the Prince to disperse. The site was originally occupied in the latter half of the 14th cent. by a castle stronghold of the Comyns and the Wolf of Badenoch.

James Macpherson (1738–96), the translator-creator of "Ossian", was born at the nearby village of Ruthven (pronounced "riven") and for a time was parish schoolmaster.

The Highland Folk Museum, Am Fasgadh, in Kingussie, displays a remarkable collection of tools, domestic utensils, furniture, dresses, pottery, and other items illustrating Highland customs in the past two centuries. Founded by the historian Dr I. F. Grant in 1935, the collection is now owned and maintained by four Scottish universities.

The town is an excellent base for walking, touring excursions, and fishing, it has a pleasant golf course, and is a shinty stronghold. Shinty is a game similar to hockey; it is played in parts of Scotland and Northern England.

KINLOCH BERVIE, *Sutherland* (Map 5, ref. 22²95⁷). Situated on Loch Inchard, and on the isthmus between it and Loch Clash, Kinloch Bervie is the base of a considerable fishing fleet for vessels operating in the Northern Minch, the sea between the Outer Hebrides and the mainland.

Kinloch Bervie is now a "specified port". It is gratifying in these days, when you hear so much of the lamentable decline in the Western Fisheries, to learn that the building of the new plant here and the reconstruction of roads has been justified by continuous notable landings of herring and white fish.

Angling visitors to Kinloch Bervie will find a variety of fishing – salmon, sea-trout and brown trout; and they can pursue their pleasure in the finest W. Highland scenery dominated by the peaks of the Reay Forest.

For some 4 m. NW. of Kinloch Bervie the road continues to end at the Atlantic by the small fishing village of Sheigra. After that there is only a peat track, but it is one well worth walking over, for it leads to the far-famed beauties of Sandwood Bay and Sandwood Loch. Sandwood is uninhabited, but those who visit it are unlikely to forget it. Here too is some outstanding sea-trout angling.

KINLOCHEWE, *Ross and Cromarty* (Map 5, ref. 20³86¹). The township of Kinlochewe stands at the head of Loch MAREE. It is the centre of outstanding W. Highland scenery, and is excellently placed for angling sea-trout, salmon, and brown trout. There is good climbing on the Torridon Hills, and it is near the National Nature Reserve of BEINN EIGHE.

KINLOCHLEVEN, *Argyll/Inverness-shire* (Map 5, ref. 21⁸76¹). Situated at the E. end of Loch Leven, Kinlochleven is surrounded on three sides by mountains. At the beginning of this century, Kinlochleven as a village did not exist, but in 1908 an aluminium works started

building plant here; and this, along with the hydro-electric scheme on the R. Blackwater behind the town, provides work for more than 700 men. The rows of pipes ascending to the reservoir, and the industrial activity in the village, contrast strangely with the serene loch and the quiet splendour of the W. Highland scenery, making Kinlochleven a unique spot.

A pleasant walk may be taken following the old military path across the hills, over the Devil's Staircase to Kingshouse in the Pass of GLENCOE.

The village is administered by two county councils.

KINLOCHMOIDART, *Inverness-shire* (Map 4, ref. 17²77³). This village lies at the head of Loch Moidart on the new road (formerly a bridle path) that gives motorists a magnificent cirular tour of Ardgour, Sunart, and Moidart, linking up with the main road at Lochailort.

Kinlochmoidart House is built near the site of a previous one, burnt after 1745, in which Prince Charles Edward Stuart stayed on his way to raise the standard at GLENFINNAN in August 1745. A line of seven beech trees near the house commemorates the seven men of Moidart who landed with the Prince. One tree was blown down in a winter storm, but has been replaced.

The steep hills above Kinlochmoidart House are crowded with lochs containing some excellent brown trout, but permission to fish them must be obtained from the house.

KINLOCH RANNOCH, *Perthshire* (Map 5, ref. 26⁶75⁸). This village at the E. end of Loch Rannoch, at the point where the R. Tummel flows out of the loch, is at the centre of an area of great scenic beauty. From the village, roads run on either side of Loch Rannoch. Along the N. shore, the views westward to the summits that guard the entrance to GLENCOE are magnificent. Though today the road ends at Rannoch Station on the edge of RANNOCH MOOR, this is the route celebrated in song as "The Road to the Isles". At Camusericht a vast power station brings water by pipeline from Loch Ericht and the catchment area of Ben Alder forest.

On the S. shores near Dall, the road skirts the verge of the famous Black Wood of Rannoch. Here the Scots pines of the primeval Caledonian forest are regenerating themselves, thanks to conservation work by the Forestry Commission. The forest was almost extinguished in the 17th and 18th cents. to provide timber for a variety of purposes, including the building of many houses in PERTH. Today, the remaining mature pines are as much as 60 to 70 ft in height and 14 ft in girth; they may be anything up to 250 years old.

Dall House, now a boys' public school, is known as Rannoch School. It was founded in

1959, and is run on lines inspired by GORDON-
TOUN.

At Lassintullich are the remains of an early
chapel dedicated to St Blane, who died in
A.D. 590. Just SW. of the ruin is a slab of stone
with a cross carved in relief, and nearby stands
a crude holy-water stoup.

A nine-hole golf course, now disused, was
laid out on the site of the early village of
Bunrannoch. Many house foundations can be
traced, including at the E. end the footings of a
circular building, which is probably an Iron
Age ring-fort similar to those in GLEN LYON.

There is a small factory here that produces
Highland souvenirs.

KINLOSS, *Moray* (Map 6, ref. 30⁷86¹). This
village on the E. side of the estuary of the R.
Findhorn is now near an R.A.F. station; but in
the past the place was associated with heaven-
ward aspirations long before the flying-machine
was invented.

There are ruins of an abbey that was founded
in 1150 by David I for Cistercian monks from
MELROSE, which became rich and prosperous
on the very good land in this district. The most
famous abbot was Robert Reid, 1526–40, later
Bishop of ORKNEY. He ran a school at which
many of the Highland chiefs of the time were
educated, and he also introduced to Moray
from France the art of grafting fruit trees. After
1643, the lands came into the hands of Brodie
of Lethen, and the abbey was used as a quarry
for stones, giving yet another example of the
way in which the decay of a religious building
in Scotland has been brought about by indifference or neglect rather than by reforming
zeal. It shows now only the foundations and
the cloister wall, the prior's chambers, and part
of the abbot's house.

About 2½ m. NE. is Milton Brodie, with an
old abbey garden, which has a well and a
hexagonal tower.

KINNAIRDS, *Aberdeenshire* (Map 6, ref.
40⁰86⁷). In the very heart of the N. part of
FRASERBURGH is Kinnairds or Kinnairds
Head. On this slate rock, rising 60 ft above the
sea as a projection from the town, stands a
square machicolated tower of four storeys
built by Sir Alexander Fraser in 1574. He was
of the family that was later to be known as the
Frasers of Saltoun, who should not be confused with the Frasers of Lovat, though of
course they were distant kinsmen. The castle on
the top of Kinnairds Head proved too exposed,
and the family of Fraser later moved to
Philorth. On the rock now stands the first
lighthouse established by the Commissioners of
Northern Lighthouses. It was put up in 1787.

KINNEFF, *Kincardineshire* (Map 6, ref.
38⁵77⁴). Between INVERBERVIE and DUN-
NOTTAR, the main road to the N. passes
through the united parishes of Kinneff and

Aberdeen Press and Journal
Kinnaird Head Lighthouse

Catterline. Kinneff has a special niche in
Scottish history, for it was the place where,
during the Cromwellian occupation, the
honours of Scotland – the regalia consisting of
the crown, sceptre, and sword of state – were
safely concealed beneath the pulpit of an
ancient parish church and denied to the
usurping power of the Commonwealth soldiery.
That church survived into the first quarter of
the 18th cent. It was described as "a very old
fabrick, the walls thereof being supported by
eight strong butrishes of stone and the roof by
pillars of wood so that probably it is the oldest
countrey church presently possess'd and in use
of any in Scotland". But, unfortunately, it was
demolished and superseded in 1738 by the
present old parish church, now itself almost
pensioned off.

Almost, but not altogether. For services are
still held here one Sunday in the month during
the summer, and the visitors' book bears witness to the hundreds of pilgrims who view the
memorials within it to the Rev. James Grainger,
the parish minister who buried the regalia
under the spot where he had most authority
and security in a troubled world, and to Sir
George Ogilvy of Barras, who, as Governor of
DUNNOTTAR Castle, had discharged his trust
by denying the honours to the invader.

Who in fact actually conveyed the emblems
of Scottish sovereignty from Dunnottar Castle,
at some time between November 1651 and
May 1652, and gave them into the charge
of the minister of Kinneff, while General
Overton and his successors were besieging that
fortress and endeavouring to obtain possession

Kinnoull Hill above Perth

Scottish Field

of them, will probably remain for ever in doubt. There are two stories. According to the first, it was Grainger's wife, Christian, who went to the castle in person and, somehow secreting the crown and sceptre in her belongings, bore them safely through the lines of Cromwell's investing soldiers and rode along the coastal cliffs with them to Kinneff. The second and more probable version recounts how it was arranged that Mrs Grainger's servant should go to the seaward side of the castle rock on the pretence of gathering dulse on several occasions. By doing this frequently, she succeeded in making the besiegers take her visits for granted – and then she carried off the regalia hidden under dulse and other coverings in a creel, and so bore them to the waiting Graingers at Kinneff church, where they remained until the King came into his own again.

Unfortunately, this brilliant episode of the Royalist resistance was very inadequately acknowledged at the Restoration, and the result was a great deal of sordid bickering between the Keiths, the official guardians of the honours, and the Ogilvys of Barras, in which the veracity of the lady of the manse was called in question. There are, of course, always post-war inquests that leave nobody satisfied.

It is, however, Catterline, some 3 m. to the N., that in the past two decades has become the showplace of the parish. This delectable fishertown, perched on a long wedge-shaped bluff of land, forming an elevated cliff-top ridge above the rocky crescent of its picturesque little bay, is famous for its colony of artists, its enterprising line fishermen, its old-world Creel Inn – and latterly for the water-skiers, who have found the pier-sheltered little bay a perfect amphitheatre for their sport.

Best-known of the Catterline artists was the late Miss Joan Eardley, a leader of the modern GLASGOW school. James Morrison, from Glasgow, also discovered Catterline, and he has made his home there. And various others, not surprisingly, find irresistible the half-moon of the bay, scalloped by temptingly irregular fragments and gripped in the pincers of towering old red sandstone cliffs. Catterline first appears on record in the 12th cent. as Katerlin. Relics of the old pre-Reformation church dedicated to St Catherine still survive in the old kirkyard, where the rude aumbry and the fragment of a coffin slab bearing an incised cross and sword are built into the wall of the enclosure. The remoteness of this little haven made it the favourite resort of smugglers in the 18th cent. Today a small group of about half a dozen salmon and line fishermen keep alive its ancient fishing traditions, and with them the artists find a true affinity.

KINNEIL, *West Lothian* (Map 2, ref. 29⁸68⁰). The House of Kinneil, about 1 m. W. of BORROWSTOUNNESS, is on the high ground overlooking the Firth of FORTH, and was originally a seat of the Hamiltons. The old keep had wings added in the 17th cent.

Later it was occupied by Dr John Roebuck, co-founder of the CARRON Iron Works, and also by Professor Dugald Stewart, a considerable figure in EDINBURGH during her Golden Age at the end of the 18th cent. and the beginning of the 19th. In the grounds of Kinneil is an outhouse where James Watt developed his steam-engine with encouragement from Roebuck. Set up outside as a memorial is a cylinder designed by Watt for a colliery pump.

Part of the house is preserved as an Ancient Monument; it has mural and ceiling decorations, the earlier ones done for the Regent Arran in the middle of the 16th cent. These include the Parable Room and the Arbour Room.

KINNOULL HILL, *Perthshire* (Map 6, ref. 31⁴72⁴), the southern outlier of the SIDLAW HILLS, rises to 632 ft on the E. bank of the R. TAY and overlooks the city of PERTH. From the top is a superb panoramic view of the foothills of the Highlands and a bird's-eye view of the estuary of the Tay and the valley from Perth northwards. There are as good views elsewhere in Scotland, but none quite like this one from Kinnoull Hill. An indicator at the summit gives a mass of historical and topographical information. To the S. the face of the hill is rugged and precipitous, falling sheer for 500 ft. At the top of the cliff is a ruined tower built in the 18th cent. by the 9th Earl of Kinnoull in imitation of the castles on the banks of the Rhine.

Agates are found on the hill. It was given to the city of Perth in 1924 by the Hon. John Dewar.

KINROSS, *Kinross-shire* (Map 3, ref. 31¹70²). The county town of its shire, Kinross is near to the shores of the world-famous angling waters of Loch LEVEN. Its tolbooth dates from the early 17th cent., and was repaired in 1771. The steeple standing by the Town House finds itself in its rather odd position owing to the 18th cent. "steeple committees" of Kinross. When a church was designed in 1742 without a steeple, a committee was formed to raise money for this necessary adjunct to a church. The money was raised, but the church moved, leaving the steeple behind it.

Between the town and the loch with its gates in the centre of the town is Kinross House, built in 1685–90 by Sir William Bruce.

Now being by-passed by the new trunk road (see GLENFARG), Kinross is an important agricultural centre. Its traditional woollen industry has greatly expanded, now including the largest spinners of cashmere and fine yarns in Britain. Newer trades include mushroom-growing and light engineering. Nearby, on the S. shore of Loch Leven, is the now famous Vane Farm Reserve of the Royal Society for the Protection of Birds with its great variety of duck, geese, and other birds. A ferry runs from Kinross to Castle Island on Loch Leven.

KINTAIL, *Ross and Cromarty* (Map 5, ref. 19⁴82¹), is a small district in the superbly scenic Mackenzie and Macrae country at the head of Loch Duich on the main route to KYLE OF LOCHALSH and SKYE. The Clan Macrae came to the district in the 14th cent. to serve the Mackenzies, later earls of Seaforth, as fighting men, becoming known as the "Mackenzies' shirt of mail".

The Five Sisters of Kintail rise dramatically

The peaks of Kintail

from the head of the loch to heights of over 3,000 ft. They are among the steepest grass-sloped mountains in Scotland, and offer extensive views from their summit ridges, from which can be seen a striking profile of the CUILLINS of Skye.

KINTORE, *Aberdeenshire* (Map 6, ref. 37°81⁴). A river winding about the mounds in a wide valley bottom – this was the skeleton that nature clothed with rich meadowlands, creating the lovely haugh you see today if you approach Kintore as you are best advised to do, not by the Great North Road, but by the braes of Balbithan to the NE.

Most people, however, pass through Kintore, an ancient if tiny royal burgh strung out on either side of the highway from ABERDEEN to INVERNESS, without noticing anything particularly worthy of remark except the Town House in its tiny square, notable for its two quaint curving flights of stone forestairs. This building was erected in the years from 1737 to 1748. The rest of the little town is much more modern, with the exception of a pre-Reformation sculptured stone sacrament-house now placed on the stairway of the parish church on the opposite side of the main street from the Town House.

Kintore's first extant charter was granted by James IV in 1506, but it claims to have acquired its heraldic emblem, a branch of the oak tree, as the result of assisting Kenneth II to triumph over Norse invaders in A.D. 854. The tale is the rather familiar one of how cattle dressed in oak leaves were driven on to the scene of battle and thus deceived the enemy into thinking that reinforcements had arrived. At a later date, however, Kintore had its royal castle, in the heart of a royal forest, and from it Alexander III issued various charters.

The forest was granted by Robert Bruce in 1309 to Sir Robert de Keith, Marischal of Scotland, and about this time was built Hallforest Castle (1½ m. SW.), a keep that strongly resembles the tower of DRUM on Deeside. Twice vaulted and 60 ft high, the great oblong tower has walls 7 ft thick. Two lofty barrel-vaults, one on top of the other, were each subdivided to make four storeys, containing cellar, kitchen, hall and solar. Hallforest was inhabited until 1639, but is now a very precarious ruin.

The handsome old Town House, with its clock-tower and ogival-slated roof, was built at a cost of £850 Scots, largely subscribed by the Earl of Kintore, and contained originally a council room, a tolbooth, a school, and school-house, and a meal girnal – where the grain of the tenants on the Earl of Kintore's estate who paid their rents in kind was deposited.

Visitors to Kintore should know of one of the most interesting castellated buildings in Scotland; it lies in a quiet and retired glen on the other side of the R. DON from the royal burgh. This is Balbithan Castle, built by William Chalmers about 1667, the last of the turreted L-plan manors in the country. Belonging to a period when castellated houses had become thoroughly domestic, it has a captivating grace and charm. It is moving to think that at a time when great magnates of the Restoration era, such as the Earl of Kintore and the Earl of Middleton, were building in a style that looked forward to the 18th cent. and had none of the old tower-house characteristics, Chalmers of Balbithan preferred the native tradition that had lasted 400 years, and gave it a sweetness that it has retained unspoilt to the present day. Balbithan has the projecting jamb of its L-plan extended to such great length as to deny all thought of its being just a helpful adjunct to a keep. But it is still a true tower-house, with corner turrets, steep crow-stepped gables, and predominance of wall over window. It has been most carefully preserved, and it has a sensitive and devoted chatelaine in Mrs M. N. McMurtrie.

KIPPEN, *Stirlingshire* (Map 2, ref. 26⁵69⁵). This attractive village, with its single hilly main street, has the GARGUNNOCK and FINTRY hills as a background, and looks northwards to the fine ranges of the Southern Highland hills.

It was once the home of Sir D. Y. Cameron, who painted many landscapes there.

In the old churchyard is the grave of Jean Kay, the lady abducted by Robin Oig, Rob Roy's youngest son.

The Kippen Great Vine, which, it was claimed, was one of the largest in the world and was over 70 years old, covered 5,000 sq. ft and yielded more than 100,000 bunches of grapes (about 2,000 per year). Eventually the vine was sold; it died early in 1964.

KIPPFORD, *Kirkcudbrightshire* (Map 2, ref. 28³55⁶). This village of whitewashed cottages lies on the rugged and exceptionally beautiful estuary of the Urr, looking across to the impressive ridge of Screel and Bengairn, and down the firth to HESTAN ISLAND.

Smuggling and fishing were formerly important; now holiday-making and yachting are the principal concerns, though mussels are still gathered on Hestan. There is a nine-hole golf course.

A little S. of the village is the smaller resort of Rough-Firth, with a shell beach; beyond this lies ROCKLIFFE.

KIRKBEAN, *Kirkcudbrightshire* (Map 2, ref. 29⁷55⁹), is a village a little inland from the Solway Firth and dominated by Criffel (1,866 ft). In the church is a memorial font presented in 1945 "by the officers and men of the U.S. Navy who served in Great Britain under the command of Admiral Harold R. Stark" to Paul Jones (1747–92), who was born at ARBIGLAND, 2½ m. SE. of Kirkbean. One panel of the font commemorates the *Bonhomme*

Kirkcudbright: the river and the castle

Richard, the ship in which Paul Jones, a native of Kirkcudbrightshire and later founder of the American Navy, fought the battle off Flamborough Head. In the churchyard is a stone erected by him to his father.

Also born at Kirkbean was Dr James Craik, a friend of George Washington and the organizer of the medical service of the American Army.

The Rev. Thomas Grierson, minister here from 1824 to 1855 and author of *Autumnal Rambles Among the Scottish Mountains*, was a famous pedestrian and hill-walker. His record was from Loch LOMOND to the farthest end of the Moor of RANNOCH in one day.

KIRKCALDY, *Fife* (Map 3, ref. 32⁸69³). The industrial town of Kirkcaldy on the N. shore of the Firth of FORTH is best known for the manufacture of linoleum. Indeed, at one time the distinctive smell of linoleum pervaded the whole place; when the train stopped at Kirkcaldy station you knew where you were solely by your nose. This pervasiveness of linoleum has now ceased, but in Coal Wynd are the remains of the little factory where Michael Nairn started the industry in 1847. Kirkcaldy now has many other industries including engineering, boiler-making, rope-spinning, and linen-weaving.

Once described by Defoe as "one street a mile long", Kirkcaldy still has a promenade whose length is well over a mile, but now the town has deepened behind it. Yet the old name "Lang Toun" is still sometimes used. There are early buildings at Sailors' Walk; overlooking the harbour is an attractive group of houses whose earliest parts date from the late 15th cent. Kirkcaldy also has good modern buildings – the Town House (opened in 1956), a very

up-to-date high school, and a museum and art gallery. Adam Smith was born in Kirkcaldy, and a plaque in the High Street marks the site, though the house has gone.

Though Adam Smith decorated the intellectual society of Augustan EDINBURGH in the latter half of the 18th cent., he continued to reside much in Lang Toun. It is said that he used to look across the firth at the smoke of "Auld Reekie" (such was the Fife name for the capital) as a stimulus for his work.

At the N. end of the town is Ravenscraig Castle, founded by James II in 1460 – an imposing ruin on a rocky promontory. It has claims to have been the first castle in these islands systematically designed for defence by firearms.

KIRKCUDBRIGHT,   *Kirkcudbrightshire* (Map 2, ref. 26⁹55¹). An old royal burgh on the estuary of the DEE, Kirkcudbright is the capital of the Stewartry, and houses several of the county administrative departments, though the modern town of CASTLE DOUGLAS is developing faster.

Some of the streets are unwidened and unchanged since the 18th cent.; the 17th-cent. tolbooth still stands, and the great pile of McLellan's Castle, built in 1583, still dominates the harbour. The Stewartry Museum houses a fine, well-displayed collection of local antiquities; Broughton House, the 18th-cent. seat of the Murrays of Broughton, in High Street, was latterly the home of the artist E. A. Hornel, and is now a Hornel museum, the rooms being displayed as he left them; it houses many of his paintings.

The town has long been the home of an art colony – painters, weavers, and potters; many summer courses in art are held in the town, and a whitewashed cottage beside the harbour is now a gallery for exhibitions.

Kirkcudbright was an active port in the late Middle Ages and in the 17th and 18th cents. In the 1570s it was much troubled by Leonard Robertson, pirate, and burgess of Leith and Kirkcudbright; the Council made repeated efforts to get his "Men of Weir and Marinaris" to cease their "tuelyeing and harlotrie" and leave the town. He had captured a rich merchant cargo in the Chester Dee and sold it to the lairds around Kirkcudbright. When Queen Elizabeth of England complained to King James VI of Scotland, he appointed a commission consisting of those same lairds to look into the matter.

About ½ m. S. of the town is the mound of the 13th-cent. castle (partly excavated in 1906) of Castledykes, and the site of the priory of St Mary of Traill, at St Mary's Isle.

A little over 1 m. N. of the town is the pretty site of Tongland Abbey beside the rocky Dee gorge; its abbot was murdered at the altar in 1235 by the Scottish forces after the Galloway revolt. Its most famous abbot was John Damian, Dunbar's "Fenyent Freir", a charlatan and alchemist noted for his attempt to fly from the battlements of STIRLING Castle. This Scottish Icarus made his attempt in the presence of James IV; it was no doubt an effort to please and startle this superstitious Renaissance Prince who was King of Scotland at that splendid yet fateful time. A fine 14th-cent. arch, richly carved, stands at the entrance to the later church and a few yards from the present church.

KIRKHILL, *Inverness-shire* (Map 5, ref. $25^5 84^5$), is a village on the S. shore of the BEAULY Firth. On a hill above stands Wardlaw Chapel, the burial place of the Frasers of Lovat until 1815. This was the church of the Rev. James Fraser, author of the Wardlaw Manuscript (an account of the Frasers and local life in the 17th cent.).

KIRKINNER, *Wigtownshire* (Map 2, ref. $24^2 55^1$). Between WIGTOWN and WHITHORN, Kirkinner lies among pleasant, gently rolling country, 2 m. inland from the W. side of Wigtown Bay. Its churchyard contains, about 30 ft S. of the W. end of the church, a fine 10th-cent., wheel-headed cross, with interlace work.

Baldoon Castle, an early 17th-cent. building, the seat of the Dunbars, just S. of Bladnoch, is only a stump; but its fine entrance gate, erected in the late 17th cent., is a good example of Renaissance work. David Dunbar, of Baldoon, was the original of the bridegroom in Scott's *Bride of Lammermoor*.

Ring Hill, just E. of North Balfen farmhouse, bears on its western end a fine oval fort, 190 ft by 135 ft. In the field to the W. of Balfen farm road, some 200 yds WNW. of the farmhouse, is an outcrop of rock with a smooth surface, some 15 ft long by 4 ft broad, exposed for almost 10 ft, and bearing 11 striking cup-and-ring marks and several cup-marks.

KIRKINTILLOCH, *Dunbartonshire* (Map 2, ref. $26^5 67^4$). An ancient burgh with Lenzie adjacent on the S., Kirkintilloch is in a detached portion of its county. The town was once a station on the ANTONINUS' WALL; and some stones from the Roman wall were included in the castle built by the Comyns. Kirkintilloch was a royal burgh in the 12th cent. St Mary's church, dating from 1644 on an earlier chapel site, has been restored and is now used as a historical centre and museum.

Kirkintilloch's older industries were connected with iron foundries and coal, but it is a lively modern place, and recently it has been attracting new industries. It was awarded the Saltire Society's first prize as "most alive community" of the small burghs 1945–61.

Lenzie is largely residential and composed of business and professional people.

KIRKLISTON, *West Lothian* (Map 3, ref. $31^2 67^4$), is a village on the main EDINBURGH–LINLITHGOW road. Its parish church includes some 12th-cent. material, but is specially notable for its carved Romanesque doorway, while the W. tower has a steep saddle-back roof and shallow buttresses, rarely found in Scotland. The bell-cote on the eastern gable dates from the 17th cent. In Newliston Aisle are buried the 1st Earl and Countess of Stair.

Some 2 m. SW. of the village is Newliston House, which originally belonged to the Stair family in the early 18th cent. The 2nd Earl was responsible for laying out gardens, ornamental lakes, and woodlands on the French model, as he did at LOCHINCH, and for having a plan made for a new mansion by William Adam, who, however, died in 1747 before anything was done. Later, the property was acquired by the Hog family, and Thomas Hog employed Robert Adam to build the present house in 1789–92. Adam's house was much smaller than his usual ones; in 1845, wings were added to it by Bryce.

The village was once called Templeliston, after the Knights Templar who settled there.

About 2 m. W. of the village is the ruin of Niddrie Castle, where Queen Mary spent her first night of freedom after escaping from Loch LEVEN.

KIRKMADRINE, *Wigtownshire* (Map 2, ref. $20^8 54^7$). WHITHORN is justifiably renowned as one of the oldest centres of Christianity in Britain; but here, in a slight hollow among gently rolling meadows, 2 m. SW. of Sandhead, and 200 yds along a lane from a good secondary road, is the site of a religious settlement which, in the 5th and 6th cents., may well have been more important than Whithorn. As against Whithorn's two

Plate 11   *Sheep-dipping at Lairg, Sutherland (see p. 325)*
Scottish Tourist Board

arly inscribed stones, one of about A.D. 350 and one near A.D. 700, Kirkmadrine has four tones (including the lost Ventidius Subdiaconus tone), covering the period from near A.D. 500 o near A.D. 700, and all (like the Whithorn tones) purely continental and late-Roman in ettering and language, and in the church organization they indicate. All the surviving tones bear the Chi-Rho; the Initium et Finis tone also has the Alpha (almost worn away) and the Omega. All three of the presently available stones bear a unique ligature for ET, with the centre bar of the E forming the top bar of the T; as they cover 150 or 200 years by style, his implies the existence of a strong scriptorial tradition, and a considerable body of literate priests.

There are several crosses covering the early Northumbrian period; this period is also represented at Whithorn; thereafter only a few examples cover the late Northumbrian and Scots–Norse period, which at Whithorn sees a great efflorescence of crosses. It seems, therefore, that Kirkmadrine sank to minor status some time in the 9th cent.

Eight of the stones are preserved in a recess in the W. end of the mortuary chapel, which incorporates part of the old parish church.

KIRKMAIDEN, *Wigtownshire* (Map 2, ref. 21³53⁷). This parish occupies the tip of the Mull of GALLOWAY, and so is the most southerly parish in Scotland. Like many parts of Scotland, it is unexpectedly S. of northern England and Kirkmaiden is opposite Hartlepool in County Durham on the E. coast.

In the SE. corner of the parish is St Medan's Chapel, a coastal cave converted to a chapel in the Middle Ages. Excavation by the Marquess of Bute in 1870 yielded a sandstone statue of a draped female figure, with the arms crossed in front of the breast, brass mountings from a small book, and many coarse, narrow roofing-slates, with a great deal of animal-bone food-waste; near the chapel are the holy wells associated with it – natural pot-holes filled by the sea at high water of ordinary tides. The water was held in great repute for curing "back-gane bairns", and people flocked to the place from long distances on "Co' Sunday" – Cave Sunday, the first Sunday of May – to immerse weakly children in the water.

The chapel probably has an early Dark Age origin. It lies across Luce Bay from another Kirkmaiden, an old church site, also with a holy well; St Medana was said to have crossed from there to the Mull on a floating rock.

KIRKNEWTON, *Midlothian* (Map 3, ref. 31¹66⁶). The parish and village of Kirknewton, on the verge of the once prosperous shale district of West Lothian, might have suffered more, with other towns, in the recession in that industry had not the Ministry of Defence property nearby been chosen as an American base for the "692nd Security Group", which brought substantial trade and cash. The Americans departed some years ago, and the barracks, now Ritchie Camp, are occupied by a battalion of the Black Watch. There is also a gliding station much used by the Air Cadet Force. Kirknewton, nestling neatly at the foot of the Pentland Hills, only 8 m. from Edinburgh and convenient for growing centres in the industrial belt of Scotland, has a residential population of some 1,500.

KIRK O' SHOTTS, *Lanarkshire* (Map 2, ref. 28⁴66⁸). The old township of Kirk o' Shotts stands just off the main EDINBURGH to GLASGOW road 5 m. ESE. of AIRDRIE. There is evidence of a church here dedicated to St Catherine of Sienna, dating from before 1450; the present building was put up in 1821, a little to the W. of the old one.

This old village is now a familiar one, for on the high ground above the church stands the B.B.C. television mast, 750 ft high. The Independent Television Authority also has a mast in this district. The choice of Kirk o' Shotts for a TV transmitting station lay in its nearness to the most densely populated areas in Scotland. But when the B.B.C. mast went up in 1952, the cottages around it were still lit by paraffin lamps and had an outside village tap.

KIRKOSWALD, *Ayrshire* (Map 2, ref. 22⁴60⁷), is an old village about 4 m. S. of MAYBOLE. It contains the ruins of a pre-Reformation kirk replaced in 1777 by the present building, which was designed by Robert Adam at the behest of the Earl of Cassillis. In the middle of the village street stands Soutar Johnnie's cottage, now preserved by the National Trust for Scotland. Soutar Johnnie, alias John Davidson the village Soutar or cobbler in the late 18th cent., was, of course, one of the characters in Burns's *Tam o' Shanter*, referred to under MAIDENS. The graves of the two cronies – Tam and Johnnie – are in the kirkyard. The cottage contains a varied collection of Burnsiana and contemporary tools of the cobbler's craft; it is an interesting reflection of the ways of village life in Burns's day. In the small garden behind the cottage life-size stone figures of the Soutar, Tam, and the ever-hospitable Innkeeper and his wife sit in silent tableau: these are the work of a local self-taught sculptor, James Thom. The cottage and garden are open to the public on afternoons only during the summer.

KIRKPATRICK-IRONGRAY, *Kirkcudbrightshire* (Map 2, ref. 29¹57⁸). Kirkpatrick Cro, as it used to be known (Cro being one of the divisions or "eadrey" of Galloway in Scoto-Norse times), is a very large parish including much hill and moorland; its church, churchyard, and manse nestle in the valley by the Cairn, or Cluden, Water. In the churchyard,

Above *Summer on Loch Earn* (*see p. 341*)

Scottish Tourist Board

Below *Near Loch Inver: Cul Mor across Sionascaig Loch* (*see p. 342*)

Scottish Tourist Board

among 17th- and 18th-cent. stones, is the grave of Helen Walker, prototype of Scott's Jeanie Deans in *The Heart of Midlothian*, the Scots lass who walked to London eventually and successfully to plead with the Queen for the life of her sister, who had been condemned to death – easily Scott's most successful fictional female creation. The table-stone was erected by Sir Walter and bears an epitaph he composed.

In the W. of the parish, above Glenkiln reservoir, Johnnie Turner's monument rises on top of a prominent hill; he was an eccentric farm-worker and shepherd whose fear of body-snatchers led him to excavate his own grave in the solid rock on the hill-top at 1,306 ft; part of the rhymed epitaph is Johnnie's own doggerel. He came into DUMFRIES every day during the cholera epidemic of October 1832, when hundreds died in the town, with milk, and everyone spoke fair to him, for it was said if one annoyed him one would be dead by night.

The roadside past Glenkiln reservoir and the meadow slopes above it bear, mounted on rocks on the hillside, Epstein's "Visitation", Henry Moore's "King and Queen", "Torso", and "Strugglers", Renoir's bust of his wife, and, at the head of the reservoir, Rodin's fine "St John the Baptist"; all these were mounted here by Mr Keswick, the proprietor. About ¼ m. W. of Irongray Church is a monument marking the grave of two Covenanters hanged nearby, and 4 m. W., on Skeogh Hill, an obelisk set up in 1870 commemorates the great Conventicle of 1687; the stones are set on the side of a natural basin in the hills to form seats, and an altar can still be seen.

KIRKWALL, *Orkney* (Map 7, ref. 34⁴01¹), is the capital town of ORKNEY Northern Islands

(*see* "The Shape of Scotland"). This fine and ancient town – or city, for it contains a venerable cathedral – is, and always has been, the capital of Orkney. Even in prehistoric days, this site, in so well protected a bay of the main island of this group, must have been used by early inhabitants – and there is evidence of this. It was, in the days of the Norse occupation of Orkney and SHETLAND before 1462 (*see* "Scotland in History"), their prime seat in these Northern Islands, and it was the Norsemen who, nearly nine centuries ago, built its cathedral, which still stands as a reminder of how they spread civilization as well as ruthlessness in their conquests.

The great Norman cathedrals that strode up the length of England and as far as Durham remind us of the abiding power of Norman rule after the conquest of Saxon England in 1066. They built to last. At the same era, their remoter northern cousins were doing the same in St Magnus's Cathedral in Kirkwall.

When the Norsemen left, and Scotland took over in the reign of James III, Kirkwall kept its position, but felt the heavy hand of foreigners much more disliked than any Norsemen had been. The cruel Earl Patrick Stewart, of odious memory, built a palace near the cathedral, and the remains still stand to recall to us "the finest relic of domestic Renaissance architecture in Scotland".

After the Stewart earls had lost their hold on Orkney, Kirkwall inevitably continued to flourish as the county capital and royal burgh. Its position as a port, as the centre of a growingly agricultural entity, and as trading centre to the Baltic ensured that. Kirkwall, however, withdrew from Scottish politics, being untouched by the domestic upheavals of the 17th and 18th cents. When the British Navy

Sunshine in St Magnus's Cathedral, Kirkwall
Scottish Tourist Board

Kirkwall: the nave of St Magnus's Cathedral
Scottish Tourist Board

grew to its once pre-eminent position, Kirkwall re-entered the southern consciousness because of the nearness of the splendid harbour of SCAPA FLOW. Sailors of both world wars were very familiar with Kirkwall.

Today it is a lively town unrivalled in this respect amongst Scotland's island communities, save by STORNOWAY in LEWIS. It is as much of an island centre as Stornoway, but at the height of summer it attracts more tourists and foreign visitors.

The old town of Kirkwall clusters round the cathedral, and is notable for its solid stone, picturesque rather than beautiful, Scandinavian-type building. Some of the streets have no pavements, but contain massive paving-stones to form one comprehensive thoroughfare between facing houses. It is this, combined with occasional Dutch crow-stepped building, that most strongly helps to give to visitors from the south the feeling of a foreign air about Kirkwall.

Outside the old town, Kirkwall has spread in the modern manner, and there is every facility for the visitor who wishes to go sailing, to explore the island by bus, or to go sea fishing, or angling in the splendid brown-trout lochs of Orkney. There are good hotels and guest-houses. Kirkwall is and looks a flourishing little modern town, self-sufficient, yet in touch with the outer world and welcoming to visitors.

Apart from the Cathedral (of which more below), the only really ancient relics of Kirkwall's past buildings are the earl's palace already referred to and the bishop's palace of pre-Reformation days, now in ruins.

The Cathedral, which would be an impressive building anywhere in Scotland, gains added stature in its island position. Apart from GLASGOW, Kirkwall is the only city in Scotland to preserve structurally undamaged its pre-Reformation cathedral. The old statues, ornaments, and other signs of the Catholic past are, of course, long gone, but the building remains as it was. It has one unique qualification. Though the services in it today are those of the Protestant Church of Scotland, and though it is the "parish church of Kirkwall and St Ola", the building itself does not belong to the Established Church; it is the property of the town. The Town Council of Kirkwall is responsible for its maintenance and repair, an obligation the burghers of Kirkwall are proud to fulfil.

Kirkwall Cathedral was built in the 12th cent. as a result of what was virtually a pagan vow. A nephew of the saintly Earl Magnus had vowed to build a noble minster in memory of his murdered uncle – this at a time when the Norse in Orkney were scarcely Christian. He fulfilled his vow, became Christian, and was buried in the Cathedral along with the remains of the great and good Magnus, who was shortly afterwards canonized. The remains of St Magnus and of his nephew were discovered all but accidentally during repairs to the building between 1919 and 1926.

Cruciform in construction, the Cathedral is of flagstone and red and yellow sandstone with a central tower and spire. Its style is uncompromisingly massive Romanesque. It is 234 ft long and 101 ft across the transepts. Though damaged by Cromwellian troops, as so many buildings were, during the Commonwealth usurpation and subjugation of Scotland, the ravages have long since been repaired. In the interior is an interesting series of tombstones marking Kirkwall's eminent men from the 16th cent. down to the present day. A plaque commemorates the 833 men lost in the *Royal Oak* in 1939 at the beginning of the Second World War. There is a rose window at the S. end. It is of the 19th cent. The "keeled" shafts of the clustered piers supporting the tower, and the mouldings of the tower arches, are of the 12th cent.

Dominating and alive, St Magnus's Cathedral of Kirkwall in Orkney speaks in its stones of the close on nine centuries it has existed. It is, in size and style, easily the most outstanding island building in Scotland. If RODEL (*see* HARRIS) is the most poignant reminder of Scotland's religious past in her islands, St Magnus's is the most impressive. It would be impressive on the mainland of Scotland. It is double impressive on the island Mainland of Orkney.

Reaching Kirkwall from Scotland is easy. There are daily flights to Kirkwall airport from GLASGOW and EDINBURGH via ABERDEEN, INVERNESS, WICK, and LERWICK, and steamer services from SCRABSTER, Aberdeen, and LEITH. Let it be repeated that the little town of Kirkwall is in many respects a capital city on its own, yet in touch with the world.

KIRN, *Argyll* (Map 2, ref. 21^{8}67^8). Now linked with DUNOON by a promenade along the East Bay, Kirn is a Firth of CLYDE resort. It has a lido and a pier of its own, and is busy as a base for yachting during the summer season.

KIRRIEMUIR, *Angus* (Map 6, ref. 33^{8}75^4). The pleasing and characteristically Scottish small burgh of Kirriemuir has picturesque narrow streets. It was once noted for its weavers. Now there is more jute-manufacturing than weaving, but the narrow streets and red houses still retain their charm. Kirriemuir is also an excellent centre for exploring the glens that run up into the GRAMPIANS.

The little town is proud of being the birth-place in 1860 of J. M. Barrie, and features as Thrums in his writings. The birthplace, No. 9 Brechin Road, is maintained by the National Trust for Scotland as an intimate personal museum. Also preserved is (behind the house) the wash-house where he had his first theatre. The "Auld Licht" Manse of the little Minister is opposite the birthplace. The cottage with the "Window in Thrums" is at the other end of the town near the junction of the GLAMIS and FORFAR roads. Barrie was buried in the cemetery here in 1937.

Some 5 m. to the W. is Airlie Castle with its beautiful gardens, often visited by the late Queen Mary when her close friend Mabell Countess of Airlie (grandmother of the present Earl) lived here. Burned in 1641, the house lay in ruins until rebuilt in 1792–3, and a new wing was added in this century Airlie Castle is occupied by Alexandra Countess of Airlie, widow of the 9th Earl.

After 1641 the Airlie family moved to Cortachy Castle, 3½ m. N. of Kirriemuir, previously bought by them in 1625. The present building has undergone various alterations, but the basis of the old castle remains. The final additions by Bryce, in 1873, almost doubled the area of ground covered by the castle. It is now the home of the 10th Earl, who succeeded on the death of his father, a prominent figure in Scottish affairs, in 1968.

KISHORN, Ross and Cromarty (Map 5, ref. 18⁴83⁹). Also known as Courthill, this township is on Loch Kishorn, an inlet of Loch Carron. The road to APPLECROSS branches off the one to SHIELDAIG just N. of Kishorn at Torna-press. This is typically wild and beautiful W. Highland countryside. The local youth hostel provides a good base for walking and climbing.

KNOCKANDO, Moray (Map 6, ref. 31⁹84¹). Near the R. SPEY at one of its most delightful winding wooded stretches, this village is dominated by Ben Rinnes (2,755 ft) on the opposite side of the river. It is in the distillery country, being contiguous with Banffshire. The parish church stands on a hill to the N. of the village. This small, galleried church has three worn sculptured slabs in the churchyard dating from the 8th to the 10th cent. One has a runic inscription on it said to be the same as one found at Sanda Södermanland in Sweden.

KNOCKFARRIL, Ross and Cromarty (Map 5, ref. 25⁰85⁷), is the name of the summit of a ridge called Druim Chat (Cat's Back), 1¼ m. E. of STRATHPEFFER. The ridge rises very steeply and is crowned by an important vitrified fort. This fort first attracted the attention of archaeologists as far back as the 1770s. The result was for us a trifle unfortunate. As Mr Richard Feachem, in his Guide to Prehistoric Scotland says, "The great size of all the remains and the blurring of outlines and details render almost all questions about this fort unanswerable as yet".

However, those not primarily interested in archaeology can console themselves with excellent views of the countryside from the Cat's Back, easily approachable by a footpath from near the centre of Strathpeffer.

KYLEAKIN, Inverness-shire (Map 4, ref. 17⁵82⁶), is a village on the Island of SKYE in the Inner Hebrides (see "The Shape of Scotland"). This is the nearest inhabited spot on the island to the mainland, and acts as the Skye end of the ferry over the short distance from Kyle in Scotland. It is for most visitors their first encounter with the celebrated "Misty Isle". A touch of Skye's past is immediately discovered in the remains of Castle Moil, a miniature Highland keep, believed to have been built by the daughter of a Norse king who, it is said, levied a toll from ships passing through the straits between Skye and the mainland. Kyleakin indubitably owes its name to Norse origins, the "akin" part of it coming from King Haakon, who sailed through the straits on his way to defeat, at the Battle of LARGS. (See "Scotland in History".)

KYLE OF LOCHALSH, Ross and Cromarty (Map 4, ref. 17⁶82⁷). This small town and tourist centre is also the terminus of the railway from INVERNESS. There is a ferry to SKYE from Kyle, and boats leave here for STORNOWAY and the "Small Isles". Kyle of Lochalsh is a good centre for touring, not only in Skye but among the sea lochs of the mainland. Roads from the S. via GLEN SHIEL, from the E. via Strathcarron, and from the N. via SHIELDAIG and STROME FERRY all meet at the water's edge at Kyle. From here one can enjoy about the best grandstand view of the CUILLINS that can be had from the mainland.

KYLE RHEA, Inverness-shire (Map 4, ref. 17⁹82⁰), is on the Island of SKYE in the Inner Hebrides (see "The Shape of Scotland"). From its island position, Kyle Rhea faces GLENELG across a very narrow strait, and is connected with the mainland by a car ferry that operates in the summer. The narrowness of the strait causes it to be swept at predictable intervals by strong rapid tidal currents. Despite this (as an old drove road shows), cattle used to be made to swim across to the mainland from this point. The road to the ferry at Kyle Rhea is steep and narrow, but it has spectacular views of the mountains of the mainland.

KYLESKU, Sutherland (Map 5, ref. 22²93³), is the name of a sheltered ferry where the road from LOCHINVER and ULLAPOOL crosses Loch Cairnbawn just W. of its division into Loch Glendubh and Loch Glencoul. From here there are spectacular views of Quinag (2,653 ft) and Glasven (2,541 ft), where the lochs penetrate deep into the land with no roads to accompany them. Near the head of Loch Glencoul is a magnificent waterfall, Eas Coul Aulin (600 ft high), which can be reached only on foot or by boat. The ferry crossing takes about ten minutes and is free, but you are liable to find queues in the summer.

LADYBANK, *Fife* (Map 3, ref. 33°71°). In the fertile Howe of Fife to the NE. of the Lomond Hills, Ladybank stands where the monks of LINDORES were granted the right in the 13th cent. to gather 200 loads of peat yearly by Roger de Quincy.

Just after the middle of the 19th cent., the railway from the FORTH to the TAY was built and linked with the line from PERTH. The junction then developed into the burgh of Ladybank, where linen-manufacturing and agricultural engineering was carried on.

Some 2½ m. N. of Ladybank is Melville House, a mansion built in 1692–1702 for the Earl of Melville by James Smith; it is now used as a boys' school.

LADY ISLE, *Ayrshire* (Map 2, ref. 22°62°), is a desolate rocky islet with a lighthouse in TROON Bay, and is a noted mark for mariners. The island, which extends to about 10 acres, is the breeding-ground of roseate and other terns, and is under the wing of the Scottish Society for the Protection of Wild Birds. It may be visited by arrangement.

LADYKIRK, *Berwickshire* (Map 3, ref. 38°64°). This charming Tweedside village has a church built by James IV in gratitude after having nearly lost his life by drowning in the TWEED in 1499. It is said to be one of the last churches built in Scotland before the Reformation. The church now has a stone slabbed roof, a three-storeyed W. tower, possibly constructed with a view to defence, and a four-sided belfry dating from 1743.

LAGGAN, *Inverness-shire* (Map 5, ref. 26°79°), is a township 7 m. NNW. of DAL-WHINNIE and near the watershed of Scotland's East and West. The SPEY rises 10 m. to the W., but the Spean flows from Loch Laggan 6 m. W. of the town. General Wade's road from CORRIEYAIRACK divided at Laggan for Dalwhinnie and Ruthven.

An ancient hill-fort must once have occupied a commanding position on the promontory ridge dividing the main Strath of Spey from Strathmashie about 2 m. SW. of Laggan.

On the southern bank of the loch lies a house that Queen Victoria considered buying as a "Highland home". It is Ardverikie, built in 1840 by the Marquess of Abercorn. Unfortunately, during the Queen's visit there, the rain never ceased and was said to "come down in sheets". Not even Queen Victoria's love for the Highlands of Scotland could survive such a downpour. She changed her plans and chose BALMORAL instead.

The Lochaber Power Scheme undertaken in connection with the INVERLOCHY works was responsible for the Loch Laggan dam, which raised the level of the loch and increased its length from 7 to 11½ m. The increased water was then taken by tunnel to Loch Treig, and thence by another through BEN NEVIS to INVERLOCHY. Later the headstreams of the Spey were diverted through a 2-m. tunnel into the loch. Work on this scheme began in 1931 and was completed in 1943.

LAGGANGARN, *Wigtownshire* (Map 2, ref. 22°57°). If you have an urge to penetrate to the back of beyond, this is it, for up in "The Moors" the very names of the farms and cottages standing alone in the remoteness round about – Dirneark, Dirvachlie, Kilquhockadale, Dirvananie, Belgaverie – are evocative enough. You reach Laggangarn usually from the Water of Luce; but, whichever way you approach, it involves 5 or 6 m. across the moors on foot.

The name means "hollow of the cairn", and there clearly has been some sanctity attached to the spot for a long time. The reduplicated crosses on the two grey standing stones are of an early type, though not precisely datable; certainly from some time in the Dark Ages. Another stone, a slab with a simple Latin cross, leans against the wall on the outside of the old garden of the ruined farmhouse of Laggangairn.

Laggangairn and its stones lies about ⅓ m. WSW. of Kilgallioch. The farmer at Laggangairn, tradition says, moved one of the stones to use as a fireplace lintel; his wife broke her arm, his dog went mad and bit him, and he was smothered in a feather-bed at his own request in the paroxysms of hydrophobia.

LAIDE, *Ross and Cromarty* (Map 5, ref. 19°89¹). A crofting village on GRUINARD BAY, Laide is in a scenically splendid situation. Visitors here will find that there are caravan and camping sites near to the beach.

LAIRG, *Sutherland* (Map 5, ref. 25°90°). This village and holiday resort, situated at the E. end of Loch Shin, is an excellent touring centre, as it lies at the junction of roads to the N. and W. It is well known for the salmon and trout fishing that can be found in the neighbourhood, and its lamb sales.

The surrounding district provides a variety of scenery, including wide expanses of moorland to the N. and the spectacular R. Shin with its waterfalls to the S. About 3 m. N. of the village, at the foot of Strath Tirry, stands a monument on a hillside commemorating the "Great Plough". This was used in large-scale reclamation works undertaken between 1873 and 1877 by the Duke of Sutherland, when 1,829 acres were turned over by steam mechanical cultivators.

LAIRIG GHRU, *Inverness-shire* (Map 5, ref. 29°80°), is the great cleft running N. and S. through the CAIRNGORMS between Deeside and Speyside (*see* SPEY). Cairngorm and Ben Macdhui rise to the E., and Braeriach and

Lairg Ghru from Rothiemurchus

Cairn Toul to the W. Near the summit of the pass (2,750 ft), the R. DEE has its source in the Pools of Dee. The length of the pass is 19 m. and walking is, for most of the way, fairly easy. (For further references to this district see the CAIRNGORMS.)

LAMBERTON, *Berwickshire* (Map 3, ref. 39⁷65⁷). The village of Lamberton is on the Great North Road from London to EDIN-BURGH on the Border (3 m. N. of Berwick and just in Scotland). At the toll-house, the toll-keepers used to conduct marriages similar to those performed at GRETNA GREEN; the spot is now marked with a tablet. It served as a "Marriage House" from 1798 to 1858.

Lamberton Church is now a ruin with only nave and chancel remaining. It was the place where Princess Margaret Tudor, sister of Henry VIII, was received by the Scottish Commissioners in 1503 on her way to Edinburgh to marry James IV. From this marriage eventually emerged the Union of the Crowns. But before that event there was to occur the disaster of Flodden. (*See* "Scotland in History".)

LAMINGTON, *Lanarkshire* (Map 2, ref. 29⁹63³). This small village on the left bank of the CLYDE looking towards Tinto Hill is connected by tradition with William Wallace.

A little N. of the village there used to be Lamington Tower, popularly called "Wallace's Tower". The reason for this was a tradition surviving from the partly legendary account of Wallace's life by the minstrel "Blind Harry". According to this tradition, Wallace's wife was Marion Bradfute, the heiress of Lamington. Some authorities, including his latest biographer, say that he was never married. The matter of the Tower of Lamington (or Wallace's Tower) need no longer concern the visitor. A local factor destroyed it in 1780 to procure building material.

Lamington Church has a fine Norman arch and a bell dated 1647.

LAMLASH, *Buteshire* (Map 1, ref. 20³63¹), is a small town on the Island of ARRAN. Along with WHITING BAY, this, after BRODICK, is the most popular holiday resort in Arran. Situated in a striking bay on the E. coast 4 m. S. of Brodick, and in the part of the island where the Highland scenery of the N. just gives place to the more Lowland contours of the S., Lamlash contains the two attractions of Arran. Its bay is protected by the small but lofty HOLY ISLAND. This protection allowed King Haakon of Norway to rest his armada before attacking Scotland (to be defeated at LARGS) in 1263 in Lamlash Bay. The bay also has been used as a base for later British naval forces, particularly just before the First World War, when there was fear of civil war in Ireland.

LANARK, *Lanarkshire* (Map 2, ref. 28⁸64⁴). The county town of Lanark grew up around a castle built by David I on a steep bank above the CLYDE. The castle was prominent in the Wars of Independence, and was probably enlarged by Bruce, who founded a chapter of Franciscans here and encouraged the building of St Leonards Hospital. Some remains of the hospital are still visible, but the castle (probably by the present "Castlegate") has totally disappeared. The town, however, was a royal burgh from the time of David I and has remained as such ever since.

The industry in the district is mainly at nearby NEW LANARK. Lanark confines itself to the knitting and hosiery trade.

The Festival of Lanimers, the riding of the marches, takes place at the beginning of July; but Lanark also claims it has the earliest race trophy in the world. A silver bell was made in 1590 and has been raced for since 1628 over a course of 1½ m. each September.

Some 3 m. NW. of the burgh is "The Lee", the seat of the Lockhart family, owners of the Lee Penny traditionally brought from the Holy Land by Sir Simon Lockhart in the 14th cent. This Lee Penny has the reputation of working wonder-cures; Sir Walter Scott used this as the basis for *The Talisman.*

Although Lanark is the county town, the county buildings of Lanarkshire are now at HAMILTON, which has been the administrative centre for many years.

LANGHOLM, *Dumfriesshire* (Map 3, ref. 33⁶58⁴) is a sizeable little town and burgh, on the R. Esk, about 8 m. from the English border. Langholm grew rapidly according to a well-developed plan, of which the shape is still visible. In the late 18th cent. the town was much involved in the cattle trade. In 1788 a cotton-mill was founded, and Langholm became important for cloth-making in 1832, when the manufacture of black-and-white check trouser-ing for shepherds began; there are now five tweed mills. The town being the centre for a wide area of good sheep and cattle country, there is also an auction market for stock.

Farther up Eskdale, at a cottage (now mere foundations) on the Meggat Water, Thomas Telford, one of the giants of the Industrial Revolution and a great builder of roads and bridges, was born and brought up; and in Eskdale he served his apprenticeship, which began his engineering career. The Malcolm brothers, from the nearby village of Burnfoot, all achieved knighthood for services to the State: one of them, Sir Pultney, was Governor of St Helena when Napoleon was a prisoner there; the tall obelisk topping Whita Hill near Langholm celebrates Sir John Malcolm, a "Knight of Eskdale". A contemporary of Nelson, Admiral Pasley, whose excellent diary was published in the 1930s, was also a Lang-holm boy. C. M. Grieve (Hugh MacDiarmid, the poet) was born at Langholm. Grieve is celebrated as the Scottish nationalist poet of our age, and his powerful verse certainly earns him that title. He has said that had he been born 8 m. to the S. he would have been the nationalist poet of England.

The town has a fiery local patriotism that reaches its climax with the Common Riding on the last Friday in July; this began as a walk round the marches in 1759, the horse-riding beginning in 1816. About 1½ m. S. of the town is the site of a series of Roman forts at Broom-holm. The Wauchope medieval motte and churchyard lie a little W. of the town; Lang-holm Castle is the remains of a Border tower.

LARBERT, *Stirlingshire* (Map 2, ref. 28⁵68²). A railway junction near FALKIRK, Larbert is a familiar name to EDINBURGH and GLASGOW travellers of the Rail Age, going N. It is also associated with the ironworks at CARRON. Some of the guns used at Waterloo were cast here.

LARGO, *Fife* (Map 3, ref. 34³70⁴). This village on the Fife coast is divided into two parts: Upper Largo, inland, and Lower Largo, washed by the bay to which it gives its name. Largo was formerly an important fishing place, but is now mainly residential and a popular holiday resort.

Upper Largo parish church has a 16th-cent. chancel and tower; its spire, dated 1623, is unique in Scotland, as it rests entirely on the arched roof of the chapel. In the church is buried Sir Andrew Wood (d. 1515), the Captain of the *Yellow Carvel,* who beat an English squadron in the FORTH in 1489 and was given lands at Largo.

Alexander Selkirk, the prototype of Daniel Defoe's Robinson Crusoe, was born in Lower Largo in 1676. After his adventures in Juan Fernandez, Selkirk returned to Largo, where he died, and a statue to his memory is erected in front of his cottage.

Just N. of Upper Largo a magnificent view of the Forth can be seen from the summit of Largo Law, which was once a volcano. Legend had it that a chief was buried in silver armour under this hill, and in 1819 a tinker digging sand found a hoard of silverware; later excava-tion produced more silver, which is now in national collections.

LARGS, *Ayrshire* (Map 2, ref. 22¹65⁹). A bustling holiday resort and sailing centre on the Firth of CLYDE, near the northern boundary of Ayrshire, Largs is, to those fond of cruising in sheltered waters, an ideal base. From it steamers ply to all the piers of the Clyde, and beyond to Loch Fyne and the Kilbrennan Sound. Sheltered by the Island of CUMBRAE, it has a safe anchorage for all craft. Near the town is the scene of the Battle of Largs, in which, on an October day of storm in 1263, Alexander III and his Western levies slaughtered the survivors of the battered Viking fleet, torn from its moorings at ARRAN. (*See* "Scotland in History".) Largs looks back to this turning-point of history with pride, and at the same time looks forward with a proprietary anti-cipation to the future of the atomic power station situated at Hunterston Bay, 4 m. to the S. To the visitor, Largs appears to be a much-churched place; but this impression is perhaps illusory, and has arisen because the town is tightly hemmed in, between the 1,500-ft escarpment on the E. and the sea. Although this puts all the goods in the shop window, it has become an embarrassment to this expanding community. The Inverclyde National Recrea-tion centre run by the Scottish Council for Physical Recreation is situated nearby.

LASSWADE, *Midlothian* (Map 3, ref. 33⁰66⁷), is a village well situated on the steep slope of the North Esk river valley, and the constant supply of water explains the variety of mills, which have provided employment for the last 200 years: paper-mills, meal-mills, and once a gunpowder-mill.

In the graveyard of the old church is the burial place of the poet William Drummond of HAWTHORNDEN, and the family of Melville, including Henry Dundas 1st Viscount, the benevolent despot and virtual ruler of Scotland, 1775–1805.

There are several literary associations with Lasswade. It was to Lasswade Cottage that Sir Walter Scott brought his bride, and spent the first happy six years of his married life, being visited here by the Wordsworths and by James Hogg, the "Ettrick Shepherd". In neighbouring Polton, 1½ m. up-river, lived De Quincey for the last years of his life, in a cottage called Mavis Bush, now known as De Quincey Cottage. Born in 1785, he died in 1859.

It is an odd reflection on the vagaries of the human body that this self-confessed opium-taker, this addict who upon coming out of his opium-trances used to delight the EDINBURGH Literary Society of the early 19th cent., should somehow have managed to live 74 years. He is said to have cured himself of his addiction by his own efforts. This is either a tribute to De Quincey's strength of character, or maybe a piece of evidence to the effect that all our bodies are not equally susceptible to certain drugs. Not many addicts today succeed in becoming septuagenarians. They make their literary reputations (if any) early, and disappear early. But it is just possible that the invigorating atmosphere of Edinburgh in her early 19th-cent. literary phase had something to do with De Quincey's recovery and longevity.

LATHERON, *Caithness* (Map 7, ref. 32⁰93⁴). There are two parts to the village of Latheron, which is a small hamlet with three churches, a school, and a post office, in the coastal strip of arable land on the E. side of the county. The other section, known originally as Janetstown, now Latheronwheel, with shops, hotel, and most of the housing, lies nearly 1 m. to the S., and stretches from the main road down to a charmingly secluded and sheltered natural harbour, where the burn meets the sea, and over the centuries has carved an inlet in the steep grey cliffs, a familiar pattern on this coastline.

At Latheron, the road to THURSO branches across the moors; a considerable length of the way was laid in a single day in the late 18th cent. in an exercise planned with almost military precision by Sir John Sinclair, utilizing every available man, beast, and stone. The old church in Latheron is down in the slope towards the sea, and on a high ridge above the village a bell-tower was built to call the faithful of the parish, the largest in the county, stretching from Bruan to the ORD, to worship.

The whole area around Latheron is rich in antiquarian remains, brochs, galleried dwellings, hut-circles and standing stones, in a variety of states of preservation, but the majority have been robbed of stones for building later houses. About 1 m. NNE. of Latheron, the oldest of several ruins recently excavated at "The Wag" at Forse is a homestead which might date from the earliest Iron Age.

LAUDER, *Berwickshire* (Map 3, ref. 35³64⁸). Situated in Lauderdale on the Leader Water, Lauder's present main attraction for tourists is angling. Its charter as a royal burgh dates from 1502, but it claims to have been a burgh since the time of William the Lion. The church, built by Sir William Bruce in 1673, is in the shape of a Greek cross and has an octagonal steeple.

In 1483 Lauder Bridge, the site of which is not now known, was the scene of the hanging of six favourites of James III, including the architect Cochrane, at the demand of nobles headed by Archibald Douglas, Earl of Angus or "Bell-the-cat".

To the NE. of Lauder, on the Leader Water, stands Thirlestane Castle, the seat of the earls of Lauderdale. The old castle was built about 1590 for the first Baron Maitland of Thirlestane; the present building of red sandstone is very imposing, being much extended in Restoration taste for the 1st (and only) Duke of Lauderdale by Sir William Bruce, the architect of many famous houses, including Drumlanrig and the modern part of Holyrood House. The long drawing-room of Thirlestane Castle is decorated in splendid Restoration style, including a plaster ceiling executed by Dutch workmen; it is said that the decoration of this room took five years and cost £1,500, and the whole house is probably the most splendidly decorated in Scotland. It also contains a fine collection of furniture, china, and paintings, including works by Reynolds, Romney, Gainsborough, Lawrence, and others.

LAURENCEKIRK, *Kincardineshire* (Map 6, ref. 37¹77¹), was intended to be a model burgh, but it has unfortunately been built too much on the ribbon development plan, so that its built-up area seems inordinately extensive for its actual size. But its long main street is not unduly narrow, and its length is seemingly lessened by interesting features at either end.

Laurencekirk lies in the heart of the Howe of the Mearns; the rich red clay is something that has to be seen to be believed. It is so deep and spongy that it is difficult to find firm foundations for any very ambitious building, apart from the intense reluctance of local landowners to part with some of the best farming land in the world. The little town extends along a ridge within a plain, but it turns its eyes to the hills – to the distant GRAMPIANS on the W., and on the E. the nearby Hills of Garvock, which separate the Howe from the Kincardineshire coastal plain. Overlooking the town on the highest point of the Garvock range (a mere 914 ft) is the Johnston Tower, a splendid viewpoint, built by James Farquhar of Johnston in the early 19th cent. when he found he had some stones left over after building his own mansion-house. It bears an indicator placed there by the National Trust for Scotland.

The original Kirkton of St Laurence, whose church was dedicated to St Laurence of Canterbury, stood round the Chapel Knap to the E. end of the present town. Modern Laurencekirk's founder, Francis Garden, the second son of the laird of Troup in Banffshire, was a successful lawyer who became sheriff of the Mearns and, in 1764, a judge of the Court of Session as Lord Gardenstone. When he bought the estate of Johnston, Laurencekirk became his passion. He encouraged settlers, and in 1779 had the place erected into a burgh of barony. The inn, the Gardenstone Arms, which he built and furnished with a library that interested Dr Johnson in 1773, still survives at the E. end of the town. At the W. end of the main street, which is 1½ m. long, lies Kinnear Square, a pleasant village square.

The most colourful of the trades that Lord Gardenstone brought to the town, hand-loom weaving and snuffbox-making, have now died out. Charles Stiven's snuffboxes, notable because the hinge and pin are concealed, are much sought after by collectors. The future of Laurencekirk probably lies in the light industries ancillary to agriculture, for the range of farming carried on in the Howe is virtually unlimited. Fat stock is the basic preoccupation, and there are famous Shorthorn herds, but the good earth here is also used to grow peas and beans on a large scale. Tulip and daffodil bulbs are also grown, and there is poultry-farming, and sheep-farming with Border Leicester flocks.

LAURIESTON, *Kirkcudbrightshire* (Map 6, ref. 37⁵76⁶), is a pleasant village in rich farming country, a few miles W. of the S. end of Loch Ken. It was called Clachanplish until the 18th cent., when the name was changed by a member of the Laurie family who bought the estate.

It was a noted centre for Covenanters; Samuel Rutherford Crockett, the novelist, was born at Little Duchrae at the N. end of Woodhall Loch, 3 m. N. of Laurieston. There is a memorial to him in front of the small whitewashed church above the village.

LAWERS, *Perthshire* (Map 2, ref. 26⁸73⁹). Colin Campbell of Glenorchy, who was born about 1406, played an important part in apprehending the men who murdered King James I at PERTH (*see* "Scotland in History"). In recognition of these services James III in 1473 granted him the barony of Lawers. Colin left Lawers to his youngest son John, from whom are descended the Campbells of Lawers, Loudon, and Shian. In 1657 the barony was pawned to pay off debts. The residence of the

lairds of Lawers lies below the present-day inn and close to the edge of the loch and can be reached by a path from the main road. Here are the ruins of a double-storied thatched house called today the House of the Lady of Lawers, and nearby are a meal-mill, the old church of Lawers, and the numerous foundations of a small clachan. The Lady of Lawers is said to have been a Stewart of APPIN; she was the wife of a younger brother of the 6th Laird. She probably lived in the latter half of the 17th cent., as a stone over the doorway of the old church next to her house bears the date 1669. The lady was famous for her gift of second sight.
(*See also* BEN LAWERS.)

LAXFORD, *Sutherland* (Map 5, ref. 22⁴94⁶). The Laxford river and sea-loch are both in EDRACHILLIS parish. Laxford Bridge, a little over 1 m. above the mouth of the river, is at the point where the road from LAIRG and the E. divides to SCOURIE and the S. and DURNESS and the N. There are no buildings at Laxford Bridge.

This is indeed a notable salmon river and flows out of Loch Stack an outstanding angling loch containing salmon, sea-trout, and splendid brown trout. Angling rights on it are obtained only by permission.

The name Laxford derives from Norse – "lax" for salmon, "ford" from fiord.

LEADHILLS, *Lanarkshire* (Map 2, ref. 28⁸61⁵). Situated 1,350 ft above sea-level, this village claims to be one of the highest in Scotland. It is surrounded by very bare hills, which yielded lead for centuries, possibly even during the Roman occupation; the lead mines were, however, closed in 1928. Gold is also found in small quantities in the neighbouring streams; James IV encouraged Dutch and German prospectors for gold here in the 16th cent. Gold from the Lower Hills to the S. of Leadhills is included in the crown of Scotland, and when the Queen opened the Daer Water scheme in 1951 she was given a brooch of local gold.

Allan Ramsay (1686–1758), the celebrated Scottish poet, was born at Leadhills, his father being the superintendent of the mines; in 1741 the poet gave the village a circulating library, the oldest of its kind in Britain.

There is a gravestone bearing the name John Taylor and the dates 1637–1770; he is said to have worked in the lead mines for over 100 years.

LECHT, The, *Aberdeenshire/Banffshire* border (Map 6, ref. 32⁵81⁹). To pass over the Lecht, the second highest driving road in the country, is a remarkable experience. This pass connects Strathdon with STRATHAVON, beginning at Cock Bridge (1,344 ft), rising very rapidly northwards to 2,114 ft ½ m. S. of the watershed, and then descending gradually to the Conglass water and to TOMINTOUL. It is not so much that the mountains on either side are very high or shapely (they rise only a few hundred feet higher than the road itself), but that in their remote barrenness they give the impression of a landscape on the moon. Few county boundaries can be more dramatic than this one between Aberdeenshire and Banffshire: it looks like a customs station between two sovereign states. Halfway down on the E. side is a tiny loch, the Lochan gun Doimhe (Bottomless Loch), into which it is the custom of travellers to throw stones, while at the brink of the Conglass is the Well of the Lecht, with an inscription dated 1754, which tells how the 33rd Regiment made the road from that point to the SPEY. About ½ m. up the vale of the Conglass on the right can be seen the grim, factory-like building built when ironstone and manganese mines were worked there in the 18th cent., the ore being carried in panniers to smelting furnaces at Balnagown in NETHY BRIDGE. As little as 1 m. lower down the Conglass on the far side of the stream is the cottage where in June 1920 the murderer, Percy Topliss, hid and shot a police party from Tomintoul, wounding two men.

But the most interesting landmark on the whole route is at the other end of the pass. Directly facing the start of the steep climb up from Cock Bridge, and on the other side of the DON, is Corgarff Castle, now restored by the Ministry of Public Building and Works and Sir Edmund Stockdale of Delnadamph. Built before 1550, it was the scene in 1571 of the pathetic incident described in the ballad "Edom o' Gordon", in our own day the subject of Gordon Bottomley's play *Towie Castle*. The confusion with Towie Castle (a ruined 17th-cent. tower-house many miles down the Don valley) arose because the victim of the tragedy

The Lecht road

was the wife of the Forbes laird of Towie, then in occupation of Corgarff.

In November 1571, when the Forbeses and Gordons were at feud, Adam Gordon of Auchindoun (*see* DUFFTOWN), who favoured the claims of Mary Queen of Scots as against the Regency operating in the name of her son James VI, supported by the Forbeses, descended on Strathdon and put Corgarff Castle to the flames − burning to death in the process Margaret Campbell, the wife of the Forbes laird, with her family and servants to the number of 27. This tragedy was not the end of the Corgarff story. The old keep was restored by the Earl of Mar, briefly housed the Marquess of Montrose in 1645, and was burnt again by the Jacobites in 1689. It was held by the Jacobites as an arms store in 1745, and, in the snowy month of March 1746, Lord Ancrum with 400 men marched thither to take it from them. They found the place abandoned, "but so lately that the fire was still burning and no living creature in the house but a poor cat sitting by the hearth".

Two years later the Castle was taken over as a barracks for the Hanoverian troops in the disarming of the Highlands. The original tower was remodelled. Low wings were added to each gable-end, and a star-shaped curtain wall was built − pierced for musketry like the ramparts at BRAEMAR Castle. It was garrisoned until 1831, latterly by a captain, subaltern, and fifty-six men detailed to help in the suppression of whisky smuggling.

LEITH HALL, *Aberdeenshire* (Map 6, ref. 35⁴83⁰). The rather out-of-the-way situation of this charming house, near the village of Kennethmont, on the road from INSCH to HUNTLY, is probably responsible for its being less well-known than it deserves to be. For it has an appeal that is rather rare in Scotland. Although the nucleus of the building, a turreted oblong tower, was built by James Leith, 13th of his line, about the year 1650, the total aspect was transformed a century later when James's great-grandson John added a low building to form three sides of a square, with the original tower as fourth, and at each corner a dainty little pavilion of two storeys.

When he married, John carved a marriage lintel with his own name and that of his wife, Harriot Stuart of Auchluncart, and a design of true lovers' knots. That is very characteristic of the Leith and Leith-Hay lairds. They have so often been loving creators of new beauty. The last alterations to the house came when, in this century, the late Mr C. E. N. Leith-Hay, the last laird but one, built a large front hall on to the E. wing and panelled it with old oak that he had been collecting for years. Although it is the product of so many different periods, Leith Hall is an organic whole. It has an air of domestic felicity that is quite captivating in its own unpretentious and friendly way.

Aberdeen Press and Journal

Leith Hall, near Kennethmont

Since its acquisition by the National Trust for Scotland, the general public have been able to share in the beguiling intimacies of this graceful house and garden. In the oldest part there are four upper floors of little low-ceilinged chambers. In the later parts the rooms are lofty and on three upper floors. The music room houses several family treasures, including Prince Charlie's étui. On the eve of CULLODEN, Prince Charles Edward Stuart gave to Andrew Hay of Rannes, whose sister married a Leith, this elegant little miniature writing-set. It contains a tiny silver pen and pencil, a set of compasses, a measuring rule in centimetres, and a silver ink-pot with a screw top. Beside this lie a pair of silver buttons worn by the Prince, while on the wall above it hangs the pardon, with the great royal seal depending from it, granted to Andrew Hay in 1780 after years of exile and proscription. He had been excluded from the indemnity granted in 1747 to many of the Jacobites.

LENDALFOOT, *Ayrshire* (Map 2, ref. 21^459^0). This township on the inhospitable Carrick shore 7 m. S. of GIRVAN, where the Lendal water enters the sea, was at one time a haunt of smugglers, but has latterly been supported by a few families of inshore fishermen. It is now a miniature holiday resort with chalet summer-houses nestling along the base of the hills, which at this point come close to the sea. Carleton Castle, a striking ruin, is perched on a rocky ridge inland from the hamlet, and was the ancestral home of the Cathcarts of Carleton, a family whose influence in Ayrshire

at one time rivalled that of the Kennedies. They were extensive landowners, being at one time Lairds of KILLOCHAN, and at Auchendrane near AYR.

LENNOXLOVE, *East Lothian* (Map 3, ref. 35^267^2). Formerly called Lethington, this beautiful house near HADDINGTON belonged to the Maitland family from the 14th cent. The main tower was built in the 15th cent. on an L-plan in a plain style. The house is connected with the story of Mary Stuart, Queen of Scots, for the Maitland of Lethington of the time was her secretary; her death mask is in the hall of the house.

In 1682 the line of the Maitlands failed, and the estate was sold to Frances Duchess of Lennox and Richmond, "La Belle Stuart", the mistress of Charles II. Despite what must have been disapproval at the time, the name of the house was changed in 1704 to Lennoxlove, thus poetically recognizing the fact of Royal Stuart amorousness. The house contains various gifts from Charles II, but the famous silver toilet service is in the Royal Scottish Museum.

Lennoxlove, in its fine park, is now the home of the Duke of Hamilton.

LENNOXTOWN, *Stirlingshire* (Map 2, ref. 26^367^8), was originally called the Clachan of Campsie. At the old parish church, abandoned in 1828, is the graveyard with the Lennox family vault and some early 17th-cent. Kincaid stones.

The new village of Lennoxtown, or Newtown of Campsie, started with the introduction of calico-printing in 1785–6, and some examples of its industrial housing date back to about 1795. A nail-works has now been established.

About 1¾ m. NW. of Lennoxtown is Lennox Castle. Erected between 1837 and 1847, after a design of David Hamilton of GLASGOW, it commands an extensive view of the area.

LENY, Pass of, *Perthshire* (Map 2, ref. 25⁹71⁰). This short, narrow, attractive, and romantic pass was shared by road and rail going northwards from CALLANDER into the Central Highlands, but this once popular line is now closed. The R. Leny leaves Loch LUBNAIG on its short journey to join its sister, the Teith, just outside Callander and by means of this pass. It is a typical rapid, tumbling, Highland stream – neither river nor burn. And on its passage southward it goes over the picturesque Falls of Leny, to which many visitors come. At the right season of the year you may see salmon attempting these falls in their journey N. to their breeding-ground in Loch Lubnaig, or even farther.

The old Leny Castle stands at the meeting-place of the rivers Teith and Leny. On a narrow neck of land between the rivers is the burial-ground of the Buchanans of Leny; this burial-ground includes the grave of Dugald Buchanan, the famous Gaelic poet. The Buchanans, usually thought of as a Lowland family, certainly inhabited this part of the Southern Highlands for many centuries, and there are plenty of them still there.

At the N. end of the Pass of Leny, and just where the river leaves Loch Lubnaig, is the ancient chapel of St Bride. Attached to this chapel is a small burying-ground in which are the graves of no fewer than six generations of McKinlays, ancestors of President McKinlay of the United States of America. The chapel was vividly described by Walter Scott in his *The Legend of Montrose*, but it had already begun to fall into disrepair. Upon the centenary of Scott's death, the citizens of Callander subscribed to a fund to repair the chapel as a memorial to the great Scottish novelist and poet.

LERWICK, *Shetland* (Map 8, ref. 44⁸14¹), the capital of SHETLAND Northern Islands (*see* "The Shape of Scotland"), is the most northern town in the British Isles, and is the one that to the eye of a newly-arrived visitor looks most foreign. It is in fact geographically nearer to Bergen in Norway than to any considerable town in the United Kingdom.

Lerwick looks foreign in a number of indefinable ways, but mostly because of various houses that are built into the sea rather in the Venetian manner, and because of the large paving-stones that lie between facing houses in the narrower and older streets. Such streets seem all pavement and no thoroughfare or,

alternatively, all thoroughfare and no pavement. The effect is odd but attractive.

SCALLOWAY, 6½ m. W., was the earlie[r] capital of the islands under the bad old rule o[f] the Scottish Earl Patrick Stewart, in the 17t[h] cent. Later, Lerwick imperceptibly drifte[d] from being a fishing village with a fine harbour into being the county town of Shetland. It ha[s] good comfortable hotels, up-to-date shops, an[d] a few cafés and eating houses. Its port connect[s] it with the Scottish mainland, and buses ru[n] regularly to SUMBURGH, where there is a[n] airport with daily connections to GLASGO[W] and thence, if necessary, to London. It is easie[r] to get from Lerwick to the main towns o[f] Scotland and England by air than it is fro[m] many Scottish or English mainland districts.

Though Lerwick was anciently but a fishin[g] village, its fine harbour, protected by the islan[d] of BRESSAY, made it an important place of cal[l] for ships. King Haakon of Norway, when h[e] made his massive attack on Scotland in 1263 which culminated in his defeat at the Battle o[f] LARGS (*see* "Scotland in History"), rested hi[s] armada at Lerwick. The town and harbou[r] were not, however, heard much of in British history until after the Union of the Crowns in 1603. In the reign of Charles II, it began to be recognized as a fortification base for the British Navy in northern waters. After having been forced by the Dutch during the wars of Charles's time, it was eventually restored and rebuilt in the comparatively peaceful era of George III.

From that period it has steadily grown in size and prosperity. If that prosperity has slightly declined in the years after the Second World War, it is partly because of the difficulties that have arisen in Scottish inshore fishing, and partly because of the centripetal force that is drawing life away from all, or nearly all, out-lying places in Britain to the great centres.

Of the old fishing village, little if anything remains. In the centre of Lerwick, and particularly by the harbour, you may, however, see the stout origins of the town that began to arise in the 17th cent., and that grew through-out the 18th and the 19th cents. This town is massively and compactly built in stone, and the word compactly is significant. Mention has already been made of the narrow streets with paving running directly between facing houses. You understand the reason for this compact huddling together of dwelling places in Lerwick if you have ever faced the full fury of a Shetland gale. Under such an assault it used to be necessary for people to pass among each other's houses with as little exposure as possible.

It was the habit of the Scottish lairds in the old days, when they owned land in the country-side of Shetland, to have a town house in Lerwick, mainly to escape from the wind. The lairds of Hayfield, for instance (only a few miles away from Lerwick), felt they could not endure the winter winds alone in their massively

Lerwick: Up-Helly-Aa

built country seat, and had a town house that is now the Queen's Hotel.

There is little of architectural style or beauty in Lerwick (nothing of the faint Regency remains still lingering in Stornoway), but there is a distinct appeal in the practical stolidity of the building in this, Britain's most northern town. It is not only practical; it is original and refreshing to look at.

The sea is ever present in Lerwick, and through the sea the outer world. Maybe, owing to the decline of Scottish inshore fishing, there are fewer native herring-boats, but vessels from all northern European countries use Lerwick as a base during their fishing in the northern seas. You can hear many foreign tongues on the quayside and in the streets of Lerwick, including Russian. Many a foreign vessel in trouble in these sometimes tempestuous seas has owed its rescue to the lifeboat service of Lerwick.

Modern Lerwick has spread well out from the huddled compact harbour, the stone-built town of the 19th cent. There are suburbs in the

Lerwick harbour and town

modern manner spreading inward. Television arrived in Lerwick in 1964, but, up to the present, there is little sign that this is preventing the Lerwick people from making their own entertainment. Lerwick is a musical town.

One cannot leave the subject of Shetland's capital without mention of the festival of "Up-Helly-Aa" that takes place on the last Tuesday in January, and is intended, in the dark short days of the northern winter, to celebrate the returning sun that will burgeon in six months into the beneficence of the "simmer dim" (*see* SHETLAND). This festival gives the modern Lerwick people the chance to go for a short while (as far as costume is concerned, and to a lesser degree in behaviour) "all Viking again".

The festival is modern in origin, but ancient in the evocation of Shetland's Norse past. Perhaps some citizens in the future will stage a festival recalling their even remoter ancestors the Picts, or the unnamed builders of JARLS-HOF who lived in these islands long before the Vikings touched them. One thing is certain. No Shetland festival will ever be staged in Lerwick to recall the memory of the oppressive Scottish lairds of the time when Scotland took over from the Norsemen. Indeed, there is now a federalist movement on foot in Shetland to give it more independence from Scotland.

LESLIE, *Fife* (just NW. of GLENROTHES). This is a small stone-built industrial town. At the E. end of the town is "Town Green", used for sports and games, and the church, rebuilt in 1869, but said to be the original of "Christ's Kirk on the Green", a 15th-cent. poem. On the green is a "bull-stone", worn dramatically thin in the middle, where the bulls were chained when baiting was in progress.

The traditional industry was once textiles alone, but it now includes plastics, pens, and paper-mills, which are mostly situated out of sight of the town in the valley of Leven. Some of the interesting small 17th-cent. houses are being restored for modern use, and there is some very imaginative new housing, making the most of the lovely view to the Lomond Hills.

To the E. of the town is Leslie House, formerly the home of the earls of Rothes. The house was built during the late 17th cent. as an attempt to rival in magnificence EDINBURGH's Holyroodhouse, and had a picture gallery 3 ft longer than the one at Holyrood. It was originally built round a quadrangle, but three sides were burnt down in 1763. The remainder is now a Church of Scotland Eventide Home.

LESMAHAGOW, *Lanarkshire* (Map 2, ref. 28¹64⁰). The village of Lesmahagow stands on the W. bank of the small R. Nethan; evidence of prehistoric dwellers has been found at the quarry at Creamery Brae nearby.

Benedictine monks travelled from KELSO and established a priory on the lands here granted by David I in 1144; the monks of Lesmahagow became well known as pioneers of fruit-growing in the CLYDE valley. After the Reformation, Lesmahagow became a centre for the Covenanters. David Steel, a farmer in the district at Skellyhill, was shot in 1686, and there is a monument that commemorates him at his farm. At Auchingelloch another monument recalls the sufferings of other Covenanters here.

1856 saw the first coal working at Auchenheath, 3 m. NW. of Lesmahagow. It is still productive, but the district continues in its main character as a farming and fruit-growing part of Scotland.

LETHENDY, *Perthshire* (Map 6, ref. 31³74²). To the SE. of the church in the village of Kirkton of Lethendy is the Tower of Lethendy. This is today a private residence, but its Victorian aspect masks an earlier L-plan house of the late 16th or early 17th cent. Indeed, there are indications that it may at one time have been surrounded by a moat. Graham of Claverhouse was descended from a daughter of Heron of Lethendy.

LEUCHARS, *Fife* (Map 6, ref. 34⁵72¹). The village of Leuchars stands 1 m. NE. of a celebrated railway station – Leuchars Junction, at which generations of golfers changed for ST ANDREWS until that line was closed.

On a hillock in the centre of the village is the church, a particularly fine specimen of Norman work, with a semicircular apse and two arches and two arcades. It was built by Saier de Quincy, who died in 1220; but in the 17th cent. a heavy tower and a belfry were added. Inside, the church is carved with grotesque heads, and in the sanctuary are Crusaders' crosses.

The R.A.F. station at Leuchars includes bases for R.A.F. volunteer mountain rescue and R.A.F. air-sea rescue organizations.

In the immediate neighbourhood is Earlshall, the house begun in 1546 by Sir William Bruce and finished in the 17th cent. by his grandson. It was restored by Robert Lorimer in 1891, that well-known Scottish architect's first job. There remains much original work still in the interior, including the famous painted ceiling dated 1620 in the upper hall.

About 2 m. S. of Leuchars is Guard Bridge. It was once a hamlet, but paper-mills made it into an industrial village. The modern bridge over the Eden stands beside one built by Bishop Wardlaw in the 14th cent.

Leuchars Junction is said to be the most wind-swept station in Scotland. A citizen of St Andrews, having made a round-the-world trip, and having been asked how he enjoyed it, replied, "Ay, it was fine once we got past Leuchars."

LEVEN, *Fife* (Map 3, ref. 33⁸70⁰). This resort and port on Largo Bay gradually grew outwards from a small weaving village. Since the 19th cent., the chief industries have been coal-mining and engineering, but despite industrialization the town has kept a pleasing appearance and attracts visitors. Many fine golfers have come from Leven, which possesses good links.

At the N. end of the town is the Durie estate, the property in the 17th cent. of Sir Alexander Gibson of Durie, Lord President of the Court of Session. The story of his kidnapping is told in Sir Walter Scott's *Christie's Well*.

LEVEN, Loch, *Kinross-shire* (Map 3, ref. 31⁵70¹), is 8½ m. in perimeter and is circular. It is especially noted for its angling, and for a particular breed of trout – Loch Leven trout – known all over the world. This sheet of water is also one of Europe's most important wildfowl resorts, and is now a nature reserve; there are geese roosting in the winter, and nesting sites for ducks on the islands and in sheltered marshes in the summer. The loch contains seven islands. The largest (80 acres) is St Serfs, on which is a ruined priory, possibly founded in the 9th cent.

Castle Island has been much increased in size by drainage operations. The tower dating from the late 14th or early 15th cent., with 16th-cent. additions includes earlier stonework, perhaps part of the castle beseiged by the English in 1325. Mary Queen of Scots was imprisoned here after Carberry in 1567–8, and escaped with the help of young Willy Douglas, who locked everyone into the great hall and dropped the keys of the castle into the loch. Those same keys were found some 300 years later.

A place of historical interest and considerable natural beauty, Loch Leven has perhaps become most famous for its unique trout-angling facilities. International trout-angling competitions are held here. In summer there is a ferry service to Castle Island from KINROSS. E. of the loch there is an important gliding station at Portmoak, which enjoys unique air currents created by the Cleish Hills to the S. and the Lomond Hills to the N.

LEVERBURGH, *Inverness-shire* (Map 4, ref. 10²88⁶), is a small town and fishing port on HARRIS, one of the islands in the Outer Hebrides (*see* "The Shape of Scotland"). Leverburgh presents a pathetic, if interesting, remnant of Lord Leverhulme's efforts to put the "Long Island" on the world fishing map. After he had retired in understandable dudgeon from LEWIS, he concentrated his efforts on the contiguous island of Harris. At Leverburgh, he endeavoured to set up a fishing port to trade with the Western world, and built houses to contain what he hoped would be the growing community. The old name of the village, "Obbe", seemed to him brusquely monosyllabic. At the suggestion of the islanders it was renamed Leverburgh. The name has stuck; so has the original condition of the little port at the head of Loch Obbe. There is an odd confusion of houses, some ancient, some relics of Leverhulme's hopes, some modern Swedish. The place has the remnants of activity in surroundings of considerable beauty, the beauty of Harris's western side.

LEWIS, Butt of, *Ross and Cromarty* (Map 4, ref. 15²96⁶), is on the Island of LEWIS in the Outer Hebrides (*see* "The Shape of Scotland"). The only building proper to stand at this most northerly point of the island, and of all the main Hebrides, is a lighthouse. It crowns this meeting-place of apparently indomitable rock and raging sea 30 m. NE. of STORNOWAY. It is all the more impressive in that, on the land here, heather gives place to grass.

The nearest regularly inhabited dwelling-places to the Butt are in the small and attractive port of Ness, just SE. of the extreme Lewis northward point. The fisherfolk here, as many visitors have remarked, show the signs of their Viking ancestry in their Scandinavian physiognomy. Scandinavian too is their occasional habit of painting the outside of their houses in the gayest of colours.

Just SW. of the Butt is the mysterious small isle of Luchubran, traditionally supposed to have been inhabited by pygmies. The small bones discovered there are not (as was believed) the skeletal remains of little men, but of animals eaten by an early Christian anchorite. Luchubran is but one example (and an impressive one) of the innumerable remote places on the Northern Hebrides chosen in antiquity by nameless hermits for flight from man and communion with God.

1 m. S. of the Butt lies the oddly named village of Europie (possibly deriving from both Norse and Gaelic). Amidst a nest of ancient teampulls, there is the chapel dedicated to St Moluag (*see* LISMORE). In the 1920s it was roofed over and restored by the Scottish Episcopalian Church, and is occasionally used for Christian worship. Stark, simple, tastefully restored, save for an obtrusively large pulpit, it is well worth a visit.

LEWIS, Island of, sometimes called the Lews, *Ross and Cromarty* (Map 4, ref. 13⁰93⁰), is the most northerly and the largest of the Outer Hebrides (see "The Shape of Scotland"). About 30 m. long NNE. to SSW., 14 m. broad at its widest part, and, on the average, some 35 m. from the mainland, it is in many respects unique. It does not merely touch but is firmly attached to another island. HARRIS, its sister, is solidly clamped on to it, not by an isthmus, but by a land-breadth of some 14 m. Yet these contiguous islands, as has already been said under HARRIS, are indubitably two entities within the Hebrides. Lewis is assigned to the

Ian Smith
Lewis: the traditional spinning-wheel

County of Ross and Cromarty, Harris to Inverness-shire.

Harris has considerable scenic effect; Lewis has less. Her insistent demands upon the attention of any visitor with ears as well as eyes comes from the quality of the people, the Lewis folk themselves. Even amidst the highly individual Celtic community they are remarkable. He would be a dull man who did not find the Lewis people exhilarating – and exhilarating in the modern context.

The two contiguous islands form the most important living entity in the Scottish Gaelic life of today – Lewis in particular. It is for this reason that we have given, in sum, a fuller

Sheep-shearing on Lewis
J. L. Rodger

entry to Lewis and Harris than to most islands and have stressed the present rather than the past life. The past will be touched on more fully in STORNOWAY and in other minor entries in connection with the Northern Outer Isles.

Lewis is unique also in the fact that it is the only large piece of well-populated, self-contained land anywhere – and this is not forgetting Ireland – that is consciously yet naturally and vitally Gaelic in culture and in native speech. We are not forgetting also the Southern Outer Hebrides, which are equally Gaelic; but these, some of which have already been mentioned, are, in the face of economic and political difficulties, hanging on to Gaeldom with admirable tenacity – but only by their teeth. The economy of Lewis is good, and the force of its internal politics is strong. This, despite the attacks on Scottish Gaeldom from without, and the internal difficulties that have beset that culture everywhere, Lewis included.

Moreover, the Gaelic life in Lewis is gearing itself to the future; it is taking on the latter half of the 20th cent. in contemporary terms. To the confirmed lover of Gaeldom, this attunement of Gaelicism to the modern world sometimes may appear brash, but more often enlivening.

Lewis's assailment of our age within the Gaelic context has been in existence since the late Lord Leverhulme's proprietorship of the island just after the First World War (of which slightly more below); but this is not a case of *post hoc ergo propter hoc*. Lewis was vitally Gaelic long before Leverhulme gave it a sadly misplaced, but highly effective, 20th-cent. stimulus to turn the island's vitality towards the markets of the outside world.

Since Leverhulme, the island has had its ups and downs, but the most effective element in its upward contemporary trend has been the return to Lewis of young natives of the island who made their way in the outer world and who have come back to the Outer Hebrides not in the least forgetting their Gaelic, yet armed with what one is regretfully compelled in this context to call the "know-how" of modern life. They have been in commerce, industry, journalism, and many other fields on the mainland of Scotland, and far farther than that, and have returned to lend their acquired knowledge to the life of the island in its traditional businesses of cloth-weaving, fishing, tourism, and other elements. This development has been entirely post-war and, for the most part, within the last ten years.

Lewis is further unique in producing by itself, in its capital, Stornoway, a spontaneous Gaelic town. The Gael, as has been said elsewhere in this book, is essentially not a townmaker. He does not care for his cheek to be too near his neighbour's jowl; and elsewhere in Gaeldom cities and towns have been imposed either by the Norse or the Saxon. For once, and for the most part, the Gael (be it admitted, fortified by Viking blood) has done the job for himself in the capital of Lewis. Today, Stornoway may be the meeting-place of Gaelic and English. But in its building and making it was natively Lewis and Gaelic.

Except in the extreme SW., Lewis is largely flat and, save where the people of the characteristically scattered townships have been reclaiming the heather-land by re-seeding, it is, anywhere away from the coast, definitely moorland. "Defiantly" is perhaps a better word. On a wet day (and, like anywhere else in the West of Scotland, Lewis can be very wet), the huge central parts of Lewis present the appearance of a drenched and unconquerable Sahara. On the many fine days of the spring and summer, this same expanse of moorland has the soft beauty of the W. Highlands of Scotland, but it does not appear any the less unconquerable. It is all the more striking, then, that all over the island the population have recently been making some notable dents in this apparent inconquerability by the modern process of re-seeding. This development has been more properly dealt with under the entry on BARVAS, a rural township within Lewis, interestingly and anciently connected with re-seeding.

Who knows but that this popular policy of re-seeding may eventually lead people into the centre? For the present, however, and for many previous centuries, almost the entire population has lived in townships on or near the coast, and, for the most part, the E. coast. This is partly because the drainage is better there, the land less naturally intractable, and, of course, because this is a seafaring people who, despite many setbacks (some of them politically contrived by wealthy combines on the mainland of Britain), have lived by fishing in these fish-abounding seas.

Apart from fishing, some 30,000 population of this Gaelic island lives by crofting and by the growing and extremely important business of cloth-weaving. It is, by the way, from the whole of the contiguous islands of Lewis and Harris that Harris tweed comes, and from this Long Island alone. It should be stressed that this weaving is essentially a peasant industry conducted by peasants in their own homes. The wool is, as we shall see when we come to Stornoway, prepared for them by modern industrial process in the charge of Lewismen in the tweed-mills of the larger centres (principally Stornoway), but the weaving is done by peasant men and peasant women by their own firesides. The economy of Lewis is a peasant economy, perhaps the only effective example in the United Kingdom. Hence its strength. The word "peasant" has today lost some of its good, strong meaning. We use it here in the best sense, and are fortified in our use by the Lewis Association Reports (*see below*), which quote it proudly.

This is the place to mention the effect of the

Above *Pitlochry: the hydro-electric dam* (*see p. 384*)   *Scottish Tourist Board*

Below *The hydro-electric dam on the River Shin* (*see p. 414*)   *Scottish Tourist Board*

ate Lord Leverhulme when, immediately after he First World War, he bought the island and endeavoured, in the end unsuccessfully, to influence its economy. Let it be enough to state here the following cardinal facts.

(1) Leverhulme bought Lewis primarily because he was in love with the island and liked and admired the people. (2) This did not prevent his incurably imperial business-mind from attempting to "better the lot" of the people with grandiose schemes for the marketing of their produce throughout the world. This inevitably entailed, though he tried to avoid it, some regimentation of this highly individual people. (3) The people of Lewis on the whole liked and admired Leverhulme, but were suspicious of this regimentation, and in their hearts supported the returning ex-servicemen who took active steps to hold the land against the dream-inspired proprietor. (4) The head-on clash between them and Leverhulme was, if not incited, at least made inescapable by the actions of politicians and civil servants on the mainland. (5) Upon his defeat and withdrawal from Lewis, Leverhulme left a testimony of his love for the place by magnanimous gifts to the island, principally in Stornoway. It should be added that these gifts, while coming from a warm heart, were also designed to leave the politicians, and those who had actively opposed him on the island, with some difficult problems to solve. (6) While Leverhulme was completely defeated and withdrew via Harris into the security of death, he unquestionably re-animated the island economy, giving the people less insular ideas, while not reducing their essential individuality.

It is not a fact but a legitimate speculation that, had politics not entered to hasten the clash, and had both Leverhulme and the Lewismen had time to know each other better, some compromise might just possibly have been reached between a likeable, warm-hearted man and a likeable, dignified, and intelligent peasantry. But it was not to be.

The visitor to Lewis who is prepared to take life in not too much of a hurry is likely to share Leverhulme's admiration and fondness for the people, while doing no more than smiling at their eccentricities and failings. They have the qualities of peasantry all the world over, good and bad – frugality, caution, conservatism in life if not in politics, suspicion, and hospitality. Unlike some peasants elsewhere, however, they have little sense of beauty in visible things. Their houses are scattered far apart on the bleak moorland or on the forbidding coast. When antique, as in the case of the converted thatched "black houses", they may appear to the city-dweller to be positively squalid. But a closer inspection may remove or modify this impression. When modern, their houses are usually unimaginative square boxes. Having committed that sentence to paper, one might well pause to ask whether the houses of any

modern suburb under the spread of our present subtopia are any better.

In one respect, however, many houses of the Lewis peasantry, especially in the northern rural districts, display a quality of imagination unknown in mainland suburbia. In nearly every village you will find some houses that, on their outsides, successfully attempt to defy the general architectural bleakness. Against a background of white, black, or grey, the owners have painted doors, windows, and even portions of the walls in the gayest scarlet, blue, or unashamed yellow. It should be remembered that Lewis, more than any other part of Gaeldom, is strongly impregnated with Norse blood. Those who have seen the Faroe Islands or the W. coast of Norway will be familiar with this bold painting of the outsides of even the humblest houses. It is significant that in the more purely Celtic portions of the mainland, or in the inner islands less directly touched by Norse influence, such mural painting is unknown.

Having said that the Lewis people have the world-wide qualities, both good and bad, of most peasantries, one thing should be added – that, in company with their slightly different neighbours in the Southern Outer Hebrides, few peasantries anywhere have the same degree of natural courtesy and good manners. It is not something assumed, it is native to them. Native too in many is a hunger for knowledge, which they ardently satisfy. The Lewisman is often very well read, and expresses himself notably in speech and writing. The local paper, the *Stornoway Gazette*, makes good reading; its subject-matter is far from parochial, yet provides an individual point of view.

The style of the intermittently published *Lewis Association Reports* is sometimes in enviably excellent English. Particularly notable was the Association's report dealing, coolly yet devastatingly, with a hostile and inaccurate book on the Outer Isles written by a disillusioned sentimentalist turned cynic by the mockery of others in print and on the radio – a book published in London after the last war. The report on that book is journalism at its most trenchant, yet wholly dignified.

Beneath the courtesy and the perhaps unexpected erudition, the perceptive visitor may be aware of a strain of wildness in the Lewisman that may discover itself in sardonic wit or sometimes, in unusual local circumstances, in less acceptable forms. This strain of wildness almost certainly derives from the Norse blood, and contrasts with the gentleness of the equally brave but quieter inhabitants of the more purely Celtic parts of Scotland. It has been well said of the Lewisman that he is a "law-abiding anarchist".

The people of Lewis are intensely religious, and are as devoted to their varying forms of Presbyterianism as are the Southern Hebrideans to Catholicism. In their vivid and affecting

Plate 12   Queensferry: the Forth Road Bridge (see p. 392)
Shell-Mex and B.P.

zeal for their faith, especially in the stricter denominations, may be perceived a touch of that Norse characteristic (we shall not in this context say wildness, but rather extravagance) mingling with Celticism. The atmosphere of the Sabbath Day in any Lewis township, and particularly in Stornoway, is palpable. It is something you feel inescapably in the very air.

The Lewis people are great fighters for what they believe in, and sometimes win their battles outright against formidable odds.

In 1960 the late Mr Kenneth Macrae, the well-known Stornoway Free Kirk minister, led a campaign against the Government scheme to establish at enormous cost, on the E Y E isthmus, an aerodrome that would not only sweep away many well-loved houses, but would act as a base for nuclear warheads, thus bringing Lewis into the range of a prime military objective for enemy attention. He carried the whole of Lewis with him, and the Government withdrew.

We may recall that a few years earlier, that other indomitable fighter, Father John Morrison, on the Catholic island of South U I S T, endeavoured without success (though he did manage to modify its less acceptable concomitants) to prevent the establishment of a rocket range there. You may deduce from this that the Uist people are not such "bonny fighters" nor so far-seeing as the Lewismen. Or you may prefer to say that the Uist objectors had already made the Government sensitive to Hebridean feelings, and that this led the way to Mr Macrae's consequently resounding victory.

You might, however, prefer a metaphor. You might say that the nuclear schemers in Whitehall were subjected to a Hebridean pincer movement of highly individual and characteristic objection. One claw of the pincer came from the S. of the islands in Catholic objection, which did at least reduce the scale of the Uist schemes. The other claw, which later bit more deeply and effectively, came from the N., from the "Lews", and was impelled by the oratory and force of the Free Kirk. It sank deep enough to succeed. If you do use this metaphor, you may reflect that this pincer operation was unique. Seldom if ever have Rome and Geneva combined in Celtic hands to make so severe a dent in Saxon subtopia.

These are matters of speculation. The facts for visitors are these. There is a daily steamer service to Stornoway from the mainland and a daily air service from G L A S G O W. A car-ferry service from the mainland has come to T A R-B E R T in Harris by which motorists may visit all the Long Island, including Lewis, without delay and in comfort. Stornoway has hotels and guest houses. In various other townships, some Lewis people take in visitors for "bed and meals".

Brown-trout fishing in Lewis is good though scattered, and is extremely cheap. Salmon fishing is of the first class, and the sea-trout

angling excellent. This is more expensive, an you should lay your plans for it in advance. Th fishing in the sea round Lewis is abundan There are many fine beaches of Hebridean san near Stornoway, and in other places, wher you may enjoy bathing in the sea. Even in thes northern latitudes, the water is surprisingl mild owing to the beneficial ministrations of th Gulf Stream. The roads across the moorland o round the island, though not wide, have goo motoring surfaces, and it is possible easily an comfortably to travel all round Lewis's highl indented coast. This improvement in roads ha been designed to meet the car-ferry traffic.

The language of the people should present n difficulty. Of the 30,000 inhabitants practicall all adults are bi-lingual. The few monoglo Gaelic-speakers are old and tend to be secluded For those curious enough to be interested i such a phenomenon in such a vigorousl Gaelic island, there are a few among th residents who are monoglot English speakers.

At any rate English will get you everywhere Indeed, so widely do the interests of Stornoway extend that it would be possible for Italian French, Polish, or Pakistani monoglots to fin someone to speak to in their own languages ir that vital little town.

LILLIESLEAF, *Roxburghshire* (Map 3, ref 35^362^5), is a secluded village lying by the Al Water; its houses used to have pretty thatched roofs; which attracted artists.

To the SW. of the village, the mansion house of Riddell stood until it was burnt down in 1943. The Riddell family dominated the distric for seven centuries until the early 19th cent To the NE. of this site are the remains of a medieval motte enclosed by a rectangular bailey; this motte is crowned by a tower erected in 1885.

LINCLUDEN, *Dumfriesshire* (Map 2, ref. 29^657^8). A Benedictine nunnery was founded here by Uchtred, Lord of Galloway, in 1164. In the 1390s it was suppressed by Archibald the Grim, the 3rd Earl of Douglas, who established a college of eight secular canons under a provost. Though some of the 12th-cent. structure remains, the greater part of the ruins represent the florid French Gothic of the Tournois craftsmen brought here by Princess Margaret, daughter of Robert II, and widow of Earl Douglas; she was also Countess of Touraine (as well as Lady of Galloway and Annandale by right of her late husband). The ruin, though small, is one of the most beautiful pieces of decorated architecture left in Scotland; the heraldic ornament and Princess Margaret's tomb are particularly notable. The tower, like the provost's house, is 16th cent. A Norman motte, later landscaped as a processional way, adjoins the church. Terracing preserves the outline of the medieval knot-garden of the college. The whole group lies in a ovely wooded setting at the junction of the Cluden Water and the R. Nith.

Lincluden is now a part of suburban DUMRIES, and usually has to be approached through a suburb. That suburb, a development of 1938 onwards, is well designed and harmonizes with the medieval work of this beautiful place.

LINDORES, *Fife* (Map 3, ref. 32⁷71⁷). The present village of Lindores is near the small reed-surrounded Lindores Loch. But the abbey (or the remains of it), connected with the name of Lindores, is situated 2½ m. to the NW. and very near to NEWBURGH. The abbey was founded by David, Earl of Huntingdon, in 1178 for Benedictine monks, and was of great importance until the Reformation, being often visited by kings. The monks promoted agriculture on lands favourably situated on the banks of the TAY estuary.

LINLITHGOW, *West Lothian* (Map 2, ref. 30⁰67⁷), is an ancient royal burgh containing one of Scotland's four royal palaces, and is the county town of West Lothian.

There was some kind of royal residence and a church here as early as the 12th cent. The present palace was started by James I of Scotland, enlarged by his successors, completed with architectural embellishments by James V, and was much frequented by the Stuarts. Both James V and his daughter Mary Queen of Scots were born here.

Adjoining the palace is St Michael's Church, founded by David I, although the existing fabric dates mainly from rebuilding in the 15th cent., restored recently with funds from a public appeal.

Distilling and paper-making are two of the principal industries of the modern town. Its attractive and convenient situation has stimulated considerable private-housing development, largely occupied by the staffs of new oil and motor industries in GRANGEMOUTH and BATHGATE.

The long, narrow High Street, which forms part of the busy EDINBURGH–STIRLING road, has been widened to ease the flow of traffic. This process has opened up new views of the palace on its knoll above Linlithgow Loch. In addition to its protective function as a bird sanctuary, the loch serves as an inland, winter rendezvous for dinghy sailors. Nos. 44–48 High Street, typical 16th- or early 17th-cent. houses, restored by the National Trust for Scotland, form one of the few surviving domestic links with the town's period of royal patronage.

Every year, however, antiquity is formally celebrated with the riding of the marches on the Tuesday following the second Thursday in June, when Linlithgow has an air of hectic carnival, and traffic has patiently to await the pleasure of the burghers. There is a fine Augustan Town Hall built in the style of the Edinburgh New Town.

LINWOOD, *Renfrewshire* (Map 2, ref. 24⁴66⁴), developed as an industrial village near the large cotton-mill built in 1792; a paper-mill was established in 1874. A large company, established here in 1947 and making a variety of railway rolling-stock and motor-car bodies, combined in 1960 with a famous motor-car manufacturer to produce cars at Linwood. Steel from GARTCOSH and tyres from INCHINNAN have been used. The town at Linwood is to accommodate 5,000 people for the new jobs provided by this project.

LISMORE, Island of, *Argyll* (Map 1, ref. 18⁵74⁰), is one of the Inner Hebrides (*see* "The Shape of Scotland"). This little island, celebrated in Scottish ecclesiastical history and in the story of Gaelic, lies in the lower waters of the sea-arm of Loch Linnhe, and at the SW. mouth of the Great Glen that divides Scotland from NE. to SW. About 6 m. NW. of OBAN, less than a furlong from the mainland at its nearest point, surrounded splendidly by the peaks of BENDERLOCH, Appin, and Morven to the E., NE., and N., and facing the heights of the island of MULL to the SW., with as much land around it as water, it only just attains its island and Hebridean status. Having attained it, however, it eminently justifies itself as one of the most pleasing of the Inner Isles.

It is popularly supposed to derive its name from the Gaelic for "Great Garden", but more probably the Gaelic for "Great Enclosure", coming from the ecclesiastical and monastic past, is its true derivation. "Great Garden" is, however, a suitable name indeed for this fertile green isle of loam soil resting on a bed of fruitful limestone. It nowhere reaches a greater height than 417 ft, is about 10 m. long and 1½ m. broad; but, as the island's historian, Ian Carmichael, Minister of Lismore, has put it, "Lismore provides a grandstand view of some of the finest scenery – landscape and seascape – in all Scotland".

It was Christianized in the 6th cent. by St Moluag, a contemporary or near predecessor of St Columba, but, being of Pictish association, he was not of the community of Irish Celtic saints. The unedifying if amusing tales of the rivalry between the two men are probably the invention of their followers. After the establishment of the Scottish episcopate in obedience to Rome, the diocese of Argyll had its cathedral in the 13th cent. on Lismore. No more than traces of this small cathedral may be seen; but Lismore was once of considerable ecclesiastical importance.

The island touched obliquely if sensationally the course of Western literature by the discovery of *The Book of the Dean of Lismore* (d. 1551). This fortified the claims of James

Macpherson's *Ossian* to be founded on genuine Gaelic ancient oral tradition.

Lismore has a good harbour in Port Ramsay to the N., and boats touch also at the Oban end. It is the resort of vigorous holiday-makers who like to land at one end of the island and walk to the other. Its now depleted native population lives on farming and grazing. Their attractive white crofts and farms scatter the island's greenery in a pleasing fashion.

LIVINGSTON, *West Lothian* (Map 2, ref. 30³66⁸), Scotland's fourth New Town, was designated in 1965 with an area of 6,700 acres. It lies 15 m. from EDINBURGH and 30 m. from GLASGOW on the M8 Motorway between the two cities and at the hub of Central Scotland's road system, the focal point of an 80-sq.-m. region and the centre of a network of major roads. (The Scottish New Town policy is described under CUMBERNAULD.)

In 1962 the population of the designated area was about 2,000, most of it in one community, and there was little employment apart from farming. By May 1971 the population had reached 14,000, 4,721 council and 44 private houses had been completed, and there were 24 new industrial firms operating, occupying 1,212,119 sq. ft of floor space and employing almost 3,000 people. Many more factories and houses were under construction. The target intake population is 70,000 by 1985, and planning is on the assumption of 100,000 population by the end of the century.

A basic requirement of the New Town was that it should take a large proportion of the Glasgow "overspill". Under the Glasgow 20-year redevelopment scheme for sub-standard property, it was estimated that 100,000 families would be displaced and only some 40,000 re-housed there; moreover by 1965 there would be a need for 1,000 more houses a year outside Glasgow than the three other New Towns and other communities could accommodate – hence Livingston, with 80 per cent of its population coming from Glasgow.

Livingston has two noteworthy original features, one concerning its churches and the other its street-naming. Designated as an "area of ecumenical experiment", the participating churches – the Church of Scotland and the Episcopal, Congregational, and Methodist Churches – undertook to plan together and share whatever church buildings were required. The first church was erected by the Church of Scotland, and other churches are being built, but already the experiment has developed far beyond the joint occupation of buildings with team ministry and joint pastoral care. The Roman Catholic and Baptist Churches, the Free Church of Scotland, and the Salvation Army are also active. The street-naming system makes it simple to find any address, in any of the four districts of the town. Thus in Howden East all streets are "avenues" with Canadian names such as "Toronto Avenue"; in Craigs hill West they are "streets" with Australian names; in Almond West Scottish loch names are used for "walks"; in Almond East we find Scottish rivers and "drives"; and i Almond South the writers come into their own with "courts", such as Burns Court With a strong emphasis on social relations social life, and recreation, Livingston seem well set to become a happy and successfu community.

LOANHEAD, *Midlothian* (Map 3, ref. 32⁷66⁶ became a burgh in 1884, but was already o some importance, having a Charter of 166 allowing a weekly market and annual three day fair. Once the centre of a busy coal minin area (with twenty-five coal seams in the barony) the town can still claim "half a pit", becaus one shaft of the twenty-year-old Bilston Gle pit is inside the burgh boundary. The principa employment for men is still in local pits, bu several new firms now complement the engin eering works, and thanks to substantial housin development Loanhead is becoming a important dormitory for Edinburgh workers

LOCHAILORT, *Inverness-shire* (Map 4 ref. 17⁷78²). This hamlet is at the head of a se loch of the same name on the "Road to the Isles", and is the centre of beautiful scenery The best-known bridle-track ran to KIN LOCHMOIDART via Glenuig, a hamlet on the peninsula. This was one of the old "coffir roads" – routes for the long Highland buria processions of the past; it has now been super seded by a motor road. Above Glenuig are cairns and a cross showing the stopping-places on the old route. Just beyond Glenuig is Samalaman, which once housed a Catholic seminary founded in the 1780s, and which moved to LISMORE in 1804 and later to Blairs, ABERDEEN. This seminary was actually encouraged by the pre-emancipation government in London in the hope of enlisting Catholic Highlanders in the army and providing them with their compatriot chaplains.

LOCHALINE, *Argyll* (Map 1, ref. 16⁸74⁴). This village at the mouth of Loch Aline stands where the new vehicle-ferry runs between OBAN, CRAIGNURE on MULL, and Loch Aline.

Lochaline sand (99% silica) became an industrial factor in 1940, when high-grade sand was needed for the manufacture of optical glass and scientific instruments, which could not be imported. Mining continues to provide work, and by 1962 a million tons had been removed.

On a point across Loch Aline is the ruin of Ardtornish Castle, the 14th-cent. seat of the Lord of the Isles. In 1461 it was the scene of negotiations between the Lord of the Isles and representatives of Edward IV of England,

Scottish Tourist Board

Springtime on Loch an Eilean

which led to the Treaty of Westminster directed against the King of Scots. This led ultimately to the forfeiture of the Lordship of the Isles.

LOCH AN EILEAN, *Inverness-shire* (Map 5, ref. 29⁰80⁷). This outstandingly beautiful loch is in the ROTHIEMURCHUS forest, itself within GLEN MORE National Forest Park.

The castle on the island in the loch is traditionally linked with the "Wolf of Badenoch", Alexander Stewart, natural son of Robert II. The blank wall facing the shore is the only one now surviving, but some towers remain and in one ospreys nested until about 1900; after an interval they have now returned to the district and nest near BOAT OF GARTEN.

LOCHARD, *Perthshire* (Map 2, ref. 24⁷70³). A well-known sheet of water in the TROSSACHS country, Loch Ard is notable for its scenery, especially for its trees. Lochard forest is a part of the QUEEN ELIZABETH FOREST PARK, which includes Loch LOMOND. Lochard forest itself in 1963 had 21,160 acres under plantation, making it the largest planted area of the Forestry Commission land in Scotland. The Commission began work here in 1929. The shores of the loch are a rich hunting-ground for botanists.

There is good trout-angling in the loch, and the fish, probably owing to the presence of freshwater shrimp as their staple form of diet, have pink flesh and silver coats like the trout at the Kinross-shire Loch LEVEN.

LOCHBUIE, *Argyll* (Map 1, ref. 16²72⁴), is a hamlet on the Island of MULL in the Inner Hebrides (*see* "The Shape of Scotland"). At the head of this sea-loch at the S. end of Mull are three houses, former seats of the Maclaines

of Lochbuie. The latest is an early 19th-cent. mansion; the house next in age is now a stables; it has a tablet recording that it was the family home from 1752–90, and that Johnson and Boswell stayed there in 1773. About 50 yds SE. is the ruin of old Moy Castle, the earliest stronghold. Readers of Boswell's *Journey* will recall what an eccentric old Lochbuie was.

To the W. along the coast are cliffs that rise to over 1,000 ft, a height exceeded, in Scotland only, by ST KILDA, FOULA, and HOY. The cliffs include the Carsaig Arches – huge, queer tunnels carved out by the sea.

LOCHCARRON, *Ross and Cromarty* (Map 5, ref. 19⁰83⁹). This fishing village is on the sea loch of Loch Carron, and is where the road to APPLECROSS and SHIELDAIG leaves the lochside road.

At the head of the loch is Glen Carron, which includes Achnashellach Forest, one of the earliest acquisitions of the Forestry Commission and the scene of research into bog-reclamation since 1921.

This is a picturesque district with fine views of SKYE across the water. Much traffic has been taken from the road on the W. side of inner Loch Carron by the new road on the E. side by-passing STROME FERRY.

LOCHEARNHEAD, *Perthshire* (Map 2, ref. 25⁹72³). Standing at the W. end of Loch Earn, and at the mouth of Glen Ogle, the village of Lochearnhead came into existence at the meeting of roads and railways going N. with the road from the E. along Loch Earn. The railways have gone, but the roads along both sides of the loch retain their well-wooded attractiveness.

Just SE. of the village, and on the shores of

the loch, is Edinample Castle, built in 1630 by Sir Duncan Campbell of Glenorchy, who is said to have built seven castles during his lifetime. This castellated mansion, with its lofty white walls in the Highland Scottish manner, stands out effectively against the coloured hill. Farther to the E. of Edinample is Ardvorlich House, associated with Scott's Legend of Montrose. Since 1580, it has been the home of the Stewarts of Ardvorlich. Nearby is a tombstone to seven Glencoe men killed trying to raid the house in 1620.

Under the guidance and encouragement of Mr Cameron, of the hotel there, Lochearnhead was the scene of the first water-skiing club in Scotland; and the British and Scottish Championships have been held here on Loch Earn.

This spot is a good touring centre. There is some angling left undisturbed by the skiers on the loch. But in the hills above Lochearnhead, and between it and BALQUHIDDER, there are some lochs containing that beautiful and highly edible rarity, the char.

The motorist, the cyclist, or the walker gets his first feeling of entering the Highlands upon leaving Lochearnhead to go N. up Glen Ogle. The hills soar on either side, and after 5 m. the glories of Glen Dochart are open, with the run down to KILLIN and Loch TAY. From the road you may see traces of the mid-18th-cent. one, sometimes sinking into the present road, sometimes branching off on its own.

Lochearnhead now has four good hotels and is justifiably popular with visitors, many of whom bring their own sailing craft.

LOCHGELLY, *Fife* (Map 3, ref. 31⁹69³). The burgh of Lochgelly owes its prosperity to coal. Once it was a market town for neighbouring parishes, but by the mid-19th cent. it was the centre of the eastern part of the Fife coalfields, and was entirely industrialized. With the decline of coal, this district is much in need of new industries.

LOCHGILPHEAD, *Argyll* (Map 2, ref. 22⁰70¹). This pleasing little burgh of whitewashed houses, which include the principal offices of Argyll County Council, stands at the head of Loch Gilp, an inlet of Loch Fyne, and on the CRINAN CANAL 2 m. N. of ARDRISHAIG. The burgh increased from being no more than a small village in the early 19th cent., probably as a result of the canal, and is well laid out and full of villas.

It lies conveniently near to the meeting of the INVERARAY and OBAN roads to the S. of the peninsula that ends in Kintyre.

LOCHGOILHEAD, *Argyll* (Map 1, ref. 18⁶68⁸). This village at the head of Loch Goil is surrounded by woods and mountains, and is part of the Argyll National Forest Park.

The church, which was well restored in 1955, has the remains of a chantry-altar founded by Campbell of Ardkinglass in 1512. A 17th-cent. memorial to that family frames the E. door.

On the W. shore of the loch are the ruins of Carrick Castle, dating at least from the 15th cent., and once a stronghold of the earls of Argyll and burnt in 1685.

The road leading NW. from Lochgoilhead to Loch Fyne goes through spectacular, rocky Hell's Glen to a summit of 719 ft.

LOCHINCH CASTLE, *Wigtownshire* (Map 2, ref. 21¹56¹). This modern castle, the home of the Earl of Stair, was completed in 1867. It was built to replace Castle Kennedy, which was destroyed by fire in 1716 – its ruins still stand on a peninsula between the White and Black Lochs. Originally it was the seat of the Kennedy family, and passed to the Stairs in the 17th cent. Lochinch .Castle is famous for its magnificent grounds, laid out by the 2nd Earl of Stair from the inspiration of Versailles. The gardens were neglected, but when the original plan was found in the mid-19th cent., they were restored to their original beauty. Rare shrubs, rhododendrons, and azaleas are specialities here.

LOCHINDORB, *Moray* (Map 5, ref. 29⁶83⁷). This loch, situated 969 ft above sea-level, lies in the middle of the desolate Dava Moor between the rivers SPEY and Findhorn. It provides excellent trout fishing. On a small island in the middle of the loch stands the ruin of a castle that covers almost the whole of it. Although once the hunting-seat of the Comyns, it is best known as a stronghold of the Wolf of Badenoch. From here he exercised a reign of terror over the Lowlands of Moray, which culminated in the burning of ELGIN Cathedral in 1390.

LOCHINVER, *Sutherland* (Map 5, ref. 21⁰92³). The fishing village of Lochinver stands on the coast of Assynt at the NE. angle of the sea loch of Inver. It is a good holiday centre with a road W. to LAIRG and attractive, twisty roads along the coast to N. and S. There is good fishing in the river and in many hill-lochs, as well as very good sea fishing. Climbing is available on the remarkable Sutherland hills, and bird watchers have the chance to see an unusual variety of birds, including the red-throated divers.

Just S. of the village is the schoolhouse beside a lochan, with the fantastic SUILVEN rising like a sugar loaf behind.

LOCHMABEN, *Dumfriesshire* (Map 2, ref. 30⁸58³). This ancient royal burgh, traditionally chartered by Bruce and certainly the caput of Bruce power in Annandale from about 1200, sits in the flat-bottomed Annan valley at the foot of its steep W. shore, surrounded by one large loch and four small ones.

Lochmaben has a very long history. Its oldest

charter dates back to 1298. It seems likely that the promontory on which the medieval stone castle across the loch now stands was the central temenos or shrine of the god Maporos in the Iron Age. A ditch, relating to the Iron-Age lake-level, crosses the promontory outside the deep medieval ditch that defines the castle-ward. Some time about the 1130s, the Bruce motte (now in the golf course on the edge of the present burgh) was erected; and in 1290 Edward of England erected his pele, or small castle in tower-form, on the promontory across the lake. A stone castle put up about 1330 on this stronghold was in English hands for most of the years between 1290 and 1385, enabling Annandale to be governed virtually as an English shire. James IV later, when Lochmaben had returned to Scotland, took a great interest in the castle. The last important siege was in 1588, when it was held by Lord Maxwell, acting with Spanish encouragement. England lent cannon to help the Scottish Government forces to seize it. It stood intact far into the next century. The original early 14th-cent. bell, called the Bruce Bell, is still used in the 19th-cent. church, as well as another old bell called Pope's Bell.

About 1½ m. N. of Lochmaben in Elshie-shields is a particularly fine tower-house built about 1600 by the same architect as AMIS-FIELD Tower. It is still inhabited – unlike Spedlin's, built in 1605, 3 m. N. of Lochmaben, and famed for the ghost that inhabited its dungeon and had to be kept there by the presence of a fine Cranmer 1548 Bible on the cellar stair. The origin of this ghost story is the belief that a 17th-cent. laird went off on business to EDINBURGH, forgetting a prisoner in the dungeon, who starved to death; his ghost then haunted the dungeon.

LOCHMADDY, *Inverness-shire* (Map 4, ref. 09²86⁸), is on the Island of North UIST in the Outer Hebrides (*see* "The Shape of Scotland"). It is the chief village of North Uist, and is its port, from which it has connections by sea with the mainland and the other Outer and some Inner Hebridean Islands. It has an excellent harbourage in its sheltering and island-studded sea-loch. There is a coastguard station, and in Lochmaddy is the Sherrif Court, presiding over all minor legal cases arising in the Outer Islands S. of HARRIS.

It was here that judgement was passed on those unfortunate enough to be caught relieving the whisky-laden ship that foundered in the Sound between ERISKAY and South UIST during the Second World War. This incident inspired the film *Whisky Galore;* though its scenes were shot in the southern Hebrides.

LOCHNAGAR, *Aberdeenshire* (Map 6, ref. 32⁵78⁵). It used to be quite easy to see this splendid mountain-ridge, which has eleven summits over 3,000 ft in height, from the western outskirts of ABERDEEN, over 60 m. away. As it is, the dwellers in the high flats at Kincorth there still have a good view of it. It lies at the western end of the Mount, just S. of Balmoral Forest and NW. of Loch Muick, and its principal tops are Cac Carn Beag (3,786 ft) and Cac Carn Mor (3,768 ft). The

The summit of Lochnagar

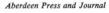
Aberdeen Press and Journal

great eastern corrie, with its crescent of cliffs and the little loch at the base, is unequalled in Scotland for stern grandeur, well earning the half-Scottish Lord Byron's apostrophe:

> England! thy beauties are tame and domestic
> To one who has roved o'er the mountains afar:
> Oh, for the crags that are wild and majestic!
> The steep frowning glories of dark Lochnagar.

The Cairngorm Club erected an indicator on the summit in 1924 that shows all the prominent points within view, from the Caithness hills on the N.; from BEN NEVIS on the W.; and on the S. from Ben Lomond, the Pentlands, the Lammermuirs, and the last Cheviot in England over 108 m. away.

The name Lochnagar originally applied only to the small loch at the foot of the eastern corrie, marked in the Gordon of Straloch map given in Blaeu's Atlas of 1662, but by the time of Byron it had been transferred to the mountain, supplanting the older name, the White Mount, now confined to the flat southern dome of the hill. The usual routes of approach are from BALLATER by Glen Muick and from BRAEMAR by Loch Callater. The other approach from CRATHIE is not open for a considerable part of the year. Towering over the loch is the Black Spout, which rises 1,200 ft, largely in sheer precipice, from the 2,575 ft level of the water.

Lochnagar is a favourite with climbers, and, as neither of the two usual approaches alone gives an adequate impression of the mountain, the traverse should if at all possible be made from one side to the other. The mountain is of coarse red granite, so weathering as to give the cliffs the appearance of gigantic masonry. Their rounded edges and absence of clear-cut fissures make them unsuitable for rock climbing, and there have in fact been many casualties involving the foolhardy. The flora of Lochnagar is of interest to botanists. In June the blossom of masses of creeping azalea give a pink tinge to great areas on the higher slopes.

LOCH NAN UAMH, *Inverness-shire* (Map 4, ref. 17°78³). The sea loch Nan Uamh is 4 m. long and is an offshoot of the Sound of Arisaig. It is famous for its associations with Prince Charles Edward Stuart, who landed here from the French frigate *Doutelle* on the 5th of August 1745 and stayed for seven days at Borrodale House before going to KINLOCHMOIDART.

After CULLODEN, during July 1746, he hid for some days in Glen Beasdale woods, and in a cave on the shore, before escaping to the Outer Hebrides. Finally, it was here that he boarded the French frigate *L'heureux* on the 20th of September and left Scotland for ever.

A memorial cairn was set up on the shore in 1956 by the " 'Forty-Five Association".

LOCHRANZA, *Buteshire* (Map 1, ref. 19³65⁰), is a village on the island of ARRAN (*see* "The Shape of Scotland"). Standing at the head of a sea-inlet at the tip of the island, Lochranza is, after the three main townships on the E. coast of Arran, the favourite of island visitors. It has a hotel, and a pier at which steamers from the mainland regularly call. A 14th-cent., half-ruined castle is amongst the places on Arran in which Bruce stayed on his return to Scotland from Rathlin at the beginning of his campaign.

LOCH RYAN, *Wigtownshire* (Map 2, ref. 20⁵56⁵). This great sheltered bay, 8½ m. long, housed a Roman naval base – probably on or near where STRANRAER now stands. A long sandbank projects from the western shore halfway up the bay, leaving a fairly narrow ship-channel.

Lochryan has long been known for its oyster-beds; a mesolithic oyster-midden of great size lies beneath the streets of Stranraer over 30 ft above the present sea-level, and dates to at least 6,000 years ago; in 1701, oyster fishing rights are mentioned in a charter; large commercial development began in the 19th cent. and lasted well into the present century, when over-fishing led to its decline and eventual cessation. Since 1954, the Scottish Marine Biological Association has been studying the beds and adding young oysters from Brittany; both native and immigrant are flourishing, and the beds are ready for controlled commercial use. They lie a little over 1 m. off Stranraer.

LOCHWINNOCH, *Renfrewshire* (Map 2, ref. 23⁵65⁸), is a small textile and furniture-making town at the SW. end of Castle Semple Loch.

At the N. end of the loch stood Castle Semple, which was once the seat of the Lords Semple, but it passed from them in 1727. The mansion house that was built in 1735 was burnt in 1924; the estate is now the property of the Department of Agriculture, and is developed as small holdings. Near the ruin of the house is a fragment of Castle Semple. The Collegiate Church was founded by John, 1st Lord Semple, in 1504 and includes an ornate monument to him. He fell at Flodden.

LOCKERBIE, *Dumfriesshire* (Map 3, ref. 31³58²). This thriving mid-Annandale town existed as a village, and lamb and horse sale-centre, back into the late 17th cent.; the lamb sales have been held annually on Lamb Hill since 1680. The village, which grew up around a 16th-cent. Johnstone tower, was by the late 18th cent. a substantial place with two streets; but the modern road and railway greatly

ncreased its importance, and it had Caledonian
Railway workshops until the First World War.
ts charter of 1863 marked its growth into a
eal town.

It is the centre of a rich farming area.
Several of the large landowners were connected
with the Jardine, Matheson Company, and so
he estates benefited from the great wealth the
China tea-trade brought to the area; fine
mansions such as Jardine Hall (recently
demolished) and Castlemilk are also a by-
product of the China trade.

The great modern road up Annandale now
by-passes the town, relieving the main street
of the incessant rumble of heavy lorries, and
giving more opportunity for the passing
tourist to appreciate the town's pleasant architecture in the red Permian sandstone from the
quarry – famed for its reptile footprints – a few
miles away.

LOGIERAIT, *Perthshire* (Map 5, ref.
29⁶75²). This village lies at the meeting-point
of the rivers TAY and Tummel. A little N. of
he road bridge and above the Tummel are the
foundations of a defensive structure, the date of
which is uncertain. On the sides away from the
steep slope to the river is a deep, dry ditch,
above which the foundations of a masonry wall
can be seen. Possibly the site is prehistoric in
origin, as it occupies a very strategic position
above the confluence of the two rivers. It is said
to have been a royal hunting-seat in the time of
King Robert II of Scotland; later, when
Logierait became the seat of the Regality Court
of the Lords of Atholl, it was the hanging-
knoll. In 1866 a tall, elaborately carved Celtic
cross was set up on the knoll in memory of
George the 6th Duke of Atholl.

Nothing remains of the hall of the Court of

Regality where judgement was passed on
offenders, but it is said to have been over 70 ft
in length, with galleries at either end. Of the
prison of the Regality, a few of the large
foundation-stones can be seen in the yard of
Logierait Hotel. Rob Roy Macgregor was
imprisoned here in 1717, but escaped after only
one night's confinement. After the Battle of
PRESTONPANS in 1745, Lord George Murray,
the Lieut.-General of Prince Charles Edward's
army, sent 600 prisoners to the gaol here.

In the churchyard several interesting things
are to be seen. There are three heavy iron
mortsafes, relics of the days of Burke and Hare,
when body-snatching was a profitable business.
There are also several very quaint tombstones,
and near the church entrance an early Christian
sculptured Pictish cross slab which for a long
time lay in the burial ground of the Stewart
Robertsons of Edradynate.

LOMOND, Loch, *Stirlingshire/Dunbarton-
shire* (Map 2, ref. 24⁰69⁰). The largest inland
water in Great Britain, Loch Lomond also has
claims to be the most beautiful. It is 24 m. long,
and varies in width from ¾ m. to 5 m. Its 30
wooded islands are towards the wider S. end,
with the exception of six small ones.

The largest island is Inchmurrin, which contains ruins of an old castle of the earls of
Lennox. Inchcaillach, or the "women's island",
has the ruins of a nunnery and is the burial-
place of the MacGregors. Five islands, including Inchcaillach and Clairinch, with part of the
mainland shore and marshy hinterland, comprise a nature reserve; the islands have semi-
natural deciduous woodland and are good for
wildfowl and rich in aquatic life. The larger
islands lie along the Highland Boundary Fault,
one of the two major structural features in

Loch Lomond

Scottish Tourist Board

Scotland, which stretches right across the country from SW. to NE.

Steamer trips from BALLOCH are a feature of the loch. Boating is enjoyed everywhere, but is more concentrated at BALMAHA. ROWARDENNAN has a large youth hostel, and is a centre for canoeing, fishing, water-skiing, and swimming. While the W. side of the loch has heavy traffic during the summer, the E. side has remained remarkably quiet, as the road ends at Rowardennan. Perhaps the most-climbed mainland mountain, Ben Lomond (3,192 ft) is usually climbed from here, a long but not difficult walk, and offers magnificent views.

In June 1971 the Queen inaugurated the first £12,000,000 stage of the Central Scotland Water Development Board's scheme to take 70,000,000 gallons a day from Loch Lomond for the industrial belt: this will later be raised to 100,000,000 gallons, but because of the great depth of the loch its level will be virtually unaffected.

LONG, Loch, *Argyll* (Map 2, ref. 23⁵69⁵), is a prolonged narrow inlet (17 m. in extent) of the Firth of CLYDE; it combines the advantages of length and shelter with exceptional depth. At Portincaple it is within 2 m. of the head of Gareloch and at ARROCHER only 1¾ m. from Loch LOMOND. It was across this narrow strip of land at TARBET, Dunbartonshire, that the Vikings pulled their boats to raid the mainland of Scotland from Loch Lomond before the Battle of LARGS. On the W. side of the loch there is much forestry work; on the E. side is the Admiralty torpedo range and port of FINNART.

LONGANNET POINT, *Fife* (Map 2, ref. 29⁵68⁷). On this site on the N. shore of the FORTH, between CULCROSS and KINCARDINE-ON-FORTH, the South of Scotland Electricity Board built its gigantic £108,000,000 coal-fired generating station, by far the biggest in the country, with a 2,400 kW. capacity and embodying several original features. Unfortunately mishaps and troubles bedevilled the station's progress. The first of the four 600 kW. turbines was scheduled to be commissioned in 1969, and the whole station to be at full capacity in 1970; but the first did not start running until January 1970; the second started in December of 1970, and while the third was being run-in during the summer of 1971 (with the fourth also in an advanced stage of readiness) faults developed in the turbines and the whole station was closed down for intensive investigations and repairs. The turbines are a prototype design and the largest operating in Britain.

But the huge, impressive Longannet power station with its enormous chimney (fitted with elaborate devices to extract polluting substance from its emissions) is only the visible manifestation of this multi-million-pound project. To feed the giant with its 10,000 tons daily of low-grade coal, which is pulverized, mixed with oil, and blown into the furnaces, three new pits were opened in the district, at Solsgirth, Bogside, and Castlehill, but their coal, unlike that of other mines, never surfaces until it reaches Longannet, being carried underground on a conveyor belt 5½ m. long (the longest continuous such belt in the world). In addition, when in full production the station will require several more thousand tons from other pits or projected open-cast schemes, unless, as has often been rumoured, it is partly converted to oil, readily available from the great GRANGEMOUTH refinery across the Forth, which is in turn fed by pipeline from the CLYDE.

The Longannet project (initiated in 1963), with its advanced computer-controlled mining complex, represents Scotland's biggest civil engineering undertaking: the power station itself employs only some 550 men, but it provides vital work for more than 2,000 miners in its immediate neighbourhood.

LONGFORGAN, *Perthshire* (Map 6, ref. 33¹73⁰). This typical lowland Perthshire village, which is now by-passed by the main PERTH to DUNDEE road, has grown around Castle Huntly, a conspicuous landmark on a rocky site to the SW. of the village.

The Castle was begun in the middle of the 15th-cent. by Baron Gray of Gray, whose family had long been connected with the district, residing first at the so-called manor of Longforgan and later at the Castle of Fowlis. In 1615, Castle Huntly was bought by the Earl of Kinghorne, and through him it came into the possession of the earls of Strathmore, who changed the name to Castle Lyon. In 1777 it was sold by the 10th Earl of Strathmore to a Mr George Paterson, a Dundee man who had made a fortune in India under Clive and married a daughter of the 12th Baron Gray.

The last member of this family, Colonel Adrian Paterson, made extensive renovations in 1937, but died before he could occupy the Castle. During the Second World War it was used as an approved school. It is now a Borstal Institution for boys.

The stone quarries at Kingoodie by the R. TAY have brought fame and fortune to Longforgan. The proprietor of Mylnefield (a mansion house that is now demolished) did much to expand this trade in the 19th cent., and the hard building stone was exported by water to England in considerable quantities. The inner stonework of the BELL ROCK lighthouse is built of Kingoodie stone. The quarries are now worked out, and an important horticultural research station has been set up on the Mylnefield estate.

LONGFORMACUS, *Berwickshire* (Map 3, ref. 37⁰65⁷). The village of Longformacus is in a sheltered cup of trees in the valley of the Dye in the midst of the moorland stretch of the Lammermuir Hills.

Some 4½ m. NW. of Longformacus, above the valley of the Dye, is a long cairn called the Mutiny Stones (previously called Mittenfall of Stones and then the Meeting Stones). It was damaged by the construction of sheep-folds and by early excavations, and appears to be part of a group of long cairns in the SE. of Scotland complementary to chambered cairns.

Longformacus is a resort enjoyed by anglers, who fish for brown trout in the burns and streams of the Lammermuirs.

LONGNIDDRY, *East Lothian* (Map 3, ref. 34⁴67⁶). A village just inland from the Firth of FORTH, Longniddry lies some 12 m. from EDINBURGH by road. It was a coal-mining village for five centuries, but mining ceased in 1924. It also used to be a centre for weaving, but now with its good communications (it is on the main E.-coast railway line), it is almost a dormitory town for Edinburgh. There is a golf course and a rocky beach, with good views across to Fife, and W. up the Forth estuary.

Longniddry House stood at the SW. of the village, but now only a circular mound and subterranean vaults remain.

To the E. of the village is Gosford House, the home of the Earl of Wemyss. Little can be seen of the house from the road, but the trees behind the policy wall on the coast road grow at an angle of 30 degrees, blown by the prevailing wind, and are a botanical curiosity.

The mansion was built by Robert Adam, and is considered to be one of the best examples of his work, although the effect of its three great arched windows has been altered by the later addition of an arcade to the front. It has a magnificent marble hall, a double staircase, and a picture gallery, and is surrounded by fine parkland.

LOSSIEMOUTH, *Moray* (Map 6, ref. 32³87⁰). This prominent fishing port, holiday resort, and police burgh at the mouth of the R. Lossie, once most widely known as the birthplace and home of James Ramsay MacDonald, the Scot who became the United Kingdom's first Labour Prime Minister, is one of the boom towns of the Moray Firth. It is expanding so fast that soon the entire peninsula on which it stands will be a built-up area. Its prosperity rests on three factors. The first and greatest of these is the fishing; the second is the Royal Naval Air Station, H.M.S. *Fulmar*, which, with the Royal Air Force base at KINLOSS, has brought much business to this coast; and the third is its holiday trade – limited only by its capacity to house the incomers lured by its great sandy beaches, luxury hotels, caravan sites, beach chalets, and golf.

In a country where ruinous and deserted harbours are only too common (in consequence chiefly of the rise and decline of the herring industry), a visit to the fish market of Lossiemouth is calculated to restore one's faith in human enterprise. For this is a harbour that has been overcrowded for decades. There is a desperate need for more accommodation here, and the overcrowded conditions are actually restricting the commercial trade that Lossiemouth might enjoy. Vast quantities of oil for the Naval Air Station are transported by road, and this and other naval cargoes might be imported by sea if the harbour were expanded. Ever since the creation of the Stotfield and Lossiemouth Harbour Company in 1814, the harbour has been operated by private enterprise, and negotiations to transfer it to a public trust have not so far succeeded.

Although the fishing fleet is somewhat smaller than it was at its post-war peak in the '50s, when 90 craft used the port, the fishermen of Lossiemouth are still the most progressive in the Firth. And what a wonderful record they have! A Lossiemouth fisherman built and designed the first Zulu boat *Nonesuch* in 1879. That was the initial step in the revolution in the design of fishing-craft which has been going on ever since. Lossiemouth also pioneered, through Peter Smith and others, the steam-drifter in the great age of the herring. Then in 1921, after a disastrous herring season due to a coal strike, Lossiemouth men first introduced the Danish seine net into this country, and the Campbells and Thomsons proved that it could open up a new era of prosperity. The urge to experiment goes on. In 1961 William Thomson of the *Kittywake* demonstrated the value of an entirely new type of seine net.

The business life of Lossiemouth is now centred in Branderburgh on its cliff-top. But down below the cliff the old sea-town with its quaint market cross jostles large areas of new housing. Here at No. 1 Gregory Place, in a "backstair room", James Ramsay MacDonald was born in 1886. The two-roomed but-and-ben, then thatched and backing on to the railway, has since been marked by a plaque of dressed Clasach sandstone from HOPEMAN. Ramsay's first school was a little Free Church General Assembly School known as "Robbie Codlin's", after a dominie who used to urge his charges when reading, "Open your mouth wide, just like a codlin'." Ramsay certainly learned the art. He then went on to Drainie Parish School, which closed in 1955 because of the danger from aircraft of the Royal Naval Air Station. The Education Committee presented to the late Prime Minister's family an old teacher's desk from this place where he not only studied but taught as a pupil-teacher.

The presence of several Service airfields somewhat restricts exploration in the immediate neighbourhood of Lossiemouth, but, providing you keep to the regulations designed to prevent obstacles to low-flying aircraft, there is nothing of interest to which access is barred. In particular there are two buildings of great architectural and historical significance in the area.

Innes House, 4 m. SE. of Lossiemouth, was designed by William Aitoun, master mason of Heriot's Hospital, EDINBURGH, and built by Sir Robert Innes of that Ilk between 1640 and 1653. It is without doubt the handsomest 17th-cent. mansion in the N. of Scotland. While the general form is the old L-plan, with the staircase set in the re-entrant angle but placed in a fine square turret, the details and decoration of the windows and chimneys closely resemble that of Heriot's Hospital. Additions forming a courtyard to the N. were added early in this century for the present owners, the Tennants.

Some 6 m. SSE. of Lossiemouth, and about 3 m. E. of ELGIN to the S. of the road to FOCHABERS, is Coxton Tower, an architectural anachronism that is yet the most perfect example of its type surviving in Scotland. Although built in the early 17th cent., it adheres to the style of the great tower-houses of over a century earlier. With corner turrets at opposite angles and an open bartizan at one of the other angles, it is a compact block of four storeys, all vaulted and with the vaults set at right angles to one another on alternate floors for strength. The stone-slab roof rests directly on the uppermost vault, so that the building is completely fireproof. It has been kept in perfect repair.

(*See also* GORDONSTOUN.)

LOTH, *Sutherland* (Map 5, ref. 29⁵91⁰). The crofting township of Loth is beautifully situated between hill and sea 6 m. N. of BRORA. Land at the mouth of Loth Burn was drained in 1818, when a new channel was cut for the burn through solid 20-ft rock.

An attractive, rough road leads 9 m. over the hill to KILDONAN. At the foot of Glen Loth is a stone to commemorate the killing of the last wolf in Sutherland about 1700.

The district is full of brochs. Some 2 m. S. of Loth between the road and the railway near Kintradwell is the ruin of Cinn Tolla broch, excavated to show an entrance passage 18 ft long, 7 ft high, and 3 ft wide, with a cell. The interior of the broch is 31 ft in diameter and 11 ft high, and has a well 7 ft deep with steps leading to it.

LUBNAIG, Loch, *Perthshire* (Map 2, ref. 25⁶71⁴). This fine loch, 4 m. long, between CALLANDER and STRATHYRE is for many visitors their first glimpse of a genuine Highland loch lying amidst steep hills. If you approach the Highlands through Callander, the "gateway to the TROSSACHS", you run along the eastern shore of splendid Loch Lubnaig.

There is, despite a tendency to over-fishing, some fair trout angling in the loch and, if you happen to strike a good run of fish, some fine salmon. One seldom passes Loch Lubnaig

without seeing fishermen either in boats or on the shore.

The shores of the loch are highly popular for campers and caravanners in the summer. Apart from the picturesque waters of the loch, they are enlivened by the height of Ben Ledi (2,873 ft) on the immediate W. This is a stimulating but not a difficult mountain to climb.

There is considerable forestry work in this district.

LUGAR, *Ayrshire* (Map 2, ref. 25⁹62¹). This is a bleak mining village; almost contiguous with CUMNOCK, it now houses the local administrative headquarters of the National Coal Board. Lugar was founded about 1840 around ironworks, which are now defunct. The village sits on the Lugar Water, the main tributary of the R. Ayr.

LUING, Island of, *Argyll* (Map 1, ref. 17⁵71⁰), is one of the Inner Hebrides (*see* "The Shape of Scotland"). Luing (the "u" is not pronounced) is the third slate-producing island lying just off the mainland S. of OBAN. Its neighbour to the N. is SEIL, which has a bridge "across the Atlantic" connecting it with Scotland. It was from Luing and from these quarrying islands that the slates were produced for roofing the restored Abbey of IONA.

LUMPHANAN, *Aberdeenshire* (Map 6, ref. 35⁸80⁴). In an agricultural district, this village is mainly supported by beef and dairy cattle.

About 2 m. SW. of the village is "Loch of Auchlossan". In 1860 James Barclay, the tenant of a local farm, leased the loch that once lay there, drained it and grew good crops of hay and straw on its former bed. By the 1920s the loch had filled up again, but since 1945 the Department of Agriculture have repaired the tunnel and ditches, and the loch is again dry and growing crops. The only people who mourned this piece of enterprise must have been the local anglers. A loch with so fertile a bed must have produced good fat trout!

To the N. of the village, on Perkhill, is "Macbeth's Cairn", on the site where he was killed by Macduff. Tradition has it, however, that he made his last stand at Peel Bog just to the S. of the village, now only a moated earthen mound, though remains of a stone building stood until the 18th cent. At any rate, it is closely within this neighbourhood that Macbeth (quite a different figure from Shakespeare's sinister creation) met his end.

LUMSDEN, *Aberdeenshire* (Map 6, ref. 34⁷82¹). This upland village in the Rhynie-Lumsden Gap, the natural passage through the hills from Donside to Strathbogie, was conjured out of a barren moor in 1825 by a local laird, Harry Leith Lumsden of Clova. It has an extensive village green and is otherwise mainly a ribbon development along the main road, but

t stands in the centre of a very beautiful and
storied countryside.

At nearby Clova there was a monastery said
to have been founded by St Moluag from
LISMORE, while 2 m. N., at the point where
the road to DUFFTOWN leaves the level strath
and climbs up into the foothills of the Cabrach
plateau, is an ancient manorial and church
centre of great interest.

Here on neighbouring mounds above the
burn stood the Motte of Auchindoir, an earth-
and-timber fortress of the Comyns, and the
original kirk of Auchindoir, succeeded in
the 13th cent. by a beautiful stone church on
the same site, whose ruins amid the kirkyard
are carefully guarded today by the Ministry of
Public Building and Works. One of the finest
specimens of Transitional or Early First
Pointed, its chief glory is the fine door in the S.
wall with its double round arch and bold First
Pointed moulding.

A short distance farther up the Den of Craig,
you come upon Craig Castle. The first glimpse
of it will be of a forbidding cliff-like block of
masonry with tiny windows and a battery of
fierce gun-loops, ready to greet any rash
attacker with a hail of fire. To the left of this
massive 16th-cent. L-plan tower-house built
by the Gordons is a gateway of rusticated-
ashlar work, erected two centuries later by
Francis Gordon, the 8th Gordon Laird of
Craig, in 1726.

Over the door of the Castle in the re-entrant
angle of the L-shape are three sunken panels
each bearing coats of arms. Just inside the
doorway, with its formidable iron yett, is a
vaulted vestibule. The ribs meet centrally in a
large foliaged boss bearing the Scottish Royal
Arms, and shields in the corbel caps of two of
these ribs show the three boars' heads of the
Gordons and a carving of the Five Wounds of
Christ, a theme also represented in the Kirk
of Auchindoir. The spiral staircase to the top of
the tower has sixty-three steps over 4 ft wide,
lit by loop-holes in the N. wall. On the first
floor is the great hall, with its pipers' gallery
(originally a chapel, like the oratory at Towie
Barclay), and high up on the S. wall of the hall
is a shield bearing a coat of arms quartered in
tinctures of gules and azure. On either side of
the helmet above the shield are the initials
F. G. and A. O., standing for Francis Gordon
(1686–1716), the 7th Laird, and his wife Agnes
Ogilvie.

LUNCARTY, *Perthshire* (Map 6, ref.
30⁹72⁹). This village, on the W. bank of the
TAY near PERTH, was in the last century
associated with the most extensive linen bleach-
field in Scotland. In the First Statistical Account
of Scotland it is recorded that 500,000 yds of
cloth were bleached annually, but by 1837 the
figure had risen to 2,000,000 yds. Today
5,000,000 yds are treated each year and over
200 workers are employed.

Just S. of Luncarty at the confluence of the
Almond and the Tay is the site of the Roman
camp of Bertha. The outlines of the fort have
been largely obliterated by ploughing, but
across the railway line the defence system can
still be traced. It has long been surmised that
the so-called Derdee's Ford marks the position
of a Roman ford or bridging of the Tay so that
there could be communication between the two
camps of Bertha and Grassy Walls.

Denmarkfield, just to the N., is the traditional site of a battle between the Scots and the
Danes in the late 10th cent. A standing stone
known as the King's Stone lies in a field beyond
the railway embankment to the E. of the main
road.

LUNDIN LINKS, *Fife* (Map 3, ref. 34⁰70³).
On Largo Bay, adjacent to the town of LARGO,
Lundin Links is a popular holiday resort with
sea fishing and excellent bathing and golfing
facilities.

Lundin House was demolished in 1876.
However, one tower of an earlier castle on the
same site remains, much altered, but originally
having the stair and one or two chambers above.

On the western outskirts of Lundin Links are
three spectacular standing stones of great
antiquity; they are 18 ft, 17 ft, and 13 ft high,
and originally they had at least one more,
forming a circle believed to have been a
Druidical temple.

LUSS, *Dunbartonshire* (Map 2, ref. 23⁶69³).
The picturesque village of Luss consists of a
single street in a very fine setting on Loch
LOMOND with a view of the wooded islands on
the loch and of Ben Lomond on the opposite
side. Glen Luss, behind, leads over the pass to
Loch LONG – a rough hill walk.

The church was built in 1875 by Sir James
Colquhoun of Luss in memory of his father,
who was drowned in the loch; it contains some
relics from the private chapel at Rossdhu,
including, in the churchyard, a hog-backed
stone sarcophagus thought to be a 10th-cent.
effigy of St Kessog, and an old stone font. The
chiefs of the Macfarlanes of ARROCHAR are
buried in the churchyard.

Rossdhu, the seat of the Colquhouns since
the 14th cent., lies S. of the village; the mansion
was built in the late 18th cent. to replace an old
castle.

The village is a tourist centre, and steamers
call here on the loch trips. There is a good
caravan site N. of the village beside the loch.

LYBSTER, *Caithness* (Map 7, ref. 32⁴93⁴).
The stranger travelling to WICK might be forgiven for passing, 8 m. to the S., one of the
largest villages in Caithness, Lybster, without
registering its existence. The road N. sweeps
past a well-known hotel, by-passing on the
right an interesting monument to that early
planner, Sir John Sinclair of Ulbster (1754–

1835). His vision of village economy, based on a balance of fishing and agriculture, has been outdated, but has left a legacy of spacious streets and solid dignified houses, which might still give a lesson in good living standards to our town planners of today. Sir John Sinclair was one of the Highland landlords who behaved with true charity during the Highland Clearances evils of the early 19th cent.

At the end of the village, a little road curves down to one of the many charming harbours that give shelter from the jagged grey cliffs and wild seas of the Caithness coast. Just NE. of the harbour is a block of yellow sandstone, measuring 3 ft by 2 ft, which has a Celtic cross, with a smaller one set within, cut across the right-hand corner.

The district round Lybster is rich in antiquities, brochs, standing stones, chambered cairns, homesteads, and (3 m. NE. at Mid Clyth) the Stone Rows. These last comprise twenty-two rows, with an average of eight earthfast boulders in each. Similar structures have been found on Dartmoor in the far SW. of the British Isles, and in Brittany, but, as no other monument in the area seems to bear any relationship to the stones, their date in history and their function remain part of the fascinating mystery that broods over the moors.

LYNE, *Peeblesshire* (Map 3, ref. 31⁹64¹). The township of Lyne has a very small church standing on a tributary of the TWEED about 4 m. W. of PEEBLES. The church is dated about 1645, and has a period pulpit and two canopied pews said to be of Dutch workmanship. Just W. of the church is the site of a Roman camp, above the road and 100 ft up a bank on a loop of the river. This is probably part of a chain of forts guarding communications through the hills.

Some 3 m. upstream are the ruins of Drochil Castle, built by Regent Morton in the later 16th cent., and intended as a palace rather than a castle; he meant to retire here, but was executed in 1581, three years after the castle was started.

MACDUFF, *Banffshire* (Map 6, ref. 37¹86⁴). BANFF has its past but Macduff has its future. So they will tell you, but, although its history under its present name has been brief, Macduff lies on the eastern Bay of Doune, across the river from Banff, under its hill-top parish church, like a jewel waiting to catch the glow of the Moray Firth's peerless sunsets. It has one of the most pleasing waterfronts in Scotland – all the more attractive because it is not merely picturesque but bustling with life and activity. Urged by the Government to be more daring, Macduff recently extended its harbour at a cost of £150,000. It was a very sure investment, because this is the safest haven for fishing-boats on the whole of the Moray Firth. It is sheltered from all the winds that blow – except those from the NW.; in consequence, its fishing-craft

lose only four weeks in the year through adverse weather, while the fishermen of other ports may lose as much as two or three months.

But although Macduff has been so called since the 16th of January 1783, after its rebuilding by the Earl of Fife, it had existed under another name for several centuries before then. Those startlingly steep streets that swoop down to the waterfront traverse what was once the fishing and crofter township of Down or Doune, part of the ancient thanage of Glendowachy belonging to the earls of Buchan, one of whom in 1528 succeeded in having Down made a free burgh of barony. The 1st Earl of Fife acquired the place in 1733. The 2nd Earl lavished a great deal of money and effort on its development, building the first harbour in 1768. The church on the Hill of Doune dates from 1805. From 1815, when herring fishing and curing began at the port, progress was spectacular.

Today Macduff has a population of 3,464 and its own permanent fishing-fleet of thirty-five seine-net boats devoted to white fishing, while the excellence of the harbour brings many visiting craft. Its chief attractions to the holiday-maker are the fine open-air swimming pool at Tarlair and the Royal Tarlair golf course.

This district is associated with *Johnny Gibb of Gushetneuk* by William Alexander, the great prose classic of the Aberdeenshire dialect. Those who are not deterred by the inevitable difficulties of reading a work like this, in which the dialogue is entirely accurate in its representation of the actual speech of country people of the North and East in the first half of last century, should certainly make a point of reading it.

MACHRIE, *Argyll* (Map 1, ref. 12¹66⁴), is on the Island of ISLAY in the Inner Hebrides (*see* "The Shape of Scotland"). This island resort is noted for its excellent golf course, laid out on the sandy turf (known as the "machair") in 1891. It lies 2 m. NW. of PORT ELLEN, and has beautiful surroundings on the bay with a 7-m.-long sandy beach and good bathing. The airport for the island lies to the N. of Machrie.

MACHRIHANISH, *Argyll* (Map 1, ref. 16⁸62⁰). The village of Machrihanish is on the W. coast of Kintyre, 6 m. W. of CAMPBELTOWN. Its bay consists of 3½ m. of sand on an otherwise rocky coast. The land between Machrihanish and Campbeltown is flat peat moss, partly drained and used for agriculture.

Till the end of the 19th cent. the village manufactured salt, which with fishing was its only industry. Now it is mainly a holiday resort with a well-known golf course laid out in 1876.

About 2 m. E. is the village of Drumlemble, with a small coal mine. Near here pits have been worked for more than 200 years. The only other coal pit in the Highlands is the privately run one at BRORA.

MAESHOWE, *Orkney* (Map 7, ref. 33³01⁴), on the Mainland of ORKNEY Northern Islands (*see* "The Shape of Scotland"), is a chambered cairn lying 4½ m. NE. of STROMNESS. According to the latest archeological research, this tomb, some 3,500 years old, represents a "standard of design and workmanship, not otherwise known to have been reached in neolithic Britain – or indeed in any place N. and W. of the Mediterranean". It may therefore claim to be among the finest of Scotland's prehistoric remains. To quote again from an acknowledged archaeological source, is a "domical mount 24 ft high and 11 ft in diameter standing on a level space varying in width from 40 to 70 ft. This is surrounded by a shallow ditch from less than 25 to 60 ft wide." The whole structure shows remarkable skill in the art of building without mortar. It is covered by a large mound of earth.

Maeshowe must have been the burial-place of remote kings or eminent persons belonging to a race at whose identity we can only guess. All we know is that they were skilled in this kind of funerary architecture, and that they were able to ornament the interior of their royal tomb with treasure, some of which can only have been gold from the Mediterranean.

We know this through the depredations of the tomb that took place during the Norse occupation of Orkney. There was a wanton invasion of Maeshowe as late as 1861, but there was no treasure for the Victorian vandal to remove; it had all gone close on 1,000 years earlier in the hands of curious and naturally greedy Norse occupiers of an island about whose ancient near-civilization they knew nothing. But these Norse depredators have left evidence of their curiosity and their awe that can interest us today.

Having admired what remains of the impressive 3,000-year-old Maeshowe tomb, the visitor may turn with curiosity to the runic inscriptions or graffiti that the Norse invaders left upon the stones and walls. Sometimes indeed one may see a trivial event of nearly a millennium ago recorded casually, yet to our eyes with startling vividness.

MAIDENS, *Ayrshire* (Map 2, ref. 22¹60⁸). Formerly called Maidens of Turnberry, this village lies close to Turnberry Point about 6 m. N. of GIRVAN. That this was a place of importance in prehistoric days is shown by the Stone Age fortresses, the remains of which still exist, that were built as outliers to the fort at TURNBERRY. It seems that the name is derived from these forts, not from the rocks in the bay, as some would have it. The modern Maidens has been a fishing village for many generations. The courage and determination of the fishing families are shown in the pier and breakwater, built largely by them from the remains of R.A.F. camps in the area that were abandoned after the Second World War.

Nearby is Shanter Farm, the traditional home of Robert Burns's hero Tam o' Shanter. Burns learnt about Tam – who was a well-known "drouth", a man fond of his dram – during his sojourn at the village of KIRKOSWALD (3 m. inland), where he had been dispatched as a youth to learn mathematics, mensuration, and surveying. Burns wrote "Tam o' Shanter" to please his antiquarian friend Captain Grose, about whose propensities for the supernatural ("A chiel's amang you taking notes, and, faith, he'll prent it!") he composed the poem "On the late Captain Grose's Peregrinations thro' Scotland", which contains the lines:

> By some auld houlet-haunted biggin,
> Or kirk deserted by its riggin,
> It's ten to one ye'll find him snug in
> Some eldritch part,
> Wi' deils, they say, Lord safe's!
>   colleaguin
> At some black art.

MAIDEN STONE, *Aberdeenshire* (4 m. SE. of OYNE). On the left-hand side of the road leading towards Oyne, a little to the NW. of the church of CHAPEL OF GARIOCH, stands this beautiful pillar of red granite, 10 ft high, with a big chip out of one side. It is a Pictish symbol stone of the second period, carved in relief, showing on the front a man between two fish monsters (sometimes called "Jonah and two Whales"), an enriched cross and shaft, and a panel with enriched disc and other decorative details. The back depicts beasts and a centaur-like figure; a rectangle and Z-rod; an "elephant" and a "mirror and comb" symbol, while the sides have panels of decorative interlacing. It is undoubtedly one of the finest of Pictish sculptured stones extant, though only one of a vast number in Aberdeenshire alone. The name Maiden Stone has never been satisfactorily explained, though many fanciful theories have been advanced. Only a few yards away on the other side of the road, at the entrance to Crowmallie House, is a modern "maiden stone", a sculpture of Primavera, by A. E. Sean Crampton, a London sculptor, who also wrought the fine memorial mosaic representing the Acts of the Good Samaritan in memory of Sir Robert Workman Smith of Crowmallie. Not far away at Newton House is the Newton Stone, which bears ogham and miniscule lettering. One theory is that it was the gravestone of St Walloch or Volocus of Logie-in-Mar, an early 6th cent. hermit, and also the burial-place of the Pictish king Aed or Eth of the Swift Foot. The Maiden Stone is under the protection of the Ministry of Public Building and Works.

MALLAIG, *Inverness-shire* (Map 4, ref. 16⁸79⁷). At the mainland end of the "Road to the Isles" lies Mallaig, which also marks the terminus of the West Highland railway. It is a convenient calling-place for Inner and Outer Hebrides steamers, and provides a motor boat link with parts of Knoydart by a route that crosses Loch Nevis to the N., where no road is available.

About 3 m. E. of Mallaig rises the hill of Cara a'Ghobhair, whose summit commands a magnificent view of the whole length of Lochs Morar and Nevis and looks out over the Sound of Sleat to SKYE and RUM.

Fishing is Mallaig's chief industry. There is a deep-freeze plant there and also lobster ponds, and the fleet is linked with markets through rail and road transport.

MAM RATAGAN, *Inverness-shire/Ross and Cromarty* (Map 5, ref. 19° 81°). The Pass of Mam Ratagan rises to 1,116 ft, with its summit acting as the boundary between Inverness-shire and Ross and Cromarty. The road runs from Shiel Bridge to GLENELG. In spite of much planting of forestry fine views can still be had over KINTAIL and to SKYE.

MANOR, *Peeblesshire* (Map 3, ref. 32²63⁸). Some 4 m. SW. of PEEBLES, the township of Manor (or Kirkton Manor) stands on Manor Water, surrounded by green Lowland hills. The site where St Gordian's Church once stood is marked by a granite cross with an old stone font at the base.

A little SW. of Kirkton is the cottage of the Black Dwarf, "Bowed Davie Ritchie", visited by Scott in 1797. The Dwarf was a legend in the Borders even before Scott's novel. There is an effigy of Davie in the garden.

MAREE, Loch, *Ross and Cromarty* (Map 5, ref. 19°85⁴). This magnificent loch, 12½ m. long and 2¼ m. broad, is overlooked on all sides by beautiful mountains. On the S. is BEINN EIGHE, the first national nature reserve in Britain. On the N. is a region of mountain and loch also of exceptional grandeur, including Slioch (3,217 ft).

Loch Maree is famous for its sea-trout fishing; there are courses of instruction in angling held here during the autumn.

There are many small wooded islands on the loch; the one named Isle Maree contains the ruins of a chapel said to be the hermitage of St Maelrubha, who came to APPLECROSS in the mid-7th cent.

MARKINCH, *Fife* (Map 3, ref. 32⁹70¹). This paper-making burgh contains a church dedicated to St Drostan (a nephew of Columba) and possessing a western tower dating from the 12th cent. In the N. wall of the church is a 17th-cent. armorial panel of a member of the Leslie family, earls of Leven. The 1st Earl, the famous General, was buried here in 1661.

About 1½ m. SE. of Markinch is Balgonie Castle, standing on top of the steep right bank of the R. Leven. Originally an early 15th-cent. tower set at the NW. angle of a later enclosure, it was reconstructed by the 1st Earl of Leven, who died in 1661 and had acquired the estates and castle in 1632–5. The SW. angle of the enclosure has a still occupied building.

Some 2 m. SE. of Markinch is Balfour House, a late 16th-cent. building with a 17th-cent. extension, which belonged to the Beaton family; the famous, or regrettably Renaissance, Cardinal Beaton was born here.

MAUCHLINE, *Ayrshire* (Map 2, ref. 25°62⁷), has been immortalized by Robert Burns and is a place of pilgrimage for Burns-lovers from all parts of the world. It would be surprising if this were not so, because, during his sojourn at Mossgiel, which is a mere stone's throw from the village, the poet attained his brighter lustre. The Jolly Beggars ranted in Poosie Nancy's; the Holy Fair was held near by. Daddy Auld and Holy Willie walked these streets and vennels, and the Mauchline Belles peeped from these windows. Fortunately the village proper is largely unspoiled, and such necessary distractions as council housing schemes and modern residential "estates" have been relegated to the perimeter. One of the great things about Mauchline (as with many another Scottish village) is that on any "simmer Sunday morn" one can stroll through the place and meet most of Burns's characters readily recognizable in spite of modern dress. If you want to know the people whom Burns wrote about, you really ought to visit Mauchline.

MAXTON, *Roxburghshire* (Map 3, ref. 36¹63⁰). The village of Maxton is on the KELSO road near the TWEED; it has a 12th-cent. church, much altered, which was formerly the property of the monks of DRYBURGH. The old shaft of the village cross marks the spot where traditionally 1,000 men of the barony were wont to assemble for war.

At Muirhouselaw, 1½ m. S. of Maxton, is an earthwork that was once a medieval homestead moat, one of three in Roxburghshire. These are much less frequently found in Scotland than earlier settlements.

MAY, Island of, *Fife* (Map 3, ref. 36⁵70⁰), in the Firth of FORTH (*see* "The Shape of Scotland"). The farthermost of the Forth islands, the May is 5½ m. SE. of CRAIL and, in pre-Reformation days after the re-establishment of the Kingdom of Scotland at BANNOCKBURN, was possessed by the see of ST ANDREWS. Like most offshore eastern Scottish islands, the May early proved attractive to pristine Christian monks. St Adrian, who had been missionizing and preaching in Fife and her islands in the 9th cent., was killed on the May by the raiding Danish heathen in A.D. 870. The remains of a later 13th-cent. chapel dedicated to the martyred saint may still be seen on the island.

The May, in the commanding position at the dissolution of the Firth of Forth into the North Sea, played varying roles of importance during the Anglo–Scottish Wars. Today this, the largest of the Forth islands, a regular oblong of 1 m. long, is from a practical point of view devoted solely to its use as an important light-house base. The May also is frequented by bird-watchers from all over the U.K. and Europe. Their energies are rewarded, for the May island is a favourite nesting-place for birds travelling N. and S. It is a nature reserve, and its soil, for one of the eastern Scottish islands so far out, is unexpectedly fertile, offering good grazing. It can be approached best from the Fife shore from PITTENWEEM, ANSTRUTHER, or Crail harbour.

MAYBOLE, *Ayrshire* (Map 2, ref. 23°60°). The ancient capital of Carrick is Maybole, and Carrick is the southern division of Ayrshire. As such, Maybole was the stronghold of the Cassillis Kennedies. No fewer than twenty-eight baronial mansions may have stood within the parish, and the old town house or "castle" still stands in the High Street. This was the Kennedy residence, and is still used by the family as the office of Cassillis and CULZEAN estates. An ancient tradition has it that the castle was the prison of a Countess of Cassillis who had eloped with Johnny Faa, King of the Gipsies. Her husband John Kennedy, 6th Earl of Cassillis, returned home in time to recapture the wayward lady and, incidentally, to hang Johnny Faa and his band. Imprisonment for life was the fate of the Countess. Unfortunately for the story, the family history reveals that John and his wife lived happily as husband and wife for over twenty years, and his letters reveal his affection and regard for her.

Maybole was created a burgh of barony in 1516, but its recorded history goes as far back as 1193, when the first church was built and dedicated to St Cuthbert. In 1371 John Kennedy of DUNURE founded a Collegiate Church, part of the ruins of which still stands. John Knox and Quintin Kennedy, Abbot of CROSS-RAGUEL, held their famous disputation in the Provost's house in 1562.

Maybole, convenient to the TURNBERRY golf courses, AYR, and splendid beaches, has grown as a residential area and with a growing population of around 5,000 and redevelopment schemes it is also attracting new industries, such as lingerie manufacture.

MEALFOURVONIE, *Inverness-shire* (Map 5, ref. 24°82³). This mountain on the W. shore of Loch NESS, 11 m. NE. of FORT AUGUS-TUS, is only 2,284 ft high, but stands alone and is conspicuous from many points; it is used as a navigation guide by ships in the Moray Firth. From its summit there are extensive

views of GLENMORE ALBIN and N. to Ross and Caithness.

MEIGLE, *Perthshire* (Map 6, ref. 32°74¹). In the village of Meigle is the most outstanding collection of early Christian Pictish sculptured stones in Scotland. These are housed in the old school, now equipped as a museum under the guardianship of the Ministry of Public Building and Works. All the stones were found in the vicinity of Meigle, and must point to an early Celtic religious foundation here. The finest of the twenty-five stones is a magnificent cross slab, 8 ft high, whose main subject is Daniel in the Lion's Den.

Another very fine collection of symbol stones of this category is housed at ST VIGEANS near ARBROATH.

MEIKLE FERRY, between *Ross and Cromarty* and *Sutherland* (Map 5, ref. 27³88⁷). This ferry across the DORNOCH Firth, from a long spit of land 5 m. NW. of TAIN to a point 4 m. SW. of Dornoch, is 1½ m. long. Now discontinued, it was once a very dangerous ferry, but was the only link with the N. until the building in 1812 of BONAR BRIDGE. The need for this was stressed by an accident in 1809 when an overloaded ferry boat was swamped, and over 100 people drowned.

MEIKLEOUR, *Perthshire* (Map 6, ref. 31⁵73⁹). The mansion-house, home of the Marquess of Lansdowne, was enlarged by David Bryce in 1869. The grounds are magni-ficently planted, culminating in the great beech hedge that stretches for 580 yds along the road running from PERTH to BLAIRGOWRIE. These beech trees were planted in 1746, and have now attained a height of 85 ft. The hedge is pruned at regular intervals, the operation being a major undertaking.

The village of Meikleour is quaint and, lying off the main thoroughfare, has retained much of its old world charm. The jougs to which local offenders were attached are still there, and in 1898 the public weighbridge for wool and other bulky farm merchandise could be seen. The original village cross, the fourth on the pilgrim road from BRECHIN to DUNKELD, was replaced in 1698 by a market cross which now stands in the centre of the village.

Just N. of the village, the Cleaven Dyke crosses the main road. This Roman *limes*, or boundary, consists of a broad bank. The work is not defensive, and yet it must be related to the great legionary fortress of INCHTUTHIL that lies behind it. Sir Ian Richmond discusses its significance in the Proceedings of the Society of Antiquaries of Scotland.

Some 3 m. S. of Meikleour is Stobhall, situated on top of a steep bank above the TAY; it is now the residence of the Earl of Perth. The house consists of four buildings set around a courtyard. The oldest part bears the date 1578 and includes a chapel with a 17th-cent. painted ceiling. But these must be on the foundations of an earlier structure, for Stobhall came into the Drummond family in 1360, when Sir John Drummond married Mary, eldest daughter of Sir William de Montifex. Their daughter, Annabella, married King Robert III of Scotland and was crowned at SCONE in 1390.

Margaret Drummond, one of King James IV's mistresses, died here most tragically in 1502.

The Dower House on the W. side of the courtyard was completed in 1671. One of the lower rooms has a particularly beautiful moulded plaster ceiling. There is a handsome entrance gateway, over which is a carved coat of arms.

All the buildings were extensively restored some years ago to make them into a modern private residence.

MELLERSTAIN, *Berwickshire* (Map 3, ref. 36⁵63⁹). Though his usual residence is at the family seat of TYNNINGHAME, the Earl of Haddington owns the splendid house of Mellerstain, which lies about 6 m. NW. of KELSO. Designed by William and Robert Adam, it is one of the great Georgian houses of Scotland. Externally it has the symmetrical dignity and well-matched proportions of its period, and inside there are all the delicate refinements of decoration – moulded plaster ceilings, mantelpieces, doorheads, light-fittings, and furniture – after the exquisite manner of the younger Adam. The library, with its broad frieze, and its ceiling resembling a piece of Wedgwood porcelain, is considered one of Adam's masterpieces. Pleasant terraced gardens run from the house to an ornamental lake.

Lady Grisell Baillie, wife of the George Baillie who started the building of Mellerstain in 1725, is remembered as a covenanting heroine and the author of a "household" book that has come to be regarded as a classic of social history.

Mellerstain is a fine setting for dances; some notable ones have been held here even in these austere post-war years.

MELLON UDRIGLE, *Ross and Cromarty* (Map 5, ref. 18⁹89⁵). This is one of the remotest townships in Wester Ross. Holiday-makers may have difficulty in finding accommodation, but if they find the beauty of this W. Highland place difficult to desert, they have not far to go to AULTBEA, where there is a youth hostel, and to LAIDE, where there are caravan and camping sites.

MELROSE, *Roxburghshire* (Map 3, ref. 35⁵63⁴). The Cistercian Abbey of Melrose was founded by David I in 1136. At Old Melrose there had been a monastery as early as the mid-7th cent., inhabited by monks who came from IONA via Lindisfarne, but it was a bare promontory on the nearby TWEED and regarded as inadequate for Cistercians, though the church continued into the 13th cent.

Melrose suffered badly in the War of Independence in 1322, and at the hands of Richard II in 1385. Finally it was much reduced in 1544 by the Earl of Hertford. The remains, however, are mainly of the 15th cent., including some of the finest decorative work and figure sculpture in Scotland.

Alas, the endemic Scottish failing of wanton rather than deliberate iconoclasm played further havoc. In 1568 the Abbey fell into the hands of the Douglas family, who used some of the stones from it to build a private house at the end of the cloisters. At length, however, it was repaired under the superintendence of Sir Walter Scott in 1822, and at the expense of the Duke of Buccleuch, who gave it to the nation. The heart of Bruce, brought back from its abortive journey to the Holy Land is said to be buried here. There was an odd confirmation of this (not made public) during some excavations in the 1920s.

The town originated from a small village called Fordel, but it achieved status as a town under the Abbey. In 1609 all the land became a temporal lordship. The mercat cross is dated 1642. Since Sir Walter Scott, Melrose has become a tourist centre for the surrounding Scott and Border country.

Darnick Tower on the outskirts of Melrose

Mellerstain

Pilgrim Press, Derby

Melrose Abbey

was until recently inhabited by the family of Heiton; the tower was built by them in 1425.

MELVICH, *Sutherland* (Map 5, ref. 28⁸96⁴). The scattered village of Melvich stands near the head of a small bay and at the mouth of Strath Halladale. There is good loch fishing and also river angling.

Bighouse, the seat of a Mackay family, is on the opposite side of the mouth of the river. The owner was the last of the clan to possess land in the old Mackay country; he sold it in 1830 to the Sutherland Ducal family when the evictions had taken place in Strath Halladale.

MEMSIE, *Aberdeenshire* (Map 6, ref. 39⁷86²), is a village and estate with a 17th-cent. mansion that belonged to the Aberdeenshire Fraser family for more than 300 years. Three cairns once stood on Memsie Muir; two of them have been removed. A third still stands to the height of 15 ft and is 60 ft in circumference at its base.

MENSTRIE, *Clackmannanshire* (Map 2, ref. 28⁴69⁷), is a hill-foot village at the western end of the Ochils, and is the usual starting-point for the ascent of DUMYAT (1,375 ft). A pleasant glen, from which Menstrie Burn runs to join the R. Devon, divides Dumyat from Myretoun Hill and is an agreeable base for children's picnic expeditions.

Glenochil distillery, with vast warehousing capacity, and its associated yeast factory are the principal industries.

Menstrie Castle, built in the 16th cent., was the birthplace of the poet and founder of Nova Scotia, Sir William Alexander, and of Sir Ralph Abercromby, hero of Aboukir Bay. Restored as housing accommodation by Clackmannan County Council, the Castle's

association with Nova Scotia is marked by two commemoration rooms featuring a heraldic display of 107 coats of arms carried by the baronets of Nova Scotia, an order of baronets founded in 1625 to raise money and to help colonize Nova Scotia.

MENTEITH, *Perthshire* (Map 2, ref. 25⁸70¹). The Lake of Menteith, maybe partly because of its round rather southern shape, partly because it contains coarse fish, including pike, rather than the indigenous Scottish trout and salmon, is the only natural sheet of water in Scotland to be called a lake and not a loch. This is not to say that the lake is not highly romantic. It contains that treasure of an island INCHMAHOME. Also, on Inchtalla, there is the ruin of a castle that was once the seat of the earls of Menteith.

That most romantic and striking of Scotsmen within living memory, that Scottish–Spanish Hidalgo, horseman, aristocrat, and supporter (a supporter to the extent of going to prison for his cause) of the early Labour movement, R. B. Cunninghame Graham, was, after his death in 1936 and at his own request as stated in his will, rowed across the waters of the lake to be buried beside the remains of his Spanish wife on Inchmahome. It was said that Cunninghame Graham had a reasonable claim to the dormant title of the earldom of Menteith. It was characteristic of his proud spirit that he never bothered to press his claim. He was content to remain "Don Roberto".

The Lake of Menteith lies in scenes of quiet Highland-Lowland beauty, with the Hills of Menteith rising gently to the westwards up to 1,289 ft. The Port of Menteith on the NE. shore of the lake, and 4 m. from ABERFOYLE, is a small holiday resort.

In the Middle Ages the waters of the lake

Curling on the Lake of Menteith

Scottish Tourist Board

were the scene of odd sporting (if that epithet is applicable) contests or displays. The clerics from Inchmahome used sometimes to catch a swan, attach a small live perch with fishing hooks on it and at the end of a longish angling line to one of its feet, and then let it loose on the water again. The struggling perch far behind the bird to which it was connected was usually an irresistible bait for pike. The ensuing contest between the bird and the fish caused much excitement. If the pike was not too large, the swan would sometimes fly away with the hooked fish dangling far below it. If the pike was a "big one", it held the swan captive on the surface. The monks then rowed out, arrested the swan, and captured the pike, which they subsequently cooked and enjoyed for their Friday dinner. Those who believe the pike to be inedible must never have tasted French *quenelles* or enjoyed the peculiarly skilful Polish cooking of this the most ferocious of fresh-water fish. The Poles have surely been long (and welcome) enough with us in Scotland for them to have taught us how to cook pike.

METHIL, *Fife* (Map 3, ref. 33⁸69⁹). The sea-port village of Methil is the oldest part of the burgh of BUCKHAVEN and Methil, and was a burgh of barony in 1665. A harbour was built about that time. The coal industry was well founded, but by the mid-19th cent. it had to stop owing to flooding of the mines; they were started again later. Methil, though primarily a port, retains some features of its origin as a mining village. The docks were especially important in both world wars when they became a convoy centre.

METHVEN, *Perthshire* (Map 6, ref. 30³72⁵). Like TULLIBARDINE, Methven had a Collegiate Church, founded in 1433 by Walter Stewart, Earl of Atholl. Only a fragment of the original building remains, but from a carved

stone built into an adjacent aisle it is possible that the church was added to by Margaret, widow of King James IV. She died at the Castle of Methven in 1540.

The present castle was finished in 1680, and is said to have been built on the site of the battle fought in 1306, when Robert Bruce was defeated shortly after his coronation by the English under the Earl of Pembroke.

About 2 m. NE. of Methven is Dalrue, a village on the right bank of the Almond. Here in 1836 was built a fine bridge with one semi-circular arch of 80-ft span.

MID CALDER, *Midlothian* (Map 2, ref. 30⁸66⁷). Under this heading, we propose to deal with East Calder and West Calder as well. All three towns lie within the shale oil district, which led to prosperity here during the late 19th and early 20th cents.

The industry has now declined and has come to a stop at PUMPHERSTON. It has, however, left its mark all round East and West Calder in the form of strange rose-coloured man-made hills or bings of shale; these are not without their mournful attractions to the eye.

Mid Calder has the largest population of the three, and the longest history. It was one of the stopping-places for coaches in the old days on what was then the main road between EDINBURGH and GLASGOW. Standing on the R. Almond, it was an obvious place for a medieval township to spring up on the E.–W. route.

The church at Mid Calder dates well back before 1541, when it was partly rebuilt, and has some flamboyant 16th-cent. window tracery. There is much modern building in this church so closely associated with the Reformation.

It was at what is now Mid Calder (though not in the church itself, but in Calder House) that in 1556 John Knox first administered Holy Communion according to Protestant rites. The Church of Scotland rightly reveres this district and this place where (though many troubles for the Kirk lay ahead of it) its most precious rites were first openly established.

MIDDLETON, *Midlothian* (Map 3, ref. 33⁷65⁸). The township of Middleton, 1 m. SW. of BORTHWICK, has now come to the fore as having near it the site of one of the residential camp schools under the Scottish National Camps Association Ltd – recognized by the Secretary of State for Scotland. Its purpose is to give town-bred children the chance of continuing their education in country surroundings. The camp school buildings have been specially designed with that intention. The Middleton Camp School (international in scope) is situated in fine Lowland Scottish parkland at the foot of the Pentland Hills and within sight of the Moorfoots. The mansion house, which was once used as a convalescent school by the EDINBURGH Corporation, has now been bought by the Scottish National Camps Association.

MIDMAR, *Aberdeenshire* (Map 6, ref. 37⁰80⁵). This pleasant wooded parish to the NE of the Hill of FARE contains one of the most original and distinctive tower-houses in Scotland. Although it is not now occupied, is unfurnished, and is not open to visitors save in exceptional circumstances and by special arrangement, it can be viewed from the public road between ABERDEEN and TARLAND a short distance to the W. of ECHT.

Midmar is on the Z-plan, with one of the large flanking towers square and its opposite number round. On the main buildings are crow-stepped gables and large rectangular turrets resting on elaborate tiers of key-pattern corbelling. The square tower has circular corbelled turrets with conical roofs, and the round tower is finished with an open battlemented parapet, while a staircase turret, rising high over the whole of the rest of the building from the re-entrant angle of the round tower is capped by an ogee roof – that is, a moulding

Midmar Castle

showing a double continuous curve. From the battlemented parapet at the top of the round tower you look down on the old walled garden. Beyond it lies a dell of sycamores, and beyond that the great encircling sweep of the northern slopes of the Hill of Fare. A second stair-turret, at the re-entrant angle of the square tower at the opposite side of the building, rises from a long cone of multiple mouldings and soars without a break to overtop the wall-head.

MILLPORT, *Buteshire* (Map 2, ref. 21⁶65⁵), is on the Island of Great CUMBRAE (*see* "The Shape of Scotland"). This holiday village rose as a resort in the late 18th cent., when the harbour was built and a ferry to LARGS provided. After 1833, when a steamer service started, the town grew as a holiday resort. Millport also had a quarry, a grain-mill, and hand-looms, and local women were well known for their embroidery. The residents now include many retired people.

The Episcopal church, built in 1851 by the Earl of Glasgow, was made the Cathedral of the Isles in 1876, which position it held for a short time.

MILNATHORT, *Kinross-shire* (Map 3, ref. 31²70⁴). Formerly a cotton-weaving and later a plaid-making town, Milnathort is now a market town with some woollen manufacture.

Just E. of the town is Burleigh Castle, a fine tower-house dating from about 1500. It is now roofless, but is otherwise complete, possessing an angle-tower with a corbelled square cap-house dated 1582. Burleigh was the ancient seat of the Balfours of Burleigh from the time that James II of Scotland gave them lands in the mid-15th cent.

MILNGAVIE, *Dunbartonshire* (Map 2, ref. 25⁵67⁴), adjoins BEARSDEN and is similarly a dormitory for Glasgow, pleasantly situated at the foot of the Campsie Fells. In addition to ample sports, shopping, and educational facilities, it has a useful variety of light industries, with a population of about 10,000. A further area has been zoned for industry to accommodate firms displaced by central redevelopment in the burgh.

MINGARY CASTLE, *Argyll* (Map 4, ref. 15⁰76³). This early 13th-cent. curtain-wall castle is sited on the rocky S. shore of ARDNAMURCHAN. It was the ancient seat of the MacIans of Ardnamurchan, a branch of Clan Donald, who were outlawed in the early 17th cent. and gradually disappeared from this district. James IV visited Mingary Castle in 1495, when he received the submission of the island chiefs. In 1644 it was captured for Montrose, and afterwards it was used as a prison for a few Covenanters.

In the early 18th cent., a barrack block was built against the inner face of the curtain wall, and this castle was garrisoned in 1745. The Governor there at that date, Campbell of Achinduin, was the first official to hear the news of the Prince's landing in Moidart.

MINNIGAFF, *Kirkcudbrightshire* (Map 2, ref. 24³56⁶), chartered as a burgh in 1619 (though no longer functioning as one), is clustered about the mouth of the Penkill Burn, ½ m. or so above NEWTON STEWART, of which nowadays Minnigaff forms a suburb. It lies among fine scenery, especially to the N., including Cumloden Deer Park, and views of Cairnsmore of Fleet and other Galloway mountains.

This very large hill parish – the biggest in Scotland, with the lowest population to the square mile – has a number of fine Neolithic cairns: Cairnderry, Bargreunan, King's Cairn, the Knappes, Boreland, and others. A 10th-cent. hoard of Anglo-Saxon coins and jewellery and an Abbaside coin from Baghdad – presumably Viking loot – was found in 1912 at Talnotry near Murray's Monument.

Some 1½ m. N. of the village is the ruin of Garlies Castle, once the seat of the Stewart family; from it the Earl of Galloway's son takes his title. It is a complex of 17th-cent. buildings centred on a 15th–16th-cent. tower.

MOCHRUM, *Wigtownshire* (Map 2, ref. 23⁵54⁷). According to pious legend, St Malachy in 1139, leaving Cruggleton, passed through "a village which they call St Michael's Church – and cured a woman mad and bound with cords". This was near Mochrum, and several stones found at the farm of Boghouse of Mochrum attest to both a Romanesque church and to an earlier church.

Mochrum village (Kirk o' Mochrum), 2 m. N. of PORT WILLIAM, has a long history, as Druchtag Mote, a well-preserved Norman motte, at the N. end of the village, also shows.

About 6 m. N. of the village is Old Place of Mochrum, owned by the Bute family, and the residence of Lord David Crichton Stuart. This is made up of two towers (the older built about 1500) 13 ft apart, joined by a modern building – built by the late Marquess of Bute at the end of the last century. Old Place was a seat of the Dunbars of Mochrum for centuries. They also had a hall on the island in Castle Loch, one of the seven moorland lochs that surround Old Place; this hall followed an earlier medieval building, which had followed a church, and even earlier Roman material has also been found. There seems little doubt that this island, heavily walled some time in the Dark Ages, housed a hermitage of the last Monastery of St Finnian, 1½ m. NW. of Kirk of Mochrum village. Chapel Finnian, a 10th-cent. building, within a 7th-cent. enclosing wall, nearby on the shore of Luce Bay, seems to have been a disembarkation place for Irish pilgrims to St Finnian's shrine.

MOFFAT, *Dumfriesshire* (Map 2, ref. 30⁸60⁵). This well-known little town is set in a deep valley among fine mountains, at the meeting of the roads over BEATTOCK Summit to GLASGOW, over the DEVIL'S BEEF TUB to EDINBURGH, and to ST MARY'S LOCH and the Border abbeys, and also to Carlisle.

Moffat was chartered as a burgh in 1648. Its chalybeate springs were discovered in 1633 and it rapidly became a noted spa, at the apex of its activity as a centre of the fashionable world in the 18th cent. The Baths House was built in 1827; the great Hydropathic Hotel, built at the end of the 19th cent., was destroyed by fire in 1921. But Moffat is still a considerable tourist centre with facilities for tennis, bowling, fishing, and golf. Moffat House was completed in 1767 for the Earl of Hopetoun.

Moffat has long been a sheep-farming centre; the Colvin fountain, erected in 1875, in the central space, which is surmounted by a huge bronze ram symbolizes the importance of this.

Among famous visitors to Moffat in the 18th cent. were Boswell, Burns, and James Macpherson, who launched his *Ossianic Fragments* in published form while staying at Moffat House, now a hotel. The controversy aroused by this work (already referred to under LISMORE) was once European in its influence. People still debate the authenticity of *Ossianic Fragments*, but scholars have largely established that there was a basis of oral tradition supporting parts of Macpherson's claims.

MOIN, The, *Sutherland* (Map 5, ref. 25³96⁰), is the moorland stretch of road between Kyle of TONGUE and ERIBOLL. At the summit is a lonely house built as a refuge when the road was first made in 1830; an inscription on the E. gable commemorates the building of a road at the expense of the Duke of Sutherland.

MONACH   ISLANDS, *Inverness-shire* (Map 4, ref. 06⁴86¹), is a group of islands in the Outer Hebrides (*see* "The Shape of Scotland").

This group, sometimes called Heisker, lies 6 m. off the SW. coast of North UIST. A lighthouse was built on Shillay, the most westerly island, in 1864, but it is an area not much frequented by shipping, and the station was abandoned some time after two of the three light-keepers had been drowned. Ceann Ear, another of the group, was also inhabited until recent times, but the last crofters left in 1943. The population of the islands ten years earlier had been thirty-three.

MONIAIVE, *Dumfriesshire* (Map 2, ref. 27⁸59¹). Set amongst particularly pleasant scenery in the hills and enclosed in Cairn Valley, Moniaive was chartered as a burgh on the 4th of July 1636. It continued to function as such for some time; but it has long ceased any burghal pretensions although the 17th-cent. mercat cross still stands in its midst. James

Scottish Tourist Board

Monifieth

Renwick, the last Covenanter martyr, executed in 1688, was a native of Moniaive, and there is a monument to him here.

The Craigdarroch and Dalwhat Waters and the Castlefairn Burn meet here to form the Cairn Water. About 3 m. SE. is Maxwelton House (not to be confused with Maxwelltown in Dumfries), dated 1641 but altered and modernized, and famous as the home of Anna Laurie, immortalized by Douglas of Fingland's song. Maxwelton House passed out of the Laurie family in recent years. "Annie" Laurie's married home was Craigdarroch, 2½ m. W. of Moniaive, built in 1729 by William Adam. She and her husband, Alexander Ferguson, are buried in Glencairn churchyard.

MONIFIETH, *Angus* (Map 6, ref. 35°73³). The coastal town of Monifieth, 6 m. E. of DUNDEE and just W. of Buddon Ness, is mostly a holiday resort. The local industries are rug- and carpet-making.

Some 2 m. N. of the town and 400 ft high on "Law Hill" is a hill-fort, which acquired some fame more than 100 years ago when it was examined in detail and written about extensively. In consequence it has been much reduced by the robbing of its stones. It is clear, however, that it was an oval of 400 ft by 200 ft with much vitrification.

MONIKIE, *Angus* (Map 6, ref. 35°73⁸). The township of Monikie is set amongst four large reservoirs providing the water for DUNDEE. The quarries of Pitairlie provide building and paving stones of excellent quality.

To the W. is Affleck Castle, a small tower-house of the late 15th cent., built on an L-plan, and still in perfect condition. It has a specially elaborate interior, with a notable upper hall, or solar, and a small chapel or oratory built into the wall of the solar.

To the E. of Monikie is Panmure House, rebuilt in 1852–5 by David Bryce.

MONKTON, *Ayrshire* (Map 2, ref. 23⁶62⁸), is a township N. of PRESTWICK at the junction of the IRVINE and KILMARNOCK roads. It is bounded on the S. by the runways of Prestwick Airport. A ruined kirk stands in the main street, with a Romanesque doorway and surrounded by a graveyard.

MONTROSE, *Angus* (Map 6, ref. 37²75⁸). Situated at the mouth of the South Esk River, and by a remarkable river-basin more than 2 m. square that, at high tide, gives the impression of an inland sea, Montrose lives up to its attractive name by being one of the most pleasing East Coast Lowland towns. With a long history, going back to the 10th cent., and a vivid life of its own today as a harbour and market town, and with native industries, it also acts as a holiday centre for golfers, anglers, and those in search of the bracing eastern air. Its name, though at first sight apparently French in origin, derives from Gaelic and has nothing to do with flowers. Nevertheless the stone of its older central part, drawing architecturally from the influence both of EDINBURGH New Town and from the Dutch and French Continental styles, has a warm blush, which it is not too fanciful to call rosy.

"Happy is the country that has no history" is a saying you may or may not agree with, but the once widespread belief that "no one could write a history of the Royal Burgh of Montrose, because nothing had happened there" is a tribute, not a sneer. It is a tribute to Montrose's long and peaceful prosperity, as compared with the savage tales of bloodshed that stain the past of so many other Scottish towns. Montrose owes its deep-rooted prosperity to the excellence of its harbour, and to the fact that during the English wars it was strategically safe, isolated behind its basin. In the 18th cent., after the Union and when strategical defence against England was no longer necessary, Montrose made up for the loss of its Scottish–Continental

Scottish Tourist Board

Montrose: the main street

trade by building the Inchbrayock or Rossie Bridge. Originally of wood, this connecting link between the near-island of Montrose and the S. crossed the narrows of the South Esk basin, touching the small island of Inchbrayock on the way. This opened up a trade route to Edinburgh and over the Border. Montrose was no longer isolated. The old wooden bridge has gone, and a modern suspension bridge has taken its place.

In a town of satisfying architecture, built in the old days to provide the county gentry of Angus with a town residence, perhaps the most arresting feature is the spacious High Street. This, almost as ample as a Flemish square or place, must be one of the widest boulevard-streets in the United Kingdom. The noble "old church" supports a graceful and characteristically Scottish spire by Gillespie Graham (the architect of Edinburgh's Moray Place), and proclaims Montrose's by no means negligible aspirations to seek the influence of the capital's New Town. There is a pleasing internal green belt called the "Mid Links" running parallel to the High Street. The ancient Castle of Montrose is now obliterated, but 4½ m. SSW. stands the interesting ruin of Red Castle in Lunan Bay.

In the 18th cent., Montrose was a spa and a town centre for county gentry who still (see Dean Ramsays' *Reminiscences*) spoke an educated old broad Scots tongue. Now it is no longer a spa but a holiday place for much of Scotland. That is not to say, however, that it has lost its prosperous small-town dignity. The gentry in it may no longer speak the Old Scots tongue, but they are unmistakably Scottish citizens in a highly characteristic Scottish royal burgh dating from the end of David II's reign in 1369.

The town's most famous son is James Graham, Marquess of Montrose, born at Old Montrose at the inner end of the basin. It is paradoxical that this most peaceful of Scottish towns should have produced the man who was, after Bruce, Scotland's most famous soldier.

MONYMUSK, *Aberdeenshire* (Map 6, ref. 36⁸81⁵). This village and parish on the DON is notable for the oldest and perhaps the finest church building in NE. Scotland. The Norman chancel arch and W. doorway of rich, red, dressed masonry from KILDRUMMY date it to around the year 1140, about which time the now vanished Augustinian priory of Monymusk, originally a Culdee house, was also built. In 1929 Monymusk Church was restored as nearly as possible to the original by Dr A. R. G. Mackenzie.

The village and the church lie in the fertile howe below Paradise Woods, and the priory stood between the church and Monymusk House, a 16th-cent. L-plan tower-house – much altered and extended – on the bank of the river.

At the SE. corner of a comparatively modern wing is a great round tower about 100 years older than the oldest part of the house. It was probably one of the angle-towers of the barmkin wall that surrounded the priory, and it is probable that stones from the priory were used to build the keep of the house.

In the original great hall, an achievement of arms in rich colour covers the whole of the wall above the great open fireplace. This was brought to light under panelling and was restored in 1937. It has a huge panel of the royal arms before the Union of the Crowns. Lesser panels display the arms of Lord Darnley, Anne of Denmark, Marie of Lorraine, and Margaret Tudor. Also preserved in the house is a carved bedpost belonging to the bed in which Bishop Elphinstone slept on his state visits to the priory, and, built into the wall of the billiard room, the Monymusk Stone, on which is carved an equal-armed Celtic cross with a base of decorative knot-work. The Monymusk Reliquary or Brecbannock, a casket for relics of St Columba, carried before the Scots army in battle and given into the keeping of Malcolm de Monymusk in 1315, was preserved in the house for centuries, but is now in the National Museum of Antiquities in EDINBURGH.

Near Monymusk: Castle Fraser

Aberdeen Press and Journal

The Forbes lairds who acquired Monymusk from the commendatory prior of the monastery after the Reformation sold it to Sir Francis Grant, later Lord Cullen, a Law Lord, in 1713, and in 1718, his son, Sir Archibald Grant, began the transformation that brought him fame as one of the great pioneers of agricultural improvement. He planted 48,000,000 trees, and enclosed the arable land, converting a "wild dreary moor" into waving cornland. His portrait, with that of his wife, Anne Potts, by Hogarth, is in a room of the house that also contains a medieval statuette of the Madonna, of Spanish provenance. It shows the Virgin standing upon the Muslim crescent, and probably came from the priory. The present laird is Sir Francis Grant, 12th Baronet.

Two poets are associated with Monymusk – Gavin Douglas, the translator of Virgil, who taught in the priory school as a young man of twenty-two; he was one of the ornaments of the poetic age of James IV. He is eminent amongst the poets of our nation. The other poet was John Skinner, who came to the place as a teacher also, and wrote one of his longest poems, "The Monymusk Christmas Ba'ing", about a local custom. About a mile N. of the village is Pitfichie Castle, a ruined Z-plan tower-house dating from the first years of the 16th cent.

By far the most spectacular castle in the area, however, is still in full and fine preservation and use. It is Castle Fraser, 3 m. SE., now the home of Major and Mrs Michael Smiley. One of the most splendid examples of the Z-plan, it is thought that in its first form, in the 15th cent., it consisted of the square tower and main block. Early in the 17th cent., the diagonally opposite round-tower and an extension were added – no doubt to the design of the MIDMAR mason, I. Bell, whose name appears on a panel bearing the date 1617. The false gun-barrel gargoyles, which form part of the decorative band at the wall-head of the main block, have no utilitarian justification, but they delight the eye, along with other sculptural details. The great hall is worthy of the splendid exterior, and it has one feature that gave Sir Walter Scott the idea for a famous passage in *The Fortunes of Nigel*. He heard about it from his friend, James Skene of Rubislaw, who, while visiting Castle Fraser, discovered the secret device known as the Laird's Lug and made a careful drawing of this machiavellian contrivance. On the second floor there is a wall-closet, the entrance to which is concealed by a window-shutter. In the stone floor of this closet a hatch leads down to a small vaulted chamber immediately above a window-seat in the great hall, and there is a hidden aperture opening on the arch of the window-recess.

MORAR, *Inverness-shire* (Map 4, ref. 16⁸79²), is a celebrated district in the W. Highlands, and also a village. The village is at the narrow neck of land between Loch Morar and the sea and beside the short Morar river, which is full of sea-trout in the right season. Loch Morar is 17 m. long and less than 2 m. wide. At the eastern end, it is by far the deepest inland water in Britain (180 fathoms), and, save for one Scandinavian lake, the deepest in western Europe. It has two or three islands, on one of which stood an 18th-cent. Catholic seminary. Simon Lord Lovat was captured hiding in a hollow tree on one of the islands in 1746.

The western end of the loch-side and village has a crofting population, which is mostly Catholic. On historical grounds partly connected with the island seminary, the Morar district is held in veneration by Scottish Highland Catholics. A small factory and instruction centre of the Highland Home Industries was opened here, including weaving, pottery, and cabinet-making.

The Morar shore is famous for its white sands. It is of weathered quartzite and sometimes conditions make it seem to "sing" as on one shore of EIGG.

The views of the islands of RUM and Eigg from the Morar area, and indeed from anywhere along this coast between ARISAIG and MALLAIG, are outstanding. This is a W. Highland seascape, landscape, and (if such a word may be coined) islandscape of the loveliest kind.

MOREBATTLE, *Roxburghshire* (Map 3, ref. 37⁷62⁵), is a village almost encircled by the windings of Kale Water; its parish boundary runs along the Border. The church of Morebattle belonged to GLASGOW Cathedral as early as the 12th cent.

Just S. of the village is Corbet Tower, burnt by the English in 1544 and restored about 1820. Whitton Tower, 2 m. S. of Morebattle, was also ravaged in the 16th cent., being rebuilt later.

Across the Kale river stands the church of Linton, Norman in origin but very frequently rebuilt. It still includes a Norman font and also a tympanum or carved stone panel, which has been set over the doorway in the modern porch. This is unique in Scotland, but is like some found in England; it has a mounted St George and various carved animals, though one tradition says that it represents Sir John Somerville, who is said to have been knighted by William the Lion for slaying a "ravening beast".

MORTON CASTLE, *Dumfriesshire* (Map 2, ref. 28⁹60⁰). About 2½ m. N. of THORNHILL, near the old Roman road, still in use, Morton Castle stands on a steep promontory over a loch that occupies part of an old glacial outflow channel. A tradition, recorded by Captain Grose, had it that the site was the seat of Dunegal, Lord of Nithsdale, and that the great standing cross, dating from the early 12th cent., now on the lawn at Friars' Carse, stood just in front of the present Castle until Riddell, Burns's friend, took it away in 1788. This would fit nicely with what we know of the kingdom Dunegal was ruling about 1120; it included Nithsdale and much of Clydesdale and this point on the Roman road near the Well Path across to Clydesdale is a native control-point for such a territory. Dunegal's grandson was first Sheriff of Nithsdale in the early 13th cent., and *his* son may have built the present Castle about 1250. It is of a type rare in Scotland, a mainly residential hall-castle, with fine windows and an ornate gatehouse just strong enough to repel a rush by a dozen or so men; otherwise the hall and undercroft are not defensible. It is therefore a much less military building than was usual in the Scotland of this period. The Castle was occupied until 1715, and is virtually complete except for the roof – a very striking ruin. It was the seat of the Douglases of Morton.

MORTON LOCHS, *Fife* (Map 6, ref. 34⁶72⁶). These lochs are a national nature reserve for the study of wildfowl. It is on the western extremity of TENTS MUIR, and is an important breeding-ground and resting-place for migrants. Surrounding the reserve is Forestry Commission land planted mainly with Corsican pine.

MOTHERWELL, *Lanarkshire* (Map 2, ref. 27⁵65⁷). This well-known industrial town originally took its name from a pre-Reformation healing well – the site is marked by a plaque in Ladywell Road. The town lies on a branch of the Roman road, and a Roman camp gives the name to "The Camp", a district of Motherwell.

Until the mid-19th cent. the area was mainly agricultural; but coal and ironworks transformed the whole district. In 1871 the Dalzell Iron Works, founded by David Colville, changed to steel, and by 1914 it was the largest steel works in Britain. This led to a mushroom growth of population.

In 1920 Motherwell amalgamated with its neighbouring burgh of WISHAW. After the slump in the 1920s and '30s, big business returned to the district with sheet steel and other works. Today (or rather tonight) Motherwell presents an exciting aspect with its glare of furnaces colouring the whole sky for miles around.

The town has been notable for producing champion swimmers, including Cathie Gibson, the Olympic Gold Medallist. Here too was started the library picture-lending service; it was the first in the United Kingdom. Motherwell led the way too in establishing a lending service for gramophone records.

To the SE. of Motherwell, near the R. CLYDE, stands Dalzell House, with its 15th-cent. peel tower; the subsequent buildings were put up in 1649. It is now a boys' school.

MOULIN, *Perthshire* (Map 5, ref. 27⁷83⁵). This picturesque village lies above PITLOCHRY on the road from STRATHTUMMEL to Strath Ardle. The site is ancient, and a traditional market called Feill Machalmaig used to be held in the field below Baledmund House.

Moulin Church has a lintel-stone with the date 1613 on it. The building was enlarged in 1704, and in 1787 it was re-seated and new windows were inserted. In the graveyard are various interesting carved stones, including two recumbent slabs that bear the incised outlines of medieval swords. At the head of one sword, much mutilated, is a Maltese cross.

The ruins of the Black Castle stand to the E. of the village. Sir John Campbell of Lochow, a nephew of Robert Bruce, was granted land hereabout in 1320, and the building of the Castle was no doubt begun about then. Sir John was killed at the Battle of Halidon Hill in 1333. The Castle is said to have originally stood in the middle of a shallow lake and to have been joined to the shore by a stone causeway.

There are two prehistoric standing stones in the neighbourhood. The first is in the field below Baledmund House. The second is at the entrance to Balnakeilly House.

MOUSA, Island of, *Shetland* (Map 8, ref. 44⁶12⁴), is one of the SHETLAND Northern Islands (*see* "The Shape of Scotland"). It is a comparatively minor island in the county group lying off the E. coast of the Shetland Mainland 11 m. S. of LERWICK. It is, however, of paramount interest through the presence on it of a broch or place of retreat and fortification, dating back about 2,000 years; yet in one respect it is contemporary. It rests on island flagstone, the same indestructible material that provides the paving-stones of Lerwick.

Despite some later occupation and well-meant restoration, the broch is unique in giving us the clearest indication of this kind of prehistoric building in Scotland. In external diameter the wall is 50 ft at the base, and just over 43 ft at the summit as it now stands. It is indeed possible that the original height of this famous broch exceeded any in Scotland. Certainly it is the most impressive example of island fortification that remains to us.

MOY, *Inverness-shire* (Map 5, ref. 27⁷83⁵), is best known as the seat of the chiefs of the Clan Mackintosh. This seat was first established in a castle on an island in Loch Moy, and was occupied from the mid-14th cent. About 1700 the chief moved to a new house at the N. end of the loch; it was burnt about 1800 and subsequently replaced by a larger house, extended in the 1860s. This was found to have dry rot, and the latest house was built in 1955-8. It is the only entirely modern chief's house in the Highlands.

The hamlet of Moy stands on the main N. road to INVERNESS. It and the loch are on a plateau between the valleys of the Findhorn and the Nairn.

The famous Rout of Moy took place on the old road to Inverness on the 16th of February 1746, when piper Donald Fraser, the local blacksmith, and four companions turned back the Hanoverian force under Lord Loudon, coming from Inverness to capture Prince Charles Edward Stuart, who was sleeping at Moy Hall.

MUCHALLS, *Kincardineshire* (Map 6, ref. 39°79¹), is a castle and a cliff-top village in the parish of Fetteresso, in the midst of a rather bare countryside, but themselves little gems. Built between 1619 and 1627 by Alexander Burnett of Leys and his son Sir Thomas, the castle has the handsomest plaster ceilings in Scotland, a secret staircase, a Green Lady, a wishing well in the courtyard, and a mysterious (and now "lost") underground passage to the smugglers' cove at Gin Shore.

It is built on the L-plan with buildings surrounding a courtyard, enclosed within a curtain-wall with triple shot-holes on each side of the gateway. The great hall has a ceiling of delicate white pargetted plaster-work of a kind also found at GLAMIS, Pinkie, WINTON, and CRAIGIEVAR; but this is without doubt the finest of them all. Its design includes six coats of arms, four medallions depicting the heads of biblical and classical heroes, and three knops with hooks for hanging lamps, all joined with a pattern of straight and curved ribs bearing floral decoration. Almost rivalling the ceiling in splendour is the overmantel dated 1624. It holds the royal coat of arms as borne in Scotland following the Union of the Crowns in 1603, with the collar of the thistle inside the garter and surmounted by the Scottish crest. There are similar ceilings and overmantels in the withdrawing room and the laird's study. In Muchalls also is the bed from Fetteresso House (now demolished) in which James Stuart, the Jacobite and *de jure* claimant to the thrones of the United Kingdom, spent a night in the campaign of 1715. The Castle, which is open to visitors on stated days, is now the home

Muchalls Castle

M. A. Simpson

of Mr and Mrs M. A. Simpson, who have filled it with antique treasures.

The 2 m. between the Burn of Elsick and the Burn of Muchalls have the finest array of rock scenery anywhere on the mainland of Scotland. The *pièce de résistance* is called the Grim Brigs, and consists of two gneiss rocks through which the waves have excavated arches 80 ft high by 50 ft wide. Other famous rocks are May Craig, Dunie Fell, the Auld Carl (often called the Old Man of Muchalls), Scart's Craig, the Castle Rock, and Tillie Tennant. The smugglers' tunnel from Gin Shore to the castle was sealed up by Lord Robertson, Lord Justice General of Scotland, who tenanted Muchalls Castle at the end of the 19th cent. and was sensitive about "illegal activities".

Muchalls was the site of an ancient fishing village called Stranathrow. It was entirely rebuilt in the middle of the 19th cent. by the "laird", an educational endowment trust, and was the pioneer of "model villages" for fishermen, but it had scarcely been completed when the trawling revolution lured away the fishermen to ABERDEEN. Its charming whitewashed cottages are now tenanted by farm and forestry workers and commuters from Aberdeen and STONEHAVEN.

Owing to the Jacobite leanings of the Keiths, earls marischal, Muchalls remained a strong centre of Episcopalian faith. The ancient church of St Ternan, still in use, and until recently lit by candles, is well worth a visit.

MUCK, Island of, *Inverness-shire* (Map 4, ref. 14²78°), is one of the Inner Hebrides (*see* "The Shape of Scotland"). The smallest of the "Small Isles" (the group including EIGG, CANNA, and RUM, standing off the coast of MORAR and ARISAIG), Muck is also the most isolated. No steamer calls there, and the few inhabitants have to rely on motor boat connection with Eigg.

Dean Monro in his *Western Isles of Scotland* calls it "Swyne's Isle"; for the Gaelic word from which Muck's unpleasing name in English derives is the only slightly less unpleasing one of "pig". This name it originally acquired because of a fancied resemblance in its shape to a sow.

Muck, however, deserves neither its Gaelic nor English name. It is a pleasing little island in superb surroundings, paternally presided over by a laird who gives employment to all the inhabitants. There are a few good sandy beaches, and some lobster fishing; and all the inhabitants seem very contented.

Not much more than 2 m. in length, it covers only 1,586 acres and rises to a height of 451 ft.

MUCKLE FLUGGA, Island of, *Shetland* (Map 8, ref. 45¹21°), is one of the SHETLAND Northern Islands (*see* "The Shape of Scotland"). This remote rock lying N. of UNST is the ultimate piece of land in the British Isles in the northerly direction. It supports a lighthouse of considerable importance in these often raging seas, and thus is the northernmost inhabited British island.

MUIRFIELD, *East Lothian* (Map 3, ref. 35º68³). Just E. of GULLANE lies the famous golf course of Muirfield. It is the home of the Ancient and Honourable Company of Edinburgh Golfers, who started playing on the links of Leith, before moving to MUSSELBURGH, which became too crowded and caused them to migrate to the turf-covered sandy hills of Muirfield, which was opened in May 1891. There has been a recent planting of coarse grass in the sand to the E. of the course to keep the sand from shifting.

Many famous matches have been played here since the first Open Championship at Muirfield in 1892, the year after the course opened.

In the old days, the Honourable Company of Edinburgh Golfers used to attribute their longevity to the fresh airs blowing in from the Firth of FORTH, and to the amount of duty-free claret they carried beneath their belts: the fresh winds still blow, but there is, alas! no duty-free claret in Scotland today.

MUIRKIRK, *Ayrshire* (Map 2, ref. 26⁹62⁷). The Kirk of the Moor was a chapel of ease of MAUCHLINE parish built about 1565, some 11 m. E. of Mauchline. It is now a bleak mining town astride the AYR–DOUGLAS–EDINBURGH road near the headwaters of the R. Ayr. The modern town grew from a settlement in the late 18th cent. that was engaged in iron-smelting. The ironworks are now defunct, and the place depends on coal. There is a live covenanting tradition; the martyr John Brown of Priesthill lived and died in the neighbourhood.

About 3 m. to the E. is Glenbuck Loch, the source of the R. Ayr mentioned by Robert Burns in his poem "The Brigs o' Ayr", which describes the river in flood and the destruction of the New Bridge:

> And from Glenbuch down to the
> Ratton Quay,
> Auld Ayr is just one lengthen'd
> tumblin' sea,
> Then down you'll hurl, deil nor ye
> never rise,
> And dash the gumely jaups up to the
> pourin' skies.

Ratton Quay was the pier-head at Ayr Harbour.

MUIR OF ORD, *Ross and Cromarty* (Map 5, ref. 25³85⁰), a village formerly called Tarradale, is in the centre of a large crofting area. On the "muir", now a golf course, there used to be great cattle-, sheep-, and horse-markets or "trysts", founded in 1820, and second in importance only to those at FALKIRK in the

mid-19th cent. Muir of Ord became the headquarters for a contracting business, which was started in 1895 by the son of a local crofter and was responsible for huge projects like the TAY Road Bridge, many hydro-electric schemes, and the INVERNESS Bridge.

Some 4 m. NE. of Muir of Ord is Kilcoy, the ancient seat of the Mackenzies, restored in the 17th cent., and a fine example of the Scottish baronial style.

The church of Kilchrist, ½ m. to the E., was the scene of a grim traditional incident of the early 17th cent. The Macdonalds, led by Allan Dubh of Lundy, plundered the lands and, so it is said, set fire to the church filled with men, women, and children, whose dying cries were drowned by the skirl of Glengarry's piper as he marched round playing his pipes.

About 2 m. SE., on the shores of the BEAULY Firth, is Tarradale House, where the geologist Sir Roderick Murchison (1792–1871) was born. It contains a notable library, and is now used as a Field Study Centre under the administration of ABERDEEN University Geography Department.

MULL, Island of, *Argyll* (Map 1, ref. 15º73⁵), is the largest of the Inner Hebrides (*see* "The Shape of Scotland"). It is an island of great variety, with its rough moorlands to the N., and its hilly centre (rising to 3,169 ft in Ben More to the W. at the BURG), and showing a bold headland to the southern townships round Loch Don, Loch Spelve, and Lochbuie, and the sandy machair at the tip of the Ross of Mull opposite IONA. Great castles, like ruined Aros and Duart (restored by the Chief of the Macleans in 1912), were strong points in their day, and the military ardour of the Mullmen is shown by a list of more than 100 officers (including seven generals) who served at the time of the Napoleonic wars, and brought countless soldiers, mostly Macleans, from the island into the ranks of the army. Although it lacks some of the grandeur and rock-climbing attractions of SKYE, Mull is to some people an equally favourite island for holidays.

Its roads are varied, though sometimes rough (and it is as well to remember that the distance from the chief town TOBERMORY to the Iona ferry is about 50 m.), and there are many attractive places at the head of the long sea-lochs that bite into the land. Tobermory, founded as a fishing village in 1788, fills a dramatic site in an islet-sheltered anchorage in the NE., and there are sandy bays such as Calgary in the NW. and Uisken near BUNESSAN in the S. The Sound of Mull, which separates the island from the mainland of Morven, is a busy and generally sheltered waterway. Steamers from OBAN to the Outer Hebrides call at the Mull ports, and a vehicle ferry connects CRAIGNURE with Oban on the mainland and LOCHALINE in Morven. Buses run throughout the island, and there are hotels in profusion, guest houses and caravan and camping sites. Campers should seek a farmer's permission, as much of the unfenced land is in fact valuable grazing. The Forestry Commission also welcomes visitors to its large tracts of land. Apart from golf, pony-trekking, sea angling, salmon and trout fishing, swimming, walking, and nature study (Mull is proud of its red and fallow deer and advertises deer-stalking for visitors on a 15,000-acre deer forest), it is a yachtsman's Mecca, and at Tobermory visitors may even join a 50-ft ketch as crew for a cruise of a week or two.

One of the attractions of Mulls is the fringe of lesser isles lying off its coast, Iona, STAFFA, TRESHNISH, ULVA, Gometra, INCH KENNETH, and others. Most of these can be visited by motor launch.

The people of Mull are great singers and musicians, and welcome visitors to their ceilidhs, impromptu or organized. A special attraction is the Little Theatre at Dervaig (the smallest professional theatre in the world, seating forty-five in a converted byre): here there are morning and afternoon performances for children – worth knowing if there is rain.

MURTHLY CASTLE, *Perthshire* (Map 6, ref. 31°73⁸), set among woods on the banks of the R. TAY 3 m. from STANLEY, is the seat of the Stewarts of Murthly or Grandtully family. Built of ash-coloured stone, like DUNKELD Cathedral, it displays a range of variously dated buildings with a terraced and formal garden. The westerly range is the oldest part, and has a five-storey tower acquired by Sir William Stewart of Grandtully (1567–1646), to which additions have been made in the 17th and 18th cents. Finally Victorian buildings were added on both the N. and S. blocks.

The 19th-cent. laird, Sir William Stewart, was a great traveller and brought home many treasures and curiosities, including two Red Indians who lived in a pagoda in the garden.

An 18th-cent. Stewart was involved in the "Douglas Case" – a matter too complicated to describe here save to say that it set all Scotland, and particularly EDINBURGH, in an uproar, an uproar in which Boswell joined.

The "Murthly Case" (Stewart *v.* Wilson or Robertson Session papers for 1874–5) was one of disputed succession following upon an alleged "Declaratory Marriage". It certainly exposed one section of Victorian Scottish society. It was hotly debated and was eventually carried to the House of Lords. It makes strange reading today; you realize that the Edinburgh of Robert Louis Stevenson's youth was truly a city of Jekyll and Hyde.

MUSSELBURGH, *Midlothian* (Map 3, ref. 33⁵67⁸). At the mouth of the R. Esk lie Fisherrow on the W. bank and the town of Musselburgh on the E. The present bridge was built by John Rennie in 1807, while the oldest one of three arches upstream is said to rest on Roman foundations. Musselburgh was a port of some significance even in Roman times, from which remains have been found in the district. On the old bridge are traces of a gate used for defence when this was the main route from SE. Scotland to EDINBURGH.

Although Musselburgh had been a burgh of regality for centuries before, it received in 1632 a charter as a royal burgh; but the Magistrates of Edinburgh are said to have persuaded Musselburgh to renounce the privileges. In 1544, part of the town and the Chapel of Loretto were burnt by the English; 1547 saw the Battle of Pinkie fought just to the E. of INVERESK, and in 1548 Musselburgh was again burnt.

The Chapel of Loretto was founded about 1533, and it had a hermitage attached. Burnt in 1544, it was restored, only to be destroyed again after the Reformation and its stones used to build the tolbooth in 1590.

At the NE. extremity of the town lies Pinkie House, of which the oldest part is the square tower. Formerly the country seat of the abbots of DUNFERMLINE, the House passed to the 1st Earl of Dunfermline, by whom it was decorated, including the ceiling in the painted gallery 96 ft long. The House now forms part of Loretto School.

Musselburgh Links have been used since 1816 as a racecourse, and the golf course is said to have been played on in 1504 by James IV. It became the home of the Honourable Company of Edinburgh Golfers, who moved from Leith in 1836, but went on to MUIRFIELD when it became too crowded in 1891. The Golf Club, founded in 1774, offered in its early days a prize of "creel and shawl" to the best player among the fishwives.

The fishing centre of Fisherrow by Musselburgh was important for broadcloth-making in the 17th cent., and cheap cloth in the 18th cent., but these have now been replaced as local industries by paper-mills and the manufacture of fish-net and twine.

MUTHILL, *Perthshire* (Map 2, ref. 28⁷71⁷). This attractive village in a wooded setting in Strathearn lies 3 m. S. of CRIEFF. The village, like others in Strathearn, was burnt by the Highlanders retreating after the Battle of SHERIFFMUIR in 1715, but was rehabilitated by the Earl of Perth, whose seat at Drummond Castle lies 2 m. NW. of the village. Many of these late 18th-cent. houses are built of local stone and have walls over 2 ft thick.

Parts of the nave and choir of the old church of Muthill exist, as well as the 70-ft tower, complete with bell and capped by crow-stepped gables whose foundations may be as old as the 9th cent. It should be compared with its counterpart at DUNNING. There exists documentary evidence that Dean Ochiltree, whose house stood on the Bishop's Green below the church, built or rebuilt the church at Muthill at the end of the 14th cent.

Drummond Castle consists of an old keep, now used as a museum, and a modern wing built early in the 19th cent. The older part was built by John, 1st Lord Drummond, in 1491. It was besieged by Cromwell, destroyed in 1689, and partly garrisoned by Government troops in 1715, but finally razed in 1745 by the Jacobite Duchess of Perth, so that the Hanoverian troops could not take advantage of it.

The gardens at Drummond Castle are one of the showpieces in the county. The original garden was laid out by John, 2nd Earl of Perth, in the 17th cent. In 1840 a more elaborate plan was completed, centred on a sundial that tells what the time is in all the principal cities of Europe. The gardens contain many rare trees and shrubs and are open to visitors at stated times during the summer.

The Roman road from ARDOCH to Strageath passes through the parish, and has been exposed at a number of places, particularly alongside the N. drive to Culdees Castle, where it is 23 ft wide.

NAIRN, *Nairnshire* (Map 5, ref. 28⁸85⁷). This popular seaside resort, known as the "Brighton of the North", has splendid beaches, a famously sunny climate, and three golf courses (two 18- and one 9-hole). It is a convenient centre for coastal and inland touring. The town stands on the border of the Highlands and Lowlands, and at one time Gaelic was spoken at the SW. end and English at the NE. end. Dr Johnson visited it in the course of his Scottish tour, and here for the first time saw peat fires and heard the Celtic tongue. The harbour was built in 1820 to Telford's plan and has since been enlarged.

About 3 m. S. of Nairn is Rait Castle, built in the early 15th cent. and notable for its round tower. Although now lacking a roof and floor, it is otherwise remarkably complete. Here the Mackintoshes massacred the Comyns in 1424. On the eastern outskirts of the town is Balblair. Here is the site where the Duke of Cumberland ("Butcher" or "Sweet William", as you care to call him) encamped before marching to defeat the Jacobites under Prince Charles Edward Stuart at CULLODEN in 1746.

NAVER, *Sutherland* (Map 5, ref. 26⁴93⁵). Some 5½ m. long, Loch Naver lies to the E. of ALTNAHARRA, with Ben Clibreck (3,154 ft) rising from the S. shore. On the N. bank are Grummore and Grumbeg, the ruins of two depopulated early 19th-cent. crofting townships; these are preserved as Ancient Monuments. The clearing of these townships in 1819 is described by Donald Sage in *Memorabilia Domestica*. Down the strath, which extends 19 m. to the sea at BETTYHILL, the land gets richer at Syre, where the Department of

Agriculture has resettled land in smallholdings. Farther N., at Skail, stands a stone commemorating the formation of the 93rd Sutherland Highlanders in 1800 – famous as the "Thin Red Line" at Balaclava.

At Truderscaig, and on the banks of the Mallart river flowing into the loch at the E. end, are remains of many hut and stone circles.

NEILSTON, *Renfrewshire* (Map 2, ref. 24⁸65⁷). On the Levern river, the town of Neilston is 2 m. S. of BARRHEAD in moorland country. In the 18th cent. it was a famous centre for bleaching cotton and calico-printing. In 1770–80 cotton-spinning was introduced, and it was so successful that the town was chosen by the authors of the *Old Statistical Account* as one of three parishes in Scotland to illustrate to the French Chamber of Commerce the status to which rural manufactures had attained in Scotland. Cotton-spinning is still the main local industry, producing fine sewing-cotton.

NESS, Loch, *Inverness-shire* (Map 5, ref. 25⁰82²). This celebrated loch is part of the Great Glen or GLENMORE ALBIN, and extends from 7 m. SW. of INVERNESS for the 24 m. to FORT AUGUSTUS; it is about 1 m. wide and 700 ft deep. There are no records of its ever having been frozen over. The W. side has a modern road built in the 1930s, and the E. side road was built by General Wade 200 years before that. The CALEDONIAN CANAL runs right through the loch.

In 1952 John Cobb, the racing motorist, was drowned here in an attempt on the water speed record; a cairn in his memory stands on the W. shore between DRUMNADROCHIT and INVERMORISTON.

All countries in Europe, and most in the Western world, have heard of the Loch Ness Monster. It was first reported as headline news in 1932, but there were local legends about it dating back to St Adamnan, Abbot of IONA in the 7th cent., who reported an *aquatilis bestia* in the loch. This is no place in which to discuss whether the monster is a fish, an animal, an illusion, or even some man-made thing, as has sometimes been suggested.

We may point out, however, that since 1932 stories about its appearance have constantly been appearing and have always obstinately remained "news"; it is a "story" that just will not lie down. Moreover it is difficult to dismiss with the phrase "mass self-delusion" the testimony of so many reputable people of all kinds and professions, within the neighbourhood and without, who have solemnly testified to having seen it.

NETHY BRIDGE, *Inverness-shire* (Map 6, ref. 30¹82⁰), is a small residential and holiday village on a tributary of the SPEY on the back road from GRANTOWN-ON-SPEY to COY-

LUM BRIDGE and the CAIRNGORMS. Strategically sited for sporting activities (climbing,
walking, fishing, and skiing), it also has a
nine-hole golf course adjoining the hotel. Considerable conifer forests extend on the high
ground behind the village. In the 18th cent.,
timber from this area was floated down the
Nethy Burn to the Spey at Broomhill and from
there in rafts down the Spey to GARMOUTH
on the Moray coast. Local timber was also
used for smelting iron brought from the LECHT.

NEW ABBEY, *Kirkcudbrightshire* (Map 2,
ref. 29⁶56⁶). Nestling in the valley of the New
Abbey Burn, among woods and dominated by
Criffel (1,866 ft) and its twin peak, Knocken-
loch, New Abbey village is a place of great
beauty. Indeed, it would be this even without
the warm red pile of SWEETHEART ABBEY,
which towers above the single-storeyed whitewashed cottages. The "New" in the name is to
distinguish it from DUNDRENNAN Abbey,
founded 130 years earlier. The old smithy in
the village has a fine 18th-cent. motto

By Hammer and Hand
All Arts do Stand

on a stone over its door; nearby, an octagonal
pillar at the corner of a house marks where the
present street passes through the precinct wall
of the Abbey – which, as a massive structure of
granite boulders, is clearly seen as you enter
the village over the New Abbey Burn Bridge.
    Abbey House, at the DUMFRIES end of the
village, incorporates 16th-, 17th-, and 18th-
cent. structural elements; it was occupied by
Gilbert Broun, the famous last Abbot of
Sweetheart.
    An attractive 18th-cent. water-mill building
sits at the end of the bridge, while, rather less
than 1 m. from the village, on a steep-faced
hillock above the Glen Burn, stands the
circular 60-ft Waterloo Tower erected "To
our Gallant Prussian Allies under Marshal
Blücher". From the summit of Criffel on a
clear day the magnificent view (mentioned by
William and Dorothy Wordsworth) includes
the Irish coast, the Isle of Man, the Galloway
Highlands, Queensberry, and the Cheviots.

NEWBATTLE, *Midlothian* (1 m. SE. of
DALKEITH), scarcely now exists as a village,
but the historic Newbattle Abbey serves a
modern function as Scotland's only residential
college of adult education. The Abbey, originally a 12th-cent. Cistercian foundation, became
a family seat of the Kerrs, later Marquesses of
Lothian, towards the end of the 16th cent.
Throughout the centuries, the Abbey has had a
recurring association with royalty. David II,
son of Robert Bruce, buried a murdered
mistress here; James IV met his bride, Princess
Margaret of England, for the first time at the
Abbey before the marriage between "the
thistle and the rose"; James V was another

Stuart visitor; and George IV started a fashion
of royal visits that has continued to the present
day. After being a family home of the Lothians
for almost four centuries, the Abbey was given
in trust to the Scottish nation by Philip Kerr,
11th Marquess of Lothian, as an adult education college.
    All that remains of the old village, which
once covered much of what is now Newbattle
golf course, is a few cottages, the architecturally
attractive but vacant Sun Inn by the Abbey
gates, and the fine old church. The gentle art of
brewing elderflower wine, once a local specialty,
has also declined.

NEWBURGH, *Aberdeenshire* (Map 6, ref.
40⁰82⁴). "A seaport village in Foveran parish,
on the right side of the R. Ythan 7 furlongs
from the sea and 5 m. SE. of Ellon Station."
So, rather quaintly, Groome's Ordnance
Gazetteer put it seventy years ago. It went on to
add: "Several schooners and steam vessels use
the estuary, exporting grain and importing coal,
timber, lime and bones". That was at the end
of the 19th cent. Newburgh is still a seaport,
though on a smaller scale. It still exports grain
from the rich farmlands of Buchan and Formartine. It still imports coal as it has done for 300
years. The Ythan estuary is the largest on the
Aberdeenshire coast, yet the stream that flows
within it is a shrunken giant, a mere 40 m.
long, in places but a burn meandering among
the reeds – yet a burn that teems with fish to a
degree unique for one of its size, a burn that,
swollen by the tide, fills a basin 700 yds across.
The secret of prehistory that explains this
paradox is that once the Ythan rolled to meet
the Rhine replete with the headwaters of
the DEVERON, the Bogie, the Shevock, and the
Ury. All these it lost by river-capture, but the
estuary it created in its heyday remains, and
few of the 1,000 visitors who come to the village
of Newburgh every year can have failed to
thrill with the strange, haunting beauty of this
wide, dune-fringed river mouth.
    Most of them come to fish for the Ythan
sea-trout, which are world-famous, though the
river also has its brown trout and salmon.
Others come to study and observe, for the
Ythan estuary offers a special challenge to the
sciences of nature, a fact catered for by
Culterty, the University of ABERDEEN's
Zoological Field Station, formerly the home
and bird sanctuary of the late Dr H. Edgar
Smith. It is equipped with laboratories, lecture
rooms, and equipment stores for rings, nets,
traps, and hides. Newburgh also possesses
raised beaches on three levels, flint-knapping
sites where prehistoric man shaped his first
tools, salt marshes teeming with every kind of
estuarine life, and the mighty dunes that pile up
to their dramatic climax on the N. side of the
estuary in the Sands of FORVIE.
    Today the tiny harbour is maintained by a
firm of meal-millers, whose vessel, the *Anno*,

assists in the export of oats for making "real porridge" all over the world. There are two fine hotels, and many boarding-houses, to cater for the influx of anglers and tourists.

NEWBURGH, *Fife* (Map 3, ref. 32³71⁸). The small royal burgh of Newburgh stands on the S. shore of the Firth of TAY. Opposite the town, the firth is divided by Mugdrum Island into the North and South Deeps. Mugdrum House, built in 1786, lies on the shore opposite the middle of the island, with Mugdrum Cross, a square pillar on a stone base believed once to have had arms as a real cross. Another similar one, Macduff's Cross, stands on the road to Strathearn; this is ruder and more antiquated, and was formerly held to mark the place of a sanctuary for any clansman guilty of murder.

Despite its name, the burgh is old, for Alexander III granted its charter in 1266, when it was called the New Burgh beside the monastery of LINDORES. Later privileges were confirmed by the Abbot of Lindores in 1457, and then by James VI and Charles I.

The hill-fort on Clachard Craig, ½ m. SE. of the burgh, is the probable site of a first settlement; there are traces of three main structural phases.

NEWCASTLETON, *Roxburghshire* (Map 3, ref. 34⁸58⁸). This pleasant village, the principal settlement on Liddesdale, lies in the flat valley bottom. It is an interesting example of late 18th-cent. planning, having been created in 1793 by the 3rd Duke of Buccleuch as a handloom-weaving village. It has a main street with a central square and small squares at each end. The side street has houses on one side only.

The surrounding countryside saw some of the earliest major activity of the Forestry Commission.

NEW CUMNOCK, *Ayrshire* (Map 2, ref. 26¹61³). Another of Ayrshire's upland mining villages, New Cumnock, is 6 m. S. of CUMNOCK on the KILMARNOCK–DUMFRIES road. Like other similar settlements, it is in two parts – "Bank" on the R. Nith, separated by 400 yds from "Path Head" on the R. Afton. This is, of course, the "sweet Afton" immortalized by Robert Burns, and it still flows gently through its glen, some 2 or 3 m. from the village.

NEW GALLOWAY, *Kirkcudbrightshire* (Map 2, ref. 26³57⁸), is the smallest of all Scottish royal burghs – a village set among delightful surroundings. Its Charter of 1633 was really a transference from nearby DALRY, which was at first intended as the new burgh, but Gordon of Kenmure wanted a burgh and market at his gates.

New Galloway stands high above the N. end of Loch Ken and just N. of Kenmure Castle,

formerly the seat of the Gordons of Lochinvar. Though much altered, there is still a little 16th- and 17th-cent. work in the present building; the site has been heavily defended by a large moat on the W. and was traditionally a stronghold of the Lords of Galloway.

In Kells churchyard to the N. of the burgh is the gravestone of a Covenanter shot in 1685, and an attractive Adam and Eve stone. Farther up the Ken valley is Glenlee power station, part of the Galloway power scheme.

NEW LANARK, *Lanarkshire* (Map 2, ref. 28⁸64³). The former manufacturing village of about 170 houses on the wooded banks of the CLYDE is 1 m. SW. of LANARK. Founded in 1783 by the philanthropist David Dale as a cotton-spinning centre and experiment in community living, it was later the scene of a far-sighted social experiment of Dale's son-in-law Robert Owen, in housing, factory management, and education. The original mill buildings are distinguished and well preserved. The village was taken over in 1903 by a rope-manufacturing company, and this is still the main industry. In 1963 the New Lanark Association was formed to maintain and modernize the interiors of the original buildings and to start a new industrial life.

NEWMILNS, *Ayrshire* (Map 2, ref. 25⁴63⁷). The middle of the three "valley burghs" of the Upper Irvine Valley, Newmilns is famous for its lace and muslin manufactures. These were introduced by Alexander Morton in the 1840s. The weavers of Newmilns sent an address to Abraham Lincoln supporting his cause in the American Civil War, and received in acknowledgment a stars-and-stripes banner. It was lost in the early 20th cent., but Congress recently presented the town with another; this hangs in the Morton Hall. The place has strong covenanting associations. The other two burghs are DARVEL and GALSTON. Darvel is separated from Newmilns only by 1 m. of road. The two towns are "twins", although Newmilns may be said to have a more attractive residential quarter.

NEW PITSLIGO, *Aberdeenshire* (Map 6, ref. 38⁸85⁵), is a large village to the SW. of FRASERBURGH. Laid out on the eastern slope of the Hill of Turlundie and intersected by a picturesque Den, New Pitsligo, which has three long parallel main streets linked by many braes, represents a miracle of human settlement. Two centuries ago the site was a wilderness, part of the "six ploughs on the moor" that formed the upper barony of Pitsligo, one of the forfeited estates of that romantic martyr of the '45 Jacobite Rising, the 4th and last Lord Pitsligo. It was cut off from the parish church of Tyrie and the sea-coast by a vast peat moss, impassable in winter, roadless and trackless. The moss still remains in the heart of the

Plate 13   The Isle of Rum, Inner Hebrides: Trallval, Ainshval, and Ruinsival, across Harris Bay (see p. 401)

A Shetland shawl (see p. 413)

Buchan plain, but is now beautiful rather than desolate. The transformation was begun by Sir William Forbes, a banker and grand-nephew of Lord Pitsligo, who determined to found a village there to perpetuate the honoured name of Pitsligo. He spent a fortune laying out the streets, making miles of roads and planting thousands of trees. He gave off feus at 5s. per annum, and much village land was offered free of rent. The houses, well-built stone and lime but-and-bens with an oot-room attached, cost £30 to build. The moss is now worked by several operators, and from it peat is exported 'or distilleries as far afield as Japan. There is a large bakery factory, and a small quarrying industry remains of what was once the principal source of employment. Life has always been hard in New Pitsligo. Its subsistence economy had to be eked out by every possible auxiliary source of revenue. One of these was the making of "pillow lace", a craft patronized by Queen Victoria, and still practised in the village today by some of the older women. The village was always a stronghold of Episcopalianism and its modern showplace is St John's Church, built entirely by New Pitsligo masons almost a century ago to designs by G. E. Street. The village itself is plain; the surrounding country-side is austere. Yet as you watch the busy trucks on the light railways that honeycomb the moss, you realize that New Pitsligo has contributed something precious to the life of Scotland.

NEWPORT-ON-TAY, *Fife* (Map 6, ref. 34²72⁸). Constituted in 1822 by Act of Parliament as the ferry station from Fife to DUNDEE (the harbour was built in the same year from designs by Telford), Newport became a popular residential area, and it has many villas dating from this period. Near Wormit, 2 m. W. of Newport, the first TAY rail bridge was broken in the gale of 1879, a train plunging into the river with the loss of ninety passengers. A new rail bridge was built in 1883–8, and in 1966 the old ferry went out of operation with the opening of the fine new road bridge, linking Fife, Angus, and the NE.

NEWSTEAD, *Roxburghshire* (Map 3, ref. 35⁷63⁴). This was a complex of Roman forts and camps of which no structural remains survive on the surface. The site is on the S. bank of the TWEED, 1½ m. E. of MELROSE on a high bluff just E. of the village of Newstead where "Dere Street" crossed the river. A memorial stone marks the site. The place was called Trimontium, and was the centre of Roman control of the area and the permanent quarters of the largest and strongest garrison in the Lowlands. It was first excavated in 1905–10; excavations continued later.

NEWTONGRANGE, *Midlothian* (3 m. S. of DALKEITH), is a mining village, and was originally the site of farmlands associated with the Cistercian monks of NEWBATTLE, themselves among the earliest workers of coal in Scotland. The Newtongrange sprint at New Year is one of the premier meetings in Scotland for professional runners.

NEWTON MEARNS, *Renfrewshire* (Map 2, ref. 25³65⁴), lies on the edge of high moorland not far from GLASGOW. It has yet retained its name and individuality since the early 14th cent. In the neighbourhood is the 17th-cent. Pollok Castle, destroyed by fire in 1882 but subsequently rebuilt. It still has its fine 17th-cent. garden layout.

NEWTONMORE, *Inverness-shire* (Map 5, ref. 27¹79⁹). This is the most southerly of the Highland holiday resorts that are known collectively as Speyside. It was here that pony-trekking was first introduced as an organized holiday sport in Scotland, and the village is also a recognized base for skiing in the CAIRNGORMS. Associations with the Clan Macpherson, who dominated the area in earlier days, are recalled in the village's clan museum. The collection includes the famous "black chanter" of the clan battle at PERTH, and the green banner under which the Macphersons never knew defeat. Adjoining the main road just S. of the village is the local shinty ground, Ellen, the scene of modern heroic encounters; dominating the view from here is the hill, Craig Dhu, that gave the clan Macpherson its rallying call. The village has a wide range of hotel accommodation. It is admirably situated as a centre for walking or car touring. Glen Banchor, running westwards through the foot-hills of the Monadhliaths, is attractive country for holiday expeditions, and farther still to the W., beyond Lagganbridge, the CORRIE-YAIRACK Pass offers a challenging walk and a classic view. Good fishing, golf, tennis courts that convert into curling rinks, and a sociable programme of ceilidhs are some of the other features of the village during its two holiday seasons.

NEWTON STEWART, *Wigtownshire* (Map 2, ref. 24¹56⁵). This busy market town and educational centre of eastern Wigtownshire is attractively situated on the Cree, just above the head of tidal water, and among hilly wooded country. It takes its name from William Stewart, the third son of the Earl of Galloway, who built a few houses and obtained a charter from Charles II for the town as a burgh of barony. The district pioneered plantations and agricultural development; the drystane dyke of modern times was developed in the Newton Stewart area from the 1690s.

There has been much reclamation of boggy land along the Cree estuary since the mid-18th cent., which has given a wide area of very fertile farmland – though, as is shown by the great cluster of cairns in the flat fields by the road approaching the town from the SE. (all but one are mere foundations now), men have found the district a good one to live in for a very long time.

The town was slow in developing after the 1677 charter, and there was much smuggling in the area during the 18th cent. In the late 1770s, Sir William Douglas, founder of CASTLE DOUGLAS, bought the estate, changed the name to Newton Douglas (which never caught on), got a new charter, and started spinning, weaving, and carpet-manufacture. But industry was not successful, although there is a hand-loom weaving industry at the present time.

The town is a splendid holiday and fishing centre. On the CREETOWN road, 3 m. SE., is Bargaly Glen, which is associated with John Buchan's *Thirty-Nine Steps*. NE. the road past Murray's Monument to NEW GALLOWAY leads through splendid mountain scenery, which is now richly forested.

NIGG, *Ross and Cromarty* (Map 5, ref. 28¹87¹). This township overlooks the Bay of Nigg on the CROMARTY Firth. In the church is a curious sculptured stone, possibly of the 7th-cent., said to commemorate one of three sons of a Danish king who were drowned nearby.

Near the North Sutor, at the mouth of the Cromarty Firth, is the green mound of Dunskaith – possibly the site of a fort erected by William the Lion in 1179. This offers a fine view of the Firth.

NORTH BERWICK, *East Lothian* (Map 3, ref. 35⁵68⁶). An ancient royal burgh situated on the S. shore of the Firth of FORTH 23 m. from EDINBURGH by road, North Berwick is a deservedly popular holiday resort as well as a pleasant place for people to live who travel daily to work in Edinburgh by rail, bus, or car.

It is famous for its two fine golf courses, has good shops, hotels, and a cinema, and is the social meeting-place for the farmers and farm-workers who live in the surrounding countryside.

There are two fine sandy bays, divided by the harbour area. Here are anchored two or three fishing boats and many privately owned yachts and dinghies, as well as the "pilot" boat that helps to ensure safe shipping up the Firth of Forth to GRANGEMOUTH and Leith. Adjacent to the harbour, in a natural rocky setting, is a heated open-air swimming-pool, filled with water from the sea.

Also near the harbour are the remains, recently unearthed, of a 12th-cent. kirk, dedicated to St Andrew. It was in the Church of St Andrew, in 1591, that the devil is said to have appeared to a congregation of local witches and wizards, as quoted in later trials of the North Berwick witches. In the garden of a house near the station called "The Abbey" (now owned by Edinburgh Corporation and used as a holiday home for old people), there is the ruin of a Cistercian convent founded in the 12th cent. The parish kirk in the High Street owns four fine silver chalices, two of 17th-cent origin, and an old hour-glass and a baptismal ewer.

In School Road stands a small museum; it is devoted largely to the history and archaeology of the district, and the natural history of the Forth. The Town House is a charming 18th-cent. building at the E. end of the High Street, and close by is "The Lodge", another 18th-cent. house, which is surrounded by park-like grounds of 25 acres, right in the centre of the town.

About 1 m. S. of the town is North Berwick Law, rising to 613 ft in a grassy pyramid, which is of volcanic origin. It is not an arduous climb to the top, where one finds the ruins of a Napoleonic watch-tower, and an archway formed by the jaw-bones of a whale. The view on all sides is magnificent, and a viewpoint-indicator helps you to pick out the many interesting points.

Offshore in addition to the BASS ROCK, with its continuous whirl of screaming, silvery gannets, are the small rocky islands of the Lamb and Craigleith, with Fidra lying off DIRLETON to the W., and in the distance the Lomond Hills in Fife. To the E. lies the massive rose-red ruin of TANTALLON CASTLE, and the fine farming land of East Lothian stretches southwards to the Lammermuir Hills.

OBAN, *Argyll* (Map 1, ref. 18⁷73⁰). This popular holiday resort and harbour at the centre of Scotland's western seaboard is one of the better examples of 19th-cent. expansion. Oban 200 years ago was of little account. Now she reverberates with life, and in the summer season offers a quite exhilarating prospect. Victorian architecture at its Scottish dreariest is inevitable here and there, but is overcome by the style of the town, and by its outstanding siting.

Indeed, few Scottish holiday towns provoke the kind of romantic sentiment with which Oban is generally regarded. All things conspire to give it a special place in Scottish affections. Perhaps these affections are primarily aroused in many of us by the fact that Oban has long been regarded as the gateway to the Western Isles, both inner and outer. Visitors who have been there do not forget too that Oban is the centre for exploration of many of the attractions in the Western Highlands of the mainland.

But Oban is more than a gateway to islands and a centre of West Highland mainland touring. It is in itself finely set in surroundings of considerable beauty, with seascape and landscape contending for attention. To stand,

Oban harbour

as one of its citizens has said, "upon Pulpit Hill overlooking the great sweep of the bay with its ornate wedding-cake hotels fringing it, to enjoy the wide prospects of the Firth of Lorne and the Sound of MULL, is an experience not easily forgotten".

Oban indeed has its own claims to hold the eye. Its position too upon the edge of a still living Gaelic island culture gives it, despite its strong holiday-town appearance, a more leisurely atmosphere than is usual in a holiday resort. There is for the English or Lowland Scots visitor to Oban a different rhythm of life here.

The town of Oban (deriving its name from a Gaelic word meaning bay or creek) stands on the coast of Lorne opposite the northern end of the Island of Kerrera, which guards the bay, and which makes of it a spacious harbour. Oban is approachable by sea and land. It is 24 miles N. of the CRINAN CANAL, just under 50 miles S. of FORT WILLIAM, and just over 90 miles N. of GLASGOW.

Though it is true that, in many cases, there are traces of ancient men who settled in the district, which supported a considerable community living off hunting and fishing; and though the town is the focal point of a neighbourhood rich in historical incident; the town itself is of no great antiquity – it is little more than 200 years old.

To develop fisheries in the Firth of Lorne, Oban was erected into a fishing station by the Government Fishery Board in 1786. As an encouragement to the fishermen, premiums were paid upon the fish caught. The venture, however, was not a success, probably through the lack of proper boats and fishing gear and the difficulty of sending the catch to market. The experiment was abandoned after a few

years, but by this time commerce had begun to extend its influence.

In 1811 Oban was raised to the dignity of a burgh of barony by royal charter granted in favour of George William, Duke of Argyll. It was not until 1817, however, that the privileges conferred by the charter were assumed and a town council and magistrates elected. The Scottish Burgh Reform Act of 1832 created a parliamentary burgh with a provost, magistrates, and councillors. In 1840, the town had sixty-four electors, and in 1855 the number had risen only by 10 per cent. The population some four years earlier was recorded as 1,742. The town was growing fast, however, and by 1881 the number of inhabitants had reached 3,986. Oban was becoming the hub of communications in the West Highlands for commerce and tourism.

The well-known steamship concern David MacBrayne Ltd maintains regular sea services between Oban and such islands as Mull, LISMORE, COLL, TIREE, BARRA, and South UIST and pleasure cruises to the islands of the West, the most popular being the thrice-weekly excursion to IONA. This trip may also be done by steamer to CRAIGNURE in Mull, and then by coach through Glenmore to FIONPHORT and by the short ferry to Iona.

In the neighbourhood there is considerable local mainland country open to tourists, to those who go by train, to cyclists and walkers. It is not without reason, therefore, that Oban has been called the Charing Cross of the Highlands.

The bay being a safe one for boating and sailing through the protection afforded by the Island of Kerrera, Oban is therefore a favourite yachting station, and the town is the headquarters of the Royal Highland Club instituted in 1881. Oban Sailing Club is also active throughout the summer months.

During the Highland Games Week at the end of August the bay and the town present their gayest aspect. During this week is held the Argyllshire (it ought to be "Argyll"!) Highland Gathering, to which thousands flock. Throughout the season Oban is never dull, and between excursions delightful hours can be reposefully spent in admiring the polychromatic sunsets, in feeding swooping gulls on the Esplanade, or in visiting a seal island by motorboat; or in listening to the Oban Pipe Band, attending a fish auction on the railway pier or a strenuous game of shinty at Mossfield Park, enjoying a snack or a cup of tea in one of the many restaurants, or studying the souvenirs in the shop windows or the flow of one's fellow tourists, so varied in garb and tongue.

The chief thoroughfare is George Street, which runs almost due N. and S.; and this, with Argyll Square towards its southern extremity hard by the Railway Station, forms the business part of the town. At the N. end of George Street, the reredos in the Scottish Episcopal Church of St John the Divine, now the Episcopal Cathedral, is a memorial of Bishop Chinnery-Haldane of Argyll and the Isles. St Columba's Church opposite has been converted into offices of the North of Scotland Hydro-Electric Board since the congregation united with Argyll Square Church. The Free Church in Rockfield Road behind Argyll Square was designed by Augustus Pugin.

Facing the bay to the N. of the pier is the Corran Esplanade, with its fine views across the water and the many hotels. Beyond lies St Columba's Catholic Cathedral, a comparatively new all-granite building designed by Sir Giles Scott. The cathedral is much frequented by Gaelic-speaking Catholics from the Islands.

Dominating the northern approach to the harbour at the end of the Esplanade is Dunollie Castle, all that now remains of the glories of the lords of Lorne, who once owned a third of Scotland. The ruins are erected upon a bold promontory overlooking the Firth of Lorne.

If you take a boat trip to Kerrera, or go by the road next to the Sound of Kerrera, you will see the MacDougalls' other castle, Gylen, which guarded the southern approach to the harbour. A farming island today, Kerrera can be reached by ferry from the Gallanach Road. It was here that Alexander II of Scotland died in 1249, when he developed a fever after fighting the lords of Lorne. It was on Horseshoe Bay on the Kerrera side of the ferry that King Haakon of Norway collected his fleet of Viking ships before sailing south to the Battle of LARGS in 1263.

About 2 m. beyond Dunollie to the N. of the town are Ganavan Sands, a popular bathing spot with an extensive caravan site. There is a sizeable car park, and during the summer months the sands are linked to the town by a frequent bus service.

Immediately behind the business portion of the town, dotted on their seaward sides by private residences, are Oban Hill and Battery Hill. Each is crowned by a structure that at once attracts attention. On Oban Hill is the skeleton of a huge hydropathic building (1880–1), which had to be abandoned for want of funds. On the neighbouring height is a vast and even more conspicuous edifice known as MacCaig's Tower. It surmounts the Bay of Oban as one of the most distinctive landmarks in the Western Highlands. There were some who thought John Stewart MacCaig, a local banker and philanthropist, a trifle foolish when he embarked on the project in 1897. His idea was to provide work for the relief of the unemployed, and he planned that the building should take the form of a museum with a lookout tower rising about 100 ft higher than the granite walls. He also proposed that a series of statues should be placed in the windows of the building to commemorate his family. Some £5,000 had been spent when MacCaig died, and the work was never completed. Today MacCaig's Tower has gained the smiling affection of the people of Oban in the same way as Edinburgh's Folly on Calton Hill has gained the affection of EDINBURGH.

Because of its reliance on traditional tourism, the town has sometimes been accused of falling behind the times, but Oban stolidly refuses to provide entertainments of the amusement-arcade variety. Paradoxically, it is this sturdy Highland independence, this refusal to dilute the town's character, which is one of the elements of Oban's popularity. People holidaying in Oban like to feel they are in the Highlands. And it is worth remembering that Oban gave birth to the National Mod – the yearly gathering of Scottish Gaels for competitions in verse and song – and that the Highland Sabbath is still a reality, though perhaps a precarious one. In various ways the tourist industry in Oban deliberately keeps the fact of the Highland attraction to the fore. It is a modern town, but unquestionably in the Highlands. That is what it has to offer.

The holiday boom does not absorb the entire working population of the town. The centre of an area in which agriculture is the principal occupation, Oban boasts an auction mart that annually handles trade worth close on £1m. At the great sales each year, 75,000 sheep and lambs and 17,000 cattle pass through its rings.

A tweed mill, established in 1946, employs between 90 and 100 operatives, and the well-known Caithness Glass firm recently set up a subsidiary here. A sizeable fishing-fleet operates from the harbour. The importance of the industry has increased steadily since the end of the Second World War, and a project to provide a covered fish market and boatshelter has been deferred only through the fact that the Town Council and the Scottish Home Department have been unable to agree over the rate of grant.

Thrusting an improbable chimney at the skies, Oban's distillery produces a potent spirit that later finds its way into some of Scotland's most famous blends.

New industry, however, would be welcome, for there is still all too little for young people to do. When Oban High School has trained their young minds to a level with the best of Scotland, they are often forced to leave the town, and there is little to tempt them back except an occasional teaching job or a position in a legal office.

Oban seems, therefore, to be at a crucial point in its history. Ought the town to continue to rely on those natural beauties that have already made it one of the most popular resorts in Scotland, or should it take its cue from the more lively CLYDE resorts with all their more metropolitan glitter?

Oban is a new town compared with most of Scotland's bigger centres. She has many problems of space for development. But, aided by her fine situation and desire to keep up with the increasing numbers who visit her, she will, if she does not lose her essential character, solve these problems.

OCHILTREE, *Ayrshire* (Map 2, ref. 25¹62⁰). A village on the AYR–CUMNOCK road, Ochiltree is just E. of Ayr. It lies in a rich dairy-farming district that is also in the heart of the Ayrshire coalfield, and the surrounding countryside gives abundant evidence of the main sources of wealth in the county – coal and cows. George Douglas Brown was born at Ochiltree in 1869. Brown was the author of the highly controversial but gripping novel *The House with the Green Shutters.* In this he endeavoured in a Zolaesque fashion to uncover Scottish provincial life at the turn of the century. It aroused a storm, but is still read and referred to. It indubitably killed the "kailyard" or sentimental Scottish country novel – so popular in the 1890s – stone dead.

The place took its name from Ochiltree House ("the lofty dwelling"), of which no trace remains. This was the home of the Stuarts, lords of Ochiltree, into whose family John Knox married in 1564. Graham of Claverhouse married into the same family in 1684.

OLDMELDRUM, *Aberdeenshire* (Map 6, ref. 38¹82⁸). This burgh was created in 1672. It has an old square dominated by the Town Hall, with tower and clock. A number of old houses still stand. Oldmeldrum is the centre of agricultural country devoted mainly to fat-stock rearing. There is also a distillery.

Just SW., the B.B.C. television transmitter called Meldrum is situated on Core Hill.

The nearby Barra Castle stands to the W. of Barra Hill, close to the site of Bruce's decisive victory over the Comyns in 1307. Nowadays it is the home of a branch of the ancient family of Irvine of Drum, connected by marriage with the former lairds, the Ramsays of Barra and Straloch. Turrets carried up from the foundations, sparse use of corbelling, and simplicity of contour make a very impressive building. It was the Ramsays who in 1755 added the "New Wing", restored by a grant from the Ministry of Public Building and Works in 1956. The buildings now form three sides of a courtyard; the fourth side is a wall surmounted by three decorative stone vases. This wall existed before 1755. The ancient vaulted kitchen is still in use but contains modern equipment.

Just N. is Meldrum House, now a hotel. The oldest part has massive stone vaulting of the 13th cent. The central portion, with its elegant external stone stairway, dates from the 17th cent., while the rest of the building dates from the early 19th cent.

Oldmeldrum stands on a westward-facing slope giving fine views across the farmlands of the Garioch towards BENNACHIE.

ONICH, *Inverness-shire* (Map 5, ref. 20³76²), lies at the entrance to Loch Leven, a sea-loch, 2½ m. W. of BALLACHULISH ferry. The village is spread along the shore and roadside below steep hillsides.

Dr Alexander Stewart ("Nether Lochnaber"), a noted Gaelic scholar, was Minister here from 1851–1901; he was one of the founders of the Mod, a yearly gathering to foster Gaelic poetry and song. His monument is in the village.

Near the ferry pier is a perforated monolith known as Clach a' Charra.

ORD OF CAITHNESS, *Caithness/Sutherland.* This abrupt, lofty granite ridge overlooking the North Sea stands in the midst of hilly country on the border of Caithness and Sutherland. The splendid new road and bridges, notable feats of engineering, have removed the terrors of what used to be known, with its unbelievably steep double-hairpin bend, as the worst hill on any main road in Britain. Now it is just a long but easy climb.

About 5 m. NW. of Berriedale, near the township of Braemore, is a monument to the Duke of Kent (1902–42), who was killed nearby in an air crash while on active service with the R.A.F.

Some 4 m. SW. of the village is Ousdale, a remote but well-preserved ruin incorporating many interesting constructional features.

Langwell Homestead lies 1 m. SW. of Berriedale. It is a round stone-walled house with an oblong chamber attached above ground. It is typical of a form of building commonly found in Caithness and Sutherland and locally called "Wags".

ORKNEY Northern Islands, *Orkney* (Map 7). This group, which should not be called the

"Orkneys" (see "The Shape of Scotland"), is a county, not a loose archipelago. True, it is a county lying some 20 m. to the N. of the mainland of Scotland by Caithness, and containing sixty-seven islands, of which about twenty-one are inhabited. It is perhaps best called an "island county", with its own mainland, in many respects more important to it than the mainland of Scotland. The city of KIRKWALL, with the Cathedral of St Magnus, almost nine centuries old, is more properly described as its capital than the county town.

The mainland of Orkney, a richly indented island with close on 200 m. of good-surfaced road, is not only the biggest island of the county but contains more land than all the other sixty-six islands together. Its capital of Kirkwall is a port on the central SE. side. The only other town, rather than township or village, on the mainland is also a port, STROMNESS, on the central SW. side. Kirkwall is an ancient city dating back to the years when these islands were part of the Norwegian dominions. Stromness did not rise above the status of a fisherman's village until the mid-17th cent., when, under the Scottish crown united with England, it became of significance as a port for the expanding trade between Scotland and the Baltic. It was also the last port of call for ships of the Hudson Bay Company and whalers bound for the Davis Straits.

Both Kirkwall and Stromness are essentially northern towns in aspect; and Kirkwall, with its roots deep in the Norse past, immediately strikes the eye of the British visitor as being foreign – foreign in a Scandinavian way.

The second largest island in the county, and the one possessing the most spectacular display of cliff and rich scenery, is HOY, SSW. of the mainland. It can be reached by a motor boat from Stromness, and is well worth a visit. In comparison with the rest of the county of Orkney, it is mountainous, and it has some fine cliffs. The Old Man of Hoy is an extraordinary isolated rock-stack, or piece of columnar rock, which rises directly to a height of 450 ft from a brief peninsula or projection of rock at the W. of the island. This noble column, which in appearance would almost seem to have been erected by man as an unilluminated lighthouse, is a well-known landmark, and on a clear day can be seen from Caithness on the mainland of Scotland. At the NW. of Hoy, St John's Head rises to as much as 1,140 ft. Near Rawick Valley is a rock-cut bomb of early Bronze Age locally called Dwarfie Stone, mentioned by Walter Scott in *The Pirate*.

Between Hoy and the mainland of Orkney is the famous island-protected naval base of SCAPA FLOW, which played such a large part in the two world wars of this century. This all but impregnable harbour is one of nature's (and Orkney's) gifts to the United Kingdom of Great Britain. It was in Scapa Flow that the German Fleet, having surrendered itself, scuppered and sank itself immediately after the First World War.

The most southerly island in the county is South Ronaldshay, highly and richly agricultural even for Orkney. This island contains St Margaret's Hope, traditionally but erroneously connected with the Maid of Norway, the infant granddaughter of King Alexander III of Scotland (see "Scotland in History"), who died in Orkney on her way to Scotland from Norway. St Margaret's Hope is more probably named after Margaret, saint and Queen of Scotland. Through the lesser island of Burray, South Ronaldshay is now connected with the Mainland of Orkney by the CHURCHILL BARRIERS.

The other islands of Orkney worthy of mention here are Stronsay to the E.; Rousay and Eynhallow, on which is a small, ruined, insular chapel; and Egilsay to the E. of Rousay, containing the remains of a round-towered church near to where St Magnus was killed in 1116. Stronsay lies to the E. of the Mainland; Westray, Eday, and Sanday to the NE. Stronsay is purely agricultural. On Westray there is the astonishing Noteland Castle built in the 16th cent. by Gilbert Balfour. From this it will be seen that the mainland, with Hoy protecting it, lies mostly to the W.

Orkney, as has been stated elsewhere here, is consciously a Norse county of islands. This is evident not only in the names of nearly all places and of some inhabitants, but in the attitude of the people, who never let you forget that they only came into the kingdom of Scotland by means of an "unredeemed pawning operation" between the Scottish and Danish crowns in 1469. And what are a mere five centuries in the minds of a tenacious peasantry or farming stock!

It would be a great mistake, however, to suppose that the Norsemen, some time in the first Christian millennium, took over uninhabited islands, or that the human story of Orkney began with them. There were Pictish, and possibly Celtic, and long before them megalithic, people from the Mediterranean, who were inhabitants of Orkney long before the first Norse galley was seen off Orcadian coasts. This is made manifest in the rich prehistoric remains that the Norse found and left for us to see today. The most noteworthy of these – such as MAESHOWE, which the Norse broke into – will be dealt with under separate headings.

The Norse possession of Orkney, vigorous and ruthless though it may have been, brought considerable civilization to the county. One has only to look at the cathedral in Kirkwall to be aware of this. Moreover, there is no evidence that, in their ruthless conquest of the islands, the Norsemen exterminated the previous inhabitants. Pre-Norse, as well as later Scottish blood, certainly mingles in the Orcadian stock today.

The Norsemen may indeed have been conquerors who would stand no nonsense, but the Scottish occupiers, particularly the Stuart earls at the time of James V, by their arrogant and cruel rule succeeded in antagonising the Orcadians of their time in a manner that is still remembered. Orkney – partly because of her Northern situation (let us not call it "remoteness"), partly because of her admirable agricultural self-sufficiency, but also as a self-consciously foreign community within the kingdom of Scotland, and later within the United Kingdom – kept clear of British affairs. She was, for instance, all but untouched by the Scottish political and dynastic upheavals of the 18th cent. Nor had she any desire to be touched by them.

There are some Scots (and not Orcadians, at that) who claim that Orkney is the finest farming county in the kingdom. Whether one admits this or not, it is certainly a very fine farming county indeed – all the more remarkably so for being an island county split up to a certain extent within itself and far away (inasmuch as most of us are concerned) in the northern seas.

Those who have visited the Outer Hebridean scene will note in this richly agricultural county group of islands that there are, in comparison, very few crofts and crofters (see LEWIS and "Scotland in History"). The Orcadian, essentially up-to-date as well as (in the better sense of the word) insularly self-sufficient, has developed his land in the farming tradition. There are some 3,000 farms, averaging thirty-five acres each. Most farmers are what would be known in England as yeomen, owning their own land. They tend to use every modern device to get everything they can out of their small farms. The tractor and the motor-car have their place. Unlike their cousins in the more northerly isles of SHETLAND, the Orcadians have not developed their local sea fishing to any great extent. No people situated as they are could have failed to produce great sailors, but they are primarily a land-cultivating race.

There were Celtic, pre-Pict, and Iron Age inhabitants, but there is no Gaelic in Orkney, nor ever has been. The speech of the Orkney people today is a pleasing sing-song kind of English, affectionate in sound rather than proud or caressing like the Hebrideans'. It is said that, till the 18th cent., the old Norse tongue survived in remote parts of the islands. It has left words and phrases in their language today.

Like most farming people, they are satisfactorily down-to-earth in manner and not much given to poetry or flights of imagination. Despite this, the fact remains that they have in our century given to the body of English literature one of the most distinguished and sensitive poets of our time, Edwin Muir, and one novelist, Eric Linklater, whose richness of fancy has delighted many readers in these islands and in Northern Europe.

The Orcadians are not as fervently religious as the Outer Hebrideans. The Reformation swept away all remnants of the old faith; and such Catholics as there are among them are the children of incomers or of converts. The Reformation did its work thoroughly here in the shadow of the great Cathedral of St Magnus (now a Protestant Kirk of Scotland church), but the people were not seized with ardent Calvinism as in Lewis.

It is much easier to visit Orkney from Scotland than it is to go to many places in the remoter Highlands of the mainland. There is a daily air service to Kirkwall and a regular steamboat connection with ABERDEEN and THURSO. The roads are good; there are hotels in Kirkwall and in Stromness. Farmers and other residents in rural districts sometimes take in visitors to bed and meals.

The attractions of Orkney to the visitor, especially in midsummer when, in these latitudes, the days seem never to darken into full night, are many. The horizons are broad and the air is invigorating. The feeling of being on holiday in a successful and go-ahead group of islands stirs one to contented action and not to introspection. Despite a small but definite and incomprehensible drainage of the population to big centres in Scotland, there is no melancholy (poetic or depressing) in Orkney.

There is good if rather brisk bathing and excellent sailing and boating from Kirkwall, Stromness, and Loughope. There is sea fishing too in abundance.

But the best fishing is in the freshwater lochs. Orkney's rich soil and limestone basis encourages the rapid growth of the brown trout. The best and most varied brown-trout fishing in all Scotland – mainland and islands – is to be found in Orkney. A record brown trout for the British Isles of 29 lb. was claimed to have been taken from the Stenness Loch on the Orkney Mainland.

The sea-trout fishing is excellent. In Scotland it is equalled, and (let it be admitted) sometimes surpassed, only in Shetland and South UIST.

There are few lairds, and no preservation of waters save on Rousay; the kindly farmer-folk will freely give permission to fish their waters to visitors who politely ask for it. Even in Association waters, the price is not heavy. The intending angler who is going to Orkney for a holiday need not make elaborate preparations in advance. He is, however, recommended, as in all other such cases, to consult the Scottish Tourist Board for details – hiring of boats, etc. But this too can often be left till after arrival in Orkney.

ORMISTON, *East Lothian* (Map 3, ref. 34¹66⁹), on Tyne Water, stands in countryside that bears the stamp of a notable 18th-cent. "improver", John Cockburn of Ormiston (1685–1758). It was his far-seeing policy that

bettered the estate by planting trees and enclosing fields with hedges instead of the old
in-field and out-field system. He founded an
Ormiston Society, which discussed farming
topics in the village inn and included several
local landlords. The gardens are still famous
for good fruit.

Ormiston Hall dates from 1745, with later
additions, but it was near the site of an earlier
house that was in the hands of the Cockburn
family from the mid-14th cent. George
Wishart, the martyr, was captured here in 1546.

OTTER FERRY, *Argyll* (Map 1, ref.
19³68⁴). A ferry used to run from this small
township on the E. shore of Loch Fyne to
LOCHGILPHEAD, but only holiday boats now
make the crossing. It lies at the shoreward end
of a very long sand-spit, about 1 m. long, and
at the bottom of the very steep zigzag road to
GLENDARUEL. Now a holiday resort in an
isolated position, it is 2 m. from the Lochgilphead shore by water, and 60 m. by road.

OYNE, *Aberdeenshire* (Map 6, ref. 36⁷82⁵),
is a village and a parish in the Garioch "whaur
Gadie rins at the back o' Bennachie". The
village provides the usual starting-point for the
ascent of BENNACHIE. On either side of the
village are two very striking castles. Harthill
(1 m. to the SE.) dating from 1601, a ruined
Z-plan tower-house with a barmkin or courtyard, the gateway to which still stands, was the
home of the Leiths, a turbulent race. John,
known as the Violent Laird, was at constant
war with authority and was more than once
warded in the Tolbooth of EDINBURGH.
When imprisoned in the ABERDEEN Tolbooth,
he set it on fire and released all the prisoners.
Westhall, to the N., with its barmkin or courtyard, is a 16th-cent. L-plan tower-house notable
for its fine label corbelling and built by the
Abercrombies, frequently at feud with the
Leiths. Ultimately it passed to another branch
of the Leiths.

The village of Old Rayne (2 m. N. of Oyne),
an ancient ecclesiastical burgh of barony with a
striking market cross, had a summer palace of
the Bishops of Aberdeen and was the site of
Lowrin (St Lawrence's) Fair, one of the
greatest of the northern markets that survived
until the '30s of this century.

PAISLEY, *Renfrewshire* (Map 2, ref. 24⁸66⁴).
An industrial burgh and administrative centre
of the county, Paisley grew up round the abbey
founded by Walter Fitz Alan, ancestor of the
Stuarts, in 1163 for the Cluniac monks. It
became an abbey in 1219, but the original
buildings were burnt in 1307, and the present
structure dates from the middle of the 15th
cent. The most notable parts are the W. front
and the nave, which is used as the parish
church; in St Murein's Chapel is an effigy that

is said to be of Marjory Bruce. Restoration
started in 1897, and was completed by Sir
Robert Lorimer in 1933. After the Reformation
the monastic buildings became the Palace of
Paisley, home of the Hamilton and later of the
Dundonald families. Deserted at a later date,
it was bought back and restored in 1904 as a
hall and manse, and the surrounding streets
were cleared so that gardens could be made.

The museum includes rooms of local history,
displaying a collection of the well-known
Paisley shawls and relics of Robert Tannahill
(1774–1810), the weaver and poet, and
Alexander Wilson (1766–1813), the American
ornithologist, who were both born here.

Paisley has a good post-war building and
development record, and among the recent
important additions is the College of Technology, still expanding. Spinning and weaving
are the traditional industries. The weaving of
the famous Paisley shawls began in the early
19th cent.; these were copies in silk or cotton of
Eastern shawls sent home by Scottish officers
in India. Now industry is varied and includes
Hillington Industrial Estate, the original
Scottish example of such a Government-
sponsored undertaking. Begun in 1937, it now
has more than 150 factories.

PALNACKIE, *Kirkcudbrightshire* (Map 2,
ref. 28²55⁷). A whitewashed village beside the
harbour on the Urr estuary, beneath the steep
wall of the Screel–Bergairn ridge, Palnackie
developed as a lively port during the 18th cent.,
and remained vigorous into the present century,
though, like most of the Solway harbours, it
now stands empty of shipping, which has been
driven away by easy road transport.

Several large buildings remain from the days
when it was an importing and processing centre.
Despite "Palnackie Treacle Works" (where
workers were paid a halfpenny a week, tramped
out the treacle, and had their feet to lick), there
never seems to have been a sugar refinery.
There is an important timber works drawing on
a richly wooded hinterland.

About 1 m. S. is Orchardton Tower, one of
the two circular 16th-cent. tower-houses in
Scotland; it was built by John Cairns about
1560. The Cairns family long dominated this
area; Kipp Cairns – Cairns of Kipp – was a
famous smuggling "laird" and eccentric of the
late 18th cent. The interior arrangements of the
circular tower are the same as in a normal
rectangular one of the period; the foundations
of a complex of buildings, mostly 17th cent.,
adjoin the tower, the parapet-walk of which
affords a fine view.

PATHHEAD, *Midlothian* (Map 3, ref.
34⁰66⁴). Although in a mining district, this
village, consisting mainly of one long, sloping,
very broad street, is prettily situated on the W.
bank of Tyne Water.

In a fine park, 1 m. N. of the village, stands

Oxenfoord Castle, formerly the seat of the earls of Stair and now a girls' boarding school. The house was built by Robert Adam round an old castle, 1780–5, and later added to by William Burn.

Between Pathhead and Oxenfoord is a magnificent bridge designed by Thomas Telford; it has five arches, each 80 ft high, which take the main EDINBURGH to LAUDER road.

PEEBLES, *Peeblesshire* (Map 3, ref. 32⁴64⁰). This pleasantly situated county town was started under the shelter of a royal castle; its charter constituting it a royal burgh was granted by David II in 1367. The town was burnt in 1545 and again by accident in 1607. Cromwell's troops were stationed here while trying to reduce Neidpath.

Cross Kirk, now in ruins, was founded by Alexander III at the spot where an old cross was found in 1261; later it had a monastery attached to it. At the Reformation the church became the parish church and was used as a place of worship until 1784. A little W. of Cross Kirk are the ruins of St Andrew's Church, which was founded in 1195. It became a Collegiate Church in 1543, but was burnt by the English; the tower was restored in 1883. The mercat cross, an octagonal column 12 ft high, now stands in the centre of the "Old Town"; it is said to date from before Robert Bruce. The old bridge at the end of the wide main street dates from the 15th cent.; it was widened in 1834 and again in 1900.

The traditional Beltane Festival, the "Riding of the Marches", used to be held annually on the 1st of May, but is now held on the last Saturday of June; James I visited it in the early 15th cent.

In the "Old Town", across the Eddleston Water, were born the brothers Chambers, William (1800–83) and Robert (1802–71), the well-known publishers who did so much for Peebles.

The main industry, which has been carried on for hundreds of years, is wool-manufacture; the town's tweed and knitwear are world-famous.

Situated as it is in attractive country and with a relaxing climate, Peebles is a popular holiday resort. Fishing is the main attraction, but there are also facilities for golf, tennis, and pony-trekking.

Just W. of the town, Neidpath Castle stands above the R. TWEED. This castle was once the stronghold of the Frasers; later it belonged to the Hays of YESTER, and later still to the Dukes of Queensberry. The walls of the oldest part are 11 ft thick; the newer portion of the castle is said to date from the early 15th cent.

PENCAITLAND, *East Lothian* (Map 3, ref. 34⁴66⁹). The village of Pencaitland is divided in two by the Tyne Water, whose bridge dates from 1510. Wester Pencaitland has an old mercat cross. In Easter Pencaitland is a church, part of whose tower and walls probably dates from the 12th cent., and the aisle to the N. of the chancel from the late 13th cent. Inside is work from the 14th, 16th, and 17th cents.; the tower is dated 1631, and the pulpit is of 17th-cent. oak.

About 1½ m. SW. of Pencaitland is Penkaet, formerly called Fountainhall, a complete example of a small 17th-cent mansion. Built by the Pringle family and originally called Woodhead, it was sold in 1685 to Sir John Lauder, who became Lord Fountainhall – possibly because Lord Woodhead might be an unsuitable title for a judge.

PENICUIK, *Midlothian* (Map 3, ref. 32⁴ 66⁰), 10 m. SE. of EDINBURGH in the folds of the Pentlands, celebrated its centenary as a burgh in 1967. Now the centre of the fastest-growing district on the E. side of Midlothian, it covers 574 acres with a population of over 13,000 and several new industries, in addition to its centuries-old paper-making. Its prosperity has been encouraged by the local lairds, the Clerks of Penicuik.

Sir John Clerk of Penicuik, Bart (1676–1755), was a patron of the arts and a man of affairs. He travelled throughout Europe, but lived as a Scottish laird on his estates.

The fine Augustan house that he designed for himself lasted till 1899, when it was accidently burnt. Its gutted façade still stands mournfully yet impressively. His descendant,

Penicuik House: the converted 18th-century stables

Tom Scott

Tom Scott

The surviving façade, Penicuik House

Sir John Clerk of today, lives with his family in what was, in the 18th cent., the stables block. These graciously designed and converted buildings are ample for the needs of a modern family. The block is about the size of a small quadrangle in an Oxford College. Penicuik House is private property.

Some 2 m. SW. of Penicuik stands Brunstane Castle, now a ruin but still impressive in its reduced state. It rises upon the bank of the R. Esk, which provides the burgh of Penicuik with the power for its paper-mills.

PENIEL HEUGH, *Roxburghshire* (Map 3, ref. 36⁵62⁷). Some 2 m. NE. of ANCRUM, upon the summit of the hill of Peniel Heugh (744 ft), stands the "Waterloo Monument", erected in 1815 by the Marquess of Lothian. It is 150 ft high; it forms a well-known landmark and has extensive views of Teviotdale and Tweeddale, the Merse, and the Cheviots. Nearby, round the base of the monument, are remains of two forts, one having been superimposed on the other. The first one is probably of the early Iron Age, while the later one may be of the Dark Ages.

PENNAN, *Aberdeenshire* (Map 6, ref. 37²86⁴). No one knows more about the fishing havens of Scotland's E. coast than Peter F. Anson, who surveyed them in their entirety in 1929. He wrote then of Pennan: "Of all the fishing villages on the east coast Pennan must come first for picturesque situation. . . . After a succession of grey villages extending all the way from Berwickshire to Buchan, broken only by the pink granite of PETERHEAD and Boddam, the mind cannot quite accustom itself to this village where everything is red, a warm purple red against crimson – red houses, red roads, red cliff, red beach, red rocks, relieved here and there by the purple of the slates". Since that was written, a large dash of white has been added to the colour scheme. Many of the walls have been painted or washed white, so that the general effect is now gayer than ever. Closely packed under the soaring wall of its red sandstone cliff, Pennan is a favourite spot for artists, who in leaner times rented many of the houses as weekend or summer cottages. But that phase has now passed.

The village is now inhabited by fishermen's families who live here all the year round, although the breadwinners may serve on fishing fleets far from home – off Iceland, Norway, and the Scottish W. coast; and it is full of young life. From Pennan itself there is a little salmon and mackerel fishing, and pleasure boating in the summer. It is the centre of a peculiar and fascinating countryside in the parish of Aberdour. Cliffs, rising to 300 ft in places, run along the whole coast from Lord Pitsligo's Cave on the E. to the mouth of the Tore·Burn at Callykhan Bay, W. of Pennan, a distance of 7 m.

Although the Quayman Cave, between the farms of Clinterty and Pennan, has a natural dock and quay wall, and a staple in the roof where smugglers hung their lanterns as they landed their contraband silk and liquor, there are only three "open" inlets in the whole seven miles suitable for fishing havens – and all three were at one time used as such. They are the Bay of Pennan itself, the Bay of Aberdour, and the inlet E. of Quarryhead. That they were all used in the 17th cent. is clear from the kirk session records. On the 21st of May 1699, the session "appointed that the boats of Penin and the boats of Aberdour and North Leslie should not stay later on the sea on Saturday night than sunset, lest they should encroach on the Lord's Day".

On the right bank of the Dour Burn that gives the parish its name, on a green saddle jutting into the red sandstone gorge of the stream about 150 yds from the beach where it runs into the sea, is the ruined medieval parish church of Aberdour. To the E. of it on the foreshore is St Drostan's Well, from which water still flows, cold, pure, and abundant. Here it is believed St Drostan, the patron saint of Buchan, accompanied by his disciples Colm, Medan, and Fergus, first landed after a voyage from Caithness that was to result in the founding of the Monastery of Deer. A version of the story is inscribed in 11th-cent. characters by monkish chroniclers on the margins of *The Book of Deer*. This tells how, when they landed at "Abbordobor", the missionaries found that "Bede the Pict was mormaer of Buchan before them and it was he who gave them that cathair in freedom forever for mormaer and toiseach". That "cathair" has been identified with the promontory of Dunarg a little to the E.

Over a long period extensive excavations have taken place at the "red fort" of Dunarg, where a picturesque modern castellated house stands in the position of a gatehouse on the seaward side of a medieval moat, guarding the approach to the ancient castellated remains on the promontory itself. There was an Iron Age fort here until at least the 4th cent. and the foundations of a building called the chapel may well be a link with St Drostan himself. In the 13th cent. the Comyn earls of Buchan built a strong stone castle within the prehistoric fort, widening the existing inner ditch to form the castle moat. This fortalice was laid low by Robert Bruce during the Harrying of Buchan in 1308; it rose again and was once more destroyed.

But the military history of Dundarg was not yet over. Two centuries later, during the War of the Rough Wooing in the infancy of Mary Queen of Scots, French fortification experts arrived on the scene and the inner gatehouse was again rebuilt, the new work being provided with gun-loops.

The threat of invasion, however, passed; the curtain rang down for the last time on the story of Dundarg as a fort. The modern "castle" was built in this century from the stones of the former Free Church in the village of New Aberdour, some distance inland. This village, with its long main street leading to the parish church, the hall, and the school, was founded in 1798 by William Gordon the laird of Aberdour.

PERTH, *Perthshire* (Map 6, ref. 31²72³), is alternatively known as the Fair City. The visitor to the place would do well to agree with the alternative as an axiom, if he would not fall foul of the vehement, but courteous, unanimity of the citizens. Yet, if you had the temerity to be objective, you might say that it is not clear whether it is the city itself that is fair, or its setting, or both. Natives of sensibility (and they are by no means few) might admit that there is not much of architectural distinction left to command the awed attention of the incomer. The ancient kirk of St John Baptist, one of the noblest of the great Scottish burghal churches of the 15th cent., with its spire "as clean as a hound's tooth", is by far the rarest of the relics, both in antiquity and in beauty. But it is condemned (as it seems, in perpetuity) to look out on the broad and ill-mannered rear of a 19th-cent. City Hall; and, on either side, it is hemmed in by warehouses, public houses, and

Perth: Marshall Place

Perthshire Advertiser

Perth and the River Tay

factories, with nothing to commend them to the eye. Elsewhere, tucked away between modern frontages, sweetly-curved small windows throw light on antiques (in South Street) and, until a most recent demolition in the High Street, on ironmongery. If you hunt for them, you will come upon vestiges of the town houses that belonged to a now long-dead nobility; well-proportioned gables recall a past more tenderly resolved to combine elegance with function. Solidity is fused with grace in the terraces and places that confront the green magnificence of the riverside inches. These terraces, in particular Rose Terrace, are reminiscent of the EDINBURGH New Town style, and are an example of how that noble style continued to flourish and push its way up the E. of Scotland deep into the 19th cent. A cheer is due no less for the new (1960) ferro-concrete Queen's Bridge than for Smeaton's old (1771) master-piece in rose-red sandstone, farther up-river. The attractions of the mid-20th-cent. City Centre (between South Street and High Street) may be considered dubious.

But take a look at Perth as you come up from the S., over "Necessity Brae" (which joins the main road from GLASGOW at Cherry-bank), or in from the E., or best of all from the summit of KINNOULL (729 ft), and the prospect is surely stirring: that of the varied, natural grandeur enfolding the place, but not less, perhaps, that of the place itself, spired and reeky, solid and studiously compact, emanating an immemorial fidelity to its bridges, which (if it did not impoverish the merchants in its medieval guilds) well served the security and wealth of bygone Scotland through many centuries.

Or walk up the river from the old bridge, look around and marvel at the continuing pleasance of the modern scene. Colonial cricketers, with (as the locals are sure) as much aesthetic discrimination as athletic distinction, have been known to testify that they never play in more splendid surroundings than those of Scotland's premier County Club on the North Inch.

Otherwise Perth is exceptionally well-furnished for its size. It has a much more than passable art gallery and museum (George St). It has the well-stocked Sandeman Library (Kinnoull St). It has the oldest-established repertory theatre in Scotland, from which many have emerged to stardom in the West End and on television. Of late it has achieved its own orchestra and choral society, which can endure the most stringent critic. It has learned societies of many sorts. It has a mint of money at its disposal for cultural and charitable objects. It is abundantly rich in open spaces and recreational facilities of every sort.

Debate about the meaning of the place-name is inconclusive. A possible derivation is from the Welsh *perth* ("bush, copse, or thicket"), but a more obvious explanation lies in the contraction and mutation of Abertay, through Bertha, to Perth. Formerly it was known as St John's Toun (see John Knox's *History of the Reformation in Scotland*), to which might be added "at the mouth of the Tay".

The theory that the place originated round a Roman camp of the 1st cent. is supported by the plan and dimensions of the old town within a city wall (of which there are still remnants), the course of which was by way of Canal St, Canal Crescent, Methven St, and Mill St.; ENE. from about the N. end of Skinnergate to the SE. corner of the front block of the Royal George Hotel (George St), thence south-eastwards to the R. TAY, N. of a medieval bridge sited near the end of High St. Though there is evidence for the national importance of nearby places (e.g. ABERNETHY, FORTEVIOT, SCONE) earlier than the 9th cent., Perth makes no appearance in records before the 12th, when it seems to have been well established. The Augustinian canons of Scone claim that a dwelling-place in Perth was amongst the first grants made by Alexander I to the monks (*c.* 1114–15). About 1126 David I gave the Kirk of Perth to DUNFERMLINE Abbey; and shortly afterwards he instructed his steward at Perth (Malbride MacCongi) that the tenths of the King's house there were payable to Dunfermline. David, too, gave an annual payment from the revenue of his mills at Perth to the Abbey at Scone. He is also reputed to have given the burgh the wide trading privileges later comprised in a charter of William the Lion.

It has been claimed that for centuries Perth was the national capital. This may be an exaggeration (yet there must be some explanation of the fact that still Perth's Lord Provost, in official precedence, ranks second only to that of Edinburgh). Kings and their courts were peripatetic in feudal times, and Perth was frequently the royal residence. Scone, nearby, was the place of many coronations. Parliaments and General Councils are known to have been convened after the accession of Alexander I (1106–7) and the death of Robert III (1406). In a 10th-cent. chronicle it is called the Royal City, and in charters of Malcolm IV and Robert III the "principal seat of our kingdom". Plainly, Perth was for long the governing centre of Scotland. It was also a preferred meeting-place for Scottish church councils from the beginning of the 13th cent. onwards. It seems possible that, had James I lived a few years longer or died a natural death, Perth might have become the permanent capital.

The city has been besieged seven times and has been the scene of many turbulent events. Among them were the Battle of the Clans (1396); the destruction of four monasteries and the altars in the Kirk (1559), consequent on the lambent preaching of John Knox that kindled the Reformation in Scotland; the Gowrie mystery (1600); the meeting of the "red" parliament, the last to be convened here (1606); the General Assembly of the Church of Scotland (1618), at which the Five Articles of Perth were approved; and Cromwell's invasion (1651). Perth was Jacobite in 1715 and 1745. Prince Charles Edward lodged at the Salutation Hotel, drilled troops on the North Inch, and here proclaimed his father King.

Surviving records include a large collection of royal charters, the oldest (1210) being that of William the Lion; a letter from John Blair, Postmaster-General, of the 7th of November 1689, explaining the beginning of the post-office system in Perth; the census of 1766, showing the population at 7,542; papers dealing with the first railway between Perth and DUNKELD (1835); a petition of Mistress Agnes Ranken (1719) for encouragement to carry on her school "much put out of its course by the late rebellion"; information about attempts to find coal (1686, 1732, 1782); an Obligation by James I of Scotland to indemnify the city for its share of his ransom (1424), and "Ane charge be King James the Secund To the toun for fanseing the burgh wyth wallis in respect of the murther of King James the First", as well as "Ane charge to mak wallis about the toun to resist the Kingis rebellis".

The city, in the past, won for itself an unenviable reputation for iconoclasm, but visible evidences of its antiquity remain. The greatest of these is the Kirk, consecrated by David de Bernham, Bishop of ST ANDREWS, in 1243. Divided for about 200 years into three separate churches, it was restored to its primitive unity (1923–6) as the memorial to men of the city and county who fell in the First World War (the architect was Sir Robert Lorimer). The walls are splendid with many examples of modern stained glass at its best, and on view in the interior is the congregation's priceless possession of old pewter, silver-gilt sacramental vessels, and a baptismal basin (16th cent.), expertly esteemed as one of the finest examples of ancient Edinburgh silver-ware. In 1936, on the initiative of Melville Gray of Bowerswell (brother-in-law of John Ruskin), a carillon of thirty-five bells, founded by Gillet & Johnston of Croydon, was hung in the tower.

No substantial remains of other historic buildings survive. The memorials of them, and of vanished activities and conditions of life, are now in the names of the streets and lanes of the city – Charterhouse, Blackfriars, Whitefriars, Greyfriars, Pomarium, Skinnergate, Guard Vennel, Flesher's Vennel, and the rest. In the courtyard of the Salutation (said to be the oldest hotel in Scotland) is a stone bearing the motto and arms of the Earls of Moray, and dated 1619; more than likely, it marks the site of a house of nobility. Inscriptions and the like are elsewhere: in the North Port, where once stood the Castle of Perth; on the Waterworks, the place of Cromwell's citadel. Inscribed pillars on the North Inch recall the Battle of the Clans, and another, at the riverside, the Monks' Tower. Tokens in the paving of the High St commemorate the old town cross and pillory, the stone of which is preserved in the Museum. Thus also John Ruskin's residence in Rose Terrace and John Buchan's in York Place are recorded. Out of immaterial legend a house, in the Curfew Row, has been conjured for Sir Walter Scott's Fair Maid of Perth.

The medieval importance of the harbour may be measured by the fact that in 1269 the customs dues amounted to what must have been then the great sum of £700. In later centuries the magistrates seem to have neglected the commercial possibilities of the river, and the shipping trade was largely alienated to places like NEWBURGH, farther downstream. Yet the number of vessels that made fast at the port in 1962 was 364 (486 in 1848). Fertilizers bulk large in the imports; seed potatoes are a major export.

British Rail are substantial employers of labour – a continuing proof of the great importance of Perth as a communications' centre. Pullars of Perth (dyeing and cleaning) have held the royal warrant since the reign of William IV. The head office of the General Accident Fire and Life Assurance Corporation (founded by the late Sir Francis Norie-Miller) is here, and the warehouses for many brands of whisky. Dewars of Perth, which began as small licensed premises in the High Street in the early 19th cent., is world-known. Linen only recently went out of production, but twine and jute are still manufactured. Beer, aerated waters, confectionery, and rat poison are other products. Much printing and publishing goes on, and the fashioning of scientific, commercial, and decorative glass. Variety of enterprise has been a feature of great strength in the industrial life of the town, which, unlike centres of heavy industry, has never seriously had to bear the effects of economic depression.

But this is, above all, a city dominated by its agricultural hinterland. Store stock sales are held every Monday, and fat stock sales every Friday; and at the peak periods, in spring and autumn, four days a week are required to dispose of the large numbers and varied selections of livestock from the county and farther afield. The annual February bull sales are now world-famous, and pack the hotels with buyers from every country. Begun in 1864, they have grown in importance ever since. The British record price for Shorthorn bulls (14,500 guineas) was set up in 1946, and for the Aberdeen-Angus breed (60,000 guineas) in 1963. At the time of the sales you may hear many languages in the streets of Perth. Predominating amongst the incoming tongues is Spanish from the Argentine.

Poverty nowhere obtrudes; the Town Council has a housing record of enterprise, if not of aesthetic excellence, that can bear comparison with any other. It is a comfortable place, and its people look comfortable, as indeed all but a minority are. Generally they look no less tidy than comfortable. And, by and large, they are contented and law-abiding. They have solid, if unexciting, reasons for their content.

PETERCULTER, *Aberdeenshire* (Map 6, ref. 38³80⁰), is a village on the N. bank of the R. DEE, which has developed from a paper-mill founded in 1751. These mills are still a major industry producing high-quality art and other papers.

The lands of Culter were divided in the 13th cent. The church on the N. side of the river is dedicated to St Peter, that on the S. side to St Mary. Peterculter parish is in Aberdeenshire; Maryculter parish is in Kincardineshire.

A coloured statue of Rob Roy above the Leuchar Burn has no historical significance; it was originally developed from a ship's figurehead that has been replaced at least twice. But it certainly adds a touch of drama to a spectacular gorge. The kilted warrior looks very real.

To the SW. of the village is Normandykes, a Roman marching camp forming a rectangle 2,900 by 1,600 ft.

Maryculter belonged in the Middle Ages to the Knights Templars and later to the Knights of St John of Jerusalem. Near the Dee are the ruins of St Mary's Chapel, built by the Templars in 1287 and enlarged by the Hospitallers.

The chapel eventually became the parish church, and it served as such until 1787, when the present parish church was built just S. of it. This last is a delightful building, set among fine old trees. Old Maryculter House is a charming 17th-cent. ha' house.

In this parish also lies the estate of Blairs long associated with the Menzies of Pitfodels; in 1827 the last Menzies laird gave the estate to the Catholic bishops for the establishment of a college. The present buildings were erected in 1897, and the Chapel of St Mary in 1901. The college is known as St Mary's College of Blairs. There are many historical documents of interest in "Blairs' College", including memorials of Mary Stuart, Queen of Scots.

In Peterculter parish the handsome 18th-cent. Culter House is now a girls' boarding-school. Both parishes have beautiful sylvan river scenery, and the Culter Paper Mills are so placed that they do not infringe the amenities.

PETERHEAD, *Aberdeenshire* (Map 6, ref. 41⁴84⁵). The modern capital of Buchan and the largest town in the county after ABERDEEN, this busy fishing port is built on a peninsula, the outermost tip of which shares with BUCHAN NESS, a little along the coast, the distinction of being Scotland's easternmost limit.

If you love the sea, you will warm to Peterhead despite the sternness of its aspect, which can hardly be denied. Built for the most part of the red Peterhead granite, it gives the impression of Spartan solidity rather than grace. The large, bare, and barn-like parish church, built between 1804 and 1806, has only one external redeeming feature, its slender steeple 118 ft high. More attractive architecturally is John Baxter's Town House, built in 1788 at a total cost of £2,000, on the highest point of land on the peninsula, at the NW. end of Broad Street, dominating the heart of the town. It has an even taller steeple than the church, with a four-dialled clock and a bell.

But the most characteristic feature of Peterhead is the harbour, formed by a succession of basins between the mainland and the island of

Keith Inch, now linked to the town by its piers, and sheltering the fishing-fleet, still the most important unit of its kind N. of Aberdeen. The town was founded by George Keith, the 5th Marischal, in 1593.

Peterhead then had fifty-six inhabitants. Now it has over 13,500. Within the town itself virtually nothing survives of the Earl's foundation. The last two houses – in Port Henry Lane, between Longate and the harbour – that provided a link with the founder, were demolished some years ago to make way for a housing redevelopment. The Keiths acquired the lands on which the town was built as the result of a deal between Robert Keith, Commendator of DEER, and the government of the day, whereby he handed over the lands of the Abbey of Deer to the Crown and received in return the Lordship of Altries.

This Robert was succeeded in possession by his nephew, the 5th Earl Marischal, and for the next century and a quarter the Keiths were the masters of the growing community. The fragmentary ruin of their stronghold, the 16th-cent. Inverugie Castle, 3 m. NW. of the town, is a melancholy reminder of the manner in which they passed from the scene.

George, the 10th Earl Marischal, born at Inverugie on the 2nd of April 1693, and his brother James, three years younger, were both great and statesmanlike men. But they were both in the first flush of youth when the Earl of Mar raised the standard of James VIII, at BRAEMAR in 1715. Influenced by their strongly pro-Jacobite mother, they joined the ill-fated rising and went into exile on its collapse. On the Continent their true qualities became apparent. James became the trusted general of Frederick the Great, and died in Prussia's service at the Battle of Hochkirchen. George, the last Earl Marischal, became Frederick's devoted adviser. Both made their peace with the Hanoverian dynasty. On the 25th of May 1759, the attainder against the Earl Marischal was reversed by the British Parliament. He bought back the estate of Inverugie, and, after an absence of almost 50 years, revisited Peterhead amid scenes of wild enthusiasm.

There is no question but that, in Peterhead and elsewhere throughout their once vast domains in the NE. of Scotland, the Keiths inspired deep loyalty and affection. When, in 1868, a statue of Field-Marshal Keith that had stood in Potsdam was presented by King William I of Prussia to the burgh of Peterhead, and was unveiled on its present site in Broad Street, the occasion was greeted with enthusiasm.

In 1728 the superiority of the estate of Peterhead was acquired by the Governors of the Merchant Maiden Hospital in EDINBURGH. Through an acquiescent town council, they virtually controlled the burgh for the next 104 years, although a mass meeting of the local feuers in 1752 secured a system of partial local

representation. Some of the stern plainness of modern Peterhead is undoubtedly due to the tensions that existed between the wishes of the local inhabitants and the over-ruling control of the Edinburgh "lairds". Burgh reform in 1833 enabled Peterhead to elect a representative town council of its own.

Incredible as it may seem, Peterhead became a fashionable spa at the end of the 18th cent., when its famous Wine Well and other springs were put to use, and elaborate warm baths were built to cater for an aristocratic clientele. As at BALLATER its first customers were ex-Jacobite gentry. In the 19th cent. the port became the "capital" of British whaling, which reached its peak in 1820, when fifteen whalers brought home 103 Arctic whales.

As the whaling industry declined, it was replaced by the great herring boom, which continued throughout the entire century and reached its maximum intensity in 1907, when 291,713 crans were landed by 420 boats. There is still more herring fishing from Peterhead than from other Scottish ports, but the entire fleet is of dual-purpose craft, and white fishing is now more important than the hunt for the "silver darlings". Food and fish-processing plants and a factory producing fuel appliances have helped to diversify the town's industry. But the incidence of unemployment is high, and there has been a large drift south of skilled labour.

The huge Harbour of Refuge was the first major public work of the kind ever undertaken in Scotland.

There is interesting countryside to explore in the vicinity of Peterhead: long sandy beaches to the N. and spectacular rock scenery to the S. The vale of the Ugie to the NW., with the ruined castles of Ravenscraig and Inverugie, has a quiet rural charm.

PITCAIRNGREEN, *Perthshire* (Map 6, ref. 30⁷72⁸). In former times there was a flax-spinning mill here, and at the end of the 18th cent. Lord Lynedoch founded a bleach-field, around which the present village grew up; it was predicted that it would be a rival to Manchester. The setting is picturesque, the houses being built around a green.

On the edge of the wood NE. of the village is a large prehistoric burial cairn built entirely of water-worn boulders. It is about 13 ft high at the centre and approximately 100 ft in diameter.

PITCAPLE, *Aberdeenshire* (Map 6, ref. 37²82⁶). Along the main ABERDEEN–INVERNESS highway on the right-hand side as one approaches the hamlet of Pitcaple, on the way N., runs a long wall that only partly screens the pleasant wooded demesne of Pitcaple Castle, a 15th-cent. Z-plan tower-house with a 19th-cent. wing attached to it, designed by the EDINBURGH architect William Burn. The incongruity of this combination is not at all oppressive, and has made possible the continuous habitation of the house down to the present day, when it is owned by Mrs M. F. Burges-Lumsden. You still catch your breath at the first glimpse of the Castle's two great round towers at diagonally opposite corners of the old rectilinear keep, one of the first and finest of examples of the Z-plan. In 1947 Mrs Burges-Lumsden discovered a box containing a series of documents that included a charter of 1457, by which James II granted the lands of "Pethapil in the sheriffdom of Abirdene" to David Lesly, son of Sir William Lesly of Balquhain. The Castle probably dates from that time. Originally it was surrounded by an outer wall with a gatehouse and an encircling moat supplied with water from the nearby R. Ury.

Mary Queen of Scots dined at Pitcaple in September 1562 and planted a thorn tree under which her great-grandson Charles II danced in 1650. It survived until 1856, and has been succeeded by a red maple that was planted by the late Queen Mary in September 1923. Throughout the 17th cent. Pitcaple lairds were at the heart of the struggle of King against Covenant and Commonwealth. In 1639 it was the headquarters of the Marquess of Huntly, the King's Lieutenant of the North, as he faced the Marquess of Montrose at the head of the Covenanters. In 1645 the Royalists captured and interned here Andrew Cant, firebrand preacher of the Covenant, along with Bailie Alexander Jaffrey of Aberdeen. On Sundays Cant preached publicly in the Castle's Great Hall, still in use as a living-room by Mrs Burges-Lumsden and her family. Eventually Cant and Jaffrey turned the tables on their jailers by seizing the Castle and standing siege within it until relieved by their Covenanting friends, who then set the place on fire. The scorched stonework of the vaulted kitchen still testifies to this conflagration.

In 1650 the Castle had two distinguished residents: first the Marquess of Montrose on his way to his execution, and then only three months later King Charles II on his way to his crowning at Scone. That poor prisoner "James Graham, a traitor to his country", as the vindictive Covenant-men declared, slept the night in what is still called Montrose's Room, and there he was visited by the Lady of Pitcaple, his own cousin, who offered him a means of escape by way of a secret staircase in the wall. He looked at the painfully narrow aperture (still shown to visitors) and replied, "Rather than go down to be smothered in that hole I will take my chance at Edinburgh." He was executed on 21st of May, and in July of that same year King Charles landed at GARMOUTH on the SPEY. He was entertained at Pitcaple, danced under the thorn tree, and slept that night in the "King's Room". The laird who was his host died fighting for him at the battle of Worcester in the following year.

PITCUR, *Angus* (Map 6, ref. 32⁵73⁶). Situated upon the edge of the Sidlaw hills, Pitcur is a village with a ruined castle. Nearby is an Earth House or Souterrain, the longest-known example, still partially roofed. The main structure is a trench, with walls corbelled inwards at a height of 6 ft, and nearly 200 ft long, with only 3 ft left between the walls. These gaps were covered with large slabs and then with turf and earth. It was occupied between the 1st and 3rd cents.

PITLESSIE, *Fife* (Map 3, ref. 33⁴70⁹). This village in the Cults parish of Fife was made famous by the picture "Pitlessie Fair" by Sir David Wilkie; it was his first picture, painted when he was only nineteen. He was born in 1785 at the Manse of Cults, just NE. of the village. The village hall, built in 1897, is known as the Wilkie Memorial Hall.

PITLOCHRY, *Perthshire* (Map 2, ref. 29⁴75⁸). This famous holiday resort lies almost at the centre of Scotland and in the beautifully wooded valley of the Tummel. The town was raised to burgh status in 1947 and has a famous tweed-mill and two distilleries.

To the E., Ben-y-Vrackie rises 2,757 ft. Golf, tennis, pony-trekking, fishing, ski-ing, climbing, and walking are all attractions for the holiday-maker, and sailing is available on Loch Tummel with club facilities at Foss, 11 m. W. of the town.

Pitlochry is an important link in the North of Scotland Hydro-Electric Board's Tummel valley scheme. From Clunie dam at the outlet of Loch Tummel, 9,158 ft of tunnelling involving the removal of 400,000 tons of quartzite schist has ensured the daily flow of 2,700 million gallons of water to feed the Pitlochry power station. Moreover, a lower dam on the Tummel at Pitlochry has created a new loch at Faskally just N. of the town and this is now a local beauty-spot. Faskally House is a Forestry Training School and in the grounds a Brown Trout Research Station was set up in 1948 by the Scottish Home Department, in cooperation with the Hydro-Electric Board. Observation chambers in a fish-pass at the Pitlochry dam enable visitors to watch the passage of salmon up-river to their spawning grounds. At Portnacraig House the Board has its Central Control, the operational centre for the whole electricity system.

In 1951 Mr John Stewart, who created a reputation in the Park Theatre at GLASGOW, founded the Pitlochry Festival Theatre, and each summer season a wide variety of plays is given. There are also Sunday concerts and exhibitions of Scottish art.

Across the river from the town, at the entrance to the mausoleum of Dunfallandy House, is a Pictish sculptured stone – one of the finest examples of this type of art in Scotland.

Above *Loch Tay* (*see p. 439*)

Scottish Tourist Board

Below *Pony trekking in the Trossachs* (*see p. 448*)

Scottish Tourist Board

PITMEDDEN, *Aberdeenshire* (Map 6, ref. 38⁹82⁷). The richness of Aberdeenshire in historic homes reaches something of a climax at the northern end of Formartine, where, cheek by jowl and virtually within sight of one another, three ancient estates are clustered: UDNY, Tolquhon, and (between these two famous old castles) the House of Pitmedden, with its great garden, which is also the headquarters of the National Trust for Scotland's representative in the North-East. Thanks to the foresight of the late Major James Keith, a farming expert and Governor of the North of Scotland College of Agriculture, the National Trust has been able to establish here a model 17th-cent. pleasance, which at the same time commemorates a remarkable Scot. Every summer many thousands of visitors pass through the stone doorway into the walled enclosure, with its legend on the lintel, FUNDAT 2 MAY 1675, surmounted by a panel bearing the initials S.A.S. for Sir Alexander Seton, over D.M.L. for Dame Margaret Lauder, his wife.

Sir Alexander was the 5th Seton laird of Pitmedden. His father Sir John was the hero of the family. His brief but brilliant life was brought to an end when at the age of twenty-eight he was shot through the heart defending the Royal Standard at the head of a detachment of Royalists at the Battle of the Bridge of Dee in ABERDEEN on the 18th of June 1639. He left two young sons, James and Alexander. James, who went abroad during the Commonwealth, returned at the Restoration and served and fell fighting in King Charles II's navy. Sir Alexander, who now succeeded, had already carved out a career for himself in the law.

He was an advocate, and had already been knighted by the King. He became a Lord of Session in 1677, and took the title of Lord Pitmedden. In 1682 he became a Lord of Justiciary, and in 1684 a baronetcy of Nova Scotia was bestowed on him. On three occasions he represented the county of Aberdeen in the Scottish Parliament. But fortune turned against him. He strongly opposed King James VII and II's moves to repeal the Test and Penal Laws, and was in consequence ejected from office. Like many a politician before and since, he retired to his estate to "cultivate his garden".

The Great Garden, closely modelled on the garden of Holyroodhouse at this period, was his creation. Restoration and re-creation was the work of the National Trust's expert, the late Dr J. S. Richardson. It is constructed in the sunken eastern half of a great square, extending to 475 ft in front of the house. Two pavilions at the N. and S. ends of the western wall of the garden have been restored to their state in Lord Pitmedden's day.

In the layout of the garden patterns in box-wood and yew, two designs were taken from a contemporary drawing of the King's Garden at Holyrood by Parson Gordon of Rothiemay. A third is now a rose garden, and the fourth,

the principal feature, is Lord Pitmedden's coat of arms flanked by panels of the saltire and the thistle for Scotland. Around the top of the coat of arms is worked the motto: SUSTENTO SANGUINE SIGNA ("I bear the Standard with blood"), in memory of the nature of Bonnie John Seton's death, and around the foot the motto is MERCES HAEC CERTA LABORUM ("This sure reward of our labours").

Much admired and perfectly accurate time-keepers at Pitmedden are the two sundials, one in the centre of the rose garden and the other on the W. wall of the N. pavilion. Above the ogee roof of this pavilion is a crest-formed weather-vane, showing the demi-figure of a Scottish soldier of horse, in late 17th-cent. uniform, holding the Standard of Scotland.

The upper apartment of the N. pavilion is now a little museum. For it were obtained copies of the portraits of Sir Alexander Seton and Dame Margaret, the originals of which are in the possession of descendants of their daughter, who married Sir John Lauder of Fountainhall in East Lothian. Also on view here is a parchment of the matriculation of arms of Lord Pitmedden, signed by Charles Erskine, the Lyon King of Arms, on the 30th of May 1678. Here too are interesting relics found during the digging and replanning of the Great Garden, including a silver coin of the 13th cent., brooch moulds of slate, and clay pipes dating from the 17th cent.

PITREAVIE, *Fife* (Map 3, ref. 31²68⁷). The mansion house of Pitreavie, 2¾ m. SE. of DUNFERMLINE, is now the R.A.F./R.N. head-quarters for the Scotland and Northern Rescue Co-ordination Centre. From here is organized air-sea rescue of service or civilian personnel for the area from Iceland to a line from N. Wales to Lowestoft. The Rescue Co-ordination Service uses helicopters, mountain rescue teams, launches, and long-range Nimrod air-craft, stationed at a variety of local bases.

PITTENWEEM, *Fife* (Map 3, ref. 35⁵70³). The picturesque seaport of Pittenweem is a royal burgh with an ancient harbour. The Priory of Pittenweem dates back to the early 12th cent., and round it the burgh grew up, a charter being granted constituting the town a royal burgh by James V in 1542. The burgh is built in steep "steps" around the harbour, and at the top of the town are the priory ruins, near the parish church with its tower, which dates from 1592. The houses, wynds, and the harbour have attracted many artists, and some of the fishermen's houses have been restored.

Near the harbour is the cave-shrine of St Fillan, re-dedicated in 1935 after its career of smuggling, since the monks venerated the place where St Fillan is said to have lived in the 7th cent.

Plate 14   The Cathedral of St Andrews, Fife (see p. 403)
Scottish Tourist Board

Paul Shillabeer

Pittenweem: Kellie Castle

About 3 m. NW. of Pittenweem is Kellie Castle, with its 15th-cent. N. tower. The E. tower was added in 1573, and in 1606 the two towers were joined by the main block with the S. tower being added. In 1878 the castle was rescued from ruin by Professor James Lorimer, father of Sir Robert Lorimer, the architect, who greatly restored it. It was on a long lease from the Earl of Mar and Kellie until 1958, when Sir Robert's son, Mr Hew Lorimer, the sculptor (noted for his "Our Lady of the Isles" at South UIST) bought it. He in turn sold it to the National Trust of Scotland. Of the interior decoration done in the 17th cent., one plaster ceiling in the drawing-room is dated 1676 and has the arms of the Earls of Kellie, while another has a magnificent design of vine leaves.

PLOCKTON, *Ross and Cromarty* (Map 5, ref. 18°83³). Established at the end of the 18th cent. as a fishing place, Plockton has now become a crofting community. On the outer part of Loch Carron between STROME and KYLE OF LOCHALSH, Plockton is a pleasant backwater with the main road passing by it behind a hill.

PLUSCARDEN ABBEY, *Moray* (Map 6, ref. 31³85⁷). Some 6 m. to the SE. of ELGIN, the original Cistercian Abbey of Pluscarden was founded in 1230 by Alexander II. In 1454 the Benedictine Order took charge, and the Abbey flourished under ecclesiastical rule until just after the Reformation of 1560. The buildings then became lay property and passed through various hands. In 1897, however, the substantial remains of the Abbey passed to the

3rd Marquess of Bute, who began renovation of the buildings. They were eventually given by his son, Lord Colum Crichton-Stuart, to the Benedictine community of Prinknash Abbey in Gloucestershire. Real and practical restoration was then begun, and the community took up residence in 1948. Work is almost complete on the church, and a block of domestic buildings is now fully used.

The monks of the community (a hospitable Order in tradition and in present fact) welcome the visitors to see the progress of their labours. The church is transitional in style between "Romanesque" and "Early English". It has an old groined roof in the aisles of the transepts.

POLMONT, *Stirlingshire* (Map 2, ref. 29³67⁸). The village of Polmont is on the main EDINBURGH to FALKIRK road, 3 m. E. of Falkirk. The line of ANTONINUS' WALL runs just N. of the village, but only very intermittent parts are visible.

Just 1 m. W. of Polmont is the Westquarter Dovecote, dated 1647, with the arms of William Livingstone above the doorway.

POOLEWE, *Ross and Cromarty* (Map 5, ref. 18°88⁰). The village of Poolewe stands at the head of Loch EWE, on the W. side of the county. The loch is well-known for its excellent salmon and sea-trout fishing. The Highland garden of INVEREWE juts into the loch on a promontory about 1 m. round the shore from the village. The approaches to Poolewe from INVERNESS make one of the most magnificently scenic touring circuits in the Highlands. The sudden vista of Loch MAREE from Glen Docherty, the golden sands of GRUINARD, glimpses of the Summer Isles, the great bulk of An Teallach, are only a few of the surprises and delights to be found on the round trip – out by ACHNASHEEN and back by DUNDONNELL. Poolewe, with the added attraction of Inverewe, which has its own restaurant service, is a natural stopping place for the touring motorist. In addition to two hotels, the village has a well-equipped camping and caravan site and information centre operated by the National Trust for Scotland.

PORT ASKAIG, *Argyll* (Map 1, ref. 14³66⁹), is on the Island of ISLAY, in the Inner Hebrides (*see* "The Shape of Scotland"). Port Askaig, though but a township, is important as one of the entrances to the island; on alternate days the steamer from West Loch Tarbert comes to Port Askaig, on the other days going to PORT ELLEN. There is also a small ferry to Feolin on JURA. No roads run to the northern tip of Islay, and only Bonahaven with its distillery and associated houses lie 3 m. N. of the township.

Just S. of Port Askaig is Dunlossit, whose gardens give magnificent views over the Sound of Islay.

PORT BANNATYNE, *Buteshire* (Map 2, ref. 20⁸66⁷), is on the Island of BUTE. This village and holiday resort on Kames Bay is almost part of ROTHESAY, but keeps its original character; its yacht slip is extremely popular.

At the head of the village is the picturesque Kames Castle, said to be 14th cent., and in its grounds is the tower-house of Wester Kames, built in the 17th cent., and rebuilt in 1900.

Just N. of Port Bannatyne, the main road crosses the island to sandy Etterick Bay with good views westwards to Kintyre and S. to ARRAN.

PORT CHARLOTTE, *Argyll* (Map 1, ref. 12⁵65⁸), is on the Island of ISLAY, in the Inner Hebrides (*see* "The Shape of Scotland"). This village was projected in 1828 and was named after the mother of W. F. Campbell of Islay, the noted Gaelic Scholar. It lies along the western shore of Loch Indaal. The street names are in Gaelic. There is a distillery just to the N. at Bruichladdich and a creamery at Port Charlotte.

Some 3 m. S. of Port Charlotte is Nereabolls, where three adjoining burial grounds have fine carved stones. About 4 m. beyond Nereabolls is Portnahaven, a semicircular village round the bay, with the Rhinns of Islay lighthouse on an island beyond.

Kilchiaran, with a roofless chapel and carved stones, lies 4 m. W. of Port Charlotte, on the W. coast. A very fine walk of about 3 m. N. along the cliffs leads to Kilchoman with a wide sandy bay. There is here in the churchyard a fine, carved stone cross.

PORT EDGAR, *West Lothian* (1 m. W. of South QUEENSFERRY), is the spot where the Saxon prince Edgar Atheling, whose sister St Margaret married Malcolm III, King of Scots, is supposed to have landed as a refugee from England about 1070 on the S. shore of the Firth of FORTH at the Binks, near the W. end of the later burgh of South Queensferry. The rocks were later hammered and chiselled down and their fissures filled in to make a more convenient landing-place for passengers, and even for cattle and carriages, using the ferry across the Forth at this point. After the passage was taken over by trustees for the public in 1809, many improvements were carried out, including the building of a commodious quay and breakwater at Port Edgar. George IV embarked here after visiting HOPETOUN HOUSE at the end of his visit to Scotland in 1822. The harbour became an important Admiralty establishment in the two world wars, and it is used as a base by the Royal Navy's fishery protection vessels.

PORT ELLEN, *Argyll* (Map 1, ref. 13⁶64⁵), is on the Island of ISLAY, in the Inner Hebrides (*see* "The Shape of Scotland"). This is the principal village on the island, and the steamer from West Loch Tarbert calls here on alternate days. The village was created by the Gaelic scholar W. F. Campbell of Islay, and was begun in 1821. There are distilleries at Port Ellen, Laphroaig, Lagavullin, and Ardbeg to the E. of the village. This island's whisky is famous.

To the W. of the village is Mull of Oa – a peninsula with high cliffs at the SW. end of the island. Near to the highest point is a memorial to American soldiers and sailors drowned in the loss of the *Tuscania* and the *Otranto* in 1918.

PORT GLASGOW, *Renfrewshire* (Map 2, ref. 23¹67⁴), was once just a fishing village called Newark, below a castle of the same name built in 1597. The port was founded in 1668, to be the harbour for GLASGOW before the CLYDE was artificially deepened in the late 18th cent. The chief customs house for the Clyde was built here in 1710, and the first graving-dock was constructed to a design by James Watt in 1762. It declined as a port in the early 19th cent. The industrial revolution, however, increased its status as a shipbuilding centre. The *Comet* was built here by James Wood in 1812.

Newark Castle was given to the nation by Sir Hugh Shaw Stewart in 1909; it has 16th and 17th-cent. features and stands between two shipyards.

PORTKNOCKIE, *Banffshire* (Map 6, ref. 34⁹86⁸), still remains a fishing village to the W. of Cullen Bay. The first houses were built here in 1677 by fishermen from CULLEN who were attracted by the excellent natural harbour. A deep-water harbour was constructed in the late 19th cent., and the place became one of the most flourishing of the Moray Firth herring ports. But it was hard hit by the depredations of foreign trawlers in the last years of the last century and in the first decades of this one. It has now declined, and the harbour is nearly abandoned. In this it has shared the fate of so much fishing in the island and inshore waters on the W. coast of Scotland.

PORT LOGAN, *Wigtownshire* (Map 2, ref. 21⁰54⁰), is a small fishing village in the Rhinns of Galloway, where cottages stand in a row behind a raised road along Portnessock Bay.

On the opposite side of Logan Bay is a remarkable tidal fish-pond, begun in 1788, taking twelve years to complete, and closed in 1939 after damage by a mine. It has, however, been functioning again since 1955. The fish are extraordinarily tame and are fed by hand, coming when a bell is rung.

Some 2 m. N. are Logan Gardens, an old walled garden containing rare shrubs, tropical plants, tree-ferns, azaleas, and rhododendrons. Logan House, built in the 18th cent., was the home of the McDoualls for many centuries until 1940.

PORTMAHOMACK, *Ross and Cromarty* (Map 5, ref. 29²88³), a former fishing village 9 m. E. of TAIN on the DORNOCH Firth, is now a holiday resort with a caravan site, and is a centre for sea bathing, fishing, and touring. The low, sandy coastline on the firth has views across to the Sutherland hills. Tarbat Ness Lighthouse, one of the highest towers in Scotland, is at the end of a low peninsula. The coastline to the E. is rocky and full of caves.

PORTPATRICK, *Wigtownshire* (Map 2, ref. 20⁰55⁴). A small fishing and holiday resort on the W. coast of the Rhinns of Galloway, Portpatrick was chartered as a burgh of barony on the 8th of February 1620, but the charter was later allowed to lapse.

It is only 21½ m. NE. of Donaghadee in Ireland, and was once of great importance as the shortest crossing-place to that country, but, owing to the danger of severe south-westerly gales at Portpatrick, STRANRAER was developed as the port for the mail-steamers to Larne in Northern Ireland, and, from 1849, the harbour that had been built in 1821 to plans of the great John Rennie gradually silted up. The railway line from Stranraer is also closed now.

Portpatrick has become a holiday centre, with beautiful coastal scenery, delightful walks, sandy bays, a golf course, and other amenities, including a large hotel. The picturesque ruins of the 15th-cent. Dunskey Castle stand in a strong position on a headland, ½ m. S., where the Craigoch Burn enters the sea.

The name "Portpatrick" is said to derive from St Patrick who "strode from Ireland" across to Portpatrick.

PORTREE, *Inverness-shire* (Map 4, ref. 14⁸84³), is on the Island of SKYE, in the Inner Hebrides (*see* "The Shape of Scotland"). The chief town, or capital, of Skye, Portree lies in a sheltered loch on the centre of the E. coast of the island. It has a harbour and a pier for steamers, some of which make tours of the island and connect Skye with its celebrated and smaller sister isle of RAASAY. There are hotels and guest houses. The name derives from the Gaelic meaning "king's haven", and recalls the visit made to Skye by James V when he was sailing through the Hebrides in an attempt to control these outlying islands of his dominions. Portree is excellently placed for tours in all directions over Skye. It is in its own right a pleasing little town with many characteristically whitewashed houses.

PORT SETON, *East Lothian* (1 m. E. of COCKENZIE). A former fishing village, and now a holiday resort, Port Seton is linked with

Cockenzie as a police burgh. The harbour, opened in 1880, was soon added to, but it is now less busy as much of the fish is dealt with at Newhaven. At Seton Sands, a 2 m. stretch E. of the village, is a holiday camp with a large modern swimming pool.

Seton Castle was built by Robert Adam in 1790 on the site of the demolished Seton Palace, a magnificent building mostly built after 1544. In the Palace Mary Queen of Scots, James VI, and Charles I were entertained by the Seton family.

Near the castle is the Collegiate Church of Seton, dating from the late 14th cent. It was never completed beyond the chancel, transepts, and unusual crossing-tower with a truncated octagonal spire. It includes a fine arched mural tomb with two recumbent effigies, probably of George, the 3rd Lord Seton, slain at Flodden in 1513, and of his lady. The foundations of the nave and of the domestic buildings have recently been excavated.

PORTSONACHAN, *Argyll* (Map 1, ref. 20⁴72⁰). The small holiday township of Portsonachan is on the S. shore of Loch AWE, with a passenger ferry across the loch to Taychreggan. The winding road along the loch side is attractive, with wooded shores and islands just off-shore, including Innis Chonell, with the remains of Ardchonell Castle, and Innis Sherrich (accessible at low water), on which is an ancient chapel and cemetery. Portsonachan is a resort for brown-trout anglers, especially at the beginning of the season.

PORTSOY, *Banffshire* (Map 6, ref. 35⁹86⁶). The story of this coastal burgh is one of great vicissitudes. In the 18th cent. the Old Harbour of Portsoy was a major commercial port. In the next hundred years fishing boomed. Today that maritime importance has all gone, but the new Portsoy shows great initiative as a holiday resort. It is not easy for a town like Portsoy to make the right decisions about town-planning. The previously shabby and rather derelict buildings round the old harbour have now been handsomely reconstructed by the Town Council, and have indeed won a Saltire Society award and a Civic Trust commendation. The Old Harbour is now an attractive amenity, and there is an active sailing club.

Portsoy boasts a highly picturesque open-air swimming-pool amid the rocks to the W. of the town, opened in 1934, and, on the E., a delightful if modest open-air theatre arena, where a wide range of plays is produced at the height of the holiday season.

Straddling two streams that run into a great rocky bay between Redhythe Head and Cowhythe Head, in a district which has been called a "geological museum", Portsoy was made a burgh of barony in 1550, but the old harbour was the creation of Patrick Ogilvie, Lord

Boyne, who developed the port from the export of "Portsoy marble" obtained from a vein of serpentine still exposed near the new swimming-pool. In 1700 he persuaded the Scots Parliament to assist this by prohibiting the import of foreign marble and the trade flourished mightily for the six years till the Treaty of Union altered the situation. There was a considerable export to France, and Louis XIV used the serpentine from Portsoy for two of the chimney-pieces of the Palace of Versailles. A magnificent fireplace of Portsoy marble can be seen today in CULLEN House. Craftsmen are still working Portsoy serpentine on a very modest scale, and paperweights, chessmen, and other small objects of this most attractive stone can still be obtained in local shops.

In 1825 the Earl of Seafield built at his own expense a new harbour alongside the old one. Its siting and construction were faulty, and it was wrecked by storms. It was rebuilt to cope with the herring boom in the 19th cent., and it still survives today, but is now used only by pleasure craft and about a dozen small lobster-fishing boats. Portsoy is within easy reach of some very striking coastal scenery and good beaches. About 2 m. W. is the picturesque fishing village of Sandend, locally pronounced "Saan-eyn".

PORT WILLIAM, *Wigtownshire* (Map 2, ref. 23⁴54³). A small seaport on the E. side of Luce Bay, with a safe harbour, Port William was founded in 1770 by Sir William Maxwell of Monreith.

About 1 m. E. from Port William is Monreith House, which was built in 1799. On a lawn near the house is a notable free-standing, wheel-headed cross, 7 ft 6 in. high; it is thought to have come from the ancient chapel of Kirk-maiden-in-Fernis (now restored), which stands on the shore of Luce Bay. In the grounds of Monreith House is the White Loch; a legend says that only half of it ever freezes. Round it were beautiful gardens and a park. The Maxwell family owned land here from the 15th cent., and lived here from the 17th cent.

Some 5 m. NW. of Port William is Chapel Finian, a small chapel or oratory dating from the 10th or 11th cent., which may be compared with other small, early chapels found in Ireland and other Celtic lands.

Monreith Bay, 1½ m. S., which is the only sandy bay on a long stretch of rocky coast, is a popular little resort.

POWFOOT, *Dumfriesshire* (Map 3, ref. 31⁵56⁶). Formerly known as Queensberry, this village on the bay at the mouth of Cummertrees Pow was noted as a seaside resort as early as the 1790s. Considerable development was carried out here early in the present century, a hotel and a fine golf course being constructed. It is now mainly a dormitory village for ANNAN, but is still a very popular holiday resort. It has a shingle and sand beach, with a wide expanse of sands at low tide. The village still has a very strong community spirit. Queensberry Terrace, on the main road 1 m. inland, was part of the development undertaken in 1911. A large chemical company has an explosives plant nearby.

PRESTONPANS, *East Lothian* (Map 3, ref. 33⁸67⁵). The prosperity of this small town, near EDINBURGH and on the Firth of FORTH, was once founded on salt pans started as early as the 12th cent. under the monks of NEW-BATTLE. These supplied the whole of the East of Scotland with salt until, in the early 19th cent., the Salt Tax was repealed. Until recently, Prestonpans salt (which is real salt, not a synthetic compound) was much relished in Edinburgh. There was also early coal-mining in the area; in the 19th cent. a colliery was re-opened.

As a result of its early prosperity, Prestonpans has a fine mercat cross dating from the 17th cent., and several houses of that period: Hamilton House, dated 1628 (well restored by the National Trust for Scotland); Northfield House, with fine painted ceilings and a sundial dated 1647; Preston House, of which only a fragment remains (also 17th cent.). At Preston Tower a 15th-cent. ruin, is a 17th-cent. dovecote with nests for over 1,000 birds.

But, for those interested in the Jacobite cause, particularly the '45, the name of Prestonpans is associated with the complete victory Prince Charles's Highland troops won over Sir John Cope on the 21st of September 1745; there is a memorial cairn 1 m. E. of the town. The battle was over in ten minutes, and General Cope fled to England, being the first, it is said, to carry the news of his own defeat. The Battle of Prestonpans was a heartening appetiser to the Jacobites, but no substantial satisfaction was to follow. There is a monument to Colonel James Gardiner, one of Cope's officers, who fell. It is in the grounds of Bankton House hard by.

There is much new building at Prestonpans, including a civic centre, and a housing estate at Inchview built by the Edinburgh University Architecture Research Unit under Sir Robert Matthew and opened in 1962. It is used for the "live study" of social conditions.

PRESTWICK, *Ayrshire* (Map 2, ref. 23⁵62⁵). Famous in this Age of Aviation, Prestwick is an ancient burgh lying immediately N. of AYR, and in fact continuous with it. The Church of St Nicholas (ruined) is thought to date from 1163, but the town probably does not take its name from the priests that served it; rather is Prestwick a reference to the splendid "split" bay on which the town sits. But the present-day Prestwick is, to all Scotland, an international airport of the first rank, dating from 1935 and attaining

Prestwick: the air terminal

importance first as the British terminal of the trans-Atlantic ferry service during the Second World War.

There are three 18-hole golf courses, the most famous, "Old Prestwick", having its origin back in the Middle Ages.

PUMPHERSTON, *West Lothian* (Map 2, ref. 30⁷66⁹). The shale oil industry that made the village of Pumpherston, and so strongly influenced West Lothian, was started in the mid-19th cent. by James Young, first at BATHGATE and BROXBURN, then around West Calder. Pumpherston refinery opened in 1884, and the maximum output of shale oil was reached in 1913. In the 1950s output was about 750,000 tons per year and the refinery employed 1,750 people. The by-products were wax, ammonium sulphate, caustic soda, bricks, and detergent. The shale-mining industry closed in 1962, but the detergent plant has been considerably expanded since the refinery ceased operations in 1964, and there is a steady market for Pumpherston bricks.

QUEEN ELIZABETH FOREST PARK, *Perthshire/Stirlingshire* (E. of Loch LOMOND). Including part of the TROSSACHS, this National Forest Park covers 41,454 acres, extending from Loch Vennacher and the head water of the R. FORTH over the summit of Ben Lomond to Loch Lomond. Plantations cover 25,000 acres, while the rest is moorland and mountain. The park includes ABERFOYLE and the "Duke's Road", built for the use of tourists attracted to this neighbourhood in the early 19th cent. by Scott's romantic narrative verse. The forest was acquired in 1928 and in 1953 received its name.

Near the Duke's Road on Craigmore Hill is a shelter built by the Carnegie Trust so that all may enjoy the view. There is a caravan site and a camping ground on Loch Lomond near ROWARDENNAN.

QUEENSFERRY, *West Lothian/Fife* (Map 3, ref. 31⁴67⁸). Under this one heading it is proposed to cover a famous narrow passage of sea-water in the Firth of FORTH between Fife and the Lothians; the vessels that have moved over it since the ferry took its name; two towns (South Queensferry in West Lothian, North Queensferry in Fife); and two bridges, both of which are triumphs of engineering and of considerable functional beauty – one has had its effect on the life of Scotland for over seventy years, the other is bound to have an effect in the future. These two are, of course, the Forth Rail Bridge (1890) and the Forth Road Bridge (1964).

THE PASSAGE

One cannot do better than quote from an article on the occasion of the opening of the Road Bridge, which looks back over the centuries. It says this: "Between the Bridge of STIRLING" (the place where Wallace won his great but solitary victory over the English – *see* "Scotland in History") "and the Isle of MAY there used to be quite a choice of 'watergangs' over the Forth, but the Queensferry has outlasted them all, just as it is probably the oldest".

Having given a list of these, it goes on to say: "It is one of the oldest lines of ferry communication in the world with 800 years of recorded history and another century of more or less continuous service. Beyond that there are only vague tales of transit for the Roman legions. . . . Queensferry's story begins with the saintly Margaret" (Queen Margaret – *see* "Scotland in History") "who found refuge in Scotland after the Norman conquest." After Margaret had married the Scottish King, Malcolm Canmore, they used this passage between EDINBURGH in Lothian and their favourite home, DUNFERMLINE, in Fife. It was over this passage that the saintly Queen's body was taken from Edinburgh Castle to be buried in Dunfermline – now a place of pilgrimage. It is because of this queenly history of over 800 years ago that the ferry bears its name.

That name of Queensferry and the occasion of the article quoted above – the closing of the ferry service, with the opening of the Forth Road Bridge – allowed the pleasingly appropriate phrase "It cam' wi' a lass, and it will gang wi' a lass". The words are those of the dying King James V, when he heard of the birth of his daughter, who was to be Mary Queen of Scots. They referred to the Stuart line of monarchs – a prophecy that was not fulfilled. In this context, of course, the well-known saying is applied to the fact that Queensferry was made by Queen Margaret at the end of the 11th cent., and that it was to be closed by Queen Elizabeth (our present monarch) in the 20th cent.

This same passage had one other royal and tragic connection with the reigning house in Scotland. In 1286 King Alexander III (the reader is again referred to "Scotland in History") mysteriously dashed through a late winter storm from the Castle in Edinburgh to join his Queen at KINGHORN in Fife. He survived the crossing, which indeed was dangerous enough, but fell from his horse in the storm and darkness on the other side, and broke his neck. He thus unwittingly plunged Scotland into the chaos of dispute that ended in the Wars of Independence and at BANNOCK-BURN.

The ferry was in constant use by sail, by rowing-boat (see Robert Louis Stevenson's *Kidnapped*), by steamboats, and finally by vessels that carried motorists in their vehicles and were themselves driven by electricity and diesel engines, until the 4th of September 1964. Now, if you are lucky enough to procure a boat, you can only row across Queensferry passage. You can, of course, if you are up to it, still swim across. For the rest, the passage is closed.

THE TOWNS

Of the two Queensferries, South Queensferry is by far the more picturesque and interesting, as it has preserved its identity and historic appearance. This ancient little royal burgh stands between a steep hill and the waters of the Firth. Seen from above (that is, by crossing either of the bridges), parts of the town appear to be wading in the sea, as they were built upon water-washed rocks. South Queensferry could expand only under the hill and along by the sea front.

Malcolm IV gave the monks of Dunfermline a grant of land in this town, subsequently confirmed by the Patriot King, Robert I. Later, a Carmelite chapel was founded by George Dundas of Dundas in 1330. The existing remains of this much-changed building date from the late 15th cent. It was restored as an Episcopalian chapel in 1890. The burgh museum retains all the old charters back to the date of its establishment. The Tolbooth was remodelled in 1720. A particularly fine house, Plewlands, built during 1643 in the main street, was threatened by modern traffic. The house was saved by the National Trust for Scotland, who now own it and have converted it into flats. The general effect of South Queensferry is pleasing both aesthetically and to the historically-minded. One of the undoubted benefits of the new Road Bridge will be to relieve South Queensferry of traffic made up of weary motorists unable to await the ferries, and who turned up-river to the far-off KINCARDINE Bridge. South Queensferry is also the site of the

well-known Hawes Inn, an ancient hostelry of more luxurious accommodation than those many inns on the N. side that used to greet the travellers after the ordeal of a northward passage.

North Queensferry is a village at the extremity of the Ferryhill peninsula. This village arose to house a colony of ferrymen and their families. Traditionally, it is said to have been established by Queen Margaret, who gave the inhabitants the exclusive right of ferrying. Difficult though it may be to believe, this little specialized place had in 1800 no fewer than thirteen inns. Most of these must have contended for the custom of north-going travellers who, at this passage, had endured their first touch of the sea.

The Tower House was built in 1809 after the ferry trustees had established headquarters there. The old burial ground at North Queensferry has a high wall with the inscription on it: "This is done by the sailers in North Ferrie 1752". The wall includes the gable-end of an old chapel dedicated to St James of Compostella, the patron saint of travellers. It was established under the patronage of James I of Scotland.

It is from North Queensferry that you may perceive the most impressive upward-looking view of the Forth Rail Bridge with all its intricacies of metal mechanism hanging almost menacingly above you.

THE BRIDGES

The Forth Rail Bridge, until recently known simply as the Forth Bridge, was opened by Edward Prince of Wales on the 4th of March 1890, seven years and two months after work had begun on it. Built on the cantilever principle, with its central cantilever resting on the historic rock of Inchgarvie, it was and remains an impressive sight. The cantilever principle is as old as the science of engineering, and was known to the ancient Chinese. Never before, however, had the system been used to practical purposes on so huge a scale.

This Forth Bridge became, and for long remained, one of the wonders of the world. Victorian and Edwardian prints, in a mannered fashion, display it alongside or rather imposed upon St Paul's Cathedral, the Porcelain Tower at Nanking, the Obelisk at the Lateran in Rome, and some seventy other buildings. Until recently, any serious visitor to Edinburgh *had* to go down to Queensferry and see the Forth Bridge; visitors continue to do so, but now see it alongside its younger sister of 1964. Its stature and impressiveness are not reduced by comparison with the slim, lovely, more ethereal lines of the Road Bridge.

From the day of the opening of the Rail Bridge, men, not only in Scotland but from all over the world, recognized that, on the largest possible scale, here was a pre-eminent kind of new beauty – functional beauty. It is still functional and shall remain so as long as the railway trains continue to run; it is still beautiful.

There had been schemes to bridge the Forth at Queensferry before – one obscure one as far back as the middle 18th cent. The great Thomas Telford, a native Scot, and constructor of the lovely Dean Bridge in Edinburgh, had schemes for building one, but was defeated by circumstances. Just before the bridge we now see was begun in 1883, an earlier scheme was abandoned because of the TAY Bridge disaster. Men did not feel like venturing on another great railway bridge across a firth until they were more sure of themselves.

However, in 1883 they did feel sufficiently confident to make the experiment. Under the impetus of the railway companies, and with the approval of Parliament, work began. The chief engineer was Sir John Fowler, assisted by the more youthful Sir Benjamin Baker, who was responsible for the bulk of the work. In carrying out the execution of the designs much of the task fell on Sir William Arrol and Mr Joseph Phillips.

The Bridge has two spans, each 1,710 ft, one over the N. and one over the S. deep-water channel. The highest part above high water is 361 ft, the total length including viaducts of approach is 1 m. 972 yds. An extraordinary amount of contraction and expansion in the metal had to be allowed for. The hitherto unsurpassed width of the central spans forced the engineers to make a bridge that could not only carry trains safely but could bear its own weight.

At least 5,000 workmen were employed on the job. Of them, over seventy years ago, Sir Benjamin Baker said: "The Forth Bridge is essentially a workman's bridge. Its successful construction was due to their collective pluck and individuality as much as to the labours of engineers and contractors. At hundreds of points each independent group of men had to use their own brains and originate expedients to overcome unlooked-for difficulties on the spur of the moment without waiting for instructions from engineers or leading foremen."

The Forth Rail Bridge, then, was a triumph not only of high engineering but of a democratic desire to get the job done.

Apart from this triumph, the results were these. The coming of the Railway Age had made Fife almost into an island, an island from which Fifers could escape only on land and by railways at PERTH or Stirling. The Forth Rail Bridge ended this. Industry in Fife immediately revived. Men were able to live in Edinburgh and work, let us say, in Dunfermline, or vice versa. The Fife holiday resorts became accessible to two generations of Edinburgh folk, who have always loved the sunny Fife coast. There was quicker communication with the N. from all up the E. side of Scotland. The effect on Edinburgh was secondary; that on

Fife was revolutionary; on DUNDEE, and even on ABERDEEN, it was perceptible.

One curious effect was on the water ferries. Almost immediately their use declined; nor did the beginnings of the Motor Age have much use for them. By 1915 the ferries were described as "almost entirely superseded". The motorist of the inter-war years must have thought of that statement with a wry smile.

After the First World War, however, there was a demand for motor-ferries across the Forth, and the increasing frustration caused by the delays they inflicted was responsible for the first agitation for a road bridge begun in 1924, an agitation with which the name of the late J. Inglis Ker must be mentioned with honour.

The car-ferry across the Forth, as it existed from between the two wars and until 1964, was an ineffectual and exasperating compromise, which even those with the most languid interest in the motor-car recognized as something that ought to be brought to an end. It was not so much the necessity for delays that was irksome, but its incalculability. Motorists going N. from Edinburgh might have accepted the delay with more equanimity if they had known that exactly half an hour, give and take either way, was what they would have to put up with. But the intolerable point was that delays varied from a quarter of an hour to over two hours.

The agitation for a road bridge grew and became something of a Scottish national issue above politics. The Government recognized this. Throughout the 1950s experiments were made for its construction; and at last, in 1958, work on it was begun, culminating in its opening in September 1964.

Lying just to the W. of the Rail Bridge and a little farther up the Firth, the lovely slender lines of this suspension bridge do not clash with or rival the impressive strides of its older sister. The Road Bridge, all questions of function apart, is complementary to that once wonder of the world, the Rail Bridge.

Work on the Road Bridge took almost exactly six years – from September 1958 till September 1964. It is the largest suspension bridge in Europe. With the approach viaducts it is a little over 1¼ m. The main towers extend 512 ft above the mean level of the Forth water. The dual 24-ft roadways on the bridge are designed to carry the heaviest loading permitted on any road bridge in the world. Some 39,000 tons of steel and 405,000 cubic ft of concrete were used in the bridge's construction.

"The men who planned and built the bridge" (these words are quoted from the official story published by the Forth Road Bridge Joint Board) "were a team working with pride and with precision on a massive engineering project. The construction of the Forth Road Bridge called for skills not used in this country before. The men at work needed every ounce of brain, dexterity and physical courage they possessed. The majority were Scots, but many came from south of the Border. Modern instruments, new devices and engineering resources saved man-power and lightened labour, but still it was a big job − a dangerous task accomplished, happily, with very few accidents."

Earlier we considered the results of the Rail Bridge. Already we can see some of the results of the Road Bridge and can speculate upon future results.

To the great benefit of trade, industry, and tourism, all motor vehicles from the SE. of Scotland, and indeed all the way down from London, can travel quickly and uninterruptedly to the NE. The main part that will benefit in this way will be Fife, to the motorist hitherto all but an island, as it had been all but an island for train-users before the Rail Bridge. Fife, with its growing industries, with its splendid New Town of GLENROTHES in particular, will receive − indeed, it has already received − a vital stimulus. Other benefits to Scotland and to the eastern portion of the United Kingdom as a whole are too obvious to require mention.

There can be no doubt that the increased traffic does present Edinburgh with a problem. This was shown on the first Fife autumn holiday, when the Fifers, always popular with us, nonetheless succeeded in paralysing the traffic of the city. This problem has particular relevance to that small but central part of Scotland's capital known as the New Town (see EDINBURGH). There is every indication that the authorities are aware of this problem, and are anxious to preserve the unique quality of Edinburgh's neo-Georgian New Town. Whether they will adopt larger and more far-reaching ring roads, or whether they will follow the methods of certain Continental cities and protect the New Town with garage space on the perimeter of it, is as yet unknown. We are, however, confident that the problem will be solved. Meanwhile, we welcome our magnificent new Forth Road Bridge.

QUIRAING, The, *Inverness-shire* (Map 4, ref. 14¹87⁰), is a collection of rock formations on the Island of SKYE, in the Inner Hebrides (see "The Shape of Scotland"). This remarkable, indeed fantastic, conglomeration of rock-pinnacle scenery lies at the N. end of the northern Skye peninsula of Trotternish. It is reckoned to be one of the most compelling sights on the island. It is a wilderness of rocks attaining at its highest peak 1,779 ft, and acts as a kind of natural fortification for anyone who would flee into it. It used to be employed as a hiding place for stolen cattle. Today it is innocent of all such matters. It is no more than rather eerie natural spectacle. It lies inland from the main road by Staffin Bay.

QUOICH LOCH, *Inverness-shire* (Map 5, ref. 20⁰80²). In one of the wettest regions in the United Kingdom, Loch Quoich is a part of the Garry−Morriston hydro-electric scheme. The

Quoich dam is the largest rock-fill dam in Britain − 1,050 ft long, with a maximum height of 126 ft.

The North of Scotland Hydro-Electric Board has built a new road past Loch Quoich by which it is possible to reach the W. coast at Kinlochhourn; the road ends there.

RAASAY, Island of, *Inverness-shire* (Map 4, ref. 15⁷84⁰), is one of the Inner Hebrides (see "The Shape of Scotland"). Some 15 m. long NE. to SW. and of uneven width, seldom more than 1 m. broad, Raasay stretches its length between SKYE and the W. mainland of Scotland.

It is dominated on either side by the peaks of Torridon and Skye, but is not overwhelmed by these tremendous circumstances. It has a special appeal that it would offer wherever it was situated. Standing, however, in the Western Seas, it ornaments all that is around it but does not attempt to reflect the dramatic quality of that which lies to the E. and W. of it. Raasay in many respects, and particularly in its not very distant past, is (as shall be shown) unique. That is why an apparently disproportionate amount of space is here given to this island, though it is by no means one of the largest of the Hebrides.

Rocky and hilly in parts, its highest hill, Dun Cann (only 1,456 ft), is oddly flattened on the top as if it had been beheaded with a huge knife. On this flat top Boswell, with characteristic exuberance, danced a reel when he visited the island with Dr Johnson. He cannot therefore have found the ascent too laborious. There used to be a certain amount of crofting land; and the people of Raasay in the 18th cent. were not impoverished nor unusually small in numbers. Conditions of the 19th cent. (including the disastrous potato famine), rather than evictions by landlords, were responsible for the tragedy of Raasay. It is indeed tragic in many aspects, but retains its appeal by means of something certainly more potent than sentimental melancholy.

At the NE. end of the island is a ruined ancient castle of the Macleods of Raasay − Brochel. To the SW. stands Raasay House, where Dr Johnson and Boswell were entertained in 1773. Enlarged in the graceful Regency style of the early 19th cent. by the last Macleods who inhabited it, it is now a hotel. There is a small harbour nearby, occasionally visited from Skye, but the population has declined even within the last ninety years from over 600 to something nearer 200.

The Secessionists or the Free Presbyterians are strong in this small population. They are the most extreme of all Presbyterians in Scotland, and disapprove of much more in contemporary life than any others do elsewhere, even in Scotland. This does not prevent them from showing the natural courtesy and gentleness of the Highlander, but it does cut them off from much of mankind.

Apart from its natural quiet beauty, the allure of Raasay to anyone who is literate and who has the history of the Highlands and Islands in his heart and blood is, quite frankly, in the past. That past may be known to be happy merely by looking at Raasay House, and by reading Boswell's inimitable pages describing Dr Johnson's and his visit there – easily the happiest adventure in all that happy pilgrimage of 1773. It is by reason of this past that Raasay has this number of words in this entry.

When Johnson and Boswell stayed on the island, Macleod of Raasay, their host, had no fewer than ten daughters in his household. They danced "every night of the year round". Dr Johnson said they were the best bred children he ever saw, and he wondered how he and Boswell would ever get away from such an island paradise. The Doctor did not, of course, join in the dancing, but merely added (in the rumbling deep bass of his happy talk) an accompaniment to the music of the dance and to the flying feet of youth.

Equally, of course, Boswell did join in every dance. It is characteristic of him that, in the midst of his openly-expressed admiration for these ten young ladies, he was "disturbed by thinking how poor a chance they had to get husbands" – on this remote island. He need not have been anxious. All of them got married.

The outstanding impression left by the Raasay of 1773 is one of contentment and gaiety, of good manners and ease, but most certainly not of indolent luxury.

The faith of Raasay, both of the laird and of his tenants, was Protestant; and, in what we read about them, we can see how, until the latter half of the 18th cent., the natural gaiety of the Celtic manner of living continued unimpeded by distress and by sectarianism. Thus in Boswell's pages we get the last glimpse of a Highland life that was soon to vanish for ever.

And then disaster struck. In the early part of the 19th cent. the rage of the Clearances afflicted all Celtic Scotland. Much of this rage sprang from the avarice of landlords; some, however, came about merely by unhappy circumstances. This was indeed so at Raasay. The agricultural quality of the island declined. The potato famine gave its savage blow. James Macleod of Raasay, son of the man who entertained the travellers of 1773, improved the estate and tried to encourage the lot of his tenants, but without avail. It was he who faced the world from Raasay with his pleasantly Regency-style reconstructed house. His son, one of the Highland lairds who emerge with honour from the whole sad story of the Clearances, ruined himself in his attempt to keep the island safe, and to keep the tenantry upon it. His labours were entirely unselfish, and he threw everything he had into the cause. But circumstances were too much for him. He left Raasay for ever and emigrated in 1846. With him there departed from the Protestant Inner Hebrides the last remnants of a true Gaelic gaiety and style. Distress and want and the Celtic inclination to sectarianism would not allow it to linger there.

There are some of the Outer Hebrides in which the Catholic faith has survived. With them there has also survived an old Gaelic culture. It has had to contend with much, but it has largely succeeded – partly because it is Catholic, therefore universal, partly because it is Gaelic, therefore local. A place, for instance, such as ERISKAY, where Father Allan Macdonald laboured so heroically in the cause of the Gaelic tongue at the end of the last century and at the beginning of this one, remains and speaks for itself.

Raasay, denuded of its population and deprived of its happy gaiety, cannot speak for itself. Its past alone speaks for it; and its past is there for those who come to look at it.

The thought of Raasay's story has haunted many writers, and some since Boswell's day have written of it well. None has written better than Neil Munro. Indeed, the fate of that ancient house came to him as a symbol of Highland grief, when, during the First World War, he heard the news of his son's death. In the name of Raasay, he invoked the memory of his dead boy, a Highland youth fallen upon the fields of France:

> O Allan Ian Og! O Allan Aluin!
> Sore is my heart in remembering the past,
> And you of Raasay's ancient gentle children
> The fartherest-wandered, kindliest and last!
> It should have been the brave dead of the island
> That heard ring o'er their tombs your battle cry,
> To shake them from their sleep again, and quicken
> Peaks of Torridon and Skye.

And then, as Gaels do when moved to their hearts' depths, he reached out to the past and mourned the whole ancient race of Raasay gone long before he, the poet and bereaved father, was born:

> Gone in the mist the brave MacLeods of Raasay
> Far furth from fortune, sundered from their lands,
> And now the last grey stone of Castle Raasay
> Lies desolate and levelled with the sands.
> But pluck the old isle from its roots deep-planted
> Where tides cry coronach round the Hebrides,
> And it will bleed of the MacLeods lamented,
> Their loves and memories.

RANNOCH MOOR, *Perthshire* (Map 2, ref. 25⁵75²). This bleak waste of 20 sq. m. of bog and lochan surrounded by mountains is one of the finest stretches of unspoilt Highland scenery. It is best seen from the road that runs from KILLIN to BALLACHULISH by CRIAN-LARICH and TYNDRUM. After Loch Tulla, the railway diverges from beside the road to cross the moor, and halfway across lies Rannoch Station at the eastern end of Loch Laidon. From here a rough and in parts dangerous track leads back westwards to join the main road again at Kingshouse Inn. Because of the boggy ground, where the peat can achieve depths of over 20 ft, the railway line is supported on bundles of brushwood.

Robert Louis Stevenson's novel *Kidnapped* gives a good description of the area, though it is now hard to believe that a regiment of horse could sweep the moor. The bogs and peat hags make it virtually impassable.

The NE. corner of the moor is a nature reserve with remarkable bog flora. Among several rare species are the tall bog-sedge and dwarf birch and plant communities associated with blanket bog-formation. Single isolated specimens of the original Caledonian Forest of Scots pine dot the moor, which must at one time have been densely forested.

Patient watching is frequently rewarded by a sight of the golden eagle or herds of red deer.

RASSAL, *Ross and Cromarty* (Map 5, ref. 18⁵84³). One of the few natural or semi-natural ashwoods in Britain, Rassal is a 202-acre nature reserve near the head of Loch KIS-HORN. The woodland only occupies about 30 acres, but the appearance of the wood is unusual, because the limestone has been weathered into slabs that have been covered with soil and turf to form hummocks, among which the trees grow. At one time copper was mined here.

RATHO, *Midlothian* (Map 3, ref. 31⁴67¹). On the S. bank of the Union Canal lies the neat village of Ratho with a number of 18th-cent. buildings in its single street; part of this street has been called Lud Gate or Lord's Gate, as it leads to the church. The ancient church was dedicated to the Virgin Mary in the 12th cent. The present church has a late Norman doorway, but the main part seems to have been built in the 17th cent., the Dalmahoy Aisle bearing the date 1683.

RATTRAY, *Aberdeenshire* (Map 6, ref. 41⁰85⁶), is today represented only by an ancient ruined chapel and graveyard dedicated to the Virgin Mary. Created a royal burgh by Mary Queen of Scots in 1564, Rattray stood at the seaward end of what is now the completely land-locked Loch of Strathbeg, and had a brief life as a port before the exit from the loch to the sea was sealed off (*c.* 1720) by a great storm

that blew a large sandhill into the navigation channel. "So sudden and destructive had been the storm," states the Old Statistical Account of 1792, "that a small ship which was in the harbour discharging slates was trapped inside and gradually went to pieces."

As a geographical curiosity, the Loch of Strathbeg is worth a visit. Recently research has shown that its gradual separation from the sea, of which it once formed a part, was a process that continued over millennia of time, as long spits of sand were built by the prevailing current and winds on this exposed coast. Apart from that, its lonely waters have a weird, unearthly beauty.

REAY, *Caithness* (Map 5, ref. 29⁶96⁴). The present village of Reay stands near the head of Sandside Bay on the N. coast of Caithness, but an earlier village was buried in the sand in the early 18th cent. The village gave its name to Mackay of Farr, chief of the Clan Mackay, in 1628, and the description "Reay Country" came to be used for great tracks of mountain and deer forest in Sutherland, once in the hands of the family. The noble family of Lord Reay went to Holland in the 18th cent. and became Dutch citizens. They returned and regained British citizenship earlier this century.

Reay Church dates back to 1739, and is of the familiar Caithness pattern with external tower-stair and contemporary loft and pulpit. In the churchyard on the opposite side of the road is the ruin of a much earlier church, with a carved Celtic cross-slab. About 4½ m. NE. of Reay, situated near the edge of the rocks, is the ruin of the oldest ecclesiastical structure in the county, St Mary's Chapel, which probably dates from the 12th cent. All that remains is the chancel and the roofless nave. DOUNREAY lies on the coast between Reay and the chapel.

RENFREW, *Renfrewshire* (Map 2, ref. 25¹66⁷), is the county town of the shire, though PAISLEY is the administrative centre. This ancient royal burgh, dating from a charter given to it in 1396 by King Robert III, gives the title of Baron Renfrew to the Prince of Wales. It was the scene of a battle in 1164 when Malcolm IV defeated and killed Somerled, Lord of the Isles.

Modern Renfrew has a wide variety of industries and manufactures, a range of products such as paint, furniture, refined oils, tyres, and cables, and also the largest boiler works in Britain. The town and PAISLEY are now almost joined by their factories.

Mention may be made of Renfrewshire's newest recreational achievement – a 30,000-acre Regional Park in the hills and moorland from above GREENOCK across to LOCHWINNOCH, the first stage of which was opened in 1970. The park is equipped with car parking space, picnic areas with rough furniture and fireplaces, an information centre and park ranger.

RENTON, *Dunbartonshire* (Map 2, ref. 23⁹67⁸). The town of Renton is on the right bank of the R. Leven. Founded in 1782 by Mrs Smollett of BONHILL, it was named after her daughter-in-law, one of the Rentons of Lammerton; the town flourished in connection with dyeing, bleaching, and calico-bleaching, the special industries of the Vale of Leven.

In more recent years Renton has been re-developed as a new village by the County Council. The novelist Tobias Smollett (1721–71) was born at Dalquhurn, ½ m. S. of Renton, where a cousin erected a 60-ft monument to him.

REST AND BE THANKFUL, *Argyll* (Map 2, ref. 22³70⁷). At the summit of the pass from Glen Croe to Loch Fyne (860 ft) stands a rough stone seat inscribed "Rest and be thankful". The road is on the military route from DUMBARTON to INVERARAY ordered by General Cope in 1744 and started in 1745; it was mostly built by Caulfield in 1746–8. The old road has a steep, zigzag course out of Glen Croe, which is still used for reliability trials and hill climbs for cars; but the reconstructed gradient is now comparatively easy.

RESTENNETH, *Angus* (Map 6, ref. 34⁶75²). The ancient parish of Restenneth contains the ruins of an Augustinian priory probably founded by David I, though claims have been made that St Boniface was its original bene-factor in the 7th cent. The priory was burnt by Edward I, but recovered through the encouragement of King Robert I. A prominent feature is the tall square tower with a broach spire; the lower part of the tower has Roman-esque work. A fine 13th-cent. chancel remains in beautiful surroundings.

Originally the priory was on a peninsula with a very narrow neck; but in the late 18th cent. the surrounding lake was drained. This was one of the many local improvements carried out by George Dempster of DUN-NICHEN, whose lands had been part of the old priory lands. At the same time (about 1788) he founded the village of Letham, 3 m. SE. of Restenneth, as a linen-weaving centre. Demp-ster was an enlightened landowner, who did much for the Scotland of his time in the High-lands as well as in his native Lowlands.

RHICONICH, *Sutherland* (Map 5, ref. 22⁵95²). A township and the place where an old inn once stood, Rhiconich is at the head of Loch Inchard, where the road to KINLOCH BERVIE leaves that for DURNESS. The district is full of small lochs lying among outcrops of some of the world's oldest rocks, and it has been described as being almost like a lunar landscape.

Some 4½ m. NE. of Rhiconich on the Durness road is Gualin House, situated on the water-shed, and originally provided by the Marquess of Stafford when the road was built in the early 19th cent., in order to give shelter to stranded travellers. Nearer Durness is a stone well, placed there in 1883 by Peter Lawson, a surveyor, as a mark of gratitude and respect to the local people for their hospitality.

RHU, *Dunbartonshire* (Map 2, ref. 22⁷68⁵). This quiet resort on the E. shore of the Gare Loch has long been a place of retreat for GLASGOW merchants and their families. Those who are familiar with the details of that *cause célèbre*, the Madeleine Smith trial for murder (1857), will recall that Madeleine's respectable father had a summer retreat at Rhu, and that some of the crucial scenes described at the trial took place there.

The club-house of the Royal Northern Yacht Club is at Rhu, and buried in the churchyard are Captain Bain, captain of *The Comet* and first man to sail through the CALEDONIAN CANAL, and Henry Bell, *The Comet*'s designer.

In the 18th and early 19th cents. Rhu was notorious for smuggling, especially whisky.

ROBERTON, *Roxburghshire* (Map 3, ref. 34³61⁵). The village of Roberton on Borthwick Water is particularly associated with Harden, which lies 2 m. to the NE. Harden House is a 16th-cent. building restored in 1864, and was the 16th-cent. home of the famous cattle-reiver, Wat Scott of Harden, whose wife, when the larder was empty, served him with a covered dish of spurs. Harden House is the seat of Lord Polwarth.

Farther up Borthwick Water are the 18th-cent. houses of the Chisholmes and the Borth-wicks. In the heart of the Border country an old church on the water has been turned into a youth hostel, from which pony-trekking takes place, with long rides into ETTRICK FOREST, arranged with another youth hostel near SELKIRK.

To the W. of Roberton the moorland road leads past Bellenden, the high gathering-ground of the Scotts (whose war-cry is "Bellenden"), then to Buccleuch and farther to meet the Ettrick Water at Tushielaw Inn.

ROCKCLIFFE, *Kirkcudbrightshire* (Map 2 ref. 28⁴55⁴). A quiet resort on the Rough Firth, Rockcliffe has small rocky and sandy bays, and a very mild climate. It is noted for its rock gardens.

Just NW. of the village is the mote of mark, an ancient hill-fort, now the property of the National Trust for Scotland. Excavated in 1913, the finds suggest that its earliest occupation carried on into the Roman period, and that it was later occupied in the period A.D. 450–700. Among the many treasures brought to light by the excavations were many fine moulds for interlace-decorated brooches, Frankish and sub-Roman pottery, and South French or Mediterranean ware.

RODEL, *Inverness-shire* (Map 4, ref. 10⁵88³), on the Island of HARRIS in the Outer Hebrides (*see* "The Shape of Scotland"). It is only just a village, yet it contains a hotel, a pier, and one finely restored early 15th-cent. church that, from the point of view of architecture, stone-carving, and evocation of the past, is the gem of the Outer Hebrides. This is St Clements Church; and for anyone who cares for the Hebridean past, and for architecture, it must be seen by any visitor to Harris, or indeed to the "Long Island" (*see* LEWIS).

Set upon a small hill, overlooking the bay and the sea between Harris and North UIST, St Clements dates from 1500. It was built as a chapel and a Macleod burial place by the 8th Macleod Chief of DUNVEGAN in SKYE, just across the water. It fell into desuetude after the Reformation, and lost its roof, but was fortunately otherwise not destroyed. It was tastefully restored and reinforced by the Countess of Dunsmore in 1873.

Built of stone upon stone, here lightly covered with grassy thin soil, it seems to rise and grow out of the island stone of Harris itself. Cruciform, and with a small square tower, containing some oddly free Celtic ornamentation, it holds a nave, a choir, and two transeptal aisles. The most remarkable of its tombs is on the S. side of the choir, recessed into the wall. It was designed and set up in 1528, and contains the body of Alastair Crotach, 8th Chief of Macleod, already mentioned. It is probable that the Chief ordered this tomb to be built for him. A richly carved arch is at its climax, showing God the Father offering up His crucified Son for the sins of the world; it also contains biblical or hagiographical scenes. Below the arch, and above the effigy of the Macleod chief in armour, there are Latin inscriptions, a fanciful religious panel, and a Celtic hunting scene. The whole, in a remarkable state of preservation, presents a proudly conceived northern tomb animated by faith and yet touched with Hebridean quirks of fancy.

St Clements, Rodel, to which the visitor can gain entrance by means of a key from the hotel, is a small church, about the size of a lesser English village church deep in the country; but the poignant intensity of this small building can be as moving as the spaciousness of a great cathedral. It is no longer used for public worship, but there is nothing to prevent the visitor, if he feels so inclined, from saying his prayers there: he will almost certainly be alone.

ROGART, *Sutherland* (Map 5, ref. 27⁴90⁴). Between LAIRG and The Mound is the small village of Rogart, which lies at the heart of a large and flourishing crofting community. The attractive tumbling waters of the R. Fleet run through the Strath, and there is a network of side roads which link the townships with Dunrobin Glen and Strath Brora.

ROMANNO BRIDGE, *Peeblesshire* (Map 3, ref. 31⁶64⁸). On the Roman road leading N. from the camp at LYNE, this village is prettily situated where the Lyne Water passes under a steep, narrow bridge, with a mill, a school, and cottages grouped round it.

Romanno Bridge was the scene of a conflict of gipsies in 1677, and there is a dovecote with an inscription on the lintel recalling the fight.

Just S. of the village, near Newlands Church, are curious Romanno terraces on the sides of the wide valley (fourteen terraces about 6 to 12 ft broad), either a natural phenomenon or possibly designed for horticulture or agriculture.

RONA, Island of, *Inverness-shire* (Map 4, ref. 16³85⁷), is one of the Inner Hebrides (*see* "The Shape of Scotland"). This small island N. of RAASAY, and between SKYE and the mainland by TORRIDON, is now inhabited only by three people who guard the lighthouse that rises to 42 ft and whose beams can be seen for 21 m. Rona has occasionally appeared in Scottish history, particularly during the divisions amongst Highland chiefs. Dean Monro in the middle of the 16th cent. says that Rona was then the home of "thieves, ruggars and reivers" who made a living by despoiling "pure pepill". This is no longer so.

This Inner Hebridean Rona should not be confused with the now utterly desolate and almost inaccessible North Rona at the tip of the Outer Hebrides.

ROSEHEARTY, *Aberdeenshire* (Map 6, ref. 39³86⁷). Approaching from the S. by the road that climbs the Peathill to the old church of Pitsligo at the side of its modern successor, descending the brae by the mouldering ruin of Pitsligo Castle, we obtain a view of the sea-town and the new town of Rosehearty that is impressive.

Many a place left in Rosehearty's position, with a harbour too shallow for modern needs and a single light industry that gives work to seven persons out of a population of 1,146, would just turn its face to the wall and die. Rosehearty has not done that yet. It is conveniently close to industrial FRASERBURGH, and many of its folk commute there.

The oldest part of Pitsligo Castle, a massive keep, was built in 1424. It consisted of three rooms, one on top of the other. In the basement was the vaulted kitchen; above it the banqueting hall, also vaulted and 25 ft high; and above that again the "sleeping apartment for the whole family, which had in it 24 beds". It was built by Sir William Forbes, the first of his line. His descendant, the first Lord Forbes of Pitsligo, improved the fishing haven of Rosehearty and secured the creation of a parish co-extensive with his barony in 1633, building the old parish kirk with its fine belfry of Dutch design, for which the carved stones imported from Holland were brought into his bedroom, and assembled in his presence, while he lay ill.

The 4th and last Lord Pitsligo is the most famous of them all. Born in 1678 and educated in France, where he became the friend of Fénelon, he succeeded his father in 1690 and took his seat in the Scottish Parliament in 1700. After the Act of Union with England, which he strongly opposed, he became a Jacobite and joined his first cousin, the Earl of Mar, in the Rising of the '15. When it failed, he fled to the Continent, but, as his name did not appear in the list of attainders, he was able to return to Scotland and live there quietly.

At the '45, he was a man of sixty-seven and had no hopes that the rebellion could succeed, but he had never renounced his old loyalty to the House of Stuart, and he gallantly threw everything into the struggle. As the best-loved landowner in the North-East, he formed a band of volunteer cavalry of the gentlemen of Aberdeenshire and Banffshire and rode into ABERDEEN on the 5th of October 1745. When the troop was mustered, he moved to the front, lifted his hat, and said, "Oh Lord, Thou knowest our cause is just. Gentlemen, march."

Lord Pitsligo is the classic example of those many highly intelligent gentlemen in the supposedly hard, calculating, and unsentimental North-East who considered the world well lost – not for love, but for a political cause that they knew in their hearts was doomed. He took part in the whole campaign, riding most of the way, and was described by Murray of Broughton as "deservedly the most popular man in the country".

Many of the North-East Jacobites went to Sweden after the '45, where they were welcomed and made a brilliant success of commercial undertakings. But this sort of new life was impossible for a man as old as Lord Pitsligo. He had, however, one great advantage. He knew that his own people would never give him away. Accordingly, when he escaped from the rout of CULLODEN, he hid himself in Mr William King's house of Greyfriars in ELGIN and a week later reached Pitsligo Castle, where he obtained a disguise from his wife. For the next four years he lived an "extraordinary, hunted, wandering life, sometimes hidden in the houses of his tenants, sometimes in caves – as in the Cave of Cowshaven at PENNAN – or under bridges".

The hunt was dropped for some while, but ten years after Culloden, when he was nearly eighty, he narrowly escaped capture in the House of Achiries, his son's house in the parish of Rathen. The family hid him in a recess, behind the bed of a woman visitor, who coughed loudly all the time the redcoats were searching her room, so as to cover up the asthmatic breathing of the old man in his hiding-place. As soon as the soldiers had left the room, Lord Pitsligo emerged and told a servant to see that his pursuers got "some breakfast and a drink of warm ale, for this is a cold morning; they are only doing their duty and cannot bear me any ill will".

The old man died aged eighty-four, on the 21st of December 1762, and was buried in the family vault in the kirk of Pitsligo. So he lies now, still close by the burgh of Rosehearty where he was adored by everybody.

ROSEMARKIE, *Ross and Cromarty* (Map 5, ref. 27⁴85⁷). A small town, Rosemarkie stands on the S. shore of the BLACK ISLE opposite FORT GEORGE and united for administration purposes with FORTROSE ¾ m. SW. It is a small holiday resort with a good beach and remarkable cliffs to the N. Also just to the N. of the town, on high ground, is the B.B.C. V.H.F. station with its prominent mast.

The church is one of those said to have been founded by St Boniface in the 7th cent. Whatever may be the truth of this claim, the church was certainly the original seat of the Bishop of Ross from about 1120 until the middle of the following century, when it was transferred to Fortrose. Beside the building is a Pictish symbol stone with a finely worked set of ornamented panels; the back includes an equal-armed cross with an elaborate border.

ROSLIN, *Midlothian* (Map 3, ref. 32⁷66⁴). Unquestionably most renowned for its chapel and castle, Roslin (also called Rosslyn) is now a mining village on the bank of the North Esk.

The castle is buttressed impressively on the lip of the cliff above the river. The oldest part was founded in the early 14th cent. by Sir William Sinclair (d. 1330); the keep was started by his grandson and enlarged by the 3rd Earl of Orkney. It was destroyed in 1544, to be restored again about 1580.

The chapel, celebrated for its sculpture and elaborately detailed carving, was founded by the 3rd Earl of Orkney in 1446, and was to have been a Collegiate Church; but only the choir, the Lady Chapel, and the beginning of the transepts were built. It was damaged by rioters in 1688, but was thoroughly restored in 1862. The beauty of the chapel is at once apparent, but it is a concentrated beauty, for the building is small, containing all its riches in a constricted space.

William St Clair, Earl of Orkney, is credited with the design of the chapel, but he ranged over Europe to procure craftsmen to carry out his ideas. The most famous feature in the chapel is the lovely pillar of entwined ribbands ascending to its top. It is called the Prentice Pillar. The story is that the chief mason, having been told of a pillar of this kind in Italy, travelled to inspect the original. In his absence his apprentice (inspired by a dream, so it is said) built the pillar. The master mason on his return was so jealously incensed by this piece of initiative on the part of his pupil that he struck him dead.

This is the popular story. Certainly there are no other pillars like this one elsewhere in the chapel or indeed in Scotland. Moreover, a certain substance is lent to the tale by the recently discovered fact that the consecration of the chapel was held up by the Bishop of ST ANDREWS because blood had been shed in the building.

ROSNEATH, *Dunbartonshire* (Map 2, ref. 22⁵68³). A small resort on the Gare Loch, Rosneath is popular as a yachting centre. In the village is St Modan's Well, indicating the spot where a church was founded by St Modan in the 7th cent., to which pilgrims came to take the healing waters of the well.

At the SE. extremity of the bay is the ruin of an old castle, which about 1630 was fitted up as the second residence of the Marquess of Argyll. Burnt in 1802, it was replaced on a new site in the following year by an Italian palace-style mansion, recently demolished, and at one time the residence of Princess Louise.

It has been suggested that Rosneath has some connections with William Wallace, a fact which may be authenticated by the nearby landmark known as Wallace's Leap, from which Wallace is believed to have jumped on horseback to make his escape across the loch to Cairndhu Point.

ROSYTH, *Fife* (Map 3, ref. 31¹68⁴). The lands of Rosyth were once a part of the old diocese of DUNKELD; later they passed to the earls of Rosebery, and then in the early 18th cent. to the Earl of Hopetoun. Finally they were sold to the Government in 1903.

The great naval dockyard and oil-storage base, begun in 1909, was vital to the Royal Navy in the two world wars and has been greatly extended since. It is now regularly visited by ships of the NATO fleet, and in addition to its important training and supply functions is Britain's only Polaris submarine re-equipping base; it was also the first nuclear re-fitting yard. The nuclear submarine *Dreadnought* was commissioned there in 1968, and *Resolution* was re-commissioned by Queen Elizabeth the Queen Mother in July 1971.

ROTHES, *Moray* (Map 6, ref. 32⁸84⁹), is a town on the bank of the R. SPEY. It was founded in 1766, but for long it was no more than a community of crofters. Today it is the centre of a distilling industry which started in 1840.

The castle, which stood in a loop of the river NE. of the town, was the seat of the Leslie family – first styled "of Rothes" in 1392. When ennobled, they took the title of Earl of Rothes in 1457-8. They also, however, owned the lands of Leslie in Fife. The Leslies of Rothes eventually sold the Moray estate to John Grant of Elchies, having resided in the N. rather than in Fife till as late as the mid-17th cent.

Rothes is alluringly placed on the Spey, between Ben Aigan (1,544 ft) and Conerock Hill. Northwards there is the pleasing Glen of Rothes. For long it had grim memories. Edward I of England went through it in characteristic style in his campaign of 1296. The great floods of 1829 did much damage to the town. Such inundations are now guarded against.

ROTHESAY, *Buteshire* (Map 2, ref. 20⁹66⁵), on the Island of BUTE is the county town. This historic town is today the famous CLYDE holiday resort.

Bute is a Lowland island, but, as it is dove-tailed into Argyll, it sees the great mountains all around it. Rothesay, in consequence, has been responsible for the well-known song written and composed by the enthusiastic Mrs Craik, "Sweet Rothesay Bay".

The area that constitutes the civic parish of Rothesay is well populated with farms, as it is mainly composed of arable and pasture land for dairy cows. The town, with its gay and beckoning wedding-cake architecture and its attractively strident shops, hugs the coast at the E. of the island looking directly across the Kyles of BUTE into Argyll. The annual Clyde Yachting Fortnight is held in what are, for its purposes, the admirable circumstances of Rothesay Bay.

In 1401 Robert III, that more than usually unfortunate Stuart King, made Rothesay a royal burgh. He had made the place a favourite summer resort. His son became the Duke of Rothesay; the title was borne by the eldest sons of the Scottish kings, and is today one of the titles of the Prince of Wales. Students of heraldry and royal genealogy have been known (without any Scottish nationalist implications) to refer to the heir to the British throne, when he is in Scotland, as the Duke of Rothesay.

Rothesay Castle was built around 1098 in the days of the Norse occupation of the Scottish Western Isles. Since then it has passed into many hands, after the restoration of the Hebrides to Scotland consequent upon the battle of LARGS (*see* "Scotland in History"). It also changed its style and building with the centuries. It is one of the most remarkable medieval castles of Scotland, and is an outstanding example of the typical 13th-cent. castles with high curtain walls fortified by protecting drum towers. The curtain walls stand to a height of some 30 ft. The castle differs from the normal plan in that the walls enclose a circular courtyard. This plan is unique in Scotland. The site is surrounded by a deep water-moat. The entrance is through a high tower that projects boldly into the moat. This fore-tower is the work of James IV and James V. Within the courtyard may be seen the foundations of sundry internal buildings, haphazardly disposed, and the roofless shell of a chapel. It may in substance be the castle captured by the Norsemen in 1230.

Rothesay

Today this large past (signs of which so impressively remain for us in the Castle) has been amiably overwhelmed by the present. Rothesay has many amenities for sport and entertainment. It contains two cinemas, and a modern pavilion for concerts and dancing. There are winter gardens, an indoor swimming-pool, three golf courses, and five bowling-greens, together with lawn-tennis courts, putting-greens, and facilities for rowing excursions and sea angling, and all the usual pursuits and pleasures of the carefree GLAS-GOW crowd on holiday "doon the watter". A staple part of their diet enjoyed out of doors while looking at the fine scenery of Argyll is fish and chips consumed out of popular Glasgow newspapers.

ROTHIEMURCHUS, *Inverness-shire* (Map 5, ref. 28⁹80⁹). Just 1 m. E. of ALVIE, the township of Rothiemurchus lies across the SPEY on the edge of the CAIRNGORMS and GLEN MORE National Forest Park. Rothiemurchus Forest is one of few stretches of natural Scots pine forest, and has been worked for many centuries – the logs were formerly floated down the Spey to GARMOUTH.

In the forest are to be found the rare but locally plentiful crested tit; on higher ground reindeer were introduced in 1952, and have bred successfully.

ROUGH CASTLE, *Stirlingshire* (1 m. E. of BONNYBRIDGE). The Roman fort of Rough Castle and the adjacent length of rampart and ditch are a part of the ANTONINUS' WALL. On a commanding site, the fort covers an acre of ground and was originally excavated in 1903.

It deteriorated owing to the weather. Now, however, it is being consolidated, for better display to the public, by the Ancient Monuments Department of the Ministry of Public Building and Works, who are also clearing the associated defence ditch.

ROUGH ISLAND, *Kirkcudbrightshire* (Map 2, ref. 28⁴55⁴) is a bird sanctuary, which can be reached on foot at low tide from near COL-VEND and ROCKCLIFFE. It extends to some 18 acres, and is the property of the National Trust for Scotland.

ROWARDENNAN, *Stirlingshire* (Map 2, ref. 23⁶69⁸), is a small village with a pier, at the end of the road on the E. side of Loch LOMOND, and from it Ben Lomond is usually climbed. It is also a calling point for steamers. It lies within QUEEN ELIZABETH FOREST PARK, and its youth hostel has facilities for canoeing.

A track from the village gives a fine hill walk of about 10 m. to ABERFOYLE via Loch Ard.

ROXBURGH, *Roxburghshire* (Map 3, ref. 37⁰63⁰). The present village of Roxburgh is 2 m. up the Teviot from the site of the castle, of which there are only some scanty remains on the grassy mound between the rivers TWEED and Teviot. The castle acted as a royal residence in the 13th cent., and as a place of strength in the 12th cent. Beside it there was once an important burgh that, along with EDIN-BURGH, STIRLING, and Berwick, was one of four royal burghs in the 13th cent. It changed hands many times, being captured by James Douglas after the siege in 1314, but by 1334 it had fallen into English hands, where it remained until 1460. James II of Scotland proceeded against it, and was killed by the bursting of a cannon, but the Scots eventually took the castle which was "doung to the ground". The new fort of 1545 had a very short life of about five years.

RUBERS LAW, *Roxburghshire* (Map 3, ref. 35⁷61⁵). The most conspicuous landmark in the county after the EILDONS, the rugged and rocky hill (1,399 ft) of Rubers Law was once a Roman signal station. There are various walls of an evidently post-Roman date.

The crag known as Peden's Pulpit recalls Alexander Peden, the Covenanter preaching to a large congregation, which was drawn to the comparative security of this place from many districts in the Lowlands.

RULLION GREEN, *Midlothian* (Map 3, ref. 32²66²), is on the E. slope of Carnethy, 1¾ m. NW. of PENICUIK. A monument marks the site of the battle that took place on the 28th of November 1666, in which 900 Covenanters, marching from the W. on EDINBURGH, were defeated by the Royalist forces under General Sir Tam Dalyell of the BINNS.

RUM, Island of, *Inverness-shire* (Map 4, ref. 13⁵80⁰), is one of the Inner Hebrides (*see* "The Shape of Scotland"). The mountainous impressive Island of Rum, lying between EIGG and CANNA, and a part of the group known as the "Small Isles" (it is much the largest of them), has a sombre appearance. Its history too, from the human point of view, is sombre. Having little arable land, it could never support the population that its size would apparently warrant. In 1772, however, there were 325 inhabitants; these were reduced to one family in 1828 by enforced or induced emigration.

Thereafter Rum became a sportsman's island, and red deer, which were said to be unknown on the island in the first decade of the last century, were brought in and bred extensively. Indeed, along with swarms of particularly vicious midges, red deer were, until recently, the two plagues of the place. Before the Second World War, proprietorship made Rum into a sportsman's private park on which no one was allowed to land.

Rum would have made an ideal national park with the advantages of seclusion, and a huge variety of sport, mountain climbing, sailing, and bathing. However, after the private ownership of this island of 26,400 acres had ended in 1957, the place was acquired by the Nature Conservancy who are pursuing studies of nature, especially the red deer. Access to the island is difficult. They have kept the herd of deer at a level and reasonable figure, though whether they have been able to do the same with the midges is unknown.

Rum stands out of the western seas in the grandest manner, and its peaks are visible from most parts of the Northern Hebrides, Inner and Outer. Askival, Sgurr nan Gillean, and Ainshval are all over 2,500 ft, and proclaim in their names the Norse as well as Celtic occupation of the island.

On the E. side of the island and at the head of Loch Scresort is the only feasible landing place on Rum. There is a small township here gathered round the Victorian-style Castle of Kinloch, which was the home of the proprietor in the days of private ownership. Here there is some woodland representing almost the only form of tree-life on the island.

The rocky coast of Rum, with its occasional beaches and ruined crofting houses still just showing themselves above the ground, provide an impressive spectacle as you sail round it. It becomes even more impressive on leaving and sailing through the Minch (the sea between the Inner and Outer Hebrides), when you perceive the whole grand scale of its mountainscape.

There is a mournfulness about Rum that is intensified by its remarkable appearance. You enjoy seeing it as you go by; you look with pleasure on its great hills across the seas and from a distance, but there is a certain sense of relief in calling at the end of one's voyage on farther islands where indigenous human beings live and where the sound of Gaelic speech is in the air.

RUMBLING BRIDGE, *Perthshire/Kinross-shire* (Map 2, ref. 30²69⁹). This beauty spot lies 3½ m. NE. of DOLLAR and consists of a spectacular gorge and falls on the R. Devon. Though the river rises only 6 m. from CAMBUS, where it flows into the FORTH, its meanderings en route stretch for 30 m.

The bridge is so called because of the noise caused by the river when in spate; the water thunders in the chasm over 100 ft below.

There are several falls, the most famous being the Devil's Mill, which is NE. of the bridge.

The earliest bridge lies below the present one. It was built in 1713 by William Gray, a native of Saline and a local mason. It has a span of 22 ft. The present bridge was built in 1816 at a height of 120 ft above the water.

RUTHWELL, *Dumfriesshire* (Map 2, ref. 31⁰56⁷). The village of Ruthwell lies a little to the S., and the church a little to the N., of the DUMFRIES–ANNAN road.

In an annexe to the church is the very remarkable Ruthwell Cross, which ranks as one of the two foremost examples of Anglian sculpture and is one of the major monuments of Dark Age Europe; the other one is at Bewcastle in Cumberland. The Ruthwell preaching cross, 18 ft high and slightly restored, dates probably from the end of the 7th cent. It is a figure sculpture, showing Hellenistic affinities in the faces, and with rich vine scrolls and birds and beasts on the sides. On the margins are inscribed, in runes (the longest runic inscription in Great Britain), portions of the famous Old English poem, *The Dream of the Rood* (the oldest poem in the English language), and also a Vulgate text in fine script.

The cross lay under the floor of the church in the 17th and 18th cents., and was set up first in the manse garden in 1823 by the minister, Dr Henry Duncan. Since 1886, it has been preserved in the church in an apse built specially for it.

The same Dr Duncan was the founder of the savings bank movement, and there is a cottage in the village still standing, which in 1810 was the first bank of this kind.

A little NW. of the village is the 15th-cent. Comlongan Castle, a rectangular tower-house, which has no projections, but whose walls are honeycombed with mural chambers, closets, and stairs.

SADDELL, *Argyll* (Map 1, ref. 17⁹63²). The village of Saddell is on the rocky E. coast of the long promontory of Kintyre that projects from the SW. mainland of Scotland.

Beside the small river are the ruins of Saddell Abbey, founded in 1160 by Somerled, Lord of the Isles, and completed by his son Reginald.

St Andrews: the first tee and last green

Little remains of the abbey now except the N. transept and portions of the choir wall, with some interesting carved effigies, which have been placed inside the ruin. Saddell has a peaceful setting of woods and rhododendrons.

SE. of the village and at the head of the bay is Saddell Castle, a large, square, battlemented tower dating from 1508 but built on the site of an earlier one.

ST ABBS, *Berwickshire* (Map 3, ref. 39²66⁸). This quaint fishing village, with its picturesque row of buildings used for storing fishing gear, is a popular holiday resort, having a good sandy beach and a magnificent coastline. A lighthouse stands on one of the rocky headlands, under which are many caves formerly used by smugglers.

About 3 m. N. of St Abbs lie the ruins of Fast Castle, a sea fortress 70 ft above sea-level, once separated by a 24-ft ditch but now accessible by a very narrow path. This castle was the stronghold of Logan of Restalrig, who was involved in the Gowrie conspiracy; it is, however, more famous as the prototype of Wolf's Crag, the tower of Edgar of Ravenswood in Sir Walter Scott's *The Bride of Lammermoor.*

ST ANDREWS, *Fife* (Map 3, ref. 35¹71⁷). Once the ecclesiastical capital of Scotland (its diocese, linked with that of EDINBURGH, is still, for the Catholic Church, *primus inter pares* in all Scotland), St Andrews has in recent centuries become the golfing capital of the world. The decrees of the Royal and Ancient Golf Club command universal respect. St Andrews too is the site of our most ancient University, founded in 1412.

It is also a little E.-coast Scottish town of singular and poignant beauty, in which the past harmonizes with the present – not only of golf but of holiday-making and of tourism. St Andrews is venerated in Scotland by all sorts of people for all sorts of reasons. Not the least of its attractions for Scottish folk from the West as well as from the East is its bracing air and its partly isolated position in this pro-

jection of Fife, protected by the North Sea on the E. side and by the Firth of TAY on the N.

St Andrews owes its early importance to its connection with the Church, a connection that made itself felt here immediately after the beginning of Christian influence on Scotland – and even before the kingdom was properly founded and defined. There is a tradition that St Regulus brought the relics and bones of St Andrew the Apostle here in A.D. 347. Historians incline to A.D. 747 as a more likely date. In any event, it will not do too lightly to dismiss the force of this ancient tradition.

In the famous Declaration of ARBROATH, 1320 (*see* "Scotland in History"), the barons solemnly averred Scotland's ancient connection with St Andrew the Apostle. They added, amidst a number of other cogent and practical arguments, what they took to be an accepted fact. They simply stated that the Scots had originally come to this country via Ireland from Scythia, which part of the world had been evangelized after Pentecost by St Andrew the Meek, the brother of blessed Peter, whom Our Lord "appointed to be our leader and patron saint for ever". The men who put forward this argument to the highly practical Pope John XXII were not remote peasants, but were learned men of the world in whom reputable tradition lived. It may be added in passing that no one has succeeded in detecting the origin of the Latin word *Scotus.* But may it not come from the latinized variation of the Greek for Scythia?

In any event, the city of St Andrews in Scotland has been held in high religious esteem over the centuries. And it is not only the Catholics who hold it so. There are distinguished members of the Presbyterian Kirk of Scotland who would not turn their backs upon the notion that St Andrews the city has an actual physical connection with the body of St Andrew the Apostle.

The town, in the purely civic sense of the word, is of great antiquity. It must have originated soon after the first settlement of the churchmen. David I granted it a charter about 1140. When the cathedral and priory were built and the university was founded, St Andrews was a very prosperous town. However, the Reformation largely destroyed the town's life; it removed its ecclesiastical *raison d'être*. The town then degenerated into a village, whose streets were "filled with dunghills, and were extremely noisome, especially on account of the herring guts exposed on them". This comes from a description in 1697; later it was said that "there was not a foot of pavement in any of the streets". Filth and squalor abounded; "cows and pigs grazed in front of the Colleges".

Considering the prestige of its antiquity as a city of learning, St Andrews was in the 17th cent. at its lowest pitch of neglect, with only its spacious streets and fine ruins to remind one of its former grandeur. In 1697 a proposal was made to move the university to PERTH since St Andrews was in such decline.

Conditions began to improve towards the end of the 18th cent., and certainly during the 19th. In 1834 Sir Hugh Lyon Playfair (1786–1861), son of Principal Playfair of the United College, retired to St Andrews and was elected Provost in 1842. During his term of office, he revolutionized the town, so that once again it built up a reputation as a university city and as a holiday resort. The modern prosperity of St Andrews depends on education, tourism, and golf, all of which bring in a steady flow of people to the town.

We see the results. Three ample streets – North Street, Market Street, and (best of all) South Street – verge upon the macabrely battered ruins of the Cathedral. Much of the architecture of these streets is in the gracious Regency style flowing from the influence of Edinburgh's noble New Town. They are all busy streets, and we are reminded at every corner of the flourishing state of the university by the red-gowned students not only from Scotland but from all over the world.

As a background to all this busy modern life in this essentially E.-coast Scottish town there stand the antiquities.

The Cathedral and Priory

The ruins of the cathedral are close to the seashore at the E. end of the town. Building was started by Bishop Arnold in 1161, but was not finished until the time of Bishop Lamberton in 1318. The Cathedral suffered various destructions by tempest and fire during the next century, but from about 1440 the building remained in all its grandeur until 1559, when it was destroyed more completely. The beginning of this destruction sprang from the Reformers' zeal, who were urged on by John Knox's famous sermons against idolatry. But it is unjust to blame the Reformers alone for the present starkly ruined state of this noble building. It is lamentable to have to record that the real villains were those citizens of the town who used the stone of the Cathedral as a kind of quarry, or as a supply of building materials.

This actually went on until the last century. In 1826 the Barons of the Exchequer took possession of the ruins and began to conserve with considerable success what remained.

Little, however, does indeed remain of what was once the largest church in all Scotland. There are some parts of the E. and W. gables, the S. wall of the nave, and portions of the choir. The foundations of the whole church have been discovered by excavation. Most of the surviving work belongs to the late 12th and the early 13th cent. In the Cathedral museum is a magnificent collection of Celtic and medieval monuments, as well as pottery, glass-work, and other relics discovered on the site.

The ruins of the Priory are near the Cathedral (founded 1144).

About 120 ft SE. of the E. end of the Cathedral is the unique little romanesque Church of St Rule with its square tower, which rises to a height of 108 ft and is well over 20 ft broad at the base. This was the first church of the Augustinian canons in Scotland, and was built by Bishop Robert (1126 to 1158) in 1144. It is possible that the tower is older and that the church was added later.

The precincts of the Cathedral and Priory, some 30 acres, were enclosed by a whole wall by Prior John Hepburn about 1516. The wall was about 4 ft thick and about 20 ft high, about 1 m. long, and was fortified by 13 projecting round towers. This wall is still a prominent architectural feature of the E. end of St Andrews.

There were three gateways, two of which still stand, one at either end of South Street. The West Port was the principal entry to the old city, and is the best surviving example of a burgh gate or "port" in Scotland. It was strengthened and refurbished in 1859. The second gate, commonly known as "The Pends", is the stately ruin of a magnificently vaulted gateway forming the principal entry to the Priory precincts.

The Castle

The ruins of the old castle stand on a rocky promontory overlooking the sea, and isolated from the land by a deep moat. The original building is said to have been erected (1188 to 1202) by Bishop Roger as an Episcopal residence. It was also a place of high military importance; in 1332 it fell into the hands of the Scottish barons and was held by them until 1336, when it was recovered for David II by Sir Andrew Moray, who dismantled it as a place of fortification.

About 1390 a new building was erected (1385–1401) by Bishop Trail. It is thought that James II was born here.

In 1546 Cardinal Beaton was murdered by a party of Reformers in the Castle. His last words as the assassins' knives fell were "Fie, fie, all is lost". But all was not lost; St Andrews still stands where it did, and the place is still venerated.

After a stormy period during the Reformation,

the Castle later passed into the possession of the Town Council, who again pursued the policy that they had applied to the cathedral – they used some of its stones to repair the pier in 1684. The sea is now encroaching upon the castle, and in 1801 some of the seaward walls were undermined and fell. But now precautions have been taken to protect it. The oldest part of the extensive ruin dates from the 13th cent., but much of the work is later than the destruction in 1547. Notable features are the rock-cut wall, about 50 ft deep, in the courtyard, and the bottle-shaped dungeon in the NW. corner beneath the sea-tower. This hideous reminder of the past, cut out of the solid rock, is in diameter 7 ft at the top and 16 ft on the bottom. Its depth is 18 ft. It was used as a prison, but very few of the unfortunates who were enclosed there could have survived more than a few weeks, or even days, in its dank and dreadful surroundings.

The University

Scotland's oldest university dates from 1410, when St Mary's College was founded by Bishop Wardlaw. Under the royal patronage of James I, the new city of learning prospered; in the time of James II, Bishop Kennedy (that wise prelate who is still remembered in St Andrews) founded and endowed a second college, St Salvator. In 1512, Prior John Hepburn and Archbishop Alexander Stewart founded St Leonard's College. In 1537 Archbishop Beaton added to St Mary's College. In 1570 (and after the Reformation) St Mary's was entirely set apart for the teaching of theology. This arrangement is still in force.

From the middle of the 17th cent., St Andrews University declined; as has been stated above, there was a proposal made to move the University to Perth, but the scheme was fortunately abandoned. By 1747, the revenues of the colleges of St Leonard and St Salvator were so diminished that the two were united in one.

In 1881 University College, DUNDEE, was founded, and in 1897 it was incorporated into St Andrews. Finally in 1967 it became the university of Dundee, with Queen Elizabeth the Queen Mother as its first Chancellor.

The buildings of the University that survive are as follows: St Leonard's is a girl's residential school, founded in 1877 for the daughters of professional men or of the upper classes from all over Scotland. It occupies some of the old buildings of St Leonard's College.

St Leonard's Chapel, the chapel of St Leonard's College, was founded in 1512, and is still in use by the University, having been recently restored.

St Salvator's is now the principal centre of university life. It incorporates the old tower and the Collegiate Church. St Salvator's Hall in the College grounds is one of the finest students' residences in Britain.

Other university buildings of note are the University Library founded in 1612, the Younger Graduation Hall presented to the University in 1929 by Dr and Mrs Younger, St Mary's College, and the Theological College.

Madras College, though connected by education with the University, is not a part of the University. It is a famous secondary school founded in 1832 by Dr Andrew Bell. The courtyard contains part of Blackfriars Church, which occupied the site in the Middle Ages.

Among other buildings from the past of St Andrews that are worthy of note is Holy Trinity Church, the "Town Kirk" founded in 1410, restored in 1909, one of the finest parish churches in Scotland. The stained glass and silver plate are particularly noteworthy.

A building also noteworthy is Queen Mary's House, a fine old 16th-cent. mansion in which Mary Queen of Scots is believed to have lived. It was restored in 1927, and is used as the library of St Leonard's School.

No one should leave St Andrews without visiting the harbour, one of the most picturesque features of St Andrews. The pier was rebuilt (one adds this with a sigh) from the stones and timbers taken from the ruined cathedral and castle.

The St Andrews Preservation Trust, founded in 1938 for the preservation of old Scottish architecture, has succeeded in some outstanding restorations. Examples are: St Joan's house in South Castle Street; 136 South Street; 141 South Street; and the Bogward Dovecot. This is one of the beehive type, and is believed to be 450 years old. It is 16 ft in diameter, 22 ft in height.

Golf

There are four full-length golf courses and five putting greens at St Andrews. Of the full-length courses, the world-famous Old Course on the natural St Andrews Links is the one to which everyone's thoughts turn. The other three courses – the New Course, the Eden, and the Jubilee – would indeed be worthy of note anywhere else than in St Andrews, but there the golfer thinks first and last of the Old Course.

The links of the Old Course are centuries old. It is said that some kind of golf was played on them in the 15th cent. Golf certainly flourished here in the 1700s, and the Royal and Ancient Golf Club was founded in 1754. The present building, in the pleasing Regency style that lingered on in Scotland until deep into Victoria's reign, was constructed a century later – in 1854. Apart from its unique amenities, and its almost sacred associations for golfers from all over the world, it houses a remarkable collection of early relics of the game of golf.

It is tempting to take the reader hole by hole, even stroke by stroke, over the hallowed ground of the Old Course. Let it suffice to say that it has two of the most famous golf-course holes in the world, the short 11th or "Sea" hole and the 17th or "Road" hole. Each of these has ruined more great golfers than any other elsewhere in the world. All dread them. All aspire to them with a kind of love. Despite its antiquity, the Old Course stands up to any changes or "improvements" in the game. The reason for this is evident: it is a course that has sprung from nature. Four centuries ago, the burghers of St Andrews played a kind of golf upon the natural links which formed what is now the Old Course. Here and there they may have smoothed out the earth around the holes to make a kind of green – or they may not have done so. What is quite certain is that they never built an artificial bunker. They let Nature scatter her bunkers where she wished to, and they are still there. The golf ball flies far farther than it did in the 15th cent.; far farther than it did at the end of the 19th cent.; farther, it is said, than it did just before the Second World War. But the Old Course retains its character and stands squarely to face any scientific or artful inventions in the game of golf.

Apart from golf, there are other amenities for the holiday visitors to St Andrews. There is bathing in the brisk and vigorous North Sea either upon the sands to the N. and E. of the town or in the open-air swimming-baths. There is riding; there are plenty of walks in the district; there is trout angling in the Lade Braes Burn and in Cameron Loch. But, in the long run, everyone in St Andrews turns back to the Old Golf Course, the University, and the city's tremendous ecclesiastical past.

One cannot leave St Andrews without mention of the Martyrs' Memorial, a stark obelisk standing at the very heart of the pleasure centre of modern St Andrews. It is on the hill behind the Royal and Ancient Golf Club, and overlooks the big swimming-pool. In summer the grass around this memorial is haunted by ice-cream vendors and others ministering to public pleasure. Yet here in the midst of them is this finger of stone pointing heavenwards and recording the names of those Protestant martyrs who suffered death for their faith in the flames nearby.

A sad reminder indeed of St Andrews, so much associated in the public mind with religious strife in the past! The visitor from outside Scotland may pause, however, to reflect that, in Scotland, where religious warring was by repute so strong, there are only seven official Protestant martyrs and only two official Catholic martyrs. In the years covering the period between the reigns of James V and James VI and I of England, there are (official martyrdom apart) believed to have been only thirty persons, Catholics and Protestants together, in the whole country who suffered death for their faith. To take London alone, with her fires of Smithfield under Mary of England, in which were burnt the Protestant martyrs, and the public butchery of Catholics at Tyburn under Elizabeth (a sum total of many hundreds on both sides), Scotland's record in comparison is merciful.

ST BOSWELLS, *Roxburghshire* (Map 3, ref. 35⁹63¹), sometimes called Lessudden, is said to be named after St Boisel, the prior of Old Melrose 2 m. NE. on the N. bank of the TWEED. St Boswells Green, a common of about 40 acres, was the scene of the greatest livestock fair in southern Scotland. This place is also the centre of the Buccleuch Hunt.

Just to the NW. is the village of Newtown St Boswells, which dates back to the days of the monks of MELROSE. The arrival of the railway in the mid-19th cent. made it the administrative centre of the county.

About 2 m. W. of the village is Bowden, a village possessing one of Scotland's earliest churches, built in 1128. It includes much 17th-cent. work and was restored in 1909, but it still keeps some of the work by the monks of KELSO who built it. A feature of the church is the 17th-cent. lairds' loft of black oak with the arms of the Cavers Kerr family carved on its panels. The 16th-cent. mercat cross was restored as a war memorial.

Some 2 m. NE. of St Boswells is Mertoun House, standing on a peninsula in the R. Tweed not far from DRYBURGH. The house was designed by Sir William Bruce 1702–3. The former house stands in the gardens; so too does a dovecote dated 1576. The Duke of Sutherland (as Earl of Ellesmere) reduced the house to its original and proper size by removing the Victorian additions. This work of architectural cleansing was performed by Mr Ian Lindsay in the 1950s. Mertoun House has an outstanding collection of pictures.

ST CYRUS, *Kincardineshire* (Map 6, ref. 37⁵76⁴), is a coastal village to the N. of the estuary of the North Esk river, and was once called Ecclesgreig. There is rocky scenery to the NE. of the village; there is also a sandy beach from which one can bathe.

About 1 m. to the NE. a ruin stands high on a cliff of refuge called Kaim of Mathers. It was built in 1421 by Barclay of Mathers, who had taken part in the slaughter of Sir John Melville. In 1795 the village was completely destroyed by an inrush of the sea at high tide during an easterly gale.

ST FILLANS, *Perthshire* (Map 2, ref. 27⁰72⁴). This village at the E. end of Loch Earn is a favourite tourist centre. Attractions include fishing, sailing, mountaineering, and walking. One of the most spectacular sights in the village is the large power station – part of the Breadalbane hydro-electric scheme. The power station is underground, hewn out of the solid rock, and is connected to the catchment area at the head of Glen Leadnock by a series of tunnels.

The burial-place of the Stewarts of Ardvorlich is in the ruined chapel near the village. The old font from this chapel is still in use in the parish church.

ST KILDA, *Inverness-shire* (Map 8 inset, ref. 01°90°). This celebrated remote place is really a little archipelago of three islands and three sea-stacks – the most westerly in the British Isles – standing out in the Atlantic 110 m. off the mainland of Scotland. The group, because of its isolation, dramatic topography, and wild life, has endless fascination for island-lovers and naturalists. Hirta, the largest of the islands, was occupied from prehistoric times until 1930, when a diminishing community who could no longer eke out a living had to be evacuated. Many monoglot Gaelic speakers from St Kilda were settled by the authorities in the Lowlands – notably Fife.

Wildfowling among the vast colonies of sea birds (fulmars, puffins, and gannets), crofting, and sheep-herding were the staples of existence, whose traces are still to be found in abundance throughout the island. Hundreds of cleitan, used for storing food, are dotted all over the hill-sides; descendants of the islanders' goat-like sheep survive in a wild state; the ruins of successive generations of dwelling houses remain above Village Bay, and distinctive species of wren and mouse also survive.

The group – including Boreray, Soay, Stac Lee, Stac an Armin, and Stac Levenish, in addition to Hirta – is now owned by the National Trust for Scotland. Service detachments, associated with the declining South UIST rocket-range, have temporarily re-populated Hirta in recent years. In co-operation with the Trust and the Nature Conservancy, the Services have helped to preserve natural features and to conduct surveys of wild life. The Trust annually organizes working holidays on the islands for the more adventurously-minded, and this is now about the only opportunity available for public access. The towering, sculptured scenery alone is a compelling enough reason to visit St Kilda. Conachair, 1,396 ft, the summit of Hirta, is impressive enough from Village Bay, but even more so on its precipitous seaward face, which forms the highest sheer cliff in the British Isles. Some 4 m. away, Boreray soars jaggedly to a height of 1,245 ft, and nearby are the spectacular rock pillars of Stac an Armin, 627 ft, and Stac Lee, 544 ft. Boreray and its stacks are the breeding ground of the world's largest gannetry, housing probably more than 40,000 pairs of birds. The largest and oldest colonies of fulmars are also to be found on St Kilda (the cliff face of Conachair alone contains some 6,000 breeding sites), and the puffin population runs into hundreds of thousands.

Although the domestic settlement, for the past few hundred years, centred on Village Bay, there is evidence that Gleann Mhor, on the NW. of Hirta, was occupied in prehistoric times. The so-called Amazon's House in this glen has excited speculation since the days of the 17th-cent. chronicler, Martin Martin.

ST MADOES, *Perthshire* (Map 6, ref. 32°72°). Well before A.D. 1000 there was probably a religious community of the Celtic church established here. In the porch of the present church is a cross slab of grey sandstone carved at the best period of Celtic art. One side is divided into five compartments, each containing representations of horsemen. On the other side the cross, accompanied by elaborate detail, occupies the entire length of the stone.

A second Celtic cross slab had been built into the wall of the church vestry, but it was removed in 1881 and is now lost. In 1945 a third carved slab was found in the grounds of Inchyra House. It seemed to be connected with a burial, which in all probability is considerably later than the slab. Among the symbols are the Christian markings of the serpent, and the fish, but these are combined with ogham writing on the edge of the stone and the pagan symbol of the double disc. This stone is now in the PERTH Museum.

The Kirk Session records of St Madoes go back to 1591. The old bell of the church is Dutch, and bears the inscription *James Burgerhuys me fecit 1671 Soli Deo Gloria.*

There is a pair of prehistoric standing stones in the western part of the grounds of Pitfour Castle. Such pairs of stones, aligned with their broad faces parallel, are typical of the Lowland Perthshire area, but they do not seem to occur with the same frequency elsewhere in the country. In many cases the stones have been chosen to contrast with one another, one stone being broad, the other narrow.

Single standing stones occur at Chapelhill and Clashbenny in the E. of the parish.

ST MARY'S LOCH, *Selkirkshire* (Map 3, ref. 32⁵62³). Some 3 m. long and ⅓ m. wide at its widest point, this loch is surrounded by steep hills, only a narrow isthmus separating it from the small Loch of the Lowes. The beautiful situation of St Mary's Loch and good fishing on both lochs attract many tourists. "There are few spots", says an anonymous writer, "where there is so little that is repulsive to man, and yet so few traces of his presence."

On a narrow neck of land between the two lochs is Tibbie Shiels, now a hotel. James Hogg (1770–1835), the Ettrick Shepherd, lived for a time at Altrive and also died there. His writings are associated with this district, and his statue stands near Tibbie Shiels.

On the NW. shore of the loch is the site of the ancient St Mary's Kirk from which the loch derives its name. This church is the scene of Blanket Preaching, an open-air service being held on the fourth Sunday of July.

Just N. of the loch is Dryhope Tower, one of the strongest peel-towers of the district; it was the birthplace in 1550 of Mary Scott, "the

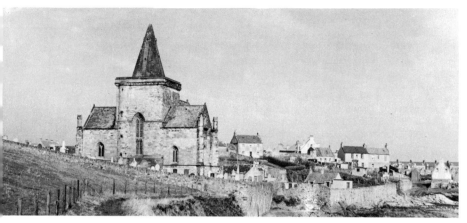

St Monance: the old church

Flower of Yarrow", bride of Watt Scott of Harden, an ancestor of Sir Walter.

ST MONANCE, *Fife* (Map 3, ref. 35²70²). The long-established fishing port of St Monance is characteristic of the small Fife seaside town at its most attractive. The old houses cluster together down to the sea's edge. And the sea is everywhere present as the source of men's livelihood here. On a day of SE. winds, the waves may break over the gravestones in the cemetery where for centuries the fishermen of St Monance have been buried. A model of a ship hangs in the sailors' loft in the church.

The age of the charming church is disputed, but it is safe to say that the present foundation existed from the reign of David II in 1362. Despite a fairly thorough restoration in 1828, much of the ancient fabric remains. Surmounted by a squat steeple, the church is built in an unusual T-plan. The name of the church is said to derive from the Irish St Mirren, whose relics were brought here in the 9th cent.

St Monance has two harbours, one inside the other; from these harbours, the little town rises in steps, wynds, and huddles of old roofs to newer houses at the top.

The pebbly shore of the town has some beautiful rose-coloured smooth stones, each one a perfect natural paper-weight.

ST VIGEANS, *Angus* (Map 6, ref. 36⁴74³). About 1½ m. N. of ARBROATH stands the village of St Vigeans. It has a cottage museum, in which there is a remarkable collection of 41 sculptured monuments of early Christian and medieval periods, including the "Drosten Stone", which bears rare inscriptions in Hiberno-Saxon minuscules. The collection is complementary to that at MEIGLE.

SALEN, *Argyll* (Map 4, ref. 16⁹76⁴). The mainland village of Salen, beautifully situated on the wooded shore of Loch Sunart, attracts holiday-makers in search of quiet and peace; its only industry, apart from a gentle form of tourism, is that of forestry. Salen stands at the junction of the roads to ARDNAMURCHAN and ACHARACLE, and is said to have originated with a pier and a bobbin mill founded by one of the Clarks of PAISLEY; the mill was burnt and Mr Clark went to England, but the village remained.

SALEN, *Argyll* (Map 1, ref. 15⁷74²), is on the Island of MULL in the Inner Hebrides (*see* "The Shape of Scotland"). Salen, which had a regularly calling steamer service, used to be passed through by many of the 19th-cent. travellers who were taking the pilgrim route to the isle of IONA. Eastwards it looks across the narrow Sound of Mull to Morven, and to the NW. is the ruin of Aros Castle, once a castle of the Lord of the Isles.

To the W. across a 2½-m. neck of land is Loch na Keal, a sea-loch on the W. coast of the island. On the S. shore of the loch is an impressive range of overhanging cliffs and caves at Gribun.

SALTCOATS, *Ayrshire* (Map 2, ref. 22⁴64²), is a holiday resort on the coast close to the town of ARDROSSAN. There is the curiosity of 26 fossilized tree-trunks visible in the harbour at low tide, thought to be the largest unrecorded forest of fossilized trees in the country.

SALTOUN, *East Lothian* (Map 3, ref. 34⁶66⁷). The two villages of East and West Saltoun are about 1 m. apart. West Saltoun is very small, with only a few houses, but East Saltoun is growing and has some attractive new buildings. Agriculture is the chief occupation in this East Lothian district.

Saltoun Hall, built about 1820 on an older site 1 m. NW. of East Saltoun, has been the home of the Fletcher family since 1643.

Andrew Fletcher (1653–1716) was born here. His tutor was Gilbert Burnet, minister of Saltoun from 1665–9 and later Bishop of Salisbury. His library is included in a notable collection in the Hall. It was Fletcher of Saltoun who, during the negotiations preceding the Union of Parliaments in 1707, pleaded eloquently but unsuccessfully for a federal rather than an "incorporating" union. Despite Fletcher's somewhat stormy political career (including exile in Holland), it was he who said, "If a man were permitted to make all the ballads, he need not care who should make the laws of a nation".

Saltoun was the first place in Scotland to establish the weaving of "Hollands", started in 1710 by Fletcher. It was also well-known for its bleach-fields.

SANDBANK, *Argyll* (Map 2, ref. 21⁶68⁰). The village of Sandbank, on the S. side of HOLY LOCH, is a holiday resort in beautiful countryside. The place, however, is world-famous for yacht- and boat-building carried on at two shipyards in the highly sheltered waters of the loch. Not only yachts come from here, but lifeboats and many naval vessels.

SANNOX, *Buteshire* (Map 1, ref. 20³64⁶), is a small village on the E. coast of the Island of ARRAN (*see* "The Shape of Scotland"), 6 m. N. of BRODICK. The main attraction of this quiet little place is its accessibility to the splendid if severe peaks of N. Arran. It lies also at the mouth of Glen Sannox, which, in complementary fashion, is as grandly dark as its rival GLEN ROSA is coloured. Though on the coast road, it yet keeps its remoteness. It has a hotel, and primarily caters for mountaineers or lovers of wild scenery.

SANQUHAR, *Dumfriesshire* (Map 2, ref. 27⁸60⁹). A small burgh on the bank of the R. Nith, Sanquhar is chiefly known in history by two Sanquhar Declarations made by Covenanters; the first was affixed to the mercat cross in 1680 by Richard Cameron, who disowned and declared war on Charles II; the second by James Renwick in 1685, against James VII and II. A granite obelisk now stands in place of the mercat cross.

Sanquhar became a royal burgh in 1484 under the protection of its castle, the seat of the Crichton family. The castle passed in 1639 to the 1st Duke of Queensberry, who built Drumlanrig, but spent only one night in it, preferring Sanquhar Castle, which, although mainly dating from 16th and 17th cents., has some 15th-cent. work. It stands S. of the town.

The tolbooth dates from 1735, and is a fine example of Scottish architecture.

This is a mining district, but there is also much dairy-farming, and a cheese factory, and milk-condensing plant.

Eliock Castle, a tower-house 2 m. S. of Sanquhar, was the birthplace of the Admirable Crichton, that 16th-cent. polymath genius who was killed in a brawl in Mantua at the age of 22. Veitch of Eliock was a famous 18th-cent. Law Lord.

SAUCHIE, *Clackmannanshire* (Map 2, ref. 29¹69⁵). Once primarily a mining village, Sauchie has become increasingly a suburb of ALLOA, as a result of new housing development. Schawpark (Alloa Golf Club), on the outskirts of the village, is a good inland golf course combining variety with an attractive setting. Sauchie Tower, on the right bank of the Devon, an early stronghold of the Schaws of Sauchie, survives as a robust ruin, dating from the late 15th or early 16th cent.

SAUCHIEBURN, *Stirlingshire* (Map 2, ref. 27⁸69⁰). As an addition to BANNOCKBURN, one might use the name of Sauchieburn, which is about 3 m. to the S. of STIRLING. It was the scene of the battle of 1488 that led to the death of James III. The King fled when his army joined action with the forces of his insurgent nobles. After being injured in a fall from his horse, he was stabbed to death by one of the rebels masquerading as a priest. The future James IV, through his presence amongst the rebels, became haunted in conscience by his supposed guilt of his father's death. In reality the boy-prince was a mere tool in the hands of the rebels.

SCALLOWAY, *Shetland* (Map 8, ref. 44⁰13⁹), is on the Mainland of SHETLAND Northern Islands (*see* "The Shape of Scotland"). This pleasing little town, on the W. coast of the island and just over 6 m. W. of LERWICK, was the ancient capital of the archipelago, and is still the seat of island justiciary.

Set in an attractive bay, and with the remains of the "wicked" Earl Patrick Stewart's castle beside it, Scalloway has a dignified, oldworld air about it. There are shops and a hotel in Scalloway, which is well placed for browntrout fishing in the excellent loch of Tingwall. In Tingwall loch there is a small island, on which in Norse times the island parliament used to meet. Once a week, if the weather permits, a boat leaves Scalloway for the remote Western Shetland island of FOULA.

SCAPA FLOW, *Orkney* (Map 7, ref. 34⁰00⁹), is an almost land-locked stretch of seawater in ORKNEY Northern Islands (*see* "The Shape of Scotland"). In 1912 the British Government decided that this unique natural harbour should be the main base of the Grand Fleet in case of a European war. Orkney therefore procured a front-line seat in the naval operations of both world wars. In 1914 a German submarine penetrated the defences of Scapa Flow. But it was in this same base in

Scottish Tourist Board

Scalloway

1919 that the defeated German Fleet scuttled their vessels or beached them. In the Second World War, Scapa Flow came in for a good deal of enemy attention, this time from the air. Defences were, however, improved; the base remained, with one or two exceptions, largely inviolate. Now this remarkable stretch of water has returned to its naturally peaceful existence.

SCHIEHALLION, *Perthshire* (Map 5, ref. 27²75⁵). This mountain, 3,547 ft high, is a conspicuous landmark, its beautiful cone dominating the Tummel and Rannoch districts. The two most famous views giving different aspects are from Loch na Craig, beside the road from DUNKELD to ABERFELDY via Glen Cochill, and from Craiganour on the N. shore of Loch Rannoch.

The name is said to mean "fairy hill of the Caledonians", and there is the usual legend of the cave from which there is no return.

A vein of limestone runs through the massif, giving fertile grazing at just below 2,000 ft on the N. shoulder. Here can be seen the extensive ruins of a deserted village.

The best approach is from KINLOCH RANNOCH via the Tempar Burn.

SCONE, *Perthshire* (Map 6, ref. 31⁴72⁶), is one of the most historic places in Scotland. Scone (pronounced "Skoon") was once the ancient capital of the Pictish kingdom and probably also a Culdee centre of Celtic Christianity.

The Stone of Destiny was brought to Scone from either DUNSTAFFNAGE or IONA, but more probably this last, during the reign of Kenneth MacAlpine, who in A.D. 843 united the Picts and Scots into a single kingdom and established his capital at FORTEVIOT. Until 1296, when the Stone was stolen by King

Edward I of England, never to be returned despite the Treaty of Northampton, the kings of Scotland were crowned upon it at Scone. The Stone is an oblong block of red sandstone 26 in. by 16 in. by 10 in., and may originally have been a portable altar belonging to some Celtic ecclesiastic or missionary.

In 1120 King Alexander I of Scotland established at Scone a monastery of Canons Regular of St Augustine. The monastery was dedicated to the Holy Trinity and St Michael, and was endowed with the lands of Liff and INVERGOWRIE. The Canons came from Nostell in Yorkshire, and were part of a wider scheme to supplant, by degrees, the Celtic churchmen in Scotland. In 1123 Robert, the Prior of the Augustinians at Scone, was consecrated Bishop of ST ANDREWS. In 1164 the Scone Priory was elevated to the status of an abbey. The site of this abbey is thought to have been towards the E. end of the terrace on which the present palace is built. The abbey was sacked and burnt by the reformers in 1559, the year in which John Knox preached his famous sermon from the pulpit of St John's Kirk in PERTH. By 1624 the abbey was a ruin.

In 1581 the lands of Scone were made a temporal lordship and were conferred on the Earl of Gowrie, but, after the Gowrie Conspiracy in 1600 when the Gowrie estates were forfeited, the lands of Scone were made over in favour of Sir David Murray of Gospetrie as David, Lord Scone. Today his lineal descendant is the Earl of Mansfield, whose heir bears the title Viscount Stormont.

In 1624 the first Lord Scone built a church, of which no more than a single aisle remains, standing on a low tree-covered mound, called Moot (or Boot) Hill or the Hill of Credulity. The mound was probably an early site for the administration of justice.

The present Palace of Scone, which replaced the house built by the Gowries and its later

17th- and 18th-cent. additions, was begun in 1803 and finished in 1808. The architect was William Atkinson. In 1805 the then Earl of Mansfield decided to move the old village of Scone, which had grown up in the neighbourhood of the early monastic buildings, to a new site 1½ m. distant. This would allow for a suitable park to be laid out around the new palace. And so today there are two villages, Old Scone and New Scone, of which the second is now almost a suburb of Perth.

Remnants of the old village can still be traced in the palace grounds. The old village cross, 13 ft high, is still there, and also the graveyard, where the right of burial can still be claimed.

About 1½ m. N. of the palace is the site of the Roman camp of Grassy Walls, lying almost opposite to another Roman camp across the TAY at Bertha on the banks of the Almond.

Below the present palace, between it and the river, is a racecourse where spring and autumn meetings are regularly held.

Between Old and New Scone is a prehistoric burial site in Sandy Road Wood (now at the centre of a housing scheme). This consists of two adjacent circles of standing stones set so that there is one particularly large stone from which the other stones decrease in size on either side until the smallest stone is opposite the largest. One of the circles has been destroyed. The other was excavated in 1962. At the centre an urn containing cremated bones was found. This type of urn belongs to the very end of the Scottish Bronze Age, and this is the first occasion on which it has been associated with a circle of such a character.

A second site consisting of two adjacent circles of standing stones occurs 1½ m. NE. of New Scone at Shianbank. Unfortunately the site was ruined by the erection of wartime defences.

In 1934 the town council of Perth decided to build a municipal aerodrome at Newlands, N. of New Scone, on the road to COUPAR ANGUS. After the outbreak of the Second World War the aerodrome was taken over, and it is interesting to record that the first experimental work done by radar experts was carried out here. In 1946 the site was sold, and since then it has been used as a training establishment for civil airline pilots. In 1960 a School of Aeronautical Engineering was set up. Students come here from all over the world.

SCONSER, *Inverness-shire* (Map 4, ref. 15²83²), is a hamlet on the Island of SKYE in the Inner Hebrides (*see* "The Shape of Scotland"). In this pleasantly placed little village at the mouth of Loch Sligachan (7 m. SSE. of PORTREE) stands Sconser Lodge. This contains portions of that rarity in the Hebrides, a genuine 18th-cent. inn. Johnson and Boswell stayed here. Above Sconser stands the pyramidal mountain of Glammaig (2,537 ft). In

front of the Lodge is a fine prospect of the Island of RAASAY.

SCOTLANDWELL, *Kinross-shire* (Map 3, ref. 31⁸70¹). The village of Scotlandwell takes its name from the springs that bubble up in the 19th-cent. stone cistern at the W. end of the main street.

In the village is Portmoak parish church, of which one minister was Ebenezer Erskine, a founder of the Scottish Secession Church.

Portmoak is the headquarters of the Scottish Gliding Union, which runs holiday courses.

In Kinnesswood, 4 m. NW. of Scotlandwell, the cottage home of the poet Michael Bruce (1746–67) has been preserved. Another native was the meteorologist Alexander Buchan, the originator of the term "cold spells".

SCOTS DYKE, *Dumfriesshire* (Map 3, ref. 33⁹57³), is an old ditch and embankment just over 3½ m. long, extending from a bend in the Esk to a bend in the Sark. Until 1552, the "no-man's-land" between the two rivers was an area of lawlessness, but in that year a low dyke was constructed across the district to form a new territorial boundary, marked with pointed stones and bearing the Royal Arms of England and Scotland on appropriate sides. These are now gone, but DUMFRIES Museum has a horn-handled Border sword found in the turf-work of the dyke.

SCOTSTARVIT, *Fife* (Map 3, ref. 33⁷71¹). About 1 m. W. of the Hill of Tarvit, Scotstarvit stands as a high and notable landmark. Ashlar-faced, embattled, and turreted, it rises to five storeys, complete with garret and roof. The panel is dated 1627, but the tower is known to have been in existence in 1579. In the 17th cent. it was the home of Sir John Scot (1585–1670), the author of the earliest topography of Scotland and *Scot of Scotstarvit's Staggering State of Scots Statesmen*. Sir John was the brother-in-law of William Drummond of HAWTHORNDEN.

SCOURIE, *Sutherland* (Map 5, ref. 21⁵94¹). The crofting village of Scourie, on its bay in the NW. of Sutherland, is surrounded by rugged hills. Angling visitors will find in these hills an unusually large number of small lochs giving ample and varied sport among brown trout. You must be prepared to walk and climb for your fish as well as to angle for them. But this, many anglers feel, is a part of the pleasure of hill-loch fishing.

Scourie House, once the seat of a Mackay family and the birthplace of General Hugh Mackay (1640–90), has a very sheltered garden characteristic of the W. coast. It contains palm trees.

SCRABSTER, *Caithness* (Map 7, ref. 31⁰97⁰). About 1½ m. NW. of the town of THURSO is the harbour of Scrabster, from

Scrabster

where the ORKNEY mail-steamer sails. It lies tucked into the NW. sweep of wide Thurso Bay, sheltered by the cliffs of Holborn Head from the wild seas of the Pentland Firth. Those jagged cliffs have been carved into curious arched chasms and stacks of rock; the highest of these, known as the Clett, is about 150 ft high, and is the haunt of many varieties of sea-birds in the breeding season.

Among the cliffs is the site of a fort on a precipitous headland, cut off and strengthened by a broad wall. Between Thurso and Scrabster, on the shores of the bay, are the ruins of the medieval castle or bishop's palace, which was seized from the Bishop of Caithness by the Earl of Caithness about the year 1544. A triangular window was taken from the ruins and built into Scrabster House. To the W. of Scrabster, near the foot of Scrabster Hill, is a broch known as Things Va.

SEIL, Island of, *Argyll* (Map 1, ref. 17^{7}71^5), is one of the Inner Hebrides (*see* "The Shape of Scotland"). To the S. of OBAN, the Island of Seil lies so close to the mainland that it is connected with it by a bridge. This attractive humpbacked bridge was designed by Telford in 1792, and is known as the Atlantic Bridge, being the only structure of its kind to cross Atlantic water.

Seil has an attractive village of whitewashed cottages roofed with the slate from the neighbouring small and much-quarried island of EASDALE. Easdale's at one time apparently inexhaustible supply of slate is now worked out. But the Balvicar quarry on Seil is still working.

SELKIRK, *Selkirkshire* (Map 3, ref. 34^{8}62^9). This royal burgh, standing on a hill overlooking Ettrick Water, was once the site of a

Tyronensian abbey founded by Prince David (later King David I) in 1113, which was moved to KELSO in 1128 for greater convenience. It also possessed a royal castle, and in 1204 King William the Lion held parliament here. Now deceptively peaceful, the town was at the centre of the Anglo-Scottish wars that raged on the Borders for three centuries. It was burnt by English forces after Flodden in 1513. A Common Riding ceremony still takes place here during which a standard-bearer, representing the town's sole survivor of that disastrous defeat, casts the colours in the market-place. A statue erected in 1913 shows him bearing a captured English standard. As late as 1540 King James V described the burgh as "often burned, harried and destroyed", and on another occasion he enjoined it to choose a "warlike" man to be provost.

In the triangular market-place stands a statue of Sir Walter Scott, who had close associations with the burgh in his capacity of sheriff of the county from 1799 to 1832. An undistinguished lawyer and a political reactionary in an age of reform, he won worldwide acclaim as author of the Waverley novels. In the Sheriff Court House his chair and some of his letters may be seen. At the other end of the High Street is a statue of Mungo Park, the African missionary and explorer, who was born at Foulshiels, 4 m. to the W., in 1771. Off the S. end of the market-place is the 17th-cent. Halliwell's Close, with its museum of ironmongery, containing old cooking and other domestic and rural implements. Near the W. end of the town is a plaque over a shop doorway marking the site of the house in which that brilliant military adventurer, the Marquess of Montrose, stayed on the eve of his final defeat in 1645 at the Battle of Philiphaugh, which was fought on the flat land 3 m. W. of Selkirk, up the valley of the R. Yarrow.

Selkirk's chief industry was formerly shoe-making, but this has now been superseded by the manufacture of tweed and other woollen goods.

SHANDWICK, *Ross and Cromarty* (Map 5, ref. 28⁶87⁴). Beside the road to this village, ½ m. S. of BALINTORE and on the N. coast of the Moray Firth, stands an ancient and battered cross slab 8 ft high and adorned with very worn bosses and figures. It was blown down by a gale in 1847 and broken into three pieces. The cross was one of three, the others being at Hilton of Cadboll and at NIGG; they were said to mark burial spots of three sons of a Danish king shipwrecked nearby.

SHAWBOST, *Ross and Cromarty* (Map 4, ref. 12⁷94⁷), is a village on the Island of LEWIS, in the Outer Hebrides (*see* "The Shape of Scotland"). About 13 m. NW. of STORNO-WAY, Shawbost has been spoken of as the "richest village in the Lews". Perhaps it would be more apt to call it a small town or township, for it straggles at considerable length along the W. coast, and contains many houses. Its reputed wealth springs largely from weaving. It has its own small wool mill, and has achieved its prosperity entirely by its own effort. This, however, is a general Lewis characteristic, shown to particular effect in Shawbost.

SHERIFFMUIR, *Perthshire* (Map 2, ref. 28²70²). The famous battle between the Jacobites under the Earl of Mar and the royal forces under the Duke of Argyll was fought here in November 1715. Mar was marching S. to attack the Lowlands, when Argyll at STIRLING heard of his plans and decided to attack before the Jacobites could reach the FORTH. The site of the battle lies on bare windswept uplands 2 m. NE. of DUNBLANE. Despite the Jacobites' great superiority in numbers, the outcome was indecisive, the right wing of each army defeating those opposing. Rob Roy and about 500 of his followers watched the battle from a safe distance. Mar retreated to PERTH, and many clansmen deserted en route. The gathering-stones of the Highland army are the main tourist attraction. Three grey boulders in close proximity to one another are now protected by an iron grille. It is said that the Jacobite standard was erected here, and that here too the clansmen sharpened their dirks.

SHETLAND Northern Islands, *Shetland* (Map 8), are sometimes known as Zetland (*see* "The Shape of Scotland"). Like ORKNEY, this group – which should never be called "the Shetlands" – forms a county set in the northern seas, and is not at all a mere archipelago in the Scottish ambit. When you look at it on the map, however, it is not, like Orkney, an obvious county huddling round one patently main island. Shetland is one of the most exciting things on the map of the United Kingdom. N. of the doucer county of Orkney and much farther N. of Scotland, its great and scattered length looks like a sword flourished towards the North Pole. It contains, indeed, the nearest piece of land in Britain to that place; there is no land between UNST (Shetland's farthest isle) and the North Pole.

Shetland lies 60 m. N. of Orkney, and consists of nearly 100 islands, of which about twenty are inhabited. Like Orkney, it possesses its own mainland, on which are its modern capital of LERWICK and the more ancient chief township of SCALLOWAY. Apart from Unst, already referred to, there is the island of Yell – considerable but, compared with the Shetland mainland, of minor importance; it is bleak and barren. To the E. of Yell is the comparatively fertile island of Fetlar, on which the world-famous Shetland ponies are bred. Far out in the Atlantic, about 30 m. W. of Scalloway, lies FOULA, which is inhabited, but is often difficult to access.

Despite its physical remoteness from the British mainland, Shetland is easily reached by regular sea services from ABERDEEN and LEITH and daily flights from GLASGOW and EDINBURGH through WICK, INVERNESS, ABERDEEN, and KIRKWALL. In 1971 new bridges connected the islands of Trondra and Burra with the Shetland mainland, and work had started on the introduction of car ferries to Yell, Unst, Fetlar, Whalsay, and Bressay to be operative by 1973–4. There are many hotels, and various guest-houses accommodate visitors in islands apart from the Shetland Mainland.

The people of the rocky, the wild, the foreign-looking Shetland have much Norse blood in them, and are Norse in sympathy, perhaps even more so than the Orcadians. As in Orkney, their speech is peppered with Norse words and even phrases, from a language that in their island-county died out in distinctive use as late only as the 18th cent. Like Orkney, Shetland was a Norse dominion until 1469, when the Northern Isles were pledged as a dowry in a Scottish–Danish royal marriage (*see* "Scotland in History", and ORKNEY).

It would be a great mistake, however, to suppose that there were no Shetlanders before the Vikings took over, or that these stern invaders obliterated all the native stock they found there. The original inhabitants were probably Picts, and they have left their memorials in the many prehistoric dwelling-places and fortifications against invaders, some of which will appear under their names in this gazetteer – JARLSHOF and MOUSA.

Today the chief source of livelihood in Shetland is from the sea. Anyone who visits Lerwick and Scalloway (the only two real

Scottish Tourist Board

Shetland ponies

towns in Shetland) will perceive this. The Orcadian has been described as a crofter with a boat, the Shetlander has been called a fisherman with a croft. This is not to say that the Shetlanders neglect their difficult northern and often intractable land; but their first thought is of the sea and its riches. In this they differ from the men of Lewis, who – also men of the sea, and also possessing naturally intractable land – have done their best with that land (*see* LEWIS).

The Shetlanders, as well as practising a certain amount of sparse agriculture, breed sheep, cattle, and their famous ponies. Their peat, of which they have an apparently inexhaustible stock, provides them with fuel. One of their most famous land industries is the

Shetland: the Giant's Leg, Bressay
Scottish Tourist Board

making of Shetland shawls and finely-spun garments from the wool of their native sheep, small, but rich in fine, distinctive wool. There is no equivalent of the Long Island (Lewis and HARRIS) male peasant weaver, but the women have developed this fine-spinning to a considerable art, an art practised in their own homes. Shetland shawls are known to be warm, but they continually surprise by the delicacy of their texture. It is no uncommon thing for a Shetland woman knitter to produce a comfortable shawl that can be drawn through a wedding-ring.

Untouched by any recognizable legacy of Celticism, the Shetlanders are without the irrepressible poetic imagination that somehow discovers itself in all Hebrideans. On the other hand, they are not nearly so ostentatiously down-to-earth as the farming Orcadians. Perhaps the strange, quiet beauty of their islands (400 m. from the Arctic Circle – which is about half the distance between them and London – and 250 m. from the drift-ice) has touched the Shetlanders with indefinable longings. Perhaps the universal call of the sea felt by all male Shetland folk has widened their horizons; and there may be other and ethnical causes, but you feel with the Shetlanders that poetry, if it is not present, is always just round the corner.

The land of their straggling county-archipelago is never flat and scarcely mountainous. Ronas Hill, the highest peak, is 1,475 ft. All islands have bays, and some are richly indented. The scene inshore is diversified with many fresh-water lochs and lochans. Nowhere is any island wide enough to contain a river in the Scottish or Hebridean sense, but there are ample burns and small cascading streams.

This, perhaps, is the place to speak of game

fishing on Shetland. Salmon are rare, brown trout in the many lochs plentiful and sporting; the Shetland sea-trout (often angled for in the "voes" or long arms of the sea) is world-famous. He may not often grow to the great size of some sea-trout on the Continent or on the mainland of Britain, but, pound for pound, he is the gamest fish that swims. In this respect the Shetland sea-trout is unrivalled. There are, as in Orkney, few lairds and little rigorously-preserved water. Much voe fishing is free, some loch fishing is free, and the charge for fishing the association waters is, for the visitor, little more than nominal. You can make your angling arrangements when you get there. The best time for the sea-trout is in August and September. The brown trout reach their climax at midsummer.

Midsummer! This is indeed a season in Shetland that one is not likely to forget. It is an error to speak of the Shetland midnight sun, but it is true that at the end of June there is no more than twilight at midnight. This twilight, with the hour or two before it, is locally and poetically known as the "simmer dim". Just before the twilight descends, the long horizontal rays of light produce a remarkable effect on the landscape, especially by the side of the lochs. Everything – heather, grass, the few flowers, and the water itself – seems to become luminous, to show colour more strongly even than at midday.

Shetland at midsummer can be an enchanted place. In winter it is never really cold in the manner of a severe winter in the heart of Scotland, but it can become an inferno of raging gales. Not even the Northern Hebrides can put on such a show of wind. In general the climate is milder than you would suppose; and really hot days each year are not uncommon.

Shetland, since it joined Scotland and then the United Kingdom, has kept out of southern affairs; but, as in Orkney, the South did touch it. The Scottish lairds, who took over much of the land after the Vikings' departure, acted tyrannically and ruthlessly. The descendants of most of these are now gone, and such as remain are benevolent. One can understand, however, the Shetlander's assertion that he is a Shetlander first, and a Scotsman only by accident. He has not happy memories of us.

The word "remote" is not an apt one to apply to an island-county containing one fair-sized and one moderate town, a county within little more than an hour's daily flight from GLASGOW and having regular sea-connection with the island of Britain and with the Continent. And you cannot call a place remote in which a large proportion of the sea-going male population has visited most of the major ports of the world. Nevertheless there is in these strange islands a quality of indefinable remoteness – self-sufficient remoteness – that for the perceptive visitor is far from displeasing.

The Reformation did its work thoroughly in Shetland, but quietly and without fuss. The old faith just fell away. It was, as in Orkney, replaced by no ardent or severe Calvinism. The religious isolationism of these islands induced (and to their credit) the English Methodists to missionize them with some effect in the early 19th cent. Unst is largely devoted to Methodism.

There is a small Catholic church (mostly for visitors) in Lerwick. It is significant of the Shetlanders' general tolerance on religious matters that this church is packed to overflowing for midnight mass at Christmas, but that in the crowds there are only a dozen or so Catholics. The rest have come to see and listen. Such a thing would be impossible in the strongly and ardently Protestant isles of the West.

SHIEL, Loch, *Inverness-shire/Argyll* (Map 5, ref. 18⁵77⁵). This narrow loch, 17½ m. long and on the borders of two counties, runs from GLENFINNAN to ACHARACLE through fine mountain and rocky scenery. A small steamer sails from one end of the loch to the other on most days of the week.

About 6 m. from Glenfinnan on the W. shore of the loch is Glenaladale, the seat of Macdonald of Glenaladale, with whom Prince Charles Edward Stuart stayed the night of the 18th of August 1745 on his way to raise the standard at Glenfinnan.

Some 6 m. farther down the loch narrows, and you come to St Finan's Isle. St Finan was a contemporary of St Columba; he had a cell there on the site of which are the ruins of a later chapel. Chained to the altar is the old Celtic bell, said to have healing powers and to fly back when stolen. There is also an old burial-place on the island.

Some 3 m. short of Acharacle on the W. shore is Dalilea House, also a Macdonald seat and once the home of the Gaelic bard Alasdair MacMaighstir Alasdair. Now it is a farmhouse with hospitable traditions.

SHIELDAIG, *Ross and Cromarty* (Map 5, ref. 18²85⁴). This crofting and fishing village is on the E. side of the sea-loch Shieldaig. Until 1963 this was at the end of the road, but with the opening in that year of the 7½-m. "Balgy Gap" road from TORRIDON it has been brought near to magnificent scenery.

The track W. from Shieldaig serving the isolated communities on the APPLECROSS peninsula has now been replaced by a good road as far as Kenmore.

SHIN LOCH, *Sutherland* (Map 5, ref. 25⁰91⁵). This, the largest loch in Sutherland, is 17 m. long and 1 to 1½ m. wide. It lies in rather bleak moorland surroundings, but provides excellent fishing.

The level has recently been raised by a dam

The River Shin at Lairg

near LAIRG. Near the NW. end of the loch is the Cassley power station, to which water is brought by tunnel from the headwaters of Cassley river.

SHIRA, *Argyll* (Map 2, ref. 21¹71²). The river and glen of Shira open into Loch Fyne just N. of INVERARAY. About 5 m. up the glen is a small house, now roofless, built for Rob Roy Macgregor by the 1st Duke of Argyll; in it Rob Roy lived for about ten years.

Farther up the glen are dams forming two reservoirs whose waters go by tunnel to a power station at Clachan at the head of Loch Fyne. The scheme includes a small-scale pumped-storage plant, forerunner of the major plant being installed at Loch AWE.

SHOTTS, *Lanarkshire* (Map 2, ref. 28⁸66⁰). A township on the high moors 6 m. NE. of WISHAW, Shotts was at one time a thriving industrial centre developed by the Shotts Iron Company. Altogether twenty-two coal pits were sunk; the last was closed in 1961, and the blast furnaces were dismantled in 1948. Since 1956 an American firm has been making diesel engines at Shotts, and here also is the only National Coal Board foundry in Scotland. Recently, other industries have been started.

SILVERFLOWE, *Kirkcudbrightshire* (Map 2, ref. 25²58⁶), is a nature reserve, 12 m. NW. of NEW GALLOWAY. It includes a unique series of seven raised bogs, undrained and virtually undisturbed by human interference, which form a series both in topography and plant communities. Samples of different types of rarer conditions are being safeguarded for scientific research. This is a remote situation in the midst of wild mountains – a countryside used by Crockett in *The Raiders*.

SKARA BRAE, *Orkney* (Map 7, ref. 32³01⁷), is an excavated prehistoric village on

the Mainland of ORKNEY Northern Islands (*see* "The Shape of Scotland"). This interesting huddle of houses, 6½ m. from STROMNESS on the W. of Orkney's main island, was built about 1500 B.C. Here is no evidence of wealth or kingly state as at the tomb of MAESHOWE (also on the Mainland of Orkney). This is a late neolithic settlement of humble folk that has been preserved for us probably because it had to be abandoned by its inhabitants on account of encroaching sand. Even had they known of its existence, Norse pirates would not have thought it worth despoiling. Skara Brae contains huts with low entrances and curious stone bedsteads. There were various primitive tools and animal bones discovered at Skara Brae. These are now mostly removed to the National Museum of Antiquities in EDINBURGH.

SKELMORLIE, *Ayrshire* (Map 2, ref. 22⁰66⁸). A small village and seaside resort, Skelmorlie is on the Firth of CLYDE 5 m. N. of LARGS and adjacent to WEMYSS BAY, one of the rail and steamer termini serving GLAS-GOW and the Clyde islands. The village was best known for its "hydropathic", which still survives, but in another form. The strange passion for building (one might almost say founding) hydropathics struck Scotland forcibly in the mid-Victorian era. Most of these large hygienic buildings are now put to other purposes. Some have become schools, some have been taken over by convents, some have transformed themselves into hotels; and this has happened very successfully at Skelmorlie.

SKENE, *Aberdeenshire* (Map 6, ref. 37⁷80⁹). This rural parish 6 m. W. of ABERDEEN is chiefly notable for two features: the beautiful, almost circular Loch of Skene; and Skene House, the oldest part of which, the Tower of Skene, is traditionally held to be the oldest inhabited dwelling in the Province of Mar. There are also within the parish, which is entirely rural, five small villages, Kirkton of Skene, Lyne of Skene, Westhills, Garlogie, and Broadstraik. From almost every elevated site in the parish, which slopes towards the S., you look down and across the loch, 3 m. in circumference, which lies in a marshy hollow on a bed of boulder clay, backgrounded by the shapely outline of the Hill of FARE. Very shallow (its greatest depth is 12 ft), it is a great resort of wild birds. Geese, wild duck, gulls, and the smaller waders all frequent it in thousands, and on a still evening the continuous high, mournful sound of their calling can be heard from afar as they gather and settle for the night. Swans go there in winter (over a hundred have been counted on a November day), and some remain to breed in spring. The loch abounds in pike and eels, and all attempts to eliminate them in favour of trout have proved unsuccessful. It is now much frequented by sailing dinghies.

The parish is co-extensive with the ancient Barony of Skene, whose lairds, the Skenes of Skene, dwelt for over five centuries at Skene House. The tower, forming the N. wing of the house of today, was built in the late 13th cent. as one of a chain of royal castles stretching northwards from the DEE at DRUM through Hallforest, KINTORE, INVERURIE, Barra, FYVIE, KING EDWARD, and BANFF. Though now much altered, it consisted of three vaulted storeys with walls over 10 ft thick. The barony was created in 1317 and the Skenes held it until the last laird died in 1827.

These are the facts, but the traditional story of how the Skenes got their name is much more picturesque. It tells how in the reign of Malcolm Canmore a son of the Lord of the Isles was in the train of the King as he went hunting in the forest of Cullerlie, which stretched at that time from the Hill of Fare till it met the forest of Stocket on the outskirts of Aberdeen. Suddenly a savage boar leapt out of a thicket and made straight for the King. The young man interposed himself. Covering one hand with his plaid he thrust it into the mouth of the boar; drawing his dirk or "sgian dubh", he cut the animal's throat. In gratitude the King granted him all the lands encompassed by the flight of a hawk, which he thereupon released. The new laird took the name Skene ("sgian") from the weapon he had so effectively used.

Even in popular imagination, this story has been eclipsed by the supposed exploits of the Warlock Laird of Skene, sometimes identified as Alexander Skene of Skene (1680–1724). He is said to have received tuition in the Black Arts from the Devil in person at Padua. His most famous feat, we are told, was to drive across the Loch of Skene in his carriage after one night's frost.

One of the features of the garden at Skene House today is an old chestnut tree, said to be 350 years old, whose branches have replanted themselves in the earth, thus regenerating the tree. On the garden wall is a fine carved stone boar, representing the animal which played its part in initiating the family fortunes of the Skenes.

SKERRYVORE Rock and Lighthouse, *Argyll* (Map 1, ref. 08⁵72⁶), is in the Inner Hebrides (*see* "The Shape of Scotland").

The remote Skerryvore often attracts the attention of those who look at the map of Scotland, but it is seldom visited. It is a low-lying rock surrounded by dangerous reefs 10 m. SW. of the Island of TIREE. It has a lighthouse built in 1838–43 (and lighted in 1844) by Alan Stevenson and called by his nephew, R. L. S., "the noblest of all extant deep-sea lights". The tower, 138 ft high (of which the first 26 ft are solid masonry), contains 4,308 tons of granite quarried in the Island of MULL.

Among the difficulties of construction, personally supervised by Stevenson, was the remoteness of the site and even of the shore station established at Hynish on Tiree. In the first season, a 60-ft wooden barrack erected for the workmen was destroyed by storm in a single November night. One of the most exposed lighthouse stations in the world, where the force of the waves has been measured up to three tons per square foot, Skerryvore is also an important landfall for ships making towards the CLYDE and Irish sea ports. In 1899 the Dominion liner *Labrador* sailing from Halifax to Liverpool, mistook the light for another off the Irish coast and became a total wreck, but all the passengers and crew were saved after 18 of them had spent 2½ days in the lighthouse. The shore station was moved to EARRAID, near IONA, after the Dubh Artach lighthouse was built, and since about 1950 the lightkeepers' families from both stations have lived at the lighthouse settlement in OBAN. The Skerryvore tower was damaged by fire in March 1954, and the light extinguished, and after renovation diesel-powered electricity was installed. A taller version of this famous lighthouse built on the Alguada Reef off the coast of Burma was lit in 1865.

SKIPNESS, *Argyll* (Map 1, ref. 18⁹65⁸). From the township on the long promontory of Kintyre, and looking over the Kilbrennan Sound to ARRAN, you obtain possibly the finest general views of that well-known island. There are ruins of a large 13th-cent. castle, which marked the southern boundary of the lands of the Campbells.

Just E. of the castle on the shore is the ruin of an ancient chapel.

SKYE, Island of, *Inverness-shire* (Map 4, ref. 15⁰84⁰), is the most northerly of the Inner Hebrides (*see* "The Shape of Scotland"). It is the largest of Scotland's Western Isles, and the

Plate 15   Loch Tay, Perthshire (see p. 439)
Scottish Tourist Board

Scottish Tourist Board

Skye: a croft near Bernisdale

Scottish Tourist Board

Cutting peat on Skye

nearest to the mainland. It combines other superlatives; it is at once on the grandest scale the most arrestingly beautiful of all Scottish islands and, in conjunction with its distant and far smaller sister of the Inner Hebrides, IONA, the most famous.

Nearly 50 m. in direct length, SSE. to NNW., Skye is 23 m. across E. to W. At KYLEAKIN, near its SE. corner, it is only a few hundred yards from the mainland, with which it is connected by a ferry that carries motor-cars. These figures give but little idea of its indented, leaping, winged shape. Even on a map, particularly if it is a relief or contour map, it is an exciting island to look at. From its brief salutation (it is no more than that) of the mainland at Kyleakin, it seems to be in the act of jumping or flying away from Scotland into the Atlantic. This cartographical impression is reinforced when you see the island itself, if you approach it from the S. by sea or from the E. by land and take a view of it from the uplands by Loch Hourn or GLENELG. The famous CUILLIN hills, as they toss the clouds away from their formidable peaks, seem to give a positively muscular effect of taking off from Scotland into the ocean.

On its western side, Skye is indented by many sea-lochs; and, save by the coast and at the NE. of the Trotternish portion of it, the island is mountainous. Its most celebrated ranges are the Cuillins in the SW. centre (some of their rocky peaks were scaled only at the end of the last century) and the Trotternish ridge in the N., culminating in STORR and the extraordinary Old Man of Storr. Skye offers to mountaineers, and in particular to intrepid rock-climbers, opportunities unsurpassed in Britain; and the reward they get upon reaching these apparently inaccessible peaks in the way of views is unrivalled. The salmon, the sea-trout, the brown-trout anglers will find good sport here too, though it is not the equal of that in the Outer Hebrides or in the Northern Isles.

The capital of the island, in a bay sheltered from the mainland by the neighbouring island of RAASAY, is PORTREE (the port of the King), so named after James V's visit to Skye. (BROADFORD and other townships have their own entries in the gazetteer.)

Skye was early inhabited by Gaels, but soon, as its place-names bear evidence, was taken over by the Norsemen. It entered the history of the Kingdom of Scotland by providing the *casus belli* that provoked King Haakon's attack on the Scotland of Alexander III. This led to

Macleod's Tables, Skye

Scottish Tourist Board

Trouting at Traquair (see p. 447)
Scottish Tourist Board

the Norse defeat at the Battle of LARGS and the cession of all the Hebrides to Scotland (*see* "Scotland in History"). Since then the ruling families in Skye have been the Macleods of DUNVEGAN, whose imposing castle still stands inhabited at the N., and the Macdonalds of Sleat in the S.

Skye remained upon the periphery of Scottish history until the Jacobite rising of 1745. Officially, the island, under the cautious leadership of its chiefs, kept out of that affair, but was – in fable, and in song – bundled into it as the scene of some of the most dramatic adventures of Prince Charles Edward Stuart when he was in hiding and in flight. It was to Skye that Flora Macdonald took him from the outer isles, disguising him as her serving woman. It was in Skye that Flora married her clansman Macdonald of KINGSBURGH. It is in Skye that this heroic, modest little woman is buried.

In common with the rest of Celtic Scotland, Skye suffered from the emigration enforced by the Clearances in the latter half of the 18th cent. and the beginning of the 19th. Both Johnson and Boswell had something to say on the melancholy subject during their memorable tour of the island in 1773. Skye, though much ravaged, did not, however, endure the full rigour of clearances, and indeed it was as a result of the vigorous action of some crofters in the 1880s that the attention of Great Britain was drawn to this question.

In 1882, in the district of Braes in the N., various crofters resisted the Sheriff's officers. Since many of the menfolk were away at the fishing, some Amazonian Celtic women, armed with stockings filled with stones, succeeded in holding up the infamous proceeding of eviction. An absurdly nervous Government at Westminster sent up a man-o'-war to deal with the situation. The happier outcome of this grotesque situation was that, under the greathearted Gladstone a commission of enquiry was set up. This resulted in the Crofters' Holding Act of 1886, which was the beginning of the amelioration of the native Highlanders' lot all over the Highlands and Islands. (*See* "Scotland in History".) This was perhaps the last occasion on which the island of Skye effectively touched Scottish history.

Skye people, as visitors before and after Johnson and Boswell have testified, are famous for their hospitality. Even in these days of universal and commercial tourism, gleams of the amiable virtue may be perceived in the remoter parts of the island. "What is it to live and not to love?" exclaimed Mistress Mackinnon at Corriechatacan when, in a spirit of pure friendliness, she embraced the venerable Dr Samuel Johnson. Few if any modern Gaelic-speaking Skye women would go as far as this; but the "pure friendliness" is there indeed.

Gaelic-speaking, dignified, courteous, the native Skye population is strongly religious and much devoted to the Free Kirk tradition. The modern traveller is asked to respect the Skyefolk's Sabbatarianism. It springs from a Christian reverence. To refrain from openly flouting that reverence one day out of the seven is a small price to pay for the beauty of the island and the friendliness of its folk.

SLAINS, *Aberdeenshire* (Map 6, ref. 40⁵83⁰). The old castle of Slains, 1½ m. N. of the village of COLLIESTON, is a spectacular but fragmentary keep on a rocky headland; it was the seat of the Hays of Erroll for close on three centuries. In 1950, the modern representative of the family, Diana Hay, 23rd Countess of Erroll, hereditary Constable of Scotland, purchased the old castle and the promontory on which it stands. She has since built for herself and her family, on the very point of the headland to seaward of the castle, a Swedish-type timber lodge of triangular end-view. Thus the romantic story of the Hays and their connection with the great estates they once owned in Buchan comes full circle.

Sir Gilbert Hay, 5th Baron, carried the mace at the crowning of Robert Bruce at SCONE. Afterwards he saved the King's life in battle, and was wounded by his side. The King thereafter gave Sir Gilbert the lands of Slains and the office of Constable of Scotland. Sir William, 9th Baron, was created Earl of Erroll and Lord Slains in 1452. The drama of Slains Castle reached its climax in the last decade of the 16th cent. when Francis, the 9th Earl, converted to Catholicism by a Jesuit kinsman, Fr. Hay of Delgatie, drew up with the earls of Huntly and Angus a bond known as the Treaty of Spanish Blanks, whereby Philip II of Spain was to assist them by landing forces on the Buchan coast. Unfortunately their envoy to Philip was captured by the English, and the plan was communicated to the ruling Protestant faction at the court of James VI. There followed the campaign ending in the Battle of GLEN LIVET, in which Francis was wounded and from which he fled to the Continent. King James marched N. and, with gunpowder collected from the town council of ABERDEEN, personally supervised the demolition of the old Castle of Slains.

On the headland near the old castle today stand, pointing out to sea beside the Countess's new Swedish lodge, two cannon from the Spanish galleon *Santa Caterina* wrecked in that fatal year of 1594. They were salvaged last century from the nearby cove known for three centuries as St Catherine's Dub. Earl Francis returned to Slains after his exile in 1597. But the old castle was beyond repair. A new Slains Castle was built several miles to the N.

SLIDDERY, *Buteshire* (Map 1, ref. 19⁴62²), is on the Island of ARRAN. Some 9 m. SW. of BRODICK at Sliddery stands an elongated, ship-like, chambered cairn exactly similar to the Curragh Mound on IONA. The sides are trenched with flag stones, and at each end stands a red sandstone monolith. The Sliddery Burn provides lively small brown-trout fishing and, in the autumn and with luck, some good sea-trout angling.

SLIGACHAN, *Inverness-shire* (Map 4, ref. 14⁹82⁹), is a mountaineering and angling resort on the Island of SKYE in the Inner Hebrides (*see* "The Shape of Scotland"). Sligachan is but a hamlet 9 m. from PORTREE, and on the main road N. from BROADFORD. Situated, however, at the head of the sea-arm of Loch Sligachan and immediately under the "black" CUILLINS, it is strategically placed for exploration amongst the hills and for sport. It has a noted hotel, much used by rock-climbers and hill-walkers. The R. Sligachan, which flows into the sea just by it, is well known in the season for its salmon and sea-trout angling.

SLOCHD, *Inverness-shire* (Map 5, ref. 28⁵82⁴). This is the summit (1,332 ft) of the road and railway route over the southern Monadhliath mountains, between the valleys of DULNAIN and Findhorn. It is a short pass emerging to the N. on a wide heather-clad hill-side. This route through the high hills was once considered very dangerous.

SLOY LOCH, *Dunbartonshire* (Map 2, ref. 22⁹71²). Once the gathering-place of the Clan Macfarlane, the name of Loch Sloy was used by them as their slogan.

This sheet of water has been changed by a hydro-electric scheme from a small loch to a very large one. Sloy has one of the highest rainfalls in Scotland, and is now harnessed so that 1 in. of rain produces more than a million units of electricity. Sloy was the first major project of the North of Scotland Hydro-Electric Board, and was opened by the Queen Mother (then Queen) in 1950.

Connected with the scheme is the dam at Allt-na-Lairige, at the head of Glen Fyne 4 m. NW. of Sloy, where the first large pre-stressed concrete dam in Britain was built.

SLUG ROAD, The, *Kincardineshire* (Map 6, ref. 37⁸79⁰). The A957 crosses the hills SE. of the town of BANCHORY, rising to close on 800 ft on the shoulder of Cairn Mon Earn (1,254 ft), and giving fine views of the DEE valley. N. of this road, within 4 m. of STONEHAVEN, is the Roman marching camp of Raedykes.

SMA' GLEN, *Perthshire* (Map 2, ref. 29⁰73⁰). This famous beauty-spot in the Southern Highlands is a narrow forbidding pass through which the R. Almond threads its way with hills rising steeply on either side to approximately 2,000 ft.

At the southern end of the pass, which is just over 4 m. long, is the Roman camp of Fendoch lying on flat open ground between the Fendoch

Burn and the Almond. This site was excavated by Sir Ian Richmond, and is described in the *Proceedings* of the Society of Antiquaries of Scotland. A mile up the pass on the W. bank, approximately 100 ft above the road, is a small Roman signal station obviously sited to give warning of any hostile forces gathering in the high rocky fastnesses of the glen.

Farther up the pass on the E. side, the river bends away from the road, and between them is a wide flat haugh on which is a prehistoric burial-cairn, the periphery of which is demarcated by a ring of boulders. Overlooking this in the same side of the glen is Dun Mor, 1,527 ft above sea-level, on whose summit is a massive stone-built Iron Age fort, sited to command the pass and yet remain impregnable to attack.

At the northern end of the pass is Ossian's Stone – a vast, ice-borne boulder, which is not now in its original position. General Wade's road, built in 1730 from CRIEFF to ABERFELDY, followed the Sma' Glen. In letters written from a "gentleman touring Scotland in the late 18th century" there is a vivid description of how, during the building of the road, the English soldiers found the line barred by Ossian's Stone, of how they eventually moved the stone and found a prehistoric burial at the base of it.

On the W. side of the glen at the northern end the hills rise very steeply; and on the summit, but over the skyline, is Kenneth's Cairn, a prehistoric burial mound of waterworn boulders, 2,000 ft above sea-level.

SMAILHOLM, *Roxburghshire* (Map 3, ref. 36¹63⁷). The village of Smailholm has a parish church dating back to 1243; having been extensively rebuilt in the 17th and 18th cents. and again in 1820, its original Romanesque character appears only in the plan. Near the church is Smailholm House, a characteristic laird's house of the early 18th cent., dated 1707, little altered and still occupied.

To the SW., Smailholm Tower stands on a rocky outcrop with magnificent panoramic views of the Border country. A rectangular building 57 ft high and 39 ft by 32 ft, it has walls 7 ft thick. Probably built in the early 16th cent. (except for the top floor, which is later), it still stands entire through five storeys, apart from the wooden floors.

At nearby Sandyknowe Farm Sir Walter Scott's grandfather lived and farmed; Sir Walter spent some of his childhood there.

SOAY, Island of, *Inverness-shire* (Map 4, ref. 14⁵81³), is one of the Inner Hebrides (*see* "The Shape of Scotland"). The flat, small island of Soay, with its village and natural harbour, lies just off the SW. coast of SKYE, and is 3 m. by 1 m. across. The island was used as a base for various shark-fishing ventures after the Second World War, but in June 1953 the local community was officially cleared and all boats and services were withdrawn from the island. By 1961, fourteen new settlers had come to the island. They sought in seclusion literary and artistic pursuits.

SORN, *Ayrshire* (Map 2, ref. 25⁵62⁷). A small village on the R. Ayr, Sorn stands some 4 m. E. of MAUCHLINE on the MUIRKIRK road. Nearby is Sorn Castle, dating from the early 15th cent. with late 18th-cent. additions. At present it is the home of Lord Sorn, retired Senator of the College of Justice; that is, a Judge of the Scottish Bench. The village church dates from 1658, and still has an outside stair to the gallery; the churchyard has a memorial to the Reverend Lewis Balfour, grandfather of Robert Louis Stevenson and minister of the parish for twenty-three years.

SOUTHEND, *Argyll* (Map 1, ref. 16⁹60⁸). The appropriately-named village of Southend lies near the southern tip of the long promontory of Kintyre. It is on a fertile coastal strip and is a holiday resort with sandy beaches and a golf course.

This was the traditional landing place of St Columba on his first mission to Scotland; a flat rock near the ruined chapel bears his legendary footsteps. A religious service is held in June every year.

Dunaverty Castle, an early stronghold of the Lords of the Isles, stood on a pyramid of rock with a sheer drop to the sea. It was captured by James IV in 1493, and again by Leslie in 1647, when the garrison was massacred. Only vestiges of the castle are to be seen now.

The island of Sanda, with its lighthouse, lies 2 m. offshore. The Mull of Kintyre lighthouse at the end of the road, the last 2 m. of which are very steep and are closed to cars, has a magnificent view of the Irish coast only 13 m. away.

SOUTHERNESS, *Kirkcudbrightshire* (Map 2, ref. 29⁷55⁴). A small but rapidly growing holiday resort on the Solway Firth. W. of the mouth of the estuary of the Nith, Southerness has extensive sand and a golf course. It was once called Satterness ("saltmakers' point"), as it had a salt-making industry. There are views towards the distant Lake District mountains.

SOUTRA, *Midlothian* (Map 3, ref. 34⁶65⁸), is a hill near the meeting-place of Berwickshire, East Lothian and Midlothian. Its summit of 1,209 ft is a well-known viewpoint on one of the main roads towards the S.

Just SW. of the summit on the side road is Soutra Aisle, the remains of a hospital founded by Malcolm IV about 1164 for pilgrims, travellers, and poor people, and dedicated to the Holy Trinity. In 1462 it was annexed to Trinity College, EDINBURGH. About 1850, all the stones were taken away to make dykes, with the exception of a small aisle now used as a burial vault by a local family.

SPEAN BRIDGE, *Inverness-shire* (Map 5, ref. 22³78¹). This township, situated 9 m. NE. of FORT WILLIAM, possesses a parish church built around 1812.

The bridge itself, built by Telford in 1819, spans the turbulent R. Spean. About 2 m. W. of this, situated 100 ft above the gorge, are the remains of High Bridge, built by General Wade in 1736 as part of his road designed to give the troops of the central government access to the Highlands. The last repairs were made in 1893, but in 1913 part of it collapsed and nothing has been done to it since. Wade's road deviates from the present one through Spean Bridge.

It was here that the first skirmish took place in August 1745, three days before the raising of Prince Charles Edward Stuart's standard at GLENFINNAN. The military associations of the area were revived during the Second World War, when commandos were trained in the surrounding hills. A fine memorial to them stands to the NW. of the township.

The road running SW. from Spean Bridge towards Fort William crosses high moorlands and gives magnificent views of Aonach Mor (3,999 ft) and the great northern corries of BEN NEVIS (4,418 ft). To the E. extends Glen Spean, giving access to Roy Bridge and the famous "parallel roads" of Glen Roy.

SPEY, River, *Inverness-shire/Moray/Banff-shire* (Map 6, ref. 33³85⁵). The second longest river in Scotland (98 m.), and draining a basin of 1,153 sq. m., Spey is the third most important salmon river after TAY and TWEED. For grandeur its scenery is said to be inferior to that of the Tay and also, in places, of the DEE; yet of all Scottish rivers, perhaps, it is the most remarkable for uniform beauty, and it carries its Highland character right from the wilds of Badenoch to its mouth in the centre of Spey Bay – this despite flowing through a considerable tract of what is properly Lowland country.

Its source is a small stream rising about 1,530 ft above sea-level on Creag a' Cleat, 5 m. from the W. shore of Loch Laggan. Its beginnings are surprisingly tame, considering the splendours which it reveals in its middle reaches. After passing through the tiny Loch Spey, it flows eastwards for 15 m. to its junction with the Truim near NEWTONMORE, at the geographical heart of the Highlands, from which point, as it swings into its NE. course, runs parallel with the great snowy wall of the CAIRNGORM plateau, between it and the less spectacular Monadhliaths. Commercially of little importance (apart from distilleries and its exceedingly expensive salmon fishings), and totally unnavigable from its mouth upwards, the Spey is yet a gateway to the largest tract of completely unspoilt mountain terrain on the mainland of Scotland. From Newtonmore, KINGUSSIE, KINCRAIG, ALVIE, AVIEMORE, Broomhill, BOAT OF GARTEN, and GRANTOWN, roads and tracks lead eastward

Scottish Tourist Board

The River Spey at Kingussie

into the heart of the GRAMPIANS and Cairngorms, the peaks of which are never absent from its vistas along this 40-m. stretch.

At Aviemore begins Strathspey, extending NE. as the territory of Clan Grant, still centred on the now virtually derelict Castle Grant at Grantown. But along the right bank of the river the influence of the powerful House of Gordon was writ large. It is seen in the ruins of Ruthven Barracks opposite Kingussie, which itself was created by the 4th Duke of Gordon after 1792, to replace the ancient burgh of barony of Ruthven, and at the lovely 18th-cent. house of Kinrara on the left bank near Alvie, which was the home of "Bonnie Jean", Jane Maxwell, Duchess of Gordon.

The whole of the Spey valley from Newtonmore to Grantown is involved in the immense development of Cairngorm winter-sports facilities, now in progress and centred on the famous Ski Road from Glenmore Lodge to Coire Cas and Coire na Ciste of Cairngorm, which, together with the Cairngorm chairlift, takes the tourist and skier to within a few hundred feet of the plateau's summit.

GLEN MORE is a National Forest Park, and there still remain within it portions of the ancient Caledonian Forest. The region also has unique flora and fauna. Spey's main right-bank tributaries in this sector, the Feshie (at Kincraig) and the Nethy (at Broomhill), come straight from the Cairngorms. Both reward exploration with magnificent mountain and moorland scenery, and both were extensively used in the 18th and early 19th cents. for floating down to the Spey, from the three forests,

the great quantities of timber that were exported from Kingston at the river's mouth, or built in one of the yards there into sailing vessels with masts 70 ft high. The floaters on the rafts that made the 60-m. voyage took anything from two days to a week to complete the journey.

Although, below Grantown, the Spey leaves behind the vista of the Cairngorms, its immediate environs are no less picturesque. Through the Haughs of Cromdale it passes into a narrowing valley between lower hills to Advie and to BALLINDALLOCH, where it receives its largest and loveliest tributary, the Avon.

The new distillery at TORMORE is a reminder that from this point northwards the production of malt whisky is Speyside's main industrial activity. From Grantown the Spey flows between Moray and Inverness-shire. Here at Ballindalloch its right bank enters Banffshire, but there is a lovely less-frequented road on the left, or Moray, bank that passes through Scootmore Forest to KNOCKANDO. And indeed it is the rule from this point that the banks of the river are gloriously wooded, while it is the upland fields above them on either side that are either arable or moorland. (Entries under Knockando, ABERLOUR, ROTHES, and FOCHABERS describe the next stages in the river's course.)

It can be said that from this point the river has not a dull moment. Even so, near its mouth at Fochabers the combination of tree and rock brought about by the imposition of the vast Forest of Speymouth (10,500 acres) upon glacially weathered old red sandstone produces spectacular scenery. Spey finally leaves Banffshire at Ordiequish, just below the famous salmon-fishing reaches at Orton and Delfur, and flows past Fochabers, GARMOUTH, and Kingston to its newly cut mouth at Tugnet. Erosion and the westward shifting of the mouth finally destroyed the commercial importance of the last-named villages.

Immediately to the E. of the river's mouth is the notable golf course of Spey Bay. Apart from Spey's allure to the angler, it is a paradise to the bird-watcher and the biologist. Over its dazzling white shingles gulls and oyster-catchers wheel all day, and the dipper darts from side to side uttering his shrill cry, and the grey wagtail bobs and flutters among the boulders.

SPEYMOUTH, *Moray* (Map 6, ref. 33³86⁰), is the name of a parish near the mouth of the R. SPEY. Here in 1087 Malcolm Canmore's army crossed the Spey to attack the invading forces of the King of Norway. The *Scotichronicon* also fixes it as the scene of a battle in 1116 between Alexander I and the people of the Mearns and of Moray who attacked him while he was building a new palace near DUNDEE. He is described as pursuing the "rebels of the River Spey". In

1296, and again in 1303, the invading King Edward I of England crossed at the ford below the church and encamped at Speymouth. The same ford that Edward used was selected by troops of Cromwell and of Montrose. Again in the 18th cent., forces under the Duke of Cumberland used this ford on their way to CULLODEN. The manse was briefly the H.Q. of Jacobite leaders during the Rising of the '45. They retired on the approach of Cumberland, who also occupied the manse for one night on the 12th of April 1746.

A distinguished native of this parish was Jane Innes, a daughter of James Innes of Redhall. She became the wife of Governor Pitt of Madras and was the grandmother of the Earl of Chatham.

SPINNINGDALE, *Sutherland* (Map 5, ref. 26⁷88⁹). At this small township, on the DOR-NOCH Firth and 7¾ m. W. of Dornoch, stands the ruin of a cotton-mill, erected in 1790 by George Dempster of Skibo, a humanitarian and what was then known as an "improver"; this mill was inspired by the example of Arkwright. It once employed 100 hands, and twenty houses were built for the operatives. Unfortunately this benevolent scheme failed, owing to the remoteness of the district and to the fact that cost of transport outweighed the cheapness of manufacture and labour. The mill was burnt down in 1808. It was never rebuilt.

SPOTT, *East Lothian* (Map 3, ref. 36⁸67⁵). This small and pleasing village 3 m. S. of DUNBAR, situated on the steep slopes of Doon Hill and Spott Dod, at whose foot Spott Burn flows in a narrow, steep-sided valley, has had rather a macabre past. Today it is a quiet place depending on agriculture, and its mode of life has not changed much in a hundred years, though there are reminders of its past in the modern church, where jougs still hang menacingly near the door. Again we are reminded of an unpleasant episode in South-East Scotland's history by the presence of an old Watch House. This was erected to house the guards who stopped body-snatchers from taking corpses.

But the most coldly macabre thing about Spott is the history of its early ministers. One in 1544 was killed in a brawl, and another was hanged for complicity in the assassination of the Regent Moray in 1571. But it was his predecessor, John Kello, who held the incumbency during 1567–70, whose misdeeds and whose end were the most spectacular. He was hanged in the Grassmarket in EDINBURGH for strangling his wife. This strange story is told in colourful old Scots in the *Historie of King James the Sext*. It tells how John Kello strangled his wife, hung her body from the roof to make it appear she had taken her own life, and then went to church (it being the Sabbath) and preached an eloquent sermon. After church he asked the neighbours back to talk with his wife, but found the door locked (he had locked it himself from the inside before leaving). The minister then went round to the back, forced an entry, let the neighbours in, and with feigned amazement and horror let them find the body of the apparent suicide. But forethought and sermonizing were of no avail. He was found out, apprehended, and hanged.

With this history, it is not surprising to learn that witch-hunts persisted in Spott later than anywhere else north of the Border. The Kirk Session records for 1705 have an entry: "Many witches burnt on the top of Spott Loan". "Witch's stone", still at Spott Loan, recalls that the last witch to be burnt S. of the FORTH suffered at Spott; she was Marion Lille, locally known as the "Rigwoody witch".

On the top of Doon Hill, General David Leslie's army lay for two days before the Battle of DUNBAR in 1650, and Cromwell is said to have spent the night after the battle in Spott House. There are relics of an oval fort on Doon Hill.

Chesters Fort is on the crest of a hill on Spott Farm. There are remains of a stone circle on the E. side of Spartleton Edge, and circles and cairns in the neighbourhood.

SPYNIE, *Moray* (Map 6, ref. 32³86¹). At one time, the sea reached to the hillock on which the ruins of Spynie Palace stand on the R. Lossie, and stretched in a broad estuary for miles on either side. Beneath the palace walls, the then town of Spynie had a safe harbour, which was mentioned in 1397 and again in 1451. In the latter year, a regality right of harbour was granted to the place. Later the sea threw up a barrier of sand and shingle and cut itself off from the inland estuary, which receded into a marsh – a bordered lake running for some 5 m. parallel to the shores of the firth. For hundreds of years it was one of the most beautiful expanses of water in the kingdom, dotted with small islands and stocked with wild fowl. According to the early Scottish historian Boece, in 1560 it was especially a habitation of swans, due to great abundance of "swangirss, whose seed is verie pleasant unto the said fowle in the eating". In 1808–12, a canal recommended by Telford was carried through the loch and on to the sea at LOSSIEMOUTH, where there were sluices to shut out the tide. These works were entirely destroyed by the great floods of 1829. In 1860, the loch was drained and the land reclaimed. Rich but monotonous flat fields now replace the former lovely loch.

On the SE. margin of the old lake basin stand the ruins of the castle-palace of the bishops of Moray. Although the cathedral was transferred to ELGIN in 1224, the bishops continued to reside at Spynie. The castle was mentioned in the survey of Moray made for Edward I of England upon his invasion of Scotland. It had loopholed walls of great thickness, a watch-tower, and a portcullis. The prominent square tower that still remains is known as Davie's Tower and dates from *c.* 1470. It was begun by Bishop David Stewart (1461–76), who had excommunicated the Earl of Huntly. Huntly and the Gordons threatened to come and "pull the Bishop out of his pigeonholes". The Bishop replied he would build a house out of which Huntly and all his clan should never be able to extricate him. His tower was one of the largest of such keeps in Scotland – four storeys high, with walls 9 ft thick.

Mary Queen of Scots "supped and slept" in the castle in 1562. After the Reformation, it continued to be occupied by the Protestant bishops of Moray; and in 1638 Bishop Guthrie garrisoned it against the Covenanters. In 1640, Major-General Munro captured it, and during Montrose's campaign of 1645 it sheltered covenanting lairds and burgesses of Elgin. Abandoned after the Revolution of 1689, it passed into the hands of the Crown in 1690, and was speedily dismantled – becoming (in the manner that we have, alas, so often to record) a "quarry" for the surrounding district.

The church of Spynie in the early 13th cent. acted as the cathedral of Moray for a short time, until the seat of the diocese was transferred to Elgin in 1224. The church was dedicated to the Holy Trinity, and remained the parish church till 1736, when the present building was erected just NW. of Elgin. The new church is plain, with the belfry and a doorway taken from the old church, of which nothing now remains but the churchyard. The bell brought from the old church seems to have been cast in the Netherlands. There is a tradition that it was the gift of Bishop John Guthrie, but that it was never hung or rung till he had left Spynie, having been deposed by the General Assembly in 1638.

STAFFA, *Argyll* (Map 1, ref. 13³73⁵), a small island of the Inner Hebrides (*see* "The Shape of Scotland"), with magnificent cliffs and caves formed of columnar basalt, lies off the W. coast of MULL and is visited each weekday by steamer from OBAN via IONA and TOBERMORY. Shaped by the cooling process associated with volcanic action, and unique in such scale and harmony, it was unknown to the outside world until, in 1772, a party of scientists called there on the way to Iceland on the recommendation of a passing traveller, and a geological description by Sir Joseph Banks appeared in a book by Thomas Pennant. After that it was visited and written about by a host of famous people, including Scott, Keats, Mendelssohn (whose "Hebrides" overture is also called "Fingal's Cave"), Turner, Wordsworth, Tennyson, and Jules Verne.

The island, which affords grazing for cattle in summer, has been uninhabited for more than a century, but, since the start of the steamboat trips in the 1820s, it has been admired by countless visitors. Those lucky enough to be able to land scramble over the tops of the six-sided columns of which it is chiefly formed, to enter Fingal's Cave. Earlier visitors went by boat from ULVA and took with them a piper, whose music contended with the waves as they flowed in and out of the cave. Even from the deck of a steamer the island is worth seeing, but a spell ashore adds to the impressiveness of the spectacle, and anyone with a boat of his own (and able to handle it skilfully) will be able to explore the "roof" of the island and the lesser-known caves. Staffa is an irregular oval, about 70 acres in superficial area, and 135 ft at its highest point.

STANLEY, *Perthshire* (Map 6, ref. 31⁰73⁴). This village on the R. TAY, 6½ m. N. of PERTH, owes its origin to cotton mills built here in 1785 by George Dempster. The fortunes of the mills have fluctuated greatly, and from 1814–23 they ceased working altogether, and again during the cotton famine of 1862, which was caused by the American Civil War.

Stanley House was a seat of Lord Nairne, and the name is said to have been given after Margaret, Lady Nairne, at the end of the 17th cent., married Lord William Murray, whose mother was Lady Amelia Stanley, daughter of the Earl of Derby.

A plaque on the present building records how the 3rd Jacobite Laird escaped from the house after 1745. The estates were twice confiscated, but parts were restored by George IV, to Major Nairne, making him 4th Lord Nairne, as a tribute to his wife, Caroline Oliphant, the Scottish poetess.

Campsie Linn, a famed beauty spot on the river, lies a short distance NE. of Stanley. Here are rapids caused by the flow of the river over a rugged basaltic dyke.

STENHOUSEMUIR, *Stirlingshire* (Map 2, ref. 28⁷68³). Now a suburb of FALKIRK and LARBERT, Stenhousemuir was once of importance in itself. It was the site, after 1785, of the largest cattle tryst in Scotland, called the Falkirk Tryst, which had been held in the W. of Falkirk since leaving CRIEFF in 1770. Stenhousemuir formed a natural centre for the drove-road system of both the Lowlands and the Highlands, and maintained this position until the end of the 19th cent.

In the area is Stenhouse, a tower-house built in 1622 and the last of this kind in the country. It underwent many alterations in 1836, and has now been reconstructed for the use of several tenants.

Kinnaird House, the home of the Bruces of Kinnaird, is the birthplace of James Bruce, the explorer and linguist (born 1730), who also died here. The house is mainly 19th cent., but the sundial on the modern pedestal is dated 1690.

Just inside the grounds of Stenhouse is Arthur's O'on or Arthur's Oven, a Roman building that survived until 1743. Built of dressed freestone, it stood 22 ft high and was shaped like a beehive. No precise parallel can be cited, but the building has been identified as a Roman temple or shrine or possibly a war memorial, since it stands 2 m. from the nearest Roman road or fort but is visible from the Antonine Wall. A replica exists at the stables of PENICUIK House.

STENNESS, *Orkney* (Map 7, ref. 32⁶01³), is a henge or group of standing prehistoric stones on the Mainland of ORKNEY Northern Islands (*see* "The Shape of Scotland"). The remains of this earthwork are now so small that it is difficult to tell to what class of standing stones this Orcadian monument belongs. The henge is now rightly noted more particularly for the four stones just within the central space defined by the inner lip of the ditch. Three of these survivors rise to heights of between 17 and 15 ft. But, remarkable though the standing stones of Stenness are, they are less striking than a similar and better preserved collection at CALLERNISH in LEWIS.

Close to this unique monument is the celebrated Loch of Stenness, in which exceptionally large brown trout have been caught.

STENTON, *East Lothian* (Map 3, ref. 36²67¹). Situated 3 m. SE. of EAST LINTON, this is a charming red stone village. The green is surrounded by houses centuries old, some with outside stairs; and nearby is the Tron, or Wool Stone, on which wool was weighed at Stenton Fair.

About 300 yards NE. of the old parish church is the well of Holy Rood, one of the best-preserved medieval wells in Scotland. Over the well is a small circular building covered with a conical roof of overlapping stone slabs, surmounted at the apex by a crocketed finial with a cable necking. The finial has been described as a "cardinal's hat", and there is a legend that the tenure of the mansion of Biel depends on the wearing of this hat. A writer in the *Pro-*

Stone circle, Stenness

ceedings of the Society of Antiquaries says, however, that a "singular amount of argument" would be needed to convince any architect that it was anything but an ordinary Gothic finial.

The ruin of the old church lies within the churchyard of the modern one. At the N. is a small sacristy, used as the burial-place of the Sydserfs of Ruchlaw. At the W. end stands a tower of two tiers, well preserved and used as a dovecote. Both the church and the tower are probably 16th cent. There is a circular font at the E. end.

The nearby mansion house of Biel, originally of great antiquity, was greatly enlarged in the 19th cent., but has recently been restored again by the demolition of much of the later buildings. The S. front is very impressive. Three beautiful terraces descend to a haugh or meadow extending from the lowest terrace to Biel Burn. The terraces were originally laid out by the 1st Lord Belhaven, who, after the defeat of Charles I, fled to England disguised as a labourer, and is said to have worked as a gardener. Employed to buy bulbs in Holland, he took the opportunity of conveying letters to Charles II. A fine stone bridge still bears the Belhaven arms and name.

There are magnificent trees in the grounds. A cedar of Lebanon, one of the largest in Britain, planted in 1707, was wrecked in a gale in 1926, but another fine specimen survives. There are also some magnificent beeches, including a splendid copper beech. Smaller than Biel, but charming, is the house of Ruchlaw, the foundations of which are 15th cent.

STEVENSTON, *Ayrshire* (Map 2, ref. 22⁶64²), is a town just inland of ARDROSSAN at the base of the Ardeer Peninsula, from which it probably derives its name ("land of the winding stream"; that is, of the sluggish Garnock). The area was evidently of importance in prehistoric days, to judge from the many weapons, implements, and other remains which have been turned up from time to time.

Stevenston has only recently acquired burgh status; nevertheless a settlement seems to have existed here from at least the middle 13th cent. As has been the case for many generations, Stevenston depends on the industries of ARDEER, and a very large proportion of the townspeople are employed there.

STEWARTON, *Ayrshire* (Map 2, ref. 24²64⁶). A country burgh on the Annick Water, Stewarton lies N. of KILMARNOCK in the centre of a rich dairy-farming area. Stewarton was at one time renowned for its making of "Tam o' Shanter" bonnets. Of this industry there is only a small remnant, some of the old firms having gone over to knitwear, woolspinning, and hosiery work. David Dale, the humane 18th-cent. W. of Scotland and Glasgow industrialist, was born here in 1739, and in

Scottish Tourist Board

Stirling Castle

1785 he began the building of his mills at NEW LANARK in which cotton yarn was first spun in Scotland.

STIRLING, *Stirlingshire* (Map 2, ref. 28° 69³), for centuries a principal centre of the FORTH-CLYDE Valley, a royal burgh and busy county town, now has its own university. Set in grounds of glorious wooden parkland, the Airthrey estate, Scotland's first completely new university for almost 400 years (Edinburgh, the youngest of the four older universities was founded in 1583) has expanded rapidly since its foundation in 1967 towards the target of 4,000 students by the mid-seventies. By September 1971 it had 1,600 students, with many of them living in tailor-made flats and halls of residence on the campus. Stirling University welcomes visitors, especially to the MacRobert Centre, Scotland's most up-to-date and superbly equipped arts centre.

Not much is recorded of the town's history before the 12th cent., although there are indications that the site was developed and occupied a good deal earlier. Alexander I, for instance, died in the Castle in 1124; and in charters of only a few years later David I refers to his "burgh of Stirling", which seems to confirm it as a place of some consequence.

Two great Scottish battles were fought in the neighbourhood of Stirling, and are always associated with the town. The first of these – both were part of the struggle for national independence – was the Battle of Stirling Bridge in 1297, at which Sir William Wallace trapped and routed an English army under the Earl of Surrey. The site of this encounter is thought to have been at Kildean, a little more than half a mile NW. of the Castle. Some years later, in 1314, it was an English attempt to relieve their beleaguered Governor in the castle that led to Bruce's victory over Edward II at

BANNOCKBURN (*see* "Scotland in History"). The Bruce statue on the Castle esplanade commands a view of both these fields of battle.

After a changeful existence throughout the early wars, relative stability came to Stirling with the reign of James I of Scotland, in the early 15th cent. From then the town grew in size and in repute, and the Castle became a regular residence of the Stuart kings. James II was born in the Castle; James III was one of its architectural improvers; Mary Queen of Scots was brought here as an infant to be crowned after the death of her father, James V, at Falkland. James V was himself responsible for erecting the palace buildings, and James VI, who was both christened and crowned here, rebuilt the Chapel Royal for the christening of his own son, Prince Henry.

The Castle is the regimental headquarters of the Argyll and Sutherland Highlanders, who in 1970 chose reduction to battalion strength rather than disbandment. Their splendid museum in the Castle is open to visitors daily. "Queen Victoria's Lookout" at the NW. corner of the ramparts covers superb views of the Campsie Fells to the W., and of Ben Lomond, Ben Venue, Ben Ledi, and Ben Vorlich to the N. Below lies the "King's Knot", one of the earliest ornamental gardens in Scotland.

The town of Stirling, like Edinburgh, can be recognizably divided into old and new. At the top of the town, on the steep approaches to the Castle in Baker Street, Spittal Street, Broad Street, St John Street, and St Mary's Wynd, can be seen survivals of the good domestic building of the 16th, 17th, and 18th cents. The Guildhall, Argyll's Lodging, Mar's Wark, and the restorations and new building carried out by the Town Council are all worthy of notice. Modern Stirling dates largely from the 19th cent., when the town grew in importance with the arrival of the railways, and developed into a thriving commercial centre, its shops and banks and law firms serving a large and prosperous agricultural hinterland. The architecture of the town centre and of the surrounding residential districts still reflects this period of late-Victorian affluence.

Today the town continues essentially as a focal point in central Scotland. It is the hub from which thousands of tourists and holiday-makers disperse annually in all directions to visit the TROSSACHS, Loch LOMOND, GLEN-COE, and the West Highlands, or Perthshire and the NE. It has, of course, its own quota of standard local attractions, ranging from golf and tennis to hill-walking and angling; and, in friendly civic rivalry with Edinburgh, it stages its own spring festival of music and drama.

STOBO, *Peeblesshire* (Map 3, ref. 31⁸63⁸). Lying in the vale of the TWEED is Stobo Church, whose tower, nave, and chancel are all Norman; but additions in the 16th and 17th cents. have given them the appearance of buildings of different periods. A barrel-vaulted porch enshrines a 13th-cent. doorway.

STOER, *Sutherland* (Map 5, ref. 20¹92⁸). On the narrow and hilly but pleasing road from LOCHINVER to KYLESKU, Stoer is one of the remoter Highland villages or townships. There is bathing, trout fishing in the many small lochs, and, from the hill of Cnoc Poll, fine views of the more celebrated Sutherland isolated peaks. Near Stoer is a broch on a low eminence bordered to the W. by the sea and to the E. by a broad expanse of turf on sand. Beyond, the sharp peaks of Quinag loom across 10 m. of low broken hills and innumerable lochs. The ruins of large rectangular blocks stand in places to a height of over 6 ft. The diameter of the interior is 32 ft, and the wall is about 14 ft thick; the outer end of the entrance passage was covered with a triangular lintel.

There is a lighthouse to the S. of Rhu Stoer, and the headland has crofting townships scattered over it. In the 18th cent. there must have been a much larger population than there is now. Traces of the vanished inhabitants remain.

STONEBYRES, *Lanarkshire* (Map 2, ref. 28⁶64¹). The Linn at Stonebyres is the last and broadest of the Falls of CLYDE, just over 1 m. below Lanark bridge; it is now utilized by a hydro-electric station. The mansion of Stonebyres is in LESMAHAGOW parish; the oldest portion of it is ascribed to the 14th cent. The estate was held by the Weir or Vere family from the 15th cent. to 1842, when the property was sold. Black Hill (now the property of the National Trust for Scotland), 3 m. W. of LANARK, is an outlook-point with a commanding view of the Clyde valley.

STONEHAVEN, *Kincardineshire* (Map 6, ref. 38⁸78⁶). Surrounded by higher land on three sides, and enclosed by Downie Point and Garron Point, two massive rocky headlands on S. and N. respectively, the county town of Kincardineshire lies in a deeply indented bay astride the mouths of the Carron and the Cowie rivers. The main centre of the town is on a small coastal plain backed by a succession of terraces rising up to the inland plateau. The beach is shingle, but, apart from the absence of sand, Stonehaven has everything needful for a seaside holiday resort giving access to a charming rural hinterland. It has an attractive golf course on the grassy shelf along its northern cliffs; a splendid, heated open-air swimming pool; a large caravan site; plentiful recreation grounds; many fine hotels and boarding-houses; and a friendly intimacy that would be impossible in a larger resort.

Stonehaven is really an amalgam of two towns – on the one hand, the Old Town round the harbour S. of the Carron, and immediately under the shadow of the massive old red sand-stone cliffs of Downie Point; and, on the other, the New Town stretched out on the little plain and the terraces between the Carron and the Cowie, with Cowie Village (on the N. of Stonehaven Bay) and its tiny harbour and rows of fisher cottages. The Cowie Village of today, picturesque "sea-toun" though it be, can have little relation to the original Cowie of the Middle Ages. It is a comparatively modern settlement. The old Cowie, it is claimed, was created a royal burgh by David I.

Stanehyve was the creation of that great master of towns and castles, George, 5th Earl Marischal, who also founded PETERHEAD. He had Old Stonehaven erected into a burgh of barony, which despite vicissitudes it remained until, in 1880, it was united with New Stonehaven, founded by Robert Barclay of Ury in 1797, to form the modern police burgh. It was this Earl Marischal, too, who built as a store-house the Old Tolbooth at the harbour, which is the town's most precious link with its first beginnings. It is situated at the base of the N. pier of the harbour, and, when recently restored, it was opened by the Queen Mother as a museum and tea-room. The picturesque old building on the quay, with its crow-stepped gables, has looked out on all the most famous incidents in Stonehaven's colourful history. Like Cowie, Stanehyve was put to the flames by Montrose in 1645. In the '15 Rising, the Old Chevalier passed through Stonehaven and was proclaimed King as James VIII at the door of Fetteresso Castle, on the 2nd of January 1716. Then again, in the '45, James VIII was proclaimed at the Cross of Stonehaven by the Procurator Fiscal of the day.

It was this same man, incidentally, who in the Old Tolbooth itself, then in use as a court-room and prison, superintended the branding of a woman and the baby at her breast with a red-hot iron. He was shot in the leg while escaping from CULLODEN, but was ultimately pardoned and resumed business as a lawyer in Stonehaven.

In 1748 three Episcopal clergymen from Stonehaven, Drumlithie, and MUCHALLS were tried and imprisoned in the Tolbooth for six months. During this period fishermen's wives from the havens along the coast were often seen trudging along the sea-beach with creels on their backs; in them were concealed babies to be christened by the jailed pastors through the stanchioned window of the Tolbooth. The scene at one of these christenings was depicted by the "literary painter" S. W. Brownlow in a famous canvas of 1865. Since this incident the Tolbooth has become something of a shrine to the Scottish Episcopal Church. They took part in its recent restoration, and one of its rooms has become a "Church Room".

At the end of the High Street in the Old Town stand the mercat cross and 18th-cent. town steeple with its Dutch roof. Old houses in its immediate neighbourhood had to be demolished, but they have been replaced by a new housing scheme specially designed to retain the ancient character of this part of the town.

The Barclays of Ury bought the estate of Arduthie for £1,500 in 1759. The site of the future New Town of Stonehaven was then largely moor-covered, with short heath, furze, and broom. To encourage settlers on a "New Town" on the N. bank of the Carron, feus, each ⅛ acre, were given off in perpetuity. Real progress came in the first two decades of the 19th cent., when the Old Town's harbour was much improved and herring fishing began. The New Town of Stonehaven has a very pleasant tree-lined square, where the Market Buildings were erected in 1827, surmounted by a steeple 130 ft high. The Town Hall, in Allardyce Street, dates from 1878. Mackie Academy, the outstanding secondary school in the county, dates from 1893.

Stonehaven, like BURGHEAD and LERWICK, has its traditional mid-winter fire-festival. It takes place at midnight on Hogmanay, the 31st of December, and ushers in the New Year. It consists of a march by the young men of the town, swinging fire-balls in the High Street. The fire-balls are carefully made according to an old recipe, and vary in size from a football to one twice as big. They consist of combustible materials encased in a sphere of wire-netting, and are swung round their heads by the marchers who promenade up one side of the High Street and down the other. The whole operation is a highly skilled performance, for which the actors are specially trained, and it seldom results in any casualties.

A small number of line fishermen still operate from Stonehaven, but the tendency is for the harbour to become the domain of pleasure craft; and, indeed, it is ideally suited to this purpose. Yachting and water skiing are now being developed here.

STONEHOUSE, *Lanarkshire* (Map 2, ref. 27⁵64⁷). Some 18 m. SE. of GLASGOW, but close to the new M74 Motorway, this previously farming and weaving township was in 1971 designated a New Town to join in Lanarkshire's rapid development as one of the key growth areas of Britain. The small population up to then found work either in the local hospital or in MOTHERWELL and WISHAW.

STORNOWAY, *Ross and Cromarty* (Map 4, ref. 14²93⁴), the port and capital town of the Island of LEWIS in the Outer Hebrides (*see* "The Shape of Scotland"). Situated about half-way up the E. coast of Lewis, this harbour town is the only example of a town purely Gaelic in its making and not one imposed by incomers. It is true that its finely protected position in tempestuous seas made it an

Stornoway from Gallows Hill

J. L. Rodger

Scottish Tourist Board
Night in Stornoway Harbour

obvious rallying point for Norse invaders, and for any who wished to take over the Western Isles, but there is no evidence that anyone except the native Lewismen established a town there, in our sense of the word today. The famous Highland chiefs, the Mackenzies of Seaforth, were lords of the island, and had their castle at Stornoway, but there was no town.

After the Norsemen the "Fife adventurers", a band of officially encouraged buccaneers, attempted in the 16th and 17th cents., but ignominiously failed, to take over Lewis and Stornoway. Later, Cromwell's troops, during the Commonwealth subjugation of Scotland, battered down the castle at Stornoway and garrisoned the present site. No town, however, arose as a result of these incursions, and, by the end of the 17th cent., Martin Martin, in his *A Description of the Western Islands of Scotland*, talks of Stornoway as a village.

The troubled state of the Highlands in the first half of the 18th cent. did not encourage town-building there; and it was not till the peace of the later Georgian era that the Lewismen began at their famous port to build a town for the future. This is manifest in early prints and in certain graceful Regency touches in the older parts of Stornoway, particularly the pleasing Regency stairways reminiscent of EDINBURGH's New Town. For the most part, Stornoway has outlived this gracious legacy. And why not? She has grown and adapted herself in the changing decades to her changing circumstances, and has always, in prosperity and adversity, remained hopeful for the future. The life of Stornoway, Lewis's single town, is mingled with the fortunes of the island.

(Much that could be said about the town has already been touched on in the entry describing Lewis. Here let us consider the appearance and character of the town today.)

At the head of a narrowing, well-protected bay, opening to the SE., Stornoway is pre-eminently a harbour. That harbour is divided by a small peninsula, on both sides of which are wharves and quays. High above the harbour to the NE. is the castle built in the 1840s in baronial style by Sir James Matheson. The castle is surrounded by a well-wooded park. Castle and park were donated to Stornoway by the late Lord Leverhulme when he left the island (*see* LEWIS). The park is worthy of a big city. The castle is now a technical college teaching those crafts and sciences suitable to Lewis – navigation, engineering, and weaving.

Education is of prime interest to Stornowegians; on the other side of the town is the well-known Nicolson Institute founded in the mid-19th cent. It exists to help young scholars to bridge the gulf between primary schools and the universities. The Stornoway people have made the Institute for themselves and have much regard for it. It is a notable example of self-help, in the best sense.

The modern town, which lies below the castle and between the two beaches of the peninsula, is lively. English predominates, but Gaelic is always beneath the surface. An internationally famous store has a branch in Stornoway that, on the days when people come in from the country for shopping, turns into something of a Gaelic "ceilidh-house". There are hotels, cafés, restaurants, and guest-houses, with a few licensed premises perhaps unfortunately concentrated in this one spot on this large island.

The most prominent thoroughfare is now, oddly enough, named Cromwell Street, after the man who battered down the old Seaforth Castle and garrisoned the site with foreign soldiery. It is a shock to learn that at an unspecified date the name was changed from Dempster Street. George Dempster was the enlightened Scot who did so much for our fisheries at the end of the 18th and the beginning of the 19th cents. Why not change the name back again to Dempster Street? It would be an act of grateful patriotism on the part of the citizens of Stornoway.

There is a modern hospital. The shops of the northern town are well-stocked and up-to-date. The most go-ahead and important tweed-mill in the islands is in Stornoway – a fascinating place of Gaelic industry to visit. Industry within the mill combines with peasant industry in the croft. The hotels cater comfortably for the visitor. There is a daily boat and air service to the town from the mainland. There are a good many well-known churches of the Kirk of Scotland and of the free denominations. There is an Episcopal and a Catholic church. In the streets of Stornoway (as has been mentioned in Lewis), you may occasionally hear other tongues than English and Gaelic.

Stornoway is sometimes called remote. But remote from what? It is in constant touch with the outer world. There is a great difference between retaining your individuality and being, in the pejorative sense of the word, remote.

Stornoway in that sense is not remote. It is self-sufficient, bustling, individual, and more in touch with the world than many a sleepy mainland town twice its size.

STORR, *Inverness-shire* (Map 4, ref. 14⁹85⁴), a mountainous ridge on the Island of SKYE, in the Inner Hebrides (*see* "The Shape of Scotland"). The northern peninsula of Skye, Trotternish, has as its backbone a 10-m.-long ridge known as Storr. Its most famous feature is the 160-ft pinnacle of rock, standing by itself, and known because of its fantastic shape, as the Old Man of Storr. The whole ridge, however, is well worth exploring for its fine views. The Storr lochs are now connected with the hydro-electric scheme.

STOW, *Midlothian* (Map 3, ref. 34⁶64⁵), is an attractive village, beautifully situated on the GALA WATER 5 m. NNW. of GALASHIELS in the most southerly part of the Lothians. To the E., a delightful road crosses the moors, climbing to 1,100 ft before descending into Lauderdale. To the W. of Stow are the lonely Moorfoot Hills, and a little farther S. rises Windlestraw Law, near the point where the counties of Midlothian, Selkirkshire, and Peeblesshire meet.

The parish, once known as the Stow of Wedale, has a wealth of antiquities, of which many are preserved. The name Wedale derives from the old race-name Goidel, or Vale of a Goidal, and here tradition tells how Arthur routed the Saxons. A more doubtful tradition was that Arthur brought a fragment of the true cross to Stow, but what seems more certain is that he founded a church that contained a highly venerated image of the Virgin Mary. The site of this original Chapel of Our Lady is under the historic seat of Torsonce, S. of the town near the Lady's Well. The old Church of Saint Mary is a ruin near the centre of the village; it was consecrated in the year 1242, and has a round-headed Romanesque doorway and a second pointed W. window. The oldest gravestone dates from the year of the Restoration, 1660, when a built-up window on the N. wall was also constructed. The modern church is a fine example of 19th-cent. Gothic with a spire 140 ft high. Opposite the church is the graceful span of one of the three remaining pack-horse bridges in Scotland, so called because of the low parapet built to prevent the pack-horses from going over the side.

About 1 m. S. of Stow, standing on level ground on the brink of a steep descent to the Gala Water, stands the broch known as Bow Castle. It is one of the ten TAY–TWEED brochs; the other two in South Scotland are Torwoodlee (2 m. away, but still in Stow parish) and Edinshall in Berwickshire. Bow Broch was originally formed by a wall 15 ft thick, surrounding a court 31 ft in diameter. Now the ruin of the wall is surmounted by a

tall modern cairn built out of the debris. The structure was excavated in 1890, when pottery, including some Roman pieces, was found. In 1922 a SELKIRK antiquary found an enamelled Roman-British bronze brooch in the form of a cock amongst the ruins of the wall. These and other small finds may be seen in the National Museum of Antiquities in EDINBURGH.

STRACATHRO, *Angus* (Map 6, ref. 36²76⁵), now a peaceful parish in the douce land of Angus, has seen much warfare and some momentous events in our history. Fordoun, the Scottish chronicler, deals with it mostly as a battleground. According to him, in 1130 Angus Earl of Moray, who had a claim upon the crown arising out of the Celtic law of succession, crossed the GRAMPIANS with an army of 5,000 men, and lost 4,000 of them when met and defeated at Stracathro by the army of David I.

In 1296 at Stracathro church, John Baliol paid homage to Edward I and was deprived of his independence. This was to lead subsequently to the wars culminating at BANNOCKBURN. In 1452 at Huntly Hill, on the Hill of Stracathro, "Earl Beardie", the "Tiger Earl" of Crawford, was defeated by the loyal clans under the Earl of Huntly. A large boulder on Huntly Hill is said to mark the spot where Huntly's standard was raised.

STRACHUR, *Argyll* (Map 2, ref. 21⁰70¹), is a small resort on the Cowal peninsula possessing a pier and facilities for holiday-makers. About 1 m. to the NW., the road from Strachur leads inland to Loch Eck, a long narrow loch surrounded by hills; the highest being Beinn Bheula (2,557 ft) to the NE., and Beinn Mhor (2,433 ft), which overlooks the W. shore of the loch.

Strachur was the ancient seat of the family of MacArthur Campbell, whose estates included ARDGARTEN, Glenfalloch, and Glendochart. General John Campbell in 1783 built a mansion-house in Strachur Park to replace his former home at Succoth. In 1897–8 the estates were sold.

Agriculture is the main occupation of the district; the Forestry Commission have acquired the largest farms, and afforestation gives local employment. There is also sawmilling and woodworking industry ranging from garden furniture to "Argyll" bungalows.

STRAITON, *Ayrshire* (Map 2, ref. 23⁸60⁵), is a charming agricultural village on the edge of the hill country 15 m. SE. of AYR on the Girvan Water. The land is fertile and well farmed, but a mere 3 m. S. it merges suddenly with bleak inhospitable moorland. This has, however, been largely taken over by the Forestry Commission, and the hill road into Galloway past Rowantree traverses an extensive forest. In the few clearings may be seen herds of the hardy Galloway cattle which thrive in these parts. The village is notable for its fine old parish church, parts of which are pre-Reformation, dating as far back as 1350; the silver communion cups were made in EDINBURGH in 1615. Nearby stands the fine mansion house of Blairquhan, on the estate of Sir James Hunter Blair.

One of Sir James's predecessors, his uncle, Sir David Hunter Blair, succeeded to the title in the 1890s and lived well into this century. He was the only baronet ever to be the abbot of a Catholic Religious House in Scotland. The order of baronets was not formed till after the Reformation. Sir David ended his days as the Lord Abbot of the Benedictine Abbey of FORT AUGUSTUS.

STRANRAER, *Wigtownshire* (Map 2, ref. 20⁷56⁰). This royal and municipal burgh at the head of the remarkable natural harbour of Loch Ryan, well placed for trade with northern Ireland, is now a busy seaport with three drive-on, drive-off car ferries plying to Larne in the British Rail Sealink services, the crossing taking just over two hours. But there is ample room in Loch Ryan for other shipping, yachts, fishing boats, small craft and water-skiing. Apart from the great volume of traffic using the ferries, Stranraer is also the marketing centre for a rich agricultural centre. The old town has attractive winding streets, but Stranraer has become one of the most popular seaside resorts in southern Scotland, with numerous hotels and guest houses, an 18-hole golf course, all the other outdoor and indoor sports, trout and sea fishing. There are two fine beaches, and the town caters specially for children with a magnificent marine lake.

The Castle, a structure of the mid-16th cent., commands a fine view from its parapet walk; it was a headquarters of Graham of Claverhouse, and many Covenanters lay and perished in its dungeons. In the 18th and 19th cents. the Castle served as the town gaol.

Craigcaffie Tower, built in 1570, lies 3½ m. NE. of Stranraer, and was a seat of the Neilsons. It is a well-preserved example of its kind, with stone gargoyles; the Neilsons claimed descent from John, son of Neil, Earl of Carrick, to whom the land of Kellechaffe (Craigcaffie) was granted by Robert Bruce.

Corsewall Point lighthouse, 9 m. N. of Stranraer, was built by the grandfather of Robert Louis Stevenson.

STRATHAVEN, *Lanarkshire* (Map 2, ref. 27⁰64¹). Originally a weaving town 7 m. SW. of HAMILTON, Strathaven still makes rayon and knitwear goods. Farm implements are also manufactured in this market town. Dungavel House, formerly a shooting-lodge of the Duke of Hamilton, was a naval hospital during the First World War and, in the later hostilities, a

convalescent depot for the W.A.A.F. It was sold when the family removed to LENNOXLOVE near HADDINGTON, and in July 1951 was opened as the first juvenile residential training centre for miners in Scotland. Dungavel was the place for which Rudolf Hess aimed in his dramatic solo flight during the Second World War.

To the W. of Strathaven stands "Lauder Ha' ", for 15 years the home of the late Sir Harry Lauder.

Avondale Castle, now a ruin, occupies a lofty isolated mound nearly surrounded by the Powmillon Burn. It was built in the 15th cent. by an illegitimate grandson of the 2nd Duke of Albany, who bore the title of Lord Avondale; the castle was designed on the plan of a parallelogram, with two towers at diagonally opposite corners. A fragment of the cornice shows characteristic 15th-cent. work.

STRATHBLANE, *Stirlingshire* (Map 2, ref. 25⁵67⁸). This small resort stands at the foot of the Strathblane Hills and the loftier Campsie Fells, in which Earl's Seat (1,896 ft) is the highest point.

Duntreath Castle, 2 m. NW. near the KILLEARN road, is partly a 15th-cent. castle, in which medieval stocks and dungeons are preserved. The building is quadrangular in plan, with an entrance through the gatehouse on the W. side, one of the most complete and extensive constructions of its kind in Scotland. The gatehouse, a three-storey structure, was built by Sir James Edmonstone, who died in 1618. This is believed to have been the last addition until modern times.

Duntreath, granted to Sir William Edmonstone of CULLODEN by James I about 1434, has remained in the possession of the same family ever since. It was abandoned and allowed to fall into ruin about 1740, but was restored as the family seat in 1857 by Sir Archibald Edmonstone.

The ruin of Mugdock Castle, 2 m. SW., was once the home of the Marquess of Montrose, who was living here before his campaign of 1644. Originally it was large, with a long narrow courtyard area; the remaining entire tower formed only the SE. corner. A large modern mansion in the neo-Scottish baronial style was built in the central area of the enclosure during the last century. Now a complete ruin, it hides traces of earlier work.

Some 3 m. W. of Strathblane at Auchineden on the GLASGOW–DRYMEN road is an A.A. viewpoint and indicator with panoramic views to Loch LOMOND.

STRATHFARRAR, *Inverness-shire* (Map 5, ref. 23²83⁸). The R. Farrar flows through Strathfarrar from the W. to join the R. Glass at Struy, where the joint river becomes the Beauly. Just downstream from Struy is Erchless Castle, dating from the 16th cent. It has been modernized and added to, and was the seat of the chiefs of the Clan Chisholm, but is no longer owned by them. In the 19th cent. there was much emigration from this district.

Strathfarrar is now part of the Affric, Farrar, and Beauly hydro-electric scheme. The main dam is at Loch Monar, W. of Struy, where an unusual arch-type dam is used. There are few of this type in Britain, because the shape of our valleys is seldom suitable for them. The two power stations in the glen are both underground.

STRATHMIGLO, *Fife* (Map 3, ref. 32²71⁰). The village of Strathmiglo, on the R. Eden 5¾ m. W. of LADYBANK, consists of one principal street on the N. side of the river and parallel to it, with four or five wynds running N. and S. On the S. side of the river are two wynds, one known as Cash Feus, which used to house the tradesmen of the village. Part of the place known as Templelands anciently belonged to the Knights Templar, then to the Knights of St John. Burgh feuars still hold the village green on both sides of the river. Originally Strathmiglo had a prosperous hand-loom linenweaving industry; two power factories are still in production, with an export trade to America.

The Castle, which stood a short distance E. of the town, is supposed to have been built in the time of James V, but was removed in 1734 as building material for the steeple in front of the Town House. This is a handsome square tower with an octagonal spire. Here the town did benefit from the Scottish tendency to pull down old buildings to make new.

Balvaird Castle, 3 m. NW., commands a fine view of the Lomonds and the valley of Eden. It was built on a 15th-cent. improved L-plan with a massive keep and square stair-tower, a feature not usually found till a century later. The hall has a fine fireplace and three large stone-seated windows. The aumbry, with late Gothic carved work, is similar to that at BORTHWICK.

STRATHMORE, *Dunbartonshire* to *Kincardineshire* (Map 6, ref. 34⁰75⁰). This great fertile valley, or band of low country, which skirts the frontier of the mountain rampart of the Highlands, lies to the SE. of them, so forming the NW. part of the central Lowlands. The Strath may be said to extend from Ardmore in Dunbartonshire to the North Sea at STONEHAVEN. At first it runs parallel with the R. TAY, and later with its tributary the Isla. Flanked by the Lennox district and the Ochil and Sidlaw hills, it comprehends a part of Stirlingshire, all Strathallan, most of Strathearn, and all the Howe of the Mearns.

In popular speech, however, Strathmore is usually said to extend from METHVEN in Perthshire to near BRECHIN in Angus. This latter region is a rich farming area, noted for arable farms, beef cattle and soft fruit.

Scottish Tourist Board

Strathpeffer

STRATHPEFFER, *Ross and Cromarty* (Map 5, ref. 24⁸85⁸). Until after the First World War, Strathpeffer was a famous spa, whose visitors included a number of foreign royalties. It is now a centre for touring, especially by coach.

The springs – four sulphur and one chalybeate – were known in the North of Scotland by the 1770s, and facilities for visitors were provided at the wells until about 1820, when the first pump-room was built and the place became known outside Scotland. In 1909 a new pump-room was added to the first and the gardens were improved. It was reopened in 1960, and the holiday centre much developed, particularly in facilities for golf, tennis, and dancing.

To the N. of the village stands Castle Leod, the seat of the Earl of Cromartie. The Castle was built on an L-plan, with a deep parapet and with bartizans at the angles, by Sir Rorie Mackenzie of Coigach in 1619. To it a S. wing was added soon after, probably by his son, and a Victorian extension and addition were built on the N. side. The Castle is set in a park with splendid trees, including two Spanish chestnuts planted in 1550 by John Mackenzie of KINTAIL, ancestor of Sir Rorie; the largest of the trees measures more than 36 ft round the base. Highland games are held in the grounds on the first Saturday in August.

Fishing is available on the Conon and the Blackwater.

STRATHTUMMEL, *Perthshire* (Map 5, ref. 29⁰75⁹). Loch Tummel, 8½ m. W. by N. of PITLOCHRY, is formed by the expansion of the river and lies 480 ft above sea-level. A wooded artificial island lies near the foot, with vestiges of a castle on it.

Tummel Bridge, 6½ m. E. of KINLOCH RANNOCH, was built by General Wade on the line of his military road from CRIEFF to Dalnacardoch.

The highest point on the N. side of the road

from Pitlochry to Kinloch Rannoch is called Queen's View; Queen Victoria visited it in 1866. From here is a prospect of almost the entire basin of the river – the river itself, the loch, and a grand array of mountains to the N. and W. in Breadalbane, dominated by the cone of SCHIEHALLION (3,547 ft), with a wooded foreground. It is one of the grandest glen views in the country.

The R. Tummel, issuing from Loch Rannoch through Loch Tummel, runs E. into the loch near Faskally, where it receives a large tributary, the Garry. Above the Garry the Tummel runs through a close and wooded glen, with rapids, cataracts, and cascades; before its confluence, it is a stately stream winding among cornfields and pastures, with many islets. This lower river joins the Tay at BALLINLUIG.

The construction of extensive hydro-electric works at Rannoch and Tummel was authorized in 1922, and was begun soon after. The hydroelectric station at Tummel opened in 1933; the Clunie Dam raised the level of the loch 17 ft and more than doubled its natural length. The ascending salmon pass through forty-three resting-pools, which allow them to surmount the dam.

In 1946 work was started on a further scheme, including a tunnel from Loch Tummel, the water going through a vast horseshoe-shaped tunnel, 2 m. long, to Clunie generating station. Here stands a commemorative arch at the mouth of the tunnel, bearing a bronze plaque in memory of the men who died in the construction. The Falls of Tummel, once a great attraction, are now known as the Linn of Tummel; the reason for this renaming is that the height of the falling water is much reduced by the raising of the water-level in the Faskally reservoir. A pleasant wooded walk along the right bank of the Garry to the junction with the Tummel leads to the Linn, which has been National Trust property since 1944.

STRATHY, *Sutherland* (Map 5, ref. 28⁴96⁴). The village of Strathy, on the headland N. coast of Sutherland, is at the mouth of Strathy Water, 17 m. SE. of THURSO. The village lies a little inland from Strathy Bay, W. of which stretches a peninsula terminating in Strathy Point, with its multitude of caves. On Strathy Point may be found the *Primula scotica*, which grows only along the N. coasts of Sutherland and Caithness, and in ORKNEY, a close rosette of leaves with a short stalk and an umbel of purple-blue flowers.

The most important feature of the place, the lighthouse, was built in 1958 on what was formerly a "dark patch" between CAPE WRATH and DUNNET – the latest lighthouse built in Scotland, and possibly the last that will be built in the country. It is of modern design, with three keepers' houses nearby, connected by covered passages to the main block, which contains a reinforced concrete tower.

STRATHYRE, *Perthshire* (Map 2, ref. 25⁷71⁷). The valley of Strathyre is the subject of the well-known song "Bonnie Strathyre"; the village of that name is not, save for a few good old 18th-cent. Scottish-style stone cottages, "bonnie" in itself, but its circumstances undoubtedly are. In the *Lady of the Lake* country between CALLANDER and LOCHEARNHEAD, on the central northern road into the Highlands, it is bonnily set amongst hills. The attractive Ben of the Fairies rises steeply – but not too steeply for climbing – to the W. Eastwards a slow slope ascends to an eminence with a good view. Farther E. is Stuc a Chrom (3,189 ft), and NE. the well-known Ben Vorlich (3,224 ft) is attainable.

Strathyre village thus lies snugly in a road and river valley, through which passes a good deal of the northward and north-westward Highland traffic. As a pleasing holiday centre, however, it has not in half a century lost its character or its charm. A few late Victorian or early Edwardian houses mingle inoffensively with the honest earlier stone cottages, to remind you that "Bonnie Strathyre" was a favourite holiday centre for our GLASGOW and EDINBURGH forefathers, who wished for an easily attainable spot in the near Highlands where they could get good but not too arduous climbing, boating, or (in the old days) steamer excursions on the larger lochs and some good trout-angling.

The epithets "tantalizing", and occasionally "exciting", should be applied to the angling immediately by Strathyre – in the deep and, for a Highland stream, oddly sluggish R. Balvaig. This abounds in really sizeable brown trout, up to three pounds and more, alluringly visible from the delightful old bridge that crosses the river E. to W. in the centre of the village. Alas, they seldom rise to fly. They can, however, be caught (rather unsportingly) on the worm during a spate; and they do occasionally take the minnow, spinned or trolled in clear water. For those traditional anglers who disclaim the "fixed spool reel", and who refrain from howking them out of the mud of a spate, these large trout are mostly unattainable.

STRICHEN, *Aberdeenshire* (Map 6, ref. 39⁵85⁵). This plain stone village, on the left bank of the North Water of Ugie and at the foot of the Hill of Mormond, has been immortalized in song, and probably most people know of it through the ballad air "Mormond Braes", by far the most popular of over 1,000 bothy ballads collected and published in his lifetime by the late Gavin Greig. Buchan – one of the plainest, sternest regions – has in fact given Scotland something like half its total tally of the traditional balladry of the bothy and the chaumer. When Gavin Greig died, a further anthology of the ballad airs he had collected was published under the editorship of Alexander Keith, and Greig's vast manuscript

"Our Lady of the Isles" by Hew Lorimer, on South Uist (see p. 454)
Paul Shillabeer

collections are preserved in the archives of ABERDEEN University.

The name Strichen derives from Strath Ugin. A succession of bridges span the stream along the western side of the village. The old bridge by the mill is perhaps the most picturesque, with its two shapely arches and its stepped parapet. The village was founded in 1764 by Lord Strichen, Alexander Fraser (1730–75), a Law Lord. He was a crony of Lord Auchinleck, James Boswell's father, and Boswell visited the place at least twice and took Dr Johnson there in 1773.

To the Frasers of Strichen the Hill of Mormond, which rises to only 769 ft but dominates the whole of Northern Buchan, owes two of its landmarks – the ruined hunting-lodge on the summit, and the famous White Horse. This last is a striking figure cut out of the turf and filled in with stones of white quartz, which gleam on the hills SW. flank above the village. The White Horse is said to have been made by Lord Strichen's grandson, a captain in the Dragoon Guards, in commemoration of a white charger that was shot under him in battle. Its length from tip of nose to tail is 162 ft.

The White Stag of Mormond – on the other, the eastern, side of the hill – covers almost an acre. It was laid out in 1870.

On this eastern side of Mormond is the picturesque New Leeds, founded as a linen-spinning village by Lord Strichen's son, and given its name in the hope – only too soon dashed – that it might one day rival Leeds in Yorkshire!

Today, the eastern summits of Mormond bear the outlines of enormous radar telescopes, part of the equipment of a weather station and distant "early warning post", an odd intrusion of the 20th century.

STROME FERRY, *Ross and Cromarty* (Map 5, ref. 18⁷83⁴), was a vital link in the conception of a scenic route up the W. coast: the passage across the mouth of Loch Carron was short, but as the ferry took only six cars there were often long, irritating delays in the tourist season. In 1970, however, a new road was opened on the E. side of the loch, by-passing the ferry and providing a new link up Glencarron by Achnashellach Forest to ACHNASHEEN, and, of course, the road, unlike the ferry, "operates" on Sundays. Overlooking the N. pier of the ferry is a fragment of the ancient Strome Castle. Originally one of the principal fortresses of the W. coast (a stronghold of the MacDonnells of Glengarry), it was destroyed by Kenneth Mackenzie of KINTAIL in 1609. The site commands a fine panoramic view across to SKYE. The road on the N. side, leading to ACHNASHEEN, was built by Thomas Telford, who, in company with the poet Robert Southey in 1819, was the first to travel over it in a wheeled carriage.

STROMNESS, *Orkney* (Map 7, ref. 32⁵00⁹), a town on the Mainland of ORKNEY Northern Islands (*see* "The Shape of Scotland"). It is one of the only five inhabited places in all Scotland's 787 islands that can properly be called a town. It is Orkney's second town after the capital, KIRKWALL. It lies in a sheltered harbour at the W. of the mainland, and is protected by the island of HOY. Not until Orkney had become well-established under the Scottish crown did Stromness achieve its town status. In the mid-17th cent., this port became a trading centre for the Kingdom of Scotland and the Baltic ports. It never succeeded in rivalling the ancient Kirkwall, but, having become established, it remained sufficient unto itself. Save for the ruins of a medieval monastery, there is nothing of great antiquity in Stromness. The town, however, was early enough to build in the Norse way with paved thoroughfares between facing houses, in the style of LERWICK, SHETLAND, and Kirkwall.

There is (as everywhere in Orkney) good trout fishing in the neighbourhood, some good walks, and some pleasant roads for bus or motor-car expeditions. For the leisurely visitor, the main attraction lies in its harbour life, its quaint wynds and old streets that owe something to a recollected Norse tradition and to an acquired Scottish manner reminiscent of EDINBURGH's Old Town and of ABERDEEN. It is 14 m. by road from Kirkwall, with its island airport and seaport connecting Orkney with Shetland.

STRONE, *Argyll* (1 m. S. of BLAIRMORE). The small holiday resort of Strone lies at the headland of Strone Point, which projects between the mouth of the HOLY LOCH and Loch LONG. It looks across to HUNTER'S QUAY, and commands a fine view of Holy Loch and the Firth of CLYDE. It was one of the clachans in this district that developed into sizeable villages entirely because of Victorian GLASGOW's taste for holidays "doon the watter".

The prominent mansion on the height at Stone Point is Dunselma, which was once the residence of the Coats family, the thread-manufacturers.

STRONTIAN, *Argyll* (Map 5, ref. 18²76¹). Some 17½ m. SW. of FORT WILLIAM, the village of Strontian is situated at the mouth of a glen on the N. side and towards the head of the salt-water Loch Sunart. The loch separates Sunart and ARDNAMURCHAN on the N. from Morven on the S. side. From the glen it is possible to climb Ben Resipol (2,774 ft), which rises NW. of Strontian.

In the disruption of the Church of Scotland in 1843 (*see* "Scotland in History"), the inhabitants of Strontian seceded almost to a man, and, when the landlord refused land to build a church, they anchored a "floating church" off

Plate 16   Weaving tartan at the woollen mills, Kilmahog, Perthshire (see p. 463)
Scottish Tourist Board

Scottish Tourist Board

Suilven and hill loch

the shore. First used in 1846, it was later blown ashore, but it continued to be used by worshippers until the Free Church built on land was completed in 1873.

This district, however, is connected with an earlier story, which has relevance to present-day affairs. Early in the 18th cent., Sir Alexander Murray of Stanhope bought land in the neighbourhood to work the local lead mines. These mines also produced mica and felspar. Strontianite was a mineral known as early as 1764, and strontium, a metallic element, was detected in it in 1787, being isolated in 1808 by Sir Humphry Davy. This element, in the form of strontium 90, is present in radio-active fall-out from atomic explosions.

STRUAN, *Perthshire* (Map 5, ref. 28°76⁵). The township of Struan lies 5 m. W. of BLAIR ATHOLL at the junction of the rivers Garry and Errochty. Across the Garry, and on the main PERTH to INVERNESS road, lies the hamlet of Calvine.

Struan (earlier spelt Strowan) Church is the ancient burial-ground of the Robertsons, though more recent chiefs have a burial-ground at Dunalastair near KINLOCH RANNOCH; the early chiefs had their home downstream from the church. The chief of the Robertsons who died in 1749 was, even in Highland Jacobite circumstances, outstanding in longevity and fidelity. Alexander Robertson of Struan fought for the Stuart Cause in 1689 at KILLIECRANKIE under Dundee, in 1715 under Mar, and in 1745 under Prince Charles Edward Stuart.

Glen Errochty had many Robertson homes, including the Georgian mansion of Auchleeks 5 m. W. of Struan, added to an older building with funds earned in the West Indies.

From the head of Glen Errochty a road runs S. over the hill to Kinloch Rannoch, and the remains of a section of General Wade's 18th-cent. road runs N. to the main Inverness road at Dalnacardoch in Glen Garry.

STRUIE HILL, *Ross and Cromarty* (Map 5, ref. 26⁸88⁵) overlooks the DORNOCH Firth, and the inland road from EVANTON to BONAR BRIDGE passing over it rises to about 700 ft where a view indicator gives a panorama of Sutherland as far as Ben More Assynt to the W.

Some 3 m. SE. of the viewpoint is Altnamain Inn, a landmark because it is the only building in a wide stretch of uninhabited moorland.

SUILVEN, *Sutherland* (Map 5, ref. 21⁵91⁸). Who is to say which is the most famous mountain in Scotland? He, however, who has seen Suilven will have no doubt as to which is the most memorable. It is situated on the W. of Sutherland 14 m. SE. of LOCHINVER, rising to a height of 2,399 ft, and stamps itself on the eye – the Sugar Loaf, the Matterhorn of Scotland, the Pillar Hill. The name Suilven is a Norse-Gaelic hybrid, meaning pillar-fell.

The dominating feature of the landscape, Suilven is one of the most remarkable mountains in Britain. Whether seen from the sea off Lochinver (or indeed on a fine day from the Northern Outer Hebrides) or from the head of Strath Oykell, the isolated, strangely-shaped peak is impressive. Although, when seen from the W. or the E., it appears as a cone, it is in reality a long, narrow ridge of about 1½ m. divided into three main peaks, so that, viewed from N. or S., it presents a triple-peaked ridge.

The great rock walls, which drop almost sheer from the summit, are named Caisteal Liath (meaning grey castle) and are tackled only by skilled mountaineers. The more modest climber ascends by the Bealach Mor – the Great Pass. Suilven lies wholly in the Glen Canisp deer forest; its upper reaches are the haunt of ptarmigan, eagles, and peregrine falcons. The view from the summit ranges over a barren landscape of isolated peaks and innumerable small lochs, and on a clear day far out into the Atlantic and over the islands.

Sumburgh Head

SUMBURGH, *Shetland* (Map 8, ref. 44°11°), on the Mainland of SHETLAND Northern Islands (*see* "The Shape of Scotland"), is a hamlet at its extreme S. It is close to the celebrated JARLSHOF prehistoric remains and to the Shetland airport connecting the island county with Scotland. There is a large, well appointed hotel, a 9-hole golf course, and one of Shetland's best brown-trout lochs. The district and the loch in particular is a favourite haunt of bird-watchers. Just S. of Sumburgh Head runs the well-known Roost, a tidal current whose roaring can be heard inland. It used to be a formidable obstacle to sea-travel in the days of small ships.

SUMMER ISLES, *Ross and Cromarty* (Map 5, ref. 19°90⁸). This cluster of islands at the mouth of Loch Broom has a variety of shapes and sizes. There is excellent sea fishing near them, but they are now virtually uninhabited. Some are used for grazing sheep, but most are simply breeding-grounds for seals and birds. Tanera More, Priest Island, and Horse Island were formerly inhabited, and Tanera, Ristol, and Isle Martin had curing stations connected with ULLAPOOL in the late 18th cent. In those days seemingly endless numbers of herring swam in and out of Loch Broom, but, after 1820, catches diminished acutely and the whole curing industry collapsed.

The largest and most fertile of the islands is Tanera Mhor (801 acres), where Dr Fraser Darling, the naturalist, lived for some time. About it he wrote *Island Years*.

Some of the islands can be visited by motor boat from Ullapool or ACHILTIBUIE. The views eastwards towards the rocky mountains of Coigach and southwards towards SKYE and the Torridons are spectacular.

SWEETHEART ABBEY, *Kirkcudbrightshire* (Map 2, ref. 29°56⁵). Known chiefly for the ruined Cistercian abbey, New Abbey or Sweetheart is one of the most beautiful monastic ruins in Scotland. It was founded in the 13th cent. by Devorgilla, Lady of Galloway, wife of John Balliol of Barnard Castle, one of the regents of Scotland. Devorgilla was the granddaughter of David, Earl of Huntingdon, brother of William the Lion, and mother of John Balliol, briefly King of Scotland. The Abbey, built in 1273, was the last pre-Reformation Cistercian foundation in Scotland. The monks came from DUNDRENNAN. Its red sandstone, brought from quarries at CAERLAVEROCK across the Nith estuary, stands out sharply against the greenery and grey granite of its situation in a typically Cistercian sequestered

Sweetheart Abbey

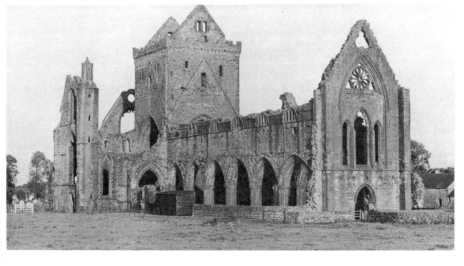

hollow among splendid scenery dominated by the looming mass of Criffel.

In 1289 the foundress was buried in front of the high altar, with the embalmed heart of her husband, which for years had been her "sweet, silent companion", encased in an ivory casket bound with enamelled silver, resting on her bosom. The original monument to Devorgilla seems to have fallen into decay by the 16th cent., when a new one was made, of which fragments were recovered at various times. They were re-assembled and set up in 1933, in the S. transept chapel, in table-form with an effigy.

Picturesque roofless remains (mainly of the 13th and 14th cents.) of the Abbey include the 90-ft central tower, with much of the nave and transepts, and a short aisleless choir that is dominated by a great rose window. A remarkable feature is the well-preserved precinct wall, enclosing 30 acres, and built of enormous boulders. Repeated finds of Iron Age or Dark Age glass beads on the Abbey site suggest an earlier settlement on this spot.

To the NE. is the isolated Abbot's Tower, and a short distance beyond is the estuary of the Nith, on the Solway Firth. The circular Waterloo Tower on Glen Hill stands to the W. To the NE. is the 16th- and 18th-cent. Kirkconnel Tower. Nearby is Shambellie Wood, containing the finest Scots pines in the county.

SYMINGTON, *Ayrshire* (Map 2, ref. 23⁸63¹). A rural and dormitory village, Symington is on the high ground between PRESTWICK and KILMARNOCK, by-passed on the E. by the AYR–GLASGOW trunk road. The village grew up around the fine old Norman church (built in 1160), which once was in the possession of the Friars of Fail. The church was restored in 1919 as a memorial of the First World War, and is open daily for inspection. On the perimeter of the village are various fine residences testifying to its popularity among the business communities of Kilmarnock and Glasgow. Thanks to its comparatively lofty situation, the village commands extensive views of Ayrshire and the Firth of CLYDE.

SYMINGTON, *Lanarkshire* (Map 2, ref. 30⁰63⁵). To the SW. of BIGGAR, this village was formerly a quiet, rural spot on the R. CLYDE, but, when the railway (now closed) came, it was an important junction. The main industry is mixed farming, but there is also tomato-growing on a large scale. In the old Symington, which stretched from Townhead to Townfoot, were many weavers, but weaving is no longer carried on, and most of the weavers' cottages have been pulled down, although a few have been modernized. The village green has, however, now lost much of its attractiveness.

The parish derives its name from Symon Loccard, progenitor of the Lockharts of Lee,

who appears to have founded its church in 1153–65. The village lies at the foot of Castle Hill, the site of an old castle of which only a few stones remain.

Just W. of Symington rises Tinto Hill, a famous landmark; from its summit the Lake District in England and the coast of Northern Ireland can be seen. On a spur projecting from the SE. skirt of Tinto lie the remains of Fatlips Castle.

The wife and mother of Dr John Brown (*Rab and His Friends*) are buried at the E. end of the parish church.

TAIL OF THE BANK, between *Renfrewshire* and *Dunbartonshire* (off GREENOCK), is the familiar name for the stretch of water at the end of the sandbank that runs down the CLYDE from DUMBARTON to Greenock.

This world-famous anchorage was especially important during the Second World War, when floating cranes, mobile grain-elevators, and several hundred London dockers moved to the many remote corners of the Clyde estuary. From here the liners *Queen Mary* and *Queen Elizabeth* ferried more than a million fighting men to and from all parts of the world.

TAIN, *Ross and Cromarty* (Map 5, ref. 27⁸88¹). This ancient royal burgh standing on the shores of the DORNOCH Firth has always been closely associated with St Duthac, who was born here about A.D. 1000. After his death in Ireland his relics were returned to Tain, which became a place of sanctuary and pilgrimage. It was in this shrine that the wife, sisters, and daughter of King Robert Bruce were captured by the traitorous Earl of Ross, who delivered them to the English. The shirt of St Duthac was reputed to possess magical properties, but these seem to have disappeared by the time it was worn by Hugh, Earl of Ross, at the Battle of Halidon Hill in 1333, when he was fatally wounded. King James IV regularly visited Tain on pilgrimage, and for that reason the road leading to the S. is still called King's Causeway. The town Collegiate Church was built in 1371, and its tolbooth in the 17th cent., but this last was restored in 1730 after suffering gale damage. It houses a curfew bell, which can still be heard. It was cast in 1630 by Michael Burgerhuys, a Flemish master founder.

Tain is the trading centre of a prosperous agricultural district, as well as a holiday resort. From it one can obtain magnificent views of Caithness and Sutherland to the N., while golf and sea and fresh-water angling and bathing may all be enjoyed in its neighbourhood.

A large expanse of sandy links known as Morrich More lie to the NE. of the town on the shore of the Dornoch Firth.

TALISKER, *Inverness-shire* (Map 4, ref. 13⁸83⁰), is the name of a bay, a district, and a distillery on the Island of SKYE in the Inner Hebrides (*see* "The Shape of Scotland"). Talisker Bay and the hamlet lie on the W. coast of central Skye, just S. of Loch Harport. The celebrated Skye distillery bearing the name Talisker is farther inland by the village of Carbost. The scenery here, just N. of the CUILLIN Hills and within sight of sea and loch, is characteristic of central Skye. Talisker district provides memorable expeditions for walking and climbing. The name Talisker, far from Skye and upon a friendly bottle of the Skye distillation, may revive such memories for many a visitor.

TALLA RESERVOIR, *Peeblesshire* (Map 3, ref. 31¹62²). An artificially-formed loch E. of the village of TWEEDSMUIR, Talla Reservoir was completed in 1905 and occupies a long narrow depression, which clearly had been an ancient lake. It provides the EDINBURGH water supply, and also brown-trout fishing.

Along the N. shore runs the hill road from Tweedsmuir to ST MARY'S LOCH.

TANTALLON CASTLE, *East Lothian* (Map 3, ref. 36⁰68⁵). This famous, rugged yet rose-coloured ruin of a castle greets the traveller from the south soon after he crosses the eastern Border, and proclaims in stone the essence of Scotland. To "ding doon" (destroy) Tantallon Castle is in popular speech put forward as the height of impossibility.

The Castle stands in a magnificent situation on the coast opposite the BASS ROCK, not far from NORTH BERWICK; and, though it is not strictly visible from the main road out of England into Scotland by EDINBURGH, it is well worth the visitor's time to make the short detour by North Berwick and DIRLETON to see Tantallon from its cliffs, facing the Bass Rock and rivalling it.

One feature of the Castle is a frontal curtain wall, flanked by round towers with an im-

posing central gatehouse; it dates from the 14th cent. and, though it is a ruin, it is a standing triumphant ruin, quite different from the mouldering fragments that sometimes pass for ruined castles elsewhere in Scotland. The rose-colour that is so striking an element in it comes from the East Lothian stone used in so many buildings here.

Tantallon was a stronghold of the Douglas family, and withstood many sieges until, in 1651, it was dismantled by General Monk during the Cromwellian occupation. Dismantled it may have been, but behind it its extensive earthworks (some dating from 1526) still remain uniquely, one might almost say impregnably, impressive.

TAP O' NOTH, *Aberdeenshire* (Map 6, ref. 34⁷82⁹). There must be few villages in Britain that enjoy a more spectacular situation than Rhynie, "at the foot o' the Tap", the "Tap" being the superb shapely cone of the Tap o' Noth (1,851 ft), a mountain that, but for its more remote situation on the extreme western fringe of Aberdeenshire, would easily eclipse BENNACHIE itself for memorable gracefulness of outline. Visible from the sea 30 m. away, it extends, with its prolonged NE. shoulder known as the Hill o' Noth, for 3 m., sheltering both the village and the vale of the Bogie from northern blasts. On the summit of the Tap is the second-highest fort in Scotland. Heavily vitrified, its immense rough rampart of loose and fused stones encloses a turfy oval basin of nearly an acre – "into which", we are told, "men and women with their families and cattle must have rushed in hot haste as the beacon fires upon it signalled the coming foe". The fort is now the property of the Forestry Commission, and within it is a constantly manned fire-watch post to keep guard on the 12,000 acres of planted timber in the Clashindarroch Forest in the Kirkney Valley on the E. side of the hill.

The village of Rhynie, with a population of about 400, is spread out along A97, the strategic highway from Donside to HUNTLY that runs through the deep geological fault known as the Rhynie–Lumsden Gap, caused by the uneven weathering of a wedge of old red sandstone. It has one superb focal point, the beautiful square, in reality a spacious village green whose grassy tree-shaded expanse is backed by the fine tower of the parish church.

In the Jacobite Rising, Rhynie gave of its men lavishly to support the "rightfu' king". During the '45 it sent much provision to feed the Prince's army. In 1746 a party of Cumberland's horse was detached to annex the belongings of these Upper Strathbogie Jacobites. But the villagers, led by the farmer of Milltown of Noth, whose sons were with the Highland army, removed the stepping stones at the ford in front of the village and set up such formidable barricades that the Hanoverian cavalry,

Tantallon Castle
Ministry of Public Building and Works

fearful of an ambush, wheeled about and galloped off, leaving Rhynie alone.

A short distance to the S. of Rhynie is the ancient castle of Druminnor, a storeyed 15th-cent. "palace house" of the Lords Forbes, restored in 1960-6 by the Hon. Margaret Forbes-Sempill, who created a museum in one of its vaulted basement rooms: it is open to the public on summer Sunday afternoons.

TARBERT, *Argyll* (Map 1, ref. 18⁶66⁸). This seaport village (not to be confused with TAR-BET, Dunbartonshire, or TARBERT on HARRIS), stands at the head of Loch Tarbert and separates that sea-loch from the other sea arm, Loch Fyne. It thus stands at the N. end of the long promontory of Kintyre. It was once a prosperous herring-fishing port, but the fishing has declined. Boat and yacht building continued in this good anchorage.

Tarbert joins Kintyre to Knapdale. Tradition has it that at the end of the 11th cent. Magnus Barefoot, son of King Olaf of Norway, dragged his ships across the isthmus, thus claiming Kintyre as an island–one of the Hebrides–and consequently at that date a Norse possession. Kintyre did remain Norse until after the Battle of LARGS in 1263.

The castle at Tarbert is the last of a series dating probably from James IV's visit to the Western Highlands and Islands in 1494.

Dun Skeig is a fort and dun on the SE. shore near the mouth of W. Loch Tarbert. This fort is oval, with a vitrified wall, the dun being 50 yds NE. of the fort, 45 ft in diameter, within a wall about 13 ft thick.

TARBERT, *Inverness-shire* (Map 4, ref. 11⁵90⁰), is a small town and port on the Island of HARRIS in the Outer Hebrides (*see* "The Shape of Scotland"). Harris's chief township lies at the constricted isthmus that connects North Harris with the southern end of the island. It is a pleasant little place, with white-washed houses reminiscent of the mainland.

Tarbert is the embarking place for the car-ferry service from the mainland via SKYE. It is also visited by a regular steamboat that touches at the Southern Outer Isles.

TARBET, *Dunbartonshire* (Map 2, ref. 23³70⁴). This Tarbet (not Tarbert) is a township on the W. shore of Loch LOMOND at the point where the road to INVERARAY crosses the narrow neck of land to ARROCHAR.

The population was increased when houses were put up by the North of Scotland Hydro-Electric Board for their maintenance staff on the SLOY scheme.

As has been described under Arrochar, this Tarbet was the scene of an astonishing feat when, before the Battle of LARGS, some Norse-men dragged their ships overland into the fresh water of Loch Lomond and ravaged the interior of Scotland.

TARBOLTON, *Ayrshire* (Map 2, ref. 24³62⁷), is a rural mining village on the same ridge of ground as SYMINGTON but lying a little farther SE. Tarbolton is known for its association with Robert Burns, who from 1777 to 1784 lived and worked with his father at Lochlie Farm some 3 m. away. Burns spent much of his free time at Tarbolton, and it was here, in 1780, that he founded his famous Bachelor's Club, now owned by the National Trust for Scotland, and here also, in 1781, that he became a Freemason. Tarbolton provided many of the scenes and characters for his earlier works, of which, perhaps, the most notable is "Death and Dr. Hornbook", a satire on the village dominie turned doctor.

TARLAND, *Aberdeenshire* (Map 6, ref. 34⁸80⁴). Between the valleys of the DON and the DEE, about midway on their journey east-wards to the sea from the CAIRNGORM massif, lies a pleasant and fertile vale called the Howe of Cromar. At its centre is the old-world village of Tarland, an ancient kirk-town of very modest dimensions with a long history.

The core of the economy of the region today lies in the 8,500 acres of the MacRobert Trust, a complicated organization comprising 2,500 acres of the MacRobert farms, 2,600 acres of let farms, 1,700 acres of woodland, and 1,700 acres of hill. The MacRobert farms have now four pedigree herds – Aberdeen-Angus, British Friesian, Highland, and Galloway – as well as two important flocks of sheep, 1,000 Black-face and 700 Greyface. Sheep are no new-comers to the Howe, for the very name Cromar derives from the Gaelic words meaning the sheepfold of Mar. This Mar, it is thought, was the name of an ancient Celtic deity, and so, in the midst of the 20th-cent. bustle of intensive agriculture, there is a link with the remote past in this sheepfold of the god.

On the fold of land overlooking the village from the S., a Ministry of Public Building and Works' notice-board points the way up a shaggy knoll to the stone circle of Tomnaverie. When, slightly breathless, you reach this double ring of monoliths and feel the breezes from Byron's "Morven of Snows" play upon your face, you are standing on anciently hallowed ground. This is classic country for stone circles. There are over 200 of them in Aberdeenshire alone, and three distinct types have been dis-tinguished. The one at Tomnaverie is said to have been the burial place of a Bronze Age "master race" who lorded it over the indi-genous peasant population of the Howe. The chieftains of the tribe would have been interred here amid rituals of purification by fire.

The village has a quiet central square with good shops and a homely and very popular hotel. At the E. end of the square is the kirk-yard, with the remnants of the old parish church dedicated to St Moluag. It is one of a chain of sites associated with the saint, stretching from DUFFTOWN, through the CABRACH to Clova, near LUMSDEN, and thence via Tarland southwards over the Capel Mounth into STRATHMORE. The handsome modern parish church stands on a site some distance to the E.

The House of Cromar, once the home of the Marquess of Aberdeen, passed in 1934 to the MacRobert family who had taken over the estate in 1918. Sir Alexander MacRobert went as a youth from ABERDEEN to India, where he became a leader of industry, and on returning to this country he settled at Douneside. On his death in 1922, his eldest son Sir Alasdair succeeded in the baronetcy. He was killed in a flying accident in 1933, and his brother Sir Roderick succeeded him. He too was killed in action with the R.A.F., in 1940, and Sir Ian, Lady MacRobert's third and last airman son, was killed four weeks later. Lady MacRobert's gift of four Hurricane aircraft and a Stirling Bomber in memory of her sons, was followed in 1943 by the turning over of the House of Cromar, now known as Alastrean House, as a "guest and rest house" for serving and former officers of the R.A.F. It is still maintained by the MacRobert Trust for this purpose.

TARVES, *Aberdeenshire* (Map 6, ref. 38⁷83¹). This modest village some 16 m. NNW. of ABERDEEN is approached through rather bare, gently undulating, and intensely cultivated countryside where the only outstanding landmark is the Prop of Ythsie, a stern finger of masonry on top of a low hill, which commemorates a local laird. The village itself is arranged round a very large central asphalt square with the old kirk and a war memorial cross at one end. It is the centre of a famous farming area, noted for its Shorthorn and Aberdeen-Angus herds and for large farms, such as Ythsie, where the very latest techniques of mechanical cultivation and animal husbandry are practised.

Some 2 m. S. of the village is one of the most interesting castellated remains in Formartine, Tolquhon Castle, now under the care of the Ministry of Public Building and Works and beautifully set in its wooded dell.

In the beginning it was a stronghold of the Prestons, lords of FYVIE, who, it is believed, built the strong rectangular keep known as the Preston Tower in the early 15th cent. Then it passed by marriage to the Forbes family.

In 1584 William Forbes, the 7th laird of his line, employed Thomas Leper or Leiper, the master mason who also built the House of Schivas and Arnage Castle near ELLON, to create the great quadrangular mansion that makes so fascinating a ruin at the present day. It is roofless, but otherwise in a very good state of preservation.

Little more than 1 m. due N. of Tarves, the road forks at the entrance gates to the great wooded estate of Haddo, the ancestral home of the earls and marquesses of Aberdeen. The Haddo estate forms an extensive oasis in the midst of a treeless land along the S. bank of the R. Ythan, with many plantations and fine parkland, including three lakes, and is centred by Haddo House, built 1731–5 to designs by William Adam for the 2nd Earl.

The house stands on the site of the former mansion, the Place of Kellie, destroyed by the Covenanters in their venom against Sir John Gordon of Haddo, the Royalist who was the first man to be legally condemned and executed in EDINBURGH for his loyalty to King Charles during the Civil War. His son, Sir George, was restored to his ancestral lands by Charles II, created Lord Haddo and, after becoming Chancellor of Scotland, the 1st Earl of Aberdeen.

Although the main façade of the house, with its classical central block and wings, is substantially an Adam creation, there have been changes, largely made in 1878 by C. R. Wardrop. These – wrote Ishbel, Lady Aberdeen – "included the introduction of bathrooms (a matter of no little difficulty when some of the walls were four or five feet thick) . . . a front hall, and a central inside staircase, the original architect having adopted the Italian idea of approaching the reception rooms on the first floor by means of stone stairs outside. This plan proved distinctly unsuitable to the Scottish climate and tended moreover to cause confusion to guests arriving from a distance, who suddenly found themselves ushered into the drawing-room with all their wraps, through what appeared to be a window."

In the long dining-room, now used only for special occasions, Gladstone, Rosebery, and many more of the great and famous sat down to dine serenaded by Andrew Cant, the Haddo House piper. The Haddo House chapel, designed by Sir George Street, was opened in 1881.

The chapel now plays a major part in the activities of the Haddo House Choral Society, led by the chatelaine, Lady Haddo, whose husband, David Gordon, Lord Haddo, is the present laird.

TARVIT HOUSE, *Fife* (Map 3, ref. 33⁹71⁴). On the Hill of Tarvit is a mansion house overlooking the Howe of Fife. The original house was built in 1696 with additions made throughout the centuries culminating in the renovation by Sir Robert Lorimer in 1906 when the owner, Mr F. B. Sharp, wanted to house his art collection there. The property, including the furniture, paintings, tapestry, and porcelains, was bequeathed to the National Trust for Scotland in 1949. The house was leased in 1952 to the Marie Curie Memorial Foundation as a convalescent home.

TAY, Loch, *Perthshire* (Map 2, ref. 27⁰74⁰), is a magnificent Highland loch lying at an altitude of 355 ft above sea-level. Surrounded by mountain scenery, it is dominated from the W. by BEN LAWERS, which rises to a height of 3,984 ft. The loch is 15 m. long, 1 m. wide at the greatest breadth, and 508 ft deep. The main road follows the N. shore, but the secondary road on the S. shore is more picturesque and commands fine views.

There are several wooded islands, particularly at the eastern end of the loch; the largest, Eilean nam Ban or the Island of Women, is ¼ m. from KENMORE Bridge. It is joined to the mainland by a causeway now under water. Sybilla, wife of King Alexander I, died here in 1122 and is said to be buried on the island. After her death Alexander gave the island to the monks of SCONE Abbey near PERTH, and decreed that a chapel should be built on it. Today ruins are visible from the adjacent road.

Spey Island, opposite Kenmore pier, is artificial and is possibly prehistoric in origin. When Queen Victoria visited TAYMOUTH CASTLE in 1842, the Earl of Breadalbane added stones to the island, thereby greatly increasing its size, and planted trees on it. The stakes that supported the gangway over which the additional material was carried can still be seen between the island and the shore.

Along the northern shore of the loch are many archaeological sites of interest to the prehistorian. Cup-and-ring markings are frequent. The best of these are on a ridge of rock between the road and the loch behind the farmhouse of Craggantoll. On the other side of the road, just before it crosses the Lawers Burn, is a circle of four standing stones with others fallen. This is a burial-place of the Bronze Age.

Loch Tay is noted for its salmon fishing. Some very large fish have been taken from its waters, mostly on the troll. For those who do not favour this type of angling, fly-fishing is an alternative.

TAY, River, *Perthshire* (Map 6, ref. 33²72⁵), is the longest river in Scotland, running a total length of 119¾ m., 15 of which are taken up by its passage through Loch TAY. It rises on the N. slope of Ben Lui, SW. of TYNDRUM, at a height of 2,980 ft above sea-level, and, before joining Loch Tay, flows under the names of Fillan and Dochart. It enters the North Sea below DUNDEE after draining 2,400 sq. m. – the largest catchment area in the country. The chief tributaries are the Ericht, Tummel, Earn, and Lyon.

Until the control of the flow of water by the hydro-electricity schemes on the Tummel and Garry, the river was liable to flood, and floodmarks from 1814 have been recorded on the westernmost pier of the old bridge at PERTH.

The Tay had no road crossing E. of Perth until 1966, when the £4,500,000 toll bridge at DUNDEE was opened by Queen Elizabeth the Queen Mother. With a length of 7,365 ft in 42 spans, including four navigational spans of 230-250 ft, it is the world's third longest con-

crete trestle bridge. It has greatly improved communication between Fife, Angus, and the NE., but with the new trunk road connecting the FORTH Road Bridge direct to Perth most tourist and heavy traffic prefers that route.

The Tay railway bridge, upstream from the road bridge, 3,500 ft longer (and the longest in Britain) was built in 1883-8 to replace the bridge broken in a gale in December 1879 when a train was crossing, with the loss of 90 passengers.

The Tay is one of the best known salmon rivers in Scotland, and to preserve this reputation the North of Scotland Hydro-Electric Board has installed elaborate salmon-ladders in connection with dams on the Tummel, so that the salmon can reach their traditional spawning grounds. There is also good trout fishing in the Tay and its tributaries.

TAYMOUTH CASTLE, *Perthshire* (Map 2, ref. 27⁹74⁶), lies just NE. of KENMORE, and was formerly the seat of the earls of Breadalbane. It is now a school.

The present Castle was erected in 1801 to replace an earlier structure known as Balloch Castle, which was built by Grey Colin, 3rd Laird of Glenorchy, about 1580. The blueish greystone of which the castle is built was obtained locally from quarries above Bolfracks House. In 1842 the W. wing was added for Queen Victoria's visit in that year.

The interior of the Castle was lavishly decorated, and the ceilings of the rooms on the S. front of the main block took over seven years to paint in the style of 14th-cent. illuminated manuscripts, while the panels of the library and adjacent gallery were elaborately carved. The entrance hall resembles a cathedral transept, and the staircase rising from it is in a Gothic style with canopied niches for the display of armoury.

The park is notable for the magnificence of its trees, especially oaks, limes, chestnuts, and larches. In 1847 the then Earl of Breadalbane reintroduced into his park that once native large game bird, capercailzie, from Sweden. In recent years these birds have increased in numbers and are frequently seen in the woods bordering the main road from DUNKELD to ABERFELDY via INVER. The native Scottish capercailzie had died out, possibly in the 18th cent. The Swedish birds were welcome to Scotland, and have flourished; they have bred well and extended northwards far into Inverness-shire. It is said that Lord Breadalbane's introduction of them to his lands and to Scotland was announced from the pulpit of the parish church.

The 18-hole golf course in the grounds of the Castle is open to the public.

TAYNUILT, *Argyll* (Map 1, ref. 20⁰73⁰). The village of Taynuilt, at the place where the Pass of Brander meets Loch ETIVE, is a holiday resort for anglers and climbers of BEN CRUACHAN. It lies across the river from BONAWE. Near Muckairn Church in the village is a monument to Lord Nelson, a large standing stone of unknown antiquity re-erected in 1805 (the year of Trafalgar) by workmen at the Bonawe furnace. This was the first of the many Nelson monuments in Britain and was put up before his burial.

TAYPORT, *Fife* (Map 6, ref. 34⁶72⁸). The burgh of Tayport was originally the ferry port across the Firth of TAY to DUNDEE from the S. With the opening of the Tay Bridge in 1888, it declined in importance. It once had its own harbour and even shipbuilding yards, and salmon fishing and weaving were carried on there. Today it contains a variety of small industries.

The church was rebuilt in 1794, and has a 17th-cent. tower that leans slightly to one side.

TAYVALLICH, *Argyll* (Map 1, ref. 17⁴68⁷), is a tourist holiday centre on a small inlet of Loch Sween, a long sea-loch with many other inlets and islands. It is a sheltered spot suitable for bathing and sailing.

TENTS MUIR, *Fife* (Map 6, ref. 34⁸72⁴). This sandy tract on the Fife coast, in the parish of LEUCHARS, is a nature reserve of 92 acres. The flat terrain lying E. of the main Leuchars-to-TAYPORT road, and extending about 7 m. S. of Tayport towards the Eden estuary, is also known as "Sheughy Dike" on account of numerous ditches.

By tradition, the former inhabitants of Tents Muir were a race of people descended from shipwrecked Scandinavian sailors, their chief occupations being wrecking, smuggling, and poaching. Today the place is practically destitute of human habitation, and is rapidly becoming a sanctuary for wildfowl. Uncommon flora abound; some 350 interesting plants have been listed here. The Forestry Commission has also planted large tracts of land.

The sea here is receding at the greatest rate in the United Kingdom. Consequently, this is an outstanding area for the study of coastal sand accretion and subsequent stages of plant colonization.

TERPERSIE, *Aberdeenshire* (Map 6, ref. 35⁵81⁹). In a little tributary glen of the Suie Burn, N. of ALFORD, stand the round towers and roofless gables of Terpersie Castle, a picturesque Z-plan tower-house, having three gunports in each of the towers at diagonally opposite angles of a crow-step-gabled main block. It was built by William Gordon in 1561, an intruder into the heart of the Forbes country. The 5th and last Laird, George, fought at CULLODEN. He afterwards lay in hiding until he succumbed to the temptation to revisit

his home. A recess in the upper part of the house near the roof was his hiding-place, but it was discovered by the troops sent to hunt him down. He was so skilfully disguised that the soldiers were unsure of his identity. They dragged him before the parish minister, who refused to identify him as the Laird. Then he was taken to a nearby farm where his own children were being lodged. They rushed towards him crying "Daddy! Daddy!", and the unfortunate rebel's fate was sealed. He was executed at Carlisle, after writing a moving farewell letter to his wife.

The road that climbs up the vale of the Suie near Terpersie, and crosses the Suie Hill at a height of 1,281 ft to Kirkton of Clatt, has what is probably the finest view in the North-East of Scotland. At Terpersie itself, the farm that now closely adjoins the castle has been tenanted by the same family, the Lumsdens, for 150 years.

THANKERTON, *Lanarkshire* (Map 2, ref. 29⁷63⁸). The village and ancient parish of Thankerton is on the R. CLYDE 5 m. S. of the CARSTAIRS junction. There is an old toll-house in the village.

The church in Covington, 1 m. away, was a religious site for about 1,000 years, but the present building dates from about the 15th cent. The Covenanter's monument in the churchyard is in memory of Donald Cargill, who suffered death for his cause in 1681.

The camp in Thankerton was originally made for prisoners of war; later it was used for a European Voluntary Workers hostel.

THORNHILL, *Dumfriesshire* (Map 2, ref. 28⁸59⁶), lies in the midst of the fertile basin of mid-Nithsdale, a little E. of the Nith; its broad street is lined with lime trees. In the centre of the town, at the crossroads, stands a column (reduced in height after a storm a few years ago) surmounted by the winged horse of the Queensberry family. This monument was erected in 1714. Near the town, the fine Northumbrian cross at Boatford marks the old ferry and ford. The famous collection of local and foreign natural history, archaeological, ethnographical, and industrial material, made in the middle of the last century by Dr Thomas Boyle Grierson and housed for nearly a century in the Grierson Museum, is now disbanded; part of the collection can be seen at DUMFRIES Museum.

At Dalgarnock, 2 m. S. of Thornhill, is a cross commemorating 57 Nithsdale Covenanters who gave their lives in various parts of the country.

Some 3 m. WSW., the village of Penpont stands on the line of the old pilgrim's track to WHITHORN. On the smithy at Keir, 1 m. SE. of Penpont, is an inscription to Kirkpatrick Macmillan, who was born there, and who invented the bicycle in 1839. The original machine is in the Science Museum in London.

Tynron Doon, a spectacular hill-fort, raises its volcanic profile 1½ m. W. of Penpont, and commands an extensive view from the top.

Some 2 m. NNW. of Thornhill, where the road forks to picturesque Dalveen Pass, is the village of Carronbridge. W. of the village across the R. Nith are the ruins of Tibbers Castle, rebuilt in 1298, garrisoned for the English, and destroyed by Bruce in 1311.

Crichope Linn, about 2 m. E. of Thornhill, is a ravine of great natural beauty in carboniferous rocks, with a natural arch and a deep cauldron.

Drumlanrig, the home of the Duke of Buccleuch, lies 3½ m. NNW. of Thornhill. The present house was built between 1676 and 1689 for the 1st Duke of Queensberry by Sir William Bruce, and nearly ruined the family. The 1st Duke spent only one night there, and then lived at SANQUHAR. The Duke of Buccleuch succeeded to lands and title in 1810. The state rooms are oak panelled, with Grinling Gibbons carving. There are portraits and fine silver, and a chandelier, which was a wedding gift from Charles II to the Duke of Monmouth.

THORNLIEBANK, *Renfrewshire* (Map 2, ref. 25⁸65⁸). Originally a textile village founded in 1778, when John Crum bought a small printing works from a bankrupt linen printer. Thornliebank by the end of the century had added muslin-weaving and other processes to its livelihood. It flourished during the first half of the 19th cent., with a large export trade in printed linen, cotton, and chintz. Walter Crum, son of John, was a noted chemist and a friend of Lord Kelvin. Walter's son Alexander extended the factory and built rows of red brick houses, which are still a feature of the village. With housing and industrial developments, this area is now virtually an extension of Glasgow.

THORNTON, *Fife* (Map 3, ref. 32⁹69⁷). The town of Thornton originated from some small coal pits and a bleach-field. The last of the village pits closed, however, in 1847; but others nearby took over production.

At about the same time railway development in Fife brought to Thornton an importance as a railway junction. It was here that the coastal lines and the main N. route by TAY met. Most EDINBURGH folk who took their holidays in Fife as children have lively memories of Thornton Junction, which now, like so many stations in Scotland, is but a memory.

THREAVE, *Kirkcudbrightshire* (Map 2, ref. 27³56²). This castle in Balmaghie parish, on an islet in the R. DEE in Kirkcudbrightshire, 1¼ m. W. of CASTLE DOUGLAS, was built by the 3rd Earl of Douglas in 1360–70. It consists of a tower four storeys high, enclosed by an outer wall with round towers loop-holed for firearms; this wall dates from 1455, when it was captured by the King's forces in the crisis of that year. It was dismantled after capture by the Covenanters in 1640. Finally it was used to house French prisoners in Napoleonic wars.

The history of Threave Castle was at first bound up with the House of Douglas. From 1455, however, when James II reduced the Douglas strongholds, Threave became a royal castle under various keepers, a part of jointure of Scottish queens. From 1473 until 1526 it was vested in the lords Maxwell as hereditary keepers, and in the 1850s was involved in Maxwell's abortive Spanish-aided revolt (*see* LOCHMABEN).

Threave House is now National Trust property possessing gardens famous for their displays of daffodils. The National Trust School of Practical Gardening has been established there since 1960. Balmaghie parish also includes the hamlets of Glenlochar and LAURIESTON. Amongst the antiquities are Dunnance Mote, which is a natural rocky hillock with signs of stone work and terraces, and Glenlochar Roman Fort.

The parish church, built in 1794, contains Covenanters' graves in its churchyard. A former minister of this parish church was the Reverend James Macmillan who founded the "Reformed Presbyterian Church". From his name a section of the Cameronians called themselves Macmillanites. This was at the very height of sectarianism and the hiving off of small bodies from the main Presbyterian Kirk of Scotland.

There is fishing in the R. Dee and in the nearby lochs of Bargatton, Glentoo, Darnell, Blates, Lochenbreck, and Grenoch; the last of these contains that rarity, the char – the ancestor of all the salmon and trout family.

THURSO, *Caithness* (Map 7, ref. 31²96⁸), is a small town of considerable distinction and interest. It has a splendid natural situation, on the sweep of Thurso Bay, with its wide stretch of sands and guarded at either point by the towering cliffs of Holburn Head and Clairdon Head, with DUNNET Head standing majestically beyond, and across the Pentland Firth the distant cliffs of HOY in ORKNEY. Thurso river flows through the town and into the bay, a long lively stretch of fine fishing water beloved of the salmon and trout fisherman; it has its source and tributaries far inland in the hills and lonely moors, and actually runs through the length of Loch More before it reaches the cultivated plateau of the NE. The town must have been an important centre for the Viking invaders of the coast of Scotland, who gave it the name Thor's-a, literally the river of the god Thor. Their power reached its height in the 11th cent. under Thorfinn, who defeated the army of King Duncan's nephew at Thurso in A.D. 1040.

To the NE. of the town is Thurso Castle, now roofless, home of the Ulbster branch of the Sinclair family. Beyond the castle, Harold's

The Thurso River

Tower, the family burial place, is said to be built over the grave of Earl Harold, who ruled over half of Caithness and half of the Orkney and SHETLAND islands. He fell in battle with Earl Harold the Wicked in the 12th cent.

There are three very clearly defined periods of development to be observed through the architecture of the town. The first is in the old streets near the harbour, where 17th- and early 18th-cent. fishermen's houses have been well restored.

The ruin of St Peter's Church, once the chapel of the bishops of Caithness, is here, with the tracery of one great window still intact. Plans are in hand for some rebuilding and preservation.

The second phase was initiated by that foresighted son of Thurso, born in the castle, and author of so many improvements in the north, Sir John Sinclair. His statue by Chantrey stands in the square named after him, and round it lie broad streets with some delightful examples of early Georgian houses, in what might be described as a worthy northern parallel to EDINBURGH's New Town.

The third phase has been necessitated by the population "explosion", caused by the influx of scientists, technicians, and other workers to the nearby DOUNREAY Atomic Reactor Station. It has led to large modern housing schemes that are being carried out by the United Kingdom Atomic Energy Authority, and parallel schemes by the local authorities. New schools and colleges have sprung up, and in only a few years Thurso has doubled in size without losing head or heart, an achievement for which all concerned are to be congratulated.

Thurso was created a burgh in 1633, and for the next 200 years was virtually the county town, and then WICK became the centre of the law and county administration. The port for large ships is SCRABSTER, which was a vital link for men and material going to SCAPA FLOW during both world wars. The Town Hall

contains a collection of fossils and botanical specimens made by Robert Dick (1811–66), the "Thurso baker" who lived in a house marked by a plaque in Wilson Street. It was he who identified the northern holy grass common in Norway, but in Scotland growing only on the banks of the Thurso river.

Thurso's Regency New Town houses remind one of how Edinburgh's noble experiment in the neo-classical style moved right up the East of Scotland. Edinburgh had derived her inspiration from the Italy of the Renaissance period. The last and most northerly examples of the Italian Renaissance style in architecture may be seen here in Thurso upon the shores of the Pentland Firth, the ultimate seas that touch the mainland of the United Kingdom. The last ripple of the stone thrown into the pool of architectural culture by Michelangelo and Bernini ends on the most northern shores of Scotland.

TIBBERMORE, *Perthshire* (Map 6, ref. 30⁵72⁴). The village of Tibbermore was the country residence of various bishops of DUNKELD from the 13th to the 15th cents.

Its name, however, is more famous in history in connection with the wars of Montrose. It was here, on the 1st of September 1644, that the Marquess met the Covenanters, who were in full strength with 6,000 men. Montrose had only about 2,000 Irish and Highlanders, yet at Tibbermore he reduced his enemy to a rabble. He immediately entered PERTH.

TIGHNABRUAICH, *Argyll* (Map 1, ref. 19⁸67²), in a picturesque wooded setting, is at one of the narrowest reaches of the Kyles of BUTE. It is a popular tourist resort for those who like sailing down the water from GLASGOW, and has a very mild climate said to resemble that of Torquay; tropical plants grow here. It is also a terminal point for some steamer trips.

Scottish Tourist Board

Tighnabruaich

TILLICOULTRY, *Clackmannanshire* (Map 2, ref. 29²69⁷). This pawkily-named town lies at the foot of the Ochils between ALVA and DOLLAR. Paper-making and woollen manufacture are its principal industries, and, like its neighbours, it has the attraction of a pleasant glen running back into the hills – the glen path here leads to the ascent of Ben Cleuch, 2,363 ft, the highest of the Ochils. The remains of an ancient circular fort can be seen on Castle Craig in the Mill Glen; legend has it that those mysterious warriors, the Picts, had a fortification here. It is also alleged that at Tillicoultry St Serf performed miraculous deeds and cures.

TIREE, or more traditionally Tyree, Island of, *Argyll* (Map 1, ref. 10⁰74⁵), is the farthest out of the Inner Hebrides (*see* "The Shape of Scotland"). If SKYE may be said to be springing out of the mainland of Scotland into the Atlantic, Tiree swings out, its farthest point being a good 10 m. W. of Skye's longest leap. Its trend is WSW. to ENE. It is just on 12 m. long, and varies in breadth between ½ m. to 6 m. The island of MULL is, at its nearest point, 15 m. to the E. OBAN, from which it is reached thrice a week by steamer, is about 50 m. directly E. of it. There are also air services to the island. Its nearest neighbour is the adjacent island of COLL to the NE. These two islands form for sea-passengers a lonely but convenient link between the Outer Hebrides and the mainland.

Tiree is easily the flattest of all the Hebrides, and it had a Gaelic nickname that called it the "kingdom whose heights are lower than the waves". Its real name comes from "tir eth", which means a land of corn. It got this reputation from Columban days, when Tiree's flat and comparatively rich surface provided IONA with grain. Today the land of Tiree is less devoted to corn-growing than to crofting and cattle-raising. By long tradition, the men of Tiree are fisherfolk, and take to the sea as easily

as to the land. The island's mild climate and exceptionally high rate of sunshine have, since the early 1950s, encouraged the islanders, and with some success, to experiment in the cultivation and growth of tulip and daffodil bulbs for export to the more inclement mainland.

In recent years, and under the inducement of a regular air service, the island has become attractive to holiday-makers in the W. of Scotland. Those who do not seek exertion and excitement, but who prefer peace, along with occasional golf and fishing, under wide skies and amidst long horizons, will find this sunny, flat island the happy source of what they want. There is a hotel at Scaranish, whose scattered houses form the only township on the island. Some of the inhabitants also take in guests.

Tiree is, like its neighbour Coll, rich in prehistoric duns and brochs, which the original islanders built as small fortresses against invaders from the sea. The best example is Dun Mor Vaul, just W. of Vaul Bay. It measures 35 ft in diameter. Within walls 13 ft thick, galleries and mural cells are apparent. The remote inhabitants of Tiree, even in defence, built to last.

TOBERMORY, *Argyll* (Map 4, ref. 15¹75⁵), is on the Island of MULL in the Inner Hebrides (*see* "The Shape of Scotland"). Capital of the large but not highly-populated Mull island, Tobermory presents an excellent safe anchorage in its bay. This anchorage led to its choice as the site of a fishing station when it was only a small village. In 1788 the British Fisheries Society built at Tobermory a planned village, with streets rising in tiers round the bay. Fishing flourished, and there was also trade in fishing gear and supplies until in the 19th cent. the capricious herring deserted the West. Now that agriculture and the tourist industry supply most of the work here, with tourism in the lead, it is a point of call on the trip to IONA.

Tobermory was undoubtedly the place where

one of the ships of the Spanish Armada was sunk in 1588 – traditionally the treasure ship. There have been several unsuccessful attempts to salvage her.

Some 4 m. NW. is Glengorm Castle, a 19th-cent. building with superb views to ARDNA-MURCHAN and SKYE.

TOLSTA, *Ross and Cromarty* (Map 4, ref. 15⁴94⁸), on the Island of LEWIS, in the Outer Hebrides (*see* "The Shape of Scotland"), a straggling and characteristic North Hebridean village, is rather strikingly out on a limb, though a beautiful one. The promontory has fine beaches and some prehistoric remains. The late Lord Leverhulme (*see* LEWIS), when he was proprietor of the island, built a road from STORNOWAY along the E. coast of Lewis that he intended would reach the Butt of LEWIS. He left the island before it could be completed, and the road peters out into the moorland just beyond Tolsta. The villagers, who live by fishing and crofting, remain deliberately secluded in their mode of life. Most of them are members of the Free Presbyterians (or "secessionists"), who are stricter even than members of the Free Kirk in doctrine and discipline. They are also denser in numbers at Tolsta than in any other place in Scotland, with the possible exception of RAASAY.

On a fine day, the view from Tolsta across the 40 m. of sea to the mainland is one of the most entrancing in Scotland. You may see all the W. coast of Sutherland, with its strangely-shaped mountains, stretched before you from CAPE WRATH down to ULLAPOOL, in Ross and Cromarty. It is well worth the drive out from Stornoway along the lonely road to see it.

TOMATIN, *Inverness-shire* (Map 5, ref. 28⁰82⁹). The main pursuits of the Tomatin district are distilling, and catering for anglers. It is situated on the R. Findhorn 13 m. SE. of INVERNESS.

Surrounded by moorland, Tomatin was once a royal hunting-ground attached to the king's Castle of Inverness.

TOMINTOUL, *Banffshire* (Map 6, ref. 31⁷81⁸). The best-known fact about this village is that, at an altitude of 1,160 ft, it claims to be the highest in the Highlands. Far more important is the fact that it is the only residential centre from which to explore the valley of the Avon. "The Avon", wrote the late Sir Henry Alexander in his guide to the CAIRNGORMS, "regarded from the point of view of river and mountain scenery, is perhaps the most perfect glen in Scotland. . . . It is rash to discriminate among the beauties of such a glen, but not the least attractive scenes are those in the middle reaches where the elder dips its branches in the singing water, and where the oyster-catcher sweeps and cries above the shingle."

Tomintoul was founded by Alexander, 4th Duke of Gordon, in 1779, and was made of local stone – limestone from Craighalkie, freestone from Achriachan and Lynaachork; and it was slated almost completely from Knockfergan Quarry. Most of the houses were built by three generations of the Stuart family of stone masons. The first brick building in the village did not put in an appearance until 1950.

Tomintoul is stretched out on a sandstone ridge on the col between the glen of the Avon and the vale of the Water of Conglass. Its basic form is that of one long single street with a square in the middle, a square that makes the perfect village green, with seats amid a grassy expanse on which visitors can sit and sun themselves within a stone's throw of the four hotels.

The history of the enchantingly beautiful country around Tomintoul – in ancient times the Lordship of Strathavon – is remarkable. Down the centuries, two quite different races of men frequented the area: those who lived on the land, and those who passed through it bent on conquest, plunder, or pacification. Landless men and outlaws "put to the horn" found hide-outs in the remote glens of the Conglass and the Avon and their tributaries long before the murderer Percy Topliss (*see* LECHT) showed what could be done by a refugee from justice in this area in modern times.

By 1377, the Lordship of Strathavon was completely in the hands of King Robert II of Scotland, who granted it to his son Sir Alexander Stewart, the notorious Wolf of Badenoch. In 1490 a grandson of the Wolf gave up most of it to the Gordons.

With brief interruptions, the Gordon family were to hold it for the next 450 years, until in 1935 the Duke of Richmond and Gordon sold the Glenavon estate of 45,000 acres to Col. Oliver Haig. Two years later the remainder of the lordship, including the village of Tomintoul, became Crown lands.

Tomintoul stands high above the actual river valley, where, until the 18th cent., all the human settlement and traffic were concentrated. The middle and lower reaches of the Avon (which is pronounced "A'an") were divided up into many small farms where black cattle were reared, but, because the home pastures were insufficient to feed the herds, each of the farms was allocated by the Gordon overlords a summer shieling high up in the Braes of Strathavon, sometimes as far as 18 m. from the main property. Every summer there was a great migration to these upland pastures. The institutional life of the area was centred round the parish church of Kirkmichael (which still stands on its lovely haugh by the Avon fronting Knockfergan) and the parish school of Tomachlaggan. These places, several miles lower down the valley than Tomintoul, should be visited to savour the lovely setting of a life that is no more. Many crofts and small farms have been amalgamated in the recent past to form larger and more economic units.

The very possibility of a village at Tomintoul was inconceivable until the making of the great military road from the Lecht pass to ABER-NETHY on the SPEY in 1754. The site chosen for the village was at the intersection of this new highway with two older roads – the track down Avonside to BALLINDALLOCH and up Glenavon to Inchrory, and the road over the Conglass to Tomnavoulin and Lower GLEN LIVET.

Although, with the inexorable process of depopulation, the economic importance of this network of roads has dwindled, it offers the visitor to Tomintoul a wonderful variety of routes from which to view some of the finest landscape in Scotland. Loch Avon, in the very heart of the Cairngorms, is a magnificent mountain tarn surrounded by the high tops (Ben Macdhui, Braeriach, Cairn Toul, and The Saddle). It lies open to the hill walker, and no one who stays at Tomintoul for any length of time will be able to resist the lure of these peaks, which beckon perpetually from every point of vantage around the village.

There is a considerable Catholic population in Tomintoul, drawn from the indigenous NE. Catholic survival. (*See* GLEN LIVET.) To quote the Statistical Account, "Protestants and Roman Catholics wholeheartedly patronize each other's social functions and live as one community unmindful of religious differences". When a convent was built in the village, "Protestant as well as Roman Catholic farmers co-operated in the carting of stones for the building, during which time the nuns were most graciously given the house of the Protestant banker for their accommodation".

TONGUE, *Sutherland* (Map 5, ref. 25⁹95⁷). The village and parish of Tongue (sometimes called Kirkiboll) is on the E. side of the Kyle of Tongue, 31 m. N. of LAIRG. The road runs along the W. shore of Loch Loyal, between the water and Ben Loyal.

Tongue House was the home of the chiefs of Mackay, but the estates were sold by the 7th Lord Reay in 1829 to the Duke of Sutherland. Tongue House is a pleasant building, sheltered by trees and with a sundial in the garden, dated 1714. The motto of the Mackays, *Manu forti*, appears on one of three pediments built into the wall of the dining-room; the overmantel bears the Mackay arms. The Lords Reay became Dutch citizens, but returned in the late 19th cent. to re-adopt British citizenship.

TORMORE, *Moray* (Map 6, ref. 31⁶83⁵), is the first distillery to have been built in the Highlands this century. Opened in 1960, and described as "the most beautiful industrial structure in the Highlands", the distillery and its associated group of houses were designed by Professor Sir Albert Richardson. Silvery

Rubislaw granite from ABERDEEN, pink BRORA stone, and Westmorland slate were the principal building materials used to achieve architectural harmony with the Speyside setting. The distillery has a capacity of 3,000,000 gallons of whisky a year.

TORPHICHEN, *West Lothian* (Map 2, ref. 29⁷67²). The village of Torphichen lies 12 m. N. of BATHGATE, and was the Scottish seat of the Knights of St John of Jerusalem. A portion of their preceptory – the tower and vaulted transepts, showing castellated architecture of the 15th cent. – survives. It has been much rebuilt, but still contains remarkable detail. In the N. transept is an inscription to the effect that Sir Andrew Meldrum, Knight of St John, had safe conducts between 1432 and 1439 to travel to Rhodes, Flanders, and England. In the transept a 16th-cent. monument of one of the last preceptors, Sir Walter Lindsay, is still to be seen. The nave, now the parish church, was rebuilt in the 17th cent.

TORRIDON, *Ross and Cromarty* (Map 5, ref. 19⁰85⁶). The magnificent sea-loch of Torridon lies on the mainland opposite the NE. of SKYE, and divides into three with Loch Shieldaig at the S. and Upper Loch Torridon through the narrow strait to the E. Ploc of Torridon is a promontory in the Upper Loch Torridon, and has three rows of large flat stones facing a larger standing stone; these are known as the Church of Ploc, and services were traditionally held there.

The mountains at the N. end of the loch are of red sandstone, some topped with white quartzite. These include Liathach (3,456 ft), BEINN EIGHE (3,309 ft), Beinn Alligin (3,232 ft), and Beinn Dearg (2,995 ft). Torridon is an excellent centre for climbing, as the mountains have serrated tops linked by narrow ridges. The views from the summits extend from CAPE WRATH to ARDNAMURCHAN and the Long Island or Outer Hebrides.

TORTHORWALD, *Dumfriesshire* (Map 2, ref. 30³57⁸), is a village lying 4 m. NE. of DUMFRIES. William Paterson, founder of the Bank of England, was born here; so too was John Paton, the missionary to the New Hebrides. There is a memorial to Paton, formerly erected on a gable of his birthplace, which has been demolished, and now on a cairn near the village.

Vestiges of two Iron Age forms on the brow of the brae show two or three concentric trenches. Torthorwald Castle stands on a series of earthworks of early medieval date. The site was, from the mid-13th cent. at least, a strong-hold of the Kirkpatricks; in 1418, William de Carleil married the heiress, and most of the time thereafter, until about 1715, the tower was in Carlyle hands. The present sturdy barrel-vaulted remains seem to have been largely built by William. In 1544 Lord Carlyle looted the castle of all its contents in a raid against his sister-in-law; little six-year-old Elizabeth Carlyle, the heiress, was abducted from here in 1574 by her uncle, Michael Carlyle, and traded for years among rival branches of the family.

Torthorwald was erected a burgh of barony on the 23rd of December 1473.

TOTAIG, *Ross and Cromarty* (Map 5, ref. 18⁸82⁴), has a pier, and lies on the S. shore of the narrows between Loch Alsh and Loch Duich opposite EILEAN DONNAN Castle. There is a ferry across the entrance to Loch Duich to the W. side of the road bridge at DORNIE, but it does not take cars. A little W. of the ferry is a broch locally known as Caisteal Grugaig, on the hillside at the foot of a precipitous rock. It is well preserved to a maximum height of 13 ft, and shows some features of broch structure very clearly; there is a triangular lintel above the outer end of the entrance passage. The natural floor is on a steep slope. The entrance on the NE. has a door-check and bar-hole. The broch has a large mural chamber in the NW. sector and a small one in the SE., together with a stair lobby and the fragment of a gallery.

TOWARD, *Argyll* (Map 2, ref. 21⁵66⁸). The township of Toward, with its pier, lies at the S. end of Cowal. Toward Point looks across to WEMYSS BAY on the E. and to ROTHESAY on the SW. Toward Castle is now a school for convalescent children.

The ruins of an older castle, 1½ m. W. of Toward Point, was once the seat of the chief of the Lamonts. Built in the 15th and 16th cents., it was destroyed by the Campbells in 1646 after a siege and much cruelty. It was never rebuilt or re-occupied.

TRANENT, *East Lothian* (Map 3, ref. 34⁰67³). A parish and police burgh, Tranent is situated 1¼ m. SE. of PRESTONPANS and 9 m. E. of EDINBURGH. It is the centre of a large mining area.

The old parish church, said to have been built about the middle of the 11th cent. and demolished in 1797, is now represented by only a small ruin used as a mausoleum. The present church, commanding a fine view of the Firth of FORTH, was opened in 1801.

Colonel Gardiner was carried to the manse from the field of Prestonpans, and was buried at the W. end of the old church in 1745, but no tombstone now marks his grave.

TRAPRAIN LAW, *East Lothian* (Map 3, ref. 36⁰67⁵). This conical hill 4½ m. E. of HADDINGTON stands "like a harpooned whale" in the heart of East Lothian. It catches the eye of the traveller, and has for long held the eager attention of the archaeologist. It was occupied as a dwelling-place and a defensive site from the late Stone Age until at least the end of Roman times. For some 300 years it carried the Celtic township of Dunpender.

In 1919 carefully planned excavations produced a hoard of native and Roman silver, indicating active trade between Dunpender and neighbouring Roman settlements. The Roman objects help to date the native ones.

The silver is now in the National Museum of Antiquities in EDINBURGH, and forms one of its most precious possessions. The large number of objects excavated from Traprain Law make it the most important native site yet excavated in Scotland.

TRAQUAIR, *Peeblesshire* (Map 3, ref. 33⁶63⁵). Just S. of INNERLEITHEN, with which it is connected by a bridge over the TWEED,

Traquair House

lies the parish and village of Traquair, which was of some importance in the 12th cent., but has now dwindled to a mere hamlet.

Traquair House is claimed to be one of the oldest inhabited mansions in Scotland. There was a royal hunting-lodge here when Alexander I hunted in ETTRICK FOREST, and it was at Traqauir that William the Lion signed the charter that gave GLASGOW its abbey lands and its foundation.

Traquair House was originally a single tower, now the NE. corner, but has been added to at various times, chiefly during the reign of Charles I. Built in château style, it looks down a broad avenue to the PEEBLES road. The gateway is flanked by two stone bears, the original of Scott's Veolan in *Waverley*.

The gates were closed in 1796 by the 7th Earl of Traquair after the death of his Countess. A more popular story, however, encouraged by Sir Walter Scott, is that they were closed after 1745, never to be re-opened till a Stuart was crowned again. Mary Queen of Scots stayed in the oldest part, the peel tower, and the house contains Stuart relics – embroidery by Mary Queen of Scots and an "Amen" glass with a toast to Prince Charles Edward Stuart engraved on it.

"The bush aboon Traquair", celebrated in song by John Campbell Shairp, stands about 1 m. above the mansion-house.

TRESHNISH ISLANDS, *Argyll* (Map 1, ref. 12⁸74²), are a small group in the Inner Hebrides (*see* "The Shape of Scotland"). These form a well-known and, to the sailor or voyager to the Hebrides, an eye-catching string of six islands off the W. coast of MULL, remarkable for their varied and curious shapes. The Dutchman's Cap, an outlier at the S. end, has a 278-ft hump surrounded by a brim; Fladda is flat, and Lunga is terraced. But the grandest are the almost inaccessible Cairn na Burg Mor and Beg, the larger with 100-ft cliffs and a fortress that was besieged more than once.

Being (as an old account says) "easily made unwinnable by crafty men", it held out under a Maclean garrison for the exiled Stuart kings in 1690 and 1715. The group is now a bird sanctuary and breeding-place of the Atlantic grey seal, and is only occasionally visited.

TROON, *Ayrshire* (Map 2, ref. 23²63¹). The name of this town derives from the same source as "Tron" and refers to the "nose" or promontory on which the burgh sits. Troon is a dormitory town for GLASGOW, to which it is connected by an excellent train service. It lies on the coast to the N. of AYR. While Troon has a fine harbour with shipbuilding and ship-breaking yards (the Ailsa Shipbuilding Company was founded by a marquess of Ailsa), it is best known for its golf courses, of which there are five. A visitor could spend a week, golfing each day on a different course of championship, or near championship, standard. Old Troon, Troon Portland, Old Prestwick, Western Gailes, TURNBERRY, and Ayr Belleisle are all comparatively close at hand and all well calculated to test the skill of the most accomplished. Troon is the W.-coast ST ANDREWS.

TROSSACHS, *Perthshire* (Map 2, ref. 24⁵70⁵). This romantic wooded defile in SW. Perthshire, between Loch Achray and Loch KATRINE, is one of the most celebrated literary beauty spots in Scotland. The reason for this is, of course, Sir Walter Scott's description in his once immensely famous poem *The Lady of the Lake*. But Scott was not the only person who has tried to describe it. Dorothy Wordsworth, when she and her brother William visited Scotland at the height of the Romantic Movement, wrote of it; so, later on, did Nathaniel Hawthorne. But Scott was easily the most successful.

The Trossachs are flanked to the N. by Ben A'an (1,851 ft) and to the SW. by Ben Venue (2,393 ft). The sides of the contracted valley are covered with hazels, oaks, birches, hawthorn,

The Trossachs: Ben Venue

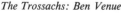

Scottish Tourist Board

and mountain ash. There is a road crossing the hills into the Trossachs from A B E R F O Y L E 4 m. S. This is still known as the Duke's Road, for it was built by the early 19th-cent. Duke of Montrose, who felt obliged to make some communication between Aberfoyle and the immensely popular Trossachs. He built the road for the sake of the tourists who had come to Scotland, and to this place, drawn by Scott's poem.

TULLIALLAN, *Fife* (at K I N C A R D I N E - O N - F O R T H). The parish of Tulliallan on the R. F O R T H contains a state forest and forest nursery.

Here are ruins of a castle that was the seat of the Blackadder family. An early 14th-cent. hall-house, it has a splendid under-croft, rib-vaulted from the central piers; it was added to in the 16th cent., and was lived in until 1662.

The mansion-house, also called the castle, was built about 1820 by Admiral Lord Keith – an odd though not unpleasing combination of Tudor, Gothic, Regency, and Victorian styles, surrounded by 88 acres of park. Since 1954 it has been the Scottish Police Training College, with residential courses for various periods of training.

TULLIBARDINE, *Perthshire* (Map 2, ref. 28⁹71⁴). This district, lying 6 m. SE. of C R I E F F, gives its name to the heirs of the dukes of Atholl, as mentioned in B L A I R A T H O L L. The Collegiate Church – one of the very few of its kind in Scotland still unaltered – was founded in 1445 by Sir David Murray. His arms and those of his wife, Dame Isabel Stewart, are on the W. wall inside the building. The church is cruciform, with a small western tower entered from the church by a narrow doorway. Both internally and externally the entrances have notable moulded detail, and the gable-ends have typical Scots crow-stepping.

William Murray of Tullibardine, the son and successor of the founder, enlarged the original foundation, and his arms and those of his wife are preserved on the exterior. At the Reformation, the provosty was suppressed and the building used as a burial vault. Lindsay of Pitscottie records that "James IV was fond of ship building and in 1511 built 'The Michael', the largest ship ever seen before. She was 240 ft long, 36 ft within the sides, which were 10 ft thick. She was a year in building and took up all the oak woods of Fife except Falkland. She had 300 mariners and carried in all about 1,000 men. Her length and breadth is planted in hawthorn at Tullibardine by the wright that helped to make her." Till the middle of the 19th-cent., only three of the original hawthorn trees had survived.

TULLIBODY, *Clackmannanshire* (Map 2, ref. 28⁷69⁵). On the S T I R L I N G – A L L O A road, Tullibody has been transformed from rural village to bustling residential mining community since the Second World War. Infusion of new population has come from the dying coalfields of Lanarkshire. Originally founded, according to an attractive legend, by Kenneth MacAlpine, King of Scots, in the 9th. cent., it is in fact probably older. In 1170 the village church and its lands were granted to the canons of C A M B U S K E N N E T H by the Macbeth family. The roofless shell of the old pre-Reformation church, as it now stands, dates largely from rebuilding in the 16th cent. It contains memorials to the family of Abercromby that produced Sir Ralph Abercromby (1734–1801), a noted soldier and military reformer. Much of the old village has been demolished to accommodate housing and shopping developments. Still surviving is the house that was the birthplace of Robert Dick (1811–66), the "Thurso baker", self-taught botanist and geologist, and friend of Hugh Miller. A sports ground for track and field events has been laid out recently in the village.

TURIN HILL, *Angus* (Map 6, ref. 35⁴75⁴), 3½ m. NE. of F O R F A R, has at its summit (814 ft) the remains of a fort known as Kemp Castle or Camp Castle, believed to be one of the oldest stone forts in Scotland. The fort appears to have been reconstructed at least once, having been begun as an oval enclosure measuring about 900 ft by 400 ft within a single stone wall. After the fort was disused, a circular dun about 90 ft in diameter, with a wall 12 ft thick, was built partly upon the northern sector of the wall of the later fort. Two similar structures are to be found within about 150 yds.

TURNBERRY, *Ayrshire* (Map 2, ref. 22⁰60⁷). The name of Turnberry properly applies to the promontory immediately to the S. of Maidens Bay, on which may be found the remains of the ancient Turnberry Castle, the childhood home of Robert Bruce. This promontory, or Maidens Bay, was the landing-place of Bruce and his little band when he came from A R R A N to Carrick and Galloway at the start of his final campaign of liberation (*see* "Scotland in History"). Today Turnberry stands for a "super" hotel and two championship golf courses that lie to the southward of the old castle. It claims a specially dry and sunny climate, a claim that appears to be well founded.

TURRIFF, *Aberdeenshire* (Map 6, ref. 37²84⁹). There is an Aberdeenshire saying, "Turra, Turra, faur the sorra idder?" This, roughly translated, means "Turriff, of course, where else, in the name of mischief, would anyone want to go?" It gives an inkling of the importance of this red sandstone town of from 2,000 to 3,000 inhabitants to the country-dwellers of western Buchan and eastern Banff-shire.

Turriff is mentioned in the 12th-cent. *Book of Deer*, and was created a burgh of barony in 1511. Its ancient ruined church, on a site occupied by a religious foundation since the 12th cent., has a belfry and a fine-toned bell dated 1559. The present church was built in 1794, and other old buildings in the town are few. It is remembered in history for the "Trot of Turriff", the first serious clash of arms in the Civil War when a band of Covenanters was routed by a Royalist force in May 1639. But Turriff, which stands on a plateau overlooking the confluence of the DEVERON and the Water of Idoch, is the centre of a district particularly rich in castles and tower-houses.

Delgatie Castle (2 m. W.) and Towie Barclay Castle (3 m. S.) are known to have been built by the same master mason in the 16th cent., although his name is not recorded. They belong to a group of four Aberdeenshire castles, all on the L-plan, built for families closely related and united by loyalty to Mary Queen of Scots and the Catholic religion; and, quite naturally in the circumstances, they show many common features. At Delgatie, an original stone keep of the 13th cent. that had been added to and extended at least three times, was completely rebuilt on the L-plan. Like its "relatives", the castles of Craig, Gight, and Towie Barclay, it was given distinctive groin-vaulting. In the solar, the laird's private room, the ribs of the groin-vaulted roof sweep up to a central boss bearing the arms of Gilbert Hay, 4th Earl of Erroll. The fireplace has the motto "My Hoyp is in Ye Lord 1570". Two of the castle's rooms have painted ceilings. In 1950 the lath and plaster was removed from the ceiling of the Tulip Room, to reveal beams dated 1592 and bearing Scottish proverbs culled from a book published early in the 16th cent. The Painted Room on the floor above also has proverbs on its beams, between which are amusingly satirical paintings in gay colours. The central keep is surmounted by open battlements with bartizan and sculptural enrichments.

In 1948 Delgatie Castle passed into the hands of the Countess of Erroll, thus returning to the Hay family who had owned it 300 years before. In 1951 it was made over as a Clan Hay centre, with Captain John Hay of Hayfield as the Countess's commissioner-in-residence. Clan Hay gatherings are held here annually, and the castle is open to the public on stated days throughout the summer.

Towie Barclay Castle was built shortly after 1587. The hall has been described as "one of the noblest and most imaginative of all the tower-house interiors". Although so late in date, it is completely Gothic and medieval in inspiration. It consists of a single high rib-vaulted chamber in two bays, with ridge and transverse ribs, diagonal ribs, sculptured corbels, and heavy pendant bosses, also sculptured. The most remarkable feature of all is a small oratory above the entrance to the

hall and separated from it only by a parapet.

Once of four storeys, this mighty keep suffered a rude curtailment in 1792, when the tenant of the adjoining farm removed the turrets and battlements, and took two storeys off the tower and roofed it with slate. This noble Gothic hall was latterly used as a Free Church sunday-school, and the chairs and forms used are still there.

Craigston Castle (4 m. NNE. of Turriff) was built between 1604 and 1607 by John Urquhart, the Tutor of Cromarty, so called because he was the tutor of his grand-nephew Sir Thomas, father of the "great" Sir Thomas Urquhart, the translator of Rabelais.

The Urquharts of Craigston are the only branch of the family still in possession of their landed estates, and the library at the very top of the house is something of a shrine commemorating those Scots who, each in their various ways, embodied the national genius.

Like so many things those Urquharts did, the house that John built was highly original, not to say peculiar, its nearest relative in appearance being the great show façade of FYVIE Castle. It consisted of a main block in two wings thrown out to the front and joined by a lofty and deep, round arch, supporting a highly ornate sculptured balcony. It is a splendid piece of Renaissance fancy.

Fastened into the 18th-cent. doors, walls, and shutters of the two rooms is a sequence of carved panels in oak, dating from the early 17th cent. In the Queen's Room at Craigston is John Urquhart's oak chest. Carved in relief in the front are the arms of the Tutor of Cromarty.

Today's laird, Major Bruce Urquhart, and his wife have done much to enhance their fine old home.

TWEED, River, *Lanarkshire* to *Berwickshire* (Map 3, ref. 39^265^0). No river in western Europe, perhaps, has been responsible for more romantic literature than Tweed. It is not so much the river itself, but rather the countryside through which it flows, that has caused this outpouring of impassioned words.

Sometimes the phrase "North of the Tweed" is used by southern writers to describe Scotland. This is inaccurate, because, for the last 2 m. before its mouth, Tweed is officially in England. Along a dozen or so more miles it acts as a division between England and Scotland, but from shortly above COLDSTREAM it is a purely Scottish river, and many of the most fervent Scots live in Peeblesshire and Selkirkshire well S. of Tweed. Yarrow Water, associated with one of the most poignant and beautiful of the Scottish Border ballads, enters Tweed by joining Ettrick Water from the W.

The Borderland is here formed by the basin of Tweed, which comprises about 1,870 sq. m.; the river runs from where it rises in the southern uplands at Tweeds Well to its mouth by a once Scottish Berwick over a distance of

Scottish Tourist Board

A good day with the salmon on the Tweed

97 m. Its source is close to the sources of CLYDE and ANNAN. As the old saying has it, "Annan, Tweed, an' Clyde rise oot o' ae hillside".

Clyde pursues its dramatic course westwards to the Atlantic, but Tweed from its beginnings wanders eastwards among the hills; and every mile of it is known and cherished by the Border folk of Scotland. It is this river scene that inspired the anonymous makers of the Border ballads. The land of Tweed was responsible for Thomas the Rhymer; at the EILDON Hills in Tweedside by MELROSE he received his mystical experience of Elfland. The countryside of Tweed nurtured James Hogg, the Ettrick shepherd poet. Tweed was to Walter Scott the most precious river in the world. By its banks he eventually settled to live, work, and die.

This river that rouses such strong emotions in the Scottish heart runs, after its source and upon achieving the character of a river, NE. through Peeblesshire, E. through Selkirkshire and Roxburghshire, and then NE. to Berwick and the sea. Its length is dotted with peel towers and with prosperous Border towns such as PEEBLES, INNERLEITHEN, GALASHIELS, Melrose, and KELSO. Some of these produce the world-famous cloth of Tweed. Oddly enough, the name does not derive from the river but from a misreading in London of the local and technical word "tweel". But as tweed the cloth became known, and as tweed it shall always be known.

Tweed is not Scotland's finest salmon river; that honour is held by GRIMERSTA in LEWIS. But as an all-rounder Tweed is unbeatable. Its spring and autumn salmon are especially good fish, and its brown and sea-trout are also excellent.

TWEEDSMUIR, *Peeblesshire* (Map 3, ref. 31°62⁴). Situated near the source of the R. TWEED, Tweedsmuir is a small, picturesque village in lovely pastoral surroundings; it lies just off the lonely road to the DEVIL'S BEEF TUB at the spot where the Tweed passes under a single-arch stone bridge.

The church, of Romanesque structure, was built in 1874–5, on the site of an earlier church built in 1648. Near the church, on a mound known as Quarter Knowe, can be seen standing stones and traces of a fort.

The village has been made famous by John Buchan's taking the title of Lord Tweedsmuir, many of his books having the neighbouring district as their background.

Near Tweedsmuir is the site of Oliver Castle, probably built in the reign of David I; it was originally the seat of the Frasers, and later of the Tweedies, and is the remotest of a chain of towers along the line of the Tweed. Oliver House, a plain modern mansion, has replaced the old castle.

TYNDRUM, *Perthshire* (Map 2, ref. 23³73⁰), is a village 5 m. NW. of CRIANLARICH in rather bleak country under the summits of Beinn Odhar, Ben Lui, and Ben Chuirn. At Tyndrum the main road branches NW. across the Moor of RANNOCH and SW. to DALMALLY and OBAN. To the SW. of the village, on the northern slopes of Meall Odhar, are abandoned lead mines. These were accidentally discovered in 1741 and worked spasmodically until 1862.

Just S. of the Free Church manse is Dail Righ, the traditional site of the battle between Robert Bruce and Macdougall of Lorne in 1306. After being defeated at METHVEN near PERTH that year, Bruce retreated to Rannoch with the remnant of his followers, but, as winter advanced in a region where supplies were short, Bruce realized that he must try to link up with his supporters in Dumfriesshire, and to this end he planned an escape towards the SW. He was ambushed in the narrow defile at Tyndrum by Macdougall and others; he barely escaped with his life and – so the story goes – he lost his brooch in the struggle. This magnificent reliquary brooch, which has a central crystalline boss and encircling pearls, and is known as the Brooch of Lorne, remained the property of the Macdougalls until 1647, when Dunollie Castle, near Oban, the Macdougall stronghold, was sacked and burnt and the brooch was looted by Campbell of Braglin. It remained with the Campbells until 1819, when it was returned to the Macdougalls.

TYNNINGHAME, *East Lothian* (Map 3, ref. 36¹67⁰). Tynninghame is a most attractive and well planned estate village, constructed out of the characteristic red sandstone of the district; the cottages have pantiled roofs.

The original Tynninghame church was founded by St Baldred (d. A.D. 756), and was destroyed by Anlaf the Dane in A.D. 941. All that remains is two 12th-cent. Norman arches, with a tomb recess and effigy, the family burial-place of the earls of Haddington. From the remains, experts deduced that it must have been one of the finest examples of parochial

Romanesque architecture in Scotland. The Manor of Tynninghame anciently belonged to the bishops of ST ANDREWS, but well after the Reformation it was obtained in chartered right (1628) by the earls of Haddington, who still hold it. The estate is famed for its woods and holly hedges. In 1705 Thomas, the 6th Earl, began planting on a grand scale. To his efforts and example – he had many imitators – southern Scotland owes many fine expanses of plantation. Binning Wood is remarkable. This was planted in 1707, the year of the Union, and remained one of the glories of East Lothian until the Second World War, when the present Lord Haddington sacrificed the wood for the war effort. Immediately after hostilities, however, he began replanting, and Binning Wood now once more decorates the scene.

Tynninghame House is the seat of the Earl of Haddington (who also owns MELLERSTAIN in Berwickshire). Tynninghame, the original house of the Haddington family, was altered and enlarged in 1829 and refaced with local red sandstone; it is a large and handsome mansion, though not the architectural equal of the splendid Mellerstain.

Whitekirk, in the same parish, contains a 15th-cent. church, square-towered and cruciform – one of the finest parochial examples of Gothic architecture in Scotland. It was gutted by fire in 1914 (thought to be incendiarism by suffragettes), but was restored by national subscription in 1917 under the direction of Sir Robert Lorimer, and is a fine piece of work.

Holy Well, near the church, was a place of pilgrimage in pre-Reformation times; it dried up, however, as a result of field-drainage in the 19th cent. The bare, narrow building behind the church is said to be one of the few remaining tithe barns in Scotland.

Mention has already been made of the mysterious and almost uncatchable sea-trout of the R. Tyne at EAST LINTON. At Tynninghame, where the same river debouches through

Tynninghame House

Aerofilms

wide plains into the North Sea, there appears an even more striking example of the peculiar elusiveness of these fish. A local clergyman has been fishing the Tyne here for years, and has only caught one sea-trout – though it did come to the net at the remarkable weight of ten pounds. Lord Binning (the Earl of Haddington's son and heir), a keen angler, has been fishing the waters at his paternal doorstep all his life but has succeeded in catching only a few sea-trout, of about three to four pounds. The shyness of the Tyne sea-trout is unaccountable.

TYNRON, *Dumfriesshire* (Map 2, ref. 28¹59⁴), is a village on Shinnel Water, 5 m. SW. of THORNHILL.

Tynron Doon, a hill with a fine multivallate fort, which was reoccupied in the Dark Ages and again in the Middle Ages, rises abruptly to 947 ft above sea-level, in a bend of Shinnel Water. There is a central enclosure of 150 ft by 130 ft, within a ruinous stone wall, and outside this are three massive ramparts. Tradition says that Robert Bruce sheltered here for a time after the murder of the Red Comyn, before going to SCONE. A 7th-cent. gold bracelet and a fine bone pin have been found on the slope.

Agriculture is the only livelihood.

There is a well-known juniper wood at Ford, in the parish, which is now a nature reserve. The church dates from about 1837, succeeding one of 1700, but Tynron has been a religious foundation from earliest times. The church possesses two silver communion cups dating from 1610, and a "ladle". Tokens are still used. In the churchyard is a memorial to William Smith, a Covenanter, shot in 1685.

Tynronkirk whisky was famous into the 1920s; for many years it held the House of Commons contract.

UDDINGSTON, *Lanarkshire* (Map 2, ref. 27⁰66¹), like STONEHOUSE close to the M74 and already a busy community, was in 1971 caught up in Lanarkshire's great expansion. Two sites have been selected for industrial development on 19 acres of woodland owned by the National Coal Board whose local activities had ceased.

UDNY, *Aberdeenshire* (Map 6, ref. 38⁸82⁶). This is the name of a parish, two villages, and a castle, all in the NE. part of Formatine, where it slopes gently down to the basin of the Ythan. The castle is approached by a handsome avenue of beech trees from the charming little hamlet of Udny Green, the ancient kirktown of the parish. Tradition has it that the great rectangular tower of Udny Castle, five storeys and over 100 ft high, crowned on one side with ornamental battlements and bartizan, and by round turrets at each of the four corners, was built by three successive lairds and completed in the 17th cent. A newel stair 8 ft wide leads to the first floor, the whole length of which – with the exception of the laird's secret passage and bedchamber – is occupied by the panelled and vaulted great hall. A concealed staircase, which was used in the old days by the ladies of the castle as a means of access to their rooms on a higher floor, leads off one corner of the hall.

The earliest mention of the family of Udny of Udny in extant records dates from 1426, and from then till the present century there were 14 Udny lairds bearing that name, until the last of them, the late J. H. Udny of Udny, was succeeded by the 11th Lord Belhaven and Stenton. The old keep was restored and integrated into a handsome modern mansion of two three-storey wings in 1875, at which time also the vaulted chamber in the basement became a domestic museum, housing among other things the ancestral "kist" or charter chest of the Udnys, rescued from a fire at Knockhall Castle in 1743 by that celebrated character, Jamie Fleeman, the laird's licensed jester.

The visitor to Udny Castle should not fail to take a look into the quiet kirkyard at Udny Green, where he will find several features of interest. There is, for example, a unique Round House or mortsafe built by subscription in 1832. Fifteen gentlemen of the parish met to discuss the panic about body-snatching that afflicted the countryside, and decided to build this impregnable fortress, with its circular slated roof, immensely thick walls, and double doors, not to mention a large turn-table inside for the accommodation of coffins. The body-snatchers would have needed an atomic bomb to get inside; but, ironically enough, the Government passed the Anatomy Act that very year, and the Round House was rendered virtually obsolete.

In the present century Cairnbrogie has been renowned as the headquarters of a famous Shorthorn cattle herd, just as in the 19th cent. the Cruickshank brothers at Mains of Udny pioneered the breed.

The Udny area, now one of the finest farming countrysides in the world, was redeemed from stony wilderness by herculean effort in the middle of last century. At the farm of Old Craig were 5 m. of drystone dykes – and every foot contained a cartload of stones collected off the fields by methods ranging from long wooden levers to a portable crane. The powerful four-horse subsoil ploughs that had been used for trenching remained on the farm until they went to make munitions in the Second World War. One farmer, describing in the year 1889 how he had cleared his land of stones, said, "After a hard day's work, with tired muscles and aching hands, I have been unable to enjoy refreshing sleep at night, but in a feverish dream repeated the work of the day". Present-day mechanical handling equipment could no doubt make light work of the whole business, but that in no way diminishes the pathos and the grandeur of this feat of human doggedness, which was repeated over vast areas of Aberdeenshire in a period still within living memory.

UIG, *Inverness-shire* (Map 4, ref. 14°86²), is the name of a glen, a bay, a village, and a small port on the Island of SKYE in the Inner Hebrides (*see* "The Shape of Scotland"). On the W. side of the Trotternish northern peninsula of Skye stands this picturesque little Hebridean hamlet. In history, it is noted as the spot at which Prince Charles Edward Stuart first touched Skye when he fled from the "Long Island" disguised as Betty Bourke, Flora Macdonald's maidservant. Today, Uig has come into prominence as the place from which motor-car ferries leave for the Outer Hebrides.

UIST, North, Island of, *Inverness-shire* (Map 4, ref. 08°87°), is one of the Outer Hebrides (*see* "The Shape of Scotland"). Though now connected with South Uist via BENBECULA by a causeway opened in 1961, and though still separated from HARRIS by a fair stretch of sea, North Uist is the beginning of the Northern Outer Hebrides. It has much more kinship with Harris than with South Uist. Its population, displaying, as everywhere in the Outer Hebrides, the native courtesy and charm, is more strongly impregnated with Norse blood than the southern islands of the "Long Island". In North Uist all the inhabitants are Protestant, in Benbecula, to the S., half the population is Protestant and half is Catholic. In South Uist, and farther S. at ERISKAY and BARRA, nearly everyone is Catholic.

North Uist, like Benbecula, is studded with lochs and lochans, giving the impression that it contains almost more fresh water than land. But it is not nearly as flat as Benbecula, and it has three sizeable hills that, viewed from the S., appear mountainous. Eaval (1,138 ft) is the highest, but South Lee (920 ft), just S. of LOCHMADDY, gives a fine prospect of the loch-filled W. of the island.

North Uist has many standing stones, stone circles (more the equal of those at CALLERNISH on LEWIS), and chambered cairns. Along its attractive W. coast are pleasing thatched houses of the blackhouse type, but conforming to this age in having chimneys. The now ruined Teampull na Trionaid, or Church of the Holy Trinity, dates from the 14th cent. and stands on a small eminence by Carinish.

The angling on North Uist is particularly good, offering excellent sport with salmon as well as notable brown and sea-trout. In this it is the superior of the southern Outer Hebrides, where salmon are rarely found.

UIST, South, Island of, *Inverness-shire* (Map 4, ref. 08°83°) is one of the Southern and Western group of the Outer Hebrides (*see* "The Shape of Scotland"). It stretches 22 m.

from N. to S., and is 7 m. across E. to W. The eastern and central parts of this long island are hilly and mountainous (Hecla 1,988 ft, Ben More 2,035 ft). The main port is in the S. – Lochboisdale; through it you approach South Uist by steamer from the mainland. There is a regular air service to the neighbouring island of BENBECULA, now connected by a road-bridge.

South Uist is one of the most characteristic and most nearly prosperous of the Southern Celtic island crofting communities; and the traditional Hebridean life may be perceived at its most natural in almost 2,500 Gaelic-speaking islanders. By Celtic tradition, these islanders do not tend to gather in townships, but are spread fairly evenly over the surface of the island. For the most part, they are a land-working and crofting rather than a fishing community. South Uist has produced many notable pipers, and its tradition is military. Napoleon's Marshal Macdonald originated in blood from South Uist. The island is 95 per cent Catholic, but the most cordial relationship exists between these Catholic and Protestant Gaels. There is one pleasant stone Church of Scotland building, together with four Catholic churches, of which those at Bornish and at Eochar are of particular architectural interest in their Celtic simplicity, being among the first churches allowed to be built after the Catholic Emancipation. A recently erected 30 ft statue, "Our Lady of the Isles", on a high and hilly outcrop of rock near the North has become a landmark for seamen. The sculptor was Hew Lorimer.

The island briefly entered British history as the scene of Prince Charles Edward Stuart's wanderings after his defeat in the '45. It was from this island that he was rescued by Flora MacDonald's heroism (see SKYE). South Uist suffered prominently in the policy of the Clearances, but eventually the tenacity of the islesmen was here happily able to overcome

these and subsequent depredations. As in BARRA and ERISKAY, they are a gay and spontaneous people of graceful manners.

One lengthy road runs down the island from N. to S. and by the side of the long machair or silvery western beach. Daliburgh, which is the nearest to a capital, is but a village. At first sight, this lack of townships gives South Uist a deserted look, which it soon loses after a day or two in exploration and conversation amongst a people easy to talk with.

South Uist possesses over 190 fresh-water lochs, of which many are filled with excellent brown trout and some with noble sea-trout, among the best and most sporting in the British Isles. Permission to angle is obtained from the factor of the South Uist estates. A man who loves fishing, and who is in sympathy with the Scottish Gaelic ethos in its most attractive form, will find South Uist a paradise for holiday-making. Loch DRUIDIBEG is full of only small trout, but is celebrated as a nature reserve. There is one hotel at Lochboisdale, and an inn at each end of the island. Some of the crofters or small farmers take in visitors.

In 1955 the British Government began to erect a rocket-range for guided missiles at Eochar. This aroused considerable controversy and opposition in the Scottish press, which was even reflected in *The Times*. The rocket-range has for some time been firing guided lumps of metal (at £40,000 a shot) to sink into the Atlantic. The controversy did, however, have the effect of making those in charge hand-pick the personnel of the range. These have taken happily to island life, and some even are learning Gaelic. The range has now extended northwards to the Island of Benbecula. Fears are expressed that rocketry may be practised all over the Outer Hebrides.

ULLAPOOL, *Ross and Cromarty* (Map 5, ref. 21³89⁴). The large village of Ullapool was founded in 1788 by the British Fisheries Society

South Uist: Bornish Church

Colin Maddox

South Uist: the Fourth Station of the Cross in Gaelic, on Bornish Church

Colin Maddox

Scottish Tourist Board

Ullapool

as an extensive fishing station, mainly for herring and white fish; Loch Broom, on whose shores Ullapool stands, had been a notable fishing ground since at least the 16th cent. The street plan and design of some of the houses were vetted by Thomas Telford. The fishing unfortunately declined in the early 19th cent., but revived during the Second World War when the E. coast was mined and dangerous. The original buildings were used once more, and the village is now a busy centre of the fishing fleet from October to March.

Ullapool is noted for its whitewashed, dignified houses and its wide streets (with Gaelic street names as well as English). It is a good holiday centre for walks, angling, boat trips, sea fishing, and pony-trekking.

ULVA, Island of, *Argyll* (Map 1, ref. 13°74°), is the largest of a cluster of islands on the W. side of MULL in the Inner Hebrides (*see* "The Shape of Scotland"). IONA and STAFFA are now more famous, but, before the steamers came, Ulva was a natural stepping-stone for visitors to Staffa, who obtained boats, men, and provisions there. It was owned for about 800 years by the MacQuarries, whose chief entertained Johnson and Boswell in a cottage that is still to be seen, and lived to the age of 102. Near his simple home is the modern mansion, built to replace one where "Macdonald of Staffa" entertained Scott and other famous visitors.

In the heyday of the kelp industry, based on the ample supply of seaweed round its shores, Ulva supported 600 people, but now has only about thirty. Moorland covers most of the island's 8 sq. m., and dense bracken engulfed the green valleys and the ruined homes after the people were evicted. The island is now a private

estate, but a rough road runs along the N. shore past the deserted townships and across a narrow sound to Gometra. On the S. shore, black basalt cliffs alternate with little bays, which offer fine views of the sea and islands, with the peak of Benmore on Mull dominating the scene. David Livingstone's father came from Ulva, and Lachlan Macquarie, remembered as the "Father of Australia", was one of the island clan. The church, built in 1827 for a larger population, has been artistically transformed by Leslie Grahame-MacDougall, and now includes a community centre.

UNST, Island of, *Shetland* (Map 8, ref. 46°20⁵), is one of the SHETLAND Northern Islands (*see* "The Shape of Scotland"). As the most northerly of the islands of Shetland, and consequently the most northerly of the British Isles, Unst has an appeal of its own. It is strange to reflect, if you climb its highest hill at HERMANESS on the NW. promontory, that, apart from a few scattered satellite rocks, there is no land between you and the North Pole.

Of the three main islands of the county of Shetland, Unst is the smallest; it is 11 m. long, N. to S., and 4 m. broad. It naturally has not the variety of the Shetland mainland, but in its smaller space is more obviously fertile. Its scenery, particularly in the northern cliff area, is grandly impressive. The island cannot be said to have a capital, but its two main straggling townships are at Baltasound and at Haroldswick; this last contains the farthest-north post office in Britain.

The people of Unst live mostly by crofting and fishing. Some of the best of Shetland's weaving comes from the cottages on Unst. There is a ferry connecting the island witn its immediate neighbour to the S., Yell, and a regular island steamer that makes a call at all ports in the archipelago and links it with LERWICK. As with nearly everywhere else in the remoter Northern and Western Isles, Unst is enduring a drainage of population to the greater centres of Britain, but the island still lives on and is well worth a visit, particularly by the Shetland island steamer.

There is some notable sea-trout fishing in Loch Cliff, and the northern promontories and cliffs are the haunt of sea-birds much prized by ornithologists. Hermaness is now a nature reserve. The Scottish Stewart earls of unhappy memory built a castle at the SE. end at Muness; it is now a ruin.

Despite its declining population, despite its northern remoteness upon the very rim of the British world, Unst, with its fertility, its alluring scenery, and its kindly folk who still remain there, gives the impression of a friendly isle. There is little accommodation, but if you visit for a full day you will be well received

UPHALL, *West Lothian* (Map 2, ref. 30⁷67²). The parish and village of Uphall used to be concerned with the now defunct shale mining. Its fortunes will be linked with the New Town of LIVINGSTON.

The old parish church contains much of its 12th-cent. beginnings, including the lower part of the tower and the main entrance, a Romanesque doorway. It also has a notable bell, one of the oldest in West Lothian, dedicated to St Nicholas in 1503.

Houston House, 1 m. away, is a crow-stepped, gabled house built in 1601, and was the home of the late Ian Lindsay, the Scottish architect, and is now a hotel.

URQUHART CASTLE, *Inverness-shire* (Map 5, ref. 25³82⁸), stands on the W. side of Loch NESS, 13 m. SW. of INVERNESS, near DRUMNADROCHIT, and occupies a commanding site on a promontory jutting out into Loch Ness. It has had a stormy and war-battered existence, and was a ruin even before the Rising of 1715.

There was probably a royal fortress on the site of Urquhart from about 1200 – and there is evidence of a prehistoric fort as well. This is not to be wondered at, for the Great Glen from Inverness to FORT WILLIAM has always been strategically important, and Urquhart's situation was tactically strong. Many buildings here have come and gone. In the wars of Bruce, the castle changed hands four times in a little over twelve years. It was repaired in the reign of James IV, who bestowed the lordship of Urquhart on John Grant of Freuchie. It was plundered in 1545, and again in 1644; in 1691 some of the buildings were blown up so that they could not be used by the Jacobites. At the time of the Rising of 1715, it was reported that "the Castell of Urquhart is blowen down by the last storme of wind, the south-west side thereof

to the laich woult". After this, the weather and the local desire for dressed stone wrought their inevitable effect upon the roofless shell of the castle. Most of the building that still remains dates from 1509. One vault is said to contain the plague, miraculously buried there; another, a concealed treasure.

URR, Mote of, *Kirkcudbrightshire* (Map 2, ref. 28³56⁴). This earthwork, 2 m. NW. of DALBEATTIE, is "a true mote, comprising a citadel, trenches and base-court, all remarkably extensive and well preserved".

Partially excavated in 1951–3 by Brian Hope-Taylor, it proved to have been destroyed by fire about 1170 and rebuilt in the 1180s. It was in the hands of the de Berclays during a good part of the later 12th cent. In addition to the fine bailey to the N., the terraces of the medieval town of Urr (recorded in 1262) can be seen on the S. slope. The river now flows to the E., but formerly contained the motte as an island. It is one of the two finest Norman earthworks in Scotland.

VALLEYFIELD, *Fife* (Map 2, ref. 30⁰68⁷). This coal-mining community lies ½ m. NE. of CULCROSS on the trunk road linking KINCARDINE-ON-FORTH with DUNFERMLINE and, via ROSYTH, the FORTH Road Bridge.

In 1663 the estate of Valleyfield and village of Low Valleyfield were made a burgh of barony, privileged to hold fairs and markets. The burgesses of Culross resented this privilege and boycotted them. There were legal battles continually between Valleyfield and Culross over the monopoly of girdle-making, till both were ruined by a cheaper product of Carron Iron Works, and from 1760 Valleyfield disappeared as a burgh of barony.

There was coal-mining here from the time of James I of Scotland. In 1644 some of the "colyears" of Valleyfield were accused by the Kirk Session of "keeping the Yule in feasting and drinking and abstaining from their ordinary work . . . and payed every one of them 20 shillings".

Valleyfield coal, recognized as the best in Scotland, does not come to the surface but travels by tunnel under the R. Forth to Kinneil colliery in West Lothian to be mixed with its coal.

WANLOCKHEAD, *Dumfriesshire* (Map 2, ref. 28⁸61³). This village is in the NW. of the country in the parish of SANQUHAR, on Wanlock Water, and on the border of Lanarkshire, just SW. of LEADHILLS and 6 m. SW. of ELVANFOOT, in the heart of the Lowther Hills; nearby is an old turf wall, known locally as the "march dyke", dividing Lanarkshire from Dumfriesshire. Wanlockhead, Leadhills, and Elvanfoot are among the highest villages in Scotland, all more than 1,300 ft above sea-level. Wanlockhead straggles at different heights, slopes, and angles, about the curve of a hill called the Dod; it is an isolated community, surrounded by high, lonely, heather-covered moorland, which in covenanting times was much used as a refuge for the holding of Conventicles.

Lead mines were opened here in 1680, closed in 1934, re-opened in 1953, and closed again in 1959. There is much association with mineral deposits in this district. Indeed, gold has been found in the streams of the neighbourhood, once referred to as "God's treasure-house in Scotland". The largest piece of gold ever discovered here weighed between 4 and 5 oz.; it is now in the British Museum. Sir Bevis Bulmer, Master of the Mint to Queen Elizabeth I, was empowered by letters of warranty both from Queen Elizabeth and from the King of Scotland, James VI, to seek for gold in this district; he is said to have employed 300 men, and to have dug gold valued at £100,100 sterling. The metal is still to be found in small quantities today.

William Symington and James Taylor, both put forward as originators of steam navigation, were born in Leadhills and lived in Wanlockhead. The first trial of steam navigation took place on Dalswinton Loch; Symington and a local blacksmith helped to build the engine. The boat was built for Patrick Miller of DALSWINTON (Burns's landlord), in whose family Taylor was tutor.

In 1948 the Ministry of Civil Aviation built a radio station on one of the highest Lowther hills − the master station of four; it provides navigation service over a large area of Scotland and the North of England and nearby seas.

While staying with his sister at Wanlockhead, Tobias Smollett began sketching out his novel *Humphry Clinker*. In Italy, in the last year of his life, he completed this entertaining, if wistful, expression of homesickness for his native land. He had gone south in search of health. He did not discover it, but instead he gave us *Humphry Clinker*.

WATTEN, *Caithness* (Map 7, ref. 32⁴95⁴). The village of Watten is 7 m. WNW. of WICK and at the SE. end of Loch Watten. This is one of the most notable inland lochs for brown trout in the North of Scotland. There are numerous brochs in the parish.

WEEM, *Perthshire* (Map 2, ref. 28⁴74⁹), is a village just NW. of ABERFELDY, from which it is approached by an avenue of Lombardy poplars planted in 1897 to mark Queen Victoria's Jubilee.

The oldest part of Weem Hotel is said to date back to 1527, and General Wade stayed here during the building of the bridge at Aberfeldy.

Castle Menzies, the seat of the Menzies family, is a short distance W. of the hotel. The Menzieses came originally from DURISDEER, in Dumfriesshire, and settled in Strathtay towards the end of the 13th cent. Their original seat was Comrie Castle, near COSHIEVILLE. When this was burnt down, the then laird began building the castle at Weem probably about 1570. Additions were made in 1840. Recently the castle has been acquired by the Clan Menzies Society, who hope to preserve the original part as a clan centre.

The old church at Weem is mentioned in charters as early as 1235. The present building probably dates from 1510. It ceased to be frequented as a place of worship in 1839, and since then has been used as a mausoleum for the Menzies family. At the back of the altar, there is an interesting mural, erected in 1616 by Sir Alexander Menzies in memory of the ladies of the house. In the church are two stone crosses from the sanctuary at DULL. These so-called "girth crosses" (of which one remains *in situ* at the centre of Dull village) marked the enclosure of Druimdain or Ridge of Protection associated with the Culdee Celtic monastery at Dull. Within the enclosure there was safety from pursuit.

On the steep face of Weem Rock, and now almost inaccessible, is St David's Well and his chapel cave, and beside the well a stone slab with a cross carved on it. Many legends are associated with the cave, which is supposed to have a subterranean connection with Loch Glassie, 1¾ m. to the N.

WEMYSS, *Fife* (Map 3, ref. 33³69⁶). The parish of Wemyss is on the Firth of FORTH in E. Fife, and contains BUCKHAVEN and METHIL, and a small part of KIRKCALDY, as well as EAST WEMYSS, a conglomeration of villages, towns, and part of a town.

WEMYSS BAY, *Renfrewshire* (Map 2, ref. 22²67²). The seaside holiday resort of Wemyss Bay has a steamboat pier on the Firth of CLYDE, and is over 24½ m. SW. of central GLASGOW.

The modern village is composed of handsome red sandstone houses. Castle Wemyss is a 19th-cent. mansion, where Trollope rather unexpectedly wrote part of *Barchester Towers* − unexpectedly, because this Clyde holiday place seems remote from the lush pasturage and ecclesiastical atmosphere of Trollope's fictional city.

There are wonderful views over the Cowal shore, and to the mountains beyond. All Clyde shipping passes Wemyss Bay, and it is a fine place from which to watch the sea-traffic of the West.

WEST KILBRIDE, *Ayrshire* (Map 2, ref. 22⁰64⁸). Modern West Kilbride comprises two villages: West Kilbride proper, which lies inland; and Seamill on the shore, about 4 m. N. of ARDROSSAN. Modern building development has made them contiguous. Close by is Portencross, a hamlet with its feet in the sea.

These villages have been transformed in recent years by the building of the nuclear electricity generating station at HUNTERSTON Bay, a short distance to the N. The surrounding countryside is pleasantly agricultural and is noted for its early crops of potatoes. The coast road to LARGS commands fine views across the Firth of CLYDE to ARRAN, BUTE, and Kintyre, with the Isles of CUMBRAE in the foreground.

WEST LINTON, *Peeblesshire* (Map 3, ref. 31⁵65²), is a parish and village on the Lyne Water 15 m. SSW. of EDINBURGH and 14 m. NW. of PEEBLES.

At one time it was a burgh of regality and had sheep markets four times a year, subsequently transferred to LANARK. According to tradition, stone-carving was introduced here by masons who had been employed building Drochil Castle, the stone being obtained from Deepsykehead quarries on the moor outside the town. At any rate, Linton carvers became the chief gravestone-carvers of the county. There is a stone figure erected over the village well representing the wife of James Gifford, known as Laird Gifford, a mason and stone carver who flourished about 1666. The story goes that the figure was originally surrounded by her four children, and that a fifth child, born after the group was completed, was added standing on the mother's head. All the children have long since disappeared.

WEST WEMYSS, *Fife* (Map 3, ref. 33³69⁴). This coastal village on the Firth of FORTH, 2 m. NE. of DYSART, was once known as the "haven town of Wemyss", and was granted a charter as a burgh of barony by James IV in 1511. The village lost its status, but retained its old-world appearance. Care has been taken in reconstruction to preserve architectural features, and the old tolbooth tower, jutting into the narrow street, is an example of this.

The harbour is now partly filled up, and is used only for pleasure-boats or by local miners who go sea fishing in their spare time.

WHITEHILLS, *Banffshire* (Map 6, ref. 36⁵86⁵). Westwards of the county town of BANFF stretches the wide sweep of Banff Links, extending into Boyndie Bay, at the far end of which one crosses the Burn of Boyndie to reach the great hump of Knock Head. Immediately on the W. side of this massive headland is the village of Whitehills, the port and principal populated place of the thanage of the Boyne, in ancient times a forest and now perhaps the most fertile farming region in Banffshire. There was a small fishing village here at the end of the 16th cent., but the present town was largely the creation of the 19th-cent. herring boom.

While many a fishing burgh along this coast has lost its fishing-fleet, Whitehills, which never aspired to burghal status, has retained both its fleet and its vitality. From this village, thirty-two seine-net boats regularly go fishing, ably supported by the salesmen and merchants of the little port. Its appearance of modernity is in a way deceptive, for families who were settled in Whitehills over 300 years ago still live in it today. The attractive name Lovie, for example, appears in the Kirk Session records in 1623, and there are still many Lovies in Whitehills. In 1842, the parish minister enumerated in the village 117 Watsons, forty-seven Lovies, twenty-five Adamsons, twenty-five Findlays, and twenty-three Ritchies. Today these families still predominate. In one single street there are seven Watsons in a row.

This continuity in the basic stock of the place has resulted in an intense spirit of independence and self-help, demonstrated many times in incidents of local history. Before the days of state education, the fishermen of Whitehills ferried in their boats all the timber required from SPEYMOUTH in Moray to roof the General Assembly school in the village. At a slightly later date, they moved, stone by stone from Banff, an entire church, which they re-erected in the village. This building, now called Trinity Church, can be inspected on the main highway leading into the village. Whitehills, though only 3 m. from Banff, operates its own famous lifeboat station, which has a long history of rescue operations.

This is surely the place to say something about the character of the close-knit fishing communities of Scotland's E. coast, a character that survives in a purer form in Whitehills than perhaps anywhere else. So important was the fisherman's wife in these societies, that they might almost be described as matriarchal.

At Inverboyndie, 1 m. E. of Whitehills, are the ruins of the ancient pre-Reformation Church of St Brandon. Its W. gable is crowned by a fine belfry with carved stonework below. The name of St Brandon the Navigator is repeated everywhere in the area in such place-names as Brangan and Pitterbrangan, and in Brangan's Stanes, which are large hornblende stones huddled together in an ancient burial site.

The second oldest building in the district is the ruined Castle of the Boyne in the glen of the Burn of Boyne, 3 m. W. of Whitehills. It had a much more ancient predecessor, the Castle of the Craig of Boyne on a cliff at the mouth of the burn.

Although to all appearances an ancient fortress on the courtyard plan, Boyne Castle is in reality an instance of "architectural atavism". It was equipped for a certain amount of defence by firearms, nonetheless, and must have looked magnificent in its heyday. Oblong, and 104 ft in breadth across the main front, it had outer walls 5 ft thick and at each of the four corners a sturdy round tower. In front is a great fosse or ditch, and the entrance to the main front is approached by a raised and walled causeway, defended by two drum towers. The main front was four storeys high.

WHITEN HEAD, *Sutherland* (Map 5, ref. 25²97⁸). Whiten Head, Kennagael, stands between Loch ERIBOLL and Kyle of Tongue on the N. coast of Sutherland. The headland (1,935 ft) rises steeply from the sea, and beneath are caverns formed by tide and storm.

WHITHORN, *Wigtownshire* (Map 2, ref. 24⁵54⁰). As distinct from the Isle of WHITHORN, this is a parish, and a royal and municipal burgh, with a charter as an ecclesiastical burgh from Robert Bruce on the 20th of May 1325; it is 9 m. S. of WIGTOWN.

The shrine of St Ninian was an object of pilgrimage, till an Act of Parliament in 1581 made this observance illegal. Bruce went on a pilgrimage there a few months before his death in 1329. James IV was a frequent pilgrim – once on foot from EDINBURGH to Whithorn, when his Queen's life was despaired of. She recovered, and both made another pilgrimage, but not on foot. Mary Queen of Scots made the last royal pilgrimage to Whithorn in 1567.

Sumptuous finds of rings, chalices, patens, and croziers have been made during Ministry of Public Building and Works excavations here in recent years. The parish church was erected partly on the ruins of a priory founded by St Ninian, and is a National Monument. St Ninian's Cave, 3½ m. SW., was the hermitage of the Whithorn community; crosses from the 7th cent. have been found there. A 16th-cent. archway leads to the 12th-cent. priory, which is believed to incorporate St Ninian's foundations. There are the remains of a camp at Rispain, 1 m. S.

St Ninian was born and educated under Roman rule, but in A.D. 397 built a church here, which is possibly the first stone-built church in Scotland, and the earliest Christian church in the country. The monastery attached to it was the Candida Casa, or White House.

Whithorn is one of the oldest Christian centres in Britain; St Ninian's mission here began traditionally in A.D. 397. In 1949 Dr Ralegh Radford excavated a 5th-cent. oratory plastered externally – perhaps the White House itself. More recently shrouded burials have been found near the sub-soil just W. of the oratory, and a Roman cremation cemetery underlying them. In the Northumbrian period the monastery was a noted cultural centre: the *Miracula Nynie* was written here in the 7th cent. And it was near here, in A.D. 880–90, that the Lindisfarne Gospel was washed up on the shore.

A cottage on the road leading up to the priory forms an excellent museum, showing the 5th- and 7th-cent. inscribed stones and many fine interlace cross-heads and shafts.

WHITHORN, Isle of, *Wigtownshire* (Map 2, ref. 24⁸53⁷). Now a coastal village in the extreme SE. of the county, 3 m. SE. of WHITHORN, this little community was built on what was once an island. There is a 12th-cent. chapel dedicated to St Ninian, a coastguard station, and a harbour.

There is a Dark Age promontory fort near the chapel, and a 7th-cent. enclosure bank outside the 12th-cent. inner bank surrounding the chapel. A pleasant tower-house stands above the harbour.

WHITING BAY, *Buteshire* (Map 1, ref. 20⁴62⁵), is a small town on the Island of ARRAN (*see* "The Shape of Scotland"). This resort on the popular holiday island lies in a shallow bay on the SE. coast. It is 3½ m. S. of LAMLASH. There are now fewer than thirty hotels and guest houses and twice as many furnished letting houses. Whiting Bay, which has good sea-fishing and bathing, is on the lip of the Lowland end of Arran. There are attractive walks, and those who do not despise burn fishing may find an allurement in the Sliddery Water, just over the hill to the SW.

WHITTINGEHAME, *East Lothian* (Map 3, ref. 36⁰67³). An old tower, built in the 15th and 16th cents. and now restored, stands to the SW. of the modern mansion. Either in this tower, or under an old yew in the garden, Bothwell and Maitland of Lethington are traditionally supposed to have plotted the murder of Darnley in 1567.

The village used to be to the SW. of the parish church, but, already decaying, it was pulled down in 1817, when James Balfour of Balbirnie bought the estate and built the present mansion in the Grecian style – it was altered in the 1870s. James Balfour was the grandfather of Arthur J. Balfour, the Prime Minister (1902–5) and 1st Earl.

The combine harvester was introduced into Scotland in 1932 by the 3rd Earl.

WICK, *Caithness* (Map 7, ref. 33⁶95⁰). It is fitting that the county town of Caithness should bear a name derived from the Norse ("vic" meaning a bay), for Wick, which is also a royal and municipal burgh, must have been an important seaport for the marauding Vikings with their eyes on the flat arable land that enriches the N. coast. It has grown round the sweep of Wick Bay, where Wick river reaches the sea, and two fine harbours were built to accommodate the once prosperous herring fishing and curing industries, which have declined sadly since 1914. One harbour, and the part of the town known as Pultneytown lying to the S. of the river, were founded early in the 19th cent. by the British Fisheries Society, and built to the plan of Thomas Telford. The harbour was later improved by Thomas Stevenson, but is still accessible only to large steamers at high tide. The part lying to the N.

Scottish Tourist Board
Unloading a catch at Wick

is known as Louisburgh. There are coastguard and lifeboat stations. The harbour is a never-ending source of interest for visitors of all ages.

As well as railway links with the S., Wick has an airport 2 m. to the NE., with regular flights to and from EDINBURGH, Aberdeen, GLASGOW, INVERNESS, Kirkwall, and LERWICK. The holiday visitor should find plenty to do – there is a golf course, an outdoor swimming-pool, tennis courts, and loch and river fishing. In addition there is a wealth of cliff and rock scenery along the coastline, with the ruins of the 14th-cent. Castle Oliphant, or Castle of Old Wick, known to seamen as the "Auld Man o' Wick", lying 1½ m. SE. Some 3 m. NE. up the coast stands the lighthouse of Noss Head, looking over the sandy shores of Sinclair Bay to the spectacular ruins of the Castles of Girnigoe and Sinclair; this last was the residence of the earls of Caithness. In Girnigoe Castle the 4th Earl, George, imprisoned his son John for seven years, after he had been accused of plotting his father's death, and until the unfortunate man died of "famine and vermine". At Keiss, farther round Sinclair Bay and standing near the modern castle, are the ruins of Bucholly Castle, which, according to tradition, was once held by that celebrated Norseman, Sweyn Asleifson.

Although rooted in the past, Wick has the busy air of a county centre, of a market town with brisk local trade. From its established light industries, the town has recently taken a step into the future with the establishment of a modern factory to produce Caithness glass. This project, originated by a descendant of the earls of Caithness, the Hon. Robin Sinclair, is coming to the fore with a product whose simple lines are compared, perhaps not un-

expectedly, with those of Scandinavia, and whose subtle colour tones bear evocative names like "peat" and "heather".

WIGTOWN, *Wigtownshire* (Map 2, ref. 24³55⁵). This ancient town was a burgh holding of the Crown before 1292; it was probably chartered in the 1260s. It is the county town of Wigtownshire, and stands on the W. side of Wigtown Bay. It has a pleasant medieval layout and a central square. There are two town crosses. The "Old Cross" dating from 1748, is a column 10 ft high, topped by a square stone with dials; the other was erected to commemorate the Battle of Waterloo.

The ancient church was dedicated to St Machitis, who died in A.D. 554. It was rebuilt in 1730, but is now a ruin. An interlace cross-shaft in the churchyard dates from the 10th cent. The parish church, adjoining the ruin, was built in 1853. The churchyard contains an inscribed stone in memory of the "Wigtown martyrs", Margaret McLauchlan and Margaret Wilson, who were tied to a stake and drowned by the rising tide for adherence to the covenanting faith. They, and other martyrs, are commemorated by the Martyrs' Monument, which stands on high ground above the town.

Some 3 m. NW. are the Standing Stones of Torhousekie, an ancient monument dating probably from the Bronze Age, and consisting of nineteen stones, which form a complete circle.

There is the mound of a medieval castle (1260) on the edge of the salt marshes beside the town.

WILSONTOWN, *Lanarkshire* (Map 2, ref. 29⁵65⁵). Formerly called Forkens, Wilsontown changed its name because in 1779 three brothers called Wilson started the first ironworks in Lanarkshire, with minerals and coal all nearby, but with a long carry to the sea. In 1807, 2,000 people were employed here, but about 1810 the work declined, and the ironworks finally closed in 1842.

Coal-mining started up at Forth, a village 1 m. SSW. of Wilsontown, and the population moved there. It is still a mining village, but many of those who work there are descendants of the ironworkers at Wilsontown.

WINTON CASTLE, *East Lothian* (1 m. N. of PENCAITLAND and 13 m. SE. of TRANENT). Built in 1619–20 by George, 8th Lord Seton and 3rd Earl of Winton, on the site of an older house, it is one of the finest examples of Renaissance architecture in Scotland. Especially notable are the spiral stonework of the chimneys, the plaster ceilings, and the fireplaces of the drawing-room and dining-room. The Castle was probably designed and built by William Wallace, King's Master Mason for Scotland, the architect and builder of Heriot's Hospital, EDINBURGH. Many of the plaster ornaments are identical with those in Pinkie House and Moray House, and are probably the work of the same plasterers.

WISHAW, *Lanarkshire* (Map 2, ref. 28°65⁵). A town in the parish of Cambusnethan, in N. Lanarkshire, Wishaw lies 14½ m. SE. of GLASGOW, and is now amalgamated with MOTHERWELL to form the police burgh of Motherwell and Wishaw. The first heavy industry was the Coltness Iron Works, founded in 1839. Once an important centre for coal, iron, and steel trades, it suffered severely in the depression between the first and second world wars. Now the basic industry has gone, but the waggon works and engineering works, the confectionery and knitting factories, still remain.

WODEN LAW, *Roxburghshire* (Map 3, ref. 37°61³). The hill of Woden Law is 4½ m. S. of HOWNAM, and has a magnificent prospect from the summit; to the W. are the Cheviots, to the N. the Lammermuirs, and to the E. the North Sea.

There is a notable group of early historical remains on the top, including a native fort, a series of Roman earthworks, and a small enclosure for the burial of incinerated bones.

YARROW, *Selkirkshire* (Map 3, ref. 33°62⁸). Lying in the vale of the Yarrow Water, this is one of the largest parishes in the South of Scotland, comprising more than one-third of Selkirkshire.

Yarrow Church, 7 m. W. of SELKIRK, was built in 1635 to replace the ruined church of St Mary on ST MARY'S LOCH; it was restored after a fire in 1922.

This is ballad country, and many poets have praised the district – notably Wordsworth.

Philiphaugh, where the glens of Yarrow and Ettrick meet, was the scene of a decisive battle between Montrose and the Covenanters in 1645, the last blow to the cause of Charles I in Scotland.

Just S. of Philiphaugh, on the right bank of the river, is the Buccleuch mansion of Bowhill, and beyond this stands Newark Castle, a 15th-cent. ruin; it was originally a royal hunting-seat, and bears the arms of James I on its W. side. It later belonged to the Scotts of Buccleuch, and it was here that Sir Walter Scott set the scene for *The Lay of the Last Minstrel*; here the minstrel is made to sing his lay to the Duchess of Buccleuch, the widow of the Duke of Monmouth.

Across the river from Newark is Foulshiels, the birthplace of Mungo Park, the African explorer.

YESTER HOUSE, *East Lothian* (Map 3, ref. 35⁵66⁷). Standing SE. of the village of GIFFORD, this is a finely proportioned mansion by William Adam, dating from 1745; it is the seat of the Marquess of Tweeddale. The house contains a great deal of fine plaster decoration, including the famous room decorated by the French artist Delacour in 1761. The lands of Yester House have been in possession of the Gifford and Hay families (joined by marriage in the 14th cent.) from at least the 12th cent. It was an early Gifford, Sir Hugo, who had a reputation as a wizard and is traditionally the builder of the famous Goblin Ha' in the 13th cent. This underground room is part of the remains of Yester Castle, in the grounds of the house. The room is 37 ft by 13 ft wide, and has a vaulted roof 19 ft high; from the main chamber a stone staircase leads down to a well, and to a bolt-hole in a nearby gully. It is also called Bo (for Bogey) Hall, and features in Canto III of Sir Walter Scott's *Marmion*, where the meeting of Alexander III and Sir Hugo Gifford in Goblin Ha' is described. The chamber is unique in Scotland, but can be compared with similar structures in old French castles.

YETHOLM, *Roxburghshire* (Map 3, ref. 38²62⁸). Some 7 m. SE. of KELSO, the "double" village of Kirk Yetholm and Town Yetholm lies on both sides of the Bowmont Water; Kirk Yetholm was the original village, Town Yetholm being first mentioned in the mid-15th cent.

The present church, curiously large for such a small place, was erected in 1836 on the site of the old one. According to tradition, a number of the Scots nobles who fell at Flodden were buried in the kirkyard at Yetholm.

The village was for a long time the headquarters of the Scottish gipsies; a writ of James V in 1540 refers to "Johnne Faa, lord and erle of Little Egypt", one of the "royal house" who held court at Yetholm. A cottage known as the "Palace" is still pointed out in Kirk Yetholm, but the gipsies have vanished, having either died out or been absorbed in the population. The last "queen", Esther Faa Blytte, died in 1883. She it was who described Yetholm as "sae mingle-mangle that ane micht think it was either built on a dark nicht or sawn on a windy ane". Her son, who became "king" in 1898, died four years later.

Jean Gordon, wife of Patrick Faa and the prototype of Sir Walter Scott's Meg Merrilies, was born in Yetholm. Three of her sons were hanged for sheep-stealing; another was murdered; her husband was transported; and she herself, in old age, died after being "ducked" by a mob at Carlisle for her Jacobite sympathies, freely expressed, soon after the Rising in 1745. Undaunted, every time she was able to get her head above water, she cried again "Charlie yet" till the mob gave up. But she died that night of exhaustion.

Yetholm used to hold a weekly market, and "Fastern E'en games" were celebrated annually; whisky-smuggling was prevalent here in olden times. Today no such disturbances occur, and the village is at peace.

Appendix 1: The Clan and the Tartan

The Clan

The Gaelic word "clann" means "children", and the central idea of a clan is kinship. Nowadays we refer as a rule only to Highland families as clans, but in earlier times even the Scots Parliament spoke of "clans . . . as well in the Borders as in the Highlands". A clan is a family, and theoretically the chief is the father of it, although, in all but the smallest, not every clansman can be a direct descendant of the founder.

No doubt many people will be surprised to learn that those who founded our present clans were not themselves always Highlanders, but included Normans (Gordon, Fraser), Bretons (Stuart), Flemings (Murray, Sutherland), Irish (MacNeil), and Norsemen (MacLeod). Concerning that early period of their settlement, which was between the 11th and 14th centuries, we must not be dogmatic on the subject of nationality; the important point is that all these were "incomers" to the Highlands. The situation came about when lands, especially in the eastern Highlands, were forfeited, either by rebellion against the crown, as in the case of 12th-century Moray, or in the early 14th century when the Comyns and their many supporters lost the struggle for power with Bruce. The disappearance of the Comyns created a vacuum into which many of Bruce's Anglo-Norman friends were drawn.

On the west the pattern is rather different, but even there the leaders were in a sense incomers. Somerled, the founder of the great clan Donald (MacDonald and the rest), was the son-in-law of Olaf King of Man. He led the people of the West against the Norsemen in the 12th century and established himself in Argyll and the Isles.

When these incomers acquired their land, whether by charter or by conquest, or occasionally by marriage with a local heiress, they virtually took over a good many people who were living on it, and who, perhaps, were already formed into a family or clan unit. Gradually the old clan came to acknowledge the protection of their new leader, and at last built up a nominal kinship with him. In course of time intermarriage made it difficult to determine how far this kinship was nominal and how far real.

Under the patriarchal system of clanship, which reached its peak in the 16th century, the order of precedence was strictly observed. First, after the chief himself, came members of his immediate family, his younger sons and grandsons, who founded "cadet" or landed families of their own. These cadets held their lands by inheritance and granted long-term feus or "tacks" to middlemen known as tacksmen, who in turn gave short-term leases to their tenants. In many cases the cadets intermarried with the tacksmen and the tacksmen with their tenants; but all, whether connected by blood or not, owned a common heritage of loyalty as clansmen. In return for the help and support of his clansmen, the chief was their leader in war and their judge and arbiter in peace. Even in the early days the king was, in theory at least, the "chief of chiefs", and as the royal power spread through the Highlands the chiefs were made responsible for the good conduct of their clansmen.

Recently a pattern has emerged in which the Highlands appear to be divided among the clans in a way made familiar by the clan maps on sale as tourist souvenirs. These maps are excellent and informative, but they should be treated with some caution. The neat red, blue, and yellow areas denote "clan countries"; most people imagine that in each "country" all the inhabitants bore the same surname, and conversely that all members of a particular clan lived within their own bounds. Unfortunately clansmen were by no means so neatly distributed as modern map-makers would have us believe.

Surnames, which tend to be the hallmark of modern clans, were not in general use throughout the Highlands until at least the 17th century, and in remote areas not for a further hundred years. Before then clansmen used patronymics such as "Donald macIain vicAlastair"; the son would be known as "Roderick macDonald vicIain". This provides no inkling of the clan to which the individual belonged, as the whole name changed in each generation. When surnames came to be adopted, some families took the name of their chief, some took recognized variants of his name, some took descriptive names or names of trades, while some probably "froze" the patronymic where it stood at the time. This explains the apparent anomaly by which one surname can figure in the lists of "septs" or followers of more than one clan. There are also cases where certain members of a clan wandered away from their original home and attached themselves to the chief of a place closer to where they settled. An example of this is the Macleans of Dochgarroch, near Inverness, who were separated by the breadth of Scotland from their chief at Duart in Mull, and associated themselves instead with the local Clan Chattan.

The great period of the clans – often called the clan system, but in fact anything but systematic – was on the decline by the beginning of the 18th century; and the failure of the Jacobite Risings in 1715, '19, and '45, with its social and economic consequences for the Highlands, completed the destruction.

But the old loyalty of a clan to its head continues, even when "mountains divide us and the waste of seas". Today clan societies flourish in Scotland and, perhaps more bravely, elsewhere in the world. The clan society movement has a long and honourable history – the earliest being the Buchanan Society, founded in 1725 as the Buchanans Charity Society to provide for the support of poor individuals of the name and clan, and to help with their education at school and university and their apprenticeship to respectable trades. Since then a wide variety of objects has attracted clansmen, and today societies are acquiring land and property in their respective clan countries, financing histories and magazines, establishing museums to preserve relics and records, founding educational trusts and prizes, and – perhaps above all – keeping alive the family spirit and providing a welcome to the ancient homeland for kinsfolk across the world.

The Tartan

Tartan is and has for centuries been the distinguishing mark of the Highlander. It has a long history. Evidence can be brought to show that as long ago as the 13th century, and probably earlier, Highlanders wore brightly coloured clothes of striped or checked material, which they called "breacan". In 1539 the Accounts of the Lord High Treasurer of Scotland included the item "For 3 ells of Heland tartane to be hoiss to the Kingis Grace – price of the ell 4s 3d., total 13s." It is recorded that King James V, the father of Mary Queen of Scots, wore the hose with a velvet coat lined with green taffeta.

The antiquity of tartan, then, is in no doubt, but there is some controversy about clan tartans as such. Traditionalists state that the Highlanders wore tartan as a badge so that they could recognize each other and distinguish friend from foe in battle. Like many theories, this looks well on paper, but in practice it seems to break down. Armorial bearings, which were evolved for the same purpose, followed certain rules, which included simplicity of design and the use of only a few basic colours in vivid combinations. Even though the old tartans were simpler than the modern ones, they could not easily be recognized at a distance, and we have much evidence that before battle the Highlanders used to take off their plaids to gain greater freedom of action, all fighting in their voluminous shirts.

On the other hand, various descriptions can be quoted to show that, in the Highlands, the patterns of the tartans were considered important. One of these is by Martin Martin, who travelled in the Western Isles during the 1690s. He wrote: "The Women are at great pains, first to give an exact Pattern of the Plad upon a piece of Wood, having the number of every Thred of the Stripe on it . . . Every isle differs from the other in their fancy of making Plads, as to the Stripes in Breadth and Colours. This humour is as different through the Mainland of the Highlands in so far that they who have seen those places are able at the first view of a man's Plad to guess the place of his residence." We notice how Martin does not say that a view of a man's plaid will supply his name, or even his clan, but that it will show where he lives; and from this conception has been built up a theory of "district" tartans. A district tartan is a very natural development in a country divided into small self-contained communities, and local fashions are still to be found in the weaving of tweeds and the special knitting patterns used in Shetland.

Some people believe that tartans are entirely territorial, but this does not appear to be the whole story. As we have seen, clans were always very closely associated with their own "countries", and by the 16th century these were becoming fairly well defined, so that the particular patterns of tartan worn in a district would gradually come to be connected with the predominant local clan; and indeed there is evidence to show that this was so. But a study of contemporary portraits shows that there was no uniformity of tartan even in the early 18th century. Members of the same family are found wearing very different tartan and, what is perhaps more surprising to modern theorists, many of the men are seen to wear a kilt of one tartan and a jacket of another.

The history of the development of tartan was sharply broken in 1747, when the wearing of Highland dress was forbidden by law after the failure of the '45. There is no doubt that this proscription was intensely unpopular. For poorer people it was a very great hardship, but by all it was regarded as a harsh political measure. At the time of the Union of Parliaments in 1707, apparently, the wearing of tartan was adopted by patriotic Scots even in the Lowlands, and the ban on its wearing in 1747 increased its significance. But, in spite of this, there was much confusion when the Act was repealed in 1782. Martin described how the women kept the patterns on pieces of wood; but many of these proved too fragile to survive the 35 years. The sticks had been lost or broken, and in many cases the memories of the people were equally unreliable, so that the experts in weaving and dyeing tartan had no direct successors.

In the early years of the 19th century efforts were made, notably by the Highland Society of London, to collect authentic patterns of each clan tartan; but this does not seem to have been very successful. The fashion for tartan was fostered by the amazing spectacle of a kilted King George IV at Holyrood in 1822, and demands for clan tartans poured into the manufacturers. The wave of enthusiasm for tartan outstripped the traditional knowledge of the Highlanders, and it was at this time and in response to popular demand that a great many of our familiar present-day tartans became associated with their respective clans. Some of the patterns had previously been identified by numbers only, while some were undoubtedly invented on the spot, as variations of the old traditional patterns. Several books of clan tartans appeared in quick succession, and it is on these that most modern books are based.

The tartan in Scotland is antique; its exact divisions as applied to many Highland clans and names is comparatively modern. It is worth pointing out, however, that most modern clan tartans dating from the Romantic Revival of the early 19th century are now at least 140 years old. They have, therefore, established a respectable tradition.

Still, even today, new tartans are being designed, and more than 250 patterns or variations can be identified. Tartan, like a coat of arms, is recorded in technical fashion; the thread-count or sett (which is always the same for weft and warp) is given with basic colours, and the details of thickness of thread, size of pattern, and shade of dye is left to the individual. The resulting cloth appears as a bewildering variety, which in a large clan gathering can, to the novice, be both fascinating and alarming. Synthetic dyes, vegetable dyes, and ancient or faded colours all have their place in the glorious tradition of Highland dress.

This term "Highland dress" has not always meant the same thing. Martin Martin, writing in the 17th century, described the making of "plads"; and in his time the kilt, as we know it, was not worn. Clansmen wrapped themselves in the "feileadh mor" – a generous length of tartan cloth some 16 feet long and 5 feet wide. The upper portion covered the wearer's shoulders, and it was belted at the waist, the lower portion hanging in rough folds to the knees. In the 18th century this belted plaid was superseded by the kilt, or "feileadh beg", in which the lower part was separated from the upper part and the pleats were sewn in. Trews, or narrow tartan trousers, were also popular, especially for those who did much riding, but they are now seldom seen except in military uniform. Modern Highland dress consists of a day-time kilt of heavy material, sometimes in a darker or "hunting" tartan, worn with a tweed jacket, while for the evening finer material, possibly in a brighter "dress" tartan, can be matched with a variety of accessories.

Tartan, though ancient in origin, has proved adaptable, and today it is admired all over the world, wherever it has been carried by the wandering Highlanders.

JEAN DUNLOP

Appendix 2: Hydro-Electric Schemes

Hydro-electric development and the spread of electricity supplies have made many changes in the Highlands and in the lives of the Highland people since the end of the Second World War.

This work is being carried out by the North of Scotland Hydro-Electric Board established by act of parliament in 1943, the object of this measure being to provide electricity supplies in the sparsely populated areas by developing water-power resources.

The Board has the duty not only of undertaking all future water-power development in the Highlands and Islands, but also of distributing electricity in three-quarters of Scotland, the 21,700 square miles north and west of a line from the Firth of Tay to the Firth of Clyde. It also sells electricity to the South of Scotland.

In its work the Board is enjoined to "have regard to the desirability of preserving the beauty of the scenery and any object of architectural or historic interest, and of avoiding as far as possible injuries to fisheries and to the stock of fish". Hydro-electric schemes have first to be approved by the Secretary of State for Scotland and laid before Parliament. There are Amenity and Fisheries Committees to advise the Board and the Secretary of State in these particular matters.

The Board is also empowered to collaborate in measures for the economic development and social improvement of the North of Scotland. This duty, unique among electricity-supply authorities, makes the Hydro-Electric Board something more than a mere producer and supplier of electricity, so that it has been involved in a variety of "sidelines", including research into raw materials, and agricultural experiments. One way in which the Board has interpreted this duty is in efforts to encourage new industry to settle in the North.

When the Board was formed, there were three hydro-power stations in the North with a capacity of 84·4 megawatts. The Board has fifty-four main hydro stations with a plant capacity of 1,052 megawatts capable of producing about 3,000 million of units of electricity in an average year, a 400-megawatt pumped storage station, and a second of 300 megawatts, planned to come into operation in 1974.

The first large-scale development promoted by the Board was the Loch Sloy scheme. A high-head, peak-load station with a capacity of 130 megawatts, Loch Sloy attracted world-wide attention while it was being built. The dam, 177 feet high, was the first of its type, and the four machines in the power-house were built on the Clyde, the first products of a new industry encouraged by the Board. Controlled from the sloy Station are two other schemes. The smaller – Allt-na-Lairige, in Glen Fyne – is noteworthy because it has the first large pre-stressed dam in Europe, a design in which steel bolts secure the structure to the rock foundations. The larger Shira scheme has two dams and two power stations, one of which has a pump to enable it to supplement the water stored in the upper reservoir by pumping from the lower reservoir.

Also promoted with the Sloy scheme were two small projects at Morar and Lochalsh, and the small power stations of these schemes, which began to produce power for the surrounding districts in December 1947, were the first fruits of this great programme.

The second large development was centred on the Tummel Valley in Perthshire, where there are today a group of eight main power stations of about 245 megawatts capacity that generate annually about 650,000,000 units of electricity. Some of the water is used to produce power four or five times on its way down the valley.

Also in Perthshire is the Breadalbane scheme, with eight power stations making use of the waters of the rivers Lyon, Lochay, Dochart, Lednock and Earn and their tributaries to produce about 390,000,000 units. The Lawers scheme, which was the first stage of this development, uses a fall of 1,362 feet between reservoir and power station.

West of the Great Glen are the Garry and Moriston schemes, with a total output of 375,000,000 units from one of the wettest areas of Britain. A feature of the Moriston scheme is a group of underground power stations, one 300 feet beneath its storage dam.

Glen Affric is another source of electricity. A second development of these waters is the Strathfarrar-Kilmorack scheme. Six power stations produce from the waters of the Beauly and its tributaries over 500,000,000 units.

The Conon Valley development was undertaken in three stages, construction being in progress for fifteen years. The work involved seven generating stations, seven main dams, 20 miles of tunnels, 15 miles of aqueducts, a main-line railway station, 2 miles of track, and about 30 miles of public and private roads. The scheme has an estimated annual output of about 440,000,000 units.

Loch Shin is the centre of the most northerly group, the three main stations of which have an average annual production of 138,000,000 units.

Cruachan pumped storage station with its reversible machines is one of the most advanced of this type in the world. At night and during the weekend, "off peak" energy from the Scottish electricity system is used to pump water from Loch Awe up 1,300 feet to a reservoir in the main corrie of Ben Cruachan. The water is let down through the power station in the heart of the mountain to produce electricity at times of peak demand.

At Foyers beside Loch Ness a 300-megawatt pumped storage and conventional hydro-electric scheme is under construction for operation in 1974. It is a redevelopment of the first sizable hydro scheme in the U.K., built by the British Aluminium Co., in 1895. To supplement water from the catchment area flowing to Loch Mhor, the reservoir formed by the original development, reversible machines will pump water from Loch Ness to Loch Mhor. The two machines are housed in two shafts each of which could accommodate the Scott Monument in Edinburgh.

All along the west coast, and on some of the islands, there are small hydro-electric schemes: Morar, Lochalsh, Ullapool, Gairloch, Storr Lochs (Skye), Gisla (Lewis), Chliostair (Harris), Lussa (Kintyre), and so on. On the islands where there are few or no water-power resources, the Board has diesel-engined power stations like those at Kirkwall, Lerwick, and Stornoway. There are steam stations at Aberdeen and Dundee.

The Board is investigating further pumped storage and thermal station sites as part of long-term planning. A nuclear power station of 1,320 megawatts has been proposed at Stake Ness in Banffshire.

To bring the power from the new stations to populated areas, the Board has built a Highland grid, which extends to 2,000 circuit miles. One stretch of this passes over the Corrieyairack Pass at a height of 2,507 feet above sea-level. A Super Grid backbone of 275,000-volt lines has been constructed from Fife via Dundee, Aberdeen, and Beauly to Dounreay on the Pentland Firth.

A distribution network of over 22,000 circuit miles serves the Board's consumers, and, to supply islands, over 50 miles of submarine cables have had to be laid.

The distribution of electricity in the Board's area presents problems without parallel in Britain. In 1971 the average consumer density was 22 per square mile compared with 313 per square mile in England and Wales. The first consumers were connected in 1946. The 1947 Act, which nationalized electricity supply, added another 100,000 potential consumers, mostly in rural districts, to the Board's area.

By 1971 over 97 per cent of all potential consumers in the North of Scotland had been provided with electricity supplies. In 1948, only 5 per cent of the farms and crofts had electricity. By the end of 1964, the figure was 86 per cent. Over 50 per cent of the householders cook by electricity.

The Board incurs a loss in supplying the consumers in remote areas, and in 1964 this was about £2m. Power is available for industry throughout the area, and since 1948 some 3,500 industrial consumers have been connected to the mains.

By-products of the hydro-electric programme include the erection of 400 houses for staff and the building or re-building of about 400 miles of road, which include about 100 miles of public highway. Some of these roads have, for the tourist, opened up areas of outstanding scenery.

A great deal of research has been undertaken in connection with fisheries. Fish-passes of various types have been built to enable the salmon to surmount dams, and the Board operates four salmon hatcheries.

GEORGE D. BANKS

Glossary

of Gaelic and other local words, as used in the text

n., noun. *v.*, verb. *adj.*, adjective. *adv.*, adverb.

barmkin, *n.* Barbican, fortified gate, outermost defence of a castle or city.

bastel, bastle, bastile, *n.* Fortified house.

biggin, *n.* Building.

bing, *n.* Slag-heap.

bonspiel, *n.* Curling match.

broch, *n.* Circular stone tower with inner wall.

but-and-ben, *n.* Two-roomed cottage.

carse, *n.* Alluvial plain.

cateran, *n.* Freebooter.

cathair, *n.* Fortified position.

ceilidh, *n.* Spontaneous gathering to tell stories and sing.

chaumer, *n.* Chamber; police court.

cist, *n.* Coffin made from stone or hollow tree.

clachan, *n.* Hamlet.

cleitan, *n.* Dry-stone chamber.

colleague, *v.* Conspire.

couthy, *adj.* Kind, comfortable.

cran, *n.* Measure of herrings.

crannog, *n.* Dwelling beside lake.

doocot, *n.* Dovecot.

dulse, *n.* Seaweed.

eldritch, *adj.* Ghostly, weird.

faem, *n.* Foam.

feir, *n.* and *v.* Fear.

fot, fut, *n.* Foot.

girnal, *n.* Granary.

grun, *n.* Ground.

gumely jaup, *adj.*, *n.* Muddy spray.

haaf-net, *n.* Deep-sea fishing-net.

haill, *adj.* Healthy.

hauff, *n.* Place of resort, inn, tavern.

haugh, *n.* River-meadow.

houlet, *n.* Owl.

howe, *n.* Valley.

joug, *n.* Iron collar for prisoners.

kyle, *n.* Strait, narrows.

lamb-bucht, *n.* Sheep-fold.

law, *n.* Isolated hill.

leister, *n.* Barbed fishing-spear.

linn, *n.* Waterfall.

loon, *n.* Lad.

machair, *n.* Coarse grass beside the sea.

mormair, mormaer, *n.* Title of honour.

mortsafe, *n.* Cast-iron frame to protect graves from body-snatchers.

mull, *n.* Promontory.

oot-room, *n.* Outer room.

papingo, *n.* Wooden parrot used as target for arrows.

quhairin, *adv.* Wherein.

reiver, *n.* Ravager, plunderer.

riggin, *n.* Roof-ridge.

roup, *n.* Auction.

seine-net, *n.* Fishing-net with floats at the top and weights at the bottom.

strake, *v.* Smooth; strike.

tarbert, tarbat, tarbet, *n.* Narrow strip of land across which boats or galleys can be drawn to the sea on the other side.

teampull, *n.* Site of church; sacred place.

tod, *n.* Fox.

toiseach, *n.* Leader.

yett, *n.* Gate.

The grid used for finding references on the maps coincides with the National Grid and, when necessary, can be related to it for larger-scale maps. The smaller squares represent 10 kilometres (6·21 miles); the larger ones, 100 kilometres.

In the Gazetteer, the heading of each entry gives (in brackets) a map reference of six figures. The first two, which are large, correspond to figures on the bottom edge of the appropriate map, and mark off 10-kilometre squares; the third figure, which is small, represents so many tenths of these squares and identifies an imaginary vertical line on the map. Similarly the fourth and fifth figures (large) represent figures at the side of the map and also indicate the 10-kilometre squares; the sixth figure (small) represents tenths of these and an imaginary horizontal line. Each reference in the Gazetteer gives two such imaginary lines on the map, where they meet is the location of the place you want.

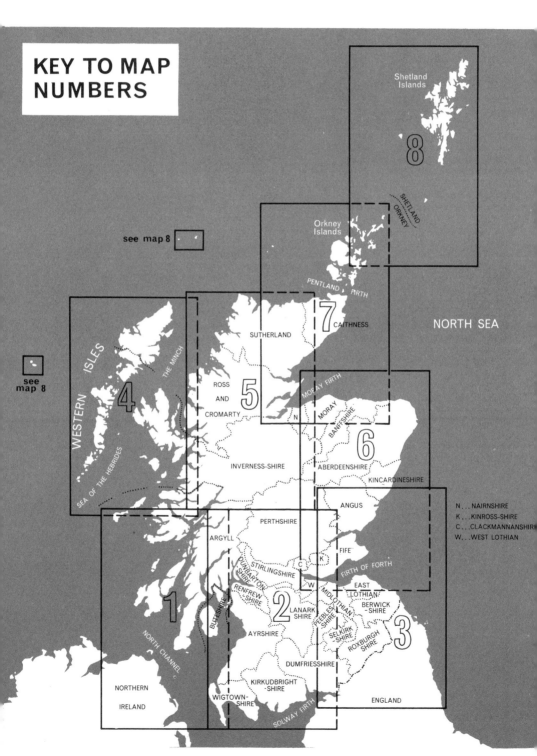

KEY TO MAP NUMBERS

Shetland Islands

8

SHETLAND ORKNEY

see map 8

Orkney Islands

PENTLAND FIRTH

7 CAITHNESS

NORTH SEA

SUTHERLAND

WESTERN ISLES

THE MINCH

see map 8

ROSS AND CROMARTY

5

MORAY FIRTH

N MORAY

BANFFSHIRE

4

SEA OF THE HEBRIDES

INVERNESS-SHIRE

ABERDEENSHIRE

6

KINCARDINESHIRE

ANGUS

N...NAIRNSHIRE
K...KINROSS-SHIRE
C...CLACKMANNANSHIRE
W...WEST LOTHIAN

PERTHSHIRE

ARGYLL

FIFE

C K

STIRLINGSHIRE

DUNBARTON-SHIRE

RENFREW-SHIRE

BUTESHIRE

W

FIRTH OF FORTH

EAST LOTHIAN

BERWICK-SHIRE

1

2 LANARK SHIRE

MIDLOTHIAN

PEEBLES-SHIRE

SELKIRK-SHIRE

ROXBURGH-SHIRE

3

AYRSHIRE

NORTH CHANNEL

DUMFRIESSHIRE

NORTHERN

IRELAND

KIRKUDBRIGHT-SHIRE

WIGTOWN-SHIRE

SOLWAY FIRTH

ENGLAND

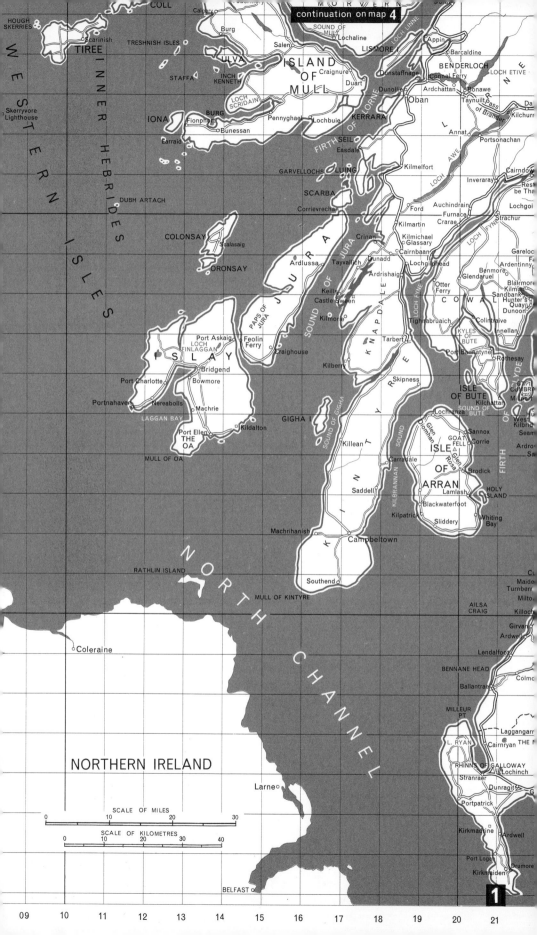

continuation on map 4

WESTERN ISLES

HOUGH
SKERRIES
COLL
Calgary
Burg
TRESHNISH ISLES
TIREE
Scarinish
INNER
HEBRIDES

SOUND OF MULL
Salen
Lochaline
MORVERN
LOCH LINNE
Appin
Barcaldine

ULVA
STAFFA
INCH KENNETH
BURG
Craignure
Duart
LISMORE I
Dunstaffnage
Connel Ferry
BENDERLOCH
LOCH ETIVE
Bonawe

ISLAND
OF
MULL
Pennyghael
Lochbuie
KERRARA
Dunollie
Oban
Ardchattan
Taynuilt
Pass
of Brander
Kilchurn
Da

LOCH SCRIDAIN

IONA
Fionphort
BUNESSAN
Bunessan

Earraid

FIRTH OF LORNE

SEIL
Easdale
SCARBA
LUNG
GARVELLOCHS
Kilmelfort

Annat
Portsonachan
LOCH AWE
Cairndow
Inveraray
Rest
be The

Skerryvore
Lighthouse

DUBH ARTACH

COLONSAY
Scalasaig

ORONSAY

Corrievrechan
JURA
Ardlussa
Tayvallich
Dunadd
Crinan
Kilmichael
Glassary
Cairnbaan
Lochgilphead

Ford
Auchindrain
Kilmartin
Furnace
Crarae

Lochgoi
Strachur
LOCH FYNE

PAPS OF JURA
Keills
Castle Sween
Kilmory
KNAPDALE
Ardrishaig
Otter
Ferry
COWAL
Benmore
Glendaruel
Blairmore
Kilmun
Sandbank
Hunter's
Quay
Dunoon

SOUND OF JURA

ISLAY
Port Askaig
LOCH FINLAGGAN
Feolin Ferry
Craighouse
Kilberry
Kilmore
Tighnabruaich
Tarbert
KYLES OF BUTE
Port Bannatyne
Colintraive
nnellan
Rothesay

Bridgend
Port Charlotte
Bowmore
Skipness
ISLE OF BUTE
SOUND OF BUTE
Kilchattan
West
Kilbri
CUMBR
Milie

Portnahaven
Nereabolls
Machrie
GIGHA I
Lochranza
Glen
Sannox
GOAT
FELL
Corrie
Seam
Ardro
Sa

LAGGAN BAY
Kildalton
Killean
KINTYRE
SOUND OF GIGHA
Glen
Diomhan
Glen
Rosa
ISLE
OF
ARRAN
Brodick
FIRTH OF CLYDE

Port Ellen
THE OA
Carradale
KILBRANNAN SOUND
Lamlash
HOLY ISLAND

MULL OF OA
Saddell
Blackwaterfoot
Kilpatrick
Sliddery
Whiting Bay

Machrihanish
Campbeltown
Maide
Turnberr
Milto

RATHLIN ISLAND
NORTH
Southend
AILSA CRAIG
Killoch

MULL OF KINTYRE
Girvan
Ardwell

NORTH CHANNEL

Coleraine
Lendalfoo

BENNANE HEAD
Colmc

Ballantrae

MILLEUR PT

NORTHERN IRELAND
Laggangarr
THE N
L. RYAN
Cairnryan

RHINNS OF GALLOWAY
Lochinch
Stranraer
Dunragit
G

Larne
Portpatrick

SCALE OF MILES
0   10   20   30
Kirkmadrine
Ardwell

SCALE OF KILOMETRES
0   10   20   30   40
Port Loga
Drumore

BELFAST
Kirkmaiden

1

09   10   11   12   13   14   15   16   17   18   19   20   21

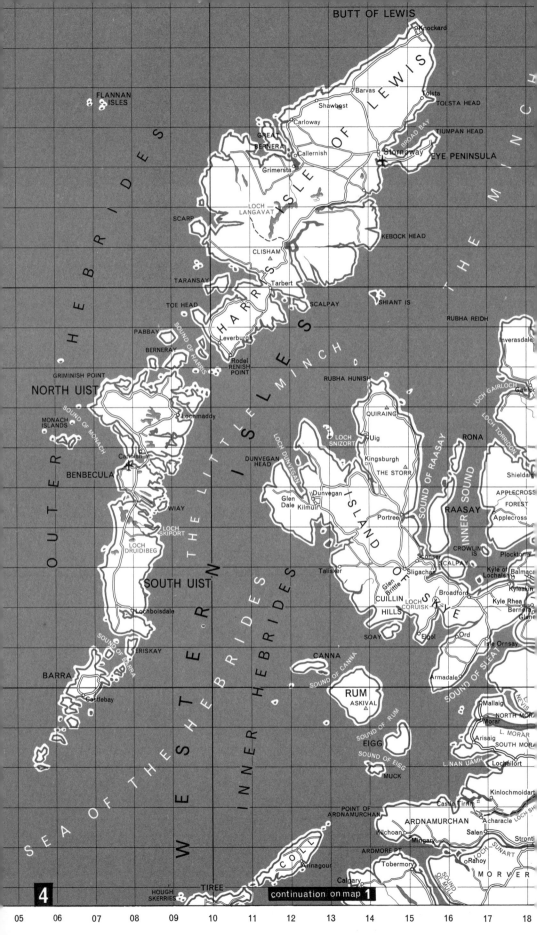

BUTT OF LEWIS
○Knockard

FLANNAN
ISLES

Barvas
Shawbost
Tolsta
TOLSTA HEAD

Carloway

BROAD BAY
TIUMPAN HEAD

GREAT
BERNERA
Callernish
Grimersta

ISLE OF LEWIS

Stornoway
EYE PENINSULA

H
E
B
R
I
D
E
S

LOCH
LANGAVAT

KEBOCK HEAD

SCARP

CLISHAM △

THE MINCH

TARANSAY

Tarbert
SCALPAY
SHIANT IS

RUBHA REIDH

TOE HEAD

H
A
R
R
I
S

LOCH OF HARRIS

PABBAY
Leverburg
Inverasdale
Gairloch

BERNERAY
Rodel
RENISH
POINT

RUBHA HUNISH

LOCH GAIRLOCH

GRIMINISH POINT

NORTH UIST

SOUND OF MONACH

Lochmaddy

RUBHA HUNISH

QUIRAING △
Uig

RONA

LOCH TORRIDON

LOCH
SNIZORT

MONACH
ISLANDS

Kingsburgh
THE STORR

SOUND OF RAASAY

Shieldaig

BENBECULA

Carinish

DUNVEGAN
HEAD

LOCH DUNVEGAN

RAASAY

APPLECROSS
FOREST
Applecross

WIAY

Glen
Dale
Kilmuir

Dunvegan
Portree

ISLAND

INNER SOUND

LOCH
SKIPORT

LOCH
DRUIDIBEG

SOUTH UIST

T
H
E

L
I
T
T
L
E

M
I
N
C
H

CROWLIN
IS

Scalpord
Talisker

OF

Sconser
SCALPAY

Plockton

Kyle of
Lochalsh
Balmaca

Lochboisdale

SOUND OF BARRA

ERISKAY

CANNA

SOUND OF CANNA

Glen
Brittle

CUILLIN

HILLS

SKYE

LOCH
CORUISK

Sligachan
Broadford

Kyleakin
Kyle Rhea
Berneray
Glene

BARRA

Castlebay

RUM
ASKIVAL △

SOUND OF RUM

SOAY
Elgol
Ord
Isle Ornsay

Armadale

SOUND OF SLEAT

O
U
T
E
R

S
O
U
N
D
O
F

B
A
R
R
A

W
E
S
T
E
R
N

H
E
B
R
I
D
E
S

I
N
N
E
R

H
E
B
R
I
D
E
S

Mallaig
NEVIS
NORTH MOR
Morar
L. MORAR
SOUTH MOR
Arisaig

EIGG
SOUND OF EIGG

MUCK

L. NAN UAMH
Lochailort

Kinlochmoidart

Castle Tirrim
Acharacle LOCH SH

S
E
A

O
F

T
H
E

H
E
B
R
I
D
E
S

POINT OF
ARDNAMURCHAN

ARDNAMURCHAN

Kilchoan
Mingary

Salen
Stronti

LOCH SUNART

C
O
L
L

ARDMORE PT
Arinagour

Tobermory
○Rahoy
M O R V E R

SOUND OF MILL

TIREE
Calgary

HOUGH
SKERRIES

continuation on map 1

4

05 06 07 08 09 10 11 12 13 14 15 16 17 18

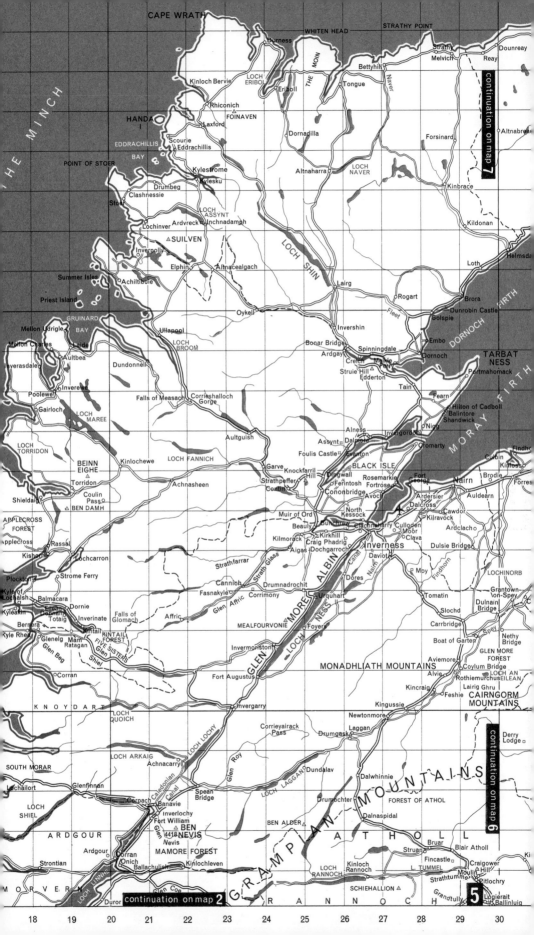

TARBAT NESS
Portmahomack

MORAY FIRTH

KINNAIRDS HEAD

Covesea
Hopeman
Burghead
Lossiemouth
Gordonstoun
Duffus
Drainie
Portknockie
Findochty
Roseheanty
Fraserburgh
SPEY BAY
Garmouth
Cullen
Whitehills
Macduff
Pennan
Gardenstown
Cairnbulg
Memsie

Findhorn
Kinloss
Spynie
Elgin
Buckie
Fordyce
Portsoy
Banff

Cullen
Urquhart
Speymouth
Deskford

RATTRAY HEAD

Brodie
Forres
Alves
Birnie
Fochabers
King Edward
New Pitsligo
Crimond
Strichen
St Fergus

Auldearn
Pluscarden
Dallas
Aberchirder
Turriff

Peterhead

Ardclach
Rothes
Keith
New Deer
DEER
Auchterless
Blackhill
BUCHAN NESS

Dulsie Bridge
Cardow
Craigellachie
Aberlour
Huntly
Fyvie
Tarves
Port Erroll

Grantown-on-Spey
Cromdale
Knockando
Dufftown
Tap o' Noth
Leith Hall
Kennethmont
Dunnideer
Insch
Oyne
Daviot
Pitcaple
Oldmeldrum
Pitmedden
Ellon
Newburgh
Udny
Slains
Collieston
Forvie
BAY OF CRUDEN

Carrbridge
Ballindalloch
Tormore
Rhynie
BENNACHIE
Chapel of Garioch
Inverurie
Harlaw
Ingliston

Boat of Garten
Nethy Bridge
Tomintoul
Lumsden
Terpersie
Kintore

BENMORE FOREST
Glenbuchat
Kildrummy
Alford
Monymusk
Don
Kemnay
Dyce

Aviemore
Coylum Bridge
Strathdon
Craigievar
Skene
ABERDEEN

Lairig Ghru
Culardoch
Lumphanan
Midmar
Echt
Cove

CAIRNGORM MOUNTAINS
Balmoral
Cambus-o-May
Tarland
Dinnet
Kincardine o' Neil
Hill of Fare
Peterculter
Findon

Derry Lodge
Braemar
Crathie
Ballater
Aboyne
Banchory
Crathes
Dee
Muchalls

GRAMPIAN MOUNTAINS
LOCHNAGAR
Cairn o' mount
Slug Road
Fetteresso
Stonehaven
GARRON PT
Dunnottar

THE CAIRNWELL
Drumtochty
Glenbervie

Devil's Elbow
Glen Clova
Alford
Fettercairn
Kincardine
HOWE OF THE MEARNS
Kinneff

Craigower Hill
Kindrogan
Glenisla
Glen Prosen
Edzell
Laurencekirk
Inverbervie

Moulin
Pitlochry
Blacklunans
Caterthun
Menmuir
Stracathro
Lauriston
St Cyrus

Tay
Logierait
Ballinluig
Kirriemuir
Brechin
Farnell
Montrose

Dalguise
Butterstone
Blairgowrie
Alyth
Meigle
Aberlemno
Restenneth
Turin Hill
Guthrie
Friockheim
Auchmithie

Inver
Dunkeld
Birnam
Lethendy
Meikleour
Rattray
Eassie
Glamis
Forfar
Dunnichen
St Vigeans
Carmyllie

Amulree
Murthly
Kinclaven
Kettins
Coupar Angus
Affleck
Monikie
Arbroath

Bankfoot
Stanley
Abernyte
Fowlis Easter
DUNDEE
Barry
Carnoustie
BUDDEN NESS

Fowlis Wester
Pitcairngreen
Methven
Luncarty
Dunsinane Hill
Inchture
Longforgan
Invergowrie
Monifieth
Broughty Ferry

Tibbermore
Huntingtower
Scone
Kinnoull Hill
Carse of Gowrie
Balmerino
Tayport
Newport
FIRTH OF TAY
Bell Rock

Inchaffray Abbey
Findo Gask
Forgandenny
Perth
Bridge of Earn
St Madoes
Newburgh
Leuchars
ST ANDREWS BAY

Forteviot
Abernethy
Lindores
Cupar
Tarvit
St Andrews

Auchterarder
Dunning
Glenfarg
Auchtermuchty
Ceres
Scotstarvit

Gleneagles
Strathmiglo
Ladybank
Pitlessie
Cults

Milnathort
Falkland
Lundin Links
Largo
Colinsburgh
FIFE NESS

Pool of Muckart
Kinross
Markinch
Kennoway
Anstruther
Crail

Cas Campbell
Drom
Beatock
LOCH LEVEN
Leven
Kilconquhar
St Monance
Pittenweem

Alva
Dollar
Cleish
Glenrothes
Kinglassie
Methil
Earlsferry
ISLE OF MAY

Sauchie
Rumbling Bridge
Blairadam
Kelty
Ballingry
Cardenden
Buckhaven
East Wemyss
West Wemyss

Clackmannan
Cowdenbeath
Lochgelly
Dysart

Kincardine-on-Forth
Valleyfield
Aberdour
Inchcolm
Kinghorn
Kirkcaldy
FIRTH OF FORTH

Culross
Pitreavie
Inchkeith
Fidra
North Berwick
Bass Rock

Grangemouth
Bo'ness
Rosyth
Inverkeithing
Dirleton
Tantallon

Kinneil
Blackness
Queensferry
Dalmeny
Gullane
Muirfield
Luffness
Aberlady
Drem
Tyninghame

Polmont
Winchburgh
Mussleburgh
Prestonpans
Garleton
East Linton
Dunbar

Linlithgow
Kirkliston
Portobello
Tranent
Longniddry
Haddington
Spott

Cairnpapple
Ratho
EDINBURGH
Inveresk
Gladsmuir
Whittinghame

Gifford
Law
Stenton
Garvald
Cockburnspath

29   30   31   32   33   34   35   36   37   38   39   40   41   42

continuation on map **8**

MULL
HEAD

PAPA
WESTRAY

NORTH
RONALDSAY

WESTRAY

.THE NORTH
SOUND

O R K N E Y

WESTRAY FIRTH

ROUSAY

EDAY

SANDAY

SANDAY SOUND

I S L A N D S

BROUGH-HEAD

Birsay

STRONSAY

SULE
SKERRY

Skara Brae

Maeshowe

SHAPINSAY

Stenness Kirkwall

Stromness

Tankerness

SCAPA
FLOW

RORA HEAD

H O Y

FLOTTA

Churchill
Barriers

SOUTH
RONALDSAY

PENTLAND

BROUGH NESS

STROMA

Castle of
Mey

John o'
Groats

PENTLAND SKERRIES

DUNNETT HEAD

Dunnet

Canisbay

DUNCANSBY
HEAD

FIRTH

STRATHY POINT

Scrabster

Thurso

Strany

Dounreay

Castletown

Freswick

THE MOIN

Bettyhill

Melvich

Reay

Nybster

Tongue

Halkirk

Watten

NOSS HEAD

Wick

Forsinard

Altnabreac

Camster

Thrumster

LOCH
NAVER

Altnaharra

Kinbrace

Lybster

Latheron

Dunbeath

Kildonan

Loth

Helmsdale

Lairg

Rogart

Brora

Inbhir

Dunrobin

DORNOCH FIRTH

Golspie

Invershin

Embo

Bonar Bridge

Spinningdale

Dornoch

TARBAT NESS

M O R A Y

Ardgay

Creich

Struie Hill

Meikle Ferry

Portmahomack

Edderton

Tain

F I R T H

Fearn

Hilton of Cadboll

COVESEA
SKERRIES

Lossiemouth

Balintore

SPEY BAY

Shandwick

CROMARTY
FIRTH

Nigg

Hopeman

Gordonstoun

Findochty

Portknockie

Assynt

Alness

Burghead

Drainie

Buckie

Cullen

Portsoy

Whitehills

Macduff

Gardenstow

Dalmore

Invergordon

Duffus

Spynie

Gaunouth

Fordyce

Pennan

Foulis

Evanton

Cromarty

Findhorn

Elgin

oUrquhart

Deskford

Banff

Dingwall

Cullen

Alves

oBirnie

Speymouth

BLACK ISLE

Rosemarkie

Nairn

Brodie

Forres

Pluscarden

Aberchirder

Ferintosh

Fortrose

Fort George

Pluscarden

Keith

Turriff

Connonbridge

Avoch

Ardersier

Auldearn

Dallas

Muir of Ord

North
Kessock

Dalcross

Cawdor

Rothes

Aberdeen

Beauly Blackburn

Clachnaharry

Kilravock

Ardclach

Craigellachie

Deveron

Kirkhill

Culloden Moor

Clava

Cardow

Aberlour

Dochgarroch

Inverness

Dulsie Bridge

Knockando

continuation on map **6**

Auchterless

7

26   27   28   29   30   31   32   33   34   35   36   37   38

continuation on map **c**

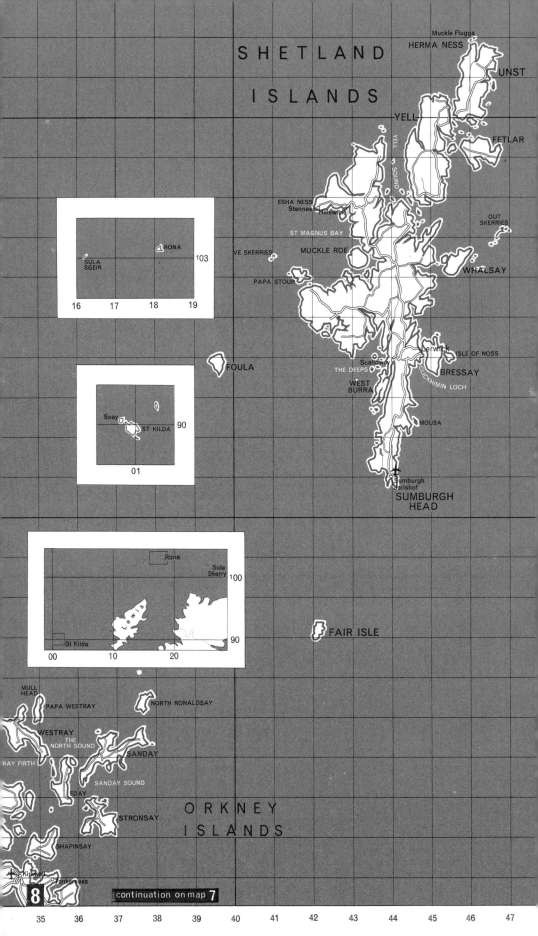

S H E T L A N D

I S L A N D S

Muckle Flugga
HERMA NESS

UNST

YELL

FETLAR

YELL SOUND

ESHA NESS
Stenness Hilliswick

OUT
SKERRIES

St MAGNUS BAY

VE SKERRIES

MUCKLE ROE

WHALSAY

PAPA STOUR

RONA

SULA
SGEIR

¹03

16   17   18   19

FOULA

Lerwick ISLE OF NOSS

Scalloway
THE DEEPS

BRESSAY

CLICKHIMIN LOCH

WEST
BURRA

Soay

ST KILDA

90

MOUSA

01

Sumburgh
Jarlshof

SUMBURGH
HEAD

Rona

Sule
Skerry

100

LEWIS

FAIR ISLE

St Kilda

90

00   10   20

MULL
HEAD

PAPA WESTRAY

NORTH RONALDSAY

WESTRAY
THE
NORTH SOUND

SANDAY

RAY FIRTH

SANDAY SOUND

EDAY

O R K N E Y

STRONSAY

I S L A N D S

SHAPINSAY

Kirkwall Tankerness

8 continuation on map **7**

35   36   37   38   39   40   41   42   43   44   45   46   47

Bibliography

BLACK, G. F., compiler. *A List of Works Relating to Scotland in the New York Public Library.* New York, New York Public Library, 1916.

HANCOCK, P. D. *A Bibliography of Works Relating to Scotland, 1916–50.* 2 vols. Edinburgh, Edinburgh University Press, 1960.

MITCHELL, Sir A., and CASH, C. G. *A Contribution to the Bibliography of Scottish Topography.* 2 vols. Scottish History Society. Edinburgh, Constable, 1917.

General

CLEMENT, A. G., and ROBERTSON, R. H. S. *Scotland's Scientific Heritage.* Edinburgh, Oliver & Boyd, 1961.

DOUGLAS, R. M. *The Scots Book: A Miscellany of Poems, Folklore, Prose and Letters, with Many Facts about Scotland and Her People.* 2nd edition. London, Chambers, 1950.

MCNEILL, F. M. *The Scots Kitchen: Its Traditions and Lore, with Old-Time Recipes.* 2nd edition. London, Blackie, 1963.

MEIKLE, H. W., editor. *Scotland: A Description of Scotland and Scottish Life.* Edinburgh, Nelson, 1947.

MURRAY, C. de Bois. *How Scotland is Governed.* Revised edition. Glasgow, Art and Educational Publishers, 1947.

RAE, G., and BROWN, C. E. *A Geography of Scotland General and Regional.* London, Bell, 1959.

Statistical Accounts of Scotland. The First Statistical Account. 21 vols. Edinburgh, William Creech, 1791–99. *The New Statistical Account.* 15 vols. Edinburgh, Blackwood, 1845. *The Third Statistical Account.* Originated in Edinburgh by Oliver & Boyd (Vol. I, 1951), and now in further preparation in Glasgow by Collins.

WATSON, W. J. *The History of the Celtic Place Names of Scotland.* London, Blackwood, 1926.

Archaeology

CHILDE, V. G. *The Prehistory of Scotland.* London, Kegan Paul, 1935.

CRAWFORD, O. G. S. *Topography of Roman Scotland North of the Antonine Wall.* London, Cambridge University Press, 1949.

FEACHEM, R. *A Guide to Prehistoric Scotland.* London, Batsford, 1963.

PIGGOTT, S. *Scotland Before History.* Edinburgh, Nelson, 1958.

ROYAL COMMISSIONS ON THE ANCIENT AND HISTORICAL MONUMENTS AND CONSTRUCTIONS OF SCOTLAND. Inventories and Reports. *Berwick.* Revised edition. 1915. *Caithness.* 1911. *Dumfriesshire.* 1920. *East Lothian.* 1924. *The City of Edinburgh.* 1951. *Fife, Kinross and Clackmannan.* 1933. *The County of Kirkcudbright.* 1914. *Midlothian and West Lothian.* 1929. *Orkney and Shetland.* 3 vols. 1946. *The Outer Hebrides, Skye and the Small Isles.* 1928. *Roxburghshire.* 2 vols. 1956. *The County of Selkirk.* 1957. *Stirlingshire.* 2 vols. 1963. *Sutherland.* 1911. *The County of Wigtown.* 1912.

Architecture

CRUDEN, S. *Scottish Abbeys: An Introduction to the Mediaeval Abbeys and Priories of Scotland.* London, Her Majesty's Stationery Office, 1960.

FLEMING, J. *Scottish Country Houses and Gardens Open to the Public.* London, Country Life, 1954.

MACGIBBON, D., and ROSS, T. *The Castellated and Domestic Architecture of Scotland from the Twelfth to the Eighteenth Century.* 5 vols. Edinburgh, Douglas, 1887–92. *The Ecclesiastical Architecture of Scotland from the Earliest Christian Times to the Seventeenth Century.* 3 vols. Edinburgh, Douglas, 1896–97.

SIMPSON, W. D. *Scottish Castles: An Introduction to the Castles of Scotland.* London, Her Majesty's Stationery Office, 1959.

See also Inventories and Reports of the Royal Commissions on the Ancient and Historical Monuments and Constructions of Scotland under "Archaeology" above.

Family History and Tartans

ADAM, Frank. *The Clans, Septs and Regiments of the Scottish Highlands.* 6th edition, revised by Sir Thomas Innes of Learney. Edinburgh, Johnston, 1960.

BLACK, G. F. *The Surnames of Scotland: Their Origin, Meaning and History.* New York, New York Public Library, 1962.

FERGUSON, J. P. S. *Scottish Family Histories Held in Scottish Libraries.* Edinburgh, Scottish Central Library, 1960.

INNES, Sir Thomas, of Learney. *The Tartans of the Clans and the Families of Scotland.* 7th edition. Edinburgh, Johnston, 1964.

STUART, Margaret, and PAUL, J. B. *Scottish Family History: A Guide to Works of*

Reference in the History and Genealogy of Scottish Families. Edinburgh, Oliver & Boyd, 1930.

Folklore

BANKS, M. M. *British Calendar Customs: Scotland.* 3 vols. London, Folk Lore Society, 1937–41. *British Calendar Customs: Orkney and Shetland.* London, Folk Lore Society, 1946.

GRANT, I. F. *Highland Folk Ways.* London, Routledge, 1961.

History

BROWN, P. H. *History of Scotland.* 3 vols. Cambridge, Cambridge University Press, 1911.

CAIRNCROSS, A. K., editor. *The Scottish Economy: A Statistical Account of Scottish Life.* London, Cambridge University Press, 1954.

FERGUSON, Tom. *Scottish Social Welfare, 1864–1914.* Edinburgh, Livingstone, 1958.

MACKIE, J. D. *A History of Scotland.* London, Penguin Books, 1965.

MACKIE, R. L. *A Short History of Scotland.* Revised by Gordon Donaldson. Edinburgh, Oliver & Boyd, 1962.

NELSON, Thomas, & Co. *New History of Scotland. Vol. 1. Scotland from the Earliest Times to 1603.* By W. Croft Dickinson. London, 1961. *Vol. 2. Scotland from 1603 to the Present Day.* By G. S. Pryde. London, 1962.

REID, J. M. *Scotland Past and Present.* London, Oxford University Press, 1958.

Literature

KINSLEY, J. *Scottish Poetry.* London, Cassell, 1955.

MILLAR, J. H. *A Literary History of Scotland.* London, Unwin, 1903.

WITTIG, K. *The Scottish Tradition in Literature.* Edinburgh, Oliver & Boyd, 1958.

Natural History

BAXTER, E. V., and RINTOUL, L. J. *The Birds of Scotland: Their History, Distribution and Migration.* 2 vols. London, Oliver & Boyd, 1953.

DARLING, F. F., and BOYD, J. M. *The Highlands and Islands.* New Naturalist. London, Collins, 1964.

FORESTRY COMMISSION. National Forest Park Guides. London. Her Majesty's Stationery Office. *Argyll.* Edited by John Walton. 3rd edition. 1954. *Border.* Edited by John Walton. 2nd edition. 1962. *Glen More, Cairngorms.* Edited by John Walton. 3rd edition. 1960. *Glen Trool.* 2nd edition. 1954.

HOLDEN, A. E. *Plant Life in the Scottish Highlands.* Edinburgh, Oliver & Boyd, 1952.

MCVEAN, D. N., and RATCLIFFE, D. A. *Plant Communities of the Scottish Highlands:*

A Study of Scottish Mountain, Moorland and Forest Vegetation. London, Her Majesty's Stationery Office, 1962.

Road and Rail

GARDINER, L. *Stage-Coach to John O'Groats.* London, Hollis & Carter, 1961.

HALDANE, A. R. B. *The Drove Roads of Scotland.* London, Nelson, 1952. *New Ways Through the Glens.* London, Nelson, 1962.

INGLIS, H. R. G. *The Contour Road Book of Scotland.* 24th edition. Edinburgh, Gall and Inglis, 1963.

NOCK, O. S. *Scottish Railways.* Revised edition. London, Nelson, 1961.

SALMOND, J. B. *Wade in Scotland.* New and enlarged edition. Edinburgh, Moray Press, 1938.

Topography

THE HIGHLANDS AND ISLANDS

ATKINSON, R. *Island-Going, to the Remoter Isles, Chiefly Uninhabited, off the North-West Corner of Scotland.* London, Collins, 1949.

BUDGE, D. *Jura: An Island of Argyll.* Glasgow, Smith, 1960.

CAMPBELL, J. L., editor. *The Book of Barra.* London, Routledge, 1936.

CLUNESS, A. T. *The Shetland Isles.* (County Books Series.) London, Hale, 1951.

FINLAY, I. *The Highlands.* London, Batsford, 1963.

FIRSOFF, V. A. *The Cairngorms on Foot and Ski.* London, Hale, 1949. *In the Hills of Breadalbane.* London, Hale, 1954.

FISHER, J. *Rockall.* London, Bles, 1956.

GILLIES, W. A. *In Famed Breadalbane: The Story of the Antiquities, Lands and People of a Highland District.* Perth, Munro Press, 1938.

HANNAN, T. *The Beautiful Isle of Mull, with Iona and the Isle of Saints.* Edinburgh, R. Grant, 1933.

KIRK, R. *St. Andrews.* (British Cities and Towns Series.) London, Batsford, 1954.

LIVINGSTONE, W. P. *Shetland and the Shetlanders.* Edinburgh, Nelson, 1947.

LODER, J. de V. *Colonsay and Oronsay in the Isles of Argyll: Their History, Flora, Fauna and Topography.* Edinburgh, Oliver & Boyd, 1955.

MACCULLOCH, D. B. *The Wondrous Isle of Staffa: Its History, Geology, Features and Associations.* 3rd edition. Edinburgh, Oliver & Boyd, 1957.

MACDIARMID, Hugh. *The Islands of Scotland.* London, Batsford, 1939.

MACKENZIE, W. C. *The Highlands and Isles of Scotland: A Historical Survey.* Edinburgh, Moray Press, 1949.

MACLEOD, D. *Oasis of the North: A Highland Garden* [Inverewe]. 2nd edition. London, Hutchinson, 1963.

MCNEILL, F. M. *Iona: A History of the*

Island, with Descriptive Notes. 4th edition, revised. Glasgow, Blackie, 1954.

MACROW, B. G. *Kintail Scrapbook: With Photographs by Robert Adam.* Edinburgh, Oliver & Boyd, 1948. *Torridon Highlands.* (Regional Books Series.) London, Hale, 1953.

MARWICK, H. *Orkney.* (County Books Series.) London, Hale, 1951.

MURRAY, W. H. *Highland Landscape: A Survey.* Edinburgh, National Trust for Scotland, 1962.

NAIRNE, C. *The Trossachs and the Rob Roy Country.* Edinburgh, Oliver & Boyd, 1961.

O'DELL, A. C., and WALTON, K. *The Highlands and Islands of Scotland.* Regions of the British Isles. London, Nelson, 1962.

PALMER, W. T. *The Verge of the Scottish Highlands.* London, Hale, 1947.

RENNIE, J. A. *Romantic Strathspey: Its Lands, Clans and Legends.* London, Hale, 1956.

SCOTTISH MOUNTAINEERING CLUB. Guide Books. Edinburgh, Scottish Mountaineering Club. *The Cairngorms.* 2nd edition. 1950. *The Central Highlands.* 2nd edition. 1952. *The Climber's Guide to Ben Nevis.* 1954. *The Climber's Guide to Glencoe and Ardgour.* 2 vols. 1959. *The Climber's Guide to the Cairngorms Area.* 2 vols. 1961–64. *Climbing Guide to the Cuillin of Skye.* 1958. *The Island of Skye.* 3rd edition. 1954. *Islands of Scotland, excluding Skye.* 2nd edition. 1952. *The Northern Highlands.* 3rd edition. 1953. *Rock Climbs at Arrochar.* 1954. *Rock Climbs in Arran.* 1958. *The Southern Highlands.* 1959. *The Western Highlands.* 4th edition revised. 1964.

SCOTT-MONCRIEFF, G. *The Scottish Islands.* 3rd edition, revised. Edinburgh, Oliver & Boyd, 1965.

SVENSSON, R. *Lonely Isles: Being an Account of Several Voyages to the Hebrides and Shetland.* London, Batsford, 1955.

SWIRE, O. F. *The Inner Hebrides and Their Legends.* London, Collins, 1964. *Skye: The Island and Its Legends.* 2nd edition. London, Blackie, 1961.

WEBSTER, D. *Scottish Highland Games.* London, Collins, 1959.

WILLIAMSON, K., and BOYD, J. M. *A Mosaic of Islands.* Edinburgh, Oliver & Boyd, 1963. *St. Kilda Summer.* London, Hutchinson, 1960.

WOOD, W. *Moidart and Morar.* Edinburgh, Moray Press, 1950.

THE LOWLANDS

BANKS, F. R. *Scottish Border Country.* (Face of Britain Series.) London, Batsford, 1951.

BLAKE, G. *The Firth of Clyde.* London, Collins, 1952.

BURNETT, G. *Companion to Tweed.* 2nd edition. London, Methuen, 1945.

CHRISTIE, G. *Harbours of the Forth.* London, Johnson, 1955.

CROCKETT, W. S. *The Scott Country.* 6th edition, revised. London, Black, 1930.

DOUGALL, C. S. *The Burns Country.* 3rd edition. London, Black, 1925.

ELDER, M. *Tell the Towers Thereof: The Ancient Border Story.* London, Hale, 1956.

FINLAY, I. *The Lothians.* New edition. London, Collins, 1963.

HOUSE, J. *Down the Clyde.* Edinburgh, Chambers, 1959.

HUGHES, J. S. *Harbours of the Clyde.* London, Johnson, 1954.

LANG, T., editor. (Queen's Scotland Series.) London, Hodder & Stoughton. *The Border Counties.* 1957. *Edinburgh and the Lothians.* 1952. *Glasgow, Kyle and Galloway.* 1954. *The Kingdom of Fife and Kinross-shire.* 1951.

LINDSAY, M. (County Books Series.) London, Hale. *The Lowlands of Scotland: Edinburgh and the South.* 1956. *The Lowlands of Scotland: Glasgow and the North.* 1953.

MCVIE, J. *The Burns Country.* Edinburgh, Oliver & Boyd, 1962.

REID, J. M. *Glasgow.* (British Cities and Towns Series.) London, Batsford, 1956.

ROBERTSON, J. F. *The Story of Galloway.* Castle Douglas, Maxwell, 1963.

RUSSEL, L. J. A. *The Book of Galloway.* Dumfries, Blacklock, Farries & Son, 1962.

SCOTT-MONCRIEFF, G. *Edinburgh.* 2nd edition. (British Cities and Towns Series.) London, Batsford, 1948.

Travel Description

BOSWELL, J. *The Journal of a Tour to the Hebrides with Samuel Johnson, LL.D., 1773.* Edited from the original manuscript by Frederick A. Pottle and Charles H. Bennett. London, Heinemann, 1963.

BROWN, P. H., editor. *Early Travellers in Scotland, 1295–1689.* Edinburgh, Douglas, 1891.

JOHNSON, S. *Journey to the Western Islands of Scotland; With James Boswell's Journal of a Tour to the Hebrides with Samuel Johnson, LL.D.* Edited by R. W. Chapman. London, Oxford University Press, 1930.

MARTIN, Martin. *A Description of the Western Islands of Scotland circa 1695.* Stirling, Mackay, 1934.

MONRO, Donald. *Western Isles of Scotland and Genealogies of the Clans, 1549.* Edited from a hitherto unpublished manuscript, with notes by R. W. Munro. Edinburgh, Oliver & Boyd, 1961.

PENNANT, T. *A Tour in Scotland, 1769; and a Tour in Scotland and Voyage to the Hebrides, 1772.* 5th edition. 1790.

Guide Books and Gazetteers

AUTOMOBILE ASSOCIATION. *Illustrated Road Book of Scotland.* Revised edition. London, Automobile Association, 1963.

CHAMBERS, W. and R. *Chambers's Guide to Scotland.* 2nd edition. London, Chambers, 1963.

GLASGOW HERALD. *Motor Touring in Scotland.* New edition. Glasgow, Outram, 1960.

JOHNSTON, W. and A. K., and BACON, G. W. *Johnston's Gazetteer of Scotland.* 2nd edition, revised. London, Johnston and Bacon, 1958.

MUIRHEAD, L. R., editor. *Scotland.* 4th edition. (Blue Guides Series.) London, Benn, 1959.

NATIONAL TRUST FOR SCOTLAND. *Seeing Scotland: An Illustrated Guide to the Houses, Castles, Gardens and Other Places of Interest Open to the Public 1965.* Edinburgh, National Trust for Scotland, 1965.

ORDNANCE GAZETTEER OF SCOTLAND. *A Graphic and Accurate Description of Every Place in Scotland.* Edited by F. A. Groome. New edition, revised. Edinburgh, Jack, 1901.

WARD LOCK & Co. *The Complete Scotland.* 8th edition. London, 1964.

Index